VOLUME 91

1987

Argus Specialist Publications Ltd.

PO Box 35, Wolsey House, Wolsey Road, Hemel Hempstead, Herts. HP2 4SS

Published by
Argus Specialist Publications
Argus Books Ltd.,
1 Golden Square,
London W1R 3AB.

On the cover: Edward Hopkins' small dressing mirror in mahogany and jacaranda was featured in the February issue – see page 152.

WOODWORKER VOLUME 91 INDEX

12 monthly copies January 1987 – December 1987

January pp 1-88
The cover features Bill Watts' beautiful burr elm and rosewood bracket clock which won a gold medal at the 1986 Woodworker Show in London. A remarkable example of work in this difficult timber.

February pp 89-176
A photograph of a Brazilian boy in the family workshop is one of a number by furniture designer/maker Lucinda Leech who contributes an article chronicling her visit to the Amazonian rainforest.

March pp 177-264
Attracting considerable attention at the London Woodworker Show was Waring Robinson's lovely little padauk collectors' cabinet photographed on the cover of this issue and drawn and detailed inside.

April pp 265-352
Leading American craftsman James Krenov made the spalted maple and red oak cabinet gracing this cover. Unusually it features a convex carcase but concave coopered doors.

May pp 353-456
Peter Stocken is renowned for his three-dimensional jigsaw puzzles and this cover illustrates one of his simpler ventures. The cover also included a free router bit sample by Bosch, normally costing £2.35.

June pp 457-552
A free booklet on cordless tools was attached to this issue's cover, but it did not obscure a charming carving of what most would take for a mouse but which is in fact an Australian feathertail glider, carved by Peter Carrigy.

July pp 553-648
John Starr, maker of harpsichords, clavichords and spinets, who runs courses in their construction and also provides prefabricated kits of parts, is shown with some of his products in his workshop.

August pp 649-744
Examples of exhibits from the 1987 Bristol Woodworker Show include a remarkable gold medal cherry and leaded glass screen which folds into a cylindrical column and prize-winning turned and carved work.

September pp 745-840
Perhaps not to everyone's taste, 'Star Table' is a sample of the type of work exhibited at the Direct Design Show; a two-part photofeature on students' work is included in this and the subsequent issue.

October pp 841-936
A 'magician's birthday clock' by Wendell Castle is shown; an article on the builder and other leading American 'trend-benders' appears on p.858. A free 3mm centre-point drill bit was attached to the cover.

November pp 937-1048
An elegant turned and black-stained African mahogany vase against a background of part of an unusual laminated ply bowl celebrates a major turning seminar. Another free sample – of Sandvik sanding plate – was attached.

December pp 1049-1152
Masur birch veneers and ash plus framed spaces make William Hepper's telephone cabinet distinctive – plans inside. Attached to the cover, yet another free gift, a Handiknife.

AUTHOR INDEX

SUBJECT INDEX

ADVERTISERS' INDEX

Woodworker

CONTENTS

design . . . craft . . . and the love of wood

January 1987
Vol. 91
No. 1

● *This delicious little serpentine-fronted chest by Wing Commander A. Landells won a silver medal at the Show: p15*

Photo Tim Imrie

On the cover: Bill Watt's magnificent burr elm and rosewood bracket clock, 'Spirit of Tompion', won a gold medal at the Woodworker Show. Photo Tim Imrie.

Editor Aidan Walker
Deputy editor John Hemsley
Editorial assistant Kerry Fowler
Advertisement manager Trevor Pryer
Advertisement production Laura Champion
Graphics Jeff Hamblin
Technical illustrator Peter Holland
Guild of Woodworkers John Hemsley, Kerry Fowler

Unfortunately we cannot accept responsibility for loss of or damage to unsolicited material. We reserve the right to refuse or suspend advertisements, and regret we cannot guarantee the bona fides of advertisers.
Published every third Friday

Editorial, advertisements and Guild of Woodworkers
1 Golden Square, London W1R 3AB, telephone 01-437 0626

ABC
UK circulation
Jan-Dec 85
28,051

Back issues and subscriptions Infonet Ltd, 10-13 Times House, 179 Marlowes, Hemel Hempstead, Herts HP1 1BB; telephone Hemel Hempstead (0442) 48434

Subscriptions per year UK £16.90; overseas outside USA (accelerated surface post) £21.00, USA (accelerated surface post) $28, airmail £48

UK trade SM Distribution Ltd, 16-18 Trinity Gardens, London SW9 8DX; telephone 01-274 8611

North American trade Bill Dean Books Ltd, 151-49 7th Avenue, PO Box 69, Whitestone, New York 11357; tel. 1-718-767-6632

Printed by Chase Web, Plymouth
Mono origination Multiform Photosetting Ltd, Cardiff
Colour origination Derek Croxson Ltd, Chesham, Bucks
© Argus Specialist Publications Ltd 1986
ISSN 0043 776X

Argus Specialist Publications Ltd

1 Golden Square, London W1R 3AB; 01-437 0626

This month

Future bench

Show visitors to the *Woodworker* stand will have had a close look at the prototype of John Green's prize-winning design in our Workbench of the Future competition, run in conjunction with Sjöbergs. If you looked at last month's full explanation of the idea, you'll realise why Sjöbergs had time only to put together a prototype incorporating a couple of John's suggestions — crammed full of clever wheezes, it was.

Many thanks to Sjöbergs for helping us with the competition, and here are a few of designer Torsten Sjöberg's comments:

'**I** have been very interested to learn of all these proposals for a workbench. Many of them accord completely with my own views when it comes to a carpenter's bench.

'The idea of a plastic film to protect the surface is excellent ... perhaps it should function like a roller blind. We are working on a panel with electric sockets and so on — it has to come ... a dust bag in a flap in the tool-well is also a good idea.

'We were attracted to the ingenious idea of a pull-out extension, widening the bench so it could easily be used for sawing board materials; the width of extension could easily be increased over the prototype's limitations (we only had these fittings available) by using double-expanding fittings and collapsible legs for support. **'**

● *Workbench of the future winner John Green (left) and Sjöberg importer Geoff Brown discuss the finer points*

Select designers

Style for '87, the 'furniture preview' show at Earl's Court in October, brought good news for Luke Hughes, designer/maker and *Woodworker* contributor; the Design Council selection committee chose his range of Ovolo oak bedroom furniture for their Design Centre label. The range is made by Juckes of Birmingham, 'recalling the traditions of the 16th and 17th centuries, when robust construction and subtle detailing were prime considerations.' There's no conventional ironmongery — pulls and hinges are all wood — and cabinet backs and undersides of drawers are all finished, an admirably detailed approach for a volume manufacturer. 'We're quite familiar,' says Juckes MD Stephen Allday, 'with having our successful designs pinched by downmarket competitors. But if they are able to follow us in this direction, the whole industry will benefit.'

● *Luke's Ovolo oak chest*

● *Robin's wishbone rocker*

'Hurrah for the untrained,' says Luke succinctly — six years ago he was starting in woodwork, putting new bits of ash on Morris Travellers. He's taught himself, largely from the pages of *Woodworker* no doubt.

Another Design Council accolade goes to Robin Williams for his 'Wishbone rocker', just two years after he left John Makepeace's School for Craftsmen in Wood in Dorset. Robin went through art college, cottage renovations, and boat rebuilding before he went to Parnham, and now makes the rocker (sold through select retail outlets and direct to clients), as well as other one-off pieces, in his Devon workshop. The chair is in laminated oak, designed so it can be batch produced; it 'allows for total relaxation when lying back, but by moving with the body, also permits the occupant to sit comfortably upright', it says here.

More of this and related topics on p24, 'Style plus'.
● Luke Hughes & Co., 1 Stukely St, London WC2B 5LQ, 01-404 5995
● Juckes Ltd, 48-52 Floodgate St, Birmingham B5 5SP, 021-772 0491
● Robin Williams, Old Brewhouse, Manor St, Dittisham, S. Devon, (080 422) 366

Hitting ITTO

The Timber Trades Federation have laid a Plan for Action on the desk of the executive director of the International Tropical Timber Organisation, ready for his first day in office.

Dr Freezailah Che Yeom of Malaysia will be looking at a call to establish an effective framework for co-operation and consultation between tropical timber producing and consuming countries, and to encourage the development of national policies aimed at sustainable use and conservation of tropical forests and the maintenance of their ecological balance. 'As a matter of extreme urgency', emphasise the TTF, should these policies be fostered. They suggest a common fund to enable the producing nations to maintain ecological and socio-economic balance.

Safety sorry

We omitted to mention that the photos of machine planing on p967 and spindle moulding on p968 of November's *Woodworker* show guarding arrangements which would not comply with the Woodworking Machines Regulations 1974, which govern professional/commercial workshops. Sorry!

William Morris

A Craft Fellowship under that august name is the new training award to raise the standard of craftsmanship in historic building repairs, arranged by the Society of Protection for Ancient Buildings. Six months' travel and study? Contact SPAB, 37 Spital Sq, London E1 6DY, 01-377 1644.

Diary

January
7-1 Feb **Timber in Architecture Exhibition**, Smith Art Gallery and Museum, Stirling, (091) 2358424
13-18 **International Furniture Fair** Cologne

February
1-3 **British Toymakers Guild 8th Toy Fair**, Kensington Town Hall, Hornton St, London W8, 01-549 1483
8-13 **Shipwright's Workshop**, traditional boat repair, West Dean College, Chichester, Sussex, (02463) 301

March
12-13 **French polishing** Charles Cliffe*
28 **Spindle moulding** Roy Sutton*
28 **Wood machining** Ken Taylor*

April
26-4 May **London International Furniture Show**, Earl's Court (26-30 trade only)

Sponsor plea

The Geffrye Museum has for 75 years been a national centre for the study of British Furniture History, and next year is mounting a six-month exhibition to celebrate 200 years of furniture making in London's East End. They are researching and producing a book, and aim to mount numerous educational activities and events such as video and oral history projects, workshops, demonstrations, a furniture festival, and a Young Furniture Makers Competition. The Inner London Education Authority is covering basic costs, but the Museum is inviting sponsors, who will benefit from the various publicity and promotions arrangements proposed. New sponsorship, they point out, may be eligible for an award under the Government Business Sponsorship Incentive Scheme.

● Geffrye Museum, Kingsland Rd, London E2 8EA; phone Julia Porter 01-739 9893, or Tish Francis 01-722 7878.

Shoptalk

Makita have found the discerning power tool user who wants professional quality and affordable price. Hence the **Power-Craft** range; drills start at £49, and top of the range is the attractive little mitre saw at a very attractive £169. Changes in employment patterns, house renovation habits — they researched it all, and decided when people trade up, Makita's where they should go. We've had a close look, and very impressive they are too.
● Makita UK, 8 Finway, Dallow Rd, Luton LU1 1TR, (0582) 455777.

Trend **Routergraph** for lettering, carving and all sorts, accepts Bosch and Elu machines 500-700w. Basic unit price £398+VAT.
● Trend, Unit N, Penfold Wks, Imperial Way, Watford WD2 4YY, (0923) 49911.

New **lathe** from well-respected Tyme Machines, the Student was seen for the first time at the Woodworker Show. Not just for students — cast iron and steel construction, ½hp motor, tailstock solid centre, two-prong drive centre, three speeds (500, 1000, 2500rpm), a hollow tailstock; and a load of accessories are available. At £199+VAT this has got to be good news for many.
● Tyme Machines, Unit 3, Halls Rd, Kingswood, Bristol (0272) 603726.

Quite a stir was caused at the Woodworker Show by Elu's two new **dust extractors** — no ordinary wet'n'dry vacuum cleaners, these. Designed for use with Elu power tools and their flip-over and mitre saws, the extractors are quiet (says the blurb), 30 and 40 litre capacity, have an easy and efficient method of cleaning the filter, a warning light to show you when your bradawl is being sucked up the tube, and a plug on the machine into which you connect your tool; so when you switch the tool on the extractor comes on — and off when you let go. Another socket switch allows you to use it independently or with two tools. Adaptors are available for the Elu tools, but you can be sure people with other brands will be fixing up their own ... The 40 litre EVE 948 costs £477+VAT, the 30 litre EVE 938

£332+VAT, and a typical adaptor — for, say, a belt sander — costs £6.38. £32.45 for the MOF 96 router adaptor, though.

● Elu, Westpoint, The Grove, Slough, Berks SL1 1QQ, (0753) 74277.

Master toolmaker Richard Kell has come up with the Anglemaster, a set of dead stable, dead accurate **angled templates** that take the headache out of angled work calculations. Machine setting, coopered work (the seventh and last template gives you 84° 22′ 30″ — need we say more?) circular and other built-up construction ... just take the angle off one of the templates. Knowing Richard's production standards, these things are certain to be accurate to a degree — or rather, a millisecond. £5.95 from specialist tool shops, or add £1 p&p from Richard himself.

● Richard Kell, 67 Newbiggin Rd, Ashington, Northumberland NE63 0TB, (0670) 351909.

Who but B&D would do a **Powerfile?** That's their new 300w abrasive 'stick' — sanding, filing, shaping. Around £30.
● Black & Decker, Westpoint, The Grove, Slough SL1 1QQ, (0753) 79311

All very scientific ... Treebridge's new cast-iron Bowl turner's **'Multi rest'** has a stepped-section profile. £26+ VAT.
● Treebridge, Mills Drive, Farndon Rd, Newark, Notts NG2 4SN, (0636) 702382.

John Sainsbury, well-known woodturner and Liveryman of the Worshipful Company of Turners, has been brought in by that historic body to help set up a London **Turning Workshop**, run in association with the Worshipful Company of Carpenters at the Carpenters Company Craft School. The evening courses will be on a continuing basis from January to April, 6-9pm, and they will be for both beginners and advanced turners.
● The Director, Carpenters Company Craft School, 153 Titchfield St, London W1P 7FR.

Shoptalking points

This month's winner of the Sandvik Centenary Handsaw below is Mr C. Hudson of Penrhyndeudraeth in Gwynedd, who suggests you get hold of the liquid soap dispensers available from chemists — you know, the pots on the wall with a little push button underneath. Apart from being a good way to put soap on grubby hands, he says, they're excellent for the workshop once they're emptied; the plunge action dispenser gives you small controlled amounts of whatever liquid or goop you are in the habit of using — machine oil, sharpening oil, linseed oil, white spirit, meths ... simple but neat, eh?

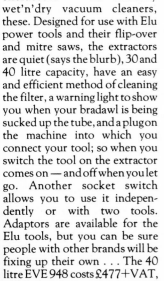

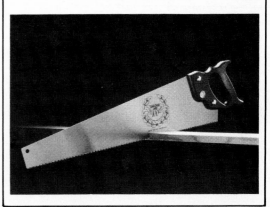

The ancient pre-fab

Dismantling, moving and rebuilding an 18th century timber-frame house is not a task for the fainthearted. But David Ouvry was more than a match for the historical craft of (re)building by numbers

In the deep countryside, mediaeval villages or thriving provincial towns, timber-frame houses are still prominent and attractive, constant reminders of our past. They have such strong visual appeal, it's encouraging to see so many oak-framed buildings still well maintained and preserved, despite changing times and fashions. For many hundreds of years oak was the most favoured building timber because of its strength and durability; traditional timber-frame houses and barns were built up to the early 19th century, when the increasing scarcity of mature oaks (thousands were felled to build wooden-wall ships during the Napoleonic wars) and the increase of brick production contributed to their decline.

A number of buildings of this kind are lately being either fully restored, or even moved complete to another part of the country. Predatory builders with an eye to the tastes of their clients have cannibalised barns for the odd beam to be added as (non-structural) 'features', and who hasn't seen a cottage with a 'wealth of exposed beams', in estate agents' jargon? Mind you, some of these old beams turn out to be well-stained papier-machè.

My own project of building a new house out of largely old materials provided the incentive to salvage part of a ruined Welsh farmhouse, a 500sq ft conventional two-storey 18th century building. It had been abandoned (probably during the 1950's), and although it was still standing, it had lost a good deal of its slate roof and most of the infill on one side. The local council had refused permission to rebuild or renovate because it was so derelict, so it was a conservationist's dream to be able to rescue and re-use a great deal of the old timber.

De-building

The traditional building frame of posts, beams and studs with mortise-and-tenon joints, pegged without any glue, means that such buildings can be taken apart without too much trouble and damage, particularly if the infilled panels are wattle-and-daub or lath-and-plaster rather than brick. Brick infilling, in fact, used to be far less common than the earlier methods, presumably because of expense. Bricks would also have

● *David Ouvry's 200-year-old timber-frame wall has a new lease of life in Berkshire,* **top;** **above,** *the ruined Powys farmhouse before removal of the timber-framing, on the left*

considerably increased the dead weight of the structure, and total weight must have been a consideration, because often there was little or no solid foundation laid beneath the floor plates. It's a tribute to the durability of timber-frame buildings that they move without disintegrating. Many old barns and even houses are still standing safely, a corner or two sunk six inches below their opposites. Imagine what would happen if a brick or stone structure subsided this much!

Taking down the framed walls proved relatively easy. Each timber was marked for re-assembly, and the dowels (pegs) were knocked out of the tenons from inside to

take advantage of their slight taper. Sometimes the pegs were end-stopped in the timber, when a brace and bit came in handy. The end tie-beam, about 12x9in section, was very heavy, but with a good deal of effort and three pairs of hands we dislodged it, and gravity did the rest. Fortunately some bushes near the house cushioned it fall. After that work went apace without mishap, except that a crumbled wall plate beneath a corner post allowed a sudden collapse — could have been nasty for anyone standing too close. We hired a lorry to take it all to east Berkshire, and the more difficult and time-consuming task of adaptation and re-assembly began.

● *Seven strong men heave the oak frame upright,* **top**; **above**, *some of the tools used in reconstruction – wide and narrow chisels, ripsaw, drawknife, mallet, spokeshave and brace and bit*

Re-building

Adaptation was necessary since the old timbers were to go into a new wall which, although only single-storey, was to be 25½ft long, almost 10ft longer than the original cottage wall. This meant 'stretching' the original ground-floor wall by inserting a section from the upper floor. The floor plate and tie-beam were both therefore doubled up, the new tenons cut with an old but well sharpened ripsaw. The mortises were hollowed out mainly with a really hefty Victorian 2in-wide mortise chisel, plus smaller chisels of course. Most

of the work on such heavy unmanoeuvrable timbers couldn't be handled easily by modern machinery, even if it had been available, so hand-tools were Hobson's choice. I used an adze, brace and bits, a draw-knife, a spokeshave, rip and crosscut saws and mortise chisels.

One of the new floor plates was wider than we needed, and had to be cut down from 8in to 6in. Wedges made a fine job of splitting the straight-grained oak, and the adze and draw-knife took care of the minimal straightening and cleaning up.

The whole central section of the frame was simply done; many of the original

6x3in studs fitted into existing mortises, followed by the oak dowels, some of which were still in good shape despite their age. The short cross-members were fitted in the same way; each stud was engaged in the floor-plate mortise, then a cross-member was added, to be joined to the next stud, and so on. The whole frame was assembled on the ground just in front of the brick foundation, on which a damp-proof membrane was bedded in mortar. The house naturally had to be built to building-regulation standards, which involved entrenching a concrete footing below brickwork.

It took seven men to slide the frame on to the foundation and heave it upright into position. Awkward and labour-intensive, this method must have been the traditional one since there's no way of assembling the frame in the upright position without making it enormously difficult to place the tie-beam. We found the timbers still had the original carpenter's numbered marks, used to identify the position of each component — probably an indication the frame was cut out in the carpenter's workshop and taken to the site by horse and waggon. Modern unit assembly isn't so modern after all . . .

Then we had to brace the upright frame temporarily, till it could be wall-tied to the inner Celcon block wall. Absurdly enough, we had to design the rafters to bear on the Celcon blocks rather than the framed wall, to keep the Building Inspectors happy. It must be fairly obvious, even to non-structural engineers, that oak posts, beams, and brick infill are at least as good load-bearers as lightweight concrete blocks.

The original timbers were of course never treated with today's stains, preservatives and anti-woodworm fluids, and the silvery-grey natural weathering over many years is attractive in its own right. Although renovators often decide to follow tradition and stain the timbers dark-brown or black, we decided simply to leave the oak in its natural weathered state on the outside, but sprayed the interior sides of the timbers against possible wet or dry rot before infilling. A number of the timbers had been attacked by woodworm at some time, but their depredations had long ceased once any sections of timber which included sapwood had been demolished. The heartwood, as the saw revealed, was magnificently solid, and is now far too hard for the teeth of even the most vicious woodworm.

The internal colour of the wood is a warm brown, somewhere between the yellow of freshly-cut oak and the black of more than 300 years of ageing. Where we had to work this fine heartwood, it was essential to use really sharp tools to get anywhere at all. The older oak is, the harder it gets — as anyone who compares a plank of new oak and an Elizabethan beam for sawing or planing will find!

So to the final stage. The foundations being more than enough to bear the weight, we completed the wall with brick infill (lath

continued

The ancient pre-fab

● *David himself at work with traditional tools – 2in mortise chisel,* **left**, *and drawknife,* **above**. **Below**, *how the component parts fit together*

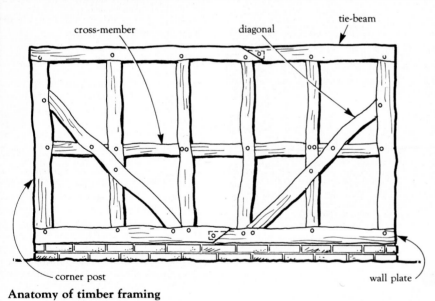

Anatomy of timber framing

cross-member

diagonal

tie-beam

corner post

wall plate

and plaster was the original finish) in a variety of traditional bondings, including vertical and horizontal herringbone. Before bricklaying could begin, we had to line the surfaces of the framework next to the brick with galvanised expanded wire; we nailed it on, providing a good key for the mortar. Wall-ties had also been inserted into the inner wall to give additional strengthening to the centre of each panel. Supported at edges and centre, the brickwork has since stayed comfortably stable, despite the inevitable slight timber movement that goes

with humidity and temperature changes.

The original cottage had stood in the heart of the Powys hills in all weathers for 200 years or more, and until it was abandoned must have needed astonishingly little structural maintenance. A little movement here or there never hurt such buildings. It is a testimony to the soundness of principle on which such houses were built, and a tribute to the quality and durability of Welsh oak trees. Our new house will give the old timbers a life which we hope will be just as long again. ■

8

Woodworker
PLANS SERVICE

JOHN THOMPSON FIELDWAY COLLECTION — OVER 40 DESIGNS

YORKSHIRE WAGON
This example is of the Vale of Pickering type, very robustly built, a handsome vehicle. Model is 16in. long.
Plan JT/40   4 Sheets   Price £3.30

HEREFORD WAGON
A small size plank sided wagon, it is now in the reserve collection at the Museum of Rural Life at Reading. Model is 15in. long.
Plan JT/14   1/8 scale, 2 large sheets   Price £2.95

HOP TUG
The high ladders fore and aft are a feature of this unusual wagon. Model is 19in. long.
Plan JT/15   1/8 scale, 2 large sheets   Price £2.95

HAMPSHIRE WAGGON
Constructed about 1900, this is an unusual wagon with double shafts. A superb subject for ??? who wants a wealth of detail. Model is 17in. long.
Plan JT/10   1/8 scale, 2 large sheets   Price £2.95

1850 EAST ANGLIAN WAGON
This massive and stately vehicle ??? 1850, now in the reserve collection at the Reading museum of Rural Life. Model is 19ins. long.
Plan JT/20   1/8 scale, 5 sheets plus sheet of photos
Price £4.50

HOW TO MAKE WHEELS
The chart MODEL WHEEL CONSTRUCTION gives step-by-step instructions to enable the average handyman to produce excellent scale wheels Available only with one other plan order.
Plan No. JT/001   Price 80p

OXFORDSHIRE WAGON
To many people this is the epitome of the English farm wagon. Used on Blackwood farm, the original is now in the Oxford County Museum this 1/8 scale model is 18ins. long.
Plan No. JT/18   1/8 scale 4 sheets plus photo sheet £3.60

GLAMORGAN WAGON
A most elegant wagon. This wagon was built around 1870, now renovated and on display at St. Fagans.
Plan JT/38   1/8 scale   Price £3.30

ASHBY DESIGN WORKSHOP — TRADITIONAL FURNITURE FOR HOUSE & GARDEN

NEW!

Chippendale Urn Stand
Another replica from Longleat House, this elegant C18 Urn Stand originally intended for flower or sculpture display may also be used as an eye catching occasional table.
Plans No. ADW 501
Price £6.75

Chippendale Urn Stand

Universal Desk
A replica of a Chippendale period desk at Longleat House Wilts, the worktop adjusts to over 1300 working positions for reading, writing painting and as a music stand.
Plans No. ADW 503
Price £8.00

18th C. Universal Desk

TAPA SYSTEM PLAN PACKS
Each Pack comprises:

A1 size Plan	2 Frameworks
3 A3 Plans	4 Chair designs
Full-size profiles	Cutting
Joint details	Schedules

Featuring a series of modern furniture designs for the home, the TAPA system of plan-packs is a new concept in woodworking projects. Each plan-pack focusses on a specific object and explores many alternatives to the original model. The Dining Chair is the ??? the series, featuring ideas based on the simple halving joint prototype.
Plan ADW401   Price £5.75

DAVID BRYANT CRAFT DESIGN PLANS
HOME & LEISURE, TOYS, SPINNING WEAVING

DRUM CARDER
Sooner or later spinners graduate to a drum carder. This design takes the toil out of hand carding. It uses a positive gear/sprocket drive which also reduces the drag which the belt drive alternative imposes. A little metalwork as well as woodwork involved. One sheet plan.
Plan No. DB54   Price £3.70

TABBY LOOM
A simple tabby loom having rollers, warp and cloth beams and fitted with a rigid heddle, and canvas aprons. Basic weaving width 380mm but plan can be adapted for other widths if desired. Ideal for beginners and it is surprising what can be achieved with warp and weft variations tufting etc.
Plan No. DB 2   Price £3.20

SLOPING STYLE SPINNING WHEEL
This design is a replica of an authentic spinning wheel doem olden days, having a 486mm (19in.) diameter wheel with bent wood rim. Plan is complete with mother-of-all, distaff, treadle operation etc. A feature of this wheel is its attractive turnings which make it a most decorative piece besides being functional. A design for the enthusiast woodturner. Two sheet plan.
Plan No. DB12   Price £5.40

UPRIGHT SPINNING WHEEL
In this vertical style spinning wheel the mother-of-all arrangement is situated above the main wheel. The latter is 460mm diameter and the rim is of segmented design. Simpler lines than the sloping wheel but nevertheless graceful in appearance and of course functional.
Plan No. DB13   Price £5.40

SPINNING STOOL
A spinning stool specially suited for use with the sloping bed wheel. Four legged arrangement, with richly carved seat and back. A good example of chip carving.
Plan No. DB20   Price ???

WARPING MILL
This warping mill design consists of a vertical revolving drum supported within a floor standing frame. The drum is fitted with pegs for securing the warp to, and the frame is complete with heck block for spreading warps up to 15-20 metres.
Plan No. DB9   Price £3.20

NEW!

SUPERB TOOL CABINET

Top notch design from Morrison Originals. 5 sheets of A3 size drawings with step by step procedures, many notes and a full cutting list. You'll never lose another valuable tool — a place for everything.
Plan No. MTC1   Price £4.75

CREDIT CARD ORDERS WELCOME
TEL: 0442-211882

Argus Specialist Publications, PO Box 35, Wolsey House, Wolsey Road, Hemel Hempstead, Herts. HP2 4SS. 0442-41221·211882. Delivery 21 days

To WOODWORKER Plans Service
(Please make cheques or P.O.'s payable to A.S.P. Ltd.,)
Please supply the following plans.   WW

Plan No .... Title .... Price ....

Plan No .... Title .... Price ....

Plan No .... Title .... Price ....

Cash total .... Name ....

Address ....

....

POSTAGE AND PACKING RATES
Inland Postage

Up to £1.40	45p
£1.40 to £5.50	55p
Over £5.50	65p

Accelerated Surface Post

Up to £4.00	£1.00
£4.01 to £7.00	£1.25
Over £7.00	£1.50

For Airmail Postage add 30% to the value of the order.

Loom service

Now that crafts are coming back home, cottage-size looms are in big demand. Leonard Markham met the McDougall clan, producing new versions of that old essential

● *Malcolm McDougall in action on one of his larger looms. Winter's the time for making them, summer the time for displaying and selling*

The home crafts revival has produced everything from furniture to figurines. But the opportunities for weaving have been restricted by the industrial characteristics of loom designs, which have rarely been adapted to home production. Now, Scotsman Malcolm McDougall has come up with a re-design, and produces hand-operated wooden looms in one of the most attractive villages in North Yorkshire.

Grewelthorpe, near Ripon, has obvious tourist appeal, and is the base for Grewelthorpe Handweavers, a weaving and retail enterprise established by Malcolm in 1970. Following a lifetime of textile mill management in Britain and South America, he used his experience of advanced British, and primitive Indian technologies, to make his first prototype loom as a woodworking project in 1965. Commercial production began in 1983, when his son Barry came into the business, and since then sales have climbed to some 20 looms a month.

The principles of weaving are based on the age-old technique of passing a thread-loaded shuttle across, and alternately over and under tensioned warp lines, until the fabric is formed. With modern hand looms, much of the tedium of weaving is removed by running the warp threads through selected metal 'healds', held in one or more raisable shafts. As the shafts are lifted, the selected warp lines rise, and the shuttle passes quickly across. The weft is consolidated by drawing the pivoted beater towards the breast beam (see the drawing). Malcolm has adapted and refined the technology for the domestic market, producing four types of loom with varying degrees of sophistication.

The designs are precisely tailored to cost and customer requirements; they have to fit into a normal living area, and the timber has to be relatively cheap hardwood, which blends, unstained, with contemporary furniture. Formerly strictly utilitarian, looms are today regarded as attractive pieces in their own right, and finish is all-important. Malcolm finds elm is the ideal material, for strength, workability, and visual appeal.

Most of the loom components are made to standard sectional dimensions for economy and manufacturing simplicity. Transport requirements — cost and size — have also influenced the loom designs.

The timber is bought green and sawn roughly to the finished dimensions before seasoning in an EBAC kiln. Costing less than £1 a week to operate, the kiln reduces moisture content from 40-60%, to around 10% in under two months. After seasoning, the timbers are planed, cut to length and jointed, using a variety of heavy-duty power tools. The components are batch-machined, as are the joints, which requires accurate planing — otherwise the joints will have to be squared by hand which costs time. A 12x9in Sedgwick gives the necessary accuracy and speed for handling multiple runs and, after planing, the components are cut to length with a DeWalt radial-arm saw; the mortise-and-tenon and dovetail joints are cut on conventional jigs.

An unusual but invaluable workshop tool is the robust and versatile Wadkin patternmaker's lathe. It's used for cloth- and warp-roller making and has a capacity of 66in between centres. Restricted by the width of the gap bed, turning diameters are limited to 28½in, but by using the rear of the headstock, the diameter is virtually unlimited (up to 7ft), using a massive free-standing tool rest. The lathe's main asset for loom making is the precision of the travelling tool-carriage which allows the turning of perfectly parallel rollers — essential for accurate weaving. The exceptional power of the lathe allows the reduction in one pass from 2½in square to 1¾in round, though a fine final cut improves the finish. The carriage is also ideal for the repetitive turning of round parts. The speed range is from 240 to 3360rpm, and the lathe weighs 17cwt.

Two pieces of identically dimensioned timber are joined to form a roller blank; semi-circular slots are spindle-moulded along the central lengths to accommodate the roller rod. The pieces are glued slot sides out, before they are turned and fitted with ratchets.

The round ratchet blanks are cogged on the bandsaw, and here Malcolm allows for the operational stresses by cross-grain laminating them. He uses Evostik Resin 'W' for jointing, although, where possible, components are bolted with galvanised roofing bolts for easy disassembly. The looms are finished by sanding, sealing, lacquering and hand waxing, and then the metal parts are fitted.

Loom production is generally confined to the winter months, when tourist interest wanes; looms sell better in the summer anyway. During the season the loom workshops and display areas are themselves promoted as attractions.

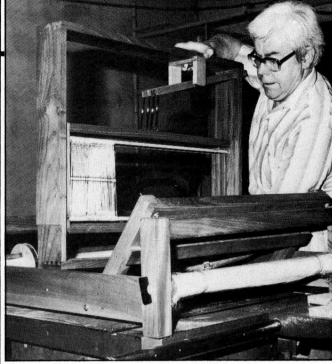

● **Left**, a small 'Mark II' loom; **above**, Malcolm assembles one. **Below left**, a peg set up in the patternmaker's lathe, and **below**, turning a hefty roller. Note the travelling tool carriage

The McDougalls used to concentrate on commercial weaving but they have given this up, although Malcolm is always on hand to demonstrate the capabilities of his machines. Varying in price from £79 for the simple Mark I to £625 for the sophisticated Mark III model, each loom offers opportunities for commercial home weaving.

The way that the McDougalls have successfully integrated manufacturing with retailing, creating a business with both craft and tourist appeal, should interest other small-workshop business people. Meticulous product design, careful organisation, and recognising the potential of a home-craft market are the keys to what will no doubt be a flourishing business. ■

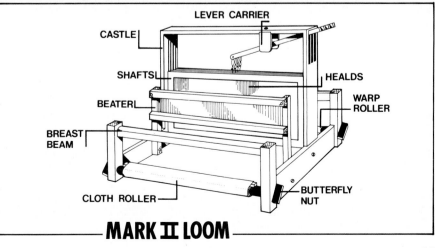

LEVER CARRIER

CASTLE

SHAFTS

HEALDS

BEATER

WARP ROLLER

BREAST BEAM

CLOTH ROLLER

BUTTERFLY NUT

MARK II LOOM

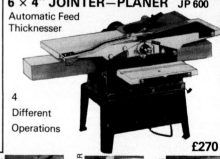

13

Showstoppers!

October's Woodworker Show had it all — the craft, the kit, the love of wood. Deputy editor John Hemsley, once an enthusiastic visitor, looks at it with equal enthusiasm from inside the fence

So what did you think of the Show? 'Same as usual, it's always the same,' muttered one tired veteran. Roy Sutton disagreed. 'There's something different about the Show this year,' he told me. 'Difficult to put a word to it . . .' He thought for a moment. 'Dynamic — that's what the Show is this year.'

Certainly the 1986 London Woodworker Show had a sparkle to it, as though somebody had applied another loving coat of wax polish to the patina. Maybe it was the crowds of people thronging the aisles — attendances up every day on last year — or their enthusiasm. Perhaps it was a slightly different mix in the trade stands that gave added interest — Black & Decker Professional, for instance, took their own stand for the first time. Or could it have been the extra dimension given by such exhibits as the wooden organ playing its tunes in the corner (tapes only, the works aren't complete yet); or the Tools for Self Reliance stand which struck a chord with many visitors who wanted their surplus tools to go to a Third World craftsman.

As well as the sparkle, there were all the familiar ingredients I associated with the Woodworker Show in the days before I was deputy editor, when I visited the Royal Horticultural Halls like any other enthusiastic reader. It always seemed to me like a song of praise to wood and to workmanship in wood; competition entries that pushed technical excellence to its furthest limits; a ready market of enticing tools and machinery; fascinating demonstrations; experts to seek advice from; and fellow enthusiasts to chat with over a coffee or beer before launching out to tour the exhibition again.

Above, familiar to Marquetry buffs and many others by now – Alan Townsend's eye-straining 'Bluebell Wood' won the gold and the World of Wood Cup. It also won the 1986 National Marquetry Exhibition overall prize . . .
left, C. Stott's natural-edged bowls in burr elm

Showstoppers!

Below, Richard Law's garden seat in iroko – a silver medal and very pretty; Stan Kimm's amazing idol shows an exploitation of sap- and heartwood little short of genius; A. C. Duncan's undercut bowls took gold and bronze, and Geoff King's charming 'Beeched whale' took gold in toys, plus the Richard Blizzard Cup. **Right**, James Gray's pitch pine lectern went gold, and we liked O. Eccleston's rugby boot; the tall side table was worth silver for W. Schilling

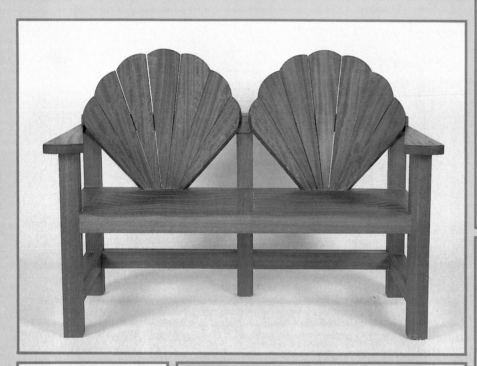

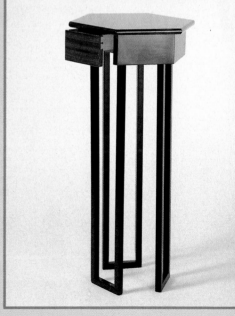

Top, Kevin Jakeway's elm desk got a Cabinetmaking gold and the Robbins Rose Bowl, and Eric Horne's marquetry alphabet monogram boggled a few minds. **Above**, nice lines for D. Russell's Japanese-style hi-fi cabinet, and a deserved Young Professionals' gold for Keith Stephenson's magnificent tool chest. **Below**, Jamie Linnwood's xylophone was well worth gold, as was Rod Smith's 'Fly fishing'

CONTINUED OVERLEAF

18

Showstoppers

It was all there at the 1986 Show, though being behind the Guild desk for much of the time gave me a rather myopic vision. I was keenly aware of the huge amount of interest aroused by the Guild of Woodworkers' London Gallery exhibits, especially the little collector's cabinet in rosewood, padauk and maple, by Waring Robinson. Keep your eyes out for a full feature on that one.

Over on the competition stands, the crowd pullers were principally the marquetry and carvings. Just why these are so popular intrigued me. Surely they are activities of a minority of woodworkers? One perceptive woman pointed out they had a double appeal; as well as being technical wonders, they form pretty pictures or shapes as a feast for the eyes. They also, of course, don't need vast amounts of expensive equipment or space.

In cabinetmaking, Kevin Jakeway's desk in elm was a deserving winner, but I must also mention Wing Commander Landell's delicious little serpentine-fronted chest with its inlaid pull-out shelf. Jamie Linwood's spectacular xylophone uses rosewood, birch, teak and bamboo — he didn't bring the mallets, perhaps advisedly! Stan Kimm's carved idol in yew showed a quite uncanny eye for the relationship between heartwood and sapwood; this piece showed just how difficult a judge's job is, for there's no doubting Stan's technical excellence and indeed the strength of his inspiration. Perhaps it didn't win a prize because it just wasn't to personal taste. Mr. A. Duncan's powder/jewellery bowls in sycamore and ebony are a delicate delight — he took gold and silver; Rod Smith's mastery of carved wildlife took him to his third gold in three years for 'Fly fishing'. We also liked Richard Law's iroko garden seat very much, though perhaps he could have cleaned the Cascamite up a bit neater.

Among the trade exhibitors the best volume business was done by a small stand selling, believe it or not, frogs on logs (little ceramic frogs on varnished slices of wood); at only 50p for a single frog, this was pocket-money material, and Artistic Woodturning sold literally thousands of them. The stand sold out each day, and every evening Sandra Pocock went home to glue and varnish more frogs till 1.30 am! The frogs were a brand new line for the firm, from Middlestoke, Rochester, who exhibit at craft fairs and county shows in the South-east. 'The Woodworker Show is the most successful for us,' said Sandra, waving at a stand almost denuded of the little knick-knacks.

● **Top right**, *Neil Pritchett's arch-top jazz guitar won gold, and W. Brimblecombe's maple and walnut stick the Theo Fossel trophy.* **Middle,** *Waring Robinson's amazaque occasional table and C. Smith's 'Zodiac clock';* **bottom,** *the incredible keyless fair organ by A. Aubrey and D. Frankham*

continued

Showstoppers

Missing from the Show this year was the familiar Myland stand, cancelled at the last moment because of illness. But there were plenty of newcomers, including Fercell Engineering who make dust-extraction equipment. Managing director Malcolm Fletcher told me his company recognised that amateur woodworkers using machines were becoming more interested in health and safety. They have developed a specific machine for this market, dubbed 'The Fly', a wall-hung ¾hp system for about £200; he sold 19 in the first two days. The wood-burning stoves on the stand (they burn shavings as well as offcuts, but not sanding dust) had aroused considerable interest but few takers. Visitors looked at the price, £199+VAT, and said they would make one themselves. Mr. Fletcher, who knows what goes into designing and making the stoves, offered a free set of plastic eyebrows to anyone who made one . . .

● *David Bailey won a gold woodturning medal for his set of three natural-edged poplar bowls. Poplar? They got a gold didn't they?*

Crownall Systems were also new to the Show, with the Italian MAGOmagh power tool system, based on a radial-arm saw. It comes in a cabinet you could put in the dining room, if you feel so inclined; you can buy the package — surface planer, lathe, jigsaw, sander, horizontal mortiser and spindle moulder — for £1800. 'We've had a fantastic response at the Show' said director Graham Hall. 'Nobody has complained about the price or the quality. But there's been a call for individual units, and we're going to look into supplying individual drive motors so people can use their existing equipment within the system.'

Also catching the eye was the Triton work centre for power tools, and its inventor, ex-journalist George Lewin, who flew from Australia to demonstrate it at the Show. The portable work table takes most makes of circular saw, router and jigsaw, and they claim it's more accurate than any similar table. On a 450mm crosscut, says George, you get an accuracy of ±1mm, using an average saw and blade, and with a router ±0.5mm. George designed it after he found he couldn't get accurate enough cuts with a hand-held circular saw, launched it in 1976 on an Australian TV inventor's pro-

gramme, and has sold 75,000 worldwide. Price in Britain for the basic unit is £165+VAT.

Near Triton was Black & Decker Professional, demonstrating Elu and DeWalt, and showing the full range of Black & Decker cordless machines. Product manager John Costello said the stand was an experiment to support their dealers in a different way; previously the company has not had a stand of its own, but has supported dealers exhibiting there. 'We've been very busy,' he told me, 'we've talked ourselves hoarse. We've had a very favourable response from visitors. What's been particularly encouraging is that people have been asking about our woodwork products, not about grass-cutters.' The Elu drills were shown for the first time at the Show, and visitors could also see the new Elu vacuum extractor — pretty, but very serious — and the power-tool table for the new Workmate.

Power-tool tables were a bit of a feature of the Show; Dunlop were also putting out their new Powerbase, and were generous enough to give three away in the prize draw on our own *Woodworker* stand.

● *Above left, David Booth's miniature hoop-back Windsor went gold; far left, Steve Turner of A-Z Tools pulls lucky Sears Craftsman radial-arm winner G. N. Sillman out of the box; left, Dunlop men Bill Shepherd (left) and Paul Edelston do the same for Peter Hunt, R. Marlow, and K. Dixom, all one Powerbase workstation the richer*

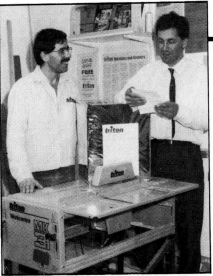

● *J. Grayson has won a Triton, inventor George Lewin is happy to hear; editor Aidan Walker is doing the spiel*

Tools for Self Reliance, also at the Show for the first time, were overwhelmed with visitors. National chairperson Jan Hoogendyk, who was on the stand every day, said they had had more than 2000 tools handed in, and scores of people had said they wanted to get involved with local groups, particularly to help with refurbishing the unwanted tools before they go abroad. 'I've been really surprised at the response. At one stage I was frightened at the amount of tools

A carver's tail

Rod Smith's beautiful wildlife carving 'Fly fishing' won the gold medal in the relief carving category, plus the Woodworker Challenge Cup; it's the third year running Rod has got a gold. Here's what he says:

'This is a one-man vote of thanks to *Woodworker* and the **Woodworker Show**, and in particular to the Woodcarving competition. If the competitions hadn't existed, my work would never have reached the standard that enabled me to take the Woodworker Challenge Cup for woodcarving at the 1986 London show.

In 1981 I entered my first and only carving, so I could compare my effort with the work of proper woodcarvers, and try to assess its quality. I had no idea I was entering the biggest, best, and only truly National Carving Competition; I also didn't realise the other advantages. Real experts would examine and assess my work; I had all the other entries to examine — and believe me I do, learning something from everything — and, of course, there is the possibility of actually winning, which gives the spur to use knowledge gained.

I won't be entering the Show competitions again; I have my 'qualifications'. I spoke to three carvers who said they wouldn't enter because their work wasn't good enough; my advice is, enter anyway. If you feel you've made a Charlie of yourself one year, you'll make doubly sure you don't do it again the next. I know — I've been there.

So thank you, *Woodworker* and the **Woodworker Show**; you've made me a woodcarver — and I like it!'

coming in; we're going to have to hire a van to get them to Southampton.' He was particularly please so many people knew of the organisation's work after reading October's *Woodworker* feature, and expects a knock-on effect as people who took leaflets get home and sort out unwanted tools.

With so many novelties, it was good to see some familiar products — especially the classic cast-iron Coronet lathes, their first year at the Show since the take-over by Record Marples.

Equally solid-looking, but in a different price bracket, were the Felder machines on the Sanlin stand. In pride of place was what director Norman Woods calls 'the Rolls Royce of combination machines' (£3500-6000), with a tilting-shaft spindle moulder. 'This has been one of our best attended exhibitions,' he said. 'We've had good business from the Show.'

AEG were even happier. 'This has been the most successful show we've attended in London,' said Jim Murray, their woodworking machines product manager. 'Our new products, including the Maxi universal, have created the interest we hoped they would, and the order books reflect that.' Helping on the stand were two visitors from France — M. Jean-Francois Boichon, export manager for the UK, and M. Patrick Sineux, ace AEG demonstrator.

In the enthusiasm stakes, nobody beat Roger Buse of Roger's of Hitchin. 'Superb,' was his one-word summing up. 'Sunday is usually a rather flat day, but it's been the busiest of the week for us.' He was also

● *Above, a quiet read in a corner; below, John Shepherd, upholstery lecturer from Manchester Central College, gets on with the job*

continued

Showstoppers

happy about the entries for the Young Professionals trophy that Roger's sponsors; 'The quality is very high,' he said. It doesn't indeed take a lot of expertise to judge that Keith Stephenson's magnificent cabinet-maker's tool chest in ash, with thuya burr veneered locking panels and rosewood inlay, is made in the true tradition of excellence. 21-year old Keith is setting up his own business and workshop in Cornwall, and made the chest as a 3-D advert in the solid — just to show what he can do.

I must confess I have a slightly sour note to strike about trade exhibitors. The majority of those demonstrating equipment paid good attention to safety, but there were those who didn't. I witnessed several examples of thoroughly unsafe practice — grooving with a circular saw, for example, with no jig, guard or even push-stick. Sales are important, and it may slow demonstrations down to refit guards, but what about the responsibility to sell safe use as well as the machine itself?

The colleges — Rycotewood, Buckinghamshire, Shrewsbury and Manchester — showed some inspiring examples of their work, and I particularly liked the bustle on the Manchester demonstration area. As one visitor remarked: 'After watching them work, I would happily give them my antiques to restore.'

Tradition was very much the theme of the demonstration stands, and the pole lathes operated by Stuart King and Mike Abbott were a hypnotic spectacle for crowds of visitors. Was it my ears, or did Stuart's country accent sound richer on Friday night's 'Six O'Clock Show', a live TV broadcast from the Pavilion? Jack Hill's display of Windsor chairmaking was also a crowd-puller, while many visitors were glad of the chance to chat with carver Maurice Lund, polisher Charles Cliffe, chair-caner Geoff Berry, lute-maker Zach Taylor and joiner *extraordinaire* Stan Thomas.

Of course, it was the visitors who made the Show come alive, queueing halfway round the building long before opening time, reluctant to leave at closing time. Gazing avidly at demonstrations, enviously at competition entries. Eagerly asking questions, incisively querying enthusiastic salesman's claims.

Then that final stroll round the hall — again — just in case something has been missed. It always has, of course, for the Woodworker Show is jammed full of interesting items. Never mind, there's always next year .... ■

NEXT YEAR

Bristol Woodworker Show, Bristol Exhibition Centre, 15-17 May
London Woodworker Show, Alexandra Pavilion, London N22, 22-25 October

Make sure your competition entries are there for the world to see!

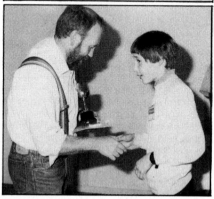

● *Top left*, lute maker and musician *Zach Taylor had his amplifier with him; left, Roger Buse shakes the hand of under-16s winner Neil Bateson, who got a gold – and a handsome gift from Roger's – for his three-legged chair; and* **above**, *Stuart (uncrowned) King of the bodgers is pretty well crowned after all!*

It was good to see so many people in wheelchairs at Alexandra Pavilion. 'Access is very good here,' said Andrew Lisicki, who was touring the Show in his battery-powered chair. 'It's good having wide aisles and it all being on one level. Parking is easy, and there are disabled toilets.'

Andrew, who lives nearby in Muswell Hill, and has been a regular visitor to the Show for years, came along on the Friday when it was less crowded so he could get close to the stands and demonstrations. He enjoyed himself so much that he came back again on the Sunday.

The increased availability of power tools at reasonable prices has opened up woodwork as a pursuit for many disabled people. Andrew pointed out that sitting in a wheelchair restricts the range of movement, and makes it impossible, for instance, to get the long sweeps you need in planing timber; so inexpensive power planers are a boon.

Even machinery has its snags, however. Andrew says many machines are made to be used at standing height, and he had difficulty finding a bandsaw without a built-in stand. With workbenches it's usually impossible to get a wheelchair underneath; he uses a Black & Decker Workmate at its low level, with extra boards placed on top to extend its small surface area.

A final word on the Woodworker Show from Andrew. 'Those of us in wheelchairs do have difficulty in seeing a demonstration when a stand is crowded. I wonder if exhibitors and demonstrators could keep an eye out for people who are low down and encourage them to squeeze through to the front?'

Competition winners

Cabinetmaking Robbins Rose Bowl & Gold Medal: Kevin Jakeway, elm writing desk
Figure carving Gold Medal: Alan Fearn, 'The Knifegrinder'
Relief Carving Woodworker Challenge Cup & Gold Medal: Rod Smith, 'Fly fishing'
Woodturning Gold Medal: A. Duncan, powder/jewellery box. Woodworker Challenge Cup & Gold Medal: David Bailey, three natural-edged poplar bowls. Gold Medal: James Gray, latticed lectern
Musical Instruments Gold Medal: Jamie Linwood, xylophone with carved frame. Gold Medal: Neil Pritchett, arch-top jazz guitar
Marquetry and Inlay The World of Wood Cup & Gold Medal: Alan Townsend, 'Blue Bell Wood'. Gold Medal: Eric Horne, 'Homeward Bound'
Toys Richard Blizzard Cup & Gold Medal: Geoff King, 'Beeched Whale'
Miniatures Stuart King Award & Gold Medal: David Booth, hoop-back Windsor armchair
Model Horse-Drawn Vehicles John Thompson Trophy & Gold Medal: R. Bates, Hertfordshire Tip Cart
Juniors under 16 £100 Roger's voucher & Gold Medal: Neil Bateson, hall chair with three legs
Juniors under 19 Gold Medal: Craig Anderson, jewel box in wenge
Long-case clocks Woodworker Challenge Cup & Gold Medal: Thor Eriksen, long-case clock
Bracket and Mantle Clocks Gold Medal: Bill Watts, 'Spirit of Tompion'
Carpentry and Joinery Woodworker Challenge Cup & Gold Medal: David Jackson, tray
Young Professionals Roger's of Hitchin Award & Gold Medal: Keith Stephenson, cabinetmaker's toolchest
Ashley Iles Carving Competition First Neville Wilson, 'The Builders'
Walking Stick Competition Theo Fossel Trophy: W. Brimblecombe, walking stick in Canadian maple and American walnut

23

Style plus one

It may be a surprise, but the Woodworker Show isn't the only interesting exhibition of the autumn. We saw and heard some interesting things at Style for 87, carving a name for itself as the 'Designer Furniture' Show, and got a look at some other outrageous work. Love it or hate it, they say, you can't ignore it . . .

● **Top**, *Paul Litton's A.L. armchair on the British Display area;* **above**, *Mark Hill of Trent Poly showed this roll-up chair.* **Above right**, *Luke Hughes and Juckes get the Design ticket for the solid oak Ovolo range*

We met the first Style show in '84, when it was called Style '84. '85 got missed out somewhere — last year's was called Style '86, for the very good reason it's in the autumn and they wanted to put a 'preview tag' on it. At Style '87, in Earl's Court last October, we saw that the Show is moving fast from strength to strength.

Flushed from the success and acclaim that British furniture design received at Milan — they actually noticed us there in '86 — members of the growingly identifiable breed of 'designer/maker' displayed yet more work, yet more quality, more imagination, and even the beginnings of a business head. Whatever next?

Last year's Style also launched the Independent Designers' Federation (*WW/Feb* 86), again there in force, and was memorable for the rousing challenge from its likeable bullish mastermind Bill Borland to the established furniture industry. Standing in the IDF's attractive (but comparatively small) corner of the Show, he was waving a hand at the acres of mass producers outside and insisting that they didn't know what was happening — here (where he was) was where it was going on. Maybe he was right.

The organiser of Style, Keith Harradine of Philbeach Events, also does the London International Furniture Show, and he is quite clearly behind British furniture designers and makers with a whole heart. At the opening press conference, he described the new consumer that people are beginning to discover; the 20-40-year old with an 'as it were, sharp, laid-back lifestyle', who wants his or her surroundings to be similarly 'with it'. No doubt of it, the market for quality 'designer furniture', whether batch-, mass-produced, or even one-off, is growing; and all power to Style, not only for recognising

it and making a noise about it (which helps to create it), but also for giving it its own special show next year. Style for '88 will be a 'designer show', held in London over 'Designers Saturday' 1987 (10 October, that means), and the volume manufacturers will get their own show too. Fine, but will the separation develop or hinder communication between the bright sparks and the people with production resources?

Another fact of the matter is that those production tie-ups are already happening. Who knows, we might ultimately get mass-produced furniture of imagination, craftsmanship and quality, though of course it's doubtful that the 'trendy' market is really a mass one. Our own Luke Hughes, *Woodworker* contributor and (trendy) Covent Garden cabinetmaker, has just landed the Design Council ticket for his Ovolo range of solid oak (yes, solid, apart from the odd bit of veneered ply, right down to the dowel-pivot hinges) bedroom furniture, which is being made by Juckes, an old-established Birmingham firm. 'A breakthrough,' says the Design Council selection committee, 'in better quality bedroom furniture, providing high design and quality at reasonable prices.' Is it eat-your-heart-out time, MFI? Not yet, but there's hope.

John Barden of the Design Council was also at the conference, saying his piece. The job, as he understood it, is to 'persuade the public to take a wider view in furniture purchase.' Just what Martin Grierson said in last month's *Woodworker*, and just what we say whenever we get the chance — why deprive the public of quality? Why raise the eyebrows and drop the portcullis when £3000 or even £1000 for a table is mentioned — fine furniture that will last for generations, appreciating in value, while £8000 is an ordinary price for a comparatively ordinary (and fast-depreciating) car? Why shouldn't furniture confer the same social status that goes with your new Ford?

But so much is down to the conservatism of the retailers, says Luke Hughes. They launched the Ovolo range at G-MEX, August's Manchester furniture trade show that's open to the public in the second week, and the poor public was all over it. Where can we get it, they wanted to know. Sorry, can't get any northern retailers interested. John Barden was in tentative agreement, but had a word to say on the retailers' side — it's very difficult for them to make significant changes year on year in such a cut-throat market. Yes, the mass market is indeed cut-throat — but are we talking about mass markets?

The furniture Colleges were well represented at Style — Ravensbourne got the Design and Industry Association/Gordon Russell Award for their stand overall — and

Peter Vickers from Trent Polytechnic, at Earl's Court to speak at one of the design seminars, hit the right note. 'The fact is that everyone blames everyone else.' The retailers, apparently, come in for a lot of stick from the makers and the designers, but they're caught in the middle, and themselves complain about manufacturing prices and distribution; the manufacturers, in turn, have got little time for the young blades with bright ideas who don't know the first thing about the economics and systems of production.

It all boils down, he went on to say, to communication between the different communities involved in designing, making selling and buying furniture. Don't forget the retail buyer — where does the public get a chance to say what it wants? This is why Style has got itself in the right position with the right idea — put everyone together and let them talk it out. Good is bound to come, but it's bound to take a time.

The Norwegian contingent meanwhile, apparently happy in a more design-oriented country with a newly burgeoning reputation for innovation and quality, played about on their foam rubber and metal trees … fun for sure, but is it furniture? ∎

Lunar movements David Swift was inspired by church carvings to create imaginary winged figures — this is one of them, recently at the Crafts Council Gallery

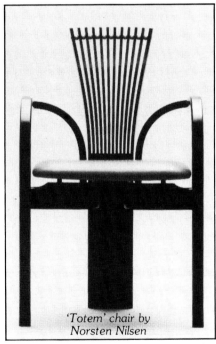

'Totem' chair by Norsten Nilsen

'Chairy tree' – is it really a seat? Peter Opsvik is responsible

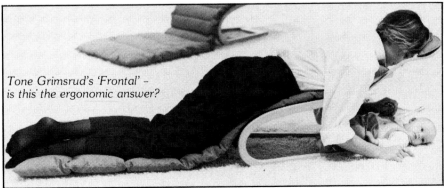

Tone Grimsrud's 'Frontal' – is this the ergonomic answer?

● *Clive Green's 'All Red' shop display cabinet is fanciful to a degree, but superbly made in flat-finished MDF*

Black is beautiful

Photos Keith Curtis

● *A cabinet to compliment any display – as much at home with Ming porcelain as motorcycle parts!*

Keith Krause's magnificent black display cabinet was one of the most talked-about pieces of recent student Shows. It's not such an ambitious project as it looks, he contends

Towards the end of my first year of the Furniture Production/Fine craft course at Bucks College in High Wycombe, I was given a brief for a small wall-hanging cabinet of specific dimensions. I designed the cabinet, but didn't actually make it. During that summer holiday I decided to use the ideas from the wall cabinet in a second-year project, and this display cabinet is the result.

Design

I have always been fascinated by glass in furniture, and the slightly less common wood finishes such as gloss black. I thought a display cabinet was the ideal project in which to combine these two attractive themes.

I decided to make the cabinet in beech, because of its strength and lack of prominent grain. Its strength enabled me to use relatively small sections, to give maximum vision into the interior, and I also thought all the sections should be chamfered to complement the bevel on the 6mm glass in the doors and side frames.

Going for the smooth black gloss pointed me towards as little decoration on the cabinet as possible. All the joints are flush, so the lacquer goes straight over them in a continuous plane. The cornice and the top of the base have a very simple profile curve, which I hoped would give interesting light reflections.

I decided to fit a fluorescent tube inside, which would illuminate the objects displayed without lighting the cabinet itself. The inside surfaces are finished in matt black to minimise reflections.

Time spent on the design stage is absolutely invaluable, and it's always a good idea to make models, since drawings can give an impression quite different from the appearance of three-dimensioned reality. But I tend to leave things till the last minute, so I didn't have time for model making or experiments. I was lucky this time, and things worked out satisfactorily.

The cabinet is really quite a simple design, a top section mounted on a base stand. The top section has three glazed doors, the centre one of which is hinged to the right-hand one; when you open them a pin on top of the centre one slides along a groove in the underside of the cornice, so the two fold together, adjoining edges outwards. I had never made doors with this type of movement before, and I was given a great deal of help by my design lecturer. The method of opening we worked out seems to operate very well.

I drew a set of full-size working drawings and had these printed, then worked from the print, which let me keep the originals in good condition for when I make another cabinet! I have scaled the drawings down for the article, but kept the same system of superimposing the end and front elevations on each other (fig. 1). This means the drawing can be done in one go, and it also keeps it to a reasonable size. There are breaks in the legs, the height of the top and the sectional plan to keep everything on the drawing board, but if you work things out, all the information is there. If I hadn't superimposed and broken it up, I would have ended up with four different and very big drawings — very difficult to work from.

The main drawing (fig. 1) looks complicated at first sight, but it is really quite simple. Possibly one confusing thing is that I have drawn a front sectional elevation on the right, showing only the top of the cabinet. I felt that if I included the legs I would end up with a jumble of straight lines, making it hard for anyone other than myself to read. I didn't need a section of the stand, as all the measurements can be taken from the elevations.

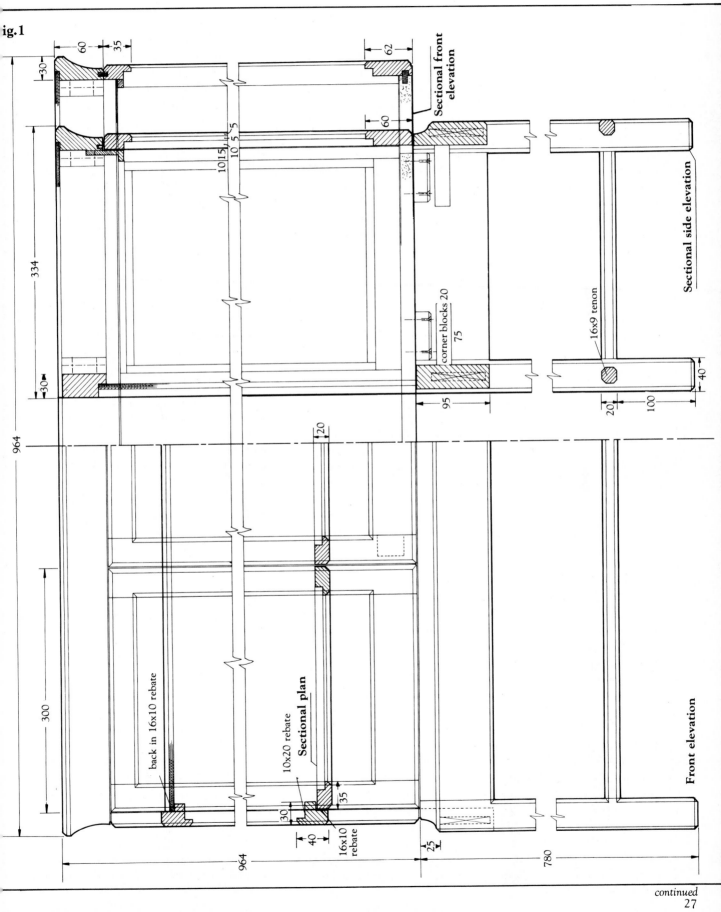

Fig.1

Sectional front elevation

Sectional side elevation

corner blocks 20

16x9 tenon

back in 16x10 rebate

10x20 rebate

Sectional plan

16x10 rebate

Front elevation

continued
27

Black is beautiful

CONSTRUCTION
Doors and side frames

I began by making the doors and the side frames — conventional mortise-and-tenon construction (figs 2, 3). I did the rebates on a spindle moulder, but they could quite easily be done with a router. I used the single-ended tenoner for the rails, reckoning there was little point in labouring over 20 tenons when there was a tenoner there to be used. Had there been any uncertainty about my ability to cut good mortises and tenons, I'm sure my cabinetmaking lecturer would have insisted on hand work!

The five pieces of glass are identical — not a matter of three of one size and two of another — and since the shoulder length for the rails of the side frames and doors are the same, only one setting up of the tenoner did the whole job.

I cut the chamfers after the doors were assembled, with the router and a 45° chamfer cutter, finishing the internal corners by hand. I would have liked to buy a chamfer cutter with a bearing guide, but they're expensive so I bought one with a fixed guide pin. The pin tended to burn the beech, so I had a close look and found its poor finish was causing a lot of friction. I polished the pin with a piece of 1200-grit silicon carbide paper, holding a length of paper against the pin with the router running. This way I could keep my fingers away from the cutter. It works, but take care if you do it not to let the paper come into contact with the cutting edge; you can blunt the edge, or the cutter can grab the paper and maybe your fingers.

Top and bottom

The next thing was to mould the cornice. I did it on a spindle moulder, but it's a very simple moulding which could quite easily be done by hand. Remember, though, the

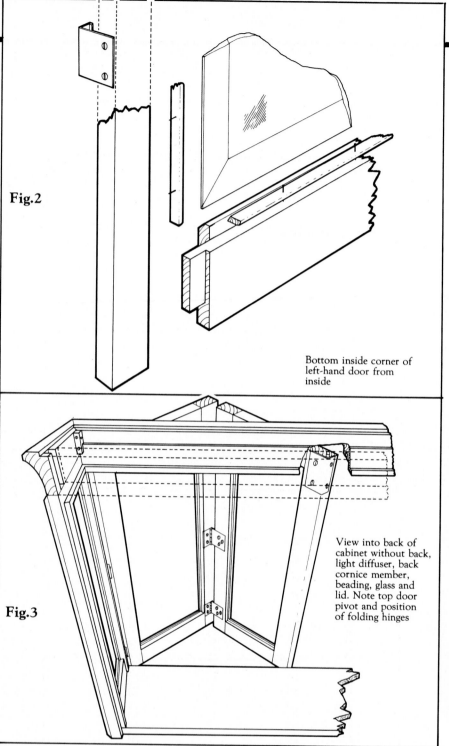

Fig.2

Bottom inside corner of left-hand door from inside

Fig.3

View into back of cabinet without back, light diffuser, back cornice member, beading, glass and lid. Note top door pivot and position of folding hinges

● Corner detail shows superb finish, cove moulding and bevel theme

black lacquered finish would show any imperfections, so take care to make sure the moulding is dead regular. I made the cornice up as a frame before I attached the sides — cornice front mitred, the back mortised and tenoned. All four corners were strengthened with screwed and glued blocks (fig. 4). The cornice and side frames are fixed to each other with loose tongues, the grooves for which I cut with the router.

The 'floor' of the cabinet is made from 18mm chipboard lipped and veneered in beech. This was fixed to the side frames with loose tongues, and assembled at the same time as the cornice. Assembly was quite simple: two sash-cramps for the bottom and two for each side. I used urea-formaldehyde glue for all the framing and assembly work.

The stand

I cut the back to size and fitted it to make sure the cabinet itself was stable, then turned my attention to the base. All the joints are mortise-and-tenoned; I made the front and back frames first, then joined them with the side rails. All the inside chamfering had to be done before assembly with the router, because it would be difficult, if not impossible, to do afterwards. I moulded the top rails of the base on the spindle moulder, then matched in the tops of the legs with moulding planes after assembly (fig. 5).

I glued a strip to the inside of the top front rail of the base to fill any gap between the top front rail and the floor of the cabinet which might be seen when the doors were

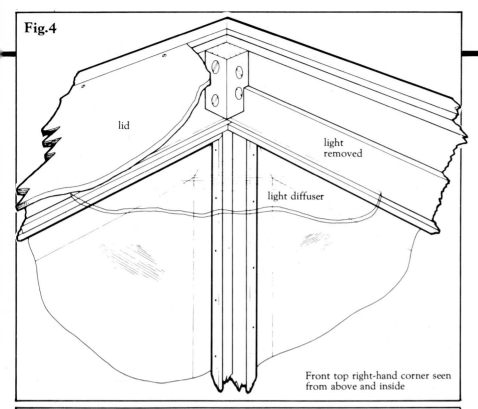

Fig.4

lid

light removed

light diffuser

Front top right-hand corner seen from above and inside

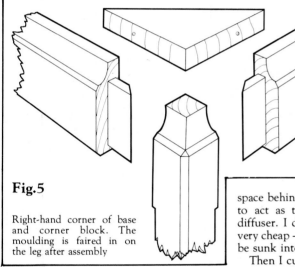

Fig.5

Right-hand corner of base and corner block. The moulding is faired in on the leg after assembly

open. I drilled and countersunk holes through this strip, to screw up through it and fix the top section to the base; three table-stretcher plates hold things together at the back.

Fitting and fixing

Back to the top section. I had cut a groove in the underside of the front cornice piece before assembly, and now I epoxy-resin glued a piece of nylon tracking into it, running from the right-hand side of the left-hand door to about 120mm from the right-hand end of the cornice. If the groove is any further to the right, it will let the doors open too far, making them vulnerable to breakage. As it is, if the doors are accidentally knocked from the right when they're open, they'll simply slide shut. If the groove let them open any further, they could fold and wrench the butts out of the side-frame stile. I also glued a shield to the front cornice member (fig. 4) to increase the

space behind the cornice for the light, and to act as the front bearer for the light diffuser. I drilled a hole for a very small, very cheap — and very reliable — switch to be sunk into the back cornice member.

Then I cut a piece of 6mm ply to fit the cornice and act as the 'lid'. I decided to hold it there with countersunk screws, which can't be seen at all from eye level, and they can easily be removed for replacement of the light tube. The light is simply screwed inside the front cornice moulding.

Then came the fitting of the doors (fig. 3). The right- and left-hand doors are hung with three brass butts each, and the centre door is hung to the right-hand one with three brass back-flap hinges. I had to fit these so the pins were as far into the right-hand door as possible. The flaps of the hinges I used were too big, so I had to cut some off to fit neatly on the door stile. You have to set the hinges so far off-centre to enable the doors to open and close smoothly. Because the right-hand door is pivoted from the front right-hand corner (with the butts) and the centre door is pivoted from the left-hand back corner (with the pin in the tracking) the doors are effectively different sizes, the right-hand one the larger. Setting the flap hinges off-centre brings the centre door to the same

effective size as the right-hand door. If the hinges weren't off-centre, the centre door would open to more than 90° to the cabinet, and wouldn't close easily if pushed from the right. Ideally, you want the doors positioned so that when they're open, all you have to do is gently push the right-hand door and the centre one will slide along the tracking and close.

I made the pin arrangement on top of the centre door myself. A brass pin fits in the tracking, set into a hole in the stile with a small spring set below it. A brass plate is fitted round the corner of the door to reinforce the pin, which lies against it. If you need to take the centre door off its track, the pin is simply pushed down into the hole against the spring and you can release the door. I used small cylindrical mortise-type magnetic catches on the left-hand and right-hand doors.

Finishing

Needless to say, the whole cabinet had to be meticulously cleaned up. The gloss black lacquer finish would accentuate any defect.

I stained everything with spirit-based black stain, very important if the cabinet got chipped, because the white timber would stick out like a sore thumb. For financial reasons, I had to make do with pre-catalysed matt black lacquer on its own to start with. Pre-cat lacquer doesn't fill the timber in the same way as sanding sealer, and it's extremely monotonous to rub down because it continually clogs the paper. I sprayed several coats until the surface was full and flat, then masked the inside, which was to remain matt. I mixed up some matt black with a melamine gloss lacquer, and gave the door-fronts and sides, and the outside of the cabinet and base, a generous coating. Denibbing and a general checkover was followed by a generous coating of melamine lacquer on its own, to re-establish a high gloss finish, and half an hour later I did all the gloss surfaces with 'pull-over'. Once the whole thing was fully dry, I went to the painstaking job of burnishing with metal polish, which I found very effective. The lacquer must be fully hardened before burnishing. Then I washed the whole job down with detergent and water to get rid of any metal polish residue, and waxed it with car polish.

Next came the fitting; the glass went into the doors and side frames, held in with beading (fig. 2). I fit the doors to the cabinet, and fit and wired the light. The wire goes out through a hole in the back cornice member after you have fixed it to the cabinet. Then the lid went on, and I put the back in and finished it.

If you can get timber to the correct sizes, I see no reason why the cabinet can't be made without machinery. Apart from the moulding, which can be done with moulding planes, the versatile router should deal with the machining. ∎

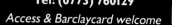

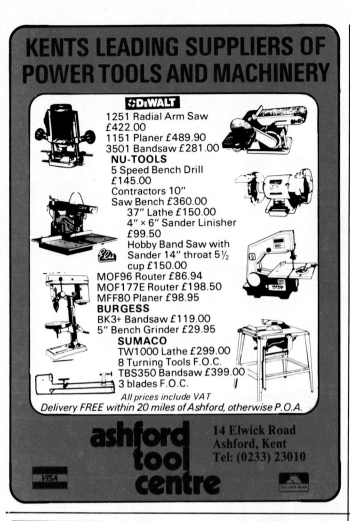

31

You only need two hands with a MAXi 26

COME AND SEE US ON STAND 286 PRACTICAL WOODWORKING EXHIBITION

Just look at the cost of some woodworking machines and what you get for your money – not to mention the size!

CAPACITY, COMPACTNESS, COST and CONFIDENCE come together in the universal Maxi 26 – the ideal woodworking machine for the light professional and the keen hobbyist.

Look at the CAPACITY. Six functions – sawing, thicknessing, tenoning, planing, moulding and mortising – all effortless, with flexibility, precision and safety, and driven by a powerful and reliable 2 HP motor.

Look at its COMPACT design. The Maxi 26 is easily moved, even in the smallest of workshops.

Look at the COST. Buy a Maxi 26 and you still get change from £1350 (plus VAT, of course).

Look at the COMPETITION – and you **must** come back to the Maxi 26.

You can have every CONFIDENCE in the Maxi 26 – in its performance, and because it comes fully guaranteed for 2 years. .

Designed and built to the highest standards, the Maxi 26 is the best value woodworking machine available today.

FULL 6 FUNCTIONS	
SAWING 90mm depth of cut, edging, mitre-cuts, panel cuts, 45° angle cutting	✓
PLANING On edge or flat, 260mm width of cut. Easy machining of any woods.	✓
THICKNESSING Up to 150mm capacity, depth of cut adjustable 0-4mm, automatic feed.	✓
MORTISING Deep, with both movements controlled by a single lever. Lateral and depth.	✓
MOULDING Moulding, rebates, grooving and all shaping tasks to a professional standard, 30mm diameter spindle shaft.	✓
TENONING Bearing mounted carriage 0-45° adjustable fence for precision square or angular cuts.	✓

AEG (UK) Limited
217 Bath Road, Slough, Berkshire SL1 4AW
Telephone: Slough (0753) 872101

AEG

Letters

Turned on

I WOULD LIKE TO say what a wonderful time my son and I had on Oliver Plant's Craft Woodturning course, advertised in *Woodworker*.

In our two days we made a tool-handle, cheese-knife, table-lamp, screw-clamp and a cotton-reel stand. This amounted to 20 separate turning tasks apart from the use of a screw-cutting thread, drilling and band-saw work. The instruction covered safety, turning between centres, proper use of tools, long-hole boring, design and decoration, face-plate turning and much more. Oliver's skill and enthusiasm and ability to share his knowledge was enormous — it was on his advice that my wife attended, and thoroughly enjoyed, a lace-making course at The English Lace School, in Honiton, whilst we got on with our turning course.

We all shared good, happy company and were delighted with what we made; there was no doubt about value for money. It was a lovely summer holiday and we've already booked up for next year!

The Joneses, Kidderminster

A dowel in time

I'D HAD TO GLUE two bits of ¼in half-round beading together to mount one of my carved foxes on its rosewood base — no dowels to hand. Perhaps not surprisingly, the makeshift dowel broke as I was twisting it into the base — so November's *Woodworker*, with its free dowels on the cover, couldn't have been more timely and more welcome. Thanks, *Woodworker* — I'm sure you'll get thousands of letters of thanks.

Vera Feldman, Birmingham
Not exactly thousands . . .

Disgusted of Chalfont

I'VE BEEN READING your magazine for 20 years, and think it has improved enormously in the past few months.

But I was surprised and hurt that you printed an article extolling sadism to saplings (*Magic wand, WW/Oct*). I had thought you were gentlemen, with your sincere approach to conservation. Have you had a brainstorm recently? You must realise that plants have feelings too. How would you like to be wrenched out of the soil at two years old, your trunk secateured at the waist, then buried alive? Worse still is the Chinese torture of twisting rope around the infant stem, restricting the natural circulation to stunt growth and produce abnormal mutations. I hope someone who loves plants will give Mr Theo Fossel a touch of his own medicine.

(Ms) Avelana Corullus, Chalfont St Giles

Rusting continued

THE FIRST PART of the 'Question Box' answer in October's *Woodworker* on rusting tools, on a well insulated workshop, is good advice; but apart from the suggestion to use rust-inhibiting paper, the rest is quite archaic. Many years ago, the answer to a similar question was — 'Use dry oil'. Ever since I have found this the perfect solution. 'Dry oil' is made in spray form by James Briggs, Lion Works, Old Market Street, Manchester M9 3DL, and it copes very well with all tools and equipment in an outside workshop.

N. Bumphrey, Norwich

Time for a change

I AM AN APPRENTICE carpenter and joiner and a regular subscriber to your usually excellent magazine, so I read about the forthcoming Woodworker Show with interest, and duly attended it.

On the whole there seemed a good variety of stands, demonstrations and videos which I found very educational. But the chauvinist attitude of many of the reps was very demoralising for me. Leaflets were being handed out — but to the men, and technical information was hard to obtain until you'd put up with initial reactions such as: 'What are you doing buying *Woodworker* — or is it for your boyfriend?'

Considering how many women are now involved in all aspects of the timber trade, it seems to me that next year's exhibitors could benefit mightily from a sexism aware-ness course. Times are changing, it's to be hoped, and I think it's also time that this kind of attitude should not be tolerated.

Nikki Greaves, London SE11

Screw-cutting

I WAS INTERESTED to read of Andrew King's screwcutting problem in 'Question Box' in October's *Woodworker*, and venture to suggest a die-box is not the only possible solution.

I recently needed to cut a screw shaft, which I did quite satisfactorily in beech, using an engineer's screw-cutting lathe. A blank was preturned to the required diameter and length, allowing a few inches extra at one end to grip in the three-jaw chuck. I mounted it in the lathe with the free end supported by the tailstock centre, then I fitted an old woodturning skew chisel to the tool-post with the point down to cut under the work, and fitted suitable gears to give the required pitch. The cut-ting action is a slicing one, and only one flank of the thread form can be cut at a time. The skew chisel is angled in the tool-post so the bevel on the cutting edge will follow the flank of the thread.

For the first cut, I positioned the chisel to begin at the tailstock end, and advanced it to the work to give a depth of cut dictated by the hardness of the timber. Then I started the lathe from the tailstock end, and engaged the feed-screw to make the first cut, stopping the machine at the end of the traverse. During all cutting operations the feed-screw nut must not be disengaged, as the continuity of the thread would be lost. Then I engaged reverse feed and took the cutter back to the starting point: and repeated the sequence until I got the required depth.

To cut the second flank of the thread I stopped the tool at the headstock end, re-adjusted it for angle and crown width, and repeated the cutting sequence, working this time from headstock. These operations result in a well incised vee being removed, which will give a strong usable thread.

The method worked well in beech, there's no reason why it shouldn't work in oak, particularly if the thread isn't required to any great accuracy.

P. E. Leedham, Uttoxeter

More spectacular safety

RECENT LETTERS ON EYE SAFETY (*WW/Oct*) and the problems of safety goggles prompted me to ask my optician about it; I was having new close-up glasses anyway, and he suggested paying an extra £9 to have the prescription made up in toughened glass. A small price to pay for comfort and protection.

Roy Benfield, Walton-on-Thames

How's that?

MIDDAY ON A FRIDAY I tightened the locking nut on my Stanley shoulder plane, there was a ping and half the curling iron flew to the other side of the workshop. The job came to an abrupt halt; my local tool stockist was out of spares — so I phoned the manufacturers, who had them in stock, ordered two, and settled down to wait. Saturday morning, bright and early, the postman arrived with a little parcel from Stanley. How's that for service?

G. L. Taylor, London EC1

34

Question box

Our panel of experts solve your woodworking problems

Minor repairs

Q *The time has come to replace the woodwork on my Morris Minor Traveller. Would you consider clear Douglas fir a wise substitution for the traditional but expensive ash? I realise it doesn't have the shockproof properties of ash but perhaps its durability would be a point in its favour.*

G. Arrowsmith, Gateshead

A Douglas fir would be entirely suitable as a replacement timber. Ash was traditionally used in coachwork, not only for its high shock resistance but also for the ease with which it could be bent into shape. In the Morris Minor, however, the curves around the wheel arches are not bent but bandsawn.

The natural desirability of Douglas fir could be enhanced by flooding the drainage holes, mortises, and other exposed endgrain with a wood preservative before assembling it all with an exterior grade glue. A penetrating organic solvent wood preservative such as Cuprinol Water Repellent Clear is suitable and you could apply it all over the wood surface before deciding upon the final finish. Such well-treated timber will then long outlast the less durable materials that comprise the chassis and wings — I speak from experience!

Michael White

● Michael White is a consultant on timber and a former Scientific Officer at the Forest Products Research Laboratory.

Have a cigar

Q *Can you tell me any special requirements for putting a humidor in a cigar box?*

A. Hinton, Larkfield, Kent

A You can make the box any size you like, but bear in mind that the larger the air space, the quicker the deterioration of the cigars. Consider how many cigars you want to store, how quickly they will be smoked, what size they are, and then make your assessment.

I make an inner lining to my boxes that has a pair of mouldings like a table rule-joint, which helps to minimise air-flow. But to make certain of an airtight seal, I use contact adhesive to stick a thin strip of white rubber draught-excluder (trimmed with a Stanley knife) into a rebate on the upper moulding. When the box is closed the rubber is compressed by the lower moulding. You can check for a proper seal by making the box — including the locks and hinges — with the bottom off. Turning the box upside down you can see whether or not the inner lining is properly in contact, and adjust accordingly before fixing the base.

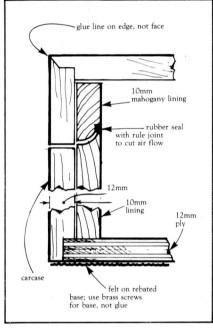

glue line on edge, not face

10mm mahogany lining

rubber seal with rule joint to cut air flow

12mm

10mm lining

12mm ply

carcase

felt on rebated base; use brass screws for base, not glue

You will also need a humidifier, which takes the form of a piece of pressed brass with a grill that holds a piece of absorbent material (it used to be asbestos but rules have changed). This must be easily removable, and is taken to a tap to be periodically topped up. You can get humidifiers from J. Shiner, 8 Windmill St, London W1 1PF.

Visit a ritzy tobacconist and ask to see some of the stock. Marvel at the prices (£300-£1500) and pinch the best idea that suits you.

Luke Hughes

● Luke Hughes is a professional cabinet-maker and contributor to *Woodworker*

Lime for church carvings

Q *I am making some lime carvings for churches, using 20x4x2in pieces edge-jointed. How can I be sure the wood (almost quarter-sawn) will not move in the damp conditions? What fillers, sealers, stains and finish should I use?*

S. Langin, Manchester

A I assume your panels have been made up of perfectly planed seasoned pieces and joined with a waterproof adhesive such as Cascamite.

There is a possibility the finished carvings will distort because of expansion and contraction of the separate pieces in the panel, which will have different profiles. This may cause the glued joints to open up. A possible solution would be to glue and screw a backing board or opposing strips behind the panels, if they are intended as wall-mounted reliefs.

Don't use filler before you begin carving. When you finish the carving work, however, it will be necessary to seal the wood. Lime is a beautiful carving wood with a natural 'buttery' colour — it would be a shame to stain it! The best finish would be to seal the entire panel after carving with a shellac sealer, followed by very fine sanding, dusting off and waxing with a hand-buffable finishing wax. The waxing should be repeated two or three times at intervals. In view of the potentially damp conditions, you might consider sealing the finished panels all over with diluted clear polyurethane varnish, applied in several thin coats and rubbed down between each coat.

A word of warning: you may find that unless the strips of lime have been carefully matched they will differ in colour after sealing, giving a striped effect to the panel. This will be particularly obvious if sections of heartwood and sapwood are next to each other in the built-up panel.

Eric Ingham

● Eric Ingham is a *Woodworker* contributor and teacher of carving.

Repairing a chess table

Q *I have been asked to repair the top of a chess table, which has white (sycamore?) and brown (mahogany, iroko?) blocks glued to a baseboard (animal glue), with an oak surround. It was made around 1940-50. It has dried out in the sun of a conservatory, the 1¼in squares now sitting with gaps of up to ¹⁄₁₆in between them. The endgrain gaps are smaller than the long-grain ones. How can I repair the table, altering/replacing as little as possible? If I use stopping, how can I prevent it cracking out? What's the best way of removing colour from the grain of the oak?*

A. Nichols, Billericay

A From your description and the aproximate date, I would think the two woods used for the squares are sycamore and mahogany.

I have assumed the squares aren't too thick, and suggest you lift the lot — black and white. Lay a damp cloth over the squares, and apply a domestic iron set at 'silk' or 'cool' until the steam softens the glue and the squares can be lifted and the old glue cleaned off. When they're dry, the pieces should then be very carefully squared up so that they are all exactly the same size (you will need to make the horizontal and vertical measurement equal to the smallest dimension you can find). At this stage you can re-stain the 'blacks' with a good oil stain such as Colron to the colour you want.

With the centre of the board free of squares you can now concentrate on the oak surround. Using finest grade wire wool and white spirit, gently clean the surface, working with the grain. Clean it off thoroughly with a cloth damped in white spirit and, when the wood is dry, it may be stained to the desired colour (possibly to match the 'black' squares).

Lay all the squares back dry into the original space, but tight up against one edge and one side. Measure the gap that now exists on the other edge and side. This will be *double* the width of a new border that you will need to cut to fit all round and fill up the gap left by the original shrinkage and your subsequent 'truing-up'. Mitre the corners for neatness. This wood should complement either the oak surround or the squares in colour and texture.

Assuming you have cut the new border exactly to size, this can now be laid — preferably with animal glue as it will be compatible with the original. Then re-lay the squares, again using animal glue. Be careful to ensure the correct sequence of black and white in each corner — there should be a black square in the left-hand corner of each player's side. Take great care to make sure they are all 'down' well; a damp cloth and domestic iron help again here. Lay a sheet of clean brown paper over the whole job, place a square of heavy plywood or something like it on top and clamp the whole package down.

After 48 hours, the job should be thoroughly dry and ready for fine sanding. Finish it with clear or white french polish and when this is thoroughly dry (allow a week in a normal room) finish it with hard wax.

If you do all this as suggested, the job should last for at least a hundred years!

David Ellis

● David Ellis is a professional restorer and teacher in Wiltshire.

Nifty hinge

Q I am looking into ways of making small boxes from 4-6mm thick solid woods, but have had a lot of difficulty getting the right hinges. I recently came across some modern professionally made boxes in which the hinge flap had been let into the edges of the carcase and lid, as shown in the drawing.

The hinges were fixed by a single brass pin in each flap, each one let into a slot which looked as if it had been cut by a miniature circular saw. The hinge flaps were no more than 1mm thick, a snug fit in the saw-slots.

Can you suggest how this was done and give me an idea of where to get the hinges and the saw?

J. R. Gentle, Norfolk

A The boxes you describe have the slots cut by a slitter saw, mounted either in a special machine or horizontally in an over-arm router. This set-up could be jigged up on a router table, but plunging the work on

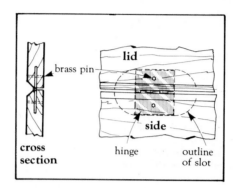

cross section — brass pin — lid — side — hinge — outline of slot

to the cutter isn't a safe practice, and I would only recommend it for the one-off, where caution tends to make one work more safely.

Oakden's of 86-89 Curtain Rd, London EC2, list three sizes of dipped brass 'Doll's House' butts which might suit your purpose.

The alternatives are: increase the box sides to 8-9mm thick and use 1in solid drawn brass butts; use lay-on fancy dipped brass hinges on the outside of the boxes — these are available from Hobby's, Knights Hill Sq, London SE27 0HH, or the Art Veneers Co., Ind. Est., Mildenhall, Suffolk IP28 7AY. Or you could copy Richard Windley's neat solution, which is to mount wooden hinges on the outside of the box. This offers design scope and would enable you to make them to suit the size of box. If you go for this solution, use a 'hard' wood like ebony or yew, with the hinge pin made from a brass escutcheon pin.

Peter Howlett

● Peter Howlett is a professional box-maker and *Woodworker* contributor.

What's the drill

Q I followed up a small ad in our local paper and came home with a small bench drill which, the vendor told me, had been untouched for many years. The drawing is a trace off a photo. It bears the name KEEN, and also M. C. Gooding, Croydon.

It seems to be in working order, but I suspect I am not using it properly. Turning the handle rotates the chuck and the horizontal 'flywheel' at the top, but I have to restrain the flywheel with my left hand to start a downward movement. I have tried adjusting the small thumbscrew under the flywheel, but without much success.

When I do get downward travel, it's rather faster than I really want. Perhaps the machine was designed for drilling metal rather than wood?

K. J. Down, Alton

A These small bench drilling machines were popular before the war. Most of them were imported from Germany, but there was one British make, the KEEN, made in Croydon. A 1936 catalogue lists them at 12s. 6d. The were described as having 'automatic feed', which may have

meant some sort of differential action to vary the speed of descent according to the load. I have spoken to two men who were familiar with them. One found that his small drills broke, but the other got on well with it, using drills about ¼ to ½in.

Unfortunately I haven't been able to find one to dismantle, so I don't know exactly what the mechanism was. It seems to have been based on two sets of threads which give a differing downward feed rate. Yours is probably gummed up with old oil, so you should give it a good wash out with paraffin, re-lubricate it, and try it out, with a ¼in drill, on a bit of brass, cast iron or mild steel. It was certainly intended for drilling metal, which requires lower speeds than wood. Once the mechanism is moving freely, the small thumbscrew under the 'flywheel' may well act as an adjustment. If the rate of feed is still too fast, the only thing to do will be to disconnect the ratchet or thread mechanism which actuates it.

Philip Walker

● Philip Walker is a founder member and former chairman of the Tools and Trades History Society.

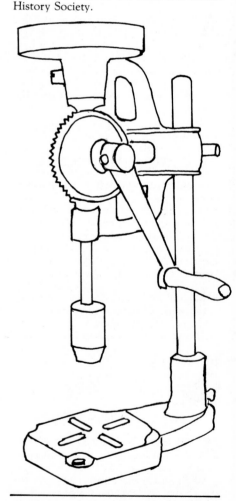

We welcome questions from readers, but it makes our lives easier if you can type them out, double-line spaced.

Only one Company offers such a range of Radial Arm Saws

More Experience
- Radial Arm Saw invented by Raymond E. DeWalt in 1922.
- No other manufacturer can match the experience that has earned DeWalt an envied reputation for quality, reliability, accuracy, versatility, safety and ease-of-use.

More Choice
- 20 different models mean both amateur and professional wood-workers can choose precisely the machine for their needs.
- The DeWalt Powershop series offers 4 different arm lengths

with 68mm max. cutting depth – from the convenient DW1201 Foldaway Powershop to the long reach DW1751 with 610mm crosscut and 880mm ripping capacity.

More Capacity
- For thicker materials, DeWalt machines with larger motors offer cutting depths of 93-125mm, crosscuts up to 1155mm and ripcuts up to 1505mm wide.
- Additionally a series of 8 double arm radials are available with automatic blade feed for large scale intensive operations.

More Sales
- More experience and more choice naturally means DeWalt has more dealers, and sells far more Radial Arm Saws than any other manufacturer.

More Details
- Your local woodworking machinery dealer will be pleased to assist you in selecting the right DeWalt machine for your needs.
- Any other details and literature are available from the address below.

DeWALT ®

POWERSHOP/RADIAL ARM SAWS

UK: DeWalt Woodworking Machines, Westpoint, The Grove, Slough, Berks SL1 1QQ. (0753) 74277
Australia: DeWalt Woodworking Machines. Maroondah Highway, Croydon, Victoria, Australia 3136.
New Zealand: DeWalt Woodworking Machines, 483 Great South Road, Penrose, Auckland 6, New Zealand.

Remember, the Guild of Woodworkers is an organisation to help all wood-workers get more out of the craft. See p39 for our current courses and local reps

---

If you work with wood you need

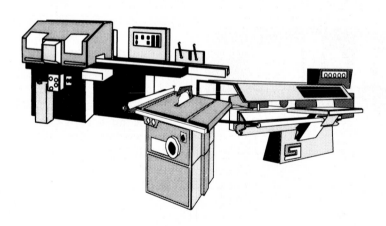

A
GUIDE TO
WOODWORKING
MACHINERY

for the smaller

BUSINESS

Write or phone for your free copy

Guild notes

Guild of WOODWORKERS

The Guild was set up by *Woodworker* to create a meeting ground for all those involved in working wood, whether professional, amateur, or enthusiastic beginner. Guild members get:

- Access to Guild courses and events
- Free publicity in *Woodworker*
- Specially arranged tool insurance at low rates
- 15% off Woodworker Show entry
- A free display area and meeting point at the Show
- 15% discount off *Woodworker* plans
- Inclusion in our register of members' skills and services

For details, please send an sae to the Guild of Woodworkers, 1 Golden Sq, London W1R 3AB.

GUILD COURSES

- **Only Guild members are eligible to go on these courses. You must book in advance, and we must have a cheque for the full cost of the course at the time of booking. If you cancel less than four weeks before the advertised date you will forfeit 50% of the cost, unless there are exceptional circumstances.**

Guild representatives — nationwide

Communication and sharing knowledge are the essence of the Guild. We have representatives throughout the UK waiting to hear from you (see the list below) — regular meetings, workshops, demonstrations and seminars are all possible if you take advantage of our network and get involved with your local group now! Collective experience and ideas can work wonders and, as they say, a problem shared . . .

So drop your rep a line, explain what you're interested in, how you'd like to contribute (workshop space, equipment or your valuable time) and any suggestions for developing Guild groups. The more members that get involved, the more everyone will benefit. If you're interested in becoming a local rep or starting a group write to: John Hemsley (Guild Administrator), *Woodworker*, 1 Golden Sq, London W1R 3AB.

Bedfordshire: John Greenwell, 1 Plumtree Lane, Leighton Buzzard
Cheshire: Ian Hosker, 1 Spring Ave, Little Sutton, South Wirral L66 3SH
G. M. Findlow, 12 Linnet Grove, Macclesfield, Cheshire
Cornwall: Mr Stoddern, 16 Woods Browning Est, Bodmin
Essex: Doug Woolgar, 49 Ascot Gdns, Hornchurch RM12 6ST
Herefordshire: Paul Smith, Dinmaur, Hope under Dinmore, Leominster HR6 0PP
Kent
East: Roy Sutton, 14 St George's Ave, Herne Bay
West: Bob Holman, Copley Dene, 8 Kippington Rd, Sevenoaks
London
South-east: M. J. Belcher, 30 Rusholme Grove, SE19 1HY
Merseyside
Central: Allan Hird, 25 Podium Rd, Liverpool L13
North: H. H. Bridge, 2 Ashley Rd, Southport PR9 0RB
Middlesex: Mike Cripps, 41 The Greenway, Ickenham UB10 8LS
Midlands
West: Bill Ferguson, 40 Quinton Lane, Quinton, Birmingham B32 2TS

Norfolk: Steven Hurrell, 70 Decoy Cottages, Woodbastwick
Northamptonshire: A. J. A. Jennings, 55 High St, Braunston, Daventry
Nottingham: B. Hamer, Westbridgeford (Nottingham 815046)
Suffolk: S. Lloyd Jones, Varne, New St, Stradbroke, Eye
Surrey
North: George Netley, 19 Manor Way, Purley
West: Morrison Thomas, 3 Oak Tree Close, Knap Hill, Woking GU21 2SA
Sussex
East: P. D. Wetherill, 'Glasfryn', Colebrook Rd, Southwick, Brighton BN4 4AL
C. J. Allen, 3 Oakhurst Close, Hastings TN34 2SE
West: Clive Green, The Lychgate, 20 Broadmark Lane, Rustington, BN16 2HJ
Wiltshire: David Ellis, Restorations Unlimited, Pinkney Park, Malmesbury
Yorkshire
South: Ken Davies, 27 Ennis Crescent, Intake, Doncaster DN2 5LL
Michael Judge, 8 Haden St, Sheffield S6 4LB
Scotland: Peter St D Boddy, Valdheim, Hatland, Carrutherstown DG1 4JX

Power routing — Roy Sutton

14 February, 10-5, Herne Bay, Kent, £25+VAT.

Roy is an expert on this subject. Starting from first principles, he covers housing, grooving, rebating, straight and circular moulding, tenoning, mortising, and rule-joint and template work; he also deals with designing and setting up your own jigs.

French polishing — Charles Cliffe

12-13 March, 10-4, Bexleyheath, £40.
This is a popular course by one of our 'Question box' experts and author of *The Woodworker Manual of Finishing and Polishing*. Charles explains preparation, staining and the techniques of French polishing itself; he'll also show you how to sharpen a cabinet scraper, so bring yours along. Charles will offer advice on any small piece of furniture you want to refinish, and can also order supplies for you to take away if you tell him in advance.

Wood-machining — Ken Taylor

28 March, 10-5, Bletchley, Bucks, £25+VAT
Ken's across-the-board course on wood-machining has something for everyone who's interested in learning more about workshop hardware. First-hand experience in table- and bandsaws, radial-arm saws, planers and thicknessers, spindle moulders, mortisers and universals.

Spindle moulding — Roy Sutton

28 March, 10-5, Herne Bay, Kent £25+VAT
What Roy doesn't know about spindle moulding simply isn't worth knowing. He'll take you through the spectrum of procedures and techniques: straight and stock moulding, grooving, rebating, moulding small components with jigs, raised-panel work, laminates, machining semi-finished work, simple circular work, and sectioning handrails. Lunch is provided.

BOOKING FORM

I wish to book for the following course(s).
- ☐ **Power routing** 14 February, £25+ VAT = £28.75
- ☐ **French polishing** 12-13 March, £40; make cheques payable to Charles Cliffe
- ☐ **Wood machining** 28 March, £25+ VAT = £28.75
- ☐ **Spindle moulding** 28 March, £25+ VAT = £28.75

Please make cheques payable to 'The Guild of Woodworkers/ASP Ltd' unless otherwise stated.

Name..

Address..

....

....

Guild no..
Send to: The Guild of Woodworkers, 1 Golden Square, London, W1R 3AB. The Guild reserves the right to cancel any course.

The grand furniture saga

The demise of Cromwell's Commonwealth was celebrated with fresh, cosmopolitan style.
Vic Taylor explains how the Restoration put comfort back into the home

'This day the month ends . . . and all the world in a merry mood because of the King's coming' — wrote Samuel Pepys on 31 May, 1660. The King was Charles II and the event, the Restoration of the Monarchy. He had returned from exile on the Continent and brought with him Continental fashions and ideas, notably from Versailles where extravagant, ostentatious luxury had become a by-word. Under his patronage and with his encouragement, the Court and the aristocracy eagerly copied the continental life-style, and nowhere was this more reflected than in architecture and furnishings.

But even wider influences were at work. Charles' wife, Catherine of Braganza in Portugal, brought with her as a dowry the city of Bombay, in the Portuguese colony in India, and there was also the influx of hundreds of Huguenot refugees, many of whom were highly skilled craftsmen, fleeing from the consequences of the Revocation of the Edict of Nantes. The Edict, originally passed in 1598 by Henri IV of France to guarantee them freedom of worship, was revoked by Louis XIV in 1685. So we had a melting-pot of French, Oriental, Portuguese, and English cultures; which arguably altered the course of English furniture development more radically than the Renaissance had done.

The impact was seen in new design features like the 'Braganza' foot, a kind of scrolled foot (also called the 'Spanish' foot), the cabriole leg, introduced from France about 1680, and the ball-and-claw foot, which came in about 1700. The last was adopted by the Dutch from China, and represented a dragon's claw clutching the pearl of wisdom. Carved ebony inlaid with ivory, and superb leatherwork for chairs, were two more innovations.

One of the most marked changes was the replacement of oak by walnut as the favoured timber for furniture — and it seems to have happened with astonishing speed. Walnut had previously been used for furniture only on a small scale — in 1536 it appears some was used for furniture in Windsor Castle, and in 1587 walnut furniture was supplied to Wollaton Hall, Nottingham — but after the Restoration it was in great demand.

Unfortunately English walnut was in short supply and most of it came from France (European walnut *Juglans regia*) but in 1709 severe winter frosts killed so many

● *An elegant card-table in Italian walnut, c1700. The legs swing open to support the open top*

of the trees that exports were prohibited from 1720 onwards. There were abundant supplies of American black walnut (*Juglans nigra*) in the American colonies, particularly in Virginia. It is a darker brown than the European wood, and has even darker striping but soon became a favourite with furniture makers. In 1786 Chambers Encyclopaedia quoted it as having been held in great esteem until 'the quantity of mahogany and other useful woods imported in the late years have almost banished its use'.

The rule of the Commonwealth in England from 1649 to 1659 had largely insulated native fashions and styles from the exuberance of the French Baroque; the Restoration came at the right time to allow expression of pent-up desires for richness and colour in life, and comfort and luxury in the home.

In terms of furniture, no better examples can be found than the cabinets which became the status symbols of the time. Above right is a cabinet on a stand, made about 1675, with the cabinet japanned in gold, silver, and red on a black ground; the stand is in pine, carved and silvered. It exemplifies two characteristics of the period, the use of japanning to imitate. Oriental lacquering, and the emergence of the wood-carver as a craftsman in his own right — rather than as a co-worker with cabinet-makers, chair makers, and joiners.

The most outstanding woodcarver of the time was the Dutch born Grinling Gibbons (1648-1721). He came to England where he was discovered in 1670 by John Evelyn at Deptford, carving a reproduction of Tintoretto's *Crucifixion*. He was brought to the notice of the King and a long and fruitful career followed. His work can be found in some of Wren's churches built after the Great Fire of London in 1666, and also in the home counties; one of his finest pieces is the frame for a portrait of Henry VIII at Petworth House, Sussex. His fellow carvers generally indulged themselves in a profusion of acanthus foliage, elongated S-scrolls, heraldic motifs, and the ubiquitous 'boyes and crowns' — chubby *amorini* (or *putti*) supporting a crown.

There was another style of cabinet on a stand which took its inspiration from the Dutch rather than the Orient; it contained numerous small drawers surrounding a central cupboard which was itself fitted with more drawers. The stand had either four or six legs which were connected by shaped stretchers. Magnificent parquetry or floral marquetry combined with oyster veneering decorated the cabinet, which was often used as a repository for valuables and documents — a convenient piece to have in the days before 'public' banking.

Letter writing had become popular

● *Lavishly opulent, this Restoration cabinet is japanned in gold, silver, red and green, against a black background; the pine stand is carved and silver-leafed*

● *High-backed chair in walnut c1685. The seat and back-splat are upholstered in velvet*

because of the improvement of postal services, and the writing-stand emerged as a piece of furniture in place of the small portable desk. It was variously called a 'scriptor', a 'scriptoire', or a 'scrutoire'; as distinct from a bureau in which the fall-front slopes when closed in — its fall-front was vertical and opened to provide a large writing surface, supported by chains. The interior was fitted with the familiar pigeon-holes and drawers.

The design of chairs also took a leap forward. Caned seats and backs were an innovation imported from Holland, and the upholsterers unsuccessfully applied to the King to have the craft prohibited, or at least reduced, as it was harming their trade. The designs invariably incorporated twisted legs or back feet, an ornately carved crest rail to the back (often with the 'boyes and crowns' motif), and a carved front stretcher rail; all of which gives us the well-known 'Charles II' or 'Restoration' chair. They were usually made in walnut, or in beech stained to resemble it.

'Wing' easy chairs (called 'easie' chairs) made their appearance about 1670 and the style soon became standardised into what we use today. An interesting variation is the famous 'sleeping chair' at Ham House, which has large, upholstered side panels, or 'ears'; and a ratchet-adjustable back. Day-beds, too, became popular after 1660 and

were modelled on the French *lit de repos*; in most cases the head-end was adjustable for slope.

The trend for a separate dining-room, rather than the communal dining-hall, was now well established, and the long, heavy Tudor draw-tables were discarded in favour of small circular- or oval-topped gate-leg tables which could be removed after dining. Sideboards began to be widely used; they were long tables (up to 7ft) with four or more legs and drawers beneath the top. They were also the right height for carving and serving up food. In the country, the dresser became an indispensable piece of furniture; the lower part had a cupboard and drawers beneath, and the top, a rack of narrow shelves for displaying and storing crockery. The original design bred a multiplicity of regional variations, including the several kinds of Welsh dresser.

It would be remiss to omit the bookcases made by Christopher Sympson, a ship's joiner from Deptford, for Samuel Pepys, Thomas Povey and others. There's one in the V&A Museum, several at Magdalen College Cambridge, and two more at Dyrham Park (one is a replica). This is probably the first instance where the name of the craftsman is identified (by courtesy of Pepys' diary); luckily, the 18th century makers have provided us with more clues than their predecessors! ■

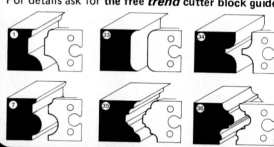
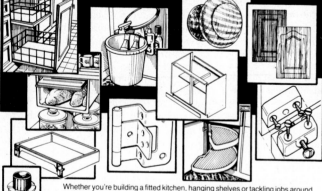
42

43

Mini folder

Folding chairs are favourite brain-befuddlers for the optimistic; all that pivotal geometry isn't as simple as it looks. Eric Coldwell has done the homework for you, and presents details of an attractive child's version

When my own daughter was just two, I noticed a neighbour's little girl using a folding chair with a plain ply back and (rather crude) swivel joints. I liked the idea, but thought I could improve on it at least aesthetically, and the result is what you see here.

● *A pretty little child's chair, whose proportions would suit full size any day of the week. This one is nearly 25 years old and has worn very well indeed*

Construction

This requires accuracy and patience, because you must constantly check for opening and closing when you are making the legs, rails and stays. The distances between centres of the holes, and the shoulder distances, are critical for smooth opening and closing, so you have to check the frame movements constantly. Other dimensions can be varied, of course; I simply followed my own picture of what seemed aesthetically and functionally right. A design drawing alone was not enough to solve all the problems, and I had to use some trial-and-error — tedious, but not difficult. Almost any hardwood can be used, even suiable offcuts, as long as you get good matching. This chair was made from beech with sycamore seat laths; it's quite likely to be used outside, so other suitable woods are teak, oak, ash, afrormosia or other 'durables', properly finished.

The seat

Fig. 1 shows the finished chair in the open position, and fig. 2 the seat details. Make the seat unit first, because this decides the widths of the other frames, and also the all-important hole positions. For the chair to fold properly, the $7/16$in spigots turned on the ends of the $5/8$in front and rear seat-frame dowels should turn freely in the side rails (fig. 2). Fig. 3 shows the profile of the seat side rails, which have a groove in them for the seat slats. Mark out the centres for

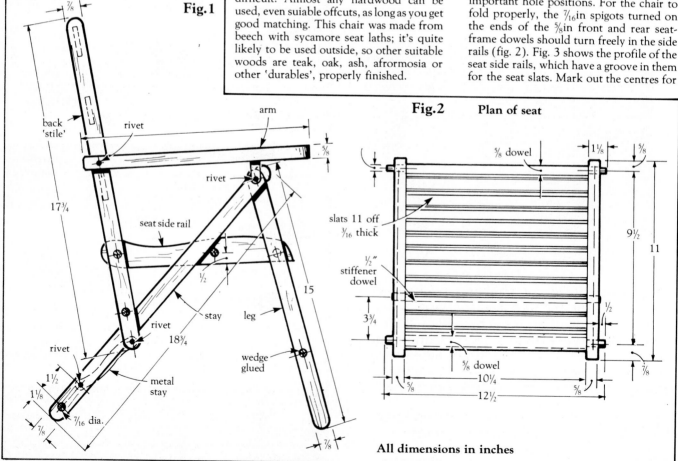

Fig.1

back 'stile'

rivet

arm

$5/8$

$17\frac{3}{4}$

rivet

seat side rail

$1/2$

15

rivet

stay

leg

$18\frac{3}{4}$

wedge glued

rivet

$1\frac{1}{2}$

$1\frac{1}{8}$

metal stay

$7/8$

$7/16$ dia.

$7/8$

Fig.2 **Plan of seat**

$5/8$ dowel

$1\frac{1}{8}$

$5/8$

slats 11 off $3/16$ thick

$1/2''$ stiffener dowel

$9\frac{1}{2}$

11

$3\frac{3}{4}$

$1/2$

$5/8$ dowel

$10\frac{1}{4}$

$12\frac{1}{2}$

$5/8$

$5/8$

$7/8$

All dimensions in inches

Fig.3   Seat side rail

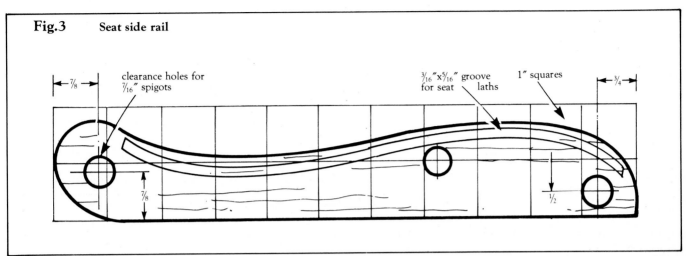

clearance holes for
$\frac{7}{16}$" spigots

$\frac{3}{16}$"x$\frac{5}{16}$" groove
for seat laths

1" squares

$\frac{7}{8}$

$\frac{7}{8}$

$\frac{3}{4}$

$\frac{1}{2}$

the $\frac{7}{16}$in spigot pivot-holes front and rear, and the $\frac{1}{2}$in stiffener dowel (fig. 2), then cut the groove — with a router and guide template is best. The top edge of the groove must not be more than $\frac{1}{8}$in below the rail top. A $\frac{3}{16}$ or $\frac{1}{4}$in cutter with bottom cut will be fine, but if you use a $\frac{1}{4}$in, make sure the front holes are positioned so the seat-frame dowels ($\frac{5}{8}$in diameter, $10\frac{1}{4}$in between shoulders) will not foul the front slat. When it's assembled, the front edge of the seat should fall away smoothly, the seat-frame dowel and the slat both on a radius. if you don't have a router, you can use a drill stand like I did — power routers were neither common nor cheap when my daughter was two! — cutting the groove with a $\frac{3}{16}$in engineer's drill. Grind the end square, then form cutting wings by grinding the bevels to make a bottom cut. Draw the outline accurately on the seat side rails, then follow that freehand, moving the work below the drill, and making light cuts at increasing depths. Drill $\frac{3}{8}$in deep holes at either end of the groove first.

Whatever way you do it, it's best to cut the groove first in oversize square-ended pieces with the profile drawn out on the inner faces, then cut them to shape afterwards. This makes routing with template and clamps easier — but be careful not to make two lefts or two rights! Also be careful to check for possible groove/hole fouling. Drill the holes after you have cut the groove — all holes, of course, should be done on a drill stand to be certain of the perpendicular.

Measure the linear length of the curving groove by bending a thin lath or a piece of wire along it, and decide on your slat width and hence number. Keep them quite narrow for a bit of flexibility; I used 11. Cut them slightly oversize and trim them to fit, bevelling the top edges to give a faint vee-groove effect. Dry-assemble the frame sides, seat-frame dowels, stiffener and slats, check everything is square, then disassemble and sand everything carefully. Make a cut in the ends of the $\frac{1}{2}$in stiffener for wedges, and wax the pivot spigots for noise-free operation; then glue up the seat, wedging the stiffener ends.

● *Detail of the front edge of the seat shows how the support dowel and front slat work in the same curve. The U-brackets are also clearly visible*

Back and arms

Now for the back frame and arms. You will see from fig. 4 overleaf that I have given $11\frac{3}{4}$in as the shoulder length for the 15x$\frac{5}{8}$in dowel that effectively decides the width of this frame; before you turn the $\frac{7}{16}$in spigots with that shoulder length, check that it will allow the seat to fold inside. The extra outside lengths bear on the back stays when the chair is folded out. If $11\frac{3}{4}$in is not right, give it a bit more (or less) and remember that that adjustment will also affect the length of the back slats. These are $1\frac{1}{2}$x$\frac{3}{16}$ (quite thin for some 'give'), with

all their edges radiused; choose pieces with a nice grain pattern for these as well as the arms and seat slats. The back slats sit in mortises $1\frac{1}{2}$x$\frac{3}{16}$in, $\frac{3}{8}$in deep.

The profile of the shaped front part of the arms is shown in fig. 5. Cut it out — 2in goes to 1in — but leave it oversize so you can do the final shaping after a dry assembly. The shaped parts should clear the tops of the back 'stiles' when the chair is folded up, of course. You will have to use the rivets loose in their holes for this and other test assemblies. It's as well to make all the rivets, washers, stays and other metal fittings in non-ferrous metal to avoid rust if

Mini folder

the chair is used outside.

Assemble and glue the back frame with the spigots of the back seat-frame dowel sitting in their sockets in the 'stiles'. Rivet the arms, but *don't close the rivets*. Glue and pin the spigots of the back seat-frame dowels in the 'stiles', making sure they turn easily in the seat frame itself. Make the U-brackets (fig. 7) and fix them to the arms as shown in fig. 4.

Front legs and back stays

Have a good look at fig. 6 and see how the front legs and back stay arrangement work. Since you have the back frame with the seat attached by its back seat-frame dowels, you can check the distance between centres of the front seat-frame dowel and top U-bracket pivot. I have shown it as 4⅝in; mark it as such and do a dry run to see that it all works before you drill. Do another dry assembly, then wedge-glue the bottom ⅝in dowel, 11¾in (approximately) between the shoulders of the turned ⁷⁄₁₆ spigots, and glue and pin the front seat-frame dowel spigots in their holes. Again, be careful that the spigots turn freely in the seat-frame rails themselves.

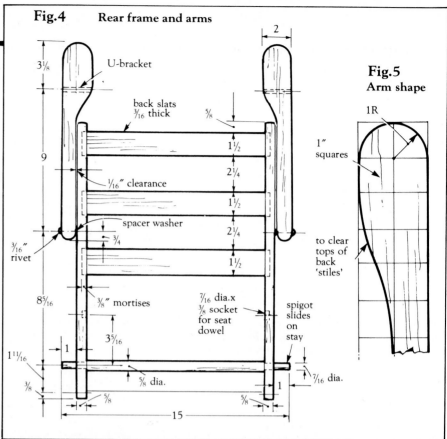

Fig.4   Rear frame and arms

**Fig.5
Arm shape**

Now make the back stays, and check that 13¼in between the spigot shoulders on their dowel will allow everything to close easily inside the stays when the chair is assembled (figs 1, 6). When you are sure, or have adjusted the shoulder length as necessary, turn the ⁷⁄₁₆in spigots on the dowel. Make the curved metal stay (fig. 8), but before you drill the rivet holes in it, check that it will control the closing of the chair so that the back stays come neatly outside and in line with the front legs. Sand and wedge-glue the dowel between the back stays.

Now put the whole chair together, rivets, washers, and all, checking that it opens and closes well. All the rivets can then be cut to length, but before you do that you must decide about the finish. Assuming the chair will be used outside, you have the choice of oil, polyurethane (staining shouldn't be necessary), or of course you can use one of the newer and rather attractive microporous 'varnish stains'. My suggested oil recipe is boiled linseed plus 10% white spirit plus 5% (maximum) terebene — 15 to 20 rag-rubbed coats with 24 hours between each, which means the young sitter-to-be could easily give up hope! If you use polyurethane I recommend doing the parts separately before final riveting. When it's ready to put together, cut all the rivets to length and get someone to help you join it all up.

My daughter's little chair has mellowed pleasantly over the years — it is stubbornly intact, a favourite family piece. If you like the idea, you can always scale it up . . . ∎

● A1 rod and washers by mail (and make your own flat-headed rivets): K. R. Whiston Ltd, New Mills, Stockport SK12 4PT, (0663 42028) are good suppliers.

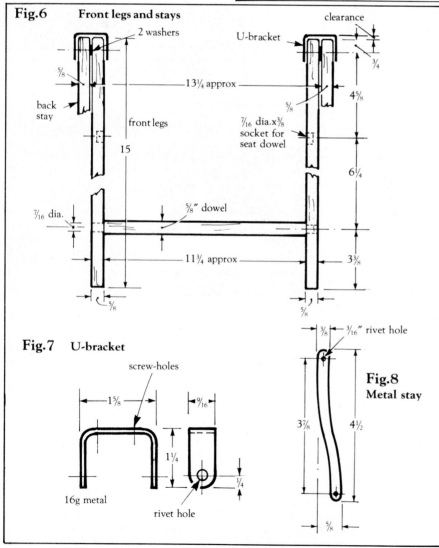

Fig.6   Front legs and stays

Fig.7   U-bracket

**Fig.8
Metal stay**

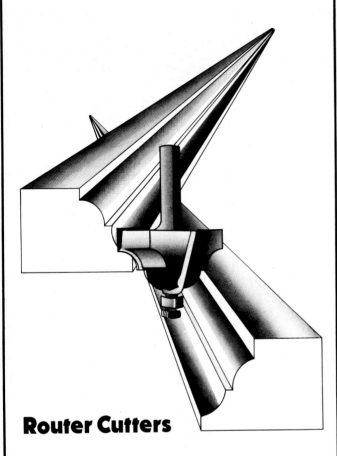

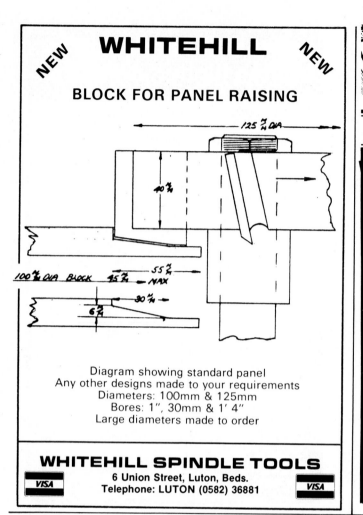

48

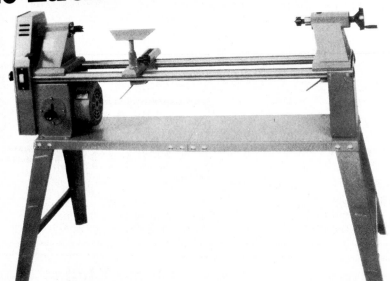

Mouths and chatter

More on wooden planes, which are making a big come-back, aided and abetted by Bob Wearing. Here are the tested remedies for two very common problems . . .

It's a common mistake to think that wooden plane mouths grow bigger because of the amount of shavings that pass through them. This is not the case. Planing narrow edges produces extra wear on the middle of the sole, which becomes hollow across its width; this is apparent when shavings taken at the sides of a wide board become thicker, even though no adjustment has been made. It's planing the sole true which steadily increases the mouth size.

Long working days on hardwoods meant that plane soles had frequently to be trued and although the slope of the escapement towards the blade helped, the plane would eventually have to be remouthed. One practice was to let in ebony or rosewood patches, which wasn't a good idea as the two

areas of the sole wore differently. Likewise the iron front didn't reduce wear behind the blade, which led to difficulties when truing did become necessary. The patch should match the body of the plane as far as possible, both in species and hardness. The patches generally glue in without any problem; I still have one from 1938, held with scotch glue. It's best to degrease with petrol or carbon tetrachloride. The final truing up should be done with a finely set steel try plane with the wooden plane's blade and wedge under working tension, and the blade slightly withdrawn. Lignum or ebony soles are best treated by the grinding method, using fine belt-sander strip held by its ends on plate glass or a machine table.

Chatter was the great bane of the workshop, and the 'favourite plane', the plane that never chattered, had great appeal. At worst it meant a considerable, unpleasant vibration, and at best, rough and crinkled shavings instead of the long sweet ribbons.

Ideally planes should have been made from quarter-sawn wood but even good stock like this would sometimes warp. This was easily corrected by planing the sole, but the same warping distorts the angle blade bed, much more difficult to remedy. The blade has to fit snugly all along the bed but when the cap-iron (it was always back-iron in those days) screw is tightened, it can distort the blade (parallel blades were less affected than tapered blades.) A distorted cap-iron could be wrenched true in a metal vice or corrected by filing.

The general solution was to glue a ½in strip of thin leather to the bed, close to the mouth. The back of the blade, not the bevel, sits on this. If the bed is badly distorted, the leather strip can be pared down at one side to compensate. (The strip needn't be leather, but must be absorbent — cardboard makes a good substitute.)

A mouth was sometimes closed by inserting a shim of thin brass behind the blade, although any metal will do. Two lugs stop it from slipping through the mouth. I can't imagine that mouths were closed and opened to suit the work; planes were relatively cheap, so cabinetmakers often had a coarse and a finely set jack and smoother to save time.

If the mouth expanded because the tapered blade was ground down, then the leather strip would be glued to the bottom of the bed. When a brand new, thick blade was fitted and the mouth was too fine, a similar strip was glued in at the top of the bed.

The demise of the wooden plane must be linked to the amount of time and effort in grinding hard, thick blades, compared with today's Stanley type. Grindstones were not freely available, and tended to be big hand-swung stone wheels. The small electric motor and water-cooled horizontal wheels have made the job easier. However, I don't recommend freehand grinding; it's better to make a jig to suit your equipment so that you can regrind at precisely the same angle as last time — a great saver of that time and effort, not to mention metal. ■

Rout and turn

Buying a Craft Supplies Precision Combination chuck, **writes Roy Benfield**, opens up a new world for the woodturner; likewise, the acquisition of a plunge router spells a different sphere of adventure for the 'flat and (occasionally) straight' woodworker. Bring both bits of gear together and you have a great team.

I find, however, that to use the expanding dovetail lathe chuck, the necessary double chucking can get a bit tedious. You have to turn the dovetail recess and then reverse for the main turning — somewhat time-consuming.

I bought a dovetail cutter for my new plunge router, and investigated the idea of using it with a sole-plate ring-guide and simple plywood rings to cut the dovetail recess for turning. The result was excellent.

I have two sets of expanding collets, 3½ and 1¾in diameter; I made two round templates of ¼in ply, oversize to match the difference between ring-guide and cutter diameter. You only need two ⅝in panel pins to hold the template in position on the work; the cutter should be set to cut ³⁄₁₆in deep, plus, of course, the thickness of the template.

It's important to plunge to full depth first and cut in one pass in the ring, or the dovetail sides will be lost because of the expanding diameter of the cutter at different heights. On average, it takes me about 30 seconds to pin on the template, cut the recess, and remove the template.

This method offers considerable savings of time and stock, quite a consideration when you get on to exotic timbers!

For green wood turning, the mounting method has great safety advantages — I'm never happy mounting those out-of-balance chunks on a 1in pin.

Wood magpies like me will have a ball sorting out all those odd bits of timber

cluttering the shelves and having a dovetail-recess routing session on them all in one go. Then when you can escape the washing up or the decorating, you can get straight into some creative turning therapy without tedious mounting and re-mounting. ■

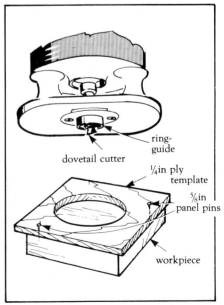

ring-guide

dovetail cutter

¼in ply template

⅝in panel pins

workpiece

A shift in time

Moisture can play havoc with solid wood furniture. Steven Hurrell explains how you can avoid cracked panels and rattling drawers

Understanding the materials which we work with is the most important woodworking skill and should be mastered long before the first dovetail is cut. Wood is a very unforgiving material and must be treated with respect to avoid later headaches. Nothing tarnishes the professional image more than comebacks caused by a failure in the product; one complaint can easily cancel out a hundred recommendations.

Much of the development of furniture and woodwork has been dictated by the need to overcome problems related to the movement of solid timber. As a classical example the frame and panel (fig. 1) illustrates how wood is allowed to move whilst maintaining stability and providing effective decoration.

The most common problem related to incorrect or unsympathetic use of wood is the appearance of splits where the movement of wood has been restricted (fig. 2). Not only are such splits unsightly but they can affect the strength and life of the piece.

Moisture content

Much ignorance surrounds the subject of moisture content of timber. To many people 'kiln dried' and '12%' are magic words which in reality are meaningless.

Wood will always come to equilibrium with the surrounding conditions (relative humidity). In a wet environment wood swells and in a dry one it shrinks. The environment includes the workshop in which the piece is made, so it's pointless stipulating wood dried to 10% if the conditions in which you work are cold and damp.

The living conditions of yesteryear were much different from today's; conditions tolerated for centuries are unimaginable in the 1980s. Those involved in antique restoration know only too well that furniture and woodwork which lived happily in those environments suffer greatly from central heating and modern living conditions. In a *normal* room today woodwork will attain a moisture content of 8-16%, and with central heating it can be as low as 4%.

Of course we have no control over our furniture and woodwork after it leaves the sanctuary of the workshop, but it's useful to know the type of situation in which it will be used. You can learn a lot from visiting the client's home; whilst clinching the deal a quick glance round will allow you to form a good impression of what's expected of your products. Note the condition of existing

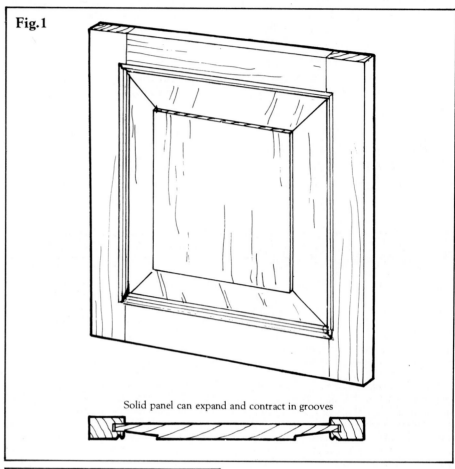

Fig.1

Solid panel can expand and contract in grooves

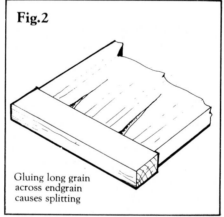

Fig.2

Gluing long grain across endgrain causes splitting

furniture and the proximity and settings of radiators.

For a more accurate picture, relative humidity can be measured by the use of a thermohygrometer, such as the Protimeter Aquant, and can then be directly related to moisture content (fig. 3). This kind of equipment for measuring relative humidity and moisture is particularly useful in such difficult situations as kitchens and bathrooms.

Matching timber and workshop conditions to those of the environment in which the piece will be used may be difficult to achieve in practice. But if you know some of the hazards your furniture will face you can take precautions in construction.

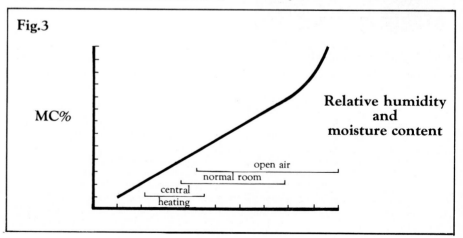

Fig.3

MC%

Relative humidity and moisture content

open air

normal room

central heating

Principles

Provided you follow the basic rules of using solid timber, changes in relative humidity will have an unnoticeable effect on such pieces as chairs, tables, beds, panelling and other framed or simple construction. You must remember that wood expands and contracts, adjusting itself to the conditions in which it is placed, no matter what, so our job is to make these movements as unnoticeable as possible.

An early indication of movement is the appearance of 'white' lines where panels have started to shrink away from stiles, revealing unfinished wood. It makes sense to stain or darken these concealed edges of the panel before assembly. With panelling, ensure no glue is inadvertently forced out of the mortises and into the grooves, cancelling out the object of the exercise. In the same way mouldings that are 'planted' around panels must be fixed to the framework rather than the panels (fig. 4).

Those well-fitting doors and drawers can easily be spoiled by a change in the surrounding conditions; nothing creates a worse impression than a sloppy drawer that rattles around in its compartment or large uneven gaps around doors.

Selection of timber is very important. Fig. 5 shows the way in which wood moves as it loses moisture and this should be taken into account when choosing wood for door stiles, drawer pieces, unsupported leaves of tables and any other area that must remain stable.

When boards are split by rip-sawing, stresses are often released that cause the pieces to bend. So it's important, especially when cutting out door stiles and the like, that bits are initially cut out oversize ($\frac{1}{4}$ in is usually enough, but it depends on the wood) so any kink can then be planed out before ripping to exact sizes.

Quarter-sawn stuff offers the most stability and least overall movement; the more pleasing grain of flat-cut timber can be exploited in panel and table-top situations where other means of support is provided.

While shrinkage is a common risk, re-

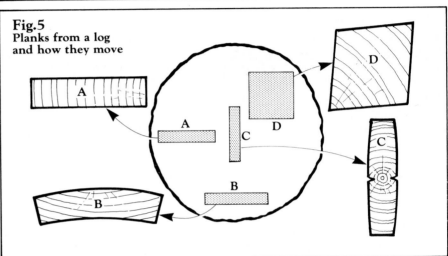

Fig.4

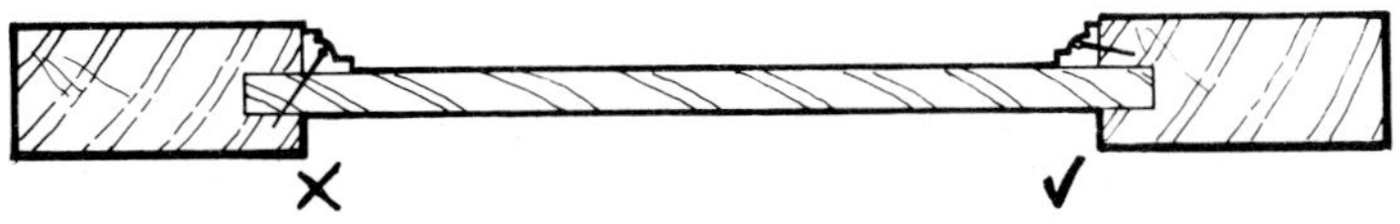

Don't nail mouldings through panels but into rails and stiles only

Fig.5
Planks from a log and how they move

Fig.6

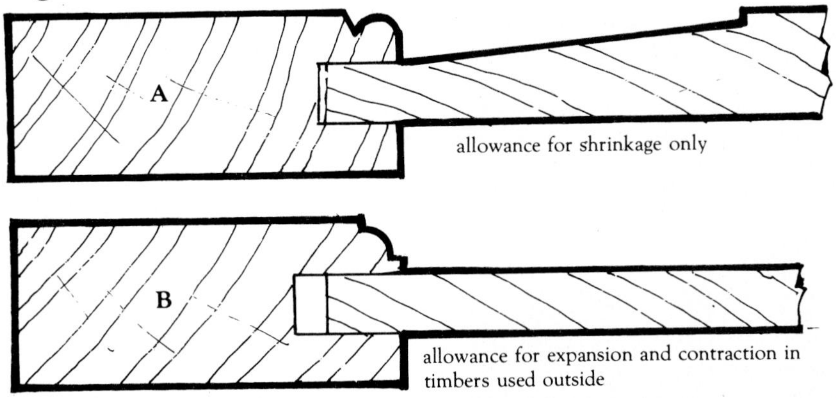

allowance for shrinkage only

allowance for expansion and contraction in timbers used outside

member that 'dry' timber used for external work will almost certainly take on moisture and swell, so allow for such expansion (fig. 6).

Obviously the finish of painted woodwork can be affected if timber isn't sufficiently dry before painting. Moisture content should be 12% for interior and 18% for exterior work.

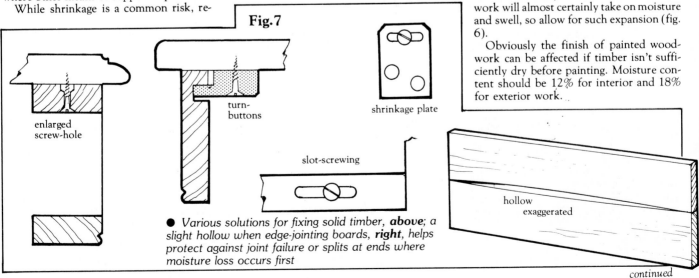

Fig.7

enlarged screw-hole

turn-buttons

shrinkage plate

slot-screwing

hollow exaggerated

● *Various solutions for fixing solid timber, **above**; a slight hollow when edge-jointing boards, **right**, helps protect against joint failure or splits at ends where moisture loss occurs first*

continued

A shift in time

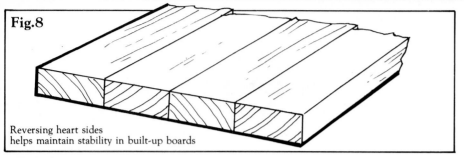

Fig.8

Reversing heart sides
helps maintain stability in built-up boards

Fig.9

Avoid problems
like this by careful
selection and machining

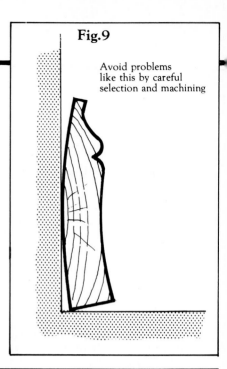

Measuring moisture content

The Protimeter 'Mini Super' illustrated here is one of a range of meters for measuring moisture in wood and probably the most useful to the average woodworker. It costs around £65.00, with the hammer electrode £39.00 extra (prices plus VAT). Despite its compact and simple appearance the 'Mini Super' is a precision instrument that offers all the features necessary in measuring moisture content and damp diagnosis. It is also well designed.

With this instrument you can gauge moisture levels above 28% by the use of the high rance scale, especially useful as a guide when drying timber. Calibration charts supplied cover 150 species of timber giving accurate correction or a quick plus or minus 2% conversion. Readings from the standard scale are compatible with such woods as oak, ash, elm, American walnut and Indian rosewood. The hammer electrode allows moisture readings to be taken to a depth of 25mm (fig. 11). Distinguishing between being dry on the surface and completely dry can mean the difference between successful deep cutting or a pile of spoiled timber.

You expect the thicker sections will be drier on the surface than at the centre (in fact most timber merchants will not guarantee sizes thicker than 3in as consistently dry) but where the differences are extreme the resawing of such timber will result in warping and surface checking of the exposed boards.

Fig.10

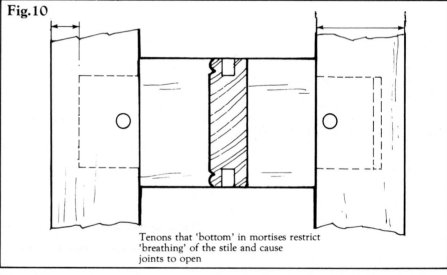

Tenons that 'bottom' in mortises restrict 'breathing' of the stile and cause joints to open

● *Checking moisture on timber in stick with the hammer electrode*

Fig.11

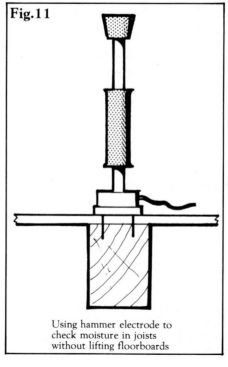

Using hammer electrode to check moisture in joists without lifting floorboards

Damp in buildings

Dampness in buildings can affect furniture and joinery, so you should be aware of the risks. Moulds, fungus, rot and wood-boring insects are all attracted to damp conditions.

Lack of ventilation is as much to blame for timber decay as the dampness itself; timber that is allowed to dry out again will not be adversely affected by the odd shower. It's when a moisture content of above 20% is maintained that decay will just be a matter of time.

This moisture meter incorporates a 'traffic light' scale of 'decay impossible', 'possible' or 'inevitable' which is both straightforward and obvious, and by carrying out regular surveys, an accurate picture of any dampness can be built up and a diagnosis formed.

For those who would like to know more about dampness, humidity and condensation related to buildings, I recommend *Dampness in Buildings* by T. A. Oxley and E. G. Gobert, Butterworths. ■

● Protimeter PLC, Meter House, Marlow, Bucks SL7 1LX, (06284) 72722.

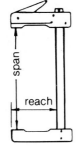

56

Tales out of steel

The sun, alas, always has to set; the last instalment of Ashley Iles' tool industry tales take us with him from Sheffield to a Lincolnshire field

The 1980s will probably go down in history as the decade of the small-firm revival. Just as the cottage industries of the 18th century moved to the cities and are now returning to the country, so the small-firms absorbed by the amalgamates over the last 30 years are breaking away again in this age of the specialist.

The mortality rate of small businesses is high and not always due to lack of moral fibre or rugged individuality. Getting suitable premises and raising workshop capital has chiselled more tombstones than bears thinking about.

Just as the road to Hell is paved with good intentions, so the road to Heaven can be paved with frustrations. In the 60s men walked the streets of Sheffield looking for workshop space and took anything they could get, often doing all the things the landlord should have done; installing mains, repairing and decorating, and all this without security of tenure.

My position was even worse. I needed premises with hammer rights and work-shops either had them or they didn't. Of course, preference was given to those who didn't want hammer rights. As a stop-gap, I took a large workshop at £2 10s. a week, owned by the Firma Chrome Plating Company in Cambridge Street, and set it up as a finishing shop. All the work had to be taken backwards and forwards to the other shop in Solly Street over a mile away. It was an impossible situation.

Eventually, inspired by the Beverley Saw Company who had set up in the middle of a field in Lincolnshire, I came across the perfect solution. A four-bedroomed modernised farmhouse in 1½ acres, with a 1500sq. ft workshop and three-phase power only three poles away. At a thousand yards from the nearest house, my hammer noise troubles were over.

I wanted the money to expand and went to the bank for help — I can tell you no stone ever put up a greater struggle to retain its blood. The manager, a retired Irish rugby star, went beserk. 'A factory in the middle of a Lincolnshire field? Really, Mr Iles, you can't expect me to put a proposition like that to my head office.' Being a Buddhist I stood firm in the knowledge that the only thing we know for certain is that we don't know. 'Try 'em', I said. Never before or since has my future hung on such a slender thread. Ten days later the manager sheepishly told me that in view of my export record his head office had agreed to finance me.

The next few weeks were a mixture of frantic buying of tackle and Teutonic planning; D-day was to be Good Friday 1967. The great move had all the romance and risk of taking a covered wagon with the 49ers; moving from one place to another, the actual distance doesn't really make a difference.

By noon on D-day all the tackle was loaded on to lorries and I led the procession out of Sheffield driving a 5cwt Morris van. I had taken one last look at the workshop where I'd worked for over 10 years, bashing my head on the banister of bureaucracy until it dawned on me that to make tools I must leave Sheffield! Two years later the block I'd been in was demolished. Some survived; some didn't — I was lucky.

When we arrived at the new site, everything was dumped on the grass outside the workshop and the battle was on. A farm labourer passing on a tractor stopped and looked at the lead pot for hardening and asked if it was for boiling up for pigs. By Whitsuntide we'd installed two power hammers, two wet grinding-wheels, two diesel-fire furnaces with blowers and fuel tanks, two anvils, a hardening pot, the electric wiring and all the air and fuel pipes. 12 men with two lorries from the electricity board installed three-phase power and I got a bill for £52, and for £8 the local architect arranged unconditional planning for industry.

In the eight weeks of fitting out the factory, I noticed with alarm that the element of a new electric kettle was furred up with lime — the water was very hard. When production started, hardening proved to be a nightmare and I seriously thought of fetching water from Sheffield. Putting in 4% of detergent softened it, but it needed constant checking, as the water evaporated but the detergent didn't.

There is most decidedly no shortage of workshop space in Sheffield today. Landlords are walking the streets looking for tenants and the banks are begging people to take their money to start a small business anywhere. How times change!

Sam Goldwyn said that a story has a beginning, a middle and an end, but not necessarily in that order — this story is no exception.

My mother was a spiritualist and when I was 15 she took me to my first — and last — spiritualist meeting. To my horror the lady medium pointed a wavering finger at me and said 'The boy in the third row, I see tools, lots of tools. Someone is telling me that if you stay with tools you'll do good.' Mother took it very seriously, but as the years rolled by I began to think that in the vast industrial complex of Sheffield and Rotherham, there was little else for a boy but tools of some sort. Perhaps she was on a better bet than me. ■

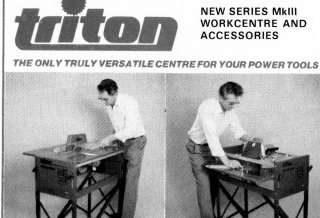
58

Brolly folly

If you need a stand for those hard-worked umbrellas, and fancy giving yourself a course in unusual coopering, try Tim Kidman's technique for built-up octagons

● Spiralling oak leaves encircle the unusual coopered cylinder, faired in to form a 'squashed' circle

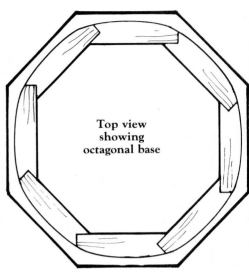

Top view showing octagonal base

I made the plank-back stool described by Alan and Gill Bridgewater in the August 1985 *Woodworker*, and almost before I'd had time to stand back and admire it, I was asked to make a matching umbrella stand.

About the same time, I saw through my 'nautical eyes' an article describing the construction of a hollow wooden spar, made by cutting right-angled rebates at 45° into the long edges of eight pieces of wood. When it was glued and pulled together, the angles and corners were self-aligning, and formed a circular wooden spar. I decided to try this technique out.

I needed a height of 16in to match the stool, and so cut eight pieces of oak 15x3x¾in; I cut the rebates into the long edges of the pieces by setting up a 45° fence — a bandsawn and planed bit of softwood — on the router table, then with a straight two-flute ¾in cutter projecting between the 45° fence and the vertical fence, all I needed to do was get the angle-fence side of the cutter to the right depth and plumb in the middle of the long edge. Once it was set up, cutting the 90° rebate was easy. The rebates are effectively 90° vee-grooves in the timber edges.

I glued the eight pieces of rebated oak together, pulling them into position with 24in plastic wire ties, for which I was lucky enough to have a tie gun. You could also use a string windlass, or 24in Jubilee clips, or extra-strong ratchet band cramps.

I made the base from an 8in square piece of oak, 1⅝in thick. While the cylinder was still square-surfaced, I marked off its outside shape on to the base piece, and then cut that out on the bandsaw. I cleaned up each side with a plane, then marked semi-circular shapes out on each face. I found the centre on the underside, and scribed a 2in circle, then drew lines from the bottoms of the semi-circles on the faces to the 2in circumference. That gave me eight triangular shapes, which I cut out with chisel and gouge, finishing off with a good woodcarving gouge. I cut a ¼in rebate round the outside of the top to fit the cylinder exactly on to the base.

I planed the cylinder not quite circular to keep the maximum gluing area and minimise the joint lines, then drew eight oak leaves in a spiral pattern, and carved them

All dimensions in inches

Dimensions: 7½ across top, 15 height, 1¼, 2¼, 3¼, 1⅛R, 8 across base

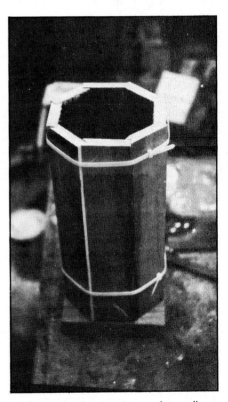

● Long plastic wire ties used to pull together the eight pieces of oak

with my woodcarving chisels, gouges and a Swann-Morton scalpel.

The inside of the stand needed a drip-tray, which I made from galvanised steel, cut into octagonal shape from an 8in square. I cut the corners to give a 1in lip when they were bent at 90°, and soldered them with aluminium/zinc solder.

Finally, the cylinder and base were stained, glued together and polished, and the drip-tray placed inside. The stand now graces our hall along with the stool, giving a traditional country air to our umbrellas.■

Underside of base

Galvanised steel tray

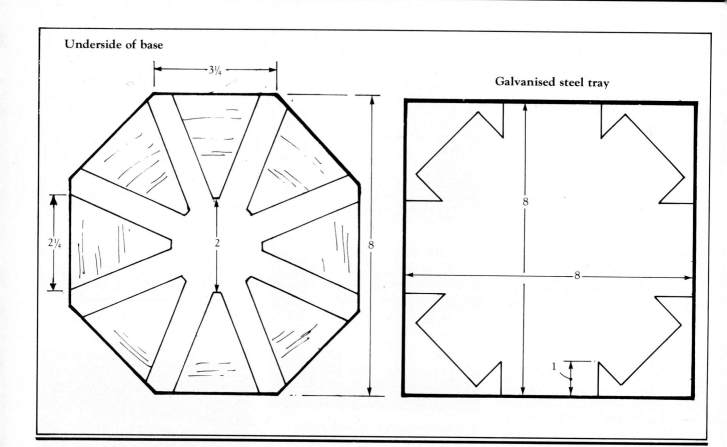

60

The heartful bodger

Green wood special: in a two-sided look at the spirit and activities of green wood and country craft specialists, we introduce Mike Abbott, chair bodger and Living Wood educator. Mike's lively Woodworker Show stand lined up with Stuart King's and Jack Hill's to create a warm centre of attraction; Keith Tutt talked to him

Before I met Mike Abbott I thought a bodger was someone who wasn't quite up to the task. That changed when Mike told me about the original 'bodgers' who lived in the woods until earlier this century, producing all the turned parts for Windsor chairs, that most popular form of 'cottage' furniture. Mike is proud to be a bodger, in fact he's one of the few people alive today who make their living entirely from this old craft. His neighbour at the Woodworker Show, Stuart King, is another one of the enthusiastic traditionalists who are putting all their energies into invigorating and promoting the art and craft of bodging.

But Mike is not in his late 70s as you might expect. He was born in 1951, seven years before the last of the old generation of bodgers is reputed to have committed suicide over the fate of the industrialised Windsor chair industry.

Mike set up 'Living Wood Training' in the summer of 1985 to pass on the knowledge and skills of this ancient wood craft to a new generation of enthusiasts. On his courses, not only do the participants learn how to make objects like stools, hay rakes, drumsticks, axe handles and Windsor chairs, they also become deeply involved in the processes by which a piece of a tree is transformed into a usable object. On many of the courses, the first task is to make a shaving horse which becomes almost indispensable as a form of vice to hold wooden parts when they are being cut, gouged or shaved. 'It's one of the perfect machines — the more pressure you exert on the piece of wood, the more the horse grips it.' I'm immediately impressed by the simplicity of the machine, and by Mike's enthusiasm for it.

Mike has an excellent collection of bodgers' tools, including the 'authentic' maul which has had five new handles and three new heads. In true bodger's style, he is not above using the tool which works best; for instance, many of the tools he uses for turning are not turning tools at all. A carving gouge here, a flat chisel there. But if his experience tells him it works better that way, so be it.

There are tools in Mike's workshop that most people wouldn't see in a lifetime — scorps, froes, beetles, side axes, a bucket shave, bow-saws, draw-knives and many others. Most of these are the original bodger's tools, though the bucket shave is in fact a cooper's tool which is used to shape the elm seats for Windsor chairs. It's tremendously exciting to see and even try these beautiful old pieces which are so often superior in quality, and more pleasurable to use than modern equipment.

But the most important tool of all, and central to Mike's approach to his craft, is his pole lathe. He compares it to a power lathe: 'For spindle turning I find it much more enjoyable. It's not as time efficient, but it's probably a lot more energy efficient. Mine runs on cider or Guinness (depending on the mood), granary bread, peanut butter, marmite and jam.' And the sound of a springy ash sapling is a lot more pleasurable than an electric motor. When all three lathes in his workshop are on the go it's a wonderful sight. 'To see a pole lathe being operated offers an almost irresistible challenge to find out if it's as easy as it looks. When people try it and turn a rough chair leg out of a piece of green sycamore, it's very difficult to get them to stop.'

Mike's self-confessed obsession with this woodland craft started about 10 years ago and developed during a number of jobs in forestry and tree nursery work. His first pole lathe was built in the attic where he was living — 'it used to vibrate the house apart'. Some time spent in Germany, where shaving horses and the products and ways of woodland crafts are often just a normal part of life, helped develop his ideas.

What emerged was the 'Living Wood'

● *Traditional country chairs, made in traditional country style with traditional techniques*

idea, originally envisaged as a woodland site with a threefold purpose. Firstly, a woodland environment where the public could see displays and exhibitions of woodland crafts, as well as simply being in the peace of the woods. Second, a place where training courses could be run. And third, an outlet for a number of products like chairs, spoons and bowls, created by old methods from the woodland's own green wood.

When Mike returned to England he took up a post as Supervisor of a Youth Training scheme set among 15 acres of mixed woodland at Abbot's Pool. Though his brief was to keep six 16 and 17 year olds out of trouble, he had more interesting aims which resulted in, among other achievements, the creation of imaginative woden projects — a bridge over a stream, picnic tables, children's play structures. And all of them showed a touch of something extra, something inspired.

Mike soon had the pole lathe working and was starting to make Windsor chairs.

● *Left, Mike and the machine at work in the woods; below, legs and stretchers from cleft stock*

continued

The heartful bodger

● *Living and working in the woods makes you more weather-aware; but there was always the old estate car to shelter in when the English summer rain came down*

The initial interest in this particular type of chair had a very appropriate logic behind it: they happen to use all the different types of timber available in the wood — elm, oak, ash, and beech. And he and his students used them because of their particular individual properties. Mike was able to learn and pass on much about these woods in the green, unseasoned state. When the project finished in 1984, he had a much better picture of how his 'Living Wood' idea might come about.

Mike talks about the men who inspired him. The original bodgers who worked in the woods were producing legs, stretchers and sticks (for the stick back) for the Windsor chair workshops, mostly round High Wycombe in Buckinghamshire. At that time it was simply easier to go to the wood rather than get the wood to come to

you. They would usually work in pairs, one preparing the leg blanks while the other turned them. There are oft-related stories that 600 turned parts could be produced each week by a pair. Great stacks of freshly turned legs could be seen drying out in the wind before being taken in sacks for sale to the nearest workshop or chair factory. There the 'bottomers' and 'framers' would carry on the work — shaping the one-piece elm seats and putting all the turned, bent and shaped pieces together to make a harmonius piece of furniture which would last for a hundred years or more.

Now Mike makes fine Windsor chairs in the authentic way, turning the legs and stretchers from green wood on a pole lathe, and steam-bending fresh ash to make the 'bow-back'. 'The Windsor is the perfect chair, both a technical marvel and a

beautiful piece of furniture,' he says. Mike's chairs look and feel much more like the old and valuable Windsor chair than today's mass-production units. The legs, for instance, are finer, made as they are from cleft rather than sawn wood. 'With cleft wood you can guarantee the strength because you know there's a core of fibres running the length of each leg. Sawing across any fibres of the wood weakens it. You might not think it makes a difference, but I can tell you which will break first.' Mike usually leaves the chairs in a natural finish, just using wax to show off the different grain of the timbers.

Some say that the hard life of the bodgers, who slept out in the forest all through the winter, was an apprenticeship for a place in the workshop. But some of them, for sure, are also known to have worked in the woods all their lives. Does Mike aspire to these hardships? This summer he embarked on a Bodging Tour from Cornwall to the Lake District, giving courses, displays and workshops to the public, to private groups and to a number of woodlands conservation schemes.

Although he didn't sleep outdoors every night, preferring the relative comfort of his old Volvo estate, he told me just how sensitive he became to the weather. 'Living like that, outdoors all the time, the weather has a very strong effect. If it's raining when you get up it can ruin your whole day.' But with a huge tarpaulin he was able to set up a mammoth bodger's hut at his tour venues, and quite a sight it made; sheltering up to 10 aspiring bodgers, three busy pole lathes, enough shaving horses to enter the Derby, and a gaggle of extraordinary tools.

He told me with much pleasure how, at one venue, he had met a group of 'swillers', as they're known, making baskets from thinly cleft oak. They had shared skills to make stools with woven elm bark seats. He had compared notes with Jack Hill, author of *The Complete Practical Book of Country Crafts* on Windsors. At Grizedale in the Lake District the Director General of the Forestry Commission came to see him. ('I think maybe he'd seen it all before.') About 100 people had participated in courses and displays, and had been initiated into the ways of the pole lathe.

It had been a great trip for meeting people, many of whom had no previous knowledge of the bodgers or their craft. For a few, the great Herbert Edlin had been an inspiration through his books on the old woodland crafts. The tour was rounded off with a week as a craftsman in residence at Bristol's Windmill Hill City Farm, where Mike has also had his temporary workshop for some months.

His next permanent venue will, he hopes, be a small woodland where he can pursue the next phase of his Living Wood idea. He is still looking for support in finding the right site and the right arrangement to create 'the poor man's Hooke Park' as he calls it, referring to John Makepeace's School for Woodland Industries in Dorset (*WW/Mar, Apr 86*). 'I would dearly love to have 20-30 acres of mixed broadleaved woodlands to take care of, where people could come and spend their time.'

Mike says he's getting to know of more and more projects involved in the regeneration and rejuvenation of woodlands — the breathing of new life into the embattled forests. People are beginning to appreciate the value, the absolute necessity to life of trees; the 'lungs of the world'. Mike is

● **Right**, all you need for bodging – and teaching it; a teepee, a pole lathe, and a forest clearing. **Below**, young aspirants succumb to the irresistible challenge; **bottom**, a handy tree-trunk with a flat area, a chair-back former, some wooden pegs and strong arms – plus, of course, green ash

wholeheartedly behind a responsible approach to forestry which will involve people, and give them both a living experience of the woodland environment and an appreciation of the splendour of trees, the Kings of the plant kingdom. 'Using green timber is a wonderful way to understand about wood and trees, their qualities and their uses. And it can be very cheap. A pound's worth of ash can give me 24 chair legs, with minimum wastage. The whole process of timber production generally is very wasteful — cutting it up into square sections only to turn it back into round sections. I'm able to use all my wood — even the shavings get the fire going.'

Mike's approach to his work is thoughtful and caring. The chairs and other pieces he makes reveal these qualities in abundance, as well as showing an affectionate understanding of wood in its raw state. It's an uncompromising approach which is hard to argue with, because it's clear it comes from a deep respect for Nature. ∎

65

Trust in green

uneconomic to their owners. Many acres have been destroyed, and such woodlands continue under threat, along with their unique and varied wildlife.

Telford Development Corporation Landscape Department recently reintroduced coppicing in old woodlands in the Ironbridge Gorge, largely with nature conservancy in mind. Large quantities of the green timber produced have been donated to local schools and colleges for design and craft work; a natural development was that a number of people saw the need for somewhere where this wood could be available to many more ordinary people who wanted to learn the old manufacturing techniques.

And so it was decided that an educational centre should be built at Coalbrookdale Station, Telford. This is an ideal woodland location away from residential areas, and Telford Development Corporation have generously agreed to make the building, its woodland site, and the timber from land management available to bring a new education concept to life.

There are many reasons for creating such a centre. Art and Craft students of all ages have a limited understanding of timber — most of them live in urban areas, and look on it as just the product of the saw-mills.

● *The nature of coppicing;* **above**, *the multiple tree-trunk in the foreground has been harvested, and* **right**, *planking on site with a portable chain mill*

Shropshire's Green Wood Trust is a complete concept in the revival of coppicing and traditional green wood crafts. David Griffith outlines its work

A burgeoning green wood project is under way in the Ironbridge Gorge and the new town of Telford. We aim to educate people in the use of green timber, in the hope that in a few years' time there will be a body of knowledge in the area, enough to revive a woodland-based, commercially viable manufacturing enterprise.

Systems do exist for manufacturing articles from green or unseasoned timber, principles which have been applied since the Middle Ages to produce a large variety of timber products — timber-frame buildings, furniture, gates, fences, hurdles, all manner of turnery, and many others in the wooden miscellany. The raw material, when it's worked unseasoned by these traditional methods, is cheap; modern production methods and seasoned timber are far more costly. Supply is regenerable, as the timber is home-grown in small woodlands which at present have little or no

commercial value. Workable green wood is produced by 'coppicing' — cut a young tree to the bole a foot or so above ground level, and allow multi-stem growths to emerge. The timber is then harvested in cycles of 1-25 years, depending on the section and size required. 25-year old trunks for building, for example, or one-year old shoots for basketry.

For various socio-economic reasons, coppicing and its related manufacturing methods fell into decline some 40 years ago. It means that many small woodlands have become overgrown, neglected, and

There's a fundamental need to bridge the knowledge gap and show the real relationship between timber and trees!

There is also a growing interest in green wood, and new creative ideas, based on old craft techniques and principles, are being enthusiastically explored. It is an interest which has been stimulated by the high-profile work of many artists and craftspeople both here and in America, but it's impractical to work green wood in centrally-heated schools and colleges, so many pupils and students have found this new area of learning closed to them.

Photos I. Hughes

● **Top**, Coalbrookdale station without windows or doors – a lot of restoration work ahead. **Top right**, the exhibition at Rose Cottage. **Above**, a range of Shropshire chairs made by John Barlow in the workshops behind the Cottage

The scheme is to construct a site at the old Coalbrookdale Station where timber from coppicing, and land-management waste from parks and social amenity areas of Telford new town, will be stored and used by students and pupils of all ages. The aim is to revive old and often forgotten skills, so people can make things for themselves, re-learn crafts or revive a joy in making for its own sake. Adult organisations, such as Young Farmer's clubs, can use the facility to learn the disciplines of coppicing woodland and the traditional tasks of gate, hurdle and fence-making. Other organisations will be able to benefit from the site's recreational value and its hobbyist potential, and individuals and enthusiasts will have the chance to extend

continued

Trust in green

their own knowledge and expertise.

The traditional ways of using locally grown timber will be investigated and adapted to present-day needs, and the old techniques of rural furniture making will be explored and developed. Much has already been done, but there's a great need for further development and research.

Renovated and restored, Coalbrookdale Station will be used for lectures and talks, and it will house displays of craft tools and equipment plus a photographic display of processes related to working with green timber. On top of this, the Green Wood Trust is undertaking a unique venture — the erection of a new timber-frame 'cruck' building, which will give us a chance to explore the skills and methods of the medieval builder. When it's finished, the barn will provide a covered outdoor work area.

During 1986 the Trust has had a temporary base at Rose Cottage in Coalbrookdale, opposite the station site. There is the office and a small exhibition, showing the many historical and contemporary uses of small-diameter timber. In the Boring Mill at the rear of the Cottage, two self-employed craftsmen, sponsored by the Trust, can be seen working every Wednesday and Friday. Frank Parker, a retired teacher, is producing chairs from green wood using the Fred Lambert techniques, now ably presented by Jack Hill and others; and John Barlow, a graduate from Wolverhampton Polytechnic, is successfully reviving the production of Shropshire chairs from green ash, as well as making his own designs.

The entire project is administered by a charitable trust, inaugurated in November 1984. The Trustees have been selected from prominent local people, and nominees come from organisations which support the aspirations of the scheme.

The restoration of Coalbrookdale Station has been financed by Telford Development Corporation and the Countryside Commission, and the work is put in by a Manpower Services Commission team. The Green Wood Trust has received some valuable sponsorship from local industry and grant aid from several sources, but the project has to be largely self-financing.

A scale of charges will be established for the casual use of the site, and money will come from the sale of wood for educational purposes, plus income from membership fees and fundraising events. It will all contribute to the expenses.

A large amount of surplus timber will be produced every year from coppicing aimed at nature conservancy, in the Lloyds coppice and Benthall Edge Woodland. The steep slopes of the gorge on which the woods lie make timber retrieval hazardous, but the labour-intensive job is done by a very competent and responsible voluntary group. The cost of all this work is of course very low, which is important when a major part of the income for the whole project will

● **Above**, *a model of the cruck barn, whose construction is going on apace;* **below**, *an artist's impression of the frame*

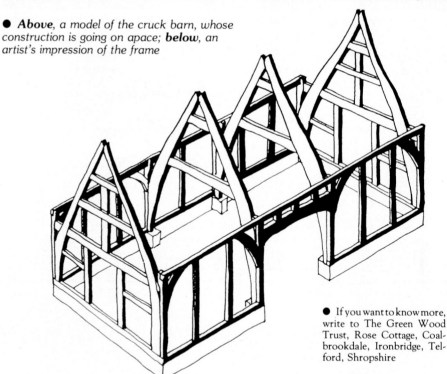

● If you want to know more, write to The Green Wood Trust, Rose Cottage, Coalbrookdale, Ironbridge, Telford, Shropshire

come from the sale of the timber.

The Trust has an active educational policy of providing inexpensive wood, advice and facilities for schools and colleges in the region. The growing membership benefits from a lecture and workshop programme, regular seasonal newsletters, summer schools, demonstrations and technical advice. Members are encouraged to get actively involved in the woodland, and of course they can take advantage of timber at lower prices.

The Trust also aims to establish a small reference library, publish information packs and produce pamphlets on the different aspects of green timber. It will record the rapidly disappearing woodland

crafts, and create an information bank for the future. Charcoal burning will be re-established to process useless 'brash', and we will be pioneering a responsible policy of timber fuel production.

The Trust hopes to sponsor more self-employed craftsmen creating objects, both traditional and contemporary, from local timber. In the long term Coalbrookdale Station will be developed as a visitor centre, providing information on past and present woodland industry.

The Green Wood Trust offers an opportunity to be part of a new educational concept, its roots firmly in the past and its sights set on the future. What better combination for wood lovers who care? ■

No holds shelved

A multi-adjustable storage system without so much as a screw or nail to wall, floor or ceiling? A couple of simple ideas make Alan Blower's shelves a triumph of flexibility

Detail of the lowest shelf shows the cut-in overlap and adjustable foot

photos Steve Mussell

Faced with building a shelf unit to cover a wall, I didn't want to take the usual approach and end up with square-ended sections, the normal type of shelf unit one comes across. No matter what goes into the design, they always somehow look the same; a variation on a theme of square box-like shelf sections. So after much doodling and pondering on how to break away from this, I decided to develop an idea that uses pillars braced floor to ceiling, the shelves resting on cross-bars on the pillars. The original scheme I heard of used eight 2x2in pillars, with a section of shelves between each pair, but I re-thought it, and decided to use four 3x3in pillars, the shelves supported by a dowel passed through as a crossbar under the shelf (fig. 1). Putting the first hole at 7in from floor level, the second at 14in up, then every 6in up to a height of 75in, or 20in from the ceiling, gave 11 possible shelf levels.

The first problem with this is that once a shelf is on the first section, you can't have a shelf on the next section at the same level, or the shelves will clash at the pillar — or can you? Fig. 2 shows how I solved the problem, but it makes another in that you have to predetermine the arrangement of shelves to some degree. By making a couple of pairs that will meet on a pillar, they can be used to change the arrangement later — it was important that the whole unit be designed to be re-arrangeable.

Making the pillars

Being a great believer in the strength of laminated timber, I made the four 3x3in pillars from four lengths of 4x1in each, planed to $^{13}/_{16}$in, which gave me an extra $^1/_4$in when the four lengths came together as one. The extra $^1/_4$in proved useful, as though the pillars came out of the clamps reasonably straight, I still had enough to finish them to 3x3in dead straight.

Making the shelves

I decided to build up an approximate 12in width from 4x1in timber; the original length of shelf I planned would have given 35in between pillars, but the timber came in either 3m or 6m lengths, so to save wood I ordered the 3m and closed the pillars up to give 33in between them. A 3m length cut into three gave one at 35in and two at 41in for each shelf (fig. 3). Realising that once the three lengths were together it would be a difficult job to end-sand the centre piece, I did this on a disc sander before I glued up, to a dead 31$^3/_4$in. The two outer pieces were cut at 41in, planed to 3$^3/_4$x$^3/_4$in, and once out of the clamps the four outer lengths' ends were trimmed to within $^1/_{16}$in, then disc-sanded to a dead 39$^1/_4$in. I finished the shelves by putting a slight rounding on all four edges of each one. I allowed $^1/_8$in round the pillars between pillar and shelf on three sides, and on reflection feel that $^1/_{16}$in would have been enough. If you go ahead with this project, I'd recommend you allow just that clearance. For the arrangement I have, I

continued

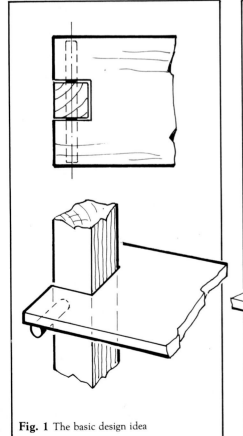

Fig. 1 The basic design idea

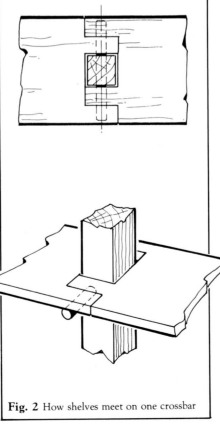

Fig. 2 How shelves meet on one crossbar

No holds shelved

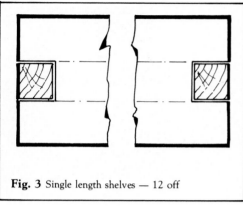

Fig. 3 Single length shelves — 12 off

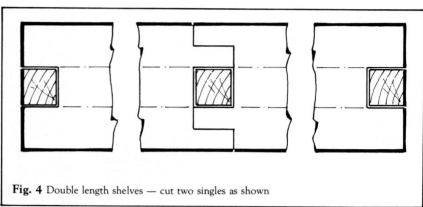

Fig. 4 Double length shelves — cut two singles as shown

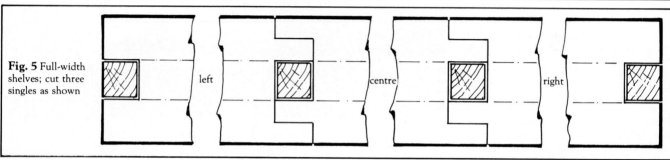

Fig. 5 Full-width shelves; cut three singles as shown   left   centre   right

made 12 shelves as shown in fig. 3, a pair as in fig. 4, and a set of three as in fig. 5 that go straight across the bottom to take large books and files. It makes a total of 17 shelves.

Drilling

For drilling the holes in the pillars I already have a very useful jig I made myself some years ago that fits on to my pillar-drill table (fig. 6), and for a job like this it really came into its own. Once the pillars were marked for holes, the drill table arranged to allow the length of the pillar to go through the jig unhindered, and a pile of offcuts ready to hold up the pillar to the same height when drilling, I found little problem completing the task. The critical part is that the holes are true through the pillar; I checked this by putting a dowel in a hole I'd drilled and trying a T-square on it off the pillar.

I know I'm not the only one that's been driven half mad trying to match imperial drills to metric dowel and vice versa, and not all dowel, as we know, comes perfectly round. But having acquired a good 1 in drill-bit I got the dowel matched on the second attempt, and although it was a little tight, I made a simple tool to sand out the holes a bit. This is merely an offcut of dowel turned down a fraction, rolled in 150-grit abrasive paper with lots of glue, and covered in elastic bands overnight. It did the trick.

Bracing

The bracings I used are really adjustable feet with a threaded M10 pin moving in a threaded spiked collar that hammers into the endgrain. They are like the ones you find on bed legs or adjustable-height kitchen units. Rocking-type hard rubber-pad feet have 15mm nuts incorporated in

the top to screw the foot in or out of the spiked collar and adjust height. I drilled a ⅜in hole in each end of the pillars, tapped the spiked collar in round it, then threaded the rubber pad in. It doesn't matter if the hole isn't dead square, as the pads will adjust. A word of warning — look for these fittings and buy them before you make your height calculations and start cutting and drilling the timber!

Construction

Bracing each pillar, I packed 3x3x½in softwood pieces between pad and floor and pad and ceiling. Once the first pillar was in

place, slightly tightened and lined up with a spirit level, I put the second pillar in line with it, using a 33in offcut between pillars and another of 4¾in to the wall. And so on until all four pillars were up.

No floor is dead flat, and my living room floor is no exception. It posed the problem of getting the shelves level, but I found that the pillars, once they were up, would turn on the pad fittings. Turning a pillar to the right raises it by winding it up the top fitting and off the bottom one, and this allowed me to raise or lower each pillar fractionally to get the shelves dead level. You only have to make sure the bottom pad fitting is

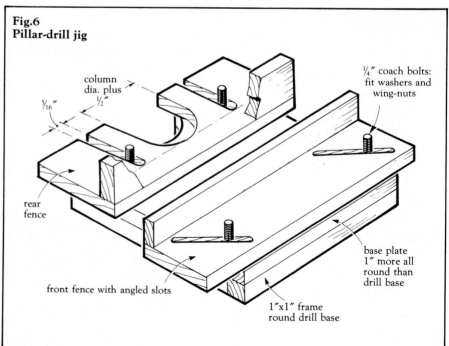

Fig.6 Pillar-drill jig

¼″ coach bolts: fit washers and wing-nuts

column dia. plus ½″

5/16″

rear fence

front fence with angled slots

1″x1″ frame round drill base

base plate 1″ more all round than drill base

unscrewed just a little before starting. After I'd completed the unit and added some weight in the form of books, the top fittings needed tightening a little as the pillars sunk into the carpet. After this I found I only needed to adjust it a little just twice, once after a week and the second time about 10 days later. Before it went up and the arrangement of shelves was decided, I expected to have a lot of empty holes about, but surprisingly enough there aren't. There are more empty holes in the two end pillars for obvious reasons, but on the arrangement I have there are 13 empty holes in all, out of a total of 44.

Conclusions

I built the unit to go against a wall in my living room, but it can also, of course, be used as a room divider. The spacing of the pillars doesn't need to be constant; one could for example have the first two pillars 30in apart, then the third 18in or whatever from the second pillar — however you want it. Of course the finish is entirely optional. I used a polyurethane finish to match my existing furniture, but it could be painted to blend in with a colour scheme.

I live in a small modern block of flats with concrete floors and ceilings, which allow the unit as it stands to work. If you live in an older house it might not be so easy — you'd have to redesign to line the pillars up with the joists and beams. First question — do the joists and beams line up? No doubt 'plates' of, say, 4x2in between pillars and floor and ceiling would spread the weight; 4x1in might be enough. But then you have great lumps of wood on floor and ceiling, which would give it a heavy look. Your problem!

Although building the unit involved a lot of work — planing up 102 metres of 4x1in

sawn was just a part of it — the entire unit, which covers a wall about 8ft high by 11ft wide, has over 46ft of shelf space between pillars, and it stands solid without a screw, nail or joint. It cost me less than £85 to build. But the nice part (next to the building) was that it has put me in domestic good books for some time to come! ∎

● **Above**, the installation is decorative enough on its own, but of course it'll hold a lot more than this. The feet work fine on strong walls and ceilings, but load-spreaders would be necessary in old and infirm structures

● **Left and above**, shelf and vertical member meeting details. The clearance round the pillars could have been less, says Alan

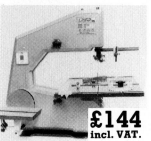

The Great Turn-up

The annual Irish Woodturners Guild Seminar is a must for any turner's diary. Lech Zielinski was there, learning some new tricks and teaching a thing or two himself

W hy is it, I wonder, that so few turners from the English side of the Irish Sea come to the Irish Woodturners Guild Seminar? If they think there's not much to turn them on in Ireland, they're mistaken. The 5th Annual Seminar, organised by the Guild in early October, proved as always a formidable event. Richard Raffan and Peter Bossom were the guest demonstrators — and this year's title? 'Turn on to Wood'. The tiny village of Letterfrack, Co. Galway, played host to some 90 woodturners.

It's been the tradition since the first Seminar in September 1982, and the foundation of the Guild in 1983, to invite one or two internationally renowned turners to demonstrate their skills, share the secrets of their techniques, and impart some of their hard-earned knowledge. The first few Seminars have seen Ray Key, Richard Raffan, Mick O'Donnell and David Ellsworth and there's little doubt about their pervasive influence on the character and style of Irish turning.

Many of the Guild members demonstrate at the Seminars, proving a match for the invited guests. Liam O'Neill, one of the Guild originators (Garth May and Bill Scott are current Guild and Seminar organisers), is now selling work in the US. Then there's Ciaran Forbes, a Benedictine monk and until recently woodturning instructor at the Connemara West Centre which hosts the Seminars. Ciaran's speciality is beautifully bulbous bowls. Michael Dickson is now an expert on miniature turnings; Keith Mosse is best known for his 3ft diameter elm bowls, and Willie Stedmond's unassuming excellence has earned him the reputation of 'quiet man of woodturning'. I'd seen Richard Raffan's exhibition (with Jim Partridge and Maria von Kesteren, *WW/Feb 86*) at the British Crafts Centre, and read his book — so to see the man in action promised to be a treat. Watching him work — boxes, scoops, green bowls and thin spindles — it was hard to imagine anyone more adept at using the skew chisel. He could turn nearly anything with this tool; at one point he was turning the outside of the bowl with it (not for novices!).

Take for example, the way he makes a scoop. A square is mounted between centres, and within seconds, with systematic, repeated cuts along the grain, it is converted into a cylinder. The wood offers no

● *Clockwise from top: Peter Bossom demonstrates a cost-effective cheeseboard on the lathe he brought with him; Tom Dunlop's delicate yew goblets; Ray Cornu's beautiful lacquered sycamore vase, and a bubinga lamp by Jerry Roche*

resistance (or so it seems) to the tool; a ¾in skew skims through the layers, leaving the surface smooth and ready for further shaping. The speed and confidence of the movements is astonishing, and all you can do is smile with amazement when Raffan says he 'never lets the wood in on the act'. I guess this is the dream of all turners . . .

Hollowing the inside was as rapidly done with a gouge. Once the opening was made, Raffan pushed the tool in and swivelled it left and right, up and down — working mainly on the up-thrust (the top right corner). Looking at the way the shavings poured out, you really believed the wood had nothing to say in the matter. Richard then turned, with similar flair and expertise, his 10in long ¼in thin spindles, with their

tiny beads.

Next came some thin-walled bowls. RR paid particular attention to the outside curves, taking time to stop and examine the shape; then, with smooth, flowing movements of the gouge, he improved the profile until he was satisfied. This meticulous attention to form is part of his philosophy. The grain configuration and the colour of the wood help to sell the work, but it's the shape that remains forever to please the eye — if it's good.

I was particularly interested in Raffan's comments on finishing. It was my modest task for the Seminar to gather, organise and impart some available knowledge about methods of finishing turned objects, and turners' finishing materials. I'm not too

continued

The Great Turn-up

sure now if I'm any the wiser; after using some fine wet-and-dry paper (on a box), Raffan amazed everyone by taking a piece of candlestick and friction-melting it. That was it — finishing finished, and a finished finish. Ideally, he says, he wouldn't finish his work at all, just let pieces gather patina with time. To put something on a piece is a compromise for the sake of the client. His preferred materials are oil and wax; leave it waxed if you want, or let it wash off with use and you can keep re-oiling it.

Peter Bossom offered us an insight into production turning. He came to the Seminar with his own lathe, ready with a (self-made) dust extractor. He makes his living doing wooden pears, apples and mushrooms, as well as cheese boards and domestic ware. He had it all worked out to the penny, cost effectiveness being his main motto. For those who earn their bread and butter from turning, the theme must be all too familiar. How many bowls, platters, apples per hour; how many £p left after deducting the overheads. Bossom spent a considerable time explaining his various time-saving devices and techniques. For example, when you're production-turning cheese boards: how do you speed up the mounting of the blanks on the lathe? Here Bossom uses contact adhesive (EvoStik type) to glue a square piece of waste to the blank. He then mounts that on a screw-chuck. Some time was also devoted to marketing and advertising techniques — a weak point for many turners, I feel.

It was good to see a variety of spin-offs from last year's inspirational displays of skills by American Del Stubbs, who showed how to make wafer-thin bowls and miniature goblets. This year Michael Dickson, last year's Guild Secretary, was invited to demonstrate making his ¼in high goblets and decanters. It is an art in itself to produce objects of this size. Michael showed one goblet with about 15 loose rings round the stem, and I thought I

overheard him saying he made one with 30... Most of these tinies are made of animal bone or tagua nut. Needless to say, all the tools for this sort of turning are home-made, often from masonry nails.

Willie Stedmond was there this year, just as before, to enlighten and help build confidence of those turning folk who think they can never make a lamp or a balustrade spindle. He has a thorough and steady approach, and the shavings flew fast to uncover a slender shape. It was a pleasure to watch him.

Liam O'Neill dealt with making platters this year. Liam is a full-time turner with a well-organised production line; his workshop is full of rough-turned bowl blanks and platter discs, all drying waiting for their turn... A small number of Guild members (I was one of the lucky ones) had an opportunity to take advantage of Liam's hospitality and organisational skills. Two days after the Seminar, he put together a mini-seminar with Richard Raffan in his workshop in Shannon. It was an

● **Top left**, *Richard Raffan's ebony bowls sell well to the Australian Japanese;* **top right**, *Michael Dickson's miniature goblets won a spindle-turning prize.* **Above**, *John Ambrose's 'brick laminated' teak and sycamore bowl.* **Below**, *a Raffan bowl from an interesting bit of holly*

opportunity to ask some more detailed questions, and sort out some problem areas in turning.

Parallel to the programme of demonstrators dealing with their tasks, the main Seminar this year put up a set of other subjects, dealt with by members. Tom and John Dunlop displayed and explained the various stages of laminated turning, Pat Hogan showed how to use a chainsaw, Terry Cromer brought some samples of exotic timbers and offered expert advice on their properties, and I had a corner bench with the finishes.

The Seminar ended with the announcement of the winners of the competition of members' work. There were three categories; Bowls or Hollow Ware, Boxes and Spindle turning. The first prizes were £50 Crafts Supplies vouchers and £50 from the Guild, and the second and third prizes were made up of finishing materials kindly donated by Rustins.

First prize in the Bowl category went to

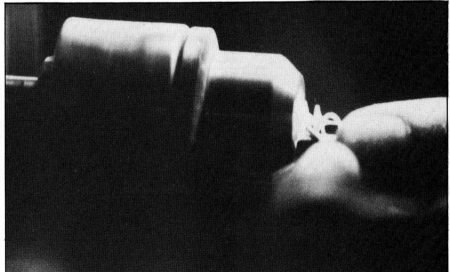

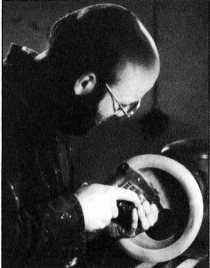

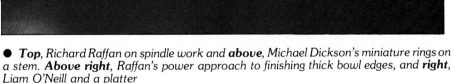

● **Top**, *Richard Raffan on spindle work and* **above**, *Michael Dickson's miniature rings on a stem.* **Above right**, *Raffan's power approach to finishing thick bowl edges, and* **right**, *Liam O'Neill and a platter*

Niall Fitzduff for a superbly turned 14x5in diameter vase (he had more work of similar quality), closely followed by Ray Cornu, who brings exciting new work each year to the Seminar. His second-place bowl was a thin-walled piece of laminated rosewood and tulipwood. Third prize went to John Ambrose for his 7in diameter ladle (quite a thing to turn, and to explain how to turn. John took some time over it . . .) John also won a third prize in the box category for his 4x9in diameter 'brick laminated' bowl with a lid. I think he should have also been commended for patience. The first prize in the Box category went to John Kelly for his unusual yew vessel, some 12x4in diameter;

an oval shape with a handled lid. There is a dish inset which you see as you lift the lid, beautifully turned and finished. John consistently produces work of quality and this and last year's awards prove it. He also won a second prize for a walking stick. It came as no surprise to see Michael Dickson scooping the first prize in the Spindle category with his miniatures. The winner was a set of six goblets about ¼in high, with loose rings and a decanter. If his talent grows any more, we won't even be able to *see* his work next year.

As it happened, another 'wood event' was taking place alongside the wood-

continued

The Great Turn-up

turning Seminar in Letterfrack. Connemara West Centre had organised, and were hosting (jointly with the Regional Arts Officer and the Sculpture Society of Ireland) a Wood Sculpture Symposium. 'The aim of the Symposium,' says the blurb, 'is to create a greater awareness of outdoor wood sculpture and to make it more accessible to the community.'·Over a four-week period, nine sculptors were working on their various pieces, mainly in the open air, and the public were free to watch the artists at work. The pieces were destined ultimately for the grounds of the

Connemara West Centre and the villages of Tullycross and Tully. The nine sculptures have been conceived and designed to reflect the local environment, history and traditions — dancing, the sea and coastline, the community. Very strong stuff.

And so, you see, the Irish Woodturners' Guild continues to provide a meeting place for craftspeople and a venue for everyone to turn up to, and turn on to each other's work. What about it, England? ■

See Woodworker Feb for an answer to that!

● *'Fish eats fish' – meal as yet unfinished*

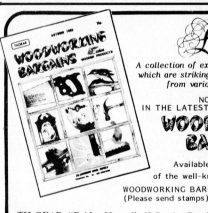

shopguide

AVON

BATH Tel. Bath 64513
JOHN HALL TOOLS
RAILWAY STREET ★

Open: Monday-Saturday
9.00 a.m.-5.30 p.m.
H.P.W.WM.D.A.BC.

BRISTOL Tel. (0272) 741510
JOHN HALL TOOLS LIMITED ★
CLIFTON DOWN SHOPPING CENTRE
WHITELADIES ROAD
Open: Monday-Saturday
9.00 a.m.-5.30 p.m.
H.P.W.WM.D.A.BC.

BRISTOL Tel. (0272) 629092
TRYMWOOD SERVICES
2a DOWNS PARK EAST, (off North View)
WESTBURY PARK
Open: 8.30 a.m.-5.30 p.m. Mon. to Fri.
Closed for lunch 1.00-2.00 p.m.
P.W.WM.D.T.A.BC.

BRISTOL Tel. (0272) 667013
FASTSET LTD
190-192 WEST STREET
BEDMINSTER
Open: Mon.-Fri. 8.30 a.m.-5.00 p.m.
Saturday 9.00 a.m.-1.00 p.m.
H.P.W.WM.D.CS.A.BC.

BRISTOL Tel. (0272) 667013
WILLIS
157 WEST STREET
BEDMINSTER
Open Mon.-Fri. 8.30 a.m.-5.00 p.m.
Sat. 9 a.m.-4 p.m.
P.W.WM.D.CS.A.BC.

BERKSHIRE

READING Tel. Littlewick Green
DAVID HUNT (TOOL 2743
MERCHANTS) LTD ★
KNOWL HILL, NR. READING
Open: Monday-Saturday
9.00 a.m.-5.30 p.m.
H.P.W.D.A.BC.

READING Tel. Reading 661511
WOKINGHAM TOOL CO. LTD.
99 WOKINGHAM ROAD

Open: Mon-Sat 9.00 a.m.-5.30 p.m.
Closed 1.00-2.00 p.m. for lunch
H.P.W.WM.D.CS.A.BC.

BUCKINGHAMSHIRE

MILTON KEYNES Tel. (0908)
POLLARD WOODWORKING 641366
CENTRE ★
51 AYLESBURY ST., BLETCHLEY
Open: Mon-Fri 8.30-5.30
Saturday 9.00-5.00
H.P.W.WM.D.CS.A.BC.

HIGH WYCOMBE Tel. (0494)
SCOTT SAWS LTD. 24201/33788
14 BRIDGE STREET ★

Mon.-Sat. 8.30 a.m.-6.00 p.m.

H.P.W.WM.D.T.CS.MF.A.BC.

BUCKINGHAMSHIRE

HIGH WYCOMBE Tel. (0494)
ISAAC LORD LTD 22221
185 DESBOROUGH ROAD KE

Open: Mon-Fri 8.00 a.m.-5.00 p.m.
Saturday 9.00 a.m.-5.00 p.m.
H.P.W.D.A.

SLOUGH Tel. (06286) 5125
BRAYWOOD ESTATES LTD. ★
158 BURNHAM LANE
Open: 9.00am-5.30pm.
Monday-Saturday.

H.P.W.WM.CS.A.

CAMBRIDGESHIRE

CAMBRIDGE Tel. (0223) 63132
D. MACKAY LTD. ★
BRITANNIA WORKS, EAST ROAD

Open: Mon.-Fri. 8.30 a.m.-1 p.m./2.00-
5.00 p.m. Sat. 8.30 a.m.-1.00 p.m.
H.P.W.D.T.CS.MF.A.BC.

CAMBRIDGE Tel. (0223) 247386
H. B. WOODWORKING K
105 CHERRY HINTON ROAD
Open: 8.30 a.m.-5.30 p.m.
Monday-Friday
8.30 a.m.-1.00 p.m. Sat.
H.P.W.WM.D.CS.A.

CHESHIRE

NANTWICH Tel. Crewe 67010
ALAN HOLTHAM K★
THE OLD STORES TURNERY
WISTASON ROAD, WILLASTON
Open: Tues.-Sat. 9.00 a.m.-5.30 p.m.
Closed Monday
P.W.WM.D.T.C.CS.A.BC.

CLEVELAND

MIDDLESBROUGH Tel. (0642)
CLEVELAND WOODCRAFT 813103
(M'BRO), 38-42 CRESCENT ROAD K

Open: Mon-Sat 9.15 a.m.-5.30 p.m.

H.P.T.A.BC.W.WM.CS.D.

CORNWALL

SOUTH WEST Power Tools

CORNWALL Tel: Helston (03265) 4961
HELSTON AND LAUNCESTON Launceston
(0566) 4781
H.P.W.WM.D.CS.A. K

CUMBRIA

CARLISLE Tel: (0228) 36391
W. M. PLANT
ALLENBROOK ROAD
ROSEHILL, CA1 2UT
Open: Mon.-Fri. 8.00 a.m.-5.15 p.m.
Sat. 8.00 a.m.-12.30 noon
P.W.WM.D.CS.A.

DEVON

BRIXHAM Tel. (08045) 4900
WOODCRAFT SUPPLIES E★
4 HORSE POOL STREET

Open: Mon.-Sat. 9.00 a.m.-6.00 p.m.

H.P.W.A.D.MF.CS.BC.

PLYMOUTH Tel. (0752) 330303
WESTWARD BUILDING SERVICES ★
LTD., LISTER CLOSE, NEWNHAM
INDUSTRIAL ESTATE, PLYMPTON
Open: Mon-Fri 8.00 a.m.-5.30 p.m.
Sat. 8.30 a.m.-12.30 p.m.
H.P.W.WM.D.A.BC.

PLYMOUTH Tel. (0752) 665363
F.T.B. LAWSON LTD.
71 NEW GEORGE STREET
PLYMOUTH PL1 1RB
Open: Mon.-Sat. 8.30 am-5.30 pm.

H.P.W.CS.MF.A.

ESSEX

LEIGH ON SEA Tel. (0702)
MARSHAL & PARSONS LTD. 710404
1111 LONDON ROAD EK

Open: 8.30 a.m.-5.30 p.m. Mon-Fri
9.00 a.m.-5.00 p.m. Sat.
H.P.W.WM.D.CS.A.

GLOUCESTER

TEWKESBURY Tel. (0684)
TEWKESBURY SAW CO. LTD. 293092
TRADING ESTATE, NEWTOWN K

Open: Mon-Fri 8.00 a.m.-5.00 p.m.
Saturday 9.30 a.m.-12.00 p.m.
P.W.WM.D.CS.

HAMPSHIRE

ALDERSHOT SOUTHAMPTON
(0252) 334422 (0703) 332288
BURCH & HILLS POWER TOOL CENTRES
374 HIGH ST. 7 BELVIDERE RD.
Open Mon.-Fri. 8.30-5.30. Sat. 8.30-12.30
Closed for Lunch 1.00-2.00
H.P.W.WM.D.CS.MF.BC.K.*

HERTFORDSHIRE

WARE K★
HEATH SAWS
16 MALTINGS
STANSTEAD ABBOTTS (near Ware) HERTS.
Open: Mon.-Fri. 8.30am-5.30pm
Sat. 8.30am-1pm. Sunday by appointment.
P.W.WM.D.CS.A.

HERTFORDSHIRE

ENFIELD Tel: 01-363 2935
GILL & HOXBY LTD.
131-137 ST. MARKS ROAD ADJ.
BUSH HILL PARK STATION, EN1 1BA
Mon.-Sat. 8-5.30
Early closing Wed. 1 pm.
H.P.A.M.MC.T.S.W.

HUMBERSIDE

GRIMSBY Tel. Grimsby (0472)
58741 Hull (0482) 26999
J. E. SIDDLE LTD. (Tool Specialists) ★
83 VICTORIA STREET
Open: Mon-Fri 8.30 a.m.-5.30 p.m.
Sat. 8.30 a.m.-12.45 p.m. & 2 p.m.-5 p.m.
H.P.A.BC.W.WMD.

HULL
HUMBERSIDE FACTORING/H.F.C.
SAW SERVICING LTD.
MAIN STREET
Open: Mon.-Fri. 8am-5pm.
Saturday 8am-12.00pm.
H.P.W.WM.D.CS.A.BC.K.

KENT

WYE Tel. (0233) 813144
KENT POWER TOOLS LTD.
UNIT 1, BRIAR CLOSE
WYE, Nr. ASFORD

H.P.W.WM.D.A.CS.

MAIDSTONE Tel. (0622) 50177
SOUTH EASTERN SAWS (Ind.) LTD. ★
COLDRED ROAD
PARKWOOD INDUSTRIAL ESTATE

Open: Mon.-Fri. 8.00 a.m.-6.00 p.m.
Sat. 9.00 a.m.-12.00 a.m.
B.C.W.CS.WM.PH.

MAIDSTONE
HENSON AND PLATT
TOKE PLACE
LINTON

Open Mon.-Fri. 8.00 a.m.-5.00 p.m.
Saturday 8.00 a.m.-1.0p.m.

H.P.W.T.CS.A.

LANCASHIRE

PRESTON Tel. (0772) 52951
SPEEDWELL TOOL COMPANY E★
62-68 MEADOW STREET PR1 1SU
Open: Mon.-Fri. 8.30 a.m.-5.30 p.m.
Sat. 8.30 a.m.-12.30 p.m.

H.P.W.WM.CS.A.MF.BC.

ROCHDALE Tel. (0706) 342123/
C.S.M. TOOLS 342322
4-6 HEYWOOD ROAD E★
CASTLETON
Open: Mon-Sat 9.00 a.m.-6.00 p.m.
Sundays by appointment
W.D.CS.A.BC.

BERKSHIRE ... CLEVELAND

PETERBOROUGH Tel. (0733)
WILLIAMS DISTRIBUTORS 64252
(TOOLS) LIMITED K
108-110 BURGHLEY ROAD
Open: Monday to Friday
8.30 a.m.-5.30 p.m.
H.P.A.W.D.WH.BC.

shopguide

LANCASHIRE

LANCASTER   Tel. (0524) 32886
LILE TOOL SHOP   K
43/45 NORTH ROAD
Open: Monday to Saturday
9.00 a.m.-5.30 p.m.
Wed. 9.00 a.m.-12.30 p.m.
H.P.W.D.A.

**All shops with an
asterisk *
have a Mail Order
Service**

BLACKPOOL
FLYDE WOODTURNING SUPPLIES   ★
255 CHURCH STREET
BLACKPOOL FY1 4HY
9.30-5.30 Monday to Saturday
H.P.W.WM.A.MF.C.B.C.D.

LINCOLNSHIRE

LINCOLN   Tel. (0522) 689369
SKELLINGTHORPE SAW SERVICES LTD.
OLD WOOD, SKELLINGTHORPE
Open: Mon to Fri 8 a.m.-5 p.m.
Sat 8 a.m.-12 p.m.
H.P.W.WM.D.CS.A.*.BC.
Access/Barclaycard

LONDON

ACTON   Tel. (01-992) 4835
A. MILLS (ACTON) LTD   ★
32/36 CHURCHFIELD ROAD W3 6ED
Open: Mon-Fri 9.00 a.m.-5.00 p.m.
Saturdays 9.00 am.-1.00 p.m.
H.P.W.WM.

LONDON   Tel. 01-723 2295-6-7
LANGHAM TOOLS LIMITED
13 NORFOLK PLACE
LONDON W2 1QJ

LONDON   Tel. (01-636) 7475
BUCK & RYAN LTD   ★
101 TOTTENHAM COURT ROAD W1P ODY
Open: Mon.-Fri. 8.30 a.m.-5.30 p.m.
Saturday 8.30 a.m.-4.00 p.m.
H.P.W.WM.D.A..

WEMBLEY   Tel. 904-1144
ROBERT SAMUEL LTD.   (904-1147)
7, 15 & 16 COURT PARADE   after 4.00)
EAST LANE, N. WEMBLEY   ★
Open Mon.-Fri. 8.45-5.15; Sat. 9-1.00
Access, Barclaycard, AM Express, & Diners
H.P.W.CS.E.A.D.

HOUNSLOW   Tel. (01-570)
Q.R. TOOLS LTD   2103/5135
251-253 HANWORTH ROAD
Open: Mon-Fri 8.30 a.m.-5.30 p.m.
Sat. 9.00 a.m.-1.00 p.m.
P.W.WM.D.CS.A.

LONDON

FULHAM   Tel. (01-385) 5109
I. GRIZZARD LTD.   E
84a-b LILLIE ROAD, SW6 1TL
Open: Mon-Sat 9.00-5.30 p.m.
Half day Thursday

H.P.A.BC.W.CS.WM.D.

MANCHESTER

MANCHESTER   Tel. (061 789)
TIMMS TOOLS   0909
102-104 LIVERPOOL ROAD   ★
PATRICROFT M30 0WZ
Weekdays 9.00 a.m.-5.30 p.m.
Sat. 9.00 a.m.-1.00 p.m.
H.P.A.W.

MERSEYSIDE

LIVERPOOL   Tel. (051-207) 2967
TAYLOR BROS (LIVERPOOL) LTD   K
195-199 LONDON ROAD
LIVERPOOL L3 8JG
Open: Monday to Friday
8.30 a.m.-5.30 p.m.
H.P.W.WM.D.A.BC.

MIDDLESEX

RUISLIP   Tel. (08956) 74126
ALLMODELS ENGINEERING LTD.   E★
91 MANOR WAY

Open: Mon-Sat 9.00 a.m.-5.30 p.m.
H.P.W.A.D.CS.MF.BC.

NORFOLK

NORWICH   Tel. (0603) 898695
NORFOLK SAW SERVICES
DOG LANE, HORSFORD
Open: Monday to Friday
8.00 a.m.-5.00 p.m.
Saturday 8.00 a.m.-12.00 p.m.
H.P.W.WM.D.CS.A.

KINGS LYNN   Tel. (0553) 2443
WALKER & ANDERSON (Kings Lynn) LTD.
WINDSOR ROAD, KINGS LYNN   K
Open: Monday to Saturday
7.45 a.m.-5.30 p.m.
Wednesday 1.00 p.m. Saturday 5.00 p.m.
H.P.W.WM.D.CS.A.

NORWICH   Tel. (0603) 400933
WESTGATES WOODWORKING   Tx
61 HURRICANE WAY,   975412
NORWICH AIRPORT INDUSTRIAL ESTATE
Open: 9.00 a.m.-5.00 p.m. weekdays
9.00 a.m.-12.30 Sat.
P.W.WM.D.BC.   K

KING'S LYNN   Tel. (07605) 674
TONY WADDILOVE WOODCRAFT   ★
HILL FARM WORKSHOPS
GT. DUNHAM
(NR. SWAFFHAM)
Tues.-Sat. 9.00am-5.30pm
H.P.W.D.T.MF.A.BC.

NOTTINGHAMSHIRE

NOTTINGHAM   Tel. (0602) 225979
POOLEWOOD   and 227064/5
EQUIPMENT LTD.   (06077) 2421 after hrs
5a HOLLY LANE, CHILLWELL
Open: Mon-Fri 9.00 a.m.-5.30 p.m.
Sat. 9.00 a.m. to 12.30 p.m.
P.W.WM.D.CS.A.BC.

OXON

WITNEY   Tel. (0993) 3885.
TARGET TOOLS (SALES,   & 72095 OXON
TARGET TOOLS   HIRE & REPAIRS)   ★
SWAIN COURT
STATION INDUSTRIAL ESTATE
Open: Mon.-Sat. 8.00 a.m.-5.00 p.m.
24 hour Answerphone
BC.W.M.A.

SHROPSHIRE

TELFORD   Tel. Telford (0952)
ASLES LTD   48054
VINEYARD ROAD, WELLINGTON   EK★

Open: Mon. Fri. 8.30 a.m.-5.30 p.m.
Saturday 8.30 a.m.-4.00 p.m.
H.P.W.WM.D.CS.BC.A.

SOMERSET

TAUNTON   Tel. (0823) 85431
JOHN HALL TOOLS   ★
6 HIGH STREET

Open Monday-Saturday
9.00 a.m.-5.30 p.m.
H.P.W.WM.D.CS.A.

STAFFORDSHIRE

**Use this space
for your
New Year Plans**

SUFFOLK

SUFFOLK   Tel. (037983) 8126
LOCKWOOD WOODWORKING MACHINERY
WHITEGATES BUNGALOW
THE COMMON MELLIS
NEAR EYE/DISS IP23
Open standard hours.
*Lathe demos every Saturday morning.
Woodcopy lathes/Dust extractors.*
H.P.W.D.A.

IPSWICH   Tel. (0473) 40456
FOX WOODWORKING   KE★
142-144 BRAMFORD LANE
Open: Tues., Fri., 9.00 a.m.-5.30 p.m.
Sat. 9.00 a.m.-5.00 p.m.

H.P.W.WM.D.A.B.C.

SUSSEX

BOGNOR REGIS   Tel. (0243) 863100
A. OLBY & SON (BOGNOR REGIS) LTD.
"TOOLSHOP," BUILDERS MERCHANT
HAWTHORN ROAD   K
Open: Mon-Thurs 8 a.m.-5.15 p.m. Fri.
8 a.m.-8 p.m. Sat 8 a.m.-12.45 p.m.
H.P.W.WM.D.T.C.A.BC.

WORTHING   Tel. (0903) 38739
W. HOSKING LTD (TOOLS &   KE★
MACHINERY)
28 PORTLAND RD, BN11 1QN
Open: Mon.-Sat. 8.30 a.m.-5.30 p.m.
Closed Wednesday
H.P.W.WM.D.CS.A.BC.

TYNE & WEAR

NEWCASTLE   Tel. (0632) 320311
HENRY OSBOURNE LTD.   E★
50-54 UNION STREET

Open: Mon-Fri 8.30 a.m.-5.00 p.m.

H.P.W.D.CS.MF.A.BC.

TYNE & WEAR

NEWCASTLE-UPON-TYNE   ★
J. W. HOYLE LTD
CLARENCE STREET
NEWCASTLE-UPON-TYNE
TYNE & WEAR
NE2 17J
H.P.W.WM.D.CS.A.BC.K.

W. MIDLANDS

WOLVERHAMPTON   Tel. (0902)
MANSAW SERVICES   58759
WARD STREET, HORSELEY FIELDS   K★
WOLVERHAMPTON, WEST MIDLANDS
Open Mon.-Fri. 9.00am-5.00pm
Sat. 8am-3pm
H.P.W.WM.A.D.CS.

YORKSHIRE

**This space is
reserved for
you!**

SHEFFIELD   Tel. (0742) 441012
GREGORY & TAYLOR LTD   KE
WORKSOP ROAD
Open: 8.30 a.m.-5.30 p.m.
Monday-Friday
8.30 a.m.-12.30 p.m. Sat.
H.P.W.WM.D.

HARROGATE   Tel. (0423) 66245/
MULTI-TOOLS   55328
158 KINGS ROAD   K★

Open: Monday to Saturday
8.30 a.m.-6.00 p.m.
H.P.W.WM.D.A.BC.

THIRSK   Tel. (0845) 22770
THE WOOD SHOP   ★
TRESKE SAWMILLS LTD.
STATION WORKS
Open: Seven days a week 9.00-5.00

T.H.MF.BC.

LEEDS   Tel. (0532) 574736
D. B. KEIGHLEY MACHINERY LTD.   ★
VICKERS PLACE, STANNINGLEY
PUDSEY LS2 86LZ
Mon.-Fri. 9.00 a.m.-5.00 p.m.
Sat. 9.00 a.m.-1.00 p.m.
P.A.W.WM.CS.BC.

**You see! They
will notice you in
'Woodworker'**

HUDDERSFIELD   Tel. (0484)
NEVILLE M. OLDHAM   641219/(0484)
UNIT 1 DALE ST. MILLS   42777
DALE STREET, LONGWOOD   ★
Open: Mon-Fri 9.00 a.m.-5.30 p.m.
Saturday 9.30 a.m.-12.00 p.m.
P.W.WM.D.A.BC.

shop guide

YORKSHIRE

HOLME UPON SPALDING MOOR Tel: 0696 60612
CRAFT TOOLS AND TACKLE LTD.
HOLME INDUSTRIAL ESTATE
Open: Mon.-Fri. 9.30 am-5.30 pm.
Saturday & Bank Holidays 9.30 am-4.30 pm.
H.P.W.D.T.CS.MF.A.BC.

CLECKHEATON Tel. (0274) 872861
SKILLED CRAFTS LTD. ★
34 BRADFORD ROAD
Open: 9.00 a.m.-5.00 p.m. Monday
Saturday Lunch 12.00 a.m.-1.00 p.m.
H.P.A.W.CS.WM.D.

HALIFAX Tel: (0422) 45919
SMITH'S WOODWORKERS LTD.
GRANTHAM ROAD
HALIFAX HX3 6PL
Manufacturer of Mortices, Tenoners and Mitre Machines.

SCOTLAND

EDINBURGH Tel. 031-337-5555
THE SAW CENTRE
38 HAYMARKET EH12 5JZ
Mon.-Fri. 8.30 a.m.-5.30 p.m.
SAT. 9.00 a.m.-1.00 p.m.
H.P.W.WM.D.CS.A.

GLASGOW Tel. 041-429-4444/ 4374 Telex: 777886
THE SAW CENTRE E★
650 EGLINTON STREET
GLASGOW G5 9RP
Mon.-Fri. 8.00 a.m.-5.00 p.m.
Sat. 9.00 a.m.-1.00 p.m.
H.P.W.WM.D.CS.A.

CULLEN Tel. (0542) 40563
GRAMPIAN WOODTURNING SUPPLIES AT BAYVIEW CRAFTS
Open Mon.-Sat. 9.00 a.m.-5.30 p.m. Sunday 10.00 a.m.-5.30 p.m. Open later July/Aug. Sept. Demonstrations SAT/SUN or by appointment.
H.W.D.MF.BC.

SCOTLAND

PERTH Tel. (0738) 26173
WILLIAM HUME & CO. K
ST. JOHN'S PLACE
Open: Monday to Saturday
8.00 a.m.-5.30 p.m.
8.00 a.m.-1.00 p.m. Wednesday
H.P.A.BC.W.CS.WM.D.

IRELAND

NEWTOWNARDS Tel. 0247 819800 or 812506
NORLYN MACHINERY
UNIT 10, MALCOLMSON IND. EST.
80 BANGOR ROAD, CO. DOWN
Open: Mon.-Fri. 9.30am-5.30pm
(Closed 1-2pm for lunch)
Any other time by request.
H.W.WM.D.T.MF.A.   24 Hour Service. K

WALES

CARDIFF Tel. (0222) 595710
DATAPOWER TOOLS LTD,
MICHAELSTON ROAD,
CULVERHOUSE CROSS
Open: Mon.-Fri. 8.00 a.m.-5.00 p.m.
Sat. 9.00 a.m.-1.00 p.m.
H.P.W.WM.D.A.

WALES

SWANSEA Tel. (0792) 55680
SWANSEA TIMBER & PLYWOOD CO. LTD.
57-59 OXFORD STREET ★
Open: Mon to Fri 9.00 a.m.-5.30 p.m.
Sat. 9.00 a.m.-1.00 p.m.
H.P.W.D.T.CS.A.BC.

CARMARTHEN Tel. (0267) 237219
DO-IT-YOURSELF SUPPLY K
BLUE STREET, DYFED
Open: Monday to Saturday
9.00 a.m.-5.30 p.m.
Thursday 9.00 a.m.-5.30 p.m.
H.P.W.WM.D.T.CS.A.BC.

CARDIFF Tel. (0222) 396039
JOHN HALL TOOLS LIMITED
ROYAL ARCADE ★
Open: Monday to Saturday
9.00 a.m.-5.30 p.m.
H.P.W.WM.D.A.BC.

WOOD SUPPLIERS

WOOD SUPPLIERS

WOOD SUPPLIERS

H. G. MILDENHALL AND SONS JOINERY AND TIMBER

Over sixty species of timber available, small quantities our speciality. From Bobbin blanks, Turning and Carving blanks. Full machining facilities available. Send s.a.e. with cutting list for quote by return. To:

H. G. Mildenhall and Sons,
Joinery and Timber, 11 Oxford Street,
Lambourn, Nr. Newbury, Berks. RG16 7XS. Tel. 0488 71481

ENGLISH HARDWOODS

Oak, Ash, Sycamore, Beech etc. Air & Kiln dried
All sizes in stock
HOUGHTON TIMBER
HIGHER WALTON TRADING ESTATE
PRESTON, LANCS.
Tel: Preston 323566

Oak

First quality kiln dried, keen prices.
Most other English Hardwoods.
Hoyle Hardwoods, Shropshire.
Ironbridge (095245) 3373 (anytime)
WEM (0939) 33006 (9am-5pm)
Suffolk, Hadleigh (0473) 823048
(Evenings & weekends only)

WOOD

NOW AVAILABLE!

VENEERS FROM 21p per sq. ft.

MARQUETRY PACKS

Containing around 20 species approx 4" x 3" including exotics such as . . .
● Burrs
● Sycamore
● Rosewoods
● Walnut
● Cerejeira
● Ash

SEND TODAY
ONLY £4.75 a pack inc. VAT
+ 95p post and packing

Fast turnaround on all orders

ROBBINS LTD.
The one stop wood shop at
Merrywood Road,
Bedminster,
Bristol, BS31 1DX.

FREE Catalogues of product ranges now available:
(tick as required)

Wood Turners ☐	Mouldings and Sheet Materials ☐
Cabinet Makers ☐	Joinery ☐
Boat Builders ☐	Veneers and Marquetry ☐

All lists include full details of support materials and supplies.
Cheque/P.O. with order.
Access/Barclaycard. Phone orders accepted
Tel 0272 633136.
NAME_____
ADDRESS _____
_____
_____

HOMEGROWN HARDWOODS

Select your own boards from our workshop in London.
17 species of British hardwoods, kiln dried to 10-12%.
Acacia, Ash, Beech, Cedar of Lebanon, Cherry, Chestnut, Elm, Burr Elm, Lime, Oak, brown Oak, London plane, black Popular, Sycamore, Walnut, Wellingtonia, Yew.
Also some turning stuff in the round.
**1-5 Chance Street,
London E1 6JT.
Tel: 01-729 5736**

English Hardwoods — kiln dried English Oak and Elm. Air dried Ash 1¼", 3" and 4". Walnut 1". Yew 1" and 2". Elm and Oak Burrs.
**M. Griffin, 'Wesleyan House',
Alstonefield, Ashbourne,
Derbyshire.**
Tel: Alstonefield (033527) 249

WELSH OAK and ASH

Kiln dried, small — medium quantities. Deliveries arranged.

**Valley Timber Company,
Cwm Cych near Newcastle Emlyn,
Dyfed. Tel: (023977) 200**

OAK 150 cubic ft. fresh sawn £6.00 cubic ft. Elm 100 cubic ft. 1-4 years air-dried. Beech 150 cubic ft. of 1 inch and 2 inch planks, 1 year air-dried £5 cube. Also on-site mobile service. Christow Mobile Saw Mill, Christow, Exeter, Devon. Tel: 0647 52531.

18TH CENTURY pitch pine, superb quality. Bandmilled to your requirements. Most English hardwoods stocked, air and kiln dry. Tel. Will Tyers, cabinet maker for price list — (0468) 21292 (Nr. Lancaster).

HARD & SPECIALIST WOODS, air and kiln dried. Priced stock list. Items prepared to your cutting list. Minns, Unit 7, West Way, Oxford (0865) 247840.

Berkshire Hardwoods
Seasoned British hardwoods for the woodworker and turner. Prime oak, ash, beech, chestnut, cherry, yew. Waney edge boards, bowl blanks or fully finished stock. Cutting lists quoted for:
Prices from £10 cu.ft. kiln dried.
**Allan Morris, Crowthorne 772157
Steve Dooley, Crowthorne 773586**

SEASONED ENGLISH OAK
BEST QUALITY AT SENSIBLE PRICES
Carefully dried to 10-12% moisture by dehumidifying process, then graded. Square and waney edged, any quantity.
**Craig MacDonald (S.C.O.P.E. Products),
Fair Meadow, Upper Farringdon, Alton,
Hants. Haslemere (0428) 52751 (office hours) or Tisted (042058) 357 (other times)**

OAK, ASH, ELM, WALNUT etc. Fresh sawn, air dried or kiln dried. Also blanks for woodturners. Thos Harrison & Sons, Launceston, Cornwall. Tel: (056 685) 322.

THE WOOD SHOP

Our Cabinetmaker and Woodturners sawmill specialises in **homegrown**, imported and exotic timbers for the small user.
We can **machine** to your cutting list and **deliver** to your home.
Open 7 days a week, 9 to 5.
Send for new brochure to Treske Sawmills, Station Works
Thirsk YO7 4NY
Tel (0845) 22770
Treske ⚙ Sawmills

SEASONED ANTIQUE PINES

Pitch and Yellow. Cut to your specification.
Ring Bernard for personal attention
(Deliveries over reasonable distances)
**Britannia Sawmills — Huddersfield
(0484) 645931/535063.**

H.B. LACEY & SON
Whitemoor Farm, Doddiscombsleigh,
Exeter, Devon. Tel: (0647) 52268
Air dried Oak £14 cu.ft. Ash £18 cu.ft.
Olive Ash £12 cu.ft. Most stock has been air dried for 2 years.
Cheap delivery and "cut-to-size" service available.

BEDS/CAMBS/HERTS BORDERS Kilned timber and small sections at competitive prices. Timber prepared, worktops to order. The Butts End. 0767 51608.

WESSEX TIMBER

OAK, ELM, WALNUT, YEW, ASH, CHERRY, CHESTNUT, CEDAR, SYCAMORE, PEAR, ACACIA, BEECH, PINE ETC. BOWL BLANKS & BURRS, NATIONAL DELIVERY.
Prices & Machining to Specification.
Any Quantity.
Inspection welcome by Appointment.

Longney, Gloucester GL2 6SJ.
Tel: Gloucester 740610 incl. evenings.

Hardwoods for the Craftsman

Send for a FREE CATALOGUE

Fitchett and Woollacott Ltd.
Willow Road, Lenton Lane, Nottingham NG7 2PR
Telephone: (0602) 700691 Telex 377401

SELL IT NOW IN WOODWORKER RING
01-437-0699

Classified Advertisements

FOR SALE

THE FINEST SELECTION ON DISPLAY IN SCOTLAND!

WOODWORKING & METALWORKING MACHINERY POWER TOOLS HAND TOOLS

THE SAW CENTRE

LARGE STOCKS COMPETITIVE PRICES. PHONE AND TRY US NOW!

Eglinton Toll, Glasgow G5 9RP Tel: 041-429-4444

38 Haymarket Edinburgh EH12 5J2 Tel: 031-337-5555

OPEN Mon - Fri 8am - 5pm Sat 9am - 1pm

WOODCARVING tools

LARGEST STOCK IN EUROPE

Henry Taylor
Arkansas Bench & Slip Stones
Strops & Strop Paste
Bench Screws, Carvers' Vices

WOODTURNING tools

Complete range of Henry Taylor handled or unhandled

send 40p in stamps for illustrated catalogue

ALEC TIRANTI LTD
70 High St, Theale, Reading, Berks RG7 5AR
27 Warren Street, London W1.

CLOCKMAKERS

Extensive range of very competitively priced German quartz clock movements, (including standard quartz, pendulum, mini-pendulum, chining, striking and insertion movements). Large selection of quality dials, chapter rings, hands, bezels, clock plans and weather instruments. *Please send 25p stamps for 20 page catalogue.*
Bath Clock Company (Dept. W), 13 Welton Road, Radstock, Bath.

USERS AND COLLECTORS tools for sale at the Old Craft Tool Shop, 15 High Street, Whitton, Middx. Telephone 01-755 0441.

ARUNDELL K150 lathe complete with Multistar chuck, used for demonstration only £230. Tel: Stevenage (0438) 358970.

BANKRUPT STOCK

Sandvik circular saw blades tungsten tipped.
5", 5½", 6" .... **£4.00** each
6½", 8¼" .... **£6.00** each
½" to 1⅜" bore any size.
P&P £1 extra per order.
**Tel: 01 672 7776
Hannett, 1A Links Road, Tooting, London SW17 9ED.**

BLADES

Spindle tooling, circular saw blades, dado sets, planer blades, router cutters and router accessories, machinery of particular merit, Forstener bits, mortise chisels, profile cutter blocks, radial arm saw accessories, etc.
Send £1 (refunded on first order) for your copy of our brochure.
Blades, Dept. WWM. Freepost, Petersfield, Hampshire. GU32 2BR (no stamp required)

RECORD Multi Plane 405 complete and unused in original box, £120. Tel: (01) 539 5638.

FOR SALE. Stanley 55 complete. Offers over £100. Tel: 021-477-9480.

Restless sleepers, Backache suffers — for a more comfortable night's sleep see advertisement below:

D.I.Y. WATERBEDS, Heater Dream Merchant Waveless Mattress, Liner and full instructions supplied. You only supply the easy-to-build (5ft. by 7ft.) timber and chipboard frame. For a more comfortable nights sleep with total support and warmth (recommended by Doctors for backache sufferers and restless sleepers). Send £149.95 to Horizontal Hold, Unit 5A Mendip Edge, Bleadon Hill, Weston-Super-Mare, Avon. BS24 9JF. This offer is for a limited period only prior to stocktaking. Complete beds, including frames also available from £480 to £1,050.

FOR SALE: 300 old copies of Woodworker from 1913-1948. Twelve complete years. Offers to Palmer: 0733-49991.

FOR SALE: old copies of 'Woodworker' dating from 1924 to 1965. Several years complete. Write to Mr. D. G. Greenaway, 30 Shandon Park East, Ballyholme, Bangor, Co. Down, N. Ireland or phone (0247) 467681. Reasonable offers accepted.

WINDSOR CHAIRS

Full size bends. 50 × 1⅜ × 1⅛" in Ash £6.95.
Childs Windsor Chair bends in Ash 36 × 1⅛ × ⅞" £4.95.
All prices include p&p.
Please send cheque/P.O. with order to:
P. Stuffin, Spurn View, North End Road, Tetney, Grimby DN36 5NA. Tel: (0472) 812576 (Afternoons)

FOR SALE: Inca Bandsaw 230/250 volt, almost new £250. Tel: 01-857-1804.

BUSINESS FOR SALE

SEDBERGH £22,000

Woodworking workshop in prominent location in Yorkshire Dales National Park.
Good communication links.
Ground floor: Workshop approx. 300 sq.ft.
First floor: Workshop and office and shower room.
Loft: storage.
Good modern equipment.
***Contact -* Thompson Matthews 70 Main Street, Sedbergh, Cumbria. Tel: 20293**

Windsor and Ladderback chair-making business, producing highest quality copies of antique designs. Machinery patterns, full technical information and continuing sales to established wholesalers included. Could be run by one craftsman from double garage or similar building — £7.500.
For further details please phone:
East Knoyle 604 (Wilts).

FRENCH POLISHING, furniture restoration business for sale, including Teaching School (if required). Situation in the Midlands, well established and known world-wide. A wonderful opportunity for a keen craftsman. All stock, fittings, etc. included in sale at £6,000 for good will and name. For further details write Box WW122 'Woodworker' Advertisement Dept., Argus Specialist Publications, 1 Golden Square, London W1.

THE WHISTON CATALOGUE

Nuts, bolts, screws, washers, bar materials. In brass, alloy, steel, stainless steel, P.T.F.E., nylon, Tufnol, sheet material, electrical and mechanical items. We could go on and on! Better to send for free catalogue No. 114 and see for yourself.
K. R. Whiston Ltd., Dept. WW, New Mills, Stockport, Cheshire. Phone: 0663 42028.

KITS & HOBBIES

HOBBY'S ANNUAL

£1·10 P&P FREE

FREE PLAN OF TOWN DOLLS HOUSE

Book-binding, pictures from sand, New plans of push along trike, London bus, kitchen furniture and Tiffany clock.
New kits, new plans, Candle making and garden moulds. Dolls house accessories.

HOBBY'S ANNUAL 1987

188 PAGES Many in colour

No 17

Hobby's (Dept. W) Knight's Hill Square, LONDON SE27 0HH 01-761 4244
From WH Smith, Menzies and leading newsagents or direct.

GUITAR KITS

For under £35 you can make your own classical guitar with our comprehensive kit. Mahogany veneered back and ribs, solid rosewood fingerboard — a quality product with superb tone. Compares with factory made guitars costing many times this price. For full details write or phone:
The Early Music Shop
28 Sunbridge Rd, Bradford, W. Yorks. BD1 2AE
Tel: 0274 393753

QUARTER SIZE GRANDFATHER CLOCK KIT

Traditionally styled in solid **mahogany** throughout. Deep etched, **solid brass** break arch dial, with tempus fugit. Easily assembled from our complete D-I-Y kit. **Ideal gift** at £19.95 + £2 p&p, or send. Just £2.50 for full scale drawing and all details. (Refundable on first order).

CRAFTWOODS WALES
Gwalia Works, Dulais Road, Portardulais, Swansea SA4 1RH Wales. Tel: 0792 884456

Everything for the home craftsman

Clock movements, hands, faces, dials, ceramic tiles kits. Woodturning accessories. Miniature power tools, etc. Send £1.95 for 128 page catalogue and £5 voucher against first order.

Toolmail (WWD) Ltd. Dept. WS, 170 High Street, Lewes, East Sussex. Telephone: (0273) 477009.

SHARPENING SERVICES

WHY throw away those expensive router cutters when they can be re-ground correctly at a fraction of new price? Ring Woodcutter Services for details. 061 4324294 (after 6pm).

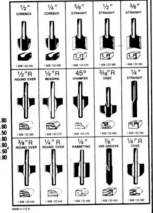
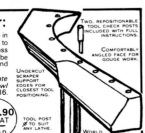

MICRO PLANES LTD.
103 LEE MOOR ROAD, STANLEY, WAKEFIELD, W. YORKS. WF3 4EQ.

DIAL YOUR THICKNESS. SET AND FORGET. EASILY FIXED. SIMPLE TO USE, ACCURATE, FROM 1/50 TO ¾".
PRICE £13.50 P.P. £1.50
FOR FURTHER DETAILS S.A.E. TO ABOVE ADDRESS.

As demonstrated at all leading exhibitions.

LANGARD
ONLY £14.99
FLEXI·DISC
SANDER/GRINDER PATENT
You'll be amazed by the performance of this new power drill accessory, due to the flexible drive and slap on, peel off discs.
Flexible/rigid drive. 125mm/5" metal plate. 3 sanding discs. One-year Guarantee.

25th Anniversary Offer £5 OFF with this ad

LL LANGDON (LONDON) LTD. ICKFORD, BUCKS. HP18 9JJ. Tel: (08447) 337
Money back if returned in 30 days.
For a superb finish with a disc sander

NEW – Extra Long Life disc pack – 2 each coarse, medium, fine, wet/dry .... **only £4.50**
Cash with order. VAT inc./we pay postage. Visa and Access phone orders accepted.

FYLDE WOODTURNING SUPPLIES
255 Church Street, Blackpool FY1 4HY

WE STOCK A FULL RANGE OF COMPONENT PARTS FROM WOOD-TURNING PROJECTS, SORBY TOOLS, LATHE ACCESSORIES, TYME LATHES, SAWTOOTH BITS ETC, CALL ROUND AND SEE OUR DISPLAY IN OUR BASEMENT SHOW ROOM OR S.A.E. FOR PRICE LIST. MAIL ORDER A PLEASURE.

WORKBENCHES

Before you buy, you must compare our benches. Heavy, rigid and truly substantial, these benches in solid beech, make many on the market look like toys. See them at the London Woodworker Show in October, or send for details to:
SALISBURY BENCHES
Twmyards, Worth, Wells, Somerset.
Tel: (0749) 72139

CIRCULAR & BANDSAW BLADES
for all applications
A. A. SMITH LTD.
63 Brighton Road, Shoreham, Sussex BN4 6RE
0273 461707
(24 hours)

WEALDEN
ROUTER CUTTERS

LOOKING FOR BIG DISCOUNTS ON CARBIDE-TIPPED CUTTERS? OUR PRICES COMPARE WITH THE BEST AROUND!
WRITE OR PHONE NOW
FOR OUR FREE LITERATURE AND RESHARPENING DETAILS.
WEALDEN TOOL COMPANY (Dept WW)
97 Tudeley Lane, Tonbridge, Kent
Tel: (0732) 357864
CUTTERS

415v from 230v house mains to run your 3-phase machines, the 'Maldon' unit **£66** 1½ h.p.

Maldon Transformers
134 London Road, Kingston-on-Thames.
Tel: 546-7534
Access – Barclaycard VISA

OMAS TOOLING
Once again available in U.K. Enormous range of solid profile and "Tigerhead" cutters. Stack system Tooling for Window and Door manufacture etc. Send now for details and address of your nearest supplier or stockist to:
WOODFRAME TOOLING (U.K.)
Halls Higher Town, Sampford, Peverell, DEVON EX16 7BP.
Tel: Tiverton (0884) 820340

AN ENTIRE WORKSHOP IN ONE CATALOGUE ...

WITH THE BIGGEST TOOL MAIL ORDER SPECIALISTS IN THE U.K.
Send 70p for 92 page Tools and Machinery Catalogue No. 12 complete with up to date price list.

J. SIMBLE & SONS
Dept. WW, The Broadway, 76 Queen's Road, Watford, Herts.   Tel: Watford 26052

SHERWOOD WOODWORKING MACHINES
All cast constructed, lathes from £93.19. Bowl Turning Heads £60.81; Motors etc. 8" Saw Benches £59.50; Pulley's Belts; 8" + 10" DIY Saw Benches from £28.50.
Send stamp for leaflets.
JAMES INNS (Engineers),
Unit 3, Welbeck Workshops, Alfred Close, Nottingham, NG3 1AD.

AUSTINS OF WREXHAM
POWER TOOLS AND MACHINERY CENTRE
Plas Acton, Wrexham, North Wales.
Tel: 261095 or 262316
Evenings and Weekends 351186
Discounted prices on Sheppach, DeWalt, Elu, Sedgwick, Warco, Naerok, Luna, Startrite, Woodworking Machinery B+D, Makita, Skil, Bosch Power Tools. Postal Service on Router Cutters, Saw and Bandsaw Blades. Converters 1 to 3 phase. Repairs to Leading makes of Power Tools.

B/DECKER, SKIL, BOSCH, MAKITA TOOLS ALL IN STOCK
NEW LUTZ SAWBENCH NOW IN STOCK ONLY £165.00

BEST QUALITY TCT SAWS, 5" DIAMETER UP TO 36" GUARANTEED PERFORMANCE
24 HOUR RETURN POST SHARPENING SERVICE.
PHONE OR WRITE TO MAYS HIGH SPEED SAWS LTD.
NEW ROAD (Nr. CHANDLER CORNER), RAINHAM, ESSEX.
TEL. (04027) 55371/21331
(7 DAYS A WEEK)
TCT   ALLOY

HARRISON GRADUATE and JUBILEE Wood Turning Lathes For Sale
Contact the specialists
L.R.E. MACHINERY & EQUIPMENT CO.
15 Upwood Road, Lowton, Warrington WA3 2RL.
Tel: (0942) 728208 day or night

PLANERS 6" × 9", planers/thicknessers, 12" × 7", 9" × 6", 12 × 7", sawbenches, 10", 12" combination woodworkers. British made. Particulars, send stamp. Dodd Machine Tools Ltd., South Woodham, Chelmsford, Telephone: (0245) 320 691.   T/C

SAWBENCHES 10" tilt arbor. Bandsaws 12" throat manufactured by Humberside Tools. Send SAE for leaflet. 98a Lambert St., Hull. Telephone: 0482 223187.

EBAC TIMBER SEASONERS, Protimeter moisture meters, always good prices and advice from the man who pioneered small scale seasoning. John Arrowsmith, 74a Wilson Street, Darlington, Co. Durham. DL3 6QZ. Tel: 0325 481970.   T/C

ROUTER CUTTERS. Save up to 60%. **LARGE** SAE for lists. MTL, Box 2, Disley, Cheshire, SK12 2NN.

SINGLE to 3 phase converters up to 20HP 18 and 21 throat bandsaws. Illustrated details. HAB Engineering Unit 24, 16-20 George St., Balsall Heath, Birmingham B12 9RG. Telephone 021-440-6266.

DeWalt Woodworking

Fantastic Savings. DeWalt reconditioned machines As new — Guaranteed.
Braywood Estates Ltd.,
158 Burnham Lane, Slough SL1 6LE. Tel: (06286) 5125

SCRU-DRILL
COMPLETE SET OF FOUR £14.00 Incl. VAT + P&P

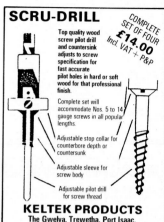

Top quality wood screw pilot drill and countersink adjusts to screw specification for fast accurate pilot holes in hard or soft wood for that professional finish.
Complete set will accommodate Nos. 5 to 14 gauge screws in all popular lengths.
Adjustable stop collar for counterbore depth or countersunk
Adjustable sleeve for screw body
Adjustable pilot drill for screw thread

KELTEK PRODUCTS
The Gwelva, Trewetha, Port Isaac, Cornwall PL29 3R.

Braywood Estates

Main stockists
Trend Router Cutters.
Augers. Forstner bits.
All at discount Prices.
Agents required countrywide.
Braywood Estates Ltd.,
158 Burnham Lane, Slough SL1 6LE
Tel: Burnham (06286) 5125

STUCK FOR 3 PHASE ELECTRICITY? If you can connect a motor then you can create your own 3 phase supply for as much as £20. For full instructions send s.a.e. + £3.50 to: D.L. Ponsonby (EM4), P.O. Box 286, 72 Weymede, Weybridge, Surrey KT14 7DH.

WOODCARVING

Second-Hand Carving Chisels
bought and sold
New Swiss Carving Chisels and Carving Sundries.
Catalogue available, SAE to:
The Woodcarvers Shop,
Rear 28 Painswick Road, Cheltenham, Glos.
Telephone: (0242) 38582

MATERIALS & FINISHES

OLD FASHIONED GLUE POTS
½ litre size.
Inner pot malleable cast iron.

Price £23.00 p&p £1 (inc. VAT)
Pearl glue or Scotch glue 500g **£2.00**
1kg **£3.75**
Pearl glue ½ kilo gross p/p 66p
1 kilo gross p/p £1.41
Crown Craft Products
22 Crown Lane, Four Oaks, Sutton Coldfield, West Midlands B74 4SU
Tel: (021) 308-2780

87

88

CONTENTS

Woodworker

design . . . craft . . . and the love of wood

February 1987
Vol. 91
No. 2

FEATURES

Photo Stan Folb

PROJECTS

REGULARS

On the cover: *one of a large Brazilian woodworking family smiles for* **Lucinda Leech's** *camera, p.104.* **Above right**: *Michael 'Lew' Lewis fine-fettles the soundboard of his Celtic harp, p.162*

Editor Aidan Walker
Deputy editor John Hemsley
Editorial assistant Kerry Fowler
Advertisement manager Trevor Pryer
Advertisement production Laura Champion
Graphics Jeff Hamblin
Technical illustrator Peter Holland
Guild of Woodworkers John Hemsley, Kerry Fowler

Unfortunately we cannot accept responsibility for loss of or damage to unsolicited material. We reserve the right to refuse or suspend advertisements, and regret we cannot guarantee the bone fides of advertisers.
Published every third Friday

Editorial, advertisements and Guild of Woodworkers
1 Golden Square, London W1R 3AB, telephone 01-437 0626

ABC
UK circulation
Jan-Dec 85
28,051

Back issues and subscriptions Infonet Ltd, 10-13 Times House, 179 Marlowes, Hemel Hempstead, Herts HP1 1BB; telephone Hemel Hempstead (0442) 48434

Subscriptions per year UK £16.90; overseas outside USA (accelerated surface post) £21.00, USA (accelerated surface post) $28, airmail £48

UK trade SM Distribution Ltd, 16-18 Trinity Gardens, London SW9 8DX; telephone 01-274 8611

North American trade Bill Dean Books Ltd, 151-49 7th Avenue, PO Box 69, Whitestone, New York 11357; tel. 1-718-767-6632

Printed by Chase Web, Plymouth
Mono origination Multiform Photosetting Ltd, Cardiff
Colour origination Derek Croxson Ltd, Chesham, Bucks
© Argus Specialist Publications Ltd 1987
ISSN 0043 776X

Argus Specialist Publications Ltd

1 Golden Square, London W1R 3AB; 01-437 0626

This month

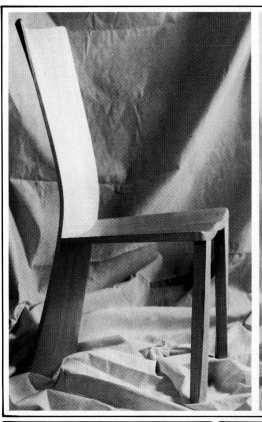

Woodworker **Design Award** The most comfortable non-upholstered chair at the Direct Design Show (Kensington Town Hall, 28-30 Nov 86) was judged to be **Andrew Whateley's** remarkable piece (far left), in steam-bent English ash. He has developed and perfected, with his partner Rebecca Myram, a unique technique for getting double curvature in wide boards.

Dr Bernard Watkin, distinguished orthopaedic physician, co-judged the award with *Woodworker* editor Aidan Walker. We liked Rycotewood student **Carl Allen's** design (near left), but thought Andrew's piece showed better use of materials.

We're dead chuffed Andrew won the award — a fine furniture maker, and far too little recognition so far for this man.

The **Direct Design Show** features designer/makers in all media — next dates 5-7 June, selection day 2 March. Contact Joe Tibbetts, Jardines Marketing, 1 Lawn Lane, London SW8 1UD, 01-587 0256.

Furniture forum

The Gulbenkian Craft Initiative's Forum, 6-7 December 86, was by all accounts a creative and exciting weekend. Participants came from a wide range of design, make and materials interests; from traditional makers in wood through metals and more unusual media to architects.

'Everyone seemed to think,' says project administrator Heather Smith, 'that it was a long overdue gathering. The main preoccupation of all the makers there is to open up their design ideas and push themselves creatively far more than they would be able to do in isolation, which they lament.'

Most of the big names in British furniture design were there, everyone with a lot to say and share. They looked formally at furniture as structures, small scale production, new uses for new timber sources, the influence of materials. 'Everyone was very interested in exploring other materials,' says Heather, 'and to see the influence they have on others' work.

'We hope that furniture designer/makers will continue to meet, mix and experiment; that's what they all want to do.'

The Craft Initiative will be running workshops in July; write with full details of yourself, work and design philosophy to Heather Smith, Flat D Langham Mansions, London SW5 9UH.

Winners of prize draws at the Woodworker Show; **top,** G. Sillman takes a **Sears Craftsman radial-arm** from Steve Turner of A-Z Tools (right); **bottom,** Paul Hardy of **Dunlop Powerbase** (right) hands over to Messrs P. Hunt, R. Marlow and K. Dixom — one each. Many thanks to A-Z and Dunlop, and Mike Payne of **Multi-Tools** Harrogate for his hospitality.

Diary

Guild courses are shown by an asterisk (*); for further details see Guild pages.

February
1-3 **British Toymakers Guild 8th Toy Fair**, London W8, 01-549 1483
8-13 **Shipwright's Workshop**, traditional boat repair, West Dean College, Chichester, Sussex, (02463) 301
14 **Power Routing** Roy Sutton*

March
4-10 April **The Young Creators**, student showcase, Haymarket, London
12-13 **French polishing** Charles Cliffe*
28 **Spindle moulding** Roy Sutton*
28 **Wood machining** Ken Taylor*

April
4 **Hammer veneering** Ian Hosker*
5 **Parquetry** Ian Hosker*
12-17 **Cabinetmaking** Manchester*
12-17 **Upholstery** Manchester*
12-17 **Modern finishing** Manchester*
26-4 May **London International Furniture Show**, Earls Court (26-30 trade only)

Shoptalk

A bunch of **courses** this month: Leading woodturner Michael O'Donnell (*WW/Dec*) is expanding his successful programme of five-day 'Exploration into **Woodturning**' courses. He's doing more of those, plus a **green wood** course entitled 'Turning Green', plus — here's an interesting one — a two-part (five days each) **Instructor Training** course. There's no proper teaching for teachers, says Mick, so why not start something with the aim of getting a nationally-recognised standard?

Then there's John Storrs' 10-day summer course in **early keyboard instrument making**. It's at Bishop Otter College, Chichester from 24 July-3 August, (residential), and you can build a clavichord, spinet or harpsichord from a Storrs kit. John is a well-known and highly respected craftsman in this specialised field. The course costs £320+VAT plus the price of an instrument kit (they start at £480).

Then there's **chair caning** and **rush seating**. 21-22 March are the dates, Upton on Severn in Worcestershire the place. Betty Fowler is the teacher — experienced in practising the craft, showing and teaching, she and her husband collect the raw materials from the banks of the River Severn! Bring a chair ready to work on; £60 for the two days including lunch.
● Michael O'Donnell, The Croft, Brough, Thurso, Caithness, KW14 8YE, (084 785) 605.
● John Storrs, Hunston, Chichester, W. Sussex PO20 6NR, (0243) 776263.
● Betty Fowler, Primrose Cottage, Longdon, Tewkesbury, Worcs, (0684) 81365.
● Don't forget the **Guild of Woodworkers'** range of courses on p138.

A Z1 and AZ2 are the new **dust extractors** from, not surprisingly, A-Z Tool Sales. Castor mounted, metal fans: 1hp does 1000cu. m. per hr for £210, 2hp does 1500 cu. m. for £345+VAT. A-Z are also looking for stockists.
● A-Z Tool Sales, Union Close, Kettlebrook Rd, Tamworth, Staffs B77 1BB, (0827) 56767.

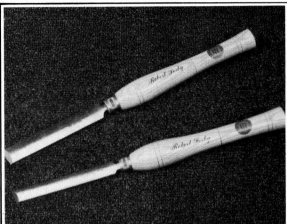

N ortec is the name of the people making **rotary planes**, not PIK Castings as we said in the December issue. Their phone number was also subject to gremlin force; the right number is 03656 21777.

On the same subject, it's only right to say that such planes have been available on a small scale for the last two years via a colleague of **Fred Lambert's**, who is credited with their origination in this country. **Jack Hill**, who is carrying on Fred's fine chairmaking tradition, was not using Nortec tools at the Woodworker Show, but versions of Fred's original design.

R epair your own bandsaw blades — it's not as hard as it sounds. Charles Hollick's **blade repair kit** consists of a metal jig and self-fluxing brazing rod for £11.50, and includes a blowlamp for a total of £19.50 inc. p&p.
● Charles Hollick, Kittisford Glebe, Wellington, Somerset TA21 0SA, (0823) 672366.

L una's new universal **router stand** has a 650x500mm pressed steel table, 350mm angle-section legs, and comes with fences, guards and a dust-extraction outlet as standard. There's also a jigsaw plate available. £125+VAT.
● Luna, 20 Denbigh Hall, Milton Keynes, Bucks MK3 7QT, (0908) 70771.

B lack & Decker's **danger detector** flashes a little light at you if you're about to drill walls with pipes and wires just where the hole needs to be — £13.50 from most trade, DIY and electrical stockists.
● B&D, Westpoint, The Grove, Slough SL1 1QQ, (0735) 74277.

B owls and other turned items without a lathe? Yes, it's possible with the Ring Master, a **concentric cutting machine** that caused a lot of interest at the Woodworker Show. It cuts rings from boards between 8 and 12in square; the cutter can be adjusted for angle so you can build up sections. Maximum thickness of the blank is ¾in. Make a vase in 20 minutes for £345+VAT with a ½hp motor; £275 without a motor.
● Ring Master (UK), 87 Abshot Rd, Titchfield Common, Hants PO14 4ND, (04895) 82633.

The new Sorby oval-shaped **skew chisel** is really a beautiful tool to handle, writes **John Buckley-Golder**. I was asked to try one out while demonstrating at the London Woodworker Show. I found it difficult to use at first, since it had been ground flat on either side. But I hollow-ground it when I got home, and it worked beautifully. It is almost elliptical in shape and glides smoothly along the tool rest. I would recommend this tool to beginner and professional alike.

The ¾in skew, handled, costs £9.50+VAT, the 1in £11.45+VAT.
● Robert Sorby Ltd, Athol Rd, Woodseats Rd, Sheffield S8 0PA, (0742) 554231.

W oodworker **Plans** Service are doing a full set of drawings and instructions for a magnificent two-tier **tool cabinet** with a load of shelves, drawers and cubby holes. £4.75 for six sheets; please quote order code MTC 1.
● Plans Service, Wolsey House, Wolsey Rd, Hemel Hempstead, Herts HP2 4SS, (0422) 41221.

1986 **Indexes** for *Woodworker*, your favourite **woodworking magazine** — the quality one — are available now for £1.25 inc. p&p from Reader Services, same address as Plans.

D ual-action **finishing sander** from Makita gives you the choice of straight or orbital action. No-load speed 7000 orbits per minute, input rating 130w, half-sheet size pad, £73 inc. VAT.
● Makita UK, 8 Finway, Dallow Rd, Luton, Beds LU1 1TR, (0582) 455777.

U sing the spindle moulder for fielding solid panels, writes **Luke Hughes**, is one of the best ways — but solid integral blocks are expensive, and there hasn't been a block available for interchangeable knives — until the new Whitehill 4in **panel-raising cutter block**. It's exceptional value (£68+VAT) and well thought out; the jaws are set at an angle for a clean finish. Rapid knife-setting; interchangeable knives allow variation in depth and pitch; and you can grind your own cutters or get Whitehill to do it for you in 48 hours for £16-20+VAT per pair. It costs less than half the equivalent solid block, and allows you far greater flexibility. An extremely useful bit of tooling for those whose work demands a range of moulded detail; 125mm block £80+VAT.
● Whitehill Spindle Tools, 6 Union St, Luton, Beds LU1 3AN, (0582) 36881.

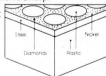

93

The craft of cabinetmaking

Edge-jointing: David Savage continues his occasional series with a detailed look at making narrow boards wider

● **Above**, Dave Gardiner of CoSIRA 'joints' new cutters to the same arc with a small slip-stone; **above right**, the safe way – pressure forward

Next door to my workshop is a small joiners' workshop run by Dezzy and Ginger. They make windows, staircases or whatever is needed at ferocious speed and with great skill. Last week Dezzy had the top joints of two fingers removed by the planer, and the effect on me and the other members of the workshop was profound. Sympathy and concern are quickly followed by shock and worry . . . After all, Dezzy is no cowboy — he knows his business and is a careful machinist. If it happened to him . . .

However, just as happens when you drive past a serious accident on a motorway, the effect of this was salutary, but temporary. It's too easy to forget the uncomfortable truth. Writing about safety is an immediate turn-off for everyone, including myself, for nobody wishes to contemplate the truth of the situation for more than a moment. We all know machines are dangerous, and accidents happen despite our best efforts to prevent them. But who would wish to dwell upon the grizzly reality of maimed hands for more than a moment? Our hands are fantastically complex manipulative and sensory mechanisms; the antics of the CNC robot or the dense complexity of the micro chip are feeble and crude compared to the wiggly bits on the ends of our arms. Because we cannot consider mutilation of ourselves for more than a moment, we deny ourselves a valuable safety mechanism.

We can guard machines fully, and I am not for one moment arguing against this; but there are occasions when the guard isn't there to protect us. How does this happen? Why does it happen? I don't pretend to know — but human fallibility has a lot to do with it. For this reason, I believe it isn't enough to say that guarding a machine is the answer to the problem. For those occasions that, heaven forbid, the guard is not in place, there must also be a secondary protection for the operator — good technique.

Good technique is simply something by which you accomplish the task in hand, pressing the job against table or fence in the necessary way, but without putting your hands in danger. If a slip, either from the job or from loss of balance, could carry your wiggly bits into the meat grinder — that isn't good technique. If you can feel the breath of the table-saw on your hand, that's too close. Use any manner of shop-made devices to control the job over the cutters; push-sticks are found on almost all my machines, and I get very ratty if they aren't put back in the same place *every time*. If you

reach out for a push-stick, it should always be there.

Finger-boards are home-made pressure blocks. Easily made from scraps of plywood, they can clamp to the fence for downward pressure, or on to the machine table for sideways pressure. When you are making one, make two more; they are invaluable aids that only get used if they are close at hand.

The final thing is to examine the existing guarding systems on your equipment. From the manufacturer's point of view, a good guard isn't always the same thing as it is to you and me. I have two Startrite table-saws in my shop, a large dimension saw and a smaller 9in saw used for joints and fitting. Both machines' guards are attached to the riving-knife, and with the guard fitted, it's impossible to bring the fence nearer than 30mm to the blade. A better system is Luna's where the crown-guard is hung above the table, allowing it to be positioned very quickly and easily. A good guard is one that gets in the way of accidents without obstructing operations to the point of frustration.

It was edge-planing a board that took Dezzy's fingertips, and it is this operation I want to examine in the context of a basic cabinetmaking technique; edge-jointing.

The joint

Almost every piece of furniture we make in the solid has edge joints in it somewhere. Even if trees grew with faultless wide boards, it wouldn't generally be good practice to use them. So we joint narrow boards together to make wide panels and carcases. The maximum width of board without a joint is usually determined (apart from the grain factor) by the width of your planer or thicknesser, and if that doesn't stop you, the stuff you plane will. We have a 16in planer/thicknesser, which allows us to take advantage of good wide boards when they

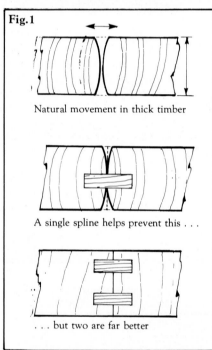

Fig. 1

Natural movement in thick timber

A single spline helps prevent this . . .

. . . but two are far better

come up; a smaller 10in machine would do good work, but make edge-jointing a more regular job. An 18in-wide panel can be made quite simply by bookmatching a 9in board, so the creative limitations of the smaller machine are very slight.

To achieve a faultless invisible joint between two boards demands considerable care and attention to detail. Producing it quickly and effortlessly is the result of practice based on faultless technique. As in most general cabinetmaking skills, the attitude of mind, the method, the procedure, all determine the result.

There are three common types of edge joint; plain butt-joints, splined joints and dowelled joints. I must confess I have never used the slot-screwed joint. A plain butt-joint, well made, will suffice for most cabinet carcase work, because a glue joint long grain to long grain has great strength. Work like this would generally be in timber less than 25mm thick.

For thicker sections, the extra strength gained from splines is an advantage. A thick section of timber has more problems to concern us; being thick, it may not be dry right through, or it may have been kiln-dried too quickly, drying in stresses that usually relax with slow air-drying. Even a perfectly behaved board may distort across the joint enough to break the glue's adhesion and ruin your perfect work. For edge-jointing timber more than 25mm thick, I generally insist that at least one spline is used. Where there's room for two splines, this gives the best joint as strength gained from the increased glue area is positioned where it is needed, near the surface (fig. 1). A spline may be fitted to a narrow board to give a location if the boards were twisted.

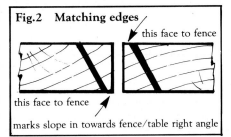

Fig.2 Matching edges

this face to fence

this face to fence

marks slope in towards fence/table right angle

Most of the splined work we do is in stopped grooves, which can be the very devil to cut. A spindle moulder with a variable grooving saw is the best solution, and a no.1299 Leitz grooving saw, which allows the width of groove to be dialled in, is a favourite but expensive toy. A router can do the job, with a jig to stabilise it on the edge of a board; a table-saw can also cut stopped grooves with a dado head fitted for the wide kerf. This is less satisfactory, as the guard and riving knife must be removed from the saw and the job dropped on to the cutter — illegal in a commercial shop. The biscuit jointer can cut a very clean groove, if like the router it can be stabilised on the narrow edge. The cutters are 4mm, so usually two passes are needed to cut the groove for a 6mm spline. (The splines themselves are best made of plywood, which takes advantage of long-grain gluing surface and cross-grain strength across the joint.) The only trouble is, the biscuit jointer is rather an unwieldy beast, which, rather than cutting perfect stopped grooves — doesn't. Stop, that is. It gallops off across the job instead, leaving a trail of toothmarks.

Dowelled edge joints are much less common than splined ones, because it's just a more complicated operation to align 20 or so dowels down the length of a board than fit two splines. Dowels do, however, have a valuable role to play in locating a board so it sits dead flush with its new neighbour. Splines do this as well, but they allow for lateral movement in the glue-up, and so if end dimensions have been determined before gluing, a dowel at each end will help to make sure everything bangs up nicely.

But the plain old, honest-to-good butt-joint, despite its simplicity, is still the most common edge joint in carcase work. Beginners often needlessly incorporate tongues and grooves, splines and dowels to overcome the butt-joint, for a good butt-joint takes a bit of skill.

The equipment

In years gone by, hairy-armed woodworkers wielded planes much longer than is common today — wooden jointers, sometimes 30in long, did the task of edge-jointing superbly. The length of the sole and the fineness of cut ensured a straight edge, and the skill of the craftsman kept it square to the job. A jointer plane was often only used for this task as it was too cumbersome for general work.

Today the name is given to the machine that does the same work. A 'jointer' is a planing machine set up for edge-jointing, which may just mean your general-purpose planer is fitted with a vertical fence and used as a jointer. We keep a separate machine for this work, with a shop-built fence permanently fitted. The main feature of a good jointer is the length of its tables, the longer the better. Many industrial jointers extend for 6 or 7ft — most of us have to be content with something less than this ideal. Edge-planing a long board on a short jointer demands the careful setting up of roll-on-roll-off tables before and beyond the machine; a large 2500mm walnut table we are currently making will need this fiddling about to ensure a perfect straight edge along its length.

The jointer needs careful setting up if it's to function correctly. Spend some time with a bright light and a *real* straight-edge, checking the tables don't twist or droop in relation to each other. The outfeed table is the important one — this should be set at a height fractionally below the top of the cutter arch, but *only fractionally*. The cutters must be set to exactly the same cutting circle, because if only one cutter is doing the work the finish will be poor. If any of these factors are ignored, indeed, the chances of getting good results are very poor.

The next task is to set up a fence at right angles to the cutter. Most jointers have adjustable fences allowing them to cant over to plane chamfers; wonderful, the chance of holding a constant 90° immediately shoots straight out of the window. Other jointer fences I have seen twist the job as it's fed across the cutters or better still, were permanently bent into a banana shape at birth. I have given up with jointer fences and made my own, but even this isn't trusted implicitly, for wood chips can get under it. Always check the fence with a square as the job proceeds.

Using the jointer accurately and safely demands a fairly high degree of co-ordination. The first thing is the length and straightness of your workpiece; if you have a fair way to go before you get a very fine and straight edge, you can set the cut quite deep, then finer. Passing the work over the

● *Apprentice Neil keeps the valuable fingers well away from the cutters*

cutters, the golden rule is *no hand should be on the work immediately over the cutter-block.* You stand with the machine to your right, your left (forward) hand pushing the work in to the fence and down to the table; push it forward, keeping your forward hand behind the cutters and feeding with your right (back) hand too, and as soon as there is a good hand-hold length on the outfeed table, transfer the pressure of your forward hand smoothly to the outfeed side. Keep the work moving all the time, but *don't let your forward hand travel on the work over the cutters.* Once the left hand is on the outfeed table side of the work, that is your reference; keep pushing in and down and forward with it, and assist with very light feed pressure from your 'infeed' hand — but don't press down on the table or fence on the infeed side, because it's the outfeed surfaces that you must work to.

The surface held against the out table will be sufficient to maintain the perfect straight right angle, and during the entire process your precious fingers will have been nowhere near the cutters. Fences are set up so the minimum of cutter is exposed and guards are there to prevent accidents, *but* the technique used by you, the operator, would have saved you had they not been there. Heaven preserve us from people who leave off guards, but wiggly bits are still being turned into dogmeat every day. Legislation prevents employers like myself from risking the very precious digits of my staff, but the home workshop has no such protection. You must tend your own meat grinder and guard your own digits; 'nuff said.

continued

The craft of cabinetmaking

So the edge has been planed square and straight; check it with a straight-edge and square. If you are doing a batch of 20, check the first three to get into the swing of it, then check every third edge. Checking means looking for trouble, not hoping for the best. If you don't want to see your poor workmanship, it's easy not to look that hard.

The problem of getting a constant right angle on a jointer with a doubtful fence can be helped by marking the boards as shown in fig. 2. The endgrain mark indicates which side has pressed against the fence, the mark pointing into the junction of fence and jointer table. Keep these marks parallel when assembling, any inaccuracy in the fence should be cancelled out, and the assembled panel will remain flat.

Finer points

On the question of marks, we come to the cabinetmaker's triangle (fig. 3). Used correctly, it can tell you which three pieces out of a pile of 50 go together. It will also tell you which way they fit, what's the inside, the outside, the top, the bottom, the right, the left. By underscoring the base of the triangle in different ways you can identify groups of components. Use white chalk on light boards, red on mahogany or padauk.

If the edges have been passed over the jointer slowly on a fine cut, the edge will butt up to give a good joint straight from the machine. Small components less than 100mm can be left straight, but with longer pieces it might be better to put a slight bow in the edge. The idea is to get the ends to come together first, and then the centre can be cramped. The amount of bow is a debatable point; I have found that one shaving, beginning and ending 100mm from either end, is enough. The plane should be finely set and keen. The iron should be slightly curved, which has two effects; firstly it allows the plane to enter the cut from the side smoothly and delicately, and secondly, the cut is slightly concave across the joint so the points to touch first are the parts you see, the outer edges.

Begin the cut to one side well into the length of the board. As you go forward, move the plane across so the shaving is centred in the throat of the plane. By pressing down it should be possible to take one continuous shaving before easing the plane off the edge. This is a skill worth acquiring, for edge-jointed boards, if they are to split, go at the ends. For this reason, I like to put the ends under a bit of compression. The end grain is absorbing and losing moisture far quicker than the centre of a board, so the ends are working harder than the middle.

Assembly

Edge-gluing a board can be tackled in one of two ways; rub-jointing or cramping. Anyone familiar with this occasional series will know my perverse fondness for animal

Fig.3

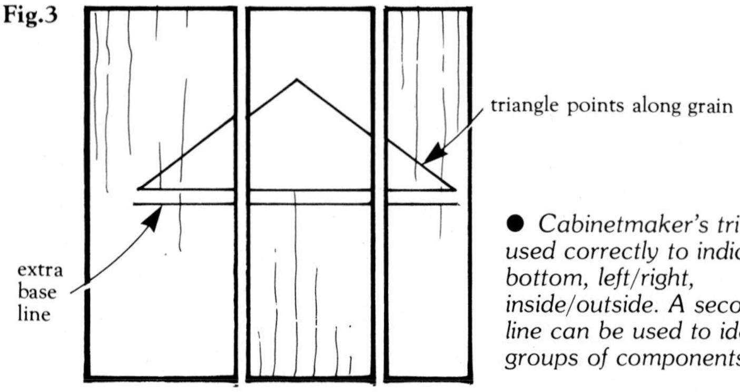

triangle points along grain

extra base line

● *Cabinetmaker's triangle used correctly to indicate top, bottom, left/right, inside/outside. A second base line can be used to identify groups of components.*

● *Not this way!*

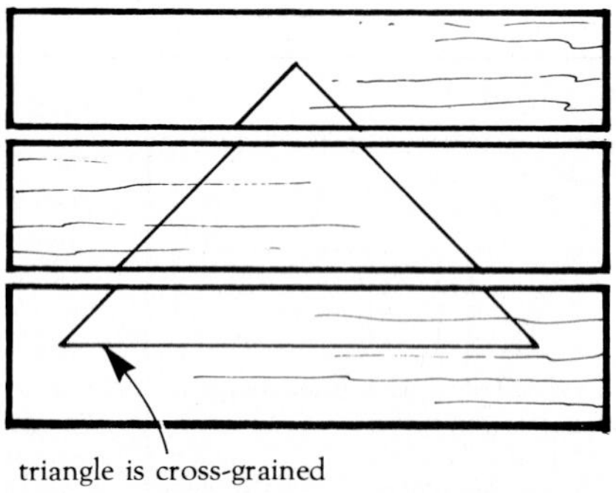

triangle is cross-grained

glue; if your job isn't very large and there are a great many edges to glue, animal glue is the stuff of life. The advantage is that a great many edges can be glued very quickly without cramps, but the disadvantage is that it takes a bit of doing if you are unfamiliar with animal glue.

The joint should be dead flat and true. Grip the bottom board upright, either in the vice or in the bench dogs. Make sure the glue is hot and not too thin. The second board can be leant against the first, so both surfaces are there together ready for the glue brush. Brush on a little glue; your first few goes will get glue dribbling everywhere, for you actually need less than you think. Now bring the surfaces together and rub. This is why it's called a rub-joint — the action of pushing to and fro coats both surfaces and expels excess glue. It should only need one or two good rubs before a stiffening is sensed, rather than felt. Now align the boards and let it stand for a moment. The test of a good rubbed joint is simple — can you now open the vice and lift the assembly, holding it by that top board? The action is that fast. Pick up the panel, and gently lay it against two stickers propped against a wall. Other panels can be piled in front, using carefully placed stickers, and then don't disturb the joint for the rest of the day. Although it's possible for very long boards to be rubbed together by two people, I prefer to see large boards put under cramps.

Cramping edge joints together demands a very flat surface on which to stand the cramps — the bench is the obvious place. I made a number of sash-cramps a few years ago when I couldn't afford the proper Record metal T-bar variety; they use much

cheaper cramp-heads and a hardwood bar. These cramps have been a great success and are now used in preference to heavier hardware. The secret, if there is one, is to make the bar from a good tough hardwood; but make it very carefully. If the holes for the locating pins aren't spot on, you will regret your carelessness for many a year.

PVA or white glue is a favourite for a cramped edge joint. There should be plenty of time to apply glue (with a brush not a finger!) to both surfaces. Successful glue-ups are about having everything to hand, a little glue, a little bit of squeeze and no fuss. Most jobs use between five and seven cramps spaced evenly along it. Alternate the position of cramps, so for every two beneath there is one cramp above the job. Then give it a very little squeeze. If the boards don't align properly, either tap them down or pull them together at the ends with a speed cramp. Now a bit more squeeze from the centre and you should be finished.

Resist the temptation to wipe away the globs of glue which shouldn't be there. The assembly can be moved from the bench, but the clamps must remain on the job for at least one hour. The panel can then be removed and stored in the same way as rubbed panels. The globs of glue are best removed when they are rubbery hard, but not yet set, for which a cranked paring chisel is a favourite weapon.

If the job has been done properly, there will be no visible glue line. The joint between the boards will be visible only by the change of figure between one board and the next. If your first attempts are less than perfect, don't despair — when you get it right, the sense of achievement will be all the more enjoyable. ■

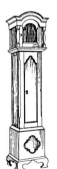

97

Big is beautiful

Many a turner's turn-on is the idea of doing things spectacularly big. Professional woodturner Mike Darlow looks at some of the do's and don'ts of setting yourself up with a giant lathe

Woodturners who take a particular direction of seriousness about their craft — going bigger — find that even the best hobby lathes impose restrictions on the size of workpiece they can turn confidently and safely. I like to do bowls and all sorts of work as big as I can, so I've needed large lathes in my professional shop; this is to give you a brief idea of what's involved in equipping yourself with the machinery you'll need, and to outline the things to watch for, the pitfalls — and, of course, the joys.

The lathe

Those brave souls contemplating the move into heavy metal need to be able to forecast the types of work they hope to do or will be able to market. The most usual categories are:

Large bowls Bowls over 24in diameter are difficult to sell, not only because of their high price, but because prospective buyers can't think where to put them. But if you are into such work, a heavy faceplate or bowl-turning lathe is cheaper and more compact than a conventional commercial lathe.

Large wall sculptures Again a heavy faceplate lathe is better.

Architectural and large furniture turnings Most of the work will be between centres, so you must assess the largest work you wish to take on. For verandah posts and columns, about 14ft capacity is enough. If you are contemplating large rollers or fluting and reeding, you should seek out lathes with carriages, and an outboard turning facility enables you to go for large bowls, bases, table tops, and circular mouldings.

Patternmaking Although patternmaking for iron foundries is declining, there is an increase in demand for patterns and moulds for plastics, ceramics, and concrete.

Although they're essential for all these kinds of work, large lathes tend to be clumsy. Accessories are heavy, tailstocks don't glide along under finger pressure, and none of the nifty gadgets for hobby lathes fit. In short, take care that you aren't making an albatross for your neck — or a piranha for your pocket!

A large lathe is rarely the only necessity, it pays to remember. You also get involved

in major materials-handling problems. One person just doesn't have enough strength, let alone enough long arms and hands. It may take three people plus a forklift to load very large turnings into a lathe. Also, much large work is glued up, so large planers, thicknessers, saws, and lots of clamps will be needed to exploit the full potential of a large lathe. Even if you just want to do large bowls, you'll require chainsaws with 3ft bars and longer, 36in bandsaws, and a helper.

Lathe sources

Relatively inexpensive hobby lathes have been both the cause and effect of the growth in amateur woodturning. To reduce costs and prices, manufacturers have naturally sought to reduce the cost of the most expensive lathe component — the bed. Commercial lathes have beds of vibration-dampening cast iron, with accurately machined bedways. In hobby lathes this has often been replaced by considerably cheaper vibration-transmitting steel sections. The sheer mass of a commercial lathe is also an important factor in reducing vibration, a particular bugbear of woodturning with its high rotational speeds and dynamically unbalanced workpieces.

● **Above**, Mike, forklift and large-diameter product. **Below**, a 1907 Oliver lathe's bed and tailstock (capacity 8ftx32in) with a Darlow chuck-plate

● *Top, the drive system for the Oliver; 5hp floor-mounted motor, double stepped pulleys, layshaft. **Above**, Mike's largest lathe takes 13ftx36in between centres; the bed weighs 3½ tons and cost £75*

Until the Second World War, there was a wide variety of commercial and pattern-making lathes on the market, but since then their number and range has diminished rapidly, with the replacement of commercial hand-turning by automatic lathes, and the substitution of plastics and metal for wood. Because they're made in limited numbers, new machines are expensive, and with most brands there has been little updating. Still, heavy machines are available new from both British and foreign manufacturers.

The most popular source of heavy lathes is the enormous pool of abandoned or little-used machinery. Dealers, auctions, liquidations, and just asking around can often turn up just the thing.

Besides woodturning and patternmaking lathes, metal-spinning lathes are a source of fine headstocks and short heavy beds. Their tailstocks aren't often suitable for wood-turning and the headstocks have no outboard turning facility, but by turning the headstock round or shortening the bed you can turn one into a splendid faceplate lathe.

Flat-bed metal-turning lathes also offer great potential, and by using specially machined blocks under banjos, V-beds can also be used.

But there are things to be on guard against:

White metal or other non-rolling friction bearings These will give endless trouble, and there is also usually not enough cast iron round the bearing to allow re-machining for replacement with ball- or roller bearings.

Excessive wear or damage to the bed Laying in fresh metal and/or bed regrinding are expensive.

Missing equipment It's unusual to find an old lathe complete. Be prepared to make your local engineering shop a place of some prosperity! Nevertheless, the cheapness, (often merely scrap value) of old lathes allows one to mix-and-match and/or customise.

Customising

Headstock This is usually the area of greatest expenditure. If there's no outboard turning facility, it's possible to re-spindle, but this will involve a redesign of the bearing and thrust-taking arrangements.

Screwed lathe noses are cheap and compact, but they offer no other advantages. Accessories unscrew if you have spindle braking, and they may also unscrew if the lathe is run in reverse to speed up bowl-sanding. Furthermore, trying to screw on several hundredweight of faceplate and workpiece assembly is no easy task. So for really heavy turning a nose such as the American long taper is ideal. It allows fittings to be pushed on, and the key prevents any problems caused by braking or reverse running. Although such a nose is expensive to have machined and so are the faceplates, at least the latter can be used on either end of the spindle.

If you are re-spindling, make sure you have an axial hole bored through the spindle. This not only allows driving centres to be drifted out, it allows vacuum and air chucks to be used and wires to be threaded through.

Drive to the headstock pulley will usually be through pulleys, for location of which a grubscrew isn't enough. A keyway will be needed. The number and grades of pulleys will need to be properly designed so the high torques of starting and braking can be transmitted without slippage.

Tailstocks When they're there, these usually demand little more than stripping down and replacing missing levers and/or handles. If the tailstock is missing, search round machinery dealers and scrapyards to find one that needs the minimum of modification.

Drive and transmission The usually accepted optimum speed of the wood relative to the tool's cutting edge is about 1200 feet per minute. One usually works at a point smaller than the workpiece's maximum diameter, so the recommended workpiece speed is based on 1600fpm at the maximum diameter. But with very large work, this would mean the work would take a long time to complete rotation, so you get the sort of problems associated with running more normal-sized work at low revs — a rippled finish, and a tendency for the tool to bounce when cutting endgrain. So you will sometimes end up turning considerably faster than the theoretical optimum, especially, say, when using a

Big is beautiful

● **Above**, the 13 footer's headstock had to be respindled for American long taper noses. **Right**, six speeds from a sliding, pivoting-mounted motor

skew to cut the end of a section that's to be left square. It's difficult to make categorical statements, but a range of headstock spindle speeds from 200 to 1500rpm would cover most eventualities.

Motors 2-5hp is usually enough. Under-powered motors will run hot and blow fuses. You can get gradual acceleration with a capacitor start, and your braking can be electric and/or mechanical, with automatic or manual operation.

Speed variation can be by stepped or diametrically adjustable pulleys (often noisy at the extremes of their range), or by motors with an inbuilt mechanical variation capacity. Motor speed can also be varied by altering the supply voltage, but this is un-satisfactory because immense fuse-blowing currents are needed to start the lathe from rest. Three-phase motors with multiple (usually two) windings offer multiple speeds, and eliminate the need for lay-shafts.

With long lathes where you could be outboard turning or working several feet away from the headstock, it's sensible to have the switching and other controls mounted on a portable console. It soon becomes apparent that the design of the drive, transmission, and controls is a major influence on the efficiency of large lathes, so professional advice is well worth obtaining. **The bed** True alignment of heastock and tailstock axes is vital if you are thinking of in-lathe drilling. A carriage is a mixed

blessing — when hand-turning it's usually in the way, but it's worth its weight in gold when fluting, reeding, or turning rollers. It's also invaluable for horizontal boring.

Clamping plates are needed beneath the bedways for locking on-bed equipment in position. For a very long lathe you may have two steadies and two long toolrests, each with three stems, so you'll need about ten clamping plates!

Accessories

Depending on your work, you may need several straight and curved toolrests (use 1¼in stems), an outboard turning stand, tail and driving centres with the appropriate Morse tapers (the driving centre will probably have to be specially made, no. 3 or 4 Morse), faceplates, and chucks. Engineers chucks are the most useful (see 'The Gripping Story', WW/Jan 86). Other types will usually have to be specially made.

Conclusion

So there it — briefly — is. I've shown that launching into the big time isn't to be taken lightly, but it does nevertheless offer satis-factions just not possible for those working at a more 'normal' scale. The majesty of the machinery is complemented by the apparently slower pace. But as I have tried to show, the grand façade is neither easily nor cheaply achieved. Having said that, I've just heard about this 25 footer . . . ■

EXCLUSIVE OFFERS

If you've got cash left over from Christmas, don't miss out on our major 'sale'.
We're continuing our special offers on a range of goodies

Dowelling set

Last month's offer continued — the Wolf-craft universal set includes jig, clamp, dowels, and drill depth-stops

Retail price £21.50

Woodworker price inc. p&p £17.95
ORDER CODE ROWW 2

Heavy-duty drill stand

The popular Wolfcraft stand is strong as an ox — and we include a machine vice and bolts

Retail price £49.95

Woodworker price inc. p&p £39.95
ORDER CODE ROWW 3

Variotec work table

Unique flip-over table: guard and fence included: and we're throwing in the extra safety switch

Retail price £107.70

Woodworker price inc. p&p £87.95
ORDER CODE ROWW 4

MASTER CLASS VIDEOS

All videos VHS only

Learn bowl turning with an acknowledged professional, teacher and artist. 120 minutes

Retail price.......£31.95
inc. p&p

Woodworker offer
price £28
Order Code WV1

Carving with experts — lettering, scallop shell, tools, tips, techniques. 90 minutes

Retail price.......£31.95
inc. p&p

Woodworker offer
price £28
Order Code WV2

Wood finishing — stain, oil, varnish, lacquer, french polish, refinishing. 100 minutes

Retail price.......£31.95
inc. p&p

Woodworker offer
price £28
Order Code WV3

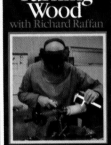

Router techniques galore — joints, jigs, a project, drawings included. 60 minutes

Retail price.......£26.95
inc. p&p

Woodworker offer
price £24
Order Code WV4

Turning wood with Richard Raffan — demonstrations from the book featured last month; tools, cutting, six projects. 117 minutes

Retail price £31.95
Woodworker offer
price £28
Order Code WV5

Small shop tips and techniques — new ideas and angles, ingenious solutions to common problems in the small workshop. 60 minutes

Retail price.......£26.95
inc. p&p

Woodworker offer
price £24
Order Code WV6

To A.S.P. Reader Services, Wolsey House, Wolsey Rd, Hemel Hempstead, Herts HP2 4SS. **Hotline** (0442) 211882
Please rush me the following goods!

Order code(s) ....

Name ....

Address ....

....Post Code...........

I enclose a cheque/PO for...

● Make cheques payable to Argus Specialist Publications Ltd   ● We accept Access/Barclaycard

Amazon question

Furniture designer/maker Lucinda Leech went to Brazil last year to explore an array of unusual and beautiful timbers for fine work, and to see what the Brazilians are doing in the face of controversial deforestation.
The Worshipful Company of Furniture Makers' travel award made her trip possible; we asked her to recount her impressions and feelings. Here's her report

Very hot, very wet and very green — that's what I noted in my diary when I went into the forest for the first time. I had flown from Miami to Belém at the mouth of the Amazon, the main timber exporting port for the area, and on to Santarém, 500km away, at the junction of the Tapajos river with the Amazon.

Then it was an hour's very bumpy ride up a dirt road into a government-owned reserve used for both commerce and research. SUDAM (Superintendência do Desenvolvimento da Amazônia), an institution concerned with commercial forestry, runs a training course in Santarém to teach appropriate methods of felling and converting trees extracted from the reserve. It is also assessing which timbers growing in that area's virgin forest are suitable for commercial purposes, looking into physical properties and whether useful species are abundant enough.

One problem with commercial exploitation of the rainforest is the way in which the trees grow. Any individual tree is generally separated from another of its own kind by quite a distance. This is a natural barrier against the spread of pests and diseases, many of which are so specialised that they are specific to one particular host. And it leads to great diversity of the forest — over 200 types of tree per acre (in Britain we have only 20 native species in the whole country). So you don't find a stand of mahogany where several valuable trees could be felled at once; harvesting can be a difficult and expensive business despite the quantities of timber.

In Belterra I saw research plantations, some planted back in 1959. Attempts to grow a number of the same native species together have frequently been foiled by pests sweeping through them. Experiments with 80 indigenous species and 40 imported 'exotics' (ie, not native to Brazil), often result in much greater resistance to attack. Melina and eucalyptus are widely grown as pulp crops, and they are looking at other trees suitable for this. Although plantations don't have the appeal of the natural forest, they reduce the pressure on it, and if they are successful they will be much easier

— and more economic — to harvest, which would mean it would no longer make sense to use the virgin forest. But the time scale is a long one.

Timber dealers see no point in clear cutting of the naturally variable forest. One told me they had been felling in the same area for 15 years. He claimed that if only 10% of the forest were cut it could regenerate naturally. In a given area of forest, only 10% of the trees are actually useful — some are the wrong types, others too small or too big. They carefully extract those they want to use, making space for smaller trees to grow up and be usable later. This copies the natural conditions where, since the trees are very shallow rooted, they frequently fall and die, creating space for new ones; within six months the space is filled with greenery. I'd like to observe this kind of felling to see if the system actually works, and maybe identify responsible suppliers acting in this way so we could buy from the 'right' people. The only felling I actually saw was ground being cleared for agricultural research north of Manaus.

The vast number of types, plus the fact that even the same tree will vary according to the conditions of its particular bit of forest, make it difficult to classify useful species for the woodworker. It's clear that many of the trees in the Amazon will never be useful as timber; they are too hard or impossible to dry without splitting and warping. SUDAM have isolated a group of about 40 on which they are working for further information, and I was given a box of samples — a range of colours, from straw yellow and white through pinks and reds to browns and blacks.

From Santarém I took a local boat to Manaus, a trip of two days and three nights. Even first class with food the fare was only £11 — so you can imagine the conditions. You had to take your own ham-

● *Are we over-exploiting the tropical forests?* **Opposite top**, *the impenetrable Amazon forest in its natural state, and after clearance,* **below**. *The flooded forest,* **above**, *and* **below**, *a small wood yard accessible only by river*

● **Below**, *unloading timber at Belém from a boat that held only 30 tons.* **Left**, *boat building on the river's edge, and* **bottom left**, *strange aerial root structures*

continued

Amazon question

mock, and there were so many strung up on deck that there was little opportunity of getting out. Humanity within an inch of me in every direction — and nothing spoken but Portuguese. I fervently wished I had taken lessons, but it's amazing what you can communicate if you have to ...

Until recently the rivers have been the only means of transport and access, so the banks are relatively highly populated and the bordering trees have all been felled. In the last few years roads linking the major cities have been built, opening up land previously unavailable for settlement. Legally a farmer may only fell half the forest on his land, but there's nothing to stop him selling the forested section on, and the new owner then felling half that. So in practice this law doesn't actually preserve the forest. New roads and better access also mean it becomes economic for larger logging operations to move in and extract the wood, but it's still very expensive to transport it to a processing point.

Brazil is a developing country with a rapidly increasing population. In the area I saw, many of the people are very poor, so it's easy to understand that the immediate problem of feeding them seems more important than world concern about ecology. Our country used to be covered in forest and we chopped it all down — do you really suppose if Wales was covered with walnut trees we'd just leave them there? The Amazon is, after all, part of the country of Brazil — we have no real right to march in and tell them what to do with it, even if certain sorts of land reform and so on seem obvious to us. Even in the short time I was in Brazil I saw evidence of concern within the country, and various related research projects; but whether all this will prove adequate is doubtful.

The main difference between forest clearance in Europe and in the Amazon is that at least here the land is usable for agriculture, long term, once it's cleared. In the rainforest each of the thousands of plants and animals are interdependent; the ecostructure is so complex that once the forest is cleared it just can't re-grow.

The soil itself has little to do with fertility. When a leaf falls from a tree here, it will take about a year to break down fully; in the rainforest it takes around six weeks before all the nutrients are reabsorbed. The soil itself is very thin, with a layer of decaying vegetation over it and — my main impression — thousands of ants, some of them huge, assisting the process.

Over half the (frequent) rainfall never reaches the ground, used by the plants and animals above before it gets there. The tree canopy breaks the force of the rain, and the vegetation as a whole acts as a sponge, holding and releasing the water in a regular rhythm. When the vegetation is cleared the rain comes down with full force, rapidly washing away what nutrients there are, eroding the soil, and causing cycles of flooding and drought.

● *Open air work preparing timber for boat building; most firms take care of the whole process from tree to broomstick*

The most devastating effects on the Amazon forest are being wrought not by logging, but by vast projects such as hydro-electric power schemes, and by big agri-business. Huge areas are burnt, making for easy clearance and adding a little extra goodness to the soil. Grass is grown for cattle for a few years before the soil is exhausted, then the ranchers move on and burn more forest, leaving semi-desert behind them. I read that this process — producing meat for export — cuts the price of a hamburger in the USA by 5 cents. Is it really worth the destruction of the forest? To a country that needs foreign money to service debts, let alone feed its people, obviously it is. If the timber itself was a valuable enough commodity, and we showed ourselves prepared to pay for it, perhaps the Brazilians would view the forest differently, to be preserved and maintained for economic reasons. They do, after all, tend to be more immediately powerful than ecological ones. Anyway, using the wood has got to be better than burning it, and harvesting it as a renewable resource should be encouraged.

At the moment Brazil has 37.3% of world reserves of timber but its level of participation in world trade, including sawn wood and plywood, is only 3.3%. The forest seems enormous, and only a relatively small proportion seems to have been lost so far. But it's extremely difficult to get figures in such an inaccessible area, and the most worrying thing is that the rate of loss appears to be growing exponentially, so that it really could be only one or two generations before the whole lot is gone.

All the trees around Belém have already been felled. The companies I visited are now getting their wood from up to 1000km away, transporting it by river, either in the traditional, slow log rafts, or by the faster barges. The timber merchants I saw were usually much more than just suppliers of planks. Local unreliability, as one (European!) owner explained to me, makes it necessary for any firm to handle the whole process itself. They have people out in their own area of forest felling the timber, barges to bring it down river — the sawmills are always at the side of the river — and unloading facilities. Then comes conversion, often with very antiquated machinery (serviced by their own small engineering shop), followed by drying, then machining some of the material into products for local use and export (flooring and panelling, for instance). The rest of the timber is exported as straight-edged boards. Laws prevent the export of round logs now, and encourage as much local work on the timber as possible for the sake of jobs. Most of the firms I saw took care of the whole process from tree to broomstick in one big company in this way, some using up to 90% of the original product in some way or other.

I saw what was said to be the largest saw in Brazil for converting logs — a bandsaw with 1.8m diameter wheels, but it all looked pretty primitive by European standards. Reciprocating frame saws are still being made there — I saw a couple in timber yards on the river's edge in a small town with no access but by river. This was a centre for boat building because suitable timber grows nearby. Most of the machining was done in the open air, sheltered by just a roof. Safety standards were minimal and few machines were guarded.

In one small workshop I visited, the average age of the workers seemed about 10 years old. This was a small family concern with the owner using his sons as labour. 'Sons' must have meant extended family — there were far too many of them for the boss to have time for producing them and organise the woodwork as well! One was quite a skilled turner, and the products ranged from fairly crude furniture to roof trusses for building work.

I saw some simply beautiful timber samples already polished up, but found the names difficult to remember — like muiracatinga and maracauba. Some of the names are taken from the native Indian tribes' words for the trees. The more finely figured ones would be lovely for details or turning. Mahogany is becoming scarce, and rosewood more or less unobtainable, though I talked to someone who is planting it further south, apparently successfully. Other species we don't see much of here will become more widely known over the next few years I think; the Brazilians have plans to promote them.

I didn't learn to tell one tree from another as standing timber — not all that surprising given that the tops are often 150ft above your head! There are a variety of fascinating root structures including great buttresses, and strange aerial root structures. There are various different sorts of forest. In the places I was in there were not many of the bright flowers one imagines, but plenty of strange noises, warnings about snakes, and glorious bright blue butterflies in the clearings when it was sunny. Much of the time, although very hot, it was cloudy and rainy — which I knew about in theory beforehand, it being a rainforest and all! But it felt quite unlike anything I had ever experienced before. I also knew that the trees were going to be huge; what I hadn't realised was that it would only be some of them. In England one often sees trees of a similar type and age together, with undergrowth of a fairly consistent size beneath. In the rainforest there are trees of all sizes and the canopy is made up of various levels, with lianas tangling all over them. The green is in many shades, a result of each tree being at a different stage in its cycle. The colours we associate with the different seasons are there all together, with some dead trees interspersed, creating a remarkable pattern.

This is the mainland forest. The other type I saw was the 'Igapo' (flooded forest) on the River Negro, near Manaus. This was extremely beautiful, and the area I was in was a reserve, with little population — just our boat, water and forest in all directions (also crocodiles, dolphins, piranha, parrots, toucans . . .). The trees of the flooded forest have adapted to grow under water for part of the year. This meant that at the time I was there, at the end of the wet season, only their tops were sticking out of

the water; 20 or 30ft of trunk were immersed, and you could swim across (despite piranhas!) and stand in the top branches — then swim away again very fast because of the ants! In the dry season the seeds germinate and the new trees start to grow, remaining dormant during the time they are covered in water. I suppose this is one area of forest not likely to be felled since the operation would be so difficult. As it is, timber in the Amazon can only be harvested in the dry season because it's impossible to pull it out and transport it when it's wet. Several roads only operate for half of the year.

My original apprehensions about 'going to the jungle alone' proved entirely (well, nearly entirely) unfounded, and I now hope to restructure my life as a self-employed furniture designer and maker. I want to see as much of the world's different sorts of forest as possible — and to assess the situation from the woodworker's point of view.

I went to Brazil with various preconceived notions about deforestation, ecological crisis, and imminent disaster, gleaned from the bits of information we are given here. I found the matter a good deal more complex than I had realised, and I also found more concern and knowledge on the spot than I expected.

As I was there such a short time I was only able to see a limited amount. I was greatly helped by IBDF, (Instituto Brasileiro de Desenvolvimento Florestal) the government department in charge of developing forestry, and also EMBRAPA (Empresa Brasiliera de Pesquisa Agropecuaria) a research establishment doing a lot of interesting work with timber.

The biggest problems seem to be a lack of co-ordination between projects, plus only very short-term funding. Some government money is being put into worthwhile schemes connected with the rainforest, but the nature of the problems means that results take a long time to appear. So six-month reviews of financial aid based on results mean that all too many projects are abandoned too early.

● *Trees soar up to 150ft above your head*

The small-scale experiments are often more successful, although they lack the political appeal of the giant schemes the Brazilians seem so fond of; for example, various manufacturing concerns have been set up in free-trade Manaus, including a company making tennis racquets. Manaus is surrounded by forest in every direction, and yet this company was importing American ash, with great difficulty and no doubt expense too, to laminate the frames. So INPA conducted experiments to find them a suitable local timber with the same properties — this sort of thing certainly seems to make better sense, at one level at any rate.

I was greatly helped in the organisation of my trip by the Forestry Department of Oxford university, by Dan Kemp of Timbmet, and of course, by the Worshipful Company of Furniture Makers whom I frequently silently thanked when things got particularly stunning!

My reasons for wanting to go to Brazil incorporated the woodworker's dilemma. On the one hand I knew there was some wonderful wood growing there and I wanted to know more about it, and find out about new materials for my own work. On the other hand I had heard a lot about the problems and way in which the resource of the rainforest is being squandered in just one generation. I thought being on the spot would make it easier to clarify these issues, but I think going there has actually confused me further. It has certainly left me with more questions to ask, and the realisation that I need a lot more time and another visit to see more. Meanwhile I read what I can, talk to people and continue to work towards further travels. ■

● *Converting to planks; the largest bandsaw in Brazil is small beer by European standards*

Luna de Luxe Belt sander

- A compact and robust universal belt sander for schools, handymen, craftsmen and industrial workshops.

- The machine is tiltable 360°, which facilitates different types of sanding operations.

- Luna de Luxe is easily adjustable from horizontal to vertical position (flat sanding, edge sanding).

- The small sanding drum can be changed from Ø 50 mm to Ø 80 mm for the sanding of different radii.

- Lateral belt adjustment by a knurled set screw.

Standard Equipment

Vertically adjustable sanding table, fence moveable 90° to 45°, fixed sanding table, two (2) sanding drums Ø 50 mm and Ø 205 mm, one (1) sanding belt and tools.

Supplied for bench mounting as standard.
Tripod for floor mounting is an optional accessory.
Available 1- and 3-phase, 1.5 hp.

For further information please contact your nearest Luna dealer or write to the address below:

Luna
Tools and Machinery Ltd

20 Denbigh Hall, Bletchley, Milton Keynes MK3 7QT. ☎ Milton Keynes (0908) 70771 Telex: 82125 Luna G.

110

111

Tabletalk

Woodworker Giant Test

Black & Decker Power Tool Table

Dunlop Powerbase

Meritcraft Powermate

The Black & Decker Workmate has long been a respected piece of equipment, and with very good reason. It's a valuable renovation and maintenance base for the home-owner with limited or no bench space; saves the kitchen table, and works better. It's also an item the professional woodworker is rarely found without, an essential part of the on-site arsenal, and very handy in the workshop as a second vice or portable work surface.

Before my workshop days I had the bright idea — along with thousands of others, I'm sure — of bolting my hand-held circular saw to a bit of ply, plunging the blade through it, clamping the ply into the Workmate — and hey presto, a saw-bench. A natural development was doing the same thing with a router — a revelation, when I'd hardly even seen a spindle moulder. Saw-table, router table and Workmate were an invaluable team, and the three put together as one for mass-production was inevitable, merely a matter of time.

DIYers are buying and using more and more hand-held power tools, getting more and more serious about them and the work they do with them, and particularly in the last couple of years seem to have discovered the router. Witness the explosion in the DIY router market. And so comes the new breed of Workmate, or 'workcentre', a stand with table or carriage or both into which you can fit a range of hand-held

power tools. Effective sole-plate size of the tool is increased, and there are usually larger fences than come with the tool as well, increasing ease of operation, control and accuracy. Some designs use an over-table sliding system of tracks as well. With various clamping and holding arrangements — usually specific plates or less specific screw-clamps — the idea, or at least the publicity blurb says it is, is to turn your power tool into a workshop machine.

Just how sensible such claims are will come clear as you read on, but suffice it to say that in the market we're talking about, with pricing and production limitations at work, most of the workcentres I looked at do not and never will turn a ratty old circular saw into a precision saw-bench. It's unrealistic to expect them to do so — partly, of course, because the manufacturers have no control over what tool you'll be using. Nevertheless, the DIYer doesn't want a 'proper' table-saw — neither the budget or the space for it — so these devices have to be attractive to that kind of user; the professional woodworker, too, should be having a close look at their site-work potential.

As we (me and my mate) went through the six different models, scrutinising, using and testing them, it became apparent that although they were there to compare one against the other, there were such wide differences of approach in design, pricing,

style, materials — and marketing — that there really is a different slot for each of the six. What you have to decide is which one should find its way into your workshop, shed, or cupboard under the stairs.

Safety

A serious question, and one which I was forced to ask very early on. Aspects of design and quality, both of basic equipment and accessories, made me think of the probable buyer, inexperienced in the use of 'upside down' tools. Blade or cutters are fully exposed, both hands are free — an unfamiliar situation to many, increasing manifold the potential for personal injury. Hand-holding a circular saw and bench-sawing need very different cutting techniques. So of course, the need for reliable and sturdy guards and fences is paramount. Lack of concentration is a big factor in most accidents, and if you have to compensate for a wobbly guard or inaccurate fence, add another direction of push and watch for the cut wandering, you are having to concentrate on too many things at once. The chances of an inaccurate cut in the work — or a messy one on your fingers — are much greater.

I've been lucky with most of my accidents — minor cuts could easily have

112

All of a sudden, there are half-a-dozen 'workcentres' on the market — tables and stands into which you fit hand-held power-tools. Will they turn your circular saw into a precision table machine? We gave six to Grant Pearce to find out

Skilten Skilmate

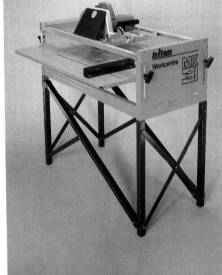

Triton Mark III

Wolfcraft Variotec

been bloody disasters — but what kind of safety protection is luck? You have to stand in the right way and the right place at a worktable for the best and safest cut; you have to use push-sticks; there is a whole catalogue of safety warnings that manufacturers should include in their literature. Most of them seemed to show an alarming lack of appreciation of the safety factor, especially considering the awkward change of mode from hand-held to table-mounted machinery. Guards that restrict the width of cut or which are fiddly or awkward to use merely invite the user to do away with them altogether. Literature that comes with such purchases should make it clear that guards are not something extra you have to deal with, they are part and parcel of using the machine. Their design should be integral, not an afterthought. I regard an easily accessible quick-action on/off switch as essential — perhaps the biggest single safety question in this whole concept of a table that uses tools whose switches normally depend on hand pressure — yet out of the six, only one machine has a switch as standard, and they aren't even available as accessories on some of the others.

As a trained mechanical draughtsman — a trade I haven't practised for some years — I also appreciated many of the ideas and developments that had gone into basic concepts. It was interesting to see the right use of materials and detail 'thinking

through' — and interesting to see that in many cases the ideas are hindered, not helped, by materials and detail. Many are a good buy considering the price and range of use, but it's also easy to see where lack of time or money, or a tight pricing policy, have forced the life out of good concepts, leading to flimsy and inadequate guards or cheap materials.

You can overcome many of the failings, of course, by reinforcing fences, adding longer bits of wood for better accuracy and safety, or drilling extra holes in the tables or sole-plates of your tools. You are also likely to find yourself making a multitude of jigs.

Tools

Circular saws and routers make most sense used upside down, and it is on these tools largely that the designs concentrate. Jigsaw mounting plates are easy to make and include, so most of the tables have that facility; I can think of only very limited use for an upside-down jigsaw, where you have really small bits of thin ply or other material you want to cut, and can't hold the tool and clamp the material. Otherwise, why bother. Planers are a different matter again; if you're looking for machined accuracy in facing and edging, don't look here. If you want to run old beams across your hand-

held planer to take the rough stuff off them, then putting your planer in a table is fine. At this stage (November 1986), only one table would take a planer, though a few of the other manufacturers are working on it.

The test

I took on the role of the average punter, looking first at the literature and trying to assemble the things from it, then going through the various operations of ripping, crosscutting, routing, planing where I could, and jigsawing. We also examined adjustments, clamping systems, fences and guards, and general safety.

One of the things you have to look at closely is how many power tools can be used in the table you like the look of; generally, adjustable clamping systems are better than plates with holes supposed to line up with threaded inserts in the tool base, because that is obviously limiting. (You can always drill extra holes, which doesn't seem to be the point.) It's also worth mentioning that almost all of these designs are under continuous development, so detail design and accessory availability is likely to have changed from the time we tested the tables to the time you're reading this. I've listed them alphabetically to show no fear or favour.

continued

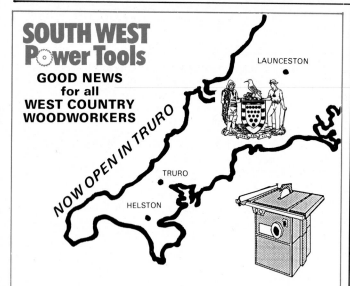

Tabletalk

BLACK & DECKER POWER TOOL TABLE

Press releases say 'all DIY jobs', so we can safely assume B&D know where they're pitching this product. It's designed to be mounted on the new Workmate 2, which I liked very much, although the increasing use of plastic in stress-bearing parts is a bit disconcerting; the power-tool table is made entirely of plastic, with a ribbed construction through which dust easily falls. But it's plastic. Some bits bend more than others, and I didn't break any, although I'm sure it wouldn't be hard to.

Literature

Very comprehensive indeed — admirable. Parts checklist, assembly instructions, all sorts of detail on how you do what sort of cut; a thorough job — and good safety advice. They suggest you make mounting templates for your tools, which hints at the strength or otherwise of the table itself.

Assembly

Relatively straightforward — everything fitted well, and everything you need for sawing, jigsawing, and routing comes as standard, except those ply templates. Good ideas were evident, though making them up in plastic killed them somewhat. The table attaches to the Workmate 2 quickly and easily, but there is also a separate stand you can get for it. The tool clamping system, a set of reach-over bars and screw-up knobs, is just about adequate.

B&D claim you can use any hand-held circular saw with a blade up to 7¼in, which I have no reason to doubt. My old Skil certainly went in OK. Saws only mount under the table. DIY routers up to 750w can be used; there is a list of saws which will go with it, in which B&D, AEG, Bosch Metabo and Peugeot all appear. It takes B&D, Elu (the little MOF 96) and Bosch routers.

Strength

When you use the saw or router without the ply 'template' they suggest — sole-plate, in other words — the table surface warps slightly. I tightened the clamps to hold the tools very carefully, worried about pulling the mounts right out of the plastic table, but it survived. The strength of the plastic fence-faces is pathetic, quite frankly; they certainly need the strong ply sole-plates that the instructions suggest. The router cutter pulled the work to the fence as it should, but the fence bent, making inaccuracy inevitable unless you stick bits of ply on it. My question is, why use plastic like this? Apart from these weak areas, it seemed adequate, but . . .

● *B&D Power Tool Table's grid is a good idea, but the crosscut/mitre fence is a long way from the saw-blade*

● *Routing/spindle moulding; guards are big and clear, and move up when you push the wood under, but catch dust. You can see the double-adjusters on the fences*

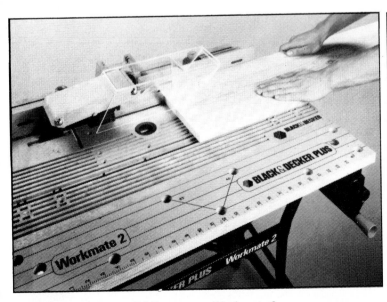

● *Ripping with the B&D, set on a Workmate 2*

● *Angle cutting – that crosscut/mitre fence needs a facing piece*

continued

Accuracy, adjustments

The main fence has two halves, in the gap between which the router will sit. The two halves are adjustable on slides with a clamping knob, and there is a fine adjustment knob on top of that which operates a cam. A nice idea in principle, but it's not really necessary to fine-adjust both fences; one would be adequate. When in position, the saw-guard stops the fence coming closer than 19mm to the blade; a false fence is necessary. For ripping, you can only get 118mm maximum distance between fence and blade — for wider cuts, you must take the fences off. The crosscut/mitre fence is small and sits in its slide too far away from the blade, because the cutout for the router in the table is between the slide for the fence and the blade. You'd have to lengthen the face of the fence with a bit of straight hardwood to get good use out of this. As it is, it's awkward and unpleasant to use.

Safety, guards

The guards are good on the whole, although perhaps unnecessarily big, and they have an angle to slide up over the wood which is moulded all in one, creating a nice deep vee-channel for dust to collect. Visibility, good to start with, might suffer, and guards might get pulled up out of the way . . . The riving-knife supports the saw top-guard, and it lines up too far over to one side, forcing the saw hard over to the plastic insert, into which of course, it wants to cut.

The various sizes of (plastic) insert for saws and routers are a good idea.

There's no separate on/off switch — you get a clamp handle with a piece of string on it, which you can clamp over the tool switch and pull off quick if you panic. Better than some, not as good as others. The literature gives a good safety awareness, and the guards do their job, if at times getting in the way of full use of the machines.

The B&D product does the job within limits, but to me an extensive use of plastic like this lowers its credibility. Well worth looking at for the DIYer with light tools and small jobs to do.

Prices

Everything you need comes as standard on
the Power Tool table: **£53.95**
B&D Workmate 2 **£79.00**
Independent leg stand **£19.95**
There is such a thing as a discount on B&D stuff . . .

DUNLOP POWERBASE

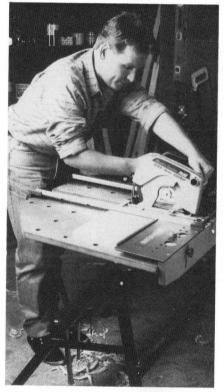

This is an interesting design, showing a breadth and depth of approach greater than most of the other products. A foldable metal stand supports a 25mm MDF worktop, which has a removable middle section allowing a sole-plate mounted circular saw, jigsaw, router and planer (when they get the planer plate out) to be used upside down. It has a long fence, 45x25mm MDF, for use as a rip-fence and a router fence in the 'spindle-moulding' mode, and comes with two rather neat adjustable clamp/stops for adjusting the fence or holding workpieces. Clamping carcases for assembly is an obvious use here, and the generous size of the table sets you up well for that. There is also a unique (amongst these six) 'control unit', basically two aluminium bars with 'wings' that fit over the table and on which you can run the tools in 'overhead' mode. Crosscutting and routing grooves, trenches and dadoes are all therefore possible.

The 'wings' of the control unit have various holes in them, all spaced on a 32mm module, for spaced drilling (drill bush supplied), and routing recesses for Blum-type hinges. Two template followers come with it for your router. I use a drill-stand for this, but the wings and fence are already lined up to give you the correct distance of these big holes from the door edge. There is also a calibrated adjustable length stop for crosscutting or routing to predetermined lengths and spacings. There is a riving-knife and top-guard for the saw, and the front bar of the stand has holes drilled for tools to sit in. All evidence of coherent and careful thought.

You can put a special drill-stand in the overhead rails for accurate vertical drilling and positioning; there's no planer facility as yet, but extension tables are available to increase the already very good size. Genuine 8x4 ripping is possible. The control system allows accurate crosscutting — large long lengths, pieces up to 64mm thick; crosscut capacity is 24in, better than many radial-arm saws. Excellent for box carcases and similar operations, and the adjustable stop should allow you accurate repeat cutting — good for routing too. Tools 'checked for suitability' are basically B&D and the smaller Bosch and Elu stuff.

Literature

An eight-page A4 booklet, comparatively well written and well illustrated, tells you all the basics you need to know. As an unusual concept, the Powerbase might perhaps have been better served by more comprehensive literature. Safety gets good mention here and there, but not as prominently as I think an unfamiliar user should have.

Assembly

Easy and straightforward — the instructions are good on this part. The whole thing folds flat, good for wall storage, and the metal stand is good and strong. It folds and unfolds quickly, and locks reassuringly into position; the tool rack is very handy.

● **Above**, crosscutting on the Powerbase's overhead guide system. You must move the tool to the right to clear its cut – 'nil tolerance' would be better. **Right**, this is what happens when you follow through, unless you want to stop the blade while it's still in the cut

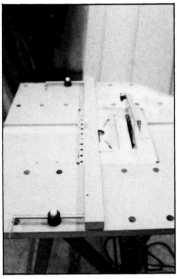

● **Above**, 'rip-fence' – not the straightest or firmest; **left**, yes, you can rip 8x4s with a table extension

● **Left**, routing dadoes for shelving; good and straight, but doubtful on groove width. **Above**, useful clamping for assembly

Strength

The stand is strong and well designed. It feels stable with the top, and makes for confidence — even if you have to stand on it yourself. But I do have serious reservations about the use of MDF for a worktop surface. Moisture makes it expand if it isn't treated (it does appear to have some sort of wax on it), and if it was stored in a damp shed or garage in the winter it would swell, making the sole-plates and table insert hard

to fit and remove. MDF is also easily mutilated, and the edges are most likely to take a beating. The sole-plate clamping system is accommodating and well made, but the plates themselves are flimsy, with too many holes. Pressed sheet steel isn't really good enough — one drop and it's a goner. The aluminium track rails are also very light and bendy; the whole tracking system, in fact, is eminently bendable or breakable, with its light plastic wings. You

have to take it off to use the underslung tools, and it's a bit of a chore to put together — so you won't want to take it apart every time; it's an awkward shape to store. Best to hang it up.

Again, the adjustable clamps, which fit into a variety of holes drilled all over the table, are a good idea but the materials are a bit cheap. Steel thread held by push-button plastic (for quick release or fine adjustment); how long will they last?

Accuracy, adjustments

The big problem for me with the overhead mode was that there is about $\frac{1}{4}$in side-to-side play in between the sole-plate and the guide rails. The blurb says 'always use the left-hand guide rail as a cutting reference', but they don't make enough mention of it; the manufacturers tell me they decided to allow this play in the design, but have built in provision for adding a nylon insert on one side of the sole-plate so you can get 'nil tolerance'.

You're supposed to make a cut along the left rail, move the saw over to the right and withdraw it, but if you're cutting repeat lengths, the offcut on the right is as valuable as the one on the left, and you'd have to push your right-.hand cut piece away before you moved the saw back — while the saw itself is on the far side of the workpiece, just about to tip off the table. If you're using a 15mm router cutter for 15mm grooves to fit 15mm chipboard or whatever as shelves, nil tolerance is what you need — any more and you've got horrible slop.

The rip-fence is not really serious. The clamps hold it well in position, but the fence itself is bendy anyway (not helped by the cutout for the router), and I'd reckon at

continued

117

Tabletalk

least four clamps would hold it straight, not the two supplied. It's also fiddly to line it up parallel to the saw-blade — no calibration system on table or fence. Maximum distance between blade and fence is enough for most work. The saw-plate has an insert for underslung mode — again a bit cheap and thin — but it works with its own guard for overhead, so you leave out the insert. This means you have two alignments in the plate, one with insert and one without, and there are lines scribed on the plate to help you with that alignment. It's a bit fiddly. There are three clamping-bolts for the tools in the plates, but four would have been better.

The height of the overhead guide rails adjusts very easily; just a matter of twiddling knobs and pushing the assembly hard down on the work. Spring washers would have been good — power tools do vibrate, and knobs on threads have been known to fall off. I think there ought to be a separate sole-plate for the router, since the universal one is full of holes, which don't help bendiness. There's an extra few bits and pieces you have to buy for using the router upside down.

Safety

A safety switch is available, but it's an extra. All the necessary guards for routing upside down are again extras. The overhead guide rails finish at the far end of the cut — on top of the 'anti-spelch' insert in the back fence, which you can replace when it's cut to bits — so to complete the cut the tool and sole-plate end up hanging half in the air on the other side of the table. They should really extend so the plate and machine are secure right through their travel. The top-guard for the saw in underslung ripping mode is adequate; it doesn't tilt, however, which means you can't rip bevel cuts.

All in all, the Powerbase is a well-thought out design, a bit let down by too-cheap materials. It's a borderline case for serious machining, and a handy workbench as well, with a particular advantage of good table area.

Prices

No rrp as yet; expected range as follows:
Basic Powerbase — folding bench, worktop, clamping system, overhead guide rails, length stop, universal sole-plate (for circular and jigsaw, router), bench clamps, routing templates — **£125**
Extra sole-plates — **£10**
Extension table — **£25**
Set of four bench dogs (non-adjustable) — **£2**
Safety switch — **£20**
No-volt release safety switch — **£30**
Router kit — **£25**
Drill-stand and attachments — **£30**
Mitre and dowelling systems also on the way; most of the accessories above should be available early spring '87.

MERITCRAFT POWERMATE

A neat, well-finished cast aluminium alloy table on short legs, which takes four plates for circular saw, jigsaw, router, planer and two B&D belt sanders. The planer wasn't available for test, but will be out mid-February. A full-height work stand comes as an optional extra; apart from the nice appearance of the worktable itself, it's quite small, only about 30x18in. No chance of 8x4s here without a lot of setting up extra supports.

Literature

Skimpy, but they do give you an accurate guide for the tools you can use, which are mainly from the B&D and Bosch ranges, with a Makita and a Hitachi here and there. 'In order to simply improve every DIY job and leave your hands free', it says — a key to market positioning. Safety gets a mention in a checklist at the back of the book, which is OK as far as it goes — not very far, in other words. What's a pushstick look like to someone who has never used one? It also so happened we had a Bosch POF 52 to fit on the router plate, and thus found a shortcoming in the instructions; you're supposed to fit bars with a multitude of cutouts over the base of the machine to hold it on, as well as screw through the plate into threaded inserts in the base, but the bars won't work with a POF. We struggled for some time before a phone call to Meritcraft elicited the information that screws through the base were all the POF router needed to fix it. The instructions do actually indicate this, but it's not easy to work out. We also understand the range of suitable tools is expanding. Perhaps a re-write would be a good idea.

● **Above**, stud-and-bar fixing system for tools on the Powermate is fiddly and limiting. **Right**, good safety switch – it's an extra

Assembly, strength

The cast alloy table is basically complete — no nuts and bolts; it's designed to stand on an existing bench or table. The accessory leg stand, into which tool plates sit neatly for storage, took a bit of putting together; I had to bend bits at the corners so the angle section steel would go together, and drill out some of the bolt holes to get all the bolts in. Once it was put together, it's perfectly sturdy enough for the job.

One of the more unusual things about the Powermate is that it has a 25mm diameter hole in it for a drill-stand column. This worked fine with my drill-stand, but you need a 25mm column — and a round one at that. The table and stand were strong

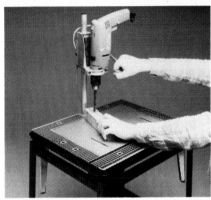

● **Above**, *crosscut/mitre fence travels to right of blade – why?* **Above right**, *the workpiece end can drop into angle-fence slot; right, a drill-stand slots in*

enough, but the sole-plates flexed quite easily out of the table. Depends on the weight of your tools.

Accuracy, adjustments

The fences are all small, in scale with the table-top itself; both the mitre/crosscut fence and rip-fence adjustments aren't calibrated. The rip-fence is strong and reasonably accurate, but short. Maximum distance from router fence to centre of cutter is 87mm. The sole-plates hook under at one end of the table, then sit down in a clip at the other end, which is quite a positive fixing, but the mitre/crosscut fence moves in a groove to the right of the saw-blade, which is a bit strange, and we looked to see if there was any way of turning plate or tool round to get it running on the left of the blade. There isn't. There was also

a bit of slop in the fit of the plates on their recess, which made absolute accuracy impossible.

The sole-plates, with their stud-and-bar design, are a bit limiting. The range of tools you can use is quite wide, but it could be wider with a more variable clamping system. As seems to be usual, product development is still under way to include

more tools in the range of suitables. The switch clip is unimpressive.

Safety, guards

There's no top guard for the router fence, which is not really long enough; they're bringing one out shortly, I'm told. In safety terms, the size of table and fences would make long and large work awkward unless you set up outrigger supports. The circular saw won't tilt in the plate, which is why they give you a 45° bevel rip-fence as an accessory; again, it's small, the running area being only about 2in deep. The slot in it is also slightly too long, allowing the back end of your cut piece to slip down against the blade and potentially ruin the full-length accuracy of the bevel. There's a good on/off switch available as an extra.

O verall, the Powermate looks good, in its silver, black and red livery, but it's not really a serious machining centre, if that's what you're after. More for the adventurous hobbyist.

Prices

Basic bench, circular saw plate, jigsaw plate, mitre/crosscut fence, top guard and riving knife, guide bar for rip-fence, rip-fence	**£69.95**
Router plate, fence and fixing bars	**£24.45**
Preset 45° angle rip-fence	**£5.95**
Safety switch, extension lead, 3m cable	**£24.95**
Planer plate, fixing bars, top guard (available mid-Feb)	**£21.95**
Full-height workstand	**£26.95**

SKILTEN SKILMATE

I was impressed by this comparatively simple-looking table when I first saw it at the Woodworker Show — it looks quite like a B&D Workmate, but the top isn't a vice. It's made of first-class materials, a good thick ply top, a section of which hinges down for use as a shelf; the stand is solid rectangular-section steel. No problems servicing your V-8 engine on this one.

It could certainly take you standing on it; thought has gone into extended use, because the legs are height-adjustable, which means you can crank up one side and use it as a drawing board. There is a coverall aluminium plate available to make it a strong and well-protected table.

Tool plates drop into a recessed section, one long side of which is exposed when you hinge the opening section down; you can use circular saw, jigsaw, router and planer, all in underslung modes. The table is drilled for inserts, and the holes also take the long overhead top-guard for the saw, the planer top-guard, router fence and two metal stops

— stronger versions of the familiar Workmate variety — which go with a good-quality machine vice. All of which gives good evidence of sound and careful thinking.

The problem we had with the Skilmate was that the only model available for test was a development prototype, so a lot of the detailing was hand finished, and there were literal and metaphorical rough edges to much of it. The makers claim you can fit almost any power tool; the existing planer plate will take half the planers on the market, they say. You can fit a circular saw with up to a 210mm blade, which is bigger capacity than most of its competitors. The existing bracketing arrangements will fit 90% of the circular saws on the market, and the makers say if you have a tool which doesn't fit, they will make up the brackets for you at no extra cost.

Literature

All I can say about this is I hope the customer gets something better. There is a leaflet with a number of photos showing the Skilmate being used in its various modes; and another one which supposedly explains the brackets and fixing plates. Position

● *Oops! Bendy plate on the Skilmate – but a support rebate is on the way*

no.1, position no.6, locking bracket 8, diagram 4 — it's all over the place. Having used the thing I still have difficulty working

continued

out what they're trying to tell you. They're the sort of instructions that invite people to abandon them and work it out for themselves. There's a safety note on the first page which tells you that tools must be securely fixed to the plates, and plates to the bench, and to check this regularly. 'When using the circular saw,' it goes on to say, 'a clip is required to lock the button on. Alternatively this can be achieved with tape or string.' They are working on an electronically controlled safety switch, but this wasn't available at the time of writing.

Assembly

You don't really need assembly instructions, because it's ready assembled. Just fold out the legs and drop in the tool tray beneath, which locks them apart. I felt a holding mechanism for that would be an improvement.

Strength

As I said, first-class materials; it'll be interesting to see what compromises have been made for mass production. The first batch were delivered to Texas Homecare, apparently, on the day I wrote this.

The sole-plates — good solid 3mm steel — were, however, awkward to fit tools to; and quite a serious point is that the fourth one of the long sides had no support at all. This is the one which goes against the hinging section. It would surely be quite easy to put a rebate on that edge too, so the sole-plates are supported all round. As it was, there was flex along that edge with a saw, jigsaw or router, and with the planer, well. The cut-out in the plate for the wide blade allows only about a ½in strip along that one long unsupported edge, which is further weakened by two countersunk screw-holes. Accurate machining with a hand-held planer? Not with this design.

The mounting bar at the end of the table on which the rip-fence fits could also have been a great deal stronger. It allowed the fence to move about under pressure, especially from hefty workpieces. The long overhead mount for the top-guard on the saw was more like it; 25mm-diameter steel tube, the business.

Accuracy, adjustments

The mitre/crosscut fence was tiny, uncalibrated, and wouldn't slide all the way along the obviously hand-routed groove in the ply top. Mass production should sort this out. Our rip-fence was different from the one in the leaflet pictures, and different again, I understand, from the production version; what we had wasn't really long or high enough. Bevel ripping is with an angled fence, like the Powermate; as it was, we couldn't get it near enough the saw-blade to make any sense at all. Add a bit of thick ply to it and it will work. The overhead saw-guard arm didn't bring the guard directly above the blade, however we fiddled about with the position of the saw, and the sole-plates fit with varying degrees of accuracy,

● **Above**, unimpressive plane guard is now improved; **left**, clamping brackets are now also better than this

● **Middle left**, planing's OK if it's rough stuff; **middle right**, router fence has no guards. **Above left**, good clamps and vice; **above right**, adjustable legs, aluminium cover (extra) and you have a drawing board

leaving ridges where the workpiece goes from table to plate and back again. Again, all details I would expect to be sorted out for production.

The clamping arrangements for the tools are based on a 'universal' idea — nuts, spring-washers and bolts hold little clamps that locate over the ridges of the tool sole-plates — but they fix through holes rather than slides in the universal plate, so depending on the size of your tool sole-plate, the pressure the bolts can exert on the plate transfers well or badly to the tool

itself. They could have done with being bigger section, with a greater height so you got better leverage.

The saw we fitted remained a bit wobbly, as did the router — a POF 52, which like the Powermate relied only on screws through into threaded holes in the router base. It wobbled, because, as we found, both sole-plate and the base of the router itself weren't totally flat. The odd bit of garnet paper slipped in here and there sorted it out. I couldn't mount my big Elu MOF36 on this plate.

Safety, guardings

The saw mounting was designed so the saw's own full-cover blade guard came up through the plate. Again, I understand this system will differ from production, and it's basically a good safety idea, but as it was the spring-mounted guard flipped over on to the last couple of inches of the workpiece as it passed the blade on completion of the cut. The spring guard jammed against the top guard, which jammed the work, plus the spring guard wanted to push the work upwards. A wider top-guard would solve this, which is apparently the change that has been made for production. The planer top-guard was difficult to fit and barely adequate; it didn't line up over the blades, because you couldn't move it back and forth on the length of the plane, only round on its pivot arm.

Despite the cavalier-sounding advice to tape up or tie with string your saw switch, there is no alternative at the moment with the Skilmate. The electronically controlled safety switch they're working on sounds an excellent idea.

I must be fair to the Skilmate. It's basically an excellent design, with a great advantage of excellent-quality materials; it has the sort of strength that an everyday on-site user would ask for. Most of the problematic details we found in use should be sorted for production, and if Texas Homecare have already bought the idea — and a great number of Skilmates — then it must be serious. Even if the sole-plate flex and inaccurate seating, with its bumps and ridges, is sorted out, I still wouldn't expect planing to be any more than taking real rough surfaces off real rough work.

Prices

Bench, plate for circular and jigsaws, brackets, screws, guide bar, overhead saw guard, jigsaw guard, 6in metal vice, two stops, tray	**£114.95**
Router plate, router fence, fixings	**£19.55**
Planer plate, cover, fixings	**£19.55**
Extra tray	**£14.95**
Aluminium worktop	**£14.95**
45° angle rip-fence plus mitre/ crosscut fence	**£14.95**
Electronic safety switch, 5m cable	**No price yet**

TRITON MARK 3

This product is markedly different from all the rest, in more ways than just the obvious ones. It is basically an open-sided box construction, with two aluminium parallel tracks at the top. A carriage slides between those tracks for a circular saw in overhead crosscut mode; a different plate (or the saw one with some add-ons) carries a router, for grooving and trenching over the work. Pretty much any tool will fit, including my big Elu. A worksurface slots in below the tools in 'overhead' mode. Flip the carriage over in its tracks and lock it into one of two positions along the length of the table, and you have an underslung saw for ripping and crosscutting with a sliding fence — the table fits in an upper position. Same with the router to become a spindle moulder. The whole affair sits on a stand, which costs extra.

They make no bones of the fact that you will lose depth of cut if you use the router kit in the standard carriage, and so tell you that ½in-shank machines are best; there is an extra router kit which includes another small table if you don't want to buy another router, for ¼in-shank machines. This loses you less depth. You can get extension tables and even a set of wheels.

Literature

Comprehensive to a degree. 28 pages, 120 photographs, clear, well written, easy to read . . . 'You are about to assemble your Workcentre', it says on the front page; 'There's a right way of doing it and very many wrong ways (bold type). Follow the instructions step by step . . . and you should have it properly set up in an hour or two. Ignore or skim through this manual, and you could spend a whole day putting it together, and still not get it right. The choice is yours.' Fair warning. Everything has been thought through in detail, and explained clearly and simply in detail. Assembly of machine and stand is easy if

● *Top, Triton saw 'chassis' flips easily for over or under modes; above, first-class rip-fence*

you follow the blurb; then the booklet takes you through fitting and using each tool in their different modes. Large numbers of suggestions for jigs, fence extensions, operations you can perform and so on are suggested; safety is a continuous and recurring theme, well documented and well emphasised.

You can also rent or buy a three-hour video, which fills in other details and covers the use and potential of the machine; more jigs than the booklet. Most important, it's an excellent way of illustrating safety points, showing the dangers and pitfalls of machine woodworking of this kind; first-class safety education.

Assembly

Procedure is clear, and all the parts — there are a lot of them — fit together well. The kind of attention to detail the Triton displays throughout is in evidence in the different kinds of washers — lock, spring or flat — which are provided to go where they're specifically needed. There's also three different kinds of nut. As you put the thing together you just see more and more of the quality of the design and appropriate use of materials.

Strength

All the bits and pieces are made from the right material for the job, all are sturdy and sensible. The aluminium track for the sliding carriage is well hefty enough; any longer and it would have begun to flex. The sliding carriage is a tight fit, and slides as smoothly as you would expect on a £1500 table saw, though the nylon sliding lugs will probably wear, especially if you catch them on sharp aluminium corners. The table top is pressed steel with strong cross-bracing, hefty and confidence-inspiring; the stand is 25mm-square channel steel, well braced. The adjustable saw carriage is cast alloy, again very carefully and thoughtfully designed. This product is engineered, and moreover by people who understand woodwork and woodworkers. All the fences and guards are solid, weighty and easy to use. As a mechanical draughtsman, I can see the detailed approach, and appreciate it.

Accuracy, adjustments

When you use the table-top underneath the saw or router, there's calibration for setting height, and a guide in the booklet to tell you where to set it according to your blade or cutter projection. You can adjust table height or cutting depth, of course, for dadoing with a router.

The booklet describes some uses where it suggests you line the table with a false board; angle cutting with the saw, for instance, and compound mitres. When you adjust the table up hard, it stays up hard. In its top slots for using the saw or router

continued

Tabletalk

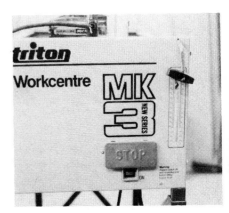

● **Top left**, *simple and strong crosscut/mitre fence on the Triton has non-slip faces and dual calibration;* **above left**, *excellent top-guard and no-fuss fitting;* **above right**, *hooray for a standard safety-switch.* **Left**, *2hp router in overhead mode with the worktable beneath*

underslung, there are 90° locking keys which both locate it and push it up tight. A neat little idea, but very loseable — drill and wire them to the table yourself.

The adjustable saw-plate would take, as far as we could see, just about any size of sole-plate; you can slide bits around in it so the whole thing fits accurately and comfortably. Aligning the blade with the rip-fence in the table is easy, and all the instructions are there. The sliding carriage, as I said, is an excellent fit. Basically the machine itself is so tuneable, you'd soon find your limitations came from your tools, not the table.

Safety guards

The rip-fence is the business, far and away the best of any I looked at. A simple, strong aluminium U-channel, the full length of the table, sits over two slots in the table which are calibrated so you can easily get and keep the fence parallel to the blade. The router

fence screws on to this rip-fence; two pieces of less solid U-section steel, the outfeed one with a fine adjustment so you can set it nearer the cutter than the infeed one for 'spindle-moulder planing'. They sit either side of the cutter, and adjust in and out towards or away from it along the fence; one of them was bent when we got it, which meant I couldn't rout a straight cut. An interesting little side feature of these fences is that the dust gets thrown into the U-section and spews out the far end — I doubt that was designed into it!

The clear plastic top-guard for the router functions perfectly well, as does the top-guard and riving knife for the saw when underslung; serious stuff, easy to use, and they don't tempt you into doing away with them. The locating lug for the riving knife, for instance, drops into the saw-blade channel in the table, turns, and tightens up; no fiddling about trying to thread nuts on bolts from underneath.

The crosscut/mitre fence is a good size, strong, and calibrated for angles to both the rip-fence and the 90° axis of the blade. Both working faces of the crosscut mitre fence are faced with abrasive paper to stop slip — a nice touch.

Video and booklet together do a great job on safety education, and perhaps best of all a simple but totally effective safety switch comes as standard — just at knee height where you can knock it off if you're in

trouble with both hands above.

The table is a good height for working when you've got the saw or router underslung, but on overhead crosscut, the position is slightly awkward, because you have to stand to the left and hold the work with your left hand while you push with the right, or stand on the right and lean over while you push the saw with your left.

Enough said? The Triton is definitely the business if you want to transform your saw or router into a precision machine. Jigsaw too, of course, though as I've said that application is limited. Just make sure your blades, cutters and bearings are in good nick because this machine will show them up if they aren't. It's thoroughly designed and made to high engineering standards, not a low market pricing policy — and here's the rub. If you want the stand and the router table as well as the basics, it set you back £257. And whatever else it is, it isn't really a Workmate-style bench.

Prices

Workcentre with saw carriage	£189.75
Folding stand	£35.25
Router and jigsaw kit (standard table,	£32
½in shanks recommended)	
Router and jigsaw table (extra table,	£41
¼in shanks OK)	
Extension table (rip 4ft from blade	£80
Wheels kit	£10

WOLFCRAFT VARIOTEC

This is really a general contractor's type of saw-bench, with basic guides and guards. The clamping system for the tools is highly accommodating — perhaps the easiest to use, and pretty much any tool would go on. Mounting is made easier by the swing-over table. You can use a router and jigsaw — the router kit is extra, but includes an overhead

arm that comes above the cutter for template following. The adjustable mitre/crosscut fence, which slides on a bar along the left-hand side of the table, is also an extra, as is the very good safety switch. A table extension is also available, and if you had two you could easily crosscut long pieces. The basic table isn't foldable.

Literature

You get quite a thick booklet, which looks impressive until you realise it's in nine languages and your bit is two pages — plus

an addendum page, telling you about the saw insert they've obviously added to the design. Photos at the back show you how bits and pieces go together, and outline the operations you can perform; safety gets a mention, but the whole effect is rather less than impressive.

Assembly

The 1mm galvanised pressed steel components bolted together quickly and easily to make a sturdy stand. A few washers would have helped; a nut fell off

continued

while I was using the table. The 2mm steel table-top, pivoting in its own length, is the surface to which the tools themselves are clamped.

Strength

The stand is strong enough, and the table will take a good bit of punishment; the clamping system distorts it, though, which can't be very good news. The T-bar nuts for the tool-holding clamps, in themselves quite a good design, need severe cranking up, which moves the table; trying to get a good firm grip on the jigsaw, I actually split the T-bar tightener off the splines on its threaded insert.

None of the guides and fences are really strong enough in themselves, nor is the bar on the left of the table to which the mitre/crosscut fence is attached.

Accuracy, adjustments

The saw insert plate, apparently a design afterthought, assists in lining up the saw-blade with its calibrations, but you still need to check it against the rip-fence.

The slotted clamping fingers which fix to the underside of the table have different positions for smaller sole-plates like jigsaws, but have to reach a bit far in these situations and leverage is reduced, which is why you have to crank them up so hard.

The rip-fence is held by one clamping bolt in a slot in the back edge of the table, and the fence itself is a bit wobbly. We had problems lining the crosscut/mitre fence up to run accurately at 90° to the rip-fence, and it was also wobbly because it stretches out on quite a long arm. The bar it runs on also contributed to the general feeling of minimum accuracy. The surface of the crosscut/mitre fence was also extremely slippery, which made holding work against it difficult, particularly when cutting angles.

The straight router fence is a disaster. It's plastic, and flexes quite easily, putting one

● **Top**, *Variotec's safety switch – an extra.* **Above**, *ripping width is limited by vertical arm;* **left**, *good clamps, but nylon parted from brass.* **Below**, *router 'guard' leaves a lot to be desired.* **Below left**, *template-following with the overhead guide*

side out of alignment with the other, plus the wing-nut fixings in the back are awkward to tighten up. The fence is also rather too short, but I could have lived with all this if there had been more adjustment. 3mm maximum distance from fence to centre of cutter? I could hardly believe it. But no, everything was in the right place, and there were no other holes I'd missed. Clearly a case for drilling your own.

Safety, guards

The clear plastic guard for the circular saw and jigsaw comes overhead from the right-hand far corner of the table, on a pivoting bar, which limits the maximum rip to the right of the blade to about 15in. OK for pieces no more than about 12in front to back, but if you were into panel materials the obvious solution would be to butcher the saw slot to allow its own guard up through it, or take the guard off altogether. Not very clever — a riving-knife mounted guard has to be the answer.

The clear plastic guard that comes with the router fence isn't really a guard at all. Its edges are square to the table, which means you have to lift it away from the cutter to get the work through, otherwise the work just jams up to it; it's open at the top, so the dust spews straight upwards, or if you raise it to let the work through, out behind the fence.

The template-follower arrangement uses the overhead saw-guard, which works fine as long as your pieces aren't likely to get too near the right-hand far corner and hit the mounting pillar.

The (extra) safety switch is excellent, but I can't say I was impressed with the general safety standard. No rubber feet on metal legs . . .

At least the Wolfcraft Variotec isn't pretentious. Despite PR blurb, it is basically a rough-and-ready contractor's site tool, and highly useful at that price for that sort of work. A few holes drilled here and there and bits and pieces of ply for the fences — make your own, even — and it would be fine within its limits.

Prices

Variotec basic table, rip-fence, guard	£85.15
Crosscut/mitre fence and guide bar	£24.45
Safety switch	£29.55
Table extension	£30.67
'Milling set' for parallel and shaped router work	£24.23

● **Above**, *standard wing-nuts foul the router fence and make it hard to tighten;* **below**, *crosscutting with two table extensions*

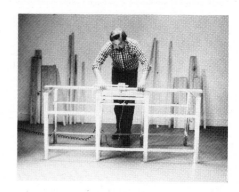

Conclusion

So there it is. Comparisons are odious, so they say, and there's no doubt that the products we tested differ enormously in market position, claims and price. If you want a durable precision machining centre, there's only one — the Triton. The Power-base takes a decent second, but I'd be prepared to pay more for better materials that looked like they were going to last longer. The Skilmate was a difficult one, because the prototype I had was so clearly still a prototype; a serious contender, and many good ideas. The Variotec stands on its own, rather, looking every inch a work-centre for the builder or perhaps shopfitter

as a back-up; which reminds me to say that despite the fact you can get wheels for the Triton, it's not that portable. The Power-mate and B&D Power Tool table are definitely DIY, and within their limitations will do the jobs asked of them. Almost all the workcentres are being worked on and improved, and there are many little things you can do yourself that will make most of them perform better. When it comes down to it, it's a matter of what you can afford and what you want to do with it. ■

● Grant and *Woodworker* would like to thank the manufacturers and suppliers of the workcentres loaned for test, and express appreciation of their co-operation:

Black & Decker, Westpoint, The Grove, Slough SL1 1QQ, (0753) 74277
Dunlop Powerbase, 140 Fielden St, Glasgow G40 3TX, 041-554 3811
Meritcraft (Powermate), Martindale Ind. Est, Hawks Green, Cannock, Staffs WS11 2XN, (054325) 73462
M&M Distributors (Triton), PO Box 128, Bexhill-on-Sea TN40 2QT, (0424) 216897
Skilten Tools (Skilmate), 36 Reynards Rd, Welwyn, Herts AL6 9TP, (043 871) 6949
Wolfcraft (Variotec) Brimarc, PO Box 100, Leamington Spa, Warwicks CV31 3LS, (0926) 882 727

NOW READ THIS: We asked the manufacturers for their replies and to tell us of developments

Black & Decker

The Power Tool Table is made of 'non-traditional' materials, some of the most technologically advanced now available in our industry. Let there be no doubt about the toughness of this tool and its ability to stand up to the rigours of woodworking.

The top is injection-moulded in structural-grade foamed polystyrene, as used in business-machine housings and other load-bearing items. The beauty of this material is it is immune to moisture and will not split, blister or rust like wood or metal. The process also enables extra features such as the dust extraction facility to be built into the table. To shear the T-bolts through the top when clamping tools would require a loading of more than ¼ ton — the weight of an average car engine!

Sawing: B&D are making ongoing improvements, and the riving knife ('spreader') in all models now in production is now positioned in the centre of the blade-slot.

We have also improved our instruction leaflet — which Mr Pearce praises — and it includes instructions on how to make a face-piece for the fence for ripping closer than 19mm to the blade. The instructions which Mr Pearce had, explain that for ripping wider than 118mm, you take the fences off and cut to the line.
Mike Webb, Group Marketing Manager

Dunlop Powerbase

Grant was using a very early production unit, and a number of the points he has raised are already being tackled for future units. A revised instruction book is being printed, and it is intended to produce further 'techniques and projects' leaflets by early 1987.

Key design criteria were the need to provide a portable unit which folds flat for easy storage, at a price to meet the budget of the average DIY enthusiast. Obviously the product could be constructed of different materials, but care has been taken to ensure that those used are suitable for normal DIY use. Engineering plastics have been used, for example — extremely tough and durable. A professional version is contemplated for the future, but this will inevitably cost more. Dunlop Powerbase's key distinguishing feature is the overhead guidance system — we recommend it is clamped to the unit for easy storage. The facility to accurately and repeatedly crosscut 610mm-

wide board (standard unit depth) is, we believe, unique in this price range.

Dunlop Powerbase is aimed principally at the DIY enthusiast, but early indications are that its portability, versatility, simplicity and accuracy appeal to the tradesman, craftsman and householder alike.
William M. Shepherd, Chief Executive

Skilten Skilmate

This professional workbench has been in production in Germany for many years and thousands have been sold. Skilten, via the German manufacturers, have adapted it, via the power insert, into a power centre, and there's no reason to suppose the manufacturer will alter the quality from that which he has always maintained — solid, strong and workmanlike.

● The production Skilmates have a rebated leading edge on the hinged section to support the sole-plate on all edges.

● The rip-fence will be changed to a solid panel adjustable fence 600mm long, locked by metal inserts in the table.

● Production versions already have the crosscut/mitre fence rebated the full length of the table. Accurate degree marks will be available on the adjustable guide by early spring.

● The 45° angle fence needed its adjustable slide guide to be 25mm longer; this has been done.

● The overhead saw-guard's gap has been increased from 10 to 40mm, alleviating any problem with the positioning of the guard bracketing.

● The Universal plate in production will take the Elu MOF96 router — all routers, in fact, up to 2000w. The hole positions have been modified.

● The planer guard in production will be twice the size of the one tested, and will cover all planer cutters.

● The universal brackets as they are now give a more secure fixture than suggested, since more of the clamp bracket is in contact with the sole-plate. Increasing its height would weaken the clamp. Both versions have been tested and the strongest used; these clamping brackets are slide-adjustable. By having a single hole in the plate rather than slots, we also strengthen the plate.

● The Universal plate also incorporates the

router position as well as circular and jigsaw positions. All Skilmates sold will incorporate this fixture, together with the router fence, at the price quoted. A separate router plate will be available.

● We are now able to accommodate virtually all planers on the market.

● The existing Universal plate will take most popular DIY saws, and a new large one 200mm wide will take most professional saws of up to 215mm blade size. This will be available in the spring, when the worktop area is altered to accommodate the larger plate.
S. R. Skarsten, Managing Director

Triton

The nylon sliding bearings are unconditionally guaranteed against wear for five years, and are made of nylon 66, so we don't expect wear to take place for a considerable time. They are easily replaced for under £5 for all four, should such a situation arise.

I'm sorry one of the router fences was bent when Grant received the test kit, but we operate a 'without quibble' policy of instant replacement for faulty parts.

The price may seem high but as Grant Pearce says the Triton is thoroughly designed and made to high engineering standards with quality heavy-gauge steel construction throughout and baked-on epoxy powder paint — all designed to give years of accurate service.

The Triton will fit into the back of most cars and with only two journeys from the car to the site can be erected in two minutes for a cutting operation. The Triton is made predominantly of 16-gauge steel, so it's heavy. The wheels add mobility, even to the extent of allowing the Triton to climb stairs!
Paul Merry, Managing Director, M&M

Wolfcraft Variotec

We believe this will be an objective and most useful article for the consumer. The constructive criticisms have been noted.

We submit that the Wolfcraft Variotec succeeds in offering both DIY and professional user excellent value for money.

Further improvements will be announced in early '87, to the rip-fence, milling attachments and switch.
Geoff Brown, Managing Director, Brimarc

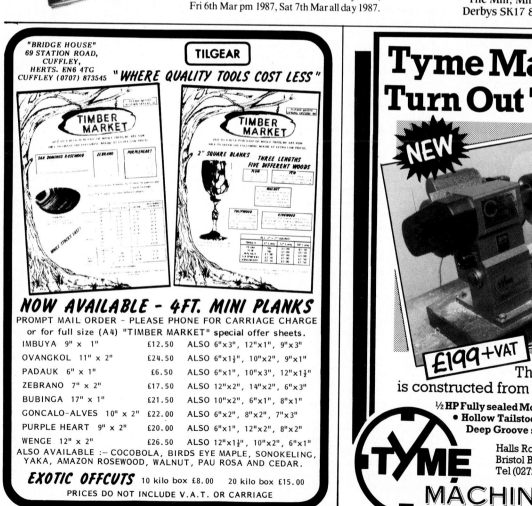

Coker coaler

Scuttle is too dull a word for Don Solman's compact coal box, made in oak to a traditional design. Just the thing for the open grate

Last winter I opened up the fireplace in the lounge and had the first 'real' fire since the central heating was installed 20 years ago. What a pleasant focal point it makes on a cold dark winter's night! I hadn't realised how much I'd missed the warmth and glow over the years.

Having done the hard graft my wife and I discussed how to bring coal in from the bunker and keep it at hand for burning. There are copper, brass, plastic and mild steel scuttles, 'helmet' and various other styles; but we decided the old fashioned wooden coal box we remembered from our childhood days would be most suitable, and it would blend in with the other furnishings.

The search was on. After three weekends covering many miles visiting the newly opened shops catering for this 'new' craze of open fires I had found no coal boxes. Next we turned to junk and antique shops, where we finally located a total of three — but they cost an arm and a leg. Not one of them had a liner (long since corroded away), and they were also in a bad state of repair, requiring many hours of work to bring them up to standard. So I decided to make my own.

I intended using a piece of oak I'd had for some time, so the size of the box was governed by the width of the board; it so happens the finished size was about perfect.

You'll get the basic idea of the box from fig. 1, which shows the front and end elevation with shape and sizes indicated.

I used the router with a 12mm straight bit to cut stopped housings in the sides for the top, front and bottom pieces and I also rebated for the back (fig. 2). Using the same bit I rebated both ends of the front and top to fit the housings (fig. 3).

Changing bit, I coved all the outside edges except the bottom of the sides, and also the front and top edges on the inside only, as well as the back edge of the top.

When I had fitted all these pieces and sanded them I glued and clamped them together. I made the door with a fielded panel; using a 10mm straight router bit I cut the grooves to take the panel, and tenoned the ends of the rails. I shaped and fitted the panel, applying the traditional stopped chamfer to the inside of the frame. Using a pair of 50mm brass butt hinges, I fitted the door and hinged it to the box.

I stained the box with dark oak to match existing furniture, sealed it with Danish Oil, then rubbed with wire wool and wax polished it. I screwed a brass carrying handle on the top, after locating the

● Solid oak and solid brass – grace your open fire with this neat and functional design

position of balance, and a brass handle for the door. When I find a suitable shovel I'll make a bracket for the back to retain it.

Coal box liner

Often coal is wet so you need a liner to protect the wood. Cost can be a deciding factor; I used 22swg (0.7mm) galvanised mild steel sheet. The liner has over-folded seams joining the sides to the body and a wired edge around the opening (fig. 4).

The construction of the body and sides is shown in figs 5 and 6. The over-folded seam allowance is 5mm, which is added twice down the sides of the body and once on the edges of the sides. The wiring allowance is $2\frac{1}{2}$ times the diameter of wire; I used 10swg ($\frac{1}{8}$in) wire, so the allowance was $\frac{5}{16}$in.

The notches shown in figs 5 and 6 are essential to ensure the seams lay flat when made up. Clamp the sheet between a length of angle iron and a piece of wood or two pieces of wood as folding bars, and knock over 5mm at 90° with a boxwood or hide mallet, making sure the side pieces are made left- and right-handed. Then flatten the 5mm edges of the body on a piece of metal a little thicker than the 22swg as in fig. 4a.

Fold up the body with the turned-over edges on the inside, making sure you don't

squash them. Now fit the side pieces into the body (fig. 4a), and pein them down tight. Supporting the inside of the sides either on a metal bar clamped to the bench or with a hand-held metal block, knock over the joint (fig. 4b), dressing it to make it neat and tight. You won't need to solder.

For wiring around the opening, bend your wiring allowance over on a piece of wood or metal block, making a radius bend (fig. 4c). Starting your wire in the centre of the bottom edge, tuck the metal right round the wire. Bend the wire at the corner and tuck the side over, and so on. Finally you can make two folding wire handles, riveting one at each side, inside the liner; I used 10swg wire, with the end of each handle curved to a 12mm radius, and 70mm straight sections. Around one of the straight sections I bent a suitable piece of the sheet metal, pre-drilled for the rivets.

If you don't have facilities for sheet-metal work you could make a liner from WBP plywood (fig. 7). Apply a couple of wood preservative treatments and I'm sure it will give admirable service; the outside dimensions are the same as the metal liner.

And then, of course, having scrabbled round in the coal-hole, all you have to do is sit back in the easy chair and toast your toes — or sit forward and do the muffins! ■

Cutting list

Finished sizes

Sides	2	out of	660mm	x	300mm	x	20mm
Top	1		320		195		20
Front	1		320		80		20
Back (ply)	1		320		260		10
Bottom (ply)	1		320		320		10
Door stiles	2		280		32		20
Door rails	2		250		32		20
Door panel	1		250		235		12

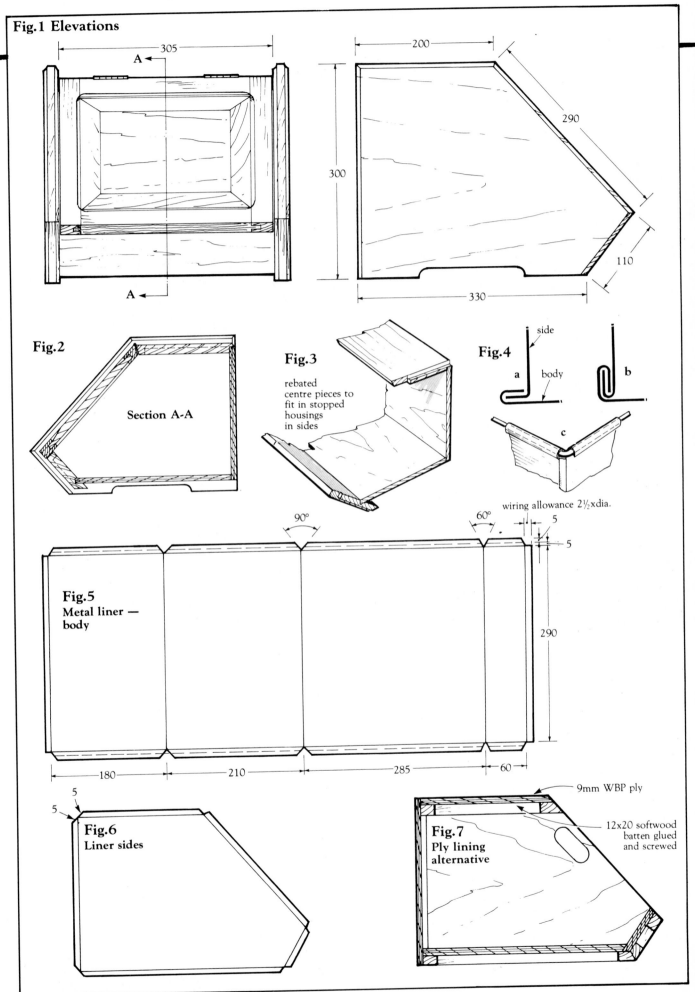

Fig.1 Elevations

305

A

300

200

290

110

330

Fig.2

Section A-A

Fig.3

rebated
centre pieces to
fit in stopped
housings
in sides

Fig.4

side

a

body

b

c

wiring allowance 2½×dia.

90°

60°

5

5

Fig.5
Metal liner —
body

290

180

210

285

60

5

5

Fig.6
Liner sides

9mm WBP ply

Fig.7
Ply lining
alternative

12×20 softwood
batten glued
and screwed

129

SUBSCRIPTION SAVINGS FOR YOU!

Take advantage of these fantastic money saving subscription offers to these magazines. Hurry, this amazing offer is for a limited period only.

	UNITED KINGDOM			OVERSEAS (Accelerated surface post)		
	Normal Price	*Sale Price*	*Please Tick*	*Normal Price*	*Sale Price*	*Please Tick*
A&B Computing	£21.80	**£18.00**	☐	£26.00	**£20.80**	☐
Computer Gamer	£16.00	**£13.00**	☐	£21.50	**£17.20**	☐
Your Commodore	£16.00	**£13.00**	☐	£21.50	**£17.20**	☐
ZX Computing Monthly	£15.00	**£12.00**	☐	£18.00	**£14.40**	☐
Citizens' Band	£16.90	**£13.52**	☐	£22.00	**£17.60**	☐
Ham Radio Today	£17.30	**£14.40**	☐	£21.00	**£16.80**	☐
Electronics Digest	£11.30	**£ 8.30**	☐	£14.00	**£11.20**	☐
Electronics Today International	£18.10	**£14.40**	☐	£22.50	**£18.00**	☐
Video Today	£16.90	**£13.52**	☐	£21.00	**£16.80**	☐
Which Video?	£16.90	**£13.52**	☐	£21.00	**£16.80**	☐
Photography	£16.00	**£12.00**	☐	£21.50	**£16.00**	☐
Photoplay	£17.90	**£14.32**	☐	£21.50	**£17.20**	☐
Clocks	£30.80	**£24.64**	☐	£35.00	**£28.00**	☐
Woodworker	£16.90	**£13.52**	☐	£21.00	**£16.80**	☐
Popular Crafts	£17.90	**£14.32**	☐	£21.50	**£17.20**	☐
Winemaker & Brewer	£13.70	**£10.96**	☐	£17.00	**£13.60**	☐
Aeromodeller	£25.10	**£20.08**	☐	£29.00	**£23.20**	☐
Military Modelling	£16.90	**£13.00**	☐	£21.00	**£16.80**	☐
Model Boats	£16.10	**£13.00**	☐	£20.00	**£16.00**	☐
Radio Control Model Cars	£19.10	**£14.00**	☐	£21.50	**£17.20**	☐
Model Engineer	£27.40	**£22.00**	☐	£32.50	**£26.00**	☐
Radio Control Boat Modeller	£ 8.50	**£ 7.50**	☐	£11.50	**£ 9.20**	☐
R C M & E	£15.80	**£12.00**	☐	£20.00	**£16.00**	☐
Radio Control Scale Aircraft Quarterly	£ 9.70	**£ 8.00**	☐	£11.50	**£ 9.20**	☐
Radio Modeller	£16.10	**£13.00**	☐	£20.00	**£16.00**	☐
Sea Classic International	£10.30	**£ 9.00**	☐	£12.50	**£10.00**	☐
Scale Models International	£18.00	**£13.00**	☐	£20.00	**£16.00**	☐
Your Model Railway	£16.00	**£12.00**	☐	£25.00	**£20.00**	☐

(Offer ends 30th April 1987)

Please commence my subscription(s) with the . . . . issue.

I enclose my cheque/postal order for £. . . . . made payable to Argus Specialist Publications Ltd.

or debit £. . . . . from my Access/Barclaycard No. ☐☐☐☐☐☐☐☐☐☐☐☐☐☐☐☐

valid from . . . . to . . . . Signature . . . .

Name . . . .

Address . . . .

. . . .

Send this form with your remittance to: *Subscriptions Savings Offer (S.O87)*
INFONET LTD., Times House, 179 The Marlowes, Hemel Hempstead, Herts. HP1 1BB.

The grand furniture saga

Dutch and Oriental influences abounded in the late 17th and early 18th centuries. Vic Taylor's furniture time travel takes in imported tea, lacquer, and mirror glass . . .

Before we come to what is called the 'Golden Age of Cabinetmaking' in the 18th century, we must look at the William and Mary and Queen Anne periods (1689-1702 and 1702-1714), when the Continental styles which had accompanied Charles II across the Channel were first absorbed by English craftsmen, and then grafted on to their own native ideas.

Queen Mary's Dutch husband, William of Orange, brought with him his own set of followers, and that, coupled with a steady stream of Huguenot immigrants, led to a strong Dutch influence. The inevitable results were changes in architectural and furniture styles, both of which enriched English culture.

The chief furniture designer of the period was a Huguenot, Daniel Marot (1663-1752), who followed William to England and stayed until 1698. He had been head designer to Louis XIV of France, but was forced to flee to Holland to escape religious persecution. Many of his drawings still exist; they are basically his personal interpretation of Louis XIV style — his chair designs were gracefully curvilinear, the backs with compound curves, the arms and stretchers boldly shaped, and the legs either turned with a distinctive motif like an inverted cup near the top, or a flowing cabriole leg with a hoof foot. His forte was the use of draperies, and one of his most famous designs was the 'Angel' bed with a flounced tester (or canopy) suspended from the ceiling, thus dispensing with foot posts. The valance and the base were elaborately draped and the whole piece could be enclosed by a huge 'case curtain' which formed a protective covering for the more delicate and expensive fabrics beneath.

Marquetry, which had travelled from Italy through France to the Low Countries, was enthusiastically taken up by the Dutch. The national love of flowers led them to become specialists in floral marquetry and produce some of the finest specimens ever; most known was Jan van Merkeren, who worked between 1690 and 1735. They were also expert in 'seaweed' or 'arabesque' marquetry which is made from intertwining, sinuous fronds of foliage, vaguely resembling seaweed.

Another fashion was the use of 'oyster' veneers made from laburnum, yew, walnut, and others. Oysters are thin slices of wood

● *A fine and rare William and Mary walnut bureau, c1695. The sloping fall front opens to reveal pigeon-holes and drawer compartments*

By kind permission of Mallett & Son (Antiques) Ltd

cut transversely across a small log or branch; a right-angled cut gives a roughly circular oyster, and an oblique cut an elliptical one.

The Dutch had a passion for ceramics and so display cabinets for showing collections of jars, bowls, and dishes became popular — Mary had several made to house her collection of Delft pottery and porcelain. Generally, the cabinets were mounted on stands and the glazed doors were fitted with small oblong panes of glass mounted into wooden glazing bars. In later Georgian times such cabinets became more ornate, with swan-necked or broken architectural pediments and fluted columns or pilasters flanking the doors.

It was at this time that both East India Companies (British and Dutch), approached the peak of their activities and a love-affair with all things Oriental, in both countries, developed. It lasted well into the 18th century but began to dwindle about 1760 and its last belated manifestation was the Brighton Pavilion, begun in 1815 for the Prince Regent.

There was a fascination with lacquerwork, then called 'japan' or 'lac'. Lacquered cabinets-on-stands had become status symbols and such was the desire to have everything 'japanned' that 'ready-to-assemble' panels were imported from China, often of poor quality. Good lacquer needs time for its manufacture (up to a year is not too long) and Chinese merchants were so anxious to cash in on the boom that considerably less than perfect goods were shipped to the undiscerning buyers in the West. A favourite trick of those who wanted instant fashion was to break up imported lacquered screens and use the panels to embellish other furniture with scant regard for the continuity of design or the overall appearance. The well-known book by John Stalker and George Parker, *A Treatise of Japanning and Varnishing*, published in 1688, purported to be 'a Compleat Discovery of Those Arts . . . and the Method of Guilding, Burnishing, and Lackering', and its contents were eagerly read and put into practice by thousands of ladies who were persuaded that it was a suitably ladylike pursuit.

The truth is that European countries rarely produced any lacquer work which was comparable with the Chinese or Japanese — despite the importing of Chinese craftsmen who, no doubt with an eye to the main chance, never did reveal the secrets of true lacquering. The best English work suffered from over-repetition of motifs, from the symmetry of designs (Oriental designs were always asymmetrical), the pairing of motifs as mirror-images, and the paucity of colours. The overall finish, moreover, of true Oriental lacquer was more brilliant, the details finer, and the general effect more jewel-like.

Another fashion adopted from the East was tea drinking. The first tea came to England via Holland early in the 17th century, but it's not until 1658 that we find it referred to as 'that excellent drink called by Chinese Teka, by other nations Tay alias Tee'. Pepys mentions his wife drinking it (as a cure for her cold!) in his diary for 1667, and in 1679 the Duchess of Lauderdale is reported to have had 'a tea table carved and gilt'. It was at first regarded as a kind of herbal medicine and its cost was prohibitive. Even when the price came down it was still too dear for the general population, so much so that tea-leaves were infused three times: first for the mistress of the house and her family and guests, second for the servants, and third for the relatives and friends of the servants.

The first tea tables (about 1710) were simply side tables with low galleries of fretcut wood or metal to stop cups and saucers sliding off. By 1730, the familiar tea poy appeared (variously called a 'tripod', a 'claw', or a 'pillar and claw' table).

After the exuberance of Restoration carved and gilded decoration, fashion swung in the opposite direction, and figured wood was allowed to be its own glory, usually in the form of veneers. These were, of course, saw-cut and much thicker than modern knife-cut veneers; they could be up to $\frac{3}{16}$in thick. Walnut remained the favoured timber, both in the solid and as veneer (particularly walnut burrs), and was often laid on a groundwork of oak or pine. Not always with happy results, one might add, as both timbers are notoriously unstable and prone to shrink dramatically (especially in modern centrally-heated surroundings).

The double chest, or chest-on-chest, made its appearance at the end of the 17th century and gradually grew in height to 6ft 6in, adorned with walnut veneers and fluted pilasters at the front. The single chest of drawers was also much in evidence and usually had walnut burr-veneered drawer fronts with the drawer rails cross-veneered. The 'secretaire' also developed into what is now the accepted form of bureau (it was then called a 'buro') with a sloping front enclosing a compartment fitted with pigeon-holes and small drawers.

About 1658 the first longcase (Grand-

● *A William and Mary walnut side table: note 'trumpet' legs*

● *A walnut dressing table with typical faceted legs*

● *A carved walnut chair after Marot, with early 'hoofed' cabriole legs*

father) clocks were offered for sale by Ahasuerus Fromanteel, who was a resident in London's Dutch Colony. The invention caught on and by 1700 there were many other makers such as Edward East, Joseph Knibb, and William Clement, but they only made the clockwork movements and pendulums. The case-makers are unknown, possibly because clocks' status value lay in the movements, not the cases.

The Restoration (1660), with its outlook of luxury and self-indulgence, encouraged the use of cosmetics by both sexes; a practice much frowned upon in Common-wealth times. At first, cosmetics were contained in small chests or caskets but it was obvious they needed to be mounted on a base and brought to a convenient height; so the dressing or toilet-table came into being.

A necessary adjunct to a dressing-table is a mirror. Before 1660 mirrors had to be imported from Venice, which had a jealously guarded monopoly on how to make mirror glass. After that date, the Duke of Buckingham was granted a sole patent to produce mirror glass and he set up a glassworks at Vauxhall, London. The size of the mirror plates was limited to about 36in, and the backing was raw silver, which could be easily marked or scratched — as opposed to the amalgam of tin and mercury used by the Venetians. In 1665 a group of Venetian glassmakers was attracted to Paris by Jean-Baptiste Colbert, a French patron of the Arts, and a factory was set up which later moved to Gobain. The process of casting glass plates was re-discovered by

French glassmaker Thevart, about 1693, and so plates up to 50x84in could be made; the manufacturers held the monopoly for over 100 years.

Elsewhere glass plates were made by blowing a long cylindrical bubble, which became unmanageable if it exceeded the standard 36in. The end of the bubble was cut off with a piece of red-hot wire to form a long open-ended cylinder; the hot wire was then used again to cut a straight line along the length so the cylinder could be opened out and flattened on a stone bed. Obviously, the overall size was determined by the size of the bubble.

Consequently, the large mirrors often placed above overmantels usually consisted of two plates at the bottom with a third at the top — a single mirror in a piece of the period suggests a modern replacement. Larger cast plates did not become readily available until the end of the 18th century; by then the tin and mercury amalgam backing material was also being used.

Mirror glass was in fact known in England before the Duke of Buckingham set up his factory — Shakespeare mentions (1597) that the mirror which Richard II dashed to the ground was 'cracked in a hundred shivers'. Sir Robert Mansell, a retired naval officer, started making them in 1615 but neither his nor any of the several previous attempts lasted. The French king Henry II granted letters patent to a Venetian in 1552 to make mirrors in the Venetian fashion, but again, the venture seems not to have been long-lived. ∎

TABWELL TOOLS, BRIDGE STREET, BAKEWELL, DERBYSHIRE

HAND AND POWER TOOLS

Tel: 062981 3885 or 062981 4681
(VAT included, carriage extra)

HAND TOOLS
MARPLES — RIDGWAY — HENRY TAYLOR STANLEY

RECORD VICES — WOODWORKERS
52ED... £38.09	52½ED £44.81
53E £47.15	52P £25.00
52E £35.00	

RECORD 'T' BAR CRAMPS
42" ....£34.57   48" £34.92
54" ....£35.41   66" £38.63
78" £45.77

HENRY TAYLOR TURNING TOOLS
TT3 Set £15.00   TT5 Set £27.00
TT8 Set £44.00   Super 5 £17.40
Riffler Set £37.00

NOBEX SAWS
202 Pro £74.95   303 Pro £44.50

SANDERSON PAX SAWS
20 x 10" £21.00
24 x 7" £23.36
26 x 6" £24.40

SPEAR & JACKSON 'PRO'
22" x 10" £26   10" x 15" £19
26" x 6" £28   12" x 15" £20

KLEMSIA KLAMPS
110 x 200 .... £3.75
110 x 400 .... £4.50
110 x 600 .... £5.30
110 x 800 .... £6.10
110 x 1000 .... £7.10
200 x 200 .... £6.80

RECORD 'G' CRAMPS (120)
4" .... pair £5.17/£10.00
6" .... pair £7.27/£14.00
8" .... pair £10.77/£20.00

RIDGWAY POWER EXPANSIVE BITS
Heavy Duty ⅞" to 2" £25.00
Heavy Duty 1⅜" to 3⅛" £29.00

NEW PRODUCTS — ALL MADE IN ENGLAND
4" Inside Caliper £3.52
6" Inside Caliper £4.04
8" Inside Caliper £4.96
Coping Saw £2.86
4" Outside Caliper £3.52
6" Outside Caliper £4.04
8" Outside Caliper £4.96
4" Divider £3.52
6" .... Divider £4.04
8" Divider £4.96

STANLEY YANKEE SCREWDRIVERS
135B 13" £12.86
130B 20" £14.17
131B 27" £18.86

MARPLES ROSEWOOD CABINET SCREWDRIVERS
M1968 3" £4.19
M1968 4" £4.42
M1968 5" £5.25
M1968 6" £6.66
M1968 8" £7.75
M1968 10" £12.25

RECORD SASH CRAMPS — 135 SERIES
18" .... £17.00   24" £17.49
30" .... £18.19   36" £19.17
42" .... £19.80   48" £20.22

ESTWING DELUXE HAMMERS
20oz. Leather Claw £18.12
20oz. Vinyl Claw £18.12
24oz. Vinyl Claw £20.00
Flat Head Claw £19.40

TENON SAWS (SANDERSON)
12" x 12 TPI £19.40
24 x 7" £23.36
12" x 12 TPI £19.40
10" x 14 TPI £20.00
14" x 12 TPI £20.40
8" x 20 TPI £21.00
6" Backsaw £5.25
8" Backsaw £5.99

RECORD PLANES — BENCH
03 ......£19.10   06 .... £32.75
04 ......£16.99   07 .....£37.75
04½ ...£18.61   010 .....£0.00
05 ......£21.00   020C ...£69.00

BLOCK
060½ . £16.18   09½ ... £17.24
Stanley 93 .... £28.00
Stanley 92 .... £23.00

MISCELLANEOUS HAND TOOLS
Record 153 Floorboard Cramp £74.95
Record 145 Holdfast £12.99
Record 146 Holdfast £14.99
Weller Woodburning Iron £8.99

STANLEY BRACES
No. 73 10" sweep £23.00
No. 73 8" sweep £23.00
No. 73E Mk4 .... £22.00
Footprint Brace £15.00

ROUTER CUTTERS — RIDGWAY & TREND — ALL LESS 30%

TREND PROFILE SCRIBER SETS — LESS 30%

NICHOLSONS RASPS
Half Round Wood - 12" £6.46
Half Round Wood - 10" £4.38
Half Round Wood - 8" £3.73

ECLIPSE SAWS
Piercing Saw £5.95
Coping Saw £3.95
Fretsaw £4.50

HAND DRILLS
Stanley 805 .... £14.00
Record 423 .... £12.50
Footprint £11.25

MARPLES MARKING GAUGES
M2049 ...£3.14   M2083 ...£7.11
M2050 ...£4.27   M2153 £10.26
M2154 .... £16.19
Silex Die-cast Butt Gauge £15.99

POWER TOOLS
FULL RANGE OF ELU, DeWALT, ELEKTRA, KITY, LUNA, MINIMAX

LATHES
Coronet No. 1 .... £239.00
Coronet Elf £379.00
Coronet Major £599.00
Elu DB180 .... £297.00
Elektra HDM 1000 .... £275.00
Minimax T100 .... £465.00
Coronet Chuck Set £65.00
Woodfast Superchuck £75.00

GRINDERS — DRY BENCH
Burgess 5" £29.95
Skil 5" £39.50
Skil 6" £64.00
Wolf 5" £64.00
Wolf 6" £105.00
Wolf 8" £152.00
Elu EDS 163 .... £62.95
Elu EDS 164 .... £66.95
Elu MWA 149 .... £81.95

CIRCULAR SAWS
Skil 1805 6" £67.00
Skil 1865 7¼" £69.95
Skil 1886 9¼" £138.00
Skil 1873 8¼" £127.00
Skil 1899 10¼" £149.00
Wolf 7¼" £103.00
Wolf 9¼" £135.00
Elu MH65 .... £114.95
Elu MH85 .... £160.95

CORDLESS DRILLS/ SCREWDRIVERS
Wolf 5 Stage Clutch Driver/Drill £77.00
Skil 'Twist' £19.99
Skil 2001H 10mm Drill £41.00
Bosch 1921.8 External Torque £124.77
Bosch 1920.8 Drill £108.50
Bosch 19201 ⅜" Drill £95.60
Skil 200H Screwdriver £34.50
Bosch Cordless Jigsaw £159.00

BELT SANDERS
Elu MHB 157 .... £95.00
Elu MHB 90 .... £161.00
Skil 1200H £49.00
Skil 1400H £122.00
Wolf 4" £165.00
Elu MHB 90K £181.00

FINISHING SANDERS
Elu MUS 500/501 .... £53.95
Elu MUS 94 .... £101.95
Elu MUS 47 .... £110.95
MUS 156 .... £65.95
MUS 156E £77.95
Skil 663 .... £38.00
Wolf 5205 .... £86.00
Skil 662 .... £29.00

SDS PLUS DRILLS
Kango 285 .... £85.00
Kango 422 .... £150.00
Kango 426 .... £170.00
Bosch 11210.6 .... £118.00

ROTARY DRILLS
Bosch 1126 2-speed £83.00
Bosch 1159.7 Variable £96.00
Bosch 1102.1 2-speed £169.00

MORTICERS
Smiths Bench Model £399.00
Smiths Floor Model £499.00
Charnwood Bench £465.00
Charnwood Floor £580.00
Ridgway Stand £140.00
Ridgway Mortice Stand £169.00
Wolf Mortice Stand £131.00

RIDGWAY CHISEL & BITS
ALL LESS 30%

WHETSTONES
Scanslib 150 .... £79.00
Scanslib 200 .... £95.00
Scanslib 400 .... £295.00
Lion Horizontal £139.00
Kiruna 350mm £190.00
Kiruna 275mm £135.00

DREMEL MINI POWER TOOLS — ALL AT SPECIAL PRICES
238 Moto Flex £66.00
338 Variable Speed Moto Flex £72.00
229 Router Attachment £9.95
358 Moto Tool £47.00
358 Kit £57.00
258 Moto Tool £31.00
318 Moto Tool £43.70
576 Moto Shop Scrollsaw £69.00
Drill Press £22.00
558 Table Saw £93.00

BANDSAWS
DeWalt 3401 .... £273.00
DeWalt 3501 .... £281.00
DeWalt 100 .... £149.00
Burgess BK3 Plus £115.00
Burgess BK3 .... £99.00
Luna BS320 .... £339.00
Minimax P32 .... £380.00
Elektra BAS315 .... POA
Elektra BAS450 .... POA

PLANERS
Elu MFF 80 .... £98.95
Elu MFF 80K £114.95
Elu MFF 40 .... £156.95
Skil 94 .... £39.00
Skil 97 .... £42.00
Skil 98 .... £92.00
Wolf 8614 .... £94.00
Wolf 8657 .... £140.00
Elu Inversion Stand £17.50

ROUTERS
Elu MOF 96 .... £86.50
Elu MOF 96E £106.95
Elu MOF 31 .... £136.00
Elu MOF 177 .... £173.00
Elu MOF 177E £198.00
Elu MOF 112 .... £165.00
Accessory Kit £63.00
Dovetailer £66.00

IMPACT DRILLS
Skil 60438H £49.95
Bosch 1182 .... £90.00
Bosch 1182.7 .... £99.75
Bosch 1198.7 .... £110.25

TABWELL TOOLS, BRIDGE STREET, BAKEWELL, DERBYSHIRE

Tel: 062981 3885 or 062981 4681
VISA OR ACCESS MAIL ORDER

134

Question box

Garden afrormosia

Q *Some time ago I was given some afrormosia, and I am now making two large
garden seats with it.*

*How should I finish the completed seats? I
want to bring out the lovely grain and preserve
the timber, but I don't want the finish to peel off
after a few years.*

*Also, I had to supplement my gift with some
bought wood which is light straw, while what I
had is dark brown. A teak stain helps on the
lighter wood, but I don't really want to do this as
I want a natural finish. Will exposure bring the
two colours closer together? Finally (a bit late
this) is afrormosia really suitable for the project?*

P. H. Kent, Newark

A Afrormosia is highly suitable for
making garden seats. It's a strong hard
wood with excellent durability. It takes glue
very well and is good with screws, though
it's advisable to pre-bore for the larger sizes.

Cascamite is a strong glue and I would
recommend it for outside situations such as
this.

Although there are numerous exterior
grade varnishes available, most of them are
inclined to peel when damp enters the joints
and creeps behind the varnish film. I would
advise you to get Sadolin stain/preservative
from a builder's merchant and brush it well
in to your seats. Carry out the manufacturer's instructions about intervals between
applications and you should have a most
attractive durable finish which will enhance
the beauty of your wood. You can also, of
course, try the microporous varnish stains,
some of which have an attractive flat finish;
if they live up to the manufacturers' claims,
they should be excellent, and won't peel
like polyurethane.

Charles Cliffe

● Charles Cliffe is a professional polisher,
author and teacher.

Swimming-pool ceiling

Q Can you tell me what type of cladding to
use for the ceiling of an indoor swimming-
pool? The ceiling joists are treated wood
(300x50mm) with 200mm insulation, and
there is a ventilated flat roof. I was planning to
use foil-backed plasterboard sealed against
moisture penetration before installing the cladding. The walls and floors will be covered with
ceramic tiles.

S. L. Manson, Caithness.

A Provided that the heating and ventilating system for your swimming pool
has been properly designed, you can use any
material which will tolerate high humidities
to clad the ceiling. This does, however,
exclude plasterboards, some mineral fibre
and all cellulose fibre acoustic tiles or
boards. Timber is quite satisfactory as long
as it does not contain fire retardant salts.
Plastic can be used, but metal must be
treated as for external use.

However, the ceiling construction you
describe will be quite unsatisfactory and I
strongly advise you to seek professional
assistance in designing not only the roof
construction but also the heating and
ventilating system, without which the roof
cannot properly function.

James Smith

● James Smith is a swimming pool and
dampness expert for the Building Research
Advisory Service.

Wheel table

Q I want to make a 24in-diameter circular
table top with a rim and spokes, like
a wheel. The wide 'spokes' are tenoned
into the 2in-thick rim. How many segments
should I use to make the rim? Is a bridle joint the
right one to join the segments, and how should I
mark it out? What is the minimum diameter of
hub I can use? Should I use a mortise jig for the
rim/spoke joints, or will it be enough to do them
'by eye', as I usually do with mortise faces? I am
using oak – is it suitable? If not, what is a good
alternative?

C. A. K. Brightman, Kingston

A Your first requirement is a sheet of
ply or hardboard on which to set out
the job full size. The outer diameter is to be
24in; draw this circle with a bit of lath
(about ¾x¼in) with a pin through it 12in
from one end. Drive the pin into the ply,
and draw the circle. Now cut away 2in from
the compass lath (trammel) and draw the
inner circle, then again for the hub.

For an 'open' curve, I would say eight
segments minimum for the rim; but in this
case, short grain is completely protected
when the job is complete, so six will be
quite all right.

To set out the six, step out the radius
round the circle; lines from these points to
the centre of the circle will give the joint
lines between the segments. You say 'bridle
joints', but this is a misnomer here; what
you mean is an 'open tenon', commonly
confused with a bridle. A good method here
would be as shown in the diagram, while
intermediate spokes, if you want them, can
be plain mortise-and-tenon. These joints
are shown 'stopped', but they can of course
go through.

The hub would of course be far more
accurate off the lathe than by hand, but for

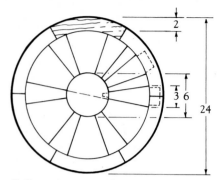

all dimensions in inches

the spokes and segments ('felloes' pronounced 'fellies'!), ply templates should be
cut, ignoring the tenons. All we want is to
be able to knife-cut (against the template)
the shoulder lines, for vertical chiselling.
Intermediate mortises, if any, can be
'picked up' off the setting-out with a set-
square, and then gauged and so on in the
normal manner.

Having cut out the pieces, take two
segments and butt them together on the
full-size setting-out, to keep overall curvature correct, and to get good butt joints.
The mortises can now be cut, (sawn across
the corner, and finished with the chisel)
then a spoke tenoned and fitted into this
assembly. These three pieces should now be
glued and left to set, after which you can go
to the next segment, and so on. Don't forget
the hub; this would have to be positioned
on fitting spoke no.2. The inner shoulders
of the spokes can, if you prefer it, be cut
straight, and relevant flats made upon the
hub; but the curve is the nicer of the two
methods.

There is no problem in cramping up the
spokes, but for the segments, glue a paper
block, a cramping block to take the pull,
near the butt end of each on the surface.
When they are set hard, cramp off these. As
the paper is between the blocks and the job,
they are easily knocked off on completion;
even without paper, they could be chiselled
and planed. Yes, 2in oak would be very
suitable — but expensive nowadays!

Stan Thomas

● Stan Thomas is a first-class joiner of the
old school, with 50 years' experience.

Fixing window boards

Q I am having the window frames of my
house replaced with double glazed units
in Brazilian mahogany frames, and
have it in mind to renew the inside window
boards, at present 96x9x1¼in painted softwood.

I need advice on a suitable wood for the new
boards, ideas on fixing without drilling through
the top face, and on types of finish.

Brazilian mahogany seems to be readily
available at the moment, but I'm really looking
for something lighter, possibly oak or sycamore,
that would contrast with the mahogany frames
and look attractive.

G. A. Butler, Henfield

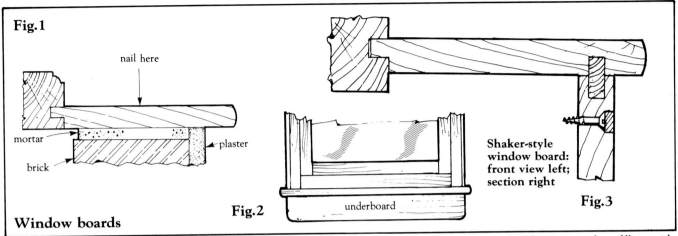

Fig. 1

nail here

mortar

brick

plaster

Fig. 2

underboard

Shaker-style
window board:
front view left;
section right

Fig. 3

Window boards

A One has to be very careful about mixing hardwoods, and the more so in joinery. Oak and mahogany in any case is a bad mix. I would certainly make the window board from Brazilian mahogany, relying for contrast on the adjacent wall finish and carefully chosen curtains. The mahogany must be kiln-dried, and should be stored in the room for a while to condition it — particularly important where there is central heating. The most suitable finish for the entire window would be a minimum of three coats of a clear one-pot polyurethane varnish in satin (or

eggshell) finish. Rub down between coats with wet-and-dry paper, 320-grit or finer, dipped in white spirit.

The normal method of fixing (fig. 1) is to tongue the window board into a groove in the cill. This is not glued, the idea being that the board is allowed to move with humidity. In practice this movement is generally prevented, many layers of paint effectively gluing the two parts together. The board is nailed either to a wood wedge or pad, or else to dovetailed blocks set into the mortar.

You can conceal the fixing by counter-

boring for the screws, then filling with carefully matched mahogany plugs made with a plug cutter.

Fig. 2 shows an alternative style used by the American sect, the Shakers. An underboard is glued to the window board, either tongued or dowelled. This is screwed and plugged to the brickwork, the screws concealed with plugs (fig. 3). The screws beneath the overhanging window board will not be as conspicuous as on top.

Bob Wearing

● Bob Wearing is a regular *Woodworker* contributor of encyclopaedic experience.

Guild notes

Guild of WOODWORKERS

The Guild was set up by *Woodworker* to create a meeting ground for all those involved in working wood, whether professional, amateur, or enthusiastic beginner. Guild members get:

- Access to Guild courses and events
- Free publicity in *Woodworker*
- Specially arranged tool insurance at low rates
- 15% off Woodworker Show entry
- A free display area and meeting point at the Show
- 15% discount off *Woodworker* plans
- Inclusion in our register of members' skills and services

For details, please send an sae to the Guild of Woodworkers, 1 Golden Sq, London W1R 3AB.

BOOKING FORM

I wish to book for the following course(s).

☐ **Power routing** 14 February, £25+ VAT = £28.75

☐ **French polishing** 12-13 March, £40; make cheques payable to Charles Cliffe

☐ **Wood machining** 28 March, £25+ VAT = £28.75

☐ **Spindle moulding** 28 March, £25+ VAT = £28.75

☐ **Hammer veneering** 4 April, £37 inc. materials; make cheque payable to Ian Hosker

☐ **Parquetry** 5 April, £39 inc. materials; make cheque payable to Ian Hosker

Please make cheques payable to 'The Guild of Woodworkers/ASP Ltd' unless otherwise stated.

Name ....

Address ....

....

....

Guild no. ....

Send to: The Guild of Woodworkers, 1 Golden Square, London, W1R 3AB. The Guild reserves the right to cancel any course.

GUILD COURSES

● Only Guild members are eligible to go on these courses. You must book in advance, and we must have a cheque for the full cost of the course at the time of booking. If you cancel less than four weeks before the advertised date you will forfeit 50% of the cost, unless there are exceptional circumstances.

Spindle moulding — Roy Sutton

28 March, 10-5, Herne Bay, Kent £25+VAT

What Roy doesn't know about spindle moulding simply isn't worth knowing. He'll take you through the spectrum of procedures and techniques: straight and stock moulding, grooving, rebating, moulding small components with jigs, raised-panel work, laminates, machining semi-finished work, simple circular work, and sectioning handrails. Lunch is provided.

Wood-machining — Ken Taylor

28 March, 10-5, Bletchley, Bucks, £25+VAT

Ken's across-the-board course on wood-machining has something for everyone who's interested in learning more about workshop hardware. First-hand experience in table- and bandsaws, radial-arm saws, planers and thicknessers, spindle moulders, mortisers and universals.

Power routing — Roy Sutton

14 February, 10-5, Herne Bay, Kent, £25+VAT.

Roy is an expert on this subject. Starting from first principles, he covers housing, grooving, rebating, straight and circular moulding, tenoning, mortising, and rule-joint and template work; he also deals with designing and setting up your own jigs.

French polishing — Charles Cliffe

12-13 March, 10-4, Bexleyheath, £40.

This is a popular course by one of our 'Question box' experts and author of *The Woodworker Manual of Finishing and Polishing*. Charles explains preparation, staining and the techniques of French polishing itself; he'll also show you how to sharpen a cabinet scraper, so bring yours along. Charles will offer advice on any small piece of furniture you want to refinish, and can also order supplies for you to take away if you tell him in advance.

Veneering weekend — Ian Hosker

April 4-5, 9.30-5, Chester

You have a choice; spend the whole weekend with Ian, or opt for one of the two individual day courses on offer.

Hammer veneering: 4 April

You'll learn about preparation of veneers and ground, laying the balancing veneer, laying veneer with a join, and laying stringing crossbanding. The course costs £25, materials an extra £12 per person.

Parquetry: 5 April

The skills of producing geometric patterns in wood veneer are covered in this one-day course, including preparation, laying balancing veneer, and making a parquetry jig. You'll find out how to lay a chess board with stringing and crossbanding. This course costs £25, plus £14 for materials. Book for one of these day courses, or spend the whole weekend veneering.

Lively thriver

The West Midlands branch continues with its lively programme of local meets. In December they had well known amateur woodworker Ralph Fellows along discussing and illustrating his work, and on January 21 Mark Golder will be visiting for the third time, covering box and goblet turning on this occasion.

The Birmingham meetings take place in the Quinborne Community Centre, Ridgacre Rd, Birmingham B32 2TW, starting at 7pm; a charge of £2 is made towards room hire and postage/printing costs.

Swap shop

Mr I. R. Du'Kett has been collecting back-numbers of *Woodworker* dating back to the early 1950s. He has got some spares he wants to swap, in exchange for the issues he has missing. If you are interested in doing a deal, write to him c/o Guild of Woodworkers and we'll put you in touch.

Craft attraction

The first National Festival of Crafts took place over four days in November at the National Exhibition Centre, Birmingham, and was a great success, writes **Stuart King**.

Every exhibitor I spoke to praised the organisers, ICHF (International Craft & Hobby Fair Ltd) for their promotional efforts which had visitors flocking in and many making return trips.

Considering the aircraft hanger appearance of the NEC, the atmosphere was amazingly 'crafty', which was largely down to the many demonstrations.

Dave Sherwood, the Sussex trug-maker, is a master at pulling in a crowd to his basket-covered stall; he makes the trugs in the traditional way, from sweet chestnut and willow, and he finds a ready market among gardeners (for collecting vegetables) and shopkeepers (for display).

Windsor chair maker John Parkin entertained visitors by adzing chairseats and bending Windsor bows, while Theo Fossel was telling folk what they should do with their blackthorn and hazel and when to do it. Cooper Bob Kohler was making barrels of every shape and remodelling old barrels from distilleries.

Turning was well represented. Ian McGregor was making bowls of immense variety, while Jeremy Blake-Roberts displayed an eye-catching burr elm bowl. For sheer excellence and art it takes a lot to beat Peter and Michael Bossom, who produce exquisite turned 'fruit'; Michael's toadstools turned from gorse are a joy.

Richard Ainsworth's carved birds were perfection, and his creations reflect his infectious enthusiasm for carving. John Holman's lovely inlaid marquetry boxes were snapped up — his stand was empty by the final day.

So you can see woodworkers were well to the fore at Birmingham. I was there, too — demonstrating a newly restored Victorian wheel lathe!

Easter School — Manchester

Here's your chance for a solid six days on a course. In association with the School of Furniture, Central Manchester College, we have arranged three different courses, all running 12-17 April, 9.30-5, and costing £140.

Introduction to Cabinetmaking — Robert Cooksey and Keith Parry

A course for enthusiastic beginners and those with some experience who want to improve. It includes an introduction to basic machine preparation and hand-tool techniques in fine furniture making, and you'll be making a small item during the course.

Traditional upholstery — John Shepherd

Introducing the use of traditional methods and materials (tacks and webbing, not foam and staples!) and developing your hand skills. You can practise on a basic frame (supplied), or take a small item of your own, stripped, repaired and ready to work on.

Modern wood finishing — Eric Lyons

All your questions answered about using stains and modern finishes, including mixing stains and colour matching.

● Richard Hill, Senior Lecturer at the College is administering the courses, and **all enquiries should go to him** at the School of Furniture, Central Manchester College, Lower Hardman St, Manchester M3 3ER, (061) 831 7791, extn. 346. **Not to the Guild!**

Yet more reps

Since our comprehensive list of local reps was published last month, we've had three more volunteers, in Hertfordshire, North Avon and the far north of Scotland. If you live locally, please contact them.

● I. Macdonald, 7 Pendock Rd, Winterbourne, North Avon BS17 1EF
● I. E. Waigh, 61 Roundwood Lane, Harpenden Lane, Harpenden, Herts.
● John Lochore, Tulachard, Fountain Rd, Golspie, Sutherland KW10 6TH

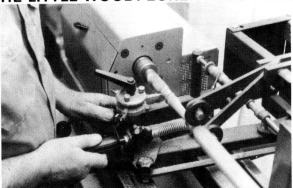

Angle wrangle

Quick'n'easy hexagons and octagons — plus a micro-course in trigonometry for those who think logarithms are musical forests

Angles of 90°, 45°, 30° and 60° are readily available as try-squares — even large ones if you go to art suppliers — and even bigger ones can be made quite easily. So squares, rectangles and triangles present no particular problems.

The hexagon is also quite easy for practical workshop purposes; simply step a radius six times round the circle (fig. 1). Accurate enough for most work, although of course the larger the area the more careful you must be. Octagons too are not enormously difficult; we differ from the mathematician, who would have us draw the inscribing circle and construct tangents where diagonals of the outside square cross the circle (fig. 2). All very well on exam paper, but not on the endgrain of a bit of 2x2.

A better method for the bench is to set a compass to half the diagonal of the timber, and draw arcs from each corner. Join up the points where the arcs meet the faces of the work (fig. 3). On square stock, you don't even have to draw the arcs; simply set a gauge to half the diagonal and gauge along the sides from all edges, so you get double sets of lines on each face. Join them on the endgrain where they meet the end and you have your shape.

Fig.1

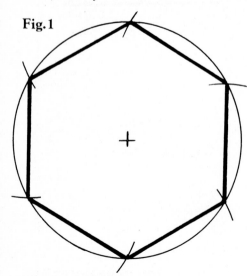

● *Rough-and-ready way to hexagons for woodworkers; step a radius six times round a circle*

Fig.2

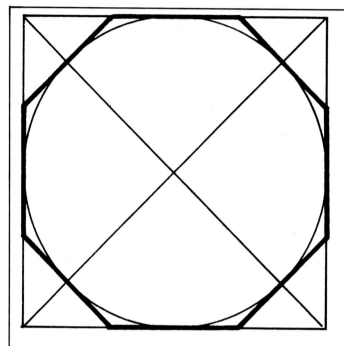

● *The geometrician's octagon; circle in a square, tangents where the diagonals cross the circumference*

Fig.3

● *For oblong-section stock, scribe arcs the radius of half the diagonal from each corner and join up the meeting points; for square stock, just set a gauge to half the diagonal, scribe two lines on each face and join up the points*

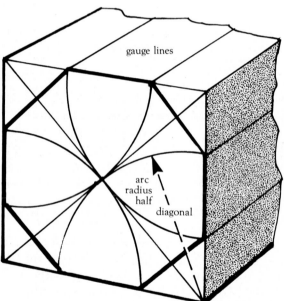

gauge lines

arc radius half diagonal

Angles by trigonometry

This is not so frightening as may at first appear to those with but the haziest school-day memories of the subject. The simplified table gives enough accuracy for woodworking purposes. Of course the bigger the project, the greater the accuracy will be — the small protractor is quite innaccurate for large scale work. Very great accuracy can be obtained using the tan tables (or a suitable calculator). The principle is this:

The tan of an angle is $\dfrac{\text{opposite side}}{\text{adjacent side}}$

Suppose the angle is 9°: the tan of 9° is .1584, therefore

$$\frac{\text{opposite}}{\text{adjacent}} = .1584 \text{ or } \frac{.1584}{1}$$

So opposite = .1584 and adjacent = 1. For workshop purposes two decimal places are enough, so the tan is taken as .16. The method of use on the bench, then is:

1 Look up the tan of the angle, e.g. 9° = .1584
2 Correct this to two decimal places ie.16
3 Multiply this by 100 (or 500) = 16 (or 80)
4 Draw a line 100 units (or 500) long
5 At right angles at one end, draw a line 16 (or 80) units high
6 Join the ends to get the angle required.
Fig. 4 shows the idea. In practice, multiply by the largest number which will fit on the workpiece. ∎

Natural tangents

	0′	30′		0′	30′		0′	30′
0°	0.0000	0087	31	0.6009	6128	62	1.8807	9210
1	0.0175	0262				63	1.9626	0057
2	0.0349	0437	32	0.6249	6371			
3	0.0524	0612	33	0.6494	6619	64	2.0503	0965
			34	0.6745	6873	65	2.1445	1943
4	0.0699	0787	35	0.7002	7133	66	2.2460	2998
5	0.0875	0963				67	2.3559	4142
6	0.1051	1139	36	0.7265	7400	68	2.4751	5386
7	0.1228	1317	37	0.7536	7673	69	2.6051	6746
			38	0-7813	7954	70	2.7475	8239
8	0.1405	1495	39	0.8098	8243	71	2.9042	9887
9	0.1584	1673						
10	0.1763	1853	40	0.8391	8541	72	3.0777	1716
11	0.1944	2035	41	0.8693	8847	73	3.2709	3759
			42	0.9004	9163	74	3.4874	6059
12	0.2126	2217	43	0.9325	9490	75	3.7321	8667
13	0.2309	2401						
14	0.2493	2586	44	0.9657	9827	76	4.0108	1653
15	0.2679	2773	45	1.000	0176	77	4.3315	5107
			46	1.0355	0538	78	4.7046	9152
16	0.2867	2962	47	1.0724	0913	79	5.1446	3955
17	0.3057	3153	48°	1.1106	1303			
18	0.3249	3346	49	1.1504	1708	80	5.671	5.976
19	0.3443	3541	50	1.1918	2131	81	6.314	6.691
			51	1.2349	2572	82	7.115	7.596
20	0.3640	3739				83	8.144	8.777
21	0.3839	3939	52	1.2799	3032			
22	0.4040	4142	53	1.3270	3514	84	9.51	10.39
23	0.4245	4348	54	1.3764	4019	85	11.43	12.71
			55	1.4281	4550	86	14.30	16.35
24	0.4452	4557				87	19.08	22.90
25	0.4663	4770	56	1.4826	5108			
26	0.4877	4986	57	1.5399	5697	88	28.64	38.19
27	0.5095	5206	58	1.6003	6319	89	57.29	114.6
28	0.5317	5430	59	1.6643	6977			
29	0.5543	5658						
30	0.5774	5890	60	1.7321	7675			
			61	1.8040	8418			

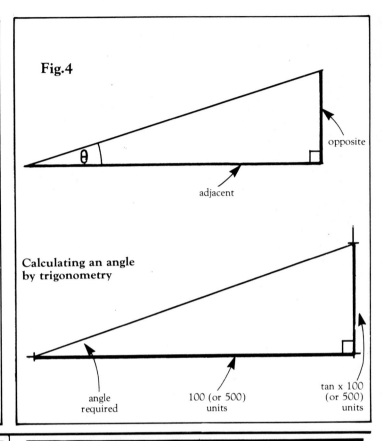

Fig.4

opposite

adjacent

Calculating an angle by trigonometry

angle required

100 (or 500) units

tan x 100 (or 500) units

   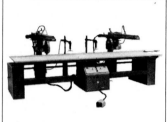

Only one Company offers such a range of Radial Arm Saws

More Experience
- Radial Arm Saw invented by Raymond E. DeWalt in 1922.
- No other manufacturer can match the experience that has earned DeWalt an envied reputation for quality, reliability, accuracy, versatility, safety and ease-of-use.

More Choice
- 20 different models mean both amateur and professional woodworkers can choose precisely the machine for their needs.
- The DeWalt Powershop series offers 4 different arm lengths

with 68mm max. cutting depth – from the convenient DW1201 Foldaway Powershop to the long reach DW1751 with 610mm crosscut and 880mm ripping capacity.

More Capacity
- For thicker materials, DeWalt machines with larger motors offer cutting depths of 93-125mm, crosscuts up to 1155mm and ripcuts up to 1505mm wide.
- Additionally a series of 8 double arm radials are available with automatic blade feed for large scale intensive operations.

More Sales
- More experience and more choice naturally means DeWalt has more dealers, and sells far more Radial Arm Saws than any other manufacturer.

More Details
- Your local woodworking machinery dealer will be pleased to assist you in selecting the right DeWalt machine for your needs.
- Any other details and literature are available from the address below.

DeWALT®
POWERSHOP/RADIAL ARM SAWS

UK: DeWalt Woodworking Machines, Westpoint, The Grove, Slough, Berks SL1 1QQ. (0753) 74277
Australia: DeWalt Woodworking Machines, Maroondah Highway, Croydon, Victoria, Australia 3136.
New Zealand: DeWalt Woodworking Machines, 483 Great South Road, Penrose, Auckland 6, New Zealand.

---

2 VALUE FOR MONEY OFFERS FROM ASLES

NEW
10" HOBBY SAW BENCH

FEATURES INCLUDE:
- ★ 10" blade, depth of cut 90° 75mm 45° 63mm
- ★ Big 17" x 27" cast alloy quality table
- ★ Complete with mitre guide and double locking rip fence
- ★ Independent rise/fall and tilt handles
- ★ Fully guarded with anti-kickback
- ★ Powerful 1½hp motor with overload cut-out.

INTRODUCTORY PRICE INC. VAT & DELIVERY £144

★ *PERSONAL CALLERS AT OUR SHOWROOMS WELCOME* ★

5 SPEED ROUND BED LATHE

£144 incl. VAT.

LOOK AT THESE FEATURES!
- ★ 37" Centre to Centre
- ★ 12" Turning Capacity
- ★ Bowl Turning Facility
- ★ Complete with long and short tool rest, face plate, four prong centre and live centre

★ 5 Speeds ★ ¾h.p. induction motor ★ Lockable safety switch ★ Major construction cast iron ★ Quick release locking handles on tool rest and tail stock ★ Indexing spindle lock ★ Complete range of accessories.

FREE 8-piece turning set if you order both machines together

☏ TO ORDER phone & quote Visa or Access card number or post order with cheque.

We reserve the right to charge prices and specifications.

VINEYARD RD., WELLINGTON, TELFORD, SHROPS.
0952 — 48054
Open Mon.-Fri. 8.30-5.30
Sat. 8.30-3.30

Lurem C268
the last word in Combination Woodworkers With 3 Powerful Motors

STAND 263
Practical Woodworking Exhibition

TECHNICAL DATE:
- 12" SAW BLADE
- 10"-7" PLANER-THICKNESSER
- SPINDLE MOULDER
- SLOT MORTISER
- LARGE TENONING TABLE
- TRIPLE DRIVE
- 3 MOTORS • TENONING

LIST PRICE

£2,995.00

(plus VAT)

Please send for leaflet and full quotation of machine and range of accessories. Plus other combinations in stock.

CECIL W. TYZACK LTD.
TOOLS AND MACHINERY

SHOP & HEAD OFFICE
DEPT. W, 79/81 KINGSLAND ROAD, SHOREDITCH, LONDON E2 8AG.
Tel: 01-739 2630/7126

DEMONSTRATION CENTRE
DUNLOE ST (Behind Geffrye Museum)
SHOREDITCH, LONDON E2
Tel: 01-739 2630

142

Winter warmer

It costs a great deal to keep a workshop warm — yet we all have quantities of waste wood, writes **James Reid.** Thinking about this reminded me of the method of disposing sawdust and shavings during my woodworking apprenticeship 30 years ago. A large cylindrical sheet metal heater 4ft high and 2½ft in diameter was filled each morning with waste, apart from a central core through which the slow-burning shavings, packed down, were fed with air. This type of heater burned for up to eight hours and at no cost — a great advantage even in those apparently fuel-inefficient days.

The wood-waste burning stove I've designed consists of an aluminium beer keg 2ft high and 18in diameter (a chat with your friendly publican may produce a similar keg), a length of cast-iron rainwater pipe to act as a chimney and various other bits and pieces usually found in workshops.

The most difficult job is cutting various holes in the keg, as follows (fig. 1):

A 3in diameter in the top for the chimney
B 5-6in diameter in the base; the size of this hole regulates the rate of burning
C A small rectangular hole for stoking, about 3x6in. This opening should be about one-third from the top of the keg to allow any gathering smoke to escape.

These openings are easily cut in the aluminium using an electric drill, hacksaw and cold chisel, finishing off with a file. I cut the chimney exit to ensure a tight fit with the chimney protruding into the top of the keg by about 1in.

I made a door from sheet material to overlap the stoking hole by ½in all round. I cut another piece of metal accurately to fit into the hole and riveted it (you could use self-tapping screws) into the back of the door to provide a fairly smoke-free tight fit. A hinge and an old casement fastener completed the stoking door.

Lay a piece of wire grid, or alternatively a piece of sheet metal with a series of holes, over the hole in the base of the keg. The rate of burning will be dictated by the amount of air passing through this aperture.

Before installing the stove, I prepared the surrounding area carefully, as my workshop is made entirely of timber. I placed heavy sheet metal (old road signs) immediately under the heater and put a sheet of corrugated iron behind it, fixed to the wall; this gives adequate protection to the floor and wall. I put the heater itself on three bricks about 6in from the wall. I cut a hole through the wooden roof to take the chimney, allowing a clearance of 1in round the opening. Later I fitted a 6in square of lead as flashing on the outer surface of the roof to provide a watertight finish.

Around the junction between the chimney and the top of the keg I laid some metal putty (for repairing car exhausts) to provide a heatproof seal. A bracket fixed the chimney in position to the wall of the workshop and held the whole structure in position. As an extra precaution, I laid a hearth of bricks around the base to prevent stray ash from coming into contact with the timber floor.

The basic principles of firemaking will ensure success. Light a few dry sticks, then put some sawdust/shavings on top; you'll soon find the correct level of topping-up. I find a single stoking of sawdust/shavings on top of a few well ignited sticks will burn quite happily for two hours or so with little or no attention.

This heater provides lots of free heat, takes up little room and is ideal for keeping my scotch glue on the boil. A few hours' work with virtually no cost will provide warm working conditions through the winter and get rid of unwanted waste. ■

Safety

- **Don't** throw light handfuls of sawdust in the stove — it can flash back and/or explode. Wrap it up in newspaper to stoke it in
- **Make sure** all walls and floors that come anywhere near the heat are adequately protected
- **Keep all your stored timber** and off-cuts, as well as **finishes** and other flammable materials, well away from the stove, and preferably in a different room

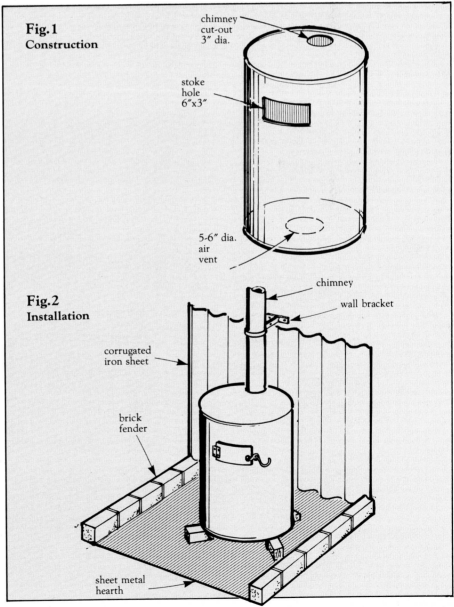

Fig. 1
Construction

chimney cut-out 3″ dia.

stoke hole 6″x3″

5-6″ dia. air vent

Fig. 2
Installation

chimney

wall bracket

corrugated iron sheet

brick fender

sheet metal hearth

A case of honour

Desmond Sant's display cabinet, meticulously made in solid oak, was designed for a Book of Remembrance in a church — but you can follow his ideas for a piece which, with its unusual detailing, will grace any museum or gallery

● *Clean lines and correct proportions for this memorial display cabinet hide an ingenious secret-access drawer*

After making three paschal candle-sticks for my parish church, I was asked to construct a display case for a book of remembrance for another church. The first step was to visit the building and discuss the project with the vicar and the lady donating the book in memory of her parents. The church is only about 10 years old, so a fairly modern design was called for. English oak, with natural waxed finish, was specified; this delighted me, for I fiercely object to staining this lovely timber.

The actual design seemed to grow of its own accord. The starting point was my desire to keep the edges of the top flush with the line of the carcase, rather than have the traditional overhang. To conceal the junction I applied a small rebate all round the top edge of the box carcase, which created a pleasant feature. This rebate was complemented by a small groove along the bottom edge of the box, and a similar groove down each external face of the legs and along the stretcher rails; the rebate and grooves are of similar proportions, and the leg groove is offset outwards from the centre line (fig. 3).

I struck a snag with the sloping top; the case should be as dust-tight as possible, and with a hinged lid this would be difficult, however perfectly the lid was seated on the frame. A sloping lid meeting a vertical side also presented practical problems in fitting a lock; in any case I was determined to keep the sight line of the glass at the back vertically down to the bottom of the case (fig. 2 shows what I mean), and I didn't want the clean lines of the case marred by fittings. These considerations drove me to a completely different solution — to make the interior a drawer which enters from the back. This means the top can be permanently sealed and fixed to the framework; when the case stands against a wall you can't see the drawer or how you can get inside the case.

Construction

This piece is quite demanding, and unless you set it out accurately and strictly observe certain sequences you could find yourself in deep water. If you want to follow the design

Fig. 1

front elevation — 762 — 940

side elevation — 457

See Fig. 3

All dimensions in mm

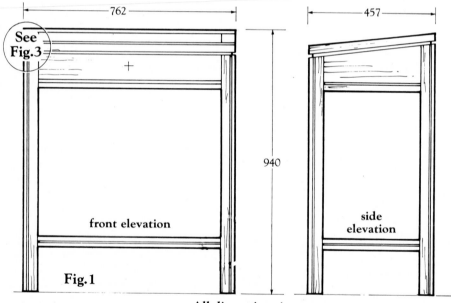

Fig. 2 Side sectional view

- lid-frame rail
- screwed bead
- ¼" plate glass
- glass 'sight line' in line with drawer
- internal drawer-front
- drawer 'back'
- cabinet front
- book stand
- external drawer-'front'
- drawer bottom
- front leg
- drawer runner
- back leg
— 457 —

Fig.3   Groove details

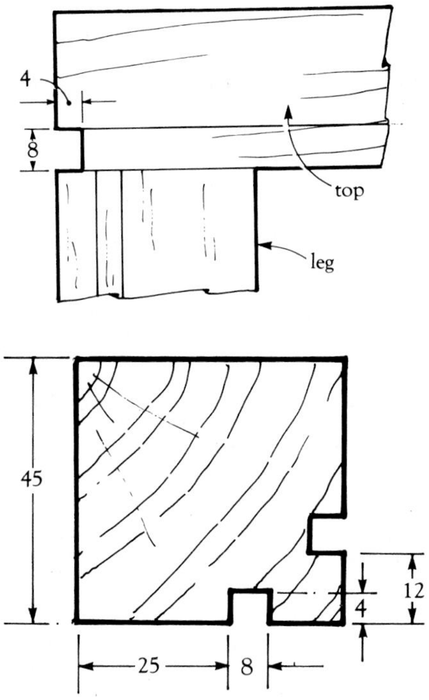

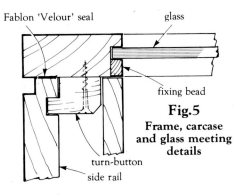

4

8

top

leg

45

12

4

25

8

to make a cabinet for displaying a book or similar-shaped item, in a church, or indeed a gallery or museum, the first stage is to prepare a full size setting-out plan based on the size of the specific book or piece to be displayed, opened out. Allow an appropriate margin around the book for the stand, and then a suitable margin around the stand to the inside faces of the drawer. Make an allowance for the thickness of the drawer sides, front and back and finally the thickness of the legs. This will give you the overall size of the cabinet. The height of the unit should be about 900mm at the back.

I have not given a cutting list here, and the dimensions on the drawings are specific to the book for which the case was designed. Obviously, your own measurements will relate to your own display object. From your drawing you can work out a cutting list; select your timber carefully, for oak can vary considerably from plank to plank.

I must point out that though the drawer-front takes the place of the back rail of the unit, and is at the back of the case in use, it's still technically the drawer-front, and this is what I am calling it throughout.

Legs
Start by setting out the legs and framework. Ignore the rebating and grooving details until later, and forget about the slope of the top for the time being; at this stage, keep the top rails all the same width.

Mark out mortises for the two side rails, the front rail and stretcher rails. To avoid the risk of penetrating the mortise when rebating and grooving later, I used bare-faced tenons (fig. 4). Make sure you mark and cut the mortises in the front rails

shorter, to allow for the slope of the top. When marking the shoulder lines on the front rail, mark out the 'drawer-front' at the same time, so the lengths are identical. You don't need mortises, of course, at the back where the drawer fits.

Cut the mortises and tenons in the usual way, fit each joint separately, adjusting as necessary, and then assemble the legs and carcase framing dry. It's best here to trim the 'drawer-front' precisely to length, put it in position and hold it lightly with a sash-cramp.

After deciding what degree of slope you want for the top — I had a drop of 50mm — strike a line along the top of the front rail to the depth; return the line round each end with a try-square and a pencil tick. Do the same with the top edge of the 'drawer-front'. Use a straight edge to join pairs of ticks across the ends to get the slope set out accurately.

Now dismantle the unit and carefully cut the side rails to the rake, clean up with a plane and check for squareness. Reduce the width of the front rail, but remember to cut first to the slope line on the back of the thickness — say 2-3mm full — as the top edge slopes upwards. Plane the splay carefully, checking with a bevel set to the end

Fig.4
Bare-faced tenon

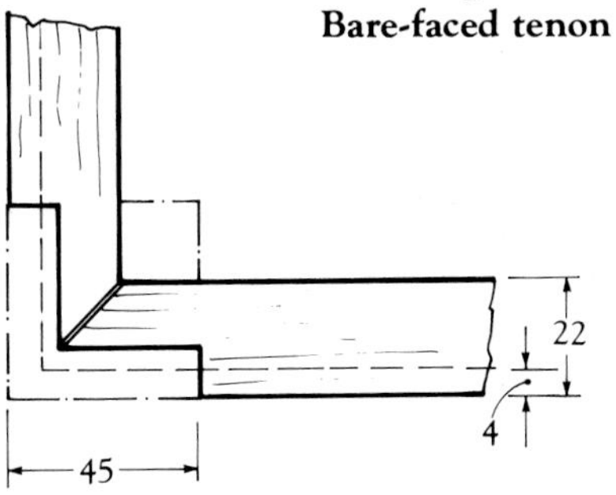

22

4

45

Fablon 'Velour' seal   glass

fixing bead

Fig.5
Frame, carcase and glass meeting details

turn-button

side rail

slope. Then plane a similar bevel on the top edge of the drawer-front, but this time down towards the front. Then cut the ends of the legs to the splay before reassembling the framework again, lightly cramping up and checking for squareness.

If your setting out and cutting has been accurate, the sloping top edge should be

perfectly in line and true; if not, trim with a plane and check with a straight-edge.

For the rebates and grooves I used a router with a tungsten carbide cutter. Dismantle the framework, and neatly run a rebate around the top edge of the carcase framing, not forgetting the drawer-front. Leave the rebate across the end of the legs for the time being; you can best do this after assembly. Cut the grooves, including grooves inside the top edges of the front and two side rails for the top turn-buttons (fig. 5).

Now clean up all the faces of the various pieces of wood, slightly softening the arrises with sandpaper, but don't smooth away the crisp corners too much. Incise the cross or decorative motif on the front rail at this stage, if you want it, and then you can glue up, placing the drawer-front in position as before for stability.

Drawer
Glue and screw the drawer-guides and runners to the side rails (fig. 6), leaving them short by the thickness of the drawer-front to act as stops. With the drawer itself, you want to aim for a fairly easy and smooth run in up to the last inch or so, when it should tighten slightly to a glove-like fit, so there is just a hairline where the ends of the drawer-front meet the legs. Cut the top edges of the drawer-sides to the same slope as the carcase. I used standard drawer construction, with lap dovetails to the drawer-front and through dovetails to the sides and back; the bottom, of 6mm plywood, is grooved in.

Here we come to an interesting feature of the drawer; it has an inner 'false front' just behind the outer back rail/drawer-front (figs 2, 7) which maintains the sight-line of the glass along and down inside the back. Thinking ahead, the inner face of this false piece should align vertically with the inner

Fig.6   Draw-runners

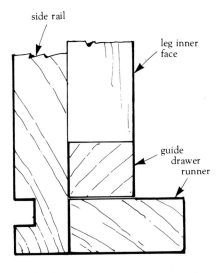

side rail

leg inner face

guide

drawer runner

continued

 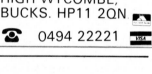

A case of honour

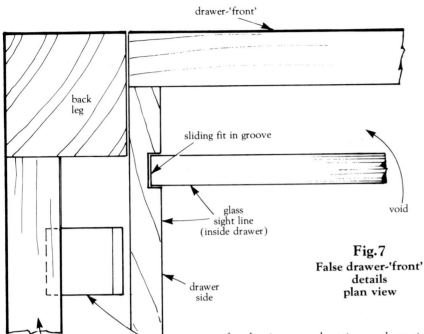

drawer-'front'

back leg

sliding fit in groove

glass
sight line
(inside drawer)

void

Fig. 7
**False drawer-'front'
details
plan view**

drawer
side

side rail

turn-
button

edge of the top-frame rail. Figs 2 and 7 show how it works. I fitted this inner piece loosely in grooves in the sides, in case the lock ever needs to be removed, and stuck a small label in the gap pointing this out, for the benefit of some ham-fisted person of the future who might try and take the drawer to pieces. Before assembling the drawer I recessed in the drawer-lock and fitted the escutcheon. After gluing up, I lined the drawer with Fablon 'Velour' self-adhesive felt.

Top

The top is left to last since its measurements are determined by the inside of the framework and drawer. The interior edges of the frame should coincide with the interior of the drawer, and the width of the stiles and rails will be from the insides of the drawer to the outside of the frame, plus a margin

for cleaning up and cutting neatly to size.

After cutting the mortises and tenons, I rebated the underside for the glass, which is fixed with plain screwed beads. I used 6mm polished plate glass, bedded with wash-leather; you can buy it as adhesive strip and it's cleaner and neater than mastic. Before glazing, cut a mortise for the lock bolt.

I fastened the top in place using turn-buttons (fig. 5), after sticking some narrow strips of the self-adhesive Fablon 'Velour' felt along the top edge of the framing as a dust seal.

The bookstand itself is straightforward.

To finish the cabinet I used sander sealer, cut back with 4/0 steel wool, and waxed with Briwax. The result is a superfine finish which reminds everyone who touches it that there is nothing like 'real wood'.

This was a very satisfying project to make, and the real reward came when I handed it over to the donor. She looked at it in silence for a few seconds, muttered 'It's lovely', and shed some quiet tears.

The display case stands in St John's Church, Pleck, Walsall. ∎

● Without the lid frame, the inner drawer details and leg/side joints can be clearly seen

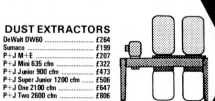

Photo finish

There are almost as many turners' finishes as there are turners, says Lech Zielinski — here's a general view and some personal findings

A lot's been written about finishing turned wood objects, and I doubt if there are two turners who have exactly the same approach and techniques. A definitive book, chapter or article on the subject can't be written — and so much the better. This area of the craft is very subjective. Much can be learned from experiment, and the exchange of information among turners is important. Ultimately it remains your personal choice of how you want the object to look and feel, and how to go about achieving it.

The most commonly accepted procedure is to turn, sand, then finish. Sounds simple enough, but the variations on the theme are nearly infinite, depending on your personal philosophy, the timber used, the final destination (use) of the turned object, and other factors. For example you could skip the latter two stages completely if you want, although you couldn't avoid the first! A reproduction staircase spindle will probably only need to be sanded, leaving the final choice of finish to the customer, while a box or bowl may need wax, oil, or maybe both.

I had the task at last October's Irish Woodturners Guild Seminar in Letterfrack (*WW/Jan*) of providing information and advice about finishing techniques and materials, and as I soon found out, I was learning fast myself. Most of the professional turners had clearly worked out methods of preparing and finishing their surfaces, and the Seminar provided an excellent forum for exchange of ideas, approaches, techniques and philosophies.

I must admit my own ideas about finishing have lately been greatly influenced by the simplicity and the effectiveness of Richard Raffan's methods, as described in his book *Turning Wood with Richard Raffan*, and as demonstrated by him at the Seminar. He would like to see most of his work unsanded and even unfinished, as he believes wooden objects which are used gradually acquire their own sheen (patina) from constant handling, and will soon look beautiful enough. Obviously, this approach needs a nearly-finished surface straight from the tool — which Raffan produces with ease. Since the majority of clients like at least some kind of finish, he found a happy compromise with light sanding and oil-and-wax. Should the client prefer it shiny, he or she can keep rewaxing and buffing the piece; if they want to use it when the wax washes off, it's back to bare wood which can then just be re-oiled if and when.

Sanding and abrasives

Most turners use abrasives, grit particles embedded in a layer of glue and attached to a paper or cloth backing. The size (and density) of grit determines the grade. There are occasions when I use as coarse as 40-grit to cope with very torn fibres on a wet-turned bowl, but generally I start sanding with 80-grit, going progressively through 100, 180, 240 and even sometimes 400 and 600. I've used aluminium oxide papers for some time, but I find silicone carbide not only cuts better, it's also a great deal more durable. If you skip a grade when sanding, you'll probably end up wasting a lot of time because you won't have removed the marks left by the previous one. Sometimes this doesn't become apparent until you've used your finest abrasive, and then you have to go back one or two grades to remove the scratches. I tended to be rather impatient with sanding until I learned to value my efforts and time — well-turned bowls showed blemishes which spoiled the whole effect.

● *Richard Raffan's no-nonsense approach involves the occasional candlestick . . .*

If I come across a particularly nasty area of torn grain, I often apply some oil to the spot and leave it for a few minutes to soak in, then I can sand the grain off. Apparently paste wax works just as well.

I turn a lot of faceplate work; bowls, platters, plates and so on, all with quite large areas to sand. To speed up production, there's nothing like power sanding. It has been used in the USA for some years, but for some reason it has only been accepted as a legitimate method here quite recently. You can use an ordinary electric hand drill, or an angle drill which gives better control, as it has a shorter shaft and

you can keep it tight against your body. A piece of abrasive is held on a round 2in or 3in pad with a steel shaft, the pad of soft foam supported by harder rubber. What you get is an elastic form that gives and changes shape as you sand the curves of your work.

There are a number of ways of attaching the abrasives to the pad. I make my own abrasive discs and squares, and I used to use double-sided tape, but the discs would fly off when they heated up with the friction. There's a system available from the USA in which pad and disc have a male and female interlocking 'catch', making it very easy to change to another grit. I think the most effective system is the 'Velcro' hook-and-loop tape one; you glue the tape on to the sanding pad and abrasive disc, and change the abrasive simply by peeling it off the pad. You can buy Velcro discs and pads from your woodturning supplier, but they work out at about 14p each.

I have been making my own Velcro system, and discovered some other advantages besides the much lower cost of 5p per piece. I buy Velcro tape straight from the manufacturer, and glue it to a sheet of abrasive with contact adhesive. Then I cut the sheet into 2x2in or 3x3in squares to fit my pads. Cut the corners off to make a disc, but I found that with care I can use the corners of the squares very effectively to sand undercut curves of bowl rim which would otherwise have to be done by hand. With a bit of practice, it's also possible to sand a difficult patch of torn grain with the drill held against the body for control and the work rotated to and fro by hand. Natural-edged green-turned bowls are notorious, and this is often the only way to get a smooth surface. Plenty of room for experimenting with the drill! If you have a lathe which reverses, you'll find less problem with sanding. As the work rotates in opposite directions, applying the usual sequence of grits will more effectively remove raised fibres.

With power sanding less heat is generated, as the rotating disc is constantly moving across the surface of the wood. There's little chance of heat-cracks, but it is possile to start sanding a green-turned bowl and have your face covered with sap, then end up with plenty of dust as the sanding itself dries the wood in front of your eyes.

On the subject of dust, for the sake of your only pair of lungs you should have a dust-mask as an *absolute minimum*. A dust extractor with the tube close to the sanded wood won't necessarily transform your workshop into a dust-free laboratory, but at least you won't have to use a shovel to look for your tools after a week's work!

Finishes

It's often difficult to decide on an appropriate finish, and to my knowledge there is no all-purpose universal mixture or wonder-chemical. When I was getting ready for Letterfrack, I made a selection of finish-

continued

Photo finish

ing materials commonly used by turners. The list included shellac sanding sealer, mineral oil, corn oil, Rustins Danish and Teak oils, beeswax, carnauba wax (and a mixture of both), Craftlac Melamine and others.

You could say there are three categories of surface treatment: penetrating finish (treatment *in* the surface), coatings (treatment *on* the surface), and no treatment at all. A combination of the first two seems very common with turners.

When turning a platter, for example, I brush on a liberal coat of shellac sanding sealer. Shellac is dissolved in denatured alcohol, and when applied to wood it stays in and seals the pores while the alcohol evaporates. It takes about 15 minutes for the coat to dry but I often leave it for much longer. You can cut back the surface with fine sandpaper or 4/0 wire wool dipped in oil, if you want that to be your final finish. If you want the piece to be purely decorative, you can apply just wax. I often use my own mixture of 75/25 beeswax and carnauba wax; you dissolve them together in turpentine, in a double boiler on a cooker. Beeswax on its own is too soft and tacky, while carnauba is too hard. Apply the mixture by holding a lump against the rotating wood and friction-melting it. The final shine is achieved by buffing with a well-worn cloth, which helps to spread the wax evenly on the surface.

● *Keith Mosse, giant bowl specialist, discusses a natural treatment for an elm piece at the Irish Woodturners Guild Seminar, Letterfrack October 86*

Amongst the penetrating finishes there is one (it could be called a 'coat' finish, in fact) that deserves some attention, despite a rather lengthy application process — Rustins Danish Oil. It is a commercially prepared penetrating finish that contains polymerising resins, which set permanently in the wood and provide a durable and water-resistant seal. You can apply it on to the bare prepared surface with a cloth or brush. Drying time is four to eight hours, and I normally apply the second coat within

They form an impenetrable layer between your fingers and the object; the wood will never change, it's eternally preserved. You often find polyurethaned boxes or small bowls in gift/craft shops, and you're never too sure they aren't moulded plastic from Taiwan. It's undeniable, though, that these 'modern technology' finishes produce a surface highly resistant to water and alcohol. Rustins Plastic Coating, a two-pack 'cold-cure lacquer', offers durability beyond expectations. It can even be used for floors!

Another useful finish is Craftlac Melamine, its main advantage being that it's very quick drying. It's best applied with a cloth, and the coat dries in minutes. You need to flatten the surface before applying a second coat, which has to be applied very fast and the excess wiped off to prevent build-up. You then have a choice of buffing the dried surface for a pleasant sheen or applying, for example, a coat of paste wax to achieve a higher gloss.

The last category: the no-treatment finish. To quote Raffan's book: 'We are surrounded by examples of what use can do for a surface.' You can start by looking round your house: old kitchen knife with a worn handle, breadboard, handrails, garden tools . . . They have all been continuously handled, touched; they are smooth and shiny (no polyurethane!) and they have all been *used*.

Shouldn't the best reward for hours spent in the workshop be that someone could have pleasure in handling and using your product — and that it could become better with time? If the shape is good, the object well turned, then it will continue pleasing for years after the colours darken — if you let them. ∎

● Velcro: Selectus Ltd, Biddulph, Stoke-on-Trent

● Rustins, Waterloo Rd, London NW2, 01-450 4666

● Turners' materials from Craft Supplies, The Mill, Millers Dale, Buxton, Derbys SK17 8SN, (0298) 871636, and other *WW* advertisers.

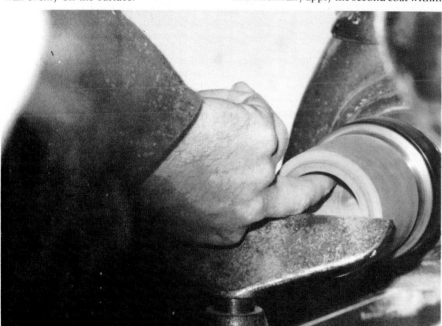

● *Testing the inside of a bowl to see how far the finish off the tool has come*

Another mixture is one of Richard Raffan's preferences; first he applies a penetrating coat of corn oil, and then friction-melts whatever wax he has handy — often just a candlestick (paraffin). The result is washable and useable, or decorative if you don't touch it. There are numerous such combinations; shellac/wax, shellac/mineral or cooking oil, and so on.

that time, but it's better to leave it overnight if you can, especially with the third coat on. You will need to cut the surface back with 4/0 wire wool, dipped in oil for lubrication. The efforts pay off, as you can get an attractive low lustre but the wood still feels like wood.

It's impossible to say the same about the finishes that remain *on* the surface of wood.

photos courtesy Ray Key

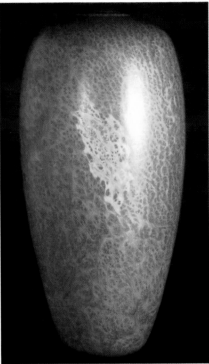

● **Above left**, Ray Key's African blackwood bowls are melamined and waxed: **left**, Jim Partridge's distinctive shapes are charred, wire-brushed and waxed; **above**, David Ellsworth spreads oil inside by spinning a vase, then friction-burns more on the outer surfaces

Turning—From Craft to Art

At last, the serious event British woodturners have been waiting for. Ray Key introduces this summer's seminar/conference

The first major Woodturning Seminar/Conference to be held in Britain for seven years takes place in August at Loughborough College of Art and Design. It is long overdue, since the last significant event like this was the International Seminar on Woodturning held at Parnham House in 1980.

This current seminar, 'From Craft to Art', has its origins in a visit to the American National Event in Arrowmont, USA, in 1985; Mick O'Donnell and I came back determined to do something for woodturning and woodturners in Britain. Margaret Lester, who organised the Parnham House event in 1980, agreed to help.

The three of us have been putting in considerable work behind the scenes, and we must acknowledge the financial backing from the Crafts Council, Robert Sorby Ltd and Craft Supplies Ltd, without whose help the seminar would not have got off the ground.

What we've got together is a package that will titillate, encourage and fire the imagination of everyone interested in turning. Our line-up includes lecturers and demonstrators who are leaders in their fields, and whose names are associated around the world with distinctive work and individual style.

At the seminar will be:

● **David Ellsworth** (USA), President of the American Association of Woodturners, a true artist/craftsman specialising in hollow forms so delicate they're unbelievable

● **Ed Moulthrop** (USA), known for his giant bowls and spheres (*WW/June 86*)

● **Mick O'Donnell** (UK), noted for his delicate wet-turned bowls and particularly the 'Bird' bowls created with his wife Liz (*WW/Dec 86*)

● **Jim Partridge** (UK), who pioneered wet turning in Britain; Jim's an innovator who cocks snoots at traditional sacred cows, and his work always provokes discussion (*WW/Feb 85*)

● **Ray Key** (UK), (me!) known particularly for boxes, work in exotic woods and writing.

We hope to have other leading personalities in turning, including a spindle turner.

Alongside the seminar/conference will be a small exhibition of turning craft and art, with international entries selected.

This is an event not to be missed if you're serious about woodturning. We hope the lectures and demonstrations will generate a fresh direction and a climate of greater creative awareness among British turners. It will also be a forum to exchange ideas, between professional and amateur alike, and there'll be a room for you to display your own work.

If you want to know more, send a sae to **'Satyrs', 5 Bridport Rd, Beaminster, Dorset DT8 3LU.** Places are strictly limited, and will be reserved on a first-come-first-served basis. ■

● 'From Craft to Art', 14-16 August, Loughborough College of Art & Design

Mirrorman

Edward Hopkins reflects on the varied career that brought him to furniture making, and explains how to make his delightful dressing mirror

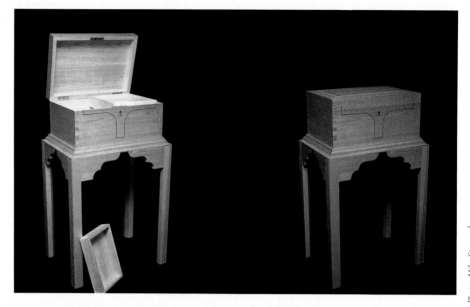

● Hopkinalia: **top**, a speculative chest on strand in pine and ebony; **above left**, a photographer's Wellington in blockboard and yew; **above right**, the extraordinary chess table entered for the Bristol Woodworker Show 'Squares & Rounds' competition

Photos Mike Stannard

This photo Colin Wilson

The pleasure of a woodwork shop first hit me long ago when my father bandsawed all four sides of my fort at once. Instant perfection! I played with wood and later spent hours doing peculiar things with spokeshaves and gouges. At school I was systemised into sawing straight, planing square and cutting accurate angles; what I acquired was not skill, but fear. Until relatively recently, wood was my adversary not my friend. To start a job was to march into battle prepared to subjugate the enemy. But it must have done some good — it was considerably better than Latin.

On leaving school I excelled myself at art; then sank out of sight in Religious Knowledge and for reasons difficult to understand now, headed into college and up the aisle towards ordination. I dismantled my hereditary beliefs, assembled my faith and found I did not conform. But before I left I made a 7ft high crucifix in pine and sapele. It was hung in chapel — an unconventional, dramatic, geometric piece expressing the bridging of two worlds, the eternal ascending and descending of Christ, permanently impaled on the horns of the altar. It took days to design, a vacation to make. But the crucifix provoked objection and was taken down; later I saw it, broken in the bicycle sheds. Much later I stole it back; it remains my favourite piece.

I moved to a job in Wiltshire where a local antique dealer gave me a few repair jobs, stripping, gluing and polishing. They worked out. I enjoyed them. I took more. They paid. I knew very little but with a combination of helpful friends, trial and error, I learned. I began to quote (i.e. under-quote) for more substantial jobs. Then an empty old shop with room to live came up for sale. On a wing and a prayer I resigned my job with the County Council and wrote my name on the door.

And lo, the work kept coming in. For the next few years I became an Antique Restorer. I learned from a varied supply of loose, broken, scratched and stained furniture, and there was a lot to learn — so

many skills, from construction to colouring, carving, gluing and patching veneers to mending metalwork. For some reason I was never confronted with an insuperable problem, although many times my finest French polishing demanded the up-ending of the meths bottle, the complete swabbing off and the return to square one. Being your own boss means being your own novice.

I learned about furniture itself — its quality, its weaknesses . . . and its style. By no means all of our antiques are beautiful, but some have fine balance and proportion, a rare feel. I don't particularly want to possess fine furniture, but I like to see it and have it pass through my workshop. When a customer staggers in with an armful of grey wood covered in dust and littered with pigeon droppings, and you return him a bow-fronted golden oak panelled corner cupboard originally made in the 18th

century, the satisfaction is considerable. You return his potting table to his dining room; you make the dull shine.

But I had a growing frustration that all restoration is essentially self-effacing. The very best work is not even noticed. Clever yes, but creative — no.

One of my first commissions was in exchange for our wedding rings. Trevor wanted a table and delivered to my bench a 15ft slab of 3in mahogany. I made a massive trapezoidal refectory table which grew out of the floor like a site of standing stones.

Commissions came, they vied with restoration and a turning point came. I still don't refuse restoration (unless it is clearly futile) but mercifully not so much comes in. Instead I am blessed with a steady stream of discerning customers who want something made — something original and distinct. We discuss the requirements and come up with sketches. As long as the budget is fairly realistic there will be a good chance for a good design. I find the financial constraint is as helpful as functional and dimensional parameters in forging the overall shape, form and idea; it inspires invention.

Coming up with a radical solution is exciting, but as often as not, the answer is straightforward, a reworking of a conventional theme. These pieces stand in line with antique design but they are in no sense 'reproduction'. They are not copies, they are not 'aged' or 'distressed'. There's no need for such deception. Neither do I get fancy. There is enough latitude in forthright lines and constructional detail, I think, to establish the overall mood. I like it to be strong and honest. And after all that repairing repairs, I like it to last.

There are several real pleasures for me in woodwork. One is the 'concept' and the scale drawing which tells you it will work. Another is standing in a timber yard grandly selecting boards. Planing is exciting,

like tearing off wrapping paper. And then there is a pleasure which is easy to miss; you can take a break, stand back and think 'Goodness! Where did that spring from?' A piece of furniture has popped into existence. The idea has metamorphosed into fact. Of course there's pleasure in satisfying customers, but better yet is coming across one of your older pieces and finding it still looking good.

My workshop has become very efficient. I depend on other people's table-saws and planers but from there on, I'm equipped. There's a large bandsaw, radial-arm and treadle fretsaw, a heavy lathe and a clutter of small machines — routers, a sander and a planer — all more useful when table or wall-mounted. The most recent acquisition is a mortising machine, a magnificent hunk of cast iron, with a chisel on a 12:1 lever which crunches oak like celery. With all this hardware, I turned to batch production.

I tapped a few retail outlets, made prototypes and took orders. It worked but with limited success. Stationery racks, spice racks, trays and boxes rolled off the line and most of them sold, especially at Christmas.

But keeping cost controlled is critical. If you lose on one piece, you multiply that loss by 10 or 20 or whatever. If you're successful then the logical extension is more orders, more machines, more operators and a room where you shut yourself away from the noise and the dust and the repetition — a neat office with a telephone.

From time to time I've indulged in speculative pieces. Here too, the fortune is mixed. There can be nothing better for a designer to sit down unhindered and uninhibited to think 'What springs to mind? What shall I make now?' This stimulates totally original design which belongs to the designer alone — your truest work and likely to be your best. But having made it, it helps the common good if you can sell it, and if you can't, it begins to look unnaturally like a stuffed parrot — very interesting and very useless.

So far, I've been lucky. How lucky is still coming home to me as I search around for another larger workshop. I'll settle for anything, but I've got a rather pleasant image of a stone barn overlooking a cow pasture. High on a wall in a niche stands a statue of Joseph, gazing over a lot of space in the middle of which stands a gleaming planer. Music plays and coffee steams. It's a simple dream, I tell myself, a totally plausible fantasy.

Small dressing mirror

A project in mahogany and jacaranda

Designed as a retail batch production exercise, this mirror stand will hold all your miniature clutter . . . and still look decorative

Small houses need small furniture. You may not have room for a dressing table, but you need something for the everyday clutter. This dressing mirror, which was originally intended to be produced in batches of five, with shelves and drawers, is designed to hang or stand and to absorb bottles, boxes, jewellery and flowers.

For the carcase I jig-dovetailed ⅝in mahogany. The various mouldings that cover the joints I cut by router, bandsaw or scratchstock. The drawer-sides are ¼in mahogany, glued and brass-pinned to the fronts — dovetailing seems unnecessary for the scale and expensive for a general market.

The turnings are from what was sold to me as jacaranda, heavier than water and in time as red as berries. The knobs are slender but strong, shaped like inverted cups and saucers. The finials (for hooking necklaces), the pillars and balustrades reflect classical architecture, while the balcony suggests Juliet.

The cork pinboard with its contrasting marble patterns is fixed to the balcony's sides, while the back is boarded up with ³⁄₁₆in solid stuff and brass screws. I used ⅛in

continued

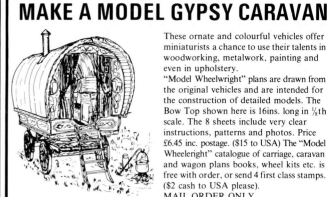

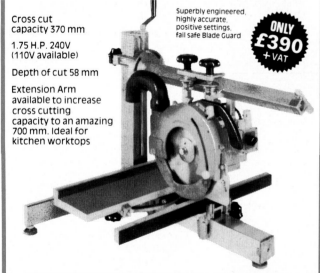
154

Mirrorman

Side and front elevations

here, but basically with these sections go as thin as you can. The hanging plates are fixed through the backboarding, distributing the weight evenly.

To build the piece you'll need $\frac{5}{8}$in mahogany at least 7in wide, $\frac{3}{16}$in for the drawer bottoms and backboards, and $\frac{1}{4}$in thick for the drawer sides and horizontal drawer dividers, and pediment.

Construction is quite straightforward. Start with the drawer-box carcase; I used a router and dovetail jig where I could and

half-thickness housings to join the upright drawer carcase to the long one. All the joints will be covered by mouldings so take your pick as long as the joints are strong. The jigged dovetail seems to me the strongest, neatest and fastest solution — it takes about as long as sharpening a pencil. The radial-arm saw does the same job on the housings.

Cut a dado half the thickness of the top-box verticals in the top piece of the long bottom box where the left vertical meets it;

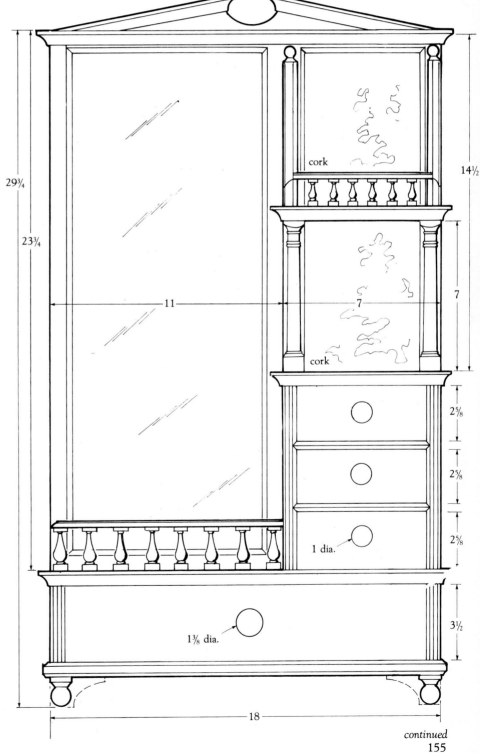

all dimensions in inches

continued

Mirrorman

this will be a half-thickness housing. The right vertical of the top box goes right down to the bottom piece of the bottom box, where they are dovetailed together. In the right vertical of the top box you must cut a half-thickness dado for the half-thickness tongue of the top piece of the long bottom box, and also dadoes in both verticals the full thickness of the horizontal drawer-dividers, which in my case were ¼in. Glue up the double carcase, then fit the horizontal dividers, which also serve as dustboards.

Make the frames for the mirror and the cork so they can sit on the carcases side-by-side, flush all round. Allow rebates behind and chamfer the front a little to soften up the 'picture frame' effect. Mitre the corners; I can't seem to get on with mitre cramps so I nailed together a holding block for gluing and pinning the corners.

The frames can be screwed into place but it's worth finishing them before they are finally glued.

Now splatter the piece with mouldings. True up a long piece of ⅝in mahogany, run off the profile (I use a table-mounted router) and rip the lengths off on the bandsaw. I removed the bandsaw marks by pulling them over a jack plane held upside down in a vice — effective enough but likely to be frowned on for some reason. This procedure works well for the 'Scotia' strips and the double-chamfered ones along the base and, while you're at it, the jacaranda balcony 'handrail'. A hand-held router cuts the ovolo moulding down the balcony sides, but then the industrial revolution hiccups and stalls. For the vertical reeding I have no substitue for a scratch-stock. It's a Stanley no.66, passed down from my grandfather, and it makes you think that every tool should be a hand-tool.

The fitting and gluing of these mouldings (I used minute pins as well) takes time. Be as precise as possible, for the purpose of these details is to bring the eye in; inspection of a tiny area leads to seeing the standard for the whole work. Mitre the reeding between the small drawers. It's neat; it shows care and attention.

So too with the turnings. If your lathe is more of a GXL Turbo than my coal lorry, you'll probably do them yourself and positively enjoy not making miniscule errors which split, chip and whizz chunks past your ear. If not, sub-contract. But insist on identical height for each set of items. Have accurate ¼in shafts on either end — holes can then be drilled into the mahogany and, ideally, into the handrail; I confess I relied solely on Cascamite here. I used jacaranda for these turnings; mahogany would do but the knobs would have to be beefed up a bit which might detract from their elegance. They can all be shellacked on the lathe. Scrape or finely sand. Seal with shellac and cut back with finishing paper. Polish again and cut back with fine wire wool; wax.

Fit the mirror, of course, and the cork. Then use more of the 3/16in planks (vertically) to board up the back, peppering it with small brass screws. These boards are of structural importance, tying the whole thing together more firmly and, crucially, taking the strain from two brass hanging plates (screwed into the back below the pediment) right down to the drawers and the shelves.

Finally, sit down and be glad you didn't stain it because in quite a short time the mahogany will ripen to a warmer and more natural hue than could ever be poured from a bottle.

An unexpected (!) bonus was the mirror reflection which enlarges the 'courtyard' and makes the 'colonnade' more inviting. It offers entry and accommodation. It asks to be occupied, decorated, draped and stuck with pins. A friendly little property; fountains and roof-garden extra. ■

● Edward Hopkins, 4a Bath Rd, Beckington, Bath BA3 6SW, (0373) 830632.

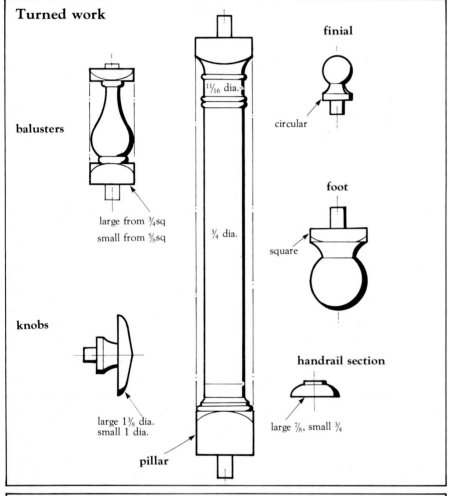

Turned work

finial

circular

balusters

large from ¾sq
small from ⅝sq

¹¹/₁₆ dia.

¾ dia.

foot

square

knobs

large 1⅜ dia.
small 1 dia.

handrail section

large ⅞, small ¾

pillar

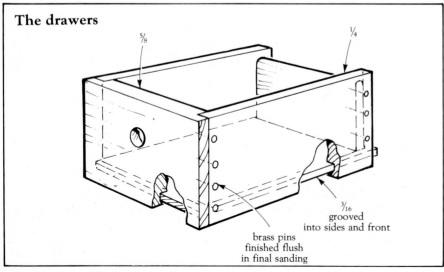

The drawers

⅝

¼

brass pins
finished flush
in final sanding

3/16
grooved
into sides and front

156

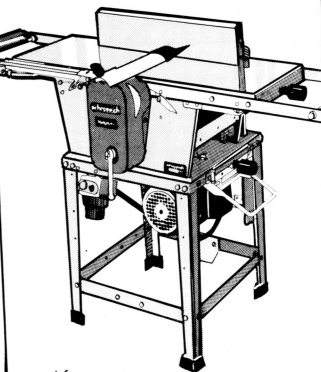

Textiles touch timber

One of *Woodworker's* near neighbours is a gallery with a high line on textiles and top taste in furniture. Aidan Walker had a look

Room sets in galleries are not by any means a new thing, of course; but coming at it from the textile end, the contemporary Textile Gallery ('This Month,' *WW/Dec*) thought like this; as the leading textile gallery for modern fabric design in the country — functional items like carpets as well as wall hangings that work like paintings — why shouldn't we expand into furniture?

The result of which was the Designer Showcase, a monthly room set at the CTG which concentrates on the two basic furnishing needs; the soft bits we cover walls and floors with, and the wooden bits we sit on, eat off, and use every day in every way. Committed to promoting the highest standards of art and craft as they are, the Gallery has chosen for their first Designer Showcase the work of Martin Grierson (*WW/Dec 86*) and Jennie Moncur. Grierson's furniture, arguably the finest being hand-made in Britain today — some would say ever — is complemented and offset by large-scale tapestries, full of bold shapes and bright colours. The designs are picked up in the upholstery of the chairs that go with a magnificent Cuban-mahogany veneered table designed by Grierson for his own home. He made a set of the chairs for a private commission, and duplicated them so he and his family could sit on them too. Jennie Moncur's textiles, says the blurb, 'echo the patterns and scales of the Mediaeval and Jacobean periods. Her designs in tapestries, embroideries and printed fabrics also carry the romanticism of the early French Renaissance'.

The CTG's parent company is one of Britain's largest importers of Oriental rugs, and has moved from there into antique carpets and tapestries. Next step furniture — but, says gallery administrator Pauline Bates, there is an identifiable decrease in the quality of craftsmanship in furniture as well as fabrics from the 1880s onwards. If you take antique as meaning at least 100 years old, we are now beginning to get on to the pieces which are indeed old, but that's about all. Before you start thinking through the early 20th century into Gimson and Barnsley country — high craft if ever there was — it's the antique market we're looking at, and special work from the Cotswold and Arts and Crafts schools already has its own special value. So as a response, in a sense, to the dwindling supply of first-quality antique craft, the Contemporary Textile Gallery was set up to display and deal in the antiques of the future. Certainly in the case of Martin Grierson's furniture, the 'production values' he and his colleagues Robin Furlong and Jonathan Baulkwill operate would put Chippendale or Sheraton to shame. No rough-sawn backs for cabinets here.

It's a matter of educating the public, says Pauline — a favourite theme at the moment, one of Grierson's own and indeed, of other leading makers like Alan Peters, plus the people at the Style furniture shows (*WW/Jan*); why shouldn't people buy functional items of first quality? They tend to buy mass-produced furniture and carpets, then tart up the effect with expensive or unusual decorative artefacts like glass, ceramics, paintings, *objets d'art*; the CTG is working for designer/makers by exposing the (necessarily well-heeled) purchasing public to basic furnishings that are superbly designed and made. Why buy a vase when the table you put it on is an object of rare beauty in itself? A telling argument for designer/craftspeople who realise that they must sell to survive. Another persuading factor, of course, is that modern one-off pieces are just as good an investment, if not better, than antiques of doubtful provenance. Antique may mean old, but it doesn't necessarily mean excellent.

Other designer/craftspeople in wood who have shown or are showing at the gallery are Jeremy Broun (*WW/May 84*), who we mentioned in this general context in 'This month' in December's issue; Anthony Bryant, whose breathtaking bowls made a cover feature for our December '84 issue; Bert Marsh, who won woodturning gold medals at the Woodworker Show so many years in succession that he decided to stand down and let other people get some limelight; and Peter Stocken, whose amazing three-dimensional puzzles will shortly grace these pages. The gallery's own plans for the future include some more names familiar to regular *WW* readers; it's a bit like the list of Britain's best. David Colwell (*WW/Nov 86*), Alan Peters (*WW/June 86*), Fred Baier, John Coleman, Robert Williams and Rupert Williamson (*WW/Apr 85*). Excellent exposure for admirable craftspeople, with the solid idea behind it that people must be shown they need quality in their domestic basics before they'll buy it.

It's still more than a little rarefied, it must be said; a gallery is not a place where average people with average incomes go to look for furniture or carpets. But it's grist to the mill, and after all there's usually at least a couple of really special purchases to make in life . . . why not a future antique? ∎

● Contemporary Textile Gallery, 10 Golden Sq, London W1R 3AF, 01-439 9071.

Opposite page, clockwise from top left:
Anthony Bryant's daring thin-turned bowls are heated to shape them into something more like shells. The eagles above seem to fit . . . Martin Grierson's 'Carlton House' desk and 'Chinese' chair, offset by Jennie Moncur's 'romantic' fabric, hung on a screen made in the Grierson workshops. Bert Marsh's distinctive bowls nestle amongst luxurious cushions; plus another shot of the room set, showing the Grierson table (Cuban mahogany with rosewood edge-banding) and macassar ebony display cabinet, plus chairs. Walls graced by Jennie Moncur's colours and shapes

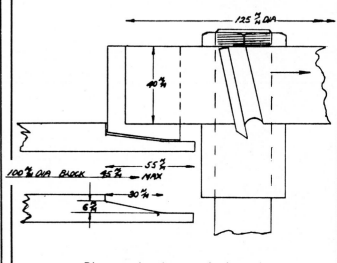

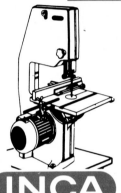

161

Two in tune

Two contrasting items on musical instrument makers. Christopher Elliott relates how shell-shocked trees of the Great War became a violin, while photographer Stan Folb tells how he was confronted with an amateur harp-maker

● *Shattered Somme tree-stumps yield a sweet melody;* **above**, *one of Kenneth's miniatures*

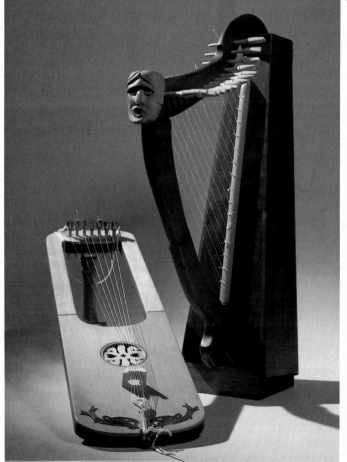

● *Lew's Saxon lyre and Celtic harp,* **left**, *and* **below** *the carved oak head on the harp in close-up*

● *Kenneth Popplewell with the 'Great War' violin he made and now plays*

The Somme guns echo down through time, transmuted into sweet music by a violin made from timber growing in the centre of the battlefield. In one day in 1916 20,000 British soldiers died in No-man's Land; only a few shattered stumps of trees were left in this devastated and shell-pitted landscape. Some of the pine and sycamore sent up new growth, and timber from these trees has been crafted into a unique violin by Kenneth Popplewell, of West London, as a tribute to the men who died on the Western Front.

Named 'The Western Front Violin', the instrument is completely playable, and Kenneth — a former member of the Royal Philharmonic and BBC Symphony Orchestras — has played arrangements of 1914-18 Great War songs during a war veteran's meeting.

Kenneth himself was not born until 1914 but was fascinated by the Somme devastation, and wanted to make his personal tribute to the men who died. The pine and sycamore trees were from two wooded areas that were the scenes of the most bitter conflicts during the Great War. The pine tree grew between La Boisselle and Authuille; the sycamore at Bois Quarante,

through which ran the German Front Line, three miles south of Ypres. Both trees are thought to be over 80 years old.

Kenneth found the timber to be slightly softer in texture than is generally used for violins, so he worked the centre front to $9/64$in and the centre back to $11/64$in; the Somme pine is medium-grained, while the figure of the Ypres sycamore is of a modest feathery appearance, unlike the zebra-like markings found on most violins.

The violin has been judged a fine instrument by celebrated violinists, and Kenneth's performance of Vaughan Williams' beautiful 'Lark Ascending' with orchestral accompaniment impressed Richard Baker, the BBC music personality. Kenneth now hopes to give a grand concert using the violin to benefit war charities.

He has made several other violins, including a miniature just three inches long, which has been much admired. Kenneth has a family link with Edward Popplewell, who worked in the Leeds/Manchester area around 1840-75 and who made first-class instruments.

The Western Front Violin is Kenneth's proudest accomplishment, and he hopes its music will keep alive the memory of those who died on the Somme. ∎

Lew, the gent who delivers photographic material to my studio, tried to attract my attention. 'Your're interested in woodwork, aren't you?'

'Go away, I'm busy,' I said, turning back to the bird in the bathing costume in front of my camera (she was three, and getting impatient).

'Don't be like that,' said Lew, 'I've just made a harp.'

'You'll need one where you are going,' I said, 'if you don't . . . you've just made a what?'

Michael Lewis (Lew to his friends) started his working life as an apprentice toolmaker; later he was a camera repairer for several years. Then, perhaps claustrophobic about working indoors, Lew turned to driving a delivery van for a photographic supplier.

His interest in woodwork started about 10 years ago when his wife needed bobbins for lacemaking; so he bought a small lathe and taught himself to make bobbins. He went to an exhibition of musical instruments at Merton Technical College, got interested and joined the evening class there. His first instrument was a lyre; his harp demonstrates the use of available materials — a soundboard made from a piece of an old piano; the bridge made from a bit of bone pinched from his dog (Lew told me this with a dead straight face). The harp's neck and arms are from a door, and the body from some mahogany which was just laying about.

'Now,' says Lew, 'I suppose I had better learn to play them.' ∎

● *The Celtic harp (left) is the sixth instrument made by Lew since he started with the lyre which he's holding, loosely based on an Anglo-Saxon lyre at the British Museum*

Letters

Scrub planes

I WAS VERY INTERESTED in the article by Rik Middleton, 'Soled on Wood' (*WW/Nov '86*), for it took me right back to my apprenticeship days in the early 1920s. The tool he calls a scrub plane was frequently used by cabinetmakers for roughing out the solid panels, such as ends, tops and bottoms, which were usually made up of two or three unplaned planks of mahogany, walnut, oak or other timber. These planks could vary in thickness by as much as ⅛in at times; they were almost always rub-jointed, no mean feat when they were up to six feet long.

When these joined panels were dry they would be roughly levelled with this plane to some mean thickness, before planing with the jack and smoother. This was highly skilled and very hard work indeed. But there was a cry of protest when the Guv'nor hinted one day that he was going to send the panels to the trade mill for planing. Even after the 'makers' grudgingly accepted the inevitable, they used this plane to clean off excess glue — which blunted the machine cutters — and high points created by the differing thicknesses of the planks.

However this plane was known throughout the cabinetmaking area of London as the 'Rice-ooble' (my attempt at phonetic spelling).

Many years later I discovered the actual word is German, made up from *reis* (to tear) and *huble* (a plane) — hence rice-ooble — and had been brought into Britain by the many mid-European cabinetmakers immigrating here in the early part of this century. This is an apt name, and much more descriptive than scrub plane, for its function is literally to tear off large chunks of wood from the rough planks.

There was no need to modify the tool to make it work; it did its job perfectly provided the blade was kept sharp, a challenge in itself. I can't see the need of such tools these days, so I should think they are, as Rik Middleton says, adorning the shelves of collectors. They are too light in weight and too expensive to be used as door stops.

Mark Kenning, Evesham

Sole thickness

THE SOLE THICKNESS of the E. C. Emmerich stable of wooden planes (*WW/Nov '86*) has seemed excessive to me. There's an obvious aesthetic quality in such a sole, and a mouth that promises to retain its tightness for many years of use. However, as it may be necessary to relieve the front of the throat to facilitate the passage of shavings, the mouth of the non-adjusting models may open up faster than anticipated.

But a thick sole of such material as lignum vitae has one serious disadvantage, as Rik Middleton discovered. If the thick section of this dense material moves, it will take the whole plane with it. In an extreme case I have seen a plane body and sole part

company — but this is unlikely in an Emmerich plane because of the complex sole/body joinery.

As a maker of Krenov-style planes, I use much thinner soles, typically 3-5mm, of iron bark (*Eucalyptus* sp), Amazon bloodwood (*Brosimum paraense*) or lignum vitae. This ensures a beautifully burnished working interface, but the plane body is not dominated by the movement whims of the sole. Further, choosing a well-seasoned, suitably weighty yet stable timber such as doussie (*Afzelia* sp) for the body will give a fine plane only marginally affected by atmospheric vagaries.

Rodney Hayward, Bundandon, Australia

Third leg

THANKS FOR THE WONDERFUL article on working walking sticks (*WW/Oct '86*). I had thought I was quite mad making these all on my own. Now I know I am not alone in making the third leg, so to speak; it was quite a fillip, I can tell you.

I carve most of my sticks with an old pocketknife, and I then give them to OAPs in the area.

Carry on with the good work; let's have a follow-up on this subject, please. Sorry, Theo, I can't afford the book.

Alfred Gardiner, Dudley

Hold on

THE IDEA OF LOOPING a belt through a hole in the bench as a holdfast ('Shoptalking points', *WW/Nov '86*) is good — but it's also very old. Cobblers used this method to hold boots and shoes on the last; saddlers used it to hold the saddle tree for cart saddles and other work while dressing it before padding (dressing is fitting the straps fore and rear, the leather flaps and back band slide). I saw this method being used in the early 1920s.

J. Booth, Derby

● *Choking a router - see below*

Bad practice

IN 'TAKING THE BISCUIT' (*WW/Nov '86*) a photograph on page 931 shows a router being used with the operator's left hand completely blocking the air intake.

Having spent a number of years inves-

tigating the failure of aircraft electrical equipment, I may be more conscious than most that this malpractice can have serious effects on the life of electric motors.

On no account should the carefully designed area of the air intake of any motor, or its housing, be reduced or obscured. The resulting rise in temperature often causes melting or reduced viscosity of lubricants with catastrophic effects on the bearings.

W. Battersby, Wirral

Propcraft

I WAS INTERESTED IN the airscrew article by Jim Kingshott (*WW/Nov '86*). As a member of the Vintage Aircraft and Flying Association I was involved in the 1960s with making two replica flying aircraft, a Vickers Gun Bus and a Vickers Vimy. The Gun Bus was given an original WWI propeller, but new ones were designed and made for the Vimy. These four-bladed mahogany laminated screws, about 10ft diameter, were made in much the same way as those in the article. Much of the roughing out was done with a hand-axe, and the final work with scrapers. Finally they were balanced by being placed on knife edges; when a cigarette paper was placed on the blade at 90° to the vertical, the whole airscrew revolved. After being flown, the aircraft were presented to the RAF Museum, Hendon.

L. Wild, Walton-on-Thames

shopguide

AVON

BATH   Tel. Bath 64513
JOHN HALL TOOLS   ★
RAILWAY STREET

Open: Monday-Saturday
9.00 a.m.-5.30 p.m.
H.P.W.WM.D.A.BC.

BRISTOL   Tel. (0272) 741510
JOHN HALL TOOLS LIMITED   ★
CLIFTON DOWN SHOPPING CENTRE
WHITELADIES ROAD
Open: Monday-Saturday
9.00 a.m.-5.30 p.m.
H.P.W.WM.D.A.BC.

BRISTOL   Tel. (0272) 629092
TRYMWOOD SERVICES
2a DOWNS PARK EAST, (off North View)
WESTBURY PARK
Open: 8.30 a.m.-5.30 p.m. Mon. to Fri.
Closed for lunch 1.00-2.00 p.m.
P.W.WM.D.T.A.BC.

BRISTOL   Tel. (0272) 667013
FASTSET LTD
190-192 WEST STREET
BEDMINSTER
Open: Mon.-Fri. 8.30 a.m.-5.00 p.m.
Saturday 9.00 a.m.-1.00 p.m.
H.P.W.WM.D.CS.A.BC.

AVON

BRISTOL   Tel. (0272) 667013
WILLIS
157 WEST STREET
BEDMINSTER
Open Mon.-Fri. 8.30 a.m.-5.00 p.m.
Sat. 9 a.m.-4 p.m.
P.W.WM.D.CS.A.BC.

BERKSHIRE

READING   Tel. Littlewick Green 2743
DAVID HUNT (TOOL
MERCHANTS) LTD   ★
KNOWL HILL, NR. READING
Open: Monday-Saturday
9.00 a.m.-5.30 p.m.
H.P.W.D.A.BC.

READING   Tel. Reading 661511
WOKINGHAM TOOL CO. LTD.
99 WOKINGHAM ROAD

Open: Mon-Sat 9.00 a.m.-5.30 p.m.
Closed 1.00-2.00 p.m. for lunch
H.P.W.WM.D.CS.A.BC.

BUCKINGHAMSHIRE

MILTON KEYNES   Tel. (0908) 641366
POLLARD WOODWORKING
CENTRE   ★
51 AYLESBURY ST., BLETCHLEY
Open: Mon-Fri 8.30-5.30
Saturday 9.00-5.00
H.P.W.WM.D.CS.A.BC.

SLOUGH   Tel: (06286) 5125
BRAYWOOD ESTATES LTD.   ★
158 BURNHAM LANE
Open: 9.00am-5.30pm.
Monday-Saturday.
H.P.W.WM.CS.A.

HIGH WYCOMBE   Tel. (0494) 24201/33788
SCOTT SAWS LTD.   ★
14 BRIDGE STREET

Mon.-Sat. 8.30 a.m.-6.00 p.m.

H.P.W.WM.D.T.CS.MF.A.BC.

BUCKINGHAMSHIRE

HIGH WYCOMBE   Tel. (0494) 22221
ISAAC LORD LTD   KE
185 DESBOROUGH ROAD

Open: Mon-Fri 8.00 a.m.-5.00 p.m.
Saturday 9.00 a.m.-5.00 p.m.
H.P.W.D.A.

CAMBRIDGESHIRE

CAMBRIDGE   Tel: (0223) 63132
D. MACKAY LTD.   ★
BRITANNIA WORKS, EAST ROAD

Open: Mon.-Fri. 8.30 a.m.-1 p.m./2.00-
5.00 p.m. Sat. 8.30 a.m.-1.00 p.m.
H.P.W.D.T.CS.MF.A.BC.

CAMBRIDGE   Tel. (0223) 247386
H. B. WOODWORKING   K
105 CHERRY HINTON ROAD
Open: 8.30 a.m.-5.30 p.m.
Monday-Friday
8.30 a.m.-1.00 p.m. Sat.
H.P.W.WM.D.CS.A.

shopguide

CAMBRIDGESHIRE

PETERBOROUGH   Tel. (0733)
WILLIAMS DISTRIBUTORS   64252
(TOOLS) LIMITED   **K**
108-110 BURGHLEY ROAD
   Open: Monday to Friday
   8.30 a.m.-5.30 p.m.
H.P.A.W.D.WH.BC.

CHESHIRE

NANTWICH   Tel. Crewe 67010
ALAN HOLTHAM   **K★**
THE OLD STORES TURNERY
WISTASON ROAD, WILLASTON
   Open: Tues.-Sat. 9.00 a.m.-5.30 p.m.
   Closed Monday
P.W.WM.D.T.C.CS.A.BC.

CLEVELAND

MIDDLESBROUGH   Tel. (0642)
CLEVELAND WOODCRAFT   813103
(M'BRO), 38-42 CRESCENT ROAD   **K**

   Open: Mon-Sat 9.15 a.m.-5.30 p.m.

H.P.T.A.BC.W.WM.CS.D.

CORNWALL

SOUTH WEST Power Tools

CORNWALL   Tel: Helston (03265) 4961
HELSTON AND LAUNCESTON   Launceston
   (0566) 4781
H.P.W.WM.D.CS.A.   **K**

CUMBRIA

CARLISLE   Tel: (0228) 36391
W. M. PLANT
ALLENBROOK ROAD
ROSEHILL, CA1 2UT
   Open: Mon.-Fri. 8.00 a.m.-5.15 p.m.
   Sat. 8.00 a.m.-12.30 noon
P.W.WM.D.CS.A.

DEVON

BRIXHAM   Tel. (08045) 4900
WOODCRAFT SUPPLIES   **E★**
4 HORSE POOL STREET

   Open: Mon.-Sat. 9.00 a.m.-6.00 p.m.

H.P.W.A.D.MF.CS.BC.

PLYMOUTH   Tel. (0752) 330303
WESTWARD BUILDING SERVICES   **★**
LTD., LISTER CLOSE, NEWNHAM
INDUSTRIAL ESTATE, PLYMPTON
   Open: Mon-Fri 8.00 a.m.-5.30 p.m.
   Sat. 8.30 a.m.-12.30 p.m.
H.P.W.WM.D.A.BC.

PLYMOUTH   Tel. (0752) 665363
F.T.B. LAWSON LTD.
71 NEW GEORGE STREET
PLYMOUTH PL1 1RB
   Open: Mon.-Sat. 8.30 a.m.-5.30 p.m.

H.P.W.CS.MF.A.

WEYMOUTH   Tel. (0305) 770303
WEYMOUTH HIRE & SALES LTD.   **K**
5 KENT CLOSE
GRANBY INDUSTRIAL ESTATE
   Open 7.30 a.m. - 5.30 p.m. Mon.-Fri.
   Sat. 8 a.m. - 1 p.m.
H.P.W.WM.D.CS.A.K.

ESSEX

LEIGH ON SEA   Tel. (0702)
MARSHAL & PARSONS LTD.   710404
1111 LONDON ROAD   **EK**

   Open: 8.30 a.m.-5.30 p.m. Mon-Fri
   9.00 a.m.-5.00 p.m. Sat.
H.P.W.WM.D.CS.A.

GLOUCESTER

TEWKESBURY   Tel. (0684)
TEWKESBURY SAW CO. LTD.   293092
TRADING ESTATE, NEWTOWN   **K**

   Open: Mon-Fri 8.00 a.m.-5.00 p.m.
   Saturday 9.30 a.m.-12.00 p.m.
P.W.WM.D.CS.

HAMPSHIRE

ALDERSHOT   **SOUTHAMPTON**
(0252) 334422   (0703) 332288
BIRCH & HILLS POWER TOOL CENTRES
374 HIGH ST.   7 BELVIDERE RD.
Open Mon.-Fri. 8.30-5.30. Sat. 8.30-12.30
   Closed for Lunch 1.00-2.00
H.P.W.WM.D.CS.MF.BC.K.★

HERTFORDSHIRE

WARE   **K★**
HEATH SAWS
6 LEESIDE WORKS
STANSTEAD ABBOTTS (near Ware) HERTS.
SG12 8DL
   Open: Mon.-Fri. 8.30am-5.30pm
   Sat. 8.30am-1pm. Sunday by appointment.
P.W.WM.D.CS.A.

ENFIELD   Tel: 01-363 2935
GILL & HOXBY LTD.
131-137 ST. MARKS ROAD ADJ.
BUSH HILL PARK STATION, EN1 1BA
   Mon.-Sat. 8-5.30
   Early closing Wed. 1 p.m.
H.P.A.MM.MC.T.S.W.

HUMBERSIDE

GRIMSBY   Tel. Grimsby (0472)
   58741 Hull (0482) 26999
J. E. SIDDLE LTD. (Tool Specialists)   **★**
83 VICTORIA STREET
   Open: Mon-Fri 8.30 a.m.-5.30 p.m.
   Sat. 8.30 a.m.-12.45 p.m. & 2 p.m.-5 p.m.
H.P.A.BC.W.WMD.

HULL
HUMBERSIDE FACTORING/H.F.C.
SAW SERVICING LTD.
MAIN STREET
   Open: Mon.-Fri. 8am-5pm.
   Saturday 8am-12.00pm.
H.P.W.WM.D.CS.A.BC.K.

KENT

WYE   Tel. (0233) 813144
KENT POWER TOOLS LTD.
UNIT 1, BRIAR CLOSE
WYE, Nr. ASFORD

H.P.W.WM.D.A.CS.

MAIDSTONE   Tel. (0622) 50177
SOUTH EASTERN SAWS (Ind.) LTD.   **★**
COLDRED ROAD
PARKWOOD INDUSTRIAL ESTATE
   Open: Mon.-Fri. 8.00 a.m.-6.00 p.m.
   Sat. 9.00 a.m.-12.00 a.m.
B.C.W.CS.WM.PH.

KENT

MAIDSTONE
HENSON AND PLATT
TOKE PLACE
LINTON
   Open Mon.-Fri. 8.00 a.m.-5.00 p.m.
   Saturday 8.00 a.m.-1.0p.m.
H.P.W.T.CS.A.

LANCASHIRE

PRESTON   Tel. (0772) 52951
SPEEDWELL TOOL COMPANY   **E★**
62-68 MEADOW STREET PR1 1SU
   Open: Mon.-Fri. 8.30 a.m.-5.30 p.m.
   Sat. 8.30 a.m.-12.30 p.m.
H.P.W.WM.CS.A.MF.BC.

ROCHDALE   Tel. (0706) 342123/
C.S.M. TOOLS   342322
4-6 HEYWOOD ROAD   **E★**
CASTLETON
   Open: Mon-Sat 9.00 a.m.-6.00 p.m.
   Sundays by appointment
W.D.CS.A.BC.

LANCASTER   Tel: (0524) 32886
LILE TOOL SHOP   **K**
43/45 NORTH ROAD
   Open: Monday to Saturday
   9.00 a.m.-5.30 p.m.
   Wed. 9.00 a.m.-12.30 p.m.
H.P.W.D.A.

All shops with an asterisk * have a Mail Order Service

BLACKPOOL   **★**
FLYDE WOODTURNING SUPPLIES
255 CHURCH STREET
BLACKPOOL FY1 4HY
   9.30-5.30 Monday to Saturday
H.P.W.WM.A.MF.C.B.C.D.

LINCOLNSHIRE

LINCOLN   Tel. (0522) 689369
SKELLINGTHORPE SAW SERVICES LTD.
OLD WOOD, SKELLINGTHORPE
   Open: Mon to Fri 8 a.m.-5 p.m.
   Sat 8 a.m.-12 p.m.
H.P.W.WM.D.CS.A.★.BC.
   Access/Barclaycard

LONDON

ACTON   Tel. (01-992) 4835
A. MILLS (ACTON) LTD   **★**
32/36 CHURCHFIELD ROAD W3 6ED
   Open: Mon-Fri 9.00 a.m.-5.00 p.m.
   Saturdays 9.00 am-1.00 p.m.
H.P.W.WM.

LONDON   Tel. 01-723 2295-6-7
LANGHAM TOOLS LIMITED
13 NORFOLK PLACE
LONDON W2 1QJ

LONDON

FULHAM   Tel. (01-385) 5109
I. GRIZZARD LTD.   **E**
84a-b LILLIE ROAD, SW6 1TL
   Open: Mon-Sat 9.00-5.30 p.m.
   Half day Thursday

H.P.A.BC.W.CS.WM.D.

LONDON   Tel. (01-636) 7475
BUCK & RYAN LTD
101 TOTTENHAM COURT ROAD W1P 0DY

   Open: Mon.-Fri. 8.30 a.m.-5.30 p.m.
   Saturday 8.30 a.m.-4.00 p.m.
H.P.W.WM.D.A..

WEMBLEY   Tel. 904-1144
ROBERT SAMUEL LTD.   (904-1147
7, 15 & 16 COURT PARADE   after 4.00)
EAST LANE, N. WEMBLEY   **★**
   Open Mon. 8.45-5.15; Sat. 9-1.00
   Access, Barclaycard, AM Express, & Diners
H.P.W.CS.E.A.D.

HOUNSLOW   Tel. (01-570)
Q.R. TOOLS LTD   2103/5135
251-253 HANWORTH ROAD

   Open: Mon-Fri 8.30 a.m.-5.30 p.m.
   Sat. 9.00 a.m.-1.00 p.m.
P.W.WM.D.CS.A.

MANCHESTER

MANCHESTER   Tel. (061 789)
TIMMS TOOLS   0909
102-104 LIVERPOOL ROAD   **★**
PATRICROFT M30 0WZ
   Weekdays 9.00 a.m.-5.30 p.m.
   Sat. 9.00 a.m.-1.00 p.m.
H.P.A.W.

MERSEYSIDE

LIVERPOOL   Tel. (051-207) 2967
TAYLOR BROS (LIVERPOOL) LTD   **K**
195-199 LONDON ROAD
LIVERPOOL L3 8JG
   Open: Monday to Friday
   8.30 a.m.-5.30 p.m.
H.P.W.WM.D.A.BC.

MIDDLESEX

RUISLIP   Tel. (08956) 74126
ALLMODELS ENGINEERING LTD.   **E★**
91 MANOR WAY

   Open: Mon-Sat 9.00 a.m.-5.30 p.m.
H.P.W.A.D.CS.MF.BC.

NORFOLK

NORWICH   Tel. (0603) 898695
NORFOLK SAW SERVICES
DOG LANE, HORSFORD
   Open: Monday to Friday
   8.00 a.m.-5.00 p.m.
   Saturday 8.00 a.m.-12.00 a.m.
H.P.W.WM.D.CS.A.

You see! They will notice you in 'Woodworker'

shopguide

NORFOLK

KINGS LYNN   Tel. (0553) 2443
WALKER & ANDERSON (Kings Lynn) LTD.
WINDSOR ROAD, KINGS LYNN   **K**
Open: Monday to Saturday
7.45 a.m.-5.30 p.m.
Wednesday 1.00 p.m. Saturday 5.00 p.m.
H.P.W.WM.D.CS.A.

NORWICH   Tel. (0603) 400933
WESTGATES WOODWORKING   Tx
61 HURRICANE WAY,   975412
NORWICH AIRPORT INDUSTRIAL ESTATE
Open: 9.00 a.m.-5.00 p.m. weekdays
9.00 a.m.-12.30 Sat.
P.W.WM.D.BC.   **K**

KING'S LYNN   Tel. (07605) 674
TONY WADDILOVE WOODCRAFT   ★
HILL FARM WORKSHOPS
GT. DUNHAM
(NR. SWAFFHAM)
Tues.-Sat. 9.00am-5.30pm
H.P.W.D.T.MF.A.BC.

NOTTINGHAMSHIRE

NOTTINGHAM   Tel: (0602) 225979
POOLEWOOD   and 227064/5
EQUIPMENT LTD.   (06077) 2421 after hrs
5a HOLLY LANE, CHILLWELL
Open: Mon-Fri 9.00 a.m.-5.30 p.m.
Sat. 9.00 a.m. to 12.30 p.m.
P.W.WM.D.CS.A.BC.

OXON

WITNEY   Tel. (0993) 3885
TARGET TOOLS (SALES,   & 72095 OXON
TARGET TOOLS HIRE & REPAIRS)   ★
SWAIN COURT
STATION INDUSTRIAL ESTATE
Open: Mon.-Sat. 8.00 a.m.-5.00 p.m.
24 hour Answerphone
BC.W.M.A.

SHROPSHIRE

TELFORD   Tel. Telford (0952)
ASLES LTD   48054
VINEYARD ROAD, WELLINGTON   **EK**★

Open: Mon. Fri. 8.30 a.m.-5.30 p.m.
Saturday 8.30 a.m.-4.00 p.m.
H.P.W.WM.D.CS.BC.A.

SOMERSET

TAUNTON   Tel. (0823) 85431
JOHN HALL TOOLS   ★
6 HIGH STREET

Open Monday-Saturday
9.00 a.m.-5.30 p.m.
H.P.W.WM.D.CS.A.

STAFFORDSHIRE

TAMWORTH   Tel: (0827) 56188
MATTHEWS BROTHERS LTD.   ★
KETTLEBROOK ROAD
Open: Mon.-Sat. 8.30-6.00 p.m.
Demonstrations Sunday mornings by
appointment only
H.P.WM.D.T.CS.A.BC.

SUFFOLK

SUFFOLK   Tel: (037983) 8126
LOCKWOOD WOODWORKING MACHINERY
WHITEGATES BUNGALOW
THE COMMON MELLIS
NEAR EYE/DISS IP23
Open standard hours.
Lathe demos every Saturday morning.
Woodcopy lathes / Dust extractors.
H.P.W.D.A.

IPSWICH   Tel. (0473) 40456
FOX WOODWORKING   **KE**★
142-144 BRAMFORD LANE
Open: Tues., Fri., 9.00 a.m.-5.30 p.m.
Sat. 9.00 a.m.-5.00 p.m.

H.P.W.WM.D.A.B.C.

SUSSEX

BOGNOR REGIS   Tel. (0243) 863100
A. OLBY & SON (BOGNOR REGIS) LTD.
"TOOLSHOP," BUILDERS MERCHANT
HAWTHORN ROAD   **K**
Open: Mon-Thurs 8 a.m.-5.15 p.m. Fri.
8 a.m.-8 p.m. Sat 8 a.m.-12.45 p.m.
H.P.W.WM.D.T.C.A.BC.

WORTHING   Tel. (0903) 38739
W. HOSKING LTD (TOOLS &   **KE**★
MACHINERY)
28 PORTLAND RD, BN11 1QN
Open: Mon.-Sat. 8.30 a.m.-5.30 p.m.
Closed Wednesday
H.P.W.WM.D.CS.A.BC.

TYNE & WEAR

NEWCASTLE   Tel. (0632) 320311
HENRY OSBOURNE LTD.   **E**★
50-54 UNION STREET

Open: Mon-Fri 8.30 a.m.-5.00 p.m.

H.P.W.D.CS.MF.A.BC.

NEWCASTLE-UPON-TYNE   ★
J. W. HOYLE LTD
CLARENCE STREET
NEWCASTLE-UPON-TYNE
TYNE & WEAR
NE2 17J
H.P.W.WM.D.CS.A.BC.K.

W. MIDLANDS

WOLVERHAMPTON   Tel. (0902)
MANSAW SERVICES   58759
WARD STREET, HORSELEY FIELDS   **K**★
WOLVERHAMPTON, WEST MIDLANDS
Open Mon.-Fri. 9.00am-5.00pm
Sat. 8am-3pm

H.P.W.WM.A.D.CS.

YORKSHIRE

SHEFFIELD   Tel. (0742) 441012
GREGORY & TAYLOR LTD   **KE**
WORKSOP ROAD
Open: 8.30 a.m.-5.30 p.m.
Monday-Friday
8.30 a.m.-12.30 p.m. Sat.
H.P.W.WM.D.

HARROGATE   Tel. (0423) 66245/
MULTI-TOOLS   55328
158 KINGS ROAD   **K**★

Open: Monday to Saturday
8.30 a.m.-6.00 p.m.
H.P.W.WM.D.A.BC.

YORKSHIRE

HOLME UPON   Tel: 0696 60612
SPALDING MOOR
CRAFT TOOLS AND TACKLE LTD.
HOLME INDUSTRIAL ESTATE
Open: Mon.-Fri. 9.30 am-5.30 pm.
Saturday & Bank Holidays 9.30 am-4.30 pm.
H.P.W.D.T.CS.MF.A.BC.

CLECKHEATON   Tel. (0274)
SKILLED CRAFTS LTD.   872861
34 BRADFORD ROAD   ★

Open: 9.00 a.m.-5.00 p.m. Monday
Saturday Lunch 12.00 a.m.-1.00 p.m.
H.P.A.W.CS.WM.D.

HALIFAX   Tel. (0422) 45919
SMITH'S WOODWORKERS LTD.
GRANTHAM ROAD
HALIFAX HX3 6PL
Manufacturer of Mortices, Tenoners and
Mitre Machines.

THIRSK   Tel. (0845) 22770
THE WOOD SHOP   ★
TRESKE SAWMILLS LTD.
STATION WORKS
Open: Seven days a week 9.00-5.00

T.H.MF.BC.

LEEDS   Tel. (0532) 574736
D. B. KEIGHLEY MACHINERY LTD.
VICKERS PLACE, STANNINGLEY
PUDSEY LS2 86LZ
Mon.-Fri. 9.00 a.m.-5.00 p.m.
Sat. 9.00 a.m.-1.00 p.m.
P.A.W.WM.CS.BC.

HUDDERSFIELD   Tel. (0484)
NEVILLE M. OLDHAM   641219/(0484)
UNIT 1 DALE ST. MILLS   42777
DALE STREET, LONGWOOD   ★
Open: Mon-Fri 8.00 a.m.-5.30 p.m.
Saturday 9.30 a.m.-12.00 p.m.
P.W.WM.D.A.BC.

SCOTLAND

EDINBURGH   Tel. 031-337-5555
THE SAW CENTRE
38 HAYMARKET EH12 5JZ
Mon.-Fri. 8.30 a.m.-5.30 p.m.
SAT. 9.00 a.m.-1.00 p.m.
H.P.W.WM.D.CS.A.

GLASGOW   Tel. 041-429-4444/
THE SAW CENTRE   4374 Telex: 777886
650 EGLINTON STREET   **E**★
GLASGOW G5 9RP
Mon.-Fri. 8.00 a.m.-5.00 p.m.
Sat. 9.00 a.m.-1.00 p.m.
H.P.W.WM.D.CS.A.

SCOTLAND

CULLEN   Tel. (0542) 40563
GRAMPIAN WOODTURNING SUPPLIES AT
BAYVIEW CRAFTS
Open Mon.-Sat. 9.00 a.m.-5.30 p.m. Sunday
10.00 a.m.-5.30 p.m. Open later July/Aug.
Sept. Demonstrations SAT/SUN or by
H.W.D.MF.BC. appointment

PERTH   Tel. (0738) 26173
WILLIAM HUME & CO.   **K**
ST. JOHN'S PLACE
Open: Monday to Saturday
8.00 a.m.-5.30 p.m.
8.00 a.m.-1.00 p.m. Wednesday
H.P.A.BC.W.CS.WM.D.

IRELAND

NEWTOWNARDS   Tel. 0247 819800
NORLYN MACHINERY   or 812506
UNIT 10, MALCOLMSON IND. EST.
80 BANGOR ROAD, CO. DOWN
Open: Mon.-Fri. 9.30am-5.30pm
(Closed 1-2pm for lunch)
Any other time by request.
H.W.WM.D.T.MF.A.   24 Hour Service **K**

WALES

CARMARTHEN   Tel. (0267) 237219
DO-IT-YOURSELF SUPPLY   **K**
BLUE STREET, DYFED
Open: Monday to Saturday
9.00 a.m.-5.30 p.m.
Thursday 9.00 a.m.-5.30 p.m.
H.P.W.WM.D.T.CS.A.BC.

SWANSEA   Tel. (0792) 55680
SWANSEA TIMBER & PLYWOOD CO. LTD.
57-59 OXFORD STREET   ★

Open: Mon to Fri 9.00 a.m.-5.30 p.m.
Sat. 9.00 a.m.-1.00 p.m.
H.P.W.D.T.CS.A.BC.

CARDIFF   Tel. (0222) 595710
DATAPOWER TOOLS LTD,
MICHAELSTON ROAD,
CULVERHOUSE CROSS
Open: Mon.-Fri. 8.00 a.m.-5.00 p.m.
Sat. 9.00 a.m.-1.00 p.m.
H.P.W.WM.D.A.

CARDIFF   Tel. (0222) 396039
JOHN HALL TOOLS LIMITED   ★
ROYAL ARCADE

Open: Monday to Saturday
9.00 a.m.-5.30 p.m.
H.P.W.WM.D.A.BC.

WOOD SUPPLIERS

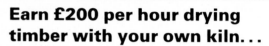

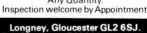

WOOD SUPPLIERS

169

WOOD SUPPLIERS

SEASONED ENGLISH OAK
BEST QUALITY AT SENSIBLE PRICES
Carefully dried to 10-12% moisture by dehumidifying process, then graded. Square and waney edged, any quantity. Craig MacDonald (S.C.O.P.E. Products), Fair Meadow, Upper Farringdon, Alton, Hants. Haslemere (0428) 52751 (office hours) or Tisted (042058) 357 (other times)

H.B. LACEY & SON
Whitemoor Farm, Doddiscombsleigh, Exeter, Devon. Tel: (0647) 52268
Air dried Oak £14 cu.ft. Ash £8 cu.ft. Olive Ash £12 cu.ft. Most stock has been air dried for 2 years.
Cheap delivery and "cut-to-size" service available.

WELSH OAK and ASH
Kiln dried, small — medium quantities. Deliveries arranged.

Valley Timber Company,
Cwm Cych near Newcastle Emlyn, Dyfed. Tel: (023977) 200

HOMEGROWN HARDWOODS
Select your own boards from our workshop in London.
17 species of British hardwoods, kiln dried to 10-12%.
Acacia, Ash, Beech, Cedar of Lebanon, Cherry, Chestnut, Elm, Burr Elm, Lime, Oak, brown Oak, London plane, black Popular, Sycamore, Walnut, Wellingtonia, Yew.
Also some turning stuff in the round.
1-5 Chance Street,
London E1 6JT.
Tel: 01-729 5736

THE WOOD SHOP
Our Cabinetmaker and Woodturners sawmill specialises in **homegrown**, imported and exotic timbers for the small user.
We can **machine** to your cutting list and **deliver** to your home.
Open 7 days a week, 9 to 5.
Send for new brochure to Treske Sawmills, Station Works
Thirsk YO7 4NY
Tel (0845) 22770
Treske Sawmills

REMEMBER!
CRAFTWOODS OF DEVON
Have increased stocks of Tropical and Home grown hardwoods, for Woodturners, Carvers, Cabinet makers, Bobbin and Jewellery makers. Also available, a large selection of Veneers, for Restoration work, and packs for Marquetry.
Please send S.A.E. for catalogue to:
Thatchways, Thurlestone, Kingsbridge,
S. Devon TQ7 3NJ.   Phone 0548 560721

ENGLISH HARDWOODS
Oak, Ash, Sycamore, Beech etc. Air & Kiln dried
All sizes in stock
HOUGHTON TIMBER
HIGHER WALTON TRADING ESTATE
PRESTON, LANCS.
Tel: Preston 323566

Phone Simon Evans on 01-437 0699 for details of our series discount.

Classified Advertisements

WANTED

CAPACITY WANTED

Companies with capacity to manufacture under licence exclusive furniture and upholstery designs of leading interior design studio.

Write giving full details to:
Box WW123A, c/o Argus Specialist Publications, Classified Advertisement Dept., No. 1 Golden Square, London W1R 3AB.

BOOKS wanted on Gothic Woodworker/carving. Mr. Davis (0782) 629555.

URGENTLY required to copy and return, instructions for 2½hp. Stanley router. Postage gladly paid. Humphrey, Tanygraig, Ystrad Meurig, Dyfed. SY25 6AD. 09745 263.

01-437 0699
=
RESULTS

WORKWEAR

WORKWEAR
Smocks to protect clothing in washable polyester/cotton twill. Unisex fitting size range. For leaflet and colour swatch send S.A.E. to:
Geinine Brown (Styled Garments)
8 Belmont Road, Malvern, Worcs.
WR14 1PL.

PYROGRAPHY

PYROGRAPHY MACHINES
Decorates wood, leather & shapes plastic foam. Light, precise pencil, Calibrated heat control.
£41.40 (all inclusive)
SAE for brochure.
The Old Hyde,
Great Yeldham,
Halstead
Essex CO9 4QT
Tel: (0787) 237291

P E T E R C H I L D

DEMONSTRATIONS

INCA
Woodworking Demonstrations
Jan. 29th/30th. Williams Distributors, Peterborough. Tel: 0732 64252
20th/21st Feb. Pollards Woodworking Centre, Bletchley. Tel: 0908 641366.
26th/27th/28th Feb. W.M. Plant of Carlisle. Tel: 0228 36391.
Please phone for confirmation

**Our next copy deadlines are
11th February
April Issue
10th March
May Issue**

Classified Advertisements

FOR SALE

THE FINEST SELECTION ON DISPLAY IN SCOTLAND!
WOODWORKING & METALWORKING MACHINERY POWER TOOLS HAND TOOLS
THE SAW CENTRE

LARGE STOCKS COMPETITIVE PRICES. PHONE AND TRY US NOW!

OPEN Mon - Fri 8am - 5pm Sat 9am - 1pm

Eglinton Toll, Glasgow G5 9RP
Tel: 041-429-4444

38 Haymarket Edinburgh EH12 5J2
Tel: 031-337-5555

WINDSOR CHAIRS
Full size bends. 50 × 1⅜ × 1⅛" in Ash £6.95.
Childs Windsor Chair bends in Ash 36 × 1⅛ × ⅞" £4.95.
All prices include p&p.
Please send cheque/P.O. with order to:
P. Stuffin, Spurn View, North End Road, Tetney, Grimby DN36 5NA.
Tel: (0472) 812576 (Afternoons)

WOODCARVING tools
LARGEST STOCK IN EUROPE
Henry Taylor
Arkansas Bench & Slip Stones
Strops & Strop Paste
Bench Screws, Carvers' Vices

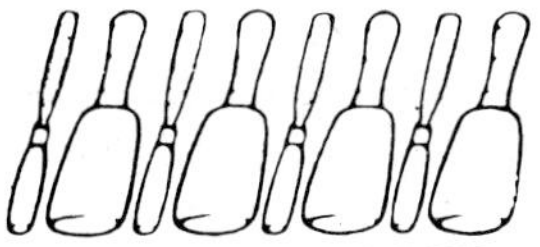

WOODTURNING tools
Complete range of Henry Taylor handled or unhandled

send 40p in stamps for illustrated catalogue
ALEC TIRANTI LTD
70 High St, Theale, Reading, Berks RG75AR
27 Warren Street, London W1.

Quality Movements for Quality Cases
Eight Day Long case clock movements hand made of traditional design and very high quality, suitable for fitting in reproduction clock cases. These should appeal to the craftsman who requires the quality of the original Long Case movements. Dials and hands available made to your requirements. Brassware for clock cases including, capitals, escutcheons, etc. available.

RICHARDS OF BURTON
Woodhouse Clockworks
Swadlincote Road, Woodville
Burton-on-Trent   Tel: (0283) 219155

BLADES
Spindle tooling, circular saw blades, dado sets, planer blades, router cutters and router accessories, machinery of particular merit, Forstener bits, mortise chisels, profile cutter blocks, radial arm saw accessories, etc.
Send £1 (refunded on first order) for your copy of our brochure.
Blades, Dept. WWM. Freepost, Petersfield, Hampshire. GU32 2BR *(no stamp required)*

SHEPPACH HMO Solo single-phase £450. Lathe attachment £143. Rebate block 100mm, 30mm bore £34. Minirad rebate block £55. Adjustable spindle sence £40. All new. Phone 0833 50566 (after 6pm).

WADKIN 14" CIRCULAR SAW with two blades £380 ono. Tel: 0425 53562.

FOR SALE: Woodworking Lathe Union Graduate, excellent condition, fully equipped £690. Tel: day: Swindon 613 642, evening: 826560.

STARTRITE 9" circular saw, almost new £580. Various chucks for Myford ML8 — other Woodworking tools. SAE for details. J. Struthers, 5 Hole Farm Road, Greenock. PA16 9EA.

FOR SALE: One No. 7 Steel Jack Plane £30 ono. Three wooden block planes 17", 8", 7". Good condition. £25. Sedgley 64168.

TEAK SLAB slight split one end. Approx. 9", 51" x 30" x 1½" £35. Phone 0323 870021.

BANKRUPT STOCK
Sandvik circular saw blades tungsten tipped.
5", 5½", 6" .... **£4.00** each
6½", 8¼" .... **£6.00** each
½" to 1⅜" bore any size.
P&P £1 extra per order.
Tel: 643 0244
Hannett, 11 Lind Road, Sutton, Surrey.

THE WHISTON CATALOGUE
Nuts, bolts, screws, washers, bar materials. In brass, alloy, steel, stainless steel, P.T.F.E., nylon, Tufnol, sheet material, electrical and mechanical items. We could go on and on! Better to send for free catalogue No. 114 and see for yourself.
K. R. Whiston Ltd., Dept. WW, New Mills, Stockport, Cheshire. Phone: 0663 42028.

CLOCKMAKERS
Extensive range of very competitively priced German quartz clock movements, (including standard quartz, pendulum, mini-pendulum, chining, striking and insertion movements). Large selection of quality dials, chapter rings, hands, bezels, clock plans and weather instruments.
Please send 25p stamps for 20 page catalogue.
Bath Clock Company (Dept. W), 13 Welton Road, Radstock, Bath.

EUMENIA UNIVERSAL RADIAL ARM SAW hardly used. Still under guarantee £275.00 o.v.n.o. 01-552 3297.

BANDSAW BLADE REPAIR KIT. Repairs blades in minutes £19.50 including blowlamp, £11.50 excluding blowlamp. Includes P&P. Cheques payable to: Charles Hollick Enterprises, Kittisford Glebe, Wellington, Somerset. TA21 0SA. Tel: 0823-672366.

SECOND-HAND Industrial Woodworking Machinery. Woodcutter Services, Stockport. Telephone: 061-432 4294. (After 6.00pm)

MARQUETRY

MARQUETRY stars, shells and fans, made to order inlays for restoration and reproductions. Send design and colour scheme for quote to: S. Rockwood, 13-15 Seel Street, The Courtyard, Liverpool L1 4AU or Telephone 051-708 5200. Send large S.A.E. for details.

GENERAL

HIGH QUALITY SOLID BRASS period cabinet fittings. Including all types of hinges, plate and drop handles, catches, clock ornaments and door and window fittings. All reasonably priced. For further details telephone Keighley 605741.

SHARPENING SERVICES

WHY throw away those expensive router cutters when they can be re-ground correctly at a fraction of new price? Ring Woodcutter Services for details. 061 4324294 (after 6pm).

KITS & HOBBIES

HOBBY'S ANNUAL

£1·10 P&P FREE
FREE PLAN OF TOWN DOLLS HOUSE

Book-binding, pictures from sand, New plans of push along trike, London bus, kitchen furniture and Tiffany clock.
New kits, new plans, Candle making and garden moulds. Dolls house accessories.

HOBBY'S ANNUAL 1987
No 17 188 PAGES Many in colour
Hobby's (Dept. W) Knight's Hill Square, LONDON SE27 0HH   01-761 4244
From WH Smith, Menzies and leading newsagents or direct.

MOTOR POWERED FRETSAW KITS
All Components for Home Construction. Full 12" Throat. Uses Standard Blades. Free sanding hub. **Kit only £30.25** inc. P&P (Standard kit requires 1400-1500rpm motor) Suitable ex-Equipment **Motor — £12-25**
(Kit excluding base mounting board). S.A.E. or Phone 0242 — 62252
KIT PROJECTS
Dept. W, The Workshop, Gt. Washbourne, Nr. Tewkesbury, Glos. GL20 7AR.

GUITAR KITS
For under £35 you can make your own classical guitar with our comprehensive kit. Mahogany veneered back and ribs, solid rosewood fingerboard — a quality product with superb tone. Compares with factory made guitars costing many times this price. For full details write or phone:
The Early Music Shop
28 Sunbridge Rd, Bradford, W. Yorks. BD1 2AE
Tel: 0274 393753

QUARTER SIZE GRANDFATHER CLOCK KIT

Traditionally styled in solid **mahogany** throughout. Deep etched, **solid brass** break arch dial, with tempus fugit. Easily assembled from our complete D-I-Y kit. **Ideal gift** at £19.95 + 2p p&p, or send. Just £2.50 for full scale drawing and all details. (Refundable on first order).
CRAFTWOODS WALES
Gwalia Works, Dulais Road, Portardulais, Swansea SA4 1RH
Wales.   Tel: 0792 884456

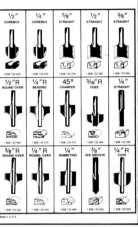

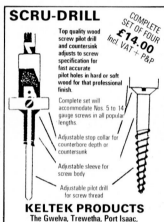

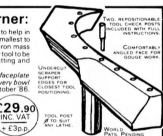

As demonstrated at all leading exhibitions.

LANGARD

ONLY **£14.99**

FLEXI·DISC

SANDER/GRINDER PATENT

You'll be amazed by the performance of this new power drill accessory, due to the flexible drive and slap on, peel off discs.

25th Anniversary Offer **£5 OFF** with this ad.

Flexible/rigid drive. 125mm/5" metal plate. 3 sanding discs. One-year Guarantee.

LANGDON (LONDON) LTD. ICKFORD, BUCKS. HP18 9JJ. Tel: (08447) 337

For a superb finish with a disc sander

Money back if returned in 30 days.

NEW - Extra Long Life disc pack - 2 each coarse, medium, fine, wet/dry .... only £4.50

AN ENTIRE WORKSHOP IN ONE CATALOGUE . . .

WITH THE BIGGEST TOOL MAIL ORDER SPECIALISTS IN THE U.K.

Send 70p for 92 page Tools and Machinery Catalogue No. 12 complete with up to date price list.

J. SIMBLE & SONS

Dept. WW, The Broadway, 76 Queen's Road, Watford, Herts.   Tel: Watford 26052

W. HOSKING

28 Portland Road, Worthing, Sussex

Tel: **0903-38739**

TRY HOSKING FIRST FOR COMPETITIVE PRICES ON

Bosch, Burgess, Coronet, DeWalt, Emco, Elu, Eumenia, Inca, Kity, Naerok, Triton, Tyme, Warco.

+ large range of power tools + hand tools.

 Telephone orders welcome   VISA

WORKBENCHES

Before you buy, you must compare our benches. Heavy, rigid and truly substantial, these benches in solid beech, make many on the market look like toys. See them at the London Woodworker Show in October, or send for details to:
SALISBURY BENCHES
Twmyards, Worth, Wells, Somerset.
Tel: (0749) 72139

MICRO PLANES LTD.

103 LEE MOOR ROAD, STANLEY, WAKEFIELD, W. YORKS. WF3 4EQ.

DIAL YOUR THICKNESS. SET AND FORGET. EASILY FIXED. SIMPLE TO USE, ACCURATE, FROM 1/50 TO ¾".

PRICE **£13.50** P.P. £1.50

FOR FURTHER DETAILS S.A.E. TO ABOVE ADDRESS.

WARNER'S MACHINERY CENTRE

Unit 10, Finedon Road, Irthlingborough, Northants.

Telephone:
0933 651296-316812-651284

For all types of New & Used Woodworking, Engineering and Sheet Metal Machinery. Wadkin, Multico, Startrite, Luna, Myford, DeWalt, Scheppach, Edwards, Colchester, Bridgeport, Black & Decker, Lurem, Ryobi, Trend, Elu, Ridgeway, etc.

Open 6 days a week.
Part Exchange Welcome.

Please write for a free stock list.

415v from 230v house mains to run your 3-phase machines, the 'Maldon' unit **£66** 1½ h.p.

**Maldon Transformers
134 London Road,
Kingston-on-Thames.
Tel: 546-7534**
 Access – Barclaycard VISA

OMAS TOOLING

Once again available in U.K. Enormous range of solid profile and "Tigerhead" cutters. Stack system Tooling for Window and Door manufacture etc. Send now for details and address of your nearest supplier or stockist to:
**WOODFRAME TOOLING (U.K.)
Halls Higher Town, Sampford, Peverell, DEVON EX16 7BP.
Tel: Tiverton (0884) 820340**

SINGLE to 3 phase converters up to 20HP 18 and 21 throat bandsaws. Illustrated details. HAB Engineering Unit 24, 16-20 George St., Balsall Heath, Birmingham B12 9RG. Telephone 021-440-6266.

EBAC TIMBER SEASONERS, Protimeter moisture meters, always good prices and advice from the man who pioneered small scale seasoning. John Arrowsmith, 74a Wilson Street, Darlington, Co. Durham. DL3 6QZ. Tel: 0325 481970.   T/C

ROUTER CUTTERS. Save up to 60%. **LARGE** SAE for lists. MTL, Box 2, Disley, Cheshire. SK12 2NN.

Furniture Restoration Materials

Everything you need to give your furniture that professional restoration look. Waxes, cleaners, french polishes, traditional upholstery supplies and many more items. Send sae for full price list:–
Furniture Restoration Supplies,
42 Acacia Avenue, Hale,
Cheshire WA15 8QY. Tel: 061-928 3903.

FYLDE WOODTURNING SUPPLIES
**255 Church Street,
Blackpool FY1 4HY**

WE STOCK A FULL RANGE OF COMPONENT PARTS FROM WOODTURNING PROJECTS, SORBY TOOLS, LATHE ACCESSORIES, TYME LATHES, SAWTOOTH BITS ETC. CALL ROUND AND SEE OUR DISPLAY IN OUR BASEMENT SHOW ROOM OR S.A.E. FOR PRICE LIST. MAIL ORDER A PLEASURE.

HARRISON GRADUATE and JUBILEE Wood Turning Lathes For Sale

Contact the specialists

**L.R.E. MACHINERY & EQUIPMENT CO.
15 Upwood Road, Lowton,
Warrington WA3 2RL.
Tel: (0942) 728208 day or night**

THE TOOL SHOP, BOSHAM WALK, Bosham, Chichester, Sussex. For collectors and second hand tools. Tel: 0243 572937/572475.

OLD WOODWORKING TOOLS bought, exchanged and sold. Paul Rougetel, 77 Watergate Row, Chester. Tel: 0244 — 318782.

HANDTOOLS & MACHINERY. Antique and modern. Wood and metalworking. Bought and sold. The Tool Box, Craft Centre, Umbourne Bridge, Colyton, Devon. (0297) 52868.

SECONDHAND/TRADITIONAL tools — bought & sold. Norris, Spiers, Preston, Stanley, Record, Addis, etc., and our own. List £1. Bristol design, 14 Perry Road, Bristol. Tel: (0272) 291740.

ANTIQUE and modern woodworking tools bought and sold at Woodworkers World, 77 Shakespear Street, Derby. Tel: Derby (0332) 761779.

FINE COLLECTION Antique Woodworking tools for sale. S.A.E. details: Pollard, 92 Penrhyn Ave., Rhos-on-Sea, Clwyd.

COME INTO OUR WORLD OF VENEERS AND . . .

discover an Aladdin's Cave of over ½ million sq. ft. of selected decorative veneers featuring at least 100 of the world's most prized and exotic species.

The key to the treasure is our fully illustrated veneering Manual and Catalogue.

The Manual is your "Open Sesame" to the master craftsman's methods and know-how whilst the Catalogue reveals an astonishing range of traditional tools and materials side by side with the latest innovations appealing to expert and enthusiast alike.

Fred Large is your guide who, with a lifetime's experience of helping fellow craftsmen, is waiting to share his expertise with you.

Take your first step on this road today by sending for the Manual/Catalogue only £1.30: or Catalogue with Mini Wood collection (three cards containing 45 sample veneers) £4.00

SPECIAL OFFER: Catalogue plus introductory Marquetry Kit (7" x 7" floral plaque) £7.00. All offers include post and packing.

WORLD OF WOOD **The Art Veneers Co. Ltd.,** Dept. W27
Industrial Estate, Mildenhall, Suffolk. IP28 7AY.
Tel: (0638) 712550

OLD FASHIONED GLUE POTS

½ litre size.
Inner pot malleable cast iron.

Price £23.00 p&p £1 (inc. VAT)
Pearl glue or Scotch glue 500g £2.00
1kg £3.75
Pearl glue ½ kilo gross p/p 66p
1 kilo gross p/p £1.41

Crown Craft Products
22 Crown Lane, Four Oaks, Sutton Coldfield, West Midlands B74 4SU
Tel: (021) 308-2780

HAVE YOU

COMPARED OUR PRICES FOR:-

Turning tools, Ceramic Tiles, Eggtimers, Table Lighters, Hourglasses, Barometers, Cheese Blades, Peppermills, Polishes, Waxes, etc. PRICE LIST S.A.E.

COUNTRY CRAFT STUDIO LAWSHALL, BURY ST. EDMUNDS, SUFFOLK.

Tel: (STD 0284) 828661

Give a **'STRIPPED PINE'** look to new pine furniture etc. This remarkable NEW staining DISCOVERY makes "antique-ing" of Pine Furniture and Kitchens easy & quick, just wipe it on — no fear of "tide marks." Makes your work look authentic. Repair old furniture with new wood. Use our special wax for final colour, finish & patina. Prices include P&P. Trade supplied.

	250ml	1 Litre	5 Litres
Stain	£1.85	£4.50	£17.30
Sealant	£1.95	£5.75	£22.90
Old Pine Wax	180g £2.25	450g £4.50	

Complete Starter Kit £6.00.
Orders under £5 add 50p.
THORP & CO.
30 St. Lawrence Lane, Ashburton, Devon.

CLOCKMAKING

Grandfather clocks to kitchen clocks for the widest range of Quartz and Mechanical Movements, Plans, Kits, Dials, Bezels, Brassware, Barometers etc., etc.

SAE for FREE 20 page catalogue to:
Kingswoode Clocks (W4), 14 Riverside, Eynsford, Kent DA4 0AE.

CLOCKMAKERS!!

Yes! Believe it or not. Quartz movements from **£1.59** + VAT. Pendulum, Melody, Striking & Chiming movements Dials — card, metal, brass, ceramics, kits, plans, mechanical movements etc. Send 50p in stamps for brochures. Refundable on order.
To Yorkshire Clock Builders,
300 Attercliffe Common,
Sheffield S9 2BS. Tel: 0742 441022

VENEERS

SHORT AND FULL LEAVES
In all popular timbers. Send S.A.E. for FREE price list or £1 for samples of 12 pieces 4" x 3" to:
ELLIOTT BROS
Four Winds, Moorwoods Lane, Dore
All letters to PO Box No. 6, Glossop, Derby. Reg. No. 2064782

LEATHER TOPS RENEWED

Replace your old damaged tops with a new Leather Skiver, choice of ten colours available in an antique finish with an embossed gold finish patterned border. Send for samples to:
DORN ANTIQUES, Tew Lane, Wooton, Woodstock, Oxon OX7 1HA. (0993) 812023
Send 9 × 4 s.a.e. for samples.

TIMECRAFT

Have you ever thought of building a clock case? A project which will delight the eye for generations. Its easier than you think. Send for our colour catalogue illustrating our complete range of URGOS and HERMLE springwound and weight driven movements, plans, dials, chapter rings and brassware. Send £1 deductible from first order to:

TIMECRAFT, Dept. W, 10 Edinburgh Road, Formby, Liverpool L37 6EP.

MARKING STAMPS — name stamps branding irons supplied to your requirements SAE for details. Davey, 37 Marina Drive, Brixham, Devon TQ5 8BB.
T/C

VENEERS, inlay bandings, stringing and marquetry panels. Largest selection.
Mail order and callers welcome. S.A.E. for details.
R. AARONSON (VENEERS) LTD
45 Redchurch St., London E2.
Tel: 01-739 3107

RUSH good quality flat rush for chair seating. Phone or write for quotation. I & J L Brown Ltd., 58 Commercial Road, Hereford HR1 2BP. Tel: 0432-58895.

CHAIR CANE

Pre-Woven cane
Rush — Fibre Rush
Seagrass — Tools
Books — Advice

SAE for list to:
BERRYCRAFT
Acadia, Swansbrook Lane, Horam,
Heathfield, East Sussex TN21 0LD
Tel: 043 53 2383 (anytime)

ANTIQUE FURNITURE RESTORATION MATERIALS, including veneers, brass, stains, polishes, leathers. Table Desk, leathers by post. All other items personal shoppers only. Weaves and Waxes, 53 Church St., Bloxham, Banbury, Oxon (0295) 721535.

LACE BOBBIN turning blanks. Extensive range of exotics, ivory, lathes, miniature tools, sundries, lace supplies. SAE J. Ford, 5 Squirrels Hollow, Walsall WS7 8YS.

STEPHEN SMITH

Woodturning tools, finishing materials, clock movements, saltmills, peppermills, coffee grinders, barometers, circular tiles & clock faces, cheese domes, sealers & polishes.
MAIL ORDER SERVICE.
We also stock a small selection of English Hardwoods.
Shop Open: 9.30-5.30pm Mon.-Sat.
Stephen Smith, Shipon Turnery, Eccleston Street, Failsworth, Manchester M35 9PP. Tel: 061-682 3613 till 9 p.m. 061-6818671 (Day)

TUDORCRAFT WOODTURNERS SUPPLIES

Junghans clock movements. 20 different hands to choose from. Reverse and chiming clock movements, barometers, weatherstations, jewellery box lids with embroidered inserts. New designs in ceramic tiles and clock faces. Superb new range of copper and brass ware. Bezels, polished, candle lamps and glass shades etc. Please send 50p for new catalogue to:
TUDORCRAFT
49 Moor Hall Drive, Four Oaks, Sutton Coldfield,
West Midlands B75 6LN.
Tel: 021 308 1193

Eric Tomkinson Woodturner

Lathes, Bandsaws, Grinders, Woodturning tools & chucks, screw boxes, peppermills, saltmills, coffee grinders, barometers, lighters, hourglasses, quartz clock movements, circular tiles & clock faces, cheese domes, sealers & polishes, fast and efficient mail order service + competitive prices. S.A.E. for catalogue.
Shop Open: 9-5 Mon.-Sat.
ERIC TOMKINSON, 86 Stockport Road, Cheadle, Cheshire SK8 2AT. Tel: 061-491-1726.

CLOCKMAKING & WOODTURNING SUPPLIES
Junghans quartz movements from £1.78 inc. VAT. Wide selection of hands, barometers, clockfaces, ceramic tiles, polishes, waxes. We aim to provide the best service at the lowest prices. You could save £££'s on your very first order. Send SAE for illustrated catalogue to:
Clock Robin
16 Wimpstone, Stratford-on-Avon, Warks. CV37 8NS

ADVERTISING:
01-437 0699

 Caranda Crafts
Cross Lane, Alkborough, Nr. Scunthorpe, S. Humberside. Tel: (0724) 720614
Shop Open Mondays to Fridays 10 a.m. to 5 p.m. Sundays 2 p.m. to 5 p.m.
Other times by appointment.
Mail Order Service available.
Send Now for our 25 page catalogue (50p + SAE). Fast friendly service; very competitive prices.
We supply a complete range of woodturners supplies including attractive, unusual lamp glasses from £1.80 each inc. VAT. Clock movement, faces, barometer insertions, & lots, lots, more.

NEW! The Carpentry & Joinery Home Study Course

Now at Home in Your Spare Time, you can learn all about carpentry and joinery. Turn an interest into a well-paid profession. Enjoy expert tuition in the comfort of your own home and learn at the pace that suits you. No previous experience needed. ICS has over 90 years experience in home study courses and is the largest Correspondence School in the world.

Find out how we can help you! Simply post or phone today for your **FREE INFORMATION PACK.**

I·C·S INTERNATIONAL CORRESPONDENCE SCHOOLS

NAME: _____

ADDRESS: _____

P. Code _____

DEPT. K1027, 312/314 HIGH ST., SUTTON, SURREY SM1 1PR or phone 01-643 9568 or 041-221 2926 (both 24 hours).

GILDING COURSES

At our workshops in South London. 5 day courses in oil and water gilding.
For details please send SAE to:
**Frances Binnington,
65 St. John's Hill,
London SW11 1SX.
Tel: 01-223-9192**

REG SLACK

Practical Woodturning courses. 1-3 days duration. Max 2 students. Professional tutor backed by 30 years full time experience. Closed Thursday, Friday. Open all other days including Sunday.
For details write or phone.
Saracens Head Coaching House Yard, Brailsford, Derbyshire (0335) 60829. Evenings (0332) 519563.
Also Woodturning Supplies.

WEEK-END COURSES
IN BASIC CABINET MAKING

David Savage FURNITURE MAKER

PLEASE SEND S.A.E. FOR DETAILS TO:
DAVID SAVAGE CABINET MAKING
21 WESTCOMBE, BIDEFORD, DEVON EX39 3JQ

EXPERT TUITION

Peter Hibbard's creative woodcarving, woodturning and sculpture courses.
SAE for brochure.
Old School Arts Workshop, Middleham, Leyburn, North Yorkshire DL8 4QG or Phone: Wensleydale (0969) 23056

NORFOLK WOODTURNING CRAFT CENTRE

One and two day courses in fully equipped workshop by professional instructor.
**Tony Waddilove Woodcraft,
Hill Farm Workshops,
Gt. Dunham, King's Lynn,
Norfolk. Tel: 07605 674.**

Profit from the use of Woodworking Machinery

A ONE DAY 'Wood Machining Course' to arm yourself with the necessary knowledge to enable you to:

- Make the correct choice of machine for YOUR purposes
- Use that particular machine to gain maximum efficiency, safely
- Open up new opportunities for you to profit from a small workshop

IPSWICH	Fox Woodworking	12th Feb. 1987
READING	Sarjents Tool Stores	18th Feb. 1987
CARLISLE	W. M. Plant	25th Feb. 1987
ALDERSHOT	Burch and Hills (Machinery) Ltd.	26th Feb. 1987
WARE	Heath Saw and Cutter Repairs	5th March, 1987
PERTH	Wm. Hume and Co.	26th March, 1987
SOUTHAMPTON	Burch and Hills (Machinery) Ltd.	23rd April, 1987
MIDDLESBROUGH	Cleveland Woodcraft	30th April, 1987

EIGHT VENUES TO CHOOSE FROM
One must be near to you.

 Telephone now for place availability and full timetable.
Rawdon Machine Sales Ltd., 6 Acorn Park, Charlestown, Shipley, West Yorks BD17 7SW.
Telephone 0274 597826

P.S. These are *NOT* exhibitions or demonstrations of a particular manufacturer's machinery, but a general eight-hour 'HANDS ON' instruction course showing the techniques of using machinery. You will find your time well spent.

JOHN GOLDER

Woodturning courses day/evening. Personal tuition with Registered Professional Turner in fully equipped workshop.
**76 Burntwood Road, Norton, Canes, Cannock, Staffs.
Telephone (0543) 79137**
On the register of the Worshipful Company of Turners.
Demonstrator for Liberon Waxes.

Creative Woodcarving

Courses in Cornwall. Beautiful Helford River Area. Experienced Instructor & Craftsman offers short courses ideal for beginners or the more advanced. Tuition limited to three students per course and each receives a detailed 50 page manual.
Details from: Jeremy Williams, Sycamore Cottage, Trabae, St. Martin, Helston, Cornwall TR12 6EA.
Tel: 032-623-609

CRAFT WOODTURNING

A two-day residential woodturning course for beginners in a fully modernised 17th century Devon coaching inn. Teaching limited to two students per course, accommodation for families if required.
S.A.E. for brochure to:
Oliver Plant, Hartford Barton, Gittisham, Honiton, Devon, EX14 0AW or Phone Honiton 44155.

WOODTURNING COURSES

2 Day courses, mid-week or weekend. Expert personal tuition in modern well equipped workshop. Comfortable accommodation available in pleasant surroundings.
SAE for details to
**Cliff Willetts, Gables, Frisby On The Wreake, Melton Mowbray, Leics.
Tel: Rotherby (066 475) 246**

FULL TIME COURSES
IN FINE CABINET MAKING

David Savage FURNITURE MAKER

Two places exist for a one year course, leading to work of exhibition quality

FOR PROSPECTUS APPLY TO:
DAVID SAVAGE CABINET MAKING
21 WESTCOMBE, BIDEFORD, DEVON EX39 3JQ

WOODTURNING IN NORTH WALES

Courses, Beginner/Intermediate, weekdays, weekends • Turning blanks in natural/exotic finishing materials. Tyme lathes & accessories.
Keith Lawrence, Old Stables Turnery, Tri Thy Centre, Coed Talon, Nr. Mold, Clwyd. Tel: 0352 771771.

OULDER HILL COMMUNITY SCHOOL, Hudson's Walk, Rochdale. Starting 5th January, 1987 until March (10 weeks) or Monday 7-9pm. £11.00 or £4.00 (reduced fees) per term. David Milne 0706 353643.

MIDLANDS School of French Polishing 'Learn the Trade'. 4 day, 4 week, long-term courses. SAE to Mr. A. V. Fry, DLC, LCG, MCollP, 18A Mansfield Road, Eastwood, Notts. Tel: (0332) 553505.

ROY SUTTON'S COURSES

Two-day woodmachining and one-day routing or spindle moulding courses. Enjoy a day or two with a craftsman who has had over forty five years experience. Absolute beginners welcome. Special private tuition given on most aspects of machine woodworking. Machines available from Startrite and Multico. Main stockist of Elu machines and Trend cutters, all at competitive prices.
Free tuition given on any machine purchased – we won't let you struggle!
For details send SAE to:
**ROY SUTTON, 14 St Georges Avenue, Herne Bay, Kent CT6 8JU
or Ring (0227) 373297 or (0227) 272136 evenings and weekends.**

WOODTURNING COURSES

One and two day Woodturning Courses in a fully equipped studio, under the expert tuition of:

ALLAN BATTY

Maximum of 2 students
Please write or phone for details.

Allan McNair Woodturning Studio
St. James Sq. Boroughbridge N. Yorks YO5 9AR
Telephone (09012) 4064

MERSEYSIDE'S COMPLETE WORLD OF WOODTURNING

Two day courses by Ray Jones demonstrator of Tyme lathes £25 per day, 3 students or for locals evening tuition 7-10. £3 per hour. Shop open for Tyme lathes and accessories. Sorby tools turning blanks and sundries plus gifts. For details ring 051-420-3379 or write to: **Dept. WW, The Balister, 102 High Street, Wavertree, Liverpool 15.** *Free Saturday tuition with every lathe sold.*

WOODCARVING COURSES IN SOMERSET

Professional tuition in pleasant well-equipped studio, maximum five students, beginners especially welcomed. 6-day, 5-day and week-end courses throughout the year.

SAE: **Zoe Gertner, Dean's Cottage, Bagley, Wedmore. Tel: 0934 712679**

Woodworker

CONTENTS

March 1987
Vol. 91
No. 3

design . . . craft . . . and the love of wood

FEATURES

● **Right**, *A half-finished decoy fascinates a young mind . . . see p248*

REGULARS

On the cover: *Waring Robinson's superb padauk cabinet – full details on p242. Photo Tim Imrie*

PROJECTS

Editor Aidan Walker
Deputy editor John Hemsley
Editorial assistant Kerry Fowler
Advertisement manager Trevor Pryer
Advertisement production Laura Champion
Graphics Jeff Hamblin
Technical illustrator Peter Holland
Guild of Woodworkers John Hemsley, Kerry Fowler

Unfortunately we cannot accept responsibility for loss of or damage to unsolicited material. We reserve the right to refuse or suspend advertisements, and regret we cannot guarantee the bone fides of advertisers.
Published every third Friday

Editorial, advertisements and Guild of Woodworkers
1 Golden Square, London W1R 3AB, telephone 01-437 0626

ABC
UK circulation
Jan-Dec 85
28,051

Back issues and subscriptions Infonet Ltd, 10-13 Times House, 179 Marlowes, Hemel Hempstead, Herts HP1 1BB; telephone Hemel Hempstead (0442) 48434

Subscriptions per year UK £16.90; overseas outside USA (accelerated surface post) £21.00, USA (accelerated surface post) $28, airmail £48

UK trade SM Distribution Ltd, 16-18 Trinity Gardens, London SW9 8DX; telephone 01-274 8611

North American trade Bill Dean Books Ltd, 151-49 7th Avenue, PO Box 69, Whitestone, New York 11357; tel. 1-718-767-6632

Printed by Chase Web, Plymouth
Mono origination Multiform Photosetting Ltd, Cardiff
Colour origination Derek Croxson Ltd, Chesham, Bucks
© Argus Specialist Publications Ltd 1987
ISSN 0043 776X

Argus Specialist Publications Ltd

1 Golden Square, London W1R 3AB; 01-437 0626

This month

Antique restorer Michael Barrington puts the finishing touches to the casing of an 18th century organ in Lulworth Castle chapel, Dorset. 'It is right out of the Chippendale period,' he points out. 'The original workmanship is beyond criticism. From a furniture man's point of view it is perfect.' After making a 1:10 scale drawing and cataloguing all the parts, he started recarving mouldings from old wood in his Warmwell workshops. Michael has had CoSIRA help in setting up.

It's not often we have space to do a 'pre-contents' blurb, telling you a little about what's in your new issue of Britain's quality woodworking journal. But this month we happen to have some things we think it's well worth bringing to your preliminary attention.

First, 'Sit down design' describes in detail some of the **chairs** we looked at the Direct Design Show last November, and explains why the one that won the **Woodworker Award** did so. We asked the orthopaedic physician who did the judging to say his piece, and what he has come up with is a pretty frightening indictment of some ostensibly good-looking design. Uncomfortable reading.

'Who is AWARE?' is one concerned and conscientious woodworker's statement about what he wants to do about the tropical **deforestation** problem; it's a statement from the heart, but we thought we should ask other interested parties their views to go along with it. TRADA expert, Timber Trade Federation representative, and timber importer seemed a good combination; read what they have to say.

Then we have something we've been cooking up for a while, and are very proud to present; as comprehensive a guide to setting up, running and making a success of your own **Woodwork Business** as we can muster. It'll go on for some months, and we'll be looking at many aspects, including marketing, motivation, planning, organisation and methods, design for production; we've got some well-known people lined up to offer their experience, and we think there'll be a lot of help from our pages for the many of you out there who want to make a go of it but are stuck for woodwork-specific business information.

Also, our warm thanks to **Sandvik UK** for sponsoring a monthly prize of £60 worth of tools from their range for the best **Woodworking Wheeze** of the Month. We'll now be printing a range of ingenious hints and tricks that make almost any sort of woodwork easier, quicker, more enjoyable, more efficient and more profitable; the 'Wheeze' page in its new form will be called **'Hands on'**. Naturally, there's a whole lot more . . . hard information, interesting and entertaining reading . . . well, do we cram it in or what?

A million words and 50,000 biographies make up the *Dictionary of English Furniture Makers 1660-1840*. It took 400 volunteers and seven years to compile; few pieces had makers' labels (**above**). Price £100 from Maney, Hudson Rd, Leeds LS9 7DL.

Same place, new name

Contemporary Applied Arts is the new name of the British Crafts Centre in London's Covent Garden; they've changed it for various reasons. 'The word "craft"', they say, 'carries with it a great number of associations, some of which . . . are very unhelpful indeed, and totally inapplicable to the kind of work produced by our membership.' They display work by, among other woodworkers, Jim Partridge, Maria van Kesteren, Richard Raffan, Richard La Trobe Bateman, Erik de Graaff, Guy Taplin — and 'applied artists' in other media. They are also setting up a commissioning service with a slide library and information resource. The exhibition to launch the service finishes on 28 February.
● Contemporary Applied Arts, 43 Earlham St, London WC2H 9LD, 01-836 6993.

Diary

Guild courses are shown by an asterisk (*); for further details see Guild pages.

March
24 **Early Woodwork Techniques** lecture, Victoria & Albert Museum, London
28 **Spindle moulding** Roy Sutton*
28 **Wood machining** Ken Taylor*

April
4 **Hammer veneering** Ian Hosker*
5 **Parquetry** Ian Hosker*
12 **The Importance of the Woodworking Woodland Ancient and Modern** seminar, The Theatre, Bucks College, Newland Pk, Gorelands Lane, Chalfont St Giles, Bucks, (0923) 772755
12-17 **Cabinetmaking** Manchester*
12-17 **Upholstery** Manchester*
12-17 **Modern finishing** Manchester*
26-4 May **London International Furniture Show**, Earls Court, London (26-30 trade only)

May
7-8 **French polishing** Charles Cliffe*
9 **Design and Workshop Drawing** Bob Grant*
10-14 **Interior Context**, Olympia 2, Earls Court, London
26-29 **Countrychairmaking**, Jack Hill*

Shoptalk

A novel device to turn your bench plane into a **precision thicknesser**; designed by a miniaturist, the micro plane will be welcomed by anyone who wants accurately dimensioned timber in small quantities. Skids screw either side of your plane, with micro-adjusters. Price is £13.50+VAT+£1.50 p&p.

● Micro Planes Ltd, 103 Lee Moor Rd, Stanley, Wakefield, W. Yorks WF3 4EQ.

Charles Stirling of Bristol Design, maker of new **planes** in traditional styles, writes to tell us of the detail improvements made since David Savage's 'Tools of the trade' series last June and July. Handles are now fully contoured and shaped on the finished planes; the lever-cap holding screws are now machined flush, the soles are now surface ground to 1/1000in 'or better', and the panel plane soles are even worked on a surface plate and individually hand scraped. Castings, kits and finished tools are all available; finished prices range from £40 for the 3½x1in bullnose to £155 for the 14½x3in panel (jack) plane. You can also get bits and pieces, irons, and even special steel soles.

● Bristol Design, 14 Perry Rd, Bristol BS1 5BG, (0272) 291740.

People got a first look at it at the Woodworker Show in October, but now it's officially launched — the Lurem C268 **universal woodworking machine** (below right) really does look a treat. Three motors, cast and machined (and long) tables, central control panel, and you can get a tenoning attachment. Serious business for around £3000.

● AEG, 217 Bath Rd, Slough, Berks SL1 4AW, (0753) 872101.

If you're serious about **dowelling** — if you buy 8mm dowels by the 1000, that is — you'll be glad to hear your gluing problems could be over, courtesy of Ashwood. The clever people are putting just the right blob of glue in little plastic bullets, which you drop into the hole and then drive the dowel in. Must be used with grooved dowels so the glue travels up; perfect amount every time, no cleaning problems, no mess. Great for the volume manufacturer and even interesting for the smaller workshop at £6.45+VAT per 1000; 8mm only available at present.

● Ashwood Timber and Plastics, Plyfa House, Leven Rd, London E14 0LN, 01-987 6461.

Short **courses** in fine woodworking from Lucinda Leech (*WW*/Feb, Oct '86) at her workshops go from basic joint making to laminating; time is allowed to focus on your own enthusiasms. Three full days £115, next dates 3-5 July; five-day 'summer school' projected for 24-28 August, £175.

● Lucinda Leech, King St, Jericho, Oxford OX2 6DF, (0865) 56376.

Shows and fairs reminders ... **BRISTOL WOODWORKER SHOW**, 15-17 May, the organisers, Wolsey House, Wolsey Rd, Hemel Hempstead HP2 4SS, (0442) 41221; June's **Direct Design Show** selection date is 2 March —01-587 0256; **Chelsea Crafts Fair**, 7-21 October, is now run by the Crafts Council, 12 Waterloo Place, London SW1Y 4AU.

● The Lurem C268 – see above left

A new bench-mounted **fretsaw**, the Bri-Ton BT250 above, uses standard coping or fretsaw blades, tungsten and spiral-tooth. Cuts materials up to 73mm deep at 0-2000 strokes per min. £465+VAT, carriage paid from Bri-Ton.
Wall or ceiling-mounted **extractor** for small workshops left, the Fly costs £178+VAT+ carriage.

● Bri-Ton Tools, 26 The Square, Dobcross, nr Oldham, Lancs OL3 5AA, (04577) 3045.
● Fercell Eng., Unit 60, Swainsland Dve, Crayford Ind Est, Crayford, Kent DA1 4HU, (0322) 53131.

Definitive and comprehensive — that's the new Woodworker Dictionary by our former editor Vic Taylor. £12.95+£1.30 p&p from Argus Books, Wolsey Hse, Wolsey Rd, Hemel Hempstead, Herts HP2 4SS, (0442) 41221.

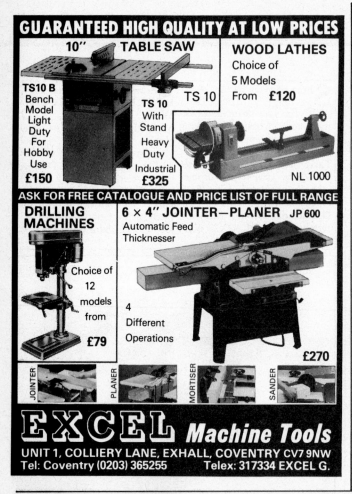

180

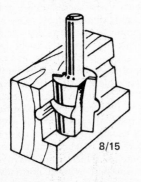 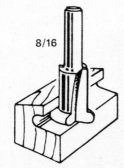

181

The grand furniture saga

Photo courtesy Victoria and Albert Musem

● *Exquisitely carved and engraved, the throne of the 18th-century Chinese Emperor Ch'ien Lung once graced the Summer Palace, Peking. The red lacquer work is superb*

Harmony and balance were overriding themes of Chinese furniture design. Vic Taylor explains why the definitive Chinese style enjoyed a long and happy life

Although the Chinese were renowned for their lacquer work, they had a fine style of furniture which reflected their long-established cultural and social practices. Originally the Chinese used the floor for sitting cross-legged, or reclined leaning on one elbow, and so there was no need for chairs or stools. Floors are not the most hospitable of places to squat or lie on and by the time of the Chinese Chou dynasty (1122-225BC) the *k'ang* had evolved.

This was a kind of raised brick platform built along one side of a room and heated by hot air passing through flues underneath. Here they'd lie on rush mats and chat, drink tea, and conduct their daily business — a definite improvement on damp, draughty floors. By 1000BC wooden *k'angs* had been developed and were often built into the walls; they were massive and heavy, with backs and arms. During the Han dynasty (206BC-AD220) they were supplemented by small tables, and stools for sitting on cross-legged.

The first chairs as such were introduced, probably by Buddhists, towards the end of the dynasty. The seats were higher than modern chairs, and they were meant to be used with foot-stools, indicating that they were reserved for people of high status. Some early examples had box-like frames with arms and back rails arranged in a continuous curve which met the seats; the backs were supported by solid curved splats in the middle. There were other designs which retained the box-like frame and had tall straight backs (reminiscent of the famous Charles Rennie Mackintosh chair). All chair seats were perfectly horizontal, with the backs strictly vertical; the designs were formal and decoration was confined to combinations of differently coloured woods, or low relief carving.

Status chairs were covered with furs or decorative fabrics — the higher the status, the more luxurious the covering. Arm-chairs were greatly outnumbered by chairs without arms, which were judged suitable for men of lower rank, while women were relegated to stools. By the 18th century a combined design of a chair and a small couch called a *hua-li ch'uang* (*hua-li* is a kind of rosewood) had been developed from the earlier *ch'uang* which was the narrow Chinese equivalent of a European settee. It was particularly popular among mandarins and highly-placed officials who regarded it as a sort of throne. And there was even a 'drunken lord's chair' which had an adjustable back and an extending foot-rest!

The Chinese used a variety of tables, but side and dining tables were the most common. It's interesting that Chinese furniture was designed to be arranged at right angles to the walls and not against them or free-standing, as in the West. This was to achieve a symmetrical harmony in both the horizontal and vertical planes; even in large rooms where, at first glance, the grouping appears to be asymmetrical you'll usually find it has a complementary counterpart elsewhere in the room. So the side tables, which were massive, rectangular, and narrow, were normally arranged in pairs to display choice works of art.

There were no dining-rooms as such; tables and chairs were simply set up in any convenient room. The diners served themselves with chopsticks from the food in the centre of the table, so the tables were comparatively small and square, or circular, so that everyone could reach without rising from their seats. The tables were brought in for each meal and removed afterwards, so they had to be of light construction. The *t'iao-an* or altar table was a side table made to venerate the spirits of the dead and was either situated in a place of honour (in the centre of the reception room's rear wall) or in a room set aside for worship. The *k'ang* tables (used alongside the *k'ang*) were light-weight and only 8 or 9ins high — rather like our modern coffee tables. In addition there were tables for special purposes like the 'lute' table which supported a Chinese zither; gaming-tables with recesses for counters, and large, flat writing tables which were also used for painting. Calligraphy and painting were, of course, the two great arts of Chinese culture.

● *More decorative than comfortable, this richly ornamented status chair uses the favourite Chinese motif of clouds for its carved back*

The Chinese bedroom had a box-like bed enclosed by curtains and fitted with a canopy; it was often built over a *k'ang*. By the time of the Ming dynasty (1368-1644) the bed resembled a European bedstead, except that it was fitted with a railing all round, with an opening in the middle of one side. In daytime the bedding quilts were folded away and replaced by a large pad so the bed became a large couch.

The bedroom also contained various wardrobes and chests. There were travelling chests for clothes (*ting kuei*) and larger chests (*t'ang hsiang*) for heavy fur-lined garments. Wardrobes were made in pairs and were comparatively narrow; they had two tiers, the lower being a cupboard and the upper consisting of a pair of *ting kuei* with front-opening doors. Most wardrobes had a unique method of keeping the doors tightly closed and locked — a removable central bar with a loop on each end was slotted into place on the front and the doors closed on to it so that the loops protruded through slots; Chinese-style horizontal padlocks were then inserted through the loops to lock the wardrobe.

Screens were found in any house of importance and varied from the small two-panel design to one containing six, eight, or even twelve panels. The finest are generally reckoned to have been produced in the *K'ang Hsi* period (1662-1722), and were of superb workmanship in lacquer. There were also small table-screens which could be moved from room to room and slotted into heavy bases prepared for them.

There are two distinguishing features of Chinese furniture. One is that they never invented the lathe and so any cylindrical or rounded parts were not turned, but benched by hand. The other is that screws and nails were never used: the components were slotted and fitted to each other by joints, usually mortise-and-tenon and sometimes dovetails, with glue used only sparingly. This method overcame the effects of the high humidity levels by accommodating any swelling or shrinkage of the wood. Hardwoods such as *hua-li* (rosewood), *chi-ch'ih* (ormosia) and *wu-mu* (ebony) were among the most popular timbers — hardwood is actually more resistant to termites.

● An 18th century chu'ang, a combined chair and couch, in hua-li (rosewood) with hua-ma (burr figure) panels

● Chinese eating tables were lightweight, small, and easily transportable; this 18th century example is in the widely used hua-li (rosewood)

Tracing the provenance of Chinese furniture is frustrating in the extreme. The pieces were never signed and many were destroyed during the frequent wars; in any case, furniture making was regarded as a lowly craft and not worthy of special mention. The best sources came from literary references; picture and illustration references are often misleading as it was the practice to depict archaic furniture and not the contemporary styles.

As with most countries, indigenous Chinese furniture had one style for the rich and privileged and another for the working masses. The style adopted for the Imperial Household and the nobility was sumptuous and ornate; furniture for ordinary people was strictly utilitarian but nevertheless elegant in its simplicity. There were cultural influences at work, too; the Confucian upper class liked formal and classical Chinese designs, while the followers of Tao, who believed in the harmony of man and nature, liked a more naturalistic and freer treatment of design. In the warmer south of China, bamboo was widely used and was so popular that any timber which could be painted or made to simulate it was in great demand.

Chinese culture was extremely conservative and by the time of the Tang dynasty (618-906AD) most of the basic designs and styles had appeared, and continued to be used (with minor variations) until the present century. The finest examples were probably made during the late Ming dynasty (1368-1644) and the Ch'ing dynasty (1644-1912).

Not all Chinese furniture was of a high standard (much of the exported production was pretty poor stuff) but the reputation of Chinese lacquer finishing was so high that European furniture was sometimes sent to China just for lacquering. This applied to longcase clocks, too, and the optimism of their owners has to be admired — exposing treasured goods to such a long and dangerous return sea-journey. ■

184

Woodworker
PLANS SERVICE

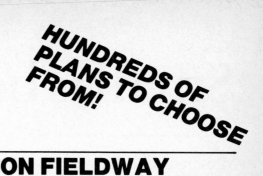

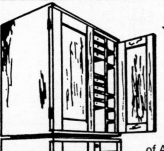

185

Small is beautiful

Miniature but not micro, Robert Cutler's design for a small lathe allows you to turn both very small and 'normal size' pieces

● A little lathe with big ideas; the bell chuck is mounted here, plus the perspex cover

If, like a friend of mine, you are looking for a woodturning lathe suitable for delicate miniature work but which also has enough strength and motor power to handle the odd bowl and, say, 1½in diameter stuff between centres, there are a few possibilities. You have cheap (usually Far Eastern) lathes, small metal-turning lathes, combination machines for around £1000, lathe beds on to which you can fit a power drill, and machines like the medium-sized Picador Pup, about £100 without the motor.

My friend wanted a combination machine, but nothing available suited him or his pocket; he needed disc-sanding and precision sawing (a fine 4in blade) for hardwoods up to ⅜in. I decided to have a go at building the lathe he needed, particularly because I was interested in using an induction motor itself as a headstock. I found an industrial type that runs at 2750rpm (it is sometimes shown as 2800), which is the ideal single speed to cover the range of work we were talking about, and its horsepower range — ¹⁄₁₂ to ⅛ — was also perfectly adequate. (I test this by running the motor and pinching the shaft between finger and thumb of a strongly gloved hand. If you can't stop it the power is fine.)

With this motor as a building starting point, I set to making a machine which would be good for the obsessional miniaturist who likes to do the odd 'normal size' turning. Strength, compactness and portability are all advantages of the design, as I hope you'll agree.

The major expense is, of course, the motor. Once you've got that sorted out, you'll be looking at making the bed and 'bodywork', most of which will be fine in good, stable, straight-grained hardwood. There are parts to be made in metal, of course, which you can either put out, have a go at yourself, or get a metalworking friend involved. If you only want to turn between centres or on a screw-chuck on the headstock, you won't have to deal with much metalwork anyway; if you want to go for the combination version — sander, saw-table and flexible drive — then you need greater precision. I recommend the Picador saw-table, which doubles as a sanding table, and this needs exactly 2½in between the centre of the motor shaft and the top of the lathe bed. With the motor I used — available from the address at the end of the article — this is no problem, because this type has a shaft centre height of 2in over the feet, which gives you room for a ½in base.

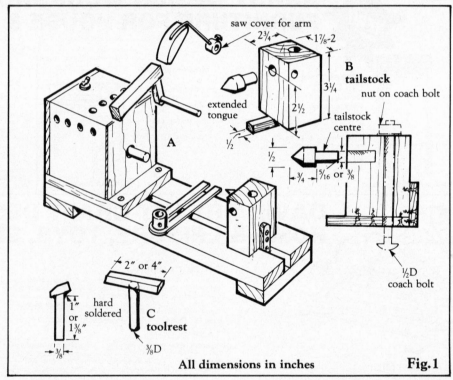

saw cover for arm

B tailstock

nut on coach bolt

extended tongue

tailstock centre

A

½D coach bolt

hard soldered

C toolrest

⅜D

All dimensions in inches   **Fig.1**

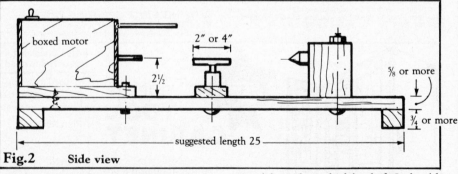

boxed motor

2" or 4"

suggested length 25

Fig.2   Side view

The motor as headstock

By far the most suitable is a capacitor start/capacitor run induction motor, the condenser built in or separate. It should be foot-mounted, with a drive shaft around ⁵⁄₁₆in diameter and not less than ¾in long. The rotation should be anti-clockwise, as viewed from the end of the shaft. It should run at 2750rpm and be rated at between ¹⁄₁₂ and ⅛hp. Height of the shaft above the base should be around 2in. Platform-based models with the motor flexibly mounted aren't really suitable in view of the modifications required. Series wound motors are sometimes available as 'surplus' or secondhand, but these tend to have a high no-load speed, and need a speed controller to bring them into a useful range. What are known as 'shaded pole' motors are not suitable. Good quality motors usually have ball-race bearings, and naturally, as the motor functions as the headstock, the more rugged the construction the better.

The bed

Two lengths of seasoned hardwood, 2in wide and at least ⅝in thick, form the bed. True up one side edge of each, using a plate-glass mirror or straight-edge. Screw end crosspieces, not less than ¾in thick, to the first length, trued side inward, then take a distance piece of ½in diameter rod, tubing or dowel, lay it along the edge of the first length, and offer up the second length firmly, trued side also inward. Glue and clamp it firmly on to the end pieces, remove the spacer rod, and working while the glue is wet, check the gap with a caliper, or better, a 5in length of truly parallel hardwood. It should slide along smoothly without shake. Adjust the gap if you need to, then screw up to the end pieces. Check for warping of the top face, and if necessary rub down (on wide glasspaper pieces taped together perhaps) on any flat surface such as plate glass.

The motor base

This must be of dead flat hardwood (fig. 3), of a thickness that puts the centre of the motor drive shaft not less than 2½in above the bed. Not much more, as at this height the stems of the Picador saw-table and tee-rest can comfortably sit in the boss of the lathe-bed bolting plate. The stem of the saw-table may need cutting down to allow the table to sit down fully to the saw-shaft.

At this stage you have to decide whether to box in the motor. It's purely a matter of choice, but if you do it you can extend the box rearwards to house the condenser, if it's separate, and switchgear. The front end of the box should be thin so as not to reduce the projecting length of the shaft too much. The motor base should extend ¾in beyond the front of the box. Then scribe a longitudinal centre-line top and bottom of the base, with right-angle cross lines on the upper face for the positions of the motor feet. Screw a short round peg the same diameter as the bed gap (½in) on at the underneath front end of the centre-line. Then bolt the motor down along the centre-line of the base, the bolt heads countersunk beneath; a line vertical to the motor end of the shaft (use a try-square) is the front of the box, which should come as near to the motor body as possible to expose the maximum amount of shaft (fig. 3). The boxing can now be completed.

The tailstock

This is a block of hardwood; don't vary it much if at all from the dimensions shown in fig. 1B. It must have a dead flat base and a

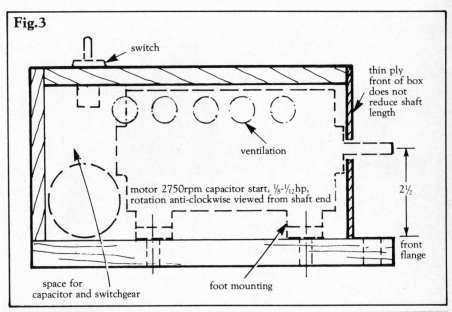

● *A rear view of the motor boxing, with the extension rod for the swing-over saw-cover arm shown in detail*

centre-line scribed all round. Drill a ½in vertical clearance hole right through in the centre of the rear third of its length to house the bed clamping-bolt, which can be a standard ½in coach-bolt. File the square under the head of the bolt for an easy siding fit in the bed gap. Now glue and screw the hardwood tongue (the 5x½in spacer you used to set the bed gap) along the centre-line of the tailstock base, and add a rear short vertical strengthening piece as shown in fig. 1B; a section is cut away to clear the clamp bolt. Make a Jacobs-type chuck fitting for the motor, or failing that, a simple motor-shaft arbor with a projecting drive screw (fig. 8). Assuming you've done the latter, slide it on the motor shaft and position the motor at the end of the bed with its underneath circular peg lying in the gap of the lathe bed. Then offer the tailstock up to the point of the arbor screw, and

clamp it firmly with its coach-bolt. Then, holding the whole motor firmly downwards, slew it round on its peg, scribing an intersecting line on the vertical centre-line of the tailstock. Centre the motor and base, clamp the front projecting ledge of the base firmly to the bed, and drill right through base and bed for ¼in bolts; enlarge *only* the ledge holes to ⁵⁄₁₆in to allow for final adjustments. Coat the motor base and bed with glue, insert the bolts but don't nip them up fully, and check the centring again. Then tighten the bolts hard home, turn the whole thing upside down, and screw a pair of stout woodscrews in at the rear end, giving four-point contact. When the glue has set you'll have an immensely strong structure. The tailstock centre is described later.

If you have already fitted a Jacobs chuck, insert, say, a ¼in drill, bring up the

continued
187

Small is beautiful

● **Above**, *tailstock and tee-rest bolting plate bits and pieces. Note the hardwood guide fixed to the bottom of the tailstock*

Fig.4 Arbor

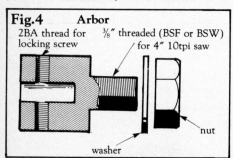

2BA thread for locking screw

⅜" threaded (BSF or BSW) for 4" 10tpi saw

washer

nut

● **Right**, *a Jacobs chuck with adaptor for a parallel shaft, plus a small drive-screw arbor*

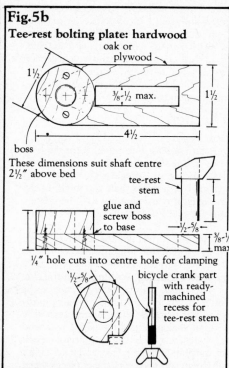

Fig.5b
Tee-rest bolting plate: hardwood

oak or plywood

1½

⅜-½ max.

1½

4½

boss

These dimensions suit shaft centre 2½" above bed

tee-rest stem

1

glue and screw boss to base

½-⅝

⅜-½ max.

¼" hole cuts into centre hole for clamping

½-⅝

bicycle crank part with ready-machined recess for tee-rest stem

---

tailstock, hold it firmly down, and feed it into the drill. This pilot hole can later be enlarged to, say, ⅜in, to a depth just short of the clamping hole. If you don't have a chuck, set the tailstock up in a vice for truly vertical drilling at the scribed intersection; a drill-stand is a great help. Making a drill-chuck fitting is the most demanding part of the metalwork, but apart from using it for the set up, you can put a large woodscrew with the head cut off in it, as a drive screw for heavy work. A fine one, similarly treated, will do for turning delicate sections between centres. Otherwise just make a couple of simple arbors (fig. 8), to carry different-size wood screws.

The tee-rest bolting plate

A Picador tee-rest is suitable, though its ⅜in diameter stem is on the short side. It is 4in long, and you can easily make a shorter one with a longer stem. Best to make a dummy bolting plate in ¼in ply with a section of cotton reel for the boss to the dimensions shown in fig. 5a; then you can determine whether the height of the 'boss' is enough to house the clamping screw for a good grip on the Picador tee-piece stem when the bar is just below centre height. Once you're sure of this, see that it isn't too high to prevent the Picador saw-table, also on a ⅜in stem, from sitting low enough. (This is apart from the need to shorten the saw-table stem itself.) In general, the tee-rest has to be at

centre height or just below, and for turning very thin sections, brought close to the work. The plate itself must therefore be as short as possible, so it can be slewed round without fouling the tailstock base. Make the plate in mild steel plate, slotted for the clamping coach-bolt, bored ⅝in to fit the recessed base of the boss with its ⅜in clearance hole. The diameter of the boss should be ⅜in, plus ½in to give the thickness for the ¼in clamping screws. The boss should be lightly press-fitted and soldered, using blow torch heat.

The bed mounting plate, the tee-rest supporting boss and the tee-rest itself could, of

course, all be made completely in hardwood (fig. 5b), which means the only parts that need to be metal are the arbors and the tailstock centre.

The tailstock centre

Assuming the body of the tailstock has been drilled ⁵⁄₁₆in for the centre, you can use a hexagon head bolt, the head turned down to a conical point; or you can make one with a degree of projection by turning down a ½in section to a thinner stem, which will fit the tailstock (fig. 1B). If you feel like minimising the metalwork, just take a piece of steel rod and grind it conical freehand.

You can try turning something at this stage, with a drive-screw arbor in position and the tailstock centre locked with adhesive or a set-screw. A spot of graphite grease on the tailstock centre is helpful, and allows firm pressure on the workpiece centre when you clamp up the tailstock.

Fig.5a Tee-rest bolting plate: metal

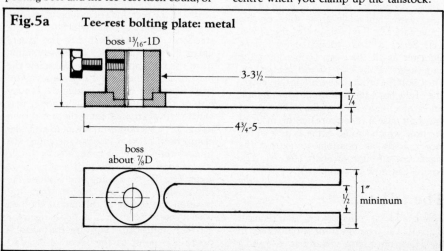

boss ¹³⁄₁₆-1D

1

3-3½

¼

4¾-5

boss about ⅞D

1"
½ minimum

The sander

This can be made of a mild steel disc soldered to a standard arbor (fig. 6); if you use Dural, fix it to the arbor with 'Hyperbond' (Bostik). If you have a Jacobs chuck, fix a stem to the back of the disc and turn that to fit the chuck. The saw-table with its fence removed makes an excellent sanding table, and if you turn the tee-rest bolting plate upside down, so the boss comes downwards, the table can be brought down to centre level.

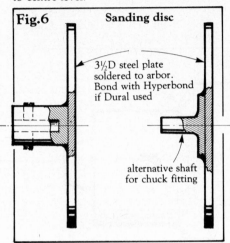

Fig.6   Sanding disc

3½D steel plate soldered to arbor. Bond with Hyperbond if Dural used

alternative shaft for chuck fitting

The saw-table

If you make one, you must have saw protection. A cover is available from Picador, but if the motor is boxed, a ⅜in rod can be screwed to the top at the back and a tilting arm fitted, locked by a binding screw. You can see this arrangement in the photograph below — the cover itself is Perspex. A saw arbor up to 3in long needs no support, but if you make it longer to cut wide material, fix up support from the tailstock to a threaded extension to avoid whip (fig. 7).

Flexible shaft

For convenience, a Jacobs-type chuck will be necessary to accept the drive pin of the shaft. DIY models are quite cheap, though the handpieces are usually clumsy; quality

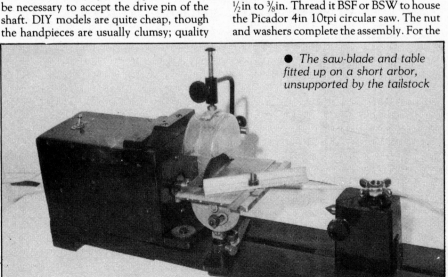

● The saw-blade and table fitted up on a short arbor, unsupported by the tailstock

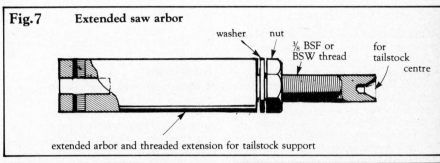

Fig.7   Extended saw arbor

washer   nut   ⅜ BSF or BSW thread   for tailstock centre

extended arbor and threaded extension for tailstock support

● A Picador saw-blade and rip-fence with home-made mitre fence

models like the ones used by dental technicians are also available. They have foutain-pen shaped handpieces, and are essential for fine work (see 'Addresses').

Arbors and fittings

Arbors can be from brass or mild steel round stock; the diameter should be ½in plus the diameter of the motor shaft, to allow ¼in thickness to carry opposing locking grub screws or round-head setscrews. 2BA thread is suitable. If the only material available is smaller diameter, you can solder a brass collar on to give depth for the locking screws.

Circular saw arbor

Drill and ream it and turn down the final ½in to ⅜in. Thread it BSF or BSW to house the Picador 4in 10tpi circular saw. The nut and washers complete the assembly. For the

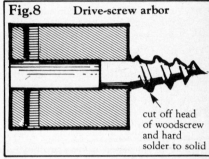

Fig.8   Drive-screw arbor

cut off head of woodscrew and hard solder to solid

tailstock support you will need for cutting wide pieces, extend the turned-down section of the arbor, thread the whole length and countersink the extremity to match the tailstock centre (fig. 7).

Drive-screw arbor

Drill and ream it to fit the shaft, and drill the final solid section to house a woodscrew after you've cut off the head. Best to hard solder the screw (fig. 6).

Bell chuck

2in diameter Dural bar is very suitable; reduce it to the profile shown in fig. 9, set out holes at 90°, and thread them for ¼in studding or set-screws. Slot the studding so you can use a screwdriver on it.

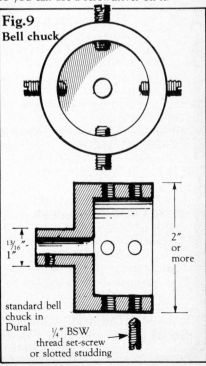

Fig.9 Bell chuck

13/16 1"

2" or more

standard bell chuck in Dural   ¼" BSW thread set-screw or slotted studding

continued

Small is beautiful

Jacobs-type chucks

Adapt these for useful drive-screw arbors, as they will take any size woodscrews with their heads cut off for large or very small work. Capacities of 0-¼in or 0-⅜in are suitable. If you can get a female Morse taper chuck, the arbor (preferably mild steel) can be taper-turned for a wringing fit. Usually only Jacobs-type chucks with a female ⅜in 24tpi thread are available, but you can adapt them without threading (fig. 10). Drill and ream an arbor and reduce all but the first quarter to around ⅜in diameter. Cross-drill and fit locking screws to the unreduced part. Chuck a short length of mild steel rod, and reduce it to fit the reamed arbor; slide the latter on and lock it up, then continue the reduction until the threaded chuck *just* slides on and butts firmly against the shouldered end of the arbor, where it will run truly. Remove the assembly carefully from the lathe and soft-solder the steel back of the chuck to the shoulder of the arbor, using a small blowtorch to heat the arbor from underneath. Use an acid flux, and clean and oil it afterwards. Brass is desirable for this arbor, for ease of soldering and turning to fine limits.

Tee-rest

A pair is best, with cross-pieces 2in and 4in wide. The Picador model is 4in, with a short 1in stem. The item is easily made from ⅜in rod, ⅜in long, with a ½x³⁄₁₆in cross-piece hard-soldered at a slight angle and bevelled in front (fig. 1C). ∎

Addresses

● Remember this design is based on a motor as headstock; general dimensions can be altered, but the ones given allow fittings of the Picador tee-rest and saw-table. The best source for motors conforming to this design is:

F. Smith, 26 Victoria Rd, Pinxton, Nottingham. Other possibilities:

Batwin Electric Motors, 331 Sandycombe Rd, Richmond, Surrey

Beatson Electric Motors, 17-21 Mowbray St, Sheffield

The Fan and Motor Centre, 65 Sidney St, London E1

Harrisons Electrical, 17 Chigwell Rd, S. Woodford, London E18

K. R. Whiston, New Mills, Stockport, Cheshire

Other sources

Picador Engineering Co., Unit 8, Leeway Court, Leeway Ind. Est., Gwent

Flexible drives: FCA Products, First Floor, Unit 7, 1-7 Corsica St, London N5 1JD

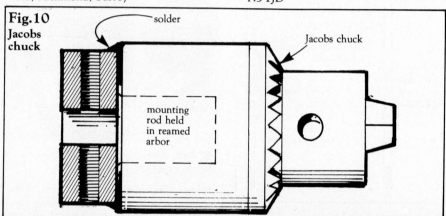

Fig. 10 Jacobs chuck

solder

Jacobs chuck

mounting rod held in reamed arbor

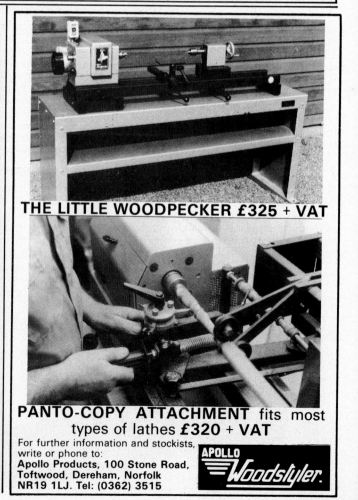

Sit-down design

Last November's Direct Design Show, a sales-and-display extravaganza for more than 100 designer makers in a multitude of media, was another move in establishing the breed and putting its products before the buying public. *Woodworker* sponsored an award for the most comfortable non-upholstered chair of the Show; here's the winner and the judges' comments, plus a few notes

Naturally, we were interested most in the furniture at the Direct Design Show in Kensington Town Hall last November, and more specifically the chairs. Many of the designer makers were already familiar to us — Rebecca Myram and Andrew Whateley's innovative steam-bent chairs have had a good deal of publicity recently (though perhaps not all they deserve), while Timothy Freeman's 'Shogun' table found its way into our September '86 College show report. Ex-Parnham Timothy was finding business slow, and toying with the idea of going to Milan next year . . . we hope he comes back.

Daniel Reynolds was there, with his rough-hewn and bean-decorated (yes, beans) cabinet that caused former *WW* editor Peter Collenette a fit of apoplexy in print in our November '85 issue ('Nothing to show'). Perhaps the fact that the said cabinet is still being touted round indicates it hasn't been sold yet. *WW*'s current position on outrageous student experimentation is that there's definitely a place for it — when can you go wild if not then, after all? — but surely Daniel could have applied some of his obviously abundant energy to making the drawers work properly.

In ceramic and textile design, well represented at the Show, there are less exacting functional requirements than in furniture. Sure, it's no good if your teapot lid falls off every time you pour a cuppa, and 'experimental' shapes can be the devil to clean; the former is hardly excusable, but people will put up with the latter. But furniture really needs to work.

Or does it? Charles Rennie Mackintosh's chairs and many seminal Bauhaus pieces are notoriously uncomfortable, anatomical disasters — yet they're classics of design. When it comes down to it, an enormous amount of very common production furniture is uncomfortable to the point of actual harm. We're just used to it, that's all. Furniture as art is OK as long as you don't have to sit on it. Distinguishable current themes popular with young furniture designer makers hark very closely — slavishly, even — back to Mackintosh and Bauhaus, with a bit of Oriental lip-service paid along the way; nothing new under the sun, perhaps, however hard you try.

But with all this effort and attention paid to the visuals, it's still more astonishing to find people who've only recently finished a training in furniture design going all out for appearance and producing, in some cases, chairs that are literally a pain to sit on. It's enlightening to examine such work in the company of a specialist like Dr Bernard

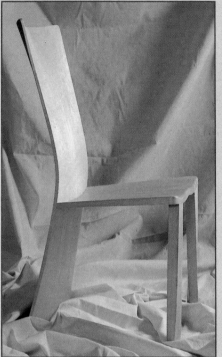

● **Above left**, Andrew Whateley's graceful and innovative double-steam bent ash chair, and **right**, Carl Allen's laminated ash and wicker runner-up. **Below left**, Rebecca Myram's oak design is also double-steam bent – Andrew's chair is a development of this. **Below right**, Timothy Freeman's chair in maple looks unusual but does the sitter no favours

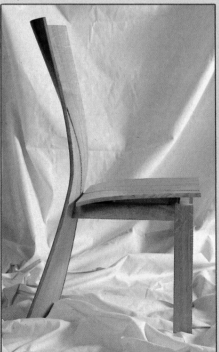
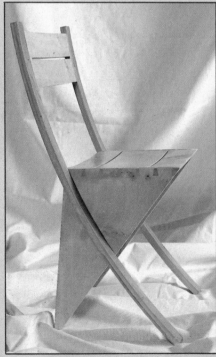

continued

Sit-down design

Watkin, Harley St orthopaedic physician and seating research consultant to the civil aircraft industry and military and earth-moving vehicle manufacturers. (Comfortable foam is a fire hazard; the airline seats of tomorrow will be lined with about ¼in of foam and still be comfortable on a 14-hour flight.) He didn't look at the aesthetics of the chairs at all; was it comfortable, was it sittable? Was it a 30-second chair, was it a 3-minute chair?

Coming from the world of design and make, of course, we couldn't but look at the looks and construction of the chairs as well as what they did to our sit-upons. Kodama's knock-down laminated ply design was striking but possibly short-lived in fashion terms, and it definitely hurt to sit on. Designer Zyg Staniaszek (a computer science graduate who has learnt his design skills 'as he has gone along') explained it was actually conceived with a cushion seat, but they put a non-upholstered one together for entry into the award. Not wise, perhaps. Adaptation of the sprung backrest piece, which sticks into the wrong bit of your back, is already under way.

Timothy Freeman's slab-sided and laminated maple chair is well balanced and neat to look at, and superbly made, but, alas, Dr Watkin didn't need to spend more than about 30 seconds on its 'anatomics'. The position of the backrest is crucial . . . surely you can get it to look right and still be comfortable? There was a hint of desperation about some of the designers' in-

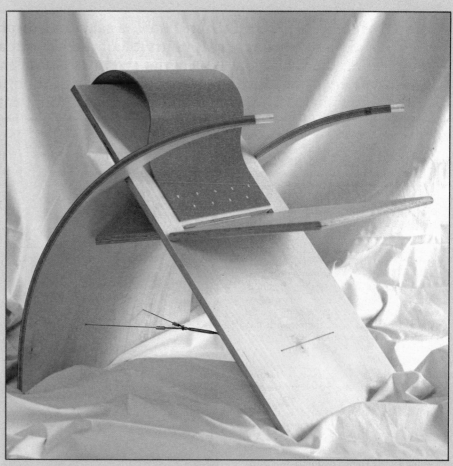

sistence that their pieces were comfortable; self-persuasion born of that unfortunate familiarity with the less-than-acceptable norm.

Which is why both WW and Dr Watkin really had eyes only for 19-year old Rycotewood student Carl Allen's laminated ash and wicker design, and the fascinating steam-bent pieces of Rebecca Myram and Andrew Whateley. Carl's we felt, worked quite well anatomically for the sitter, although the lower back rail should have been yet lower; of Rebecca and Andrew's pieces, Andrew's was more comfortable and quite a lot tidier to look at. (It is both visually and technically a development of Rebecca's.) Dr Watkin thought the inward curve at the top of the back should have been at the bottom, in the lumbar area, whereas at the moment the shoulders are hunched round; but he wasn't looking at the extraordinary technical achievement — steam bending in double curvature on a single (jointed) wide board. Both chairs are pretty and beautifully made; Andy's is lighter in line (no underframe), a visual whole and represents an exciting development in the use of materials. A worthy winner indeed.

● **Above**, *Zyg Staniaszek of Kodama produced this knock-down idea; would the shape work if it was actually comfortable?* **Left**, *Tom Fisher's ply and solid prototype also put the lumbar support where the lumbar ain't*

An important point — a slippery seat isn't comfortable. If it's to be non-upholstered, don't lovingly lacquer and steel wool your chair seat to a minimum co-efficient of friction, or your unfortunate sitter will be constantly slumping down, sitting up, bracing his or her legs to stay upright, and cursing you, the chair maker.

The orthopaedic physician's view — Dr Bernard Watkin

I was particularly pleased to be asked to judge the exhibition for the *Woodworker* most comfortable non-upholstered chair award, because of my own background in research into unpadded and foam-reduced seating for civil aircraft and military vehicles, where padding, especially foam, is now thought to be a disadvantage in safety terms.

It's worth noting backache is now considered to be a sedentary disease. Recent work shows that pressure in the discs of the spine is least in lying down, increases in standing, and is at its greatest in the sitting position — hence the need for correct design.

My judging criteria were founded on anatomically correct shaping. Good lumbar support with proper follow-through into the chest region, putting the spine into its natural S-shape — where stresses are least when sitting; plus how was the pressure distributed on the seat pan or bottom? Was

it correctly shaped to follow the human femur?

I found only two chairs could be considered to have any anatomical shape and a degree of comfort. The remainder I found hard and uncomfortable; they did not use the constructional material to advantage, being more concerned with appearance, and ignored the fundamentals of sitting down. One chair even reminded me of the Ashley-Cooper Victorian child's 'correction chair', famously uncomfortable. The chair which came second (Carl Allen's from Rycotewood) was perhaps the more comfortable of the two, considered just on the strength of the first sitting down; it had reasonable lumbar support and paid some lip service to chest shape. The bottom was shaped moderately like a human femur. But I felt there was little or no room for development in the design, and the winning chair (Andrew Whateley's) had made some attempt to use the shaping of the wood anatomically — although the particular shapes chosen require a lot of improvement.

The chair designer does have a duty to the sitter in terms of both long- and short-term comfort, and a study of simple anatomy and the basic principles of seating would pay dividends.

From a personal point of view, I did a review of chairs at the Victoria & Albert Museum for BBC TV's 'Horizon' some years ago; and concluded that the most comfortable chair was in fact the most aesthetically pleasing. Perhaps there's a double lesson to be learned. . . . ∎

● *Much more restrained; Nick Dyson looks towards the classical with a library study chair and a display dresser*

● *Far cry from chairs . . . Nick Allen of Inventive Design (WW/May '86) is still inventively designing marquetry extravaganza tables, among other things . . .*

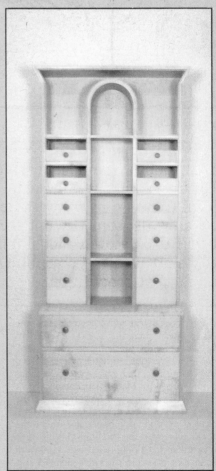

Who is AWARE?

● Are we really out on a limb?

Last month Lucinda Leech described her journey in Brazil, looking at unfamiliar timbers and gauging the local response to deforestation issues.
Meanwhile, someone out there was also thinking hard. Chris Cox, a professional joiner and cabinetmaker, explains his own perception of the problems and makes a practical proposition

About a year ago, I started to become aware that the world's rainforests were disappearing at an alarming rate. The various statistics were indeed frightening . . . 1.3 acres per second has been quoted. My information pack explained the supreme importance of the forest to the Earth's climatic system; soaking up and recycling water under the sun's heat, turning carbon dioxide into oxygen and helping maintain optimum balance of gasses in the air, which sustains all life forms. These alone seemed pretty

good reasons for looking after and maintaining the rainforest. It became obvious to me it was performing a vital function for the whole world — apart from the importance of its unique plant and animal life.

And yet, it seemed, this vital global resource is being chopped away, burned down, sold off, for short-term profit and short-term solutions to long-term problems. The human race has done some daft things in its time, but this seemed to me to be one of the daftest; one our descendants would be least likely to thank us for,

particularly if they knew we knew what was happening and what were the likely consequences.

I gathered that only a small percentage of the forest loss could be directly attributed to the logging operations of the timber companies. A much greater part results from a misguided attempt to open up more land for exploding local populations — misguided because the land works only as a forest. As Lucinda Leech said last month ('Amazon question'), the soil and the trees operate together as a single unit. Take away the trees, and the thin topsoil washes away in the rain that the trees would otherwise have soaked up and recycled. In a couple of years the land is a useless desert. The policy (or lack of it) is doubly misguided because with proper sustainable management the whole forest eco-system could provide many times more useful biomass to sustain a human population than cleared land on its own.

As I read all this from armchair safety in the UK, what was wrong seemed to me desperately obvious. But it was also clear that the main thrust of change had to take

Illustration Maggie Ling

place in the national policies of the countries where rainforest exists. As a UK resident, I could hardly hope to influence politics in Brazil or Indonesia.

My immediate response to all this information was akin to that of a meat eater who is shown a film of an abattoir in action and becomes a vegetarian overnight. Suddenly the thought of proceeding with those solid mahogany bookshelves just wasn't on. I could not be aware of and bemoan the erosion of the rainforest, and simultaneously make use of the product of that forest for my own profit, knowing its method of production had destroyed a part — however small — of that same forest.

To begin with, a personal boycott of all

My dilemma as an individual joiner was acute and uncomfortable . . .

tropical rainforest hardwoods seemed the only consistent response, and I decided to take that step. But I'm a practising joiner, and this decision immediately caused problems and raised a number of secondary questions.

- European and North American hardwoods are comparatively expensive and not always appropriate.
- If everybody switched overnight from using mahogany and parana pine to beech and oak for joinery, who would be able to satisfy the sudden surge in demand for these timbers?
- Are those timbers sustainably produced anyway? Do we know where they come from and under what circumstances?

It rapidly became clear there wouldn't be a temperate hardwood tree left standing in Europe if a total tropical timber boycott were to take effect. And that day would come a great deal sooner than the day the last of the rainforest was cut down, even without the contribution of the timber importers.

My dilemma as an individual joiner was acute and uncomfortable. After a lot of thought and discussion with like-minded friends a way out began to emerge. In the end it seemed to come down to adopting a 'holistic' approach; the argument runs something like this.

Timber is one of the planet's great **potentially renewable** treasures, both for energy and as a material. Oil, coal, gas and most metals will eventually run out. The energy for tree production comes from the sun. So long as the greater part of the wood we take from trees is burned and released back into the air (at the moment this is so and will be for the foreseeable future — most wood products, globally speaking, are for cooking and firewood), the carbon cycle can theoretically continue indefinitely. The same cannot be said, even theoretically, for oil, gas, coal and metals. Thus timber as a global resource assumes a massive importance; the link between the

inexhaustible energy of the sun and our insatiable appetite for energy and materials on earth.

The way forward becomes clear. We bear a global responsibility to make sure that the conditions for that renewability are observed, protected and enforced, by whatever means at our disposal. To do anything else is in the long term and maybe even in the medium term is to commit global suicide. Any action, however small, which conspires even accidentally to hinder that renewability is effectively aiding and abetting that suicide. To be ignorant of the law is no defence in law, and we cannot allow it to be a defence in this case also. This may seem like strong stuff, but I believe it's nothing less than the truth.

The key word is **sustainability**. We have to plant at least as much as we cut down, preferably more to make up the deficit. We have to think in terms of harvesting rather than mining timber. We harvest grain and fruit, we don't mine them.

When global ecology is added as a 'factor' in the trade equation — the old principles of a free market economy and unrestricted trade based solely on principles of demand and the ability to supply — that equation begins to break down. Until now we have been able to get away with not taking the the ecology factor into account in the course of our economic activity. The earth has been sufficiently forgiving to absorb the damage; but those days are now over. The global ecology factor is going to have to be taken into account in nearly every sphere of economic life from now on, and a lot of cosy and established ideas are going to have to change. Cutting down and not replacing trees is the one that concerns us here, but the same principles apply to other industrial/economic/ecological issues. In many cases the argument for doing nothing about the problem is that action is too expensive and would put up the cost of the product concerned. But add the global ecology factor, and you see that to do nothing about it now is in the long term the most expensive option of all. We are all part of and contribute to the system whether we like it or not.

The global ecology factor has to be taken into account in economic life

So what can the individual do about it, the small joiner, the woodworker at home, the customer in the High Street buying a mahogany sideboard or coffee table? The consumer on his/her own can do little, but thousands of consumers exercising choice have an awesome power. We in the trade have to begin to exercise that choice. If the choice isn't there yet, we have to demand it.

I see pages of advertisements for timber from suppliers in the back pages of this

magazine. There is not one that makes a virtue of the fact that the timber sold comes from a sustainable source. This is probably because:

- They don't know whether it does or not
- They do know — and it doesn't
- They don't care about whether it does or not
- They've never thought about it, because no one ever asked them:
 Or a combination of all four.

Action?

What I believe we have to do is to start asking questions of our suppliers, start creating a demand for timber from sustainable supplies. The chances are your supplier doesn't know. You should suggest they should make it their business to know. We need to know under what circumstances our timber was produced in the same way we want to know its quality, colour and price. If we can create a market

To do nothing now is the most expensive option in the long run . . .

niche, sales will eventually fill it. If there are enough customers out there who want to buy mahogany from a sustainable source, but don't want it otherwise, eventually this will filter back up through the industry to the people who *can* do something about it. It worked for real ale, it worked for real bread. It worked for people who wanted to know what the food they bought in packets consisted of. I'm sure it will eventually work for sustainably harvested timber. One thing is certain: it won't work unless we ask for it. And not to ask fo it is to have a hand, albeit indirect but a hand nevertheless, in the global suicide.

In the meantime, to help things along a bit I propose that we in the trade should operate a temporary boycott or at least a severe cutback in our tropical timber usage, to show we are serious about this. Always remembering to *explain*, trying to convince the sceptics and being positive on behalf of the *future* of the industry.

Remember, it's not the hardwoods themselves we object to, only the non-sustainability of the operation. It will require a little courage at first. Your customers will think you're crazy to turn down business and will go to your competitor up the road. But if he or she turns them down as well . . .

I propose an 'in-house' ('in-trade'?) pressure group, called **AWARE** (Association of Woodusers Against Rainforest Exploitation). Come out into the open and declare your support and concern. Add the logo to your business letters and cards to show whose side you're on. Maybe this way we can begin to get something done! ∎

- If you want to know more, write to **AWARE**, PO Box 92, London N5 2JJ.

continued

Reactions

Here's how the timber industry reacted to Chris Cox's proposition. You can also read a synopsis of a comprehensive report from TRADA on the threat to tropical forests

Forest industry expert

Dr Peter Hansom
Forest Industries Consultant, Timber Research and Development Association

Thank you for the opportunity to comment on Chris Cox's article. I support his targeting of sustainable yield as a principle, but take issue with him on the practical effect of his proposed action.

I am one among very many people who have contributed to the responsible development of the tropical forest industry and the marketing of its products, sponsored by FAO, UNIDO, Commonwealth Secretariat and the like, for the social and economic benefit of Third World peoples. I regret anything that puts the results of this work at risk.

Certainly the irresponsible use of resources puts them at risk, but so to my mind would sanctions based on criteria that cannot possibly be determined fairly or applied effectively, except through some international body that can take account of the overall problems of the forest, fuel wood, agriculture and the socio-economics of forest industries. If this organisation should by any chance be ITTO then let's work strongly through them with sustainability as a key issue. Put the pressure on them if you like, but don't put at risk individual forest industries, their workers and the benefits of foreign exchange from exports, on the basis of criteria we in the UK couldn't possibly know how to apply fairly or effectively.

The UK has a good record of importing forest products rather than raw materials, and our 1¾% share of world trade in tropical logs and wood products provides much greater socio-economic benefit than the global average. We have a 6% share of trade in products but only 0.5% of trade in logs. Sanctions against UK imports could be very damaging to individual countries. I believe we should be supporting trade in forest products because the responsible care of the forest in tropical countries is more likely where there is prosperous local industry with its investment and future to be protected. Harming an industry because its current resource base may arguably be unsustainable could easily be self-defeating in any terms as slash-and-burn takes over more easily.

The trade federation

Chris Holmes-Smith
Hardwood executive, Timber Trade Federation

I can only wonder what effect Mr Cox's proposed 'pressure group' would have in reducing that most alarmist statistic of 1.3 acres per second with which he excites the reader at the very beginning of his article. I would suggest no effect at all in any area of the producing countries where the problem lies. However, I can see a considerable effect on life in this country. There would be redundancies in the docks, in road haulage and in the manufacturing side of the timber trade and its customers and I suspect that Mr Cox himself would be unemployed before long.

This is equally emotional supposition and to be practical let us understand what he is going to ask his suppliers — 'Does this timber come from a sustainable source?' The only possible answer he can receive is 'Yes'. All forests are sustainable if all the people and all the governments in these countries so wish; and they are more likely to so wish if the forests have an increasing value. If the world stopped using tropical timber the forest product value would be

More positive thinking and less hysterics saves timber . . .

negligible and even less care would be taken by the fast-increasing populations of South-East Asia, South America and Africa. (Brazil's 140 million will increase to 280 million by 2050.) The forest would just go quicker.

How then can a specialist joiner and cabinetmaker do something really positive rather than merely negative and passive?

I suspect that the writer selects his mahogany to make his bookshelves by picking over a stack of timber to choose the pieces which in his opinion are perfect — no knots, no pin holes and no colour variation. And in crafting the bookshelves, he thought that he had been very clever. However, he was just adding to his own frightening statistic because in order to

meet his demanding standards of perfection still further areas of forest will have to be worked to keep to that standard. Trees are natural products and all are different. The beauty of wood is in these differences and not in its monotony like plastic. So why, I must ask Mr Cox, doesn't the manufacturing side of the trade accept timber as it comes instead of demanding only the best 20% of any tree? The importer must buy what he can sell and currently that is a minute proportion of a very small number of species. Greater skills in using timber and greater use of available species would add value to the forest — and protect it. If Mr Cox as a user of tropical hardwoods asked more positive questions of suppliers in the utilisation of 'Standard' and 'Better' grades or even 'Select' and 'Better PHND' (Pin Holes No Defect), he would already be making a most positive contribution to solving the overall problem.

The use of lesser-known species that grow in the forest which is already being worked gives a greater yield per acre. This means fewer acres cut and gives value to other areas that would otherwise just be burnt because the timber has no value. More positive thinking and less hysterics saves timber.

Another thought comes to mind concerning the status of the UK in the market. Recently the International Tropical Timber Organisation came into being and the trade believes this organisation to be very capable of persuading the tropical countries to take more account of their actions for the long term. Now the voting in ITTO is based on involvement in the trade; any reduction in imports by the UK would reduce voting power. Already one third of the votes go to Japan on the consuming side, as they import over 50% of all tropical timber traded internationally. Any reduction in UK trade volume would weaken this country's voice and forest destruction would continue.

The answer for Mr Cox the craftsman would be to improve his skills to reduce the wastage of timber by upgrading the timber he employs and by being more adventurous. Try new species and the volume of timber used in the UK may increase but the forest area worked will be much reduced and the UK will have a more powerful voice to solve the real problems.

However, the problem may already be overtaken for it must be realised that only 8% of all tropical timber felled is exported out of producing countries. Of that total only 1.4% comes to the UK. It is in local use and sovereign employment of space that the damage is done. After all, who told Britain not to destroy its own forests when stripping these islands of every suitable tree to build ships for the Napoleonic War and to make charcoal for gunpowder? All we can do is to persuade, to influence, to help and to guide. To do this we must be a customer of the tropical forests — not a 'late' customer as Mr Cox promulgates.

Timber importer

Dan Kemp
Director,
Timbmet Ltd, Oxford

The signatories to the International Tropical Timber Agreement agreed to co-operate in all aspects of the tropical timber economy about two years ago. As the International Tropical Timber Organisation, they are now getting down to the real work.

The forestry contractors, sawmillers and other wood processing and ancillary industries employ very large numbers of people who would otherwise be unemployed, especially in the Philippines, Indonesia and parts of Brazil.

The most important tropical deforestation is caused not by exploitative timber importers in the western world, but by:
● Governments capitalising on natural resources to finance politically attractive developments, such as prestige airports or hospitals lined with marble and filled with sophisticated medical equipment which local personnel are untrained to use.
● Governments moving populations to sensitive political borders, establishing villages and allocating forest lands for farming at their boundaries.
● Farmers moving in after roads have been built for timber extraction, instead of leaving smaller trees for natural regeneration, complete the deforestation. Over 90% of the timber felled worldwide is used for fuel. It is therefore of paramount importance to educate local populations to the benefit of wise use of resources, not to slash and burn each time a new crop is to be planted.

It is only in small parts of Brazil that the soil has turned into a dust bowl after all the timber had been cleared for agricultural use. It was done in one or two instances with government consent; it was not appreciated at the time that only strips of land should have been cleared for planting.

In most tropical countries forest areas intentionally cleared for farming have been successful. The Republic of the Ivory Coast and the southern islands of the Philippines are the best examples. Therefore for whatever reason land clearance has to be undertaken by governments, we in the western world should help make use of the secondary species which so many of our customers even refuse to try when free samples are provided.

Natural regeneration in most tropical countries is possible if forest contractors obey their National Forest Officers.

I can only hope that the ITTO will

We should make use of the secondary species . . .

gradually make an impact on the members of the producing countries to preserve the forest with selected felling and providing fertilisers for the farmer so they do not have to slash and burn. Above all, the governments in the Third World must ensure that the laws which exist to protect the forest are obeyed and licences granted for the felling are not exceeded.

I can only recommend those who have a bad conscience for buying and using tropical hardwoods to try and utilise hardwoods and softwoods from the North American continent, where good forestry

Other countries would continue to buy tropical hardwoods . . .

is practised and the sustained yield is much larger than the quantities cut annually. In the north-eastern states of the USA hardwoods regenerate much faster than the volume felled annually, and a good forestry policy prevails, controlled by the government. A very much larger quantity could be cut annually without any risk of deforestation or damage to the timber lands. The western world is already importing larger volumes of USA hardwoods, and we in this country have done likewise. Our consumption is about 8% of the total hardwood used in the UK annually in a great variety of species.

I am also pleased to be able to state that in the peninsula of Malaysia, Burma and Java, forest management ensures that the quantity harvested each year is balanced by replanting and natural growth.

If we in Great Britain have scruples, many other countries have not, and in any case, they would continue to buy tropical hardwoods.

Way through the wood

Woodworkers and wood lovers are concerned but confused about tropical forest issues. We present a digest of a TRADA report that sets them out in detail

Tropical forests are under threat. That much everbody knows. But with little real information available about the size of the problem and how best to deal with it, a controversy had flared between conservationists and those in the international timber industry.

Now the Timber Research and Development Association's major 1985 report, *The Tropical Closed Forest*, has been reprinted to clarify the situation presenting facts and figures which at least illuminate the discussion area.

Dr. O. P. Hansom, an industrial consultant who has written the comprehensive document, appears to understand the views both of the trade and the conservationists. He makes it clear that this was the aim of the exercise — to enable both parties to understand the other's position.

Those in the international timber trade, he points out, see themselves as benefiting people working in forest industries as well as themselves, and would regard any reduction in trade as harming both, as well as the overall economies of the producing countries.

Conservationists may see some reduction in trade as a good thing, and might encourage timber buyers to avoid tropical hardwoods or products made from them. 'Is such a step of any actual benefit from a conservationist's viewpoint,' he asks, 'or is it a worthwhile gesture? Is its effect on the other hand to cause economic harm to developing countries?'

From the preservationist point of view, the first problem is the loss of the irreplaceable virgin forest, its flora and fauna. While it is generally felt that adequate areas of virgin forest should be preserved, some conservationists feel that the only answer is to phase out the industrial use of virgin forest altogether. They fear that any disturbance of an ecosystem can have contingent effects that may not be predictable, and they seek to avoid irretrievable loss.

Ecologists point to the lush variety of life, particularly in lowland rain forests where a few hectares often contain more species than the whole of the European continent.

Additionally, they point to fears about the environment; tropical forests are catchment areas for clean water supplies and irrigation, and prevent soil erosion.

Dr Hansom claims that secondary forest can provide this protective role as well. While conceding there can be conflicts between ecological considerations and the socio-economic benefits derived by developing countries from forest indus-

continued

Way through the wood

tries, he appeals for a broader definition of 'conservation' to include in its overall objectives the need for economic development.

Dr Hansom offers a possibility of conciliation between these viewpoints by using the United Nations' definition of conservation: 'The management of human use of the biosphere so that it may yield the greatest sustainable benefit to present generations, while maintaining its potential to meeting needs and aspirations of future generations'.

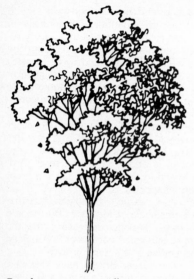

But his most compelling points come from the facts he reveals:

Fact 1: More than 80% of wood taken from tropical forests is used as fuel, taken by local people for their own use. This mainly happens in 'open' forests rather than the less accessible 'closed' forests. Only one quarter of 'industrial wood' is exported.

Fact 2: The main cause of forest depletion is uncontrolled agricultural expansion. The problem is that the fertility of the tropical forest (unlike our temperate forests) is not in the soil, but in the vegetation, mostly above ground level. Often the transfer of forest to agricultural land results from local people desperate to feed themselves; then farmers take over the 'slash and burn' territory for cash crops.

Fact 3: Governments of developing countries see the industrial development of forests as a way of improving living standards of their people; they want to maximise the forest's productivity by using the many secondary species of timber as well as the few primary species.

'Most tropical forests will before long be left with only small quantities of currently sought-after species, which may be expected to achieve a scarcity value,' warns Dr Hansom. *'Only major changes in the species accepted by users will enable these areas to continue to supply wood in the longer term to current markets.'*

So work needs doing urgently to come up with suitable replacement woods.

Fact 4: As well as timber, the forests yield constructional materials like fibres and canes, chemicals, pharmaceuticals and oils or exudates of various kinds. Apart from how to conserve these, there are problems of integrating their supply with logging and ensuring local people don't lose their own extraction of these products.

Dr Hansom says technological research is needed into the effects of logging and how disturbed forest can be encouraged to regenerate into natural forest. It ought to be possible to plan and control logging so the level of disturbance is no more than an acceptable degree of degradation that falls short of deforestation and which can be the basis of a productive secondary forest. So far this has been very difficult or impossible. Plantations, particularly where trees of one species are planted, are susceptible to pests and disease, and mixed species plantations are not as popular, probably because of their lower economic return.

Dr Hansom identifies the main causes of tropical deforestation as:
1 Conversion and use for agriculture
2 Fuel wood gathering
3 Poorly managed industrial logging.

How fast is tropical forest being depleted? The United Nations estimated in 1980 there was a total of 1800 million hectares of tropical forest, and that between 1980-85 $2\frac{3}{4}$% of tropical closed forest would be deforested, and 4% of 'productive undisturbed' and unproductive forest. The area of tropical closed forest is expected to have reduced by about 12% by AD2000, largely through clearance for agriculture. Comments Dr Hansom: 'It is less than has been thought by some, but will seem too much for most people as a continuing figure.'

He points out that logging contributes to deforestation in two ways: by excessive degradation, and by opening up an infrastructure providing access to the area inviting immediate further exploitation.

Avoiding excessive degradation, he suggests, requires the fixing of conservative production targets, and pressure on the land after clearance should be reduced by planned colonisation rather than spontaneous migration or squatting. He advocates productive forest management, perhaps linked with reforestation. Currently little forest management is practised; local populations have been little involved, which adds to the difficulty of enforcing conservation. 'Above all, however, the need for local populations to feed themselves is the dominant factor,' he adds.

Dr Hansom concludes that from an ecological point of view reducing international trade in timber would not generally be a good thing, because the ecological problem is much more related to the agricultural exploitation that comes after the logging of forests areas.

He says the international timber trade has profited in the past from the overlogging of forests in South East Asia, with some damage to the ecology; and that particular species have been overlogged in West African forests, but the effects have been to the long term economic disadvantage of the countries rather than broad ecological damage. The more accessible forests of the Amazon region have been heavily exploited for popular species, he says, but again claims the consequences are economic rather than ecological except for the possible loss of the species altogether.

Virgin forests that have been only partly degraded could become similar to primary forests again after 60-80 years of undisturbed growth, it is suggested.

He urges the international tropical timber trade to recognise that its own interests are best served by the sustained productivity of the forest based on responsible logging practices as part of proper forest resource management — including reforestation — and that they actively encourage this.

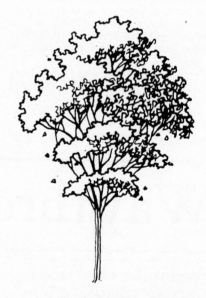

Solutions to the problems of deforestation are political as much as anything else, Dr Hansom says, and points out that conservation strategies and policies can only be established and developed by or through the governments of independent countries. These governments will need to determine the relative priorities between industrial and agricultural development on the one hand, and preservation on the other, while conserving their tropical forest resource overall.

Meanwhile, Dr Hansom says, reforestation and better forest management are most important objectives for the trade. ■

● *The Tropical Closed Forest*, TRADA Research Report 6/85 is available at £2 from Publications Department, TRADA, Stocking Lane, Hughenden Valley, High Wycombe, Bucks HP14 4ND.

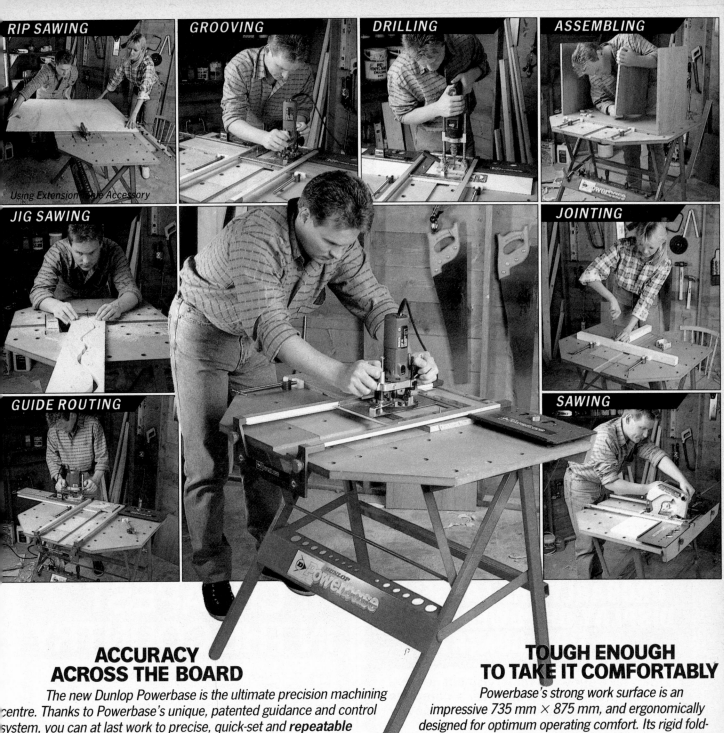

ACCURACY ACROSS THE BOARD

The new Dunlop Powerbase is the ultimate precision machining centre. Thanks to Powerbase's unique, patented guidance and control system, you can at last work to precise, quick-set and **repeatable** measurements on virtually any workpiece.

You can use it with most domestic power tools, and because Powerbase provides a stable work surface and clamping system, you'll find working with hand tools easier too.

TOUGH ENOUGH TO TAKE IT COMFORTABLY

Powerbase's strong work surface is an impressive 735 mm × 875 mm, and ergonomically designed for optimum operating comfort. Its rigid fold-away base frame is fabricated in steel. Lots of innovative technical features – including Powerbase's versatile soleplate – mean safer, more consistent, more accurate working. Whatever the job, Powerbase measures up. At a price that fits your pocket!

Anything you can do you can do better

Makes things easier

Dept WW, 140 Fielden Street, Glasgow G40 3TX.

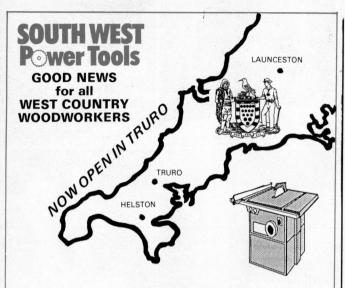

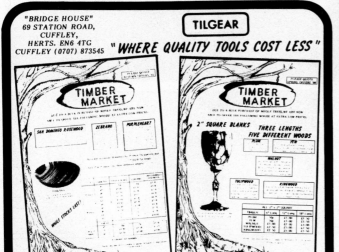

Boxing clever

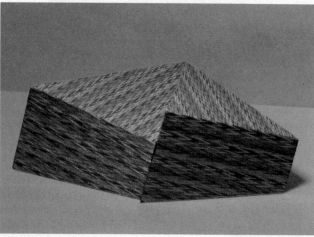

● *Boxes galore from Peter Howlett.* **Above,** *'A view of a hill' in ebony and masser birch;* **below,** *spiral box – glued isosceles triangles in Mexican rosewood, Amazon rosewood and kingwood*

● **Above,** *'Leaning triangles' in livieux and manmade veneer from Italy;* **below,** *detachable boxes in walnut and yew*

Fig. 1

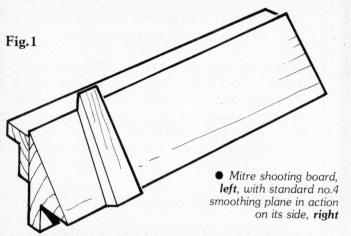

● *Mitre shooting board,* **left,** *with standard no.4 smoothing plane in action on its side,* **right**

Peter Howlett makes boxes — just boxes. He shares his professional expertise and infectious enthusiasm for the craft

I consider myself an artisan rather than an artist, with perhaps a little flair and talent for matching beautiful timbers and balancing taste with excess. I make boxes to be touched, handled, used and coveted; I hope precious without an artificial preciousness. The basic principles of jointing and putting a box together are those used in the Sheffield cutlery box-making trade. Mitre joints are efficient and easy to produce by hand; feather-keying gives added strength to larger boxes.

By their nature, boxes are 'plain', so I make a point of carefully matching timber grain and figure, and where possible use only the finest and most exotic timbers. I use both solid wood and veneers. Not because veneers are cheap — the ones I use are rare and definitely expensive. Many of the woods I use are either horrendously expensive, unobtainable in the solid or unusable in any other form but veneer. Even the ground on which these are laid is costly, and the old tag that veneers are used

Fig.2

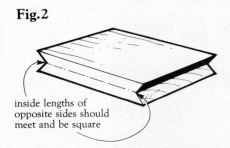

inside lengths of opposite sides should meet and be square

to hide inferior materials just doesn't apply in my boxes.

Perfect mitres are essential. I use the traditional box-maker's shooting-board to produce accurate mitres (fig. 1). This presents the timber at a specific angle to the sole of the plane, which is used on its side. For rectangular and square work this angle is normally 45°, but accuracy in the shooting-board itself is not super-critical because the lateral adjustment on metal planes allows the blade to be angled to compensate for error. Notice that the stop is housed in a compound taper, so it's held by friction; you can trim the end when it gets worn.

Bear in mind that boxes are traditionally made in one piece and then sawn in two to give base and lid.

As well as perfect mitres, you need to match the grain extremely carefully. With solid timber you can do this by re-sawing, preferably on a bandsaw. I use metal cutting blades, with three points to the inch, which cut very true and simply chew through the dense exotics I favour.

I tend to thickness boards before sawing, so I can cut dead in the middle, with very little to remove in the thicknesser. This is particularly important if you use boards which come from the outside of the log, as you can easily lose grain-match on tangential surfaces.. With the halves opened out in sequence on the bench, show-side up, I number them to identify assembly order (I put a tail on the '1' to avoid confusion which is easy on quarter-sawn timber).

Shooting the mitres

I use a standard no.4 smoothing plane on its side with the cap-iron set close to the cutting edge. To set the plane, I shoot two trial corners first; then I bring them together and check the internal angle with an engineer's square. If they aren't perfect I adjust the angle of the plane blade and re-shoot the ends until I get a precise right angle.

Once the plane is set up, I tend to work on all the mitres to avoid shortening two pieces of wood in my effort to get it right; if the wood gets shortened, you lose grain continuity. You should shoot the four sides to the same internal length if you want a square box, or match opposite sides for a rectangle. Check these lengths (fig. 2).

Gluing up the sides

I used to use sisal string to clamp up the boxes (the blisters have only just disappeared from my hands) until I found some useful nylon strap-clamps. They apply phenomenal pressure uniformly, and are particularly ideal for the more unorthodox shapes I produce. All corners should be protected with thick card, obviously.

For feather-keying the mitres of larger boxes I use a special jig and a portable router with a 1.5mm cutter, inserting a cross-grained tongue in the key-way. Glue alone is enough to hold the corners of small boxes, the lid and base adding to the strength. This works fine with exotics, whose high density tends to prevent rapid endgrain absorption.

When you have glued and clamped the sides, check the internal dimensions. You may have produced perfect mitres, but discrepancies can creep in, and a slight squeeze before the glue has set will often remedy these minor errors; otherwise you might be disappointed and frustrated later.

Lids and bases

Solid boxes usually have solid lids and bases dropped into rebates in the sides. Traditionally (and masochistically) a side fillister was used, but today rebates are easily machined with a router inverted on a simple stand.

You can inlay a contrasting veneer between the drop-in lid and the sides if you undersize the lid by two veneer thicknesses, and insert veneer before gluing the lid in place. The corners of the inlay should be mitred, and they should fit perfectly; if you aren't careful here you'll find the lid top buckles up the line instead of just sliding in neatly.

Personally I no longer taper the lid-tops from the underside to ensure a tight fit; the exotics I use don't have a lot of give. I glue the lid-top on first so I can remove any glue dribbles from the underside before inserting the base; any runs at the base will be masked by the linings.

Veneered boxes

The bulk of my veneered boxes are for stationery, and are generally 250x 200x60mm. It would be wasteful and ex-

● *Above*, *nylon strap-clamps used to hold sides in position after gluing*

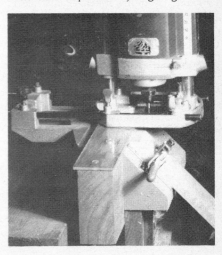

● *Peter's jig used with a router to cut slots for keys in mitres*

pensive to make these in solid ebony (over £160 a cube); many of the burrs and rosewoods I use are obtainable or usable only in veneer form.

Buying veneer can be rather intimidating, as it's quite a different market from solid wood. You generally buy veneers in 'bundles' per square foot. The best value are 'shorts' — small-leaved bundles which result from merchants buying a log where some bundles were trimmed of all their defects. Because the leaves are small, you can often buy a bundle at half the price of full leaves. A bundle has 12-32 leaves. I've found I can buy ebony, burr oak, poplar, myrtle and the pseudo-burr, masser birch, in this way. But you'll never find Rio rosewood sold as half-price shorts!

You'll also find prices vary for the same species; the charge relates not only to the age of the stock, but also to what the merchant paid. There's some scope for bargaining, too.

Before buying, check through the bundle to make sure it hasn't already broken down, and that any minor defects on the cover leaves don't expand into ugly holes in the middle of the bundle. Don't waste your merchant's time with asking questions; he

continued

Boxing clever

won't know how it will glue or polish. I recommend Crispin's and Aaronson's in London, both of which give an excellent service and carry some beautiful stock.

When I get my veneers back home I store them on bulldog clips hanging from nails on my workshop wall. Then if I get the blues I look up at the lovely wood and sigh, think how lucky I am, and feeling refreshed, get on with the job.

Grain matching is similar as for solid wood boxes, using paired leaves for a running match.

For large boxes I lay up veneers for the lids and bases six at a time, in a 12x10in letter press, each panel separated by a thin sheet of aluminium, and the top and bottom plates supported by 9mm ply. I use Cascamite glue mixed 3:1 for the correct viscosity. With this system I can lay up 12 panels every 24 hours. These old presses were made quite accurately, with pretty hefty screws, so the result is as good as the commercially pressed panels I used to put out to contract.

You almost always need to prepare veneers before you lay them down. All cross-grain edges need to be taped, and splits and faults 'stitched' with veneer tape. Cut the veneer oversize, so it projects from the groundwork about 3mm all round, with the groundwork itself 6mm oversize.

You'll need to press very distorted veneers flat before they join in the press, which involves damping them and sandwiching them between clean dry boards in the press. It's essential they are completely dry before you subsequently lay them.

Once the panels are glued and pressed (12 hours), take them out and immediately trim off excess rubbery Cascamite with a knife — it saves your fingers getting ripped, and makes it easier on the plane.

For sides of large veneered boxes I generally use Brazilian mahogany as ground for dark woods and sycamore for light ones. After gluing up the sides, I plant the lid-tops and bases directly on, then when they're dry trim them flush with a suitable cutter in the router. For laying ghastly burrs on box sides, I use a special press, and 'glue-film' for quartersawn and tamer stuff. Purists may support the hammer, but with the outrageously distorted burr veneers I use I'd never prevent the veneer from tearing as I hammered it down.

If you like, you can rebate the base of the box to protect the fragile edges. For the top edges I recommend lipping, but it must be applied on the 'try and fit' principle. First cut a suitable rebate, then mitre the slightly oversize lippings in sequence around the box, starting first with a 'dummy' corner taped in place. Offer the next lipping up to this, and mitre its opposite end, using the adjacent lipping to meet it. This way you'll get the exact length and a perfect corner joint. It sounds complicated, working with two pieces of lipping at once, but it works. Use gummed tape to hold each lipping in place, and glue each piece when you have fitted it.

With the first three edges done, you'll have to take care to get the last piece exactly right; even a perfect mitre is wasted if the final gluing is skewed. Use glue sparingly so you can still see the three-way meeting corners, and tape from the centre outwards. Be warned that a bad joint in holly or boxwood is impossible to cover up.

Sawing off the lid

When you have glued on the lid and base, and given the whole thing a cursory clean-up, you're ready to saw the lid off. The traditional method is to gauge two lines at the appropriate distance — allowing for the saw kerf plus a couple of fag papers — and then saw between them with a fine dovetail or beading saw. I use a slitting cutter in my overarm router and do the job in a fraction of the time.

With veneered boxes you need to back-mill — feed with the rotational cut rather than against it; this breaks the surface of the veneer cleanly rather like the scoring cutter on a panel saw, and minimises 'spelching' of the veneers. This is a very delicate operation, however, and you should cut only to the depth of the veneer or a fraction below.

With solid lids I put the whole thing aside for a month to allow the wood to settle down. Curls, burrs and 'wild effect' are particularly susceptible to movement and will often cause the lid to distort if used in the solid; to overcome this, I use very thin sections and fit the lid so the rebate stands proud, which gives added rigidity to the lid sides.

Linings

Now you can make and fit the inner pieces which stand proud of the body of the box around the sides, holding the lid in place. I use 2.5-4mm wood, planed to a precise fit on the mitre shooting-board. Resist making these too tight a fit, for the feather-edge of the mitre is easily crushed on such thin wood. Work round the box to fit them, slightly tapering the final mitre so that it slides comfortably into place, 'biting' only at the last 10mm.

Finishing

As you gently place the lid into position and push it home, the moment of truth arrives, with the accompanying mixture of satisfaction/irritation, pleasure/frustration. If

● *A slitting cutter in the router makes easy work of cutting lid from base*

it has gone well, a few strokes with a crisp, sharp smoothing plane, followed by careful glasspapering will bring the work to polishing stage. Work around the box, and turn the lid frequently to check you're not trimming off excessive amounts. Planing can rectify slightly skewed lids on solid boxes, but you haven't got much scope for adjustment with veneered boxes. Don't be in too great a hurry to slap the polish on, but concentrate on getting the fine details right for this stage.

Polishing

Boxes are ideal practice pieces for French polishing; you get fast results, and the obvious difficulties of getting that smooth even shine are minimised over such small areas.

Before polishing, chamfer all the edges, using the mitre shooting-board. Your best bet is to make a feature of the joint-line between the lid and the body of the box — I've been trying to get a perfect fit here for ages, but work schedules prevent me from pursuing this course as far as I'd like. This doesn't mean that I sacrifice perfection, but that I have found a way to achieve a good appearance, accepted by my clients at the price they will pay. Of course, my personal collection of boxes are given just that little bit more attention . . .   ■

● Aaronson Bros, 45 Redchurch St, London EC2, 01-739 3107
● J. Crispin & Son, 94 Curtain Rd, London EC2, 01-739 4857

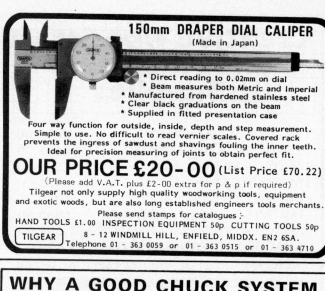

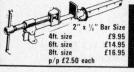

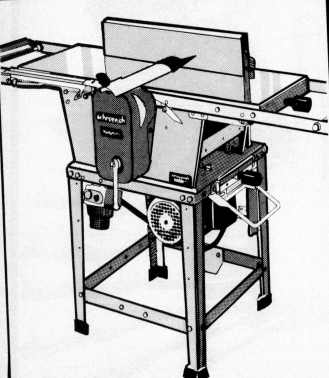

Books

Two turning videos

Turning Wood with Richard Raffan
  (Home Workshop, £29.95 plus p&p)
Dennis White Teaches Woodturning,
  Part I: The Basics (Knowhow Productions,
  £29.95 plus p&p)
Reviewed by Ken Cooper

Richard Raffan's video-cassette, 'Turning Wood', is intended to be a supplement to his book of the same name. A useful list relates each section of the tape to the appropriate passage in the book, with timings which make it comparatively easy to move to the right part of the tape if you wish to have another look at a particular sequence.

The cassette starts with a demonstration of the fundamentals of stance and movement with particular reference to between-centres turning, and then shows how to sharpen and use gouges, chisels, and scrapers. Some of this doesn't always make for particularly effective teaching. The camera angles aren't always well chosen, while a few close-ups would have worked wonders; image quality is far from ideal, so for instance, a black chisel tends to merge with the dark tool-rest on the grinder. I wish the tape included some of the excellent diagrams in Mr Raffan's book to reinforce the points which don't always emerge very clearly from either the commentaries or the live pictures.

In the next few demonstrations several lumps of green cherry are turned into continuous ribbons of shavings — the sort we lesser mortals know we should produce but never quite achieve. We're shown how to use the basic tools and we're told why as well. He demonstrates how to make simple objects; a light-pull, a box, a breadboard, a bowl, and several practical points of more general application emerge. Richard Raffan doesn't scorn the use of the scraper, or the use of other tools in the scraping mode, on the right occasion; he even uses a disc-sander for fast finishing, a production-orientated, if somewhat dusty, approach.

In Richard Raffan's hands woodturning is more of an art form than a craft, but he never forgets the practical details: why you should use a particular tool or method, for instance. Much of the material can be viewed time and again with advantage, something new emerging each time.

This videotape, which lasts for 119 minutes, is a very useful complement to Richard Raffan's book, and could be used on its own by some students. It is by no means perfect, but most of its faults are flaws of production and are more irritating than serious.

The other cassette, 'Dennis White Teaches Woodturning, Part I: The Basics', is from a new company, Knowhow Productions, and has a different approach. Dennis White is a craftsman woodturner who has been turning for 65 years and whose skill is fascinating to watch. The photography is excellent, the picture definition is good, and the shots are nicely lit and well composed. Unfortunately the commentary and the teaching content generally are not nearly so good.

The opening sequence has Dennis White talking straight to camera, obviously feeling awkward. Later on we are shown how to sharpen tools using free-hand grinding and ignoring the tool-rest; I doubt if this is a very sound way of instructing the novice, a method neither accurate nor very safe in unskilled hands. Frequent cooling in water is advocated, although this isn't always shown. We are also told that 'you must hone the cutting edge', the inference being that if we don't, the penalty will be dire; but there is no further explanation.

This programme, unlike Richard Raffan's, is the first in a series of six, yet practically intended to be used entirely on its own. In fact, the opening captions urge us to 'use it as another tool in your workshop'. It is supposed to be about the basics, but novice woodturners viewing this cassette could be forgiven for wondering what these basic concepts are. The commentary is patronising and of the 'you must do it like this' variety, although what 'this' may be is rarely obvious from the picture. It deals repetitively with trivia, but ignores important things. The last part of the programme has no commentary when in fact much could be made of some very elegant, well photographed turning.

Of these two the Raffan video is bound to be the most effective, particularly if it's used with his book. The Knowhow production could be improved with a better commentary; a few diagrams and a little editing to produce a more logical flow of ideas would help. As it stands it's unlikely to improve anyone's theoretical understanding of woodturning, or practical skill.
● Ken Cooper is a professional antique restorer and ex-producer/director of educational videos.

Desmond MacNamara
Picture Framing: a Practical Guide from Basic to Baroque
David & Charles, £10.95
Reviewed by Frances Binnington

This guide to practical framing is comprehensive and thorough. The profusion of diagrams and photographs amply support the descriptive text, which is clearly aimed at the amateur.

The chapters on basic mitre cutting, as applied to all mouldings, and on mount cutting are exhaustive and very thorough. The author demonstrates how old frames can be repaired, new lengths of moulding run off from old frames, and how new 'antique' frames can be reproduced from drawings and photographs. He also shows many ways of decoration, from plaster and paint to bronze powders and gold leaf. The weakest chapter is on gilding, where instructions are limited and confused.

Mr MacNamara explains that interest from his evening class students drove him to explore ways of framing pictures cheaply, effectively and quickly; the book is a result mostly of his own experiments and discoveries. His own work is interesting technically, but it would have been good to have more illustrations of the beautiful work by contemporary framers such as Paul Levy and Vilmo Gibello.

The book deals with period framing, reproduction and repair and the photographs of antique frames are welcome, despite occasional poor cropping.

Some omissions are disappointing; no guide to acid-free boards and adhesives, no warnings about the use of inappropriate mounting materials or against trimming prints and watercolours.

This book does give careful consideration to the various aspects of framing a picture, print or drawing, going through every stage. He discusses taste, stressing that he can only point the way to aesthetic judgement. A list of suppliers, bibliography, index and an excellent glossary complete the book.
● Frances Binnington is a professional framer, gilder and restorer.

David Hawkins
The Technique of Wood Surface Decoration
Batsford, £12.50 hardback
Reviewed by John Hemsley

Don't be misled by the title of this book. It is not about gilding, graining or painting, the subjects you might associate with decorating the surface of wood. But it is a really superb guide for woodworkers interested in veneer, marquetry and inlay work.

Author David Hawkins is a restorer of great experience who also has a firm grasp of the history of each technique — he lectures and teaches for the V&A, the National Trust and at Christie's Fine Art Course. (You may have seen him on BBC TV's 'The Antiques Roadshow'.) Obviously it is fine art orientated and therein lies its interest, for the author supplies fascinating background material on the origins of each technique and the early methods of producing them. The skills involved are generously illustrated with line drawings, 200 black-and-white, and a handful of carefully chosen colour photographs.

The book covers the origins of veneer work, marquetry, parquetry, oyster work, bandings and Tunbridge ware, and the techniques of wood inlay; it also includes chapters on metal and repetition inlay and Boulle work. As well as a useful bibliography, it has a short list of suppliers which includes merchants of such exotic materials as raw horn, pearl and ivory.
● John Hemsley is *Woodworker*'s deputy editor.

THE WOODWORK BUS

Woodwork is thriving, and WOODWORKER is thriving; but are woodworkers thriving? All the time we are meeting and talking to people intending to turn their hobby into a profession (or semi-profession); to students about to leave college and set up on their own; or to professional woodworkers experiencing varying degress of success. The common theme is: there's plenty of advice about, but where is it specific to woodwork? Which is where we come in. This is the first in a series of articles in which we examine making a living (and profit) in woodwork. We've asked **Hugh O'Neill**, a professional management consultant and craftsman woodturner, to set the agenda and introduce the themes, and we'll be using comments and add-ons culled from the experience of professional woodworkers great and small, of all reputations and specialities. Plus we have contributions lined up from agencies who hand out information, advice — and money. In short, if you're a professional, semi-professional, intending professional or even a serious enthusiast who sells the odd item, and you want to know how to do it better — look no further. It starts here.

Look before you leap

First: Hugh O'Neill suggests you examine your motivation

So you're a budding entrepreneur determined to make your first million within five years? I thought not. For most craftsmen setting up on their own, becoming a tycoon is the last thing on their minds. What most want is to exercise their craft — and hope they will make enough money to live on.

The result is that some do earn sufficiently, but many don't. Almost every book I've seen on becoming self-employed starts with the topic of money — how much you'll need and where you might find it. These books are concerned with 'setting up a business' — any business. Authors seem to believe every reader is bursting to become an entrepreneur, and will take delight not only in making money but also the very activity of business management and running the show. Even the Crafts Council's excellent publication *Running a Workshop* has something of this flavour.

I think these books have got it wrong. Money is not the starting point of thinking about running a business. But even more at fault is the craftsman who dives in without

thinking through some of the key aspects of what self-employment means.

There was a delicatessen in Pinner High Street, a nice little business. Run by a Jewish family, it sold some kosher products, but most of the stock was aimed at the predominantly gentile, wealthy residents of this London suburb. In its quiet way, it was one of the most successful shops in the High Street.

Sunday morning saw one of its busiest periods. The shop was close to the Anglican parish church, and worshippers from there, and from the Catholic church just round the corner, queued to get in. Some wanted a cup of coffee in the café section, some wanted fresh bread, some milk; but most went away with fancy meats, salads, and cheeses.

Not far away was an up-market grocer's and there was some small overlap, particularly on the cheeses. But with no Sunday opening they had to rely on the people who made planned shopping trips during the week. So the two co-existed happily.

Someone noticed the delicatessen business, saw its success, and (probably) thought: 'I could do better than that — just look at their prices!' So they opened a new delicatessen just round the corner. It was bigger, didn't open on Sunday, and didn't have the same family feel about it; but, being cheaper, and with a wider range of stock, it did attract some custom.

'Gosh!' thought another trader, 'delicatessens are obviously "in" — there must be a lot of trade for them and I've always wanted to run one.' So a third establishment opened. It was new, and people tried it.

Twelve months later there were none. All three had gone out of business — there just wasn't enough trade to support them all.

Competition is fine, but three delicatessens within 300 yards of each other is lunacy. The only time that setting up in someone else's patch is totally justified is when there is a hope of making the village, town, area, or whatever, a world centre for the particular trade. Hence every other shop in parts of Fulham is an antiquery, and we have the world-famous centre for second-hand books at Hay-on-Wye on the Welsh border.

Many craftsmen's problems start on holiday. It's a time to relax, to think, 'perchance to dream'. You see a good craft retail outlet or two, a potter, and a woodturner or cabinetmaker. Probably the potter and the turner live in idyllic cottages set in their own patch of garden. The dairy or an outhouse has been white-washed and converted into an airy, light, studio/workshop/display area. You look at their wares and sometimes you're enchanted. They have originality, design flair, superb execution, and an enviable price.

More often, though, you find run-of-the-mill work. A few bowls, small tables and chairs, an odd interesting vase; but then masses of serviette rings, light-pull bobs, lace bobbins and polished eggs. Perhaps there's a bowlful of turned apples in a range of varnished exotics, marked at prices that seem exorbitant, but then you've never had to make a living selling your own craft.

That dream that had been lying quiescent in the back of your mind suddenly takes a step nearer to becoming a reality — or a nightmare.

People go into business for a variety of reasons — often the wrong ones. It's something that's worth doing. It's satisfying, interesting and rewarding — or, at least, it can be. But it can also be hell if it isn't done properly.

Marketing is where so many people setting up in business go wrong . . .

Just what does 'doing it properly' mean? Talk to any bank manager or accountant, and they'll tell you that the first thing that you'll need is capital, and only second a good idea. Yes, money does help, and you'll be surprised just how much it can take to set up even the simplest of craft-based businesses. And, make no mistake about it, BUSINESS is what it is, and what it has to be if it isn't going to be hell. Doing it properly is a lot more than 'money'. In fact, if I were to put the requirements in order of importance, the list might read:

1 Motivation
2 Idea
3 Marketing
4 Money
5 Management
6 Skill

As I said, the reasons why people make such a move are many, some right and some wrong. But actually almost every reason can be a good one, which is just made wrong by the way we implement it.

Let's look at some of the reasons given during a recent workshop run for people interested in setting up on their own:
. . . because I like furniture making.
. . . because I'm good at woodturning.
. . . because I've always wanted to make things.
. . . because I fancy the life of a craftsman.
. . . because there seems to be a market for the things I make.
. . . because my friends tell me I'm good enough to make a business out of my hobby.
. . . because I've always wanted to live in the country.

Of this list probably only the fifth item — a market for the things I make — comes near to being a reasonable motive; but even the others could be made to work.

Today we also get another set of reasons. There are young people who haven't been able to find employment but have embryonic skills they think they might be able to use. There are many people who are made redundant and find they suddenly have no employment prospects, but have a little capital. A third and rising category are those given early retirement, some with quite substantial severance monies — the

former Director General of a major army corps is now making dolls' houses, and a retired RAF senior flying instructor is turning out beautiful clocks on a commercial basis.

Others think about it and decide not to go into business for themselves, expressing reasons such as:
. . . I cannot make anything.
. . . I've no craft skills.
. . . I'm too old to learn new tricks.
. . . The only piece of furniture I ever made was a kitchen cabinet and that fell apart.
. . . I can't take the risk.
. . . I don't have any money.
. . . I couldn't run a business.

With the possible exceptions of the early retirees, almost all the reasons given, for and against, are only the tip of the iceberg. We may have a skill that has increased with experience, our friends tell us that we are 'good enough' — but there are usually many other factors that tip our own personal scales. We've worked for inefficient bosses, we've seen our skills under-utilised for years, we're fed up with the 8-to-5 routine and so on.

Our **motivations** are often complex: but unless we go into things completely blind they also have to be powerful if the 'pros' are to outweigh the 'cons'.

And there are plenty of disadvantages. Any business is risky — we may have to put all our savings into it before we see any return. We may run up debts — at least an overdraft. In all probability we have to put our assets, even our home, on the line. We are going to work longer hours than we have ever done in our lives. We may have to spend a part of each day selling: that means we do our production in the evenings and weekends, doing the book-keeping after the telly has closed down. We probably have to forget holidays; we eat irregularly (and badly), we get niggling or massive doubts and tiny or traumatic ulcers.

The smaller the business the greater the range of tasks for each individual . . .

Even working on overload, motivation alone is not enough. We have to have an **idea** — something that will differentiate us from the also-rans. This isn't necessarily something on which to build an empire, just something of enough substance to allow us to survive. It may be for a particular approach, a particular range of designs, a particular quality of execution, a particular attitude to marketing, a particular area of need to meet; or, as in the case of people like John Makepeace, a combination, even a super-abundance, of all of these. But it does have to be at least one of these things, and it does have to be 'particular'.

The 'idea' and '**marketing**' are, inevitably, totally interwoven. Only when we've got these things sorted out should we start to think about **money**.

Marketing is the one thing that the second and third delicatessen in Pinner overlooked. Marketing is where so many people setting up in business go wrong. I'm not talking about advertising, leaflets, open days selling over the counter, and the like, but fitting what we wish to do into the marketplace, to the local area and community, to the competition, to the overall need, to the purchasing money available, and to many other factors. Before a single wheel turns and before you take the bank manager from the cupboard for a light dusting down, you have to have a plan of what you're going to make; how you're going to market it; and where, in what quantities, and for how much, it's going to be sold. Once you actually get started you may have to change some of your ideas, but this in no way negates the need for the preparatory thinking.

So the beginning is not, as the books might have us believe, with money. If you have a good idea and have really done your marketing analysis, it's usually possible to

Exercising your craft is often only a tiny part of running a business . . .

find money. One might almost say if you can't find the money, then don't do it; you probably haven't got a good enough idea in the first place. Equally, if you can find the money, it doesn't necessarily mean you are half-way to success and that your idea is a sound one: you may have convinced some gullible person that it is (perhaps they liked your face), but you still have to make the whole thing work in the real world.

Making it work is what **management** is all about. The word management has two connotations. One is the controlling of affairs to achieve a required end, and the other is, more specifically, controlling people.

If we take the broader view of management, it's something we will have to become involved in, although we may never have other people to manage. Businesses don't just happen, nor do they run themselves. The basic principles of running a business are much the same whatever its size or nature. Obviously there's more similarity between the individual woodturner and a garden furniture factory than there is with, say, ICI; but there are still some common principles.

Common to all businesses is the need for finance and financial control, and particularly for managing **cash flow**. Indeed the smaller the business the more the need for careful cash flow management. There are then common principles of marketing, stock control, production scheduling and quality control, and certainly of selling (as distinct from the broader marketing).

The major differences between businesses can probably be boiled down to three key elements. The first is in the

continued

THE WOODWORK BUSINESS

employment of other people (if any) and the numbers and the typs of skills required. The second is in the quantity/quality split — whether the emphasis is on volume production (kitchen furniture, light-pull bobs and serviette rings), or on one-off craftsman-produced items (fine cabinets, spinning wheels, harps, etc.).

The third area of difference is that the smaller the business, the greater the range of tasks each individual will have to under-take. In the single person business, the single person has to do it all — financial control, marketing, production, selling, packaging, dispatch, stock ordering, paying the bills, and back to financial control in an endless circle. *Actually exercising your craft is only a part, often a tiny part, of the whole*. Yes, there are differences — financial control may be one cash book, a VAT record and a ledger, instead of the hundreds of documents of ICI. The total filing system may be three shoe boxes and the stock control system a blackboard and chalk — but we do have to have something; and it does have to be 'managed'.

Next month I'll look at some of the basic marketing questions upon which the whole business will depend. Later I'll review some of the sources of assistance; look at questions of finance, record keeping and administration, promotion and selling, and even of managing staff . . .

Editors' Notes

Aidan Walker and John Hemsley have both been professional woodworkers, and both have some personal points to make

I firmly believe that craftspeople must put out of their minds the notion that profit is a dirty word. During the years I was running my own one-man furniture making business I made a load of mistakes, all but one of which I needn't go into here. That one was crucial; I didn't think I could price my stuff for profit as well as for a living. My wages, OK; but profit on top of that? How would I ever get the work? The answer — and it's a tough one — is, if the client doesn't accept a price with a profit element built in, don't do the job. There's nothing more soul-destroying than doing the work you love for almost nothing; it makes you hate yourself and ultimately hate the work. As a small business person, your responsibility is to feed yourself, and to feed your business. They are not one and the same thing; your wages are what you get out of your business, your profit is what you put into it, and it's vital insurance.

As much precision as you can get into your planning, your workshop practices, as much pizazz as you can get into your presentation (of self, portfolio, work), as much perfection as you can get into the product itself, all are wasted unless you aim at profit. Look at it this way; running a business is a craft, a skill, which you must learn and take pride in as much as in the development of your technical skills. Can't make wooden things without timber can you? No more can you make a business work without building profit into it. It's my hope this series will tell you how.

Aidan Walker

I had toyed with the idea of turning my lifelong hobby into a business for several years, but being cautious I considered the appropriate start was to make products part-time and ease my way in, testing the ground before the big launch. In fact, I was precipitated into a decision when I was made redundant. Short of moving 300 miles, no comparable post existed, so I decided to do woodwork three days a week and freelance writing the rest.

Income guaranteed; outcome uncertain

The government's business start-up scheme cushions unemployed people in their first 12 months, explains Tony Draper

If you're unemployed and fancy starting your own business, the government's Enterprise Allowance Scheme (EAS) could get you launched. Provided you meet all the conditions, you receive £40 a week for the first 12 months' trading. This covers the loss of unemployment benefit during the start-up period and gives at least a guaranteed basis for income in the early days of self-employment.

The scheme also provides access to free business advice; a one-day session introducing EAS, and individual counselling with experienced businessmen of the Small Firms Service (run by the Department of Trade and Industry). This assistance could help you develop the fundamental business management skills which are often lacking in craftspeople; this weakness is a major cause of failure among small firms.

I must stress that the scheme is not a general subsidy for new small businesses — only those who would otherwise be drawing unemployment or supplementary benefit are able to join.

And there's no test of your business's likely success, or otherwise; the responsibility remains yours and yours alone.

However, the positive news is that the majority of the 185,000 people who have joined the scheme since it was launched nationally in August 1983 are still in business. Surveys have found that for every 100 people who joined, 88 were still trading at the end of the first 12 months (the 12 who dropped out may not be through failure, but because they found suitable full-time employment). Three months after the end of the payments, 74 were still trading, and six months after leaving the scheme 68 remained in business. In the longer term, 54 of the 100 who started were still self-employed three years later.

Your first step is a visit to your local Job Centre to pick up leaflet EAS 102, 'The Enterprise Allowance Scheme Guide' and leaflet EPL 171, which gives the complete eligibility conditions. The most important of these conditions are:

● You must have been unemployed and actively seeking work for at least eight weeks
● You must be receiving unemployment or supplementary benefit
● You must have at least £1000 available to invest in the business
● You must be over 18 and below state pension age
● You must agree to work full-time (at least 36 hours a week) in the business
● Your proposed business idea must be approved by the Manpower Services Commission
● You must not have started to operate the business until your application is aproved

If the condition of having £1000 available causes you problems, Job Centre staff will guide you towards banks, many of which are sympathetic towards EAS candidates. And don't forget your family and friends; I persuaded my family to loan the money and I survived to repay it. A useful guide to raising finance is the Bank of England book *Money for Business*.

Premises were no problem because I had a house large enough to use one broad reception room as a workshop and a tiny bedroom as an office/drawing studio. An answerphone was a priority for me (useful when gluing up as well as when out on a job) and so was the simplest accountancy system I could devise (a 3-in, 9-out account book for banking and a petty cash book).

I recognised that nobody has all the myriad skills necessary for self-employment, but I had what I considered the most important — self-discipline to work even when I didn't feel like it, and the ability to market myself and my products/services. I decided I would offer only skills I had mastered, more or less, and that most learning would have to be in my own time. I also decided not to produce speculative pieces at first, just offer my skills to whoever wanted them.

So I put advertisements in newsagents' windows, 'Anything in Wood' (12p a week, four weeks at a time, keeping a careful record of which windows produced most enquiries as I appeared in a different four windows each month) and put the word round my friends and acquaintances.

It worked too. I asked for anything and got it, from designing and making side-gates and hanging garage doors to putting in fitted wardrobes and building hi-fi/video units. A few interesting jobs, too.

Some jobs I turned down as being beyond my skills or ingenuity (I got a local reputation for solving problems — satisfying, but not profitable), or because prospective clients were not prepared to pay a fair price ('No, madam, I cannot make you a solid oak corner cabinet for £40'). I got a useful tie-in with a local builder for carpentry and joinery and narrowly escaped the metropolitan cowboy scene where small firms undercut each other to gain business and nobody makes a profit.

Pricing was always the most difficult problem and even hardy professionals continue to underestimate how much time a project will take; in the end I would double the time span I first thought of, and it was usually about right. I worked on a materials plus time basis, time including initial consultation, design time, problem-solving time, making and installation.

I don't really recommend turning a hobby into an occupation. With a hobby you can choose which projects you want to take on and how you do them; I had to calculate what kind of 'real' joints I could afford at the price I had quoted. And many clients have banal design sense.

Some people find they are not cut out for self-employment because they need imposed discipline; they can't get out of bed in the mornings! Others find it difficult to break away from domestic things — they find they are the ones expected to take the car in for a service, or pick up the dog from the vet — until they put up a notice saying 'Dad is working from 8 till 5 — and that's all he is doing'.

My own biggest difficulty was social isolation. Working from home by oneself all day suits some people, but not me. And I worked too many evenings and weekends to build up a good social life away from the work environment.

In my experience, self-employment involves all the snags and tedium of being employed — plus plenty more. For the first time in 20 years of work I found I did not easily switch off in the evenings or at weekends.

I actually managed to scrape a living, to my satisfaction if not to my accountant's, but after three years I decided enough was enough. I'd rather earn money working for somebody else and indulge my hobbies in my free time . . . .

John Hemsley

Books and Addresses

Running a Workshop, Crafts Council, 12 Waterloo Place, London SW1Y 4AU, £4.95 inc. p&p. Reviewed in WW Dec '85

Money for Business, Bulletin Group, Bank of England, Threadneedle St, London EC2R 8AH, £3

Enterprise Allowance Scheme, contact your local Job Centre

Small Firms Service, 13 regional centres, 100 Area Counselling Offices, ask operator for FREEFONE ENTERPRISE

Manpower Services Commission, Head Office, Moorfoot, Sheffield, (0742) 753275

Department of Trade and Industry, 1-19 Victoria St, London SW1, 01-215 7877

The scheme won't support just any kind of business, but the exemptions aren't likely to apply to woodworking. The Manpower Services Commission (MSC) reject business ideas that 'might bring the scheme into public disrepute', such as nightclubs, licensed drinking clubs, gambling establishments, those involving the promotion of particular political or religious views, those involving nude or semi-nude modelling or offering sexual services. Hardly woodwork-linked, any of these . . .

However enthusiastic you are to get started, don't launch until you have been accepted on to the scheme. You must **not**:
● sell products or services
● manufacture products for sale
● buy stock for use in the business
● enter into contract with suppliers or customers
● advertise for staff
● advertise your products or services.

If you do any of these before approval you are ineligible.

You can do some preparation without losing out on the £2,080. You can obtain premises, get planning permission if necessary, contact suppliers to check on availability and price of materials, produce samples of work and approach potential customers to gauge the level of demand (market research).

If you comply with all these rules, the Job Centre will put you on one of their information sessions. These are mandatory, are held at local centres and fall into two parts. First an MSC official explains in detail the eligibility conditions (by this time you'll probably be fed up with hearing about them). Then a counsellor from the Small Firms Service lays out some of the pitfalls of running your own business. This session is the best time to raise any questions you have about the scheme.

You leave this session with an information pack which includes the all-important application form, on which you have to briefly describe your business proposal and specify a date when you want to start. Soon after you send the form back the MSC will write to tell you whether you've been accepted. There shouldn't be any problem if you have examined the conditions closely.

If you are accepted, then you're in business. It's a big step to take, but I found I got plenty of support on the EAS, particularly from using the Small Firms Service and the MSC courses on improving business skills.

During the 12 months the MSC sends staff round twice to monitor that you still satisfy all the conditions of the scheme.

The MSC concludes their guide to the scheme with a word of caution:

'Starting a new business involves a risk. Many people will succeed — but some will fail.

'The MSC does not require you to prove that your business is a sound commercial proposition. Acceptance on to the scheme should not be taken as an indication of the expected success of your business proposal. Nor is acceptance an indication in any way of official approval for the business you operate. And while Job Centre staff and the Small Firms Service will do everything they can to help you, the responsibility for the step you take is yours and yours alone. We want you to succeed. But the decision to go into business on your own is a big one. All we ask you to do is to think it through — carefully please.'

There's never been a better time to start in business, with many organisations working for the small businessman. The Enterprise Allowance Scheme gives a financial push to any new business and the advice offered is both practical and realistic. Take a careful, close look at your work and ask yourself whether it will sell; they're waiting to help those who help themselves. ■

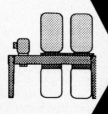

214

AXMINSTER POWER TOOL CENTRE

WOODTURNING LATHES — *OUR PRICE INC. VAT*

TYME STUDENT 10" swing 30" centres (With accessory voucher £20) **£219**
CORONET HOBBY 10" swing 39" centres 1MT ½HP 3 speed **£179**
CORONET No. 1 12" swing 3 Speed 24" ctrs ..... **£218** 36" ctrs ..... **£239** 48" ctrs **£295**
CORONET No. 1 22" Bowl Rest Assbly .. **£39** 48" Bed Extension for existing 24" lathe .. **£59**
ELU DB180 39" centres 15" swing 1½HP motor 3 speed **£299**
TYME CUB 30" centres (With accessory voucher £30) **£296**
TYME AVON 36" centres (With accessory voucher £45) **£419**
MYFORD ML8B 36" centres 9" Rear turning .... **£432** ML8C 42" centres **£467**
KITY 663 3 Speed Lathe 1.0M Centres .... **£554** 1.5M Centres **£576**
KITY 664 Var. Spd. Lathe 1.0M Centres .... **£649** 1.5M Centres **£669**
MINIMAX Centre lathes T90 ...... **£421** T100 ...... **£497** T120 ...... **£538** Legs **£67**
MINIMAX COPIERS for above lathes CT90 .... **£484** CT100 .... **£514** CT120 .... **£560**
LUNA SPKA 900 COPIER medium duty copier for all lathes **£256**
CORONET CMB600 33" Centres 23" bowl cap .... **£589** Bowl rest **£49.95**
HARRISON GRADUATE 30" Centres .... **£1175** 42" Centres .... **£1232** Shortbed **£1037**

WOODTURNING FITMENTS CHISELS & ACCESSORIES (State m/c)

Coronet collet chuck sets (state m/c) **£65**
Coronet collet bodies .... only **£29**
Collets ⅝", ¾", 1" .... each **£12**
Expanding Jaws 3", 2", 1" .... each **£27**
Spigots ⅝", ¾", 1" .... each **£14**
Speedaneez polish std/wht **£5**
Coronet planer blades 4½" .. **£20** 7" .. **£23**
Revolving centres 1MT or 2MT **£18**
0-½" Drill chuck 1MT or 2MT **£15**
Craft supplies chuck **£58**
Long hole boring kit 5/16" **£32**
2½" Woodscrew chuck **£22**
Sorby sizing tool **£8**
Carnuba wax turning stick **£1.80**

WOODTURNERS "AT LAST PERFECTION"

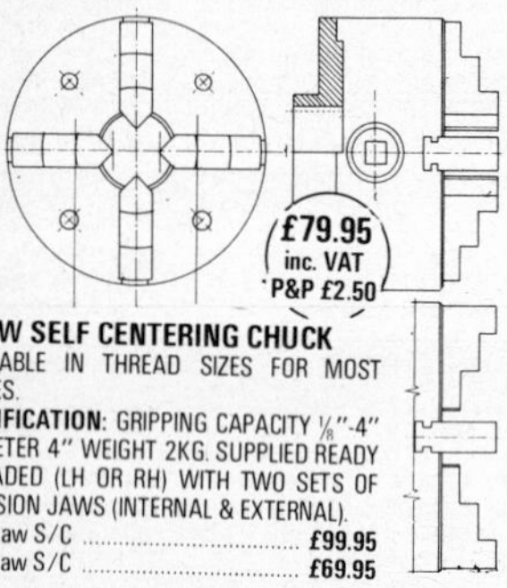

4 JAW SELF CENTERING CHUCK
AVAILABLE IN THREAD SIZES FOR MOST LATHES.
SPECIFICATION: GRIPPING CAPACITY ⅛"-4" DIAMETER 4" WEIGHT 2KG. SUPPLIED READY THREADED (LH OR RH) WITH TWO SETS OF PRECISION JAWS (INTERNAL & EXTERNAL).
5" 4 Jaw S/C **£99.95**
4" 3 Jaw S/C **£69.95**

HENRY TAYLOR HSS CHISELS

(P&P £1.20 per order)

GOUGES		PARTING TOOLS	
HS1 Superflute	**£24**	HS2 Fluted	**£15**
HS3 ¾" D/Fte	**£14**	HS11 ¼" Std.	**£5**
HS4 1½" D/Fte	**£24**	HS12 ⅜" Std.	**£7**
HS5 ¼" Spindle	**£5**	HS13 ¾" × ½"	**£10**
HS6 ⅜" Spindle	**£7**	HS33 Diamond	**£13**
HS7 ½" Spindle	**£9**	HS32 ½" × ⅛"	**£6**
CHISELS		**SCRAPERS**	
HS8 ½" Skew	**£7**	HS26 ½" Rnd	**£7**
HS21 ¾" Skew	**£8**	HS38 ¾" Rnd	**£8**
HS22 1" Skew	**£9**	HS27 1" Rnd	**£10**
HS9 1¼" Skew	**£14**	HS28 ½" Sq	**£7**
HS23 ½" Square	**£7**	HS29 ¾" Sq.	**£8**
HS24 ¾" Sqre	**£8**	HS30 1" Sq.	**£10**
HS25 1" Sqre	**£10**	HS15 HD Round	**£20**
HS10 1¼" Sqre	**£15**	HS16 HD Domed	**£20**

ALL PRICES INCLUDE HANDLES
LUNA Ring Gouge 16mm **£17** 25mm **£19**

WOODTURNING CHISEL SETS (P&P £1.80)

HENRY TAYLOR Carbon Steel Sets, 3 Piece .... **£17** 5 Piece .... **£29** 8 Piece **£46**
SORBY Carbon Steel Sets 5 Piece (51c) .... **£26** 6 Piece (61c) .... **£45** 8 Piece (82c) **£63**
SORBY High Speed Sets 5 Piece (51h) ...... **£40** 6 Piece (61h) ..... **£81** 8 Piece (82h) ... **£107**
LUNA Swedish Steel Sets GOOD VALUE 3 Piece ..... **£14** 4 Piece ..... **£27** 5 Piece **£37**
MINIATURE SETS SORBY HSS set of 5 .... **£28** HENRY TAYLOR SUPER FIVE **£18**

BANDSAWS

BURGESS BK111+ 45° 3" cut jigsaw fretsaw .... (inc. P&P) **£115**
7" Sanding attachment for Burgess ..... **£23.50** Mitre fence ..... **£8.50** Rip fence **£7.50**
DeWALT DW100 45° tilt 4" cut c/w sanding table .... (P&P £2.50) **£149**
DeWALT 6" cut 14" throat 45° DW3401 .... **£273** DW3501 .... **£289**
MINIMAX P32 45° tilt 6" cut 14" throat cast iron table **£367**
Mitre fences for above .... **£12** Stands for above **£29**
KITY 613 8" cut Large table 1½HP Very Sturdy .... **Special Price**
MINIMAX S45 45° tilt 10" cut 17" throat **£676**

★ ★ ★ SPECIAL OFFERS ON STARTRITE 301 — 351 — 352 ★ ★ ★
5 FREE BLADES WITH EACH MACHINE

STARTRITE 301 45° tilt 6" cut c/w rip & mitre fence floor standing **£399**
STARTRITE 351 45° tilt 8" cut c/w rip & mitre fence floor standing **£495**
STARTRITE 352 45° tilt 10" cut c/w rip & mitre fence floor standing **£699**
STARTRITE 502 14" cut 20" throat 1PH .... **£1204** 3PH **£1111**

★ ★ Carriage To Be Advised Mainland Each Startrite Bandsaw ★ ★

★ ★ ★ ★ ★ ★ ★ SWEDISH STEEL BANDSAW BLADES ★ ★ ★ ★ ★ ★ ★ ★ ★ ★

THE FINEST RANGE OF SWEDISH STEEL BANDSAW BLADES WELDED AND PRECISION GROUND FOR PERFECT RUNNING ENSURING ONLY THE BEST PERFORMANCE FROM YOUR BANDSAW. WHY SETTLE FOR LESS?
SEND NOW FOR CURRENT PRICE LIST
OVER 4000 BLADES IN STOCK FROM 57" — 144" IN ALL WIDTHS

METAL BLADE GUIDES for DeWalt DW100, 1310, 3401, 3501, Luna & Minimax **£5.20**

RADIAL SAWS

EUMENIA 9" blade 1¾HP 15" C/cut .... **£339** 24" C/cut **£399**
EUMENIA Stand .... **£112** Router Bracket .... **£76** Wobble Washers **£14.50**
DeWALT 1201 Portable 10" TCT Folding Radial Saw 1½ HP **£295**
DeWALT DW1251 10" TCT blade 1½ HP 16" C/cut .... **£422** Stand **£25**
DeWALT DW1501 10" TCT blade 1½ HP 18" C/cut **£496**
DeWALT DW1751 10" TCT blade 1½ HP 24" C/cut **£571**
DeWALT DW8001 12" TCT blade 2HP 18" C/cut floor standing **£616**
DeWALT DW8101 12" TCT blade 2HP 24" C/cut floor standing **£703**
DeWALT DW1600S 14" TCT blade 24" C/cut 1PH .... **£993** 3PH **£956**

PORTABLE AND WORKSHOP SAWBENCHES

MAKITA 2708 8" Portable tilt arbor bench saw **£229**
ELEKTRA 12" Sawbench floor standing TCT blade 3HP **£189**
SCHEPPACH TKU 12" Sawbench floor standing TCT blade 3HP **£229**
Elektra & Scheppach Sliding Table .... **£90** Panel Cutting Extension **£75**
ELU TGS Sawbench/Mitre Saws c/w TCT blade TGS 172 .... **£405** TGS 171 .... **£331**
Sliding table for TGS .... **£98** Aluminium cutting kit **£60**
KITY 618 10" tilt arbor sawbench floor standing .... **SPECIAL PRICE**
MULTICO NTA300 3HP 12" .... **£1099** Sliding table 48" cap. **£316**
WADKIN AGS250/300 3HP 1PH ..... **£1199** Sliding table 35" cap. **£450**
STARTRITE Scoring Saw 1PH .... **£1377** Sliding table 48" cap. **£327**
LUNA L18 12" 3HP 1PH .... **£840** Sliding table 24" cap. **£140**

ROLLER SUPPORT STANDS (P&P £3.00)

LUNA 10" support roller adjustable height sturdy construction **£28**
LUNA 16" combined roller support adjustable height **£39**

INDUSTRIAL QUALITY T.C.T SAWBLADES

ALL PRICES. INCLUDE V.A.T. AND P&P
GENERAL DUTY (MADE IN SHEFFIELD) PREMIUM QUALITY FOR CONTINUOUS USE (MADE IN W. GERMANY)

BLADE DIAMETER	6"				7"-7 1/4"				8"				9"-9 1/4"			
NO OF TEETH	16	24	36	48	18	30	42	56	20	36	48	64	24	40	54	72
GENERAL DUTY	£16	£17	£20	£26	£16	£17	£21	£26	£20	£25	£27	£32	£24	£26	£25	£36
PREMIUM QUALITY	-	£26	-	£34	-	-	-	-	-	£31	£36	£42	-	£39	£44	-
BLADE DIAMETER	10"				12"				14"				16"			
NO OF TEETH	24	40	60	80	32	48	72	96	36	60	84	108	28	36	60	96
GENERAL DUTY	£23	£26	£35	£38	£28	£36	£42	£48	£34	£42	£50	£57	-	-	-	-
PREMIUM QUALITY	£32	£36	£41	£50	£36	£42	£51	£60	£41	£48	£59	£68	£47	£50	£60	£70

PLEASE STATE BORE SIZE WHEN ORDERING

MORTICING MACHINES — *OUR PRICE INC. VAT*

SMITHS BCM 75 bench morticer c/w lateral table ¾" cap. **£399**
SMITHS CM75 floor standing morticer dual table movement ¾" cap. **£499**
MULTICO HM bench morticer ⅝" capacity precision morticer **£356**
MULTICO HMT bench morticer dual table movement **£499**
MULTICO M floor standing 1" capacity dual table movement 1PH **£626**
WADKIN EDA-2 floor standing 1" capacity dual table **£599**
RYOBI portable chain morticer .... **£365** Portable chisel morticer **£395**
WOLF Drill mortice stand C/W ½" chisel & sharpener **£135**
RIDGEWAY mortice/drill stand (requires ½" power drill) **£165**

MORTICE CHISELS & BITS

JAPANESE ¼" .... **£16** ⅜" ...... **£17** ½" ...... **£20** ⅝" ...... **£25** ¾" ...... **£37** 1" **£45**
8mm **£21** 10mm **£24** 12mm **£25** 16mm **£29** 20mm **£44**
RIDGEWAY ¼" .... **£19**; ⅜" .... **£23**; ½" .... **£24**; ⅝" .... **£35**; ¾" .... **£37**; 1" **£45**
6mm ... **£21**; 8mm ... **£22**; 10mm ... **£25**; 12mm ... **£26**; 16mm ... **£31**; 20mm ... **£46**
CHISEL BITS ONLY ¼" ..... **£6**; ⅜" ..... **£7**; ½" ..... **£8**; ⅝" ..... **£10**; ¾" ..... **£14**; 1" **£18**
MORTICE CHISEL SHARPENING SETS set 1 (¼"-½") .... **£21** Set 2 (⅜"-¾") **£26**

DUST EXTRACTORS

LUNA SPSS400 460m/hr portable suitable for low volume waste **£215**
LUNA W178 975m/hr excellent general purpose extractor c/w hose **£324**
LUNA NF243 1500m/hr mobile 5" hose ideal for high volume waste **£429**
LUNA NF259 2000m/hr heavy duty suitable for up to 3 machines **£599**
LUNA 4" × 3m hose ...... **£18** 5" × 4m hose ..... **£36** LUNA dust bags (per 10) **£3**
MULTICO DEA 960m/hr mobile extractor 4" hose **£335**
DeWALT DW60 500m/hr 5" hose .... **£265** ELEKTRA 1000m/hr 4" hose **£199**
STARTRITE CYCLAIR 55 960m/hr 4" .... **£399** CYCLAIR 75 1800m/hr 6" **£499**

MITRE CUTTERS & MITRE SAWS

ELU PS174 8" Portable mitre crosscut saw 10" crosscut **£298**
DeWALT DW250 Portable mitre saw 1¼HP 10" Blade **£194**
HITACHI CF10A 10" Portable precision mitre saw **£259**
ORTEGUILLE MITRE CUTTERS ORC55 .... **£230** ORC80 .... **£259** ORC100 .... **£430**
LION MITRE TRIMMER Excellent for clean cuts and mitres **£249**
NOBEX 202 PRO Hand Mitre saw .... **£72.95** NOBEX 303 .... **£44** (P&P £2.50)
NOBEX 202 Replacement Blades 12T, 18T or 24T .... **£4.30** each

PLANER THICKNESSERS

DeWALT DW1151 10" × 6" 2HP 2 speed power feed .... **SPECIAL PRICE**
Stand for DW1150 .... **£25** Slot Morticer .... **£65** HSS knives **£18.90**
ELECKTRA 10" × 6" floor standing power feed **£490**
SCHEPPACH HMO SOLO 10" × 6" 2HP floor standing Adjustable fence **£490**
STARTRITE PT260 10" × 7" floor standing ⅝" rebate capacity **£834**
STARTRITE SD310 12" × 7" 3 cutter block 1PH .... **£1299** 3PH **£1260**
LUNA 3HP Planers 10" × 9" .... **£1399** 12" × 9" .... **£1499** 16" × 9" **£2299**
MULTICO NS300 surfacer 3 cutter block 2HP 1PH .... **£1388** 3PH **£1271**
MULTICO THA300 12" × 10" thicknesser only 1PH .... **£1399** 3PH **£1299**
MULTICO CPT 12" × 8" Combined planer/thicknesser ¾" rebate 1PH .. **£1749** 3PH .. **£1649**
WADKIN BAOS 12" × 7" Heavy duty planer 3PH (1 only to clear) **£2699**

DRILLING MACHINES

WARCO HOBBY ½" 5 speed rack and pinion table bench mounting **£139**
WARCO ⅝" cap 2MT 12 speed 2B12 bench mounting ... **£189** 2F12 floor standing **£222**
FOBCO STAR ½" precision drill bench mounting .... **£340** floor standing **£385**
STARTRITE SP250 ½" 5 speed bench mounting .... **£356** floor standing **£398**
Morticing attachments Warco 2B/2F .... **£24** Fobco .... **£61** Startrite **£110**

SPINDLE MOULDERS AND TENNONERS

SCHEPPACH HF33 3HP 30mm 3 speed with adjustable fences **£499**
ELEKTRA TF100 3HP 30mm 3-speed 4" Rise and fall. With free cutter set **£479**
KITY 623 2HP 3 speed 4" Rise and fall C/W sliding table **£776**
STARTRITE T30 30mm C/W sliding table 1PH 2HP .... **£943** 3PH 3HP **£915**
LUNA L28 30mm 3 speed 3HP Heavy duty 1PH 3HP .... **£999** 3PH 3HP **£988**
WADKIN BURSGREEN BEL 5HP (3PH only) 4 speed 30mm **£1999**
MULTICO TENNONER TM1 240v twin motors (excluding tooling) **£1579**

SPINDLE MOULDER TOOLING (State bore size P&P £1.50)

OMAS "TIGER" BLOCKS 392 .... **£46** BLOCK in wooden case with stone etc. **£56**
OMAS cutter profiles .... **£11.50** CUTTER BLANKS .... **£6** SAW SEGMENTS **£16**
KITY PROFILE Door set .... **£96** OMAS ART 176D1 DOORSET complete **£139**
WHITEHILL BLOCKS 4⅞" × 15/16" .... **£47** 5⅜" × 15/16" .... **£66** Panel Raising Block **£92**
LEITZ 488 Cutter block 100mm .... **£56** 40mm blanks ...... each **£2.80** 60mm ...... ea **£5**
TUNGSTEN REBATE BLOCKS 125mm × 50mm ...... **£98** 6" Wobble saw 3-21mm .. **£89**
LUNA MINI POWER FEED 2 speeds **£299**
LUNA MASTER COMBINATIONS 240v W59 .... **£2599** W64 .... **£3100** W69 .... **£3899**

COMBINATION MACHINES (Carriage £10.00 UK Mainland)

STARTRITE K260 saw spindle planer etc. FREE TIGER HEAD SET **£1990**
STARTRITE TZ30 saw spindle only FREE TIGER HEAD only **£1170**
LUNA MASTER COMBINATIONS 240v W59 ..... **£2650** W64 ..... **£3100** W69 ..... **£3899**
SCHEPPACH HM2 COMBI saw spindle planer (other accs. available) **£969**
LUNA Z40 light duty combination saw planer spindle morticer **£685**

★ ★ ★ ★ ★ ★ ★ ★ ★ KITY COMBINATION MACHINES ★ ★ ★ ★ ★ ★ ★ ★

K5 COMBINATION K5 BASIC K704 TABLE COMBINATION K704 DIRECT DRIVE AND ACCESSORIES ALL AT SPECIAL PRICES SEND FOR LATEST PRICE LIST.

BORING BITS (inc. P&P)

CLICO SAW TOOTH & FORSTNER BITS (State type) 6" long ½" shank ⅜" .... **£7.70**; ½" **£7.90**
⅝" .... **£8.70**; ¾" .... **£9.50**; ⅞" .... **£10.20**; 1" .... **£10.90**; 1⅛" .... **£12.80**; 1¼" **£15.60**;
1⅜" ... **£16.20**; 1½" ... **£17.10**; 1⅝" ... **£19.70**; 1¾" ... **£22.40**; 1⅞" ... **£24.80**; 2" ... **£26.20**;
2¼" .... **£32.90**; 2½" .... **£43.70**.
CLICO PLUG CUTTERS ⅜" .. **£20** ½" .. **£23** ⅝" .. **£26** ¾" .. **£28** 1" .. **£34** 1⅓ .. **£37.80**
CLICO SAW TOOTH set ½", ¾", 1" .... **£25** ECONOMY 5 piece set ½"-1½" × ¼" **£53**
RIDGEWAY ADJUSTABLE FORSTNERS WR10/2 ½"-1¾" ...... **£14** WR10/3 ⅞"-3" **£16**
RIDGEWAY ADJUSTABLE FORSTNER (h/duty) WR20/2 ⅞"-2" **£25** WR20/3 1⅜"-3" **£29**

ROUTERS AND ROUTER ACCESSORIES

ELU MOF96 ¼" 600W **£98.50**
ELU MOF31 ¼, ⅜, ½" 1200W **£152.50**
ELU MOF177 ¼, ½" 1600W **£193.50**
HITACHI TR8 ¼" 730W **£79.95**
RYOBI R150 ¼" 730W **£75.95**
HITACHI FM ¼" 550W **£46.95**
MAKITA 3600B ¼, ½" 1500W **£168.95**
ELU MOF96E ¼" Var. speed **£119.50**
ELU MOF11/2 ½" 2000W c/w base **£337.33**
ELU MOF177E ½" Var. speed **£218.50**
HITACHI TR12 ¼, ½" 1300W **£137.95**
RYOBI R500 ¼, ½" 1500W **£113.95**
BOSCH POF 52 ¼" 520W **£55.00**
BOSCH 1604 Fixed base 1300W .. **£163.95**

ROUTER ACCESSORIES

ELU DOVETAIL KIT TCT cutter **£74.00**
ELU MOF96 Accessory kit **£74.00**
STAIR JIG (General duty) **£69.00**
ELU ROUTER BRKT. for DeWalt **£39.00**
ELU 96 Dust extraction kit **£36.00**
ELU MOF96 Height adjuster **£3.95**
RYOBI Dovetail jig fits above **£99.95**
ELU ROUTER COMBI BENCH **£97.00**
STAIR JIG (heavy duty) **£160.00**
ELU 12 piece Guide bush set **£35.00**
ELU MOF 98, 31, 177 Height adjuster **£16.95**
ELU 96 177 side fence adjuster **£6.90**

★ ★ ★ ★ ★ ★ ★ ★ ★ ELU ACCESSORIES ★ ★ ★ ★ ★ ★ ★ ★ ★

10% OFF ALL ELU ACCESSORIES 90% STOCK AVAILABILITY POST PAID ON MOST ITEMS. EXCELLENT RANGE OF ROUTER ACCESSORIES SEND NOW FOR FREE LIST.

HSS ROUTER BIT SETS (inc. P&P)

SAVE 30% ON HSS ROUTER BIT SETS AND GET A FREE ROUTER BIT CASE.
13 PIECE SET £59.95
8 PIECE SET £37.95
5 PIECE SET £21.95
ROUTER BIT CUTTER BOX .... ONLY **£4**

ROUTER CUTTERS
20-25% OFF LEADING BRANDS EXCELLENT STOCKS OF HSS & TCT ROUTER CUTTERS OVER 500 PROFILES IN STOCK. SEND NOW FOR FREE CUTTER CHART:- TECHNIQUES OF ROUTING £7.95 (inc. P&P)

IMMEDIATE DESPATCH ON CREDIT CARD PHONED ORDERS — CREDIT TERMS AVAILABLE OVER £120

0297 33656 CHARD STREET AXMINSTER DEVON EX13 5DZ 6.30-9pm 34836

BARCLAYCARD VISA

AXMINSTER POWER TOOL CENTRE

HORIZONTAL WETSTONE GRINDERS
OUR PRICE INC. VAT

JAPANESE Wetstone grinder £129.00
180G stone for above £40.00
1000G stone for above £40.00
6000G stone for above £43.00
PRECISION grinding jig £43.00

SHARPENSET Wetstone grinder £240.00
SHARPENSET 150G stone £18.40
SHARPENSET 280G stone £20.41
SHARPENSET Green stone (TCT) . £18.40
10" Planer Knife grinding jig £65.00
15" Planer Knife grinding jig £78.00
CHISEL grinding jig £67.00

VERTICAL WETSTONE GRINDERS
SCANGRIND 150 6" wetstone £69.00
SCANGRIND 2008" wetstone £88.00
SCANTOOL COMBI WET AND DRY STONES
COMBI SC150 6" wet & dry £80.00
COMBI SC200 8" wet & dry £128.00
LUNA KIRUNA 11" wet & 4" dry £118.00
LUNA KIRUNA 14" wet & 5" dry £185.00

BENCH GRINDERS
ELU EDS163 6" 360W £73.95
ELU EDS164 7" 390W £77.95
ELU MWA149 6" Honer grinder .. £90.95
LEROY SOMER 5" 180W £33.00
LEROY SOMER 6" 250W £44.00
LEROY SOMER 6" with chuck £49.00
WARCO 5" 180W (European) £33.00
WARCO 6" 380W (European) £43.00
WARCO 8" 570W (European) £69.00

GRIND STONES (state bore size)

	5"	6"	7"
COARSE 36G	£6.60	£7.90	£11.40
FINE 60G	£6.60	£7.90	£11.40
WHITE 60G	£7.20	£8.50	£13.50
GREEN (TCT)	£7.20	£8.50	£13.50

JIGSAWS (Light Duty)
Bosch PST50 Single Speed £29.95
Bosch PST50E Var. Speed £38.50
Bosch PST55PE Var. Speed Pend ... £68.50
Hitachi FJ50SB Single speed £27.50
Hitachi FJ50VA Var. speed £36.50
Hitachi FCJ55V Var. Speed Pend. Act £58.95

JIGSAWS (Heavy Duty)
Elu ST142 2 speed £101.95
Elu ST142E Var. speed £110.95
Elu ST152 2 speed £98.95
Elu ST152E Var. speed £106.95
Cases for above Jigsaws £10.00
Hitachi CJ65 2 speed £98.95
Hitachi CJ65VA Var. speed £104.95
Hitachi CJ65V Var. speed £104.95
Bosch 1581.7 Var. speed £109.95

DISC AND BELT SANDERS
Picador 10" Disc Sander £219.00
Warco BDS460 6" Disc 4" Belt £86.00
Warco BDS690 9" Disc 6" Belt £179.00
Holmes 6" 2HP £399.00
Luna Favourite 4" £285.00
Luna De-Lux Sander 4" £599.00
Luna YKV Pad Sander £647.00
Luna YK1500 Pad Sander 1PH .. £1564.00
Luna YK1500 Pad Sander 3PH .. £1509.00
Picador Unmotorised 3" Belt £49.00
Picador Unmotorised 3" Belt £65.00
Holmes 4" Belt Sander £94.00
Holmes 6" Belt Sander £120.00

CIRCULAR SAWS
HITACHI FC5SA 6" TCT 710W £42.95
BOSCH PKS46 6" TCT 600W £53.50
BOSCH PKS66 7⅞ TCT 1200W £90.95
HITACHI PSU6 6" 1050W HSS £74.95
HITACHI PSU7 7" 1600W HSS £99.95
HITACHI PSU9 9" 1759W HSS £124.95
HITACHI PSM7 7" 1200W TCT £141.95
HITACHI PSM9 9" 1600W TCT £154.95
ELU MH151 6" 850W TCT £90.95
ELU MH65 7" 1200W TCT £131.95
ELU MH85 9" 1600W TCT £177.95
ELU MH182 8" 1400W TCT £148.95
ELU 550 COMBI (for MH182) £130.00
ELU 555 Snip saw (for 182) £179.00
WOLF 9" CIRCULAR SAW £135.00

FINISHING SANDERS
(DB Dust Bag)
BOSCH PSS230 1/3rd Sheet £29.95
HITACHI FS10SA 1/3rd Sheet £25.95
HITACHI FSV12 ½ Sheet DB £47.95
BOSCH PS280A ½ Sheet DB £59.95
B&D P6303 ½ Sheet £59.95
ELU MVS156 1/3rd Sheet DB £73.95
ELU MVS156E Var. Speed DB £85.95
ELU MVS 94 ½ Sheet DB £111.95
ELU MVS47 ½ Sheet £123.95
HITACHI SV12 ½ Sheet £109.95
HITACHI SOD110 ½ Sheet DB £95.95
HITACHI SO110 ½ Sheet £86.95
BOSCH 1288.9 ½ Sheet DB £99.95
WOLF ½ Sheet DB £85.95

DRILL STANDS (43mm collar)
BOSCH S2 Light duty £21.00
BOSCH S7 Heavy duty £52.95
BOSCH S8 Milling attachment for S7 £24.50
RIDGEWAY Very heavy duty £145.95

EXTENSION CABLES
50 Metre on sturdy drum £28.95
Jo-Jo 6 Metre 30 foot £9.95
Jo-Jo 12 Metre 40 foot £14.26
Jo-Jo 18 Metre 60 foot £17.95

OUR PRICE INC. VAT

POWER PLANES (Light Duty)
BLACK & DECKER DN710 ..... £29.95
BOSCH PHO100 82mm 450W £47.95
HITACHI FP20SA 82mm 320W .. £38.95

HEAVY DUTY
ELU MFF80 82mm 850W £109.95
ELU MFF80K (in kit box) £127.95
ELU MFF40 82mm 1000W £189.95
INVERSION Std. for MFF80 ..... £20.95
INVERSION Std. for MFF40 ..... £29.00
HITACHI P20SA 82mm 720W £95.95
HITACHI FU20 82mm 620W £88.95
HITACHI F30A 92mm 900W £124.95

BELT SANDERS
ELU MHB 157 3" 600W £106.95
ELU MHB 157E 3" var. speed £119.95
ELU 157 FRAME £35.00
ELU 157 inversion stand £28.00
ABRASIVE BELTS FOR MHB 157/pkt. 3 40G, 60G, 80G, 100G, 120G, 150G £3.00
BOSCH PBS75 3" 620W £71.95
ELU MHB 90 4" 850W £193.95
ELU MHB 90K With frame £234.95
HITACHI SB75 3" 950W £116.95
HITACHI SB110 4" 950W £144.90
HITACHI SB110T 4" 950W £129.00
HITACHI SB110V 4" var. speed £134.00
MAKITA 9401 4" 1040W £169.00
MAKITA 9924DB 3" 950W £117.00

BISCUIT JOINTER
ELU DS140 Biscuit Jointer £197.95
No. 20 Biscuits (1000 off) £19.95
No. 10 Biscuits (1000 off) £19.50
No. 0 Biscuits (1000 off) £18.63
Mixed Box 0, 10, 20 (500 off) £12.50
DS140 saw blade 12T Std. £29.95
DS140 saw blade 30T Fine £29.50
DS140 Dust Tube adaptor £5.95
BOSCH Biscuit Jointer £124.95

★ ★ WOODSCREWS ★ ★
Twin Fast Zinc Plated GKN 1600 Woodscrews from 1" × 6 to 2" × 10 with Free Screwdriver. (State slotted or pozidrive)
ONLY £19.99 inc. VAT and P&P

★ ★ ★ NEW ★ ★ ★
BOSCH INDUSTRIAL HOT AIR PAINT STRIPPER 2000w Electronic Control 100°-600°C. ..... Special Price £79.95

MARTEK DRILL SHARPENER
Excellent for Sharpening all Drill Bits ..... ONLY £24.95 inc. VAT and P&P

S.D.S. POWER DRILLS
Hitachi DH16v £103.95
Hitachi VRV16 ..... £164.95
B&D PB020 ..... £112.95
B&D P8020T (c/w 110v Transformer) £185.95

DRILL/BREAKERS
Hitachi DH28Y £272.00
Hitachi DH500A £443.00
HAMMERS
H55 SA £375.00
H90 SA £756.00

HAMMERS
Hitachi H55 SA £375.00
Hitachi H90 SA £756.00

POWER DRILLS (K-Kit box)
NEW ELU POWER DRILLS
ECD304K 420W V/S 10mm Compact £73.95
EMD400K 600W 2 Speed 13mm £81.95
ESD705K 320W V/S & Rev. 10mm . £102.95
EMD403K 500W V/S/R Ham. 13mm £90.95
EMD405K 500W V/S/R Ham. 13mm £114.95
EMD406K 550W V/S Hammer 13mm £106.95

B&D 2162 KM V/S RW 450v £63.95
B&D P2264K 13mm 2 Speed 550W £74.95
B&D P2266K 13mm V/S Rev. 480W £69.95

BOSCH 400-2 10mm 440W £29.95
BOSCH 500RLE 13mm 500W V/S Rev. £49.95
BOSCH 7002E 13mm 700W £79.95
BOSCH 850RLT 13mm 850W V/S Re £111.95

HITACHI FV12VA 13mm 420W V/S £37.95
HITACHI FV16V 13mm 600W V/S/R £59.95
HITACHI FV20VA 13mm 710W V/S/R £86.95
HITACHI VTP13K 13mm 2 Speed 460W £74.00
HITACHI VTP16AK 2 Spd. 800W £103.00

ANGLE GRINDERS
HITACHI PDP100C 4" £44.85
HITACHI G13SB 5" 750W £66.81
HITACHI G23SC 9" 2000W £89.00

PALM GRIP SANDERS
(DB Dust Bag)
ELU MVS500 1/6th Sheet 135W DB £60.95
ELU MVS501 1/4 Sheet 135W DB £60.95
B&D P6301 1/6th Sheet 136W DB £51.50
B&D P6302 1/4 Sheet 135W DB ... £51.50
HITACHI SV12SA 1/4 Sheet 180W £46.95
MAKITA BO4510 1/4 Sheet £43.95

LIBERON WAXES
Waxes Sealers Stains Polishes Etc. All Your Requirements In One Send for Free Price List
GLUE POT ..... £23.00 inc. P&P
470 FLUTED DOWELS 6mm 8mm 10mm ..... £5.75 inc. P&P

HITACHI 10mm CORDLESS DRILL-SCREWDRIVERS
Our price inc. VAT

DTC 10 6 cell 2 spd. & rev. £65.00
DRC10 as above torque adjustable . £89.95
DTC10K 6 cell 2 spd. & rev. in case . £69.00
D10DB 6 cell variable spd. & rev. £80.95
D10DD 8 cell 2 spd. & rev. £82.95
D10D as above torque adjustable .. £101.95
DV10D 8 cell 2 spd. & rev. hammer £107.95

MAKITA 10mm CORDLESS DRILL SCREWDRIVERS
6012DWK 6 cell 2 spd. & rev. in case £92.95
6012HDW 8 cell 2 spd. torque adj. £111.95
8400DW 8 cell 1 spd. & rev. hammer £119.95
MAGNETIC Screwdriver kit 7 piece .. £5.95
REPLACEMENT BITS (state type) £0.50

CORDLESS TOOLS
Our price inc. VAT

HITACHI CK12D Knife cutter £103.84
HITACHI C6DA 6" Circular saw ... £143.95
MAKITA 5600DW 6" circular saw £179.95
MAKITA 4300DW Jig saw £119.95
B&D INDUSTRIAL Jig saw £110.95
B&D SPOTLIGHTER Torch £14.95
B&D DUSTBUSTER Cleaner £17.95

MISCELLANEOUS POWER TOOLS
KEW HOBBY PRESSURE WASHER £239.00
DREMEL D576 FRETSAW £69.95
BOSCH WET 'n' DRY Vacuum cleaner £93.95
BOSCH 520 HOT AIR paint stripper £23.95
BOSCH 560 HOT AIR paint stripper £32.95
NEW ELU DUST EXTRACTORS
EVE 938 ..... £275 EVE 948 ..... £395

SASH CRAMPS (P&P £2.00 per order) may be mixed for quantity

	1 off	5 off
RECORD 135-24"	£20	£18
135-36"	£21	£19
135-42"	£22	£20
135-48"	£23	£21
DRAPER 18"	£14	£12
30"	£17	£15
42"	£19	£17
T bar 66"	£30	£28

RECORD CRAMP HEADS M130
1 off £10.70 5 off £10.20 P&P £1.50)

PARAMO CRAMP HEADS
1 off £10.00 5 off £9.00 (P&P £1.50)

G CRAMPS (P&P £1.50 per order) may be mixed for quantity

	1 off	5 off
RECORD 120-3"	£5.76	£4.80
120-4"	£5.91	£4.90
120-6"	£8.31	£6.90
120-8"	£12.31	£9.80
120 10"	£18.15	£17.00
RECORD DEEP THROAT 4"	£13.27	
PARAMO 3"	£5.30	£5.00
4"	£5.55	£5.18
6"	£7.76	£7.24
8"	£11.41	£10.66
10"	£16.90	£15.77
PARAMO DEEP THROAT 4"	£12.45	

KLEMSIA QUICK CLAMPS
(P&P £1.50)

SPAN	REACH	1 off	5 off
200mm	110mm	£3.75	£3.56
300mm	110mm	£4.10	£3.89
400mm	110mm	£4.50	£4.27
600mm	110mm	£5.30	£5.03
800mm	110mm	£6.10	£5.79
1000mm	110mm	£7.10	£6.74
200mm	150mm	£5.70	£5.41
200mm	200mm	£6.80	£6.46

SADVIK SCREW CLAMPS
(P&P £1.50)

SPAN	REACH	1 off	5 off
100mm	50mm	£5.24	£4.93
160mm	80mm	£8.17	£7.69
200mm	100mm	£8.86	£8.34
250mm	120mm	£10.21	£9.61
300mm	140mm	£11.74	£11.05
400mm	175mm	£13.53	£12.73
500mm	120mm	£15.79	£14.86
600mm	120mm	£17.25	£16.24

RECORD HAND PLANES
(P&P £1.50/Order)
03 Smoothing 240×45mm £20.10
04 Smoothing 245×50mm £17.00
041/2 Smoothing 260×60mm £19.50
05 Jack 355×50mm £26.75
051/2 Jack 380×60mm £29.50
06 Jointer 455×60mm ... £34.50
07 Jointer 560×60mm .. £39.75
778 Rebate 215×38mm ... £30.80
010 Rebate 330×44mm ... £39.50
020C Circular Plane £69.50
0601/2 Block Plane £16.50
073 Shoulder Rebate £42.50
CLIFTON 420 Rebate Plane £57.00
CLIFTON Multi-Plane £189.00
CLIFTON Cap Iron 2" or 2⅜" £5.00

STANLEY HAND PLANES
(P&P £1.50/Order)
3 Smoothing 240×45mm £23.60
4 Smoothing 245×50mm £20.00
41/2 Smoothing 260×60mm £21.60
5 Jack 355×50mm £27.00
51/2 Jack 380×60mm £28.00
6 Fore 455×60mm £37.80
7 Jointer 560×60mm .. £39.40
78 Duplex Rebate £21.50
10 Rebate 330×44mm ... £40.50
80 Scraper £9.50
601/2 Block Plane £21.00
92 Rebate Plane £24.80
CLIFTON 3 in 1 Rebate Plane £67.00

WOODWORKING VICES (P&P £4.50)
RECORD V175 7" Width £12.50
52½ED 9" Quick Release £58.95
53E 10" Quick Release . £64.95

DRILL BIT SETS

	Lip & Spur	HSS Std.
1/16"-½" x 64ths	—	£21.00
1/16"-½" x 32nds	£42.00	£17.00
1-13mm x 0.5mm	£54.00	£19.00

JAPANESE WATER STONES (P&P £1.00)
KING BRAND 800G WETSTONE £8.00
KING BRAND 1200G WETSTONE ... £8.00
SUPER FINISHING STONE 6000G ... £8.90
COMBINATION WATER STONE £10.80

MISCELLANEOUS HAND TOOLS (P&P £1.50 PER ORDER)
RECORD Dowel Jig £36.20
140 Corner Cramps £5.20
145 Hold Fast £13.00
Floorboard Cramp .. £74.95
18" Extension Rods . £4.95
141 Corner Cramps £19.40
146 Hold Fast £15.50
169 Bench Stop £7.50
Drill Bushes £1.90
Spare Collars £3.20
Priory Bench Stop ... £2.95
STANLEY Web Clamp £7.99
Stanley Yankee Screwdrivers 13" ..... £12.86 20" ..... £14.17 27" £18.50

HANDSAWS (P&P £1.50)
DISSTON D8 22" 10pt . £24 DISSTON D8 24" 8pt .. £26 DISSTON D8 26" 6pt .. £27
ROBERTS & LEE 10" DOVETAIL BRASS BACK £21 ROBERTS & LEE DORCHESTER 10" £27

SANDERSON KAYSER "PAX" HANDSAWS (P&P £1.50)
BRASS BACK TENNON SAWS 8" £18.50 10" .. £19 12" £19.50 14" £20 D/Tail .. £25
HANDSAWS 20" × 10pt £21 22" × 8pt £22 24" × 7pt £23 6" × 6pt £24 26" × Rip £24

CHISEL SETS (State bevel edge or firmer P&P £1.00/Order)
MARPLES CARVERS ASH 4 piece .. £13.60
MARPLES SPLITPROOF 4 piece .. £24.50
MARPLES BOXWOOD 5 piece .. £38.50
PARAMO ROSEWOOD 4 piece .. £29.50
STANLEY 5001 6 piece .. £33.39
MARPLES BLUE CHIP 4 piece .. £17.42
MARPLES BLUE CHIP 5 piece .. £23.00
SORBY BOXWOOD 5 piece .. £26.00
PARAMO ROSEWOOD 6 piece .. £42.50
STANLEY 5002 5 piece .. £23.68

CARVING CHISEL SETS (P&P £1.00/Order)
Marples M155 3pce £12.00
Marples M153 6pce £25.58
H. Taylor PW1 3 pce £17.07
Woodcarvers Screw .. £5.99
Marples M152 6pce £35.50
Marples 153B 3pce . £12.79
H. Taylor PW4 3 pce £16.64
3½" Lignum Mallet £10.00
Marples M60A 6pce £41.00
Marples M260 5pce £44.23
H. Taylor CT6 6 pce £32.14
3½" Beech Mallet £5.55

ABRASIVES (West German top quality P&P £1.00/Order)
SANDING BELTS resin bonded aluminium oxide cloth belts (price each)

Size (length width)	M/C	40G	60G	80G	100G	120G
75 × 480mm — 3" × 19"	(Elu)	£1.11	£1.02	£0.98	£0.95	£0.95
75 × 510mm — 3" × 20"	(B&D)	£1.13	£1.04	£1.00	£0.97	£0.97
75 × 533mm — 3" 21"	(Bosch Hit)	£1.18	£1.08	£1.03	£1.00	£1.00
100 × 560mm 4" × 22"	(Elu 90)	£1.30	£1.25	£1.20	£1.16	£1.15
100 × 610mm 4" × 24"	(Wolf Hit)	£1.38	£1.33	£1.28	£1.24	£1.23
100 × 915mm — 4" × 36"	(Coronet)	£2.10	£1.86	£1.82	£1.78	£1.72
150 × 1090mm — 6" × 42"	(Coronet)	£3.90	£3.50	£3.30	£3.20	£3.20

★ ★ OTHER SIZES AVAILABLE ON REQUEST MANY IN STOCK ★ ★

ABRASIVE SHEETS (P&P £0.50 PER ORDER) state grit when ordering 100G and finer

Type	Description	60G/10	60G/50	80G/10	80G/50	100G+/10	100G+/50
PGF	GARNET FINISHING	£1.70	£8.20	£1.55	£7.10	£1.45	£6.40
GCAB	GARNET CABINET	£2.52	£11.60	£2.20	£10.04	£2.00	£9.06
PSF	SILICON FINISHING	£2.50	£12.14	£2.30	£10.51	£2.10	£9.47
WS	WET 'n' DRY	£4.80	£23.80	£4.20	£20.00	£2.80	£12.99

★SPECIAL OFFER★ 50 Sheets of asstd. Abrasives £5.99 inc. P&P Garnet-Glass-W/Dry

WIRE WOOL OIL FREE

	0000 Fine	00/0 Medium	1/2 Coarse	3/4 V Coarse
1 KG ROLLS	£4.73	£4.35	£4.25	£4.13
250g ROLLS	£1.50	£1.45	£1.42	£1.38

SAVE 20% ON ALL HAND TOOLS SEND NOW FOR NEW HANDTOOL CATALOGUE £1.50 (REFUNDED ON 1st ORDER)

0297 33656 CHARD STREET AXMINSTER DEVON EX13 5DZ 6.30-9pm 34836 BARCLAYCARD VISA

Hands on

When Sandvik tools offered prizes of their Centenary handsaw for clever ideas for handtool users, we were surprised and pleased to find what a well of ingenuity and enthusiasm we had tapped. So pleased, in fact, we couldn't bear the thought of 'Shoptalking Points' just fading away.

So we got talking with Sandvik, who have come up with a truly generous and a very enticing offer. 'Shoptalking Points', as from this issue, becomes **HANDS ON** — and we have £60 worth of Sandvik tools to give away every month! Instead of one **Woodworking Wheeze**, we will now be regaling readers with a whole page full of neat and tidy tricks for the workshop, the site, the machinist, the handtool specialist, the turner, the carver. Whoever or whatever kind of woodworker you are, we aim to have a 'Hands on' idea for you — *and from you*.

But it depends on you. Send in your ideas for making your woodwork easier, neater, quicker, more precise, more productive, more enjoyable, more efficient, more profitable . . . any useful hint, tip or trick that you have devised or picked up. There's £60 worth of goodies waiting for the winning wheeze every month!

● *Just a taste of the enormous Sandvik range you could choose from*

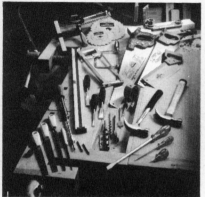

● *Hand tools, circular saws . . . win £60 worth from Sandvik's enormous range*

Easy planing

Planing difficult or wild-grained timber, try reversing the iron so the honed bevel edge is uppermost, as it is on a block plane. It increases the cutting angle so the action tends to be more of a scraping one than a wedge-splitting one. Also, keep a tin or container of cotton waste or something like it on the bench, lightly dampened with linseed oil, and draw the sole of the plane across it occasionally. It reduces the effort needed.

N. K. Milne, Margate

WOODWORKING WHEEZE
of the month

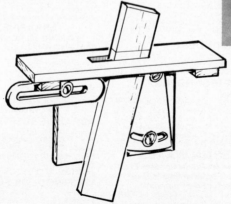

First Sandvik winner

Angle-tenoning jig

This is a version of an old French chair-maker's jig I once saw in a photograph. It consists of a vertical clamping board with an adjustable clamping stop on a pivot and slide; a perfectly flat 10x6x1in top, screwed to the vertical board at a perfect right angle, with a 3½x2in aperture in the centre; and an adjustable backstop. It is all made in accurately dimensioned and well-seasoned beech.

The 'saw' is a 24tpi 12in double-edged hacksaw blade, set in a groove in the side of another piece of perfectly flat well-seasoned beech. The groove to take the blade must be absolutely parallel to the sole of the saw 'block', to make sure the cut is parallel to the surface of the top. The blade is held in the saw-block with a tapered wedge piece.

Set your angle on the angle stop — you can use a bevel gauge through the opening — clamp the workpiece hard to the vertical board and to the angle stop, protruding through the opening at the right height to bring the saw-blade to the tenon shoulder line, and make all four cuts by simply sliding the saw-block back and forth on the true table surface. You can set the saw-blade to give the right shoulder depth. The handles aren't strictly necessary, but make it easier to use and nicer looking.

David Hodge, London E11

Calling all creatives!

● *David is **Hands on**'s first proud winner of our generous prize. Send your wheeze in as described above and you too may be the lucky one!*

Depth stops

A depth stop for a constant depth in holes drilled with a brace-and-bit is easily made by cutting a part circle out of two scraps and screwing them together either side of the bit. It will work for a range of bit sizes. If space is restricted, drill a hole of the bit size in a piece of rod or dowel and tighten it to the bit with a flat-bottomed machine screw.

Charles Cliffe, Bexleyheath

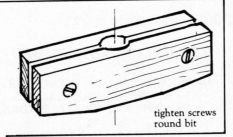

tighten screws
round bit

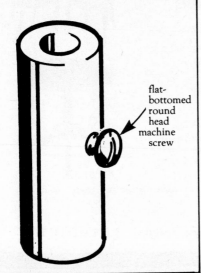

flat-bottomed round head machine screw

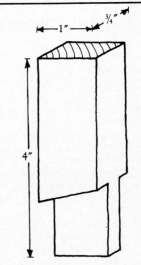

1"   ¾"

4"

Gluing the fiddly bits

Assembly of small components on the bench is a lot easier if you use a piece of thick mirror glass (without a frame) as your working surface. It provides a true, flat surface; the reflected light from the mirror lets you examine the dry fit of the joints very closely — arrange a lamp such as an Anglepoise to help; protects the bench from glue blobs; keeps the gluing process sawdust-free; prevents the assembled components from sticking to the bench; and acts as a tray to carry the assembly away from the bench to dry. You can also draw helpful construction lines on the mirror to check accuracy as you work — but do it in a medium that neither wood nor glue will absorb. Also make sure you're using the lines themselves and not their reflection!

Brian Cox, Cranleigh

Dovetail template

Instead of setting and resetting a bevel gauge for marking out dovetails, just cut an angled shoulder in an accurately dimensioned piece of hardwood, using the common 1:8 slope, or whatever pleases you. It is flipped for lines going in the opposite direction. It must be accurately made, though — or all your dovetails will exhibit the same wonkiness as your template.

Charles Cliffe, Bexleyheath

220

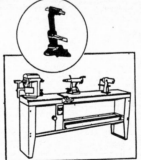
221

To be precise

An economical and accurate drilling 'engine' for dowels — a good substitute for a drill-stand with a versatility bonus. Designer Robert Smith explains

I designed this dowel jointer so that holes for jointing wood could be drilled accurately and safely by my pupils at Guthlaxton College, Leics, where I was head of the Creative Design and Handicraft department. It gives precise alignment for a series of dowel holes, and has been used by both boys and girls from first year admission to sixth form without any mishap, helping maintain a remarkably high standard of work. I think the jointer is ideal for schools, recreational courses, and also, obviously, individual woodworkers who prefer dowelling.

I used a small industrial motor, which has a great capacity for hard work and will last a lifetime, but you could easily rig up a portable electric drill on a horizontal stand, as long as the chuck will take a $^{25}\!/_{64}$in Morse drill.

The dowel jointer, which is mostly made of 12mm ply, consists of three main components:
● the base for holding the motor and jointer
● the jointer body
● the sliding surface table.

The components, together with shims, allow material to be lined up accurately, and holes to be drilled at precise right angles to the surface.

● Robert Smith's versatile dowel jointer is simple and safe to use, giving accurate results every time

Base

I used ¾in blockboard covered with 12mm ply for the base, which is 24x8½in; I stuck them together with PVA glue and suitable screws. The motor is secured to a built-up plinth of four rectangles (you may need more if you use a different motor) of 12mm ply, each 7½x6½in. I glued and screwed the first piece to the baseboard with four screws in the corners, and then glued and screwed the others systematically on top.

Once the glue had set I carefully marked a centre-line along the 7½in length of the plinth, squaring it over the front edge and then along the centre of the ply base. I made a cut line and went over it with red ballpoint pen.

Then I made up the hole-depth stop, which is a bolt going into a nut welded to the back of a metal plate. The plate is fixed to the front of the plinth, and screwing the bolt in and out alters the travel of the surface table. I cut the 2½x1½in plate from ⅛in mild steel, drilling a $^{25}\!/_{64}$in centre-hole and two countersunk screw holes for fastening. I welded a ⅜in BSF nut behind the centre-hole; I had at hand a matching 3x⅜in BSF bolt with locknut.

You need a 4in deep hole in the plinth to take the end of this bolt. This hole is centred on the red zero line in the middle of the third piece of ply up. I drilled this $^{25}\!/_{64}$in hole by hand, then screwed the metal plate on horizontally over the hole.

I glued the vertical backing board at the other end of the plinth, reinforcing with three 1½in x no.6 steel screws through the backing board into the plywood base.

Finally I fitted the runners on which the jointer body slides. I made these of 1½in wide ply with two 16x⁹/₁₆x½in hardwood

---

Fig. 1   Jointer base

7½

centre line

6½

plinth for motor

plan

side elevation

24

7½   16

4

plate with welded nut: stop bolt in hole

ply
ply
blockboard

12mm
12mm
¾
¾

front elevation

6½
1½   1½
2
¾R
hardwood strips

⁹/₁₆
⁹/₁₆

4

12mm

8½

45°

All dimensions except ply thicknesses in inches

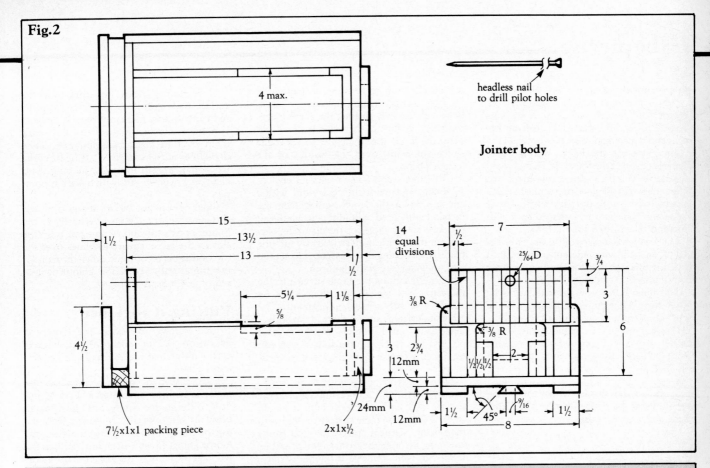

Fig.2

headless nail
to drill pilot holes

Jointer body

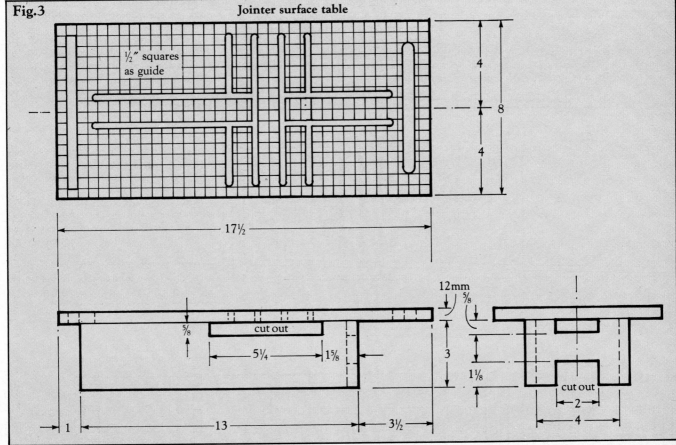

Fig.3   Jointer surface table

½" squares
as guide

cut out

cut out

strips (replaceable) planed at 45° on their inside edges.

Jointer body

The body consists of two box-like constructions. The outer box has a base 13½x8in. I fastened the 3x1in reinforcing pieces with glue and pins to the inside fronts of each side. Then I fixed the sides to the base with glue and 2in long deep-drive panel pins. I had previously drilled pilot holes using one panel pin, head removed, in an electric drill chuck. I used a similar technique elsewhere in the construction, driving panel pins in dovetail fashion. To the underside of the base I glued and pinned1½in ply strips flush with the outer edges, as runners, and a hardwood dovetail slide accurately along the central line.

Now to the inner box. I cut sections from the tops of the inner pieces; these cut-outs were 5¼x⅝in, and started 1⅛in from the back end. I also made a similar notch in the 3x3in piece for the back, cutting out a central section at the top of 2¼x⅝in. I glued and pinned this back piece between the two inner sides. Then I glued and pinned a small packing piece on to this, and finally cut to shape and fastened the T-shaped back with glue and two 1¼in x no.5 screws.

The 7x6in front piece of this inner box is also T-shaped, with side cut-outs 3x2in. I fastened this into the front end of the inner box, gluing and pinning.

This inner box is now fastened inside the outer box. After gluing, I pinned it to all four edges from underneath the base.

I shaped the front by rounding off the top corners to ⅜in radii. I glued on the packing piece (I used abura, but any accurately-squared 1x1in hardwood is suitable) and pinned it to the box base, and finally glued and pinned the shaped front, using long panel pins to go right through the packing piece and into the base.

Surface table

The underframe of the surface table is made first, followed by the working surface itself, and these are fastened together while in position on the jointer body.

Cut the back end of the surface-table 'underframe' from 4x3in ply, with cut-outs top and bottom to form an H-shape. Cut 5¼x⅝in sections from the two side pieces before gluing and pinning the three pieces together, ensuring that the internal dimension is no less than 4in so the table slides smoothly over the insides of the jointer body.

Cut the table itself accurately to 17½x8in, and mark the centre line with a cut-line down the length, going over the incision with a red ballpoint pen. Mark out the slots in the table for the clamping bars and cut them with an electric jigsaw and fine blade before using fine glasspaper to get top and undersurface really smooth.

Before fastening the table surface to the underframe, I made some thin shims, by which you get vertical adjustment. The table underframe sits on them in the body. I made four from 12mm ply, two from 9mm ply and two from ⅛in hardboard, but you may want to make extra to give more flexibility.

Now place the jointer body on the workbench, put the shims in position and sit the surface table underframe on them; it should fit well. Place the table surface on top, with the front vertical piece of the body emerging through the front slot of the table. If all fits well, remove the table surface, leaving the underframe in position; glue the exposed edges of the underframe, replace the table surface and pin through, keeping it all in position in the jointer body. Punch the pins well home, and fill the holes. Wipe any surplus glue off both surface table and jointer body.

Now you're ready to mark out the surface table grid lines. Working from the red central line, mark out parallel lines at ½in intervals; incise the lines and mark them over in black ballpoint pen. Then draw lines at right angles, starting from the front end, at ½in intervals, incising them and going over the cuts with black ballpoint pen.

Once you have marked the grid on the surface table, run the lines vertically up the jointer body projection coming through the slot in the table; square the lines over the top of this projection and down the front of the jointer body projection, colouring in in red or black as appropriate.

Putting it together

I used screws to fasten the Compton Parkinson 0.25hp silent electric motor, with a plinth and red warning light, on the jointer base.

I then placed the jointer body and surface table in position and fitted a 25/64in Morse drill to the motor chuck. I put in shims to bring the centre of the drill to ¾in from the top of the jointer body front; setting the motor going, I just touched the drill on the wood at the front of the jointer body, giving an accurate centre mark. I squared this mark to the top, and then drilled right through the wood.

I made the slotted clamps from 6½x1in x12mm ply; the guide clamping screws are easily made — at a metalworking class, for instance, if you don't have the facilities.

Finishing

I finished the jointer by glasspapering each piece and then giving all parts a thin brush coat of 'Gleem' plastic polish. For the bits that slide, the base guide and dovetail slide, I rubbed down with fine glasspaper before wax polishing. On the rest of the jointer I applied two more coats of plastic polish allowing 12 hours between coats. I kept wax well away from the top working surface and the clamps, since I didn't want them to slide about in action.

To make the motor motion obvious I stick pieces of coloured tape on the chuck. That's the only precaution you need for

Fig.4   How the parts fit together

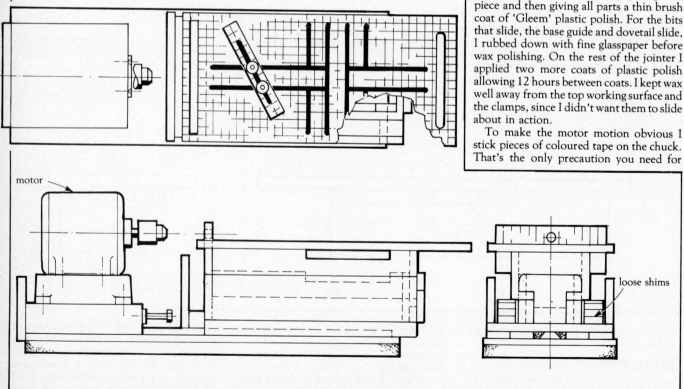

motor

loose shims

safety with this device, though I also recommend goggles and a cap for people with long hair.

Dowelling on the jointer

Material to be jointed should be marked clearly on the face side, so even if your dowels are not dead centre, they will still be precisely in line if the wood is put face-side-down on the table surface. Using a square, mark across both pieces together where the centres of the dowel holes are to be. If you are using a series of dowels, mark the positions of all the holes at once, clamping the wood lengths to be joined carefully together.

Decide what size dowels to use, and select an HSS Morse drill fractionally larger ($\frac{1}{64}$in or metric equivalent — for $\frac{3}{8}$in dowels use a $\frac{25}{64}$in drill). Fit the drill in the motor chuck and adjust the horizontal bolt depth-stop so the drill projects a suitable amount for your depth of cut.

Now adjust the table vertically by placing shims between the table surface and the jointer body. Thin shims tend to compress, so if you can, use one thick one instead of several thin ones. The clamps can be used in various ways to hold wood in position or to act as fences.

To drill holes, set the motor running, and holding the jointer top and material together, feed them forward gently into the moving drill. Give just a touch at first so you can check the drilling centre is accurate. Then, with the wood clamped in position, you can feed it firmly into the revolving drill, using your hands and stomach for forward pressure.

Dowel joints are very effective if the joint is properly designed and precision made. Use the appropriate number, diameter of dowel and length. I don't use dowels more than $\frac{3}{8}$in diameter, however thick the material. My rule of thumb is to use a dowel of half the thickness of the material to be jointed, or a little less — so $\frac{3}{8}$in will suit $\frac{3}{4}$in, $\frac{7}{8}$in and 1in material. For thicker materials I arrange the dowels in series, and stagger them if necessary. The length of dowel varies according to the material to be joined.

I prefer beech for dowels, but ramin is more commonly available. Plastic and nylon dowels also have their uses, but they hold by pressure alone, so select a suitable drill size so they hold snugly.

A smooth-surfaced dowel should be roughened, either on a lathe by running a thread-chaser down the dowel while revolving slowly, or roughening by hand with a rasp or the teeth of an old tenon saw.

Holes and dowels both need to be soaked in glue before the edges of the material are glued and cramped up; I find Flexibond is satisfactory for most woods and manufactured materials, though teak needs a one-shot Cascamite glue.

Remember to polish your construction after cleaning up but before gluing; a single coat of polish is enough to stop glue and dirt causing frustration when finally finishing the item.

When gluing up, I try to do as much of the construction as possible at one go — frame, leg and rail or the complete carcase — but you need enough cramps.

I first put glue in all the holes, putting a piece of Sellotape over each to stop it escaping. Then I soak the dowels in a pool of glue for 5-10 minutes. Finally I remove the tape systematically, glue the edges of the material, push the dowels in place by hand and cramp up so all joints are tightened simultaneously. This method pressurises glue into dowels and the material being jointed. Before leaving the construction to dry, test for squareness and winding.

Extra uses for the jointer

If your work is too large to drill directly on the jointer, you can quickly make a dowelling template on the machine. Such templates — ideally made from 1x1in or $\frac{7}{8}$x$\frac{7}{8}$in beech — quickly wear when you use a hand-held electric drill, but with the jointer you can make new precise templates at the first sign of wear.

You can also use the jointer for accurate countersinking or counterboring. ∎

Fig.5   Guides and clamps

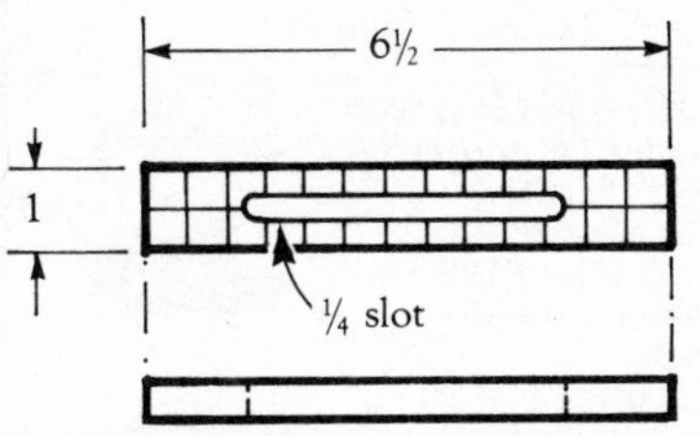

6½

1

¼ slot

12mm ply guide: two off

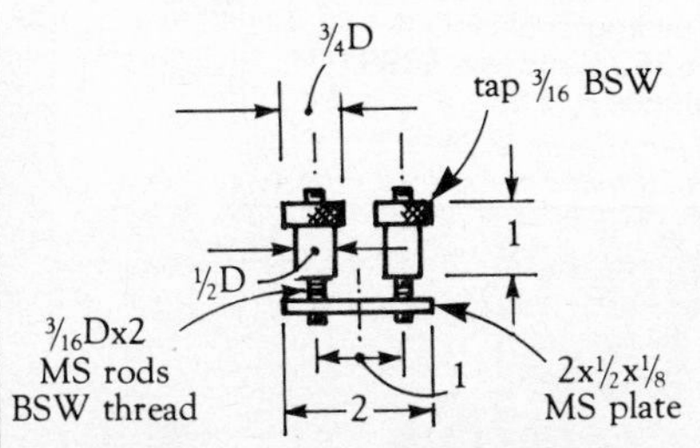

¾D

tap $\frac{3}{16}$ BSW

1

½D

$\frac{3}{16}$Dx2
MS rods
BSW thread

1

2x½x⅛
MS plate

2

Guide clamp screws: two pairs

Cutting list
Finished sizes

Jointer base

Base	1	24in	x	8½in	x	¾in Blockboard
Base	1	24		8½		12mm Ply
Runners	2	16		1½		12mm Ply
Runners	2	16		⁹⁄₁₆		½in Hardwood
Back	1	6½		4		12mm Ply
Blocks	4	7½		6½		12mm Ply
Plate	1	2½		1½		⅛in Mild steel
Nut, bolt and locknut						

Jointer body

Base	1	13½	8	12mm Ply
Sides	2	13½	2¾	12mm Ply
Front	1	6	7	12mm Ply
Front	2	2¾	1	12mm Ply
Runners	2	13½	1½	12mm Ply
Dovetail slide	1	15	1⅛	½in Hardwood
Inner sides	2	13	3	12mm Ply
Back end	1	3	3	12mm Ply
Shaped back	1	4	3	12mm Ply
Back packing	1	2	1	12mm Ply
Front packing	1	7½	1	1in Abura
Front	1	8	4½	12mm Ply

Surface table

Top	1	17½	8	12mm Ply
Sides	2	13	3	12mm Ply
Back end	1	4	3	12mm Ply
Clamps	2 or 4	6½	1	12mm Ply
Guide clamp screws, 4 or 8, as illustrated fig. 5				

Thick shims	4	13	1⅜	½in Ply
Medium shims	2	13	1⅜	⅜in Ply
Thin shims	2	13	1⅜	⅛in Hardboard

All dimensions in inches, unless specified otherwise. Note: these are finished sizes. For rough sawn sizes increase length and width by ¼in; with hardwood also add ⅛in for thickness.

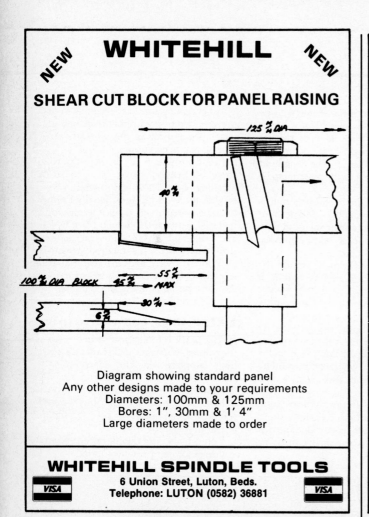

226

Guild notes

Guild of WOODWORKERS

The Guild was set up by *Woodworker* to create a meeting ground for all those involved in working wood, whether professional, amateur, or enthusiastic beginner. Guild members get:

- Access to Guild courses and events
- Free publicity in *Woodworker*
- Specially arranged tool insurance at low rates
- 15% off Woodworker Show entry
- A free display area and meeting point at the Show
- 15% discount off *Woodworker* plans
- Inclusion in our register of members' skills and services

For details, please send an sae to the Guild of Woodworkers, 1 Golden Sq, London W1R 3AB.

BOOKING FORM

I wish to book for the following course(s).
- ☐ **French polishing** 12-13 March, £40; make cheques payable to Charles Cliffe
- ☐ **Wood machining** 28 March, £25+VAT = £28.75
- ☐ **Spindle moulding** 28 March, £25+VAT = £28.75
- ☐ **Hammer veneering** 4 April, £37 inc. materials; make cheque payable to Ian Hosker
- ☐ **Parquetry** 5 April, £39 inc. materials; make cheque payable to Ian Hosker
- ☐ **French polishing** 7-8 May, £40; make cheque payable to Charles Cliffe
- ☐ **Design and workshop drawing** 9 May £25+VAT = £28.75

Please make cheques payable to 'The Guild of Woodworkers/ASP Ltd' unless otherwise stated.

Name..

Address..

....

....

Guild no...
Send to: The Guild of Woodworkers, 1 Golden Square, London, W1R 3AB. The Guild reserves the right to cancel any course.

GUILD COURSES

● **Only Guild members are eligible to go on these courses. You must book in advance, and we must have a cheque for the full cost of the course at the time of booking. If you cancel less than four weeks before the advertised date you will forfeit 50% of the cost, unless there are exceptional circumstances.**

French polishing — Charles Cliffe

12-13 March, 10-4, Bexleyheath, £40.
This is a popular course by one of our 'Question box' experts and author of *The Woodworker Manual of Finishing and Polishing*. Charles explains preparation, staining and the techniques of French polishing itself; he'll also show you how to sharpen a cabinet scraper, so bring yours along. Charles will offer advice on any small piece of furniture you want to refinish, and can also order supplies for you to take away if you tell him in advance.

Wood-machining — Ken Taylor

28 March, 10-5, Bletchley, Bucks, £25+VAT
Ken's across-the-board course on wood-machining has something for everyone who's interested in learning more about workshop hardware. First-hand experience in table- and bandsaws, radial-arm saws, planers and thicknessers, spindle moulders, mortisers and universals.

Spindle moulding — Roy Sutton

28 March, 10-5, Herne Bay, Kent £25+VAT
What Roy doesn't know about spindle moulding simply isn't worth knowing. He'll take you through the spectrum of procedures and techniques: straight and stock moulding, grooving, rebating, moulding small components with jigs, raised-panel work, laminates, machining semi-finished work, simple circular work, and sectioning handrails. Lunch is provided.

Veneering weekend — Ian Hosker

April 4-5, 9.30-4.30, Chester
You have a choice; spend the whole weekend with Ian, or opt for one of the two individual day courses on offer.

Hammer veneering: 4 April

You'll learn about preparation of veneers and ground, laying the balancing veneer, laying veneer with a join, and laying stringing crossbanding. The course costs £25, materials an extra £12 per person.

Parquetry: 5 April

The skills of producing geometric patterns in wood veneer are covered in this one-day course, including preparation, laying balancing veneer, and making a parquetry jig. You'll find out how to lay a chess board with stringing and crossbanding. This course costs £25, plus £14 for materials. Book for one of these day courses, or spend the whole weekend veneering.

Easter School — Manchester

Here's your chance for a solid five days on a course. In association with the School of Furniture, Central Manchester College, we have arranged three different courses, all running 12-16 April, 9.30-5, and costing £140.

Introduction to Cabinetmaking — Robert Cooksey and Keith Parry

A course for enthusiastic beginners and those with some experience who want to improve. It includes an introduction to basic machine preparation and hand-tool techniques in fine furniture making, and you'll be making a small item during the course.

Traditional upholstery — John Shepherd

Introducing the use of traditional methods and materials (tacks and webbing, not foam and staples!) and developing your hand skills. You can practise on a basic frame (supplied), or take a small item of your own, stripped, repaired and ready to work on.

Modern wood finishing — Eric Lyons

All your questions answered about using stains and modern finishes, including mixing stains and colour matching.
● Richard Hill, Senior Lecturer at the College is administering the courses, and **all enquiries should go to him** at the School of Furniture, Central Manchester College, Lower Hardman St, Manchester M3 3ER, (061) 831 7791, extn. 346. **Not to the Guild!**

French Polishing — Charles Cliffe

7-8 May, 10-4, Bexleyheath, £40.
Another chance to learn with an expert. You'll find out about preparation, staining and techniques of French polishing itself, with plenty of hands-on experience. Charles shows the correct way to sharpen a cabinet scraper — bring yours along — and will offer advice on any small piece of furniture you want to refinish.

Design and workshop drawing — Bob Grant

9 May, 9.30-5, Oxford, £25+VAT
If putting your design on paper doesn't come easy, here's the course to learn how. Bob will help you gain confidence in freehand sketching, show you how to use grid paper and drawing boards, and lots more.

Country chairmaking with Jack Hill

You've seen Jack working at our Wood-worker Shows. Now you can join him at Dartington in glorious Devon in May for our intensive introduction to the mysteries of traditional chairmaking. Cleaving green wood, shaping and jointing with 'rounders' and on the lathe, angle drilling, seat shaping, rush seat weaving, assembling and finishing — all will be fully covered and everyone will make something to take away.

The course, 26-29 May, includes day and evening sessions, and is fully residential at an all-in fee of £141 inc. VAT (three nights' accommodation, all meals, light refreshments); there's also a small charge for materials. The venue is part of the Dartington Hall complex close to the A38 extension of the M5 and a main-line station at Totnes.

● **Full details** direct from Rick James, The Old Postern, Dartington, Totnes, Devon TQ9 6EA — **not from the Guild.**

Calling Avon woodworkers

The Jobstart project in Bristol is carrying out a survey of craft workers in the Avon area in order to establish a register to promote their work, and to identify common problems among craftworkers. The agency, for instance, might encourage courses specifically geared for craftspeople about to become self-employed. Future plans include establishing an exhibition circuit for mixed crafts and small individual shows in new locations; a central marketing

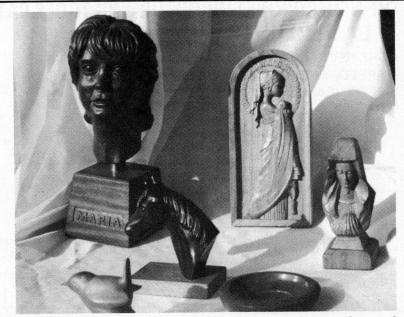

Emerging talent

We have deep sympathy with everyone who faces the trauma of unwanted redundancy; sometimes, though, even that cloud has a silver lining, as evidenced by this letter from Mrs Hubbard, of Birmingham:

When my husband Derek was sadly made redundant he was asked by a friend to carve a 'Madonna and Child' for a local nursery school. He was quite nervous, but his attempt was, in my opinion, fantastic. The original was about 30in high; a scaled-down version is in the photograph.

He had received no tuition until enrolling in a local evening carving class. He was 43 years old when he discovered his talent, and I'm so proud of him.

It took redundancy to reveal my husband's talent. Maybe this letter will encourage other men to see what they can do.

He is now happily back at work, but he still finds time for his hobby.

agency, possibly with an in-house gallery or permanent exhibition space; and producing a slide index or group catalogue.

If you're based in the Avon area, it's to your advantage to fill in a questionnaire, available from Sheila Sim, The Robinson Building, Norfolk Place, Bedminster, Bristol BS3 4NQ. Please include a stamped addressed envelope.

New course venue

Yet another long course to announce this month, 'Country chairmaking with Jack Hill'. This is at Dartington Hall, a new venue for us, and is fully residential at a very reasonable all-in price. New to us it may be, but it's been part of the Arts and Crafts scene since 1925, and has its own impressive programme of courses including woodturning and carving. For details of what's going on there, write to Rick James at the address given under 'Country chairmaking'.

Hampshire rep

A semi-professional woodturner in Southampton has volunteered to become local Guild representative for Hampshire. If you live in the area, please contact Robin Maddock, 25 Chessel Avenue, Bittern, Southampton SO2 4DY.

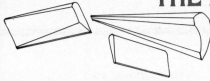

231

Question box

Our panel of experts solve your woodworking problems

We will try to answer any questions you can throw at us, but the ones we publish are the ones of most general interest to readers.

Please type your question double-spaced with generous margins, and include a stamped self-addressed envelope. Send it to: Question Box, Woodworker, 1 Golden Sq., London W1R 3AB.

Gadrooning

Q *Can you tell me the proper way to go about nulling or gadrooning edges of table tops and suggest any books?*

P. P. Butler, Dublin

A By gadrooning I take it you mean cutting a series of convex shallow relief patterns, curves and motifs on a moulding. The first thing to do is settle on a moulding section and a carved motif. Let's say you want to work a simple repeat ribbon-and-leaf pattern on a traditional astragal moulding — a full convex nicely rounded section.

First cut the moulding with plane, scratchstock, spindle moulder or whatever. No matter, as long as you finish up with a well rounded crisp-edged section.

Take a trip to a museum or grand house and get to see as many examples of gadrooning as possible, see how variedly the designs are worked so that they are repeated, cut in at depth, shallow-worked, pierced and so on. Now take your sketch book, settle on one design and a single repeat, and then make a careful pencil drawing; you might also make a full-size Plasticine maquette of the detail.

When you get back to the workshop, reduce or enlarge your chosen design so that it fits your piece of moulding, then make a good tracing. Now pencil-press transfer the lines of the design through to a piece of kitchen foil. When this has been done, look to your drawings, and note the areas of the moulding that need to be lowered and carved. Now go back to the foil, and with a fine-point craft knife very carefully cut away this part of the design. You should now have, as it were, a foil stencil plate with a number of cut-out 'windows'.

When you have achieved such a stencil plate, shape and bend it over the moulding, then take either a felt-tip pen, or better still a brush and a stiff water-colour paint, and work round or along your chosen moulding, stencil-printing the design. If you are working on a table edge, then you will need to modify and adjust the stencil printing to fit. For the carving, take a knife or a chisel of your choice and, taking note of the depth of the carving, cut in the lines of the design. Finally, (use anything from a knife, a small spoon-bent gouge, a V-tool, through to a

skew chisel), slice in at an angle and meet your initial cuts. And so you can continue, cutting in and then lowering the wood until you have achieved a miniature, shallow relief carving, on the curved moulded surface.

As to a good book, try *Practical Woodcarving and Gilding*, by William Wheeler and Charles Hayward, published by Unwin and Hyman.

Alan Bridgewater

● Alan Bridgewater is a multi-skilled craftsman and author who works with his wife Gill.

Safe toy finishing

Q *Can you suggest a good quality finish for hardwood toys so they are safe for children to handle? I am interested in both coloured paints and clear wood finish. I've tried varnish, but this is a lengthy process needing two or three coats.*

L. Williams, Co. Down

A Paints and finishes for children's wooden toys . . . quite a problem! A great many paints and finishes contain lead and other toxic materials, so you do have to be wary. I am told that all modern paints, or at least those used commercially in the UK for painting toys and other child-related goods, are required by law to meet certain non-toxic lead-free standards. Now for the tricky bit: when I first made contact with a well known paint manufacturer, they said that although their paints came within the safety standards, they didn't necessarily come up to the standards as required by the British 'Toy Safety Act'. My advice is to play it safe and use either Humbrol or Airfix modelmakers' paints — they come in small tins, they are fast drying and brilliantly coloured, and most important of all, they are designed with children in mind.

But have you tried using Deca or Pebeo acrylic paints? These are completely non-toxic, they are water based, there are special varnish and wax finishes, and they are very quick-drying.

There are no short cuts to achieve a good quality finish. Start by making sure your working area is well organised and all your tools and materials are comfortably to hand. For a painted finish, first lay on a primer, making sure you work it well into edges, grain, joints and holes, then let it dry before you rub it down with fine paper. Next lay on an undercoat, and let this dry before you rub it down. Finally lay on a thin topcoat and the job is done.

Of course there are any number of possible problem areas; the wood to be painted must be well prepared, no dust, splinters or greasy finger marks; you mustn't mix paints of a different brand or type, say car paint on top of household paint; you shouldn't paint in a wet, damp atmosphere — and be careful of fumes, toxic brush cleaners, eating or smoking while you are painting and so on.

Alan Bridgewater

Neutralising salt

Q *I am stripping an old pine dresser and refinishing in polyurethane, and I have a problem. When I found the dresser in a farm out-building it had an empty packet of salt on one shelf; the damp appears to have dissolved the salt, which seeped into the wood around that area. The result became apparent when I went to work on the dresser. I used Blackfriars self-neutralising paint stripper, then fine wire wool to clean up and rub down. The affected panel had a film of liquid, presumably water, in the area where the salt packet had stood.*

Can I apply some sort of neutralising agent and then varnish, or can I just varnish without the salt 'burning' through? Is there another finish which may solve the problem?

John Crosby, St Helier, Jersey

A Your problem can be solved by following the procedure outlined in the strict order given:

1 Wash the affected 'salted' areas of the pine dresser with a mixture of warm water and a little detergent and scrub it into these areas liberally.

2 While the wood is wet, apply a solution of mild acetic acid or undiluted white vinegar and leave this solution to lie on the wood for at least one hour.

3 Wash down the surfaces treated with clean water — if possible by using running water from a hose pipe and a scrubbing brush.

4 Allow to dry out naturally for a day or so.

5 Bring the dresser into a warm dry atmosphere at a temperature not less than 65°F and leave to dry out for a further 48 hours.

6 Apply heat from a hair dryer to the 'salted' areas until you are sure that the wood is bone dry: this is important.

7 Sand down using 100-grit garnet papers and finishing off with 240-grit papers.

8 Apply two coats of dewaxed shellac sanding sealer to the whole dresser and leave to dry out for 48 hours.

9 Re-sand slightly using 320-grit Lubrisil abrasive papers and dust off.

10 You can now apply any good quality clear gloss or satin internal varnish — preferably NOT a polyurethane type. Two coatings should be sufficient. Leave to dry out for three-four days in a temperature not less than 65°F. You should now have no further trouble.

Noel Leach

● Noel Leach is a professional wood finisher and lecturer.

Monkey-puzzle puzzle

Q *During the last gales a Monkey-puzzle tree became uprooted in a friend's garden. Is it possible to make use of the wood, perhaps in a piece of furniture, for sentimental reasons?*

Hywel Evans, Aberystwyth

A The tree known as the 'Monkey-puzzle in England is indigenous to

South America. The wood is pale brown, of even texture, and resembles Parana pine in appearance. Small brown flecks, resembling pin knots, are a common feature. Timber grown in the UK is liable to contain knot clusters, from the many groups of small branches.

The wood is similar in working qualities to Parana pine, with a slightly higher resistance to cutting. It works easily but has a tendency to crumble when working endgrain. The wood polishes well but may absorb stains unevenly.

To avoid fungal staining, the tree should be converted as soon as possible and the boards open-stacked for drying. During drying, small knots may tend to split slightly, but other splitting and distortion is usually mild.

The wood should be quite satisfactory for small items of furniture and joinery.

Ron Hooks

● Ron Hooks is a professional timber consultant.

Satin finish

Q *I am making some Swedish-style wall furniture in black ash. Can you tell me how to achieve a satin finish like that of commercially-made furniture, which stain/polish to use, and suppliers of these finishes?*
J. Turnbull, Sunderland

A The satin finish you require is achieved commercially by spraying with a cellulose or pre-catalysed lacquer which dries to the desired sheen (matt, satin or gloss). You can arrive at this effect quite easily using either of the following methods. The important thing is to have a warm dust-free environment and best quality brushes which are used only for clear finishes. Those previously used for painting will contaminate the work.

1 Eggshell or satin polyurethane. Thin the first coat by about 10% with white spirit and allow to dry overnight. Cut back with fine glasspaper or garnet. The second and third coats are unthinned. Smooth the second coat with very fine wet-or-dry, used wet with a drop or two of washing-up liquid. There is no need to flood the work. A good brushing technique is essential (see the books listed below).

2 Shellac-based sanding sealer. You may be able to obtain this locally, otherwise Horological Solvents, Proctor St, Bury is a reliable mail-order source. You can use cellulose sealer but over the large areas envisaged the fumes would be rather overpowering. Brush on two coats of sealer and allow a couple of hours between for drying. Avoid runs; they are difficult to eliminate. After overnight drying cut back with OOO wire wool dipped in wax polish, rubbing along the direction of the grain. Take care

not to cut through to the colour below.

I presume the colour you want is either dark grey or black. To arrive at this nothing works better than the aniline dyes. They are sold in powdered form which you then mix with a solvent. I prefer the water soluble variety because they don't dry too quickly while you work and leave a tide mark. They will raise the grain so wet the work and sand it back first. Watch out for glue-lines when staining. The work must be perfectly clean of any traces of glue. The strength of solution is a matter of experiment on samples of ash, but I suggest starting with a stock solution of 1oz to a pint of warm water and dilute or strengthen according to trial and error. This dye is also available from Horological Solvents. Strain the dye through a pair of old tights before use to remove undissolved crystals (they can be reused).

I recommend the following books:
Staining and Polishing, Charles Hayward.
Complete Manual of Wood Finishing, Frederick Oughton.
Wood Polishing and Finishing Techniques Aidan Walker.
Working with Wood Mitchell Beazley (Publishers).

Ian Hosker

● Ian Hosker is a professional restorer and teacher.

Lathe hammer

Bob Wearing's Workshop

Take the grind out of chuck changeovers with this natty little lathe device

Removing lathe centres and drill chucks is always a bit of a nuisance. For a moment's work, you've got to find a piece of metal which is just the right thickness and length to go through the head or tailstock — without bending — and track down a hammer. You can avoid all this by making a 'lathe hammer' which will hang conveniently with all your other lathe tools. (The lengths given are for the Myford ML8 lathe but they can be modified for any lathe.)

You'll need a good hefty block of mild steel — a cast-iron or brass doorknob, or a round mild steel bar will do the job. Drill and tap, or weld, it to take the steel rod. The rod should project ½in from the head or tailstock, which ever is the longer. Turn down the business end of the stem; this is a small step which stops the stem spreading with wear and jamming in the bore. Protect the threads on the headstock ends with a thick leather or rubber washer fixed by an epoxy resin like Araldite.

Make this little time-saver and you'll wonder how you managed without it. ■

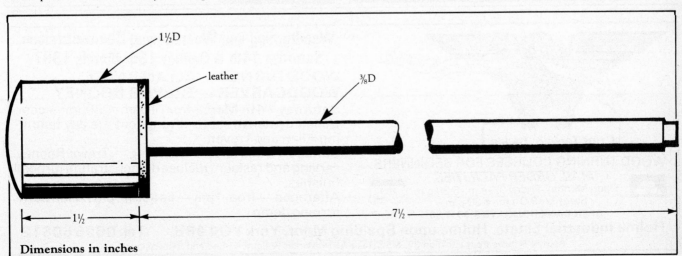

1½D

leather

⅜D

1½

7½

Dimensions in inches

Find some time

Old but solid mechanical movements make good innards for elegant bracket clocks — like this design of Bill Walker's

They lurk in attics, turn up frequently in second-hand shops and you might even find one at a jumble sale for a few pence — mechanical clock movements in old-fashioned cases. They were mass-produced, but nonetheless are well made and good reliable timekeepers.

This basket-top bracket clock case based on a late 17th century English design was built to house one of these old movements, an eight-day pendulum clock with gong striking on the hour and half hour. This movement is about 40 years old, and was originally in an oak-veneered plywood case, stained and polished. It sat on the mantelpiece for years with a wedge under one side of the case, otherwise it wouldn't go in beat (a fault that's not too difficult to correct or have corrected if you can't do it yourself). When the central heating came and we lost the mantelpiece, it disappeared into the attic.

Until, that is, I wanted a movement for this case, which is made from sycamore and cherry. You could use any hardwood, but try to choose something with a bit of character to the grain, figured rather than plain.

The dimensions of a clock case are governed by the pendulum length and size and type of dial. Set the movement up, in going order, on a temporary stand (fig. 1). This must be placed on a perfectly level base — I use an old mirror plate and level it both ways carefully. Pendulum clocks will not go well unless they are level and very steady; any rocking about will stop the clock.

My movement was originally fixed by four woodscrews through metal brackets to the inside front of the case, with a dial ring stamped from thin brass and pinned to the case front. Movements are fixed in a variety of ways, and you may have to use some ingenuity in re-fixing it in a new case.

In my case I removed the hands and took out the four woodscrews to lift the movement out of its old case. I used the original metal brackets to fix the clock to its temporary stand. I decided the dial wasn't suitable for the new case, so I would make my own, but you can buy various types from horology suppliers. Whatever you choose, you must decide the size and type of dial as well as the method of fixing it to the front of the movement before you start making the case.

With the movement fixed to its temporary rig, you can determine the internal measurements required for the case. Allow plenty of clearance between the pendulum and the bottom; you may have to adjust the

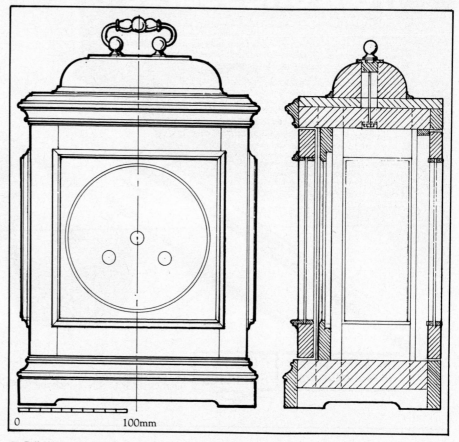

● Bill Walker's bracket-clock case: front elevation **left**, section **right**

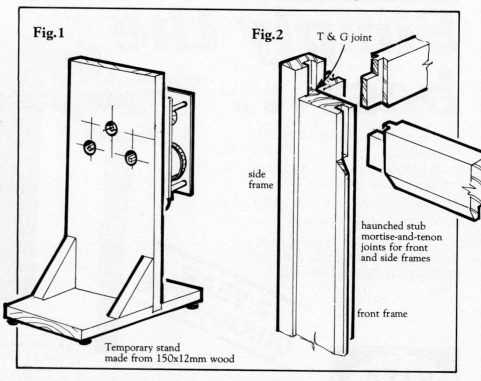

Fig.1

Temporary stand made from 150x12mm wood

Fig.2

T & G joint

side frame

haunched stub mortise-and-tenon joints for front and side frames

front frame

pendulum length, and you don't want it to scrape — about 30mm clearance will be fine. You must allow room for fixing the gong or chimes behind the movement. All these measurements vary with different movements, so check carefully —

otherwise you might find you can't shut the back door of the case later.

Once you have determined the internal measurements — height, width and depth to accommodate the complete movement with adequate clearance all round — you can make a full-size drawing of the front and side elevations. Do this on a piece of hardboard or thick card, so you can use the drawing as a rod to take off sizes when marking out individual parts.

Carcase construction

The cutting list gives net thicknesses of the timber I used, but obviously dimensions may have to be adjusted to suit your movement.

First prepare the solid pieces of timber for the inside top and base pieces. Then make the two side frames, using haunched mortise-and-tenon joints (fig. 2). Plough grooves for the front frame.

Make the front dial frame, rebated, with tongues on both stiles for joining to the side frames.

Test fit the front and side frames to the top and bottom, checking that the assembly is dead square.

Before gluing up, clean up and finish all these components, masking out with tape the parts to be glued. I used two or three coats of transparent shellac, cutting this back with OOO wire wool between coats, and finishing with wax.

Next make up the mouldings (fig. 3). I made these up by hand, using a plough plane, shoulder plane and scratch-stock. As indicated, I cut the small mouldings on thick pieces, cutting them off after shaping and cleaning up. I shellacked and polished all the mouldings, again protecting gluing surfaces.

The top is made up of top frame, basket and capping (fig. 4). I mitred the timber for the top frame and basket and glued them together, then glued on the one-piece capping and the scotia moulding.

I mitred, glued and pinned the top moulding and skirting on to the sides and front, pre-drilling holes for the veneer pins to avoid splitting. Cut the head off a veneer pin and use it in the chuck of a wheel-brace to drill the holes; if the chuck won't grip, wrap some masking tape round the pin. Hide the pins in the quirks of the moulding, punching the heads in and stopping the holes with the right coloured wax stopping.

For the front and back door-frames I used haunched stub mortise-and-tenons. I didn't use pins for fixing the mouldings around the inside edges; any springy pieces I wedged in place until the glue set. I hung the doors on 25mm solid drawn brass butts, and fitted a stop fillet inside the back door.

The glazing for the doors and the sides is fitted with mouldings and fillets.

Handle and catches

I made up my own handle (fig. 5), but you can also buy them from horology suppliers. I made a mild steel mandrel for turning the handle top and lugs, as shown. I finished the handle shaping with a graver, hand-held on the tee-rest. I annealed the 4mm brass before bending round a jig; heating the pieces to cherry red and quenching them quickly in cold water. I drilled the trans-

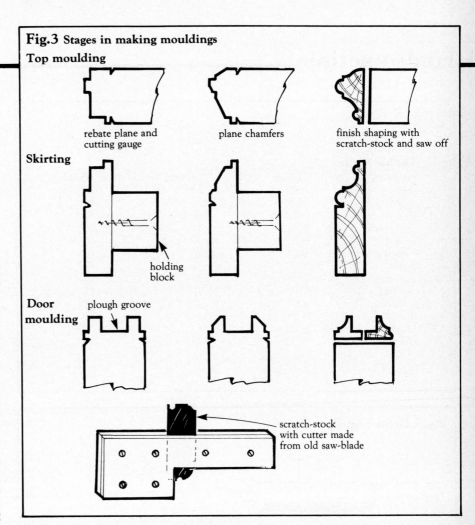

Fig.3 Stages in making mouldings

Top moulding

rebate plane and cutting gauge

plane chamfers

finish shaping with scratch-stock and saw off

Skirting

holding block

Door moulding

plough groove

scratch-stock with cutter made from old saw-blade

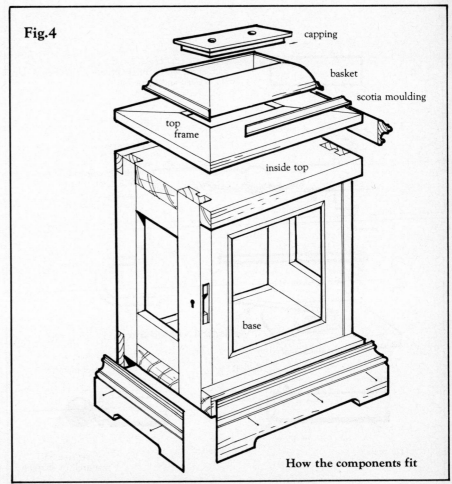

Fig.4

capping

basket

scotia moulding

top frame

inside top

base

How the components fit

continued

Cutting list

Thicknesses net

Inside top	220mm	x	130mm	x 20mm
Base	220		130	25
Side frames	1400		30	10
Dial frame	800		30	10
Top frame	600		65	10
Basket	500		30	30
Capping	100		30	10
Scotia	500		9	9
Top moulding	550		25	12
Skirting	550		45	15
Front door	800		30	12
Back door	800		30	10
Mouldings for glass	2000		12	9
Fillets	2000		6	4

Fig.5 Brass handle

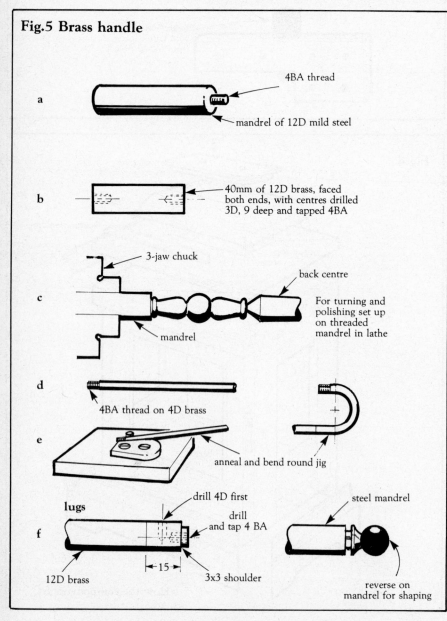

a
4BA thread
mandrel of 12D mild steel
b
40mm of 12D brass, faced both ends, with centres drilled 3D, 9 deep and tapped 4BA
c
3-jaw chuck
back centre
For turning and polishing set up on threaded mandrel in lathe
mandrel
d
4BA thread on 4D brass
e
anneal and bend round jig
f
lugs
drill 4D first
drill and tap 4 BA
steel mandrel
15
12D brass
3x3 shoulder
reverse on mandrel for shaping

verse 4mm holes in the handle lugs before shaping, then polished all the parts well and finally lacquered them with transparent lacquer for brass.

For the back door I used a simple turn-catch (fig. 9). I wanted a locking catch for the front door, but couldn't find anything suitable, so I made my own (fig. 9), based on a larger version I found in my box of old locks. It's not difficult to make, but I found some trial and error was necessary before the wards worked smoothly.

Dial

I fancied a hand-made dial for this clock so I made the dial plate from a 150mm square of 9mm plywood (fig. 6), filling the grain and applying several coats of flat white paint, cutting back each coat before applying the next. Finally I smoothed the surface with wet-and-dry paper to eliminate all brush marks.

I drew the dial rings and figures lightly in pencil first; you might study the layout of a good dial to see how the Roman numerals are set out.

I used slightly thinned matt black paint with an old-fashioned ruling pen compass for the minute rings. Then with a fine sable brush and bated breath, I used the same medium for the letters — definitely not a time for interruptions!

Assembly

The winding arbor holes must be drilled in exactly the right position; check this on the temporary stand, and drill the holes with a lip-and-spur drill. I lined the winding and centre arbor holes with brass bushes (fig. 8).

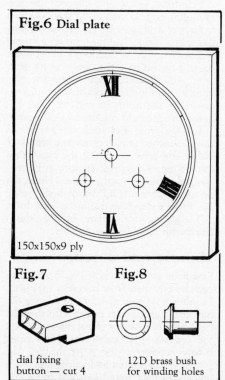

Fig.6 Dial plate

150x150x9 ply

Fig.7

dial fixing button — cut 4

Fig.8

12D brass bush for winding holes

Fig.9 Locking catch

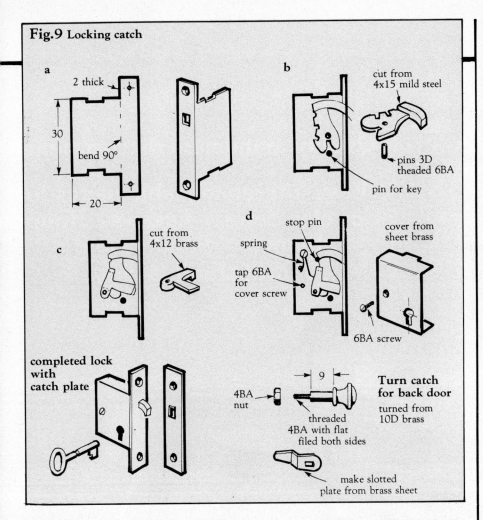

a

2 thick

30

bend 90°

20

b

cut from
4x15 mild steel

pins 3D
theaded 6BA

pin for key

c

cut from
4x12 brass

d

stop pin

spring

tap 6BA
for
cover screw

cover from
sheet brass

6BA screw

**completed lock
with
catch plate**

4BA
nut

9

threaded
4BA with flat
filed both sides

**Turn catch
for back door**

turned from
10D brass

make slotted
plate from brass sheet

The clock movement is screwed to the back of the dial. I put two keys on the winding arbors to ensure the movement was correctly positioned before inserting the fixing screws. I secured the dial and movement in the case with four wooden buttons; it's essential that the movement is firmly in the case and the clock level.

I used two lengths of 4BA studding, washers and nuts to fix the brass handle through the top of the case.

And there you have it — a clock to grace any sitting room, created in antique style with a not-so-antique movement. ∎

239

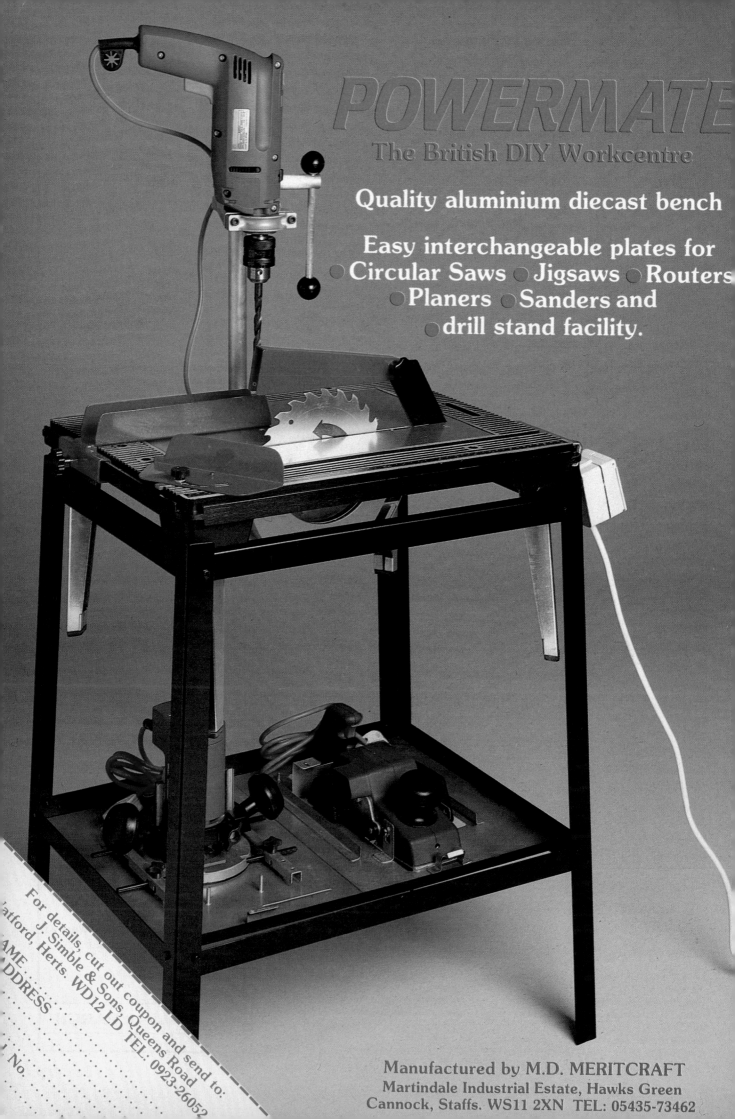

POWERMATE

The British DIY Workcentre

Quality aluminium diecast bench

Easy interchangeable plates for
- **Circular Saws** • **Jigsaws** • **Routers**
- **Planers** • **Sanders and**
- **drill stand facility.**

Manufactured by M.D. MERITCRAFT
Martindale Industrial Estate, Hawks Green
Cannock, Staffs. WS11 2XN TEL: 05435-73462

Collector's cocktail

This beautiful little chest by Waring Robinson uses no less than four hardwoods; ring your own changes or follow his instructions to reproduce a subtle marvel

Unobtrusive good proportion, fine cabinet work and the feel of the maker is a mix which never fails to excite. This is always how I am affected when I look at James Krenov's books and anticipate the problems his designs suggest. A small chest with a bow door offered an opportunity to try and emulate his principles, and our local art exhibition created the spur to make it.

I decided to make the chest from African padauk and Indian rosewood, which I felt would be a rewarding mixture. The visual effect of recently re-cut padauk is quite startling, and planing the surface exposes the full brightness and colour of the wood. The proportions were established by determining the height which would accommodate the six rosewood drawers (I had some offcuts from a previous piece). I then applied the 'geometric' or 'golden rule' of proportion to find the width and depth of the cabinet.

The construction is interesting and presents some unusual problems associated with the bow door, including the sequencing when fitting the door to the top and base of the carcase, and the correct positioning of the hinges to get an accurate pivot at the top and base of the door. The concave surface allows the door to close and still clear the protruding handles, which in turn complement the visual effect. Continuity is achieved when they form a mitre joint with the drawer-runners.

Construction

Prepare the padauk for the carcase work, which includes finishing the sides and back to the final dimensions. The top and base are left oversize in depth for final fitting at the front.

Cut the four tenons for the top and base, and grooves for the shelves, drawer-runners and back in the two sides. I did this with a router, guide-bush and template. Then I prepared five maple shelves, planing them to correct dimensions and making sure they fit snug in the grooves.

The concave fronts of the shelves were marked out with a template and bandsawed into shape, then finished with a spokeshave and fine garnet paper. Then I glued the shelves to the sides and clamped them in position.

I mortised the top and base to accept the tenons, and cut a groove for the back, then cut the back to size and rebated it to fit in the grooves. I checked the assembly dry with the sides and shelves to make sure I had an accurate fit at the back.

● *This delicately proportioned and beautifully designed little piece makes the most of the subtle beauty of a variety of hardwoods. The rose shows scale*

Photos Tim Imrie

The door

The coopered door is made up of six pieces of padauk, flat and accurately thicknessed. Ideally, these should be quarter-cut and matched for colour and grain. The edges are planed to 88°. Two halves of the door are formed by rub-jointing and clamping the segments individually, ensuring that the surface edges are in alignment. When the two halves were complete I joined them in the same way.

I planed the door to approximate dimensions, using a flat smoothing plane on the convex surface and an old moulding block plane for the inside, which approximated to the concavity. Then I finished the convex surface with a plane, scraper and fine garnet, and when I was satisfied, scribed the edges with a marking gauge to give the thickness. Ideally the concave surface should be finished with an accurately dimensioned plane, but I was able to get a satisfactory result with my moulding plane, a convex scraper and garnet paper held on a wood block which I shaped to fit the curve. I checked both surfaces regularly against accurate templates.

The hinges

Commercial pivot hinges are much too crude for the door, so I decided to make them out of 1.5mm brass, which I found surprisingly easy. The plates are two pieces 34x8mm for each hinge, and the posts are 3.5mm diameter steel rod, which fit in a hole at the 4mm centres. They can be brazed or riveted in position, and an 8mm thin steel washer should be included on the

lower hinge post to act as a spacer. I filed the exposed part of the hinge round to match the washer, and drilled two countersunk holes in each plate for the screws. I finished the brass with abrasives, first paper and then a rubbing compound to produce a polished surface.

Fitting the door

This is probably the trickiest part of the construction, bearing in mind it is the shape of the fitted door which will give the line of the top and bottom front edges, so you have no outside position to work to on the

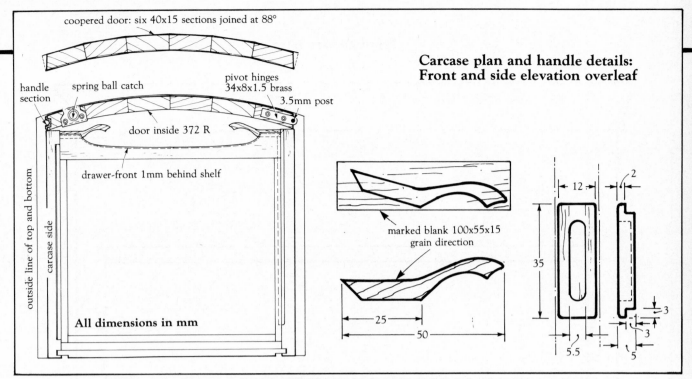

coopered door: six 40x15 sections joined at 88°

**Carcase plan and handle details:
Front and side elevation overleaf**

handle section

spring ball catch

pivot hinges
34x8x1.5 brass

3.5mm post

door inside 372 R

drawer-front 1mm behind shelf

outside line of top and bottom

carcase side

All dimensions in mm

marked blank 100x55x15
grain direction

25

50

12

2

35

5.5

3

3

5

carcase for the door. Krenov describes how to use a 'pivot-positioning jig' so the centre of the hinge post is accurately placed in the top and bottom of the carcase; I followed his advice, although there must be other simpler ways which would work equally well.

Separate the hinge plates from their pivot posts, and mark and scribe the door plates of the hinges into the top and bottom edges of the door, measuring exactly to the centre of the pivot and making sure the hinges protrude precisely the same amount top and bottom. Then cut the 'positioning jig', which is in fact no more than a piece of wood the same thickness as the door. Hold it in the door position against the front edge of the hinging side, and offer the door up to it, marking the exact pivot centre of the hinge. Then, knowing how wide the hinge plate is and how far out the pivot centre protrudes, you can mark and cut the recess for the carcase plates of the hinges in the relevant surfaces of the top and bottom pieces. Once those recesses are cut you can check how the door works, dry-assembling top and bottom again and clamping them up while you check that no adjustment is needed. If it is, be very careful and cheat the thickness of the door a bit. Don't try and re-position the hinges!

I drilled a hole in the bottom edge of the door for the brass ball-catch, fitted it, and closed the door. This left a mark on the wood for the striking plate, which I cut out of 1.5mm brass (commercial ones are too thin) and carefully fitted it in position. I closed the door again and the ball marked the exact position for the hole to be cut. The unobtrusive handle is made from rose-wood, fitted into a mortise in the vertical edge of the door.

The outside convex surface of the door is used as a pattern when it's closed to mark the front line of top and base with a pencil. I cut them oversize by the width of the mould detail, made a template and used my router and guide bush to cut the moulding along

the front edges, and the same section on the sides. I gave the surfaces a final finish and waxed the door well, polishing to a finish. With the hinges screwed in position, I glued and clamped the top and base in final position. The door closed with a satisfactory click without any chatter.

The drawers

The drawers are made in the traditional way; I completed the dovetailing before shaping the fronts. Accurate marking-out is essential, as the groove for the drawer-runner must be in the middle of the centre pin. The drawer-fronts are marked out to set back 1mm from the shelves. I bandsawed them to shape and finished them with spokeshave, scraper and fine garnet. I fitted the completed drawers, working from the back to the front and then cut the grooves in the drawer side for the runner. Accuracy is essential; having made a template for the size and shelf positions of the carcase, I found it possible to use the

same one for positioning the grooves in the drawer sides.

The handles are made out of one piece of wood. I marked out the outline on two edges against a template, making sure the grain ran in the direction of the narrowest section. The shape was carved out, checked for uniformity and then sanded smooth. Finally I sectioned them on a bandsaw and finished them to fit in a groove on the drawer-front, making a mitre joint with the drawer-runner. I glued them in position.

I made the chest over a period of three months in my available spare time. The finish was wax, apart from the drawer handles which I finished with Rustin's plastic coating and then polished them.

The proportions and the colour of the padauk are very satisfying, but a word of warning for padauk lovers. Ultra-violet light is unkind to African padauk and turns it a rather murky brown — so keep it away from the sunlight. ∎

Cutting list

Carcase

Sides (padauk)	2	330mm x	203mm x	13mm
Top (padauk)	1	240	247	19
Base (padauk)	1	240	247	19
Back (padauk)	1	322	210	6.2
Door (padauk)	6	316	40	15
Shelves (maple)	5	210	193	6.2

Drawers

Fronts (Indian rosewood)	6	203	47.5	23
Sides (English cherry)	12	181	47.5	6.2
Backs (English cherry)	6	203	38	6.2
Bottoms (maple)	6	196	172	2.5
Runners (English cherry)	12	175	6.2	6.2
Drawer handles (rosewood)	1 (12)	100	55	15
Door handle (rosewood)	1	35	12	5
Pivot hinges (brass)	4	34	8	1.5
Striking plate (brass)	1	24	16	1.5

continued

Collector's cocktail

Front elevation

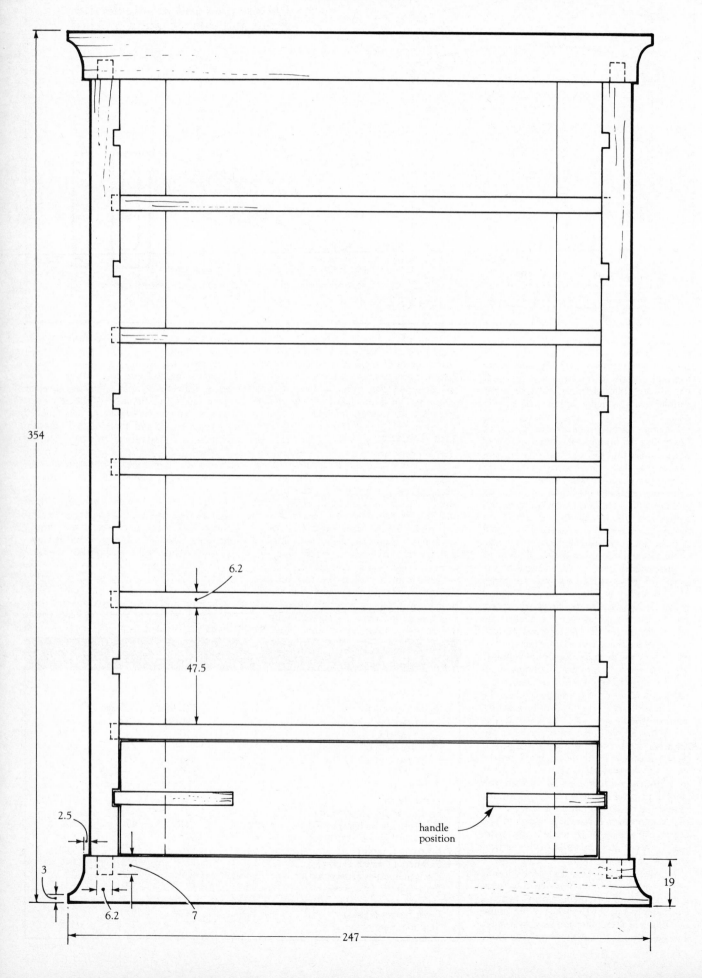

Carcase side — elevation

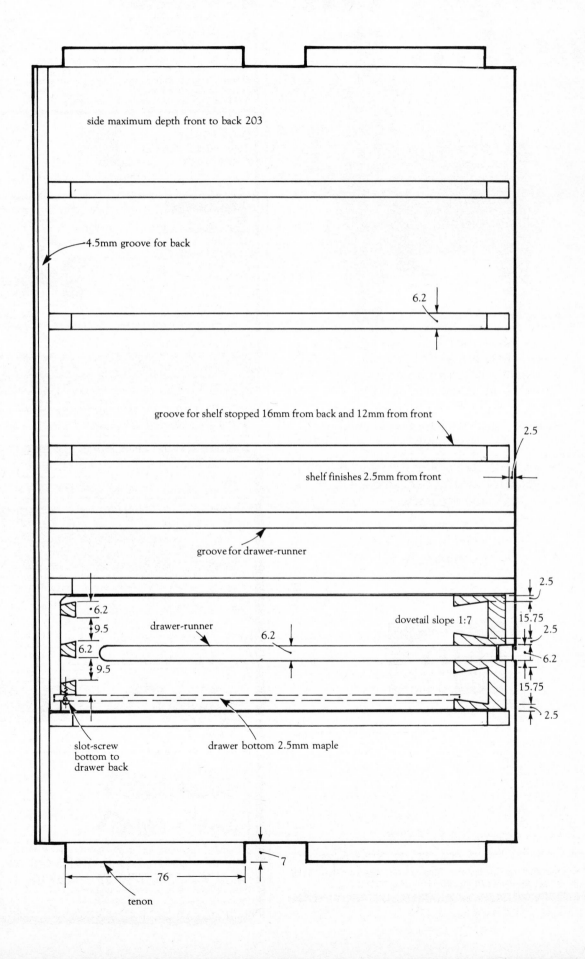

side maximum depth front to back 203

4.5mm groove for back

6.2

groove for shelf stopped 16mm from back and 12mm from front

2.5

shelf finishes 2.5mm from front

groove for drawer-runner

2.5

dovetail slope 1:7

15.75

2.5

6.2

6.2

9.5

drawer-runner

6.2

6.2

9.5

15.75

2.5

slot-screw
bottom to
drawer back

drawer bottom 2.5mm maple

7

76

tenon

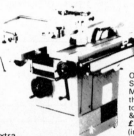

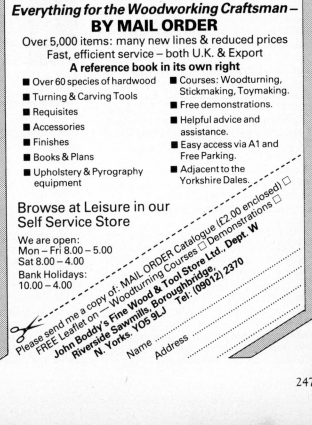
247

Wood, glorious wood

Margaret Lester is a woman with a passion for wood, a talent for communication, and a new line on education. Kerry Fowler watched her 'Touchwood' workshop

It was artist and marquetry wizard Kit Williams who first put me on the trail of Margaret Lester. He'd been bowled over by this 'extraordinary woman' and her unique workshop 'Touchwood'. I was equally impressed with his enthusiasm and went to meet her (with some trepidation) on London's South Bank when she was running Parnham House's summer exhibition. 'Touchwood,' said Margaret, 'was lots of ideas I'd had for a long time, but it took one event for it all to come together.' That event was an exhibition she visited for the partially sighted; not only were there no special facilities, most of the exhibits were behind glass.

'Touchwood' emerged as a travelling workshop which would allow people to handle and appreciate wood in many forms; from its raw state to fine work by the likes of carvers Guy Taplin and Howard Raybould, Robin Williams, and turner Ciaran Forbes. Her dislike for the look-but-don't-touch attitude of galleries and museums put her thoughts into a novel framework, but she emphasises it is a very simple idea. When I saw her in action during an intensive three days of workshops at Cleveland Crafts Centre, it did indeed seem a simple idea, but one with endless possibilities.

Margaret runs the workshops single-handed, driving to venues all over the UK with her precious sacks of 6000-year old bog-oak shavings, hand-planed and machined sycamore, fantastic redwood bark, burr elm and myriad exotic timbers. She also transports her collection of desirable objects — Howard Raybould's painted wooden fruit, Bob Ridges' decoy ducks and Richard La Trobe Bateman's stark collapsible chair. Within five minutes of arriving at the Crafts Centre she had turned the workspace into a veritable celebration of wood. Every conceivable colour and texture of the stuff, in various states and forms, emitting the unmistakable fragrance, awaited Margaret's first class of the day.

The children from Ormesby Secondary School were wheeled in 20 minutes late; Margaret was psyched up and raring to go, and with a bit of quick thinking condensed her schedule so they could experience as much as possible. Integrating physically handicapped children into 'able-bodied' schools is a fairly recent scheme; Ormesby School adopted it over a year ago and obviously felt that Touchwood had something to offer the disabled pupils. They do

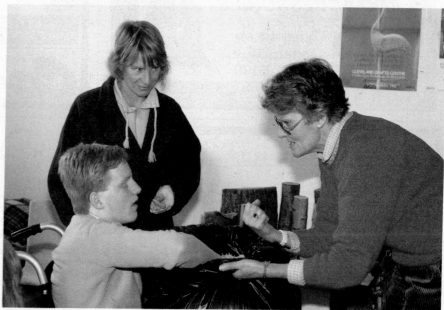

● **Top**, *lip-smacking good! An irrepressible little girl finds Bob Ridges' wooden water-melon almost good enough to eat;* **above**, *'feel the texture, appreciate the wood' – Margaret strikes her message home*

have woodwork classes, but not all of the pupils can co-ordinate fully; wheelchair-bound as they all are, they can't reach out and touch trees or pick shavings off the floor. But they can appreciate wood when it's put in their grasp, as well as understand its relevance in a social and aesthetic context, which Margaret puts across with her endless supply of stories and analogies.

They were soon up to their elbows in sacks of sawdust and shavings or holding substantial chunks of bark to their faces, learning that bark is the tree's protective skin and wrinkles like ours, that burrs are like scabs, and how the wonderful spaghetti shavings are produced. Through careful planning, Cleveland Crafts Centre was holding a 'Painted Wood' exhibition in the gallery next door where the children caught

up on their lost time enjoying working models like Frank Nelson's 'Hartlepool Monkey' (the real-life monkey was actually tried and hanged as a French infiltrator during the Napoleonic Wars). David Swift's delightfully bizarre mobiles and Guy Taplin's preening birds were amongst the exhibits, which were creatively and sensibly arranged by the centre's administrator, Susan Hoyal. But the showstopper (and there were no 'Please don't touch' signs to stop play) was a pyjama'd crocodile automaton who brushed his teeth on command, made by Frank and Bridget Egerton.

The teachers enjoyed it at least as much as the children and the trip had certainly created a lot of excitement. There are restrictions on teachers, not just in finding amenities for outings like this, but in tight curricula and exam schedules. Margaret has the time and energy to open up different dimensions to education and translate a potentially boring natural history lesson into a totally new experience that heightens awareness and widens scope. She's knows that the only contact some children have with wood is the veneer round the television screen and that the TV-age child is automatically encouraged to take a one-step-removed approach to life, strictly one-dimensional and passive. Through going back to basics, she can enliven the senses of smell and touch, the effects of form and light, and the desire to discover things for yourself.

The second shift that morning, six- to seven-year olds, had the full session. Margaret's first question was 'How many of you have touched a tree recently?' One boy put his hand up but quickly retracted in case he was put on the spot. The massive concrete and gas-jet ICI plant in Cleveland (on what was open fields 20 years ago) is the landscape the children are used to. The Yorkshire moors are a coach ride away but most of the schools found this trip into Cleveland town centre difficult enough to arrange.

She took the group through various stages of woodwork (planing, sawing and turning) explaining how big pieces of wood are made into usable, attractive items. 'When you saw wood, what do you get?' — answer, sawdust. All very elementary stuff, but chipboard can then be made by adding glue and Robin Williams' jigsaws are made of just that. The inevitable free-for-all as the sacks of shavings were passed round was constantly checked by Margaret throwing in questions like: 'How old is the *very* old bog-oak?' One girl dated it at 1981 ... well, 6000 years is hard to imagine if you're only six yourself.

The response to the tree barks, particularly the glorious velvety redwood, was loud and varied; then Margaret moved on to an African spirit drum, tapping out a beat as she explained that it was used to summon 'good ghosts' to help out when a village has problems. The children were transfixed —

● *What's this in here? Exploring hands pile into sycamore shavings galore*

and silent. Margaret strongly believes in the sixth sense and our ability to develop it. Using the simple device of the drum and the picture of these good ghosts helping out their descendants, she broached telepathy and the ideal of common good through working together. I was stunned at how quickly she progressed from the practicalities of making wooden artefacts to the intangible appeal and magic of wood.

As anyone who works with wood knows, it does have a magic about it: it can be made to resemble virtually anything; it floats, burns, decays, it looks and smells wonderful; it's a warm, living material. It also provides heat and shelter and has been important to most cultures for furniture, for religious worship — and consequently for craft.

Margaret's family have worked with wood for generations and although she's worked with John Makepeace on international woodturning and carving seminars and is administering this year's 'From craft to art' woodturning symposium with Ray Key, she makes it plain that she's technically unqualified. 'I'm not a craftsman, I'm not a teacher — I don't have formal training and I have to keep thinking one step ahead to satisfy myself that what I do is worthwhile for the students'.

The way she expresses the nature of wood, particularly in her use of folklore, is similar to the unofficial apprenticeship carpenters' children used to have. They would play about with shavings, hear the woody anecdotes, help carry the timber and see an end result to the carpenter's labours. Crafts are being revived but because they don't have the same unbroken tradition as before, Margaret feels we have to be careful that the turned bowl or hand-woven rug isn't seen as just another consumer acquisition — without understanding the work that's gone into it.

Margaret has two of Paul Caton's splendid bowls, one unfinished, rough-hewn, the other carved and polished. The students feel both and begin to realise the

● *Wood is fun: David Swift's jaunty 'Sea Salt' mobile flew high at Cleveland Crafts Centre's 'Painted Wood' exhibition*

● *Margaret raves about Guy Taplin's work - it just asks to be touched*

Photos courtesy Crafts Council Shop, V&A Museum

continued

Wood, glorious wood

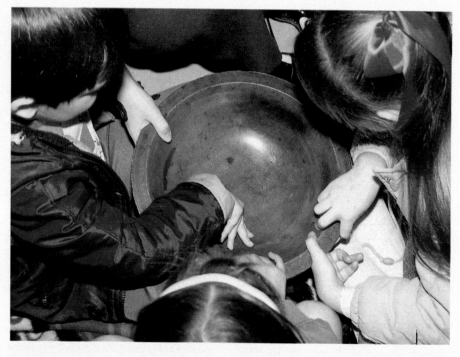

● **Left**, *'It's just like an orang-utang' – the redwood bark caused a real stir;* **above**, *young connoisseurs of wood sample Paul Caton's sensual bowl;* **below**, *food for thought; Howard Raybould's 'Fruit bowl' gave false hope for early lunch*

effort required in making them. The finished bowl is cracked — but it's one of Margaret's prize possessions. 'Just like people,' she explains to her audience, 'It's not perfect but it's still pleasing and wonderful.'

The finale of the workshop is when the children get their hands on the life-size swan, decoy ducks, netsuke mice, painted fruit and the drums. The swan won by a neck. One little girl wanted to take it home for her grandfather's pond — it's just the sort of response that keeps Margaret consistently enthusiastic. Imaginations have run riot and spawned questions and discoveries, the redwood has become an orang-utang, the dried shavings were wheat flakes and doll's hair and the rich black bog-oak (courtesy of John Makepeace) smells like pot-pourri. Unlikely, but Margaret doesn't squash any of their ideas.

All the workshops for the younger children were run on the same lines but evolved differently as new stories and angles emerged from both the class and Margaret. Touchwood is not just for the young who want to know more about wood; Margaret has presented it to Art colleges, PTAs and Art galleries, as well as to children at all levels of education and capability. I didn't see her with the older children but she said they gave her a chance to expound on sixth sense, Art and ecology — she has tremendous energy, and never stops thinking up new projects. She's now

hoping to translate Touchwood into ceramics and maybe even fabrics. When I left her she was taking in the ceramics section of the Craft Centre's gallery, wondering how such enormous pots were thrown.

Put crudely, Touchwood has found and filled a hole in the crafts/teaching market. More realistically, it's brought the beauty of the forest into the urban jungle and opened doors, maybe even careers and hobbies, for some children who may not even know what real wood looks like. So next time you're sweeping up shavings in the

workshop, or pick up some peeled bark, apply the Touchwood maxim — appreciate. ■

● Information on the Touchwood workshops can be obtained from Margaret Lester, 5 Bridport Rd, Beaminster, Dorset DT8 3LU, (0308) 862566.

● Work by Guy Taplin, David Swift, Howard Raybould is available at the Crafts Council Shop, V&A Museum, London SW7 2RL, 01-589 5070.

Letters

Carving school

THANK YOU for the most interesting article on the 'Magical mystery school' (WW/Dec '86). Although not a student there at any time, I remember several names of outstanding carvers who trained there in the period that you query. These came to my attention whilst carving in the workshop of Robert M. Cross (Architectural Carver) of Seaton Place, which was then in the somewhat dingy backwaters of the Euston Road area. Here I had the good fortune of working under foreman carver Harry Wilmore; he had been a foremost student at the South Kensington School, entering with a scholarship. We deeply admired his technique and artistry in our lovely and ancient craft. In time we became close friends, although I always remained a little envious of the obviously sound and thorough training of his student days. He often spoke of fellow students, in particular A. J. Ayres, who eventually achieved fame as a sculptor.

The principal, or chief tutor of the carving school at one time was W. H. Grimwood; he had been a notable carver in his day, and the more elderly of those in the carving trade always spoke very highly of his contribution to carving.

Although I enjoyed the work at Seaton Place, I was avid for more experience of the various styles in carving, and I felt an urge to carve figures. Each workshop tended to specialise in one aspect or another, and carving is a long row to hoe. So I left Seaton Place and went the rounds of the workshops.

The years passed and eventually came the sad news of Harry's death. I was deeply moved to find his wife wanted me to have his carving tools; she thought this was what he would have wanted. I still treasure them, and the memories of happy days with a good benchmate.

Gino Masero, Battle

Rotary planes

FOLLOWING RECENT 'Shoptalk' announcements and advertisements for rotary planes in *Woodworker*, I'd like to set the record straight.

Close on 30 years ago a Yorkshireman called Fred Lambert developed a range of tools which he simply called rounders, but which some people now call rotary planes. After a lot of design work and pattern-making and trial casting, he got it right, really right. The tools were initially made for use in schools, and enabled even the most 'less able' youngsters to make 'turned' items of furniture with well-fitting joints. Less able adults found them useful, too, including a certain Lancastrian chairmaker by the name of Jack Hill!

Fred never made the tools commercially; he didn't even patent the designs. But he ran courses showing how to make the tools, how to sharpen the blades and set them up to work efficiently. For a period the school supplies firm, Griffin & George, made and marketed the tools by agreement with Fred (their handles were dipped in black plastic, Fred's had wooden handles).

When Fred finally retired he passed the toolmaking over to another Yorkshireman who trades as Ashem Crafts of Worcester; he has been making rounders, or rotary planes, for several years now. He doesn't run courses, but sells the tools in 17 different imperial sizes, which can be bought individually and all matched up to appropriate-sized drill bits for accurate jointing. They haven't been extensively advertised because production is limited; they are handmade to order and individually set and tested before dispatch.

Which brings me to the main point of this letter. The rounders or rotary planes which I use for chairmaking, which I have demonstrated at Woodworker Shows and elsewhere for several years and which my students use on my chairmaking courses, are the genuine 'Fred Lambert' variety, made either by myself, with Fred's help, or for me by Ashem Crafts. The tools which I advertise and recommend at Shows and to students and in publications are those made only by Ashem Crafts, 2 Oakleigh Ave, Hallow, Worcester WR2 6NG, tel. (0905) 640070.

Jack Hill, chairmaker, Manchester

Jumping switch

I WONDER WHETHER anyone can help me find a replacement switch for my Coronet lathe. I have a red Consort which is fine except that vibration frequently causes the switch to jump off. I can find no way of correcting this fault, which is mechanical and inside the sealed part of the unit.

Surprisingly, Record Ridgway, the new owners of the Coronet company, say they don't have any replacement to offer, or even one that might be adapted.

I should think that somebody, somewhere, has one or two of these switches — or at least a similar one with a mounting that could be adapted. I'd be pleased to hear from anyone who might have a suitable replacement, or can suggest a solution.

Details are: MEM single phase start switch with no-volt release, catalogue no. 2SPS, also 27 SPH on block. The power unit is a Gryphon by Brook Motors, Class E, 1hp, 50Hz, 750w, 220/240v, FL amps 5.8.

G. A. Holliday, Little Hawthorn, Southwick, Dumfries DG2 8AP

Pillars and presses

I WAS INTERESTED in K. J. Down's 'Question box' query on his old pillar drill (WW/Jan), and am gathering information (I am a member of TATHS) on these very items. I have seen two types of feed mechanism on old machines; one relies on friction and the second on a cam and rachet. The former works as follows: the end of the spindle is threaded and holds a 'wheel'. As the spindle revolves in the 'no-feed' state, the wheel revolves with the spindle. To create a feed, a screw is screwed on to a spring which in turn compresses a metal rod against the wheel. This creates friction and results in the wheel turning on the thread of the spindle. If the drill cannot advance, the wheel turns with the spindle. By adjusting the compression of the spring, the friction is adjusted and so the feed force. This is so variable that holes of $\frac{1}{16}$-$\frac{1}{2}$in can be drilled in wood and metal (steel)!

I saw the other method on a drill in a junk shop. The spindle is driven by bevel gears; the driving spindle has a cam mounted between the driving gear and the handle on a short spindle. This drives a rocker arm which in turn drives a rachet cut in the top of the 'wheel'. For each turn of the spindle, the rachet turns the wheel back a determined amount. Since the cam and rachet were as far as I remember fixed, it seems the feed rate was also not variable.

I would appreciate it if Mr Down — or anybody else, come to that — could let me have any details of old drills, as I intend to write an article for the TATHS Newsletter/ Journal. Photos and sketches, preferably with an indication of size, would be very much appreciated.

A. Nichols, 39 Tyelands, Billericay, Essex CM12 9PA

Rusting tools

FOR PROTECTING TOOLS and machinery from rust (QB, WW/Oct '86) I recommend 'Waxoil' from car accessory shops. This is sprayed or brushed on, and can easily be removed with turps substitute when required.

A. Cliffe, Manchester

252

shopguide

AVON

BATH   Tel. Bath 64513
JOHN HALL TOOLS   ★
RAILWAY STREET

Open: Monday-Saturday
9.00 a.m.-5.30 p.m.
H.P.W.WM.D.A.BC.

BRISTOL   Tel. (0272) 741510
JOHN HALL TOOLS LIMITED   ★
CLIFTON DOWN SHOPPING CENTRE
WHITELADIES ROAD
Open: Monday-Saturday
9.00 a.m.-5.30 p.m.
H.P.W.WM.D.A.BC.

BRISTOL   Tel. (0272) 629092
TRYMWOOD SERVICES
2a DOWNS PARK EAST, (off North View)
WESTBURY PARK
Open: 8.30 a.m.-5.30 p.m. Mon. to Fri.
Closed for lunch 1.00-2.00 p.m.
P.W.WM.D.T.A.BC.

BRISTOL   Tel. (0272) 667013
FASTSET LTD
190-192 WEST STREET
BEDMINSTER
Open: Mon.-Fri. 8.30 a.m.-5.00 p.m.
Saturday 9.00 a.m.-1.00 p.m.
H.P.W.WM.D CS.A.BC.

BRISTOL   Tel. (0272) 667013
WILLIS
157 WEST STREET
BEDMINSTER
Open Mon.-Fri. 8.30 a.m.-5.00 p.m.
Sat. 9 a.m.-4 p.m.
P.W.WM.D.CS.A.BC.

BERKSHIRE

READING   Tel. Littlewick Green
DAVID HUNT (TOOL   2743
MERCHANTS) LTD   ★
KNOWL HILL, NR. READING
Open: Monday-Saturday
9.00 a.m.-5.30 p.m.
H.P.W.D.A.BC.

READING   Tel. Reading 661511
WOKINGHAM TOOL CO. LTD.
99 WOKINGHAM ROAD

Open: Mon-Sat 9.00 a.m.-5.30 p.m.
Closed 1.00-2.00 p.m. for lunch
H.P.W.WM.D.CS.A.BC.

BUCKINGHAMSHIRE

MILTON KEYNES   Tel. (0908)
POLLARD WOODWORKING   641366
CENTRE   ★
51 AYLESBURY ST., BLETCHLEY
Open: Mon-Fri 8.30-5.30
Saturday 9.00-5.00
H.P.W.WM.D.CS.A.BC.

SLOUGH   Tel. (06286) 5125
BRAYWOOD ESTATES LTD.   ★
158 BURNHAM LANE
Open: 9.00am-5.30pm.
Monday-Saturday.
H.P.W.WM.CS.A.

BUCKINGHAMSHIRE

HIGH WYCOMBE   Tel. (0494)
SCOTT SAWS LTD.   24201/33788
14 BRIDGE STREET   ★

Mon.-Sat. 8.30 a.m.-6.00 p.m.

H.P.W.WM.D.T.CS.MF.A.BC.

HIGH WYCOMBE   Tel. (0494)
ISAAC LORD LTD   22221
185 DESBOROUGH ROAD   KE

Open: Mon-Fri 8.00 a.m.-5.00 p.m.
Saturday 9.00 a.m.-5.00 p.m.
H.P.W.D.A.

CAMBRIDGESHIRE

CAMBRIDGE   Tel: (0223) 63132
D. MACKAY LTD.   ★
BRITANNIA WORKS, EAST ROAD

Open: Mon.-Fri. 8.30 a.m.-1 p.m./2.00-5.00 p.m. Sat 8.30 a.m.-1.00 p.m.
H.P.W.D.T.CS MF.A.BC.

CAMBRIDGE   Tel. (0223) 247386
H. B. WOODWORKING   K
105 CHERRY HINTON ROAD
Open: 8.30 a.m.-5.30 p.m.
Monday-Friday
8.30 a.m.-1.00 p.m. Sat.
H.P.W.WM.D.CS.A.

PETERBOROUGH   Tel. (0733)
WILLIAMS DISTRIBUTORS   64252
(TOOLS) LIMITED   K
108-110 BURGHLEY ROAD
Open: Monday to Friday
8.30 a.m.-5.30 p.m.
H.P.A.W.D.WH.BC.

CHESHIRE

NANTWICH   Tel. Crewe 67010.
ALAN HOLTHAM   K★
THE OLD STORES TURNERY
WISTASON ROAD, WILLASTON
Open: Tues.-Sat. 9.00 a.m.-5.30 p.m.
Closed Monday
P.W.WM.D.T.C.CS.A.BC.

CLEVELAND

MIDDLESBROUGH   Tel. (0642)
CLEVELAND WOODCRAFT   813103
(M'BRO), 38-42 CRESCENT ROAD   K

Open: Mon-Sat 9.15 a.m.-5.30 p.m.

H.P.T.A.BC.W.WM.CS.D.

CORNWALL

SOUTH WEST Power Tools
CORNWALL   Tel: Helston (03265) 4961
HELSTON AND LAUNCESTON   Launceston
         (0566) 4781
     K
H.P.W.WM.D.CS.A.

CUMBRIA

CARLISLE   Tel: (0228) 36391
W. M. PLANT
ALLENBROOK ROAD
ROSEHILL, CA1 2UT
Open: Mon.-Fri. 8.00 a.m.-5.15 p.m.
Sat. 8.00 a.m.-12.30 noon
P.W.WM.D.CS.A.

DEVON

BRIXHAM   Tel. (08045) 4900
WOODCRAFT SUPPLIES   E★
4 HORSE POOL STREET

Open: Mon.-Sat. 9.00 a.m.-6.00 p.m.

H.P.W.A.D.MF.CS.BC.

PLYMOUTH   Tel. (0752) 330303
WESTWARD BUILDING SERVICES   ★
LTD., LISTER CLOSE, NEWNHAM
INDUSTRIAL ESTATE, PLYMPTON
Open: Mon-Fri 8.00 a.m.-5.30 p.m.
Sat. 8.30 a.m.-12.30 p.m.
H.P.W.WM.D.A.BC.

PLYMOUTH   Tel. (0752) 665363
F.T.B. LAWSON LTD.
71 NEW GEORGE STREET
PLYMOUTH PL1 1RB
Open: Mon.-Sat. 8.30 am-5.30 pm.
H.P.W.CS.MF.A.

DORSET

WEYMOUTH   Tel. (0305) 770303
WEYMOUTH HIRE & SALES LTD.   K
5 KENT CLOSE
GRANBY INDUSTRIAL ESTATE
Open 7.30 a.m. - 5.30 p.m. Mon.-Fri.
Sat. 8 a.m. - 1 p.m.
H.P.W.WM.D.CS.A.K.

ESSEX

LEIGH ON SEA   Tel. (0702)
MARSHAL & PARSONS LTD.   710404
1111 LONDON ROAD   EK

Open: 8.30 a.m.-5.30 p.m. Mon-Fri
9.00 a.m.-5.00 p.m. Sat.
H.P.W.WM.D.CS.A.

GLOUCESTER

TEWKESBURY   Tel. (0684)
TEWKESBURY SAW CO. LTD.   293092
TRADING ESTATE, NEWTOWN   K

Open: Mon-Fri 8.00 a.m.-5.00 p.m.
Saturday 9.30 a.m.-12.00 p.m.
P.W.WM.D.CS.

HAMPSHIRE

ALDERSHOT   **SOUTHAMPTON**
(0252) 334422   (0703) 332288
BIRCH & HILLS POWER TOOL CENTRES
374 HIGH ST.   7 BELVIDERE RD.
Open Mon.-Fri. 8.30-5.30. Sat. 8.30-12.30
Closed for Lunch 1.00-2.00
H.P.W.WM.D.C.S.MF.BC.K.★

HERTFORDSHIRE

WARE   K★
HEATH SAWS
6 LEESIDE WORKS
STANSTEAD ABBOTTS (near Ware) HERTS.
SG12 8DL
Open: Mon.-Fri. 8.30am-5.30pm
Sat. 8.30am-1pm. Sunday by appointment.
P.W.WM.D.CS.A.

ENFIELD   Tel: 01-363 2935
GILL & HOXBY LTD.
131-137 ST. MARKS ROAD ADJ.
BUSH HILL PARK STATION, EN1 1BA
Mon.-Sat. 8-5.30
Early closing Wed. 1 p.m.
H.P.A.M.MC.T.S.W.

HUMBERSIDE

GRIMSBY   Tel. Grimsby (0472)
     58741 Hull (0482) 26999
J. E. SIDDLE LTD. (Tool Specialists)   ★
83 VICTORIA STREET
Open: Mon-Fri 8.30 a.m.-5.30 p.m.
Sat. 8.30 a.m.-12.45 p.m. & 2 p.m.-5 p.m.
H.P.A.BC.W.WMD.

HULL
HUMBERSIDE FACTORING/H.F.C.
SAW SERVICING LTD.
MAIN STREET
Open: Mon.-Fri. 8am-5pm.
Saturday 8am-12.00pm.
H.P.W.WM.D.CS.A.BC.K.

KENT

WYE   Tel. (0233) 813144
KENT POWER TOOLS LTD.
UNIT 1, BRIAR CLOSE
WYE, Nr. ASFORD

H.P.W.WM.D.A.CS.

MAIDSTONE   Tel. (0622) 50177
SOUTH EASTERN SAWS (Ind.) LTD.   ★
COLDRED ROAD
PARKWOOD INDUSTRIAL ESTATE

Open: Mon.-Fri. 8.00 a.m.-6.00 p.m.
Sat. 9.00 a.m.-12.00 a.m.
B.C.W.CS.WM.PH.

MAIDSTONE
HENSON AND PLATT
TOKE PLACE
LINTON
Open Mon.-Fri. 8.00 a.m.-5.00 p.m.
Saturday 8.00 a.m.-1.0p.m.
H.P.W.T.CS.A.

LANCASHIRE

PRESTON   Tel. (0772) 52951
SPEEDWELL TOOL COMPANY   E★
62-68 MEADOW STREET PR1 1SU
Open: Mon.-Fri. 8.30 a.m.-5.30 p.m.
Sat. 8.30 a.m.-12.30 p.m.

H.P.W.WM.CS.A.MF.BC.

shopguide

LANCASHIRE

ROCHDALE Tel. (0706) 342123/
C.S.M. TOOLS 342322
4-6 HEYWOOD ROAD E★
CASTLETON
Open: Mon-Sat 9.00 a.m-6.00 p.m.
Sundays by appointment
W.D.CS.A.BC.

LANCASTER Tel: (0524) 32886
LILE TOOL SHOP K
43/45 NORTH ROAD
Open: Monday to Saturday
9.00 a.m-5.30 p.m.
Wed. 9.00 a.m-12.30 p.m.
H.P.W.D.A.

**All shops with an
asterisk *
have a Mail Order
Service**

BLACKPOOL
FLYDE WOODTURNING SUPPLIES ★
255 CHURCH STREET
BLACKPOOL FY1 4HY
9.30-5.30 Monday to Saturday
H.P.W.WM.A.MF.C.B.C.D.

LINCOLNSHIRE

LINCOLN Tel: (0522) 689369
SKELLINGTHORPE SAW SERVICES LTD.
OLD WOOD, SKELLINGTHORPE
Open: Mon to Fri 8 a.m-5 p.m.
Sat 8 a.m-12 p.m.
H.P.W.WM.D.CS.A.*.BC.
Access/Barclaycard

LONDON

ACTON Tel. (01-992) 4835
A. MILLS (ACTON) LTD ★
32/36 CHURCHFIELD ROAD W3 6ED
Open: Mon-Fri 9.00 a.m-5.00 p.m.
Saturdays 9.00 am.-1.00 p.m.
H.P.W.WM.

LONDON Tel. 01-723 2295-6-7
LANGHAM TOOLS LIMITED
13 NORFOLK PLACE
LONDON W2 1QJ

FULHAM Tel. (01-385) 5109
I. GRIZZARD LTD. E
84a-b LILLIE ROAD, SW6 1TL
Open: Mon-Sat 9.00-5.30 p.m.
Half day Thursday

H.P.A.BC.W.CS.WM.D.

LONDON Tel. (01-636) 7475
BUCK & RYAN LTD
101 TOTTENHAM COURT ROAD W1P 0DY
Open: Mon.-Fri. 8.30 a.m-5.30 p.m.
Saturday 8.30 a.m-4.00 p.m.
H.P.W.WM.D.A..

LONDON

*Capture both local
and national
markets here.
01-437 0699*

HOUNSLOW Tel. (01-570)
Q.R. TOOLS LTD 2103/5135
251-253 HANWORTH ROAD

Open: Mon-Fri 8.30 a.m-5.30 p.m.
Sat. 9.00 a.m-1.00 p.m.
P.W.WM.D.CS.A.

MANCHESTER

MANCHESTER Tel. (061 789)
TIMMS TOOLS 0909
102-104 LIVERPOOL ROAD ★
PATRICROFT M30 0WZ
Weekdays 9.00 a.m-5.30 p.m.
Sat. 9.00 a.m-1.00 p.m.
H.P.A.W.

MERSEYSIDE

LIVERPOOL Tel. (051-207) 2967
TAYLOR BROS (LIVERPOOL) LTD K
195-199 LONDON ROAD
LIVERPOOL L3 8JG
Open: Monday to Friday
8.30 a.m-5.30 p.m.
H.P.W.WM.D.A.BC.

MIDDLESEX

RUISLIP Tel. (08956) 74126
ALLMODELS ENGINEERING LTD. E★
91 MANOR WAY
Open: Mon-Sat 9.00 a.m-5.30 p.m.
H.P.W.A.D.CS.MF.BC.

NORFOLK

NORWICH Tel. (0603) 898695
NORFOLK SAW SERVICES
DOG LANE, HORSFORD
Open: Monday to Friday
8.00 a.m-5.00 p.m.
Saturday 8.00 a.m-12.00 p.m.
H.P.W.WM.D.CS.A.

KINGS LYNN Tel. (0553) 2443
WALKER & ANDERSON (Kings Lynn) LTD.
WINDSOR ROAD, KINGS LYNN K
Open: Monday to Saturday
7.45 a.m-5.30 p.m.
Wednesday 1.00 p.m. Saturday 5.00 p.m.
H.P.W.WM.D.CS.A.

NORWICH Tel. (0603) 400933
WESTGATES WOODWORKING Tx
61 HURRICANE WAY, 975412
NORWICH AIRPORT INDUSTRIAL ESTATE
Open: 9.00 a.m-5.00 p.m. weekdays
9.00 a.m-12.30 Sat.
P.W.WM.D.BC. K

KING'S LYNN Tel. (07605) 674
TONY WADDILOVE WOODCRAFT ★
HILL FARM WORKSHOPS
GT. DUNHAM
(NR. SWAFFHAM)
Tues.-Sat. 9.00am-5.30pm
H.P.W.D.T.MF.A.BC.

NOTTINGHAMSHIRE

NOTTINGHAM Tel. (0602) 225979
POOLEWOOD and 227064/5
EQUIPMENT LTD. (06077) 2421 after hrs
5a HOLLY LANE, CHILLWELL
Open: Mon-Fri 9.00 a.m-5.30 p.m.
Sat. 9.00 a.m. to 12.30 p.m.
P.W.WM.D.CS.A.BC.

OXON

WITNEY Tel. (0993) 3885
TARGET TOOLS (SALES, & 72095 OXON
TARGET HIRE & REPAIRS) ★
TOOLS SWAIN COURT
STATION INDUSTRIAL ESTATE
Open: Mon.-Sat. 8.00 a.m-5.00 p.m.
24 hour Answerphone
BC.W.M.A.

SHROPSHIRE

TELFORD Tel. Telford (0952)
ASLES LTD 48054
VINEYARD ROAD, WELLINGTON EK★

Open: Mon. Fri. 8.30 a.m-5.30 p.m.
Saturday 8.30 a.m-4.00 p.m.
H.P.W.WM.D.CS.BC.A.

SOMERSET

TAUNTON Tel. (0823) 85431
JOHN HALL TOOLS ★
6 HIGH STREET

Open Monday-Saturday
9.00 a.m-5.30 p.m.
H.P.W.WM.D.CS.A.

STAFFORDSHIRE

TAMWORTH Tel: (0827) 56188
MATTHEWS BROTHERS LTD. ★
KETTLEBROOK ROAD
Open: Mon.-Sat. 8.30-6.00 p.m.
Demonstrations Sunday mornings by
appointment only
H.P.WM.D.T.CS.A.BC.

SUFFOLK

SUFFOLK Tel: (037983) 8126
LOCKWOOD WOODWORKING MACHINERY
WHITEGATES BUNGALOW
THE COMMON MELLIS
NEAR EYE/DISS IP23
Open standard hours.
*Lathe demos every Saturday morning.
Woodcopy lathes/Dust extractors.*
H.P.W.D.A.

IPSWICH Tel. (0473) 40456
FOX WOODWORKING KE★
142-144 BRAMFORD LANE
Open: Tues., Fri., 9.00 a.m-5.30 p.m.
Sat. 9.00 a.m-5.00 p.m.

H.P.W.WM.D.A.B.C.

SUSSEX

BOGNOR REGIS Tel. (0243) 863100
A. OLBY & SON (BOGNOR REGIS) LTD.
"TOOLSHOP," BUILDERS MERCHANT
HAWTHORN ROAD K
Open: Mon-Thurs 8 a.m-5.15 p.m. Fri.
8 a.m-8 p.m. Sat 8 a.m-12.45 p.m.
H.P.W.WM.D.T.C.A.BC.

WORTHING Tel. (0903) 38739
W. HOSKING LTD (TOOLS & KE★
MACHINERY)
28 PORTLAND RD, BN11 1QN
Open: Mon.-Sat. 8.30 a.m-5.30 p.m.
Closed Wednesday
H.P.W.WM.D.CS.A.BC.

TYNE & WEAR

NEWCASTLE Tel. (0632) 320311
HENRY OSBOURNE LTD. E★
50-54 UNION STREET

Open: Mon-Fri 8.30 a.m-5.00 p.m.

H.P.W.D.CS.MF.A.BC.

NEWCASTLE-UPON-TYNE ★
J. W. HOYLE LTD
CLARENCE STREET
NEWCASTLE-UPON-TYNE
TYNE & WEAR
NE2 17J
H.P.W.WM.D.CS.A.BC.K.

W. MIDLANDS

WOLVERHAMPTON Tel. (0902)
MANSAW SERVICES 58759
WARD STREET, HORSELEY FIELDS K★
WOLVERHAMPTON, WEST MIDLANDS
Open Mon.-Fri. 9.00am-5.00pm
Sat. 8am-3pm
H.P.W.WM.A.D.CS.

YORKSHIRE

SHEFFIELD Tel. (0742) 441012
GREGORY & TAYLOR LTD KE
WORKSOP ROAD
Open: 8.30 a.m-5.30 p.m.
Monday-Friday
8.30 a.m-12.30 p.m. Sat.
H.P.W.WM.D.

HARROGATE Tel. (0423) 66245/
MULTI-TOOLS 55328
158 KINGS ROAD K★

Open: Monday to Saturday
8.30 a.m-6.00 p.m.
H.P.W.WM.D.A.BC.

HOLME UPON Tel: 0696 60612
SPALDING MOOR
CRAFT TOOLS AND TACKLE LTD.
HOLME INDUSTRIAL ESTATE
Open: Mon.-Fri. 9.30 am-5.30 pm.
Saturday & Bank Holidays 9.30 am-4.30 pm.
H.P.W.D.T.CS MF.A.BC.

CLECKHEATON Tel. (0274)
SKILLED CRAFTS LTD. 872861
34 BRADFORD ROAD ★

Open: 9.00 a.m-5.00 p.m. Monday
Saturday Lunch 12.00 a.m-1.00 p.m.
H.P.W.A.W.CS.WM.D.

THIRSK Tel. (0845) 22770
THE WOOD SHOP ★
TRESKE SAWMILLS LTD.
STATION WORKS
Open: Seven days a week 9.00-5.00

T.H.MF.BC.

254

WOOD SUPPLIERS

WOOD SUPPLIERS

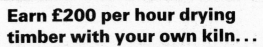

Classified Advertisements

All classified advertisements under £30.00 must be pre-paid: Cheques/PO made payable to A.S.P. Ltd. (WW). **Private and trade rate** 52p per word (VAT inclusive) minimum £7.80. **Display box rates s.c.c.** £8.60+VAT (minimum 2.5×1). All advertisements are inserted in the first available issue.
Copy to Classified Dept. (W.W.), A.S.P. Ltd., 1 Golden Square, London W.1.
There are no re-imbursements for cancellations.

**Telephone
Simon Evans
01-437-0626**

FOR SALE

THE FINEST SELECTION ON DISPLAY IN SCOTLAND!

WOODWORKING & METALWORKING MACHINERY POWER TOOLS HAND TOOLS

THE SAW CENTRE

LARGE STOCKS COMPETITIVE PRICES. PHONE AND TRY US NOW!

Eglinton Toll, Glasgow
G5 9RP
Tel: 041-429-4444

38 Haymarket
Edinburgh
EH12 5J2
Tel: 031-337-5555

OPEN
Mon - Fri
8am - 5pm
Sat 9am - 1pm

WOODCARVING tools

LARGEST STOCK IN EUROPE

Henry Taylor
Arkansas Bench & Slip Stones
Strops & Strop Paste
Bench Screws, Carvers' Vices

WOODTURNING tools

Complete range of
Henry Taylor
handled or unhandled

send 40p in stamps for illustrated catalogue

ALEC TIRANTI LTD
70 High St, Theale, Reading, Berks RG7 5AR
27 Warren Street, London W1.

BANKRUPT STOCK
Sandvik circular saw blades tungsten tipped.
5", 5½", 6" .... **£4.00 each**
6½", 8¼" .... **£6.00 each**
½" to 1⅜" bore any size.
P&P £1 extra per order.
**Tel: 643 0244
Hannett, 11 Lind Road,
Sutton, Surrey.**

RECORD MULTI PLANE 405, 22 Tungsten steel cutters, original box, excellent condition, £120. Tel: 022 023 2665.

RETIRING WOODTURNER has quantity of timber for sale, cheap, buyer collects. Telephone 0234 720270.

SCHEPPACH Universal, 10" x 6" Planer Thicknesser, 12" Saw, 4 blades, 1 TCT, Slot Morticer. All tools v.g.c. £545. Ring Maidstone 673988.

CLOCKMAKERS

Extensive range of very competitively priced German quartz clock movements, (including standard quartz, pendulum, mini-pendulum, chining, striking and insertion movements). Large selection of quality dials, chapter rings, hands, bezels, clock plans and weather instruments.
Please send 25p stamps for 20 page catalogue.
**Bath Clock Company (Dept. W),
13 Welton Road, Radstock, Bath.**

BLADES

Spindle tooling, circular saw blades, dado sets, planer blades, router cutters and router accessories, machinery of particular merit, Forstener bits, mortise chisels, profile cutter blocks, radial arm saw accessories, etc.
Send £1 (refunded on first order) for your copy of our brochure.
Blades, Dept. WWM. Freepost, Petersfield, Hampshire. GU32 2BR (no stamp required)

BARGAINS GALORE!

Genuine once only sale of high quality cabinet makers and woodturners tools, finishing materials and many hard to find items at fantastic prices. For details send SAE to:
Corbett Tools, 111 St Johns Avenue, Kidderminster, Worcs. DY11 6AX.

CONTENTS of 3 school workshops, engineering and woodworking machines and various tools. For detailed list write to: Warners Machinery Centre, Unit 10, Finedon Road, Irthlingborough, Northants.

RADIAL ARM SAW DW1751 less than one years light use, router bracket, drum sander, TCT blade, £450. Canterbury 472449.

STARTRITE K210 Multi Saw + Myford Woodlathe. Highest offer secures 01-228-1817.

LATHES: Coronet, Myford, Arundle from £250. Also Coronet Imp Bandsaw, Kity Morticer, Multico 12" Sawbench. All 240v. Phone 0902 743675.

WINDSOR CHAIRS

Full size bends. 50 × 1⅜ × 1⅛" in Ash £6.95.
Childs Windsor Chair bends in Ash 36 × 1⅛ × ⅞" £4.95.
All prices include p&p.
Please send cheque/P.O. with order to:
**P. Stuffin, Spurn View, North End Road, Tetney, Grimby DN36 5NA.
Tel: (0472) 812576 (Afternoons)**

ZYTO Universal Woodworker 15 inch saw, 9 inch planer, slot mortiser. Excellent condition £600. Phone Consett 0207 503767 or 0207 504167.

WOODWORKER magazines very good condition, 1938-39, 14 copies and 1947-56, 108 copies. Offers: Sedgley (09073) 64168.

THE WHISTON CATALOGUE

Nuts, bolts, screws, washers, bar materials. In brass, alloy, steel, stainless steel, P.T.F.E., nylon, Tufnol, sheet material, electrical and mechanical items. We could go on and on! Better to send for free catalogue No. 114 and see for yourself.
K. R. Whiston Ltd., Dept. WW, New Mills, Stockport, Cheshire. Phone: 0663 42028.

BUSINESS FOR SALE

HOUSE AND CABINET MAKING WORKSHOP IN RURAL AYRSHIRE

This former smithy comprises a two bedroom house and fully equipped workshop set-up, including three phase Wadkin Bursgreen machines, showroom and timber drying shed.
**Offers over £63,000.
For detailed schedule
Phone (0292) 591365**

WANTED

WANTED URGENTLY No. 52 Chute-board plane in good condition. Tel: Sean Collins after 6pm. 01-450-5700.

MARQUETRY

MARQUETRY stars, shells and fans, made to order inlays for restoration and reproductions. Send design and colour scheme for quote to: S. Rockwood, 13-15 Seel Street, The Courtyard, Liverpool L1 4AU or Telephone 051-708 8961. Send large S.A.E. for details.

EVENTS

NEW WOODCARVING CONTEST

**at the Lincolnshire Show
24th & 25th June, 1987**

TOP CARVING TOOL SETS FOR WINNERS
OPEN TO ALL.

FOR SCHEDULE AND ENTRY FORM SEND S.A.E. TO:
A. SISSONS
Lincolnshire. Showground,
Grange-de-Lings,
Lincoln, LN2 2NA.

MINIATURA

THE SHOWCASE FOR DOLLSHOUSE CRAFTS

in one-twelfth and related scales

at The Pavilion Suite,
County Cricket Ground
Edgbaston Road, Birmingham

FREE PARKING

1987 EVENTS
Sunday, March 22nd to
Saturday, September 26th
10.30am-5.00pm
Adults £1.75,
Children (accompanied) 50p
41 Eastbourne Ave., Hodge Hill,
Birmingham B34 6AR.

WOODCARVING

Second-Hand Carving Chisels
bought and sold
New Swiss Carving Chisels and Carving Sundries.
Catalogue available, SAE to:
**The Woodcarvers Shop,
Rear 28 Painswick Road,
Cheltenham, Glos.
Telephone: (0242) 38582**

CARVERS why not carve in comfort seated on my substantial adjustable carvers horse? Details SAE please. Dalton, 26 Erith Crescent, Collier Row, Romford, Essex RM5 3JP.

**Carve yourself a niche
with 'Woodworker'**

260

262

Profit from the use of Woodworking Machinery

A ONE DAY 'Wood Machining Course' to arm yourself with the necessary knowledge to enable you to:
- ● Make the correct choice of machine for YOUR purposes
- ● Use that particular machine to gain maximum efficiency, safely
- ● Open up new opportunities for you to profit from a small workshop

READING	Sarjents Tool Stores	18th February, 1987
CARLISLE	W.M. Plant	25th February, 1987
ALDERSHOT	Burch and Hills (Machinery) Ltd.	26th February, 1987
WARE	Heath Saw and Cutter Repairs	5th March, 1987
PERTH	Wm. Hume and Co.	26th March, 1987
SOUTHAMPTON	Burch and Hills (Machinery) Ltd.	23rd April, 1987
MIDDLESBROUGH	Cleveland Woodcraft	30th April, 1987

SEVEN VENUES TO CHOOSE FROM
One must be near to you.

 Telephone now for place availability and full timetable. Rawdon Machine Sales Ltd., 6 Acorn Park, Charlestown, Shipley, West Yorks BD17 7SW. Telephone 0274 597826

P.S. These are *NOT* exhibitions or demonstrations of a particular manufacturer's machinery, but a general eight-hour 'HANDS ON' instruction course showing the techniques of using machinery. You will find your time well spent.

NEWARK TECHNICAL COLLEGE

The Department of Music & Musical Instrument Technology offers the following full-times courses for the practical student.

MUSICAL INSTRUMENT ELECTRONICS
(2 years)

PIANO TUNING MAINTENANCE & REPAIRS
(3 years)

VIOLIN MAKING & REPAIRING
(3 years)
(Newark School of Violin Making)

WOODWIND MAKING & REPAIRING
(3 years)

For details and application forms please write to The Principal, Newark Technical College, Chauntry Park, Newark, Notts. Tel: 705921.

 Nottinghamshire County Council Education

SPECIAL CRAFTSMAN'S COURSE IN TRADITIONAL FRENCH POLISHING OF 6 MONTHS DURATION

COVERING: Surface preparation, repairs, staining, matching-up colours, french-polishing to full bodied finishes, including dull, eggshell and antique etc.

PIANO WORK: requiring spiriting-out, and 'Acid and Chalk' finishes.

Vacancies for this course will be limited.

Early bookings are advisable.

ALSO: Normal 5 day or longer courses.

PLUS: Special "Solo" courses for intensive tuition.

S.A.E. to:
'Midland School of French Polishing'
18A Mansfield Road, Eastwood, Notts.

WOODTURNING COURSES

2 Day courses, mid-week or weekend. Expert personal tuition in modern well equipped workshop. Comfortable accommodation available in pleasant surroundings. SAE for details to
Cliff Willetts, Gables, Frisby On The Wreake, Melton Mowbray, Leics.
Tel: Rotherby (066 475) 246

FULL TIME COURSES IN FINE CABINET MAKING

Two places exist for a one year course, leading to work of exhibition quality

David Savage FURNITURE MAKER

FOR PROSPECTUS APPLY TO:
DAVID SAVAGE CABINET MAKING
21 WESTCOMBE, BIDEFORD, DEVON EX39 3JQ

GORDON STOKES

Author of six books on woodturning, international demonstrator, and long established instructor, offers two day, one day, or hourly tuition for beginners. Maximum three students. No previous knowledge required. Benefit from forty years practical experience. More than two thousand satisfied students. Ring us on BATH (0225) 22617, or send S.A.E. (A4 size) for full details to:
202 THE HOLLOW, BATH, AVON BA2 1NG.
Act today – start a creative and lucrative hobby.

Creative Woodcarving
Courses in Cornwall.
Beautiful Helford River Area.
Experienced Instructor & Craftsman offers short courses ideal for beginners or the more advanced. Tuition limited to three students per course and each receives a detailed 50 page manual.
Details from: Jeremy Williams, Sycamore Cottage, Trabae, St. Martin, Helston, Cornwall TR12 6EA.
Tel: 032-623-609

Restorations Unlimited
FURNITURE RESTORATION
Specialised weekend courses in all aspects of antique furniture restoration. Maximum of three students in well equipped Cotswold workshops.
RESTORATIONS UNLIMITED
Pinkney Park, Malmesbury, Wilts.
Tel. Malmesbury 840888.

TWO-DAY PRACTICAL WOOD TURNING COURSE IN RURAL LINCOLNSHIRE
Comfortable accommodation arranged if required.
S.A.E. for details to: Peter Denniss, Cabinet Maker & Turner, The White Bungalow, South Reston, Louth, Lincolnshire. LN11 8JL or Phone: Withern 50429
S.D.T. Code 0521.

CRAFT WOODTURNING
A two-day residential woodturning course for beginners in a fully modernised 17th century Devon coaching inn. Teaching limited to two students per course, accommodation for families if required.
S.A.E. for brochure to:
Oliver Plant, Hartford Barton, Gittisham, Honiton, Devon, EX14 0AW or Phone Honiton 44155.

Cane and Rush Seating
Weekend Courses
21/22 March 1987
at Upton-on-Severn
further details from:
Betty Fowler, Primrose Cottage, Longdon, Tewkesbury, Gloucs. GL20 6AR. Tel: 068 481 365

David Stanley Auctions
1080 LOTS OF ANTIQUE WOODWORKING & ALLIED TRADES TOOLS, TREEN & BYGONES.
on Tuesday, 24th February, 1987
(View Monday 11am-8pm and Tuesday from 8am)
at THE KINGS HEAD HOTEL LOUGHBOROUGH, LEICS.

To include: 18th Century ploughs & moulding planes, early measuring devices and gauges, miniature and other mitre planes, rare planes by STANLEY, NORRIS, SPIERS, MATHIESON etc. a rare boxwood filled ultimatum brace by MARPLES, plus the usual interesting selection of antique tools in silver, ivory, boxwood, ebony, rosewood etc.

The colour catalogue includes 1,000 illustrations, estimated prices and postal bidding instructions, £5 (SAE for prices realised list to follow) to:

DAVID STANLEY AUCTIONS
OSGATHORPE, LEICS. LE12 9SP.
TEL: 0530 222320

Important Auction of Quality Antique Woodworking & Craft Tools at Kensington New Town Hall, London, on Tuesday March 24th 1987 at 11.30 a.m. Viewing Monday 23rd, from 12 noon to 8 p.m. & Sale Day from 8 a.m. to 11.30 a.m.

Tyrone R. Roberts offers for sale over 1060 lots of tools of the wheelwright, cooper, cabinet maker, saddler, sailmaker, bookbinder, carver, shipwright, pattern maker & the complete workshop of a gold & silversmith, plus good vintage tools, including many Disston saws, 1000 chisels & gouges, 30 Norris planes, 100 Stanley tools etc., etc.

Large size 44 page profusely illustrated catalogue, with full instructions for postal bidders, £3.50 (send S.A.E. if prices realised list required), from:

TYRONE R. ROBERTS
35 High Street, Heacham, King's Lynn, Norfolk PE31 7DB.

Ring 01-437 0699 to advertise in the market leader.

Woodworker

Lineage 52p per word (inc. VAT). Minimum £7.80. Semi-display £8.60 per single column + VAT. Minimum 2.5 x 1. No reimbursements for cancellations. All ads must be pre-paid.
Write your advert in BLOCK CAPITALS in the grid below, ticking the section you wish it to appear under, INCLUDING YOUR NAME AND ADDRESS IN THE WORD COUNT and send it to: 'WOOD-2WORKER', ASP ADVERTISEMENT DEPARTMENT, No. 1 GOLDEN SQUARE, LONDON W1R 3AB.

☐ W/S/E ☐ FOR SALE ☐ MATERIALS & FINISHES ☐ WOOD SUPPLIES ☐ COURSES ☐ PLEASE STATE

CLASSIFIED COUPON

ALL CLASSIFIED ADVERTISEMENTS MUST BE PRE-PAID. THERE ARE NO REIMBURSEMENTS FOR CANCELLATIONS.

I enclose my Cheque/Postal Order* for £................. for .... insertions, made payable to Argus Specialist Publications.
(*Delete as necessary) or
Please debit my Access/Barclaycard No.

| | | | | | | | | | | | | | | | |

Expiry Date

£ .... for .... insertions.

Name ....
Address ....
.... Post Code ....
Day Time Tel. No. ....
Signature .... Date ....

Woodworker

CONTENTS

April 1987
Vol. 91
No. 4

design . . . craft . . . and the love of wood

FEATURES

PROJECTS

REGULARS

● **On the cover**, James Krenov's cabinet in spalted maple and red oak has coopered concave doors and a convex carcase; **above**, benefit from Harry Turner's carving wisdom on p330

Editor Aidan Walker
Deputy editor John Hemsley
Editorial assistant Kerry Fowler
Advertisement manager Trevor Pryer
Advertisement production Laura Champion
Graphics Jeff Hamblin
Technical illustrator Peter Holland
Guild of Woodworkers John Hemsley, Kerry Fowler

Unfortunately we cannot accept responsibility for loss of or damage to unsolicited material. We reserve the right to refuse or suspend advertisements, and regret we cannot guarantee the bone fides of advertisers.
Published every third Friday

ABC
UK circulation
Jan-Dec 85
28,051

Editorial, advertisements and Guild of Woodworkers
1 Golden Square, London W1R 3AB, telephone 01-437 0626

Back issues and subscriptions Infonet Ltd, 10-13 Times House, 179 Marlowes, Hemel Hempstead, Herts HP1 1BB; telephone Hemel Hempstead (0442) 48434

Subscriptions per year UK £16.90; overseas outside USA (accelerated surface post) £21.00, USA (accelerated surface post) $28, airmail £48

UK trade SM Distribution Ltd, 16-18 Trinity Gardens, London SW9 8DX; telephone 01-274 8611

North American trade Bill Dean Books Ltd, 151-49 7th Avenue, PO Box 69, Whitestone, New York 11357; tel. 1-718-767-6632

Printed by Chase Web, Plymouth
Mono origination Multiform Photosetting Ltd, Cardiff
Colour origination Derek Croxson Ltd, Chesham, Bucks
© Argus Specialist Publications Ltd 1987
ISSN 0043 776X

Argus Specialist Publications Ltd

1 Golden Square, London W1R 3AB; 01-437 0626

This month

Star turn Nick Davidson of **Craft Supplies** with Malaysia's PM, Dr Mahathir, who took a place on a beginner's turning course early January. He was better than a beginner ... **WOODWORKER SHOW** turners note: Craft Supplies and Sorby are sponsoring **turning prizes** this year to the tune of £600 total value tools and equipment! Entry forms — phone 0442 41221.

Warning — read this

Anyone intending to follow James Reid's 'Woodworking wheeze' advice that appeared under the title 'Winter warmer' in WOODWORKER February, please note that:

1 'Tampering with beer containers — casks and kegs — can be extremely dangerous, as they often contain gas under pressure, sometimes in the form of a pressurised compartment.

2 'The casks and kegs are the property of the brewing companies and anyone accepting them without authorisation from the brewing companies concerned lay themselves open to possible prosecution for dishonestly handling stolen goods.'

This is a verbatim quote from the Technical Secretary of the Brewers' Society. Allied Breweries Ltd would also like us to point out that any beer kegs marked Allied Breweries, Allied Breweries (UK), Alloa, Ansells, Ind Coope or Tetley are the property of Allied Breweries Ltd and may not be used for any purpose other than the dispensing of beer without their prior written permission.

Gimme the beat
Furniture maker Jonathan Hawkes (*WW/Dec '86*) made this bureau in English ripple ash for Dave Hill, manager of rock'n' roll group the Pretenders. Jonny rubbed carbon paste into the grain to accentuate the figure.... he is at 1 Church St, Pewsey, Wilts SN9 5DL, (0672) 62878.

Chair's fair

In the March issue of WOODWORKER we featured a maple slab-sided and dovetailed chair in the Direct Design show report, 'Sit-down design'. It was entirely the work of **Susi Janus**, and not Timothy Freeman as we said. We apologise to Susi for any inconvenience this may have caused. She can be contacted at Parnham House, Beaminster, Dorset DT8 3NA, (0308) 862445.

Medal boats The Paris Mint's medal in honour of the boatbuilder: £13.15 bronze, £178.15 silver plus p&p from Monnaies et Medailles, 11 Quai de Conti, 75279 Paris 6e, France.

Safe machining On p94 of February's WOODWORKER, Dave Gardiner of CoSIRA is shown HONING the cutters of a jointer with a small slipstone, not jointing them as the caption said. The machine was, of course, isolated at the mains.

Tropical timber hopes

'Against the background of the continuing scarcity of traditional species,' runs the introduction to a feature in *Cabinet Maker and Retail Furnisher*, 30 January, 'the desire of tropical timber producing countries to export a wide range of secondary species remains undimmed.' The author, independent consultant Geoffrey Pleydell, introduces a few timbers from the main exporting regions, and — writing for the larger-scale manufacturer — explains: 'Few of the woods written about here can be bought ex-stock in the UK. However, a little pressure on the importers and their agents ought to spark their co-operation in the patient process of getting some trial quantities from shippers for commercial testing.'

Crafts fair change

The Crafts Council has taken over the running of the Chelsea Crafts Fair from Lady Philippa Powell, who has been the organiser for the last seven years. Dates for the fair this year are 7-21 October; it will be held as usual at the Old Town Hall, King's Rd, London SW3. If you're interested in exhibiting, send a large SAE for details to the Crafts Council (Marketing), 12 Waterloo Place, London SW1Y 4AU.

Cabinetmakers' forum

CoSIRA have organised a forum for any or all cabinetmakers on 14 April at the Bear Hotel, Market Place, Devizes, Wilts. It starts at 10am, and takes the form of individual consultations — a sort of 'clinic' — with CoSIRA experts. From 6.30-8.30 in the evening there is open discussion, where people can exchange views and ideas.

Diary

Guild courses are shown by an asterisk (*): for further details see Guild pages

April
4 **Hammer veneering** Ian Hosker*
5 **Parquetry** Ian Hosker*
11-12 **Spring Crafts Fair**, Alexandra Palace, London, (0727) 23176
12 **Woodworking Woodland Ancient and Modern** seminar, The Theatre, Bucks College (0923) 772755
12-16 **Cabinetmaking** Manchester*
12-15 **Upholstery** Manchester*
12-16 **Modern finishing** Manchester*
14 **Cabinetmakers' Forum**, Devizes (see 'This Month')
26-4 May **London International Furniture Show**, Earls Court, London (26-30 trade only)

May
7-8 **French Polishing** Charles Cliffe*
9 **Design and Workshop Drawing** Bob Grant*
10-14 **Interior Context**, Olympia 2, Earls Court, London
22-26 **INTERZUM** International Furniture Trade Fair, Cologne
26-29 **Country Chairmaking** Jack Hill*
27-2 June **LIGNA** International Trade Fair for Wood Machinery, Hanover

June
13 **Routing** Roy Sutton*

Shoptalk

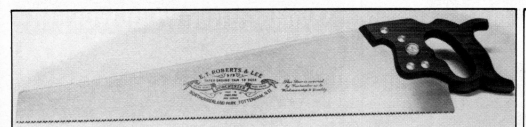

E. T. Roberts & Lee's new addition to their top 'Dorchester' range of **handsaws** — a 'bellied' version of the walnut-handled taper-ground saw. 10 Northumberland Pk, London N17 0TX, 01-808 2486.

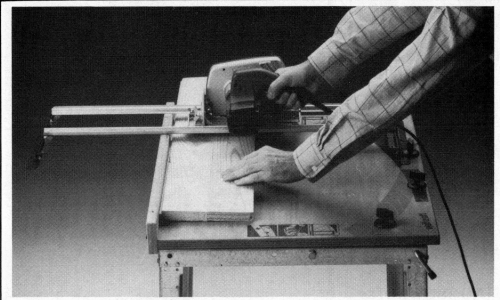

The Wolfcraft **VarioCut** is a 680x594 base table with adjustable guide rails to suit saw plates 116-220mm. Straight or any angle cuts; angle graduation scales, snap locks for 45° and 90°: £49.96 inc. VAT. Wolfcraft also announce improvements to the **Variotec**: better underplate, rip-fence now fixed at both ends, safety switch now has knee-height panic button, parallel router fence now with better fixing and far greater adjustment range, curved routing guide now with top bearing. Brimarc, PO Box 100, Leamington Spa CV31 3LS, (0926) 29262.

New 'Hy-line' **safety specs** from Iles Optical — browguard, side shields, 'revolutionary hinged design', choice of lenses. From £2.40+VAT.
● Iles Optical, Walmgate Rd, Perivale, Middx UB6 7LG, 01-998 6600.

W hen you've finished that fine cabinet, how do you get it to the customer? ATK Specialist Moving Service, personally run by Anthony Keil from west London concentrates on **moving fine furniture** for craftsmen. This caring carrier operates in the London area, but will do runs all over UK and Europe.
● ATK Transport, 8 Birkbeck Rd, Ealing, London W5 4ES, 01-568 4115.

Extended range of router **profile/scriber cutter sets** for all scribed mortise-and-tenons; £138.50 a set.
●Trend, Unit N, Penfold Works, Imperial Way, Watford WD2 4YY, (0923) 49911.

PRODUCT DIGEST

Mainly power tool news this month — apart from a useful addition to the popular Jet Clamp range; a **Holdfast Kit** to turn your Jet Clamp into a bench holdfast, £3+VAT.

AEG have a new **screwdriver/drill** with a pressure-operated clutch and a detachable and adjustable depth gauge; the electronically speed-controlled and reversible UBSE 8 RL costs £109+VAT.

Bosch announce an electronically variable five-speed **jigsaw** with a choice of three orbital cutting actions; a see-through blade-guard helps safety, visibility, and extraction — you can hook it up to a vacuum cleaner. £91.80 inc VAT. They're also bringing out a **cordless screwdriver/drill** with a 4.8v nickel-cadmium battery (12 hours to charge from flat); reversing, 10mm chuck, and a 'unique recharging facility' which enables it to be charged 'directly' or through a special wall bracket. £66 inc. VAT.

Ryobi, marketed by Luna in the UK, are going petrol powered; heavy industrial-rated tools with 16cc motors and 45 minutes' use per tank of two-stroke include a **reciprocating saw** at £230, an **impact drill** at £245, and a **rotary hammer drill** at £336, all prices plus VAT. New meaning to cordless?

Makita are coming up with 13 additions to their power tool range, over and above the Power-Craft models they recently introduced; 6½ and 9½in circular **saws**, a belt-driven laminate **trimmer**, palm **sander**, a 7in **sander/polisher** with 'soft start', five more **drills**, some with screwdriving, some cordless; and a cordless compact ratchet **wrench**. Range from £65 for the palm sander to £175 for the 9½in circular saw.

● Jet Clamps from TMT, Queensway Trading Est., Leamington Spa, Warwicks, (0926) 312033: AEG, 217 Bath Rd, Slough, Berks SL1 4AW, (0753) 872101: Robert Bosch, PO Box 98, Broadwater Pk, N. Orbital Rd, Denham, Middx UB9 5HJ, (0895) 833 633: Luna, 20 Denbigh Hall, Milton Keynes, MK3 7QT, (0908) 70771: Makita UK, 8 Finway, Dallow Rd, Luton, Beds LU1 1TR, (0582) 455777.

Shoptalk special

Abrasive extra

Two new products that will make your abrasive life easier

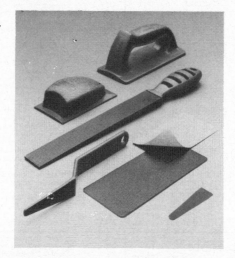

SANDVIK SANDPLATE

'An entirely new product . . . a completely new sanding concept . . . designed to compete with sandpaper . . . ' amidst the PR-speak, Sandvik really do seem to have something significant. 'Sandplate' is a wafer-thin, flexible sheet of special steel, which comes in various shapes and sizes and is etched in regular patterns and various grades. There is a peel-off sticky back, which allows you to fix whatever plate you please to one of a range of their own tools, or indeed to one of your own gizmos.

The implications are enormous, of course; it does bear a striking resemblance to the Cintride discs which made a splash some years ago, and faded out of sight when everyone realised they weren't going to replace sandpaper; but it's more flexible, and not so cloggable. Also Sandvik's own 'Abrader' comes to mind, which came up more recently but was apparently dogged by consumer confusion.

Sandvik are trying really hard to get it right this time. We've used the stuff and we have to say we're impressed. Sandvik's own packaging claims it cuts five times faster than sandpaper and lasts 100 times as long; they said their lab tests made it last 200-250 times longer than ordinary sandpaper, but they couldn't push consumer credibility that far. It's a dream for decoration pre-paration, and there's no doubt that's where Sandplate is principally aimed — at all those DIY decorators who rightly think preparation is a pain and wrongly skimp on it. With the various tools you can get in nooks and crannies, and you don't have the problem of edges and corners of sandpaper crinkling up and ruining your fingers. You can use the flexible sheet without a backing tool to get round shaped components — turners and carvers note — and you can cut the stuff with a pair of (old!) scissors to fit it to ingenious devices for abrading the awkward internals of your latest wonder project. What about clogging? Drop it in turps or hot water and just brush the crud out.

Power tools? The shapes and patterns of the cutting 'points' make that a difficult one — orbital sanders are the obvious choice — but they're working on it. At the moment you can only get coarse, medium and fine grades, which roughly correspond to 80, 100 and 120 grit; so forget it if you're after everlasting 320-grit garnet. But for initial fast removal of waste, comparatively coarse rubbing down between coats of finish, and numerous other applications for which your imagination is the only limit, this is definitely worth the couple of quid it takes to start. Turners and carvers just can't afford to ignore it.

The nicely shaped fingernail-friendly 'Hobby sander' costs £2.49 with a fine plate; replacement 'hobby' plate is £1.79. The 'File sander' with a medium plate costs £4.49; replacement plates are £2.29. A 4x3in plate on its own, which you cut to requirements, is £3.49; all prices inc. VAT. And before you gasp, we reckon it'll save you money and suffering on sandpaper, if not garnet.

● Sandvik UK, Manor Way, Halesowen, W. Midlands B62 8QZ, 021-550 4700.

B&D POWERFILE

We've also been having fun with the latest Black & Decker brainchild — the Powerfile, a sort of mini-belt 'sander on a stick'. The 300w motor is housed in a tough plastic moulding with a handle; belts, which come in ½in and (soon) ¼in widths, move at 150m/min on the 'stick' end, which is about 6in long. To compare: a hefty hand-held belt sander like the Elu MHB 90 has a 350m/min belt speed.

Claims for its applications include wood-carving, shaping tiles, derusting metal, sharpening tools, and more. It's very light and easy to control, and at the risk of wearing out the edges of the narrow belts too quickly you can use it for surprisingly finicky work. Don't try and sharpen chisels with it — it moves too fast — but it'll clean up a cold chisel or axe edge very nicely. It's another one for carvers; you can actually carve with it, as well as get power sanding into the nicks and notches where only sand-paper-on-a-stick has gone before.

It will take a lot of material off in a short time — keep it moving if you're working on wide surfaces, for which a wider belt is probably better anyway — and for things like quick and controllable chamfering it's right handy. It's a tool in its own right, plus it fills a definite if small gap in the power sanding range. The kind of thing you can get on without quite well, and find yourself using a lot once you've got one; almost to the point of dreaming up things to do so you can use it.

The 'clever dust extraction system' doesn't blow or suck; like most belt sander extraction systems, it relies on the move-ment of the belt to carry dust into a bag, which in this case is underneath the handle. Not exactly extraction, more like collection. The breathing air, at least, is better with the bag than without, especially if you're taking off a lot of wood in a short time. It's another obvious temptation for gadget-crazy DIYers — decorating would be a lot easier with one — but at around £30, it's almost worth buying one for one job and then seeing what else you can do with it.

One thing that did strike us was that the Powerfile is so easy and light to use, some-one inexperienced in sanding with a moving

belt might be likely to use it with less care than it needs. You can hold it upside down or wrong way round and still do the work, but catch the round end of the 'stick' on a corner or surface, and the thing could easily leap. You will soon be able to get a stand, and cranked arm to widen the range of uses.

● B&D Indoor, West Point, The Grove, Slough SL1 1QQ, (0753) 79311.

Lightweight thicknesser

For all those people who've experienced the frustration of needing a packing or scribing piece to a precise thickness on site — and baulked at the marking gauge and hand-plane, without time or a decent workbench — the Ryobi AP-10 is your answer. It's also the answer for workshop workers who need a small and (comparatively) cheap thicknesser — model makers, perhaps, or a business with a full complement of heavy machinery in another room, where there is sometimes a need to thickness a piece near the bench here and now.

This little 10x5in capacity thicknesser, with a 1350w motor driving rubber feed rollers and a two-cutter block, is about as heavy (57lb) as a well-filled carpenter's tool box, and only slightly more awkward to shift. It's definitely portable, and it's definitely neat — no problem in the back of the van.

A Luna press release (they sell it in the UK) calls the AP-10 an 'industrial planer', but in truth it's not a surface planer, nor is it industrial. Not, anyway, in the sense that it will take the place of a heavy three-phase cast iron machine; nor in the sense that it will be any more use surfacing than that same heavy machine. Thicknessing only, unless you want a smooth surface on a lumpy board. The safety instructions on the operator's leaflet — clear and comprehensive enough, despite the odd bit of 'Japspeak' gobbledegook — actually take the trouble to say in capital letters 'This tool is intended for residential use only'.

We borrowed Luna's demonstration model to have a good close look, and bearing in mind the limitations of such a small piece of equipment, could hardly fault it. It's not supposed to take off more than 2.5mm at a time, but naturally we had to see how it would behave given the abuse anyone on site with a job to do in a hurry would be likely to hand out; it will handle 3.5mm, but under protest. The infeed 'mouth' is cleverly designed so you can't get timber into it that needs a deeper cut than that.

We started (in a cold workshop) with 19x19mm softwood, and found the feed rather jerky on a 2mm cut on the sawn surface. It would grab, feed, then stop again; we needed to pull through from the other side first time round. Then as the rollers warmed up, and once they had a smooth, consistent surface to work on, things got better. Mainly, the problem was caused by the accumulated shavings compressed on the rollers; once we cleaned them up, the feed was only hindered when we asked the machine to do more than it should. A smaller cut is better anyway — 1-1.5mm is about right. The calibration for setting thickness isn't dead on, but we've used machines costing five times as much where

it isn't either. Digital readouts are OK if you have that sort of money to invest — otherwise, test on scrap. There is no provision for adjusting the little pointer against the depth scale, but you could enlarge the hole which holds it to the body of the machine if you really wanted. Half a millimetre out isn't bad.

Next was 65x40mm beech, with which the AP-10 coped very well. Two and 2.5mm cuts certainly slow the motor down, but this is also only to be expected with a comparatively small single-phase unit. Potential bearing and brush wear both suggest that the 1.5mm limit is a good one to set yourself. As a comparison, the AP-10's 1350w motor gives away 500w to the electronic MOF 177 Elu router! How long a light machine like this lasts is obviously dependent on how you and your colleagues or employees use it.

The acid test was a 10in jointed-up board of ¾in maple. One and 1.5mm cuts were fine, 2mm was pushing it — the machine needed hand help — and a naughty 3mm cut was just too much. The piece stuck and we had to wind the cutter up to get it out — not really a reasonable request for the little machine. The brushes for the motor are extremely easy to replace; a good feature, and perhaps also an indication that you can expect to be changing them fairly often.

You are advised not to thickness pieces of less than 5mm in the AP-10, a warning of which you would do well to take heed. Go thinner and you could damage the cutters, plus there is always the danger of missing the kickback fingers. It's common practice to put a false wooden bed on the thicknessing table of larger machines for really thin pieces, and there's no reason why this shouldn't be done on the AP-10 as well, but make sure it's securely fixed. The applications to which this machine is suited are likely to include thicknessing pieces of less than ¼in.

The designers have thought carefully about cutter changing and adjustment, which could hardly be easier. The kit that comes with it includes a setting jig, a solid piece of plastic into which you slot the knife and its 'blade binder', an L-shaped metal section which sits with the knife itself in the block. Fit the new or reground knife finger-tight into the binder, put them both in the jig and tighten the cutting edge to the notch in the jig; tighten up the screws, then set knife and binder back into the block. Dead simple. They also give you a 'manual sharpening holder', which holds both knives in alignment if you want to grind your own. OK for dressing slightly dull edges, perhaps, but we prefer to keep the specialist cutter doctors in business for a real sharpening job.

One slight misgiving we had was about motor cooling when the machine is running at its maximum thickness, 5in or thereabouts. The motor and cutters move up and down as a unit, and at the top of the travel the air outlets come high up into the top of the body pressing. Airflow could be restricted — something to watch out for, particularly if you're making it work hard. There is an outlet for dust extraction, to which you would probably fit a hose from an industrial-type vacuum cleaner, but many an AP-10 will be used without extraction. Which makes inner cleanliness — particularly of the rubber feed rollers — all the more important.

Other bits and pieces you get include all the Allen keys you need, a T-wrench for cutter changing, and extra rollers. You also get lumps of 2x2 to mount the machine on, which extend its base area and reduce the possibility of it falling over when you're cramming a 12ft piece of 8x4in pitch pine through it (not recommended).

For the money, the little AP-10 is going to make a lot of friends. It's certainly worth it for the shopfitter or someone who works a lot on site; better if you're in a partnership of two or three, or employ a handful of people, all of whose efficiency it would improve, because it's quite an investment for a single worker when the occasions it would be used are comparatively few. A cheap alternative to a heavy thicknesser it is not, nor is it intended to be. The serious non-professional with a limited budget should also look carefully at it, but many of you will want a surface planer as well. It's a good little machine, does its limited job admirably, and will serve the careful and sympathetic user well. Solid as a rock it isn't, and it shouldn't be treated as if it is.

● The Ryobi AP-10 costs £395+VAT. For your nearest stockist contact Luna Tools and Machinery, 20 Denbigh Hall, Milton Keynes MK3 7QT, (0908) 70771.

AXMINSTER POWER TOOL CENTRE

HORIZONTAL WETSTONE GRINDERS
OUR PRICE INC. VAT

JAPANESE Wetstone grinder £129.00
180G stone for above £40.00
1000G stone for above £40.00
6000G stone for above £43.00
PRECISION grinding jig £43.00

SHARPENSET Wetstone grinder £240.00
SHARPENSET 150G stone £18.40
SHARPENSET 280G stone £20.41
SHARPENSET Green stone (TCT) . £18.40
10" Planer Knife grinding jig £65.00
15" Planer Knife grinding jig £78.00
CHISEL grinding jig £67.00

VERTICAL WETSTONE GRINDERS
SCANGRIND 150 6" wetstone £69.00
SCANGRIND 2008" wetstone £88.00
SCANTOOL COMBI WET AND DRY STONES
COMBI SC150 6" wet & dry £80.00
COMBI SC200 8" wet & dry £128.00
LUNA KIRUNA 11" wet & 4" dry £118.00
LUNA KIRUNA 14" wet & 5" dry £185.00

BENCH GRINDERS
ELU EDS163 6" 360W £73.95
ELU EDS164 7" 390W £77.95
ELU MWA149 6" Honer grinder .. £90.95
LEROY SOMER 5" 180W £33.00
LEROY SOMER 6" 250W £44.00
LEROY SOMER 6" with chuck £49.00
WARCO 5" 180W (European) £33.00
WARCO 6" 380W (European) £43.00
WARCO 8" 570W (European) £69.00

GRIND STONES (state bore size)

	5"	6"	7"
COARSE 36G	£6.60	£7.90	£11.40
FINE 60G	£6.60	£7.90	£11.40
WHITE 60G	£7.20	£8.50	£13.50
GREEN (TCT)	£7.20	£8.50	£13.50

JIGSAWS (Light Duty)
Bosch PST50 Single Speed £29.95
Bosch PST50E Var. Speed £38.50
Bosch PST55PE Var. Speed Pend ... £68.50
Hitachi FJ50SB Single speed £27.50
Hitachi FJ50VA Var. speed £36.50
Hitachi FCJ55V Var. Speed Pend. Act £58.95

JIGSAWS (Heavy Duty)
Elu ST142 2 speed £101.95
Elu ST142E Var. speed £110.95
Elu ST152 2 speed £98.95
Elu ST152E Var. speed £106.95
Cases for above Jigsaws £10.00
Hitachi CJ65 2 speed £98.95
Hitachi CJ65VA Var. speed £104.95
Hitachi CJ65V Var. speed £104.95
Bosch 1581.7 Var. speed £109.95

DISC AND BELT SANDERS
Picador 10" Disc Sander £219.00
Warco BDS460 6" Disc 4" Belt £86.00
Warco BDS690 9" Disc 6" Belt £179.00
Holmes 6" 2HP £399.00
Luna Favourite 4" £285.00
Luna De-Lux Sander 4" £599.00
Luna YKV Pad Sander £647.00
Luna YK1500 Pad Sander 1PH .. £1564.00
Luna YK1500 Pad Sander 3PH .. £1509.00
Picador Unmotorised 3" Belt £49.00
Picador Unmotorised 3" Belt £65.00
Holmes 4" Belt Sander £94.00
Holmes 6" Belt Sander £120.00

CIRCULAR SAWS
HITACHI FC5SA 6" TCT 710W £42.95
BOSCH PKS46 6" TCT 600W £53.50
BOSCH PKS66 7⅞ TCT 1200W £90.95
HITACHI PSU6 6" 1050W HSS £74.95
HITACHI PSU7 7" 1600W HSS £99.95
HITACHI PSU9 9" 1759W HSS £124.95
HITACHI PSM7 7" 1200W TCT £141.95
HITACHI PSM9 9" 1600W TCT £154.95
ELU MH151 6" 850W TCT £90.95
ELU MH65 7" 1200W TCT £131.95
ELU MH85 9" 1600W TCT £177.95
ELU MH182 8" 1400W TCT £148.95
ELU 550 COMBI (for MH182) £130.00
ELU 555 Snip saw (for 182) £179.00
WOLF 9" CIRCULAR SAW £135.00

FINISHING SANDERS
(DB Dust Bag)

BOSCH PSS230 1/3rd Sheet £29.95
HITACHI FS10SA 1/3rd Sheet £25.95
HITACHI FSV12 ½ Sheet DB £47.95
BOSCH PS280A ½ Sheet DB £59.95
B&D P6303 ½ Sheet £59.95
ELU MVS156 1/3rd Sheet DB £73.95
ELU MVS156E Var. Speed DB £85.95
ELU MVS 94 ½ Sheet DB £111.95
ELU MVS47 ½ Sheet £123.95
HITACHI SV12 ½ Sheet £109.95
HITACHI SOD110 ½ Sheet DB £95.95
HITACHI SO110 ½ Sheet £86.95
BOSCH 1288.9 ½ Sheet DB £99.95
WOLF ½ Sheet DB £85.95

DRILL STANDS (43mm collar)
BOSCH S2 Light duty £21.00
BOSCH S7 Heavy duty £52.95
BOSCH S8 Milling attachment for S7 £24.50
RIDGEWAY Very heavy duty £145.95

EXTENSION CABLES
50 Metre on sturdy drum £28.95
Jo-Jo 6 Metre 30 foot £9.95
Jo-Jo 12 Metre 40 foot £14.26
Jo-Jo 18 Metre 60 foot £17.95

POWER PLANES (Light Duty)
OUR PRICE INC. VAT

BLACK & DECKER DN710 ..... £29.95
BOSCH PHO100 82mm 450W £47.95
HITACHI FP20SA 82mm 320W .. £38.95

HEAVY DUTY

ELU MFF80 82mm 850W £109.95
ELU MFF80K (in kit box) £127.95
ELU MFF40 82mm 1000W £189.95
INVERSION Std. for MFF80 ..... £20.95
INVERSION Std. for MFF40 ..... £29.00
HITACHI P20SA 82mm 720W £95.95
HITACHI FU20 82mm 620W £88.95
HITACHI F30A 92mm 900W £124.95

BELT SANDERS
ELU MHB 157 3" 600W £106.95
ELU MHB 157E 3" var. speed £119.95
ELU 157 FRAME £35.00
ELU 157 inversion stand £28.00
ABRASIVE BELTS FOR MHB 157/pkt. 3 40G, 60G, 80G, 100G, 120G, 150G £3.00
BOSCH PBS75 3" 620W £71.95
ELU MHB 90 4" 850W £193.95
ELU MHB 90K With frame £234.95
HITACHI SB75 3" 950W £116.95
HITACHI SB110 4" 950W £144.90
HITACHI SB110T 4" 950W £129.00
HITACHI SB110V 4" var. speed £134.00
MAKITA 9401 4" 1040W £169.00
MAKITA 9924DB 3" 950W £117.00

BISCUIT JOINTER
ELU DS140 Biscuit Jointer £197.95
No. 20 Biscuits (1000 off) £19.95
No. 10 Biscuits (1000 off) £19.50
No. 0 Biscuits (1000 off) £18.63
Mixed Box 0, 10, 20 (500 off) £12.50
DS140 saw blade 12T Std. £29.95
DS140 saw blade 30T Fine £29.50
DS140 Dust Tube adaptor £5.95
BOSCH Biscuit Jointer £124.95

***** WOODSCREWS *****
Twin Fast Zinc Plated GKN 1600 Woodscrews from 1" × 6 to 2" × 10 with Free Screwdriver. (State slotted or pozidrive)
ONLY £19.99 inc. VAT and P&P

* * * NEW * * *
BOSCH INDUSTRIAL HOT AIR PAINT STRIPPER 2000w Electronic Control 100°-600°C. ..... Special Price £79.95

MARTEK DRILL SHARPENER
Excellent for Sharpening all Drill Bits ..... ONLY £24.95 inc. VAT and P&P

S.D.S. POWER DRILLS
Hitachi DH16v £103.95
Hitachi VRV16 ..... £164.95
B&D PB020 ..... £112.95
B&D P8020T (c/w 110v Transformer) £185.95

DRILL/BREAKERS
Hitachi DH28Y £272.00
Hitachi DH500A £443.00

HAMMERS

H55 SA £375.00
H90 SA £756.00

HAMMERS
Hitachi H55 SA £375.00
Hitachi H90 SA £756.00

POWER DRILLS (K-Kit box)
NEW ELU POWER DRILLS

ECD304K 420W V/S 10mm Compact/ £73.95
EMD400K 600W 2 Speed 13mm £81.95
ESD705K 320W V/S & Rev. 10mm . £102.95
EMD403K 500W V/S/R Ham. 13mm £90.95
EMD405K 500W V/S/R Ham. 13mm £114.95
EMD406K 550W V/S Hammer 13mm £106.95

B&D 2162 KM V/S RW 450v £63.95
B&D P2264K 13mm 2 Speed 550W £74.95
B&D P2266K 13mm V/S Rev. 480W £69.95

BOSCH 400-2 10mm 440W £29.95
BOSCH 500RLE 13mm 500W V/S Rev. £49.95
BOSCH 7002E 13mm 700W £79.95
BOSCH 850RLT 13mm 850W V/S Re £111.95

HITACHI FV12VA 13mm 420W V/S £37.95
HITACHI FV16V 13mm 600W V/S/R £59.95
HITACHI FV20VA 13mm 710W V/S/R £86.95
HITACHI VTP13K 13mm 2 Speed 460W £74.00
HITACHI VTP16AK 2 Spd. 800W £103.00

ANGLE GRINDERS
HITACHI PDP100C 4" £44.85
HITACHI G13SB 5" 750W £66.81
HITACHI G23SC 9" 2000W £89.00

PALM GRIP SANDERS
(DB Dust Bag)

ELU MVS500 1/6th Sheet 135W DB £60.95
ELU MVS501 1/4 Sheet 135W DB £60.95
B&D P6301 1/6th Sheet 136W DB £51.50
B&D P6302 1/4 Sheet 135W DB ... £51.50
HITACHI SV12SA 1/4 Sheet 180W £46.95
MAKITA BO4510 1/4 Sheet £43.95

LIBERON WAXES
Waxes Sealers Stains Polishes Etc.
All Your Requirements In One
Send for Free Price List

GLUE POT ..... £23.00 inc. P&P
470 FLUTED DOWELS 6mm 8mm 10mm ..... £5.75 inc. P&P

HITACHI 10mm CORDLESS DRILL-SCREWDRIVERS
Our price inc. VAT

DTC 10 6 cell 2 spd. & rev. £65.00
DRC10 as above torque adjustable . £89.95
DTC10K 6 cell 2 spd. & rev. in case . £69.00
D10DB 6 cell variable spd. & rev. £80.95
D10DD 8 cell 2 spd. & rev. £82.95
D10D as above torque adjustable .. £101.95
DV10D 8 cell 2 spd. & rev. hammer £107.95

MAKITA 10mm CORDLESS DRILL SCREWDRIVERS
6012DWK 6 cell 2 spd. & rev. in case £92.95
6012HDW 8 cell 2 spd. torque adj. £111.95
8400DW 8 cell 1 spd. & rev. hammer £119.95
MAGNETIC Screwdriver kit 7 piece .. £5.95
REPLACEMENT BITS (state type) £0.50

CORDLESS TOOLS
Our price inc. VAT

HITACHI CK12D Knife cutter £103.84
HITACHI C6DA 6" Circular saw ... £143.95
MAKITA 5600DW 6" circular saw £179.95
MAKITA 4300DW Jig saw £119.95
B&D INDUSTRIAL Jig saw £110.95
B&D SPOTLIGHTER Torch £14.95
B&D DUSTBUSTER Cleaner £17.95

MISCELLANEOUS POWER TOOLS
KEW HOBBY PRESSURE WASHER £259.00
DREMEL D576 FRETSAW £69.95
BOSCH WET 'n' DRY Vacuum cleaner £93.95
BOSCH 520 HOT AIR paint stripper £23.95
BOSCH 560 HOT AIR paint stripper £32.95

NEW ELU DUST EXTRACTORS

EVE 938 ..... £275 EVE948 ..... £395

SASH CRAMPS (P&P £2.00 per order) may be mixed for quantity

	1 off	5 off		1 off	5 off
RECORD 135-24"	£20	£18	DRAPER 18"	£14	£12
135-36"	£21	£19	30"	£17	£15
135-42"	£22	£20	42"	£19	£17
135-48"	£23	£21	T bar 66"	£30	£28

RECORD CRAMP HEADS M130
1 off £10.70 5 off £10.20 P&P £1.50)

PARAMO CRAMP HEADS
1 off £10.00 5 off £9.00 (P&P £1.50)

G CRAMPS (P&P £1.50 per order) may be mixed for quantity

	1 off	5 off		1 off	5 off
RECORD 120-3"	£5.76	£4.80	PARAMO 3"	£5.30	£4.60
120-4"	£5.91	£4.90	4"	£5.55	£4.78
120-6"	£8.31	£6.90	6"	£7.76	£6.60
120-8"	£12.31	£9.80	8"	£11.41	£9.50
120 10"	£18.15	£17.00	10"	£16.90	£15.77

RECORD DEEP THROAT 4" 1 off £13.27
PARAMO DEEP THROAT 4" 1 off £12.45

KLEMSIA QUICK CLAMPS
(P&P £1.50)

SPAN	REACH	1 off	5 off
200mm	110mm	£3.75	£3.56
300mm	110mm	£4.10	£3.89
400mm	110mm	£4.50	£4.27
600mm	110mm	£5.30	£5.03
800mm	110mm	£6.10	£5.79
1000mm	110mm	£7.10	£6.74
200mm	150mm	£5.70	£5.41
200mm	200mm	£6.80	£6.46

NEW RECORD 132 SPEED CRAMPS
(P&P £1.50)

	Reach	1 off	5 off
Record 132/30	12"	£12.00	£10.00
132/40	16"	£13.00	£11.00
132/50	20"	£14.00	£12.00
132/60	24"	£15.00	£13.00
132/80	32"	£16.00	£14.00
132/100	40"	£18.00	£16.00

RECORD HAND PLANES
(P&P £1.50/Order)

03 Smoothing 240×45mm £20.10
04 Smoothing 245×50mm £17.00
04½ Smoothing 260×60mm £19.50
05 Jack 355×50mm £26.75
05½ Jack 380×60mm £29.50
06 Jointer 455×60mm £34.50
07 Jointer 560×60mm £39.75
778 Rebate 215×38mm £30.80
010 Rebate 330×44mm £39.50
020C Circular Plane £69.50
060½ Block Plane £16.50
073 Shoulder Rebate £42.50
CLIFTON 420 Rebate Plane £57.00
CLIFTON Multi-Plane £189.00
CLIFTON Cap Iron 2" or 2⅜" £5.00

STANLEY HAND PLANES
(P&P £1.50/Order)

3 Smoothing 240×45mm £23.60
4 Smoothing 245×50mm £20.00
4½ Smoothing 260×60mm £21.60
5 Jack 355×50mm £27.00
5½ Jack 380×60mm £28.00
6 Fore 455×60mm £37.80
7 Jointer 560×60mm .. £39.40
78 Duplex Rebate £21.50
10 Rebate 330×44mm ... £40.50
80 Scraper £9.50
601½ Block Plane £21.00
92 Rebate Plane £24.80
CLIFTON 3 in 1 Rebate Plane £67.00
RECORD 3 in 1 Plane £39.00

WOODWORKING VICES (P&P £4.50)
RECORD 52½E 9" Quick Release .. £44.00
52½ED 9" Quick Release £47.00
53E 10" Quick Release ... £69.00

DRILL BIT SETS

	Lip & Spur	HSS Std.
1/16"-½" x 64ths	—	£21.00
1/16"-½" x 32nds	£42.00	£17.00
1-13mm x 0.5mm	£54.00	£19.00

JAPANESE WATER STONES (P&P £1.00)
KING BRAND 800G WETSTONE £8.00
KING BRAND 1200G WETSTONE £8.00
SUPER FINISHING STONE 6000G ... £8.90
COMBINATION WATER STONE £10.80

MISCELLANEOUS HAND TOOLS (P&P £1.50 PER ORDER)
RECORD Dowel Jig £36.20
140 Corner Cramps £12.00
145 Hold Fast £13.00
Floorboard Cramp .. £56.95
18" Extension Rods . £4.95
141 Corner Cramps £19.40
146 Hold Fast £15.50
169 Bench Stop £7.50
Drill Bushes £1.90
Spare Collars £3.20
Priory Bench Stop ... £2.95
STANLEY Web Clamp £7.99
Stanley Yankee Screwdrivers 13" ..... £12.86 20" ..... £14.17 27" £18.50

HANDSAWS (P&P £1.50)
DISSTON D8 26" 6pt ..... £27 RIDGWAY SPEED SAW 22" or 26" £19
ROBERTS & LEE 10" DOVETAIL BRASS BACK £21 ROBERTS & LEE DORCHESTER 10" £27

SANDERSON KAYSER "PAX" HANDSAWS (P&P £1.50)
BRASS BACK TENNON SAWS 8" £18.50 10" ... £19 12" £19.50 14" £20 D/Tail ... £25
HANDSAWS 20" × 10pt £21 22" × 8pt £22 24" × 7pt £23 6" × 6pt £24 26" × Rip £24

CHISEL SETS (State bevel edge or firmer P&P £1.00/Order)
MARPLES CARVERS ASH 4 piece .. £13.60
MARPLES SPLITPROOF 4 piece .. £24.50
MARPLES BOXWOOD 5 piece .. £38.50
PARAMO ROSEWOOD 4 piece .. £29.50
STANLEY 5001 6 piece .. £33.39
MARPLES BLUE CHIP 4 piece .. £17.42
MARPLES BLUE CHIP 5 piece .. £23.00
SORBY BOXWOOD 5 piece .. £26.00
PARAMO ROSEWOOD 6 piece .. £42.50
STANLEY 5002 5 piece .. £23.68

WOODTURNING CHISEL SETS (P&P £1.80)
HENRY TAYLOR Carbon Steel Sets, 3 Piece ..... £17 5 Piece ..... £29 8 Piece £46
SORBY Carbon Steel Sets 5 Piece (51c) ..... £26 6 Piece (61c) ..... £45 8 Piece (82c) £63
SORBY High Speed Sets 5 Piece (51h) ..... £40 6 Piece (61h) ..... £81 8 Piece (82h) £107
LUNA Swedish Steel Sets GOOD VALUE 3 Piece ..... £14 4 Piece ..... £27 5 Piece £37
MINIATURE SETS SORBY HSS set of 5 ..... £28 HENRY TAYLOR SUPER FIVE £18

ABRASIVES (West German top quality P&P £1.00/Order)
SANDING BELTS resin bonded aluminium oxide cloth belts (price each)

Size (length width)	M/C	40G	60G	80G	100G	120G
75×480mm — 3"×19"	(Elu)	£1.11	£1.02	£0.98	£0.95	£0.95
75×510mm — 3"×20"	(B&D)	£1.13	£1.04	£1.00	£0.97	£0.97
75×533mm — 3" 21"	(Bosch Hit)	£1.18	£1.08	£1.03	£1.00	£1.00
100×560mm 4"×22"	(Elu 90)	£1.30	£1.25	£1.20	£1.16	£1.15
100×610mm 4"×24"	(Wolf Hit)	£1.38	£1.33	£1.28	£1.24	£1.23
100×915mm — 4"×36"	(Coronet)	£2.10	£1.86	£1.82	£1.78	£1.72
150×1090mm — 6"×42"	(Coronet)	£3.90	£3.50	£3.30	£3.20	£3.20

★★ OTHER SIZES AVAILABLE ON REQUEST MANY IN STOCK ★★

ABRASIVE SHEETS (P&P £0.50 PER ORDER) state grit when ordering 100G and finer

Type	Description	60G/10	60G/50	80G/10	80G/50	100G+/10	100G+/50
PGF	GARNET FINISHING	£1.70	£8.20	£1.55	£7.10	£1.45	£6.40
GCAB	GARNET CABINET	£2.52	£11.60	£2.20	£10.04	£2.00	£9.06
PSF	SILICON FINISHING	£2.50	£12.14	£2.30	£10.51	£2.10	£9.47
WS	WET 'n' DRY	£4.80	£23.80	£4.20	£20.00	£2.80	£12.99

★SPECIAL OFFER★ 50 Sheets of asstd. Abrasives £5.99 inc. P&P Garnet-Glass-W/Dry

WIRE WOOL

	0000 Fine	00/0 Medium	1/2 Coarse	3/4 V Coarse
1 KG ROLLS	£4.73	£4.35	£4.25	£4.13
250g ROLLS	£1.50	£1.45	£1.42	£1.38

SAVE 20% ON ALL HAND TOOLS SEND NOW FOR NEW HAND TOOL CATALOGUE £1.50 (REFUNDED ON 1st ORDER)

0297 33656 CHARD STREET AXMINSTER DEVON EX13 5DZ 6.30-9pm 34836

BARCLAYCARD VISA

Mr Universe

Felder's universal machines have a top-of-the-market reputation for performance — and price. Luke Hughes has been working with one for more than a year

● Felder's Big Boy, the BF4/41. A solid chunk of universal for the professional or really serious enthusiast

I run a small workshop in central London. Three of us work flat out, making prototypes for industry, exotic one-offs, and hunky architectural woodwork. We have two floors of 250sq ft, where to manoeuvre an 8x4 sheet requires deft footwork and considerable tolerance from everyone else. The 'universals vs individual machines' debate doesn't enter into it. For three years I used an old Lurem universal which irritated me daily by inefficient belt changes, inaccurate fences, inadequate power, and little design thought behind making it 'user-friendly'. It had to go. But what should replace it? What had the accuracy, versatility, and robustness for us? Pricewise, it was between a big Luna and the Felder, and you don't have to be Einstein to perceive light years between the two. The solid cast construction and the thought behind some of the design features convinced me — Felder. And the biggest one they could deliver: the BF4/41, with a 16in planer, three-phase motors, and no mortiser.

You've probably seen it at WOOD-WORKER Shows; glistening, robust and permanent-looking. What is it like after 15 months of hard, professional, continuous use? Here are some of the things potential purchasers may like to consider.

Who should be interested

This is a professional machine. It is ideally suited to Research and Development workshops in factories, small professional businesses like my own, designer makers who are setting up and trying to put together the kit they need (here it is, all in one), schools and colleges, and ambitious amateurs who know a good thing when they see one.

Things to consider

Expense. Around the £5,000 mark, you need to be certain it's right for you. For us, not having the daily irritations of a cheaper machine, being sure of the solidity, the accuracy and the ease of operation have saved thousands of pounds over one year alone. The beefiness of the power and the capacity of the fences, the planer and the

moulder have added a new dimension to the work we thought possible. As for keeping its value, that will stand the test of time. Felder claim that in Austria, over a five-year period, a serviced machine will sell for 85-90% of the current market price (prices increase by 4% per year, but for the UK, exchange rates are also part of the equation). If you are setting up, and can tell that to your Bank Manager, you may find a slightly more sympathetic ear when it comes to loan facilities.

What it can do

See the full list of technical specifications, but salient points include a saw with 12in

blade (3¾in cut), which tilts to 45°; a 16in planer with spring-loaded knife adjustments and 7½in thicknessing capacity; and a spindle with three speeds, which tilts to 45°, allowing endless permutations with a limited range of cutters. Better still, the top surface of all the beds is entirely level, so you can extend the fences over the whole surface. This gives a maximum cutting width on the saw of 36½in. There are independent motors, so no belts need to be changed. Brake motors are an extra. I've got them, and I recommend them. I cannot vouch for the mortiser, but I refer you to the specifications.

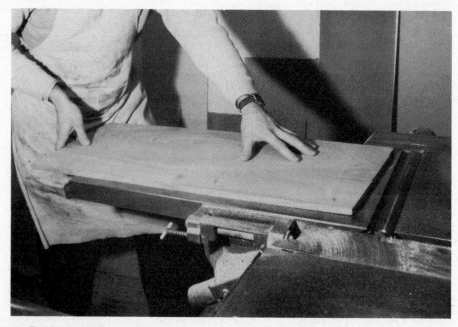

● Taking panels up to 16in wide, the planer substantially reduces the need for gluing up narrow boards

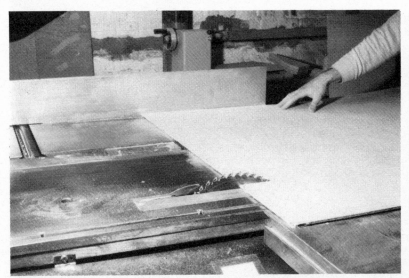

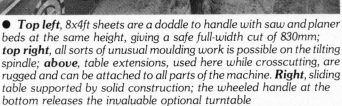

● **Top left**, 8x4ft sheets are a doddle to handle with saw and planer beds at the same height, giving a safe full-width cut of 830mm; **top right**, all sorts of unusual moulding work is possible on the tilting spindle; **above**, table extensions, used here while crosscutting, are rugged and can be attached to all parts of the machine. **Right**, sliding table supported by solid construction; the wheeled handle at the bottom releases the invaluable optional turntable

Accessories

These are all first-rate, and as solid and sensible as the machine. There are table extensions, fence supports, precision adjustments, rip-fence extensions, mitre fences, slot and bore chuck spindles, precision moulding fences, support stands, rolling carriages (for moving round the workshop) a turntable, vacuum attachments, sawblades, ring fences, pressure springs, power feeders and a hold-down attachment for the moulder . . . and that's only a few. There is every attachment that I have seen available for any other machine on the market, and they are all reasonably priced. Particular mention must go to the turntable; the whole machine swivels in the workshop so you get the benefit of the length of the building

● Moulding small pieces becomes a pleasure with the hold-down attachment, 'one of the best ancillaries of any machine ever'

continued

Mr Universe

when mitring skirtings or moulding end-grain — a revolution; to the hold-down for the spindle moulder: this is a power feeder (except you provide the power and save yourself £300), which keep pieces tight up against the spindle fence and held down on the table — a snip at £51+VAT when I bought it; and to the table extensions. These bolt on in a second and can extend any table in any dimension. A simple idea brilliantly executed.

Transformations in our life

1 Sawing big clumsy panels using the table extensions gives a convenience compatible with a dimension saw.
2 Having all the tables at the same level, all contributing to the operation in hand, means you can use the machine as an extra surface in the workshop. I often put one of the table extensions on to the saw table, and clamp my home-made router table between it and the planer's infeed table; it's just right for the job, and I can use the dust-extraction outlet of the planer for the router.
3 Having the immediate changeover switch and three motors beats belt-changing between functions hands down. To be fair, competitive universals (and cheaper ones) generally have this feature nowadays.
4 Having the hold-down attachment for the spindle moulder has given me a renewed confidence with that aspect of machining, which came just in time — I've had a few scares in the past.

Related acquisitions

First — dust extraction. I never thought we could fit it into the workshop, but now we have, I can't think how we managed before. Apart from all the health implications and the time spent sweeping up, it does help the machine operate at its optimum. In particular the bearings of the sliding table used to gather pernicious lumps of MDF dust, which were a pig to shift. Similarly, the interior of the carcase casting used to fill up with dust and shavings and had to be periodically scooped out. All this has changed.

Second — three-phase. I bought the machine with three-phase motors in the belief that one day I would get a supply connected. In the meantime I would use an AC converter. Despite the protestations of the converter manufacturer, this was not as much of a success as I'd hoped. It worked reasonably well for about nine months until the capacitor of the converter kept blowing. It wasn't really strong enough for our kind of work, though for a less intensive requirement it is still infinitely better than single-phase. But I've finally drawn a deep breath and installed a mains three-phase supply, and for the first time I really understand what advantages it can bring. For those uninitiated in these mysteries, three-phase gives a much more constant supply, appreciable when motors are under load — sawing 4in oak up the grain, for example, or thicknessing a 16in lump of iroko. With single-phase, the power dips, the motor complains, the whole system is put under tremendous strain and wear occurs dramatically. With three-phase, the power is more constant, the motors more efficient, and that lump of iroko is munched away contentedly. A converter converts a normal single-phase into a three-phase supply, and enables a three-phase machine to be run from a normal 13-amp ring-main. A converter costs about £150-£200, and the manufacturers will tell you it is 95% efficient. Well, it's not, but it works. If you are strapped for cash having bought your Felder, then buy a three-phase machine and get a converter as a stop-gap. Within a year or so you'll be able to afford to have a proper supply installed, which costs £500-£1000, depending on cable runs and other variables.

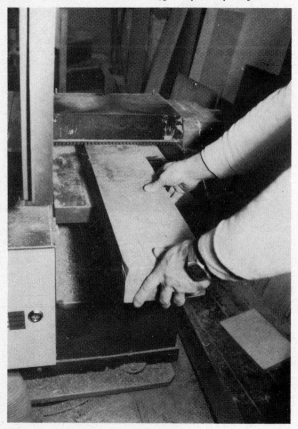

● *Top right*, 'awkward' saw tilt adjustment lever; *below*, the thicknesser has 7½in depth capacity

Technical specifications

Planer/thicknesser	BF4/31	BF4/41
Cutter width	310mm/12¹³⁄₁₆in	410mm/16⅛in
Thicknessing depth	0-190mm/7½in	0-190mm/7½in
Table length	1300mm/51³⁄₁₆in	1500mm/59¹⁄₁₆in
Max. depth of cut	5mm/³⁄₁₆in	5mm/³⁄₁₆in
Saw		
Arbor diameter	30mm	
RPM	4800	
Blade diameter	150-300mm/6-12in	
Saw-blade max. height	95mm/3¾in	
Tilt	90°-45°	
Cutting width	0-830mm/32½in	0-930mm/36½in
Spindle		
Diameter	30mm or 1¼in	
RPM	4000, 5600, 8300	
Tilt	90°-45°	
Mortiser		
Max. depth	150mm/5⅞in	
Max. height	120mm/4¾in	
Electrics		
Motors	3	
Standard size	380v 50Hz, 3ph 3HP	
	4hp optional	
Dimensions		
Height	830mm/32½in	
Min. transportable width	950mm/37⅜in	
Max. gross weight	830kg/1830lbs	
Crate dimensions		
Length	1450mm/58in	
Width	1130mm/44½in	
Height	1050mm/41½in	

Prices
Exchange rates and optional accessories vary the final figures, but a basic price for the BF4/41 without mortiser is £5000+VAT; for the BF/31 without mortiser £4300+VAT.

Problems

1 It's big. The BF4 needs a 45in doorway — I widened mine, there was no option.

2 It's heavy. It weighs nearly a ton, so if you aren't on the ground floor, you may need reinforcement.

3 The saw-tilt adjustment is awkward. It uses a lever, which is inferior to the revolving wheel arrangement on earlier models. I'm hoping Felder will amend this.

4 There is no standard-equipment switch that can be operated while you are standing behind the planer. The manufacturers tell me that machines made to German and Austrian specifications have such a switch because of their regulations, but British regulations don't require it. However, this is apparently likely to be changed in the near future.

5 The adjustment on the thicknessing table on my machine seemed quite stiff until I learnt the knack of using two hands.

6 Using the machine without dust extraction is likely to clog certain moving parts unless they are swept clear frequently.

7 It's not possible to wind the spindle below the level of the table because of rise-and-fall tolerances, so you have to take the spindle out of its mounting (a turn of a lever detaches it) to use one of the other functions. This irritated me initially, but there is in fact an advantage in that you can leave all the tooling set up on the shaft between operations.

But these are small problems, and Felder have taken in all my criticisms willingly and constructively — and, I trust, to everyone's benefit.

Backup

Felders are sold in the UK by Sanlin (see box), under the auspices of Norman Woods. Norman is proposing to run a service arrangement which is still in embryo stage, but it should be of special interest to institutions. My own experience: when I first bought my machine, I had problems with the levels on the planer beds. They were fractionally out (well within most people's tolerances). I had a gentle moan to Norman. Blow me if there wasn't an engineer from Felder flown out from Austria to come and sort it out. It was better for a while, but wasn't perfect. It seemed likely that the machine had been mishandled in transit. But fault or no fault, Rheinhard the engineer was back on his plane to London to iron out the problems. Service of a very special kind, indeed. A British-based engineer is being trained, but something that cannot be handled here will be referred to Austria.

My grandfather married (second time round) a woman who was able to keep him in a manner to which he had never become accustomed. He used to drive her Rolls-Royce round Europe, and it once broke down outside Nice. He telephoned the nearest RR dealer, and before he got back from the phone box there was a helicopter waiting beside the car, ferrying one of their engineers. All was put to rights in a jiffy. There is something about the Felder which harks back to an age when there was no skimping on quality, and the aftercare is as thorough as the manufacture. It is an exceptional machine; would it were made in Britain. ∎

● Sanlin, 23 Church Sq, Toddington, Beds LU5 6AA, (05255) 2259.

Postscript

Since writing this article, I bumped into Felder again at WOODMEX '86. To my surprise and delight, they have taken all the criticisms to heart and have spent a lot of time and trouble sorting out some of the imperfections of the design that I, and presumably others, have fed back to them over the last year. The result is an even better machine, and the continued assurance of Felder's pursuit of excellence.

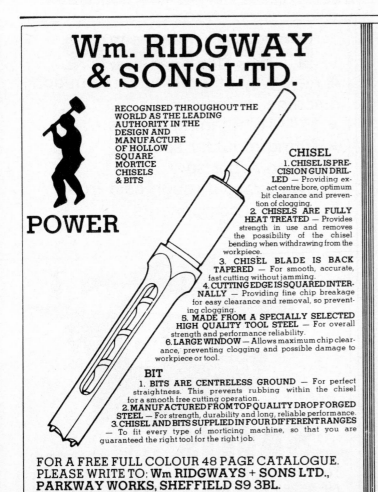

Gentle giant

James Krenov's uniquely warm, reflective approach to his craft has earned him a special place in the hearts of woodworkers all over the world. Englishmen Ted Hawke and Kelvin Mather went to study with him in California; here's their experience

Above James Krenov's bench in the corner of his teaching workshop is pinned a sentence cut from a cardboard packing case:

LOOK FOR CONCEALED DAMAGE.

The multiple meanings of the phrase indicate the ethos of Krenov's School for Fine Woodworking, where the two of us from England met when we enrolled in September 1984. Ted has a fine art background, Kelvin came to woodworking via architecture; we had both earlier discovered Krenov's books, and their enticing voice of sanity beyond technique. An uncompromising attitude quickly became first base for us all — things were what you were capable of making them and the time taken was the time needed, no cheating allowed.

The deeply personal style of his books — *A Cabinetmaker's Notebook*, *The Impractical Cabinetmaker*, *The Fine Art of Cabinetmaking*, and *James Krenov: Worker in Wood* — reflects his approach, summarised by Michael Stone in *Contemporary American Woodworkers*:

'He advocates a return to the values traditionally associated with cabinetmaking, such as integrity, durability and independence. He personalises each facet of his craft: every board he selects, every joint he cuts, every detail he creates is performed in a way to immerse himself in the process of making. The result is a craftsman totally inseparable from his work and secure in knowing he has done his best and done it by himself.'

● **Left**, *Krenov and cocobolo clock on a laminated cherry stand. An hour and a second hand only – no minutes. 'Very relaxing, a sort of clock mobile . . .'*

● *A showcase cabinet by Krenov, in pear with a pecanwood frame. Glass doors front and 'back'; 'There is no actual back – the piece should stand free.'*

James Krenov trained in Sweden under Carl Malmsten, who followed the principles advocated by the Arts and Crafts movement, in a direct line from the philosophy of Morris and Ruskin.

Krenov's approach, however, is neither consciously 'historical' nor overtly 'intellectual', but is rather instinctive and poetic, a personal expression within the canons of high quality hand-made furniture.

He doesn't feel that work has to be 'original' to be valid — 'All too often', he writes, we are prone to use quick, purely visual effects to bypass skill and dedication. If you can't make it good, make it weird.' And he points out some of the dangers and contradictions: 'There is a new role for the craftsman. He is both craftsman and artist, although not necessarily in that order. In fact many craftsmen are able to do well by being artists first and craftsmen second. To do so they must above all be 'imaginative' which often means being eccentric . . . It is a pressured existence into which most of the really successful craftsmen are forced.' For Krenov there is another kind of originality or uniqueness: the 'fingerprints' on the object of the person who made it, the result of the patient weaving together of sensuous material and method, the craftsmanship of risk and personal discovery.

'Is there a connection between crudeness of hand and the over-emphasis on technical points in our craft? Don't some of us get greater satisfaction from 'saving' work than from actually doing it? . . . There is in some of us the need for a balance between a method we use and the satisfaction it can give.'

K renov's school is in Mendocino County in north California, which has become a Mecca for all kinds of woodworkers and their customers over the past decade or so. Krenov's presence there is as a result of and, lately, a contributing factor to this phenomenon. The interests of the craftsmen in the area are promoted by the local Woodworkers Association, an active body which was instrumental in organising a series of summer workshops with Krenov in the picturesque coast town of Mendocino. These successful seminars prompted the Community College of the Redwoods to provide a full-time programme in 'Fine Cabinetmaking' under Krenov's direction in Fort Bragg, a small fishing and logging town of wide roads and low timber buildings in the 'New England' style, some four hours' drive north of San Francisco.

California is a wealthy state with plenty of people prepared to buy handmade furniture of modern inspiration — there's a growth in the number of artist/craftspeople producing speculative one-offs and of small batch producers and workers to commission. The quality of work ranges from mediocre to superb, and stylistically from Shaker/neo-antique, Chinese, Japanese, European, through 'Green and Green' to modern/post-modern, etc. — the nest of an energetic and enthusiastic magpie. We saw a few 'lava-flows' in purpleheart and zebrano, and some vast 'conspicuous-consumption' executive desks 'all-over round-over', but these were less ubiquitous than we'd feared.

The School

The College of the Redwoods Fine Woodworking Programme is housed in a well-lit spacious workshop, purpose-built on a wooded rise at the eastern edge of Fort Bragg. Its west-facing entrance lobby allows views over town to the Pacific Ocean and of spectacular winter sunsets — the gathering point for relaxing smokes, coffees and chats.

The benchroom has space for 22 students, a few of whom may be invited to do a second year. Krenov has his bench in one corner. There's adequate cupboard space at each bench for the hand-tools which each student must supply him or herself. The temperature is thermostatically controlled, and humidity is maintained at around 7%.

The timber store is fully enclosed but with open access direct from the benchroom. There is a good stock of cabinet quality hardwoods which may be purchased as required. Students are encouraged to obtain timber from other sources, in quantities limited by the storage space beneath their benches, at their lodgings, or, of course, by the state of their bank balances.

The machine room, through swing doors at one end of the bench room, contains: one 5hp Oliver bandsaw (a beautiful machine) and two other smaller bandsaws: two surfacing planers and one thicknesser: two table saws: two horizontal mortisers: one spindle moulder: one fixed vertical router: one pillar drill: one large veneer press, and a varied selection of hand routers. Apart from the Oliver, there's nothing exceptional about any of the machines, but they are kept clean, tuned and sharp.

The Curriculum

The nine-month programme draws heavily on Krenov's experience and techniques as outlined in his books. The school has published its aims as follows:

'It's a programme for the aspiring cabinetmaker who hopes to combine sensitivity with personal expression, patiently striving towards a goal best described as fine craftsmanship . . . Our aim is to 'go into' our material, discover its richness when worked with finely tuned tools and intimate methods. Although machine tools will in no way be neglected, the emphasis in this programme is on hand, eye, and workbench.'

To this end, the first term is devoted to a close study of the classic techniques of cabinetmaking and furniture construction, as well as the aesthetic and practical design aspects peculiar to wood. Much time is spent in the making and subtle use of tools, fine planes, chisels, knives, and so on, and the ways in which the caring craftsman can tune these essential instruments. As the term progresses, ideas for a modest first project are personally proposed and developed to deploy some or all of the techniques covered. The second term continues exploring more advanced tech-

continued

Gentle giant

to the look and feel of the finished piece, wherein each part is adjusted/tailored to the demands of the whole. In his hands it results in an all-round understated 'rightness', rather than the often over-emphatic, first-glance 'sharpness' of furniture derived from two-dimensional graphics. Nor does Krenov need drawings and/or templates as records — if he repeats a piece it will be because he's had some new thoughts about it, and it will probably be in a different wood — factors which will produce a different equation, new proportions, altered curves and other subtle changes. The consequences will reverberate throughout the piece — it will not be a repeat. It's an approach he encourages:— although, aware of and sympathetic to different needs and skills, he has arranged extra-mural classes in drawing.

Practical techniques are taught to the gathered students via blackboard lectures, slide-shows and demonstrations at the bench or in the machine room. These are followed up by a great deal of individual consultation and regular informal critiques.

● *With student Garrett Klugertz in the workshop. 'A shared sense of purpose . . . our lives revolved around the workshop.'*

niques including the sawing and use of veneer and joinery at other than 90°. A more ambitious project is developed and undertaken in consultation with the staff. During the final term a single piece of fine cabinetmaking may be undertaken.

The school sees this learning process as one of an 'upward spiral' in which the student is constantly returning to and refining techniques previously learned, progressing in skill-with-integrity towards that ever-changing personal goal.

The Teaching

Students are required to put in a minimum of 48 hours per six-day week. Krenov is assisted by two part-time instructors and one instructional aide, all ex-students. There is neither a formal classroom nor a drafting room. Krenov doesn't rely on drawing, preferring to work with full-size mock-ups roughly scaled from thumbnail sketches, composing a piece in three dimensions — a sculptural methodology integral

Krenov's lectures are particularly riveting; he's an intense yet amusing raconteur with a facility for off-hand colloquialism which drives home the point. He takes pains to ensure that students do not feel pressured, that they work in a reflective way. He excites and focuses curiosity about subtleties, 'the little things' which can contribute so significantly to the whole. Furniture making for him is a tactile as well as a visual and functional craft. The sense of touch can tell you not only about proportions, three-dimensional form, and textures, but also unexpected things such as temperature. There are some things your eyes cannot tell you.

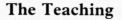

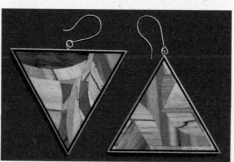

● *Far left, Ted Hawke's mahogany cabinet on a stand sold quickly; left, one of Ted's 'venearring' designs. Below, a bird's-eye maple jewellery box – Ted again*

While not denying that one can learn from mistakes, Krenov feels it can be a time-consuming and depressing route — much better to learn from one's successes. His guidance is geared accordingly, and with appropriate tact; he rarely said outright that he didn't like something or that something wasn't good, preferring to preface his criticisms with 'I wonder if . . .'. He did not seek to impose any particular 'style' of work, although there was an understandable hesitancy on the part of some students to venture outside the areas mapped by Krenov for himself. He was not dogmatic, merely aware of his own pre-delictions and limits, and insisted only that a piece be the result of honest thought and feeling and a striving for quality.

It's a common misconception that Krenov does all his work by hand. We had fallen victim to this too, because we were initially surprised at how much of our work was done by machine. It must have been our romantic, anti-machine sub-conscious which had edited out the due emphasis on machine work which Krenov gives in his books. Machines were used with discretion to remove donkey work, and with jigged finesse for repeatable tight fits. Settings were arrived at after many test cuts and fittings with scrap wood. No part of a piece was left as finished direct from the thick-nesser or surfacer; hand-planing removed ripples and produced finished dimensions — there was pleasure here as gossamer shavings curled from a plane built by one-self, as one listened for the characteristic 'whistle' tell-taling its efficiency. Sanding, if used, was by hand only and kept to a minimum. Tenons and corner bridles were cut on the table-saw or, if preferred, on the bandsaw suitably jigged to counter blade drift. A similar fence adjustment permitted the cutting of veneers on the bandsaw, a revelation to us both.

Japanese hand-tools figured largely among the students' kits — they were no doubt influenced by Krenov's reference to them in his books (and by recent commer-cial hype?). By the end of the year some had reverted to, or were seeking as additions, good English back-saws and chisels. Krenov has a smallish collection of hand-tools, of various origins including Japan. They are tuned and, where appropriate, altered to suit his needs. He's not a tool fetishist. His self-made planes are his 'violins' with which he, as he says, 'attempts to make music'. At his relatively low-tech school the impor-tance and potential of finely tuned hand-tools came as an eye-opener: no fighting, no sweat — a kind of liberation.

Atmosphere

The workshop was friendly and co-operative. The generosity of Krenov and his assistants with time, tools and information was infectious and became the norm. There was a shared sense of purpose, of difficul-ties, of successes, despite the international flavour — students had come from

England, Norway, New Zealand, Alaska, Hawaii. 'Dusty', the resident black Labrador, somewhat arthritic, lay around between benches polishing the floor, scrounging food and offering odd noises and smells during critiques — a relaxing presence.

We were all strangers to Fort Bragg and it was difficult to get to know the locals except in a superficial way. Our lives revolved around the workshop. Inevitably, the single-minded dedication to the work plus a certain isolation from 'normal' life gave rise to tensions. But the greatest demands were those which we made upon ourselves, that came from within. It was easy to overdo things, to work 10 or even 12 hours a day, seven days a week, to burn out. Krenov, who played tennis, advised the same for us, or volley-ball, or a bike ride, a walk on the beach, anything for a change of pace.

Ted took to beachcombing and dis-covered abalone shell for the first time, which later became inlay material. Behind the school is a park of deep ravines and meandering water courses. Lofty redwoods provide welcome grabs when skittering down the inclines or, for the cautious, rough timber stairs snake amidst the foliage. It was a favourite place for quiet reflection.

In summer all doors and windows were thrown open and sometimes humming birds and variegated newts would find their way into the workshop. They'd be gently rescued and returned to their world. Early in the course, when all was new and strange, and the pressures few, Sundays were often spent rambling or searching for mushrooms which grew in great variety in the area or, in winter, standing on the headlands braced against the wind searching the sea for the tell-tale water spouts of the migrating grey whales south-bound for the breeding grounds of Baja. Some months later they would return, the spouts of the parents now punctuated by the weaker sprays of the calves.

Our social life tended to be somewhat incestuous, involving mutual invitations to 'pot-lucks' — parties to which guests brought the bulk of the food and drink. Friday night was 'Elephant Night' — whoever had completed a piece bought Carlsberg 'Elephant' lager for everyone else. If no piece had been finished, there was a whip-round and 'elephants' were drunk anyway. 'Elephants' was essentially an opportunity to unwind and, over the year, became quite a social event with food, slide-shows and live music provided by the students.

Krenov partook willingly but modestly in these affairs. The lager was pretty strong stuff and one had to be wary — Saturday was a working day, starting as usual at 8.30am. Sundays could be worked too, if you so chose. Krenov usually appeared on Sundays and, in the relative quiet, worked on his own current piece or contemplated the speculative mock-up of the next. He would sometimes seek our thoughts on his

● *Top*, and details *above*: a 'showcase walkaround' in Italian walnut, made in 1985-6 by Krenov, preceding the pear and pecan piece on the previous pages. Note the attention to visual detail in the handles, and the subtlety of the curves

continued

Gentle giant

progress; impromptu, intimate discussions of the aesthetic and structural options would ensue. He was no guru, but a human being with problems and doubts like the rest of us. He had, however, an energy of feeling and an enthusiasm for the work which drew us along.

We don't feel qualified to offer an opinion on USA woodworker training in general or how it compares with such training in the UK. No doubt it varies from state to state to state and from school to school. Conversations led us to believe that Krenov's school is unique, contrasting, for example, with the two-year programme offered by Wendell Castle at his school in New York State. Castle seeks to train woodworkers who could build the designs of others or work in industry. Castle's curriculum is highly structured, with emphases on problem solving, rigid design briefs, all kinds of drawing, as well as good practical

skills. This sounds very much like the kind of curriculum one could find in Britain.

Course fees for an out-of-state student at Krenov's school are around $1000 per term, three terms in the year. Accommodation, food, materials and tools are all extras. Ted sold his house in East London to finance the year and Kelvin used personal savings.

While we were there, the school held two exhibitions of students' work. The first, in Mendocino at a craft gallery, was a relative financial success — pieces were sold and commissions placed. Ted was among these successes, selling the mahogany cabinet-on-a-stand on the first day and getting a commission for a repeat on the second. The second exhibition, in a public gallery in Walnut Creek near San Francisco, was a relative financial disaster. So it goes.

Krenov is an individualist. He left Malmsten's shop in Sweden in order to

pursue his craft free from as many unwanted pressures as possible. He does not underplay the difficulties of his path. His work is a fact and a reminder, an exemplary demonstration, that his way is possible and has a place in the world.

'As to the work itself, there are things one does, and likes to do, that cannot be explained by efficiency. Are those enjoyable moments gained at the price of efficiency or is there a commonsense and a feeling in our odd ways that is more rational than any efficient engineering . . .? Wood is a rich, sensuous material. One can do the most exquisite and refined things with it. Or hack out impulsive, naive messages. Work hours, days, months on one single object. Or sit and carve a toy, a whistle, anything or nothing. Just make shavings.' (From *The Fine Art of Cabinetmaking*: for stockist of all the books mentioned in this article, see box.). ∎

Personal summing-up

Ted

It was an intense year, a period of serious play realistically undertaken against the economic and psychological pressures which inclined me to abandon this path in craft. One had to gain a capacity for discrimination, for resistance, a sense of value, a sense of self. Technique was prized but not above a certain feeling. Through all previous years something had been missing — a sense of conviction and reassurance that comes from witnessing a master working material with great confidence and understanding. I found this in James Krenov who had no need of defensive irony.

At one stage I became concerned that, in pursuing my own notions, I was remaining unfamiliar with many cabinet-making techniques. I spoke with Krenov about this. His reply was deliberately encouraging to me and indicative of his own essential outlook. He said, smiling, 'Stay ignorant, I have' — shorthand in that context for 'Use imagination, intuition, feeling; leave the academics on the shelf for reference as needed.' It was always a

question of emphasis. Under his eye my self-confidence grew. Meanwhile, back in the constrained UK, under the auspices of the Enterprise Allowance Scheme, I've set up a small shop in Manchester.

Kelvin

At the moment I'm taking stock of the year, gathering tools and machines around me and keeping a paternal eye on a workshop under construction in Cornwall. I began the year with a great many questions. I have no answers even now, but I do have a greater awareness of what may be achieved if you put your heart, mind and energy into it. I feel better able to face that challenge. My work advanced five years during the course.

● Krenov's four books and *Contemporary American Woodworkers* by Michael Stone from Stobart & Son, 67-73 Worship St, London EC2A 2EL, 01-247 0501.
● For more details of the Krenov course, write to College of the Redwoods Woodworking Programme, 440 Alger St, Fort Bragg, California CA 95437, USA.

● *Above* and *below*, a maple side-table by Ted Hawke shows Krenovian influence, but perhaps not his restraint

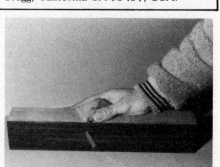

● *Kelvin's shooting plane, 'showing the logic of the pimple grip'. The bar and wedge remain square to the skewed blade. Maple body, partridgewood wedge, ironbark running sole, lignum vitae shooting sole!*

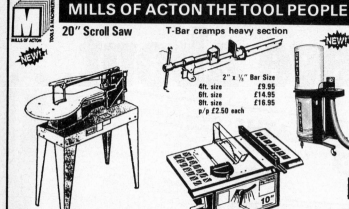

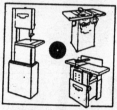

Contemporary cabriole

Graham Cooke's daring design casts a quizzical look at reproduction furniture

● Bright red legs, grey plastic finish, blue PVC foam and false wood drawers – but is it truer to the spirit of the 17th century than modern 'reproduction' furniture?

My aim was to design a cabinet which took the most outstanding features of historic design and interpreted them through contemporary materials and structural elements without producing banal 'reproduction' furniture.

The cabinet as such first appeared in this country during the 16th century as a technical development of the medieval chest. Cabinets really became important in the 17th century as 'Japanned' cabinets begun to be imported from the Orient; this marked the beginning of a craze for decorative domestic cabinets with no truly defined function except as a strong-box to hold papers, relics or any artefacts.

Traditionally Oriental cabinets were constructed as straightforward storage boxes. A base or stand was generally added as an afterthought in England to house the cabinet for convenience. The cabinet itself would be smothered in highly decorative Oriental lacquer work, while the base

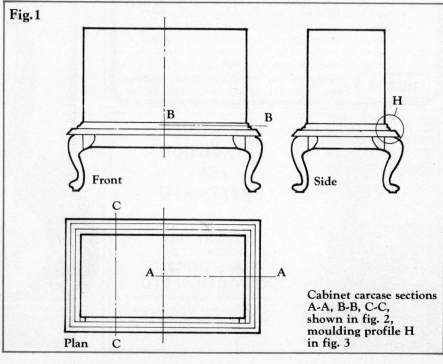

Fig. 1

Front

Side

H

B   B

A   A

C

C

Plan

Cabinet carcase sections A-A, B-B, C-C, shown in fig. 2, moulding profile H in fig. 3

Fig.2

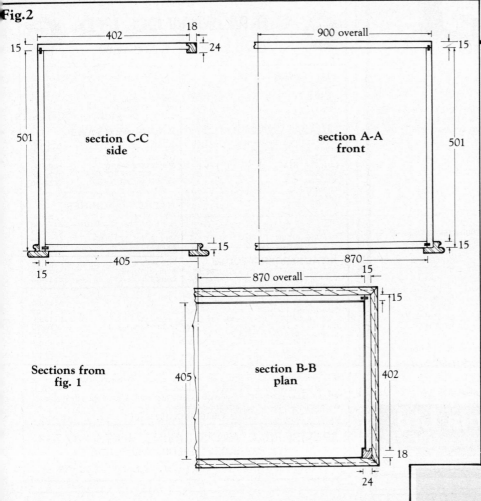

section C-C side

402   18
15   24
501
405
15
15

section A-A front

900 overall
15
501
870
15

Sections from fig. 1

405

section B-B plan

870 overall
15
15
402
18
24

Fig.3

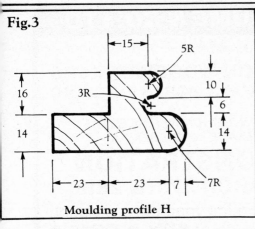

15
5R
16
3R
10
6
14
14
23   23   7   7R

Moulding profile H

grooves for biscuit joints, gluing each panel in place and clamping securely. Next I applied a beech lipping to the front of the carcase from which the doors would hang; the top and side panels of the carcase were already tongued on the overhead router to join to the lipping (the front and side faces of which were laminated before assembly, as was the floor panel inside).

The carcase was now ready to laminate externally. I chose grey 'Colorcore' laminate by Formica to cover the cabinet as it could provide a uniform colour with no nasty black seams which are usual with regular laminates; it's also a good contemporary alternative to lacquer work. I cut the laminate oversize and clamped pieces to each panel in turn, shaving away the excess using a hand-held power laminate trimmer.

Next I made up the beech moulding on a spindle moulder, and fitted it to the base before masking off the cabinet and spraying the moulding with red polyurethane paint. After cutting the doors, I laminated them in grey and black and fixed them by piano hinges to the carcase. I turned two beech

● *Exploded diagram **below** shows construction; the interior boxes are free-standing*

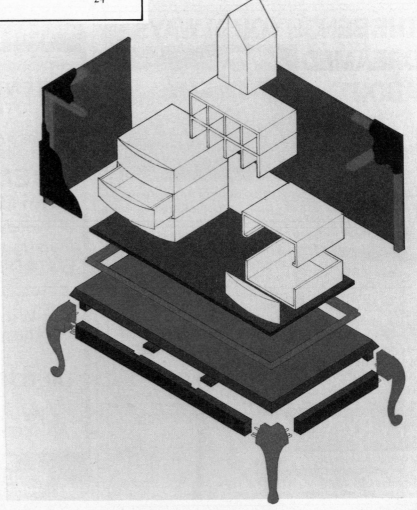

would be constructed in the English style of the day, usually 'Queen Anne' — hence the use of the cabriole leg.

For my cabinet I took these traditional references and applied them to the demands of the 20th century. I wanted an adaptable piece of furniture which would be capable of housing anything from a computer to a butterfly collection. The primary need was to make a construction which would, as far as possible, abandon the conventionality of 'reproduction furniture'.

Construction

Wherever possible I deliberately used contemporary materials and treatments, and mass-production techniques for construction. I made the carcase from 15mm chipboard, cutting the panels to size, cutting

continued
289

Contemporary cabriole

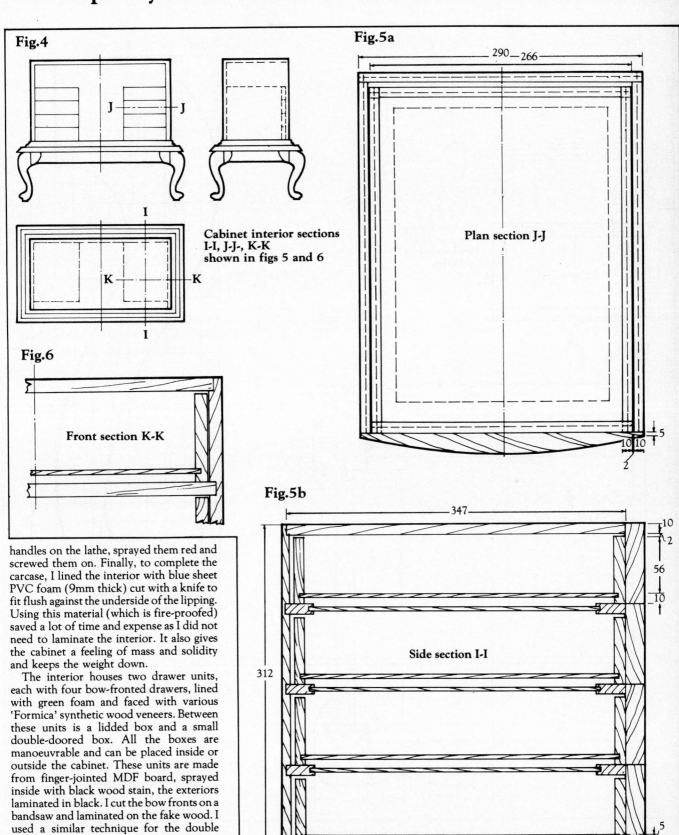

Fig.4

J — J

I

I

K — K

Cabinet interior sections
I-I, J-J-, K-K
shown in figs 5 and 6

Fig.6

Front section K-K

Fig.5a

290 — 266

Plan section J-J

5

10 10

2

Fig.5b

347

10

2

56

10

312

Side section I-I

5

10

5 5

5 10 6

307

372

5 20

10

5

5

handles on the lathe, sprayed them red and screwed them on. Finally, to complete the carcase, I lined the interior with blue sheet PVC foam (9mm thick) cut with a knife to fit flush against the underside of the lipping. Using this material (which is fire-proofed) saved a lot of time and expense as I did not need to laminate the interior. It also gives the cabinet a feeling of mass and solidity and keeps the weight down.

The interior houses two drawer units, each with four bow-fronted drawers, lined with green foam and faced with various 'Formica' synthetic wood veneers. Between these units is a lidded box and a small double-doored box. All the boxes are manoeuvrable and can be placed inside or outside the cabinet. These units are made from finger-jointed MDF board, sprayed inside with black wood stain, the exteriors laminated in black. I cut the bow fronts on a bandsaw and laminated on the fake wood. I used a similar technique for the double doors and the box lid.

Base and legs

The base is not attached to the cabinet, so it can be used in its own right as an occasional table. I laminated black Colorcore on to chipboard with a beech underframe (also laminated), which connects to the set of

Contemporary cabriole

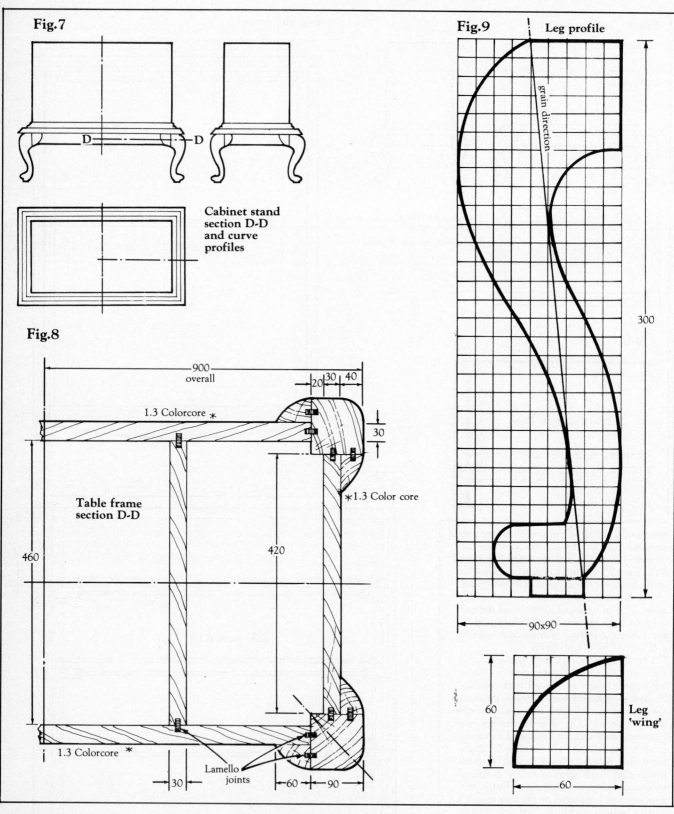

Fig.7

D — — D

Cabinet stand section D-D and curve profiles

Fig.8

900 overall

1.3 Colorcore ✳

20 30 40

30

*1.3 Color core

Table frame section D-D

460

420

1.3 Colorcore ✳

Lamello joints

30   60   90

Fig.9   Leg profile

grain direction

300

90x90

60   Leg 'wing'

60

cabriole legs. In the field of mass-produced furniture the cabriole leg has been over-used to the point of insignificance; cabriole legs tooled by machine lose much of the sculptural properties which should be inherent to a good leg. So I chose to hand-tool the legs myself, which proved to be a far simpler operation than one would imagine.

I exaggerated the form almost to its structural limitations to obtain the desired effect. I drew a template of the shape I needed, cut the leg with a bandsaw, and finished off with a rasp, spokeshave and glasspapers. Then I cut out the wings and dowelled them to the legs; finally I sprayed the leg pieces red and dowelled them to the table frame.

I hope the resulting cabinet goes one step beyond the banality of reproduction furniture. It combines modern materials and methods with traditional motifs, and I hope will complement a contemporary interior, while making an ironic comment on English furniture 'iconology'. ■

Probably the foremost six-function woodworking machine currently available to the professional joiner and the enthusiastic home worker

C268 six-function three-motor universal.

The new C268 from AEG is a full six-function machine with three motors – giving triple-drive power, capacity, convenience, handling, safety and the very latest in design.
Packed with superb features, the C268 is a truly precision machine – placing in the hands of the professional and the skilled hobbyist the means of producing the full range of good joinery from basic carpentry to fine woodworking.

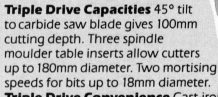

Triple Drive Capacities 45° tilt to carbide saw blade gives 100mm cutting depth. Three spindle moulder table inserts allow cutters up to 180mm diameter. Two mortising speeds for bits up to 18mm diameter.

Triple Drive Convenience Cast-iron tables give 1.4×0.7 metre working space and guarantee extra safety capacity, accuracy and quality. Vacuum nozzle for each function. Choice of accessories to meet every need.

Triple Drive Handling Electric control gives instant function switching. Settings are simple, straightforward and accurate with quick set-up fittings.

Triple Drive Safety Carefully-designed guards combine safety and ease of work. Microswitches on all vital components and emergency stop buttons at work stations for all-round safety. Braked motor on spindle moulder ensures practically immediate stopping.

Triple Drive Design Superb working conditions with move-away mortiser for easy surface planing, two-way swivel-back planer tables for easy thicknessing, and sawing/tenoning carriage glides on ball-bearings and v-ways built into the moulder table.

AEG Woodworking

AEG (UK) LIMITED
217 Bath Road, Slough, Berkshire SL1 4AW
Telephone: Slough (0753) 872101

Fully illustrated descriptive leaflet, together with price list and the address of your nearest AEG stockist available on request.

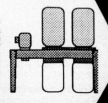

Guild notes

Guild of WOODWORKERS

The Guild was set up by *Woodworker* to create a meeting ground for all those involved in working wood, whether professional, amateur, or enthusiastic beginner. Guild members get:

- Access to Guild courses and events
- Free publicity in *Woodworker*
- Specially arranged tool insurance at low rates
- 15% off Woodworker Show entry
- A free display area and meeting point at the Show
- 15% discount off *Woodworker* plans
- Inclusion in our register of members' skills and services

For details, please send an sae to the Guild of Woodworkers, 1 Golden Sq, London W1R 3AB.

GUILD COURSES

● Only Guild members are eligible to go on these courses. You must book in advance, and we must have a cheque for the full cost of the course at the time of booking. If you cancel less than four weeks before the advertised date you will forfeit 50% of the cost, unless there are exceptional circumstances.

Veneering weekend — Ian Hosker

April 4-5, 9.30-4.30, Chester
You have a choice; spend the whole weekend with Ian, or opt for one of the two individual day courses on offer.

Hammer veneering: 4 April

You'll learn about preparation of veneers and ground, laying the balancing veneer, laying veneer with a join, and laying stringing crossbanding. The course costs £25, materials an extra £12 per person.

Parquetry: 5 April

The skills of producing geometric patterns in wood veneer are covered in this one-day course, including preparation, laying balancing veneer, and making a parquetry jig. You'll find out how to lay a chessboard with stringing and crossbanding. This course costs £25, plus £14 for materials. Book for one of these day courses, or spend the whole weekend veneering.

Easter School — Manchester

In association with the School of Furniture, Central Manchester College, we have arranged three different courses, all running 12-16 April, 9.30-5, and costing £140.

Introduction to Cabinetmaking — Robert Cooksey and Keith Parry

Traditional upholstery — John Shepherd

Modern wood finishing — Eric Lyons

● Richard Hill, Senior Lecturer at the College is administering the courses, and **all enquiries should go to him** at the School of Furniture, Central Manchester College, Lower Hardman St, Manchester M3 3ER, (061) 831 7791, extn. 346. **Not to the Guild!**

Timber!

Guild member Phil Brownlees of Stetchford, Birmingham, has a variety of timber for sale. He is prepared to do a deal with anyone who cares to contact him on (021) 784 7038.

French Polishing — Charles Cliffe

7-8 May, 10-4, Bexleyheath, £40.
Another chance to learn with an expert. You'll find out about preparation, staining and techniques of French polishing itself, with plenty of hands-on experience. Charles shows the correct way to sharpen a cabinet scraper — bring yours along — and will offer advice on any small piece of furniture you want to refinish.

Design and workshop drawing — Bob Grant

9 May, 9.30-5, Oxford, £25+VAT
If putting your design on paper doesn't come easy, here's the course to learn how. Bob will help you gain confidence in freehand sketching, show you how to use grid paper and drawing boards, and lots more.

Country chairmaking with Jack Hill

Our intensive introduction to the mysteries of traditional chairmaking. Cleaving green wood, shaping and jointing with 'rounders' and on the lathe, angle drilling, seat shaping, rush seat weaving, assembling and finishing.

The course, 26-29 May, includes day and evening sessions, and is fully residential at an all-in fee of £141 inc. VAT (three nights' accommodation, all meals, light refreshments); there's also a small charge for materials. The venue is part of the Dartington Hall complex close to the A38 extension of the M5 and a main-line station at Totnes.
● **Full details** direct from Rick James, The Old Postern, Dartington, Totnes, Devon TQ9 6EA — **not from the Guild.**

Power routing — Roy Sutton

13th June, 10-5, Herne Bay, Kent, £25+VAT.
Roy is an expert on this subject. Starting from first principles, he covers housing, grooving, rebating, straight and circular moulding, tenoning, mortising, and rulejoint and template work; he also deals with designing and setting up your own jigs.

Tool trip

The indefatigable West Midlands branch is now planning a day trip to see Ashley Iles, the renowned tool manufacturer (and popular WOODWORKER contributor), at his labours.

Branch member Ralph Fellows has agreed the idea with Ashley, but the date and costs can only be confirmed when they know how many of you are interested. If you fancy the trip then contact Bill Ferguson, 40 Quinton Lane, Quinton, Birmingham B32 2TS.

The grand furniture saga

Photo courtesy Phillips Fine Art Auctioneers

● **Above**, *the much-prized lacquer on a 17th century Japanese cabinet;* **opposite page**, *the Tea Ceremony is prepared in a sparsely furnished 19th century house*

The mystique of Japanese lacquering baffled the West. Vic Taylor looks at the origins of this exquisite craft and its European equivalents

The traditional Japanese house was entirely different in concept from the Chinese; it was made principally from wood, not stone, (probably because of earthquake risk) and the sparse furniture was light and portable to suit the floor-orientated life-style. Chairs were virtually unknown; people squatted on the floor, or on thick straw mats called *tatami*, or on cushions (*zabuton*) and used small arm-rests (*kyosoku*), which resembled very small stools, as support when lying down. These were made from hardwood which was either highly polished or exquisitely lacquered. Such chairs as there were, were reserved for the Buddhist priests; these chairs originated in China and appeared in

Japan during the Nara period (AD710-794) but weren't in general use until much later.

Japanese culture attached more importance to the quality of objects, rather than quantity, and even the smallest artefacts were virtual works of art — a phrase incomprehensible to the Japanese who made no distinctions between Fine, Applied, or Decorative Arts but considered that every object produced should be of the highest craft.

The most valued items were the screens which they used not just to prevent draughts but to sub-divide their rooms; they were often fitted into channels in the floor, and could be moved to alter the internal disposition of the house, which didn't have internal walls. The multi-panelled folding screens, called *byobu*, were used for sub-division; they varied from two to eight panels and were about 5ft tall. The *byobu* was usually constructed of paper covered with gold leaf (*shoji*), stretched over a light framework.

A smaller screen, called a *tsuitati*, had a single panel and was often placed at the entrance to a room for privacy, or to conceal food and dishes during the serving

of a meal, and was more substantial than the *byobu*, in pine or hardwood, and lacquered. Two smaller screens, the *furosaki byobu*, and the *kembyo* (which originated in China) were also in wide use. The former was a small two-fold screen which protected the brazier from draughts when brewing tea for the Tea Ceremony, and the *kembyo* was used by artists to stop dust from blowing on to their work.

All screens were superbly decorated, often with calligraphy painted on to gold leaf, and unlike the symmetrical Chinese designs, the motifs were always asymmetrical. The cultivation of asymmetry stemmed from the Zen Buddhist principles of 'balanced unbalance' and was firmly established by the Momoyama period (1576-1600). It also distinguishes true Japanese and European work — Europeans preferred symmetry.

Larger pieces of furniture were obviously needed for storage, like the *tansu* or chest, which often resembled the Chinese travelling chests. It was either a simple design in pine with little or no decoration, or elaborately lacquered and often mounted on a *bukhe* — (a cabinet with sliding doors

enclosing nests of drawers). Another large piece was the family household shrine, or *Butsudan*, which, unlike other furniture, was given a permanent place in the house.

The smaller items included kimono racks (kimonos were draped over them like clothes on a clothes-horse), reading stands, the *bon*, which was a smoker's companion (tobacco had been introduced into Japan by the Portuguese), and trinket and toilet boxes — all of which were exquisitely lacquered.

Lacquering, a vast and complicated subject, originated in China during the Shang dynasty (c1600-1027BC) and soon spread to Japan, where it was exploited in ways the Chinese never contemplated — the Japanese even lacquered leather to be used as a kind of armour!

Raw lacquer (or lac) is obtained from the lac tree (*Rhus vernicifera*), like latex from rubber trees: the bark is cut with horizontal incisions and the resin which exudes is collected. It changes from transparent to grey and then black on exposure to air and can cause painful rashes if it touches bare skin. An inferior lacquer is made by boiling down the smaller branches. Both kinds of lacquer are stored in wooden pails to protect them from light and dust; they're boiled for hours to skim off any impurities, strained and then simmered slowly to remove excess moisture.

True lacquer has the strange characteristics of reaching its maximum hardness in a damp atmosphere, so the best work was carried out in cellars and caves. The foundation entailed 22 coats of the inferior lacquer, and each coat was polished after intervening 12 hour to three-day drying periods. At least three coats of the best lacquer were applied and polished, allowing the same drying intervals. Finally a minimum of seven coats of clear lacquer were laid on; each coat was allowed to dry thoroughly before being polished with deer-horn's ash, oil, and the craftworker's fingers. Even after all these coatings, the residual lacquer was only a thin layer; each successive coat was polished away almost to extinction. Colour pigments were often mixed in for coloured lacquers, and sometimes a filler like finely powdered slate was used to bulk it up for incised work.

This laborious process could not be hurried, but the results were worth it. The finish was brilliant and gem-like in hardness, and it could not be scratched or scarred. It was also the despair of the Europeans who tried to imitate it.

The lacquer could be applied to achieve a variety of effects. The most common was covering a wooden article (free from knots and resin, cracks and splits filled and smoothed) with cloth or paper stuck down with lacquer. This was then smoothed down. The cloth or paper also strengthened the joints and prevented any sap in the wood from rising up through the lacquer which was applied later. (*See the list opposite for further Japanese lacquering techniques.*)

In Europe they tried to reproduce the Oriental lacquer using various processes. The English method was to apply several coats of a mixture of whiting and size followed by a coating of varnish, which was coloured by adding lampblack (for black) and dragon's blood or alkanet root (for red). A design in relief could be built up with a paste of whiting, gum arabic, and size which was applied to the outlines of the design and incised or carved. (Incidentally, English work was almost always black with gilt embellishment.) Such work was called 'Japanning' or 'Lac', and in 1694 a small book, 'The Closet of Beauty', gave the following definition: 'A Japannian work is anything Japanned, or Varnished, or China polished, or the like.' The quality of English work varied from pieces which were almost as beautiful as the Oriental originals down to crude paintwork covered with varnish.

In the 18th century, the French brothers Martin invented '*vernis Martin*' — a highly esteemed imitation lacquer. The secret of the formula has never been fully discovered, but it appears to have been a copal varnish laid over numerous coats of colour (usually blue or green) embellished with transparent gold, either in waves or striations; the completed work was then subjected to heat. In 1740 a royal decree granted the brothers monopoly of production, no doubt because of the work they did for Mesdames du Pompadour, du Barry, and Marie Antoinette.

Italian lacquer finish was generally inferior to other European countries, but they made up for it with their flair for the artistic. The decoration was vivid, stylish and used the full range of colour (as opposed to the black, red, green, and gold which the English used almost exclusively).

At the end of the 17th century, the first flush of enthusiasm for all-things-Oriental began to subside, but re-appeared by the 1750s in the guise of the *Chinoiserie* beloved of Chippendale. Lacquer work had virtually disappeared by the beginning of the 19th century, but it wasn't the end of Japanese influence on English furniture. In 1853 Japan opened up trading links with the West, and the proliferation of bamboo occasional furniture in the Victorian era was proof of the Oriental influence. ∎

● A good source on lacquering techniques and painted decoration is: *The Art of the Painted Finish for Furniture and Decoration* by Isabel O'Neil, from Stobart & Son Ltd, 67-73 Worship St, London EC2A 2EL.

How the Japanese used lacquer

Raden — lacquer inlaid with mother-of-pearl. Originated in China during the Tang dynasty (AD618-906), adopted by Japan in the Nara period.

Kamakuri-bori — wood carved in low relief and covered with red lacquer.

Hyomon — inlaying thin metal sheets into a lacquered surface.

Coromandel — combining lacquering, carving, and painting. A wooden base was covered with fine white clay, a layer of fibrous grasses laid on as a binder, covered with more clay and then rubbed perfectly smooth. Coats of lacquer were applied and polished and the design was incised or carved out to reveal the white base. The white parts were painted with bright colours: gamboge, red ochre, cinnabar and gilt.

Negoro nuri — coats of black, and then red, lacquer were applied, usually to bowls. The red was polished away, in part, to contrast with the black.

Bantam ware — incised lacquer-ware, similar to *Coromandel*. 'Bantam', after the port it was shipped from in Dutch Java.

Maki-e — a common decoration (literally 'sprinkled picture'). The design was painted on to a lacquered surface and gold or silver powder blown across while the lacquer was tacky. Variations: *Togidashi Maki-e* — a coat of black lacquer was applied over the finished design and partially rubbed away to give tonal effects; *Taka maki-e - maki-e* in relief. A thick coat of raw lacquer and yellow ochre was built up and covered with gold leaf.

Kin-gin-e — lacquer painted with silver, gold, or both.

Lac burgauté — black lacquer inset with tiny slivers of mother-of-pearl. The slivers were deposited when the lacquer was tacky to give a shimmering effect. Perfected in the Ryu Kyu islands.

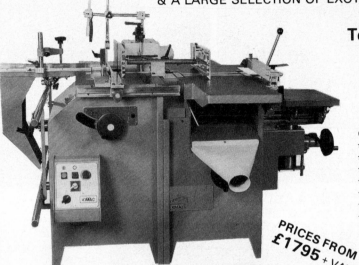
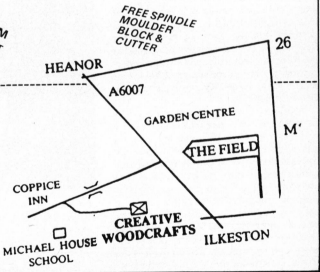

Bows 'n' arrows

The ancient skills of the bowyer and the fletcher come together in one Yorkshire craftsman — whose insistence on truth to tradition is tempered with an irreverent talent for improvisation. Leonard Markham spent some time with him

THE BOW

Lemonwood and lancewood are among tropical timbers used for longbow making, but George Thorley prefers traditional English yew. This slow-growing tree is susceptible to twisting in high winds, so George, bowyer and fletcher of Hull, seldom gets long enough staves of good grain quality to make one-piece longbows. Usually he chops short identical pieces with an axe from the bole of the tree while the timber is still wet, and splices them together later. With yew staves you must have at least a ¼in of highly tensile sapwood, destined for the back of the bow for flexibility. Very compressive heartwood at the front gives resilience and strength. After cutting, the staves are seasoned for five to seven years, turned every six months to ensure straightness.

George, who is a founder member of the Longbow Society, has collected bows by such past masters as Muir of Edinburgh and Ayres of London, using them to study construction. He backs this practical side with research into archery records and literature, in order to produce superior weapons using traditional skills.

Each longbow is tailor-made for the person using it, adjusted to height and physique, which is where the skill of the bowyer really comes in. The strength of the archer determines the 'weight' of the bow — the weight in this case being the force in pounds required to draw the finished bow. The other crucial measurement is the 'fistemele', the dimension of the archer's clenched fist with the thumb extended; this gives the distance between the undrawn string and the bow handle.

After seasoning, George joins the yew staves as necessary to make up the length required; identical 3-4in 'V' or 'W' cuts made in the ends are coated with Aerolite 306, and the staves clamped together to set. Then he marks the taper of the bow on the length in pencil, and uses a small axe to cut out the basic shape, making sure he leaves ¼in thick sapwood.

Next he taps pins into each end and runs a taut string between them. Using this line as a guide, he marks the centre point and the

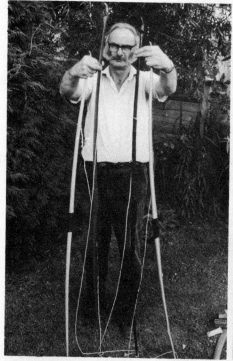

● **Above left**, George with lemonwood, lancewood, orangewood and yew bows; **above**, the shape starts. **Left**, using the 'tiller' to test the action; **below**, a piece of reamed horn and a completed nock

position of the handle. The handle runs from 3in below the centre point to 1in above, to suit the dynamics of the bow; the lower limb takes marginally greater strain than the upper part.

In order to produce the desired pyramid cross-section, with the back square or slightly rounded, George uses a variety of tools — old block planes, spokeshaves, scrapers, razor planes and pieces of broken glass. He constantly flexes the bow while he works to identify any flaws in its action; erratic movements are remedied by carefully paring wood from the belly — the inner surface of the bow, facing the archer. Now the bow is ready for proving, and George cuts temporary nocks and strings it.

The bow is proved on a device called a tiller, which is a primitive but effective stress gauge. George constructed his tiller to a medieval prototype, so it is a genuinely traditional way of testing the bow's action at progressive increments of draw. After fixing the bow to the tiller, George marks the flexed bow along its length at 3in

intervals, and then places a long steel straight-edge across the tiller from nock to nock. Using the straight-edge and 3in points as reference, he can take measurements to work out consistency of taper, working from the tips inwards. Because the upper limb is longer it is more flexible, so the measurements on the straight-edge are shorter. The idea is to maintain a constant thickness differential on the bow's length, to get a smooth, 'complete' action. Irregularities are rectified by carefully removing wood from the belly.

The weight of the bow's 'pull' is determined using a conventional spring balance; George draws the bow to arrow length and takes a reading, which determines the number of strands in the bowstring.

Next step is making the horn nocks, hooked pieces which house the bowstring ends. This gives licence for artistic flair; some bowyers carve grotesque heads and faces, and George is working on a design for a nock in the shape of a garrotted face with its tongue hanging out — the bowstring nooses the poor creature's neck.

English cow horn was traditionally used for nocks, but it isn't common, and George uses African buffalo horn instead. He saws 2in triangular sections from the tips and drills pilot holes in the bases. Then he enlarges the holes with a brace and a special bit, adapted to ream conical holes. A scraper is used to trim the tips of the bow if necessary; then the notches are cut and trimmed on a bandsaw, the nocks are glued in place and finished off with wire wool.

George prefers hemp for stringing, though it wears more quickly than modern sythetics such as Dacron. The strings are woven together, using one strand per pound weight of 'pull'. The completed composite string, waxed to keep inherent moisture, is attached to the bow with a loop wound at one end for the lower nock, and a timber hitch at the other end for the upper nock.

After finishing the bow with successive coats of linseed oil, George adjusts the string to the fistmele of the archer and fits a fabric or leather hand grip. Then it's ready for the arrow . . .

THE ARROW

Just as longbows are made to suit the archer, arrows too are geared to individual physical characteristics. George uses a long rule to measure the distance from the archer's jawbone to the knuckles. Diameter and weight of arrow are determined by this length; for arrows above 26in, the average diameter of the shaft is $^{11}/_{32}$in, while shorter arrows are about $^{9}/_{32}$in.

George doesn't have to worry about the heads; traditionally these were made by arrowsmiths, whose skills complemented those of the fletcher, but today machine-made bladeless heads or 'piles' have made the arrowsmith virtually redundant. The murderous bladed heads that could 'draw blood from a weathercock' are made only for demonstration purposes.

Having measured up the archer, George chooses suitable timber from a wide variety, including poplar, spruce, Columbian or Norway pine and cedar, all cut into ½in square lengths. George incorporates 'footings', 6in inlays of more densely grained timber at the arrow's business end, which give an attractive appearance and enhance the arrow's performance. Dense woods such as maple, beech or keruing, give forward weight to the arrow and help absorb the shock of impact.

The footing is fixed before the shaft is rounded. The square-sectioned shaft is planed on opposite sides to form a 6in tapering end; then George takes a V-cut

● **Above**, all fletched and ready to fly; **below**, preparing the footing for the pile on the home-made 'lathe'

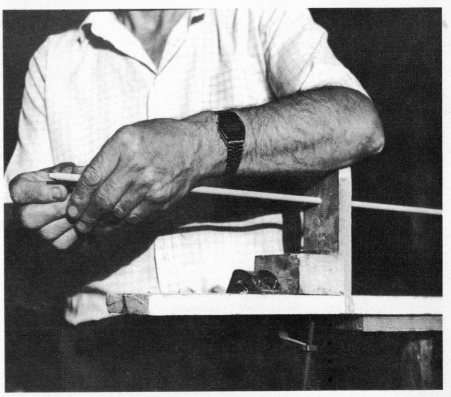

from an 8in length of footing using a thin-bladed gents saw, before gluing with Araldite 306 and inserting the shaft. To hold the timbers together, George uses strips of inner tube, leaving the binding on for at least three hours; then the projecting wings of the footing are planed flush with the shaft.

To round the shaft, George uses a special arrow plane, which has a semi-circular channel along the length of its base, into which is set a curved blade. These tools are rare, but you could use a metal razor plane, a smooth based plane with very thin blades for cutting. An ordinary block or chisel plane would do. George uses a vernier caliper to ensure accuracy, and continually examines the shaft for straightness and truth of taper; the taper begins 6in from the tip.

The metal pile needs to fit snugly over the tip, and George has an improvised lathe that would have made Heath Robinson smile. A small electric drill is fixed into one end of a special frame; the chuck holding the flight end of the arrow. The pile end is pushed through a hole at the other end of the frame, which steadies the revolving tip, and allows George to reduce the diameter with a knife to precisely the right sizes. Then the pile is glued into place.

Now George prepares the arrow nock and its mount — a tapered point at the tip of the shaft. He uses cow horn for the arrow nocks, since this material is less susceptible to splitting than buffalo horn. He cuts a $^{5}/_{16}$in piece of horn, and reams a conical shaped hole in it. The shaft end is tapered, using a conventional pencil sharpener, and finishing off with a scraper to ensure a tight fit. He shapes the nock, grooves it to take

continued

Bows 'n' arrows

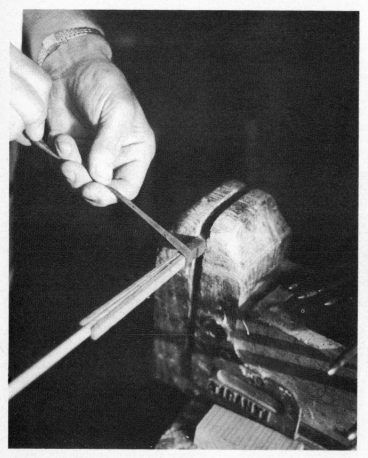

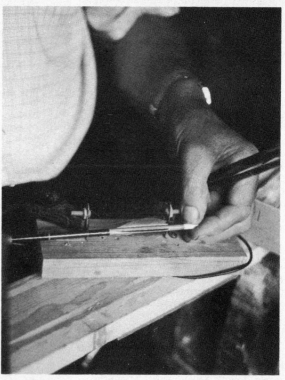

the bow string, and then glues it in position so that the groove lies at 90° to the parallel grain (the reed) of the shaft. This exploits the arrow's full dynamic potential. Then he smoothes the fitted nock with wire wool.

The art of fletching takes its name from the next stage — fastening the feathers. Like a bird, the arrow is said to be fletched when it is capable of flight. Attaching the feathers is the most fascinating stage, a process steeped in history and folklore, and requiring adherence to age-old design principles.

Flight feathers from swans, geese and turkeys are all suitable, though feathers from one wing only must be used, because feathers usually have a right or left hand curve, depending which wing they come from, and mixing them up causes erratic flight.

He cuts the feathers down the middle of the quill with a sharp knife. From the split feathers he cuts with scissors three identical parabolically-shaped sections, each with a quill base of 2in. One section is chosen for its contrasting colour.

Before gluing the feathers to the shaft, their quill bases must be smoothed level. George has his own method here, sandwiching the feathers one by one between small metal plates held together with a bulldog clip. Thus the strips of uneven quill are left protruding so he can smooth them on fine sandpaper.

The feathers aren't fastened right at the end, but enough space is left below the nock

● *Above left*, gluing and clamping the footing with inner tube; *above right*, the precious arrow plane. *Right*, burning the feather shape

for the archer to grasp the arrow. The essential element in fletching is the fixing of the colour contrasting 'cock' feather, which is fastened at right angles to the nock groove so the arrow is always lined up to the bowstring the same way, and doesn't deflect. Having glued the cock feather correctly (with ordinary household Bostik!), George mounts the other two at 120°, each with its compatible curve.

George goes one step further in preparing the feathers; he burns the edges of each over

a red hot wire to give identical profiles, improving both how the arrow looks and how it flies.

Finally he varnishes the shaft, and embellishes or 'crests' it with coloured bands for decoration and recognition in the field. He uses masking tape and enamel paints fo this.

George's beautiful arrows are the fruition of more than 500 years of arrow technology. The result is the English arrow, a weapon of deceptive ability — fast, accurate and deadly. ∎

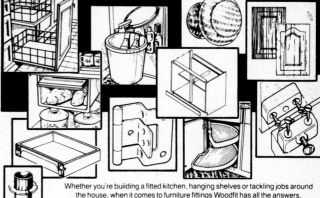

Hearth-way

Use Tony Lord's basic construction principles for an unostentatious fire surround, or add carved and applied decoration for a Rococo look

When I decided to make a fire surround, I wanted a design that was not too ornate; but there's ample surface for decoration here, such as carvings or applied motifs, if that's your taste. I used English oak, but many hardwoods are suitable, and so, of course, is pine. Obviously the size can be adjusted to suit your particular fireplace. The surround is held to the wall with brass mirror-plates, and is finished in matt polyurethane and wax. I worked the mouldings myself with router, scratch-stock and moulding planes, but you can always get a joinery shop to spindle-mould them for you.

Before starting, measure your fireplace, and adjust the overall dimensions accordingly; individual components could be wider or narrower, as well. Then buy and prepare your timber. The construction follows a logical sequence, from making the 'end boxes', then the front cross rail and finally the top moulding and mantelpiece.

End boxes

The two uprights are made as boxes without a back. You can use grooved fronts and tongued sides, or opt for a simpler alternative of using screwed fillets only. For grooved joints, work the groove on the reverse side of the two front pieces. Then run a tongue along the front edges of the side pieces to fit the groove. Now cut the notch from the top of the inner sides to accommodate the front cross piece.

Glue the end boxes together, making sure you use enough cramps for a good joint.

Cut and mitre the pieces that make up the skirting, and run a moulding along the top edges. Then you can glue these pieces and screw them from the inside of the end boxes.

Front cross-rail

The cross rail is secured to the uprights at each end by a housing joint and by screwing to a square fillet fixed inside the outermost corner of the end boxes. Measure the length you need, then mark where the housing joint will go to fit over the notch in the inner end box sides. When you have cut this housing, you can determine what dimension the square fillet should be; glue and screw the fillet in place, then drill the ends of the cross rail and screw this into place.

● *Pretty in oak, plain in pine – or go for a fancy treatment*

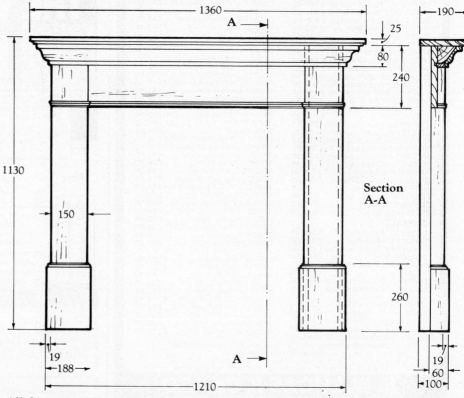

Section A-A

All dimensions in metric

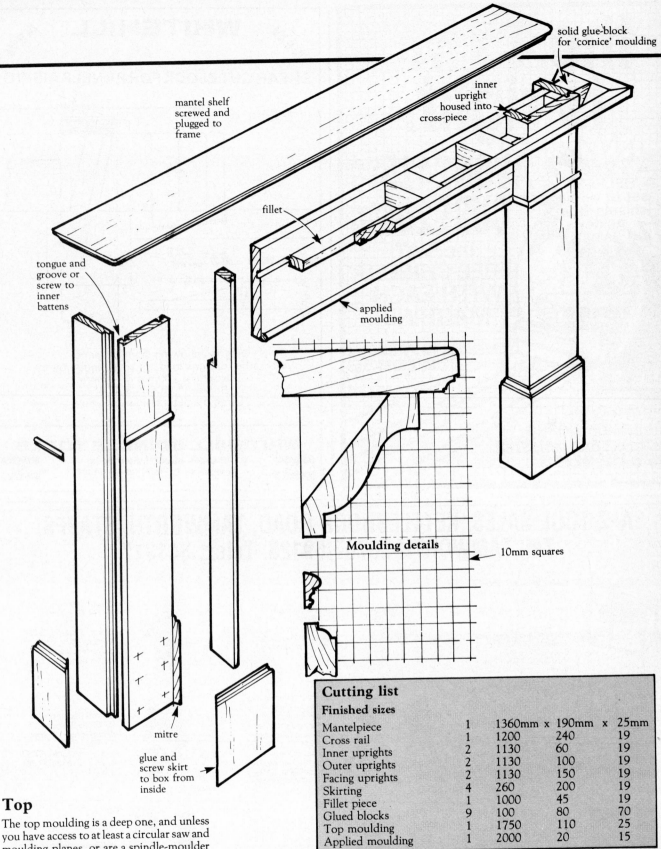

solid glue-block for 'cornice' moulding

inner upright housed into cross-piece

mantel shelf screwed and plugged to frame

fillet

applied moulding

tongue and groove or screw to inner battens

mitre

glue and screw skirt to box from inside

Moulding details

10mm squares

Cutting list						
Finished sizes						
Mantelpiece	1	1360mm	x	190mm	x	25mm
Cross rail	1	1200		240		19
Inner uprights	2	1130		60		19
Outer uprights	2	1130		100		19
Facing uprights	2	1130		150		19
Skirting	4	260		200		19
Fillet piece	1	1000		45		19
Glued blocks	9	100		80		70
Top moulding	1	1750		110		25
Applied moulding	1	2000		20		15

Top

The top moulding is a deep one, and unless you have access to at least a circular saw and moulding planes, or are a spindle-moulder expert, you should ask your local joinery shop to spindle-mould it for you. This moulding needs careful mitring, and you might want to sort out the correct angle by trial and error on spare pieces — so be sure to run up enough extra.

I fitted a fillet piece along the front cross rail, grooving the rail, and cutting a tongue along the fillet piece. I cut blocks at a suitable angle to hold the top moulding to both the cross rail and the end boxes. I glued the blocks to the framework first, and then applied the moulding once the glue had set.

Finishing

Having cleaned up the wood, I mitred the applied moulding, and then ran the pieces round the bottom of the cross rail and round the two end boxes. I cut the mantelpiece to size, and ran a moulding round its bottom edge at the front and the two ends. Then I screwed it to the blocks with coun-tersunk screws through the mantelpiece, concealing them with wooden plugs.

I gave the whole fire surround one coat of matt polyurethane and then finished it with Briwax before fastening it to the wall.

I didn't intend to make this design elaborate, but there's plenty of scope for adding as much decoration as you wish; you can buy applied decorative features for this kind of thing from good hardware suppliers to the trade. ∎

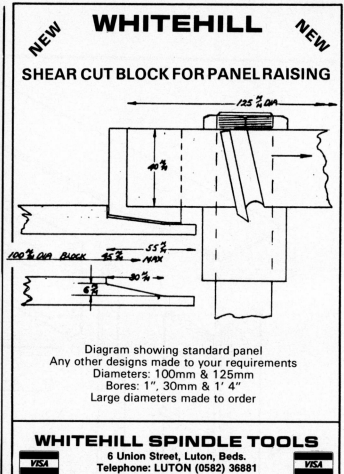

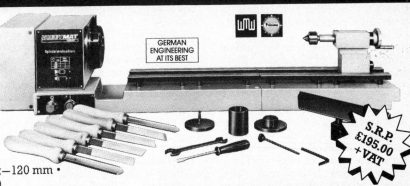

THE WOODWORK BUSI[NESS]

Marketing

Hugh O'Neill slices through the mystique of marketing, Chris Yonge tells you how to get your name known, and Alan Peters examines the ins and outs of working to commission

Marketing graft Hugh O'Neill

Marketing may be a mystery to you at the moment, but it is an essential part of any business. Don't confuse it with buying and selling. Marketing is fitting what you can profitably produce to what customers want and will buy.

Customers buy for a variety of reasons:
- They like what they see: it is aesthetically satisfying or it demonstrates the highest level of craftsmanship.
- They need it — it will be useful to them personally, or it makes an ideal gift for somebody they are buying a present for.
- There's nothing better within their price range: usually applicable to souvenirs and gifts.
- They are collectors at heart — obtaining a complete range of all the woods available, the widest variety of shapes of candlestick or whatever.
- You have pressured them into it.
- They feel sorry for you for some reason.

You'll need to do some research, analysis and planning before you can be sure you can provide what the market place wants.

That's one side of the marketing equation. The other is producing, distributing and selling in sufficient quantities to put profit in your pocket.

If you are seriously considering starting up in business, you should do the following exercise BEFORE you read on. Take a piece of paper and write a few lines to answer each of the following questions:

1 Why I want to set up in business.
2 Why I've chosen the product, range, approach, idea or whatever that I intend to base the business on.
3 Why I've chosen to locate the business in . . .

When you've done this, look carefully at what you've written. Are the statements merely pieces of self-indulgence — 'because I want to'? Or do they reveal a real drive? Is there a clear indication that you've got

something to offer, and that what you're offering is what the market needs and will pay for? You may have written something between these two extremes, such as 'because I've got to, there's no other employment available'.

The closer your response is to the self-indulgent end, the more strongly I would say: 'Stop dreaming: give up now before you land yourself in deep trouble.'

This series in WOODWORKER is dedicated to those who have good reason to start up, and who have a real driving inner urge that will be satisfied in no other way. You have to be single-minded to survive in business.

Look at your first answer again, and tick off the ONE possible reply below that comes closest to your answer:

I wish to set up a business because:
1 I have no alternative — I can find no other employment and therefore cannot make a living in any other way.
2 I have an idea (design, product range, etc.) that people will buy (and I know this because . . .).
3 I have skills which I know people will pay me to use (by commissioning me or by buying the craftwork that I can produce); (and I know this because . . .).
4 I can see a need or a gap in the market place (either for a unique product or to supply a shortage in a particular geographical area) which I know I could meet or fulfil.
5 I want to be my own boss and be as independent as possible (despite heartaches and low income).
6 I have always fancied making a living by doing something that I enjoy.

If you have ticked off number 2 you might as well skip the next few paragraphs: you are there already. Numbers 3 and 4 aren't too bad either. If you have chosen 1 or 5 then you have a lot of hard thinking to do until you can also find a close identity

with statement 2, 3 or 4. If you have chosen 6 then forget about reading this article.

Marketing 'thrust'

This exercise will help identify where your basic marketing thrust is, and you need to do this first as the whole shape and location of your business will depend upon it. There are choices of thrust. The first one that most marketeers consider is number 4 above — meeting the needs of a specific area. You'll be making what is needed (and at a suitable price for that area): you also have to have a level of skills adequate for the area. It's the only viable route if you don't have a unique product or an extraordinary level of skill. So you might meet a need for architectural woodwork, builders' joinery, home or garden furniture, even souvenirs (not every tourist area has enough to fully meet the needs).

There are some needs which aren't specifically local, but may have a particular local significance because the needs aren't being met in that area. Basic furniture is a universal need, but if there isn't a local supplier where residents can go to touch, feel and select then it becomes a viable local need.

An obviously viable thrust is where you have a product which because of its design and/or quality will appeal to a discerning buyer. It is less likely to be an 'essential' item, and the success of the business, particularly in the early years, depends heavily on where you sell. If one of the sales outlets is also the production point (the workshop) then you must choose both the area and the specific location of the production point with extreme care; it's pointless being in an idyllic cottage on the road between Middle Wollop and Lesser Widdeling if no one travels that road.

The next basic thrust is where you have a particular level of skill that is marketable —

and in the arty/crafty world this usually means being within the top five per cent of the craft. This is often the starting point for many a time-served craftsman or an experience-served hobbyist. Even with the highest level of skills, certainly when making a start, you have to consider the actual products that you will make your name on and the location which will provide enough customers for you to become established.

If none of these thrusts match your drive, then please think further: acquire some more skills, and research to find a hole in the market.

A student on a woodturning course had never before done any turning. Dennis was not the most talented of the group, but he had a drive. He and his wife run a post office and general store in rural Scotland where there are a reasonable number of tourists. The wife was already into china decoration, and he is now going to produce small turned-ware items for sale in the shop (the only one for miles) as local souvenirs. Clearly this will only be a sideline, but it will meet a need and add an extra impetus to general sales.

It will also provide him with an extra dimension to his life in that turning is a very different activity from anything else that he does; particularly when seen against the very demanding job of shopkeeping. So here was Dennis on the course, starting to learn; he bought tools and gained skills; he wasn't aiming for art work or fancy bowls in exotics at £40 plus a time, but at scoops, rattles, egg cups and items that retail for £2-3. His wife's decoration might add value to some.

It's going to be tough, and he doesn't depend upon his craft for basic income. To start with he won't have the high-speed skills that are required to make such items quickly enough to be really viable. He will certainly be turning in the few spare hours that he has and late into many winter nights.

Unfortunately many people start up a business with too little thought, and too much blind optimism in their ability to be able to make a go of it. They ignore questions of location, uniqueness, competition, and almost everything else.

In the next feature in this series, I shall be looking closely at competition and the factors in locating your business.
● Hugh O'Neill is a professional business consultant and craftsman woodturner.

One-off or batch? Alan Peters

Back in 1962 when I set up there was not much choice of action if one wanted to break through and make a living. There were no noticeable retail outlets for craftsmen's work beyond the British Crafts Centre in London. There were no craft markets, fairs or shows, and exhibition opportunities were very rare. So the choice was only between providing either a personalised service (commissioned work) direct to the public, or as a service to architects, interior designers and sections of industry on a sub-contract basis.

Now one does have a wider choice. It is possible to produce furniture without a particular customer in mind and provided the product is good and the price right, sell it at one of the numerous craft shops, galleries, markets or exhibitions up and down the country, as well as from one's own premises.

You might be tempted, in order to hedge your bets, to combine both one-off and batch work equally, but I don't advise it. For success, one area must take overall preference over the other and it is largely a question of individual temperament and ability as to which area one concentrates on.

In batch production and retail sales you will have to limit your sights to a few well thought-out designs and exhibition pieces. You will have to enjoy jig-making, machining and organisation. You may have to spend a lot of time away from the workshop promoting sales and in most cases you will not know who buys your work, but you will have the satisfaction that generally the design and creation is 100 per cent in your own hands.

In commissioned work you will be constantly, almost daily, tackling and solving design and technical problems. For if you employ other craftsmen and include unsuccessful enquiries you could easily be designing a hundred or more items a year.

● A magnificent commission – Alan Peters' boardroom table and chairs in olive ash, 1985

In return you will be giving personal pleasure and satisfaction to individuals who will become well-known to you and even good friends over the years.

You will never succeed in this area of commissioned work unless you readily accept that you are providing a service to the public in return for work and your livelihood, and that simple fact must never be forgotten however successful you may become. If, on the other hand, you secretly consider yourself God's gift to the world of art and design and that it is an honour for anyone to possess your work you will not last long unless you really are brilliant.

In some people's eyes, working to commission, working within the requirements of others, is not considered truly creative and is considered to be second-best and a compromise of integrity and standards. Frankly, after 20 years of designing both for private clients and my own unfettered instincts, I have yet to see how one can design and create anything successfully without the important element of compromise. I'm convinced that working to commission can be as exciting, stimulating and creative as you choose to make it.

From *Cabinetmaking – the professional approach*, Stobart & Son Ltd, 1985. We are grateful for permission to use this extract: Stobart & Son, 67-73 Worship St, London EC2A 2EL, 01-247 0501.

● Alan Peters is one of the country's leading furniture designer craftsmen.

continued

THE WOODWORK BUSINESS

Reaching the client Chris Yonge

The first step to getting work is making your name readily available to the many potential clients within a necessarily limited budget. The second, once you've found a reliable way of reaching the right people, has to do with achieving the optimum number and appropriate timing of serious replies. Marketing for a small workshop is an exercise in the possible: you have to balance two equations within the company's resources of cash and time while finding the amount and type of work you want.

You can best start by analysing the areas, professions, and groups where your preferred clients are concentrated, and then reach them through precise advertising in specialised journals or mailing shots based on Yellow Pages and trade directories. Advertisements must be simple, of high quality (including photographs where possible), and, to encourage serious enquirers, should invite the reader to write in for further details. This gives you three things: the chance to send out a full description of your products and services to an interested person; feedback on the readership and effectiveness of your ad; and another address for your mailing list.

This mailing list can be used at regular intervals to send out material on recent workshop commissions and improvements to a selection of individuals, retail firms, architects and interior designers. In my case this information includes furniture design and making facilities as well as the current range of batch-produced pieces. Remember you can send a good deal of paper within the 60gm limit, but to be effective it must be relevant and easy to read: too much information is as bad as too little.

So far as timing goes, don't send out hundreds of letters whenever there's a gap in the order book; so many each week on a regular basis allows you to adjust the number as need be. You want an even flow of genuine enquiries, not so many that you're always putting interested people off, or taking on so much that reliability and quality suffer. (In a specialised professional market reputation is the best way to find steady work, but be aware it cuts both ways if you're in trouble.)

You can reduce the frequency of expensive mailings by maximising the quality and permanency of your written material. This covers: your style of writing; content and its permanent usefulness; quality of paper and printing; and format.

Clearly it's no use sending out brochures that don't tell the client what you can do and how long you've been doing it; equally you will gain little by posting expensive publicity material that goes straight into the bin after a single reading. Make it simple

● *Chris Yonge's Japanese-style coffee-table in American ash, featured in 'Making it in Scotland', WW/July '85*

and pleasant to read, for a start, and incorporate something useful as an anchor: a list of the names and addresses of some of the professional groups you belong to, for example, or the sources you use for specialised supplies like veneers, finishes and hardware. Professionals often file such information, and your name will be stored along with the rest. Or a table of metric-to-traditional timber measures (get it right) with your name at the foot of every sheet. Even a brief list of local trees and forest walks where they can be seen growing — anything you think might add permanent interest and use to your material.

For private clients, the general aesthetic appeal of the whole will be as important as the content. And in both cases, the use of several sheets of paper rather than one for the same amount of information will not only repeat your name but increase the chance of one being around when it's needed. Take a leaf from the mail order companies' book: the next time you get some junk mail have a good look at it. By using several pieces of paper, simple sentences, high quality printing, and personalised addresses these organisations maximise the chance of the text being read and of interested persons replying fast. I wouldn't go so far as to advise copying their style of writing, but the format's certainly worth thinking about.

Before going to the expense of advertising it's always worth approaching the magazines your potential clients might be expected to read, sending photographs to the features editors as well as publicity material. Though only one in 20 may be

interested enough to print anything, that free publicity will repay the time and expense involved. But take a moment to examine it from the magazine's point of view: stress the individual and newsworthy points of your business, its products, and clients so that it's easy for them to make an interesting feature.

As far as direct contact with the public goes, I would advise steering clear of trade and craft fairs until you have a good range and stock of batch-run items for sale. With nothing for people to buy on impulse, you're losing half your potential sales in a situation where one pays normal workshop overheads plus stand fees to do nothing for several days.

Exhibitions are a different matter. Never refuse a chance to display photographs, samples or sketches, no matter in what surroundings or company, and have a selection of recent large-format mounted prints and sketches available for display at short notice.

And finally, don't forget to learn from experience. I make a habit of talking to clients after the work is done as well as before; asking them why they came to me, what they were looking for in commissioning an independent designer maker, how they choose other professional services, and if they have any suggestions for improvements. They are not only the best sources of marketing information but prime future customers: treat them well, and the help they can give will repay any extra effort many times.

● Chris Yonge is a professional furniture designer and maker who runs a small workshop on the Scottish border.

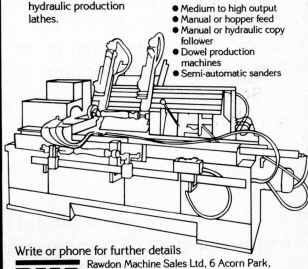

"ALL FOR THE LOVE OF WOOD"

Plan your visit now

BRISTOL WOODWORKER SHOW

Bristol Exhibition Centre
Canon's Road, Bristol

15TH – 17TH MAY 1987

— An opportunity to buy exotic woods and veneers as well as the latest woodworking machinery, tools and supplies on the many stands.

— Listen to the advice and knowledge of the experts as they demonstrate their skills.

— Admire the craftsmanship of the many competition entries from marquetry to cabinetmaking.

Opening Times:
May 15th, 16th . 10 a.m.-6 p.m.
May 17th .... 10 a.m.-5 p.m.

Admission Prices:
Adults £2.50
Child/OAP £1.75

Further information available from:
Argus Specialist Exhibitions Ltd., Wolsey House, Wolsey Road, Hemel Hempstead, Herts. HP2 4SS. Tel: 0442 41221.

The London and Bristol Woodworker Shows are organised by Argus Specialist Exhibitions and sponsored by Woodworker Magazine

Hands on

Win £60 worth of Sandvik tools!

Each month, the best **Woodworking wheeze** — the neatest, cleverest idea that makes any sort of woodwork quicker, easier, more precise, more productive, more enjoyable, more efficient, more profitable — will win £60 of tools from Sandvik's enormous range.

Send your ideas to:
Hands on, WOODWORKER, 1 Golden Sq, London W1R 3AB. If we print any wheeze you send in on these pages, you get a small fee — so write today!

HOW TO DO IT

We want to publish as many wheezes as possible, so we must use only the barest bones of the ideas. Be as precise and brief as possible; type your words if you can, double-spaced on one side of an A4 sheet; make drawings, if any, as few and as clear as you can, and annotate them clearly.

● *From the comprehensive Sandvik range, just a selection of screwdrivers*

Cable self-tidier

Annoyed — possibly endangered — by uncoiled extension leads lying round the floor of the workshop, yet always forgetting to tidy them up neatly, I hit on this idea; taking the cable retractor unit from our defunct domestic vacuum cleaner, I mounted it on a wooden backing plate, which I fixed to the wall at head height, and fitted it with a 13amp rubber outlet.

If you do this, remember that these units do not usually include an earth, so you must only use them with DOUBLE INSULATED tools — most modern power tools are wired like this. It's very convenient, a joy to use, and ensures no more loose and dangerous cables are left lying round.
Roy Benfield, Walton-on-Thames

Vice liners

Tired of constantly damaging the wooden liners for the jaws of my vice by holding bits of metal in them for cutting or filing, I took some old angle iron — the kind with a sharp outside corner such as you find in old beds — and cut it into two lengths the same as my vice jaws. Now when I need to work metal in my vice I just slip these 'false jaws' over the wooden liners; I get more precise holding and no damaged jaws.
Andrew Webb, Keswick

WOODWORKING WHEEZE
of the **month**

Sandvik winner
Pegboard holdfast
For a versatile, easy-to-make and use work-piece-holding surface, take three sheets of pegboard, cut them to suit your bench, and fix two battens to the underside of the lowest layer. An extra L-shaped 'false jaw' for the vice brings the top of the jaw level with the pegboard surface; dowels and wedges do the rest.

Holding awkward — or ordinary-shaped — pieces for almost any kind of work thus becomes dead easy. I use my pieces of pegboard as a bench hook, for routing, planing thin stock, rebating; anything, in fact, where the face and edge of a piece need to be kept clear. The bottom battens hook over the corner of the bench, and the dowels hold the pieces of pegboard together. They aren't fixed so you can take them apart to get the dust out.

Cheap, easy to make, quick to set up — and no risk to tool steel or bench surface.

Philip Davies, Reading

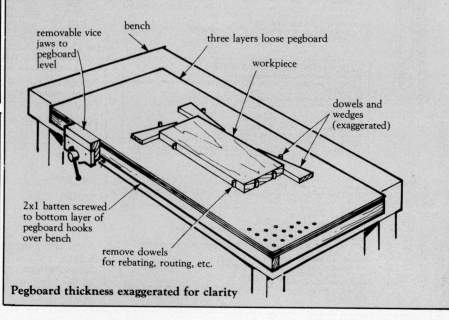

removable vice jaws to pegboard level

bench

three layers loose pegboard

workpiece

dowels and wedges (exaggerated)

2x1 batten screwed to bottom layer of pegboard hooks over bench

remove dowels for rebating, routing, etc.

Pegboard thickness exaggerated for clarity

Long hole-borer repairs

Ridgways long hole-boring drills are fairly expensive, and they often need repair because of incorrect sharpening, over-filing or collision with unsympathetic objects:
1 Holding the drill in an engineer's vice with about 1in protruding above the jaws, heat it bright red with a propane torch, and, keeping the heat playing on it, 'up-set' the end of the drill with gentle taps from a 4oz hammer. When it has cooled down it can be filed back to original shape; a fine file removes excess outside diameter, and a Swiss-type knife-edge file for the cutting edge. An alternative method:
2 File the end of the drill flat, removing all the old cutting edge. File a small piece of ¼in-diameter silver steel to the shape of a Woodruff key about ³⁄₃₂in thick — basically a semicircle. File it to fit the inside edge of the curved drill end, silver solder or braze it in place, then file the new cutting edge to the original shape.

John Buckley-Golder, Cannock

Door chock

When hanging doors on unfinished frames, before the architraves are fixed or painted, I find it very useful to fix a piece of 3x1 on the other side of the frame from the rebated side I'm working on, about 27in up from the floor, with two vertical blocks screwed to it. The distance between these two blocks is the thickness of the door plus a bit of clearance, and they are fixed off-centre towards the right-hand side of the frame.

Then you just offer up the door, mark where it needs planing, swing it and hold it between the two blocks, plane, and swing it back to offer it up again. Once it's a good fit the two blocks will hold it while you cut the rebates for the hinges. You can use the same fixed position of the 3x1 for more than one door in the same room or even flat.

A. M. Highfield, Wolverhampton

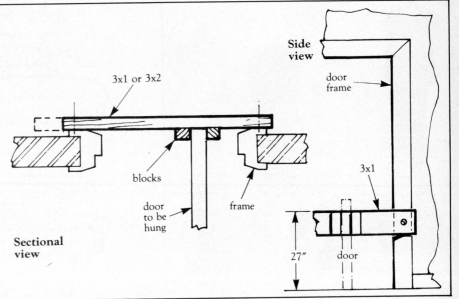

3x1 or 3x2

blocks

door to be hung

frame

Sectional view

Side view

door frame

3x1

27″

door

NEXT MONTH SPECIAL!!

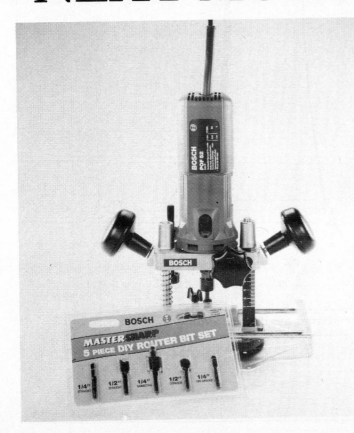

May's WOODWORKER, latest in a long line of superb issues, has got to be the best ever.
Apart from the fact that it's another 100-pager, with more colour than ever before, we have an absolutely unbeatable combination of **FREE GIFT** and **SPECIAL OFFER**.
How does a **free router cutter** worth £2.35 retail sound to you? Enough to make you buy WOODWORKER next month? It should be — we're giving away a **Bosch Mastersharp** ¼in straight cutter with every copy! And if that wasn't enough, wait till you turn to the Exclusive Offer — a **Bosch POF52 router** plus a set of five Mastersharp bits at a saving of over £33! Can you wait?
All that for the price of a copy of Britain's best — and best-selling — woodwork journal. Don't, whatever you do, miss your WOODWORKER of May 1987 — it's historic!

ON SALE 16 APRIL

Pass the checkmate

Frustrated by conventional peppermill designs, John Hipperson adapted a chess classic to add some spice

Since I first started turning pepper mills, I've been unhappy about the nondescript shape of the ones produced commercially. I looked round shops and in books in search of alternatives, but found no attractive variations in the outside shape or the general design. So I followed the conventional style, which was good practice, until I wanted to make Christmas presents for keen-eyed and discriminating relatives; conventional designs were just too dreary and unimaginative.

My first idea was to adapt the Eiffel Tower shape, but the knob on top would be too small in proportion to be a practicable capstan.

Then I thought of using classic Staunton design chess pieces, and it soon became obvious that by distorting the proportions somewhat, I would have a mill that worked without losing too much of the original feeling of the piece. All I had to do was to increase the height-to-width ratio by about

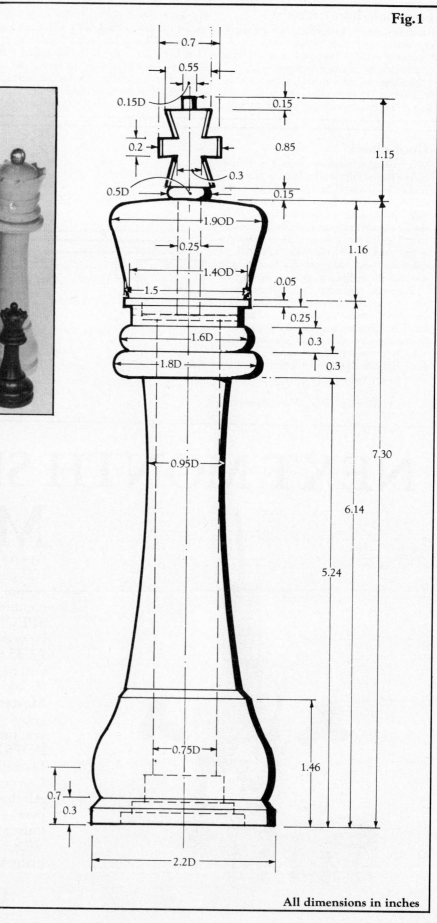

Fig. 1

All dimensions in inches

2:1, and the top diameters in relation to the base by about the same amount, to give a reasonable handful to grasp at the top for grinding.

Just about the worst atrocity perpetrated by some pepper- and salt-mill mechanism manufacturers is the little chromium screwed knob which secures the capstan to the drive shaft, often proudly displaying the cryptic capital letter 'S' or 'P'. It has as much aesthetic appeal as a moustache on the Mona Lisa. Why not use a dark wood for the pepper and light for the salt? That should speak for itself. However, with mills chessmen-style, you have to throw away the screwed knobs that are sold with the mill mechanisms anyway, because special shapes are necessary.

The easiest mechanisms to use for the present purposes were found to be those stamped 'Coles and Mason', sold by Eric Tomlinson, although those sold by Craft Supplies and others are probably equally good. However, the Coles and Mason ones I obtained had drive shafts which could be easily modified to suit any height of mill simply by cutting down an overlong drive shaft to the exact length required, without having to re-thread the top end. Shortening can be done as a last operation from the bottom end, and the aluminium drive shaft re-riveted over with a simple round-headed tapping hammer.

Before starting work, examine the actual mechanism to be used, because there are slight variations in arrangements and dimensions, depending upon the manufacturer. But the outside dimensions given in the sketches allow the use of most types of mechanism, and slight variations are then only necessary to the inside dimensions.

The general procedure for making all the chesspieces here is similar, except for the capstans, where major differences in design occur, and a few items of fancy or unusual technique are required. Let's take the King as the specific example. I used rosewood for this; a nice dark colour, an attractive grain, and easy to turn. I turned a block 2¼in square and 18in long between centres to just over 2.2in diameter. This was long enough to provide material for the Bishop, also to be made later. I parted off 9½in for the King, giving an allowance for the circular tenon or spigot on the base of the capstan, chuck holding, and waste (see fig. 1 for dimensions).

Next, I set up the rough turned blank for the King in a six-in-one chuck — any suitable chuck is acceptable — centred, and drilled with an ordinary ½in high speed twist drill just as far as the length of the drill would allow. I opened this out to ¾in using a saw-tooth machine bit, producing a nice clean hole the size required for holding the pepper. This should be done fairly slowly, clearing swarf whenever necessary, to whatever depth can be obtained with the tool to hand, up to a maximum of 6in, nearly the overall length of the body of the King. A good, true, and accurate hole is required to permit mounting on a ¾in-diameter mandrel later.

Square off the base of the King, and then prepare the three shoulders necessary for accepting the stator fittings (fig. 1). The diameter of the first rebate is exactly the same as the length of the stator retaining bar to be used, and deep enough to give clearance for the screw heads which are to hold it in place, plus say ¹⁄₁₆in to be on the safe side. The next rebate accepts the flange of the stator, and this should be accurate both in diameter and depth; try the stator the wrong way round at this stage to double-check that the stator flange accurately fits the rebate. The third rebate is to fit the diameter of the body of the stator, but it is best to make it over-deep to give positive clearance, and also win a bit of extra capacity for pepper. The Coles and Mason stator requires a 1in-diameter hole, and a depth exceeding ³⁄₈in.

You can now part off the body of the mill 6¼in long, but you can save much work later if you do it as follows. Make a

● *Top of the mill mechanism, showing capstan with disc drive plate to the left, drive shaft protruding from pepper holder, and King's cross retaining nut at right*

● *Capstans and retaining nuts for the four different salt and pepper mill designs*

● *Mill mechanism base, showing (top to bottom) stator and rebate in pepper holder, drive shaft, stator retaining bar and screws*

continued

Pass the checkmate

light cut extending from 6¼in to 6¾in from the base surface (½in long), and then take this recess down further to finish with a diameter of exactly 1.187in, the diameter required for the spigot on the base of the capstan head. If you do the final parting off with a fairly narrow tool, leaving at least a circular tenon length of ³⁄₁₆in, a little will be

left on the top surface of the body to serve as an accurate guide to the diameter of the rebate which will accept the spigot on the capstan. Accuracy is important here if most of the final outside shape of the chesspiece is to be worked with the capstan head tightly assembled on the body. Then complete the underside of the capstan head,

the circular tenon 1.187in diameter and ³⁄₁₆in deep, and let the disc drive plate with the square hole in to the appropriate depth (⅛in or a little more) and diameter (1in). Before parting off the capstan head to an overall length of about 1½in, drill the ¼in-diameter hole through which the drive bar passes when assembled.

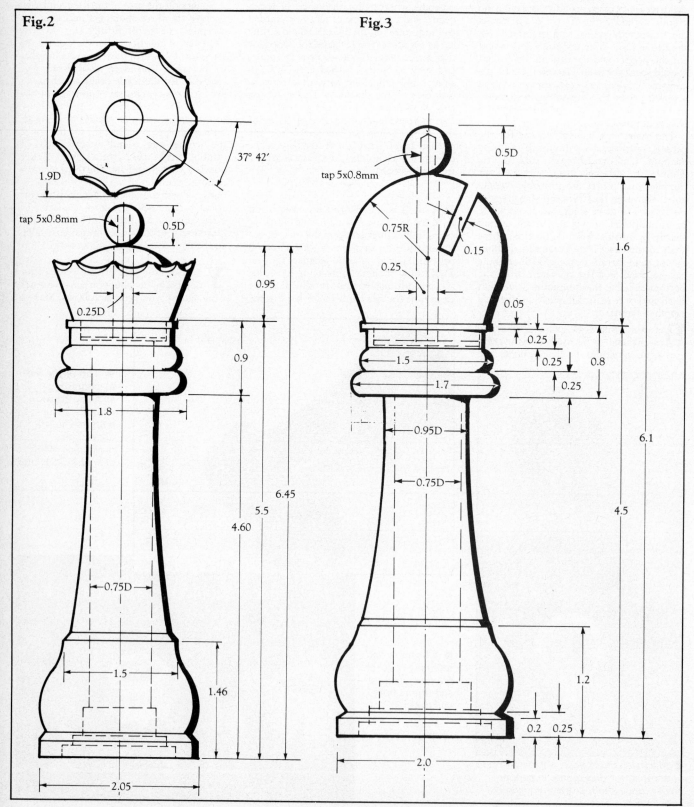

Fig.2

Fig.3

Fig.4

Remove the waste end from the lathe, and if you don't have a ¾in mandrel make one out of scrap wood mounted in the chuck, 5in long and dead parallel, making the final diameter a good snug fit for the previously bored hole in the body of the King. Mounting the King the other way round, you can complete the ¾in-diameter hole through the body. Now make the rebate to accept the circular tenon on the capstan as a good tight fit, aided by the guide left when parting off. With the capstan thus fitted, bring up the revolving centre in the tailstock, and finally turn the whole thing to shape.

The retaining nut which screws on to the top end of the drive shaft forms part of the design of the chesspiece, and could also be made from hardwood, although I made mine in brass, which looks better and is more serviceable. I drilled a piece of ¾in-diameter hard brass 4mmx½in deep, and tapped 5mmx0.8mm, to suit the thread on the end of the drive shaft. By screwing this on to a screwed spigot on the end of a piece of ½in-diameter brass held in the chuck, the cross shape shown can be shaped first as a solid cylindrical knob, and then hack-sawn to ¼in thick (except for its ⅛in high circular base). If this is carefully filed, polished and lacquered, you'll achieve an impressive finishing touch.

The Queen (fig. 2) is made in a way much like the King, using a hard white wood if it is intended for salt; the major difference is that a ½in-diameter brass ball is made as a top securing nut, and the edge of the crown requires special ingenuity in producing 11 scallops round its edges. I have not discovered what reason Howard Staunton had in mind when he decided on 11 instead of 12, but there must have been a jolly good one, otherwise John Jaques, the prospective manufacturer, would have persuaded him otherwise. A spacing of 37° 42′ is required; it is best to lay this out on a piece of card first, using a simple pair of compasses and a protractor, or simply by trial and error, using the compasses set first to just more than half the circle radius 0.5in. Transfer this spacing to the cusp of the Queen's crown by marking it in pencil. Use these as a guide for producing the scallops, simply by applying a ½in-diameter abrasive cylinder in an electric drill held at 45°; or alternatively, a ½in-diameter file would do the job.

Construction of the Bishop is again much the same as the King, paying special attention to the peculiar capstan shape, and the slanting slot which has to be carefully hand cut (fig. 3). Similarly, the castellations in the Castle's capstan have to be cut and finished by hand, but their setting out presents no particular problems because their spacing is 60°, so their peripheral spacing is simply the radius of the top (fig. 4). All other details should require no special explanation if the photographs and sketches are studied in conjunction. ■

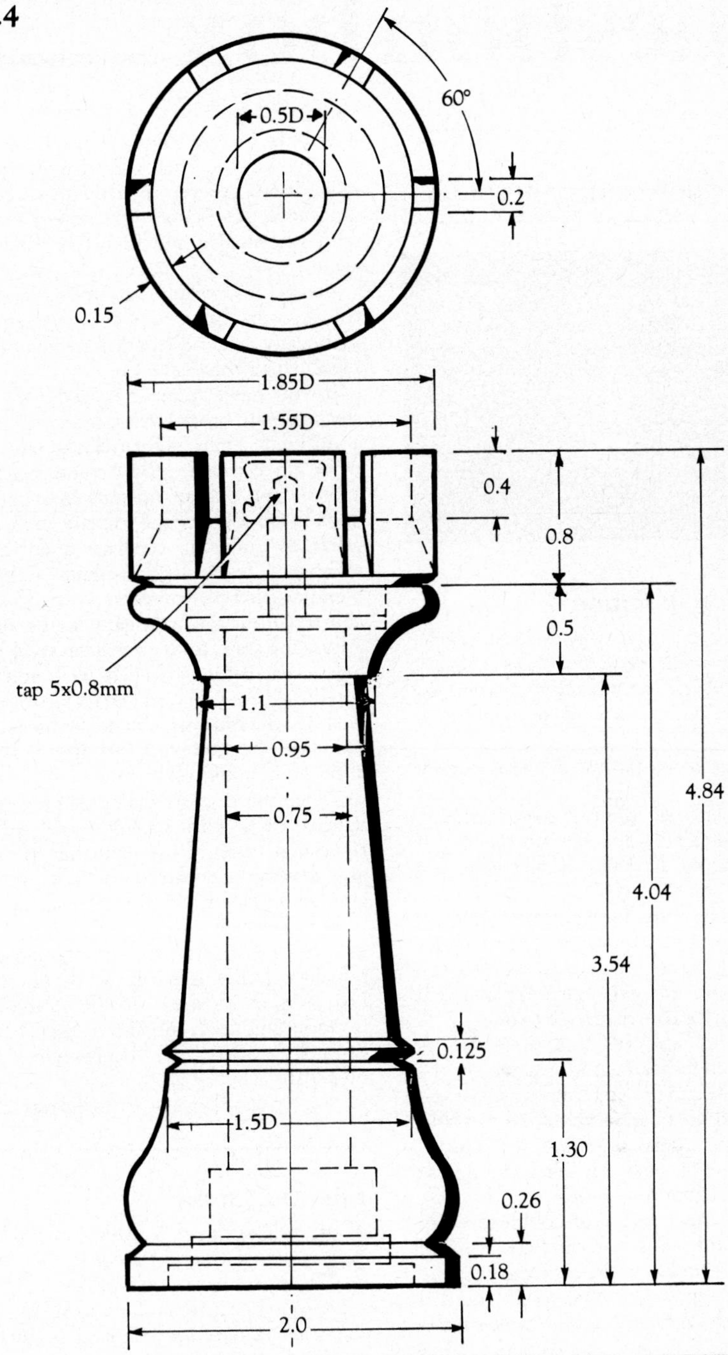

Authentic Staunton chess set design

After having made my pepper and salt mills, I checked back with John Jaques of John Jaques and Son Ltd, to find out what it was about the design of the authentic set of Staunton chessmen I own that is so fascinating. Indeed, there is a good reason.

It transpires that the great great great great grandfather of the present John Jaques cooperated with Howard Staunton, British and World chess champion 1843-1851, to design and market a set of chessmen with each piece easily recognisable but not over-ornate.

That design has remained unchanged for nearly 150 years. The chess pieces in my set are identical to those used by Spassky and Fischer during the World chess championship in 1972 and by Karpov and Korchnoi in 1978, and were made on the same equipment as was used 150 years ago. With each set, Howard Staunton permitted Jaques to supply a special green label, signed by Staunton as authentication, and present sets are still supplied with a label carrying a facsimile of his signature.

My thanks to John Jaques for his permission to mention the name 'Staunton' in relation to chess piece design.

● John Jaques, White Heather Works, White-horse Rd, Thornton Heath, Surrey
● Eric Tomlinson, 86 Stockport Rd, Gatley,

Cheadle, Cheshire SK8 2AJ
● Craft Supplies, The Mill, Millers Dale, Bux-ton, Derbys. SK17 8SN, (0298 87 1636)

Question box

Our panel of experts solve your woodworking problems

We will try to answer any questions you can throw at us, but the ones we publish are the ones of most general interest to readers.

Please type your question double-spaced with generous margins, and include a stamped self-addressed envelope. Send it to: Question Box, Woodworker, 1 Golden Sq., London W1R 3AB.

Tumbling machine

Q I built a tumbling machine to tumble-finish small wood parts, but found it didn't do what I wanted. Can you advise me how to 'sand' pine blocks in a tumbler?

K. Barnes, Whitstable, Kent

A The size of tumbler (or 'rumbler' as we call it) depends on the size of components you want to sand. Mine is a 24x14in hexagonal box with one detachable face, held in place with suitable catches or straps. It is mounted horizontally between a pair of tripod-type 'legs', (spindles on the box turning in metal sockets) with a 16in disc fixed to one end. A motor from an old Vent-Axia fan is mounted underneath, and bearing on the disc, turns it and the box simply by friction. It is geared to turn at about 20rpm, but speed is not crucial as long as it's slow.

The inside of the box is lined with coarse glasspaper. Mounting, motor, and drive are all a matter of what you can cobble together from bits and pieces you can find. You will have to experiment with gearing to keep the speed low, and of course you'll need a motor with enough power to turn the weight of the box plus your average number of components.

Dave Kemp

● Dave Kemp is a professional cabinet-maker and antique restorer in North London.

Ammonia antidote

Q I am repairing a balloon-style chair in what looks like mahogany, and after stripping the back and repairing the breaks, I applied an ammonia-based water dye. The wood went black at first, then dried out to the colour I wanted, but when I applied a polyurethane varnish it turned black again. Why is this and what can I do about it?

A. Bellis, Denbigh, Clwyd

A Adding a little ammonia to a water stain is sometimes advised because it drives the stain further into the wood. Ammonia has a darkening effect on both mahogany and oak, and it is likely that the ammonia in your stain is responsible for turning the wood black. Even after the stain has dried, there is evidently enough ammonia left behind to cause a reaction with the varnish and turn the chair black again.

Oxalic acid would normally bleach out the colour but there are varieties of mahogany, notably Spanish, which can't be bleached in this way.

If you have some mahogany left from repairing the breaks, experiment on it with a different stain before doing any more work on the chair. Buy some mahogany crystals and walnut crystals from a polish house. Dissolve some of the crystals in water to make up separate quantities of mahogany stain and walnut stain. By blending these two stains you should be able to colour the mahogany as you want it. Allow the stain to dry for at least 24 hours before varnishing. If all is well, and I am sure it will be, you can then tackle the chair. Remove the old varnish and all traces of the old stain. Restain with mahogany crystals, allow to dry and revarnish.

When the varnish has hardened you can lightly rub it with OOOO steel wool to remove a little of the brilliance and then give several applications of wax polish to give depth and warmth to the sheen.

The following firms will supply small quantities of crystals and tins of quality wax polishes: James Jackson & Co (London) Ltd, Major Works, 76-89 Alscot Rd, London SE1 5SX, and Henry Flack (1860) Ltd, P.O. Box 78, Beckenham, Kent BR3 4BL.

Charles Cliffe

File that stain

Q I believe there's a method of producing a stain for wood by soaking iron filings or steel wool in vinegar.

Do you have a recipe for making this stain and what colours are produced on differing woods? I've heard it turns oak grey, and mahogany purple.

A. Gerard, Bramhope, Leeds

A This sort of stain is made by placing a handful of rusty nails in a pint of vinegar.

Frequently agitate the bottle to speed up matters and after two or three days the stain should be ready for use. The final black colour is often used for drawing-in the grain on walnut and oak, particularly where a repair has been made and the grain of the repair has to match the original piece.

For staining other woods, you'll need to experiment, adjusting the strength of the stain by adding more vinegar to see what colours can be obtained. But I don't think that it will turn mahogany purple.

Oak can be turned grey by dissolving blue copperas in vinegar and brushing it on.

Charles Cliffe

● Charles Cliffe is a professional polisher, author and teacher.

Burr elm

Q I have some very wet pieces of burr elm; the dark centres are about 3/4-1in deep.

I intend to slice through one of the burrs to give a bookmatched inlay of about 10x8in, 1/4in thick, and mount it in an oak frame as a sewing-box lid.

What is the best way to cut, dry, plane and glue the wood, and how should I finish it?

K. B. Dennison, Acharacle, Argyle

A Burr elm is one of the most attractive woods available, but also one of the most difficult to use. Even when you've stored it for a long time, you only have to start cutting to see how unstable it can be. Fixing the slice on a ground of stable oak will of course help.

I suggest you cut the burrs with a bandsaw and glue them straight away on the oak ground. The sawn face can be glued to the oak unsmoothed and the small irregularities will make a good key. Resin 'W' by Evode Ltd, will suit your purpose; it retains a certain elasticity even when set, which allows for any small movement during drying. But I would be inclined to take a chance and not wait for the wood to dry — any small cracks that appear can be filled with a darker colour material.

The burr, once it's fixed on the ground, can be planed very well on a planer/thicknesser provided the blades are sharp. However, by its very nature the burrs will lift even on the finest setting, so I would finish with a well-honed smoother. I use the Rogers 'Peerless' with a Japanese iron.

Fiddes A & B Solution bleaches burr elm marvellously. The result is a rich golden colour the like of which I've never seen in any other wood. I made a dresser using bookmatched burr elm panels which I polished using polyurethane varnish, flattened and waxed.

I wouldn't use french polish, as its delicate high gloss isn't in keeping with the robust nature of the burrs. (This is a personal preference and by experimenting you will hit on your ideal finish.)

William Watts

● William Watts is a professional clockmaker whose burr elm bracket clock, 'Spirit of Tompion', was featured on the cover of January's WOODWORKER.

Honing disc

Q I intend to fix up a disc to a slow-speed motor and cover it with a piece of leather to use as a tool-honing disc. Does it need treating before it's impregnated with abrasive, and what sort of abrasive should I use? Any other advice on this quick method of finishing edge tools (as opposed to the laborious water-stone method) would be welcomed.

S. A. Butler, Burnham, Bucks

The leather will already be treated and any further oiling will impair adhesion with the backing plate. Car-engine valve-grinding paste, available from garages and motor-spares shops, is a suitable abrasive and comes in several grades. The grease in it will soak into the leather after gluing.

I doubt that this method is as good as using oil- or water-stones, although it may give some success on the bevel side. The flat side of the cutter must always remain truly flat and stones are dressed from time to time to ensure this, but the give in the leather may spoil the flatness, and also the speed of the disc may be a handicap in holding a wide cutter dead flat on the disc.

Some woodworkers, particularly carvers, use a rigid strop, similarly dressed, instead of (dangerous habit) stropping on the palm of the hand — but only after honing on the stone first.

I wouldn't call honing on a stone a laborious process — 30 seconds to a minute should be enough for a well-maintained chisel. In conventional honing the oil or water washes away the swarf which would stay on a greasy leather disc.

Making a horizontal disc honer requires quite sophisticated engineering metalwork, and a sizeable sub-structure, which is too elaborate to explain here.

Some of the Japanese horizontal water-cooled grinders have a very fine honing stone but even then a normal rectangular stone is required for the flat side of the cutters.

Overall, I don't think the results will warrant the effort involved.

Bob Wearing

Tambour slats

Q *I am making a roll-top desk in oak using sawn timber for the tambour slats. The slats will have to open and close in different directions to follow two opposite curves on the desk-top; the slats in the plan I am using are in a capital 'A' shape.*

I have made a trial tambour with eight slats but I'm not pleased with its appearance. Any ideas? Also, which is the best adhesive to use for fixing the backing to the slats?

J. McKay, Alloway, Ayr

A This is a rather difficult question to answer without illustrations of the shapes you mention.

With a concave curve, the slat must taper in section towards the front; on a convex curve the visible gap will increase considerably. This, I imagine, is the problem.

American and Canadian roll-top desks of the turn of the century coped with this by shaping the tambours something like **A**. Both the convex and concave curves were relatively gentle. To allow movement in both directions the slats weren't glued to fabric, but drilled at the centre height of the small half-circle and a flexible wire like a cycle-brake cable was threaded through. This was fixed to a threaded rigid piece at the back and a nut pulled the slats together. The number of wires depended on the width of the job. The hole must be generous enough for flexibility but not so large as to show.

This is a difficult shape to produce with a small hand router, but if the piece of furniture is not too large you can try the alternative shown in **B**. The shapes can be worked with small standard router cutters; again, the hole should be rather generous. The sharp arris can be rounded or slightly chamfered. A simple jig with a length stop can easily be devised for drilling the holes accurately.

Tambour slats should always be polished before assembly. Wax in the joints prevents the slats from being accidentally stuck together. Scotch glue was used traditionally, but you can use PVA glues which are quite satisfactory as they are slightly flexible. Don't use synthetic resin glues, they're too brittle. A good backing material is unbleached calico — use a piece dense enough for the size of the tambour.

For power routing, the simplest holding method for small-scale work is to use the small Bosch router in a stand, with baseboard and adjustable fence; otherwise a router table with a fence will do. In both cases a pressure plate or pressure fingers are needed to keep the work firmly against the fence.

Bob Wearing

● Bob Wearing is a woodwork lecturer of vast experience and a regular contributor to WOODWORKER.

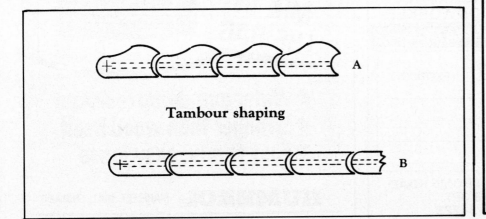

Tambour shaping

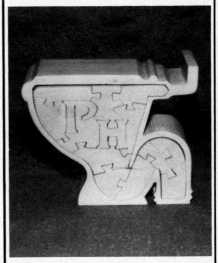

322

Lightweight sash-cramps

Making your own sash-cramps is not as difficult as you think

You can never have too many sash-cramps, and I suppose the smallest number you need in a workshop is four of 48in capacity. Cramps of this size are rather massive and awkward for small jobs such as cupboard doors, frames and drawers, but it's hard to justify buying extra cramps for smaller work.

These light sash-cramps are within the capacity of the average woodworker; a metal-turning lathe is handy but not essential. This cramp is modelled on a type common at the turn of the century, but uses a casting available in aluminium or gunmetal. A ½in thread in the aluminium casting should give an 'owner driver' years of service — I have avoided cast iron for weight reasons.

Before preparing the casting, buy suitable bar material, bright drawn steel 1x³⁄₁₆in or 25x5mm, between 18 and 24in long (for longer lengths a heavier cramp is needed).

The castings saw into two to make both ends for one cramp, but don't saw at this stage. Instead file up one narrow face of the casting square to the sides. The holes already cast in for the bar should be a fairly tight fit, so very cautiously file these out until the bar will just pass through (file the end of the bar free of any roughness before trying).

Now you need to spare a small piece of the bar, about 1½in long, to make a drilling aid. Hold this vertically in a drilling vice or between two wood blocks, and slide on to it the double-ended casting with its filed edge downwards. Using a drilling machine or drill-stand, drill a hole 10.5mm (or ²⁵⁄₆₄in) into one end; start with a small drill and use successively larger ones in order to get centred holes. Once this hole is the correct size, place the other end on the jig and drill a 12mm (or ½in) hole. This way you make sure the drilled holes are parallel with the slots for the bar.

Saw the casting into two, filing the cut surface and the other end-face flat. Get a length of ½in threaded rod for the fixed end, and a piece of 12mm (or ½in) diameter rod for the moving end. Tap the fixed screw-end casting ½in BSW for the threaded bar.

If you have a lathe, turn the two identical pressure 'feet'; you can devise a simpler form for making without a lathe. Drill right through and countersink them, the one for the screw end rather more countersunk than that for the sliding end.

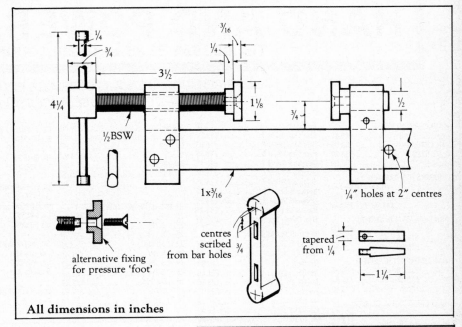

All dimensions in inches

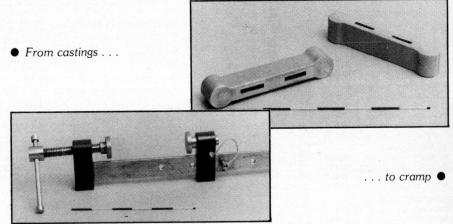

● From castings . . .

. . . to cramp ●

To fit the feet, turn or file the ends of the screw thread and the round bar. The foot for the sliding end is riveted to the round bar and turned or filed flush. The screw end is drilled and heavily countersunk (an engineer's centre drill does this well); alternatively the foot can be fixed with a countersunk screw, later secured with a touch of 'Loctite'. With luck, the plain bar in the sliding end will be a tight fit and can be pressed into the casting; if you don't have such luck,you'll need to drill and secure it with a pin.

Turn the other end of the threaded rod down to remove the thread, then silver-solder or braze a drilled boss to it. Clean it up with file, emery and wire brush, then drill a ¼in hole for the tommy bar, the ends of which you can crimp later in a vice or with a hammer. You can make the bosses on a metal-working lathe if you have access to one. Fit the revolving foot at this stage, once the screw-threaded bar is in place in the casting. If you rivet the screw that holds the foot on to the threaded bar, use a very obtuse-angled punch, because you must make sure the foot still revolves.

Now you can drill the flat bar for the peg holes, with a ¹⁵⁄₆₄in or 5.5mm drill. A tapered ¼in/6mm peg won't fall out.

Now rivet the fixed end to the bar with ³⁄₁₆in or 5mm rod. Slide the casting on to the end of the bar, make sure the threaded rod is parallel with the bar, then drill through both in two places with an undersize drill. Take them apart again and drill them out to the right size, then reassemble and rivet them together. If you did all the drilling through both components at the same time, the holes in the softer casting would enlarge too much.

Drill and tap the bar for the end-stop screw, and make the tapered pin. Both the pin and the sliding end can be drilled for a piece of retaining cord or lightweight chain. Two coats of enamel on the aluminium parts give a professional look. ■

● Castings are available from Bloxwich Alm. Casting Co., Straight Rd, Short Heath, Willenhall, W. Mid WV12 5QZ, for £2.99 (al.) and £4.19 (gunmetal), inc. p&p; quote casting no. RW43. Remember — you only need one casting for the cramp. All the other materials, if you have no local suppliers, are readily available from K. R. Whiston, New Mills, Stockport SK12 4PT.

Rattan pattern

New to caning, but want to try it? No question of punishment if you follow Ronald Snell's clear instructions

● *Hand-woven rattan caning, with its minor irregularities, gives character to the simplest chair seat*

Cane chairs first appeared in Britain in the mid-1660s. They were imported from Holland, the Dutch having learned the craft in the Orient. They became popular after the Great Fire of London destroyed household contents and inexpensive chairs were needed as replacements. The popularity of cane has ebbed and waned several times since then, reaching a peak with bentwood, and undergoing another resurgence in the past 10 years.

Caning may appear to be highly expert, but (I hate to admit) it is simplicity itself to cane a basic chair seat; you need only written instructions and plenty of patience. Expertise is needed when tackling more complex patterns, curved chair backs, double caning and so on.

The kind of cane you need comes from rattan creepers, imported mostly from south-east Asia. The creepers, which grow to enormous lengths, are harvested, dried and split along the length to a variety of sizes, ranging from no. 1 to no. 6 (the widest or thickest). For best work two or three different sizes of cane are used, which looks more attractive than a single-size weave.

For this project I used a half-kilo bundle of no. 4 cane, costing around £4. A bundle like this has about 18 strands, ranging from 4-10ft long, and for ease of handling I separate the strands, coiling them loosely and tying each with a paper-covered wire tie (like those used for closing plastic bags).

The only tool you need is a thin-bladed knife or a pair of scissors, but you will also need about a dozen tapered wooden pegs (about 1½in long, tapering from ⅜in down to about ⅛in) to trap the canes as you work. You can either push these in with the palm of the hand or tap them with a 4oz cabinet hammer (less painful!).

Some caners wet the cane before weaving, but you should avoid soaking it as the cane may discolour; it's enough to wet the cane in a bowl a few feet at a time as you work. If it tends to dry out too quickly, redamp the underside, not the top shiny side.

Whether you wet the cane or not, take an odd short length and flex it back and forth so you get the feel of its potential curvature before fracturing, and observe how it splits. You'll notice that it fractures quite easily, and that splits can run right down the length of the strand. If pieces split when you are weaving, discard them, for they will detract from the appearance.

Project

This chair uses the 'Seven Step Traditional', probably the most common and simplest of the weaves, made up of the following steps:
1 First vertical
2 First horizontal
3 Second vertical
4 Woven horizontal
5 First diagonal
6 Second diagonal
7 Beading

I assume you're tackling caning for the first time, and that you're caning a new frame rather than restoring an old chair.

Preparation is easiest carried out before gluing up the seat frame. You need to cut a ¼x¼in gutter under each rail, with the centre running ½in from the inside edge (I used a rebate plane); this gutter will take the underside of the weaving and the tying-in of the loose ends.

After gluing up the frame, put your finish on — stain, polish, or what you will. Now you need to mark the positions for the ¼in-diameter holes which go from the top of each frame component into the gutter. Run a pencil line along each rail ½in in from the inside; find the exact centre of the front rail, mark it in pencil, and then mark hole positions each ¾in out towards the side rails. Repeat with the back rail; if the seat tapers, there'll be fewer positions to mark. Mark off the side rails in a similar way. Finally, mark out the four corner holes equidistant between the last holes in each adjoining rail.

After marking up, drill the holes, which should pass centrally through the gutter beneath. Very lightly chamfer the sharp edges of the holes with a countersink.

Step 1: First vertical

Starting at the back rail, pass a length of cane through the back left-hand hole, leaving about 3in loose beneath (fig. 1). Insert a peg from the top to hold the cane firmly in position. Keeping the shiny curved side of the cane uppermost, bring it across the seat and down through the equivalent hole in the front rail, keeping the cane taut and inserting another peg. Loop the cane up through the adjacent hole, making sure it doesn't twist in the gutter, and peg it in place. Take the cane to the opposite hole in the back rail and peg in again. Now you can remove the pegs from the front rail. Continue working backwards and forwards, keeping the tension fairly taut and even, but not too tight, as subsequent weavings will tend to tighten the weave further.

If the cane runs out or breaks, leave the end protruding from beneath and peg. Then start again with new cane from the adjacent hole, pegging in position. When you come to the final hole, cut off the cane about 3in overlength and peg in position. It depends on the number of holes in the rails whether you finish on the back or front rails.

continued

Rattan pattern

Step 2: First horizontal

This is virtually a copy of the first step, but laying the cane from left to right and right to left, starting and finishing in the same way as before (fig. 2). The canes lie on top of the first verticals and are not interwoven.

Step 3: Second vertical

Start the second vertical at the back right-hand hole, pegging in and laying the cane slightly to the right of, but parallel to, the first vertical, and on top of the first horizontal (fig. 3). Whenever you reach a hole that is pegged, remove the peg, thread through the cane and re-peg both canes. As you take the working cane up through the next hole, loop in the loose strand in the gutter, trapping it tightly beneath the working cane. Peg in from the top and carry on caning.

Step 4: Woven horizontal

This is another horizontal course, but is woven under and over verticals instead of just being laid on top (fig. 4). Start at the hole directly opposite where you started the previous horizontals, passing the cane over one vertical and under the next. The shiny curved side must always face up, and keep the cane lines parallel with about $\frac{1}{32}$in between canes.

You'll have to concentrate on the weaving at first to get a consistent pattern, but the routine soon becomes automatic. Keep the canes quite taut, applying tension after every three or four pairs of weaves, and straighten up the cane lines as you weave. Remember to tie in any loose ends by looping them into the gutter.

Step 5: First diagonal

Start at the back left-hand hole, pegging in the cane, and weave over the first pair of horizontals, then under the first pair of verticals, over the next set of horizontals and so on, until you reach the front right-hand hole (fig. 5). Peg in and continue by passing the cane up through the first hole in the right-hand rail, repeating the weaving pattern exactly back to the second left-hand hole in the back rail. The pattern must be consistent, or the canes will not be properly locked together when complete. The length of the cane you need will become shorter and shorter as you proceed, until you finish on the end holes of the back and side rails. Pull the cane taut after each three or four pairs to get regular tension on each length.

When you've completed one half of the seat, do the opposite half, starting again at the back left-hand hole and finishing at the end hole of the left side rail.

Step 6: Second diagonal

This is the mirror image of the previous step, starting from the opposite corner hole, and weaving the cane **under** the first pair of horizontals and **over** the first pair of verticals.

Step 7: Beading

Beading or lacing as a method of finishing off the outside of the caned area is a relatively recent innovation; previously wooden pegs were jammed in each hole to hold the loose ends. The technique of looping in the loose ends means all pegs are removed as you reach the end of the caning proper, allowing the beading step to be applied.

Start by pushing a loop of cane up through any end hole, so the loop stands about $\frac{1}{2}$in above the rail. Slip a second cane through the loop, shiny side up, to lay along the line of holes, pushing the end of this cane into the adjacent corner hole and pegging in place. Tighten the loop by carefully pulling the long end down, thus pulling the beading cane down into the hole a fraction; don't pull it right into the hole, just taut enough for neatness.

Form a second loop and push it up through the next hole, pulling the beading cane through the loop and tightening up as before. Continue around the seat until you reach the corner you started at. Remove the peg, push both ends of the beading cane down through the hole and cut off to about 3in. Sharpen the ends of both canes and coax them under other canes in the gutter; pull tight and cut off neatly.

I usually finish off by cutting $\frac{1}{2}$x$\frac{1}{8}$in strips of wood and pinning them over the gutters with $\frac{3}{4}$in brass pins; with each corner mitred carefully and stained and polished to match the rest of the chair they make a neat finish.

Not all chairs have square seats: if the seat is wider at the front than the back, start caning at the centre hole of the back rail, working one half at a time for the first vertical step. When you reach the last hole in the back rail there'll still be empty holes in the front rail. Continue caning the front rail, taking the cane back into a hole in the side rail, choosing a suitable hole so the cane lies parallel with previous verticals.

If you are caning a circular seat, like a bentwood, carefully mark out the holes equidistant all the way round roughly $\frac{3}{4}$in apart, and then mark off four diagonally opposed holes to act as reference for your 'front', 'back' and 'side rails'. Start caning from a 'centre' hole and carry on as though it were a square seat. You'll notice that lengths of cane you need will reduce until you reach a 'side rail'; you then peg out and start caning from the 'centre' hole again.

When you've finished a chair seat, the caning should be tight and firm, with all settings and weavings in correct place, so the crossings bed in properly. I hope you find the process as satisfying as I do. ■

● *On the last lap: bottom view shows the gutter along all four frame edges, one diagonal in position, and the 'tying in' along the nearest gutter*

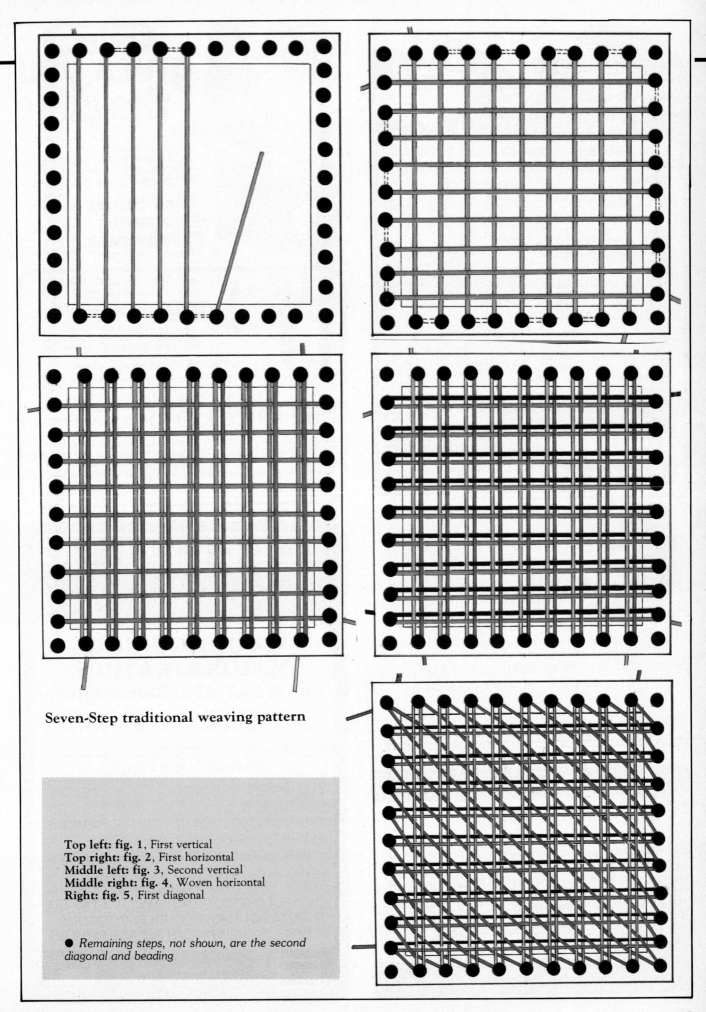

Seven-Step traditional weaving pattern

Top left: **fig. 1**, First vertical
Top right: **fig. 2**, First horizontal
Middle left: **fig. 3**, Second vertical
Middle right: **fig. 4**, Woven horizontal
Right: **fig. 5**, First diagonal

● *Remaining steps, not shown, are the second diagonal and beading*

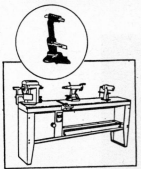

Carving anatomy

● *In classical stance, right, or dynamic in form, the human torso is a challenge to the carver-turned-sculptor*

Fig. 1   **How muscles and bones affect the outward appearance**

 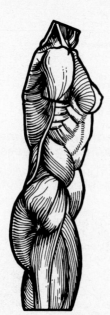 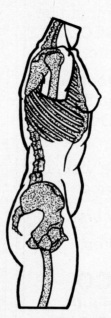 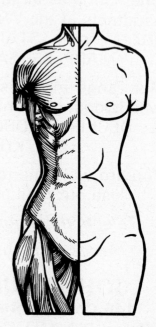

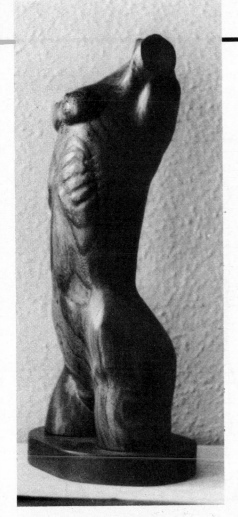

● *Skin is like a fabric draped over the internal structures of the body; undulations, indentations, flat facets and angles are governed by bones and muscles beneath the surface*

Harry Turner argues that at least a basic study of human anatomy is vital in figure carving

Most carvers work to a reduced or miniature scale — but not necessarily by choice. Limited as we are by size and price of available timber, we nevertheless aspire to work in more sculptural proportions — say half or three-quarter full size — and to do it, what's more, without joining on separate pieces or laminating. Those solutions have their own restrictions, and they are obvious in the finished work too.

I got my chance of producing something larger than usual when I acquired two pieces of well seasoned, disease-free, elm log, complete with bark. They were both about 9½in diameter, one piece 21½in long, the other 18½in.

Looking at the timber, I started thinking about a suitable subject. The pronounced grain made me decide to avoid fine detail, as it would be incompatible with the type and texture of the wood.

My subject matter became obvious — a torso of the female human form. And since I had two logs available, I thought it would be a challenge to carve the torso in two different poses, one dynamic and the other in classical stance.

Carving on a bigger scale brings its own problems — the larger the scale, the greater the margin for error. So it's even more important than usual to understand and consider how the muscles and bone structure affect the surface by their very presence, and by their movement.

If you want to carve the human body, you have to learn what produces the undulations, the indentations, the flat facets and the angles, and how they fit in with the exterior rounded form. These surface features are governed by the underlying structures, and ignoring this can lead to regret when you look at your finished carving.

Skin, after all, is rather like a fabric or covering material draped over the internal structures of the body. You'll get the idea if you cover a collection of household objects with a cloth and observe the new form created.

With this in mind, my starting point in the carving was to refer to studies of human anatomy for artists; it is less complicated than you think, and you do need to study some human anatomy if you want to carve the human figure. Fig. 1 shows the direct relationship of muscle and bones, coupled with the adjacent surface or skin drawings.

Another useful approach I found was looking at the photos in body-building magazines. The surface anatomy is exaggerated by normal standards, but it's better to start off with an exaggerated form and then refine it than miss the underlying form altogether.

I prepared full-size drawings on grid paper (figs 2 and 3), for visual reference and for transferring dimensions.

The work

Usually with a carving I trim a log into a square section, so I can transfer the drawings to two flat sides. Not in this case, for as you see from fig. 4, the portions at the

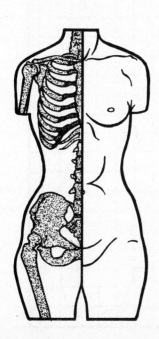
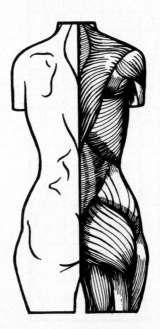
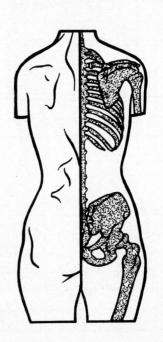

continued
331

Fig.2 Classical stance: front, side and back views

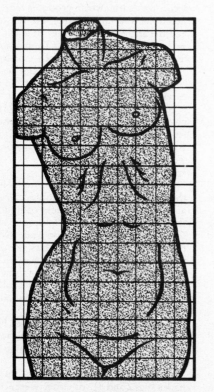
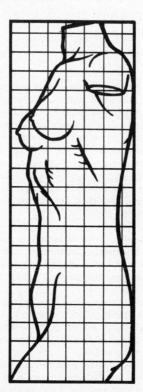
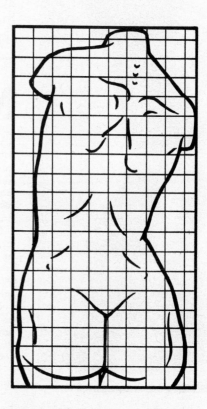

Fig.3 Dynamic pose, from front, side and rear

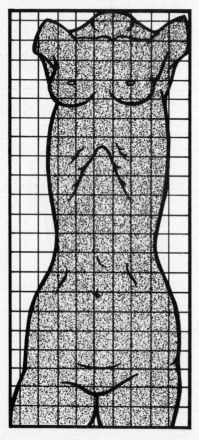
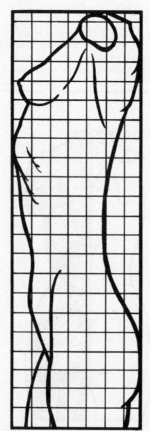
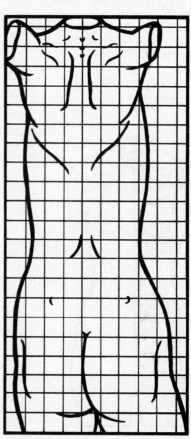

top would have been wasted; by departing from my usual system, I could allow wider body dimensions for the arms.

I cut a slice off the front of the log from top to bottom, along the initial cutting line (fig. 4b) and a parallel slice off the back, working to the maximum overall dimensions of the drawing. On the front flat surface I marked changes of direction of the torso, **A, B** and **C** (fig. 4a), and cut back appropriately. I also cut back at the top, making sure that dimension **D** was constant across the width of the log.

Then I was ready for my first marking lines. I drew the vertical measuring line, which corresponds with a grid line from the drawing — it may not necessarily be the centre line. I transferred points where the drawing crosses grid lines on to the wood, using a tape measure for vertical and calipers for horizontal dimensions, finally joining up the points freehand.

Now I could hew away excess wood from the two sides, except at the top which I left full width at this stage (fig. 4b). The result was a roughly square cross-section.

When hewing, keep outside the drawn line until the surfaces you are trimming have been flattened with a flat chisel to produce a plane surface for marking and lines. This is a continual process — marking, shaping, then marking again — until all the finer detail has evolved.

You might think this study-related approach to carving is superfluous if you're only going to produce one large torso, but if you work through this exercise you'll find the knowledge you gain will stand you in good stead for smaller scale work. ∎

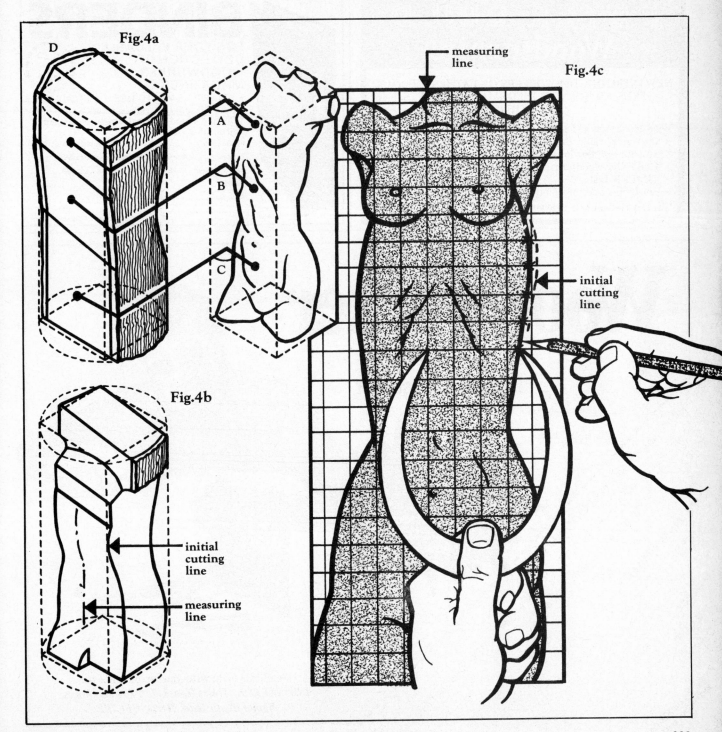

Fig.4a

Fig.4b

Fig.4c

measuring line

initial cutting line

measuring line

initial cutting line

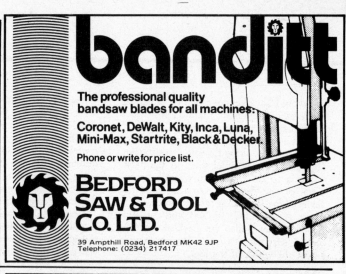

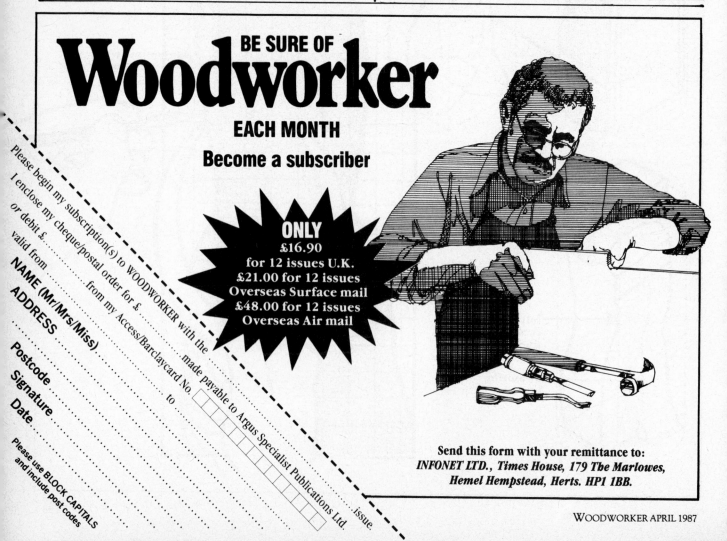

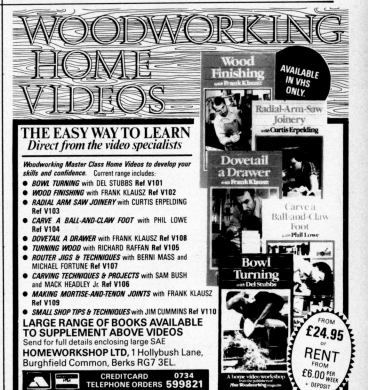

Carver's homage

● Masks, **left**, are the most famous of Balinese carvings. **Above**, craftsmen squat on a rush mat in the open air, holding their work between their feet

On the fabled island of Bali, David Saunders found skilled carvers with an eye on more than their work

The morning of the world — that's how Bali was described by the late prime minister of India, Jawaharlal Nehru. If he meant it was one of the last fresh and unspoiled beauty spots left in a rapidly diminishing and spent planet, he was right. This fabled island off the eastern tip of Java, with its three million gentle and artistic people, is surely the jewel in Indonesia's crown — the ultimate destination for any tourist of the ex-Dutch colonies. Carvings of wood and stone with religious significance abound throughout the land, giving rise to its other name — 'The island of a thousand temples'. Some people feel that maybe 10,000 would be a more realistic figure. From the simple to the intricate, each mini-temple is a reflection of the island's foremost religion, Hinduism.

Last year I visited Bali (pronounced *bally* and not *barley* as some people insist on calling it) to fulfil a boyhood dream. Unlike most ventures of this type the reality was no disappointment: the dream was fulfilled, and more besides.

As soon as I left the airport, it was clear that this was a very different world from my own. The small roadside temples, ornately carved mostly in wood, some top heavy with colourful gifts and gay cloths, were the first hint to the inner nature of the Balinese. The real Bali is not concealed along side-streets and off beaten tracks; it is all around, colourful, pungent and tinkling musically, enveloping the visitor like some exotic cloak.

To anyone like me who professes to carve wood, Mas, a village 20km north of Denpassar, the island's capital, is the Mecca. A single visit made me wonder if I'd ever carved anything of consequence in the past 15 years. Reached by a fairly easy if hot coach journey, here the most respected and skilful carvers practised their art. I saw portrayed every subject I had anticipated and a few surprises as well. Old men, women, fishermen, dancers, praying monks, birds of every description and Hindu gods, all mostly in the round. Wall plaques in deep relief of religious character for hanging on a dwelling to ward off sundry evil spirits. The choices of wood were as diverse as the subjects, with much ebony, teak, tamarind and sugarwood in evidence.

In the village I watched a group of carvers sitting outside one of the workshops, shaded from the hot noonday sun by a rickety wood and leaf lean-to. The first thing I was intrigued by was that there seemed to be very little marking or physical planning of the finished article, save for the occasional flick of white chalk against the dark wood. Roughing or blocking-out is done with a small axe or adze, nimble fingers turning the piece quickly to receive each accurately placed razor-sharp blow. The craftsmen sat on a large rush mat, mostly cross-legged; vices and holdfasts appeared to be non-existent, their only bench their laps or the mat. Dressed in shorts and colourful shirts, they were the envy of every onlooker as they worked with a creativity and dexterity most of us can only dream of. In the leafy courtyard under the shady dais where the only real sound that mattered was that of keen blade kissing wood, modern man with his shaky life-style seemed of another era.

continued

Carver's homage

Photos Applied Photographics

● *Plays and dances, involving masks, are part of everyday life;* **inset**, *fisherman, a traditional subject for carving*

Around the circle of menfolk sat an outer circle of women workers quietly and apparently contentedly finishing off the carvings with glasspaper and buffers. Here the true character of the piece is revealed, its grain, its inner light, an inherent life which no carver can create — merely enhance.

The carvers themselves used the tools familiar to us all — chisels, gouges, needle files and small rasps and scrapers. Only one tool was very different, a double-ended gouge; like nothing I'd met before, but quite practical for lighter detail.

In contrast with the west, here the portrayal of worldly and unworldly subjects in wood is more than a pursuit of leisure or profit. Self-expression through a tangible object is paramount; more, it is homage paid to the unseen world. The word artist doesn't exist in Balinese the way we use it. To call a Balinese an artist would be like describing him as a man; it would convey nothing of him beyond his gender.

Most famous of the island's carvings are the masks. Whether a mask is for ceremonial or religious use, great reverence is used throughout the process of its creation.

Once a tree is selected it is blessed by the local elders, and homage is paid to this living thing given to all human beings. Care is taken even at the initial stages when it is cut down, and prayers offered. Once reduced to suitable sizes each piece is carefully placed in the same relative position as it was when it was still part of the whole tree. Never is it placed on its side or upside down as this would not allow its life force to flow in the right direction; even worse, it could flow out and be lost for ever. The masks are used in plays and dances, which are of great importance in everyday life, usually portraying the perpetual and universal fight between good and evil. Compared with western ideas, the events display a more realistic view of the constant struggle in that the powers of good are not always the victor. The mask when completed goes beyond being merely a substitute for make-up; it is in itself good or bad depending on the role for which it is carved, the wearer not merely assuming the role of a devil, but becoming evil personified. Perhaps a little frightening to western eyes, rather like Christopher Lee actually being Dracula, and not a well respected and amiable actor we all know.

Perhaps I can best sum up and illustrate the Balinese attitude to art and carving by relating this particular experience. One day the guide pointed out carvers working on stone pillars destined for the porch of a rich man's house. Each block was painstakingly carved with ornate faces in various attitudes. I asked if such objects were ever cast, thinking it was after all a fairly low-tech process (witness the regiment of gnomes that march across the gardens of England). The guide's smile turned to puzzlement and in fractured English he told me no, never, after all what would be the point? For a moment my mind was filled with the image of a passing conveyor belt of identical duplicated pillar blocks, originality and creativity long since lost. In that moment I had another insight to these people's attitudes to their art and indeed to their whole way of life. I couldn't think how to answer the guide, and felt a little ashamed of having suggested such a thing.

Then I realised that in the originality of these carvings, the carvers give a fragment of themselves. Perhaps something of that attitude comes across in English, when we say: 'You only get out of life what you're prepared to put into it'. ■

Letters

Mystery solved

THE SCHOOL OF WOODCARVING ('*Magical Mystery School*', *WW/Dec*) was indeed a 'magical school'. I had the honour of studying there for three years, from 1924-1927, under the celebrated woodcarver, Herbert Grimwood, and was subsequently known in the trade as 'Young Grimwood'. After the death of Mr Grimwood the school was transferred to the Hammersmith School of Art, and was closed soon after.

I remember the photograph of the class being taken — it was in the middle-room of the school. The lady in the foreground is the renowned model for R. L. Sims R.A., the portrait painter; the piece of wood in front of her is a carved frame for one of his portraits. The student on the right is me. I would imagine that I am among the last of the few survivors who studied at the school — if not the only one. At no time were there more than 21 male students and about 10 ladies; we had very individual attention, the result being not quantity but quality.

I am 79 years old and still teach 60 students weekly. In my spare time I work professionally, mostly on church work. I am now the master of the Essex Guild of Woodcarvers, and still look back with a thrill at having studied at the school, knowing my work is all over the world, and in the hands of our Queen and King Hussein of Jordan.

Frederick H. Appleton,
Woodham Ferrers, Essex

Need a bias

I AM TURNING two flat-green bowls down to crown-green size; no difficulty on the between-centres turning, but I am beaten when it comes to the bias. Does any reader know how to deal with this?
E. P. Haddock, Sheffield
● Please write to the *Woodworker* office if you can help Mr Haddock; 1 Golden Sq, London W1R 3AB

Startrite safety

I WAS VERY SURPRISED to see David Savage's remarks about safety on Startrite tilt-arbor sawbenches in 'The craft of cabinetmaking' (*WW/Feb*). I feel I must put the record straight.

He comments that Startrite's riving-knife mounted guard is not as safe or easy to use as a guard mounted from a remote arm. We are a principal UK manufacturer of these machines and have designed a guard system

in close consultation with the Health and Safety Executive. The guard can easily be positioned relative to the saw-blade, covering the gullets of the teeth, which it does at whatever height the blade is set, whether it is tilted or not. This is fundamental for safety.

Mr Savage also makes the point that the rip-fence on the Startrite machines can only be brought to within 30mm of the blade when the guard is fitted. Unlike some manufacturers, we fit a general-purpose wooden faceplate to the fence to give a deep surface for accurate ripping. It is generally accepted that alternative faceplates can be fitted to the rip-fence for various tasks, and if you fit a low-section one, it can be moved underneath the guard and right up to the blade. If David Savage were using a rip-fence faceplate the same depth as our standard item, it means his guard was not in the correct position when cutting off small pieces and could therefore be dangerous.

The Startrite TA300 and TA300PS tilt-

arbor sawbenches are fitted as standard with a two-position fence system which means a low profile edge can be used so the guard is no longer in the way. The system is versatile, safe and works well, with the added advantage that there is no restriction to the size of board that can be cut, as there is with an overhanging guard system.

At Startrite, we make sure the operator gets a machine with features that satisfy the requirements of all relevant safety regulations.
John Wellings, Sales & Marketing Director,
Startrite Machine Tool Co. Ltd

Dry comment

I READ WITH INTEREST Mr Bumphrey's letter in January's WOODWORKER extolling the virtues of our 'Dry Oil'. This is in fact a silicone based lubricant that, although not designed as such, acts as a rust inhibitor (when sprayed on) for tools kept in outside workshops. It can also be used as a general purpose lubricant where a thin low-friction coating is required, on sawbenches and planers, for instance.

I must make it clear, however, that this product should not be used on any article that will require subsequent painting, staining or varnishing, as the silicone will inhibit adhesion.

Thank you to the readers who have written to us. The product is available through our agents: R.P.M. Marketing, 11 Cranston Rise, Bexhill-on-Sea, E. Sussex.
Brian Cliffe, Sales Development Manager,
James Briggs & Sons Ltd

shopguide

AVON

BATH   Tel. Bath 64513
JOHN HALL TOOLS   ★
RAILWAY STREET

Open: Monday-Saturday
9.00 a.m.-5.30 p.m.
H.P.W.WM.D.A.BC.

BRISTOL   Tel. (0272) 741510
JOHN HALL TOOLS LIMITED   ★
CLIFTON DOWN SHOPPING CENTRE
WHITELADIES ROAD
Open: Monday-Saturday
9.00 a.m.-5.30 p.m.
H.P.W.WM.D.A.BC.

BRISTOL   Tel. (0272) 629092
TRYMWOOD SERVICES
2a DOWNS PARK EAST, (off North View)
WESTBURY PARK
Open: 8.30 a.m.-5.30 p.m. Mon. to Fri.
Closed for lunch 1.00-2.00 p.m.
P.W.WM.D.T.A.BC.

BRISTOL   Tel. (0272) 667013
FASTSET LTD
190-192 WEST STREET
BEDMINSTER
Open: Mon.-Fri. 8.30 a.m.-5.00 p.m.
Saturday 9.00 a.m.-1.00 p.m.
H.P.W.WM.D.CS.A.BC.

BRISTOL   Tel. (0272) 667013
WILLIS
157 WEST STREET
BEDMINSTER
Open: Mon.-Fri. 8.30 a.m.-5.00 p.m.
Sat. 9 a.m.-4 p.m.
P.W.WM.D.CS.A.BC.

BERKSHIRE

READING   Tel. Littlewick Green
DAVID HUNT (TOOL   2743
MERCHANTS) LTD   ★
KNOWL HILL, NR. READING
Open: Monday-Saturday
9.00 a.m.-5.30 p.m.
H.P.W.D.A.BC.

READING   Tel. Reading 661511
WOKINGHAM TOOL CO. LTD.
99 WOKINGHAM ROAD

Open: Mon-Sat 9.00 a.m.-5.30 p.m.
Closed 1.00-2.00 p.m. for lunch
H.P.W.WM.D.CS.A.BC.

BUCKINGHAMSHIRE

MILTON KEYNES   Tel. (0908)
POLLARD WOODWORKING   641366
CENTRE   ★
51 AYLESBURY ST., BLETCHLEY
Open: Mon-Fri 8.30-5.30
Saturday 9.00-5.00
H.P.W.WM.D.CS.A.BC.

SLOUGH   Tel: (06286) 5125
BRAYWOOD ESTATES LTD.   ★
158 BURNHAM LANE
Open: 9.00am-5.30pm.
Monday-Saturday.
H.P.W.WM.CS.A.

BUCKINGHAMSHIRE

HIGH WYCOMBE   Tel. (0494)
SCOTT SAWS LTD.   24201/33788
14 BRIDGE STREET   ★

Mon.-Sat. 8.30 a.m.-6.00 p.m.

H.P.W.WM.D.T.CS.MF.A.BC.

HIGH WYCOMBE   Tel. (0494)
ISAAC LORD LTD   22221
185 DESBOROUGH ROAD   KE

Open: Mon-Fri 8.00 a.m.-5.00 p.m.
Saturday 9.00 a.m.-5.00 p.m.
H.P.W.D.A.

CAMBRIDGESHIRE

CAMBRIDGE   Tel: (0223) 63132
D. MACKAY LTD.   ★
BRITANNIA WORKS, EAST ROAD

Open: Mon.-Fri. 8.30 a.m.-1 p.m./2.00-
5.00 p.m. Sat. 8.30 a.m.-1.00 p.m.
H.P.W.D.T.CS.MF.A.BC.

CAMBRIDGE   Tel. (0223) 247386
H. B. WOODWORKING   K
105 CHERRY HINTON ROAD
Open: 8.30 a.m.-5.30 p.m.
Monday-Friday
8.30 a.m.-1.00 p.m. Sat.
H.P.W.WM.D.CS.A.

CHESHIRE

NANTWICH   Tel. Crewe 67010
ALAN HOLTHAM   K★
THE OLD STORES TURNERY
WISTASON ROAD, WILLASTON
Open: Tues.-Sat. 9.00 a.m.-5.30 p.m.
Closed Monday
P.W.WM.D.T.C.CS.A.BC.

CLEVELAND

MIDDLESBROUGH   Tel. (0642)
CLEVELAND WOODCRAFT   813103
(M'BRO), 38-42 CRESCENT ROAD   K

Open: Mon-Sat 9.15 a.m.-5.30 p.m.

H.P.T.A.BC.W.WM.CS.D.

CORNWALL

SOUTH WEST Power Tools

CORNWALL Tel: Helston (03265) 4961
HELSTON AND LAUNCESTON   Launceston
(0566) 4781
   K
H.P.W.WM.D.CS.A.

CUMBRIA

CARLISLE   Tel: (0228) 36391
W. M. PLANT
ALLENBROOK ROAD
ROSEHILL, CA1 2UT
Open: Mon.-Fri. 8.00 a.m.-5.15 p.m.
Sat. 8.00 a.m.-12.30 noon
P.W.WM.D.CS.A.

DEVON

BRIXHAM   Tel. (08045) 4900
WOODCRAFT SUPPLIES   E★
4 HORSE POOL STREET

Open: Mon.-Sat. 9.00 a.m.-6.00 p.m.

H.P.W.A.D.MF.CS.BC.

PLYMOUTH   Tel. (0752) 330303
WESTWARD BUILDING SERVICES   ★
LTD., LISTER CLOSE, NEWNHAM
INDUSTRIAL ESTATE, PLYMPTON
Open: Mon-Fri 8.00 a.m.-5.30 p.m.
Sat. 8.30 a.m.-12.30 p.m.
H.P.W.WM.D.A.BC.

PLYMOUTH   Tel: (0752) 665363
F.T.B. LAWSON LTD.
71 NEW GEORGE STREET
PLYMOUTH PL1 1RB
Open: Mon.-Sat. 8.30 am-5.30 pm.
H.P.W.CS.MF.A.

DORSET

WEYMOUTH   Tel. (0305) 770303
WEYMOUTH HIRE & SALES LTD.   K
5 KENT CLOSE
GRANBY INDUSTRIAL ESTATE
Open 7.30 a.m. - 5.30 p.m. Mon.-Fri.
Sat. 8 a.m. - 1 p.m.
H.P.W.WM.D.CS.A.K.

ESSEX

LEIGH ON SEA   Tel. (0702)
MARSHAL & PARSONS LTD.   710404
1111 LONDON ROAD   EK
Open: 8.30 a.m.-5.30 p.m. Mon-Fri
9.00 a.m.-5.00 p.m. Sat.
H.P.W.WM.D.CS.A.

GLOUCESTER

ILFORD   Tel: 597 7461
CUTWELL WOODWORKING   ★
776 HIGH ROAD
GOODMAYES IG3 8SY
H.P.W.WM.D.CS.A.

TEWKESBURY   Tel. (0684)
TEWKESBURY SAW CO. LTD.   293092
TRADING ESTATE, NEWTOWN   K

Open: Mon-Fri 8.00 a.m.-5.00 p.m.
Saturday 9.30 a.m.-12.00 p.m.
P.W.WM.D.CS.

HAMPSHIRE

ALDERSHOT **SOUTHAMPTON**
(0252) 334422   (0703) 332288
BIRCH & HILLS POWER TOOL CENTRES
374 HIGH ST.   7 BELVIDERE RD.
Open:Mon-Fri. 8.30-5.30. Sat. 8.30-12.30
Closed for Lunch 1.00-2.00
H.P.W.WM.D.C.S.MF.BC.K.★

HERTFORDSHIRE

WARE   Tel: (0920) 870 230
HEATH SAWS   870 636
6 LEESIDE WORKS   K★
STANSTEAD ABBOTTS (near Ware) HERTS.
SG12 8DL
Open: Mon.-Fri. 8.30am-5.30pm
Sat. 8.30am-1pm. Sunday by appointment.
P.W.WM.D.CS.A.

ENFIELD   Tel: 01-363 2935
GILL & HOXBY LTD.
131-137 ST. MARKS ROAD ADJ.
BUSH HILL PARK STATION, EN1 1BA
Mon.-Sat. 8-5.30
Early closing Wed. 1 p.m.
H.P.A.M.MC.T.S.W.

HUMBERSIDE

GRIMSBY   Tel. Grimsby (0472)
58741 Hull (0482) 26999
J. E. SIDDLE LTD. (Tool Specialists)   ★
83 VICTORIA STREET
Open: Mon-Fri 8.30 a.m.-5.30 p.m.
Sat. 8.30 a.m.-12.45 p.m. & 2 p.m.-5 p.m.
H.P.A.BC.W.WMD.

HULL
HUMBERSIDE FACTORING/H.F.C.
SAW SERVICING LTD.
MAIN STREET
Open: Mon.-Fri. 8am-5pm.
Saturday 8am-12.00pm.
H.P.W.WM.D.CS.A.BC.K.

KENT

WYE   Tel. (0233) 813144
KENT POWER TOOLS LTD.
UNIT 1, BRIAR CLOSE
WYE, Nr. ASFORD

H.P.W.WM.D.A.CS.

MAIDSTONE   Tel. (0622) 50177
SOUTH EASTERN SAWS (Ind.) LTD.   ★
COLDRED ROAD
PARKWOOD INDUSTRIAL ESTATE
Open: Mon.-Fri. 8.00 a.m.-6.00 p.m.
Sat. 9.00 a.m.-12.00 a.m.
B.C.W.CS.WM.PH.

MAIDSTONE   Tel. (0622) 44350
HENSON AND PLATT
TOKE PLACE
LINTON
Open Mon.-Fri. 8.00 a.m.-5.00 p.m.
Saturday 8.00 a.m.-1.00 p.m.
H.P.W.T.CS.A.

shopguide

LANCASHIRE

PRESTON Tel. (0772) 52951
SPEEDWELL TOOL COMPANY E★
62-68 MEADOW STREET PR1 1SU
Open: Mon.-Fri. 8.30 a.m.-5.30 p.m.
Sat. 8.30 a.m.-12.30 p.m.

H.P.W.WM.CS.A.MF.BC.

ROCHDALE Tel. (0706) 342123/
C.S.M. TOOLS 342322
4-6 HEYWOOD ROAD E★
CASTLETON
Open: Mon.-Sat 9.00 a.m.-6.00 p.m.
Sundays by appointment
W.D.CS.A.BC.

LANCASTER Tel: (0524) 32886
LILE TOOL SHOP K
43/45 NORTH ROAD
Open: Monday to Saturday
9.00 a.m.-5.30 p.m.
Wed. 9.00 a.m.-12.30 p.m.
H.P.W.D.A.

**All shops with an
asterisk *
have a Mail Order
Service**

BLACKPOOL ★
FLYDE WOODTURNING SUPPLIES
255 CHURCH STREET
BLACKPOOL FY1 4HY
9.30-5.30 Monday to Saturday
H.P.W.WM.A.MF.C.B.C.D.

LONDON

ACTON Tel. (01-992) 4835
A. MILLS (ACTON) LTD ★
32/36 CHURCHFIELD ROAD W3 6ED
Open: Mon-Fri 9.00 a.m.-5.00 p.m.
Saturdays 9.00 am-1.00 p.m.
H.P.W.WM.

LONDON Tel. 01-723 2295-6-7
LANGHAM TOOLS LIMITED
13 NORFOLK PLACE
LONDON W2 1QJ

FULHAM Tel: (01-636) 6109
I. GRIZARD LTD. E
84a-b-c LILLIE ROAD, SW6 1TL
Open: Mon.-Sat. 9.00-5.30 p.m.
Half day Thursday

H.P.A.BC.W.CS.WM.D.

LONDON Tel: (01-636) 7475
BUCK & RYAN LTD ★
101 TOTTENHAM COURT ROAD W1P ODY

Open: Mon.-Fri. 8.30 a.m.-5.30 p.m.
Saturday 8.30 a.m.-4.00 p.m.
H.P.W.WM.D.A..

LONDON

HOUNSLOW Tel. (01-570)
Q.R. TOOLS LTD 2103/5135
251-253 HANWORTH ROAD

Open: Mon-Fri 8.30 a.m.-5.30 p.m.
Sat. 9.00 a.m.-1.00 p.m.
P.W.WM.D.CS.A.

MANCHESTER

MANCHESTER Tel. (061 789)
TIMMS TOOLS 0909
102-104 LIVERPOOL ROAD
PATRICROFT M30 0WZ
Weekdays 9.00 a.m.-5.30 p.m.
Sat. 9.00 a.m.-1.00 p.m.
H.P.A.W.

MANCHESTER Tel: 061 834 0714
TILL AND WHITEHEAD ★
ELLESMERE STREET, M15 4JX

Open: Mon.-Fri. 8.00 a.m.-5.00 p.m.

H.P.W.A.BC.

MERSEYSIDE

LIVERPOOL Tel. (051-207) 2967
TAYLOR BROS (LIVERPOOL) LTD K
195-199 LONDON ROAD
LIVERPOOL L3 8JG
Open: Monday to Friday
8.30 a.m.-5.30 p.m.
H.P.W.WM.D.A.BC.

MIDDLESEX

RUISLIP Tel. (08956) 74126
ALLMODELS ENGINEERING LTD. E★
91 MANOR WAY

Open: Mon-Sat 9.00 a.m.-5.30 p.m.
H.P.W.A.D.CS.MF.BC.

NORFOLK

NORWICH Tel. (0603) 898695
NORFOLK SAW SERVICES
DOG LANE, HORSFORD
Open: Monday to Friday
8.00 a.m.-5.00 p.m.
Saturday 8.00 a.m.-12.00 p.m.
H.P.W.WM.D.CS.A.

KINGS LYNN Tel. (0553) 2443
WALKER & ANDERSON (Kings Lynn) LTD.
WINDSOR ROAD, KINGS LYNN K
Open: Monday to Saturday
7.45 a.m.-5.30 p.m.
Wednesday 1.00 p.m. Saturday 5.00 p.m.
H.P.W.WM.D.CS.A.

NORWICH Tel. (0603) 400933
WESTGATES WOODWORKING Tx
61 HURRICANE WAY, 975412
NORWICH AIRPORT INDUSTRIAL ESTATE
Open: 9.00 a.m.-5.00 p.m. weekdays
9.00 a.m.-12.30 Sat.
P.W.WM.D.BC. K

KINGS LYNN Tel: 07605 674
NORFOLK WOODTURNING CENTRE ★
UNIT A, HILL FARM WORKSHOPS
GREAT DUNHAM (Nr. Swaffham)
Tues.-Sat. 9.00am-5.30pm

H.P.W.D.T.MF.A.BC.

NOTTINGHAMSHIRE

NOTTINGHAM Tel: (0602) 225979
POOLEWOOD 227064/5
EQUIPMENT LTD. (06077) 2421 after hrs
5a HOLLY LANE, CHILLWELL
Open: Mon-Fri 9.00 a.m.-5.30 p.m.
Sat. 9.00 a.m. to 12.30 p.m.
P.W.WM.D.CS.A.BC.

OXON

WITNEY Tel. (0993) 3885
TARGET TOOLS (SALES, & 72095 OXON
TARGET HIRE & REPAIRS)
TOOLS SWAIN COURT
STATION INDUSTRIAL ESTATE
Open: Mon.-Sat. 8.00 a.m.-5.00 p.m.
24 hour Answerphone
BC.W.M.A.

SHROPSHIRE

TELFORD Tel. Telford (0952)
ASLES LTD 48054
VINEYARD ROAD, WELLINGTON EK★

Open: Mon. Fri. 8.30 a.m.-5.30 p.m.
Saturday 8.30 a.m.-4.00 p.m.
H.P.W.WM.D.CS.BC.A.

SOMERSET

TAUNTON Tel. (0823) 85431
JOHN HALL TOOLS ★
6 HIGH STREET

Open Monday-Saturday
9.00 a.m.-5.30 p.m.
H.P.W.WM.D.CS.A.

STAFFORDSHIRE

TAMWORTH Tel: (0827) 56188
MATTHEWS BROTHERS LTD. ★
KETTLEBROOK ROAD
Open: Mon.-Sat. 8.30-6.00 p.m.
Demonstrations Sunday mornings by
appointment only
H.P.WM.D.T.CS.A.BC.

SUFFOLK

SUFFOLK Tel: (037983) 8126
LOCKWOOD WOODWORKING MACHINERY
WHITEGATES BUNGALOW
THE COMMON MELLIS
NEAR EYE/DISS IP23
Open standard hours.
*Lathe demos every Saturday morning.
Woodcopy lathes/Dust extractors.*
H.P.W.D.A.

IPSWICH Tel. (0473) 40456
FOX WOODWORKING KE★
142-144 BRAMFORD LANE
Open: Tues., Fri., 9.00 a.m.-5.30 p.m.
Sat. 9.00 a.m.-5.00 p.m.

H.P.W.WM.D.A.B.C.

SUSSEX

BOGNOR REGIS Tel. (0243) 863100
A. OLBY & SON (BOGNOR REGIS) LTD.
"TOOLSHOP," BUILDERS MERCHANT
HAWTHORN ROAD K
Open: Mon-Thurs 8 a.m.-5.15 p.m. Fri.
8 a.m.-8 p.m. Sat 8 a.m.-12.45 p.m.
H.P.W.WM.D.T.C.A.BC.

WORTHING Tel. (0903) 38739
W. HOSKING LTD (TOOLS & KE★
MACHINERY)
28 PORTLAND RD, BN11 1QN
Open: Mon.-Sat. 8.30 a.m.-5.30 p.m.
Closed Wednesday
H.P.W.WM.D.CS.A.BC.

TYNE & WEAR

NEWCASTLE Tel. (0632) 320311
HENRY OSBOURNE LTD. E★
50-54 UNION STREET

Open: Mon-Fri 8.30 a.m.-5.00 p.m.

H.P.W.D.CS.MF.A.BC.

NEWCASTLE-UPON-TYNE ★
J. W. HOYLE LTD
CLARENCE STREET
NEWCASTLE-UPON-TYNE
TYNE & WEAR
NE2 17J
H.P.W.WM.D.CS.A.BC.K.

W. MIDLANDS

WOLVERHAMPTON Tel. (0902)
MANSAW SERVICES 58759
WARD STREET, HORSELEY FIELDS K★
WOLVERHAMPTON, WEST MIDLANDS
Open Mon.-Fri. 9.00am-5.00pm
Sat. 8am-3pm

H.P.W.WM.A.D.CS.

YORKSHIRE

SHEFFIELD Tel. (0742) 441012
GREGORY & TAYLOR LTD KE
WORKSOP ROAD
Open: 8.30 a.m.-5.30 p.m.
Monday-Friday
8.30 a.m.-12.30 p.m. Sat.
H.P.W.WM.D.

HARROGATE Tel. (0423) 66245/
MULTI-TOOLS 55328
158 KINGS ROAD K★

Open: Monday to Saturday
8.30 a.m.-6.00 p.m.

H.P.W.WM.D.A.BC.

HOLME UPON Tel: 0696 60612
SPALDING MOOR
CRAFT TOOLS AND TACKLE LTD.
HOLME INDUSTRIAL ESTATE
Open: Mon.-Fri. 9.30 a.m.-5.30 pm.
Saturday & Bank Holidays 9.30 am-4.30 pm.
H.P.W.D.T.CS.MF.A.BC.

CLECKHEATON Tel. (0274)
SKILLED CRAFTS LTD. 872861
34 BRADFORD ROAD ★

Open: 9.00 a.m.-5.00 p.m. Monday
Saturday Lunch 12.00 a.m.-1.00 p.m.
H.P.W.A.CS.WM.D.

THIRSK Tel. (0845) 22770
THE WOOD SHOP ★
TRESKE SAWMILLS LTD.
STATION WORKS
Open: Seven days a week 9.00-5.00

T.H.MF.BC.

**Use this space
for your
Summer Plans**

344

WOOD SUPPLIERS

Earn £200 per hour drying timber with your own kiln...

My seasoners need so little attention that your time could hardly be better spent than by drying your own timber. Can you afford to invest a few hundred pounds in order to guarantee your work is stable in central heating and ensure that your English hardwoods will cost half as much for many years to come.

No need to keep large untidy stacks of timber slowly drying and spoiling for years and years — these machines work from green in a few weeks and cost only a few pence per cubic foot to run.

The smallest seasoner costs less than £400 and will dry enough timber to keep several people busy or make you some money selling surplus timber. It can live outside and does not usually need a box much larger than 8' × 4' × 4'. As I am the man who developed these machines, I hope that my information, prices, references etc., are second to none.

Write for details or ring me any time for answers to your questions completely without obligation.

JOHN ARROWSMITH
74 Wilson Street, Darlington,
Co. Durham DL3 6QZ. Tel: 0325 481970

NOW AVAILABLE!

VENEERS
FROM 21p per sq. ft.

WOOD

MARQUETRY PACKS

Containing around 20 species approx 4" x 3" including exotics such as . . .
- Burrs
- Sycamore
- Rosewoods
- Walnut
- Cerejeria
- Ash

SEND TODAY
ONLY £4.75 a pack inc. VAT
+ 95p post and packing

Fast turnaround on all orders

ROBBINS LTD.
The one stop wood shop at
Merrywood Road,
Bedminster,
Bristol, BS31 1DX.

FREE Catalogues of product ranges now available: (tick as required)

Wood Turners ☐	Mouldings and Sheet Materials ☐
Cabinet Makers ☐	Joinery ☐
	Veneers and Marquetry ☐
Boat Builders ☐	

All lists include full details of support materials and supplies.
Cheque/P.O. with order.
Access/Barclaycard. Phone orders accepted.
Tel 0272 633136.
NAME _____
ADDRESS _____

COUNTY HARDWOODS OF TAUNTON

English oak, Ash and Elm, Brazilian Mahogany and all hardwoods. Competitive prices, machining service available.
Tel: (0823) 443760
Creech Mill, Creech St. Michael, Taunton. *Delivery Anywhere.*

HOMEGROWN HARDWOODS

Select your own boards from our workshop in London.
17 species of British hardwoods, kiln dried to 10-12%.
Acacia, Ash, Beech, Cedar of Lebanon, Cherry, Chestnut, Elm, Burr Elm, Lime, Oak, brown Oak, London plane, black Popular, Sycamore, Walnut, Wellingtonia, Yew.
Also some turning stuff in the round.
1-5 Chance Street,
London E1 6JT.
Tel: 01-729 5736

THE WOOD SHOP

Our Cabinetmaker and Woodturners sawmill specialises in **homegrown**, imported and exotic timbers for the small user.
We can **machine** to your cutting list and **deliver** to your home.
Open 7 days a week, 9 to 5.
Send for new brochure to Treske Sawmills, Station Works
Thirsk YO7 4NY
Tel (0845) 22770

Treske Sawmills

MACKINTOSH CRAFT WOODS

HOMEGROWN, IMPORTED, EXOTICS
AMAZIQUE TO **ZEBRANO**
ASH TO **YEW**
Sold by the Plank or Cut and Machined to your specification.
Polishes and Accessories.
Turning blocks and discs always in stock.
SAE for Price List.
Open 9-5 except Wednesdays.
(Nr. HMS Collingwood), Newgate Lane, Fareham, Hants. PO14 1AH
Tel: Fareham (0329) 221925

Hardwoods for the Craftsman

Send for a FREE CATALOGUE

Fitchett and Woollacott Ltd.
Willow Road, Lenton Lane, Nottingham NG7 2PR
Telephone. (0602) 700691. Telex 377401

OAK AND ELM

Prime oak and elm kiln dried, also other British hardwoods. Cutting and Planing Service. Large or small quantities. Table tops and work tops made to measure.
NEW HALL TIMBER, Duddleston, Ellesmere, Shropshire.
Tel: (0691) 75244

Oakridge Sawing Service

English oak, walnut, yew, elm, ash, chestnut, fruitwoods and others.
Fresh sawn, air-dried, kiln-dried.
£6.00-£30.00 per cube.
Machining service available.
Phone: 0293-84-424 (nr. Gatwick)
evenings or daytime - answerphone.

SCOTTISH HIGHLANDS: Kiln dried Ash, Beech, Oak and Chestnut in small quantities, machining service, delivery arranged. R. H. Raynor, Kilmuir, Kessock, Inverness IV1 1XS. 0463 73666.

SEASONED ANTIQUE PINES

Pitch and Yellow. Cut to your specification.

(Deliveries over reasonable distances)
Britannia Sawmills — Huddersfield
(0484) 645931/535063.

What is selected,
Wax sealed both ends,
Delivered by Securicor
EXOTIC and 4ft. long?

MINI PLANKS BY TILGEAR

SEE DISPLAY ADVERT

Berkshire Hardwoods
Seasoned British hardwoods for the woodworker and turner. Prime oak, ash, beech, chestnut, cherry, yew. Waney edge boards, bowl blanks or fully finished stock. Cutting lists quoted for:
Prices from £10 cu.ft. kiln dried.
Allan Morris, Crowthorne 772157
Steve Dooley, Crowthorne 773586

HARDWOOD blanks for turning. SAE for lists. G. W. Monk Pantllidiart W, Brynafnan, Llanafan, Aberystwyth, Dyfed, Wales.

HARD & SPECIALIST WOODS, air and kiln dried. Priced stock list. Items prepared to your cutting list. Minns, Unit 5, 7 West Way, Oxford (0865) 247840.

OAK, ASH, ELM, WALNUT etc. Fresh sawn, air dried or kiln dried. Also blanks for woodturners. Thos Harrison & Sons, Launceston, Cornwall. Tel: (056 685) 322.

To advertise ring
01-437 0699

YEW, CHERRY, WALNUT, CEDAR, quartersawn oak, lime, olive, ash, red oak. Air-dried 1"-4". Flint, The Needles, Hindon, Salisbury, Wilts. Telephone (074789) 237.

VENEERS, all types. SAE list. S. Gould (Veneers), 22 Spencer Road, N. Wembley, Middx. HA0 3SF. 01-904-7954. T/C

Classified Advertisements

All classified advertisements under £30.00 must be pre-paid: Cheques/PO made payable to A.S.P. Ltd. (WW). **Private and trade rate** *52p per word (VAT inclusive) minimum £7.80.* **Display box rates s.c.c.** *£8.60+VAT (minimum 2.5×1). All advertisements are inserted in the first available issue.* **Copy to Classified Dept. (W.W.), A.S.P. Ltd., 1 Golden Square, London W.1.** There are no re-imbursements for cancellations.

Telephone Simon Evans 01-437-0626

FOR SALE

EVENTS

THE FINEST SELECTION ON DISPLAY IN SCOTLAND!

WOODWORKING & METALWORKING MACHINERY POWER TOOLS HAND TOOLS

THE SAW CENTRE

LARGE STOCKS COMPETITIVE PRICES. PHONE AND TRY US NOW!

Eglinton Toll, Glasgow G5 9RP
Tel: 041-429-4444

38 Haymarket Edinburgh EH12 5J2
Tel: 031-337-5555

OPEN Mon - Fri 8am - 5pm Sat 9am - 1pm

WINDSOR CHAIRS
Full size bends. 50 × 1⅜ × 1⅛" in Ash £6.95.
Childs Windsor Chair bends in Ash 36 × 1⅛ × ⅞" £4.95.
All prices include p&p.
Please send cheque/P.O. with order to:
P. Stuffin, Spurn View, North End Road, Tetney, Grimby DN36 5NA.
Tel: (0472) 812576 (Afternoons)

NEW WOODCARVING CONTEST
at the Lincolnshire Show
24th & 25th June, 1987

TOP CARVING TOOL SETS FOR WINNERS

OPEN TO ALL.

FOR SCHEDULE AND ENTRY FORM SEND S.A.E. TO:
A. SISSONS
Lincolnshire Showground, Grange-de-Lings, Lincoln, LN2 2NA.

WOODCARVING tools

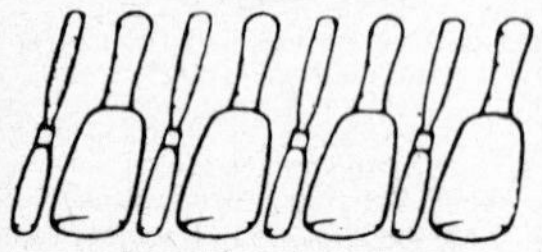

LARGEST STOCK IN EUROPE

Henry Taylor
Arkansas Bench & Slip Stones
Strops & Strop Paste
Bench Screws, Carvers' Vices

WOODTURNING tools

Complete range of Henry Taylor handled or unhandled

send 40p in stamps for illustrated catalogue
ALEC TIRANTI LTD
70 High St, Theale, Reading, Berks RG7 5AR
27 Warren Street, London W1.

DO YOU HAVE A BANDSAW?
Then you must have a bandsaw blade repair kit **£11.50** inc. P&P.
Charles Hollick Enterprises, Kittisford Glebe, Wellington, Somerset TA21 0SA.
Tel: 0823 672366

THE WHISTON CATALOGUE
Nuts, bolts, screws, washers, bar materials. In brass, alloy, steel, stainless steel, P.T.F.E., nylon, Tufnol, sheet material, electrical and mechanical items. We could go on and on! Better to send for free catalogue No. 114 and see for yourself.
K. R. Whiston Ltd., Dept. WW, New Mills, Stockport, Cheshire. Phone: 0663 42028.

QUALITY MOVEMENTS FOR QUALITY CASES
Eight Day Long case clock movements hand made of traditional design and very high quality, suitable for fitting in reproduction clock cases. These should appeal to the craftsman who requires the quality of the original Long Case movements. Dials and hands available made to your requirements. Brassware for clock cases including, capitals, escutcheons, etc. available.
Catalogue on castings + parts U.K. £1.25. Overseas £2.50.
RICHARDS OF BURTON
Woodhouse Clockworks
Swadlincote Road, Woodville
Burton-on-Trent   Tel: (0283) 219155

MULTICO chisel mortising machine, Model 'HM', 6 months old. Paid £367, accept £300. Including ½ inch chisel and auger. Used twice only. Phone 0883 844086, evenings.

WOODCARVING

SECOND-HAND carving chisels bought and sold. New Swiss carving chisels and carving sundries. Catalogue available. S.A.E. The Woodcarvers Shop, Rear 28 Painswick Road, Cheltenham, Glos. (0242) 38582.

Sale by Auction of
Lathes, Tools, woodworking machinery, sawmilling equipment, workshop contents; some 1500 cu.ft. English Hardwoods & Exotics in small lots; ivory and collector's items . . .

on Saturday, 9th May, 1987

Thos Harrison & Sons (Est. 1830) Maxworthy Cross, Launceston, Cornwall. Tel: (056685) 322

List of contents from the vendor or, Kivells, Holsworthy, Devon. Tel: (0409) 253888

CLOCKMAKERS
Extensive range of very competitively priced German quartz clock movements, (including standard quartz, pendulum, mini-pendulum, chining, striking and insertion movements). Large selection of quality dials, chapter rings, hands, bezels, clock plans and weather instruments. *Please send 25p stamps for 20 page catalogue.*
Bath Clock Company (Dept. W), 13 Welton Road, Radstock, Bath.

CONTENTS of 3 school workshops, engineering and woodworking machines and various tools. For detailed list write to: Warners Machinery Centre, Unit 10, Finedon Road, Irthlingborough, Northants.

OWING TO BEREAVEMENT for sale Coronet Major lathe with chisels £500. Ring Neath 2067 between 9 a.m. to 5.30 p.m.

BANKRUPT STOCK
Sandvik circular saw blades, tungsten tipped.
5", 5½", 6" .... **£4.00** each
6½", 8¼" .... **£6.00** each
½" to 1⅜" bore any size.
P&P £1 extra per order.
Tel: 643 0244
Hannett, 11 Lind Road, Sutton, Surrey.

BLADES
Spindle tooling, circular saw blades, dado sets, planer blades, router cutters and router accessories, machinery of particular merit, Forstener bits, mortise chisels, profile cutter blocks, radial arm saw accessories, etc.
Send £1 (refunded on first order) for your copy of our brochure.
Blades, Dept. WWM. Freepost, Petersfield, Hampshire. GU32 2BR *(no stamp required)*

TITMANS finger joint cutter perfect condition, used once £50. Tel: 0206 864881.

THUMB PLANES, polished gunmetal convex sole, centre screw adjustment 1'4" LG £14.50, 1¾" lg. £15.50 2¼" lg. £16.50. Boxed set of 3 £45. All post free U.K. Illustration on request. G.E. Scarr, 87 New Road, Brixham, Devon TQ5 8NL.

THE TOOL SHOP, BOSHAM WALK, Bosham, Chichester, Sussex. For collectors and second hand tools. Tel: 0243 572937/572475.

SECONDHAND/TRADITIONAL tools — bought & sold. Norris, Spiers, Preston, Stanley, Record, Addis, etc., and our own. List £1. Bristol Design, 14 Perry Road, Bristol. Tel: (0272) 291740.

CRAFT/ANTIQUE/ SECONDHAND TOOLS

HANDTOOLS & MACHINERY. Antique and modern. Wood and metalworking. Bought and sold. The Tool Box, Craft Centre, Umbourne Bridge, Colyton, Devon. (0297) 52868.

OLD WOODWORKING TOOLS bought, exchanged and sold. Paul Rougetel, 77 Watergate Row, Chester. Tel: 0244 — 318782.

ANTIQUE and modern woodworking tools bought and sold at Woodworkers World, 77 Shakespear Street, Derby. Tel: Derby (0332) 761779.

QUALITY TOOLS for craftsmen and collectors, order list £1. All types of woodwork tools wanted, particular paring chisels, pre-war carving tools, wooden planes. The Old Tool Store, Kirkby Fenside, East Kirkby, Spilsby, Lincs. PE23 3DD. Phone 07903 372.

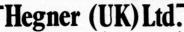

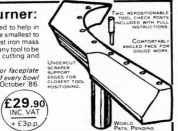

THE "DIAMOND" HEAVY-DUTY FRET SAW
One of the world's finest saws

19" Throat model.
  Type AF-19 **£235 inc. VAT**
24" Throat model.
  Type AF-24 **£295 inc. VAT**
British Made machines with
¼ HP motors
Large 18" × 18" tilt table.
Takes fret, coping &
hacksaw blades
From a 4" Max cut down to
the finest veneers.

Send large S.A.E. for illustrated brochure
**J.D. WOODWARD, Power Tool Specialists, 6 The Narrows,
Hinckley, Leics. LE10 1EH.
Tel: 0455 613432**
Trade enquiries invited.

FYLDE WOODTURNING SUPPLIES
**255 Church Street,
Blackpool FY1 4HY**

WE STOCK A FULL
RANGE OF COMPONENT
PARTS FROM WOOD-
TURNING PROJECTS,
SORBY TOOLS, LATHE
ACCESSORIES, TYME
LATHES, SAWTOOTH
BITS ETC. CALL ROUND
AND SEE OUR DISPLAY
IN OUR BASEMENT
SHOW ROOM OR S.A.E.
FOR PRICE LIST. MAIL
ORDER A PLEASURE.

Braywood Estates

Main stockists
Trend Router Cutters.
Augers. Forstner bits.
All at discount Prices.
Agents required countrywide.
Braywood Estates Ltd.,
158 Burnham Lane, Slough SL1 6LE
Tel: Burnham (06286) 5125

415v from 230v house mains to
run your 3-phase machines, the
'Maldon' unit **£66** 1½ h.p.

**Maldon Transformers
134 London Road,
Kingston-on-Thames.
Tel: 546-7534**
Access – Barclaycard

WARNER'S MACHINERY CENTRE

**Unit 10, Finedon Road,
Irthlingborough, Northants.**

**Telephone:
0933 651296-316812-651284**

For all types of New & Used Wood-
working, Engineering and Sheet
Metal Machinery. Wadkin, Multico,
Startrite, Luna, Myford, DeWalt,
Scheppach, Edwards, Colchester,
Bridgeport, Black & Decker, Lurem,
Ryobi, Trend, Elu, Ridgeway, etc.

Open 6 days a week.
Part Exchange Welcome.

Please write for a free stock list.

DeWalt Woodworking

Fantastic Savings.
DeWalt reconditioned machines
As new — Guaranteed.
**Braywood Estates Ltd.,
158 Burnham Lane, Slough
SL1 6LE. Tel: (06286) 5125**

RESTORATION

Furniture Restoration Materials

Everything you need to give your furniture
that professional restoration look. Waxes,
cleaners, french polishes, traditional
upholstery supplies and many more items.
Send sae for full price list:–
**Furniture Restoration Supplies,
42 Acacia Avenue, Hale,
Cheshire WA15 8QY. Tel: 061-928 3903.**

SITUATIONS VACANT

TWO HIGHLY skilled cabinet makers required
for work of highest quality in Organ Builders
case making shop. Wood machining
experience, highly desirable. Applicants must
be able to work from drawings with minimum
supervision. Apply to: J.W. Walker and Sons
Ltd., Wimbledon Avenue, Brandon, Suffolk.
Tel: (0842) 810296.

CABINET MAKER/JOINER must be
proficient in all aspects of trade with high
degree of skill. Mr Kay 0689 55549.

KITS & HOBBIES

"PGS" BALL BEARING PLANER UNITS

Build your own Planer using these
superb units, independent housing
to allow for thicknessing if required.
Rebate to a depth of ½". Planers up to
8". Free drawing of planer with every
enquiry. SAE to:
P. SERGENT *Precision Engineer*,
6 Gurney Close, Costessey, Norwich.
Tel: (0603) 747782 Prestel No. 603 747 782

GUITAR KITS

For under £35 you can make your own
classical guitar with our comprehensive kit. Mahogany veneered back and
ribs, solid rosewood fingerboard — a
quality product with superb tone. Compares with factory made guitars costing
many times this price. For full details
write or phone:
The Early Music Shop
28 Sunbridge Rd, Bradford, W. Yorks. BD12AE
Tel: 0274 393753

HOBBY'S ANNUAL

£1·10
P&P FREE

FREE PLAN
OF TOWN
DOLLS
HOUSE

Book-binding, pic-
tures from sand, New
plans of push along
trike, London bus,
kitchen furniture and
Tiffany clock.
New kits, new plans,
Candle making and
garden moulds. Dolls
house accessories.

**188
PAGES**
Many
in
colour

Hobby's (Dept. W) Knight's Hill Square,
LONDON SE27 0HH   01-761 4244
From WH Smith, Menzies and leading newsagents or direct

QUARTER SIZE GRANDFATHER CLOCK KIT

Traditionally styled in solid **mahogany** throughout. Deep etched,
solid brass break arch dial, with
tempus fugit. Easily assembled
from our complete D-I-Y kit. **Ideal
gift** at £19.95 + £2 p&p, or send.
Just £2.50 for full scale drawing
and all details. (Refundable on first
order).

CRAFTWOODS WALES
Gwalia Works, Dulais Road,
Portardulais, Swansea SA4 1RH
Wales.   Tel: 0792 884456

Hobbies 1987 EDITION!
**SEND 75p STAMP
POSTAGE INCLUDED (No Cheques please)**

FOR LEISURE, PLEASURE AND PROFIT!
Make Wheeled Toys, Dolls Houses, Forts, Garages,
Clocks, Musical Novelties etc. A host of spare-time
ideas on model making and fretwork. Plus catalogue
of Hobbies Plans and sets of fittings for above with
details of fretwork
outfits, machines
and Hobbies tools.
7 free plans incl.

**HOBBIES
HANDBOOK
1987**

**HOBBIES
(DEREHAM)
LIMITED**
20 ELVIN ROAD
DEREHAM
NORFOLK
NR19 2DX

PLANS

"MAKING PINE FURNITURE"

Our outstanding traditional designs now published
in a book. Includes clear step-by-step instructions,
photos and diagrams for making:
*Welsh Dressers, 2 and 3 doors; *Corner Dresser;
*Refectory Table and Benches; *Refectory style
Coffee Table, PLUS Section on *Working with Scots
Pine. Price £4.95. Also available: Guide to starting
your own moneymaking business, £2.00. NEW! Book
of 10 plans containing bedroom and kitchen items,
£5.25. Prices include postage.

L. GILMORE, 124 NORTH ROAD, BELFAST BT4 3DJ

Pine Furniture Plans

*A range of attractive traditional designs including:
Chest of Drawers, Corner Cabinet, Dressing Table,
Wardrobe, Shelf Racks, Bed etc. Complete with
construction details and cutting list.*

free list & details send s a e to:

C Rogers, 5 Derfel Cottages, London Rd,
Frodsham, WA6 7DS.

BUILD YOUR OWN SNOOKER/POOL TABLE TOP

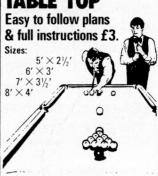

**Easy to follow plans
& full instructions £3.**

Sizes:
  5' × 2½'
  6' × 3'
  7' × 3½'
  8' × 4'

*We can supply all accessories, cloth,
rubber, balls, cues, etc.*

**Send £3, for plans to:
BILLIARD TABLE TOPS, Dept. WW8,
58 Eastwick Drive, Gt. Bookham,
Surrey KT23 3PS.
Tel: 0372 52349**
Despatched within 7 days. Mail order only.

Over 90 Woodworking Plans
FOR PLEASURE AND PROFIT
Send £1.75 for catalogue/magazine
'Planscope' and list of stockists.
Clockplans:
'Sexton Bracket Clock' — £4.15
'Vienna Regulator' — £5.75
'Grandfather Clock' — £4.90
'Grand-Daughter Clocks' — £6.00
Toyplans
'Toytrains' — £4.65
'Toy Wagons' — £6.10
'Toy Cars' — £4.65
'Rocking Horse' — £4.65
'Novelty Toys [3]' — £4.65
Furniture Plans
'Welsh Dresser' — £4.90
'Corner Shelves' — £3.90
'Spice Racks' — £3.90
'Workbenches' — £3.90
Send cheque/P.O. to:
Ashby Design Workshop,
349 Catherine Hill, Frome, Somerset BA11 1BY.

WOODWORKING PLANS

Traditional style — Cutting list, full-size
and construction details.

Bracket Clock (Georgian)	£2.25
Bureau Bookcase	£3.95
Chest of Drawers	£2.00
Corner Cabinets 35", 40" & 74"h *New*	£4.95
Corner Display Cabinet 71"h	£3.25
Cot (Drop-side)	£2.25
Four-poster Bed (Double)	£3.00
Linen Chests *New*	£4.95
Longcase Clock, Break arch dial, 81"h	£3.25
Longcase Clock, Square top, 78"	£3.25
Rocking Cradle	£2.25
Rocking Chair	£3.00
Spinning Wheel (Upright)	£4.25
Video Cabinet	£2.50
Welsh Dresser (2 & 3 door)	£3.25
Windsor Chair	£3.00

Postage is FREE. For Airmail to addresses
outside Europe, add £1.00 per plan.
Send orders, or for details to:
**CULLEN & OVENDEN(WW), P.O. BOX 76
Canterbury, Kent, CT1 2YB.
Tel: (0227) 458505**
D. Cullen (Prop.) 1 Reed Ave., Canterbury.

MAKE YOUR OWN super insulated wooden
workshop. Three sizes 8' × 12', 7' × 10' or 6' × 8'
detailed instructions on 24 sheets £10 per set
post free. Brian Ashby (WW), 21 Dane Court,
Coxheath, Maidstone, Kent ME17 4HJ. Tel:
0622 45625.

Profit from the use of Woodworking Machinery

A ONE DAY 'Wood Machining Course' to arm yourself with the necessary knowledge to enable you to:

- Make the correct choice of machine for YOUR purposes
- Use that particular machine to gain maximum efficiency, safely
- Open up new opportunities for you to profit from a small workshop

PERTH	Wm. Hume and Co.	26th March, 1987
LEEDS/BRADFORD	Rawdon Machine Sales Ltd.	9th April, 1987
SOUTHAMPTON	Burch and Hills (Machinery) Ltd.	23rd April, 1987
MIDDLESBROUGH	Cleveland Woodcraft	30th April, 1987
CARMARTHEN	D.I.Y. Supply	6th May, 1987
IPSWICH	Fox Woodworking	13th May, 1987
TEWKESBURY	Tewkesbury Saw Co.	20th May, 1987

SEVEN VENUES TO CHOOSE FROM

One must be near to you.

Telephone now for place availability and full timetable.
Rawdon Machine Sales Ltd., 6 Acorn Park, Charlestown, Shipley, West Yorks BD17 7SW.
Telephone 0274 597826

P.S. These are NOT exhibitions or demonstrations of a particular manufacturer's machinery, but a general eight-hour 'HANDS ON' instruction course showing the techniques of using machinery. You will find your time well spent.

A new profession for you in 1987
One-year course starting in September 1987

Learn to conserve and restore antique furniture with Bruce Luckhurst, qualified teacher and restorer for 25 years.
Applications are invited for this one-year course starting in September 1987. Previous cabinet making and polishing experience not essential for entry.

For prospectus and further details please send 9" × 12" s.a.e. to: Bruce Luckhurst, Little Surrenden Workshop, Bethersden, Kent TN26 3BG.

JOHN BODDY'S FINE WOOD AND TOOL STORE LTD.

Woodturning Chairmaking Pyrography Toymaking Signmaking Woodfinishing and Polishing	COURSES FOR 1987	Woodcarving Chaircaning Yarnspinning Stickmaking Gunstock Finishing Lace Bobbin Making

Held in our custom built schoolroom with specialist tutors.
Send or ring for free course/demonstration programme and course leaflets: *Jim Beadle. Tel: 09012 2370*
FINE WOOD AND TOOL STORE LTD.
Riverside Sawmills, Boroughbridge, North Yorks. YO5 9LJ.

NEW! The Carpentry & Joinery Home Study Course

Now at Home in Your Spare Time, you can learn all about carpentry and joinery. Turn an interest into a well-paid profession. Enjoy expert tuition in the comfort of your own home and learn at the pace that suits you. No previous experience needed. ICS has over 90 years experience in home study courses and is the largest Correspondence School in the world.

Find out how we can help you! Simply post or phone today for your **FREE INFORMATION PACK.**

I·C·S INTERNATIONAL CORRESPONDENCE SCHOOLS

NAME: _____
ADDRESS: _____
P. Code _____

DEPT. K1047, 312/314 HIGH ST., SUTTON, SURREY SM1 1PR or phone 01-643 9568 or 041-221 2926 (both 24 hours).

JOHN GOLDER

Woodturning courses day/evening. Personal tuition with Registered Professional Turner in fully equipped workshop.
76 Burntwood Road, Norton, Canes, Cannock, Staffs.
Telephone (0543) 79137
On the register of the Worshipful Company of Turners.
Demonstrator for Liberon Waxes.

TREVOR ROONEY

A trained and approved carver from the famous York Minster Cathedral. Offers personal and instructive WOODCARVING Courses for everyone Hourly, Half day, Full day and Two day courses available. No previous knowledge required. For further details Ring us on YORK (0904) 426767 or send S.A.E. (A4 size) to "GRAVESEND" 21 Wolfe Avenue, Heworth, York North Yorks. YO3 0SF (Carve easy plans also available)

WOODTURNING COURSES

One and two day Woodturning Courses in a fully equipped studio, under the expert tuition of:

ALLAN BATTY

Maximum of 2 students
Please write or phone for details.

Allan McNair Woodturning Studio
St. James Sq. Boroughbridge N. Yorks YO5 9AR
Telephone (09012) 4064

WOODCARVING COURSES. Weekends in Cotswolds overlooking Severn Vale, adjoining common land, max. 3 students, tuition by professional woodcarver, Peter Walwin, Fir Tree House, Rodborough, Stroud, Glos. 04536-2591.

FULL TIME COURSES
IN FINE CABINET MAKING

Two places exist for a one year course, leading to work of exhibition quality

David Savage FURNITURE MAKER

FOR PROSPECTUS APPLY TO:
DAVID SAVAGE CABINET MAKING
21·WESTCOMBE, BIDEFORD, DEVON EX39 3JQ

WEST DEAN COLLEGE
The Edward James Foundation

1 Year Course in the Restoration of Antique Furniture in conjunction with the British Antique Dealers' Association.
3 Year Apprenticeship run by West Dean College in the making of Renaissance and Baroque plucked and bowed instruments.
Commencing September 1987
Further information from:
The Principal, West Dean College, Chichester, West Sussex PO18 0QZ. Telephone 0243 63 301.

GORDON PETERS (FICW)
One and two day woodturning courses; weekends if desired.
ONLY ONE STUDENT PER COURSE.
Lunches and refreshments included.
Evening meal and overnight accommodation if required.
SAE for details to:
14 Southmead Close, Folkestone, Kent CT19 5LH.

WOODTURNING COURSES

2 Day courses, mid-week or weekend. Expert personal tuition in modern well equipped workshop.
Comfortable accommodation available in pleasant surroundings.
SAE for details to
Cliff Willetts, Gables, Frisby On The Wreake, Melton Mowbray, Leics.
Tel: Rotherby (066 475) 246

The world's finest woodturning tuition centre
The home of woodturning

- Internationally known course tutors
- Finest facilities in the country
- Most up to date workshop
- Shop with everything you may ever need
- Gallery of finished work from respected woodturners
- Superb Derbyshire setting
- First class accommodation

Send for an excellent leaflet giving complete details or telephone:-
Craft Supplies, The Mill, Millers Dale, Buxton, Derbyshire SK17 8SN.
Telephone: Tideswell (0298) 871636

350

GILDING COURSES

At our workshops in South London. 5 day courses in oil and water gilding.
For details please send SAE to:
**Frances Binnington,
65 St. John's Hill,
London SW11 1SX.
Tel: 01-223-9192**

EXPERT TUITION

Peter Hibbard's creative woodcarving, woodturning and sculpture courses.
SAE for brochure.
Old School Arts Workshop, Middleham, Leyburn, North Yorkshire DL8 4QG or Phone: Wensleydale (0969) 23056

NORFOLK WOODTURNING CRAFT CENTRE

One and two day courses in fully equipped workshop by professional instructor.
**Tony Waddilove Woodcraft,
Hill Farm Workshops,
Gt. Dunham, King's Lynn,
Norfolk. Tel: 0303 76212**

REG SLACK

Practical Woodturning courses. 1-3 days duration. Max 2 students. Professional tutor backed by 30 years full time experience. Closed Thursday, Friday. Open all other days including Sunday.
For details write or phone.
**Saracens Head Coaching House Yard, Brailsford, Derbyshire (0335) 60829.
Evenings (0332) 519563**
Also Woodturning Supplies.

WEEK-END COURSES IN BASIC CABINET MAKING

David Savage FURNITURE MAKER

PLEASE SEND S.A.E. FOR DETAILS TO:
DAVID SAVAGE CABINET MAKING
21 WESTCOMBE, BIDEFORD, DEVON EX39 3JQ

CRAFT WOODTURNING

A two-day residential woodturning course for beginners in a fully modernised 17th century Devon coaching inn. Teaching limited to two students per course, accommodation for families if required.
S.A.E. for brochure to:
Oliver Plant, Hartford Barton, Gittisham, Honiton, Devon, EX14 0AW or Phone Honiton 44155.

MERSEYSIDE'S COMPLETE WORLD OF WOODTURNING

Two day courses by Ray Jones demonstrator of Tyme lathes £25 per day, 3 students or for locals evening tuition 7-10. £3 per hour. Shop open for Tyme lathes and accessories. Sorby tools turning blanks and sundries plus gifts. For details ring 051-420-3379 or write to: **Dept. WW, The Balister, 102 High Street, Wavertree, Liverpool 15.** *Free Saturday tuition with every lathe sold.*

INDIVIDUAL TUITION for woodturning or wood machining. Also courses in furniture manufacture. Accommodation if required. SAE for details to Ernest Smith, Ty'n Rhyd, Bethel, Trefenter, Nr. Aberystwyth, Dyfed, Wales. Tel: 097-46 298.

ROY SUTTON'S COURSES

Two-day woodmachining and one-day routing or spindle moulding courses. Enjoy a day or two with a craftsman who has had over forty five years experience. Absolute beginners welcome. Special private tuition given on most aspects of machine woodworking. Machines available from Startrite and Multico. Main stockist of Elu machines and Trend cutters, all at competitive prices.
Free tuition given on any machine purchased – we won't let you struggle!
For details send SAE to:
ROY SUTTON, 14 St Georges Avenue, Herne Bay, Kent CT6 8JU
or Ring (0227) 373297 or (0227) 272136 evenings and weekends.

WOODTURNING TUITION in Southampton by a professional teacher, all equipment and materials provided, evening or weekends. Enquiries Robin Maddock 0703 433569.

TWO-DAY PRACTICAL WOOD TURNING COURSE IN RURAL LINCOLNSHIRE
Comfortable accommodation arranged if required.
S.A.E. for details to: Peter Denniss, Cabinet Maker & Turner, The White Bungalow, South Reston, Louth, Lincolnshire. LN11 8JL or Phone: Withern 50429
S.D.T. Code 0521.

WOODCARVING COURSES IN SOMERSET

Professional tuition in pleasant well-equipped studio, maximum five students, beginners especially welcomed.
6-day, 5-day and week-end courses throughout the year.
SAE to: **Zoe Gertner, Dean's Cottage, Bagley, Wedmore. Tel: 0934 712679**

WOODTURNING IN NORTH WALES

Courses, Beginner/Intermediate, weekdays, weekends ● Turning blanks in natural/exotic finishing materials. Tyme lathes & accessories.
Keith Lawrence, Old Stables Turnery, Tri Thy Centre, Coed Talon, Nr. Mold, Clwyd. Tel: 0352 771771.

Christopher Faulkner

LONG ESTABLISHED PROFESSIONAL WORKSHOP
Two places available annually for intensive one year course in fine furniture making with master craftsman.
Prospectus: Ashridge Workshops, Tigley, Nr. Totnes, S. Devon, TQ9 6EW
Tel: (0803) 862861

MOTOR POWERED
FRETSAW KITS

All Components for Home Construction. Full 12" Throat. Uses Standard Blades. Free sanding hub. **Kit only £30.25** inc. P&P (Standard kit requires 1400-1500rpm motor) Suitable ex-Equipment **Motor – £12-25** (Kit excluding base mounting board).
S.A.E. or Phone 0242 — 62252
KIT PROJECTS
Dept. W, The Workshop, Gt. Washbourne, Nr. Tewkesbury, Glos. GL20 7AR.

START AT THE TOP, TAKE A WOODTURNING COURSE IN THE HIGHLANDS OF SCOTLAND WITH

Michael O'Donnell WOODTURNER
Adventure into Woodturning, 5 days
Turning 'Green' Wood, 5 days
Instructor Training Courses
Other courses from 2 days to 4 weeks arranged to suit individual requirements.
**Phone 084 785 605 or write for the 1987 programme
The Croft, Brough, Thurso, Caithness, Scotland KW14 8YE.**

MIDLANDS SCHOOL OF FRENCH POLISHING

LEARN THE TRADE
5 days or longer courses.
SAE to Mr. A. V. Fry DLC, LCG, M CollP
18A Mansfield Road, Eastwood, Notts.
(0773) 715911 after 5pm

MID-NORFOLK woodturning courses by professional woodturner instructors in fully equipped workshop.
Norfolk Woodturning Centre, Unit A, Hill Farm Workshops, Great Dunham, King's Lynn. Tel: 07605 674

STEPHEN SMITH

Woodturning tools, finishing materials, clock movements, saltmills, peppermills, coffee grinders, barometers, circular tiles & clock faces, cheese domes, sealers & polishes.
MAIL ORDER SERVICE.
We also stock a small selection of English Hardwoods.
Shop Open: 9.30-5.30pm Mon.-Sat.
Stephen Smith, Shipon Turnery, Eccleston Street, Failsworth, Manchester M35 9PP. Tel: 061-682 3613 till 9 p.m. 061-6818671 (Day)

TUDORCRAFT WOODTURNERS SUPPLIES

Junghans clock movements. 20 different hands to choose from. Reverse and chiming clock movements, barometers, weatherstations, jewellery box lids with embroidered inserts. New designs in ceramic tiles and clock faces. Superb new range of copper and brass ware. Bezels, polished, candle lamps and glass shades etc. Please send 50p for new catalogue to:
**TUDORCRAFT
49 Moor Hall Drive, Four Oaks, Sutton Coldfield, West Midlands B75 6LN.
Tel: 021 308 1193**

Eric Tomkinson Woodturner

Lathes, Bandsaws, Grinders, Woodturning tools & chucks, screw boxes, peppermills, saltmills, coffee grinders, barometers, lighters, hourglasses, quartz clock movements, circular tiles & clock faces, cheese domes, sealers & polishes, fast and efficient mail order service + competitive prices. S.A.E. for catalogue.
Shop Open: 9-5 Mon.-Sat.

ERIC TOMKINSON, 86 Stockport Road, Cheadle, Cheshire SK8 2AT. Tel: 061-491-1726.

NEW WOODWORKERS' SMOCK with SAFETY FEATURES
● Instantly adjustable collar to keep out dust and chippings.
● Top-fastening, 'pinch close' cuffs for maximum safety with machinery.
● Large, **rear** hip pockets to avoid collecting machine waste.
● 'Clean', uncluttered front with no flaps etc. to snag on work projections.
● Close weave, hard wearing **cotton** drill keeps dirt out but lets you breathe.
● Available in BROWN, NAVY or D. GREEN.

CHEST	38"	40-42"	44"	46"
PRICE	£13.95	£14.25	£14.60	£14.95
POST & PACKING (ALL SIZES) £1.25				

P. LOVELL (WORKWEAR)
3, HEOL ESGYN, CYNCOED, CARDIFF . CF2 6JT
TEL: (0222) 753014

Ring 01-437 0699 to advertise in the market leader.

CONTENTS

Woodworker

design . . . craft . . . and the love of wood

May 1987
Vol. 91
No. 5

FEATURES

More pages . . . more colour . . . more value

PROJECTS

REGULARS

● **On the cover,** get inside Peter Stocken's head on p376; **above,** plans for this beautiful chair are on p404 (cover photo Ed Davis)

Editor Aidan Walker
Deputy editor John Hemsley
Editorial assistant Kerry Fowler
Advertisement manager Trevor Pryer
Advertisement production Laura Champion
Graphics Jeff Hamblin
Technical illustrator Peter Holland
Guild of Woodworkers John Hemsley, Kerry Fowler

Unfortunately we cannot accept responsibility for loss of or damage to unsolicited material. We reserve the right to refuse or suspend advertisements, and regret we cannot guarantee the bone fides of advertisers. **Published every third Friday**

Editorial, advertisements and Guild of Woodworkers
1 Golden Square, London W1R 3AB, telephone 01-437 0626

ABC
UK circulation
Jan-Dec 86
32,849

Back issues and subscriptions Infonet Ltd, 10-13 Times House, 179 Marlowes, Hemel Hempstead, Herts HP1 1BB; telephone Hemel Hempstead (0442) 48434

Subscriptions per year UK £16.90; overseas outside USA (accelerated surface post) £21.00, USA (accelerated surface post) $28, airmail £48

UK trade SM Distribution Ltd, 16-18 Trinity Gardens, London SW9 8DX; telephone 01-274 8611

North American trade Bill Dean Books Ltd, 151-49 7th Avenue, PO Box 69, Whitestone, New York 11357; tel. 1-718-767-6632

Printed by Chase Web, Plymouth
Mono origination Multiform Photosetting Ltd, Cardiff
Colour origination Derek Croxson Ltd, Chesham, Bucks
© Argus Specialist Publications Ltd 1987
ISSN 0043 776X

Argus Specialist Publications Ltd

1 Golden Square, London W1R 3AB; 01-437 0626

This month

From these workshops — Martyn's of Cheltenham — came decorative carving for the world's liners, public buildings and the Speaker's Chair. (From BBC Radio 4 programme 'The Best'.)

Student showcases

Students from 26 colleges are entering the 1987 London International Furniture Show College Trophy (26 April-4 May, Earls Court). Judging criteria include innovation, visual impact, craftsmanship and technical understanding of materials and ergonomics.

'The largest degree show in Britain' is being held at the Business Design Centre, London, 21-23 July. A new Design Council show, 'Graduate Designers for Industry', will have up to 50 colleges showing, while at the same venue will be the long-established House & Garden/IDDA Decorex Young Designers of the Year exhibition.

32,849!

Well, if we don't blow our own trumpet, who will? **Woodworker's** audited UK circulation in 1986 shows a **17% rise** over 1985 of 4,798 copies a month — from 28,051 to 32,849. Our overall circulation is **up by 16%** to 36,880, from 31,711 in 1985. In the UK, that puts us more than 3,900 copies a month ahead of our nearest competitor. Thanks to you all, especially new readers for taking us on — stay with us, there's more to come!

Cherry veneers on MDF and solid wood drawers; the 'Sweet L.A.' desk by Parnham-trained Philip St Pier, recently selected by the Design Council.

Furniture maker's first

Moves have been made to form Britain's first National Association of Furniture Makers to serve those in the small-batch and hand-made furniture business.

A 10-strong council was formed on 4 March from the potential members (Crafts Council Index-listed, IDF and independents) who attended the third meeting to get the association off the ground. The Crafts Council came up with the idea in early 1986, but the impetus was left up to the volunteer working-party of three who will now be the association's chairman, secretary and treasurer respectively: Chris Simpson (Rycotewood's head of fine craftsmanship and design), Andy Varah and Lucinda Leech (both prominent furniture maker/designers).

By necessity, furniture makers work in isolation, and the general consensus was that an association would be a good breeding ground to develop technology, share information and contacts and provide group benefits in the form of discounts, co-operation from existing trade and research organisations and insurance packages.

The provisional annual membership fee was set at £100 but eligibility (yet to be decided) has obvious problems; open-to-all could invite 'sharks and cowboys' to undermine integrity, but a proposal for selected membership raised cries of 'elitism' — a tendency that needs checking.

Cert. WW?

The Institute of Carpenters is trying to introduce a nationally recognised school certificate in woodwork. The initiative is in response to schools moving away from teaching basic craft skills, with the integration of Craft Design and Technology into the new GCSE examinations.

The Institute, which has been running examinations for craftsmen since it started in 1890, now has more than 3000 members in 17 regional sections. Many of its members are full-time teachers in schools of building, technical colleges and MSC training schools.

Recently the Institute became aware that the introduction of CDT might deny some youngsters the chance to exercise their skills in woodwork. A simple examination of basic skills and knowledge was devised by Ron Parker, secretary of the Institute's East Anglian section, combining a 90 minute theory paper, a three-hour practical test and continuous assessment.

About 4000 schools and colleges were mailed about the proposed examination, and 500 students enrolled from schools, colleges and training centres for the 1985-86 course; the results published last May showed 80% qualified, 11% with distinction, and 50% with a credit grading.
● The Institute of Carpenters, 45 Sheen Lane, London SW148AB.

Diary

Guild courses are shown by an asterisk (*) for further details see Guild pages

April
26-4 May **London International Furniture Show**, Earls Court, London (26-30 trade only)

May
1-30 Sept. **Viking Ships Exhibition**, St Saviour's Archaeological Resource Centre, York; bookings, Viking Ships/CRM Ltd, United House, Picadilly, York YO1 1PQ, (0904) 643211
2-4 **Weald of Kent Craft Show**, Penshurst Place, contact (04252) 72511
7-8 **French Polishing** Charles Cliffe*
9 **Design and Workshop Drawing** Bob Grant*
10-14 **Interior Context**, Olympia 2, Earls Court, London
17 **Tools of the Trade**, Weald and Downland Open Air Museum, Singleton, Chichester, Sussex (024363) 348
22-26 **INTERZUM** International Furniture Trade Fair, Cologne
23-26 **Wessex Craft Show**, Wilton House, contact (04252) 72511
23-7 June **Oxford Artweek '87**, contact (0865) 722184
26-29 **Country Chairmaking** Jack Hill*
27-2 June **LIGNA** International Trade Fair for Wood Machinery, Hanover

June
5-14 **Fine Art and Antiques Fair 1987**, Olympia, Earls Court, London
13 **Routing** Roy Sutton*
16-22 **Shrewsbury College Furniture Exhibition**, contact (0743) 231544
29-3 July **London College of Furniture Summer Show** 41 Commercial Rd, London E1 1LA, 01-247 1953

July
2-3 **Rudiments of Restoration** Barry Honeyborne*
18-19 **French Polishing** Ian Hosker*

Shoptalk

Woodturning — from Craft to Art

More big names lined up for the seminar (14-16 Aug) at Loughborough College of Art & Design include Albert LeCoff (USA) and Stephen Marchant (UK). LeCoff is one of the best-known names in American woodturning, founder/director of The Woodturning Centre, Philadelphia, and curator of The International Turned Object Show 1988 which will tour worldwide. Stephen Marchant, a highly versatile turner who works mainly in interior design, will demonstrate spindle turning.

Carving contest

An open woodcarving competition is being held at the Lincolnshire Show, 24-25 June, with three prizes from **Ashley Iles**. Details from Lincolnshire Agricultural Society, Lincolnshire Showground, Grange-de-Lings, Lincoln LN2 2NA.

Queen Victoria

Queen Victoria has been cured of wet rot in her right arm . . . and other parts of her anatomy. The 128-year old 10ft 6in solid yellow pine ship's figurehead was restored by the specialist firm Herbert Read of Topsham, Exeter. A thick layer of weather-proofing fibreglass had split, letting in moisture; the restorers took off 20-30 layers of paint, made good the rotting wood and re-painted her before she went back to the Royal Naval Engineering College, Plymouth.

New Forestor 'Baby' **bandmill** weighs 165lbs but saws 23in logs. The thin blade (0.032in) wastes less wood; it converts into a vertical bandsaw. £2800+VAT.
● Forestor, 2 Bloswood Lane, Whitchurch, Hants, (025682) 2280

The Japanese-style 'impulse hardened' teeth on Bridgedale's 'Turbocut' Professional **Saw** looked good. Here, we thought, was a neat little tool promising an excellent finish and an easy action. The blurb certainly showed confidence . . . 'DIY Man's' dream . . . unbelievably smooth surface . . .' So we put it to work.

The 6in blade is about 1¼in deep at its deepest; the teeth have no set, but are laid in two rows across the thickness, and have the characteristic Japanese shape, which on the back-pull does indeed produce an unbelievably smooth cut. But the Turbocut just doesn't live up to its promise. Try as we might, we couldn't get it to work smoothly — in hard or softwoods; we think it's because the blade is thick — more than 1mm — and not deep enough to have its own strength. The way it's held into the handle is frankly a joke. It folds away into a cheap plastic handle; a cheap snap-catch holds it in the open position. Nothing to hold it closed.

Careful and sensitive pull-back strokes could get the blade to work half decently, but it seems the undoubtedly advanced impulse hardening metal technology isn't matched by a solid understanding of blade design. Useful in an overall pocket if you're up a ladder hacking away at ceilings, or for pruning; but at £14.95, hardly the buy of the month. Their £7.95 impulse-hardened **scissors**, on the other hand, are a real marvel.
● Bridgedale, Samuel St, Leicester LE1 1RU, (0533) 27161.

Courses

Jeremy Williams is offering five day courses in Creative woodcarving in Cornwall at £155, maximum three students; the course excludes decorative carving of furniture.
● Jeremy Williams, Sycamore Cottage, Traboe, St Martin, Helston, Cornwall TR12 6EA.

Open days

Lancashire readers may like to visit Horological Solvents' open weekend on 9-10 May to look at and buy books, clockmakers' tools, clock parts, brassware, woodcarving and turning tools, cleaning fluids and wood finishing products.
● Horological Solvents, Proctor St, Bury, Lancs.

John Boddy's at Boroughbridge, North Yorks, are expanding their range of short courses and free demonstrations. In their purpose-built woodturning centre they offer woodcarving, chairmaking, gun stock finishing, lace-bobbin making, wood finishing and polishing, chair caning, signmaking and pyrography, both as free demonstrations and as courses. Also demos of tool sharpening and care, and you can see the Coronet lathe and Multistar in action. Courses are around £35+VAT per day, full details of programme from John Boddy's.
● Jim Beadle, Fine Wood & Tool Store, Riverside Sawmills, Boroughbridge, North Yorks YO59LJ.

PRODUCT DIGEST

The DeWalt DW1201 Fold-away Powershop **Radial Arm Saw** is currently on special offer at £220+VAT.

A new **circuit breaker** that plugs into any standard 13amp socket protects you against electrocution when using powered hand tools; by Superswitch, it's available from shops at £24.95 inc. VAT.

Want to know how to use your **router**? Elu have produced a **video**, being sold through service centres and Elu distributors at £12.70+VAT.

Interested in making a **Norris-type plane**? Ralph Fellows, who won a gold award in the 1984 Woodworker Show, still has drawings for his winning design, price £3.50 plus large sae.

Don't get confused, but Black & Decker have just launched a new range of **power tools** aimed at tradesmen and self-employed professionals. Called Proline, the range is nothing to do with the 'Professional' range of products. B&D say the seven tools have been designed 'to avoid the complications of expensive professional tools but to give the high performance and long-term durability required in a demanding environment'. In other words, tough tools, easy to maintain but with no frills. The PL30 Jigsaw costs £80, PL10⅜in hammer drill £65, PL50 palm grip sander £56, and the PL40 7¼in circular saw £87.50, all prices including VAT.
● Circuit breaker, Superswitch, Houldsworth St, Reddish, Stockport, Cheshire SK5 6BZ; Ralph Fellows, Ellen Vale, 67 Colwall End Rd, The Straits, Dudley, West Midlands DY3 3EJ; DeWalt, Elu and Black & Decker all at Westpoint, The Grove, Slough, Berks SL1 1QQ.

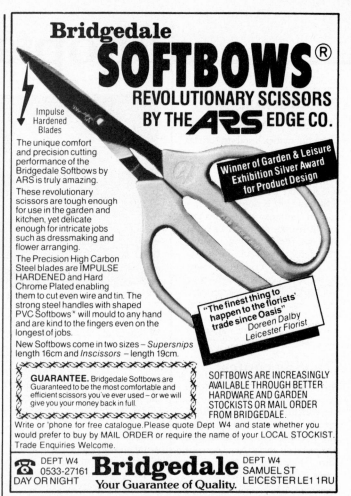

WOODWORKER SHO

BRISTOL
15-17 May
Bristol Exhibition Centre, Canon's Rd
LONDON
22-25
October
Alexandra Pavilion, London N22

ALL ENQUIRIES TO THE ORGANISERS — ARGUS SPECIALIST EXHIBITIONS WOLSEY HOUSE, WOLSEY RD HEMEL HEMPSTEAD, HERTS HP2 4SS (0442) 41221

It's think-ahead time for entering your work to the country's only truly national display of woodworking craft in all its forms. Junior, senior, professional or amateur — everyone can enter, everyone can display. Write today for your entry forms to the address above!

● *See Trevor Rooney, whose carved work adorns York Minster, demonstrating at Bristol*

These are the classes in which you can enter your work:

WA **Cabinetmaking** — including our new **PRE-PROFESSIONAL AWARD**
WB **Woodcarving**
WC **Woodturning**
WD **Musical instruments**
WE **Marquetry and inlay**
WF **Toys and miniatures**
WG **Model horse-drawn vehicles**
WH **Juniors**
WJ **Clocks**
WK **Carpentry and joinery**
WL **Young professionals**

All classes have sub-sections; your work is bound to fit in somewhere. Get more details from the organisers.

THE AWARDS

This year we introduce a new judging system, based on standards rather than a restricting 'first, second, third' approach. There will still be only one gold medal in each class, but there are more silvers and bronzes to be won — so you have a better chance.

And for the **LONDON SHOW, 22-25 OCTOBER**, we have some very, very special sponsored prizes lined up:

CABINETMAKING

WOODWORKER and AEG Woodworking proudly announce the **PRE-PROFESSIONAL AWARD** for furniture students in their final year. Submit your best final-year piece — you may win an **AEG MAXI 26 Universal** woodworking machine, worth over £1700 retail! Plus all the **publicity** you can handle to trade and consumer publications — what a set-up for a brilliant career. Jointly sponsored by AEG, WOODWORKER magazine and Argus Specialist Exhibitions.

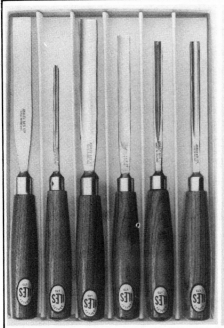
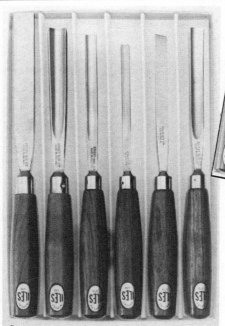

WOODCARVING

The **Ashley Iles** Carving Awards. The famous name in British carving tools is giving away three unique sets of specially selected, hand forged and polished tools, based on their Westminster (18-pc), Canterbury (12-pc) and York (6-pc) sets. Total value of these mouthwatering prizes — more than £230!

WOODTURNING

More enticements yet for the lucky woodturners; **Robert Sorby Ltd** and **Craft Supplies** are generously donating **£600 worth of tools and equipment** in the two classes — spindle work and faceplate work. For the spindle turners, there is **£100 worth of Sorby HSS tools** as a first prize, two more prizes of £50 worth of tools for another winner and runner-up, and another £50 worth of runner-up prizes. The new Sorby **oval skew chisel** will feature prominently among the goodies! Plus for the faceplate turners, **Craft Supplies Ltd** are putting up a total of **£350 worth** of desirable equipment; **£100 worth of precision combination chuck and accessories** for the outright winner, three more sets of £50 worth of chucking equipment and accessories, and a further £100 worth of tools for the best amongst the other entries. Watch out for the new **Sorby ring gouge** — there's a number to be won!

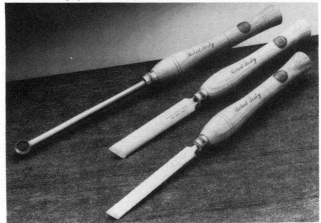
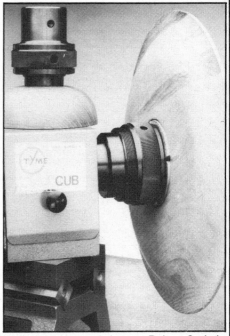

●*Left, ring gouge, oval skews – Robert Sorby's finest; above, Craft Supplies' excellent combination and collet chucks*

WOOD FINISHING

And of course, we have a set of prizes that everyone, no matter what their chosen skill, can have a crack at. **Henry Flack**, makers of Britain's most popular finishing wax, **Briwax**, are putting up a total of **£300 worth of Henry Flack** products for the best-finished items in the show. That's at trade prices — and they do a whole range, so it's not only wax we're talking about. Worth all the elbow grease, indeed!

There are **WOODWORKER Challenge Cups** in most of the classes; there's the **Robbins Rose Bowl** for Cabinetmaking donated by Robbins of Bristol, there's the **World of Wood Cup** for marquetarians and inlay specialists, donated by the **Art Veneers Company** of Mildenhall; toymakers can win the **Richard Blizzard Cup**, miniaturists can walk away with the **Stuart King Award**; model horse-drawn vehicle makers, the **John Thompson Trophy** is for you, and of course **Roger's**

the specialist tool supplier is offering the **Juniors** and the **Young Professionals** yet more desirable tools; **£100 worth of vouchers** for tools for the Juniors, and a set of **10 Japanese chisels** to the Young Professionals. And then, for those who practise the fine art of Stickmaking and growing, the **Theo Fossel Trophy** could be yours to keep.

With all that to be won, how could you stay away? Don't delay — write or phone for your entry form today!

AXMINSTER POWER TOOL CENTRE

WOODTURNING LATHES
OUR PRICE INC. VAT

TYME STUDENT 10" swing 30" centres (With accessory voucher £20) **£219**
CORONET HOBBY 10" swing 39" centres 1MT ½HP 3 speed **£179**
CORONET No. 1 12" swing 3 Speed 24" ctrs ..... **£218** 36" ctrs ..... **£239** 48" ctrs **£295**
CORONET No. 1 22" Bowl Rest Assbly .. **£39** 48" Bed Extension for existing 24" lathe .. **£59**
ELU DB180 39" centres 15" swing 1½HP motor 3 speed **£299**
TYME CUB 30" centres (With accessory voucher £30) **£296**
TYME AVON 36" centres (With accessory voucher £45) **£419**
MYFORD ML8B 36" centres 9" Rear turning .... **£432** ML8C 42" centres **£467**
KITY 663 3 Speed Lathe 1.0M Centres .... **£554** 1.5M Centres **£576**
KITY 664 Var. Spd. Lathe 1.0M Centres .... **£649** 1.5M Centres **£669**
MINIMAX Centre lathes T90 ..... **£462** T100 ..... **£534** T120 ..... **£564** Legs **£75**
MINIMAX COPIERS for above lathes CT90 ..... **£519** CT100 ..... **£551** CT120 ..... **£599**
LUNA SPKA 900 COPIER medium duty copier for all lathes **£256**
CORONET CMB600 33" Centres 23" bowl cap .... **£589** Bowl rest **£49.95**
HARRISON GRADUATE 30" Centres ... **£1175** 42" Centres ... **£1232** Shortbed ... **£1037**

WOODTURNING FITMENTS CHISELS & ACCESSORIES (State m/c)

Coronet collet chuck sets (state m/c) **£69**
Coronet collet bodies .... only **£29**
Collets ⅝", ¾", 1" .... each **£12**
Expanding Jaws 3", 2", 1" .... each **£27**
Spigots ⅝", ¾", 1" .... each **£14**
Speedaneez polish std/wht **£5**
Coronet planer blades 4½" .. **£20** 7" .. **£23**
Multistar Duplex Chuck 32mm Jaws **£65**
Multistar Duplex Chuck 45mm Jaws **£66**
Multistar Duplex Chuck 75mm Jaws **£68**
Screwchuck Set (for above) **£22**
Faceplate Ring 60mm **£7**
Pinchucks (State size) **£8**
Revolving centres 1MT or 2MT **£18**
0-½" Drill chuck 1MT or 2MT **£15**
Craft supplies chuck **£58**
Long hole boring kit 5/16" **£32**
2½" Woodscrew chuck **£22**
Sorby sizing tool **£8**
Carnuba wax turning stick **£1.80**
Dovetail Jaws for 4 Jaw Chuck ... **£49.95**
Sorby Super Skew ¾" **£11.00**
Sorby Super Skew 1" **£13.00**
Sorby ¾" HSS Roughing Gouge ... **£18.00**
Sorby Scraper (with 3 Heads) **£24.00**
Janik Pyrographer **£48.00**

WOODTURNERS "AT LAST PERFECTION"

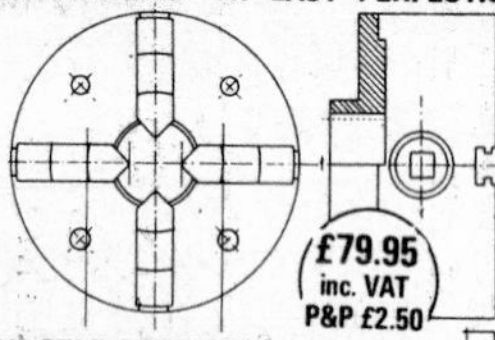

(£79.95 inc. VAT P&P £2.50)

4 JAW SELF CENTERING CHUCK
AVAILABLE IN THREAD SIZES FOR MOST LATHES.
SPECIFICATION: GRIPPING CAPACITY ⅛"-4" DIAMETER 4" WEIGHT 2KG. SUPPLIED READY THREADED (LH OR RH) WITH TWO SETS OF PRECISION JAWS (INTERNAL & EXTERNAL).
5" 4 Jaw S/C **£99.95**
4" 3 Jaw S/C **£69.95**

HENRY TAYLOR HSS CHISELS
(P&P £1.20 per order)

GOUGES		PARTING TOOLS	
HS1 Superflute	£26	HS2 Fluted	£17
HS3 ¾" D/Fte	£16	HS11 ¼" Std.	£6
HS4 1½" D/Fte	£27	HS12 ⅜" Std.	£8
HS5 ¼" Spindle	£6	HS13 ¾" × ½"	£11
HS6 ⅜" Spindle	£8	HS33 Diamond	£15
HS7 ½" Spindle	£11	HS32 ½" × ⅛"	£7
CHISELS		**SCRAPERS**	
HS8 ½" Skew	£8	HS26 ½" Rnd	£8
HS21 ¾" Skew	£9	HS38 ¾" Rnd	£9
HS22 1" Skew	£10	HS27 1" Rnd	£11
HS9 1¼" Skew	£16	HS28 ½" Sq	£8
HS23 ½" Square	£8	HS29 ¾" Sq.	£8
HS24 ¾" Sqre	£9	HS30 1" Sq.	£10
HS25 1" Sqre	£11	HS15 HD Round	£22
HS10 1¼" Sqre	£17	HS16 HD Domed	£22

ALL PRICES INCLUDE HANDLES.

CORONET HSS CHISELS IN STOCK.

★★★ CORONET WOODTURNING AIDS & FITMENTS ★★★

10% off all Coronet Woodturning Aids & Fitments (P&P £1.20/order)
Many Fitments Available for All Makes of Other Machines
20% off all Coronet Woodturning Chisels (P&P £1.20/order)
NB. Discounts do not apply to the above already discounted prices.
THE COUNTRY'S ONLY IN DEPTH STOCKIST OF CORONET MACHINES, FITMENTS AND SPARES.

★★★★★★★★★★★★★★★★★★★★★★★★★★★★★★

BANDSAWS (Send for Free Bandsaw Blade List)

BURGESS BK111+ 45° 3" cut jigsaw fretsaw .... (inc. P&P) **£115**
7" Sanding attachment for Burgess ..... **£23.50** Mitre fence ..... **£8.50** Rip fence **£7.50**
DeWALT DW100 45° tilt 4" cut c/w sanding table .... (P&P £2.50) **£149**
DeWALT 6" cut 14" throat 45° DW3401 .... **£273** DW3501 .... **£289**
MINIMAX P32 45° tilt 6" cut 14" throat cast iron table **£367**
Mitre fences for above .... **£14** Stands for above **£29**
KITY 613 8" cut Large table 1½HP Very Sturdy .... **Special Price**
MINIMAX S45 45° tilt 10" cut 17" throat **£676**

★★★ **SPECIAL OFFERS ON STARTRITE 301 — 351 — 352** ★★★
5 FREE BLADES WITH EACH MACHINE

STARTRITE 301B 45° Tilt 6" cut Bench Mtg. **£329**
STARTRITE 351 45° tilt 8" cut c/w rip & mitre fence floor standing **£495**
STARTRITE 352 45° tilt 10" cut c/w rip & mitre fence floor standing **£699**
STARTRITE 502 14" cut 20" throat 1PH .... **£1204** 3PH **£1111**
METAL BLADE GUIDES for DeWalt DW100, 1310, 3401, 3501, Luna & Minimax .. **£5.20**

RADIAL SAWS

EUMENIA 9" blade 1¾HP 15" C/cut .... **£339** 24" C/cut **£399**
EUMENIA Stand .... **£112** Router Bracket .... **£76** Wobble Washers **£14.50**
DeWALT 1201 Portable 10" TCT Folding Radial Saw 1½ HP **£295**
DeWALT DW1251 10" TCT blade 1½ HP 16" C/cut .... **£422** Stand **£25**
DeWALT DW1501 10" TCT blade 1½ HP 18" C/cut **£496**
DeWALT DW1751 10" TCT blade 1½ HP 24" C/cut **£571**
DeWALT DW8001 12" TCT blade 2HP 18" C/cut floor standing **£616**
DeWALT DW8101 12" TCT blade 2HP 24" C/cut floor standing **£703**
DeWALT DW1600S 14" TCT blade 24" C/cut 1PH .... **£993** 3PH **£956**

PORTABLE AND WORKSHOP SAWBENCHES

MAKITA 2708 8" Portable tilt arbor bench saw **£229**
ELEKTRA 12" Sawbench floor standing TCT blade 3HP **£189**
SCHEPPACH TKU 12" Sawbench floor standing TCT blade 3HP **£229**
Elektra & Scheppach Sliding Table .... **£90** Panel Cutting Extension **£75**
ELU TGS Sawbench/Mitre Saws c/w TCT blade TGS 172 .... **£496** TGS 171 .... **£399**
Sliding table for TGS .... **£98** Aluminium cutting kit **£60**
KITY 618 10" tilt arbor sawbench floor standing .... **SPECIAL PRICE**
MULTICO NTA300 3HP 12" .... **£1099** Sliding table 48" cap. **£316**
WADKIN AGS250/300 3HP 1PH .. **£1299** Sliding table 35" cap. **£496**
STARTRITE Scoring Saw 1PH .... **£1377** Sliding table 48" cap. **£327**
LUNA L18 12" 3HP 1PH .... **£950** Sliding table 24" cap. **£170**

ROLLER SUPPORT STANDS (P&P £3.00)

LUNA 10" support roller adjustable height sturdy construction **£28**
LUNA 16" combined roller support adjustable height **£39**

PREMIUM QUALITY INDUSTRIAL SAWBLADES
THE BEST IN QUALITY T.C.T. SAWBLADES LEITZ & SPEAR & JACKSON

BLADE DIAMETER	6"				7"-7¼"				8"				9"-9¼"			
No. OF TEETH	16	24	36	48	18	30	42	56	20	36	48	64	24	40	54	72
SPEARTIP	£16	£17	£20	£26	£16	£20	£23	£26	£20	£26	£28	£32	£24	£26	£29	£36
LEITZ	—	—	—	—	—	—	—	—	—	£37	£43	£49	—	£41	£51	—

BLADE DIAMETER	10"				12"				14"				16"			
No. OF TEETH	24	40	60	80	32	48	72	96	36	60	84	108	28	36	60	96
SPEARTIP	£23	£26	£35	£38	£28	£36	£42	£48	£34	£42	£50	£57	£39	£44	£54	£63
LEITZ	£39	£43	£51	£59	£42	£52	£61	£70	£48	£57	£70	£81	£54	£59	£70	£92

PLEASE STATE BORE SIZE WHEN ORDERING.

MORTICING MACHINES
OUR PRICE INC. VAT

SMITHS BCM 75 bench morticer c/w lateral table ¾" cap. **£399**
SMITHS CM75 floor standing morticer dual table movement ¾" cap **£499**
MULTICO HM bench morticer ⅝" capacity precision morticer **£356**
MULTICO HMT bench morticer dual table movement **£499**
MULTICO M floor standing 1" capacity dual table movement 1PH **£625**
WADKIN EDA-2 floor standing 1" capacity dual table **£626**
RYOBI portable chain morticer .... **£365** Portable chisel morticer **£395**
WOLF Drill mortice stand C/W ½" chisel & sharpener **£135**
RIDGEWAY mortice/drill stand (requires ½" power drill) **£165**

MORTICE CHISELS & BITS

JAPANESE ¼" ..... **£16** ⅜" ..... **£17** ½" ..... **£20** ⅝" ..... **£25** ¾" ..... **£37** 1" **£45**
8mm ..... **£21** 10mm ..... **£24** 12mm ..... **£25** 16mm ..... **£29** 20mm **£44**
RIDGEWAY ¼" ..... **£19** ⅜" ..... **£23** ½" ..... **£24** ⅝" ..... **£35** ¾" ..... **£37** 1" **£45**
6mm .. **£21** 8mm .. **£22** 10mm .. **£25** 12mm .. **£26** 16mm .. **£31** 20mm .. **£46**
CHISEL BITS ONLY ¼" ..... **£6** ⅜" ..... **£7** ½" ..... **£8** ⅝" ..... **£10** ¾" ..... **£14** 1" **£18**
MORTICE CHISEL SHARPENING SETS set 1 (¼"-½") .... **£23** Set 2 (⅜"-¾") **£28**

DUST EXTRACTORS

LUNA SPSS400 460m/hr portable suitable for low volume waste **£215**
LUNA W178 975m/hr excellent general purpose extractor c/w hose **£324**
LUNA NF243 1500m/hr mobile 5" hose ideal for high volume waste **£429**
LUNA NF259 2000m/hr heavy duty suitable for up to 3 machines **£599**
LUNA 4" × 3m hose ..... **£18** 5" × 4m hose ..... **£36** LUNA dust bags (per 10) **£3**
MULTICO DEA 960m/hr mobile extractor 4" hose **£335**
DeWALT DW60 500m/hr 5" hose .... **£265** ELEKTRA 1000m/hr 4" hose **£199**
STARTRITE CYCLAIR 55 960m/hr 4" .... **£399** CYCLAIR 75 1800m/hr 6" **£499**

MITRE CUTTERS & MITRE SAWS

ELU PS174 8" Portable mitre crosscut saw 10" crosscut **£298**
DeWALT DW250 Portable mitre saw 1¼HP 10" Blade **£207**
HITACHI CF10A 10" Portable precision mitre saw **£259**
ORTEGUILLE MITRE CUTTERS ORC55 ..... **£238** ORC80 ..... **£299** ORC100 ..... **£439**
LION MITRE TRIMMER Excellent for clean cuts and mitres **£249**
NOBEX 202 PRO Hand Mitre saw .... **£72.95** NOBEX 303 .... **£44** (P&P £2.50)
NOBEX 202 Replacement Blades 12T, 18T or 24T .... **£4.30** each

PLANER THICKNESSERS

DeWALT DW1151 10" × 6" 2HP 2 speed power feed .... **SPECIAL PRICE**
Stand for DW1150 .... **£30** Slot Morticer .... **£69.95** HSS knives **£18.90**
ELECKTRA 10" × 6" floor standing power feed **£490**
SCHEPPACH HMO SOLO 10" × 6" 2HP floor standing Adjustable fence **£490**
STARTRITE PT260 10" × 7" floor standing ⅝" rebate capacity **£834**
STARTRITE SD310 12" × 9" 3 cutter block 1PH .... **£1299** 3PH **£1260**
LUNA 3HP Planers 10" × 9" .... **£1399** 12" × 9" .... **£1499** 16" × 9" **£2299**
MULTICO NS300 surfacer 3 cutter block 2HP 1PH .... **£1388** 3PH **£1271**
MULTICO THA300 12" × 10" thicknesser only 1PH .... **£1399** 3PH **£1299**
MULTICO CPT 12" × 8" Combined planer/thicknesser ¾" rebate 1PH . **£1749** 3PH . **£1649**
WADKIN BAOS 12" × 7" Heavy duty planer 3PH (1 only to clear) **£2699**

DRILLING MACHINES

WARCO HOBBY ½" 5 speed rack and pinion table bench mounting **£139**
WARCO ⅝" cap 2MT 12 speed 2B12 bench mounting ... **£189** 2F12 floor standing **£222**
FOBCO STAR ½" precision drill bench mounting .... **£340** floor standing **£385**
STARTRITE SP250 ½" 5 speed bench mounting .... **£356** floor standing **£398**
Morticing attachments Warco 2B/2F .... **£24** Fobco .... **£61** Startrite **£110**

SPINDLE MOULDERS AND TENNONERS

SCHEPPACH HF33 3HP 30mm 3 speed with adjustable fences **£499**
ELEKTRA TF100 3HP 30mm 3-speed 4" Rise and fall. With free cutter set **£479**
KITY 623 2HP 3 speed 4" Rise and fall C/W sliding table **£776**
STARTRITE T30 30mm C/W sliding table 1PH 2HP .... **£943** 3PH 3HP **£915**
LUNA L28 30mm 3 speed 3HP Heavy duty 1PH 3HP .... **£999** 3PH 3HP **£988**
WADKIN BURSGREEN 5HP (3PH only) 4 speed 30mm **£1999**
MULTICO TENNONER TM1 240v twin motors (excluding tooling) **£1579**

SPINDLE MOULDER TOOLING (State bore size P&P £1.50)

OMAS "TIGER" BLOCKS 392 .... **£50** BLOCK in wooden case with stone etc. .. **£56**
OMAS cutter profiles .... **£12** CUTTER BLANKS .... **£7** SAW SEGMENTS **£17**
KITY PROFILE Door set .... **£96** OMAS ART 176D1 DOOR SET complete **£139**
WHITEHILL BLOCKS 4⅞ × 15/16 ..... **£51** 5⅜" × 15/16" ..... **£69** Panel Raising Block **£92**
LEITZ 488 Cutter block 100mm .... **£59** 40mm blanks .... **£3** 60mm .... ea. **£5**
TUNGSTEN REBATE BLOCKS 125mm × 50mm ..... **£98** 6" Wobble saw 3-21mm **£89**
LUNA MINI POWER FEED 2 speeds **£299**

COMBINATION MACHINES (Carriage £10.00 UK Mainland)

STARTRITE K260 saw spindle planer etc. FREE TIGER HEAD SET **£2390**
STARTRITE TZ30 saw spindle only FREE TIGER HEAD only **£1359**
SPECIAL OFFER LUNA W59 2HP 240v c/w sliding table slot morticer **£2299**
LUNA Z40 light duty combination saw planer spindle morticer **£685**
LUNA MASTER COMBINATIONS 240v W59 ..... **£2599** W64 ..... **£3100** W69 ..... **£3899**

★★★★★★★ KITY COMBINATION MACHINES ★★★★★★★

K5 COMBINATION K5 BASIC K704 TABLE COMBINATION K704 DIRECT DRIVE AND ACCESSORIES ALL AT SPECIAL PRICES SEND FOR LATEST PRICE LIST.

BORING BITS

CLICO SAW TOOTH & FORSTNER BITS (State type) 6" long ½" shank ⅜" . **£8.10** ½" . **£8.35**
⅝" .. **£9.20** ¾" .. **£10.00** ⅞" .. **£10.50** 1" .. **£11.55** 1⅛" .. **£13.55** 1¼" .. **£16.50**
1⅜" . **£17.20** 1½" . **£18.15** 1⅝" . **£20.90** 1¾" . **£23.75** 1⅞" . **£26.30** 2" . **£27.80**
2¼" .. **£34.95** 2½" .. **£46.35**
CLICO PLUG CUTTERS ⅜" . **£22** ½" . **£24** ⅝" . **£28** ¾" . **£30** 1" . **£36** 1½ . **£40.00**
CLICO SAW TOOTH set ½", ¾", 1" .... **£28** ECONOMY 5 piece set ½"-1½" × ⅛" **£58**
RIDGEWAY ADJUSTABLE FORSTNERS WR10/2½"-1¾" ..... **£16** WR10/3⅞"-3" **£18**
RIDGEWAY ADJUSTABLE FORSTNER (h/duty) WR20/2⅞"-2" **£29** WR20/3 1⅜"-3" **£34**

ROUTERS AND ROUTER ACCESSORIES

ELU MOF96 ¼" 600W **£98.50**
ELU MOF31 ¼, ⅜, ½" 1200W ... **£152.50**
ELU MOF177 ¼, ½" 1600W **£193.50**
HITACHI TR8 ¼" 730W **£79.95**
RYOBI R150 ¼" 730W **£75.95**
HITACHI FM ¼" 550W **£46.95**
MAKITA 3600B ¼, ½" 1500W ... **£168.95**
ELU MOF96E ¼" Var. speed **£119.50**
ELU MOF11/2 ½" 2000W c/w base **£337.33**
ELU MOF177E ½" Var. speed **£218.50**
HITACHI TR12 ¼, ½" 1300W **£137.95**
RYOBI R500 R500 ¼, ½" 1500W **£113.95**
BOSCH POF52 ¼" 520W **£55.00**
BOSCH 1604 Fixed base 1300W **£163.95**

ROUTER ACCESSORIES

ELU DOVETAIL KIT TCT cutter **£74.00**
ELU MOF96 Accessory kit **£74.00**
STAIR JIG (General duty) **£69.00**
ELU ROUTER BRKT. for DeWalt **£39.00**
ELU 96 Dust extraction kit **£36.00**
ELU MOF96 Height adjuster **£3.95**
ELU TRACKING SET **£35.00**
RYOBI Dovetail jig fits above **£99.95**
ELU ROUTER COMBI BENCH **£123.00**
STAIR JIG (heavy duty) **£160.00**
ELU 12 piece Guide bush set **£35.00**
ELU MOF98, 31, 177 Height adjuster **£16.95**
ELU 96 177 side fence adjuster **£6.90**
ELU ROUTING VIDEO **£12.00**

★★★★★★★★★ ELU ACCESSORIES ★★★★★★★★★★

10% OFF ALL ELU ACCESSORIES 90% STOCK AVAILABILITY POST PAID ON MOST ITEMS. EXCELLENT RANGE OF ROUTER ACCESSORIES SEND NOW FOR FREE LIST.

★★★★★★★★★★★★★★★★★★★★★★★★★★★★★★

HSS ROUTER BIT SETS (inc. P&P)

SAVE 30% ON HSS ROUTER BIT SETS AND GET A FREE ROUTER BIT CASE.
13 PIECE SET **£59.95**
8 PIECE SET **£37.95**
5 PIECE SET **£21.95**
ROUTER BIT CUTTER BOX .... ONLY **£4**

ROUTER CUTTERS

20-25% OFF LEADING BRANDS EXCELLENT STOCKS OF HSS & TCT ROUTER CUTTERS OVER 500 PROFILES IN STOCK. SEND NOW FOR FREE CUTTER CHART:- TECHNIQUES OF ROUTING £7.95 (inc. P&P)

IMMEDIATE DESPATCH ON CREDIT CARD PHONED ORDERS — CREDIT TERMS AVAILABLE OVER £120

0297 33656 CHARD STREET AXMINSTER DEVON EX13 5DZ 6.30-9pm **34836** BARCLAYCARD VISA

AXMINSTER POWER TOOL CENTRE

HORIZONTAL WETSTONE GRINDERS
OUR PRICE INC. VAT

JAPANESE Wetstone grinder £129.00
180G stone for above £40.00
1000G stone for above £40.00
6000G stone for above £43.00
PRECISION grinding jig £43.00

SHARPENSET Wetstone grinder £240.00
SHARPENSET 150G stone £18.40
SHARPENSET 280G stone £20.41
SHARPENSET Green stone (TCT) . £18.40
10" Planer Knife grinding jig £65.00
15" Planer Knife grinding jig £78.00
CHISEL grinding jig £67.00

VERTICAL WETSTONE GRINDERS
SCANGRIND 150 6" wetstone £77.95
SCANGRIND 200 8" wetstone £99.00
SCANTOOL COMBI WET AND DRY STONES
COMBI SC150 6" wet & dry £89.00
COMBI SC200 8" wet & dry £112.00
LUNA KIRUNA 11" wet & 4" dry £125.00
LUNA KIRUNA 14" wet & 5" dry £195.00

BENCH GRINDERS
ELU EDS163 6" 360W £73.95
ELU EDS164 7" 390W £77.95
ELU MWA149 6" Honer grinder .. £90.95
LEROY SOMER 5" 180W £33.00
LEROY SOMER 6" 250W £44.00
LEROY SOMER 6" with chuck £49.00
WARCO 5" 180W (European) £33.00
WARCO 6" 380W (European) £43.00
WARCO 8" 570W (European) £69.00

GRIND STONES (state bore size)

	5"	6"	7"
COARSE 36G	£6.60	£7.90	£11.40
FINE 60G	£6.60	£7.90	£11.40
WHITE 60G	£7.20	£8.50	£13.50
GREEN (TCT)	£7.20	£8.50	£13.50

JIGSAWS (Light Duty)
Bosch PST50 Single Speed £29.95
Bosch PST50E Var. Speed £38.50
Bosch PST55PE Var. Speed Pend £68.50
Hitachi FJ50SB Single speed £27.50
Hitachi FJ50VA Var. speed £36.50
Hitachi FCJ55V Var. Speed Pend. Act £58.95

JIGSAWS (Heavy Duty)
Elu ST142 2 speed £101.95
Elu ST142E Var. speed £110.95
Elu ST152 2 Speed £98.95
Elu ST152E Var. speed £106.95
Cases for above Jigsaws £10.00
Hitachi CJ65 2 speed £98.95
Hitachi CJ65VA Var. speed £104.95
Hitachi CJ65V Var. speed £104.95
Bosch 1581.7 Var. speed £109.95

DISC AND BELT SANDERS
Picador 10" Disc Sander £219.00
Warco BDS460 6" Disc 4" Belt ... £86.00
Warco BDS690 9" Disc 6" Belt . £179.00
Holmes 6" 2HP £399.00
Luna Favourite 4" £285.00
Luna De-Luxe Sander 4" £599.00
Luna YKV Pad Sander £647.00
Luna YK1500 Pad Sander 1PH £1564.00
Luna YK1500 Pad Sander 3PH £1509.00
Picador Unmotorised 3" Belt £49.00
Picador Unmotorised 3" Belt £65.00
Holmes 4" Belt Sander £94.00
Holmes 6" Belt Sander £120.00

CIRCULAR SAWS
HITACHI FC5SA 6" TCT 710W £42.95
BOSCH PKS46 6" TCT 600W £53.50
BOSCH PKS66 7⅞ TCT 1200W ... £90.95
HITACHI PSU6 6" 1050W HSS £74.95
HITACHI PSU7 7" 1600W HSS £99.95
HITACHI PSU9 9" 1759W HSS .. £124.95
HITACHI PSM7 7" 1200W TCT .. £141.95
HITACHI PSM9 9" 1600W TCT .. £154.95
ELU MH151 6" 850W TCT £90.95
ELU MH65 7" 1200W TCT £131.95
ELU MH85 9" 1600W TCT £177.95
ELU MH182 8" 1400W TCT £148.95
ELU 550 COMBI (for MH182) £130.00
ELU555 Snip saw (for 182) £179.00
WOLF 9" CIRCULAR SAW £135.00

FINISHING SANDERS
(DB Dust Bag)
BOSCH PSS230 1/3rd Sheet £29.95
HITACHI FS10SA 1/3rd Sheet £25.95
HITACHI FSV12 Sheet DB £47.95
BOSCH PS280A ½ Sheet DB £59.95
B&D P6303 ½ Sheet £59.95
ELU MVS156 1/3rd Sheet DB £73.95
ELU MVS156E Var. Speed DB £85.95
ELU MVS 94 ½ Sheet DB £111.95
ELU MVS47 ½ Sheet £123.95
HITACHI SV12 ½ Sheet £109.95
HITACHI SOD110 ½ Sheet DB £95.95
HITACHI SO110 ½ Sheet £86.95
BOSCH 1288 9½ Sheet DB £99.95
WOLF ½ Sheet DB £85.95

DRILL STANDS (43mm collar)
BOSCH S2 Light duty £21.00
BOSCH S7 Heavy duty £52.95
BOSCH S8 Milling attachment for S7 £24.50
RIDGEWAY Very heavy duty £145.95

EXTENSION CABLES
50 Metre on sturdy drum £28.95
Jo-Jo 6 metre 30 foot £9.95
Jo-Jo 12 Metre 40 foot £14.26
Jo-Jo 18 Metre 60 foot £17.95

POWER PLANES (Light Duty)
OUR PRICE INC. VAT

BLACK & DECKER DN710 ..... £29.95
BOSCH PHO100 82mm 450W £47.95
HITACHI FP20SA 82mm 320W ... £38.95

HEAVY DUTY
ELU MFF80 82mm 850W £109.95
ELU MFF80K (in kit box) £127.95
ELU MFF40 82mm 1000W £189.95
INVERSION Std. for MFF80 ..... £20.95
INVERSION Std. for MFF40 ..... £29.00
HITACHI P20SA 82mm 720W £95.95
HITACHI FU20 82mm 620W £88.95
HITACHI F30A 92mm 900W £124.95

BELT SANDERS
ELU MHB 157 3" 600W £106.95
ELU MHB 157E 3" var. speed £119.95
ELU 157 FRAME £35.00
ELU 157 inversion stand £28.00
ABRASIVE BELTS FOR MHB 157/pkt. 3
40G, 60G, 80G, 100G, 120G, 150G £3.00
BOSCH PBS75 3" 620W £71.95
ELU MHB 90 4" 850W £193.95
ELU MHB 90K With frame £234.95
HITACHI SB75 3" 950W £116.95
HITACHI SB110 4" 950W £144.90
HITACHI SB110T 4" 950W £129.00
HITACHI SB110V 4" var. speed . £134.00
MAKITA 9401 4" 1040W £169.00
MAKITA 9924DB 3" 950W £117.00

BISCUIT JOINTER
ELU DS140 Biscuit Jointer £197.95
No. 20 Biscuits (1000 off) £19.95
No. 10 Biscuits (1000 off) £19.50
No. 0 Biscuits (1000 off) £18.63
Mixed Box 0, 10, 20 (500 off) £12.50
DS140 saw blade 12T Std. £29.95
DS140 saw blade 30T Fine £29.50
DS140 Dust Tube adaptor £5.95
BOSCH Biscuit Jointer £124.95

★ ★ ★ SPECIAL OFFER ★ ★ ★ ★
WOODSCREWS
Twin Fast Zinc Plated GKN 1600 Woodscrews from 1" × 6 to 2" × 10" with Free Screwdriver. (State slotted or pozidrive).
ONLY £19.99 inc. VAT and P&P

RIDGWAY DRILL MORTICER
c/w Free Hitachi Drill ½" Chuck and ¼" Chisel and Bit ... £186.00 inc. VAT and P&P

MARTEK DRILL SHARPENER
Excellent for Sharpening all Drill Bits
..... ONLY £24.95 inc. VAT and P&P

S.D.S. POWER DRILLS
Hitachi DH16v £103.95
Hitachi VRV16 ..... £164.95
B&D PB020 ..... £112.95
B&D PB020T (c/w 110v Transformer) £185.95

DRILL/BREAKERS
Hitachi DH28Y £272.00
Hitachi DH500A £443.00
HAMMERS
H55 SA £375.00
H90 SA £756.00

HAMMERS
Hitachi H55 SA £375.00
Hitachi H90 SA £756.00

POWER DRILLS (K-Kit box)
NEW ELU POWER DRILLS
ECD304K 420W V/S 10mm Compact £73.95
EMD400K 600W 2 Speed 13mm . £81.95
ESD705K 320W V/S & Rev. 10mm £102.95
EMD403K 500W V/S/R Ham. 13mm £90.95
EMD405K 500W V/S/R Ham. 13mm £114.95
EMD406K 550W V/S Hammer 13mm £106.95
B&D 2162 KM V/S RW 450v £63.95
B&D P2264K 13mm 2 Speed 550W £74.95
B&D P2266K 13mm V/S Rev. 480W £69.95
BOSCH 400-2 10mm 440W £29.95
BOSCH 500RLE 13mm 500W V/S Rev. £49.95
BOSCH 7002E 13mm 700W £79.95
BOSCH 850RLT 13mm 850W V/S Re £111.95
HITACHI FV12VA 13mm 420W V/S £37.95
HITACHI FV16V 13mm 600W V/S/R £59.95
HITACHI FV20VA 13mm 710W V/S/R £86.95
HITACHI VTP13K 13mm 2 Speed 460W £74.00
HITACHI VTP16AK 2 Spd. 800W £103.00

ANGLE GRINDERS
HITACHI PDP100C 4" £44.85
HITACHI G13SB 5" 750W £66.81
HITACHI G23SC 9" 2000W £89.00

PALM GRIP SANDERS
(DB Dust Bag)
ELU MVS500 1/6th Sheet 135W DB £60.95
ELU MVS501 1/4 Sheet 135W DB £60.95
B&D P6301 1/6th Sheet 136W DB £51.50
B&D P6302 1/4 Sheet 135W DB £51.50
HITACHI SV12SA 1/4 Sheet 180W £46.95
MAKITA BO45 10 1/4 Sheet £43.95

LIBERON WAXES
Waxes Sealers Stains Polishes Etc. All Your Requirements in One Send for Free Price List
GLUE POT ..... £23.00 inc. P&P
470 FLUTED DOWELS 6mm 8mm 10mm
..... £5.75 inc. P&P

HITACHI 10mm CORDLESS DRILL-SCREWDRIVERS
OUR PRICE inc. VAT

DTC 10 6 cell 2 spd. & rev. £65.00
DRC10 as above torque adjustable £89.95
DTC10K 6 cell 2 spd. & rev. in case £69.00
D10DB 6 cell variable spd. & rev. £80.95
D10DD 8 cell 2 spd. & rev. £82.95
D10D as above torque adjustable £101.95
DV10D 8 cell 2 spd. & rev. hammer £107.95

MAKITA 10mm CORDLESS DRILL SCREWDRIVERS
6012DWK 6 cell 2 spd. & rev. in case £92.95
6012HDW 8 cell 2 spd. torque adj. £111.95
8400DW 8 cell 1 spd. & rev. hammer £119.95
MAGNETIC Screwdriver kit 7 piece £5.95
REPLACEMENT BITS (state type) £0.50

CORDLESS TOOLS
OUR PRICE INC. VAT

HITACHI CK12D Knife cutter £103.84
HITACHI C6DA 6" Circular saw . £143.95
MAKITA 5600DW 6" circular saw £179.95
MAKITA 4300DW Jig saw £119.95
B&D INDUSTRIAL Jig saw £110.95
BOSCH INDUSTRIAL PAINTS STRIPPER £82.95
BELLE ELECTRIC CEMENT MIXER £135.00

MISCELLANEOUS POWER TOOLS
KEW HOBBY PRESSURE WASHER £259.00
DREMEL D576 FRETSAW £69.95
BOSCH WET 'n' DRY Vacuum cleaner £93.95
BOSCH 520 HOT AIR paint stripper £27.00
BOSCH 560 HOT AIR paint stripper £39.00
NEW ELU DUST EXTRACTORS
EVE 938 ..... £275 EVE948 ..... £395

SASH CRAMPS (P&P £2.00 per order) may be mixed for quantity
RECORD 135-24" 1 off .... £20 5 off £18
135-36" 1 off .... £21 5 off £19
135-42" 1 off .... £22 5 off £20
135-48" 1 off .... £23 5 off £21

DRAPER 18" 1 off ..... £14 5 off £12
30" 1 off ..... £17 5 off £15
42" 1 off ..... £19 5 off £17
T bar 42" 1 off ..... £30 5 off £28

RECORD CRAMP HEADS M130
1 off £10.70 5 off £10.20 (P&P £1.50)

PARAMO CRAMP HEADS
1 off £10.00 5 off £9.00 (P&P £1.50)

G CRAMPS (P&P £1.50 per order) may be mixed for quantity
RECORD 120-3" 1 off .. £5.76 5 off .. £4.80
120-4" 1 off .. £5.91 5 off .. £4.90
120-6" 1 off .. £8.31 5 off .. £6.90
120-8" 1 off £12.31 5 off £9.80
120-10" 1 off £18.15 5 off £17.00
RECORD DEEP THROAT 4" 1 off . £13.27

PARAMO 3" 1 off .... £5.30 5 off £4.60
4" 1 off .... £5.55 5 off £4.78
6" 1 off .... £7.76 5 off £6.60
8" 1 off .... £11.41 5 off £9.50
10" 1 off . £16.90 5 off . £15.77
PARAMO DEEP THROAT 4" 1 off £12.45

KLEMSIA QUICK CLAMPS
(P&P £1.50)

SPAN	REACH	1 off	5 off
200mm	110mm	£4.30	£4.00
300mm	110mm	£4.75	£4.50
400mm	110mm	£5.20	£4.90
600mm	110mm	£6.20	£5.80
800mm	110mm	£7.20	£6.84
1000mm	110mm	£8.20	£7.79
200mm	150mm	£6.70	£6.37
200mm	200mm	£8.60	£8.17

NEW RECORD 132 SPEED CRAMPS
(P&P £1.50)

	Reach	1 off	5 off
Record 132/30	12"	£12.00	£10.00
132/40	16"	£13.00	£11.00
132/50	20"	£14.00	£12.00
132/60	24"	£15.00	£13.00
132/80	32"	£16.00	£14.00
132/100	40"	£18.00	£16.00

RECORD HAND PLANES
(P&P £1.50/Order)

03 Smoothing 240 × 45mm £20.10
04 Smoothing 245 × 50mm £19.95
041/2 Smoothing 260 × 60mm £19.50
05 Jack 355 × 50mm £26.75
051/2 Jack 380 × 60mm £29.50
06 Jointer 455 × 60mm ... £34.50
07 Jointer 560 × 60mm ... £39.75
778 Rebate 215 × 38mm ... £30.80
010 Rebate 330 × 44mm ... £39.50
020C Circular Plane £69.50
0601/2 Block Plane £16.50
073 Shoulder Rebate £42.50
CLIFTON 420 Rebate Plane £57.00
CLIFTON Multi-Plane £189.00
CLIFTON Cap Iron 2" or 2⅜" £5.00

STANLEY HAND PLANES
(P&P £1.50/Order)

3 Smoothing 240 × 45mm £23.60
4 Smoothing 245 × 50mm £20.00
41/2 Smoothing 260 × 60mm £21.60
5 Jack 355 × 50mm £27.00
51/2 Jack 380 × 60mm £28.00
6 Fore 455 × 60mm £37.80
7 Jointer 560 × 60mm £39.40
78 Duplex Rebate £21.50
10 Rebate 330 × 44mm £40.50
80 Scraper £9.50
601/2 Block Plane £21.00
92 Rebate Plane £24.80
CLIFTON 3 in 1 Rebate Plane £67.00
RECORD 3 in 1 Plane £39.00

WOODWORKING VICES (P&P £4.50)
RECORD 52½E 9" Quick Release £44.00
52½ED 9" Quick Release £47.00
53E 10" Quick Release . £69.00

DRILL BIT SETS

	Lip & Spur	HSS Std.
1/16"-½" × 64ths	—	£21.00
1/16"-½" × 32nds	£42.00	£17.00
1-13mm × 0.5mm	£54.00	£19.00

JAPANESE WATER STONES (P&P £1.00)
KING BRAND 800G WETSTONE £8.00
KING BRAND 1200G WETSTONE .. £8.00
SUPER FINISHING STONE 6000G £8.90
COMBINATION WATER STONE £10.80

MISCELLANEOUS HAND TOOLS (P&P £1.50 PER ORDER)
RECORD Dowel Jig £36.20
140 Corner Cramps £12.00
145 Hold Fast £13.00
Floorboard Cramp . £56.95
18" Extension Rods £4.95
141 Corner Cramps £19.40
146 Hold Fast £15.50
169 Bench Stop £7.50
Drill Bushes £1.90
Spare Collars £3.20
Priory Bench Stop ... £2.95
STANLEY Web Clamp £7.99
Stanley Yankee Screwdrivers 13" ..... £12.86 20" ..... £14.17 27" £18.50

HANDSAWS (P&P £1.50)
DISSTON D8 26" 6pt ..... £27 RIDGWAY SPEED SAW 22" or 26" £19
ROBERTS & LEE 10" DOVETAIL BRASS BACK £21 ROBERTS & LEE DORCHESTER 10" £27

SANDERSON KAYSER "PAX" HANDSAWS (P&P £1.50)
BRASS BACK TENNON SAWS 8" £18.50 10" £19 12" £19.50 14" £20 D/Tail £25
HANDSAWS 20" × 10pt £21 22" × 8pt £22 24" × 7pt £23 6" × 6pt £24 26" × Rip £24

CHISEL SETS (State bevel edge or firmer P&P £1.00/Order)
MARPLES CARVERS ASH 4 piece .. £13.60
MARPLES SPLITPROOF 4 piece .. £24.50
MARPLES BOXWOOD 5 piece .. £38.50
PARAMO ROSEWOOD 4 piece .. £29.50
STANLEY 5001 6 piece .. £33.39
MARPLES BLUE CHIP 4 piece .. £17.42
MARPLES BLUE CHIP 5 piece .. £23.00
SORBY BOXWOOD 5 piece .. £26.00
PARAMO ROSEWOOD 6 piece .. £42.50
STANLEY 5002 5 piece .. £23.68

WOODTURNING CHISEL SETS (P&P £1.80)
HENRY TAYLOR Carbon Steel Sets, 3 Piece ..... £17 5 Piece ..... £29 8 Piece £46
SORBY Carbon Steel Sets 5 Piece (51c) .... £26 6 Piece (61c) .... £45 8 Piece (82c) £63
SORBY High Speed Sets 5 Piece (51h) ..... £40 6 Piece (61h) ..... £81 8 Piece (82h) £107
LUNA Swedish Steel Sets GOOD VALUE 3 Piece ..... £14 4 Piece ..... £27 5 Piece £37
MINIATURE SETS SORBY HSS set of 5 ..... £28 HENRY TAYLOR SUPER FIVE £18

ABRASIVES (West German top quality P&P £1.00/Order)
SANDING BELTS resin bonded aluminium oxide cloth belts (price each)

Size (length width)	M/C	40G	60G	80G	100G	120G
75 × 480mm — 3" × 19"	(Elu)	£1.11	£1.08	£0.99	£1.05	£1.02
75 × 510mm — 3" × 20"	(B&D)	£1.14	£1.12	£1.03	£1.07	£1.02
75 × 533mm — 3" × 21"	(Bosch Hit)	£1.28	£1.17	£1.07	£1.09	£1.05
100 × 560mm 4" × 22"	(Elu 90)	£1.58	£1.43	£1.40	£1.37	£1.32
100 × 610mm 4" × 24"	(Wolf Hit)	£1.67	£1.53	£1.48	£1.43	£1.38
100 × 915mm — 4" × 36"	(Coronet)	£2.22	£1.99	£1.88	£1.85	£1.81
150 × 1090mm — 6" × 42"	(Coronet)	£4.20	£3.80	£3.65	£3.45	£3.40

★ ★ OTHER SIZES AVAILABLE ON REQUEST MANY IN STOCK ★ ★

ABRASIVE SHEETS (P&P £0.50 PER ORDER) state grit when ordering 100G and finer

Type	Description	60G/10	60G/50	80G/10	80G/50	100G+/10	100G+/50
PGF	GARNET FINISHING	£2.13	£8.90	£1.85	£7.70	£1.67	£6.94
GCAB	GARNET CABINET	£3.02	£12.59	£2.61	£10.90	£2.35	£9.82
PSF	SILICON FINISHING	£3.16	£13.17	£2.73	£11.40	£2.46	£10.27
WS	WET 'n' DRY	£6.19	£25.81	£5.28	£22.03	£3.59	£14.99

★SPECIAL OFFER★ 50 Sheets of asstd. Abrasives £5.99 inc. P&P Garnet-Glass-W/Dry

WIRE WOOL

	0000 Fine	00/0 Medium	1/2 Coarse	3/4 V Coarse
1 KG ROLLS	£4.73	£4.35	£4.25	£4.13
250g ROLLS	£1.50	£1.45	£1.42	£1.38

SAVE 20% ON ALL HAND TOOLS SEND NOW FOR NEW HAND TOOL CATALOGUE £1.50 (REFUNDABLE ON 1st ORDER

0297 33656 CHARD STREET AXMINSTER DEVON EX13 5DZ 6.30-9pm 34836 BARCLAYCARD VISA

THE WOODWORK BUS

Design and marketing — John Makepeace

Creative business management can develop the market for creative craft-and-design skills

Craftspeople frequently have difficulty in grasping the relevance of marketing. Mass-production, on the other hand, has developed in response to extensive market analysis and promotion through mass media. The principle of asking pertinent questions, really understanding the answers, and the interpreting these into designs is all part of an important two-way communication. Business on any scale is all about that.

Just 30 years ago, I was leaving school. At that time, my overriding concern was to learn the practical skills of woodworking — not that it seemed to offer a promising future. The values identified by William Morris, and sustained for a century, seemed to be finally withering in the face of mass-production; the direction and enthusiasm had gone. Yet, against this gloomy backdrop, the discovery of positive signs

shone out like beacons. Whether through discussion, reading or gut-feeling, each pointed the way ahead into new and unfamiliar territory.

At 18, I was too old for an apprenticeship with Edward Barnsley, who encouraged me to get a job in the furniture industry. I eventually persuaded Keith Cooper, the designer-craftsman, to let me work for him. He recommended I also study to be a teacher, so that when my business failed I would have an alternative career.

My fascination with the superb craftsmanship I had seen at the age of 11 received no obvious encouragement. When it became apparent during my training that practical skills were no assurance of survival, the necessity for design as a means of effective communication became self-evident. My early days of self-employment came dangerously close to disaster, but when I discovered the concept of directing events through business management, I felt on much firmer ground. From this stronger position, it became possible to create a market for quality at realistic prices, or, in marketing terms, to raise the perceived value of fine furniture making.

The demand for my work certainly did grow, and so did the requests for jobs from

those students leaving college who wanted a period of practical experience and education in my business before starting their own workshops. For too long, woodworking in Secondary and Further Education had been regarded with disdain. The belief that the less able are best suited to practical work tended to deprive industry of the abilities needed to stimulate its progress. So in 1977, I founded the School for Craftsmen in Wood at Parnham to teach practical, design, business and marketing skills to those best suited to establishing new enterprises.

It's tempting for the young maker or designer to assume that careful work deserves to be appreciated. It's worth considering that in a competitive world each of us has to select those 'messages' which catch our imagination and sustain our interest. That is the challenge. If our making is to have significance to other people, we need to check that we are clearly expressing our message — and in terms which are appreciated by our chosen audience. ■

● John Makepeace is one of the country's leading designer craftsmen and founder of the School for Craftsmen in Wood in Dorset.

● *Inspired by Nature – John Makepeace's dining table and chairs in English wild cherry and burr elm. The table top is laid with cherrywood veneer 'petals' and the central base is carved from solid burr elm*

The key: be unique — Hugh O'Neill

Market awareness, competition and location are all vital ingredients of a marketing recipe with an irresistible flavour

A *little* competition can be a good thing; but if it can be avoided, so much the better. If your skills and ideas are much the same as those of other people and you set up to exercise those skills in an area where somebody else is already operating, then you're heading for the breadline. The only time when setting up somewhere where the products you make are already being made and sold is at all justifiable, is where the existing operator can't meet even half of the actual demand.

However bad you are you will always take a little business away from the competition, and however good you are you'll never take it all. If you are particularly good you may eventually win more than half. Whatever the split, both competitors will end up operating at a lower level of business than if there were only one. You will both feel the pinch until one of you decides you have to increase the amount of business you're doing, which again can only be done at the expense of the other. So you cut prices, or offer some other cost-incurring incentive, which increases the level of your business; but you do it at a higher cost and therefore a lower return. The profit drops, and while one of you struggles to make ends meet the other goes out of business. So you have won? Not a bit of it. In order to survive you have taken on debts and loans, now you struggle to pay the interest and can make no inroads into the capital debt. For the rest of your life you work every day, every week — almost every hour — just to support the bank manager.

Of course it's only this cut and dried where there is a finite market, as in supplying joinery to local builders. Whatever you do, you can't increase the amount of joinery used in a given area.

But with products such as normal domestic furniture and fittings, the position isn't quite so clear. Although there is still basically a finite market — only so many people are likely to need wall cupboards at a given moment — you can, by the quality of your work and some nice little design features, tempt a person who already has a cupboard to change for one of yours. The further you move along the 'craft' scale, the less finite the market becomes.

While materials exist from which to make craftwork, and while there is any discretionary purchasing money in the economy, then there is capacity for making and selling art or superfine craftsmanship. Hence good carvings, turnery, cabinet-work, and 'designer' craft furniture will always sell. The factors most effecting the sale of such items are less connected with competition.

The product has to appeal to the discerning potential customer (not necessarily the producer!); and the goods have to be displayed and/or advertised in such a position and location that they will be seen — perhaps accidentally — by enough of the sort of people who have, and are prepared to spend, money on non-essential items. People to whom quality, artistry and natural wood appeals, in other words. Here the price matters much less; the real concern is with quality and uniqueness of design and execution. But we still depend upon location and visibility. For those selling by display, the ambience of the area is important, and the number and type of people passing through are vital.

A stall in Covent Garden Market is a good example. Not only do thousands of impecunious students and young people pass through each day, but so also do many wealthy tourists. There are many people whose idea of a souvenir of a holiday in a country is not a gaudily dressed plastic doll but a highly individual piece of that country's indigenous art. Here you can sell fine wooden jewel boxes at £200-£300. Try the same from a shop on the seafront at Clacton and see what happens!

Wealthy people buy both expensive souvenirs and exclusive pieces. Wealthy Americans actively seek traditional British craftsmanship. Both only feel that they have got good value if it was bought in the right area and at a price high enough to indicate quality. Country lovers buy country crafts, often something with 'taste' at a price they may have to think twice about. All holiday makers buy gifts. Some holiday centres attract people who will buy the more expensive, 'tasteful' items — others attract those who are themselves attracted to the less expensive, even garish. Most people will buy some inexpensive mementoes, anything that catches the eye — and it may eye-catch by its quality, its usefulness, its gimmickry, or a host of other things.

Location — your business

There are three main questions on this topic, primarily addressed to those currently considering setting up.
1 Where am I presently located — Where is my home? Where is my workplace?
2 Where would I like to be located?
3 Where should I be located (both general area and specific site) for the type of business that I wanted to do?

In answering the third you need to be honest and consider carefully the fit between your product, its unique aspects (and its price) and the general area. Also, what's the specific site like in terms of giving you the right sort of visibility and access to enough suitable customers? If the answers to the three questions coincide, then you are fortunate indeed.

Of course there are ways around the problems if the answers are not all one and the same.

If you have a skill you wish to exploit, you have to consider whether that skill has to be employed locally or not. Take into account the local demand, the 'portability' of the skill, the transportability of the end product, and similar factors.

Carpentry and joinery, for instance, are increasingly either very special local services or nationwide mass-production activities. Some of the products aren't transportable (full flights of stairs don't readily fit in the back of the van); some are, but cost more in transport than they do to make. Increasingly, with the need to use workshop-based machinery in order to stay competitive, skills in this area are less portable. There is less scope for the journeyman as we become increasingly tied to fixed workshops. So we have to work in an area where there is a substantial requirement for such skills; where there's a significant population density, substantial building activity (new or refurbishment) and insufficient competition.

If you're in this type of trade — particularly if you are starting up — you may have brought some contracts with you, but don't doubt you will have to go out selling. Circulars, leaflets through doors, Yellow Pages may bring in some business, but getting started and getting known requires door-knocking. And, of course, while you're out selling you're not actually exercising your craft and making products. It is a basic, simple scenario that many, painfully, fail to recognise or admit to; that's the way it is.

Some skills, like carving, for instance, are more transportable. A green felt roll of

THE WOODWORK BUSINESS

carving chisels, a mallet, a few hand-tools, and you're away — more or less. Now you can become a journeyman and travel to where the work is. One enterprising carver from St Albans uses a lay-by on a busy Watford road. Once established you will get commissions offered to you, but again until this happy time arrives you still have the self-promotion and door-knocking to do. Some even make turning more portable by demonstrating and selling items off the lathe at Craft fairs and shows.

The more transportable the product, the less important the location of the production point; but here we aren't just talking of transportability in terms of physically moving an item. Again you must take account of viability in a particular market. You are faced now with a very important decision; it almost comes before the issue of where you personally wish to locate yourself.

Location — the product, the outlet

In your marketing analysis, you have to resolve the interplay between location and methods of sale. Very few craftspeople make enough sales to casual visitors to their studios to make enough income to reach even the survival level. If this is all you intend to do, forget it now. Some craftspeople enjoy meeting people. They like to have people coming into their studio/workshop, and they're always ready for a chat. Fine, if that's what you want; but unless the chat moves the sale along, it's unproductive time. Visitors have an unhappy knack of arriving just at that critical moment when you're too involved to talk, and they often only want a chat or to pick up some wrinkle from the 'expert' and then leave without buying anything. You end up doing most of your productive work after shop hours.

You will have to do some other form of selling, whatever your idea or product is, but the question is, how you wish to market your output. Fundamentally, do you wish to sell retail or wholesale — if, indeed, you think there is any option for your product in the quantities you can produce. Retailing means selling direct to the final customer, wholesaling means selling through one or more middlemen.

Of course it will depend on the product and, to an extent, on your basic motivation.

Even if you intend to remain an individual craftsman operator, you may still sell all or most of your output through agents or other shop outlets. If you produce quality work, even in small quantities, outlets at the top end of the market (such as Harrods) may be interested. Then there are the local craft shops who are solely retailers (producing nothing), and even some retailers who go round the craft markets. Retailing may mean going to some of those same craft fairs yourself, and it will also almost certainly mean having a display area or showroom attached to your own workshop.

. . . be unique . . .

But! Selling to a wholesaler or to a retail outlet takes more time and skill than does selling direct to an end customer. Unfortunately, the end customer only buys one item. So, in terms of location, if you are going to retail yourself, then you have to be in your marketplace, and it must be a *market place* and not just somewhere nice to live. If you're selling wholesale it's less important, but don't forget the cost of transport, and the costs (including time) involved in making those essential visits to your markets.

Sometimes you find a location where the market comes to you. Some areas attract the sort of visitors who are more likely to buy fine pieces and craft ware. But you do still need to pick and choose with care. There is, for instance, the 'craft complex', a group of buildings occupied by a group of craftspeople. Most have a policy of 'only one of each sort of craft', so there's no direct competition. There is also the advantage of collective advertising, although this may often cost more than you would spend if operating alone. They bring in people who are interested in craft, and at seasonal gift-buying times they can be very popular.

However, the rentals of some are high, and although there may not be another wood-based craft operator within 100 miles, every other craftsperson on the site is competing for the same pound in the visitor's pocket. As much as 15% of all visitors to a centre do buy something, but the vast majority buy only a postcard or two or a jar of honey.

If you're going to rely on casual and passing trade, then you have to be in one of two places. The first is a suitable site in a town where people already have shopping and buying on their mind — but it still needs to be a tourist town in a tourist area. The other is a regular tourist route, preferably at or near a tourist site. Here you have to have easy access and a safe exit; and be able to be seen from far enough away for the car passengers to have seen you and gone through the involved process of deciding to stop.

Location — the bottom line

There is one theme, the basis of all marketing, which you must always bear in mind when considering your product, your outlets, and your own position: uniqueness. Somewhere in what you do, in your product or design, in where you are, in the way you do things, in your selling method, whatever; there has to be an element of uniqueness. If you haven't got this, and you can't build it in in some way, then please, please, stay a hobbyist.

You need to be unique in at least one of the following:
● The quality of your work — significantly better than anyone else in the area, and charging a deliberately high price to tell everybody you are quality and you recognise your worth
● The quantity of your output — such that you can sell in large quantities at prices which make the product uniquely attractive to those with less to spend, yet which by the very volume of turnover still makes a reasonable profit
● Your designs — very different from everything else available in your field. Different enough to be eye-catching and to demand attention, yet not so outrageous or impractical as to actually put people off
● Your location — there's no one else there to supply a clearly identified need
● Your siting — such that customers come to your door, and in fact can't really avoid it
● The way that you operate — such that the product is almost irrelevant, but the money is made by the way the business operates (franchising, etc)
● You can survive without bread, and what you actually make and sell doesn't really matter.
● Or, of course, unique in that you have already made it! You are a world-recognised master and spend as much time lecturing internationally as you do actually producing. People come begging for your masterpieces. There must be all of a handful of such craftspeople about. Only then are they above marketing, and you can be sure they didn't get where they are without their own or someone else's marketing skills. ■

● Hugh O'Neill is a professional business consultant and craftsman woodturner.

Guild notes

Guild of WOODWORKERS

The Guild was set up by *Woodworker* to create a meeting ground for all those involved in working wood, whether professional, amateur, or enthusiastic beginner. Guild members get:

- Access to Guild courses and events
- Free publicity in *Woodworker*
- Specially arranged tool insurance at low rates
- 15% off Woodworker Show entry
- A free display area and meeting point at the Show
- 15% discount off *Woodworker* plans
- Inclusion in our register of members' skills and services

For details, please send an sae to the Guild of Woodworkers, 1 Golden Sq, London W1R 3AB.

BOOKING FORM

I wish to book for the following course(s).

☐ **French polishing** 7-8 May, £40; make cheque payable to Charles Cliffe

☐ **Design and workshop drawing** 9 May £25+VAT = £28.75

☐ **Power routing** 13 June, £25+VAT = £28.75

☐ **Rudiments of restoration** 2-3 July, £54; make cheque payable to Barry Honeyborne

☐ **French polishing** 18-19 July, £50; make cheque payable to Ian Hosker.

☐ **Decorative techniques** 12-13 September, £55; make cheque payable to Ian Hosker

Please make cheques payable to 'The Guild of Woodworkers/ASP Ltd' unless otherwise stated.

Name...

Address...

....

....

Guild no...
Send to: The Guild of Woodworkers, 1 Golden Square, London, W1R 3AB. The Guild reserves the right to cancel any course.

GUILD COURSES

● Only Guild members are eligible to go on these courses. You must book in advance, and we must have a cheque for the full cost of the course at the time of booking. If you cancel less than four weeks before the advertised date you will forfeit 50% of the cost, unless there are exceptional circumstances.

French polishing — Charles Cliffe

7-8 May, 10-4, Bexleyheath, £40.
Another chance to learn with an expert. You'll find out about preparation, staining and techniques of French polishing itself, with plenty of hands-on experience. Charles shows the correct way to sharpen a cabinet scraper — bring yours along — and will offer advice on any small piece of furniture you want to refinish.

Design and workshop drawing — Bob Grant

9 May, 9.30-5, Oxford, £25+VAT
If putting your design on paper doesn't come easy, here's the course to learn how. Bob will help you gain confidence in freehand sketching, show you how to use grid paper and drawing boards, and lots more.

Country chairmaking with Jack Hill

26-29 May, Dartington, Devon, £141 inc. VAT.
A fully residential course (three nights' accommodation, all meals and light refreshments) introducing traditional chairmaking.
● Full details direct from Rick James, The Old Postern, Dartington, Totnes, Devon, TQ9 6EA, quoting ref. NC3 — **not from the Guild.**

Power Routing — Roy Sutton

13th June, 10-5, Herne Bay, Kent, £25+ VAT.
Roy is an expert on this subject. Starting from first principles, he covers housing, grooving, rebating, straight and circular moulding, tenoning, mortising, and rule-joint and template work; he also deals with designing and setting up your own jigs.

Rudiments of restoration — Barry Honeyborne *NEW*

2-3 July, Leominster, Herefordshire, £54. Bring along your antique and learn how to restore it. From initial cleaning to repairs and final polishing, Barry will show you all the steps — he has been 25 years in the trade. This two day course is an introduction to every aspect of restoration, plus a chance to make a start on your own piece under expert supervision.

French polishing — Ian Hosker *NEW*

18-19 July, 10-5, Chester, £50.
One of our most popular course subjects, led by Ian, a teacher and a practising professional. It covers preparation of old and new pieces, staining and colouring techniques, grain filling, shellac finishes, fadding, bodying in, spiriting off and giving new life to existing polished surfaces. The fee includes course materials. Ian will make up a polishing kit to take away at £9.50 if you order in advance.

Decorative techniques — Ian Hosker *NEW*

12-13 September, 10-5, Chester, £55.
Another chance to learn all sorts of wonderful decorative techniques, including dragging, lining, sponging, rag-rolling, marbling, spattering and tortoiseshelling. The fee includes materials, but bring a few paintbrushes and jam-jars.

Putting heads together

West Sussex Guild members who met recently for the first time soon found they were comparing notes about where to buy timber locally; one member mentioned how helpful a sawmill had been at converting timber. The general feeling was that tools and equipment purchased in West Sussex tend to be more expensive than buying in London or by mail order. Now members are hoping to organise visits to wood-related places of interest.

If you haven't met up with other local Guild members yet, why not contact your local representative? See WOODWORKER January for contact names and addresses.

Bucks fizz

Guild members in Buckinghamshire should throw their caps in the air, for Jeff Trowe has volunteered to be your local Guild representative. Please contact Jeff at Groveleigh, Langley Park Road, Iver, Bucks SL0 0JG and get your first meeting organised!

☐ **Annuals, books:** Argus Books, Wolsey Hse, Wolsey Rd, Hemel Hempstead, Herts HP2 4SS, (0442) 41221

☐ **Woodworker Shows, competition forms:** Argus Specialist Exhibitions, PO Box 35, Wolsey Hse, Wolsey Rd, Hemel Hempstead, Herts HP2 4SS, (0442) 41221

☐ **Back issues, subscriptions:** Infonet Ltd, 10-13 Times Hse, 179 Marlowes, Hemel Hempstead, Herts HP1 1BB, (0442) 48434

☐ **Binders, indexes, plans, special offers, videos:** Readers Services, 9 Hall Rd, Maylands Wood Est, Hemel Hempstead, Herts HP2 7BH, (0442) 211882

☐ **Editorial enquiries** WOODWORKER editorial, 1 Golden Sq, London W1R 3AB, 01-437 0626

CONTACTS: CUT OUT AND KEEP

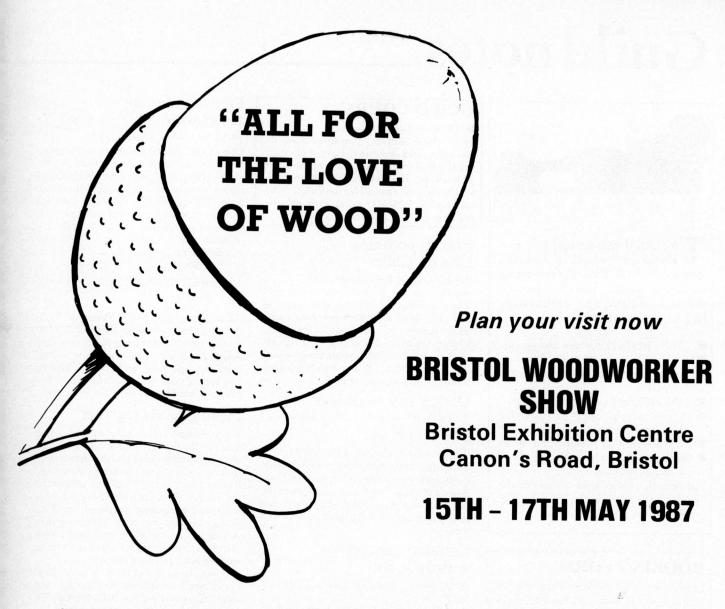

"ALL FOR THE LOVE OF WOOD"

Plan your visit now

BRISTOL WOODWORKER SHOW
Bristol Exhibition Centre
Canon's Road, Bristol

15TH – 17TH MAY 1987

— An opportunity to buy exotic woods and veneers as well as the latest woodworking machinery, tools and supplies on the many stands.

— Listen to the advice and knowledge of the experts as they demonstrate their skills.

— Admire the craftsmanship of the many competition entries from marquetry to cabinetmaking.

Opening Times:
May 15th, 16th . 10 a.m.-6 p.m.
May 17th .... 10 a.m.-5 p.m.

Admission Prices:
Adults £2.50
Child/OAP £1.75

Further information available from:
Argus Specialist Exhibitions Ltd., Wolsey House, Wolsey Road, Hemel Hempstead, Herts. HP2 4SS. Tel: 0442 41221.

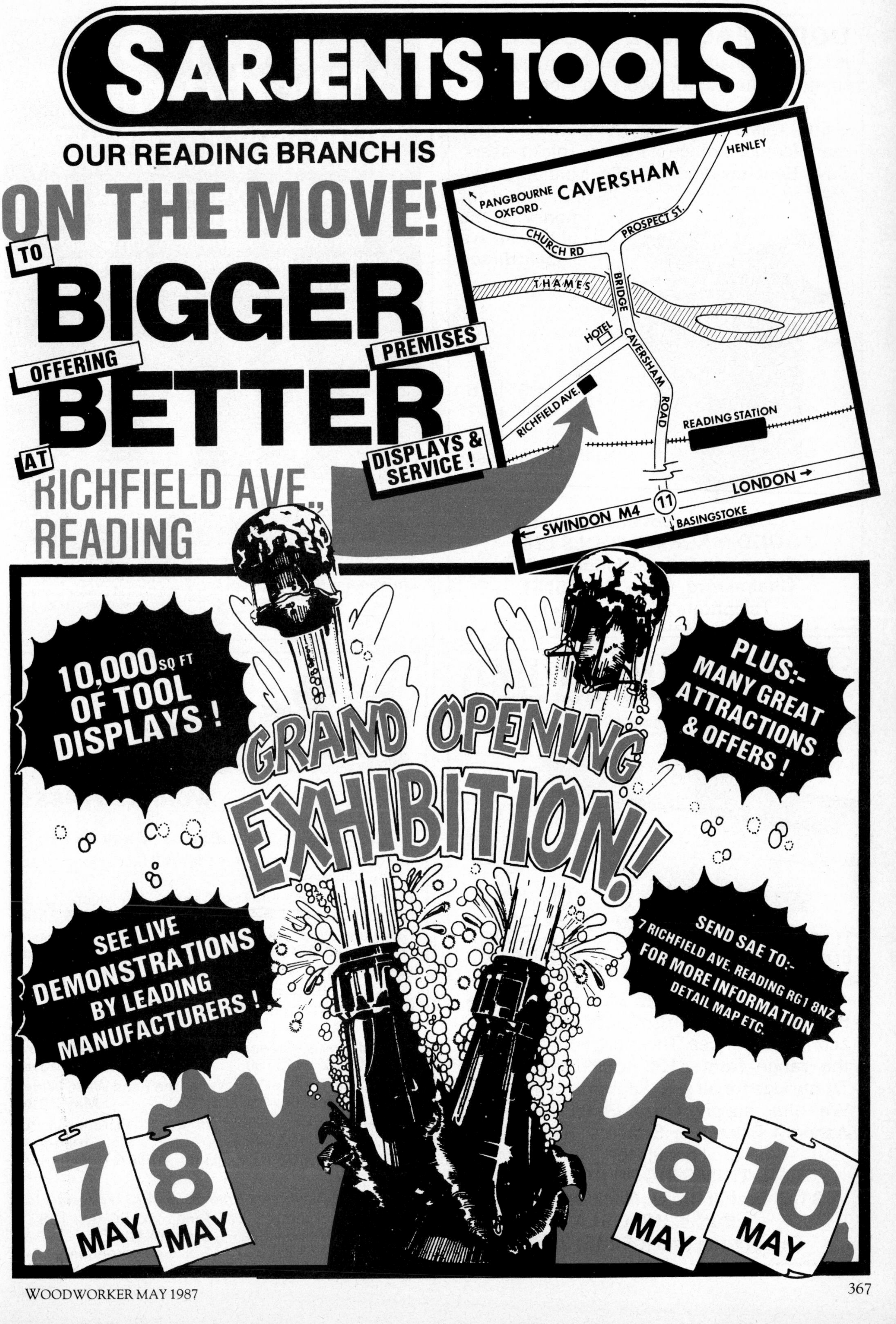

SARJENTS TOOLS

OUR READING BRANCH IS

ON THE MOVE!

TO BIGGER

OFFERING BETTER

PREMISES

AT RICHFIELD AVE., READING

DISPLAYS & SERVICE!

10,000 SQ FT OF TOOL DISPLAYS!

PLUS:- MANY GREAT ATTRACTIONS & OFFERS!

GRAND OPENING EXHIBITION!

SEE LIVE DEMONSTRATIONS BY LEADING MANUFACTURERS!

SEND SAE TO:- 7 RICHFIELD AVE. READING RG1 8NZ FOR MORE INFORMATION DETAIL MAP ETC.

7 MAY 8 MAY 9 MAY 10 MAY

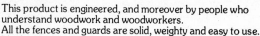
 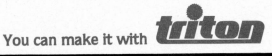

Pedal power

Alexi Clarke's cycle truck
is easy to make, handy to
use, and healthy to ride

Oxford is a cycling town, so when I
needed to carry collected waste
paper for recycling (!) to Friends of
the Earth, the idea of a trailer towed behind
a bike emerged naturally. I designed it to be
strong but light, so heavy loads could be
towed at up to 15mph with the bicycle
remaining stable. It had to carry a substantial volume but be as narrow as possible.
The finished product weighs 26lb and can
carry up to about 1cwt. It also had to
double up as a handcart.

The trailer is built almost completely out
of wood, but the towbar and cycle linkage
need welding to give enough strength; a
local engineering workshop can do this for
you.

The design proved to be surprisingly
tough and quite flexible.

Some of the 15 trucks we built are still in
regular use, and no particular problem has
emerged, except the occasional overload
bending the tow bar.

● *Humanity or hardware; the
cycle truck is stable with loads of
1cwt at up to 15mph*

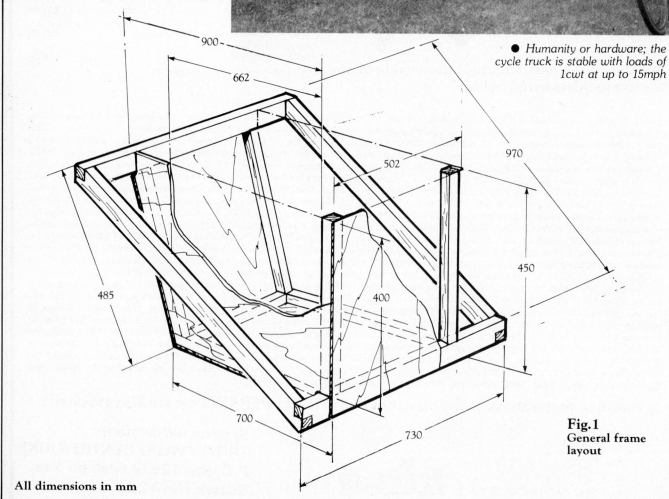

All dimensions in mm

**Fig. 1
General frame
layout**

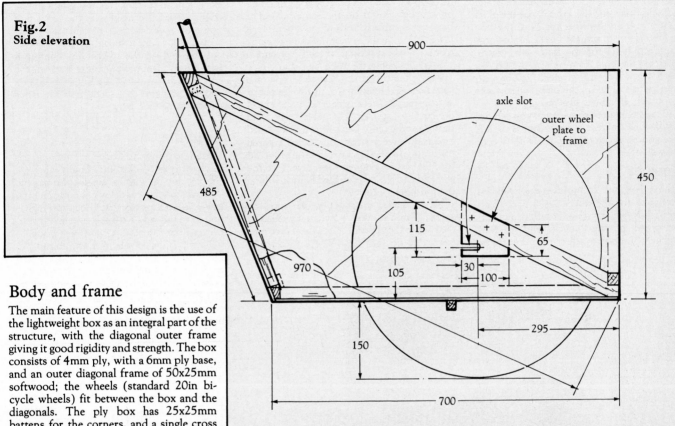

Fig.2
Side elevation

900

axle slot

outer wheel
plate to
frame

450

485

115

65

970

105

30

100

150

295

700

Body and frame

The main feature of this design is the use of the lightweight box as an integral part of the structure, with the diagonal outer frame giving it good rigidity and strength. The box consists of 4mm ply, with a 6mm ply base, and an outer diagonal frame of 50x25mm softwood; the wheels (standard 20in bicycle wheels) fit between the box and the diagonals. The ply box has 25x25mm battens for the corners, and a single cross batten underneath to stiffen the 6mm ply base.

I cut the plywood sides and the corner battens, gluing and screwing them to the side pieces; staples or pins could also be used. Then I cut the front and rear components for the outer frame, carefully marking out and cutting the lap joints the right way round so the joint takes the load. I also cut the battens for the base.

I treated all timber with preservative before gluing and screwing the box together, with the front and rear outer frame members in place, but not the diagonals at this stage. I glued and screwed the base ply beneath the horizontal base battens, with a single cross batten for reinforcement glued and screwed across the centre.

The towbar is to be secured inside the box in two places, with a metal fastening at the top frame, and a wooden block at the bottom. I shaped this block from 30x25mm section to a suitable angle, and drilled a 25mm-diameter hole into it about 15mm deep. I glued and screwed this to the lower front batten inside the box. Then I applied several coats of varnish to the superstructure, and bitumen paint underneath.

Wheelplates and diagonals

The axles of the bicycle wheels fit into slots cut in aluminium wheel plates, on the frame and box each side of the wheels. I used 4mm thick aluminium for the plates on the outer diagonal frame members, and 2mm thick

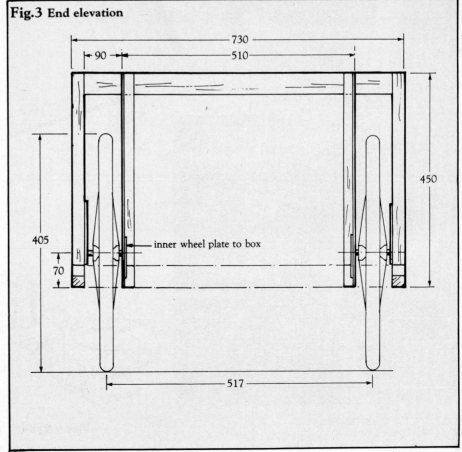

Fig.3 End elevation

730

90

510

450

405

70

inner wheel plate to box

517

Pedal power

for the ones on the box sides. After drilling suitable holes for the axles, I cut the slots before bolting the wheelplates to the box and the frame diagonals. I used 20mm large flat head bolts for the inner box plates, inserting the bolt from outside the box so the flat heads clear the wheel. You have to be careful to line up the outer wheelplates so the wheel is held straight.

Once the plates are fastened, you can cut the diagonals to size, lap-joint the ends and glue and screw them in place with 50mm screws.

Towbar

I chose 18-gauge 25mm-diameter seamless steel tube for the towbar as it has a high strength-to-weight ratio. It is flattened and reinforced at the bicycle end, and is attached by bolts to the truck outer frame through a welded-on box section (a brazed-on bracket would do the same job). The box end is inserted into the wooden block fastened inside the bottom of the box at the front. This attaching method meant I wouldn't weaken the tube by drilling it.

I bent the tube to the correct angle on a pipe bender, being careful not to flatten or corrugate. To reinforce the bike end I inserted a smaller diameter tube and flattened the end between two V-ended blocks to give a strong V-shaped tapered transition from flat to round section. To fuse the reinforcing sections, I rounded the end and had the edge welded before drilling the pin hole.

Next I shaped the short box section (18-gauge, 25mm square), and had it welded to the tube in the appropriate place. You could braze this on, but however you do it the bond must be strong as the safety of the trailer depends crucially on the towbar. If you are welding, I recommend oxy-acetylene or Mig to avoid burning holes.

I finished off the towbar by painting it with silver 'Hammerite' before inserting the end into the wooden block inside the box and bolting the box section to the front upper frame member.

Coupling

I tried various methods of coupling the towbar to the bike and finally chose a simple design with a single pin passing through the flattened towbar end. The pin is welded to a car exhaust U-clamp which is bolted to the saddle tube, with a split pin to prevent the towbar lifting off the hook.

First I drilled a hole in the 8mm rod and then had it welded to a small L-shaped strip of 3mm-thick mild steel; in turn this was bolted to the U-clamp so it would swivel and allow the bike to lean on curves. You could weld the pin straight to the U-clamp, but this doesn't give much play; if the bike

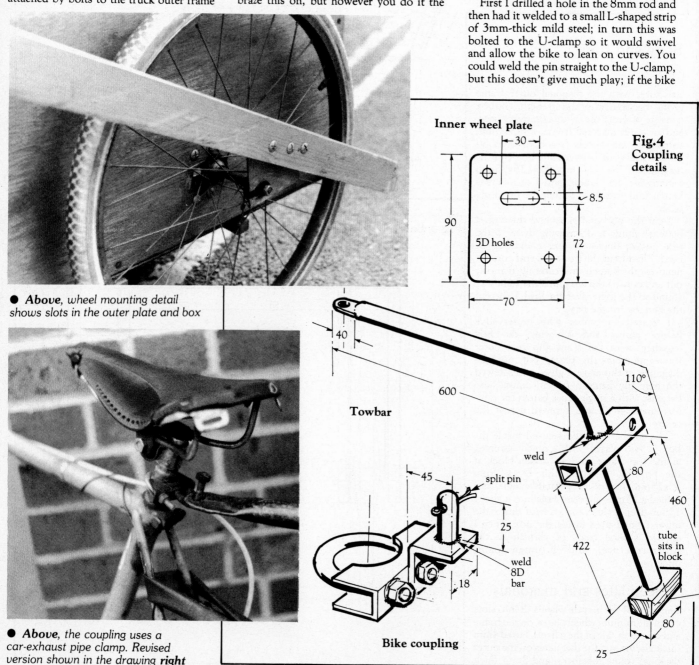

● *Above*, wheel mounting detail shows slots in the outer plate and box

● *Above*, the coupling uses a car-exhaust pipe clamp. Revised version shown in the drawing *right*

Inner wheel plate

Fig.4 Coupling details

5D holes

Towbar

weld

split pin

weld 8D bar

Bike coupling

tube sits in block

fell over when attached to the trailer, you might bend the pin or towbar.

I finished the coupling with a coat of Hammerite. The pin has a rubber ring pad (a tap washer) around it at the base, so the towbar can rest on it. Fitting the cycle wheels into the wheelplate slots between the outer frame and box required a bit of squeezing; to finish off I used aluminium channel to stiffen the upper edge of the ply box, and fixed rubber bumpers to the corners to prevent grazing. I attached a reflector and strips of reflecting material at the rear.

Trailer use

You'll find using the trailer is straightforward. It's surprisingly easy to pull, but obviously you won't want to travel more than two or three miles with a full load. The stability of the bike is hardly affected, and the outfit is still very manoeuvrable. But remember your 'vehicle' is rather longer and wider than the bike by itself. When you're not using it, you can store the trailer on end, with the U-clamp hitch left on the bike.

Having used it for some time, I recommend this useful freight transport to people without access to a car. ∎

Materials list

Wood

4mm exterior ply	2	900mm	x	450mm	
	1	450		502	
	1	485		502	
6mm exterior ply	1	662		502	
Outer frame	2	970		25	50
	2	730		25	50
Battens	2	485		25	25
	2	450		25	25
	2	662		25	25
	1	502		25	25
Bottom bracing	1	500		25	25
Block for towbar	1	100		30	25

Screws

40	25mm x 8 plated, or equivalent pins or staples
15	50mm x 8 plated
8	75mm x 8 plated

Aluminium

3.5mm plate	2	115	x	100
2mm plate	2	90	x	70
3mm gap channel		2030		

Steel tube

25mm-diameter 18 gauge seamless tube	1310mm
25mm box, 18 gauge	90

Bike coupling

25mm or 32mm U-bolt (car exhaust clamp)
3mm mild steel, 18 x 75mm
8mm-diameter rod for pin, 40mm long
Large split pin
Rubber washer

Nuts and bolts

Coach bolts	6	45mm	x	5mm
Coach bolts	2	65		5
Large flat head bolts	8	20		5

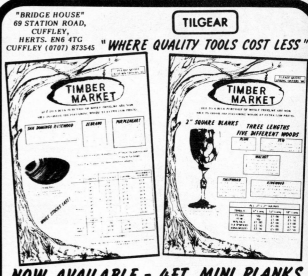

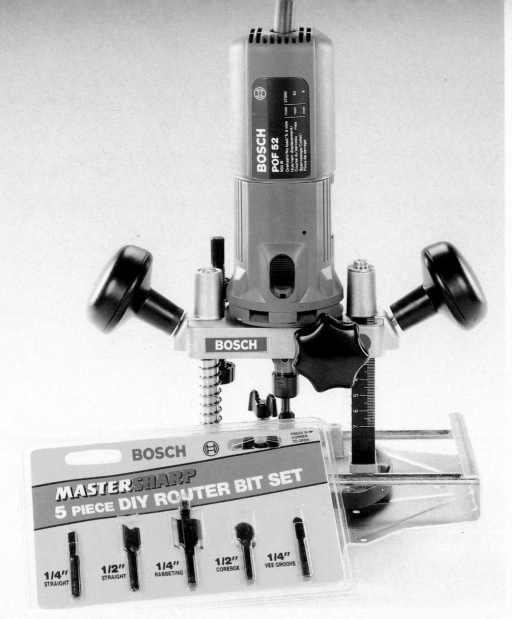

The Puzzleman

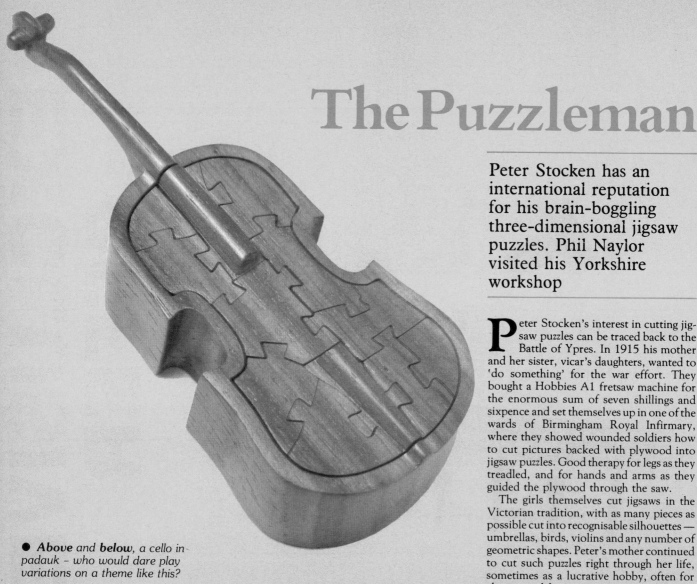

● **Above** and **below**, a cello in padauk – who would dare play variations on a theme like this?

Peter Stocken has an international reputation for his brain-boggling three-dimensional jigsaw puzzles. Phil Naylor visited his Yorkshire workshop

Peter Stocken's interest in cutting jigsaw puzzles can be traced back to the Battle of Ypres. In 1915 his mother and her sister, vicar's daughters, wanted to 'do something' for the war effort. They bought a Hobbies A1 fretsaw machine for the enormous sum of seven shillings and sixpence and set themselves up in one of the wards of Birmingham Royal Infirmary, where they showed wounded soldiers how to cut pictures backed with plywood into jigsaw puzzles. Good therapy for legs as they treadled, and for hands and arms as they guided the plywood through the saw.

The girls themselves cut jigsaws in the Victorian tradition, with as many pieces as possible cut into recognisable silhouettes — umbrellas, birds, violins and any number of geometric shapes. Peter's mother continued to cut such puzzles right through her life, sometimes as a lucrative hobby, often for charity, and from time to time as a full-time business.

Peter cut his first jigsaw at the age of seven; he learnt very quickly how to master the treadle machine, and achieve the exacting co-ordination of leg, eye and finger. He wasn't allowed to draw the shapes on the paper; every intricate shape had to be cut by eye alone. He continued cutting puzzles at school and university, to supplement his pocket money and meagre student grants. Slowly, imperceptibly, his style was developing, though at this stage he had no eye to a future with a fretsaw.

After graduating in English Literature from Trinity College, Dublin, Peter spent five years travelling the world for a large multinational company, 'always,' as he wryly puts it, 'at their expense, and occasionally on their behalf'.

He's amused by articles written about him which describe his disillusion with the rat-race and the determination he had to 'do his own thing' in the space and solitude of North Yorkshire. The reality was rather different. After a disagreement with his employer and a squalid wrangle in the Industrial Relations Court, he found himself on the dole with three children under five years, and a fourth on the way. He knew an awful lot about literature and a certain amount about business, but the only immediate way he could think of to bring in

● **Above**, *an Imperial Polish eagle in yew;* **right**, *a 95th birthday-present 'filigree' puzzle – note the dates – and* **below**, *Peru in Indian rosewood, commissioned for Paddington Bear's 25th birthday*

money was turn his hand to jigsaws again.

He told his friends: it was just before Christmas, and they were delighted to help him and at the same time solve some of their gift problems. Peter's jigsaws were certainly out of the ordinary; he cut certain pieces into letters that spelt out a message, not so obvious as to spoil the completed picture, but clear enough when the jigsaw was being put together.

The idea quickly caught on. His friends told their friends, their friends told others, and the orders rolled in for jigsaws with messages custom-made for the recipient. Sometimes it was a family photograph with a message such as 'Happy Christmas, Auntie', sometimes a reproduction of an Old Master with a classical quotation included, sometimes a *Playboy* centre-spread with a quite unrepeatable message.

The demand continued after that Christmas, and Peter and his wife realised they had a very marketable commodity on their hands. So, selling their house in Essex at a tidy profit, they threw their children into the car, strapped the fretsaw machine to the roof-rack and hightailed it for Yorkshire.

They found a totally delapidated farm-house that had been condemned 16 years before — the owner was waiting for it finally to crumble so he could use the rubble around his farm. It was perfect for Peter's needs. Though it is close to the

The Puzzleman

snapshots to enormous travel posters, scenes of Scottish lochs and Bavarian castles, Old Masters from Botticelli to Van Gogh (he would dearly have loved to cut up an original . . .). He found himself looking at pictures in his friends' houses not for their artistic merit, but purely to see whether they would cut up into good jigsaws. He was increasing the complexity of the puzzles in order to daunt his customers, but he felt he was coming to the end of this particular road.

His first move away from conventional jigsaws was what he describes as 'Filigree' puzzles, intricate and delicate tracery designs cut from slabs of highly polished hardwoods about ⅜in thick; at first he used yew and walnut, later palisander, Madagascar rosewood and Honduras rosewood. These were picture-less puzzles, with up to 200 pieces which could be either face up, and caused a great deal of puzzlement to customers.

● **Left**, *a bee in olive, and* **below**, *a selection from other inhabitants of the Stocken menagerie*

industrial conglomeration of Doncaster, Sheffield and Rotherham, the nearest village is two miles away and the next house a full mile. More importantly, while there might be coal-mining directly underneath, all the pits were at least two miles downwind.

Making that house fit for living in took 18 months of nearly full-time work. He knew nothing about building when he started, and the two ex-miners he employed as labourers knew even less. So he approached the project as if it were a jigsaw: that bit must go there, since it certainly doesn't go anywhere else. He chuckled when the local paper, the Doncaster Evening Post, printed an article about him under the headline 'Peter Stocken makes puzzles . . . and his biggest puzzle is his house'.

During this building period, the family lived in a rented hovel, with the front room reserved for puzzle production, the other for four children, two cats and two dogs. The situation eased in the summer when it was warm enough to move the puzzle-making out to the garage. Not that this made life any easier for the rest of the family; a winter of dust, glue and puzzles had rendered the front room virtually uninhabitable.

Despite these less than satisfactory conditions, this period was a very creative one for Peter's work. By the summer of 1973 he felt he had reached an artistic cul-de-sac with flat jigsaw puzzles. He'd stuck and cut every possible picture, from family

His second invention at this time was a vertical name puzzle, christened 'The Dongle'. The concept was simple; he cut the letters of somebody's name in such a way that the serifs on each letter held the pieces above and below together. He used 7mm ply — birch to reduce splintering to a minimum — and dyed the letters. Twelve years later these remain as popular as ever, and Peter wistfully admits that if he had wanted to make a lot of money, he would have employed an army of nimble-fingered Taiwanese to churn them out by the thousand.

But it was his third invention which established him — the three-dimensional puzzle. Again, the principle was simple. Take a piece of attractive wood, cut a slice off the bottom and then cut out an inside shape; glue the bottom back on so the grain matches and no-one can tell it was ever removed; cut the outside shape, make a puzzle out of the inside, and there it is — not only a puzzle, but an attractive piece of 'furniture'. And since the puzzle is contained within its outside shell, the pieces are less likely to be lost, broken or chewed by the dog.

This original idea came to him in a fit of bad temper one hot July afternoon. He was fed up with cutting jigsaws, and grabbed the first piece of wood that came to hand — a piece of yew he had intended to make into a toy for one of his children. First he cut a piece in the heart shape of one of his typical jigsaw designs; it was too chunky, so he turned it on its side and cut again. Before long he had cut it into 20 pieces with as many fitting together vertically as horizontally. There was no handy bath to jump out of an announce his find to the world; even his family was sceptical . . . but it was the start.

He continued to use his original fretsaw — not the A1, since his mother (now well into her 70s) was still using it — but the A1's direct descendant, the Hobbies Gem. It did the job equally well, though it lacked the charming wrought ironwork and Victorian stylishness of the A1. The treadle mechanism had been very satisfactory for cutting the three-ply of the conventional jigsaws, but cutting through 1¾in of tropical hardwood was tricky and wearisome — though not actually impossible.

For the new jigsaws, he attached a motor to the machine, replaced the old friction joints with ball-races, and strengthened the two arms that hold the blade. And here's the surprise: this is still the machine he uses for the cutting of the puzzles. It's a fact that staggers every visitor to his workshop. Over the years Peter has experimented with all manner of high-tech and fancy machines, but he has always returned to his original as being the best machine for the job. It cost him just under £10 in 1966 and, apart from paying the local garage to weld the odd bit of metal on from time to time, it has cost him practically nothing since. He is himself

● *Peter and the old faithful fretsaw – plus expression of concentration*

surprised that he has found no other machine that even approaches the flexibility of this curious hybrid: normally, using grade OO blades, he cuts depths up to 1½in, but he has cut lignum vitae up to 2in and Indian ebony of 2¼in.

Apparently the strength of the blade and the hardness of the wood are less important than the manner in which they are cut. It's not the really hard woods that cause him problems; one saw normally lasts through at least two Indian rosewood puzzles, but a puzzle cut from walnut — one of the lightest of native hardwoods — may require four or five blades. Fruitwoods are the same — apple is particularly difficult — but in Peter's Rogues' Gallery of woods there is a special spot for bonewood, an immensely dense timber from Nicaragua. Often confused with anjan because of its similar grain, it varies considerably in density, some planks cutting like butter, others weighing as much as lignum vitae. Because of the texture of the wood, the pieces are actually much more difficult to cut even than lignum vitae, and in producing one fairly straightforward puzzle he broke 46 blades.

Once Peter had got the farmhouse into a livable state, he was set up for expansion. Apart from the large house he had constructed from knocking the original cottage and three adjoining stable blocks into one, there was a huge barn and innumerable outhouses. The top floor of the barn became the store for seasoned home-grown woods and the more valuable imported timbers, while the drying timber was either kept in the outhouses or in the

open air.

In the early days, when petrol was cheap, he would drive the length and breadth of the country picking up trunks of any wood that took his fancy (the chainsaw beside him in the cab of his truck suggesting he was not that fussy where they came from). These days he can afford to be more selective and now finds it more economical to buy in rather than cope with the cutting and drying himself.

The ground floor of the barn became the production unit, with one room — heated and with all modern conveniences — for the cutting of the final puzzles, together with sanding and polishing, while the remainder houses the normal woodworking machinery for the initial preparation of the wood. Here also, stacked in box-upon-box against the wall are the offcuts he sells to anyone who is prepared to search through them; at the last count, he had bits of 154 different woods, including 15 rosewoods and 6 species of ebony.

Sometimes he finds a use for the offcuts himself. The dining room of his house is in yew blocks, while the drawing room has what must be the most magnificent floor in Yorkshire — 36x1½in planks of Madagascar rosewood, whose dark crimson austerity is alleviated by a symmetrical diamond pattern in a lighter wood.

Most of the machinery and equipment was acquired secondhand from sales of building and timber firms forced into bankruptcy — planer, circular saw, lathe and sander — though he had to invest in a new bandsaw, the machine he uses most. The extraction system is primitive but

● *Two 'filigree' puzzles made for St Valentine's Day*

continued

The Puzzleman

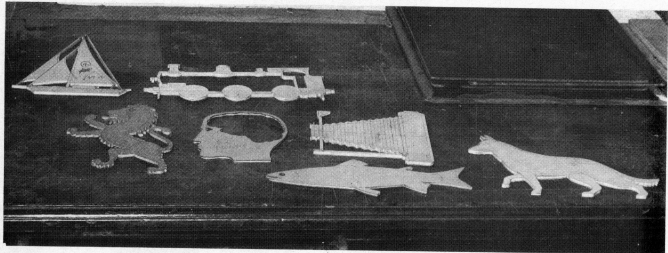

● *A selection of templates for the famous brain, animals, a camera, forms of transport...*

effective; a stainless steel chimney liner is connected to the main machinery and the dust is propelled out through the wall of the barn. So far from civilisation, the dust upsets no-one, though in windless spells the flowers in his front garden develop rosewood-tinted leaves!

The puzzles themselves are extremely intricate. Peter reckons the average person should be able to assemble the average puzzle within 3½ hours; there are some puzzle freaks around who can do the most difficult in 20 minutes flat, but they are rare. At the other end of the scale are people who would never complete a puzzle if they had all the time in the world. Luckily most people like this never take the puzzle apart, either leaving them intact upon their mantelpieces, or, like one collector, locking them up in a glass case so that neither he or anybody else can touch them. This is fortunate for Peter, for he gives an undertaking that he will always put customers' puzzles back together for the price of the return postage; he gets about 30-40 back each year, usually accompanied by some good-humoured reflections on the marital status of his parents.

Peter maintains the cutting of the puzzles is simple; to the layman, it looks positively labyrinthine. Faced with the solid inside of the puzzle, he first draws on to the top surface of the puzzle any initial or motif that he has been asked for; using this as his starting point, he cuts the piece in two, making sure the two halves interlock at several points. Then he turns the larger piece through 90° and cuts off an interlocking layer, cutting this into several pieces, one of which will be the initial. He turns the remaining chunk through 90° and cuts a further section, repeating the process until all is in pieces. Often he will be asked to hide initials or shapes deep within the puzzle; one customer wanted a dachshund-shaped puzzle, with no initials but as many internal pieces as possible shaped like

bones! This sort of thing takes more planning, of course.

Regular customers require special attention, and he varies the technique to make each successive puzzle that bit more difficult. Peter has met his Waterloo only once, with renowned puzzler Edward Hordern, who has the world's largest collection of puzzles, including nearly 50 of Peter's. For this man, Peter reached a point when he could devise no more difficult puzzle.

Since he shaped that first primitive heart-shaped puzzle one summer's evening in 1973, Peter has made over 7,000 three-dimensional puzzles: each has been unique inside, and he has created more than 150 different designs. They are sold in shops from Tokyo to San Francisco, and grace the drawing rooms of cabinet ministers, pop-stars and royalty.

His own favourite puzzle? He still prefers simple geometric shapes, preferably made from yew — partly from sentimental reasons since it was the first timber he ever used, and partly because it cuts so easily and finishes so exquisitely. His favourite design is the Human Head with the brain as the puzzle; the idea for this came to him in a bar in Co. Wexford at four in the morning when he was asked to think of a suitable puzzle for an Irish brain-surgeon. It's been one of his most popular puzzles ever since.

But he rates his best work as the gargantuan collection of European countries, made for a scrap metal merchant. Each country is a different puzzle, made from a specific wood, and the whole thing is set in a velvet-lined box, each country in its correct geographical location. Russia, even the European bit, proved too large for one puzzle, so, indulging in a piece of political whimsy, he cut Georgia and the Ukraine into separate puzzles and 'liberated' Estonia, Latvia and Lithuania.

His wife, who is now a full-time solicitor (very useful for chasing unpaid bills) still handles all the book-keeping and is a considerable help in sandpapering and

polishing; apart from this, he has never employed anyone full-time. Nor does he want to; apart from other factors, employing others would considerably cramp his individual life-style, since he reckons he is most productive after midnight.

His children can all cut conventional jigsaws, and his daughter now supplies not only her father's old customers, but also those of her grandmother; otherwise Peter does not encourage them to be involved in the business.

For the future, Peter intends to gradually reduce his output, concentrating on creating more and more exotic designs. He now uses both silver and gold worked into the puzzles, sometimes as solid pieces of precious metal interlocking into the neighbouring wooden pieces, and sometimes as inlay; he sees this as an area with great scope for development. He's also dabbled in the field of laser technology, but more for amusement than with any serious intention of moving away from his traditional methods.

What started out as merely an attempt to get himself off the dole has now entirely taken over his life. Strangers who get lost looking for Stubbs Farm get looks of blank incomprehension when they ask for Peter Stocken's house. Ask for the Puzzleman and everybody knows who you're looking for. He even received a letter from America addressed simply to 'The Puzzlemaker, Yorkshire', though he insists this was less due to his fame than to the fact that all the local postmen are puzzle aficionados.

Yet he still describes himself as 'just a craftsman' — and visitors to his workshop have their attention drawn to his vast display of graffiti scribbled on the walls rather than to his puzzles.

With some justification. Having left Peter Stocken, his incredible puzzles, and Yorkshire far behind, one of his workshop-wall graffiti sticks in my mind, a quotation from Dylan Thomas — 'Art is an accident of Craft'.

∎

Woodworker PLANS SERVICE

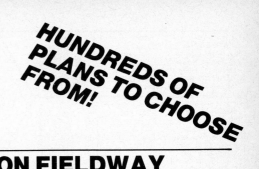

JOHN THOMPSON FIELDWAY COLLECTION — OVER 40 DESIGNS

OXFORDSHIRE WAGON
To many people this is the epitome of the English farm wagon. Used on Blackwood farm, the original is now in the Oxford County Museum this 1/8 scale model is 18ins. long.
Plan No. JT/18   1/8 scale 4 sheets plus photo sheet £3.60

GLAMORGAN WAGON
A most elegant wagon. This wagon was built around 1870, now renovated and on display at St. Fagans.
Plan JT/38   1/8 scale   Price £3.30

YORKSHIRE WAGON
This example is of the Vale of Pickering type, very robustly built, a handsome vehicle. Model is 16in. long.
Plan JT/40   4 Sheets   Price £3.30

HEREFORD WAGON
A small size plank sided wagon, it is now in the reserve collection at the Museum of Rural Life at Reading. Model is 15in. long.
Plan JT/14   1/8 scale, 2 large sheets   Price £2.95

HOP TUG
The high ladders fore and aft are a feature of this unusual wagon. Model is 19in. long.
Plan JT/15   1/8 scale, 2 large sheets   Price £2.95

HAMPSHIRE WAGGON
Constructed about 1900, this is an unusual wagon with double shafts. A superb subject for someone who wants a wealth of detail. Model is 17in. long.
Plan JT/10   1/8 scale, 2 large sheets   Price £2.95

1850 EAST ANGLIAN WAGON
This massive and stately vehicle dates from 1850, now in the reserve collection at the Reading museum of Rural Life. Model is 19ins. long.
Plan JT/20   1/8 scale, 5 sheets plus sheet of photos
Price £4.50

HOW TO MAKE WHEELS
The chart MODEL WHEEL CONSTRUCTION gives step-by-step instructions to enable the average handyman to produce excellent scale wheels. Available only with one other plan order.
Plan No. JT/001   Price 80p

ASHBY DESIGN WORKSHOP — TRADITIONAL FURNITURE FOR HOUSE & GARDEN

18th Century Gateleg Table
The convenience of the traditional gateleg table is admirably suited to the home of today. This design, which is based on an actual antique, features elegant turnings to a superbly designed profile. The original cable was built in brown oak, but any English hardwood or fruitwood would give a most satisfactory result.
ADW 103   Price £4.25

Workshop Accessories
Nineteen various tools & accessories are detailed on this drawing, including a plan for a saw horse. All the tools may be made with ease and economy and they will become valued additions to your workshop equipment.
ADW 109   Price £3.50

Lap or Table Desk
This compact item will be a favourite with all the family for letter writing & homework. The basic design offers good storage for papers, pens etc. Construction may be on a simple screw & glue basis or could incorporate dovetails or comb joints as desired. Build in solid wood or use plywood and veneers.

ADW 115   Price £3.50

Magazine Racks
This plan offers an open magazine rack and an alternative version with a table top. There is scope for decorative variations on both versions and suggestions are shown on the drawing. Construction incorporates simple housing joints.
ADW 116   Price £4.00

TAPA SYSTEM PLAN PACKS
Each Pack comprises:

A1 size Plan	2 Frameworks
3 A3 Plans	4 Chair designs
Full-size profiles	Cutting List
Joint details	Schedules

Featuring a series of modern furniture designs for the home, the TAPA system of plan-packs is a new concept in woodworking projects. Each plan-pack focusses on a specific object and explores many alternatives to the original model. The Dining Chair is the first in the series, featuring ideas based on the simple halving joint prototype.
Plan ADW401   Price £5.75

DAVID BRYANT CRAFT DESIGN PLANS HOME & LEISURE, TOYS, SPINNING WEAVING

No. 59 SPINDLE WHEEL
An alternative to the Great Wheel No. 47, this non flyer wheel offers a smaller version with a 660mm (26")

diameter hoop rim wheel. This type of wheel was in common usage before the flyer type was invented, and the example here is a measured drawing of an original on display at Quarry Bank Mill, Styal (N.T.) and in daily use. Parts list and instructions.
DB 59   Price £4.25

No. 60 FRENCH SPINNING WHEEL
This design is of an unusual French spinning wheel. The original comes from the Loire valley, and is known to have been used in the last war when clothing was scarce. Wheel diameter 442mm (17⅜"). The triangular base is typical of French style wheels. The flyer has been slightly adapted to suit modern day useage. Parts list, instructions etc.
DB 60   Price £7.13

DRUM CARDER
Sooner or later spinners graduate to a drum carder. This design takes the toil out of hand carding. It uses a positive gear/sprocket drive which also reduces the drag which the belt drive alternative imposes. A little metalwork as well as woodwork involved. One sheet plan.
Plan No. DB54   Price £3.70

SLOPING STYLE SPINNING WHEEL
This design is a replica of an authentic spinning wheel doem olden days, having a 486mm (19in.) diameter wheel with bent

wood rim. Plan is complete with mother-of-all, distaff, treadle operation etc. A feature of this wheel is its attractive turnings which make it a most decorative piece besides being functional. A design for the enthusiast woodturner. Two sheet plan.
Plan No. DB12   Price £5.40

UPRIGHT SPINNING WHEEL
In this vertical style spinning wheel the mother-of-all arrangement is situated above the main wheel. The latter is 460mm diameter and the rim is of segmented design. Simpler lines than the sloping wheel but nevertheless graceful in appearance and of course functional.
Plan No. DB13   Price £5.40

SPINNING STOOL
A spinning stool specially suited for use with the sloping bed wheel. Four legged arrangement, with richly carved seat and back. A good example of chip carving.
Plan No. DB20   Price £2.20

ANOTHER SUPERB MORRISON DESIGN

AUDIO CABINET RACK
A must for the woodworker who likes to take pride in his work, build this superb cabinet 1 sheet of explicit instructions and materials.
MTC 3   Price £4.00

SUPERB TOOL CABINET
Top notch design from Morrison Originals, 5 sheets of A3 size drawings with step by step procedures, many notes and a full cutting list. You'll never lose another valuable tool — a place for everything.
Plan No. MTC1   Price £4.75

Also available in metric
MTC 2   Price £4.75

CREDIT CARD ORDERS WELCOME
TEL: 0442-211882

Argus Specialist Publications, PO Box 35, Wolsey House, Wolsey Road, Hemel Hempstead, Herts. HP2 4SS. 0442-211882. Delivery 21 days

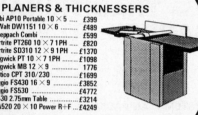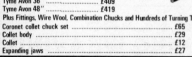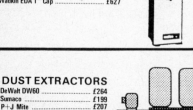

CARVING '87

● Left, Mabel Packenham-Walsh's 'At the Ark', carved and painted wood relief (1510x510mm). Below, two more painted carvings from Eleanor Glover: below left, birds; below right, 'Leaping Figure' (470mm high).

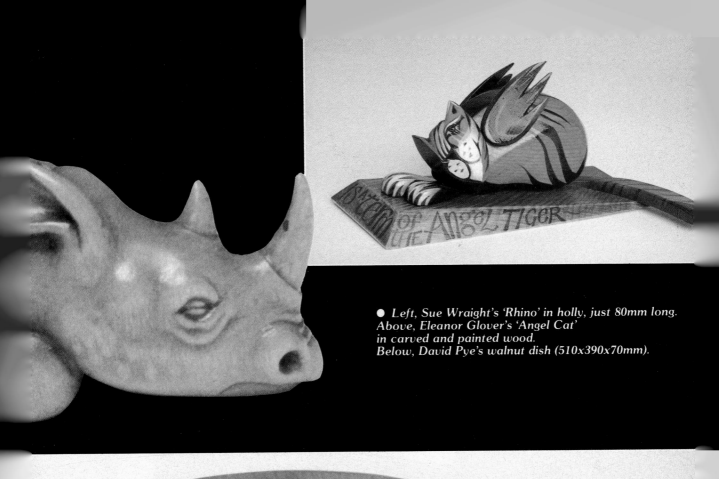

● Left, Sue Wraight's 'Rhino' in holly, just 80mm long.
Above, Eleanor Glover's 'Angel Cat'
in carved and painted wood.
Below, David Pye's walnut dish (510x390x70mm).

Carving is abuzz with vitality in 1987. Not only is WOOD-WORKER finding a growing interest among readers, but Contemporary Applied Arts is devoting its current exhibition to 'Carved Wood' — acknowledging 'an upsurge of vigour in this field at the present time'. On these pages are some examples of the work on show.

The living traditions of carving in many challenging aspects: Sue Wraight's exquisite small animals, Bryan Illsley's gaudily energetic sculptures, Eleanor Glover's carved and painted figures; Guy Taplin's estuary birds, Gerard Rigot's menagerie of animals, Howard Raybould's furniture, and Mabel Pakenham-Walsh's relief-carved wall pieces. Paul Caton's lavishly sensuous bowls contrast with Jim Partridge's haggard and haunting work.

● Carved Wood, 10 April-9 May Contemporary Applied Arts (formerly British Crafts Centre), 43 Earlham St, Covent Garden, London WC2; gallery open Mon-Fri 10-5.30, Sat 11-5.

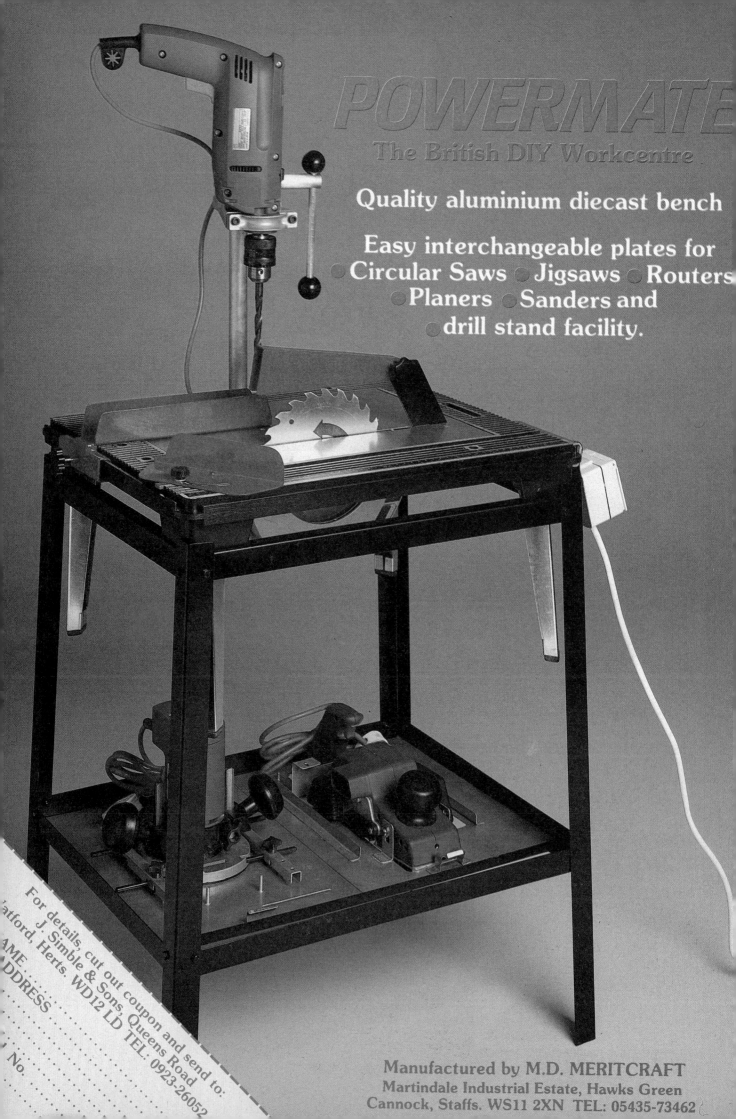

Raise the roof

The mysteries of the steel roofing square explained: Paul Curtis introduces a classic pre-technology tool and its application to basic roof carpentry

Photo courtesy Redland Roof Tiles Ltd.

The steel roofing square is the carpenter's cunning calculator. With the square in one hand and a pencil in the other, you can set out all the components of a roof in double quick time. The markings on the sides, once understood, enable you to determine the lengths of the various rafters for any pitch of roof, and to mark out the appropriate cuts.

The square has two arms at precise right angles. The blade is 24in long and 2in wide; the tongue is 18in long and 1½in wide. Both the blade and the tongue are divided into inch and ½in divisions, which represent feet and inches, like a scale. Some models have other scales in addition, and also various tables engraved on the face to determine the length of rafters.

Roofs

A roof is a primary building element. As well as being weathertight and durable, it must have the strength and durability to support both dead and live loads. The dead loads are the weight of the construction materials plus any extra loads imposed by the householder. Live loads are mainly wind and snow.

Roofs also play a part in giving a building character. There are three main types:
- Simple gable or pitch roof, with two slopes meeting at the ridge, and with triangles of brickwork forming the ends.
- Hipped roof, with all four sides sloping up at the same angle to meet at the centre line.
- Mansard roof, with steep sides hung with tiles or slates and a shallow pitched roof on top (looking in section a bit like an upside-down boat); this style may have either gable or hipped ends.

Whatever the overall shape of the roof, the structure derives its strength not just from the size of the timbers used, but also from its geometry. A roof consists of a series of triangles, the strongest straight-edged shape that exists; stressed to its limits, a triangle will not distort, unlike a square or any other polygon. It's important to remember this structural basis when you make alterations to any roof; whatever you change, you must not destroy the triangular geometry.

There are a few basic terms used in roofing that you should understand at this stage (other terms are given in the glossary):

Span The distance from wallplate to wallplate, measured on the outside (wall-

● **Above**, two pitched roofs meet forming a valley with a double pitch, plus a straight dormer. **Left**, the steel square – Stanley's metric version

plates are the timbers laid on top of the brick walls).

Run Shortest horizontal distance measured from a plumbline through the centre of the ridge to the outer edge of the wallplate (in equal pitched roofs the run is half the span).

Rise The distance from the top of the ridge to the level of the foot (for working out correct rafter length it is reckoned as slightly less than this, as explained later).

The square

You'll see from fig. 1 how the square is used to give accurate lengths and angles for cutting the corners of the triangles. Remember that one inch on the scale represents one foot. With the blade held horizontal, a run of 8ft on the common rafter is represented by 8in on the blade; a rise of 5ft on the roof is represented by 5in on the tongue of the square. Thus on the square you have a miniature representation

of the roof, with its right-angled triangle, and the hypotenuse (the line joining the 8in mark on the blade and the 5in mark on the tongue) gives the rafter length required to $\frac{1}{12}$ size. The square also gives you the angles at which the ends of this rafter have to be cut, the vertical 'plumb' cut on the tongue, and the horizontal 'seat' cut on the blade.

To improve accuracy when applying the steel roofing square to the timber you can make a fence (fig. 2) from two parallel strips of timber screwed together at each side of the square to form an adjustable hypotenuse.

Roof carpenters generally make use of this hypotenuse measurement by 'stepping' the square, set to rafter run and rafter rise, 12 times along the timber (fig. 3). The accuracy of this method depends on the skill of the operator, who uses fingers and thumbs to keep tally of the measurement, and marks each step with a pencil.

You can get increased accuracy by tightening the hypotenuse gauge and using a

16in
tongue

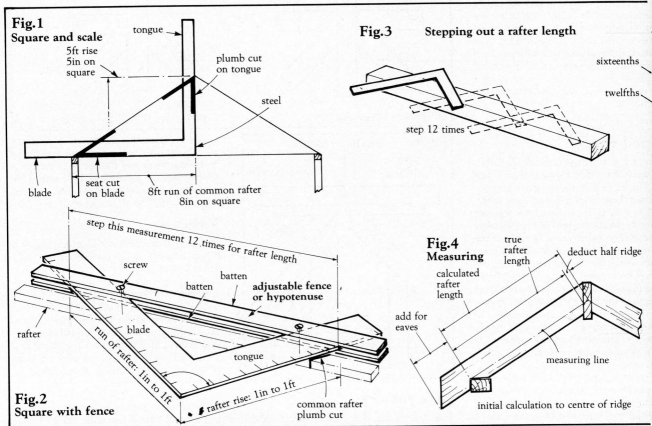

Fig.1
Square and scale

tongue

5ft rise
5in on
square

plumb cut
on tongue

steel

blade

seat cut
on blade

8ft run of common rafter
8in on square

step this measurement 12 times for rafter length

Fig.2
Square with fence

screw

batten

batten

**adjustable fence
or hypotenuse**

rafter

run of rafter: 1in to 1ft

blade

tongue

rafter rise: 1in to 1ft

common rafter
plumb cut

Fig.3 **Stepping out a rafter length**

sixteenths

twelfths

step 12 times

Fig.4
Measuring

true
rafter
length

deduct half ridge

calculated
rafter
length

add for
eaves

measuring line

initial calculation to centre of ridge

tenths

twelfths

sixteenths

twelfths

marking knife instead of the thick pencil
usually used by carpenters.

The alternative, of course, is to measure
the hypotenuse on the square and multiply
it by 12.

Whenever possible measurements
should be taken on site, for bricklayers
don't work to such degrees of accuracy as
woodworkers. The full span of the roof,
from the outside faces of each wallplate,
should be measured in situ, and halved to
give you the run.

The measurements are taken along the
centre lines (fig. 4) and therefore
allowances must be made for half the thickness of the ridge which is measured square
from the plumb cut of the common rafter.

Gable roof

For an overhanging eave, you should
lengthen the rafter by the amount of the
overhang and form a birdsmouth in the
rafter. Use the ridge plumb cut for the
plumb cut of the birdsmouth at the wallplate and the seat cut to form a birdsmouth
at about half the depth of the rafter (fig. 5).

Use the plumb- and seat-cut angles again
at the foot of the overhang to provide fixing
points for the fascia and soffit boards. You
need bracketing fixed flush with the bottom
of the rafter to support the soffit. Nail
tapered pieces of timber, called sprockets,
to the top edge of the rafter to provide tilt
for the tiles and to give more support to the
fascia.

For a simple gable roof only common
rafters are used. The ceiling joists are

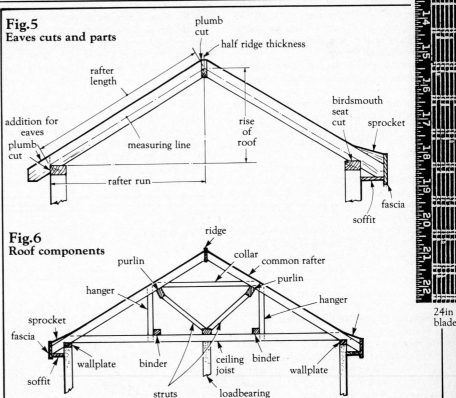

Fig.5
Eaves cuts and parts

plumb
cut

half ridge thickness

rafter
length

rise
of
roof

birdsmouth
seat
cut

sprocket

addition for
eaves
plumb
cut

measuring line

rafter run

fascia

soffit

Fig.6
Roof components

ridge

purlin

collar

common rafter

purlin

hanger

hanger

sprocket

fascia

soffit

wallplate

binder

ceiling
joist

binder

wallplate

struts

loadbearing
partition

generally used to tie the rafter feet and
prevent them spreading under the weight.
These joists are nailed to the rafter feet and
to the wallplate. Where extra height is
needed the ceiling joists may be fixed as

collars at any point up to one third of the
rafter length, measured from the wall plate.
(fig. 6). The collar can be placed higher, but
there will be a greater tendency for the
rafter feet to spread.

24in
blade

WOODWORKER MAY 1987

continued
389

Raise the roof

Where there is no collar, and the ceiling joists are used as tie beams, the rafters are supported in the middle by a purlin running the length of the roof. This is fixed at right angles to the slope of the roof and may itself need supporting by props from an internal wall. These props should also be at right angles to the slope of the roof, or as near as is practicable.

Hipped roofs

Almost all the suburban semis of the 1930s were designed with hipped roofs. The bevels for hipped roofs are more complicated than those needed for a simple gable-end roof. You find the bevels for the seat and plumb cuts of the hips in the same way as the common rafter cuts. The run of the hip is measured on the blade of the square and the rise of the roof is measured on the tongue. The tongue then gives the plumb cut and the blade the seat cut. You could get the length of the hip by stepping the square, set to the run and rise measurements, 12 times along the hip, but brickwork is not as accurate as carpentry, and site carpentry is not as accurate as cabinetmaking, so check the building diagonals if possible.

The most accurate way of obtaining hip lengths is to erect the common rafters and brace them in position so that you can take an accurate measurement from the apex of the roof to the wallplate corner. A better fit can be made if this corner is cut off to receive the hip, but if this is done allowances have to be made if the hip length is not measured on site.

There are various ways of connecting the hips to the apex of the roof; one is to allow the ridge to run through just far enough to take the hips (fig. 7A). However, the hips are usually wider than the ridge so if this method is used, the hips have to be notched so that they will fit against each other under the ridge.

The end rafter, which is a common rafter, is then fitted between the hips. Again, this rafter has to be shortened to take into account the projection of the ridge.

An alternative is to fit a deep saddle board at the apex of the common rafters, to take the deeper hip rafters (fig. 8). When this is done the hips have to be shorter than the calculated length in order to allow for the thickness of this board. The board should be measured across its thickness at the same angle as the hips; another good reason for taking site measurements.

Having got the accurate length of the hip, this measurement is used to find the cross-cut of the hips (the angle across the top edge of the hip). This angle is obtained by taking the run of the hip on the blade of the square and length of the hip on the tongue. It is the angle this makes at the tongue that is required.

The end common rafter is then cut to fit between the hips or, more likely, it is omitted and the jack rafters are spaced evenly across the end of the roof.

Jack rafters

Jack rafters are those diminishing rafters which fit between the hip and the wallplate (fig. 9). They diminish in length the same amount for each successive rafter. To find their lengths, when the wallplate has been set out, the number of jack rafters is counted and the pattern rafter is divided into equal spaces to give the required number of rafter lengths (this will be the centre of the rafter as all measurements are to centre lines).

The wallplate cuts for these rafters are the same as those used for the common rafters. The plumb cut where the jack meets the hip is also the same as that used for the plumb cut of the common rafter.

The crosscut (across the 2in edge of the jack) is the only new cut to find. It is found by taking the run of the common rafter on the blade of the square and the length of the common rafter on the tongue. The required angle is found on the tongue.

Valleys

Where a pitched roof turns at right angles, a hip is required on the outside corner and a valley is formed on the inside (fig. 10). The cuts for the valley rafter are found in the same way as those for the hip.

The cuts for the valley jack rafters are also the same as for the hip jack rafters, except the common rafter top cuts are used where the valley jacks meet the ridge; and the compound angle for where the hip jacks fit against the hip is used at the bottom of the valley jacks where they fit against the valley rafter.

An alternative method of forming a valley is often used where a smaller pitched roof joins a main roof, as for instance, where a dormer window has a small pitched roof (fig. 11). Here lay boards are lined up between the position of the ridge of the small roof and the wallplate. Jack rafters are then cut to fit on to these boards. Again, the top cut of these little jack rafters is the same as those used for the small common rafters. The common rafter seat cut is used for the side cut of the jack and the crosscut is found in the usual way by taking the run of the small roof rafter on the blade of the square and the length on the tongue; the tongue gives the cut. This provides the compound angle to fit on to the lay board.

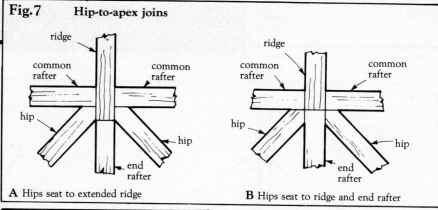

Fig. 7 Hip-to-apex joins

A Hips seat to extended ridge

B Hips seat to ridge and end rafter

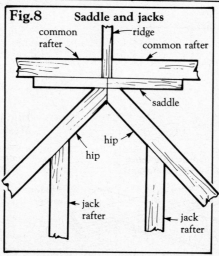

Fig. 8 Saddle and jacks

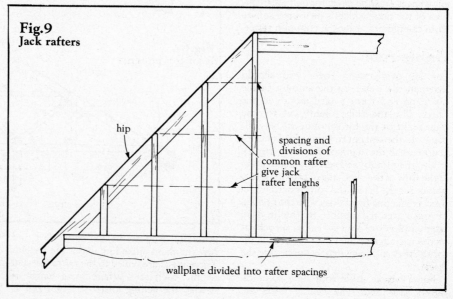

Fig. 9
Jack rafters

spacing and divisions of common rafter give jack rafter lengths

wallplate divided into rafter spacings

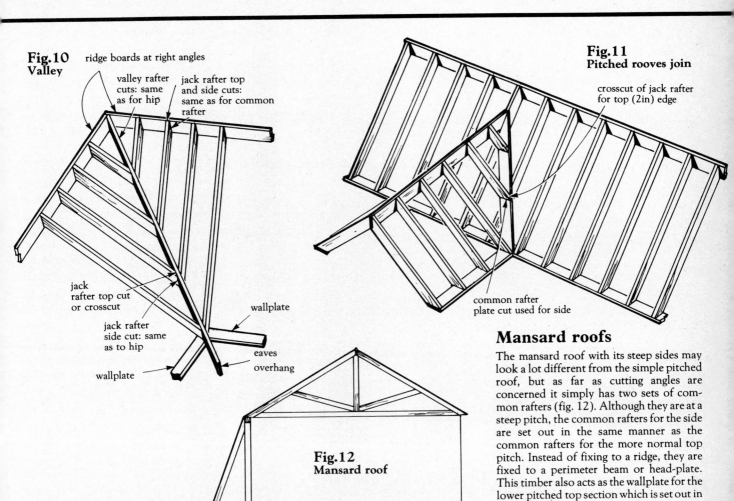

Fig.10 Valley

ridge boards at right angles

valley rafter cuts: same as for hip

jack rafter top and side cuts: same as for common rafter

jack rafter top cut or crosscut

jack rafter side cut: same as to hip

wallplate

wallplate

eaves overhang

Fig.11 Pitched rooves join

crosscut of jack rafter for top (2in) edge

common rafter plate cut used for side

Fig.12 Mansard roof

floor joists

Mansard roofs

The mansard roof with its steep sides may look a lot different from the simple pitched roof, but as far as cutting angles are concerned it simply has two sets of common rafters (fig. 12). Although they are at a steep pitch, the common rafters for the side are set out in the same manner as the common rafters for the more normal top pitch. Instead of fixing to a ridge, they are fixed to a perimeter beam or head-plate. This timber also acts as the wallplate for the lower pitched top section which is set out in the normal way.

The steel square can also be used for setting out staircases and many other structures; it's a wonderful device. ∎

Roofing table

Common rafter plumb cut	Run of rafter on blade, rise of rafter on tongue; tongue gives cut	**Hip seat cut**	Run of hip on blade, rise of hip on tongue; blade gives cut
Common rafter seat cut	Run of rafter on blade, rise of rafter on tongue; blade gives cut	**Hip crosscut**	Run of hip on blade, length of hip on tongue; tongue gives cut
Hip plumb cut	Run of hip on blade, rise of hip on tongue; tongue gives cut	**Jack rafter crosscut**	Run of common rafter on blade, length of common rafter on tongue; tongue gives cut

Purlin side cut	Length of common rafter on tongue, rise of rafter on blade; blade gives cut
Purlin cross cut	Run of common rafter on blade, length of common rafter on tongue; tongue gives cut

Roofing terms

Bargeboard	decorative board at verge or gable
Birdsmouth	a notched joint where rafters are joined to the wallplate
Binder	timbers which span load-bearing walls to which ceiling joists are attached to prevent sagging
Blade	the wide leg of a steel roofing square
Bracketing	light timber framing which supports the soffit
Common rafters	the inclined timbers fixed between the wallplate and the ridgeboard
Collar	a tie beam
Eaves	the lower part of the roof usually including rafter feet, wallplate, ceiling joists, soffit, fascia
Fascia	Vertical board at rafter foot, supporting the gutter
Gable	the triangular end of the roof
Hangers	timbers which take the strain in tension
Hip	rafter fixed at the corner of a roof
Jack rafter	diminishing rafters fixed to the hip and wallplate or valley
Pitch	the angle of the roof
Plumb cut	a vertical cut
Purlin	a strong beam which supports the rafters
Run	a rafter in plan
Ridgeboard	the apex board to which rafters are fixed
Soffit	horizontal board fixed to rafter feet
Sprockets	tapered timbers fixed to the
	top of the rafter foot to give an upward tilt to the eaves tiles
Struts	timbers which take loads in compression
Tie beams	timbers which span the building and hold the feet of the rafters to prevent them spreading (ceiling joists usually perform this task)
Tongue	the narrow leg of the steel roofing square
Valley	the intersection of two pitched roofs which forms an internal angle
Verge	the edge of a pitched roof at the gable
Wallplate	timber bedded on to the top course of bricks to take roof members

Tick top bubble

A most extraordinary clock is catching eyes and telling time in Cheltenham

Saturdays in Cheltenham's Regent Shopping Arcade have become a problem for the local police. The 45ft 'Wishing fish' clock, towering 60ft above one end of the arcade, is drawing such crowds that they have to be moved on. Hundreds of people stand gazing at the fantasy timepiece on weekdays; in the first few weekends after the clock's January inauguration the gazers were there in thousands.

Lloyd's Bank Pension Scheme, owners of the £23m development, wanted to commission a clock to make the arcade a meeting place, somewhere that would draw people as a natural rendezvous. Mike Harding of Sinclair Harding, renowned Cheltenham clockmakers, was asked to make one to an agreed design, but turned several proposals down as both impossible to make and unlikely to work. So they went to Kit Williams (*WW/Jan 86*), author, painter, and creator of the 'Masquerade' search for a bejewelled golden hare which became a national — and international — obsession.

'The architects,' says Kit, 'felt the building had the classical Cheltenham style, and wanted a piece with that feeling. The clients were more disposed towards a funfair sort of treatment — a bit of Disneyland perhaps. I wanted something that would attract both the sort of people who are fascinated by push-buttons and flashing lights in the Science Museum, and also those who just want to be surprised and delighted. Most mechanical clocks are a bit dead, actually coming into action only once an hour, but I was after something that

● *Towering above Cheltenham's elegant modern arcade, the Wishing Fish clock provides an absorbing mixture of visual illusion, mechanical ingenuity, and outright fantasy . . . **right**, the golden balls descend and appear to tip into the great wheel*

● **Above**, the mouse appears, the snake lunges . . . but to the children's delight he'll always be hungry

moved and could be looked at and wondered about all the time — something that was alive all the time. I stayed awake four days and four nights working on the idea, and when I took the drawing into a meeting with Mike Harding, he said not only that it would work, but he wanted to do it.'

The illusion

'I was transfixed as a child', Kit explains, 'by the "suspended tap" water illusion — where a tap is suspended above a bowl of water just by string, but there is a constant stream of water flowing from it. Where is the water coming from? I used to think it must be hydrogen flowing up one string and oxygen up the other, mixing to make water, but of course when I put my hand in the constant flow of "water", I felt the Perspex tube in the centre of the stream up which the water is pumped. This was the basic illusion I took as a theme.

'At the very top of the 45ft structure, we start with a white wooden duck. It "lays" a constant stream of golden 8in-diameter "eggs" into a row of cups fixed to a continuous length of motorcycle chain, which takes them down to the top housing for the gears that drive the chain. The cups with balls go into that housing, but come out again empty — go up again, and the duck lays another golden ball. Where do they come from? How does the duck keep all those balls inside? The balls appear to drop out of the cup, into the "cupola", and out of that into a spiral of wire, from which they drop into an 8ft-diameter "water wheel", which drives most of the mechanism — apart from the timekeeping. The wheel is on a long shaft with another counter wheel at the other end, and revolves on a planetary gearing system around the vertical axis of the clock as well as on its own central axis. Each time a ball drops off this lower water

● Kit Williams applies one of numerous coats of polyurethane to the fish body: note the grain match. **Below**, the sun's orbit shows the hours

continued

Tick top bubble

wheel into the large main case of the clock which carries the face — it happens about every 12 seconds — a mouse pops out of one of numerous doors on the main case, washes its whiskers, and pops back in again. They appear in random order, pneumatically powered and computer-controlled, so the children have a great time trying to work out where the next one is going to come. There's a snake on top of the case which tries to grab a mouse when it comes out of the door nearest to him, but he never quite gets there. The illusion of the endless stream of golden balls works so well that of course people spend time there, getting a crick in their necks.'

What's the secret? 'The golden balls in the cups are actually hemispheres pivoted in the cups, which turn themselves over as the cups go through the chain housing, so they appear to go up empty. There's another vertical column of solid balls inside the octagonal mahogany column above the case, which is moved up pneumatically each time the "water wheel" drops one into the case; one is pushed out of the top and runs down the wire helter skelter and on to the wheel, while the one at the bottom is pushed into its place at the base of the mahogany column.'

All this is happening all the time. What about when it strikes the hour? 'Well, that's a bit more drastic. The face of the clock — a painting with animals, the sun and moon acting as hour and minute hands — revolves very fast, and the fish at the bottom — the wishing fish — blows bubbles for 40 seconds, waggling fins and tails, and playing "I'm for ever blowing bubbles". People go crazy.' One is led to wonder how crazy the nearby shopkeepers will be after years of this.

The fish

Kit made the fish and painted the clock face, but the overall design is his. He is full of praise for Mike Harding, for the quality of whose work he has obvious respect. 'The design decisions and problem solving came back to me, but Mike was very inventive and enthusiastic, particularly with problems. I wanted the mice, for instance, to be driven by electric motors, but Mike said he would prefer a pneumatic system, which is smooth, powerful and silent. Sinclair Harding made all the other parts; the 8ft wheel is very Brunel, like something from a huge pumping engine in mahogany, brass and steel.'

The fish uses 2mm strips laid diagonally, over each other at 90°, on bulkheads, a techniqe common in racing sailboats. There are two layers of 2mm strips, mahogany for the inner and alternated mahogany, walnut and hornbeam for the outer. But the lines are more complex than an ordinary boat; there is no curve on a boat's keel like the compound curve of a fish's belly. 'And the curve on the "keel" compounded all the other curves, of course. I made the frame of bulkheads fairly straight, as if I were making

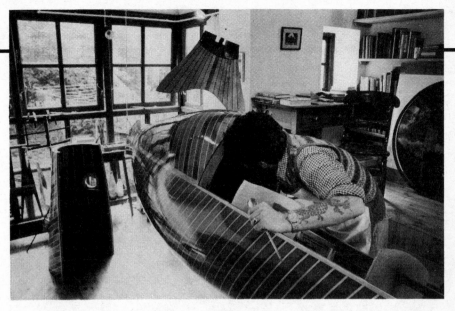

● *Inside the fish . . . the upstanding section gives a clear idea of the construction*

an aircraft, then drew a "floor" inside like you would get on an ordinary boat, took a central longitudinal axis, and positioned the centres of the bulkheads above or below that in gradual increments. So I got a continuous curve, like a sine curve.

'The diagonal laying of the strips proved an enormous challenge of matching grain and colour, which I wanted to work as a continuum the whole length of the body. For the top I used 1¼in thick boards about 14in wide, deep-cut them on a bandsaw to 2mm thick, then cut the curves so they fit next to each other, offering up, marking and fitting all the way along. But I started in the middle — the piece of walnut I used, for instance, was dark one side and light the other, so I laid the strips from the darkest side in the middle, adding at each side alternately so the colour gets lighter to each end and you have a side-to-side grain match as well.

'The underside, which is all mahogany, has a ripply, curvy effect purely from alternating grain; I cut a 1in-tapering-to-nothing wedge of the board (24in long was about right for each quarter-round section) and cut the 2mm strips on the 1¼in thickness. I ran the "tapering" edge against the fence, and the grain thus goes diagonally through the 2mm thickness at a fine angle. Then I laid them on the carcase one end up, one end down, so you get consistently alternating reflections and light picked up in opposite directions.

'I used Cascamite to glue all the strips down, and the final structure is immensely strong, but of course I couldn't machine-sand veneer thickness on curves like that — you'd go straight through it. So I made some cricket-bat sized sanding blocks and hand-sanded with wet'n'dry, all day every day for a week and a half. It's finished with Blackfriars polyurethane.

'The gills and fins are parana pine, and the tail is lime and mahogany strips, laminated over a former — all the pushrods and "waving mechanism" is inside the body, so you just see a perfectly smooth line from nose to tail. The mouth was a bit like making a loo seat. The bubble machine

● *The planetary gears by which the great and small wheels are driven on two axes*

inside is fairly common — the sort of thing you used to see at rock'n'roll concerts — but I lined the whole forward end inside with lead and made a drip tray to drain any wet. Not having that machine ruin my woodwork!'

Kit quoted for three months' work on the fish, but it took him eight, working seven days a week. It was finished in time. Clock maintenance? 'It should run for years and years on end. I like and trust the quality of Sinclair Harding's work, and Mike Harding trusts mine. The Arcade security man has to fill the bubble machine up every four days or so, and give it a wipe.'

The entire clock cost £80,000 and took a year to make. Not a lot for a community facility that will surprise, delight and fascinate the good citizens of Cheltenham — and its visitors — for years to come. Who cares if the crowds stand in front of it for hours on end? ∎

The grand furniture saga

Eighteenth-century architect William Kent had a flair for the flamboyant. Vic Taylor examines his achievements and maps the history of furniture finishing

● *A design of Kent's for a table for Houghton Hall, 1731. The under-the-table clerics have no relation to the piece; a typical Kentian whimsy*

The Italian architect and designer Andrea Palladio (1508-1580), had a profound influence on the Renaissance movement. His ideas were taken up and used by William Kent (1686-1748) on some of England's most grandiose and palatial houses: Holkham Hall (belonging to the Earl of Leicester) and Houghton Hall (Sir Robert Walpole's house), both in Norfolk, are particularly notable.

Kent was born in Bridlington, Yorkshire, and, so the story goes, was apprenticed to a coachbuilder in Hull. In 1709 he was sent by a consortium of patrons to Italy to study art and perhaps acquire profitable works of art for them. In 1719 he was brought back to England by the art-connoisseur and gifted amateur architect Lord Burlington, dubbed the 'Apollo of the Arts'. He became Kent's life-long patron — and it was a patronage of the best kind, which included George Frederick Handel among its beneficiaries.

Kent designed his furniture as a foil to his architectural achievements and both were characterised by his exuberance and panache. His work was decorated with all the classical ornamentation of Palladianism, plus some of his own. He favoured the scallop shell, 'imbrication' (rendering a surface to resemble fish scales) and a kind of reverse scroll leg. In addition he used heavy, ornate swags of leaves and flowers, satyrs' masks, foliated scrolls, and cabriole legs embellished with animal motifs carved on the knees and with claw and ball, eagle talon, or dolphin's head feet. He was also fond of using large amounts of gesso, carved and gilded, to attain some of his most opulent effects.

In those days (when professional qualifications didn't exist) it was possible for one man to embrace several professions — and this Kent did brilliantly. Let Horace Walpole (who criticised everybody and everything, and called Kent 'The Father of Modern Gardening') tell us how: '[Kent's] oracle was so much consulted by all who affected taste, that nothing was thought compleat without his assistance. He was not only consulted for furniture, as frames of pictures, glasses, tables, chairs, etc., but for plate, for a barge, for a cradle. And so impetuous was fashion, that two great ladies prevailed upon him to make designs for their birthday gowns.' (The barge referred to was the royal one now in the National Maritime Museum at Greenwich.)

This early part of the 18th century saw the publication of the first English books of furniture designs. Kent published two folio volumes in 1727 which contained a variety of designs, mainly architectural, and also collaborated in John Vardy's book *Some designs of Mr Inigo Jones and Mr William Kent* (1744). William Jones' *Gentleman's or Builder's Companion* (1739) contained some 20 designs of pier glasses and side tables — a pier glass was an upright mirror fitted on the pier between two windows and used with a pier table, which supported a candelabra whose light was reflected by the glass. Then, of course, came Thomas Chippendale's *The Gentleman and Cabinetmaker's Director* in 1754.

Kent's furniture was expensive to produce, and its almost vulgar pomposity could only be shown to best advantage in the great mansions of the wealthy. But it was only natural that the Palladian influences would filter down to 'ordinary' homes. Everyday furniture began to show classical architectural styles in form and decoration, the latter included architectural pediments, pilasters, split columns (turned and split vertically into halves, each half fixed to a surface), and the use of dentils, Grecian key ornament, Vitruvian scrolls, and egg-and-dart mouldings more suited to stonework than wood.

The most marked development was the change from walnut to mahogany as the most widely-used cabinet wood, a change hastened by severe winters on the Continent which seriously depleted the supply of French walnut. Exports were prohibited from 1720 onwards.

In 1721 the duties on some imports, including mahogany, were removed to help British ship-owners, and in 1733 Sir Robert Walpole abolished the duties on all imports of timber, and used mahogany for the panelling in his new house at Houghton Hall, Norfolk.

Jamaican mahogany (then often called 'Jamaica wood') was one of the first to be imported and was soon followed by Spanish mahogany from Cuba ('Havanna wood'). African mahogany, which is the species *Khaya* and distantly related to the true mahogany species *Swietenia*, was not imported until the middle of the 19th century.

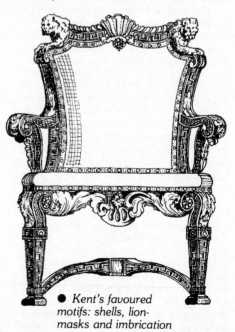

● *Kent's favoured motifs: shells, lion-masks and imbrication*

● *A very rare Windsor chair c.1720, in ash with an elm seat*

Cabinetmakers found this new timber had many advantages. Apart from its rich red colour, it was less likely to split or warp than other woods; it carved well and was very strong even in small sections; it was available in much wider planks than walnut; and it took a superb finish. Add to this the fact that it was highly resistant to woodworm, and it's easy to see why it soon became the most popular of cabinet woods; it's said that some unscrupulous makers tried to imitate mahogany by staining oak with bullocks' blood!

Another innovation of the time was the Windsor chair. This seems to have been a hybrid from the union of the triangular 'thrown' or turned chair of the early 17th century; the Carolean walnut chair which had twist legs, backfeet and stretchers, with a caned seat and back; and the 17th century reading chair. In 1724 the Duke of Chandos had seven japanned Windsor chairs made for the library at his house, Canons, and thereafter such chairs begin to be mentioned frequently in bills of sale and advertisements.

How the name originated is a mystery. There is a theory that there was a family of that name living in High Wycombe where most of the chairs were made, but I prefer the explanation that the chairs were taken to Windsor by horse-and-cart and carried by boat down to London.

The earliest design was the 'comb-back': the sticks in the back protruded beyond the arm-bow and were capped by a crest rail or yoke, resembling a comb; the back contained only sticks and no splat. The original design has developed over the years into well over 100 variations, and the Windsor remains one of the most popular chairs here and in the United States, where the early colonists quickly adapted it and evolved their own designs.

Finishing methods over the centuries make a fascinating history and it may come as a surprise to learn that medieval furniture was frequently painted (not only furniture, but castles as well!). It's quite possible that the milk-paint used by the early American colonists was formerly used on rough country furniture in the old countries, although lead-based paint was also well-known. The earliest method of preserving wood seems to have been by rubbing it with linseed, poppy, or nut oil, which darkened the surface as they oxidised, particularly on oak; this was soon followed by a waxing process which consisted of rubbing on a mixture of beeswax and turpentine. Evelyn describes wax polishing in his book *Sylva*, 1664: 'Melt some beeswax, mixing it with your lampblack and size, and when tis cold, make it up into a ball and rub it over your former black [stain], lastly with a polishing brush (made of short stiff Boars bristles) labour it till the lustre be to your liking'.

Tripoli powder and linseed oil made into a paste was used to rub down the varnish finish on 17th century walnut furniture, and the same time-consuming process was later used on mahogany and satinwood, but confined to more expensive pieces. Ordinary work was given either a finish of linseed oil which was often dyed with alkanet root to give a red colour, or simply wax polished. Alkanet root comes from the garden plant *Anchusa tinctoria* or borage; if you want to simulate an authentic 18th century finish, consult Sheraton's *Cabinet Dictionary* (1803), under 'alkanet'.

Sheraton also explains several different methods of finishing (pp 289-290) which can be summarised: (a) (for inside work such as the interiors of cupboards or drawers) rub hard wax into the wood by means of a cork pad, and clear away 'clemmings' left by the wax with powdered brick dust on a cloth; (b) a mixture of soft beeswax and turpentine with, if necessary, the addition of a little alkanet oil, the whole being polished off with a cloth; (c) (for plain cabinet work) apply linseed oil (either plain or stained) with brick dust and rub down with a cloth so that a kind of putty is produced 'which will infallibly secure a fine polish by continued rubbing'; (d) (for chairs) work a hardish composition of wax, turpentine, a little copal varnish, red lead, and Oxford ochre for colour into a ball and rub into the grain with a stiff-bristled brush (not to be undertaken with bare hands).

French polish, which now seems to be applied to any kind of furniture regardless of its period or style, didn't arrive from France until after 1820. G. A. Siddons' *The Cabinet-Maker's Guide* (1830) includes his recipe for making true French polish: 'To one pint of spirits of wine [alcohol — we would use methylated spirits], add a quarter of an ounce of gum-copal, a quarter of an ounce of gum-arabic, and one ounce of shell-lac. Let your gums be well bruised, and sifted through a piece of muslin. Put the spirits and the gums together in a vessel that can be close corked, place them near a warm stove, and frequently shaking them, in two or three days they will be dissolved: strain it through a piece of muslin and keep it tight corked for use.' ∎

RIP SAWING
Using Extension Table Accessory

GROOVING

DRILLING

ASSEMBLING

JIG SAWING

JOINTING

GUIDE ROUTING

SAWING

ACCURACY ACROSS THE BOARD

The new Dunlop Powerbase is the ultimate precision machining centre. Thanks to Powerbase's unique, patented guidance and control system, you can at last work to precise, quick-set and **repeatable** measurements on virtually any workpiece.

You can use it with most domestic power tools, and because Powerbase provides a stable work surface and clamping system, you'll find working with hand tools easier too.

TOUGH ENOUGH TO TAKE IT COMFORTABLY

Powerbase's strong work surface is an impressive 735 mm × 875 mm, and ergonomically designed for optimum operating comfort. Its rigid fold-away base frame is fabricated in steel. Lots of innovative technical features – including Powerbase's versatile soleplate – mean safer, more consistent, more accurate working. Whatever the job, Powerbase measures up. At a price that fits your pocket!

Anything you can do you can do better

DUNLOP Powerbase ®

Makes things easier

Dept WW, 140 Fielden Street, Glasgow G40 3TX.

Table d'haute

● *Luscious cocobolo used to extravagant effect. The deep colours are admirably set off by the unusual sycamore framing*

First find your rosewood . . . That was the challenge to Sean Feeney with this magnificent commissioned table. Supply problems turned him to cocobolo; and here's what happened

---

We were asked to design and make a prestige table (and suite of chairs) to seat 16 people, with no obstructions from either legs or underframe. The top must be at least 54ins wide, and the chair seats and arms should fit under the table top when not in use. The final design requirement was that a dark timber, preferably rosewood, should be used.

Now obtaining rosewood (*Dalbergia nigra*) logs in a suitable quality and quantity is difficult; prime timber is converted into veneers. Not only is the supply of solid

timber into the UK inconstant, but the logs that arrive are generally small in girth, irregular in shape and short in length. Plantation-grown Indian rosewood boards (*Dalbergia latifolia*) are available, in random rather than matching boards, but if you want anything else you are doomed to time-wasting searching through sawmills and timber merchants and a great deal of disappointment on the way.

We had a stroke of luck when visiting a northern hardwood importer. The firm had recently received two veneer quality cocobolo logs, each 102in long, 16-20in wide, clean and straight along the log length, compared with the irregular-shaped Mexican and Brazilian logs we had looked at before. They were exactly what we needed.

Cocobolo (*Dalbergia retusa*)

Though it's related to the rosewood species, cocobolo is quite distinct in colour. It grows on the Pacific seaboard of Central America, from Mexico down to Panama — our logs were apparently shipped from Nicaragua.

We had the logs sawn into 1¼in and 2in boards at our local sawmills in Cubbington, near Leamington Spa. After cutting, we found the timber had a 'rainbow' hue, with a definite reddish tinge to the heartwood; this darkened during the drying to a deep orange-red with purple stripes which had areas of mottled grain. The sapwood, initially a distinct white like most rosewoods, dried to a creamy straw colour.

When the sawn timber arrived at the workshop, we loaded the boards into the dehumidifier. The initial average moisture

content was surprisingly low, 18-20%, indicating that the logs had been felled for some time or the trees had been ring-barked before felling.

We found there was very limited information about drying cocobolo, and we were breaking new ground in attempting forced drying. Its natural oiliness and incredible density suggested this would be a slow process. We monitored the temperature and moisture extraction rate each day, to overcome possible degrade and case-hardening of this particularly rare and very valuable timber.

The 1¼in boards took 12 weeks of controlled drying to reduce the moisture content to an average of 9%. We left the thicker boards in the kiln for a further four weeks, adding some 2in thick sycamore which had previously been end-reared but still had more moisture than the cocobolo. We found the two species dried well together, the extra moisture from the sycamore preventing the cocobolo from surface checking; we had raised the temperature 10° higher after removing the 1¼in boards.

Base construction

The table was to be 16ft long and 54in wide, to allow for the 16 chairs. We started by making the two pedestals, the feet and the adjoining bottom centre rail. These were laminated from 2in boards to the required thickness. The pedestals were 10in square, and the centre rail 4x4in. The timber was cut from consecutive boards and bookmatched to give continuity of grain and colour.

● *Left*, ant's eye view shows the elaborate framing, designed to give maximum leg room all round the table

45° from the base, are stop-mortised and tenoned into the sycamore. The two pedestals are held together at ground level by an 8ft length of 4x2in cocobolo inlaid with sycamore, also mortised and tenoned into the sycamore base. With all these joints we used pegs to lock the tenons in place.

Table support

The tabletop rests on an underframe which in turn is supported at each pedestal by three cantilevered arms, made of 4x2in sycamore. They are dovetailed into the cocobolo uprights at the top; the two short arms project at 90° from the pedestal, the third and longest projects at 180° and is braced with additional support rails to create a triangular frame.

The main central body of the underframe is two 8ft lengths of 4x2in sycamore, tapering from 4in thick in the centre to 2in where they meet the 90° arms of the pedestals, and are through-dovetailed across the arms to connect the pedestals together. Spanning the rails along their length are three equally spaced crossbars, mortised into each rail and tying the rails together.

Carcase framing

The top carcase framing, which houses the individual panels of cocobolo, is from carefully selected quarter-sawn sycamore, cut and planed to 2x2in square section for the inner and outer framing.

The inner framing is a series of three equal sized crosses or X-frames, which hold

We found when machining cocobolo that it gave off a strong fragrance; the dust and natural oil stained our hands orange, so we had to use respirators and surgical gloves. It machined extremely well, but proved difficult to hand plane, so we scraped instead.

The cold marble-like surface of the timber was also difficult to glue; our attempts with several brands of urea formaldehyde adhesive soon confirmed the timber textbook information that it's a difficult wood to glue.

We'd had adhesion problems previously when using particularly oily rosewoods, but after degreasing the surface and then 'toothing' a substantial joint, we'd found urea formaldehyde worked. Not in this case.

After consulting the British Adhesive Manufacturers' Association we sent samples of the timber and adhesive to the Ciba Geigy plastic and chemical laboratories to analyse and test. The laboratory's report told us we had applied too great a clamping pressure! They recommended we try 'Aerodux', a resorcinol formaldehyde resin. Aerodux is a two-part adhesive, which turns a chocolate brown when mixed, which is a distinct advantage when using dark timber.

We tried this glue on further samples, again degreasing the surface with carbon tetrachloride and scoring the joint before gluing. It worked beautifully. After allowing the glue to dry for 24 hours, we put the samples under immense stress. The wood shattered before the glue line!

Having solved that problem, we glued up the sections and started work on the base. We cut the upright sections of the pedestals to an octagonal shape from the square on the circular saw, and planed to finished sizes. We then mortised and tenoned it down into the sycamore base, wedging from beneath. The legs or feet, which project at

Table base
Exploded view

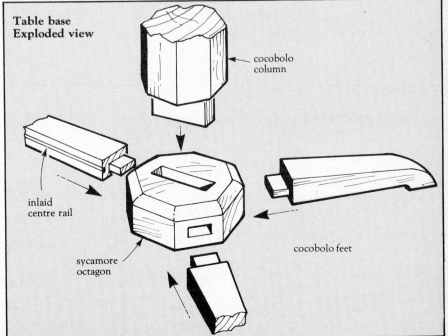

cocobolo column

inlaid centre rail

sycamore octagon

cocobolo feet

Table d'haute

● *Test-assembling the carcase framing: the outer curved members are ready to slot on to the inner diagonals*

the four central square panels of the top. We machined a ½x½in groove in both side faces. Two shorter rails of the same section were attached to the crosses at each end of the table to complete the rectangular framing.

The outer framing is six separate pieces of wood, four side rails and two curved ends. We jointed the two side rails together to make up the overall length and shape of one side of the top, connecting at each end to the curved end rails. We used loose tongues to connect these, leaving them unglued at this stage.

Now the outer framing was ready to joint to the inner X-frames; these joints had to be strong and accurately made, as well as decorative.

We first mitred the ends of the X-frames where they met the inside edge of the outer framing. Then with the inner frame resting on the outer frame, the positions of the crosses were marked out. A birdsmouth or V-section was cut from the outer frame, allowing the cross ends of the inner one to sit in the right positions on the outer. The drawing shows how it works.

To secure the frames together and lock the mitred points into the V-section, we inserted a rosewood tongue 4x2x½in. We cut a through mortise out of the birds-mouth cutout, and then inserted the tongue from the outside of the outer framing right through into the mitred points of the inner framing. This locked all three sections of the framing together and created an interesting feature of the jointing technique.

This unique joint provided the flexibility to remove the outer framing from the inner crosses by sliding the outer framing mortise off its locating tenon, enabling us to fit the panels in their frames.

Panels

The cocobolo panels for the top were made up by tongue-and-grooving three boards together before gluing (the tongue and groove increased gluing area as an added precaution on the resistant timber). After jointing and planing, the panels were rebated on their edges to produce a ½x½in tongue, which houses into the locating groove machined on the sycamore framing.

The first panels to be worked on were the four central squares, the timber for which had been carefully selected and book-matched for maximum impact from the exotic grain. We fitted all the panels into their respective housings while the entire sycamore frame was sitting on the table underframe.

The top carcase framing was designed to drop into slots relieved from the table underframe; we carefully positioned the panelled top framing on the base precisely where we wanted it, and marked the under-frame and then cut housings in the under-frame rails, so the top frame rested within the table sub-structure.

We polished the cocobolo panels individually with a melamine-based shellac, applied with a rubber in the traditional way and finished over several days. When complete, the panels were positioned within their individual frames, zig-zagging the centre panels up the length of the top. With the side and end panels, the grain runs the length of the table.

We used PVA adhesive to glue the sycamore framing together, starting at the centres of the crosses, progressing to the three-way joint where the mitres join the outer framing, and finally the shaped outer rail. As gluing progressed we inserted the appropriate polished cocobolo panels into their grooves, without gluing them.

Final task was to trim the rosewood tongues which projected through the side of the outside rail. After planing them flush with the sycamore, we polished the frame and waxed to a satin sheen.

The table took nine months from conception to completion, with the actual construction taking over 600 man-hours. It was made possible by a client with vision, and the assistance of Michael Feeney and Mark Fletcher, without whose dedication and perseverance it would not have been achieved. ∎

● We are grateful to the Building Research Establishment at Princes Risborough and the Furniture Industry Research Association for information about cocobolo and its properties, and to J. K. Arrowsmith for information on drying dense tropical hardwoods.

Three-way loose-tongued frame joint

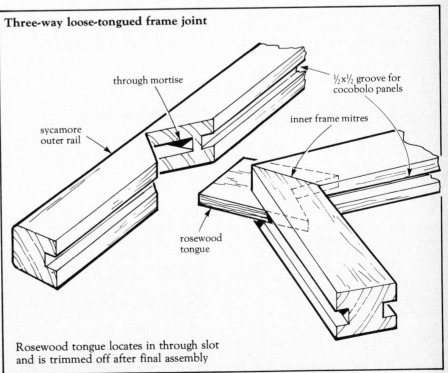

through mortise

½x½ groove for cocobolo panels

inner frame mitres

sycamore outer rail

rosewood tongue

Rosewood tongue locates in through slot and is trimmed off after final assembly

Upholstered Hepplewhite

Classic elegance in authentic style; Vic Taylor's drawings are true to the spirit of this beautiful chair

Hepplewhite would recognise this design as one of his. It's a simplified version of an armchair illustrated in Plate 9 of Hepplewhite's *Cabinet Maker and Upholsterer's Guide*, published by his wife in 1788 after he died.

I drew the chair from one in the Chair Museum at High Wycombe. The decorative details are slightly different from the *'Guide'* illustration; the legs are square tapered instead of being turned, and the arms are omitted, but the overall similarity is there. Almost certainly it was made up by a chairmaker who altered the original design to suit his skill and his customer's pocket. The function of such guides was to provide the craftsman with a basic idea that he could adapt to his own needs, and it's been said that guides by such as Chippendale, Hepplewhite, Hope and so on — but possibly not Sheraton — provided so few details of construction, dimensions and shapes that craftsmen of the time must have been very highly skilled to have made them up at all.

This particular design is in mahogany and has a shaped banister with two vertical curved stays at each side of it, all meeting in a curved shoe at the foot of the shield. The front face of the shield frame is moulded (see section in fig. 2), while the back is benched (rounded off) all round. The front legs are square and tapered, with the outside faces moulded to the section given in fig. 2. The seat is stuffover-upholstered, with a slightly serpentine-shaped front seat rail.

You need to take care with the joints, for the back in particular is quite delicate. You'll also have to thnk about the most economical way of marking and cutting the various curved members (fig. 3B), to avoid short-grained pieces; the diagram shows the directions of the grain.

Construction

I've shown an exploded view of the chair with the parts in blank form (unworked) in fig. 3A. You'll see the seat consists of a serpentine front rail, deep-cut from 2in wood to the shape shown in the plan (fig. 1). The two slightly curved side seat rails are cut similarly, while the back seat rail is straightforward. When marking out the various shapes, nest them together to save timber.

Mortise and tenon these rails into the front legs and backfeet; although I show plain stub tenons, you could mitre the ends of the tenons so they meet inside the mortise. Save the offcuts when you cut the

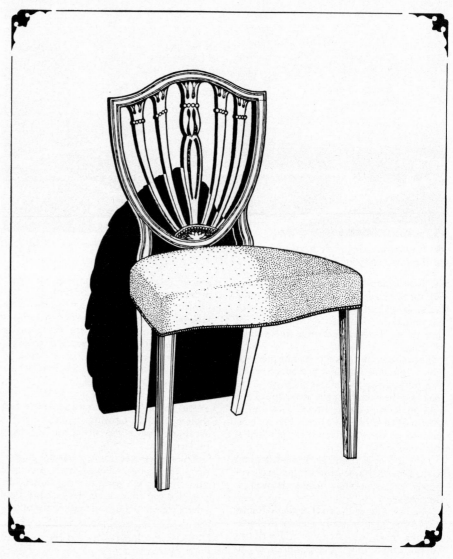

● *Eighteenth-century style for 20th century sitting; Hepplewhite's elegance abides*

rails as they can be used as cramping blocks when you assemble the seat frame.

You'll find the backfeet difficult to cut as they are curved in two planes. You'll need two straight-grained pieces, each 3½x2½x36½in; bandsaw the shape as viewed from the front first, followed by the side profile (shown in front and side elevations, fig. 1). Again, keep the offcuts for use as cramping blocks.

The lower curved piece of the back is tenoned into a notch cut in each backfoot (fig. 3C). This curved piece is grooved centrally to accept the tongue which is worked under the shoe, and this shoe is also mortised to accept the lower ends of the back stays; the stays are mortised in whole, without a tenon cut at the ends. The upper ends of the stays are tenoned into the underside of the top back rail, which is serpentine-shaped (often called a 'camel back'). Complete these joints before you start any carving; the size and shape of each

stay is shown in fig. 2.

You'll also have to make tenons at the upper ends of the backfeet to fit into mortises on the underside of the top back rail. This rail is all in one plane, so it can be cut from 1¼in wood, saving the offcut as a block again.

Details of the carving are shown in fig. 2. You could cut the channelling on the front legs with a spindle moulder if you have one, or with a moulding plane; notice that the legs are slightly tapered. With the curves of the backframe you'll probably have to resort to a scratch-stock and a few carving tools such as a fine chisel and a suitable gouge. It's difficult to show the carving of the stylised husks, and it's a good idea to look at some actual examples in a museum.

Before you start the upholstery, glue and screw in the corner brackets (fig. 1), locating them at the lower edges of the seat rails so they are clear of the webbing, and finish the wood.

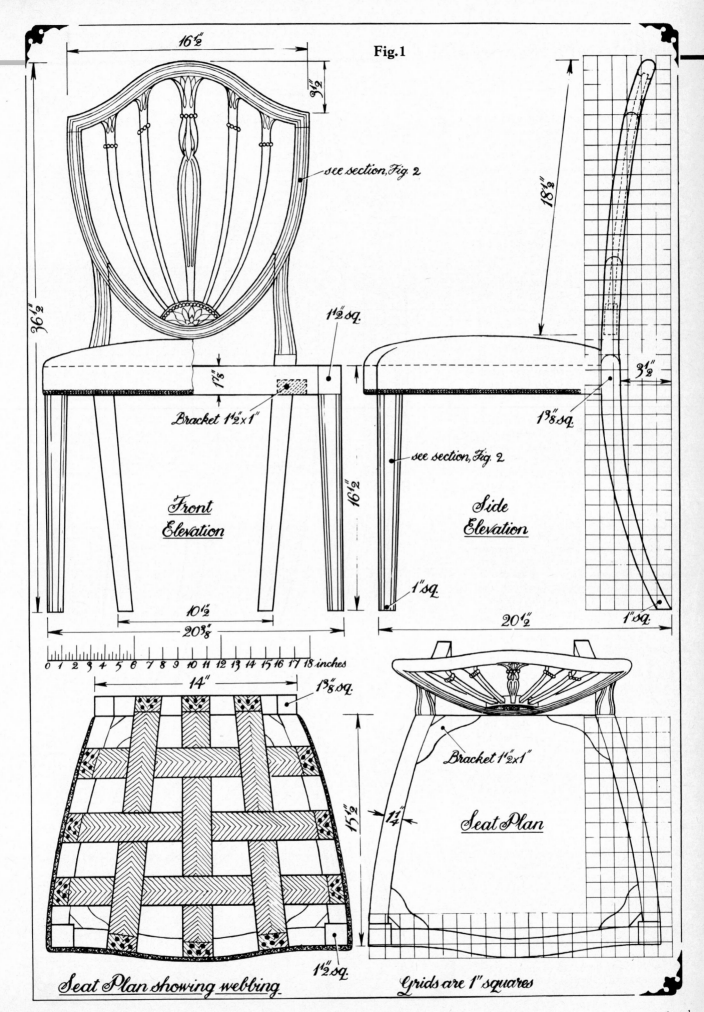

Fig.1

16½"

3½"

36½"

see section, Fig. 2

1½" sq.

1⅛"

Bracket 1½"×1"

16½"

Front Elevation

10½"

20⅜"

18½"

3½"

1⅜" sq.

see section, Fig. 2

1" sq.

Side Elevation

20½"

1" sq.

0 1 2 3 4 5 6 7 8 9 10 11 12 13 14 15 16 17 18 inches

14"

1⅜" sq.

1½" sq.

15½"

1¼"

Bracket 1½"×1"

Seat Plan

Seat Plan showing webbing.

Grids are 1" squares

Upholstered Hepplewhite

Upholstery

Begin by webbing up the seat with best quality 2in webbing, folding back the ends of the webs by 1-1¼in, and tacking through the double thickness. Use a webbing stretcher to apply tension, tacking down the central web first at the back and then at the front, and then continue with the rest, interlacing them as shown (fig. 1). Use ½in tacks.

Now you have to cover the webs with hessian (fig. 4A). Start by cutting out the piece of hessian about 1½in larger all round than the seat frame. Tack down the back edge, setting the ½in tacks in about ⅜in from the edge of the hessian, and following the sequence shown; pull the hessian as taut as possible before tacking. At the back corners, cut into the free part of the hessian at 45° right up to the leg, then stretch the lips of the cut on either side of the leg and tack them down. Finally, trim the hessian to leave a surplus margin of about 1in wide all round, turning this margin inwards and tacking it down.

Upholstery fibre, readily available from upholstery suppliers, is one of the best stuffings for the seat. You'll need to anchor it in place with 'bridle ties' (fig. 4B) positioned about 3in from the edge of the seat frame; these prevent the fibre from moving about in use, forming uncomfortable lumps or ridges.

Use an upholsterer's curved needle threaded with strong twine. Start by either of the back corners, making a small knot in the twine to stop it pulling through. The ties should be long enough so there are two at each side and three along the front; the underside stitch (dotted in the diagram) need only be 1in or so long. Push handfuls of fibre under the ties, teasing it out until it covers the top to an even depth of 4in and overhangs slightly all round. If necessary fill in the centre with a small quantity of fibre.

Now cover all this stuffing with a piece of scrim (hessian will do at a pinch) and fix it temporarily with part-driven tacks. Then stitch it down, using a straight mattress needle and twine, beginning about 4in inwards from the back leg, and pushing the needle down right through the top scrim, the fibre and the bottom hessian. Allow about an inch of stitching on the underside before pushing the needle up again and making a slip knot to tie the stitch. Carry on around the seat, with long stitches on the top and small ones underneath, removing the temporary tacks as you go. Don't make any more slip knots until you come to the last stitch, which can be finished off with a slip knot close to the one you started with. Finally trim off the edge of the scrim and tack it to the sides of the seat rails (fig. 4C).

For the seat edge use a 'sink' or 'blind' stitch (fig. 4D), with a straight needle and twine. Start with a slip knot at the left-hand side close to the backfoot and seat rail; push the needle through until the eye almost disappears, and then return it,

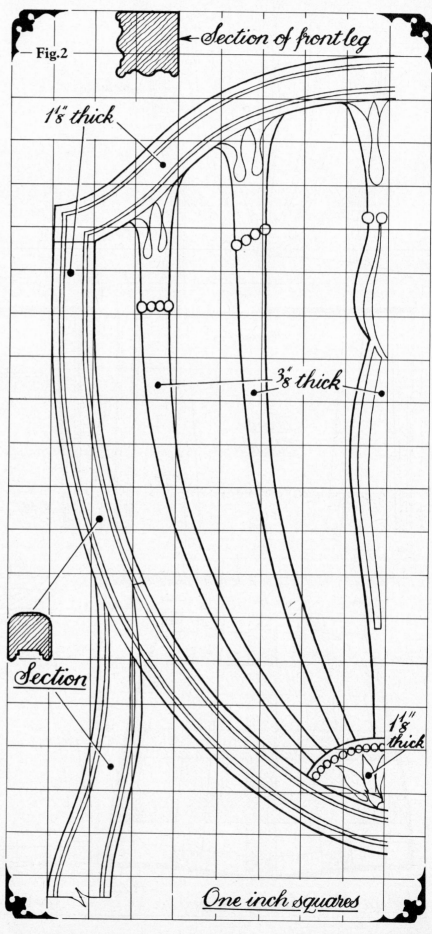

Fig.2

← *Section of front leg*

1⅛" thick

⅜" thick

Section

1⅛" thick

One inch squares

pulling the knot tight. Take the needle along about 2½in, insert it again in a similar fashion, but returning it about 1¼in behind the entry point. Twist the twine once around the needle as it emerges and pull it tight. Use a regulator (a stout knitting needle makes a good substitute) to adjust the amount of filling and keep it neat and even as you go.

Continue this process right round the seat. Then start another row of stitching about ½in above the first. For this row, thread the needle with twine and make the first stitch in one side of the seat about 1in from the backfoot, and about 1½in from the edge. Bring the needle out about 1½in in from the edge on the top of the seat, and pull it right through. Then insert again, eye first, close to the backfoot on the top of the seat, and pull it out at the side close to the loose end of the twine; make a slip knot to anchor the end. Next insert the point of the needle about 1in along from the first stitch and again bring it out on top of the seat; wind the twine twice around the needle, bring it through and pull the stitch tight (fig. 4E). Continue the stitching in this fashion all round the seat.

Upholstery fibre is also used for the top stuffing, with bridle ties to hold it in place. Tease the fibre out evenly so it covers the seat about 1in deep, although it's helpful to have it slightly thicker at the front where the wear is greatest.

The seat should initially be covered with a piece of calico or other closely woven fabric to prevent any strands of fibre

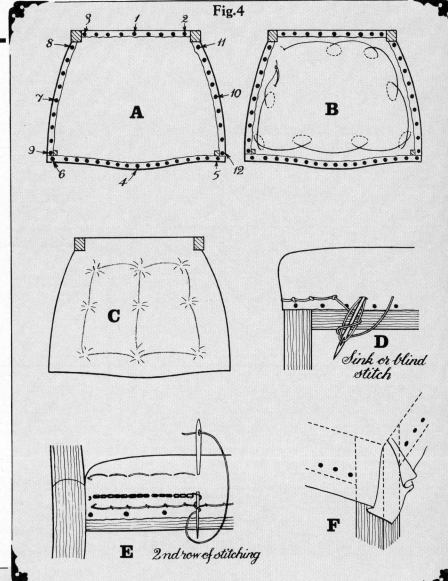

Fig.4

D Sink or blind stitch

E 2nd row of stitching

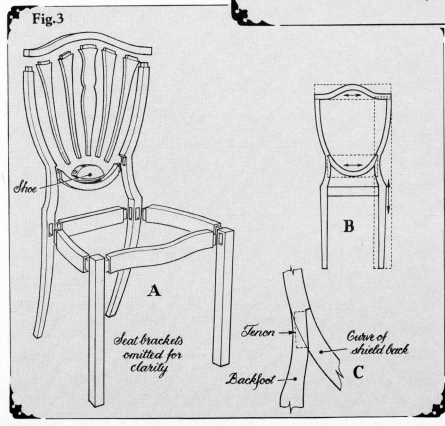

Fig.3

Shoe

A

Seat brackets omitted for clarity

B

Tenon

Curve of shield back

Backfoot

C

working through. Cut a piece large enough to cover the seat and hang down over the frame. Tack it to the outside of the back rail first, beginning at the centre and working outwards. Pull the calico taut and tack it to the front and side rails in a similar fashion. Align the tacks about ⅝in above the bottom edge of the seat rails and about ¾in apart. Fit the calico around the backfeet as you did with the hessian, and cut and fit it around the front legs (fig. 4F) in the recognised method for negotiating this kind of corner. Finally trim off the calico close to the tacks.

Before fitting the final cover, you should position a layer of cotton wadding about 1in thick on top of the calico, trimming it neatly at the corners. This wadding is held in place by the final cover, which you can now tack down in the same way as the calico. This cover must be large enough to cover not only the calico but also to lap over the undersides of the seat frame rails. When you have tacked it in place on the undersides, insert some more tacks at about 1½in intervals around the bottom edges of the rails, below those holding the calico.

Complete the job by tacking on gimp with gimp pins to hide the tack heads. Then sit down and enjoy your new chair. ■

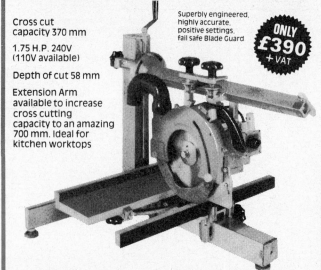

If you're starting to get serious about doing it yourself, you ought to start thinking about getting a Bosch Jigsaw.

For all those tricky jobs around your house there's probably nothing to beat one.

For example, take the Jigsaw you see on the left. It's so finely balanced it's virtually vibration free.

If you don't want a toy, get a Bosch.

This means that it's not only easy to use, but your cutting line won't become a flickering blur before your very eyes.

We've also designed an ingenious little exhaust duct over the blade to blow swarf and sawdust away, so you can always see where you're going.

The baseplate is a masterpiece in itself. It pivots up to 45° each side for cutting mitres, and retracts completely for getting into those irritatingly tight corners.

However, the real beauty of the Bosch Jigsaw is its electronic speed control.

It has a nine stage speed selector to stop you going too fast for the material you're cutting.

Slow and easy for ceramic tiles; a bit quicker for steel; even quicker for aluminium; quicker still for wood, and super quick for plasterboard.

The trigger, by the way, has an infinite speed control a bit like the accelerator on your car: the harder you press it, the faster it goes.

And of course, being a Bosch, it's a Jigsaw that'll stand the rough and tumble of workshop life, probably longer than the life of your workshop.

And it's just part of the comprehensive Bosch power tool range available from your local dealer.

So no matter what the job, be it big or small, why play around when you could have a Bosch?

BOSCH
Excellence comes as standard.

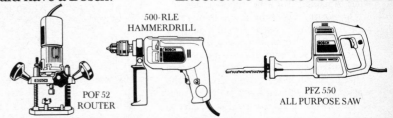

500-RLE
HAMMERDRILL

POF 52
ROUTER

PFZ 550
ALL PURPOSE SAW

P.O. Box 98, Broadwater Park, North Orbital Road, Denham, Uxbridge, Middlesex, UB9 5HJ. Tel: Denham (0895) 833633.

Fold-a-fence

This neat little gadget
from John Moseley ensures
precise routing of trenches
and dadoes

Using a straight-edge as a guide for routing rebates and shelf housings, or moulding the edges of wide boards, is fraught with hazards. You spend ages getting the straight-edge in exactly the right place, and then if your cutter isn't exactly the right width, you have to cut and set up all over again.

This simple-to-make folding wedge fence fitted to your router's guide rods eradicates the fuss. The only setting up you need is to ensure that the straight-edge is exactly parallel to the line of cut you want; it won't matter whether it's too close or too far away. As long as you have a cutter smaller than the width of the required trench, you can produce cuts precisely the size you want. Once you've got the hang of using it, you'll find a host of applications — like my latest project of routing out deeper and wider rebates in window frames for sealed unit double glazing.

I used a piece of mahogany, but any close-grained hardwood will do. Select a suitable off-cut, plane all round to a finished cross-section of 2⅜x1⅛in, and cut to length. Mark out the slope angle to the dimensions shown in fig. 2 and very carefully saw through to produce the two wedge-shaped pieces, using a fine-toothed tenon saw. Lightly plane the two sawn faces to finish square and flat so that the sliding wedge runs smoothly across the face of the fixed wedge.

Next rout out the two slots in the sliding wedge using a ⅛in cutter which will give just enough clearance for the 6mm clamping screws. This is a bit tricky but I pinned and clamped a straight-edge to the bench, held the sliding wedge in the vice, and used thin packing strips to get the slots in the right place. With the same set-up, I used a ½in cutter to relieve the top of the slots so the clamping-screw heads would be below the surface when the fence was finally assembled. My ¼in cutter didn't have enough reach to break through for the full length of the slot at the wide end of the wedge and I had to turn it over and clean out what remained from the opposite side.

The positioning of the holes for the guide rods in the fixed wedge depends on your router. On my Elu MOF96 these are 84mm apart and I set them 10mm in from the bottom face so there was a slight clearance between the underside of the fence and the workpiece, as shown in fig. 3; this reduces the 'drag' from the fence making it easier to

● *Wedges and calibration shown clearly: ¼in of slide gives ¹⁄₁₆in width difference*

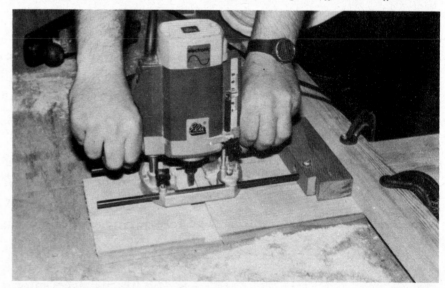

● *How a narrower cutter cuts a wider groove; make sure the board is clamped square*

● *Make your wedges as carefully as John obviously has, and you will get accurate results*

use. You need to drill these two holes quite accurately so the whole assembly will slide in and out of the router frame smoothly. I used a drill-stand for the electric drill which ensured they were square and parallel to each other, and by drilling through the holes in the adjuster-plate taken off my router's standard fence, I had a ready-made template and the holes were exactly the right distance apart; use a twist drill of the same diameter as your guide rods to obtain a nice snug fit.

Grub-screws in clearance holes, bonded with Araldite, hold the fixed wedge to the guide-rods (fig. 3); the counterbore for the 6mm hexagon nuts needs to be just the right diameter so the nuts are a reasonably tight fit. After the Araldite has cured you may find some of it has run into the threads of the nut; I used a 6mm engineer's 'tap' (£1.40 from the local ironmongers) to clean it out. Don't be tempted to leave the grub-screws in place while the Araldite cures, as you'll never get them out.

The clearance holes in the fixed wedge (fig. 2) for the clamp screws need to line up with slots in the sliding wedge and are counter-bored at the back, again for 6mm hexagon nuts, using the same drill as for the grub-screw nuts. When in use, the clamping force will pull the nuts into the counter-bore and, providing the nuts are a tight enough fit, you won't need to bond these into place.

To stop the wedges sliding against each other in use, glue a piece of 400-grit wet and dry silicone carbide paper to the face of the fixed wedge. Before the Araldite hardens, press the wedge hard on to a flat surface, and keep it under pressure for a few minutes, to squeeze out any excess glue or air bubbles so the mating face remains flat and true.

To finish off, I marked out the top face of the sliding wedge in ¼in increments, subdivided into ¹⁄₁₆in. The one-in-four slope angle of the wedges means a ¼in sideways movement of the sliding wedge increases or decreases the fence's width by ¹⁄₁₆in; if the sideways movement is only ¹⁄₁₆in, then the width only changes by ¹⁄₆₄in.

In use, this change in width is the 'cut' applied to the workpiece and highly accurate rebates and grooves become very simple and very satisfying. With 1¾in of sideways movement, the maximum change in width is ⁷⁄₁₆in and therefore any cutter can be used for cuts up to ⁷⁄₁₆in greater in width than its diameter using this adjustment alone. For larger movements, say to cut two parallel grooves or mouldings 4in apart, you can slide the guide-rods in or out of the router base and use the wedges for fine adjustment. As long as the workpiece and the straight-edge remain clamped in the same position, any number of cuts and distance apart will always be exactly parallel to each other — even if you need to change cutters in between. ■

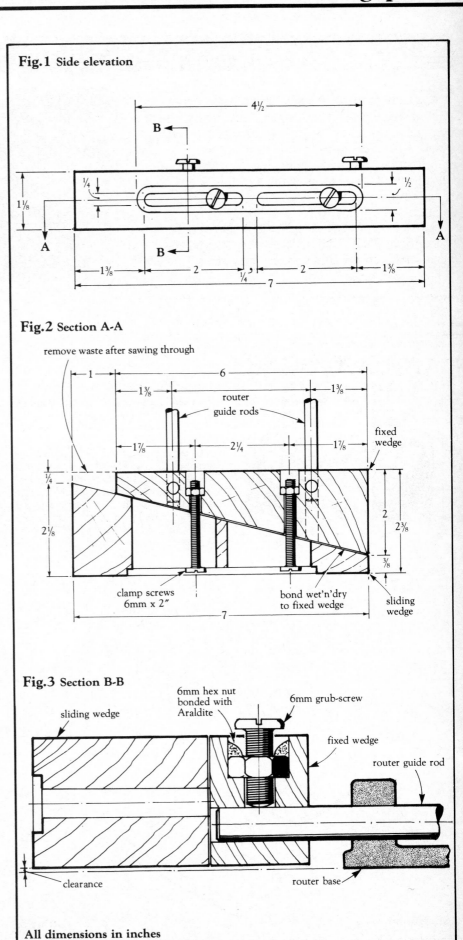

Fig.1 Side elevation

Fig.2 Section A-A

remove waste after sawing through

router guide rods

fixed wedge

clamp screws 6mm x 2"

bond wet'n'dry to fixed wedge

sliding wedge

Fig.3 Section B-B

sliding wedge

6mm hex nut bonded with Araldite

6mm grub-screw

fixed wedge

router guide rod

clearance

router base

All dimensions in inches

Hands on

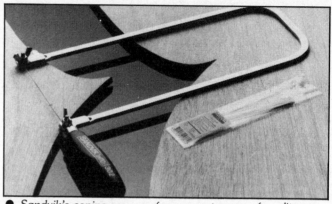
A routing theme for our special issue this month . . .

WOODWORKING WHEEZE
of the **month**

Sandvik winner

Mitre jigs

Very useful for large numbers of long mitre joints on smallish components, my two jigs are variations of the same idea, and very simple to make.

Cut the end off a block of hardwood at a perfect 45°, and fix a fence to one side of the sloping face. A piece of stout ply with a U-shaped mouth is recessed into the bottom of the block. With a straight bit in the router, mounted upside down in a table, run the ends of the U against the fence and the cutter will cut both fence and angle block in perfect alignment. Now all you have to do is clamp the work to the block and fence and pass it past the cutter, and the long mitre is cut — no need for cleaning up or 'adjustment'. The fence side acts as a stop block and prevents 'spelch'; the notch under the jig provides the right space for a cramp.

For the splined mitres you need in small decorative drawer work, make another block but this time with an angled lip at the bottom of the slope to hold the already mitred face of the work above the table. Then all you need is a slotting cutter in the router, adjusted to the right height to give the slot for the spline where you want it. You can easily cut through or stopped slots for splines.

Richard Maguire, Kincardineshire

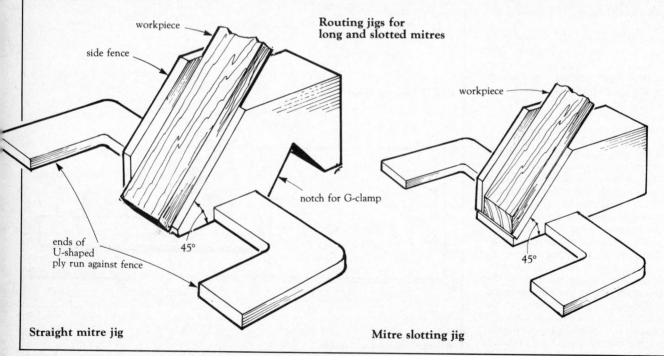

Routing jigs for long and slotted mitres

workpiece

side fence

ends of U-shaped ply run against fence

45°

notch for G-clamp

workpiece

45°

Straight mitre jig

Mitre slotting jig

Router edge-jointing

This jig is particularly useful for edge-jointing long or very thin boards — even chipboard, if you want to use up offcuts.

It consists of a baseboard with two sections screwed to it, separated by a 1½in channel, and a strong straight fence. The workpiece support boards should be about 3in wider than the two boards to be joined, and the whole thing about 6in longer. Plane the edges reasonably straight, then clamp both boards to the jig with both edges to be joined over the channel. Clamp the fence so it is accurately parallel with one board edge, positioned so a two-flute cutter about ³⁄₁₆in longer than the depth of the boards will take a ¹⁄₃₂ or ¹⁄₁₆in whisker off one edge. Make the cut, then loosen the other board but not the fence, and move it in parallel to the first edge-cut board so the cutter will take the same whisker off that. Run the router up against that edge, and the cutter will not touch the first edge. If there is a slight hiccup in the fence it will appear in both board edges, and you just move one up along the other slightly to get them to register perfectly. With curved fences, curved edges can be joined as accurately as straight ones.

H. H. Lawson, Johannesburg SA

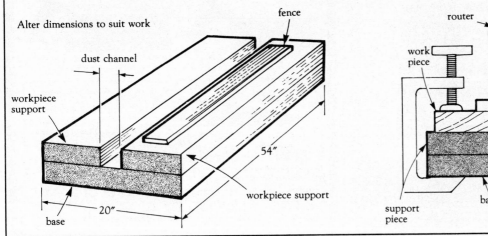

Alter dimensions to suit work

dust channel

fence

workpiece support

workpiece support

54"

20"

base

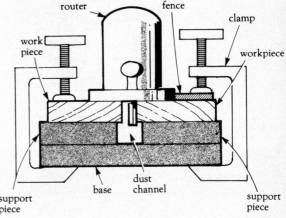

router

fence

clamp

work piece

workpiece

dust channel

base

support piece

support piece

Sash-frame marker

An easy-to-use gadget for marking out the scribed mortise-and-tenons joining moulded sections — sash frames, obviously, but any scribed joint can be done the same way. Cut the profile of the mould in both ends of a short piece of scrap moulding. Then, when you're doing windows, measure the rail for length rebate to rebate, add however much you need for the protruding tenons if you wedge them, and then lay the gadget on the rail and mark round it. Cut the rebate line and tenon with a tenon or dovetail saw, and the curve of the moulding with a coping saw, and you have a perfectly fitting joint every time.

M. J. Farman, Church Stretton

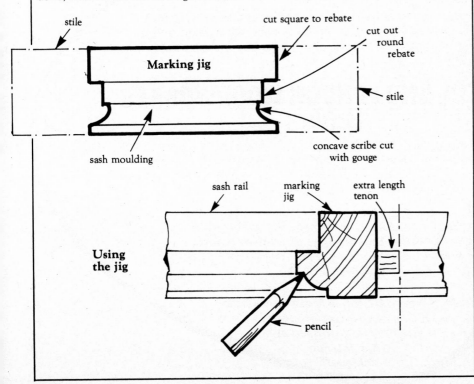

stile

Marking jig

cut square to rebate

cut out round rebate

stile

concave scribe cut with gouge

sash moulding

sash rail

marking jig

extra length tenon

Using the jig

pencil

Mallet handlebar

For a good grip on your hammers and mallets, try putting a cycle handlebar grip on the handles. I find it invaluable and comfortable on any striking tool you have to use for periods at a time.

K. T. Kettle, Northolt

The immovable box

Annoying 'slipability' of oilstone boxes while you're sharpening away on the bench can be easily eliminated by tapping panel pins into the four corners of the underside of the box and snipping them off sharp with pincers or pliers to protrude a mere 1mm or so. File the points up sharp — and your oilstone box never moves when you use it.

Charles Cliffe, Bexleyheath

HOW TO DO IT

We want to publish as many wheezes as possible, so we must use only the barest bones of the ideas. Be as precise and brief as possible; type your words if you can, double-spaced on one side of an A4 sheet; make drawings, if any, as few and as clear as you can, and annotate them clearly.

ARE YOU A WOODWORKER?

The result of all your hard work, patience and skill deserves to be displayed where it can both arouse admiration and inspire enthusiasm in others, and where better than at the

BRISTOL AND LONDON WOODWORKER SHOWS

Cabinet-making, woodcarving, musical instruments, marquetry, toys, woodturning, model horse drawn vehicles . . . there's a competition class for everyone!

Entry forms and further information available from:
**Argus Specialist Exhibitions Ltd, Wolsey House, Wolsey Road, Hemel Hempstead, Herts. HP2 4SS.
Tel: 0442 41221**

Gold, Silver and Bronze Medals available as well as certificates of merit . . . you may be surprised at what you can achieve!!

Browse at leisure in our self selection of timber
- over 60 species in boards, bowl blanks and dimensions.

Our self service Store - over 5,000 items in stock.

 JOHN BODDY'S
FINE WOOD & TOOL STORE LTD.

EVERYTHING FOR THE WOODWORKING CRAFTSMAN

- Accessories
- Barometers
- Brassware
- Books
- Carving tools
- Clock movements
- Exotic timbers
- Finishes
- Glassware
- Lathes
- Plans
- Pyrography
- Requisites
- Tools
- Turning tools
- Upholstery items
- Veneers
- Veneering tools

Over 5,000 items, over 60 species of timber
available by :

SELF SERVICE Assistance and expertise always
available. Easy access from A1. Situated adjacent
to the Yorkshire Dales.

MAIL ORDER Send for our Mail Order catalogue
- price £2.00 216 pages, many in colour.
A reference manual in its own right.

Store Opening Hours

Mon. - Fri.	Saturday	Bank Holidays
8 a.m. to 5 p.m.	8 a.m. to 4 p.m.	10 a.m. to 4 p.m.

COURSES & FREE DEMONSTRATIONS
Send for our 1987 programme and course leaflets

- Woodturning
- Chairmaking
- Pyrography
- Toymaking
- Signmaking
- Woodfinishing
- Woodcarving
- Chair Caning
- Yarn Spinning
- Stickmaking
- Gun Stock Finishing
- Lace Bobbin Making

Held in our custom built schoolrooms with
specialist tutors.
Free demonstrations given by our course tutors.

For further details,
please write or phone (09012) 2370
Riverside Sawmills, Boroughbridge,
North Yorkshire YO5 9LJ

Aerial view of our 7½ acre site.

Woodturning course in progress.

HUMBROL
CARPENTERS
ALIPHATIC RESIN
WOOD GLUE

- **Grabs fast and sets fast**
- **Stronger than wood itself**
- **Versatile, easy to use**

fix-it-fast

HUMBROL
CARPENTERS'
wood glue
FAST GRAB MULTI-GLUE

Specially
formulated
for use on
both hard
and soft
woods

HUMBROL
MARFLEET, HULL, ENGLAND.

SOUTH WEST
Power Tools

GOOD NEWS for all WEST COUNTRY WOODWORKERS

DW1201 POWERSHOP
— THE VERSATILE FOLDAWAY WORKSHOP

- Ideal for the woodworking enthusiast with limited garage or workshop space.
- Full crosscut, bevel, mitre and ripping versatility coupled with DeWalt accuracy.
- Easy to use and quick to change cutting angles.
- Quiet, yet powerful and maintenance free induction motor.
- Arm-end control switch with special safety key.
- Frame-mounted no-volt release switch with motor overload protector.
- Wide range of optional accessories for grooving, rebating, tenoning, shaping, curve-cutting, routing, sanding and drilling.

List Price £410

NEW MODEL

OUR
PRICE
£250
inc. VAT

SPECIFICATIONS — DW1201		Max. crosscut width in 25mm stock	310mm
Motor (240v)	1.0HP	Max. mitre width at 45° in 0-20/20-60mm stock	
Blade ø	250mm	— right hand	225/160mm
Blade Bore ø	30mm	— left hand	125/125mm
Max. depth of cut at 90°	68mm	Max. ripping width	505mm
Max. depth of bevel cut at 45°	50mm	Weight	32kg

DW1201 folded down and stored on wall using optional wall brackets.

AVAILABLE FROM:

Water-ma-Trout (Industrial Estate) Helston Cornwall TR13 0LW Tel: (03265) 4961	30 Ferris Town Truro Cornwall TR1 3JJ Tel: (0872) 71671	8 Western Road Launceston Cornwall PL15 7AS Telephone: (0566) 4781

Up-and-down routing

Robin Anderson decided his router had more potential mounted overhead — so he built his own precision machine

When I was given a router one Christmas I quickly discovered what a versatile tool it is. But I soon realised that its potential would be considerably increased if it were stably mounted over a worktable for moving the wood past it, rather than holding the wood still and moving the router.

This design I developed for an overhead router is largely influenced by the fact that I am an engineer by profession and have a Unimat 3 machining centre. With larger machining capacity I probably would have produced a rather different design, and if you have no metalwork facilities you could make a less complex machine — but perhaps not quite so effective.

I had the following requirements in mind:
- to work long thin sections, difficult with the router in conventional mode
- to make lap joints
- to produce transverse grooves without a straight edge
- to simplify rebating
- to make mortise joints
- to produce tapered sections in conjunction with simple jigs
- to act as a thicknesser for boards up to 6in wide, using a Trend 3-bladed cutter.

I decided it would be much easier to raise and lower the router rather than the worktable, and would also give better visibility when setting up.

The overall design is similar to a conventional vertical milling machine, as used for metal work. The work table is 40in from the floor, and measures 36x8in. Head traverse (vertical movement along the z axis) is 6in, as is the table traverse (front to rear, the y axis). There is no limitation on the movement of the work from left to right (x axis). The machine incorporates locking mechanisms for the y and z axis, and a depth stop for the head (z) axis, with clamps for holding the work during machining.

The machine consists of three main parts:
1 cabinet and head support
2 work table and its sliding and locking mechanisms
3 the head mechanism.

● *A joy to use – that's Robin Anderson's home-designed overhead router; lower picture shows his attention to detail*

Cabinet and head support

I made the base cabinet from veneer-covered chipboard and use it for storing tools and attachments; it is secured to the workshop wall to aid rigidity.

Rigidity is particularly important with the head support, which is of ¾in ply, strenthened with internal webs of ¾in ply, and faced at front, back and top with ⅜in oak, all glued and screwed; this is also attached to the wall.

Worktable

I made the worktable from ¾in ply, rebated into a fixed fence at the back to ensure both remain dead straight. I filled the grain and wax-polished the surface to produce a low-friction finish.

There are various ways of getting the table to slide backwards and forwards. A wooden dovetail slide is one possibility, but must be precise, and must also incorporate some kind of locking device.

In my prototype I used two metal rods with a V-block sliding on one, and a locking mechanism to hold the table down.

My second attempt was far more efficient, but is fairly ambitious. A 14x6in plate of 10swg MS plate has four dural blocks attached, each fitted with a brass bush, bored to be a sliding fit on ½in-diameter silver steel rods. These rods are mounted on two ½x½in MS bars in which two slots have been milled while the bars are clamped together, so they are truly parallel.

The guide bushes are fitted to the rods, the rods attached to the bars, and this assembly laid on the plate and spot drilled, the holes tapped and secured with screws; the bars are fitted with four jacking screws so you get true right-angle alignment to the vertical. This whole assembly is then screwed to a base of ½in MDF board, which in turn is screwed to the top of the cabinet, leaving the final tightening until the jack screws have been adjusted.

To lock the table I devised a caliper brake mechanism, with a lever attachment under the front of the work table.

The table was finished with clamping devices to hold the work against the fence and prevent it lifting against the cutter.

Head mechanism

You could use a standard drill-stand, provided it will hold your router, removing the base and screwing the column to the head support. Depth stop and locking could be achieved with collars above and below the head. Setting up would be a bit of a slog, but it would provide a workable machine.

I started off with this set-up, but found there was some side play. So I adapted the column and pinion from the drill-stand I had, devising a locking mechanism and depth stop.

I fitted a hinged safety guard to the front of the router mounting block, connected

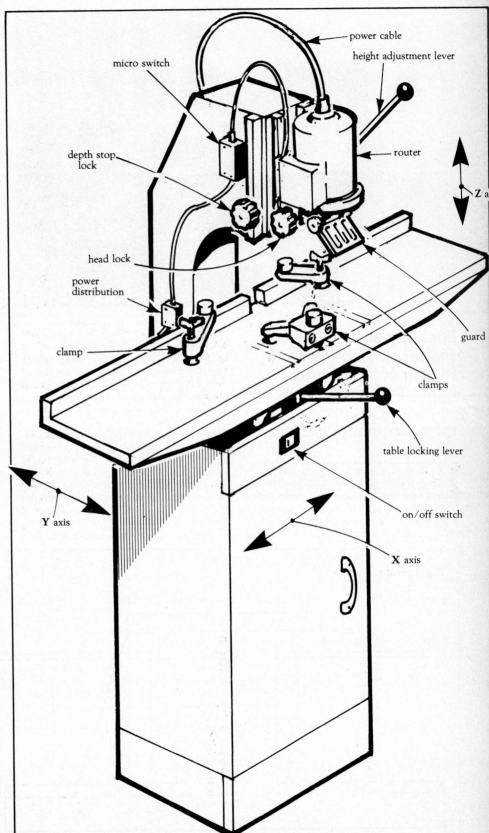

via a Bowden cable (cycle 3-speed cable) to a micro-switch to prevent operation until it is in the 'safe' position.

It took me five months to complete the machine, and it is a joy to use. ■

● Full working drawings and annotated plans of Robin's machine will shortly be available from Woodworker Plans Service, Wolsey House, Wolsey Rd, Hemel Hempstead, Herts HP2 4SS.

Pinpoint routing

For those who aren't engineers, Chris Coupe's version of the overhead router is simple to make and very effective — with the added advantage of a guide pin

It's really quite easy to make an overhead router table for your hand-held machine out of good, accurately machined hardwood. The accuracy is good enough for most woodworking applications, and as long as you're sure the wooden components will not move, you have a simple route to the vastly increased range of applications for a router which you don't have to hold. A pin or pins of different sizes, positioned in the worktable centrally beneath the cutter, give you a template effect, and you can mould or rebate with ease.

The drawings are largely self explanatory. The slideway pieces in the rise-and-fall housing column must be absolutely accurate, and fit into the housing itself with equal accuracy. I suggest erring on the side of too tight a fit, and easing with an engineer's file. Wax the slideway for a smooth action. Assemble the table, housing — with strengthening gusset but NOT THE

● A simple, solid answer to the overhead routing solution – but use stable timber and accurate dimensions

TOP YET — router support arm and slideway pieces, then turn everything over, and with the support arm clamped to the table, drill through everything for the M16 studding, which is the basis of the rise and fall mechanism. Then slide the support arm out of the top of the housing, and you can recess the underside for the M16 nut. Just thread the nut on the studding, slide the studding into the hole, and using that to keep your centre, draw round the nut. Then you can chisel (or rout, if you're confident) out the exact shape of the nut. Drill a piece of 6mm ply for a keeper plate, and set that aside until you're ready to put the whole thing together.

The device is designed to take my router — a heavy Makita — and so the dimensions shown relate to that particular machine. It's obvious you will alter things to suit your own. I couldn't be sure of accurately getting the centres for the bright mild steel bars that hold the router on the support arm, so drilled the holes oversize, then set the bars up in the router itself and laid the support arm and router, with the bars embedded in epoxy resin in the support arm holes, on a flat surface. I left the resin to cure, and had perfectly positioned and very strongly located bars.

I turned a 120mm-diameter handwheel, and a small handle to fix to it. I drilled a 16mm hole in the centre of the wheel, and using the studding with an M16 nut on it to keep the centre, drew round the nut and recessed it as I had done for the slideway. Then I drilled a 3mm hole through the side of the nut, right through the studding and out the other side of the nut, and lockwired them together with 3mm wire. I set the assembly up in the table — the 16mm hole

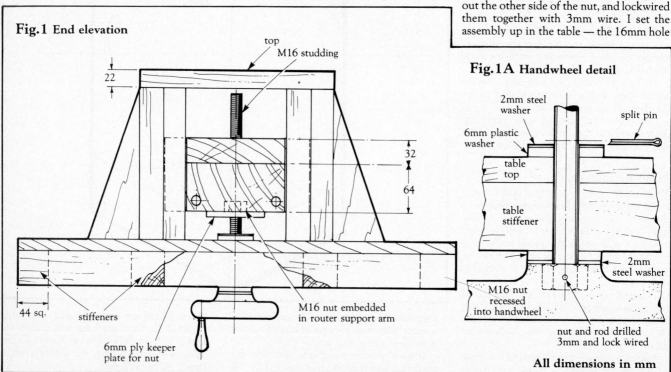

Fig.1 End elevation

top
M16 studding

22

32

64

44 sq.

stiffeners

6mm ply keeper plate for nut

M16 nut embedded in router support arm

Fig.1A Handwheel detail

2mm steel washer

6mm plastic washer

split pin

table top

table stiffener

2mm steel washer

M16 nut recessed into handwheel

nut and rod drilled 3mm and lock wired

All dimensions in mm

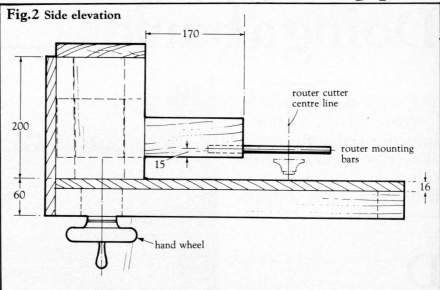

Fig.2 Side elevation

170

router cutter
centre line

200

15

router mounting
bars

60

16

hand wheel

goes through one of the 44mm stiffeners —
with 2mm and 6mm steel and plastic
washers either side as shown in the drawing,
and marked above the top washer. I drilled
through the studding there for a split pin to
keep everything tight up together.

Then it was just a matter — the trickiest
bit, this — of Aralditing the recess in the
support arm for the M16 nut, being
absolutely sure no Araldite got anywhere
near the threads, and dropping the
assembly in from the top, 6mm ply 'keeper
plate' first. I had glued this, again keeping
the glue away from the hole for the
studding, so when everything was located
on the studding all I had to do was wind the

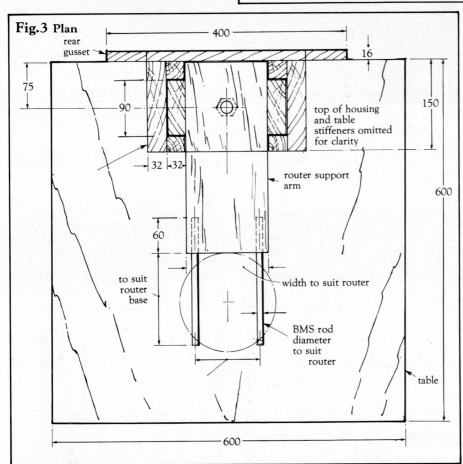

Fig.3 Plan

rear
gusset

400

16

75

90

top of housing
and table
stiffeners omitted
for clarity

150

32 32

router support
arm

600

60

to suit
router
base

width to suit router

BMS rod
diameter
to suit
router

table

600

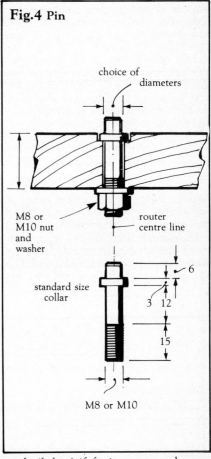

Fig.4 Pin

choice of
diameters

M8 or
M10 nut
and
washer

router
centre line

standard size
collar

6

3 12

15

M8 or M10

support arm hard down to the table to
provide clamping pressure for the ply
keeper plate. Then I glued and screwed the
top of the housing column on, and was
ready to go.

The pin

Turn a selection of pins if you're metalworking equipped; I'm not, so I got an engineering shop to make mine. You can get a
range to relate to the sizes of cutters you
have. The main thing is that the hole
through the table is a standard size — I
suggest 8 or 10mm — and the bottom
section of all your pins is always that size.

The exact location of the hole underneath the router cutter itself is a simple
matter of fitting a cutter the size of your pre-

determined pin 'shank' in the router and
plunging it all the way through the table.
The handwheel and studding give you the
major rise-and-fall adjustment, and for
micro-adjustment you can use the
mechanism on the router itself. When you
have a hole right through the table, fit a
cutter of the size of your pre-determined
pin collar, and cut a recess in exactly the
same way, merely by lowering the router on
to the table. Be careful with the depth here
— you want to allow yourself some room to
alter the height of the pin in relation to the
workpiece.

The pins themselves should have varying
diameters at the top, and standard collars
and lower threaded shanks. The pin top
section and cutter size relate to the width of

cut by 'halves'; if, for instance, you have an
8mm straight cutter with a 6mm pin, you
will get 1mm width of cut. If you need the
pin to protrude at differing heights, you can
shim it up or down with washers in the top
recess. The beauty of the pin arrangement,
of course, is that you can follow any profile
for moulding or whatever, and also that it
will work for straight rebates on straight
workpieces as well, because there is only
one point where cutter, workpiece and pin
meet, and that never changes. For the tasks
you can't perform with the pin, just take it
out and clamp a straightedge as a fence to
the table exactly where you want it. Simple,
easy to use, free hands, no clamping
problems with small workpieces; and good
visibility. But always wear safety goggles!■

Doing a bunk

The cap'n slept in style in seagoing versions of this attractive bed-with-drawers — popular with the kids as well as useful. Bob Grant shows you how

Photos Ray Clayton

● *Capacious storage, fun to use, and good looking; this solid design, with long frame members neatly picked out, suits strong-grained pine*

Designed to accommodate a standard single mattress of 75x30x6in, this piece is inspired by the fitted bunk beds of the sailing ship era; they are still popular as free-standing units in homes today. For even more storage, you could add another bank of drawers of the same size.

The original was made from pine; although it's quite a heavy piece you could also use one of the less dense hardwoods. The bed is made from three sub-assemblies; the top cot surround, the mattress framing, and the drawer unit and drawers.

The drawings show the constructional features and sizes, and you should refer to the cutting list which shows finished dimensions.

The top cot surround is simply a through-dovetailed box with a cutout in one side (fig. 1). Make sure the top edges of the surround are well rounded over.

The mattress is carried on a separate flat frame which is rebated to carry loose slats made from ½in plywood, well rounded on the top edges. At the end and over the

drawer-unit dividers, 1in thick pine members are half-lapped on to the long frame sides, then glued and screwed down (fig. 2). I used a ¼in bead or quirk moulding as a decorative feature, struck at the top and bottom of the frame edges. The mattress frame is screwed at intervals up into the cot carcase's under-edges, thus stiffening the whole construction; you'll find it best to make the cot surround first, then the mattress frame, screw the two together and then flush off the outside surfaces. Remove

the frame, work the moulding and then reassemble. The bed slats may be dropped in afterwards.

You can see how the drawer unit is constructed in fig. 3 and the photograph. The ends are made up of panels of ½in birch plywood rebated into 2x1in posts (you'll need additional ½in backing strips glued on at top and bottom to act as drawer runners). The long frame rails are lap-dovetailed on to the end posts, the top front rail set back

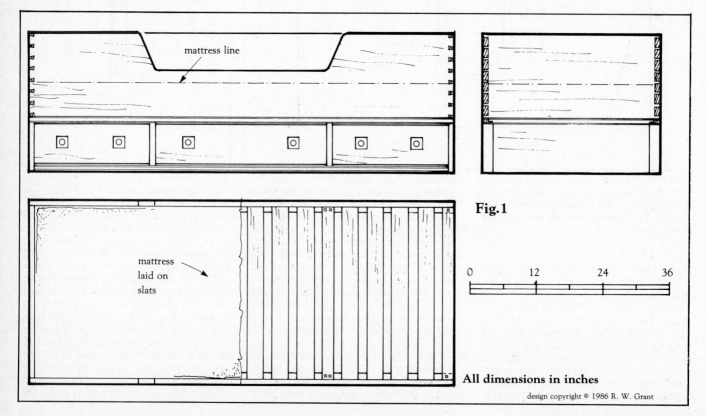

Fig. 1

mattress line

mattress laid on slats

0   12   24   36

All dimensions in inches

design copyright © 1986 R. W. Grant

Fig.3
Drawer-unit framing

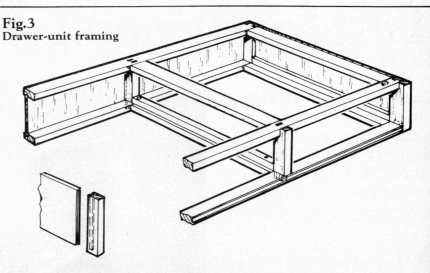

Fig.2 Mattress frame

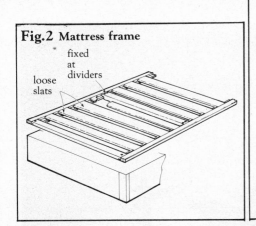

fixed
at
dividers

loose
slats

● **Above**, *slats and frame layout; note rail and post details*

Fig.4
Drawer construction

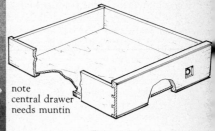

note
central drawer
needs muntin

● **Left**, *the details of the drawer-unit frame revealed. The top rail is set back*

from the carcase edge by the thickness of the drawer-front. Stub tenon the intermediate cross-members into the long rails, and twin tenon the upright drawer dividers top and bottom. Groove the back to take three panels of ¼in plywood. To prevent the drawers wandering, screw a bearer bar to the bottom cross-members between the intermediate dividers. Assemble the unit by making the top and bottom frames first then fitting the ends and the upright drawer dividers to the bottom frame, slide in the back panels, fit the drawer runners, and drop the top frame on.

The drawer construction is shown in fig. 4. Because of their size (and consequent unwieldiness) I made the drawers about 5in less than full depth. You'll have to add a central muntin to the middle drawer to support the ply bottom, because of its width. The fronts are deeper than the sides by the 1in thickness of the front drawer unit rail, which acts as a drawer stop. The drawer sides are lap-dovetailed at the front; you could dovetail them at the back as well, but I used a simple through housing.

Glue rebated drawer slips to the inner edges of the sides to carry the ply bottoms, which are housed in a groove at the front. Make sure you put this groove — which affects the thickness of the slips — to run out through the last dovetail socket, so it is hidden in the endgrain of the drawer-front. The drawer back sits on the ply bottom which is then pinned up through. The tops and bottoms of the drawer-fronts carry the same ¼in bead as the mattress frame and drawer-unit bottom rail. I fitted six brass flush ring-pull handles to the drawer fronts; these aren't cheap but they avoid the risk of catching sleepy legs!

You could use any suitable finish but only treat the fronts of the drawers; interiors of drawers can be tainted by polish smell in stale, stationary air, and polish applied to drawer sides can cause the drawer to stick — a rub with candle wax on the bearing surfaces is all you need. ∎

Cutting list
Finished sizes (all pine or suitable hardwood, except where stated)

Top cot carcase							
Sides	2	77in	x	15in	x	1in
Ends	2	32		15		1
Mattress framework						
Sides	2	77		2		1
Ends	2	32		2		1
Slats (ply)	10	30		3		½
Intermediate dividers	2	32		2		1
Drawer unit						
Long rails	4	77		2		1
Posts	8	8½		2		1
End panels (ply)	2	28½		8½		¼
Back panels (ply)	2	21½		8		¼
Back panel (ply)	1	32		8		¼
Drawer bearers	4	30		2		1
Guide bars	4	30		1		1
End guides	2	30		1		½
Drawers						
Fronts	2	21		7		1
Backs	2	21		5½		½
Bottoms (ply)	2	25		21		¼
Middle front	1	31		7		1
Back	1	31		5½		½
Bottom (ply)	1	25		31		¼
Drawer sides	6	25		6		½
Drawer slips	6	25		1		½
Muntin	1	25		2		½

Test for turners

Coronet have revitalised their operation, and added some special attractions to their new No. 1 lathe. We asked Bob Grant to take a close look

Mention the name 'Coronet' to a woodturner, and the light of recognition and admiration comes into the eyes. The long established and much respected marque, now a part of the Record Ridgway holding group, introduced in October 1986 the Coronet No. 1 lathe as a complement to the familiar Major and Elf models. More recently — in February of this year — they have added a special bowl-turning feature and introduced a range of tools.

During some 30 years of woodworking and woodturning I've worked on a variety of lathes; Coronet, Wadkin, Naerok, Harrison, Myford and others, plus my own much beloved 'Driver', a pre-war American machine inherited from my father. This lathe has proved its usefulness and versatility over the years; one can only get to know machines and their capabilities by constant use. I was able to work on the Coronet No. 1 unhindered for a good fortnight, trying out the basic machine under production conditions and also its accessories, and so was able to make a personal assessment of its performance.

So what's new about this one? Apart from its obvious newness as a product in

● Coronet's new No. 1 lathe **above**, has an ingenious versatility; re-align the bed bars at an angle and you can turn bowls up to 22in diameter, **below**

● The V-belt/pulley system gives speeds from 450-2000 rpm

the Coronet range (it's the first twin-bed lathe they have made, and employs a new production technique), it appears at first sight to be a conventional centre lathe of moderate capacity — 24in between centres and 6in swing over the bed. But all is not what it seems at first sight, as will be revealed!

Specification

From an engineering design point of view the lathe consists of a cast-iron headstock unit which carries the sealed ball-race mounted spindle with three pulleys, connected by a short poly-V belt to the pulleys on the motor shaft. This gives a speed range

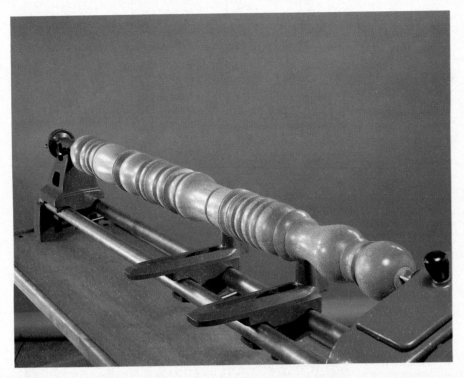

back bar and a single point on the front bar. A lever under each unit locks a baseplate securely underneath the bars. The T-rest is adjustable for height and angle by a lever that tightens downwards, clearing out of the way when you sweep and travel with the tools. A nice design detail point often overlooked in other lathes, much to the user's inconvenience. The tailstock mandrel is machined to take a morse taper for fitting centres and so on, and is also hollow, which allows long hole-boring tools to pass and be guided through. The cast parts are a pleasant dark green, which makes the bright blue Brook-Crompton motor look a bit incongruous.

This all may seem of passing interest, but it adds up to rigidity in use, rapid adjustment and ease of maintenance (the spindle bearings, for instance, are sealed for their working life). These qualities, along with high-quality engineering in an all-British product, must be balanced against the lathe's price, a prime consideration. At £297.85 inc. VAT, the Coronet No. 1 has to be taken seriously.

● **Above**, extension bars double capacity between centres. **Below**, Coronet's turning tools are 'equal to anything the serious amateur or professional could want'

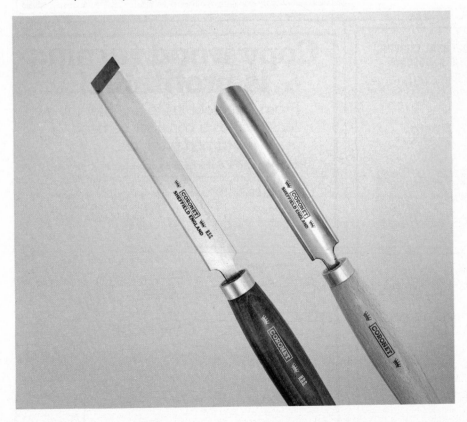

Special features

There are two 'hidden features' of the lathe, which extend both its capacity and versatility beyond the conventional and make it an attractive proposition. The first is the availability of 36 and 48in extension bar kits, immediately increasing the between-centres capacity by 100%; the second is the ingenious facility to re-orientate the head-stock and bed bars to allow faceplate turning (large bowl work, for instance) up to 22in diameter. Few manual lathes can approach, let alone exceed, this sort of capacity. You re-align the bed bars at an angle to the centre-line into pre-bored bolt holes in the stand base (or purpose-built bench top), add an extra saddle and mount the T-rest assembly to cantilever off the end. The substantial, solid bars guarantee rigidity. A special cranked tubular rest is available to allow the edges of large diameter bowls and other pieces to be worked. The headstock is simply swivelled on a pivot bolt to enable the work to swing clear over the edge of the stand.

Bits and pieces

I was supplied with a whole range of accessories that fit the lathe and a number of turning tools from Coronet's new 49-strong range, both carbon and high-speed steel. A vital complement to any good lathe, these tools are beautifully made with handles up to 16in long (nine and 12in are also available) and proved well balanced in use, equal to anything the serious amateur or professional turner could want. The large roughing gouge and the bowl turning gouge I found particularly outstanding for effortless work over sustained periods.

Fitting and removing accessories to the

of 450-2000rpm. The single-phase ½hp motor, protected by no-volt overload switchgear, is fixed to a clamp plate on the outboard end of the headstock and is easily released to change speeds through a top access hole in the casting. The twin 1½in solid steel bed bars are held in the headstock by a saddle which bolts the bars on to location bearing-points in the base of the stock. A similar technique is used to locate and hold the bars at the rear end. The tailstock and T-rest platform slide on these bars and any tendency to ride out of true is eliminated by a two-point bearing on the

continued

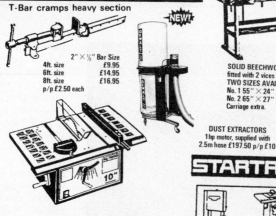
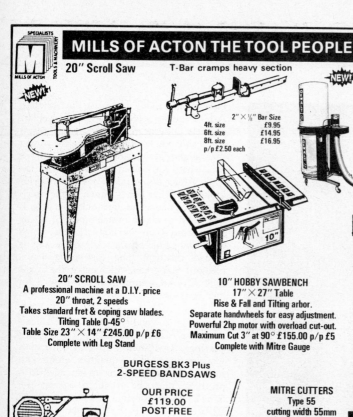
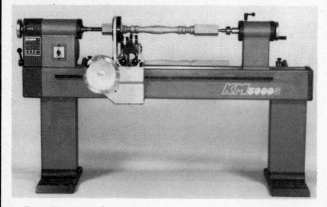
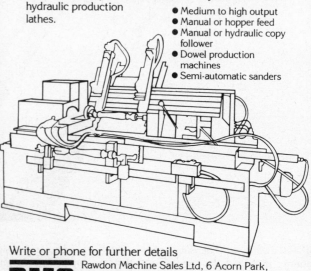

Test for turners

headstock mandrel is made easy by the thoughtfully provided spanner flats on the spindle, while the various chucks have a tommy-bar hole. The accessories, including the 6in faceplate, are precision engineered and finely finished. The woodscrew chuck is demountable *in situ* to remove finished items such as chess pieces, while the collet chuck set is a real treasure box. Easy gripping of bowls with an expanding collet, a three-jaw concentric chuck for holding circular work, a centrifugal spigot for supporting napkin rings, and so on . . . The machine will of course accept other accessories; one of the photos shows my own three-jaw chuck being used to grip a staircase newel-cap. A four-prong drive centre and a tailstock ring centre are included with the basic lathe, but medium-and heavyduty revolving centres are available for the tailstock and I must confess I prefer these, eliminating as they do the constant need to lubricate the rear end!

I was also sent a Wm. Ridgway heavyduty expansive bit which can be used on the lathe with an appropriate chuck — or in an ordinary power drill for that matter (*see* 'Shoptalk special', WW/July '86). It will bore up to 4in in depth and 2in diameter, and although not cheap it does do away with the need to carry a range of individually sized bits, as it's infinitely adjustable. It cuts extremely well in hardwoods although I found it clogged up a bit in resinous softwoods.

Coronet also sent me a bottle of their 'Speedaneez' liquid friction polish — if you haven't come across it before, it's good stuff. The frustrations of applying hard wax to turned work, when you create those irritating rings and ridges, are eliminated. Apply it with a soft cloth pad to the revolving work, and you can get a buffed superfine finish in no time.

Coronet will also supply a set of four prebored metal legs for you to make up your own lathe stand — just add a substantial top and bracing rails. But of course, there's nothing to stop you mounting the lathe on your existing or purpose-built bench. Full instructions for the lathe and its mounting come with each machine and I found that in any case help was a telephone call away. Mark Taberner is on hand at the Sheffield works to dispense expert advice and information — a service that the company takes pride in, and one that deserves to be widely known.

Gripes

I didn't set out to write a eulogy and was under no pressure to do so, and there are some (justified) moans. They're mostly small, because the quality of design thinking and evaluation that has gone into the product is consistently high. The casting of the T-rest as supplied was rough to the guiding fingers, and I removed a layer of skin at the first pass, but the roughness was easily dressed off with a bit of glasspaper.

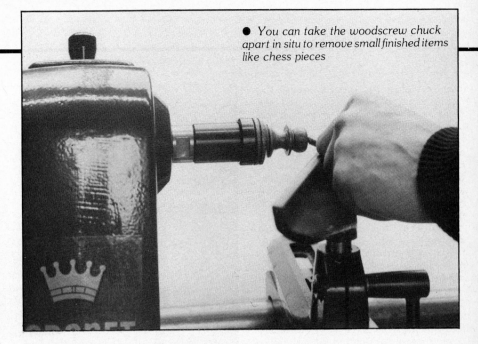

● *You can take the woodscrew chuck apart in situ to remove small finished items like chess pieces*

● *Spanner flats on the spindle and tommy-bar holes on the chucks make for easy fitting and removing of accessories*

Test for turners

That one obviously slipped through the quality control department, as did the spigot of the tubular bowl rest which was off the upright; Coronet assure me they have modified their production processing over these points and such faults are eliminated. I was disconcerted that the locking lever of the T-rest slide is designed to slide only towards the tailstock. If you happen to push it the other way — towards the headstock — the lever fouls against the headstock and tightens, so you'd have to dismantle the whole bed bar assembly to free it. Admittedly, the instructions do make this clear. Moral — always slide toward the tailstock! In the tailstock, the mandrel clamping screw is threaded through the casting to pinch into a machined groove in the mandrel itself. If the clamping screw is released by too many turns it clears the slot and the mandrel is free to revolve (there is no compensating keyway as on many lathes) and this could prove awkward when drilling via the tailstock.

All manufacturers have to monitor production costs carefully to arrive at a competitively priced item, and this often means that desirable extras become casualties at the drawing board design stage. The access cap to the spindle in the headstock is a case in point. The cap is virtually a loose plate, neither hinged nor lockable, so it might easily get misplaced and leave an open, hazardous, access hole. I understand Coronet do make a model with specially high safety standards for educational institutions, with a clamp on this cap and a micro-switch that isolates the electrics when the cap is opened. I for one wouldn't begrudge the extra expense to have this added protection on a machine for home use as well.

These reservations apart, I consider the Coronet No. 1 a good and very appealing buy. Whatever your creative fancy in this near-plastic art of woodturning, here is a machine that would be tolerant of the tyro, excellent for the serious amateur and capacious for the professional craftsman woodturner. Its many features, based on robustness and quality engineering, must give it serious advantages against potential rivals. ■

● Coronet Lathe and Tool Co, Parkway Works, Sheffield S9 3AJ, (0742) 434370.

● *Bob found the lathe would accept his own three-jaw chuck* **above**, *being used to grip a staircase newel-cap.* **Below**, *the collet-chuck set is a veritable treasure box*

Plant on top

● *Router-lathe – or 'Crafter' – ready for action*

Peter Skilton exploited his router's versatility in the decorative and constructional techniques he used for this graceful plant stand

To buy or not to buy, that is the question. It faces amateur woodworkers everytime they consider purchasing an expensive item of equipment. I mused for many months before I decided to buy a plunging router. In the years since then, my decision has been vindicated many times over, and my router has become an indispensable tool in my woodwork.

This plant stand demonstrates just how useful the router is: in this project it was used for dovetail housings and tenons, for shaping, for engraved decoration, and also for the reeding on the main column, in conjunction with my router-lathe.

Router-lathe

A router-lathe is a useful device for spiralling and fluting as well as reeding. Mine is a Router Crafter, made by the American firm Sears Craftsman. Imports have apparently dried up, but good tool suppliers might still have one on their shelves. It has a headstock, tailstock, four interconnecting bed bars giving 33in between centres, and a sliding carriage on which the router is fastened.

With the carriage stationary and an appropriate cutter in the router, you can rotate the headstock 360° using a cranked handle, keeping the router carriage stationary, to produce beads, coves, shoulders and so on.

A second option is to move the headstock through 15° of rotation, lock it at this position, and move the router carriage along the length of the workpiece to form a bead or flute, which I did with the plant stand column.

Thirdly you can lock the router carriage to a continuous steel cable attached to the headstock spindle; this rotates the workpiece and moves the carriage simultaneously, forming a spiral in the workpiece.

The headstock is cup-shaped, with four pairs of internal locating ribs to accept the corners of square-section material. The pointed tailstock locates in the centre drilled end of the workpiece; you have to be careful that the tailstock is precisely at right angles to the bed bars, and that you don't unintentionally produce a taper on the work.

You can set the depth of the router cut by adjusting the two screws that pass through the carriage and set its height above the bed bars. With a plunging router, depth of cut can also be controlled with the plunging stop. If the diameter of the workpiece is appropriate I use the carriage-height adjustment screws to align the centre line of the router with the centre of the work and the router depth control to vary the depth of the cut (fig. 1).

By attaching a template to the router-lathe you can get the router carriage to rise and fall to a prescribed pattern during its traverse of the work: this is particularly useful for repetition work, ensuring uniformity in item after item.

Column

I made this plant stand when we needed to move one of our prize botanical specimens from the gloom of a low table to be nearer a

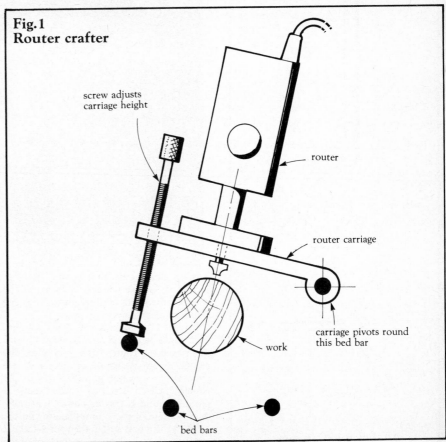

**Fig. 1
Router crafter**

screw adjusts
carriage height

router

router carriage

carriage pivots round
this bed bar

work

bed bars

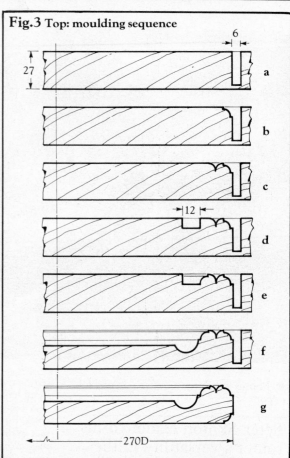

Fig.3 Top: moulding sequence

Fig.2 Dimensions

270

27

765

1020

A   A

305

520

Section A-A

52D

25

All dimensions in mm

● *Above, dovetail housings in the base of the column for the legs – tenons shaped to fit. Below, the router supported on metal bars across the width of the top to hollow out the inside; see the moulding stages right*

window, and the size of the plant container and height of the window gave rise to the overall dimensions of the plant stand. I used Brazilian mahogany throughout.

I started by making the main column. This could be turned on a lathe, of course, but I used my router-lathe to produce the reeded design. I shaped the material to a circular cross-section and then formed 24 equally spaced stopped reeds, using a pointed round engraving cutter, extending over 660mm of the column length (fig. 2).

With the wood still in the router-lathe, I cut three flats, 120° apart, at the foot of the column, and used a dovetail cutter to produce stopped housings for the legs.

Top

From the 300mm square from which I cut the circular top, I edge-jointed three 100mm pieces of mahogany. You can shape the top either on a lathe faceplate, or use the router with a radius arm and a succession of cutters (fig. 3). I used a fine depth control on the router and a series of light cuts, following the steps shown to shape the compound moulding around the circumference.

Once the moulding was complete, I hollowed out the centre of the top with a 13mm bottom-cut router bit. For this I supported the router base on two smooth metal bars firmly clamped across the top, plunging the router below and between the bars to produce the flat central area.

I cut off the remaining thin annulus of material (still with the corners of the original square) with a coping saw, before moulding the under-edge of the top, again using the router and radius arm.

Legs

I marked the shape of the legs on the prepared timber using a cardboard template (fig. 4), before cutting them out on a bandsaw and cleaning up with a spokeshave and glasspaper to match the template. Using a dovetail cutter in a stand-mounted router, I formed the 15mm deep dovetailed tenons on the shoulder of each leg to fit the main column housings.

Then I used the router machine table with a profiling (copy-follower) attachment and an ovolo cutter to form a moulding along each outside corner of the leg and along the foot. I engraved the decoration on each surface by using the router freehand, with a 5mm cutter.

Assembly and finish

After rubbing down with fine glasspaper to remove any sharp corners or cutter marks left by the router, I glued the three legs into the base of the column, and dowelled and glued the top in place, using three 6mm beech dowels.

I brushed wood stain well into the surface, removing surplus with a fluff-free cloth. Once this had dried thoroughly, I rubbed the surface down hard to remove any residue from the stain before applying the first of six sparing coats of polyurethane.

Our pot plant now seems quite at home on top of its perch and is obviously benefiting from the extra light. ∎

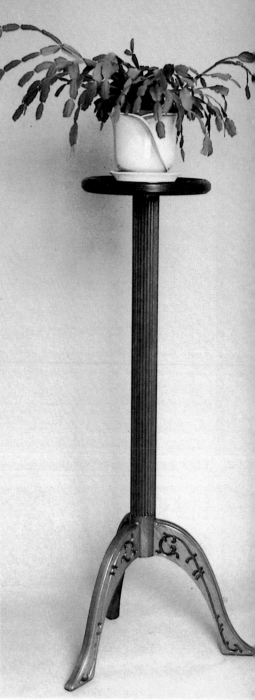

Cutting list

Column	1	765mm	x 55mm	x 55mm
Feet	3	377	100	25
Top	3	300	100	25

● Legs; edge mouldings cut with a copy follower and template, the 'carved' details routed freehand

● Routed elegance; the plant seems to like it

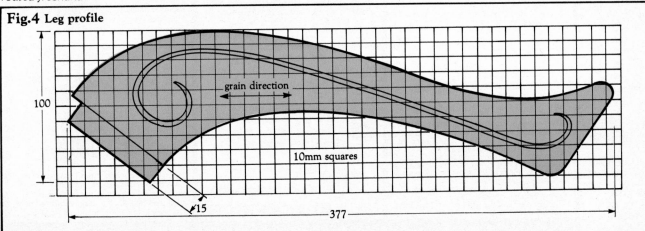

Fig.4 Leg profile

grain direction

100

10mm squares

15

377

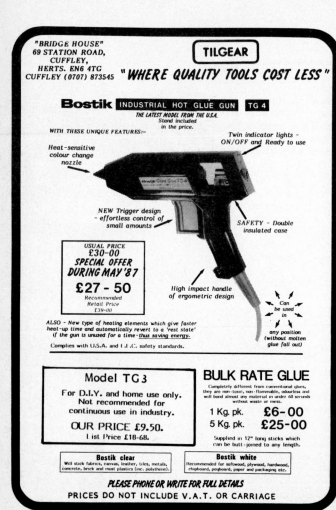

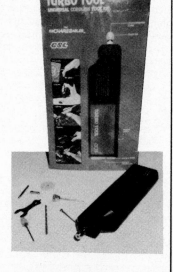

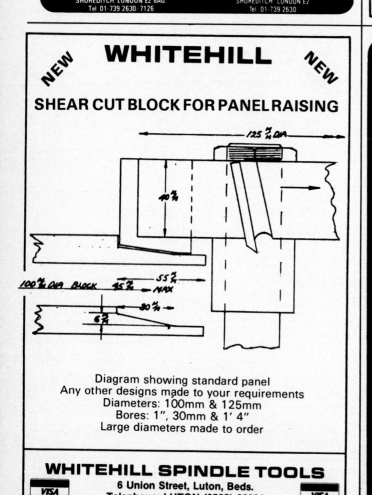
434

Very lightweight cramps

Add another cramping capability to your workshop with this ultra-light design

I produced several of these very light cramps when I had to cramp cross-grained walnut mouldings to a small clock case. They give a reasonable span with the minimum weight, with firm but not great pressure.

I first produced the hardwood blocks to exactly the same length. I ensured the holes were equally spaced whatever the size of drill by making up the simple drilling jig shown in fig. 2. The moving jaw B is thicker because it is tapped; the drawing shows a square nut let into this, though a thread merely cut in the wood will have a long life. The fixed blocks A and C are tapped in the lower holes, the upper holes being clear.

For the plain guide rod I used ¼in-diameter steel, though 6mm or even 5mm would be lighter and would do the job. I used a fairly fast thread on a thin rod, ¼in BSW. As this screw works under tension, not under pressure as with all other cramps, you can make it thinner; but as a very fine thread requires a great deal of turning, you shouldn't go below 5mm.

The lower bar is threaded at both ends, screwed into the blocks and secured with a locknut and washer. If the bar is thick enough you could drill and lock with a fine pin instead.

The threaded bar is fitted with a wingnut; for neatness this is soldered, brazed or pinned. You could use a locknut if you want to avoid metalworking, but it is rather bulky. A completely different method is to cast on the screw a knob in fibreglass resin and file or turn it to a shape which gives a good grip and a substantial shoulder; you'll need to distort the end of the screw which goes inside the knob by crimping it in a strong vice or hammering it flat.

On the inner side you'll just have to use two locknuts; try to obtain some very thin ones.

You'll have to work out how the parts assemble; it may puzzle you at first, but it will go together in several ways. Test that the cramp works, and when you're satisfied, dismantle and shape the blocks, heavily chamfering or rounding the jaws on the outside. This prevents misuse by making the screw push the sliding block instead of pulling it. Then you can oil or varnish the wood.

I've given two possible widths for the blocks, according to what you'll be using the cramps for. The end block C may have a stopped top hole for neatness; if you're making a number of blocks it's easier to take all the holes right through, so A and C are identical. Instead of wood you could use aluminium bar.

Don't make the cramps too long; I suggest you can get four 9in screws from a 3ft length of imperial bar, and slightly longer from a 1m length of metric dimension. ∎

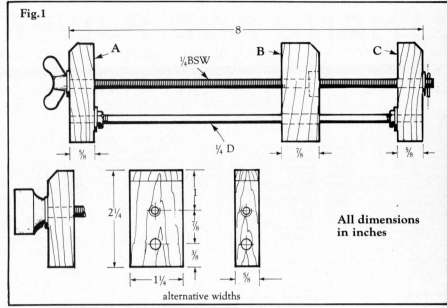

Fig.1

¼BSW
¼ D

All dimensions in inches

alternative widths

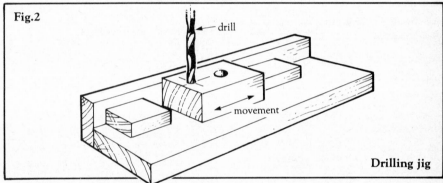

Fig.2

drill

movement

Drilling jig

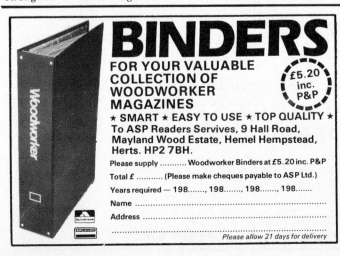

Question box

Our panel of experts solve your woodworking problems

> We will try to answer any questions you can throw at us, but the ones we publish are the ones of most general interest to readers.
>
> Please type your question double-spaced with generous margins, and include a stamped self-addressed envelope. Send it to: Question Box, Woodworker, 1 Golden Sq., London W1R 3AB.

Planing ebony

Q *I have tried to reduce the thickness of an ebony musical instrument finger-board by using a block plane with an adjustable throat set fine enough to overcome the 'wild' grain. After a few strokes the wood surface becomes greasy and resists efforts to remove any further shavings. What do you suggest?*

G. B. Bleazard, Stockport, Cheshire

A Firstly you are using the wrong plane. The sole length of a block plane is short (in comparison with the length of the fingerboard) making planing the surface flat very difficult. Instead, use a smoothing plane adjusted so the back iron is low to the cutting edge and the frog has a narrow mouth.

The cutter *must* be sharp. The greasiness is caused by the plane skating over the surface and burnishing it, instead of the cutter cutting into it. The two surfaces forming the cutting edge must be a mirror-finish for the edge to be sharp and, because of the hard granular nature of ebony, you will have to resharpen several times during the thicknessing process.

Phil Chambers
● Phil Chambers is musical-instrument making lecturer at Merton College.

Danish oil

Q *I installed a maple worktop in my kitchen and finished it with several coats of Danish oil. After some weeks of use the odd stain has begun to appear.*

Soap and water doesn't work; can you suggest what I should do?

Mark Haughton, Barnet, Herts

A It could be that you haven't applied enough Danish oil to the worktop. If the grain isn't completely sealed, it's possible that products which cause discoloration are penetrating into the wood.

I'd recommend another liberal application of Danish oil; clean off the stains you mention beforehand by rubbing along the grain with grade 0 or 1 steel wool and white spirit, and wipe down with a clean rag. Apply the oil with a clean brush or rag, and leave it to soak in for several minutes before wiping off the surplus. If there's still some discoloration after this treatment, you can wipe the surface with household bleach.

Apply the last coat of oil with a Scotch-brite pad, which will remove any nibs and leave the surface with a very smooth satiny finish.

Ronald E. Rustin

Polishing substances

Q *Could you explain what the following wood polishing materials are made from and their applications: white spirit; terebene; mineral oil; Danish oil and Watco Danish oil?*

H. H. Lawson, Johannesburg, South Africa

A **White spirit** is distilled from petroleum with a flashpoint of 78°F (25.6°C minimum). It consists of approximately 85% aliphatic hydrocarbons, and the remainder is a mixture of aromatic hydrocarbons and cyclic paraffins. It is similar to the American products, 'mineral spirit' and 'Stoddard solvent'. It was generally known in the U.K. as turpentine substitute and was originally used in place of pure turpentine. There is however, no standard for a substitute and some companies supply kerosine (paraffin) as a turpentine substitute. This has a much slower evaporation rate than white spirit and isn't suitable for thinning paint. White spirit BSS.245 has a specific gravity in the region of 0.775, an initial boiling point in the region of 155°C and a final boiling point of 201°C.

Mineralised methylated spirits is the only form of industrial alcohol on general sale in the UK and is satisfactory for dissolving spirit stains and for thinning french polish. It shouldn't be used for dissolving shellac to make your own french polish, as it has a lower alcohol content than the industrial alcohol used by manufacturers of shellac solutions. A polish made with shellac and mineralised methylated spirits would tend to 'blush' more readily when used in a cold or damp atmosphere, than one based on 'real' industrial alcohol.

Terebene/terebine was originally made by heating copal resin with linseed oil and litharge, but this method is no longer used and there can be big differences in formulation between the material made by various manufacturers. It's used for accelerating the drying of oil-based paints and linseed/boiled linseed oil, and is obtainable in small containers from paint and hardware merchants. It is completely different from turpentine, which is a solvent.

Mineral oil is a non-drying colourless non-lubricating oil obtained from petroleum, available in a range of viscosities. When the aromatic hydrocarbon content is removed, it's known commercially as white oil and is available in light and heavy grades. When it's purified for use in food and cosmetic products, it's known as liquid paraffin. This is also available in light and heavy grades. If you wish to use mineral oil for french polishing in place of linseed oil, you could use liquid paraffin, but as it is non-drying, use very small quantities.

Danish oil and Watco Danish oil — I haven't examined the properties of Watco Danish oil, but as there's no standard formula for Danish oil, it is possible that the Watco product is based on linseed oil or boiled linseed oil thinned with white spirit. Rustin's Danish oil is based on tung oil and other oils and resins to produce a hard, durable seal for wood that dries to a natural low lustre.

Ronald E. Rustin
● Ronnie Rustin is managing director of Rustin's the finish manufacturers.

Skittle balls

Q *I made some skittle balls from well-seasoned elm and soaked them in linseed oil, but they are now breaking up. Was elm the best choice of wood?*

H. Graham, Long Eaton, Notts

A I'm not quite sure what you mean by breaking up, but as the wood was seasoned, I presume you mean flaking off rather than splitting open. Flaking is a common problem with wood that receives continual shocks such as carving-mallet heads, croquet balls and skittle balls. The answer lies more in what part of the tree you choose rather than in what type, though wych elm and white poplar or willow remain good choices.

The best parts come either from just below the main branching or crutch of the tree, or from a burr or canker growth. In both cases the timber is under pressure and has become far denser than usual, as can be seen by the greatly reduced size and number of pores in the endgrain (see *The International Book of Wood*, published by Mitchell Beazley).

In the first case, the crutch should be cut

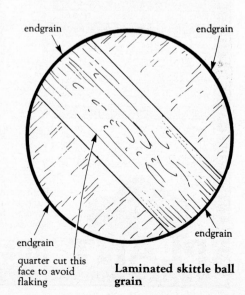

endgrain

endgrain

endgrain

endgrain

quarter cut this face to avoid flaking

Laminated skittle ball grain

down the hearts (consult *Artistic Woodturning* by Dale Nish) and the balls cut from below the main figuring from the part that supports the main branch.

In the second case, avoid wood that is too highly figured or too close to the surface, checking the endgrain to find the densest part.

Wood such as this can sometimes be obtained by contacting firewood merchants and hunting round their yards, or from the uncut supplies of sawmills; either will usually be ready to chainsaw bits to a size you can handle. For crutch timber, the bigger the bole the less the chance of splitting; for burr timber or canker (smooth burr) timber, the larger the burr the better.

Drying from wet will require rough-turning the balls to ¾in oversize and keeping 6-8 weeks in a damp, but not mouldy, place; 6-8 months in an average outdoor environment out of the sun, with some air movement but not too much (in a tea crate punched with holes for example); and 6-8 weeks indoors (similar to the environment in a skittle hall). Then finish-turn them and oil as before. Thin the oil 50/50, or to your taste, to help penetration.

Other possibilities include laminating the balls from 2in material to present as much endgrain as possible; see the drawing. A good joint with PVA should do. Don't use Cascamite, it doesn't like shocks; Cascophen, Aerolite or epoxy resin would do. You could buy some old bowling woods of lignum vitae from the bowling club if you're lucky or from an antique junk shop. This is the easiest, but costliest, solution.

Tobias Kaye

● Tobias Kaye is a professional woodturner in Devon.

Compound mitres

QCan you tell me how the compound angles are determined and cut on the sections of moulding when fitting dado rails? I can't see how a mitre box could help, since many of the angles, apart from being compound, are likely to occur only once in a job and would result in a prodigious use of boxes.

Eric Holmes, London E5

APresumably you're fitting dado rails around a stairway, and the compound mitre troubles lie at the corners. Well, if there are many mitres to be done, it would be worthwhile making a mitre box (fig. 1). But for just one or two, temporarily fix one of the rails at its correct pitch, but protruding about 6in past the corner. Assuming the turn is at 90°, the mitre now will be a vertical cut with the tenon saw at 45° (fig. 2). Use a piece of, say, 3inx1in cut at 45° one end, placed edgewise and level against the wall, to guide the saw (fig. 3). Owing to the compound nature of the intersection, some making-good with a piece of glasspaper will be necessary.

An alternative, and neater, method, is to level-off at each turn (fig. 4). You'll then just have simple mitres to contend with. Fig. 5 shows how any mitre can be found simply by drawing in the moulding widths, and joining up the intersecting points.

Stan Thomas

● Stan Thomas is a joiner of vast experience who holds a live 'Question box' and 'tool hospital' at WOODWORKER Shows.

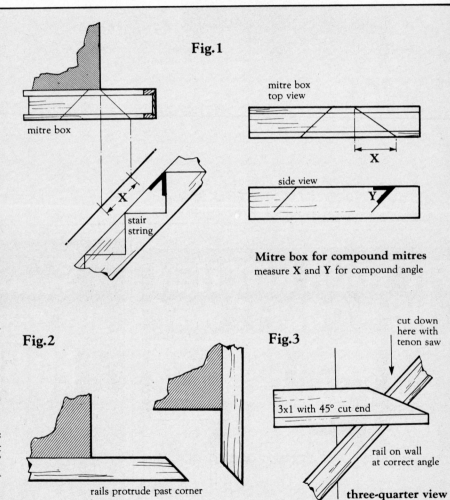

Fig.1

mitre box

mitre box top view

side view

X

Y

Mitre box for compound mitres
measure **X** and **Y** for compound angle

stair string

X

cut down here with tenon saw

Fig.2

rails protrude past corner

Fig.3

3x1 with 45° cut end

rail on wall at correct angle

three-quarter view

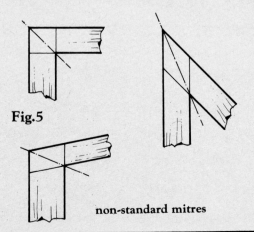

Fig.5

non-standard mitres

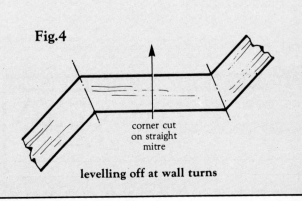

Fig.4

corner cut on straight mitre

levelling off at wall turns

CREATIVE WOODCRAFTS LTD.

EVERYTHING FOR THE CRAFTSMAN UNDER ONE ROOF

Telephone: Langley Mill (0773) 760129

NORMAL OPENING:
Monday-Friday 9-5.30
Saturday 9-4.00

See all the various machines on working demonstration at the Bristol Woodworker Show 15th-17th May 1987.

SEE THE NEW **VAMAC** UNIVERSAL WITH ADDED FEATURES, INCLUDING CAST SPINDLE MOULDER GUARD, NEW IMPROVED MULTI-POSITION SAW FENCE.

COMPARE THESE FEATURES
- ★ FOUR MOTORS
- ★ 1500mm LONG PLANER TABLES FOR STRAIGHTENING TIMBER
- ★ 3 KNIFE PLANER BLOCK FOR BETTER FINISH
- ★ MACHINE SPLITS IN TWO HALVES TO GO THROUGH 2'6" WIDE DOOR
- ★ HANDWHEEL RISE & FALL & TILT ON SAW
- ★ PRICE INCLUDES SLIDING TABLE
- ★ ALL CAST TABLES

PRICES FROM £1795 + VAT

FREE SPINDLE MOULDER BLOCK & CUTTER

PLEASE SEND DETAILS ON:

VAMAC

NAME ....

ADDRESS ....

....

.... POST CODE ....

To: Creative Woodcraft Ltd., The Field, Shipley, Nr. Heanor, Derbys. DE7 7JJ. (0773) 760129

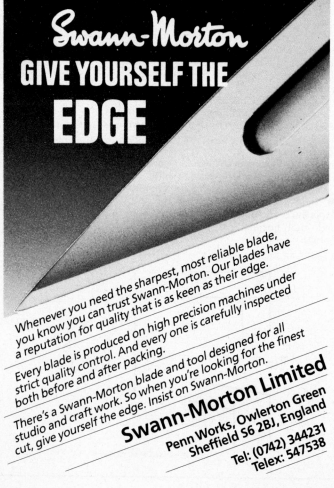

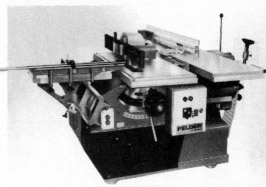

Letters

This is the drill

1 I WAS INTERESTED in Mr K. Down's 'Question box' query in January's WOODWORKER about an automatic-feed hand-powered bench drill; I have one with a smaller-than 3in flywheel, and I often have to accelerate the feed with my left hand. I wonder if Mr Down's fast-feed problem would be solved if he replaced his flywheel with a smaller one.

To quote from a one-time standard school textbook, *Technology of Woodwork and Metalwork* by Norman Rogers: 'Another self-feeding device, which has very few working parts, depends for its action upon the inertia of a flywheel. The upper end of the spindle is screwed so as to engage rather loosely with a tapped hole in the flywheel. Upward thrust on the spindle binds this screw sufficiently to spin the flywheel, but inertia prevents the wheel from ever going quite so fast as the spindle, and a feed is thus obtained which automatically adjusts itself to suit the work being done. Heavy drilling resulting in considerable thrust binds the screw so tightly that the flywheel almost keeps pace with the spindle and a slow feed is obtained; conversely, light drilling causes a quick feed.'

I would think drill breakages could be caused by the system of clamping the upper casting to the upright post. My drill uses a $\frac{5}{16}$in BSW screw for this, and when resistant material is being drilled, the whole upper part of the machine tends to swivel round the post if too much feed pressure is applied.

C. W. Miller, Rochester

2 THE ACTION OF MR DOWN'S bench drill is on this principle: Drive from the handle is transferred from the keywayed shaft **S1** via the bevel pinion key which engages the keyway in the shaft. The flywheel remains static, as does the thrust-bearing collar to which it is connected by the hollow shaft **S2**. With shaft **S1** turning and thrust-bearing collar static, shaft **S1** 'unwinds' and descends until the tip of the drill in the chuck engages the work, causing a reverse thrust. This increases the friction between the threaded part of shaft **S1** and the internal thread of the thrust-bearing collar with which it is engaged, so both bearing collar and flywheel now rotate. With collar and shaft both rotating, the 'unwinding' action tends to cease and drill-tip pressure on the work reduces. This in turn reduces the friction between shaft and collar, allowing the shaft to descend again, and the cycle of 'automatic feed' continues.

For adjustment, added friction can be applied by turning the knurled thumbscrew which increases the pressure on the spring-loaded bearing plunger against the hollow shaft **S2**. The flywheel smooths the auto-feed action by reducing the chatter between the threads of shaft and collar. There is an anti-jamming spring round the top of shaft **S1**.

My colleague Philip Walker is right to suggest a thorough clean, because excessive friction from dirt (or distortion) increases the thrust on the drill and could destroy small twist-drills if too much elbow-grease is applied. Properly adjusted, cleaned and handled, this type of drill is a joy to use.

David Carpenter, Chairman,
Tools & Trades History Society

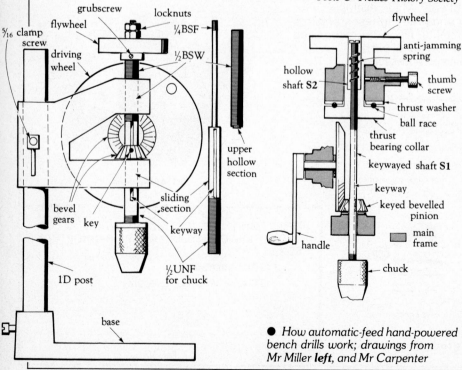

● *How automatic-feed hand-powered bench drills work; drawings from Mr Miller* **left**, *and Mr Carpenter*

Strapping idea

A SOLUTION TO Mr Butler's query ('*Question Box*', *WW/Feb*) on assembling window boards without fixings showing, is to use 'strip strap' strapping.

Cut the window board and make sure it fits. Then cut vertical slots into the plaster, say three for a 4ft window board. Nail or screw the strapping to the underside of the window board in line with the slots; offer the board in, level it up crossways, and fix the straps in the slots, making sure the straps are below the plaster. Make good as normal.

R. J. Anderson, Herne Bay

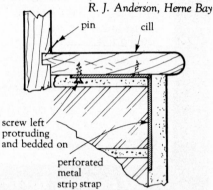

Heart of the matter

IT WAS GOOD to read Lucinda Leech's interesting and thoughtful article about her trip to Brazil (*WW/Feb*). Among the complex problems in the Amazon, there is one she didn't mention.

In 1500 there were 10 million indigenous tribal Indians in the Amazon basin. Today barely half a million survive. Their lands and way of life are now more under threat than ever before; their efforts to integrate into the modern world and simultaneously defend their cultural identity have brought poverty, disease, and (often violent) death.

I feel this information is relevant here, because it is the exploitation and destruction of the rainforests which is largely the cause of this virtual genocide.

As someone relatively new to woodwork, I feel greatly troubled that there seems to be so little we can do. I do not profess to know the answers, but one suggestion seems to make sense; we could reduce the demand for timber, and pressure on territory belonging by natural law to other people, by reverting to the great variety of timber from temperate zones. Commercial replacement of exhausted indigenous stock is well advanced here. If we do have to use tropical woods, the price should be higher.

Any money ploughed back could help countries like Brazil tackle their problems more effectively. (It might also discourage the global waste of tropical timbers if, along with higher prices, export controls forced people to appreciate the true value of this precious resource.)

Mark Haughton, Barnet
● See 'Who is AWARE?', *WW/Mar*.

On the button

I HAVE NOTICED the word 'turnbutton' creeping into your drawings (p.145, WW/Feb). Turnbuttons (**A**) are found on the doors of rabbit and 'olde worlde sideboardes'. The term should be shrinkage button. It can move in and out of or sideways in the rail mortises, but cannot turn (**B**).

Bob Wearing, Wem, Shropshire

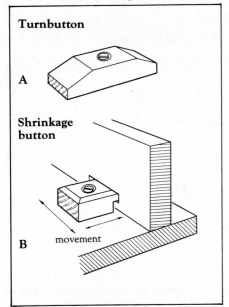

Turnbutton

A

Shrinkage button

B

movement

The sage to the bodger . . .

THE HEARTFUL BODGER (WW/Jan) showed a delightful picture of youngsters having a go at turning.

Although they were supervised, I would like to have seen them wearing safety goggles and a mask. As for the heartful bodger, he's old enough to know better.

E. J. Smith (grandad turner), Croydon

. . . and the bodger to the sage

HAVING ALSO OCCASIONALLY turned seasoned wood on a powered lathe, I can understand your concern at the photo in question. I hope by mentioning a few of the safety features of the pole-lathe, I might put your mind at rest:
● Instantaneous telepathic on-off/cut-out device. (If anything goes wrong you automatically stop treadling.)
● Built-in operator heating (you try stamping up and down on a cold day!)
● Infinitely variable speed — peripheral velocity up to 2fps (approx. 250rpm for 2in-diameter workpiece).

When I work with beginners I choose a less fibrous wood, beech or sycamore, freshly felled, and use gouges — no scrapers. If they get it right they produce pretty little 2ft long ribbons of wood. If not, they produce a kind of soggy paste on the inside of the gouge. Either way, there is a negligible chance of producing splinters, and into the bargain, I can take six-year olds

and teach them to turn 'properly' from the start.

Mike Abbott (father bodger), Bristol (Actually the girl pictured on the lathe is my daughter Hannah, and she'd like to see her name in print. And thanks to her mum Marianne for the photo.)

Good behaviour

SOME TIME AGO I signed up for a one-day wood machining course at Tewkesbury, under the auspices of Rawdon Machine Sales, W. Yorks, which I unfortunately had to cancel.

Rawdon were not only quick to answer, but they were polite and helpful. They sent me a free copy of the course notes, which have proved very helpful, and allowed me to keep the £25 voucher I was awarded as a bonus for signing on the course.

How refreshing it is to find such old-fashioned good service. This firm obviously counts future customers as valuable and I'd like to say a public 'thankyou'. Other firms, please take note.

P. R. Wallace, Banbury

Gibbons' 'Crucifixion'

THE GRAND FURNITURE SAGA in January's WOODWORKER refers to Grinling Gibbons' carving, which is a reproduction of Tintoretto's *Crucifixion*. What is believed to be that very carving may be seen in the library at Dunham Massey Hall, near Altrincham, Cheshire. The Hall was bequeathed to the National Trust by the tenth Earl of Stamford to whom it had descended from the second Earl of Warrington. He is believed to have purchased the carving from Sir George Viner and the National Trust's booklet says it was first recorded at Dunham Massey in 1758.

Geoffrey Barker, Altrincham

Gauging accuracy

I HAVE NEVER SEEN mentioned in woodworking publications a basic principle of engineering metrology which enables two of our principal gauges — the straightedge and the square — to be reliably checked for accuracy without reference to a master gauge.

Whitworth's 'Three-plate method' is a technique devised by that great engineer for avoiding the inherent problem in the usual process of finding high spots on two mating metal surfaces; smearing engineer's blue on one, rubbing it off on the other, and filing to adjust, the surfaces may fit together, but it might be because of 'mating inaccuracy' — a convex surface fitting a concave. In 'one-dimensional plane' terms (straightedges and blades of squares), you might get a fit because one square is 88° and the other 92°. but if three surfaces are worked together in rotation until any pair fit accurately, all three surfaces must be true planes, and for any pair of a set of three squares to fit

together accurately, they must all be perfect right angles.

You can easily make a set of reference straightedges and squares accurate enough for the most particular woodworker; stability of material is important but not crucial, because they can be inter-compared and corrected. Then you can use these to check your working squares and straightedges.

Robert Hedley, Settle, Yorks

Bad practice?

MR. W. BATTERSBY'S LETTER (WW/Feb) draws attention to my hand apparently blocking the air intake when using a router. The photograph may give that impression, but with the fingertips in the position shown on this Elu MOF96E router, the hand must be arched to support the motor, so an air gap exists.

The actual operation described required three short runs lasting seconds only, with the motor switched off after each run for adjusting cutting depth; the motor temperature rise is thus extremely slight.

An Elu publication, *The Plunging Router* of about 1980, shows three photographs of a similar operation with the left hand in the same position; it's clear from the pictures that the operator is making only short runs. I suggest this method of supporting the router for some operations is common practice.

Eric Coldwell, Weymouth

POWER TOOL SPECIALISTS
Contact Simon Evans on 01-437 0699

R.P.R. POWER TOOLS of WALSALL

Services and Repairs to all Power Tools including: Bosch, Makita, Wolf, B&D etc.
Free Estimates.

All work guaranteed.

Tel: 0922 642931

M.C.A. LTD.
Authorised Service Centre

BOSCH

Full range of accessories.
Mail Order
**2 Cambridge Road
St. Albans, Herts.**

Access   *Visa*
Tel: 0727 38251

W. HOSKING
28 Portland Road,
Worthing, Sussex
Tel: 0903-38739

TRY HOSKING FIRST FOR COMPETITIVE PRICES ON

Bosch, Burgess, Coronet, DeWalt, Emco, Elu, Eumenia, Inca, Kity, Naerok, Triton, Tyme, Warco.

+ large range of power tools + hand tools.

    Telephone orders welcome

---

shopguide

AVON

BATH   Tel. Bath 64513
JOHN HALL TOOLS   ★
RAILWAY STREET

Open: Monday-Saturday
9.00 a.m.-5.30 p.m.
H.P.W.WM.D.A.BC.

BRISTOL   Tel. (0272) 741510
JOHN HALL TOOLS LIMITED   ★
CLIFTON DOWN SHOPPING CENTRE
WHITELADIES ROAD
Open: Monday-Saturday
9.00 a.m.-5.30 p.m.
H.P.W.WM.D.A.BC.

BRISTOL   Tel. (0272) 629092
TRYMWOOD SERVICES
2a DOWNS PARK EAST, (off North View)
WESTBURY PARK
Open: 8.30 a.m.-5.30 p.m. Mon. to Fri.
Closed for lunch 1.00-2.00 p.m.
P.W.WM.D.T.A.BC.

Read Model Engineer for a new angle on construction & design

BRISTOL   Tel. (0272) 667013
WILLIS
157 WEST STREET
BEDMINSTER
Open Mon.-Fri. 8.30 a.m.-5.00 p.m.
Sat. 9 a.m.-4 p.m.
P.W.WM.D.CS.A.BC.

BERKSHIRE

READING   Tel. Littlewick Green
DAVID HUNT (TOOL   2743
MERCHANTS) LTD   ★
KNOWL HILL, NR. READING
Open: Monday-Saturday
9.00 a.m.-5.30 p.m.
H.P.W.D.A.BC.

READING   Tel. Reading 661511
WOKINGHAM TOOL CO. LTD.
99 WOKINGHAM ROAD

Open: Mon-Sat 9.00 a.m.-5.30 p.m.
Closed 1.00-2.00 p.m. for lunch
H.P.W.WM.D.CS.A.BC.

BUCKINGHAMSHIRE

MILTON KEYNES   Tel. (0908)
POLLARD WOODWORKING   641366
CENTRE   ★
51 AYLESBURY ST., BLETCHLEY
Open: Mon-Fri 8.30-5.30
Saturday 9.00-5.00
H.P.W.WM.D.CS.A.BC.

SLOUGH   Tel: (06286) 5125
BRAYWOOD ESTATES LTD.   ★
158 BURNHAM LANE
Open: 9.00am-5.30pm.
Monday-Saturday.
H.P.W.WM.CS.A.

HIGH WYCOMBE Tel. (0494)
SCOTT SAWS LTD.   24201/33788
14 BRIDGE STREET   ★

Mon.-Sat. 8.30 a.m.-6.00 p.m.

H.P.W.WM.D.T.CS.MF.A.BC.

BUCKINGHAMSHIRE

HIGH WYCOMBE   Tel. (0494)
ISAAC LORD LTD   22221
185 DESBOROUGH ROAD   KE

Open: Mon-Fri 8.00 a.m.-5.00 p.m.
Saturday 9.00 a.m.-5.00 p.m.
H.P.W.D.A.

CAMBRIDGESHIRE

CAMBRIDGE   Tel: (0223) 63132
D. MACKAY LTD.   ★
BRITANNIA WORKS, EAST ROAD

Open: Mon.-Fri. 8.30 a.m.-1 p.m./2.00-
5.00 p.m. Sat. 8.30 a.m.-1.00 p.m.
H.P.W.D.T.CS.MF.A.BC.

CAMBRIDGE   Tel. (0223) 247386
H. B. WOODWORKING   K
105 CHERRY HINTON ROAD
Open: 8.30 a.m.-5.30 p.m.
Monday-Friday
8.30 a.m.-1.00 p.m. Sat.
H.P.W.WM.D.CS.A.MF.BC.

shopguide

CAMBRIDGESHIRE

PETERBOROUGH Tel. (0733)
WILLIAMS DISTRIBUTORS 64252
(TOOLS) LIMITED **K**
108-110 BURGHLEY ROAD
Open: Monday to Friday
8.30 a.m.-5.30 p.m.
H.P.A.W.D.WH.BC.

CHESHIRE

NANTWICH Tel. Crewe 67010
ALAN HOLTHAM **K★**
THE OLD STORES TURNERY
WISTASON ROAD, WILLASTON
Open: Tues.-Sat. 9.00 a.m.-5.30 p.m.
Closed Monday
P.W.WM.D.T.C.CS.A.BC.

CLEVELAND

MIDDLESBROUGH Tel. (0642)
CLEVELAND WOODCRAFT 813103
(M'BRO), 38-42 CRESCENT ROAD **K**
Open: Mon-Sat 9.15 a.m.-5.30 p.m.
H.P.T.A.BC.W.WM.CS.D.

CORNWALL

SOUTH WEST Power Tools
CORNWALL Tel: Helston (03265) 4961
HELSTON AND LAUNCESTON Launceston
(0566) 4781
H.P.W.WM.D.CS.A. **K**

CUMBRIA

CARLISLE Tel: (0228) 36391
W. M. PLANT
ALLENBROOK ROAD
ROSEHILL, CA1 2UT
Open: Mon.-Fri. 8.00 a.m.-5.15 p.m.
Sat. 8.00 a.m.-12.30 noon
P.W.WM.D.CS.A.

DEVON

BRIXHAM Tel. (08045) 4900
WOODCRAFT SUPPLIES **E★**
4 HORSE POOL STREET
Open: Mon.-Sat. 9.00 a.m.-6.00 p.m.
H.P.W.A.D.MF.CS.BC.

PLYMOUTH Tel. (0752) 330303
WESTWARD BUILDING SERVICES **★**
LTD., LISTER CLOSE, NEWNHAM
INDUSTRIAL ESTATE, PLYMPTON
Open: Mon-Fri 8.00 a.m.-5.30 p.m.
Sat. 8.30 a.m.-12.30 p.m.
H.P.W.WM.D.A.BC.

PLYMOUTH Tel. (0752) 665363
F.T.B. LAWSON LTD.
71 NEW GEORGE STREET
PLYMOUTH PL1 1RB
Open: Mon-Sat 8.30 am-5.30 p.m.
H.P.W.CS.MF.A.

DORSET

WEYMOUTH Tel. (0305) 770303
WEYMOUTH HIRE & SALES LTD. **K**
5 KENT CLOSE
GRANBY INDUSTRIAL ESTATE
Open 7.30 a.m. - 5.30 p.m. Mon.-Fri.
Sat. 8 a.m. - 1 p.m.
H.P.W.WM.D.CS.A.K.

ESSEX

LEIGH ON SEA Tel. (0702)
MARSHAL & PARSONS LTD. 710404
1111 LONDON ROAD **EK**
Open: 8.30 a.m.-5.30 p.m. Mon-Fri
9.00 a.m.-5.00 p.m. Sat.
H.P.W.WM.D.CS.A.

ILFORD Tel: 597 7461
CUTWELL WOODWORKING **★**
776 HIGH ROAD
GOODMAYES IG3 8SY
H.P.W.WM.D.CS.A.

GLOUCESTER

TEWKESBURY Tel. (0684)
TEWKESBURY SAW CO. LTD. 293092
TRADING ESTATE, NEWTOWN **K**
Open: Mon-Fri 8.00 a.m.-5.00 p.m.
Saturday 9.30 a.m.-12.00 p.m.
P.W.WM.D.CS.

HAMPSHIRE

ALDERSHOT SOUTHAMPTON
(0252) 334422 (0703) 332288
BIRCH & HILLS POWER TOOL CENTRES
374 HIGH ST. 7 BELVIDERE RD.
Open Mon.-Fri. 8.30-5.30. Sat. 8.30-12.30
Closed for Lunch 1.00-2.00
H.P.W.WM.D.CS.MF.BC.K.*

HERTFORDSHIRE

WARE Tel: (0920) 870 230
HEATH SAWS 870 636
6 LEESIDE WORKS **K★**
STANSTEAD ABBOTTS (near Ware) HERTS.
SG12 8DL
Open: Mon.-Fri. 8.30am-5.30pm
Sat. 8.30am-1pm. Sunday by appointment.
P.W.WM.D.CS.A.

ENFIELD Tel: 01-363 2935
GILL & HOXBY LTD.
131-137 ST. MARKS ROAD ADJ.
BUSH HILL PARK STATION, EN1 1BA
Mon.-Sat. 8-5.30
Early closing Wed. 1 p.m.
H.P.A.M.MC.T.S.W.

HUMBERSIDE

GRIMSBY Tel. Grimsby (0472)
58741 Hull (0482) 26999
J. E. SIDDLE LTD. (Tool Specialists) **★**
83 VICTORIA STREET
Open: Mon-Fri 8.30 a.m.-5.30 p.m.
Sat. 8.30 a.m.-12.45 p.m. & 2 p.m.-5 p.m.
H.P.A.BC.W.WMD.

HULL
HUMBERSIDE FACTORING/H.F.C.
SAW SERVICING LTD.
MAIN STREET
Open: Mon.-Fri. 8am-5pm.
Saturday 8am-12.00pm.
H.P.W.WM.D.CS.A.BC.K.

KENT

**01-437 0699
= RESULTS**

KENT

MAIDSTONE Tel. (0622) 50177
SOUTH EASTERN SAWS (Ind.) LTD. **★**
COLDRED ROAD
PARKWOOD INDUSTRIAL ESTATE
Open: Mon.-Fri. 8.00 a.m.-6.00 p.m.
Sat. 9.00 a.m.-12.00 a.m.
B.C.W.CS.WM.PH.

MAIDSTONE Tel. (0622) 44350
HENSON AND PLATT
TOKE PLACE
LINTON
Open Mon.-Fri. 8.00 a.m.-5.00 p.m.
Saturday 8.00 a.m.-1.00 p.m.
H.P.W.T.CS.A.

LANCASHIRE

PRESTON Tel. (0772) 52951
SPEEDWELL TOOL COMPANY **E★**
62-68 MEADOW STREET PR1 1SU
Open: Mon.-Fri. 8.30 a.m.-5.30 p.m.
Sat. 8.30 a.m.-12.30 p.m.
H.P.W.WM.CS.A.MF.BC.

ROCHDALE Tel. (0706) 342123/
C.S.M. TOOLS 342322
4-6 HEYWOOD ROAD **E★**
CASTLETON
Open: Mon-Sat 9.00 a.m.-6.00 p.m.
Sundays by appointment
W.D.CS.A.BC.

LANCASTER Tel: (0524) 32886
LILE TOOL SHOP **K**
43/45 NORTH ROAD
Open: Monday to Saturday
9.00 a.m.-5.30 p.m.
Wed. 9.00 a.m.-12.30 p.m.
H.P.W.D.A.

All shops with an asterisk * have a Mail Order Service

BLACKPOOL
FLYDE WOODTURNING SUPPLIES
255 CHURCH STREET
BLACKPOOL FY1 4HY
9.30-5.30 Monday to Saturday
H.P.W.WM-A.MF.C.B.C.D.

LONDON

ACTON Tel. (01-992) 4835
A. MILLS (ACTON) LTD **★**
32/36 CHURCHFIELD ROAD W3 6ED
Open: Mon-Fri 9.00 a.m.-5.00 p.m.
Saturdays 9.00 am-1.00 p.m.
H.P.W.WM.

LONDON Tel. 01-723 2295-6-7
LANGHAM TOOLS LIMITED
13 NORFOLK PLACE
LONDON W2 1QJ

LONDON

FULHAM Tel: (01-636) 6109
I. GRIZARD LTD. **E**
84a-b-c LILLIE ROAD, SW6 1TL
Open: Mon.-Sat. 9.00-5.30 p.m.
Half day Thursday
H.P.A.BC.W.CS.WM.D.

LONDON Tel. (01-636) 7475
BUCK & RYAN LTD **★**
101 TOTTENHAM COURT ROAD W1P 0DY
Open: Mon.-Fri. 8.30 a.m.-5.30 p.m.
Saturday 8.30 a.m.-4.00 p.m.
H.P.W.WM.D.A.

Use this space for your Summer Plans

MANCHESTER

MANCHESTER Tel. (061 789)
TIMMS TOOLS 0909
102-104 LIVERPOOL ROAD **★**
PATRICROFT M30 0WZ
Weekdays 9.00 a.m.-5.30 p.m.
Sat. 9.00 a.m.-1.00 p.m.
H.P.A.W.

MANCHESTER Tel: 061 834 0714
TILL AND WHITEHEAD **★**
ELLESMERE STREET, M15 4JX
Open: Mon.-Fri. 8.00 a.m.-5.00 p.m.
H.P.W.A.BC.

MERSEYSIDE

LIVERPOOL Tel. (051-207) 2967
TAYLOR BROS (LIVERPOOL) LTD **K**
195-199 LONDON ROAD
LIVERPOOL L3 8JG
Open: Monday to Friday
8.30 a.m.-5.30 p.m.
H.P.W.WM.D.A.BC.

MIDDLESEX

RUISLIP Tel. (08956) 74126
ALLMODELS ENGINEERING LTD. **E★**
91 MANOR WAY
Open: Mon-Sat 9.00 a.m.-5.30 p.m.
H.P.W.A.D.CS.MF.BC.

NORFOLK

NORWICH Tel. (0603) 898695
NORFOLK SAW SERVICES
DOG LANE, HORSFORD
Open: Monday to Friday
8.00 a.m.-5.00 p.m.
Saturday 8.00 a.m.-12.00 p.m.
H.P.W.WM.D.CS.A.

KINGS LYNN Tel. (0553) 2443
WALKER & ANDERSON (Kings Lynn) LTD. **K**
WINDSOR ROAD, KINGS LYNN
Open: Monday to Saturday
7.45 a.m.-5.30 p.m.
Wednesday 1.00 p.m. Saturday 5.00 p.m.
H.P.W.WM.D.CS.A.

shopguide

NORFOLK

NORWICH   Tel. (0603) 400933
WESTGATES WOODWORKING   Tx
61 HURRICANE WAY,   975412
NORWICH AIRPORT INDUSTRIAL ESTATE
Open: 9.00 a.m.-5.00 p.m. weekdays
9.00 a.m.-12.30 Sat.
P.W.WM.D.BC.   K

KINGS LYNN   Tel: 07605 674
NORFOLK WOODTURNING CENTRE   ★
UNIT A, HILL FARM WORKSHOPS
GREAT DUNHAM (Nr. Swaffham)
Tues.-Sat. 9.00am-5.30pm

H.P.W.D.T.MF.A.BC.

NOTTINGHAMSHIRE

NOTTINGHAM   Tel: (0602) 225979
POOLEWOOD   and 227064/5
EQUIPMENT LTD.   (06077) 2421 after hrs
5a HOLLY LANE, CHILLWELL
Open: Mon-Fri 9.00 a.m.-5.30 p.m.
Sat. 9.00 a.m. to 12.30 p.m.
P.W.WM.D.CS.A.BC.

OXON

WITNEY   Tel. (0993) 3885,
TARGET TOOLS (SALES,   & 72095 OXON
TARGET TOOLS HIRE & REPAIRS)   ★
SWAIN COURT
STATION INDUSTRIAL ESTATE
Open: Mon.-Sat. 8.00 a.m.-5.00 p.m.
24 hour Answerphone
BC.W.M.A.

SHROPSHIRE

TELFORD   Tel. Telford (0952)
ASLES LTD   48054
VINEYARD ROAD, WELLINGTON   EK★

Open: Mon. Fri. 8.30 a.m.-5.30 p.m.
Saturday 8.30 a.m.-4.00 p.m.
H.P.W.WM.D.CS.BC.A.

SOMERSET

TAUNTON   Tel. (0823) 85431
JOHN HALL TOOLS   ★
6 HIGH STREET

Open Monday-Saturday
9.00 a.m.-5.30 p.m.
H.P.W.WM.D.CS.A.

Read 'Model Engineer' for a new angle on construction & design

STAFFORDSHIRE

TAMWORTH   Tel: (0827) 56188
MATTHEWS BROTHERS LTD.   ★
KETTLEBROOK ROAD
Open: Mon.-Sat. 8.30-6.00 p.m.
Demonstrations Sunday mornings by
appointment only
H.P.W.WM.D.T.CS.A.BC.

SUFFOLK

SUFFOLK   Tel: (037983) 8126
LOCKWOOD WOODWORKING MACHINERY
WHITEGATES BUNGALOW
THE COMMON MELLIS
NEAR EYE/DISS IP23
Open standard hours.
*Lathe demos every Saturday morning.
Woodcopy lathes/Dust extractors.*
H.P.W.D.A.

SUFFOLK

All shops with an asterisk ★ have a Mail Order Service

IPSWICH   Tel. (0473) 40456
FOX WOODWORKING   KE★
142-144 BRAMFORD LANE
Open: Tues., Fri., 9.00 a.m.-5.30 p.m.
Sat. 9.00 a.m.-5.00 p.m.

H.P.W.WM.D.A.B.C.

SUSSEX

WORTHING   Tel. (0903) 38739
W. HOSKING LTD (TOOLS &   KE★
MACHINERY)
28 PORTLAND RD, BN11 1QN
Open: Mon.-Sat. 8.30 a.m.-5.30 p.m.
Closed Wednesday
H.P.W.WM.D.CS.A.BC.

TYNE & WEAR

NEWCASTLE   Tel. (0632) 320311
HENRY OSBOURNE LTD.   E★
50-54 UNION STREET

Open: Mon-Fri 8.30 a.m.-5.00 p.m.

H.P.W.D.CS.MF.A.BC.

NEWCASTLE-UPON-TYNE   ★
J. W. HOYLE LTD
CLARENCE STREET
NEWCASTLE-UPON-TYNE
TYNE & WEAR
NE2 17J
H.P.W.WM.D.CS.A.BC.K.

W. MIDLANDS

WOLVERHAMPTON   Tel. (0902)
MANSAW SERVICES   58759
WARD STREET, HORSELEY FIELDS   K★
WOLVERHAMPTON, WEST MIDLANDS
Open Mon.-Fri. 9.00am-5.00pm
Sat. 8am-3pm

H.P.W.WM.A.D.CS.

YORKSHIRE

SHEFFIELD   Tel. (0742) 441012
GREGORY & TAYLOR LTD   KE
WORKSOP ROAD
Open: 8.30 a.m.-5.30 p.m.
Monday-Friday
8.30 a.m.-12.30 p.m. Sat.
H.P.W.W.WM.D.

HARROGATE   Tel. (0423) 66245/
MULTI-TOOLS   55328
158 KINGS ROAD   K★

Open: Monday to Saturday
8.30 a.m.-6.00 p.m.

H.P.W.WM.D.A.BC.

HOLME UPON   Tel: 0696 60612
SPALDING MOOR
CRAFT TOOLS AND TACKLE LTD.
HOLME INDUSTRIAL ESTATE
Open: Mon-Fri. 9.30 am-5.30 pm.
Saturday & Bank Holidays 9.30 am-4.30 pm.
H.P.W.D.T.CS.MF.A.BC.

YORKSHIRE

LEEDS   Tel. (0532) 574736
D. B. KEIGHLEY MACHINERY LTD.   ★
VICKERS PLACE, STANNINGLEY
PUDSEY LS2 86LZ
Mon.-Fri. 9.00 a.m.-5.00 p.m.
Sat. 9.00 a.m.-1.00 p.m.
P.A.W.WM.CS.BC.

CLECKHEATON   Tel. (0274)
SKILLED CRAFTS LTD.   872861
34 BRADFORD ROAD   ★

Open: 9.00 a.m.-5.00 p.m. Monday
Saturday Lunch 12.00 a.m.-1.00 p.m.
H.P.A.W.CS.WM.D.

THIRSK   Tel. (0845) 22770
THE WOOD SHOP   ★
TRESKE SAWMILLS LTD.
STATION WORKS
Open: Seven days a week 9.00-5.00

T.H.MF.BC.

Advertise here to capture both local + national markets

HUDDERSFIELD   Tel. (0484)
NEVILLE M. OLDHAM   641219/(0484)
UNIT 1 DALE ST. MILLS   42777
DALE STREET, LONGWOOD   ★
Open: Mon-Fri 8.00 a.m.-5.30 p.m.
Saturday 9.30 a.m.-12.00 p.m.
P.W.WM.D.A.BC.

SCOTLAND

EDINBURGH   Tel. 031-337-5555
THE SAW CENTRE
38 HAYMARKET EH12 5JZ
Mon.-Fri. 8.30 a.m.-5.30 p.m.
SAT. 9.00 a.m.-1.00 p.m.

H.P.W.WM.D.CS.A.

CULLEN   Tel: (0542) 40563
GRAMPIAN WOODTURNING SUPPLIES AT
BAYVIEW CRAFTS
Open Mon.-Sat. 9.00 a.m.-5.30 p.m. Sunday
10.00 a.m.-5.30 p.m. Open later July/Aug.
Sept. Demonstrations SAT/SUN or by
H.W.D.MF.BC. appointment

PERTH   Tel. (0738) 26173
WILLIAM HUME & CO.   K
ST. JOHN'S PLACE
Open: Monday to Saturday
8.00 a.m.-5.30 p.m.
8.00 a.m.-1.00 p.m. Wednesday
H.P.A.BC.W.CS.WM.D.

SCOTLAND

GLASGOW   Tel. 041-429-4444/
THE SAW CENTRE   4374 Telex: 777886
650 EGLINTON STREET   E★
GLASGOW G5 9RP
Mon.-Fri. 8.00 a.m.-5.00 p.m.
Sat. 9.00 a.m.-1.00 p.m.
H.P.W.WM.D.CS.A.

IRELAND

NEWTOWNARDS   Tel: 0247 819800
NORLYN MACHINERY   or 812506
UNIT 10, MALCOLMSON IND. EST.
80 BANGOR ROAD, CO. DOWN
Open: Mon.-Fri. 9.30am-5.30pm
(Closed 1-2pm for lunch)
Any other time by request.
H.W.WM.D.T.MF.A.   24 Hour Service K

PORTADOWN   Tel. (0762) 332546
LOCKE TOOLS   ★
50 WEST STREET BT62 3JQ
Mon.-Sat. 9 a.m.-5.30 p.m.
Any other time by request.
H.D.W.WM.D.CS.A.BC.

All shops with an asterisk ★ have a Mail Order Service

WALES

CARMARTHEN   Tel. (0267) 237219
DO-IT-YOURSELF SUPPLY   K
BLUE STREET, DYFED
Open: Monday to Saturday
9.00 a.m.-5.30 p.m.
Thursday 9.00 a.m.-5.30 p.m.
H.P.W.WM.D.T.CS.A.BC.

SWANSEA   Tel. (0792) 55680
SWANSEA TIMBER & PLYWOOD CO. LTD.
57-59 OXFORD STREET   ★

Open: Mon to Fri 9.00 a.m.-5.30 p.m.
Sat. 9.00 a.m.-1.00 p.m.
H.P.W.D.T.CS.A.BC.

Use this space for your Summer Plans

CARDIFF   Tel. (0222) 595710
DATAPOWER TOOLS LTD.
MICHAELSTON ROAD,
CULVERHOUSE CROSS
Open: Mon.-Fri. 8.00 a.m.-5.00 p.m.
Sat. 9.00 a.m.-1.00 p.m.
H.P.W.WM.D.A.

CARDIFF   Tel. (0222) 396039
JOHN HALL TOOLS LIMITED   ★
ROYAL ARCADE

Open: Monday to Saturday
9.00 a.m.-5.30 p.m.
H.P.W.WM.D.A.BC.

01-437 0699 = RESULTS

WOOD SUPPLIERS

WOOD SUPPLIERS

WOOD SUPPLIERS

Classified Advertisements

All classified advertisements under £30.00 must be pre-paid: Cheques/PO made payable to A.S.P. Ltd. (WW).
Rates: Lineage: 52p per word (VAT inclusive) minimum £7.80. **Semi-display:** £8.60 + VAT per single column centimetre (minimum 2.5 x 1). **Copy to Classified Dept. (W.W.), A.S.P. Ltd., 1 Golden Square, London W1.**
All advertisements are inserted in the first available issue. There are no re-imbursements for cancellations.

 Telephone Simon Evans on 01-437-0699 ext. 290

FOR SALE

THE FINEST SELECTION ON DISPLAY IN SCOTLAND!

WOODWORKING & METALWORKING MACHINERY POWER TOOLS HAND TOOLS — **THE SAW CENTRE**

LARGE STOCKS COMPETITIVE PRICES. PHONE AND TRY US NOW!

OPEN
Mon - Fri 8am - 5pm
Sat 9am - 1pm

Eglinton Toll, Glasgow
G5 9RP
Tel: 041-429-4444

38 Haymarket
Edinburgh
EH12 5J2
Tel: 031-337-5555

WOODCARVING tools

LARGEST STOCK IN EUROPE

Henry Taylor
Arkansas Bench & Slip Stones
Strops & Strop Paste
Bench Screws, Carvers' Vices

WOODTURNING tools

Complete range of
Henry Taylor
handled or unhandled

send 40p in stamps for illustrated catalogue

ALEC TIRANTI LTD
70 High St, Theale, Reading, Berks RG7 5AR
27 Warren Street, London W1.

BANKRUPT STOCK
Sandvik circular saw blades tungsten tipped.

5", 5½", 6", 6¼" **£4.00** each
Any bore up to 30mm.

P&P £1 extra per order.
**Tel: 643 0244
Hannett, 11 Lind Road, Sutton, Surrey.**

BLADES
Spindle tooling, circular saw blades, dado sets, planer blades, router cutters and router accessories, machinery of particular merit, Forstener bits, mortise chisels, profile cutter blocks, radial arm saw accessories, etc.
Send £1 (refunded on first order) for your copy of our brochure.
Blades, Dept. WWM. Freepost, Petersfield, Hampshire. GU32 2BR (no stamp required)

CONTENTS of 3 school workshops, engineering and woodworking machines and various tools. For detailed list write to: Warners Machinery Centre, Unit 10, Finedon Road, Irthlingborough, Northants.

CORONET MAJOR ATTACHMENTS

10" Saw Table with 2 TCT blades and wobble saw — £220.

4½" Planer thicknesser with two sets spare blades £160.

Slot morticer with four cutters — £245 or £550 the lot!

**Phone: Oxford (0865) 726383
After 6pm.**

CONTENTS OF TECH COLLEGE woodwork, engineering and sheet metal machines, some 240 volt approx 70 items. For list send s.a.e. Write only to "Trade", 155 High Street, Irthlingborough, Northants.

LATHES Coronet, Myford, Arundle from £220. Also Coronet Imp Bandsaw, Multico 12" Sawbench. All 240v. Phone 0902 743675.

MINIATURE COMBINATION LATHE described March Woodworker. Improved model available with fittings and metal bed from author, Cutler, 19 Woodland Road, Surbiton, Surrey.

MYFORD ML 8A Lathe with stand, croft chuck, chisels. Two years old, excellent condition, hardly used, bereavement forces sale £500 ono. Tel: 030-678-386. Evenings and Weekends.

WOODCARVING TOOLS. Twelve Ashley Isles unused £80 ono. Tel: 0403-54007.

CLOCKMAKERS
Extensive range of very competitively priced German quartz clock movements, (including standard quartz, pendulum, mini-pendulum, chining, striking and insertion movements). Large selection of quality dials, chapter rings, hands, bezels, clock plans and weather instruments.
Please send 25p stamps for 20 page catalogue.
Bath Clock Company (Dept. W), 13 Welton Road, Radstock, Bath.

THE WHISTON CATALOGUE
Nuts, bolts, screws, washers, bar materials. In brass, alloy, steel, stainless steel, P.T.F.E., nylon, Tufnol, sheet material, electrical and mechanical items. We could go on and on! Better to send for free catalogue No. 114 and see for yourself.
K. R. Whiston Ltd., Dept. WW, New Mills, Stockport, Cheshire. Phone: 0663 42028.

WINDSOR CHAIRS
Full size bends. 50 × 1⅜ × 1⅛" in Ash £6.95.
Childs Windsor Chair bends in Ash 36 × 1⅛ × ⅞" £4.95.
All prices include p&p.
Please send cheque/P.O. with order to:
**P. Stuffin, Spurn View, North End Road, Tetney, Grimby DN36 5NA.
Tel: (0472) 812576
(Afternoons)**

BROOKS CIRCULAR SAW and bench, good working order. Offers? Old planer needs attention. Offers? Standard geared scroll chuck 3-jawed 4" £100 ono. Elu portable saw table £40 (New) Bath 339482 Daytime.

WORKSHED 14' x 10' complete with workbench and tools. 18 months old £600. Tel: Faulkland 359 (Somerset).

RADIAL ARM SAW DW1501 with bench and various accessories, hardly used £350. Telephone: Uxbridge 35984.

KITY 10" PLANER with ¾ H.P. Dust extractor and T.C. Knives £400 ono will separate. Tel: 0749 72139.

MALDEN 1-3-phase converter. Hardly used. Paid £224, will accept £160. Bucks. (024020) 563.

COMPLETE WORKSHOP FOR SALE
Kity 636 Planer, Spindle Moulder 627, Bandsaw 612, Morticing Attachment 652, with motors and table. DeWalt Saw C/14 with two saw blades. Approximately £500 of moulding blocks, profilers, cutters and tooling equipment. The complete workshop £2,000 no offers including benches with vices. Daytime Aberystwyth (0970) 615685 evenings (097086) 436 Mark and Diana Walters, Pine Mirrors, 12-14 Glanyrafon Ind. Est., Aberystwyth, Dyfed.

BUSINESS FOR SALE

OPPORTUNITY TO LIVE AND WORK IN SHETLAND
We are offering for sale a 3 bedroom stone built family house with a workshop 30' × 20' and machinery suited for furniture making or general joinery work. Situated in a beautiful valley just 10 minutes drive from main town.
For further details write to:
**R. Dowling, Wethaburn, Wester Quarff, Shetland ZE2 9EZ.
Tel: 09503 235**

To advertise ring 01-437 0699

EVENTS

Sale by Auction of
Lathes, Tools, woodworking machinery, sawmilling equipment, workshop contents; some 1500 cu.ft. English Hardwoods & Exotics in small lots; ivory and collector's items . . .
on Saturday, 9th May, 1987
Thos Harrison & Sons (Est. 1830)
Maxworthy Cross, Launceston, Cornwall. Tel: (056685) 322
List of contents from the vendor or, Kivells, Holsworthy, Devon.
Tel: (0409) 253888

CRAFT/ANTIQUE/SECONDHAND TOOLS

QUALITY TOOLS for craftsmen and collectors, order list £1. All types of woodwork tools wanted, particular paring chisels, pre-war carving tools, wooden planes. The Old Tool Store, Kirkby Fenside, East Kirkby, Spilsby, Lincs. PE23 3DD. Phone 07903 372.

SECONDHAND/TRADITIONAL tools — bought & sold. Norris, Spiers, Preston, Stanley, Record, Addis, etc., and our own. List £1. Bristol Design, 14 Perry Road, Bristol. Tel: (0272) 291740.

HANDTOOLS & MACHINERY. Antique and modern. Wood and metalworking. Bought and sold. The Tool Box, Craft Centre, Umbourne Bridge, Colyton, Devon. (0297) 52868.

ANTIQUE and modern woodworking tools bought and sold at Woodworkers World, 77 Shakespear Street, Derby. Tel: Derby (0332) 761779.

OLD WOODWORKING TOOLS AND BOOKS bought, exchanged and sold. Paul Rougetel, 77 Watergate Row, Chester. Tel: 0244 — 318782.

THE TOOL SHOP, BOSHAM WALK, Bosham, Chichester, Sussex. For collectors and second hand tools. Tel: 0243 572937/572475.

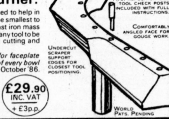
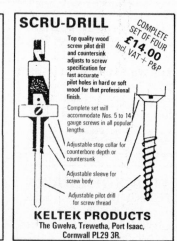

DEMONSTRATIONS & COURSES
FOR 1987 AT
FINE WOOD & TOOL STORE

WOODTURNING CHAIRMAKING PYROGRAPHY TOYMAKING SIGNMAKING WOODFINISHING & POLISHING	WOODCARVING CHAIR CANING YARN SPINNING STICKMAKING GUNSTOCK FINISHING LACE BOBBIN MAKING

Held in our custom built schoolrooms with specialist tutors.
For course/demonstration programme and leaflets,
write or phone Jim Beadle (09012) 2370,
John Boddy's Fine Wood & Tool Store Ltd., Riverside Sawmills, Boroughbridge, North Yorkshire, YO5 9LJ.

NEW!
The Carpentry & Joinery
Home Study Course

Now at Home in Your Spare Time, you can learn all about carpentry and joinery. Turn an interest into a well-paid profession. Enjoy expert tuition in the comfort of your own home and learn at the pace that suits you. No previous experience needed. ICS has over 90 years experience in home study courses and is the largest Correspondence School in the world.

Find out how we can help you! Simply post or phone today for your **FREE INFORMATION PACK.**

I·C·S INTERNATIONAL CORRESPONDENCE SCHOOLS

NAME: _____

ADDRESS: _____

P. Code _____

DEPT. K1057, 312/314 HIGH ST., SUTTON, SURREY SM1 1PR or phone 01-643 9568 or 041-221 2926 (both 24 hours).

Profit from the use of Woodworking Machinery

A ONE DAY 'Wood Machining Course' to arm yourself with the necessary knowledge to enable you to:
- Make the correct choice of machine for YOUR purposes
- Use that particular machine to gain maximum efficiency, safely
- Open up new opportunities for you to profit from a small workshop

SOUTHAMPTON	Burch and Hills (Machinery) Ltd.	23rd April, 1987
MIDDLESBROUGH	Cleveland Woodcraft	30th April, 1987
CARMARTHEN	D.I.Y. Supply	6th May, 1987
IPSWICH	Fox Woodworking	13th May, 1987
TEWKESBURY	Tewkesbury Saw Co.	20th May, 1987
LEEDS/BRADFORD	Rawdon Machine Sales Ltd.	10th June, 1987
READING	Sarjents Tool Stores	16th June, 1987
PERTH	Wm. Hume and Co.	25th June, 1987
ALDERSHOT	Burch and Hills (Machinery) Ltd.	30th June, 1987

NINE VENUES TO CHOOSE FROM
One must be near to you.

Telephone now for place availability and full timetable.
Rawdon Machine Sales Ltd., 6 Acorn Park, Charlestown, Shipley, West Yorks BD17 7SW.
Telephone 0274 597826

P.S. These are *NOT* exhibitions or demonstrations of a particular manufacturer's machinery, but a general eight-hour 'HANDS ON' instruction course showing the techniques of using machinery. You will find your time well spent.

WOODTURNING COURSES
One and two day Woodturning Courses in a fully equipped studio, under the expert tuition of:
ALLAN BATTY
Maximum of 2 students
Please write or phone for details.
Allan McNair Woodturning Studio
St. James Sq. Boroughbridge N. Yorks YO5 9AR
Telephone (09012) 4064

JOHN GOLDER
Woodturning courses day/evening. Personal tuition with Registered Professional Turner in fully equipped workshop.
76 Burntwood Road, Norton, Canes, Cannock, Staffs.
Telephone (0543) 79137
On the register of the Worshipful Company of Turners.
Demonstrator for Liberon Waxes.

A new profession for you in 1987
One-year course starting in September 1987

Learn to conserve and restore antique furniture with Bruce Luckhurst, qualified teacher and restorer for 25 years.
Applications are invited for this one-year course starting in September 1987. Previous cabinet making and polishing experience not essential for entry.

For prospectus and further details please send 9" × 12" s.a.e. to: Bruce Luckhurst, Little Surrenden Workshop, Bethersden, Kent TN26 3BG.

WOODCARVING COURSES. Weekends in Cotswolds overlooking Severn Vale, adjoining common land, max. 3 students, tuition by professional woodcarver, Peter Walwin, Fir Tree House, Rodborough, Stroud, Glos. 04536-2591.

GORDON STOKES
Author of six books on woodturning, international demonstrator, and long established instructor, offers two day, one day, or hourly tuition for beginners. Maximum three students. No previous knowledge required. Benefit from forty years practical experience. More than two thousand satisfied students. Ring us on BATH (0225) 22617, or send S.A.E. (A4 size) for full details to:
202 THE HOLLOW, BATH, AVON BA2 1NG.
Act today – start a creative and lucrative hobby.

GORDON PETERS FICW
Combine a family break with woodturning tuition. Fully qualified woodturner offers 2-day break including B+B for the whole family and 4 hours tuition per day. One student only. Learn in the morning leaving afternoons and evenings free to explore Folkestone and nearby France. SAE for details to:
14 Southmead Close, Folkestone, Kent CT19 5LH.
Tel: (0303) 76212

TWO-DAY PRACTICAL WOOD TURNING COURSE IN RURAL LINCOLNSHIRE
Comfortable accommodation arranged if required.
S.A.E. for details to: Peter Denniss, Cabinet Maker & Turner, The White Bungalow, South Reston, Louth, Lincolnshire. LN11 8JL or Phone: Withern 50429
S.D.T. Code 0521.

WOODTURNING TUITION in Southampton by a professional teacher, all equipment and materials provided, evening or weekends. Enquiries Robin Maddock 0703 433569.

SPECIAL "CRAFTSMAN'S COURSE"
IN
TRADITIONAL FRENCH POLISHING
OF 6 MONTHS DURATION
COVERING: Surface preparation, repairs, staining, matching-up colours, french-polishing to full bodied finishes, including dull, eggshell and antique etc.
PIANO WORK: requiring spiriting-out, and 'Acid and Chalk' finishes.
Vacancies for this course will be limited.
Early bookings are advisable.
ALSO: Normal 5 day or longer courses.
PLUS: Special "Solo" courses for intensive tuition.
S.A.E. to:
'Midland School of French Polishing'
18A Mansfield Road, Eastwood, Notts.
Tel: (0773) 715911

The world's finest woodturning tuition centre
The home of woodturning

- **Internationally known course tutors**
- **Finest facilities in the country**
- **Most up to date workshop**
- **Shop with everything you may ever need**
- **Gallery of finished work from respected woodturners**
- **Superb Derbyshire setting**
- **First class accommodation**

Send for an excellent leaflet giving complete details or telephone:-
Craft Supplies, The Mill, Millers Dale, Buxton, Derbyshire SK17 8SN.
Telephone: Tideswell (0298) 871636

INDIVIDUAL TUITION for woodturning or wood machining. Also courses in furniture manufacture. Accommodation if required. SAE for details to Ernest Smith, Ty'n Rhyd, Bethel, Trefenter, Nr. Aberystwyth, Dyfed, Wales. Tel: 097-46 298.

Our next copy deadlines:
12th May —
July issue
10th June —
August issue

Restorations Unlimited
FURNITURE RESTORATION
Specialised weekend courses in all aspects of antique furniture restoration. Maximum of three students in well equipped Cotswold workshops.
RESTORATIONS UNLIMITED
Pinkney Park, Malmesbury, Wilts.
Tel. Malmesbury 840888.

Creative Woodcarving
Courses in Cornwall.
Beautiful Helford River Area.
Experienced Instructor & Craftsman offers short courses ideal for beginners in carving. Tuition limited to three students per course and each receives a detailed 50 page carving manual. Beautiful Helford River area.
Details from: **Jeremy Williams, Sycamore Cottage, Trabae, St. Martin, Helston, Cornwall TR12 6EA.**
Tel: 032-623-609

CONTENTS

Woodworker

design . . . craft . . . and the love of wood

June 1987
Vol. 91
No. 6

FEATURES

PROJECTS

REGULARS

On the cover: A feathertail glider, carved by Australian Peter Carrigy in native cherry. More on p476. **Above**: Jack Hill in his coppicing element; see him at the **Bristol Woodworker Show**, read his article on p496, go on his course – p510

Editor Aidan Walker
Deputy editor John Hemsley
Editorial assistant Kerry Fowler
Advertisement manager Trevor Pryer
Advertisement production Laura Champion
Graphics Jeff Hamblin
Technical illustrator Peter Holland
Guild of Woodworkers John Hemsley, Kerry Fowler

Unfortunately we cannot accept responsibility for loss of or damage to unsolicited material. We reserve the right to refuse or suspend advertisements, and regret we cannot guarantee the bone fides of advertisers.
Published every third Friday

Editorial, advertisements and Guild of Woodworkers
1 Golden Square, London W1R 3AB, telephone 01-437 0626

ABC
UK circulation
Jan-Dec 86
32,849

Back issues and subscriptions Infonet Ltd, 10-13 Times House, 179 Marlowes, Hemel Hempstead, Herts HP1 1BB; telephone Hemel Hempstead (0442) 48434

Subscriptions per year UK £16.90; overseas outside USA (accelerated surface post) £21.00, USA (accelerated surface post) $28, airmail £48

UK trade SM Distribution Ltd, 16-18 Trinity Gardens, London SW9 8DX; telephone 01-274 8611

North American trade Bill Dean Books Ltd, 151-49 7th Avenue, PO Box 69, Whitestone, New York 11357; tel. 1-718-767-6632

Printed by Chase Web, Plymouth
Mono origination Multiform Photosetting Ltd, Cardiff
Colour origination Derek Croxson Ltd, Chesham, Bucks
© Argus Specialist Publications Ltd 1987
ISSN 0043 776X

Argus Specialist Publications Ltd

1 Golden Square, London W1R 3AB; 01-437 0626

This month

More Show prizes!

Yet another enticing set of prizes to be won at the October WOODWORKER Show — for routing enthusiasts. The **Trend Routing Award** will be made to any entrant in any class who has made the best use of a router. You can win a superb, specially made dovetailed cabinet of TCT and HSS router cutters worth £300 retail, plus Jim Phillips' book *Techniques of Routing*; or, second prize, an equally pretty cabinet with £150 worth of HSS and TCT cutters plus the book.

Judges will be looking at number of profiles, quality of finish, 'aesthetic appearance obtained through extensive use of the router in conjunction with wood and grain selection', how the router has been best used to get higher quality construction, 'innovative or subtle' use of jigs, clamps and guides, and the presentation of sketches and photos to show the techniques used. More details next month; and many thanks to Trend for their generosity.

Furniture Makers awards

New awards aimed at students were introduced by the Worshipful Company of Furniture Makers this year. Winners of the design work experience placement awards (worth £500 each) come from Leeds Polytechnic, Bucks College and Ravensbourne College of Art; three college courses group awards were made to Leeds Polytechnic (£1000), the London College of Furniture (£2700), and £1400 to Ravensbourne College of Design for various year-groups' research schemes, some involving travel.

The Gunton Award of £1000 from Formica for a laminate project goes to Garry Bennett of Leeds Polytechnic. The Company's furniture designer/craftsman awards to to Andrew Whateley, cabinetmaker at the Royal College of Art (featured elsewhere in this issue), £1000 to purchase equipment and materials for producing his own designs, and Andrew Shenton, a self-employed maker, £500 for equipment and marketing consultation.

The Company also makes awards to employees in manufacturing and retailing. This new emphasis on students will be continued into 1988, and the Company urges colleges to think early about which awards they will apply for this autumn.

Exotic timber ban?

Friends of the Earth urges a ban on importing tropical logs in a major report on Europe's involvement in the tropical timber trade, *A Hardwood Story*. The suggested phased-in ban would be a first step to developing European trade policies preventing imports of raw materials that could be processed domestically in the countries of origin.

While acknowledging that destruction of rain forest occurs for many complex reasons, this report focuses on the impact of the tropical timber trade in Europe. It claims commercial logging is the second largest cause of tropical forest loss, that Europe uses 40% of the global trade in tropical hardwood products, and that Britain is the largest consumer within the EEC. Most European imports are used for building and joinery (over 50%), plywood, furniture,

transport, packaging and water-resistant pilings.

Among its recommendations are that Europe must:

● Encourage the import of manufactured products while discouraging raw material imports
● Work towards banning products that aren't from sustainable and ecologically managed forests
● List engangered tree species and ban their import
● Create a special forest fund to help large scale re-planting
● Encourage the International Tropical Timber Organisation to develop research into sustainable management of tropical forests.

Meanwhile . . . ITTO met in Japan in March, but 16 member countries, according to confidential Secretariat documents

Stolen clocks

If you're offered German long-case clock movements from an unusual source, let Art Veneers Co. know.

Thieves stole 100 'Urgos' movements worth £12,000 from the Suffolk company in February — complete with pendulum bods, dials and weight

shells but without weights, pendulum rods or fixing screws.

So the thieves are trying to unload incomplete movements. If you hear anything contact Les Reed, Art Veneers, Ind. Est., Mildenhall, Suffolk IP287AY, (0638) 712550.

Wanted: sorcerer's apprentice

Cabinetmaker-turned-inventor Collin Camp is looking for a 'brilliant design engineer' who is also a woodworker to help him take his revolutionary planer/thicknesser through to production stage. He has used the prototype in his home workshop in Wiltshire for two years, and he claims it out-performs the conventional style on all counts. But

he hasn't found a manufacturer who'll take the idea up. Now he's determined to make a production machine for sale direct to woodworkers. Write to him if you want to help make what he fancies will be the Rolls Royce of planer/thicknessers.
● Collin Camp, 43 The Common, Bromham, Chippenham, Wilts SN15 2JJ

Marquetry on show The National Marquetry Exhibition is at Wythenshawe Hall, Wythenshawe Park, from Monday 18 May to Saturday 30 May, open from 10-6 (till 8 on 22-25 and 28-29, 3pm on 30 May).

13% increase on furniture spending over the last 10 years on average — much less than the 22% growth in total consumer spending, reveals the Henley Centre report on UK furniture retailing.

From Glos to Kent Gordon Peters, woodturning tutor, has recently moved from Cirencester, to 14 Southmead Close, Folkestone, Kent.

Diary

Guild courses are shown by an asterisk(*). For further details see Guild pages
May
17 **Tools of the Trade,** Weal and Downland Open Air Museum, Singleton, Chichester, Sussex (024363) 348
18-30 **35th National Marquetry Exhibition**, Wythenshawe Hall, Wythenshawe Pk, Manchester
22-26 **INTERZUM** International Furniture Trade Fair, Cologne
23-26 **Wessex Craft Show**, Witon House, contact (04252) 72511
23-27 **Oxford Artweek '87**, contact (0865) 722184
25-30 **38 Create**, Rycotewood final year students' show, Henley Exhibition Centre, contact Alexis James (084421) 2501
26-29 **Country Chairmaking** Jack Hill*
27-2 June **LIGNA** International Trade Fair for Wood Machinery, Hanover

June
5-14 **Fine Art and Antiques Fair 1987**, Olympia, Earls Court, London
13 **Power Routing** Roy Sutton*
16-22 **Shrewsbury College of Furniture Exhibition**, contact (0743) 321544
24-6 Sept **The New Spirit: Innovation in British Craft and Design**, Crafts Council Gallery, 12 Waterloo Place, London SW1, 01-930 4811
29-3 July **London College of Furniture Summer Show**, 41 Commercial Rd, London E1 1LA, 01-247 1953

July
2-3 **Rudiments of Restoration** Barry Honeybourne*
18-19 **French Polishing** Ian Hosker*
30-2 August **Green Wood Working** Jack Hill and Mike Abbot*

FoE claim to have seen, still hadn't paid their membership dues — to the tune of £665,000. Among the biggest debtors are listed the USA (more than $50,000) and Brazil ($134,000).

The projects — 'essential work to protect tropical forests' — would cost just over $2m; the International Timber Trade's turnover, says FoE, is worth $8 *billion*. 'By miserly skimping on the small change', FoE's Charles Secrett says, 'The defaulters are threatening the future of the one international organisation that could save the world's tropical forests.' 15 private conservation groups volunteered their 'mites' to the Special Project Fund, which runs on voluntary donations; their $12,300 moved Switzerland to pledge $1m and the Netherlands $600,000. Japan said they'd give $2m subject to Parliamentary approval.

Shoptalk

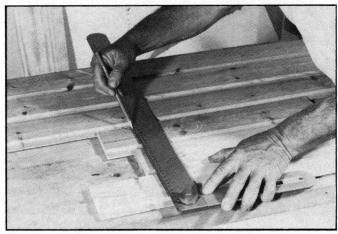

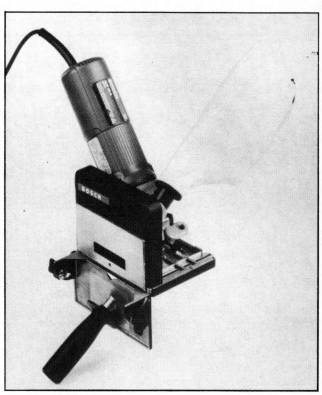

Bosch announce their new **biscuit jointer**; the GUF 22A has a 600w motor, 105mm 12-tooth cutter, 10,000rpm, dust-bag. £140+VAT including fences. Address below.

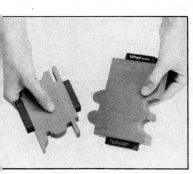

Top, Henry Taylor Tools' new **'Masterchuck'**, designed by Roy Child, has four jaws, controlled inwards or outwards by two threads at the same time. Grip internally or externally without changing the jaws: basic chuck £54+VAT. The Forge, Lowther Rd, Sheffield S6 2DR, (0742) 340282. **Above**, Wolfcraft's **Combinal** is a square, rule, straight-edge, angle-square — or, with a clamp, a guide for saw or router. Less than £25 retail. Brimarc, PO Box 100, Leamington Spa CV31 3LS (0926) 882727. **Above left**, Trend's new heavy duty machine stand will take drill or router; plunge feed is independent of the pillar, and you can get 13in throat depth. Under £275+VAT for the stand plus drill and machine mounts. Unit N, Penfold Works, Imperial Way, Watford, Herts WD2 4YY, (0923) 49911.

Left, Vitrex' popular plastic 6in Profile Gauge sells so well they've dropped the price; now £7.95 inc. VAT. There's also a 4in model for £3.99. 457 Caledonian Rd, London N7 9BB, 01-609 0011.

NEW PRODUCTS

Startrite now offer a basic bench model option to the 301 **bandsaw** at just over £300, for those who want a robust saw for basics or have limited space.

A new range of **airless spray equipment** from DeVilbiss could be useful if you use a lot of lacquer, stain or sealer. A simple tripod model delivering 3 litres/min costs £577+VAT.

Safe **craft colours** in the British-made Maestro range are now available in the UK. A range of 48 colours developed for hobby use, they dry much quicker than artist's oils but slower than tubed acrylics, so you can paint 'wet into wet', 'double loading' and use as a wash. Lead-free, they are recommended for children's toys and so on, and come in 60ml jars at £1.35 inc VAT.

Remember when the Reader's Digest *DIY Manual* was introduced in 1969? It cost £6 6s then. Now after selling 1,500,000 copies, the manual has been completely re-written as the *Reader's Digest New DIY Manual* and costs £19.95.

Iles Optical announce a new **ear defender**, the QT/EM, with swivelling cups that adjust themselves over your ears, or over your chest when you've turned the machines off. £4.15+VAT a pair.

Bosch's new 400w hammer and variable-speed reversing screwdriver **drill**, the PSB 400 RE, is the first of the company's restyled drill range for '87. It replaces the 400 RLE, and claims made for it include buzzwords like 'ergonomically optimised slimline handle' — with a lump at the bottom so it won't fall out of your hand. The switches have been designed specifically to avoid inadvertent reversing. Speeds 0-2600prm, price £59 inc. VAT.

● Startrite Machine Tool Co, Waterside Works, Gads Hill, Gillingham, Kent ME7 2SF, (0634) 55122. DeVilbiss Co, Ringwood Rd, Bournemouth BH11 9LH, (0202) 571111. Ceramic Craft & Colour Co, Unit 8, Whitebridge Lane, Stone, Staffs ST15 8LQ, (0785) 814028. Reader's Digest Association, 25 Berkeley Square, London W1X 6AB. Iles Optical Ltd, Walmgate Rd, Perivale, Middx UB6 7LG, 01-998 6600. Robert Bosch Ltd, PO Box 98, Broadwater Pk, N. Orbital Rd, Denham, Middx UB9 5HJ, (0895) 833 633.

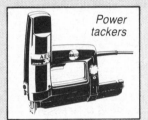
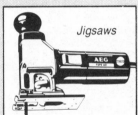

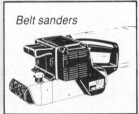
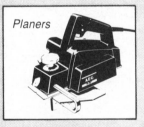

AXMINSTER POWER TOOL CENTRE

WOODTURNING LATHES — *OUR PRICE INC. VAT*

TYME STUDENT 10" swing 30" centres (With accessory voucher £20) **£219**
CORONET HOBBY 10" swing 39" centres 1MT ½HP 3 speed **£179**
CORONET No. 1 12" swing 3 Speed 24" ctrs ..... **£218** 36" ctrs ..... **£239** 48" ctrs **£295**
CORONET No. 1 22" Bowl Rest Assbly .. **£39** 48" Bed Extension for existing 24" lathe .. **£59**
ELU DB180 39" centres 15" swing 1½HP motor 3 speed **£299**
TYME CUB 30" centres (With accessory voucher £30) **£296**
TYME AVON 36" centres (With accessory voucher £45) **£419**
MYFORD ML8B 36" centres 9" Rear turning .... **£432** ML8C 42" centres **£467**
KITY 663 3 Speed Lathe 1.0M Centres .... **£554** 1.5M Centres **£576**
KITY 664 Var. Spd. Lathe 1.0M Centres .... **£649** 1.5M Centres **£669**
MINIMAX Centre lathes T90 ...... **£462** T100 ...... **£534** T120 ...... **£564** Legs **£75**
MINIMAX COPIERS for above lathes CT90 .... **£519** CT100 .... **£551** CT120 .... **£599**
LUNA SPKA 900 COPIER medium duty copier for all lathes **£256**
CORONET CMB600 33" Centres 23" bowl cap .... **£589** Bowl rest **£49.95**
HARRISON GRADUATE 30" Centres ... **£1175** 42" Centres ... **£1232** Shortbed ... **£1037**

WOODTURNING FITMENTS CHISELS & ACCESSORIES (State m/c)

Coronet collet chuck sets (state m/c) **£69**
Coronet collet bodies .... only **£29**
Collets ⅝", ¾", 1" .... each **£12**
Expanding Jaws 3", 2", 1" .... each **£27**
Spigots ⅝", ¾", 1" .... each **£14**
Speedaneez polish std/wht **£5**
Coronet planer blades 4½" .. **£20** 7" .. **£23**
Multistar Duplex Chuck 32mm Jaws **£65**
Multistar Duplex Chuck 45mm Jaws **£66**
Multistar Duplex Chuck 75mm Jaws **£68**
Screwchuck Set (for above) **£22**
Faceplate Ring 60mm **£7**
Pinchucks (State size) **£8**
Revolving centres 1MT or 2MT **£18**
0-½" Drill chuck 1MT or 2MT **£15**
Craft supplies chuck **£58**
Long hole boring kit 5/16" **£32**
2½" Woodscrew chuck **£22**
Sorby sizing tool **£8**
Carnuba wax turning stick **£1.80**
Dovetail Jaws for 4 Jaw Chuck ... **£49.95**
Sorby Super Skew ¾" **£11.00**
Sorby Super Skew 1" **£13.00**
Sorby ¾" HSS Roughing Gouge .. **£18.00**
Sorby Scraper (with 3 Heads) **£24.00**
Janik Pyrographer **£48.00**

WOODTURNERS "AT LAST PERFECTION"

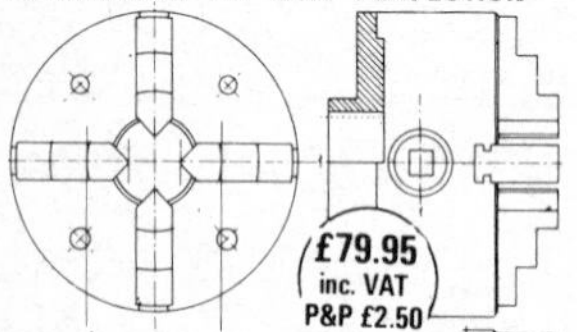

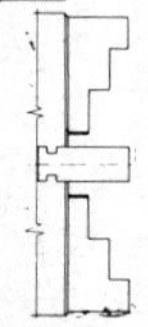

4 JAW SELF CENTERING CHUCK
AVAILABLE IN THREAD SIZES FOR MOST LATHES.
SPECIFICATION: GRIPPING CAPACITY ⅛"-4" DIAMETER 4" WEIGHT 2KG. SUPPLIED READY THREADED (LH OR RH) WITH TWO SETS OF PRECISION JAWS (INTERNAL & EXTERNAL).
5" 4 Jaw S/C **£99.95**
4" 3 Jaw S/C **£69.95**

HENRY TAYLOR HSS CHISELS
(P&P £1.20 per order)

GOUGES
HS1 Superflute **£26**
HS3 ¾" D/Fte **£16**
HS4 1½" D/Fte **£27**
HS5 ¼" Spindle **£6**
HS6 ⅜" Spindle **£8**
HS7 ½" Spindle **£11**

PARTING TOOLS
HS2 Fluted **£17**
HS11 ¼" Std. ... **£6**
HS12 ⅜" Std. ... **£8**
HS13 ¾" × ½" **£11**
HS33 Diamond **£15**
HS32 ½" × ⅛" .. **£7**

CHISELS
HS8 ½" Skew ... **£8**
HS21 ¾" Skew . **£9**
HS22 1" Skew **£10**
HS9 1¼" Skew **£16**
HS23 ½" Square **£8**
HS24 ¾" Sqre .. **£9**
HS25 1" Sqre **£11**
HS10 1¼" Sqre **£17**

SCRAPERS
HS26 ½" Rnd ... **£8**
HS38 ¾" Rnd ... **£9**
HS27 1" Rnd . **£11**
HS28 ½" Sq **£8**
HS29 ¾" Sq. **£8**
HS30 1" Sq. ... **£10**
HS15 HD Round **£22**
HS16 HD Domed **£22**

ALL PRICES INCLUDE HANDLES.

CORONET HSS CHISELS IN STOCK.

★ ★ ★ ★ CORONET WOODTURNING AIDS & FITMENTS ★ ★ ★ ★

10% off all Coronet Woodturning Aids & Fitments (P&P £1.20/order)
Many Fitments Available for All Makes of Other Machines
20% off all Coronet Woodturning Chisels (P&P £1.20/order)
NB. Discounts do not apply to the above already discounted prices.
THE COUNTRY'S ONLY IN DEPTH STOCKIST OF CORONET MACHINES, FITMENTS AND SPARES.

★ ★

BANDSAWS (Send for Free Bandsaw Blade List)

BURGESS BK111+ 45° 3" cut jigsaw fretsaw .... (inc. P&P) **£115**
7" Sanding attachment for Burgess ..... **£23.50** Mitre fence ..... **£8.50** Rip fence **£7.50**
DeWALT DW100 45° tilt 4" cut c/w sanding table .... (P&P £2.50) **£149**
DeWALT 6" cut 14" throat 45° DW3401 .... **£273** DW3501 .... **£289**
MINIMAX P32 45° tilt 6" cut 14" throat cast iron table **£367**
Mitre fences for above .... **£14** Stands for above **£29**
KITY 613 8" cut Large table 1½HP Very Sturdy .... **Special Price**
MINIMAX S45 45° tilt 10" cut 17" throat **£676**

★ ★ ★ SPECIAL OFFERS ON STARTRITE 301 — 351 — 352 ★ ★ ★
5 FREE BLADES WITH EACH MACHINE

STARTRITE 301B 45° Tilt 6" cut Bench Mtg. **£329**
STARTRITE 351 45° tilt 8" cut c/w rip & mitre fence floor standing **£495**
STARTRITE 352 45° tilt 10" cut c/w rip & mitre fence floor standing **£699**
STARTRITE 502 14" cut 20" throat 1PH .... **£1204** 3PH **£1111**
METAL BLADE GUIDES for DeWalt DW100, 1310, 3401, 3501, Luna & Minimax .. **£5.20**

RADIAL SAWS

EUMENIA 9" blade 1¾HP 15" C/cut .... **£339** 24" C/cut **£399**
EUMENIA Stand .... **£112** Router Bracket .... **£76** Wobble Washers **£14.50**
DeWALT 1201 Portable 10" TCT Folding Radial Saw 1½ HP **£295**
DeWALT DW1251 10" TCT blade 1½ HP 16" C/cut .... **£420** Stand **£25**
DeWALT DW1501 10" TCT blade 1½ HP 18" C/cut **£496**
DeWALT DW1751 10" TCT blade 1½ HP 24" C/cut **£570**
DeWALT DW8001 12" TCT blade 2HP 18" C/cut floor standing **£616**
DeWALT DW8101 12" TCT blade 2HP 24" C/cut floor standing **£703**
DeWALT DW1600S 14" TCT blade 24" C/cut 1PH .... **£993** 3PH **£956**

PORTABLE AND WORKSHOP SAWBENCHES

MAKITA 2708 8" Portable tilt arbor bench saw **£229**
ELEKTRA 12" Sawbench floor standing TCT blade 3HP **£189**
SCHEPPACH TKU 12" Sawbench floor standing TCT blade 3HP **£229**
Elektra & Scheppach Sliding Table .... **£90** Panel Cutting Extension **£75**
ELU TGS Sawbench/Mitre Saws c/w TCT blade TGS 172 .... **£496** TGS 171 .... **£399**
Sliding table for TGS .... **£98** Aluminium cutting kit **£60**
KITY 618 10" tilt arbor sawbench floor standing .... **SPECIAL PRICE**
MULTICO NTA300 3HP 12" .... **£1099** Sliding table 48" cap. **£316**
WADKIN AGS250/300 3HP 1PH . **£1299** Sliding table 35" cap. **£496**
STARTRITE Scoring Saw 1PH ...... **£1377** Sliding table 48" cap. **£327**
LUNA L18 12" 3HP 1PH .... **£950** Sliding table 24" cap. **£170**

ROLLER SUPPORT STANDS (P&P £3.00)

LUNA 10" support roller adjustable height sturdy construction **£28**
LUNA 16" combined roller support adjustable height **£39**

PREMIUM QUALITY INDUSTRIAL SAWBLADES
THE BEST IN QUALITY T.C.T. SAWBLADES LEITZ & SPEAR & JACKSON

BLADE DIAMETER	6"				7"-7¼"				8"				9"-9¼"			
No. OF TEETH	16	24	36	48	18	30	42	56	20	36	48	64	24	40	54	72
SPEARTIP	£16	£17	£20	£26	£16	£20	£23	£26	£20	£26	£28	£32	£24	£26	£29	£36
LEITZ	—	—	—	—	—	—	—	—	—	£37	£43	£49	—	£41	£51	—

BLADE DIAMETER	10"				12"				14"				16"			
No. OF TEETH	24	40	60	80	32	48	72	96	36	60	84	108	28	36	60	96
SPEARTIP	£23	£26	£35	£38	£28	£36	£42	£48	£34	£42	£50	£57	£39	£44	£54	£63
LEITZ	£39	£43	£51	£59	£42	£52	£61	£70	£48	£57	£70	£81	£54	£59	£70	£92

PLEASE STATE BORE SIZE WHEN ORDERING.

MORTICING MACHINES — *OUR PRICE INC. VAT*

SMITHS BCM 75 bench morticer c/w lateral table ¾" cap. **£422**
SMITHS CM75 floor standing morticer dual table movement ¾" cap **£528**
MULTICO HM bench morticer ⅝" capacity precision morticer **£356**
MULTICO HMT bench morticer dual table movement **£499**
MULTICO M floor standing 1" capacity dual table movement 1PH **£625**
WADKIN EDA-2 floor standing 1" capacity dual table **£626**
RYOBI portable chain morticer .... **£365** Portable chisel morticer **£395**
WOLF Drill mortice stand C/W ½" chisel & sharpener **£135**
RIDGEWAY mortice/drill stand (requires ½" power drill) **£165**

MORTICE CHISELS & BITS

JAPANESE ¼" ...... **£16** ⅜" ...... **£17** ½" ...... **£20** ⅝" ...... **£25** ¾" ...... **£37** 1" **£45**
8mm ...... **£21** 10mm ...... **£24** 12mm ...... **£25** 16mm ...... **£29** 20mm **£44**
RIDGEWAY ¼" ...... **£19** ⅜" ...... **£23** ½" ...... **£24** ⅝" ...... **£35** ¾" ...... **£37** 1" **£45**
6mm .. **£21** 8mm .. **£22** 10mm ... **£25** 12mm .. **£26** 16mm .. **£31** 20mm .. **£46**
CHISEL BITS ONLY ¼" ...... **£6** ⅜" ...... **£7** ½" ...... **£8** ⅝" ...... **£10** ¾" ...... **£14** 1" **£18**
MORTICE CHISEL SHARPENING SETS set 1 (¼"-½") .... **£23** Set 2 (⅜"-¾") **£28**

DUST EXTRACTORS

LUNA SPSS400 460m/hr portable suitable for low volume waste **£215**
LUNA W178 975m/hr excellent general purpose extractor c/w hose **£324**
LUNA NF243 1500m/hr mobile 5" hose ideal for high volume waste **£429**
LUNA NF259 2000m/hr heavy duty suitable for up to 3 machines **£599**
LUNA 4" × 3m hose .... **£18** 5" × 4m hose .... **£36** LUNA dust bags (per 10) **£3**
MULTICO DEA 960m/hr mobile extractor 4" hose **£335**
DeWALT DW60 500m/hr 5" hose .... **£265** ELEKTRA 1000m/hr 4" hose **£199**
STARTRITE CYCLAIR 55 960m/hr 4" .... **£399** CYCLAIR 75 1800m/hr 6" **£499**

MITRE CUTTERS & MITRE SAWS

ELU PS174 8" Portable mitre crosscut saw 10" crosscut **£298**
DeWALT DW250 Portable mitre saw 1¼HP 10" Blade **£207**
HITACHI CF10A 10" Portable precision mitre saw **£259**
ORTEGUILLE MITRE CUTTERS ORC55 ...... **£238** ORC80 ...... **£299** ORC100 ...... **£439**
LION MITRE TRIMMER Excellent for clean cuts and mitres **£249**
NOBEX 202 PRO Hand Mitre saw .... **£72.95** NOBEX 303 .... **£44** (P&P £2.50)
NOBEX 202 Replacement Blades 12T, 18T or 24T .... **£4.30** each

PLANER THICKNESSERS

DeWALT DW1151 10" × 6" 2HP 2 speed power feed .... **SPECIAL PRICE**
Stand for DW1150 .... **£30** Slot Morticer .... **£69.95** HSS knives **£18.90**
ELECKTRA 10" × 6" floor standing power feed **£490**
SCHEPPACH HMO SOLO 10" × 6" 2HP floor standing Adjustable fence **£490**
STARTRITE PT260 10" × 7" floor standing ⅝" rebate capacity **£834**
STARTRITE SD310 12" × 9" 3 cutter block 1PH .... **£1299** 3PH **£1260**
LUNA 3HP Planers 10" × 9" .... **£1399** 12" × 9" .... **£1499** 16" × 9" **£2299**
MULTICO NS300 surfacer 3 cutter block 2HP 1PH .... **£1388** 3PH **£1271**
MULTICO THA300 12" × 10" thicknesser only 1PH .... **£1399** 3PH **£1299**
MULTICO CPT 12" × 8" Combined planer/thicknesser ¾" rebate 1PH . **£1749** 3PH . **£1649**
WADKIN BAOS 12" × 7" Heavy duty planer 3PH (1 only to clear) **£2699**

DRILLING MACHINES

WARCO HOBBY ½" 5 speed rack and pinion table bench mounting **£139**
WARCO ⅝" cap 2MT 12 speed 2B12 bench mounting ... **£189** 2F12 floor standing **£222**
FOBCO STAR ½" precision drill bench mounting .... **£340** floor standing **£385**
STARTRITE SP250 ½" 5 speed bench mounting .... **£356** floor standing **£398**
Morticing attachments Warco 2B/2F .... **£24** Fobco .... **£61** Startrite **£110**

SPINDLE MOULDERS AND TENNONERS

SCHEPPACH HF33 3HP 30mm 3 speed with adjustable fences **£499**
ELEKTRA TF100 3HP 30mm 3-speed 4" Rise and fall. With free cutter set **£479**
KITY 623 2HP 3 speed 4" Rise and fall C/W sliding table **£776**
STARTRITE T30 30mm C/W sliding table 1PH 2HP .... **£943** 3PH 3HP **£915**
LUNA L28 30mm 3 speed 3HP Heavy duty 1PH 3HP .... **£999** 3PH 3HP **£988**
WADKIN BURSGREEN 5HP (3PH only) 4 speed 30mm **£1999**
MULTICO TENNONER TM1 240v twin motors (excluding tooling) **£1579**

SPINDLE MOULDER TOOLING (State bore size P&P £1.50)

OMAS "TIGER" BLOCKS 392 .... **£50** BLOCK in wooden case with stone etc. ... **£56**
OMAS cutter profiles .... **£12** CUTTER BLANKS .... **£7** SAW SEGMENTS **£17**
KITY PROFILE Door set .... **£96** OMAS ART 176D1 DOOR SET complete **£139**
WHITEHILL BLOCKS 4⅞ × 15/16 ...... **£51** 5⅜" × 15/16" ...... **£69** Panel Raising Block **£92**
LEITZ 488 Cutter block 100mm .... **£59** 40mm blanks .... **£3** 60mm .... ea. **£5**
TUNGSTEN REBATE BLOCKS 125mm × 50mm ..... **£98** 6" Wobble saw 3-21mm **£89**
LUNA MINI POWER FEED 2 speeds **£299**

COMBINATION MACHINES (Carriage £10.00 UK Mainland)

STARTRITE K260 saw spindle planer etc. FREE TIGER HEAD SET **£2190**
STARTRITE TZ30 saw spindle only FREE TIGER HEAD only **£1359**
SPECIAL OFFER LUNA W59 2HP 240v c/w sliding table slot morticer **£2299**
LUNA Z40 light duty combination saw planer spindle morticer **£685**
LUNA MASTER COMBINATIONS 240v W59 ..... **£2599** W64 ..... **£3100** W69 ..... **£3899**

★ ★ ★ ★ ★ ★ ★ ★ KITY COMBINATION MACHINES ★ ★ ★ ★ ★ ★ ★ ★

K5 COMBINATION K5 BASIC K704 TABLE COMBINATION K704 DIRECT DRIVE AND ACCESSORIES ALL AT SPECIAL PRICES SEND FOR LATEST PRICE LIST.

BORING BITS

CLICO SAW TOOTH & FORSTNER BITS (State type) 6" long ½" shank ⅜" . **£8.10** ½" . **£8.35**
⅝" .. **£9.20** ¾" .. **£10.00** ⅞" .. **£10.50** 1" .. **£11.55** 1⅛" .. **£13.55** 1¼" .. **£16.50**
1⅜" . **£17.20** 1½" . **£18.15** 1⅝" . **£20.90** 1¾" . **£23.75** 1⅞" . **£26.30** 2" . **£27.80**
2¼" .. **£34.95** 2½" .. **£46.35**
CLICO PLUG CUTTERS ⅜" . **£22** ½" . **£24** ⅝" . **£28** ¾" . **£30** 1" . **£36** 1⅓ . **£40.00**
CLICO SAW TOOTH set ½", ¾", 1" .... **£28** ECONOMY 5 piece set ½"-1½" × ¼" **£58**
RIDGEWAY ADJUSTABLE FORSTNERS WR10/2½"-1¾" .... **£16** WR10/3⅞"-3" **£18**
RIDGEWAY ADJUSTABLE FORSTNER (h/duty) WR20/2⅞"-2" **£29** WR20/3 1⅜"-3" **£34**

ROUTERS AND ROUTER ACCESSORIES

ELU MOF96 ¼" 600W **£98.50**
ELU MOF31 ¼, ⅜, ½" 1200W **£152.50**
ELU MOF177 ¼, ½" 1600W **£193.50**
HITACHI TR8 ¼" 730W **£79.95**
RYOBI R150 ¼" 730W **£75.95**
HITACHI FM ¼" 550W **£46.95**
MAKITA 3600B ¼, ½" 1500W **£168.95**
ELU MOF96E ¼" Var. speed **£119.50**
ELU MOF11/2 ½" 2000W c/w base **£337.33**
ELU MOF177E ½" Var. speed **£218.50**
HITACHI TR12 ¼, ½" 1300W **£137.95**
RYOBI R500 R500 ¼, ½" 1500W **£124.95**
BOSCH POF52 ¼" 520W **£55.00**
BOSCH 1604 Fixed base 1300W . **£163.95**

ROUTER ACCESSORIES

ELU DOVETAIL KIT TCT cutter **£74.00**
ELU MOF96 Accessory kit **£74.00**
STAIR JIG (General duty) **£69.00**
ELU ROUTER BRKT. for DeWalt ... **£39.00**
ELU 96 Dust extraction kit **£36.00**
ELU MOF96 Height adjuster **£3.95**
ELU TRACKING SET **£35.00**
RYOBI Dovetail jig fits above **£99.95**
ELU ROUTER COMBI BENCH **£123.00**
STAIR JIG (heavy duty) **£160.00**
ELU 12 piece Guide bush set **£35.00**
ELU MOF98, 31, 177 Height adjuster **£16.95**
ELU 96 177 side fence adjuster **£6.90**
ELU ROUTING VIDEO **£12.00**

★ ★ ★ ★ ★ ★ ★ ★ ★ ★ ★ ELU ACCESSORIES ★ ★ ★ ★ ★ ★ ★ ★ ★ ★ ★

10% OFF ALL ELU ACCESSORIES 90% STOCK AVAILABILITY POST PAID ON MOST ITEMS. EXCELLENT RANGE OF ROUTER ACCESSORIES SEND NOW FOR FREE LIST.

★ ★

HSS ROUTER BIT SETS (inc. P&P)

SAVE 30% ON HSS ROUTER BIT SETS AND GET A FREE ROUTER BIT CASE.
13 PIECE SET **£59.95**
8 PIECE SET **£37.95**
5 PIECE SET **£21.95**
ROUTER BIT CUTTER BOX .... ONLY **£4**

ROUTER CUTTERS

20-25% OFF LEADING BRANDS EXCELLENT STOCKS OF HSS & TCT ROUTER CUTTERS OVER 500 PROFILES IN STOCK. SEND NOW FOR FREE CUTTER CHART:- TECHNIQUES OF ROUTING £7.95 (inc. P&P)

IMMEDIATE DESPATCH ON CREDIT CARD PHONED ORDERS — CREDIT TERMS AVAILABLE OVER £120

0297 33656 CHARD STREET AXMINSTER DEVON EX13 5DZ 6.30-9pm 34836

BARCLAYCARD VISA

AXMINSTER POWER TOOL CENTRE

HORIZONTAL WETSTONE GRINDERS
OUR PRICE INC. VAT

JAPANESE Wetstone grinder £129.00
180G stone for above £40.00
1000G stone for above £40.00
6000G stone for above £43.00
PRECISION grinding jig £43.00

SHARPENSET Wetstone grinder £240.00
SHARPENSET 150G stone £18.40
SHARPENSET 280G stone £20.41
SHARPENSET Green stone (TCT) . £18.40
10" Planer Knife grinding jig £65.00
15" Planer Knife grinding jig £78.00
CHISEL grinding jig £67.00

VERTICAL WETSTONE GRINDERS
SCANGRIND 150 6" wetstone £77.95
SCANGRIND 200 8" wetstone £99.00
SCANTOOL COMBI WET AND DRY STONES
COMBI SC150 6" wet & dry £89.00
COMBI SC200 8" wet & dry £112.00
LUNA KIRUNA 11" wet & 4" dry £125.00
LUNA KIRUNA 14" wet & 5" dry £195.00

BENCH GRINDERS
ELU EDS163 6" 360W £73.95
ELU EDS164 7" 390W £77.95
ELU MWA149 6" Honer grinder .. £90.95
LEROY SOMER 5" 180W £33.00
LEROY SOMER 6" 250W £44.00
LEROY SOMER 6" with chuck £49.00
WARCO 5" 180W (European) £33.00
WARCO 6" 380W (European) £43.00
WARCO 8" 570W (European) £69.00

GRIND STONES (state bore size)

	5"	6"	7"
COARSE 36G	£6.60	£7.90	£11.40
FINE 60G	£6.60	£7.90	£11.40
WHITE 60G	£7.20	£8.50	£13.50
GREEN (TCT)	£7.20	£8.50	£13.50

JIGSAWS (Light Duty)
Bosch PST50 Single Speed £29.95
Bosch PST50E Var. Speed £38.50
Bosch PST55PE Var. Speed Pend £68.50
Hitachi FJ50SB Single speed £27.50
Hitachi FJ50VA Var. speed £36.50
Hitachi FCJ55V Var. Speed Pend. Act £58.95

JIGSAWS (Heavy Duty)
Elu ST142 2 speed £101.95
Elu ST142E Var. speed £110.95
Elu ST152 2 Speed £98.95
Elu ST152E Var. speed £106.95
Cases for above Jigsaws £10.00
Hitachi CJ65 2 speed £98.95
Hitachi CJ65VA Var. speed £104.95
Hitachi CJ65V Var. speed £104.95
Bosch 1581.7 Var. speed £108.95

DISC AND BELT SANDERS
Picador 10" Disc Sander £219.00
Warco BDS460 6" Disc 4" Belt .. £86.00
Warco BDS690 9" Disc 6" Belt . £179.00
Holmes 6" 2HP £399.00
Luna Favourite 4" £285.00
Luna De-Lux Sander 4" £599.00
Luna YKV Pad Sander £647.00
Luna YK1500 Pad Sander 1PH £1564.00
Luna YK1500 Pad Sander 3PH £1509.00
Picador Unmotorised 3" Belt £49.00
Picador Unmotorised 3" Belt £65.00
Holmes 4" Belt Sander £94.00
Holmes 6" Belt Sander £120.00

CIRCULAR SAWS
HITACHI FC5SA 6" TCT 710W £42.95
BOSCH PKS46 6" TCT 600W £53.50
BOSCH PKS66 7⅞ TCT 1200W £90.95
HITACHI PSU6 6" 1050W HSS £74.95
HITACHI PSU7 7" 1600W HSS £99.95
HITACHI PSU9 9" 1759W HSS .. £124.95
HITACHI PSM7 7" 1200W TCT .. £141.95
HITACHI PSM9 9" 1600W TCT .. £154.95
ELU MH151 6" 850W TCT £90.95
ELU MH65 7" 1200W TCT £131.95
ELU MH85 9" 1600W TCT £177.95
ELU MH182 8" 1400W TCT £148.95
ELU 550 COMBI (for MH182) £130.00
ELU555 Snip saw (for 182) £179.00
WOLF 9" CIRCULAR SAW £135.00

FINISHING SANDERS
(DB Dust Bag)
BOSCH PSS230 1/3rd Sheet £29.95
HITACHI FS10SA 1/3rd Sheet £25.95
HITACHI FSV12 Sheet DB £47.95
BOSCH PS280A ½ Sheet DB £59.95
B&D P6303 ½ Sheet £59.95
ELU MVS156 1/3rd Sheet DB £73.95
ELU MVS156E Var. Speed DB £85.95
ELU MVS 94 ½ Sheet DB £111.95
ELU MVS47 ½ Sheet £123.95
HITACHI SV12 ½ Sheet £109.95
HITACHI SOD110 ½ Sheet DB £95.95
HITACHI SO110 ½ Sheet £86.95
BOSCH 1288 9½ Sheet DB £99.95
WOLF ½ Sheet DB £85.95

DRILL STANDS (43mm collar)
BOSCH S2 Light duty £21.00
BOSCH S7 Heavy duty £52.95
BOSCH S8 Milling attachment for S7 £24.50
RIDGEWAY Very heavy duty £145.95

EXTENSION CABLES
50 Metre on sturdy drum £28.95
Jo-Jo 6 metre 30 foot £9.95
Jo-Jo 12 Metre 40 foot £14.26
Jo-Jo 18 Metre 60 foot £17.95

POWER PLANES (Light Duty)
OUR PRICE INC. VAT

BLACK & DECKER DN710 ..... £29.95
BOSCH PHO100 82mm 450W £47.95
HITACHI FP20SA 82mm 320W ... £38.95

HEAVY DUTY
ELU MFF80 82mm 850W £109.95
ELU MFF80K (in kit box) £127.95
ELU MFF40 82mm 1000W £189.95
INVERSION Std. for MFF80 ..... £20.95
INVERSION Std. for MFF40 ..... £29.00
HITACHI P20SA 82mm 720W £95.95
HITACHI FU20 82mm 620W £88.95
HITACHI F30A 92mm 900W £124.95

BELT SANDERS
ELU MHB 157 3" 600W £106.95
ELU MHB 157E 3" var. speed £119.95
ELU 157 FRAME £35.00
ELU 157 inversion stand £28.00
ABRASIVE BELTS FOR MHB 157/pkt. 3
40G, 60G, 80G, 100G, 120G, 150G £3.00
BOSCH PBS75 3" 620W £71.95
ELU MHB 90 4" 850W £193.95
ELU MHB 90K With frame £234.95
HITACHI SB75 3" 950W £116.95
HITACHI SB110 4" 950W £144.90
HITACHI SB110T 4" 950W £129.00
HITACHI SB110V 4" var. speed .. £134.00
MAKITA 9401 4" 1040W £169.00
MAKITA 9924DB 3" 950W £117.00

BISCUIT JOINTER
ELU DS140 Biscuit Jointer £197.95
No. 20 Biscuits (1000 off) £19.95
No. 10 Biscuits (1000 off) £19.50
No. 0 Biscuits (1000 off) £18.63
Mixed Box 0, 10, 20 (500 off) £12.50
DS140 saw blade 12T Std. £29.95
DS140 saw blade 30T Fine £29.50
DS140 Dust Tube adaptor £5.95
BOSCH Biscuit Jointer £124.95

★ ★ ★ ★ SPECIAL OFFER ★ ★ ★ ★

WOODSCREWS
Twin Fast Zinc Plated GKN 1600 Woodscrews from 1" × 6 to 2" × 10" with Free Screwdriver. (State slotted or pozidrive).
ONLY £19.99 inc. VAT and P&P

RIDGWAY DRILL MORTICER
c/w Free Hitachi Drill ½" Chuck and ¼" Chisel and Bit ... £186.00 inc. VAT and P&P

MARTEK DRILL SHARPENER
Excellent for Sharpening all Drill Bits ..... ONLY £23.50 inc. VAT and P&P

★ ★ ★ ★ ★ ★ ★ ★ ★ ★ ★ ★ ★ ★ ★ ★ ★

S.D.S. POWER DRILLS
Hitachi DH16v £103.95
Hitachi VRV16 ..... £164.95
B&D PB020 ..... £112.95
B&D P8020T (c/w 110v Transformer) £185.95

DRILL/BREAKERS
Hitachi DH28Y £272.00
Hitachi DH500A £443.00
HAMMERS
H55 SA £375.00
H90 SA £756.00

HAMMERS
Hitachi H55 SA £375.00
Hitachi H90 SA £756.00

POWER DRILLS (K-Kit box)
NEW ELU POWER DRILLS
ECD304K 420W V/S 10mm Compact £73.95
EMD400K 600W 2 Speed 13mm . £81.95
ESD705K 320W V/S & Rev. 10mm £102.95
EMD403K 500W V/S/R Ham. 13mm £90.95
EMD405K 500W V/S/R Ham. 13mm £114.95
EMD406K 550W V/S Hammer 13mm £106.95

B&D 2162 KM V/S RW 450v £63.95
B&D P2264K 13mm 2 Speed 550W £74.95
B&D P2266K 13mm V/S Rev. 480W £69.95

BOSCH 400-2 10mm 440W £29.95
BOSCH 500RLE 13mm 500W V/S Rev. £49.95
BOSCH 7002E 13mm 700W £79.95
BOSCH 850RLT 13mm 850W V/S Re £111.95

HITACHI FV12VA 13mm 420W V/S £37.95
HITACHI FV16V 13mm 600W V/S/R £59.95
HITACHI FV20VA 13mm 710W V/S/R £86.95
HITACHI VTP13K 13mm 2 Speed 460W £74.00
HITACHI VTP16AK 2 Spd. 800W £103.00

ANGLE GRINDERS
HITACHI PDP100C 4" £44.85
HITACHI G13SB 5" 750W £66.81
HITACHI G23SC 9" 2000W £89.00

PALM GRIP SANDERS
(DB Dust Bag)
ELU MVS500 1/6th Sheet 135W DB £60.95
ELU MVS501 1/4 Sheet 135W DB £60.95
B&D P6301 1/6th Sheet 136W DB £51.50
B&D P6302 1/4 Sheet 135W DB £51.50
HITACHI SV12SA 1/4 Sheet 180W £46.95
MAKITA B045 10 1/4 Sheet £43.95

LIBERON WAXES
Waxes Sealers Stains Polishes Etc. All Your Requirements in One Send for Free Price List
GLUE POT ..... £23.00 inc. P&P
470 FLUTED DOWELS 6mm 8mm 10mm ..... £5.75 inc. P&P

HITACHI 10mm CORDLESS DRILL-SCREWDRIVERS
OUR PRICE inc. VAT

DTC 10 6 cell 2 spd. & rev. £65.00
DRC10 as above torque adjustable £89.95
DTC10K 6 cell 2 spd. & rev. in case £69.00
D10DB 6 cell variable spd. & rev. £80.95
D10DD 8 cell 2 spd. & rev. £82.95
D10D as above torque adjustable £101.95
DV10D 8 cell 2 spd. & rev. hammer £107.95

MAKITA 10mm CORDLESS DRILL SCREWDRIVERS
6012DWK 6 cell 2 spd. & rev. in case £92.95
6012HDW 8 cell 2 spd. torque adj. £111.95
8400DW 8 cell 1 spd. & rev. hammer £119.95
MAGNETIC Screwdriver kit 7 piece £5.95
REPLACEMENT BITS (state type) £0.50

CORDLESS TOOLS
OUR PRICE INC. VAT

HITACHI CK12D Knife cutter £103.84
HITACHI C6DA 6" Circular saw .. £143.95
MAKITA 5600DW 6" circular saw £179.95
MAKITA 4300DW Jig saw £119.95
B&D INDUSTRIAL Jig saw £110.95
BOSCH INDUSTRIAL PAINTS STRIPPER £82.95
BELLE ELECTRIC CEMENT MIXER £135.00

MISCELLANEOUS POWER TOOLS
KEW HOBBY PRESSURE WASHER £259.00
DREMEL D576 FRETSAW £69.95
BOSCH WET 'n' DRY Vacuum cleaner £93.95
BOSCH 520 HOT AIR paint stripper £27.00
BOSCH 560 HOT AIR paint stripper £39.00
NEW ELU DUST EXTRACTORS
EVE 938 ..... £275 EVE 948 ..... £395

SASH CRAMPS (P&P £2.00 per order) may be mixed for quantity
RECORD 135-24" 1 off .. £18 5 off .. £17.50
135-36" 1 off .... £20 5 off £19
135-42" 1 off £22.50 5 off £19.50
135-48" 1 off .... £21 5 off £20

DRAPER 18" 1 off ..... £14 5 off £12
30" 1 off ..... £17 5 off £15
42" 1 off ..... £19 5 off £17
T bar 42" 1 off ..... £30 5 off £28

RECORD CRAMP HEADS M130
1 off £10.40 5 off £10.00 (P&P £1.50)

PARAMO CRAMP HEADS
1 off £10.00 5 off £9.00 (P&P £1.50)

G CRAMPS (P&P £1.50 per order) may be mixed for quantity
RECORD 120-3" 1 off .. £5.20 5 off .. £4.80
120-4" 1 off .. £5.50 5 off .. £4.90
120-6" 1 off .. £7.50 5 off .. £6.90
120-8" 1 off £11.00 5 off £9.80
120-10" 1 off £18.00 5 off £17.00
RECORD DEEP THROAT 4" 1 off £13.27

PARAMO 3" 1 off .... £5.30 5 off £4.60
4" 1 off .... £5.55 5 off £4.78
6" 1 off .... £7.76 5 off £6.60
8" 1 off .... £11.41 5 off £9.50
10" 1 off . £16.90 5 off . £15.77
PARAMO DEEP THROAT 4" 1 off £12.45

KLEMSIA QUICK CLAMPS
(P&P £1.50)

SPAN	REACH	1 off
200mm	110mm	£3.70
300mm	110mm	£4.00
400mm	110mm	£4.40
600mm	110mm	£5.20
800mm	110mm	£6.00
1000mm	110mm	£7.10
200mm	150mm	£6.70
200mm	200mm	£6.10

NEW RECORD 132 SPEED CRAMPS
(P&P £1.50)

	Reach	1 off	5 off
Record 132/30	12"	£12.00	£10.00
132/40	16"	£13.00	£11.00
132/50	20"	£14.00	£12.00
132/60	24"	£15.00	£13.00
132/80	32"	£16.00	£14.00
132/100	40"	£18.00	£16.00

RECORD HAND PLANES
(P&P £1.50/Order)
03 Smoothing 240 × 45mm £19.50
04 Smoothing 245 × 50mm £17.99
041/2 Smoothing 260 × 60mm £18.99
05 Jack 355 × 50mm £21.99
051/2 Jack 380 × 60mm £29.50
06 Jointer 455 × 60mm £33.99
07 Jointer 560 × 60mm £39.75
778 Rebate 215 × 38mm £30.80
010 Rebate 330 × 44mm £39.50
020C Circular Plane £69.50
0601/2 Block Plane £16.50
073 Shoulder Rebate £42.50
CLIFTON 420 Rebate Plane £57.00
CLIFTON Multi-Plane £189.00
CLIFTON Cap Iron 2" or 2⅜" £5.00

STANLEY HAND PLANES
(P&P £1.50/Order)
3 Smoothing 240 × 45mm £23.60
4 Smoothing 245 × 50mm £20.00
41/2 Smoothing 260 × 60mm £21.60
5 Jack 355 × 50mm £27.00
51/2 Jack 380 × 60mm £28.00
6 Fore 455 × 60mm £37.80
7 Jointer 560 × 60mm £39.40
78 Duplex Rebate £18.50
10 Rebate 330 × 44mm £33.00
80 Scraper £9.50
601/2 Block Plane £21.00
92 Rebate Plane £22.50
CLIFTON 3 in 1 Rebate Plane £67.00
RECORD 3 in 1 Plane £39.00

WOODWORKING VICES (P&P £4.50)
RECORD 52½E 9" Quick Release £44.00
52½ED 9" Quick Release £47.00
53E 10" Quick Release . £69.00

DRILL BIT SETS

	Lip & Spur	HSS Std.
1/16"-½" × 64ths	—	£21.00
1/16"-½" × 32nds	£42.00	£17.00
1-13mm × 0.5mm	£54.00	£19.00

JAPANESE WATER STONES (P&P £1.00)
KING BRAND 800G WETSTONE £8.00
KING BRAND 1200G WETSTONE .. £8.00
SUPER FINISHING STONE 6000G £8.90
COMBINATION WATER STONE £10.80

MISCELLANEOUS HAND TOOLS (P&P £1.50 PER ORDER)
RECORD Dowel Jig £34.00
140 Corner Cramps £12.00
145 Hold Fast £12.90
Floorboard Cramp .. £56.95
18" Extension Rods . £4.95
141 Corner Cramps £19.40
146 Hold Fast £14.70
169 Bench Stop £7.50
Drill Bushes £1.90
Spare Collars £3.20
Priory Bench Stop £2.95
STANLEY Web Clamp £7.99
Stanley Yankee Screwdrivers 13" ..... £12.86 20" ..... £14.17 27" £18.50

HANDSAWS (P&P £1.50)
DISSTON D8 26" 6pt ..... £27 RIDGWAY SPEED SAW 22" or 26" £19
ROBERTS & LEE 10" DOVETAIL BRASS BACK £21 ROBERTS & LEE DORCHESTER 10" £27

SANDERSON KAYSER "PAX" HANDSAWS (P&P £1.50)
BRASS BACK TENNON SAWS 8" £18.50 10" £19 12" £19.50 14" £20 D/Tail £25
HANDSAWS 20" × 10pt £21 22" × 8pt £22 24" × 7pt £23 6" × 6pt £24 26" × Rip £24

CHISEL SETS (State bevel edge or firmer P&P £1.00/Order)
MARPLES CARVERS ASH 4 piece .. £13.60
MARPLES SPLITPROOF 4 piece .. £24.50
MARPLES BOXWOOD 5 piece .. £38.50
PARAMO ROSEWOOD 4 piece .. £29.50
STANLEY 5001 6 piece .. £33.39
MARPLES BLUE CHIP 4 piece .. £17.42
MARPLES BLUE CHIP 5 piece .. £23.00
SORBY BOXWOOD 5 piece .. £26.00
PARAMO ROSEWOOD 6 piece .. £42.50
STANLEY 5002 5 piece .. £23.68

WOODTURNING CHISEL SETS (P&P £1.80)
HENRY TAYLOR Carbon Steel Sets, 3 Piece ..... £17 5 Piece ..... £29 8 Piece £46
SORBY Carbon Steel Sets 5 Piece (51c) .... £26 6 Piece (61c) .... £45 8 Piece (82c) £63
SORBY High Speed Sets 5 Piece (51h) .... £40 6 Piece (61h) .... £81 8 Piece (82h) £107
LUNA Swedish Steel Sets GOOD VALUE 3 Piece .... £14 4 Piece .... £27 5 Piece £37
MINIATURE SETS SORBY HSS set of 5 ..... £28 HENRY TAYLOR SUPER FIVE £18

ABRASIVES (West German top quality P&P £1.00/Order)
SANDING BELTS resin bonded aluminium oxide cloth belts (price each)

Size (length width)	M/C	40G	60G	80G	100G	120G
75 × 480mm — 3" × 19"	(Elu)	£1.11	£1.08	£0.99	£1.05	£1.02
75 × 510mm — 3" × 20"	(B&D)	£1.14	£1.12	£1.03	£1.07	£1.02
75 × 533mm — 3" × 21"	(Bosch Hit)	£1.28	£1.17	£1.07	£1.09	£1.05
100 × 560mm 4" × 22"	(Elu 90)	£1.58	£1.43	£1.40	£1.37	£1.32
100 × 610mm 4" × 24"	(Wolf Hit)	£1.67	£1.53	£1.48	£1.43	£1.38
100 × 915mm — 4" × 36"	(Coronet)	£2.22	£1.99	£1.88	£1.85	£1.81
150 × 1090mm — 6" × 42"	(Coronet)	£4.20	£3.80	£3.65	£3.45	£3.40

★ ★ OTHER SIZES AVAILABLE ON REQUEST MANY IN STOCK ★ ★

ABRASIVE SHEETS (P&P £0.50 PER ORDER) state grit when ordering 100G and finer

Type	Description	60G/10	60G/50	80G/10	80G/50	100G+/10	100G+/50
PGF	GARNET FINISHING	£2.13	£8.90	£1.85	£7.70	£1.67	£6.94
GCAB	GARNET CABINET	£3.02	£12.59	£2.61	£10.90	£2.35	£9.82
PSF	SILICON FINISHING	£3.16	£13.17	£2.73	£11.40	£2.46	£10.27
WS	WET 'n' DRY	£6.19	£25.81	£5.28	£22.03	£3.59	£14.99

★SPECIAL OFFER★ 50 Sheets of asstd. Abrasives £5.99 inc. P&P Garnet-Glass-W/Dry

WIRE WOOL

	0000 Fine	00/0 Medium	1/2 Coarse	3/4 V Coarse
1 KG ROLLS	£4.73	£4.35	£4.25	£4.13
250g ROLLS	£1.50	£1.45	£1.42	£1.38

SAVE 20% ON ALL HAND TOOLS SEND NOW FOR NEW HAND TOOL CATALOGUE £1.50 (REFUNDABLE ON 1st ORDER

0297 33656 CHARD STREET AXMINSTER DEVON EX13 5DZ 6.30-9pm 34836 BARCLAYCARD VISA

Radiation

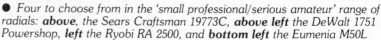

● *Four to choose from in the 'small professional/serious amateur' range of radials:* **above**, *the Sears Craftsman 19773C,* **above left** *the DeWalt 1751 Powershop,* **left** *the Ryobi RA 2500, and* **bottom left** *the Eumenia M50L*

WOODWORKER Giant Test — Radial-arm saws

The radial-arm saw market is hotting up. Four competitive machines beckon the pounds in your pocket, and naturally you want to know which one will suit. We asked John Keep to look them over

When I was approached by WOODWORKER to do a comparative test of four radial-arm saws on the UK market, I was only too happy to agree, and spent some time working out how the test should be approached. The machines we chose are as near compatible as possible — all basically in the '10in blade' slot; the DeWalt DW1751 Powership, the Sears Craftsman 19773, the Ryobi RA2500, and the Eumenia, distinguished from the others by its unusual design. Our thanks to John Costello of Black & Decker who supply the DeWalt range, Steve Turner of A-Z Tools who do the Sears, Gerry Baker of Luna who distribute the Ryobi in this country, and Craig Warren of Warren Machine Tools who import and distribute the Eumenia. Everyone readily agreed to provide their machines

for trial and we're grateful for their enthusiastic support.

Design in Wood is a six-person workshop (including myself), with two 1000sq ft areas in which we produce furniture, general joinery and specialist woodwork to commission. Everyone got involved in the test, so thanks too to Simon Guy, Trevor Findley, Jason Passco, Miles Muggleton and Lynda Franklin.

The basic idea behind the test was to evaluate the four machines for their capacity to carry out their design function in a professional/'serious amateur' workshop, and to assess their value for money.

We asked the distributors to supply their equipment as it would be received by a customer, that is, in its normal packaging. After we'd unpacked each machine we checked it for completeness and then assembled it, following the instructions. Each machine was used in the workshop for about two weeks during which time we made as full an evaluation as possible of the machine and its accessories.

It's important to point out we assessed each machine in a professional workshop, where machines are used much more frequently than by the serious amateur. Our main concern was: can it undertake the wide range of cutting requirements accurately, quickly and safely? We didn't concern ourselves in any detail with the engineering of the machines unless this affected performance. Most of the accessories provided wouldn't be required in a professional workshop, so we examined these from the point of view of the serious amateur with limited space and budget.

Value for money is more difficult to assess, not least because it's difficult to make a meaningful comparison of actual prices. The recommended retail price quoted by most of the distributors bears little relation to the prices you can get at retail outlets, especially the ones that give large discounts. So shop around, compare, and shop around again; there has to be a deal on the machine you want. But price, of course, isn't the only criterion in assessing value for money. We have of necessity to give a subjective analysis, and I hope the information and opinion we give in this article will allow you as a customer to decide what is best value, taking all factors into consideration.

DEWALT DW 1751/3 POWERSHOP

For those familiar with the DeWalt range of radial-arm saws, this is the 10in (250mm) blade Powershop but with a longer arm to give a crosscut capacity of 610mm (24in). It has a heavier duty mainframe, column and arm than the DW 1201 and 1251 Powershop. The table is deeper (930mm/37in) to allow for the longer crosscut, and a legstand comes as standard equipment. The arm is raised and lowered by a rotating handle above the column and the position of the saw for ripping and bevelling is altered at the arm/motor yoke. For mitring the arm turns on the column. Locks and setting to 90°/45° are positive and easy to locate both on the column and the yoke. A plate saw is provided as standard; the finish of all parts was good and nothing was missing.

Assembly

Murphy's Law was in operation on the day of delivery. At about 1.15pm a cheerful driver turned up and announced, 'I've got a delivery for you, Guv, have you got a fork-lift truck?' How many workshops of our size have a fork-lift truck? And everybody else was at lunch. First point — it's very heavy, so make sure you have about four big lads available when it turns up at your front door (or a fork-lift truck!) — and keep two of them to help you put it together.

Four of my big lads took about three hours to put it together, with no difficulty. The assembly instructions were straightforward, but it would have been easier if the various nuts and bolts had been packaged in separate containers to match each other.

The procedure for setting a radial-arm saw is fairly standard. It has to be done thoroughly, otherwise cutting accuracy will suffer. The instructions in the manual look a little daunting, but if you follow them carefully, you'll get a well set and tuned machine. Firstly set the crosscut travel at 90° to the fence; then the blade has to be set parallel to the arm track, and then adjusted so it is at 90° to the table. Finally the scales are adjusted. When all this had been done we each gave our first impressions:

● Mitre scale (on top of the column) difficult to read
● Didn't like the multi-purpose spanner — awkward to use
● Table too low. With the long arm it was

difficult to find a comfortable position to operate the saw; we decided we would want it raised another 6in
● The handle on top of the column which adjusts the height of the arm was difficult to reach from the front because of the long stretch over the table. The only comfortable position to do this was from a flank. On the Sears Craftsman and Ryobi, this can be done from the front.

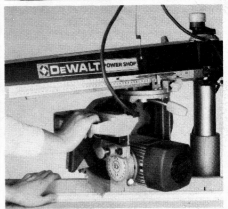
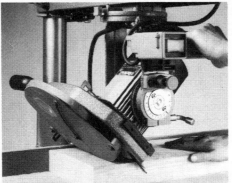
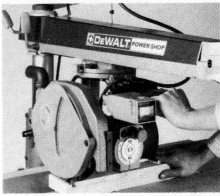
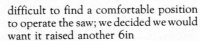

● **Clockwise from top left:** the straight-arm pull is the right technique: the 1751's anti-kickback device: mitring a moulding – clear scales, but always check on scrap: using the dado head for tenons: bevel cutting: 'out-ripping' is possible up to 880mm

Radiation

- We liked the longer arm, which would make crosscutting of panels easier
- We didn't like the mediocre plate saw provided as standard at all. This really is spoiling the ship for a ha'porth of tar. Why not supply a general-purpose TCT saw as standard?

Operation

Crosscutting With a 40-tooth TCT blade, this is smooth and straightforward. For cutting wide and thick material on radial-arm saws, you must take great care to stop the blade running away into the timber and causing a blade stall. The best method of avoiding this is to take a straight-arm stance and rotate the shoulder back as you pull the blade through. We frequently use a radial-arm saw on crosscut to cut tenons, with the arm raised to the desired height. The smooth operation of the saw back and forwards makes this easy. Crosscutting mitres is easy; the locking device on the column is simple to operate. The scale is not accurate enough for fine work, but the locks at 45° are good enough for joinery. When you're cutting mitres, it's a good idea to clamp the work to the fence to avoid a tendency for the blade to push the material out of the line of cut.

Ripping If you have to rip a quantity of thick material, it's best to change to a 24-tooth TCT blade. Set the riving-knife and anti-kickback device on the guard first; changing the yoke to the rip position is easily done, with a positive pre-set stop when the correct position is reached. We had no difficulty ripping a variety of soft and hard woods.

Accessories

Premium Quality Shaping Head and Cutters The cutters fit easily into the block and the block goes on to the motor shaft readily. The yoke is adjusted so the block is in the horizontal position; we found the guard a little awkward to fit, but when it is in position it allows a clear view of the cutter-block. You have to cut the fence to allow the cutter-block to be positioned correctly. Once the block is in position, the fence should be adjusted to allow a small clearance for the knives — if this gap is too wide, the end of the work may dig in as it passes across the cutter-block.

Our first effort at machining a piece of softwood caused excessive vibration, which to the inexperienced may be rather alarming. This was down to the slow speed of the cutter, only 2,800rpm. We reduced this vibration somewhat by taking a much small cut for each pass, and after two to three passes we got the profile.

Subsequently, we put this cutter-block on a vertical spindle moulder with a 6000rpm speed, and the cut was extremely good and very clean. So the problem isn't with the cutter-block, but with the slow speed of the saw motor, which isn't helped by the flexing of the long arm. A small point of safety: the guard seems to indicate a

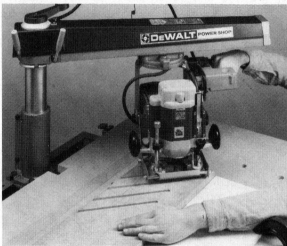

- **_Above_**: *guarding for the shaping heads – an extra £22. Cutter speeds are a drawback with almost all radial-arms.* **_Above right_**, *the drum sander in operation.* **_Right_**, *overhead routing with the mounting bracket, which fits all Elu MOFs*

direction of cut opposite to the actual rotation of the cutter-block, but we discovered it's actually a DeWalt logo! This attachment is just about adequate, but it wouldn't be suitable if you need to do quantities of shaping.

Sabre Saw A flimsy-looking attachment that didn't work well. Mounting was straightforward, but cutting was disappointing. With the blade provided, you needed to exert excessive force to feed material through. Changing the blade produced a marginal improvement, but it couldn't handle material more than ¾in thick. Not recommended.

Dado Head (Premium Quality) An excellent, robust tool which worked extremely well. The riving-knife has to be removed first before you mount it. We used it to its maximum width of cut on hard and soft woods and it gave a very clean, flat-bottomed cut.

Router Attachment The bracket fits easily to the machine after removing the guard and blade. An Elu MOF 177E router was provided for the assessment, which fitted on to the bracket with a little pushing and heaving. Having set it all up, we had to think long and hard how we could apply it! Clearly there are uses for such an arrangement, but we concluded it would be of little practical value to us. We were impressed, however, with the router, which is a delight to use, and have since acquired one for the workshop.

Drum Sander A useful accessory which works well, but we didn't like the method of locking the paper on to the drum, which works loose with time.

Shaping Head (DA 3600) Initially we had a little difficulty inserting the three cutters into the head, probably because of newness and a build-up of paint on the block. The performance of this head was a great improvement over the two-bladed moulding block. With three cutters and a higher peripheral speed, we got the desired profile in a single pass with much less vibration. For those who need a profiling capacity, this is a better option than the cutter-block.

Handbook The Powershop Handbook (not to be confused with the operating manual) is a valuable asset in the workshop. It covers setting up and operating the machine and has a very good section on techniques, concluding with information on materials and how to make a number of useful projects. The section on safety should arguably come at the beginning, and it is on this subject we have a number of criticisms about the manual. In the straightforward operation of the machine there is nothing inherently unsafe, provided normal (safe) operating procedures are followed. But this isn't the case in some of the more advanced techniques, such as dishing and cutting of circles. The inexperienced should take *very special care* when following some of the recommended techniques.

Summary

This machine and the majority of the accessories we had performed well within what we considered to be their designed functions in a professional workshop. A careful choice of accessories would give the DW1751 (1753 three-phase) the capability of a good all-round woodworking tool for the serious amateur. The inexperienced should take care when practising some of the more unusual techniques and seek experienced guidance if in doubt. The equipment is backed by a wide network of distributors and in our view represents good value for money.

But our experience of after-sales service was not so happy. Some weeks ago we asked for a small replacement item. After a couple of telephone calls a jiffy-bag arrived with one small unit and a cryptic little chit which informed us, we think, that another item was out of stock. Eventually we received it after two months of waiting.

SEARS CRAFTSMAN RADIAL-ARM SAW

This machine is made in the US, distributed in the UK by A-Z Tool Sales. It's conventionally designed, with a pillar on to which the arm is fixed. The arm carries the yoke in which is mounted the motor. It has a 250mm (10in) blade, which rotates at 2850rpm. The crosscut capacity is 420mm (17in). The arm is raised and lowered by a rotating handle at the front, under the table. For mitre cuts the arm is released and moved side to side by pulling down a handle at the operator's end of the arm. There are locks to set the arm at 45°. The head is rotated after accessible locks are released on the yoke for bevel cutting, ripping and so on. The on/off switch is mounted at the front of the arm and has a key which, when removed, makes the machine inoperable. A leg set was provided, but this is an extra. All the parts were there and the finish was good.

Assembly

This took about 2½ hours and was reasonably straightforward. The leg stand proved more difficult to assemble and on first acquaintance seemed a little flimsy. The setting up was similar to that for the DeWalt — time-consuming but straightforward enough. After it was all set up and ready to go, we sat down and discussed our first impressions, which centred mainly on a debate about machinery and aesthetics. It was generally agreed the machine had too much trim, the colour scheme was wrong, and the whole effect looked slightly 1950s American. We decided that us Anglo-Saxons are brought up in a tradition of functional austerity for machines, and have a native aversion to the flashy. Red herring perhaps, but it raises a marketing point — what looks right in one country may not look right in another. All this should not be allowed to detract from the fact that this machine is robust, well designed and functional.

First impressions:
● Liked the controls for raising, lowering and swinging the arm at the operator's end of the arm, which eliminates the need to lean over the machine
● Didn't like the alloy handle on the yoke, which would be uncomfortable on a cold morning
● Not over-impressed by the guard, which we thought had probably been designed as an afterthought for European safety standards. The trouble is the inner shroud, which is one piece, has to be

● *Above*, the Sears' handy rise-and-fall mechanism is at the front of the table. *Above right*, the anti kickback/riving knife: below right, bevel cut and angle calibration; *bottom*, the guarding looks a bit of an afterthought

put in place before the main guard is fitted. In the end we left it off
● But we did like the simple arrangement for the anti-kickback pawls on the guard
● The gauges and scales were bold and easy to read, but we still regard these with innate suspicion when it comes to fine accuracy
● We thought the safety key should be left in, otherwise it would rapidly walk
● On the whole, a workmanlike machine with a number of good features, spoilt perhaps by its looks; it's a matter of taste.

continued

Radiation

Operation

Crosscutting A-Z supplied us with a wide variety of blades (⅝in bore) so the first thing we did was to discard the horrid blade supplied as standard and fit a 40-tooth TCT blade. We experienced no difficulty cutting both soft and hardwoods, to the full capacity of the machine.

Ripping We fit a ripping blade; for those who don't wish to change blades, a general purpose TCT blade can adequately crosscut and rip, but as we often have to rip resinous softwood our practice is to use a 24-tooth rip blade. The motor assembly is easily moved into the ripping position, and the whole is locked into position on the arm. The riving-knife and anti-kickback pawls on the guard should be set at this stage.

After that cutting is easy. For both crosscutting and ripping we found the height of the table comfortable.

Accessories

A wide range of accessories is available, but we confined our evaluation to those we considered most useful or different from the accessories tested with other machines.

Saw Clamp A universal clamp for holding down irregular shaped work while machining; a useful, safety-conscious device.

Hold-Down Set A spring-loaded clamp which allows the timber to be held securely when it's fed into the machine parallel to the fence — for ripping or shaping, for example. Especially useful when feeding narrow material through cutters, we recommend for shaping/moulding operations. Both hold-down devices need holes drilled in the table before you can fit them.

TCT Adjustable Dado Head This operates as a wobble-saw, that is adjustable washers allow the blade to move side to side as it rotates. The width of cut depends on the adjustment of the washers. It was easy to fit, and the calibration reasonably accurate, although it needed a little fiddling to get a specific thickness. In operation it proved to be excellent.

Sanding Drum This fits on to the opposite end to the blade and works satisfactorily. We liked the sleeve system of fitting over an expanding rubber drum.

Three-Blade Moulding Set The cutter blades fit easily into the block, where they locate accurately. Shaping or moulding is fine as long as you make a number of passes. We don't recommend you attempt a full cut in one pass. A fairly wide gap has to be made in the fence to allow the cutters to rotate freely, but by making up a jig it's possible to use the cutter above the fence if you want. Beware of digging in the workpiece as the end passes the cutter block once it's past the end of the fence closest to you.

Rotary Planer An unusual accessory. The planer disc is fitted on the motor shaft, and then positioned so the motor shaft is turned down to point directly at the table. The disc

● **Top**, the three-blade cutter set worked OK on a number of passes; guards are extra. **Above**, the sanding drum expands to fit an abrasive sleeve. **Right**, the weird and wonderful planer accessory.

rotates in the horizontal plane, and cutting is with three cutters protruding from the bottom of the disc. We found the finish rough and the operation somewhat hairy. We didn't like this device.

Saw-Blades A wide range of blades are available, marketed by Sears Craftsman. Of particular interest is the 100-tooth TCT blade, which gave a very fine cut on sheet material.

Handbook The optional handbook appears at first glance to be rather cheaply produced compared to its more glossy rivals. Unpretentious it may be, but it's full of good sensible advice and we were impressed by its stress on safety. Definitely worth having.

Summary

This machine and some of its accessories fully meet the criteria we set in our aim. It achieved its designed function more than satisfactorily and has a number of features we particularly liked, the foremost that the main adjustment controls are at the operator's end of the machine. Good value for money.

EUMENIA SAW M50L

Made in Austria and distributed by Warren Machine Tools (Guildford), this machine contrasts markedly in design and operation with the three other radial-arm saws we tested. Its design concept is simple: the frame, support pillar and arm are made in square section steel, an austere but robust construction. Because it's designed this way, it's very flexible in use, and with a number of attachments and accessories can be readily converted to crosscut wide panels. The cutting head is mounted on four rollers which locate on to a diagonally-set square-section steel arm. Unlike the more conventional radial-arm saw, the arm is fixed, and for mitre cutting the small table is rotated to the angle you need. The arm is raised and lowered by a handle on the front of the fixed square-section pillar. There's no yoke in which the saw motor rotates. To change the position of the cutting head, it is easily removed from the arm and replaced in the right position. For bevel cutting the whole arm is rotated to an angle by loosening four bolts on a plate at the end of the arm; the plate has a simple gauge to indicate the angle. For bevel ripping the whole arm has to be removed from the pillar and set parallel to the table; a spanner releases a nut on the top cover of the pillar and allows the raise-and-lower mechanism to be removed and relocated. There's a hand-rotated nut and plate at the back of the arm which locks the arm on to the pillar. This has to be loosened before the arm will move up or down, and the plate is removed when the arm is changed for bevel ripping. If all this sounds a bit complicated, it is, and takes some practice and hunting round the floor for bits that fall off before you become 'fluent'.

Perhaps one of the more unusual features of this machine is that you crosscut by pushing the saw away from you — an interesting, and with an extra inbuilt safety feature, unique characteristic.

The machine may be bench-mounted, or placed on an adjustable (and expensive) stand. The blade is 220mm (8⅝in) in diameter, which allows a cut of about 58mm (2.3in) when the blade is at 90°. With the standard arm the maximum crosscut capacity is 370mm (14.8in) and with the extension this is increased to 700mm (27½in).

Another feature of interest is the cleverly designed guard, which is free of most of the irritating vices of guards on other radial-arm saws. Aside from the primary function of protecting you, it actually holds the wood down; a function which I will describe more fully.

Assembly

Putting this machine together is very straightforward and can be done in minutes. Unlike the procedures for conventional radial-arm saws, there's practically no need to tune up the Eumenia, certainly one of its attractive features. For those who require mobility for, say, site work, the speed of assembly without any more setting up for accuracy gives the Eumenia a considerable advantage over its competitors. In this context its light weight is also important.

Operation

There is one feature of the Eumenia we consider can be unsafe. The four rollers which allow the machine head to move along the arm have already been described. On the top of the left pair of rollers are two nuts with hand-holds on top, which hold an L-shaped bar. On one arm of the L are two holes through which go the nuts to fix the bar. The other arm of the L sits over the main arm of the saw, and bears against the stop when the head is moved to the end of the main arm nearest you. This stop ensures the saw head will not fall off the arm. It is possible and easy, when you're putting the machine together, to position this L-shaped stop bar the wrong way round. If this is done the whole head could come off the main arm while the machine is switched on,

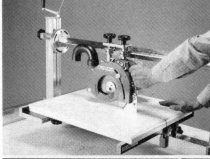
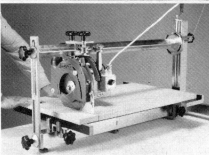

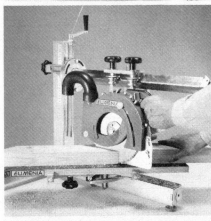
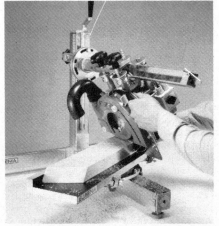

possibly causing serious injury. It must be said, however, that the knobs on top of the nuts that hold this bar are for clamping motor to arm; they don't need to be unscrewed completely to take the motor off the arm and re-position it, so it's at assembly stage the problem could arise. Confusion is possible here, and surely it's better to be totally idiot-proof.

Crosscutting The saw is pulled back from the timber to be cut, which is held on the table against the fence in the usual way. To cut, the saw is *pushed* through the material, first releasing the hold-down device on the guard by pressing the thumb-operated button. When the saw is cutting, the hold-down device, which is spring operated, automatically holds the material securely, reducing a tendency for the saw to grab into the material. Using the fence and hold-down device on the guard, cutting is inherently very safe. You can cut without having to hold the material — unique. A disadvantage of this arrangement is that it's slightly more difficult to line up the blade along the line of cut. For wider material there's a simple extension bar which moves along the bottom support and can be locked in position. To cut mitres, the table is rotated, not the arm or pillar; we found this arrangement worked satisfactorily, although it would be less useful if the saw was set up in the middle of a long wall bench, as radial-arms often are.

Ripping Setting up for ripping is quick; remove the saw from the arm, move it through 90° and replace it on the arm. Set it to the distance you want from the fence and secure the L-shaped locking plate.

Accessories

Extension Kit This increases the saw travel to 700mm (27½in) and we found it a most useful accessory. We used it throughout the test, in fact, in preference to the standard arrangement. We understand one manufacturer who needs to cut 8x4ft boards has made his own super extension kit to allow over 48in (1220mm) of travel for the saw.

Wobble Saw Similar in operation to the one previously described. At maximum setting we found it fouled the guard.

Multiprofile Cutter An interesting one-piece cutter with which, it's claimed, 33 separate profiles can be cut. This would demand great imagination and ingenuity, but could be done: a useful but expensive tool. There is no guard available, and we would sound a note of caution.

● *From top: crosscutting a 600mm worktop with the extension arm. This is a 'push-action' design; guard and hold-down raised for clarity. Out-ripping up to 850mm with the extension arm: bevel cutting: mitring and compound mitring – swivel the arm for the latter*

continued

Rebate Cutter Effective, but don't be too ambitious with depth of cut; it's only rotating at 2800rpm. Again we sound the note of caution over guarding.

Planer This device works reasonably well, but it isn't very robust. The arm of the saw has to be set in the same position as for bevel ripping, the planer is bolted to the table, and the cutter-block is connected to the motor drive-shaft through a flexible coupling.

Router Mounting This is supplied in two parts. There's the same mounting system as for the saw, plus Warren Tools will make a mounting to fit a particular router to order. Otherwise it's up to you to improvise your own mounting, which you fit to the saw mounting bracket — a little Heath Robinson. We were supplied with a router already mounted on a bracket, which worked well and would be good for those needing accurate and repetitive grooving or housing cuts. With this type of accessory, which is a poor man's overhead router, lack of hand-off control to raise and lower the router is a severe limitation.

Summary

The Eumenia grew on us as we used it. It is well designed and has a number of unique and interesting features, and also a number of limitations. We considered it achieved its design function, but its small depth of cut is a limitation, especially in a joinery workshop such as ours. We liked its flexibility, particularly the extension kit, and once we got used to the push crosscut we found this is a good and safe feature. We believe one of its great attractions is its portability, especially beneficial to the site worker. We weren't generally impressed with the range of accessories, which don't match the versatility or design of the others

● *Clockwise from above*, drum and disc sanding: 33 profiles, but no standard guard with this cutter; the large rebate cutter with guide bearing, and the little 100mm planer. The arm needs to be repositioned parallel to the back fence to use this accessory

we tested. We consider the possibility of the saw coming off the arm, if the L-shaped locking bar is positioned incorrectly, cannot be overlooked; it's really a matter of assuming that bar needs to come right off to change functions, which it doesn't. Surprisingly, there is no handbook to describe machining and operating techniques, though the manufacturer's leaflet is well illustrated.

RYOBI RA 2500

A conventional radial-arm saw, with a sturdy pillar on to which the arm is fixed, with the saw yoke travelling underneath on six bearings. The arm elevation is controlled by a crank handle on the front of the machine. The on/off switch is mounted on the front end of the arm and has a simple safety key which, when removed, renders the machine inoperable; but you can make the machine work by using a large nail or equivalent instead of the key, so this safety feature is of dubious value. The arm is moved from side to side by undoing a lock on the column and operating a release catch on top of the arm at the front end. There are positive location lugs on the column at 45°, 90°, and 45°. The yoke is located under the arm on six bearings and allows a maximum crosscut of 14½in (368mm). For bevel cuts the saw head is moved by releasing the bevel index handle, set just under the handle; use the index scale to set it to the desired

position. For mitring and ripping the saw head is moved by releasing a lock arm on the right side of the yoke and lifting the yoke knob. The saw head will automatically relocate in the correct position for ripping. The guard has been well designed, and combines the best features to be found on the Sears and DeWalt machines. The predominant colour is matt black.

Assembly

The saw arrived in a very compact package, and after removing the parts it was apparent that it was more 'knocked down' than the other saws we tested. An inspection showed no parts were missing and apart from the sanding drum (the arbor was bent) everything was clean. The assembly and setting up took longer than with the other equipment. Although verbose, the instructions were clear and easy to follow. One particular assembly operation was especially awkward; it involved locating a screw and lock washer down the main support column. In the end we turned the machine

upside down and improvised a long device to fit the screw. The procedure for setting the saw is similar to the one we described for the DeWalt, and straightforward enough if you follow the stage-by-stage instructions in the manual.
Our first impressions:
● A good-looking workmanlike machine
● We liked the main controls at the operator's end of the machine, although the locking handle for moving the arm is at the opposite end, above the support pillar
● the locking devices and index knobs on the yoke are positive and simple to operate
● We were sceptical about the safety value of the locking key
● We liked the guard
● The scales are clear and easy to read
● We didn't like the high-pitched noise of the motor
● The saw-blade provided as standard was replaced with a general purpose TCT blade

● **Right**, *view of the Ryobi's anti-kickback and guarding arrangements.* **Below**, *the dado cutter; the three-cutter moulding block is designed to spin 'vertically', on the same axis as the blade, but the motor's high speeds are good for the router adaptor,* **middle**. **Bottom**, *the sanding drum at work*

Operation

The most noticeable feature of this saw is the high-pitched noise from the motor, similar in pitch and intensity to a router. The spindle speed is a massive 17,600rpm, and there's a reduction gear to convert this to 4400rpm for the saw. The manual shows details on how to replace the motor, and we permitted ourselves to wonder whether this is an indication that motor failure is not uncommon. A high-speed low-torque saw will appear to labour as it cuts, and even with relatively small dimension timber, the Ryobi's blade speed noticeably reduces as it cuts through the timber. But we didn't manage to stall the saw either crosscutting or ripping, both of which operations are straightforward. We did encounter a slipping blade, but got rid of this by adjusting the clutch tension.

Accessories

Disc Sander A flat steel plate bolted on in place of the saw blade. The sanding discs

supplied were self-adhesive and could be stuck on either side of the plate. The saw arbor protrudes through the centre of the disc which reduces the useable area of the sanding disc; apart from this a useful and effective addition. We couldn't test the drum sander because the shaft was bent.

Three-Cutter Moulding Block This fits on the saw arbor and spins 'vertically'; we were doubtful about its quality. It gave a clean cut, but with quite a bit of vibration.

The manual advises it should be used with the existing blade guard, which is impossible if the block is used in the more normal horizontal position. Not a well-designed tool, with dubious safety features.

Three-Lip Shaper Cutter Fitting into the spindle at the other end from the saw-blade, this cutter rotates at 17,600rpm, and is used with the accessory shaping table. It worked very well and gave a clean cut. Positioning of the cutter in relation to the accessory table is restricted, because the arm has to be in the fully elevated position to allow the cutter clearance over the table. Work has to be fed across the cutter from left to right, the opposite direction from a normal spindle moulder.

Router Adaptor Using this feature, included as standard in the price, gives access to a wide range of $\frac{1}{4}$in-shank router cutters, and with its high speed of 17,600rpm the machine becomes an ideal fixed overhead router. The main limitation of this arrangement, as I have mentioned before, is the absence of any means to raise or lower the cutter from the work while you're holding the work.

Summary

On the whole, a well designed and engineered machine with a number of good features, particularly the facility for many of the adjustment controls to be operated from the user's end of the saw. We have reservations about the motor. The clutch and reduction gear seems unnecessarily complicated, and we thought a possible area for future problems.

Allied to this is the high-pitched noise of the motor, which could be a nuisance to neighbours. The advantage of a high-speed motor is when you use shaping and router cutters, but we felt this was offset by the need for a clutch and reduction gear for the saw-blade.

In comparison with other machines we tested, the range of the accessories was not as comprehensive, and the quality not as high. From our brief acquaintance with the Ryobi RA 2500 we believe the basic machine represents reasonable value — our main reservation being about the motor.

CONCLUSION

There is no doubt that each saw carried out its designed function as a radial-arm saw. Each basic piece of equipment performed well, and there is little difference between the DeWalt, the Sears Craftsman and the Ryobi, though there are variations of design and different methods of operation for each of them. The Eumenia's design is very different from the others and has a number of features which set it apart, the main one being that it is the only one of the four which would be eminently practical as a radial-arm saw for site work which involved a lot of moving about and setting up.

The accessories you can get for each saw are designed to allow the serious amateur to

continued

Radiation

enlarge the woodworking capacity of one machine. In our view the DeWalt range of accessories was the most comprehensive and best designed. The major failing of all the saws except the Ryobi is the low spindle-speed for shaping cutters. We recommend potential buyers to compare the indifferent characteristics of these machines for shaping and routers specifically designed for such work. I think one or two of the accessories are potentially dangerous, and suggest you use them extremely cautiously.

We strongly recommend that distributors supply machines with a general-purpose TCT blade as standard. The serious amateur should consider investing in separate blades for ripping and crosscut, and adding a fine-tooth blade for panel cutting.

The initial purchase of a relatively expensive piece of woodworking machinery is not the end of the story. A most important consideration is the back-up and after-sales service. A glance through WOODWORKER gives a clue to availability; DeWalt is stocked by a majority of good woodworking machine retailers. Warren Machine Tools claim 55 outlets for the Eumenia at the last count; A-Z Tools have 29 stockists for the Sears Craftsman, and Luna, the distributor of the Ryobi, certainly keep their light under a bushel — we have never seen this saw advertised anywhere. Dealers will order a Ryobi for you if you want one.

We had only one experience of after-sales back-up. We broke a small but essential item of the DeWalt saw and it took two months for the spare part to arrive. We hope this is not the usual service provided by DeWalt/Black & Decker.

'Value for money' is not an easy factor to quantify. In many cases the difference between recommended retail price and actual purchase price is considerable. Look carefully at what is offered for each machine. The basic machine, the additional cost of supporting legs and the accessories should be individually priced and compared. If saving money is a high priority, time spent shopping around won't be wasted. Secondhand value may also be a factor worth considering and a call to your nearest large wood machinery stockist will provide you with an estimate of second-hand value for the machine of your choice.

Ultimately only you can decide what suits you best, and that has to be part of the 'value for money' equation too. I hope this article has give you enough information to help you make the right decision according to your needs. ∎

REPLIES

We asked the manufacturers/distributors for their response to John's report. Here's what they said

DeWalt

Accessories I would dispute the assertion that most of the accessories would not be required in a professional workshop. Small 1-3 man companies require greater versatility; I would say 'some' of the optional accessories for the DeWalt Powershop are not particularly relevant.

Value for money Surely the principal yardstick to use (as well as those stated) would be cutting capacities relative not only to price but also to strength and rigidity in terms of standing up to the rigours of professional use.

Assembly Sorry about the inconvenience, but we do give packed and unpacked weight in our literature. The packaging of nuts and bolts is being improved.

Mitre scale does John mean illegible, or difficult to read because it's a distance from

SPECIFICATIONS (Using published data)

Make	DeWalt	Sears	Ryobi	Eumenia
Model	DW1751	19773C	RA2500	M50L
Blade diameter (mm)	250	254	220	220
Motor type	Induction	Induction	Universal	Induction
Motor power	1.5hp (output)	1.5hp (output)	1250W (input)	1.75hp
Blade speed (rpm)	2800	2850	4400	2800
Max. depth of cut in mm (90°)	68	76	76	58
Max. depth of cut in mm (45°)	50	64	57	30
Max. crosscut capacity (mm)	610	420	368	370
Max. mitre capacity (mm)	425	350	—	260
Max. ripping width (mm)	880	660	616	540
Weight (kg)	108 (incl. legstand)	54.5	48	30

PRICES

Recommended retail excluding VAT

DeWalt 1751
B&D Professional, West Point, The Grove, Slough SL1 1QQ, (0753) 74277

Saw with stand	£690.00
Premium quality shaping head with seven pairs of cutters	128.00
General duty shaping head with four sets of three cutters	38.00
Premium quality dado head	130.00
Router mounting for Elu MOF range	36.00
Drum sander	12.00
Disc sander	9.00
Sabre saw	68.00
40-tooth general purpose TCT saw-blade	48.75
Powershop Handbook	6.75

Discount: you should get a basic DW1751 and stand for around £575

Sears Craftsman 19773
A-Z Tool Sales, Union Close, Kettlebrook Rd, Tamworth, Staffs B77 1BB (0827) 56767

Saw	549.00
Stand	49.00
	£598.95
Saw clamp	16.00
Hold-down set	9.95
Cutter head and four sets of three cutters	32.72
TCT 8in dado set with 22 teeth and five chippers	59.95
Sanding drum	7.50
Sanding disc	10.37
Planer attachment	17.71
40-tooth general purpose TCT saw-blade	35.00
Handbook	4.95

Discount: saw without stand around £490

Eumenia M50L
Warren Machine Tools, Middle St, Shere, Surrey GU5 9HF, (048641) 3434

Saw	£390.00
Stand	107.00
	£497.00
Extension kit	71.00
Wobble saw (washers only)	13.50
Multi-profile cutter	77.00
Rebate cutter	66.00
Planer	68.00
Router mounting	76.00
40-tooth general purpose TCT saw-blade	29.50
Drum sander	12.00
Disc sander	14.50

Discount: you should be able to get a machine and stand for around £450

Ryobi RA 2500
Luna Tools and Machinery, 20 Denbigh Hall, Bletchley, Milton Keynes MK3 7QT, (0908) 70771

Saw with stand	£485.00
Drum sander	8.47
Disc sander	14.19
Three-cutter moulding block with three sets of three cutters	17.78
Three-lip shaper cutter	8.99
Dado cutter set with six chippers	32.01
Router adaptor	comes packed with every machine
28-tooth general purpose TCT saw-blade	27.48

Discount: at the discretion of dealers

the front of the table? Point taken, anyway — we shall look into ways of improving it. It must be said that any scale like this must only be treated as an approximate guide anyway — a fractional misreading of the mitre angle can be quite significant on wide material. The machined 0°-45°-0° locations are of course accurate.

Multi-purpose spanner This will be replaced by better-quality individual spanners.

Table height This is down to individual preference. Increasing the table height would raise the blade and control handle, which would be less convenient; adjustable table height would add to the cost of the machine. At 85cm above the floor it's a lot higher than most traditional sawbenches.

Height adjustment handle DeWalt has traditionally avoided additional linkages in the adjustment controls (except for the very large machines) as a principle. More parts means more opportunities for wear, and the necessary manufacturing tolerances in those more parts can also add to cumulative inaccuracy in use.

Standard blade We have often considered whether we should fit a TCT blade as standard, but the fact is our 40-tooth TCT GP blade is over £38 more expensive than the standard blade, and that additional cost would have to be borne by the buyer. Our view is to leave the user the choice about what blade is actually needed, given the different sorts of use. Professional woodworkers recognise that a GP blade is itself a compromise in performance terms. Certainly most of our dealers would be sympathetic in pricing a TCT blade to go with nearly £600 worth of machine!

Crosscutting Blade 'bite' is a common problem with all radials; we make a traverse control to adjust blade-advance speed if you need it.

Shaping heads Compared to the 6-9000rpm of a dedicated spindle moulder, we accept our Premium Quality Shaping head is a compromise in terms of feed speed. It still means for £185 inc. VAT (including specific guard) you can have spindle moulding for the smaller workshop. That confusing logo will be removed in future. The general duty shaping head with three cutters has better performance for a given feed speed than the premium quality block — for occasional use. It doesn't have the same mass and I wouldn't say its long-term performance and durability would make it a better buy.

Router attachment Other professional users seem to know what to do with it — 2000 have been sold since they were introduced two years ago. Mounting the router on a Powershop enables you to move either router or material — a facility you only get with dedicated overhead routers costing four figures.

Drum sander One of our biggest-selling optional accessories; I do not recall hearing criticisms before of its paper-fixing arrangement, given the space limitations.

Handbook The reader is advised to read the Safety Instructions in the appendix on the second page of the book's introduction chapter. The same safety instructions come with the manual supplied with the machine. John's comments about the safety aspects omitted from the more advanced techniques are accepted; the next edition will be amended.

After-sales service As I understand it, John's poor experience in obtaining a replacement part relates to damage (possibly due to inexperience) which occurred on the premises of the user who purchased the machine after John had used it. If that user had actually assembled the machine, he would have been better aware of how to adjust it for various cutting angles. The part involved is very rarely required. If it had been bought from a dealer as normal, the dealer would obviously have made it his business to replace the part quickly. Our extensive dealer and Service Centre network is there to assist: if anyone has difficulties of spares supply, they should feel free to speak to me direct.

Cutter speed The greater shaping-cutter speed of one of the competitors is down to the universal motor, as against our induction motor with its overwhelming noise, maintenance and operating life advantages.

Guarding One aspect which is missing is comment on the guarding of the machines. We pride ourselves on the relative safety of what we call our 'Euroguard', approved for use in all European countries, and feel the guards on some competitor models leave a lot to be desired.

John Costello, Group Product Manager, Black & Decker Professional

Sears Craftsman

Looks I feel that John's comments on the aesthetics of the machine are not relevant to the criteria of operating efficiency.

Safety key We supply 15 or 20 of these a year.

Blade The blade supplied is a grade 1 chromium-plated blade.

Steve Turner, Managing Director, A-Z Tool Sales

Ryobi

Sales growth of the RA 2500 has been quite substantial in recent months. Initially some of our dealers were concerned about the noise level from the brush-type motor, but experience has shown that apart from this, features of design, performance, price competitiveness, reliability and the standard router adaptor are accounting for the increased demand.

The motor is covered, like all Ryobi industrial power tools, by a full 12-month warranty. Our replacement motors are gathering dust; a small quantity, they have been counted at stocktaking for at least five years.

We enjoy an excellent business relationship with Ryobi, and discussions on product improvement and development feature prominently during our regular meetings. Both Luna and Ryobi welcome objective and constructive comment and criticism; such co-operation between manufacturers and users can only be of long term benefit to all parties.

Readers will soon see a new back-page advert in WOODWORKER featuring Ryobi products — including the RA 2500. We also realised it's time we took our radial-arm saw out from under the bushel!

Gerry Baker, Director, Luna Tools and Machinery

Eumenia

Table size We have a work support as standard to accommodate larger panels — no mention is made of this. Table and fence move towards you for cutting smaller sections to eliminate fatigue.

Bevel ripping It does require a spanner to release one bolt — we haven't had bits dropping on the floor! But with any equipment you need familiarity.

Crosscutting/ripping The safety guards are primarily designed for ripping. The work is held by automatic clamps either side of the blade, and you can let go during ripping without the kickback common on other radials.

Wobble saw We looked at the guard lock on the saw John had, and noticed it was distorted — the rubbing is not at all normal.

Planer This accessory is not intended for heavy work.

Router mounting We didn't want to provide a mount that limited the user to one machine, and manufacturers have not standardised router-base design. It's straightforward to adapt the mount to your own router, and we're pleased to help should there be any difficulty.

Performance We feel more mention could have been made of performance, noise level, or indeed accuracy — all of which the serious enthusiast may wish to consider.

Service We prefer to deal directly with the user on after-sales service, so we ask stockists and the user to contact our Service Department, which means we can offer a prompt response to any complaint.

Craig Warren, Director, Warren Machine Tools

Now you've read all about the radial-arm saws you're interested in, you'll doubtless be going out to buy one. Remember that dust extraction is important with all machines, and particularly that radial-arms chuck the muck about more than most. So turn to p480 for a cost-effective solution . . .

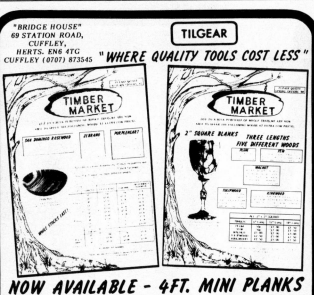
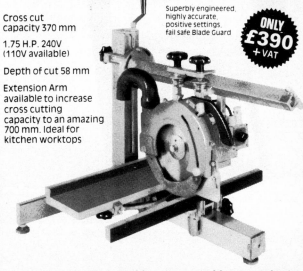

Woodworking W

English designer craftsman Jeremy Broun found himself on a four-month trip Down Under, getting to know strange and wonderful timbers and meeting craftsmen in search of the authentic Australian feel

I made friends with Paul Eliseo, an Australian furniture designer and maker, 10 years ago when he was on a scholarship at High Wycombe College. I made a vague promise that I would come out to Australia and visit him one day, but it was a stroke of good luck that made the trip possible. I was offered a seat on the flight deck of a Jumbo — a member of my family works for an airline — and so I jumped at the chance. Apart from time in Italy and Scandinavia on a Travel Scholarship, I had spent the previous 10 years in my small furniture workshop in Bath, and was beginning to get sick at the sight of a piece of wood. But in the rush of enthusiasm I did remember to pack a few slides of my work, which turned out to be a wise move; woodworking was a good point of contact with people.

Making my base with Paul at his hilltop farm in North Adelaide after an arduous coach journey across the famous Nullabor plain, I decided it would be far too ambitious to try and 'do' the whole continent in four months, so I found myself staying here and there for a while, and then moving on. Vast areas of Australia are almost devoid of trees, but there are many unfamiliar timbers, some of them hard and unforgiving like the Australian landscape. Travelling by coach round the south-west tip I passed through mile after mile of jarra and gum forest, amidst dramatic scenery. In the east, forests contain over 50 species of eucalyptus alone.

I met Australian woodworkers who use all sorts of woods — She oak, native cherry, Black Bean, Red gum, Queensland walnut, Tasmanian myrtle, silver ash, and my favourite, Huon pine — rather like a blond yew wood. I actually got to make a piece in this timber. Wood is highly treasured, and the craftsmen I met fully exploited the character of each wood both in structure and decoration. *(continued)*

● *Destination Australia - Jeremy Broun in the outback.* **Inset above**, *Henry Black's desk and chair in leather-covered MDF, fumed blackwood legs, silver ash and celery top drawer*

zards of Oz

● **Left**, Tom Graham's chest: carcase and drawer slips in Australian cedar, with silver ash drawers, ebony base and handles

● **Left**, Jeremy carved this Huon pine clock while he was in Australia. **Below**, Andy Smylie's red gum turnings

It was refreshing to meet people who have no established historical tradition, but a common desire to produce something truly 'Australian'. Of course some of the woodworkers I met were of British or German descent, but I got the impression they were feeling their way to creating a market for well designed, well made Australian furniture.

The growing momentum of interest in contemporary furniture making reminded me of Britain 10 years ago. I was particularly impressed by the formation of strong State woodworking groups, where amateurs and professionals meet to exchange ideas freely and show their work; they are enthusiastic, and people travelled long distances at short notice to attend the meetings I addressed.

Some of the woodworkers I met are self-taught, I think reflecting the original pioneer spirit of the country. I saw an enormous variety of style, and particularly liked the innovative approach of Henry Black, a pattern maker by trade, who had produced an interesting circular desk and chair in MDF on a huge lathe.

In Sydney I met members of the New South Wales Woodworkers Group, and visited several workshops in the capital. Richard Crossland, who emigrated on a £10 ticket in the sixties, showed me an ingenious wooden go-kart using a variety of Australian woods which he had exhibited in the Opera House recently; he runs a small woodworking school as well.

Robert Neville runs a small Sydney workshop with three craftsmen, dividing their time between bread-and-butter restoration work and his own speculative modern furniture designs, which include solid wood cabinets with beautiful hand-lacquered paint finishes.

I stopped off in the Adelaide area for two months (where I caught sizeable trout on Paul's farm in the North Adelaide Hills), a month in Sydney (where I ended up helping to restore an old steamship for the Americas' Cup), saw something of the Melbourne and Perth areas, and even got a taste of opal mining in the outback.

Travelling round certainly changed my preconception that all Australia is flat scorched scrubland. Ninety per cent may be, but the rest — which covers an area at least twice that of the UK — boasts some of the most dramatic scenic extremes in the world. South West Australia reminded me of Scotland, where I have my roots, and there's probably more snow in the Blue Mountains than in the whole of Europe!

Some of the Australian landscape is strikingly caught in the 'found wood' pieces of Peter Carrigy, a wood sculptor and former wildlife artist, in whose work is sensitively and skilfully expressed the power of the elements, the dryness of the South Australian landscape, and its mysterious history.

I missed seeing the woodworking activities that are going on in Tasmania and

● **Above**, Robert Neville's desk and chair in silver ash and blackwood, **right**, Ian Macpherson's pine wall cabinet, and **below**, Peter Carrigy's 'Worry Birds'. **Bottom**, Richard Crossland's go-kart really looks the business

Canberra, for instance, and my brief glimpses of what was happening elsewhere were probably fairly superficial. But I felt the woodworkers I met had a positive optimism about the future; I hope the recent severe tax reforms haven't dented their confidence too much.

I also learnt that despite the increasing tightness of Australia's immigration policy, woodworkers — particularly cabinet-makers — are in high demand. That may

appeal to those people who can labour at their craft with commitment and still make time to enjoy the great Australian lifestyle on the beach — when it's too hot to work in any case. ■

● Jeremy made a video on the work of some Australian woodworkers he met during his visit. The VHS tape is available at £15 from Jeremy Broun, Belgrave Lodge, Camden Rd, Bath.

NON-STOP GROWTH!

36,884 ABC and still rising...

For the last 5 years, WOODWORKER magazine has shown a non-stop circulation growth giving its advertisers more value per advertising £ each year.

This year is no exception. This year we are pleased to announce that WOODWORKER delivers to you its biggest ever increase, a massive jump of **16.3%**, which means another 5,180 new readers – resulting in 5,180 more opportunities for you to sell your products and services to committed woodworking enthusiasts.

Britain's best-selling woodwork magazine offers you the largest market place available to committed woodworking enthusiasts in the United Kingdom and offers you an opportunity at a price you simply can't afford to miss.

If you are interested in putting your business in front of **36,884** dedicated woodworkers (and by the time you read this advertisement, this figure will probably have grown by at least another 1,000), then phone Trevor Pryer on 01-437 0626 extension 310. He will be able to tell you how little it costs to reach them!

Woodworker

Britain's best selling woodwork magazine by
ARGUS SPECIALIST PUBLICATIONS LTD

Clever cleaner

● *Mark 1 hood with additions; mark 2 with its offset design is 90% efficient in crosscut mode*

● *For ripping, Don connects a vacuum hose to the dust spout. It's 95% efficient; detail shown opposite page, bottom right*

Extracting dust from radial-arm saws is notoriously difficult and rarely efficient. Don Solman's home-made solution is based on a classic amongst vacuum cleaners

I built my workshop to combine both woodwork and silversmithing, but they are not really compatible because of the dust. If I want to do some silversmithing it's a 45-minute task to clean away 3-4mm of dust from the silversmithing bench and tools.

Most of this dust (sawdust and fine dust) is created by the radial-arm saw, which backs up to the wall. The sawdust hits the wall and spreads everywhere. I have tried hoods with chutes to direct it into a container, but without much success.

I decided I had to get an extractor, but there were two constraints; cost (I am always reluctant to spend large sums of money on my hobbies) and — the real deciding factor — available space. There's just no room for a large but efficient free-standing extractor. The cost, depending on size, ranged from about £80 up to £450. The next stage was inevitable. The thought was already running through my mind: 'I'm sure I can make a reasonably efficient extractor for a fraction of the cost'.

Raw materials

The heart of an extractor is a good motor and fan blade, so I started looking at vacuum cleaners for an efficient motor that could also be easily adapted. I reckoned the most suitable was a Hoover 'Constellation' (I believe they're no longer made), the spherical type that glides along on a cushion of air. This particular model has excellent suction, and it could be easily modified

because it's made in two halves hinged together. The bottom half houses the motor, switch and two filters. It didn't take long to pick up a secondhand Constellation cleaner for £8.

The conversion

The basic idea is to junk the top half of the cleaner and fit the motor unit upside down on a new bin. The more I studied the cleaner the more I saw it was going to be easier than I thought. The hinge, toggle clamp and dust bag bracket had to be removed from the bottom half; they were riveted on with hollow rivets, which made it easy to drill the heads off. To do this I removed the three self-tapping screws that hold the filter plate to the bottom half, then lifted the motor about 20mm and pushed it to one side so the rivets could be drilled out. I plugged up the holes left by removing the rivets, using pop rivets — quick and simple. I removed the two small locating lugs that are spot-welded to the filter plate by centre-punching the spot welds and drilling out. An ⅛in drill was large enough.

Before re-assembling, the three round-head self-tapping screws had to be replaced with countersunk screws, as this is where the unit sits on the bin and you need a flat surface. The plate isn't thick enough to countersink normally, so it had to be press-countersunk. Get a large centre punch or something similar, hold the plate on a piece of wood (endgrain) and punch it deep enough to accept the countersunk head.

A seal was necessary between the motor housing and bin to keep up full suction. I made it by removing the rubber seal from the top half of the vacuum cleaner and cutting round the outer edge with a sharp knife to produce a flat rubber seal, which I fitted and stuck into place with contact glue. The motor housing was then complete and ready to be fitted to the bin. I did intend to remove the base ring but realised it made a perfect carrying handle, so I left it on.

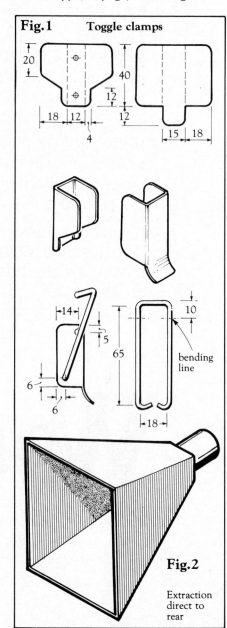

Fig.1   Toggle clamps

Fig.2

Extraction direct to rear

The bin

The bin needed to be 12in diameter, which I thought would be difficult to get — but I asked some friends who might have access to throwaway bins at work, and five were produced, all 12in diameter! I chose a tinplate one because it was the ideal height (14in); it would sit under the saw, and it has a reasonable volume.

I put the motor housing on the bin and took measurements for the toggle clamps, which I had also decided to make. Some 20swg mild steel sheet I had knocking about was suitable for all three clamps.

Fig. 1 shows the dimensions. Once I cut the metal (easily done with tinman's snips), I clamped the inside piece in the vice and bent it over a 12mm square bar (a piece of hardwood would do), and bent the outer piece over a 15mm square bar. The two pieces were then put together and drilled as a pair. The position of the holes is important, to ensure the toggle snaps over and clamps down. The size of the holes should suit the available rivet, bolt or wire. The clips were made from a 10swg (⅛in diameter) wire coat-hanger. The three toggle clamps were spaced out round the bin and pop-riveted into place.

I removed the hose connector from the top half of the cleaner by drilling out the two hollow rivets and spot welds. I used the holes created in the flange when I drilled out the spot welds for pop-riveting it on to the bin. Using the outer plate to mark the shape and position of the hole, I cut it out with tinsnips, and as the flange is flat I cut a piece of plywood the required diameter and G-clamped it on the inside, with another piece of wood on the outside. This created a flat surface so the hose connector could be pop-riveted in place.

Hoods and fitting

The dust extractor was now complete. It didn't take too long, but I did spend a great deal of time experimenting with the extractor hood for the crosscut mode of the saw. There's no doubt the most efficient is a hood that directs the sawdust to a point of extraction at the rear (fig. 2). My saw backs up to the workshop wall, so the point of extraction is at the bottom of the hood. This is where the problem was created. The first hood I made had a flat back and I thought the dust would drop down and be sucked away, but the sawdust hit the back of the hood with so much force that about 70% rebounded out.

I tried again, and made mark 2 (fig. 3) with acutely sloping top and sides to direct the sawdust to the point of extraction. This was about 70% efficient, the rest of the waste rebounding out. To overcome the bounceback I added inwardly sloping baffles (fig. 3) at the front. This has improved the unit to about 90% efficient, and unless I spend a lot more time I feel it's as good as can be expected. The photos show

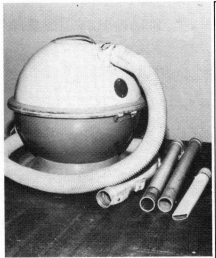

● *The Hoover Constellation – what price extraction for £8?*

● *Above, how it looks when it's ready to go. The fan and motor unit is inverted. Below, cam clamps hold the hose for in- or out-rip positions*

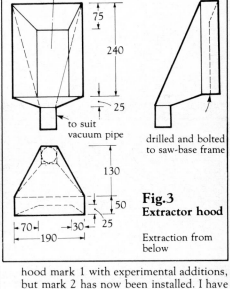

offset opening aligns with saw-blade

75

240

25

to suit vacuum pipe

drilled and bolted to saw-base frame

130

50

70   30   25

190

Fig.3
Extractor hood

Extraction from below

hood mark 1 with experimental additions, but mark 2 has now been installed. I have the facilities to gas weld, so I made the hood from 20swg. mild steel sheet, but with a little ingenuity it could be made from plywood, hardboard or any suitable sheet material.

For ripping, I put a piece of tube in the rubber dust spout on the blade guard, held with jubilee clips, and with the extractor connected at least 95% is extracted. The changeover from crosscutting to ripping only takes seconds, and to support the hose I made two simple cam clips, one for in-rip and the other for out-rip positions. It also attaches to my belt sander and power planer, a bit cumbersome but nevertheless efficient.

This was definitely a worthwhile project, and the total cost to me was £8, plus a couple of pints for the bins. It has made my workshop environment healthier, and now there is no great build-up of dust. It's efficient and portable so a general clean-up can take place more frequently; even the car gets vacuumed now! ■

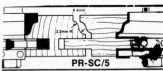

The Natural

Making the finest furniture comes deceptively easily to Andrew Whateley. Aidan Walker looks at the work of an important but unsung figure who's about to take his just deserts

● Famous furniture: the 'Gothic' chair in ebony and nickel silver uses highly-developed 'kerf lamination'

TO WHOM IT MAY CONCERN. The underlined heading on a piece of pink and now slightly tatty Parnham House notepaper is dated July 1980. 'Andrew Whateley completed his five year apprenticeship with me on 21st July, 1974. From the outset he demonstrated a natural manual dexterity; a growing awareness of sound technique and the principles of construction have been accompanied by an ability to interpret designs in a sensitive manner. As senior cabinet maker in my workshops Andrew has in recent years been responsible for the making of a number of major pieces of furniture of remarkable quality. He leaves with our warmest wished for a happy future.'

It's impossible to assess the work of one of Britain's best furniture makers (this one at least) in isolation from the work of Britain's best-known furniture designer maker — John Makepeace, the signatory of that letter. The short sentences speak volumes; Andrew has made some of the most publicised prestige furniture in the country, working in one of the country's most publicised workshops. It's to Makepeace's credit that he conceived the remarkable pieces and played an important part in spreading their fame, focusing attention the while on the species 'designer craftsman' with whose recognition he is so closely associated; it's to Andrew's credit that he gave the ideas three-dimensional reality. Always a craftsman, Andrew Whateley is just now beginning to give reality to his own

independent status as a designer maker; only now, indeed, is he actually seeking it. None too soon, say some.

Born in 1952 into a Warwickshire family of cabinetmakers and restorers, Andrew comes from a different mould than many of the furniture *glitterati*, names familiar to people who watch that particular world. Martin Grierson, Rupert Williamson, Ashley Cartwright, David Field, have all developed their work via an art and design education, usually with a final formative period at the Royal College of Art. Then there are those with a traditional apprenticeship background; Makepeace worked with Dorset cabinetmaker Keith Cooper, while Alan Peters' early working years were spent in the Barnsley workshops. Andrew, whose father had built him a bench before he was six, fits fair and square into the 'trade education' slot; plus he's never been anything other than a woodworker — naturally. He left school at 17; 'I was good at maths, physics, technical drawings . . . and of course the woodwork was always there.' No question of rebelling against the family tradition; wood, so to speak, was in the boy's blood. He resisted the Youth Employment Officer's attempts to get him into the Army; 'I suppose it's down to my mother really. She persuaded John Makepeace to take me on as an apprentice. He didn't want to at first.' This was in 1969, when Makepeace was already making a name for himself and his fine furniture in workshops at Farnborough Barn on the Oxford/Warwickshire border, 15 miles from the Whateley home.

Andrew settled in for a five-year apprenticeship, as part of which he took a City and Guilds day-release course at Wycombe Technical College (not Bucks College) which lasted three years. The training was comprehensive; hand skills, machining, metalwork, finishing, plastics, upholstery. An education for the furniture industry. His apprenticeship completed, he stayed on until 1980 as senior cabinetmaker with

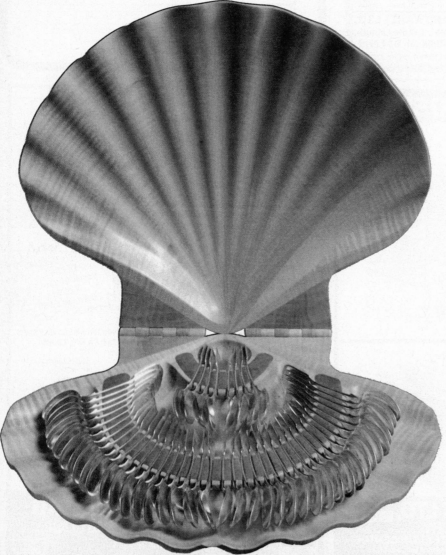

● A carved cutlery case, specially commissioned from the RCA: 'I wanted to do something a bit different'

Makepeace, moving with him to Parnham in Dorset in 1976.

'Andrew and I worked together for 13 years,' says Makepeace. 'When he joined me from school he was seeking a career in reproduction furniture making, but towards the end of his apprenticeship he really settled down to become a good craftsman, and developed continuously — it was a rare collaboration between a designer and a maker. Several of the pieces we did together will go down as landmarks in the history of furniture. It was sad but perhaps inevitable that it came to an end when the RCA was looking for a technician to take the place of Ron Lenthal, whom Andrew so much admired.'

'Collaboration' is of course the key word; the designer maker sparks off the maker, who gradually develops as a designer in his own right. Talking to Makepeace about the creation of some of the 'landmark' pieces, one also gets a clear sense of the workshop team constantly giving support and stimulation, intensifying the atmosphere of experiment and discovery. A

partnership, in many cases, of more than just two.

Of some of the most significant Makepeace designs, Andrew made the 'Liberty Centenary' dining table (1975), a 10ft-diameter four-section oak affair on built-up legs as massive as many a tree; the superb ebony and nickel silver 'Gothic' chair (1977), and the Great yew Four Poster, still to be seen at Parnham, whose four curved uprights are cut from a single trunk. There is also, of course, the Longleat table, built for the 400th anniversary of Longleat House in 1980.

As Makepeace's career has developed, he has naturally enough spent less time at the bench making things out of wood. There's not a hint of doubt in Andrew's mind about his former employer's making skills, however; 'a fine maker,' he says. Apart from his obvious purely technical skills, Andrew reckons his own strength is as an 'interpretative maker', taking an idea, perfecting techniques, 'actualising'. He describes how the design for the Gothic chair, for instance, came to him from Makepeace as a

● **Above**, Marie Pearson designed this 'Apsley House chair', now in the V&A; **below left**, the 'Longleat table' in situ

perspective sketch. It had to be in ebony and nickel silver, to blend with a chess set of gold, silver, ivory and gunmetal,and the back and arms are rounded, tapered, and curved in two planes. Not an easy wood to bend, ebony; the solution was to kerf-cut longitudinally in the sides of the arm blanks and bend them round and up on carved formers. The opened gaps were filled with slips of ebony veneer. The arms are tenoned into the outer back frame pieces, which are bent in the same way and tongued together, with the inside members, at the apex. The front legs are worked from the solid, curving up and out and ebony-dowelled to the arms just about where your knuckles would be if you laid your arm on the chair's and let your hand hang. The chair took six months to make; discussion, development, inspiration both aesthetic and technical. It was after the completion of that design that Makepeace-conceived pieces made by Andy carried both names.

The Longleat table is another such *tour de force*. It is made from holly, laburnum and robinia, all from trees grown on the Longleat estate; the 'natural' arboreal forms (which some would call a Makepeace hallmark if they didn't know his straight-and-square work) are highly developed in this piece, particularly in the multi-ribbed base, which is obviously intended to look as if it grew like that. A bit over the top for those whose tastes veer towards Modernist aesthetic puritanism, but an extraordinary technical challenge, given that drawing in a piece like this can only get you so far. Many detailed decisions could only be made (along with the designer) when the previous steps had been taken; how much, for instance, to remove from the oversize blanks for the rib/legs after they had been cut, blocked together, dowelled, glued and cramped. The top is a thick ply core laid with 22 grain-matched holly veneer segments, meeting a central 'petalled' motif of laburnum oysters. Rich fare indeed.

Design John Makepeace

continued

The Natural

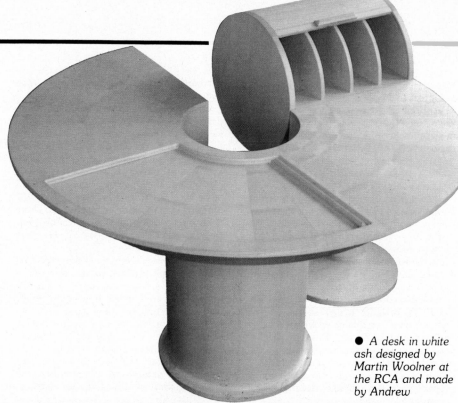

● A desk in white ash designed by Martin Woolner at the RCA and made by Andrew

When he left Parnham, Andrew took time out in Australia, where he made a conference table for Perth's University of West Australia, and returned via South East Asia to work at the Royal College of Art as cabinetmaker and prototyper with 'craftsman's craftsman' Ron Lenthal. It is another unsung but highly significant position; from playing a vital role in the establishment of a leading designer of this generation, Andrew moved to interpreting and giving form to the ideas of the next. His link with the RCA goes back to his early days with Makepeace, who employed such as David Field and Ashley Cartwright in the early 60s and 70s, when they themselves were fresh from the College. The RCA invited him to join the staff, seeing him as the natural heir to Lenthal, who was due to retire but died in 1982, much lamented, before he could do so.

Much of the work you see exhibited and publicised from the RCA's degree shows has been made by Andrew Whateley. WOODWORKER's recent coverage has

● The Liberty Centenary dining table and chairs in English oak. The four sections are joined by steel inserts

Design John Makepeace

included pieces designed by Eleanor Wood, Gavin Lindsay, Rebecca Myram, Julia Tiesteel, Michael de Caires . . . all made entirely, (or in one case more than half) by Andrew. A chair designed by Marie Pearson which he made is now in the Victoria and Albert Museum's 20th Century collection.

Students' designs go before a committee of the academic staff, who decide which one is worthy of Andrew's making skills; he enjoys the guiding role his job gives him, but it's clear he has growing frustrations about making other people's designs. 'I'm basically here to show the students what has to go into making a piece of furniture, from the point of view of traditional cabinet-making skills. I discuss the design with them and try to offer them as many alternatives as

possible, show them what can and can't be done. But the real development is up to me.' Andy says he often puts far more work into a design than the designer him or herself; designing is also problem solving, and to do that you have to have technical knowhow. It's here that he places great importance on technical drawing skills.

Andrew enjoys the technical challenges of this sort of work, but is poised now to start and run his own workshop in partnership with Rebecca Myram, whose double-curved steam-bent chairs caused a stir at the 1985 RCA Summer Show, and have been made much of since. Andrew has been heavily involved in this particular technical challenge from the outset, having been inspired at more or less the same time as the originator of the idea by a visit to David

Colwell's highly efficient steam-bending workshops in Wales (*WW/Nov '86*). There was a further step that Andrew and Rebecca wanted to take — the development of a method of steam-bending wide boards in two planes. Narrow-section components bent in one plane would not at all give the effect Rebecca wanted, and Andrew himself, naturally inclined anyway against straight lines — 'I'm not keen on them' — became fired with enthusiasm. He put a great deal of his own time into developing the jig for the first designs, and progress has continued since; working with Rebecca in her workshop, he produced the chair that won the WOODWORKER Award at last

● **Below**, the Bed of Yew in the Strode Bedroom at Parnham – from one tree

Design John Makepeace

Design John Makepeace

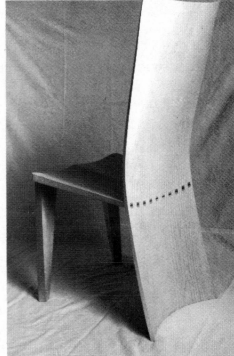

autumn's direct Design Show (*WW*/*Mar*). In February he won the Worshipful Company of Furniture Makers' Designer Craftsman Award to develop production techniques for the chairs (and perhaps a table as well) and get them down to an affordable price. If they can be sold for around £200 and produced quickly and easily, they will become the basic everyday earner that a specialised workshop needs, giving Andy the economic freedom to take special commissions and spend time designing, experimenting and developing. Being able to please himself, he will also be adding the label 'designer' to his own name of 'craftsman'.

In which context comes the unavoidable question. Most of Andrew's working life has been spent acquiring and honing skills, working in workshops; but not his own workshops. The atmosphere of his workplaces has always been rarified, and the pressure has always been on quality rather than output. The costs have never been his to bear. How will he cope when he's carrying his own can? The best answer to that is Andrew's own quiet confidence. He has done enough time sheets and cutting lists to produce realistic costings and analyse possible production problems; he is also very clear-headed about the double-curved chairs as his business bottom line. Having developed a highly unusual if not unique technique, he's politely unforthcoming about the details, recognising the singular value of a commodity which will be well marketable if the price is right. He knows that designing is more than just getting the item drawn and made; there are economics too. He's equally confident about his production capacity; retaining a familiar uncompromising commitment to quality, he'd prefer to work longer hours and keep his high standards rather than churn stuff out quickly for the sake of his hourly rate. Whether this actually answers the question about speed or not remains to be seen, but most people can motor when they know what they're doing, and the evidence suggest that Andrew is not exactly a ditherer. Nor is he the sort of traditionalist who insists on inappropriate traditional materials and techniques for their own sake; MDF and laminate 'bread and butter' lines are also on the stocks.

● **Above**, *three-way mitres in this airy display cabinet are reinforced with special steel 'claws'; yes, there's a door.* **Right**, *the double-curved steam-bent chair;* **below**, *more pieces from the Liberty dining suite*

Fame and fortune are not Andrew Whateley's overriding objectives. He wants to design and make, for himself and for others; he is not a man in a hurry, but then neither is he content to stand still. He must have challenges to conquer, and there will always be some idea developing and maturing at the back of his mind. As a designer, he has had an unusually long 'ripening' period, but now no technical problem will be insurmountable for him, and working with John Makepeace, much of whose aesthetic he obviously shares, he has observed the ins and outs of running a woodwork business. In a way it's a shame there isn't a lot of original Andrew Whateley work to show on these pages, but it would be far more of a shame if you felt there never would be. Andrew doesn't go till he's good and ready; as a maker, he's readier than almost anyone, and as an independent designer, he's good — and now, he feels, he's ready. ■

The Woodworker Guide to
HOME SECURITY

A Do-It-Yourself Manual

OUT 29 MAY

A WOODWORKER SPECIAL
Our acknowledged experience
and expertise have gone into
this useful manual, detailing
the things you can do to make
your home more secure.
Doors, windows, lighting,
alarms, fire precautions,
childproofing; it's all there.
What to buy and how to fit it
— make that burglar's life
miserable!

£1.50 from newsagents, or
£1.50 + 50p p&p from Infonet,
10-13 Times House,
179 Marlowes, Hemel
Hempstead, Herts HP1 1BB

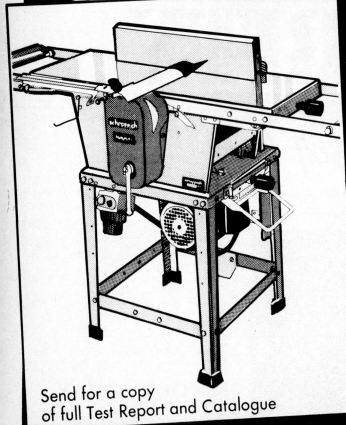
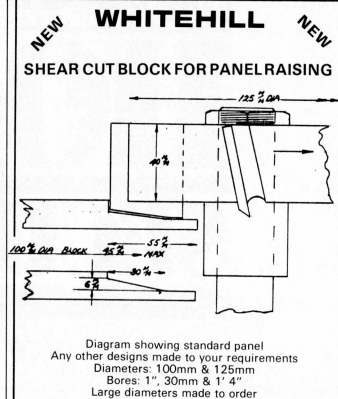
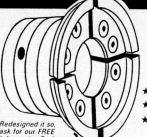

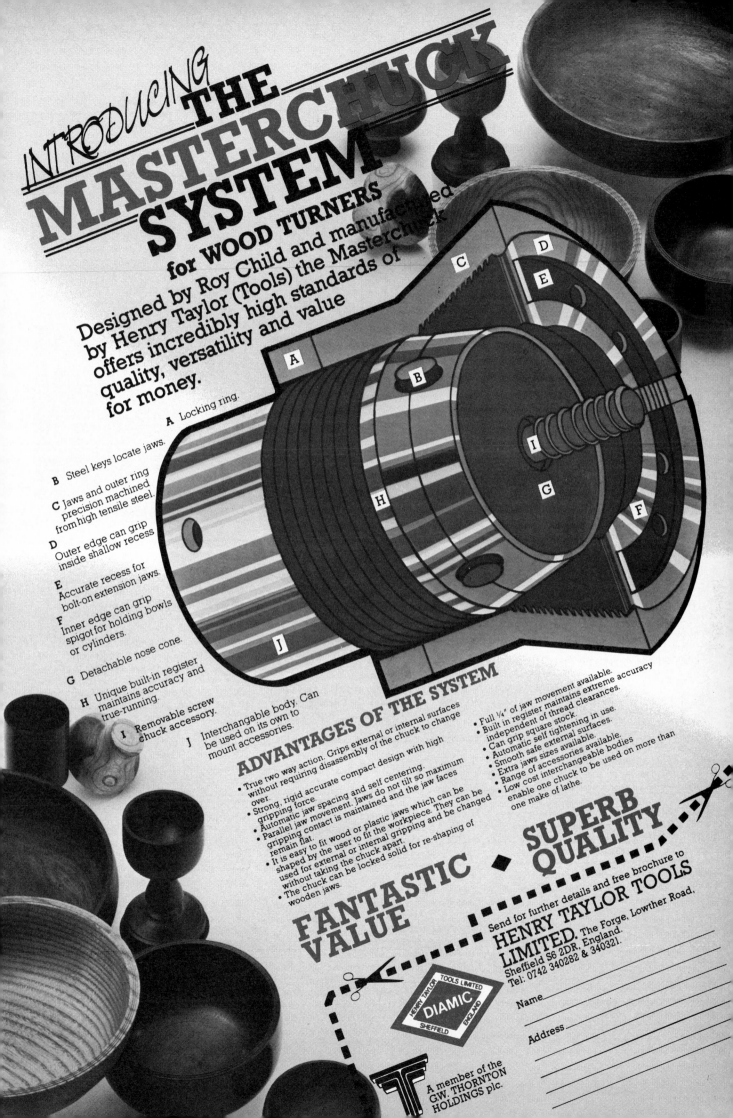

The grand furniture saga

● Early Rococo: a fine commode by Cressent with a 'crossbow' or Cupid's bow front, veneered in kingwood

Like it or loathe it, there's more to Rococo than decoration, reveals Vic Taylor — who also examines the growth of the French furniture guilds

Balance without symmetry is the quintessential ingredient of the Continental Rococo style, which seems to have had its origins in cartouches designed in the 1630s by some Italian architects. The adjective 'Rococo' was not applied to the style until 1796, when the Parisians used it as a term of disparagement: the feeling persisted, in England, at least, until well into our century when dictionaries defined it as describing meaningless and excessive decoration, anything tastelessly florid and ornate. Actually, the word is derived from the French *rocaille* which originally referred to the grottoes and rockwork at Versailles and other fashionable French gardens.

Chinoiserie, a fashion employing such motifs as Chinese figures and pagodas, was popular in France for 30 years before the arrival of Rococo, and can be found in the designs of Jean Berain and in some of the marquetry of André-Charles Boulle. It was taken up and developed by another French designer, Pierre Le Pautre, who worked at Versailles from 1699 until his death in 1716, and it reached its finest expression in the work of Meissonier.

The achievement of balance without symmetry was brought about by using a wide (some would say grotesque) variety of naturalistic motifs. This included human figures, icicles, dripping water, all kinds of fish and crustaceans, rocks, shells, fountains, and scale monsters. These were disposed on a framework of serpentine curves and C- and S-scrolls to give the desired effect of balance — not always achieved by those who arranged the motifs like hats on a rack with the sole intention of displaying their versatility.

In Europe there were three great exponents of the style: Françoise Cuvilliés (1695-1768), Juste-Aurèle Meissonier (c1693-1750), and Nicholas Pineau (1684-1754). Cuvilliés, who was of somewhat diminutive stature, was originally Court Dwarf to the Elector Max Emmanuel of Bavaria but succeeded in getting to Paris to study, afterwards becoming Court Architect at Munich. His preference was for light and delicate treatment, most effectively displayed in his Mirror Room at Nymphenburg.

Meisonnier, the finest exponent of *Chinoiserie*, was an Italian, born in Turin. About 1720 he went to Paris where he was appointed architect-designer to Louis XV; although he was primarily a silversmith, he did design some furniture. He, perhaps more than any other designer (or *ornemanistes*, as designers were then called), initiated and encouraged the more bizarre and exotic forms of Rococo known as *genre pittoresque* (literally 'picturesque style'), which included *Chinoiserie*. He travelled and worked in Poland and Portugal.

Pineau, who was born in Paris, worked in Russia from 1716 to 1726 on designs for the Peterhof of Peter the Great. On his return to Paris he became well-known for his elegant furnishing schemes in a city which was at the height of its fame as a centre of culture, fashion, and luxury.

The Rococo style came to England in the 1730s, almost certainly through the work of London silversmiths and goldsmiths. Some of these were descended from Huguenot refugees, and still in close touch with their Continental counterparts. I can give three examples: Hubert François Gravelot (1699-1773), George Michael Moser, and Gaetano Brunetti. Gravelot, who was French, arrived in London in 1732, opening his own drawing school and designing for silversmiths and furniture makers; Moser, a German-Swiss, also had a drawing school and also designed for silversmiths, while Brunetti, who was an Italian artist, published a book in London in 1736 entitled *Sixty Different Sorts of Ornament... very useful to Painters, Sculptors, Stone-carvers, Wood-carvers, Silversmiths, etc.*

This era in French furniture design is notable for the development of the various forms of *commode*. At first these took either the form of a sarcophagus, when they were called *en tombeau*, or a serpentine-fronted chest called *bombé*. They appeared massive as they had three or often four drawers with an apron piece beneath, and the dividing drawer rails were allowed to show. It was Boulle who introduced a lighter appearance by dispensing with the bottom drawer altogether and raising the carcase on to longer legs.

But the most noted of *commode* makers was undoubtedly Charles Cressent (1685-1758). He was the son of a sculptor and at first followed his father's profession; in 1719 he married the widow of Joseph Poitou, who had been cabinetmaker to the Regent (Duc d'Orléans) and a rival of Boulle's. His marriage seems to have inspired him to abandon sculpting and take up his grandfather's trade of cabinetmaking, and he himself eventually became the Regent's cabinetmaker.

Perhaps as a result of his early connections, many of his designs do have sculptured, rich, flowing lines and ornaments. One of his introductions was a new shape for *commode* fronts called *en arc d'abalete* (shaped like a crossbow) or what we would probably call today a 'Cupid's bow'. Another of his innovations (sometimes accredited to Gaudrau), was either to mask the dividing drawer front rails (*traverse perdue*) or to dispense with them (*sans traverse*): in both cases, the result is a front which presents an uninterrupted surface.

He was an enthusiastic art collector, amassing a considerable number of valuable paintings, and moved in high social circles. His finances became straightened through law suits, with the result that he had to use floral marquetry instead of more expensive ormolu mounts on his furniture.

A competitor of his, Antoine-Robert Gaudreau (c1680-1751), is considered by some authorities to have been the true originator of the *traverse perdue* and *sans traverse* commodes; his work closely resembles that of Cressent, and several pieces accredited to Cressent were actually his. You can see for yourself if you visit the Wallace Collection in London where commodes by each of them are exhibited.

French craft guilds

Craft guilds in Paris, called Corporations, have ancient origins like our own. The earliest records we have of French guilds date back to 1260 when a Provost of Paris, Etienne Boileau, summarised and formulated them.

English and French guilds were very similar in concept and aims, based on the ideals of honesty and integrity in manufacture and trade, and the training of workmen to be skilful, sober, and of good conduct. These aims were translated into hard (very hard!) reality by the fines imposed on guilty parties, and also the confiscation of goods if it was deemed necessary. Employees too were kept in their place by having their working and social lives strictly controlled and restricted.

It's a sad fact of life that the best-intentioned of activities tends to nourish the seeds of its own destruction. So it was with the guilds; one of the results was a long drawn-out series of disputes over 'who does what' amongst the various trades. Charles Cressent, for example, was involved in legal arguments in 1723, 1735, and 1743 with

● *Magnificence for Louis XV's bedroom at Versailles*

the Guilds of *Fondeurs, Ciseleurs et Doreurs* (bronze casters, chasers and carvers, and gilders). They were all engaged in making ormolu mounts and objected to his doing such work himself.

In 1743 the Paris guild of *Maîtres Menuisiers et Ébénistes* admitted *marqueteurs* (marquetry craftsmen) and strictly regulated admission to the guild by insisting on a six-year apprenticeship, followed by six years as a journeyman before the entrant could submit his *chef d'oeuvre* to the jury of masters.

But by 1751 so many anomalies and contradictions had arisen that the position had to be radically re-examined and changed. This was done by the publication of what we should today call a Code of Practice, but which was then a small book entitled *Statutes, Privilèges, Ordonnances et Règlements* under the auspices of the *Corporation des Menuisiers-Ébénistes*. *Jurés* (wardens) were appointed to see that the regulations were adhered to and the requirements met, and they were drawn from some of the most important makers of the time. Wardens had to have been masters in their trade for at least ten years and known to be skilled craftsmen and of integrity; and they had to submit a *chef d'oeuvre* for the approval of the *Maîtres*. A son, son-in-law, or assistant, who married his master's widow also had to submit a *chef d'oeuvre* and pay 100 *livres*; he also had to be born or naturalised French, and a Catholic.

The revision also had the effect of abolishing all demarcation lines between cabinetmakers who produced veneered work (*ébénistes*), marquetry workers (*marqueteurs*), and joiners who produced unveneered work such as chairs, settees, and so on (*menuisiers*). To quote: 'each one is at liberty to practise every part of the said profession'.

Another result of particular importance to furniture historians and antiquarians was that most craftsmen were required by law to stamp their work with an iron stamp (*estampille*). Such a stamp would normally show the maker's name or his initials and the approval mark of the wardens who had passed the work as satisfactory. The approval marks were either ME (*menuisiers-ébénistes*) or JME (*juré des menuisiers-ébénistes*).

Another guild closely connected with the

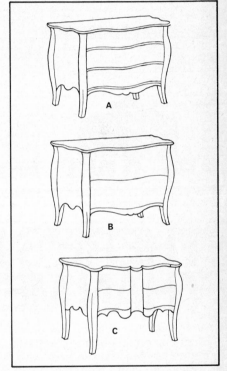

● *Examples of the* bombé *commode front: A, early type with drawer rails showing; B, without drawer rails showing (*traverse perdue*); C, rails dispensed with (*sans traverse*)*

decoration and ornamentation of furniture was formed in 1754 by the combination of the *Ciseleurs et Doreurs* (the chasers and sculptors of ormolu, and the gilders) with the *Argenteurs, Damasquineurs et Enjoliveurs sur Fer, Fonte, Cuivre, et Laiton* (the silverplaters, steel ornamenters, and embellishers of iron, cast metals, copper, and latten — a form of brass sheet). Many of these craftsmen had close associations with the making of furniture as they undertook the manufacture of ormolu mounts and gilding. Workers in these trades seem to have had a particularly raw deal as they could not leave their masters without written permission; they could not join with their co-workers in an effort to improve their positions in life; and they could not prevent their employers from taking on any other kind of worker. Hardly what one would call the best standards of labour protection! ∎

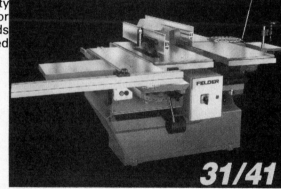

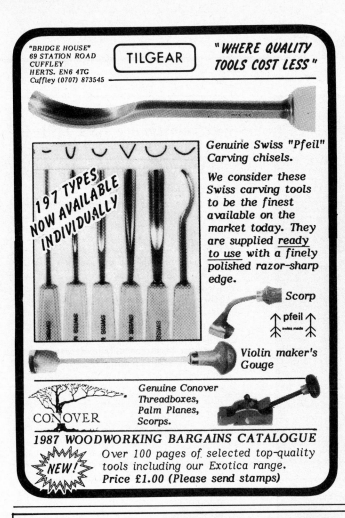

Woodworker PLANS SERVICE

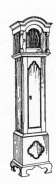

GRANDMOTHER/GRANDFATHER CLOCK CASES

Long Case (Grandmother) Clock Case WW/104
An imposing design 6ft. 9in. tall 1ft. 7in. width. Glazed front with facility for moon phase dial. **Price £3.25.**
Grandfather Clock Case WW/111
A classical design with shaped Chippendale style bracket feet. Finished with brass ball capitals and finials 8ft. 6in. high, 1ft. 6in. width. **Price £2.50.**
Grandfather Clock Case II WW/1122
A truly grand clock, 7ft. 6in. tall and 1ft. 6in. width. Authentic fretwork panel and cross banding with veneered panels. **Price £2.50.**
Grandmother Clock Case WW/113
A dignified design for a smaller clock, turned swell columns, moulded arches and base panel — 5ft. 10in. tall. **Price £2.50.**

CLOCK MOVEMENT DRAWINGS

Weight Driven Regulator Timepiece G.7
Claude B Reeve design, 2 sheets of detailed drawings for the mechanism. **Price £6.25.**
M.E. Jubilee Electric Clock G.8
An Edgar T. Westbury design modified by John Wilding. Two sheets. **Price £5.50.**
English Dial Clock G.12. Price £5.50.
Crystal Skeleton Clock G.13. Price £5.50.
Frame Template for the above. Price £1.00.
Model Engineer Musical Clock G.10
Complete set of 5 sheets of drawings including case details. **Price £10.60.**

WALL CLOCKS

Vienna Regulator WW/102
A 19th Century design pendulum clock. 3ft. 9in. high, 12in. width. **Price £3.25.**
Hooded Wall Clock WW/105
A Dutch design, popular on the Continent takes an 8 day movement. Case 22in. × 14in. **Price £2.50.**
Deborah Vienna Clock WW/117
An attractive variation of the Vienna regulator. **Price £2.50.**
Grandmother Wall Clock WW/114
Early style of clock dating back to the reign of James II. 28in. high by 15in. width. **Price £2.50.**
Grandfather Wall Clock WW/115
An imposing wall clock with arched top and fluted columns. 33½in. high, 16¾in. wide. **Price £2.50.**
English Dial Clock ADW 130
Handsome design with enclosed pendulum visible through glazed panel. **Price £4.50.**

CLOCKS

18th Century Balloon Clock ADW 132
Attractive pedestal mounted clock by Ashley Design Workshop. **Price £4.25.**
19th Century Lancet Clock ADW 131
Another design from Ashley Design Workshop. **Price £4.25.**
Bracket Clock WW/103
Classical dignity with inverted bell top 14in. high by 10in. width. **Price £1.75.**
Georgian Bracket Clock WW/109
Glazed side apertures and brass embellishments with ogee shaped facet. 19½in. high by 12¼in. width. **Price £2.50.**
Queen Anne Bracket Clock
A popular style of clock case with bracket top and glazed sides 13¾in. high, 12in. wide. **Price £2.50.**

Argus Specialist Publications, 9 Hall Road, Maylands Wood Estate, Hemel Hempstead, Herts. HP2 7BH. Delivery 21 days

Clissett comfort

● *The Clissett chair with a woven seagrass seat. It has a distinctive low-slung look but retains attractive simplicity. **Below**, the parts in assembly – front and back sections first*

Country craft exponent *extraordinaire* Jack Hill explains how to make this distinctive traditional chair in authentic style

This chair is named after a famous Herefordshire chairmaker, Philip Clissett. Born in 1817, he was making chairs from around 1838, and was still making them well into his 70s. Based upon a type directly credited to Clissett, the style is a worthy example of a traditional English 'country' chair. It is a type of ladderback, distinctive in being rather lower in height than more familiar ladderbacks, with simple lines enhanced by the graceful curve of its arms. Its components reflect the techniques of production; the round parts are just plain turnings (our 'roundings'), the back slats and arms the products of the drawknife.

The correct wood, ash, was traditionally cleft from coppice-grown trees and mostly shaped while still green. Use cleft material if you can get it, but otherwise straight-grained sawn ash is fine. The two back uprights and the back slats are bent after steaming and these should be made from air-dried rather than kiln-dried material.

The main directions here are to make the original Clissett chair with arms, but a matching chair without arms can be made to the same directions and dimensions (or smaller) simply by reducing the length of the front uprights and omitting the arms. I'll give details of these differences and some alternative methods of construction. Round components can be lathe turned or made with rotary planes.

Back and front uprights can be 1⅜in diameter — a standard rotary plane size — or 1½in diameter if you turn on the lathe. If you turn the back uprights you can top them with nipply finials which add a nice detail to the finished chair.

Whatever size or method you choose, round the back uprights and cut them to length (38in) before bending. Make up the former in the photograph to give slightly more than the curve shown in fig. 1; the back uprights are bent on it in pairs. Front uprights remain straight, 28in long for an armchair, 19in for a chair without arms.

If you wish to keep the construction simple you can have a square seat so that all the holes drilled in the uprights to take seat rails and stretchers are at 90° to each other, and most components cut initially to the same length. More correctly the seat should be wider across the front than the back but this needs angled holes of 85° and 90° respectively, and rails and stretchers of varying lengths. The chair shown has a square seat — I like to keep things simple — but instructions are given for both kinds.

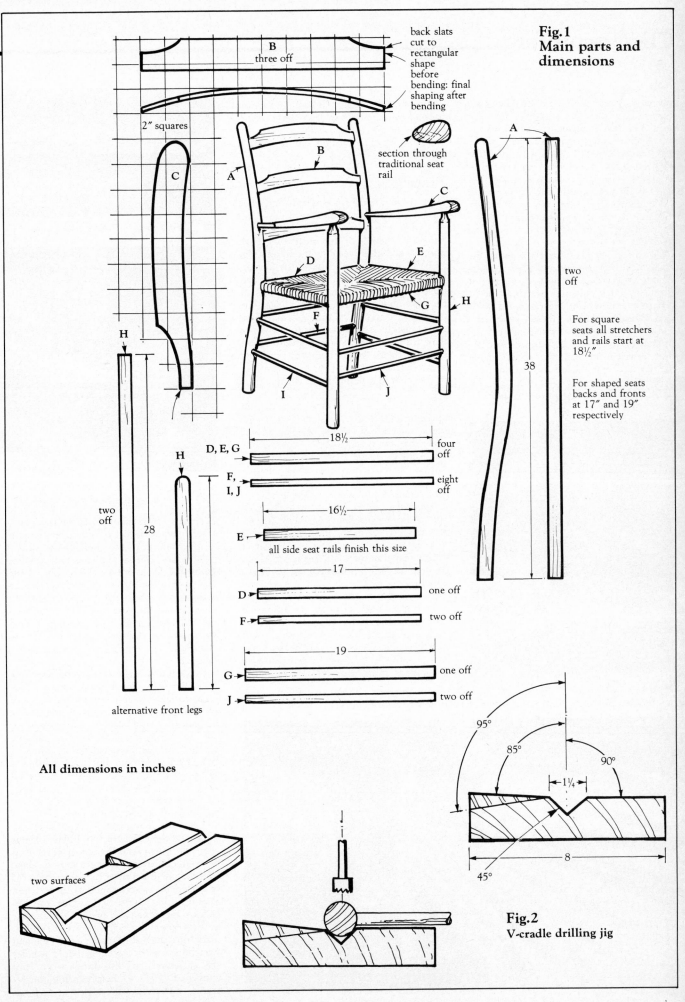

Fig. 1
Main parts and dimensions

B
three off

back slats cut to rectangular shape before bending: final shaping after bending

2" squares

section through traditional seat rail

A

two off

38

For square seats all stretchers and rails start at 18½"

For shaped seats backs and fronts at 17" and 19" respectively

C

A

B

C

D

E

G

F

H

I

J

H

H

two off

28

alternative front legs

D, E, G
18½
four off

F,
I, J
eight off

E
16½
all side seat rails finish this size

D
17
one off

F
two off

G
19
one off

J
two off

All dimensions in inches

two surfaces

Fig. 2
V-cradle drilling jig

95°

85°

90°

1¼

45°

8

Clissett comfort

You need four seat rails and eight stretchers. Seat rails are 1in diameter, reduced to ¾in at each end for jointing; stretchers are ¾in diameter reducing to ½in at the ends. For a square-seat chair, cut all rails and stretchers 18½in long at first; the two side seat rails are cut back later to 16½in in length, because at seat level the chair is shorter front to back than side to side. Side stretchers are individually adjusted for length to take account of the backward splay of the leg portion of the back upright (fig. 3).

For a seat wider at the front than at the back, make side seat rails and side stretchers exactly as described for the square seat. But front and back rails and stretchers are of different lengths, 19in at front and 17in at back. You can make all these components and their jointing tenons with rotary planes, or lathe-turn them. In traditional construction, however, the seat rails would not have been turned, but shaped with a drawknife to a roughly egg-shaped section (fig. 1), much stronger and claimed to hold the woven seat better.

● **Above**, where it all begins. Part-finished components are allowed to season before use. **Below**, a rotary plane used on the rails and stretchers

For the arms you'll need two pieces of 3x1in ash, each about 19in long, and for the back slats three pieces 2¼x¼in. Be generous with the length to begin with to allow for the bending and jointing; about 20in is suitable.

Preparation

Start by making the parts to be bent so they can be left on their formers to dry out and set while you work on the other components. Round or turn the two back uprights and after steaming them for about an hour, put them quickly on the former, bend them to shape with G-clamps and leave them to set. Steam the three back slats for only about 15 minutes — longer and they distort across the grain — and bend them quickly, one on top of the other, in their former. Don't shape the slats before bending them, keep them full size and square-edged until later. They'll take four or five days in a warm, dry environment to dry.

Meanwhile round or turn the two front uprights and all the rails and stretchers. Mark out and saw a pair of arms, to size using the arm pattern (fig. 1), then shape and smooth using a spokeshave and a scraper. Keep the joint ends a full ¾in for a tight fit with the back upright later. Aim to get a 'comfortable' shape to the arms.

Remove from the former the three back slats and draw the shape on them (fig. 1). Saw close to the line and finish to a rounded edge all round with a spokeshave. The slight wedge shape at each end ensures a close, gap-free fit when jointed into the back uprights.

Remove the two back uprights from the former and mark out the positions for drilling socket holes (fig. 3). Begin by marking the position of seat rail and stretcher holes ACROSS the back of the chair. Do this by marking to a centre line on their inside facing surfaces. Mark similar

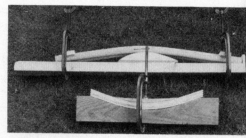

● The formers for the chairback and legs

● Drilling socket holes on the pillar drill with the component held in the V-cradle

positions across the front uprights on their inside facing surfaces. Whatever the seat shape, these holes are all drilled at 90°.

Now you can assemble, as two separate parts, the back and front sections of the chair; this simplifies the next stage of drilling, especially the angled drilling to provide for the seat wider at front than back. These socket holes are best drilled with a saw-tooth Forstner-type bit, drilling each hole to a depth of ¾in on a V-cradle (fig. 2).

Mark out and cut the slots for the three back slats on the inside facing surface of the back uprights; to allow for the curvature of the slats, these slots aren't on the centre line but located just behind it. A series of adjacent holes (chain drilling) followed by careful work with a sharp chisel is one way of cutting these slots, but you could use a slot mortiser or a router. These slots should be 1½in long, round-ended and ⅝in deep. Try each slat for fit and adjust individually as necessary to give a neat joint.

Assemble the seat rails, stretchers and slats into their appropriate holes without glue, checking that back and front sections to together correctly and are square. Make sure that all joints enter fully into the holes or slots made to accommodate them. If you assemble them on a flat surface you can check for twisting and proper alignment.

With front and back sections assembled, mark out the positions of side rails and stretchers to joint them together. The holes are staggered so the uprights are not weakened. Drill as before using the V-cradle, but check the angles to give the

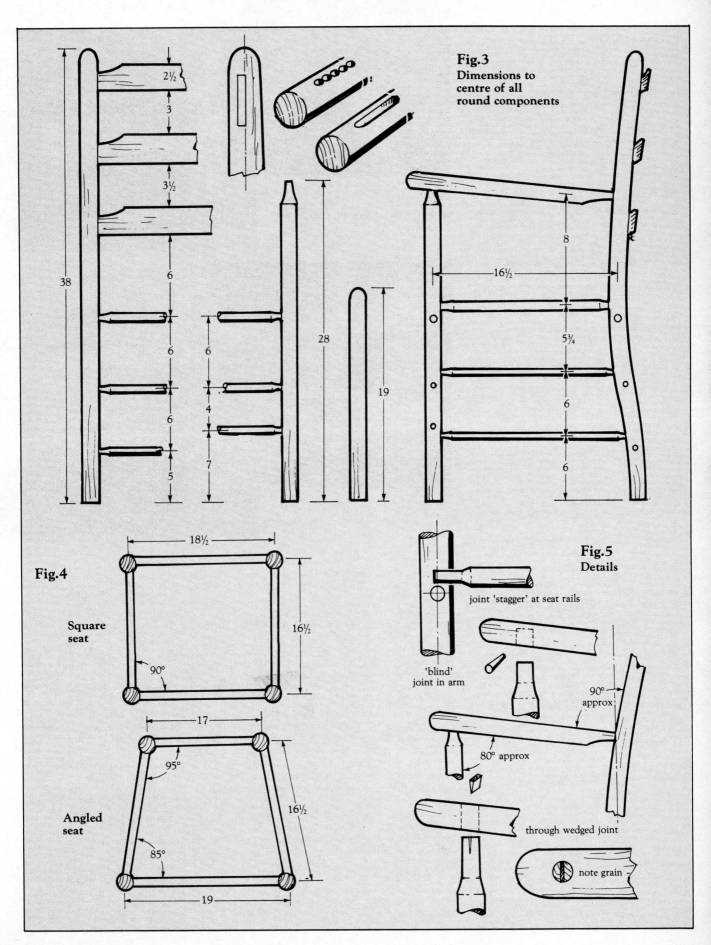

Fig.3
Dimensions to
centre of all
round components

2½
3
3½
6
6
6
5
38
6
4
7
28
19

8
16½
5¾
6
6

Fig.4

18½
Square seat
16½
90°

17
Angled seat
95°
16½
85°
19

Fig.5
Details

joint 'stagger' at seat rails

'blind' joint in arm

90° approx

80° approx

through wedged joint

note grain

Clissett comfort

correct seat shape. For the square seat, all are at 90° but for the shaped seat the holes in the back uprights angle OUT at 95° while those in the front uprights angle IN at 85° (fig. 4).

Now fit the side seat rails to their full depth. With the partly completed chair lying on its side on a flat floor ascertain how long the side stretchers should be. Fit the side stretchers, stand the chair on its four feet, and check that all goes together square and fair.

Arms

While it's all together mark the position of the arm socket holes in the two uprights; these are drilled at an upward angle for the square-seated chair and at an upward and an outward angle (a compound angle) for the shaped seat. Take the chair apart and drill these holes, ¾in diameter, ⅞in deep (fig. 5). Check carefully and make sure you drill correctly and end up with a left-hand and a right-hand arm socket and not two of the same. It happens!

Fully assemble the chair again, checking in particular that side rails and stretchers are fully home in their sockets. Then measure precisely the distance between the front face of each back upright at the hole position just drilled and the centre of the top of each front upright. Add a full ¼in to this measurement for the joint and, on the underside of the arm, use this measurement to locate the position of the socket for the uprising front upright. Note that the 1in holes at this point are also angled and take care not to drill through the arm.

The blind joint method used here is relatively simple and substantial enough if you peg it. Traditionally, however, the joint would have been a through joint, wedged from the top and not pegged, but for this some subtle changes and careful marking out are required. The front upright needs to be about 1in longer to pass right through the arm. You should drill from the top surface of the arm to avoid break-out, so you need to mark the socket positions on the arm top surfaces; this is tricky because of the angle of the arm. You also have to be careful with the saw-cut across the top of the uprights for the wedge which tightens the joint. Make this cut so the wedge lies ACROSS the grain of the arm — if it is in line with the grain, the arm will split as the wedge tightens (fig. 5).

Whatever method you use, fit the arms by entering their ends into the respective sockets in the back uprights before bringing the arm down on to its appropriate front upright.

Assembly

If all component lengths, socket hole positions, sizes, depths and angles are correct the chair should go together satisfactorily on a dry run. If it doesn't, then one or more are wrong and some adjustment will be needed. The chair has a certain amount of inherent flexibility and minor

● **Left**, spokeshaving an arm

● **Right**, dry-fitting an arm to the assembled chair

● **Left**, starting the seat with seagrass cord

● **Right**, the seat almost complete

errors can usually be accommodated. Dry runs are needed until everything is correct and ready for finishing and final assembly.

Before gluing clean up all components with a scraper or fine grade glass paper; this is easier on the separate components than on the assembled chair. It's also easier to apply a coat of sanding sealer at this stage, but avoid getting this on or in the jointing areas as this will inhibit the glue. After a further light sanding the chair can be glued up and assembled.

Begin with the back and front sections. Put glue in the socket holes and bring the parts together, using protected cramps if necessary or a soft mallet to ensure all joints are fully home. Check that both sections are out of twist and square (lay them on a flat surface again) then add the side rails and stretchers and finally the arms. Remove any glue squeezed from joints before it dries. For wedged joints put glue in the hole and make sure the top of the upright goes right through. Fit the wedge right away and tap down with a hammer; leave the protruding stub and wedge until the glue is set, then clean off flush with the arm with a sharp chisel. Give a final finish of wax polish to the chair, preferably after you've woven the seat.

The proper seat for this chair would be English rush (*Scirpus lacustris*) but this has become very expensive and not everyone can obtain it easily. Other species of rush may be used but all rush has to be worked moist and it requires some expertise, especially the twisting and knotting required. An easier and cheaper alternative is to use seagrass cord, a natural ready-twisted material stocked by most craft shops. A chair like this takes just over 2lbs of cord, and at less than £1 a pound it's worth considering. Full details of how to weave a rush seat can be found in my book *Practical Country Crafts*, published by David & Charles. ■

● See Jack in action at the BRISTOL WOODWORKER SHOW 15-17 May.

MAKING CHAIRS IN THE OPEN AIR

Jack himself and **Mike Abbott** (WW/Jan) will be running a **three-day course** on country crafts in the Forest of Dean, 31 July-2 Aug. You must be there from the Thursday evening, 30 July, and the cost will be £90 for three days' tuition. More details from the **Guild of Woodworkers** — see 'Guild notes'.

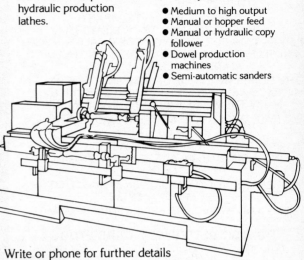

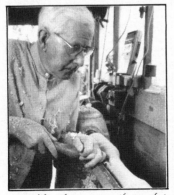

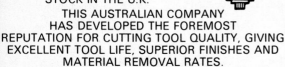

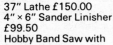

TABWELL TOOLS

TEL: 062 981 4681

TEL: 062 981 3885

BRIDGE STREET, BAKEWELL, DERBYSHIRE

WOODWORKING VICES
Record 52½ED, 9″	£44.81
Record 53E, 10½″	£69.95
Record 52ED, 7″	£34.80
Record 52E 7″	£32.00
Record 52P	£25.00

RECORD 'G' CRAMPS (120)
4″	£5.25/£10 pair
6″	£7.50/£14 pair
8″	£11.00/£21 pair
10″	£15.00/£28 pair

SPEED CRAMPS (132 SERIES)
12″	£9.50	32″	£12.53
16″	£9.90	40″	£14.19
20″	£10.55	60″	£17.50
24″	£11.20		

SASH CRAMPS (135 SERIES)
18″	£17.90	32″	£20.00
24″	£18.25	42″	£20.70
30″	£19.00	48″	£21.10

T BAR CRAMPS (136 SERIES)
42″	£36.10	66″	£40.36
48″	£36.49	78″	£47.82
54″	£37.00	Extension	£29.00

MISCELLANEOUS CRAMPS
M130 Cramp Heads	£10.40
MFC153 Floorboard Cramp	£54.00
M145 Holdfast	£12.90
M146 Holdfast	£14.70
Deep Throat Cramp	£12.50
C129 Cramp	£3.37

RECORD PLANES
No. 03	£19.50	No. 0110	£9.99
No. 04	£17.99	No. 0220	£13.50
No. 04	£18.99	No. 060½	£16.50
No. 05	£21.99	No. 09½	£17.50
No. 05½	£29.50	No. 073	£43.90
No. 06	£33.90	No. 077	£26.50
No. 07	£39.50	New 3 in One	
No. 020C	£72.00		£39.00

ESTWING DELUXE HAMMERS
16oz Vinyl Claw	£16.99
16oz Leather Claw	£16.99
20oz Vinyl Claw	£19.48
20oz Leather Claw	£19.20
24oz Vinyl Claw	£20.99

STANLEY RATCHET BRACES
No. 73 5⅞″	£20.88
No. 73 8″	£20.88
No. 73 10″	£20.88
No. 73 12″	£24.85

STANLEY PLANES
No. 75	£6.50	No. 71	£27.00
No. 90J	£10.90	No. 271	£5.99
No. 92	£22.05	No. 78	£18.00
No. 93	£26.40	No. 10½	£31.50

MARPLES BEVEL OR FIRMER CHISEL BITS
Ash set of 3	£10.95
Ash set of 4	£13.00
Blue Chip set of 3	£12.57
Blue Chip set of 4	£15.99
Blue Chip set of 5	£19.99
Splitproof set of 3	£18.05
Splitproof set of 4	£22.05
Splitproof set of 5	£26.95
Boxwood set of 5	£33.15
Blue Ribbon set of 4	£10.87

WOLFCRAFT DRILL STANDS
3403 Heavy Duty Free Vice	£29.95
4000 Super Duty	£39.95
5005 Electronic Workshop	£229.00
5120 Compass Drill Stand	£50.00

HENRY TAYLOR TURNING SETS
TT3 set	£17.00	TTS set	£28.00
TT8 set	£45.00	Superfive	£18.00
Superflute Gouge	£23.00		

MARPLES CARVING SETS
M153A Orbital	£10.99
M153	£23.39
M152	£32.40
M60	£71.99
M60A	£37.50

NICHOLSON'S RASPS (HALF ROUND)
8″	£3.67	10″	£4.65	12″	£6.35

RIDGWAY POWER EXPANSIVE BITS
⅞″ to 2″ Heavy Duty	£25.00
1⅞″ to 3⅛″ Heavy Duty	£29.00

SANDERSON PAX SAWS
20 × 10TPI	£21.29
22 × 6TPI	£22.14
22 × 8TPI	£22.14
22 × 10TPI	£22.14
24 × 6TPI	£22.90
26 × 6TPI	£23.93
26 × 8TPI	£23.93
26 × 5½TPI	£23.93
8 × 19TPI	£18.70
10 × 14TPI	£19.06
12 × 12TPI	£20.00
14 × 14TPI	£20.30
8 × 20 TPI	£21.25

NOBEX SAWS
Nobex 202 'Pro'	£74.95
Nobex 303	£54.00

DREMEL MINI POWER TOOLS
238 Motoflex	£68.00
338 Variable Speed Motoflex	£74.00
258 Mototool	£42.00
318 Suppressed Mototool	£44.50
328 Variable Supp. Mototool	£54.00
358 Variable Speed Mototool	£48.00
3235-328 in kit	£63.00
292 Engraver	£14.00
292 Drill Press	£22.50
228 Deluxe Router Attachment	£16.00
229 Router Attachment	£10.50
576 Motoshop Scroll Saw	£68.00
588 4″ Tilt Table Saw	£95.00
708 Motolathe	£48.00
709 Deluxe Motolathe	£63.00
738 Belt and Disc Sander	£85.00

SCANSLIB WETSTONES
Scanslib 150	£69.00
Scanslib 200	£88.00
Scanslib 300	£275.00

LATHES
Coronet No. 1 2ft.	£237.00
Coronet No. 1 3ft.	£256.00
Coronet No. 1 4ft.	£284.00
4ft. Conversion	£69.00
Bowl Turning Kit	£39.95
Coronet Elf	£369.00
Coronet Major	£590.00
Arundel K450	£369.00
Arundel K450 H.D.	£395.00
Arundel K600	£449.00
Luna Minimax T100	P.O.A.
Elektra HDM1000	P.O.A.
Elu DB180	£331.00

BANDSAWS
Burgess BK3 Plus	£115.00
DeWalt 100	£148.00
DeWalt 3401	£273.00
DeWalt 3501	£281.00
Minimax P32	P.O.A.
Minimax 545	£660.00
Lunabs 320	£369.00
Elektra BAS315	£299.00
Elektra BAS450	£599.00

FULL RANGE OF KITY MACHINES IN STOCK PRICES ON APPLICATION

PLANER THICKNESSERS
DeWalt 1151	P.O.A.
DeWalt Mortice Att.	£69.00
Elektra 10″ × 6″	£490.00
Ryobi Surfacer	£395.00
Luna HM31	£1399.00

RADIAL ARM SAWS
Ryobi 10″	£375.00
DeWalt 1251	£422.00
DeWalt 1501	£496.00
DeWalt 1751	£570.00

SAWBENCHES
Elu TGS 171/172	P.O.A.
Elektra Site Saw	£189.00
Elektra Deluxe	£549.00
Stirling Portable 10″ Rise & Fall	£99.95

BENCH GRINDERS
Skil 115mm	£41.50
Wolf 200mm	£169.00
Elu EDS163	£73.50
Elu EDS164	£77.50
Kiruna 11″	£118.00
Kiruna 14″	£185.00

BELT SANDERS
Ryobi 3″	£110.00
Ryobi 4″	£142.00
Skil 3″	£59.95
Skil 4″	£140.00
Elu MHB157E	£119.95
Elu MHB90	£193.95

HAND ROUTERS
Ryobi R150 ¼″	£77.00
Ryobi R500 ½″	£132.00
Elu MOF96	£98.50
Elu MOF96E	£119.00
Elu MOF177	P.O.A.
Elu MOF177E	P.O.A.
Bosch POF52	£59.00

CIRCULAR SAWS
Skil 1850 6″	£67.00
Skil 1865 7¼″	£69.95
Skil 1873 8″	£140.00
Skil 1886 9¼″	£152.00
Skil 1899 10¼″	£156.00
Elu MH182 8¼″	£148.50
Elu DS140 Biscuit Jointer	£197.00

ORBITAL SANDERS
Ryobi S500 Palm	£45.00
Ryobi LS35 Pad	£45.00
Ryobi NS40 Dust Bag	£66.00
Ryobi SU6200A Pad	£86.00
Elu MVS156	£73.50
Elu MVS147	£123.50
Elu MVS94	£111.50

MORTICERS
Smiths Floor Mounted	£549.00
Smiths Bench Mounted	£399.00
Ryobi Portable	£395.00
Ridgway Stand Plus Free Drill	£169.00

JIGSAWS (20% OFF ALL BLADES)
Elu ST142	£101.00
Elu ST142E	£109.50
Elu ST152	£98.00
Elu ST152E	£106.50
Bosch 1581	£105.00
Bosch 1581.7	£112.00
Ryobi JS60	£84.00
Ryobi JS60E	£98.00

RYOBI SABRE (Reciprocating) SAWS
RJ100V (Variable Speed)	£125.00
RJ102 2 Speed	£128.00

MITRE TABLE SAWS
Elu PS174	P.O.A.
Ryobi TS250M	£216.00
Ryobi TS251M	£235.00

PLANERS (K=KITBOX)
Elu MFF80	£109.00
Elu MFF40	£189.00
Elu MFF80K	£127.50
Ryobi L400A 4⅞″	£144.00
Ryobi L22LN 3″	£110.00
Ryobi L1323 3¼″	£86.00
Ryobi L120N 3⅝″	£77.00

Hands on

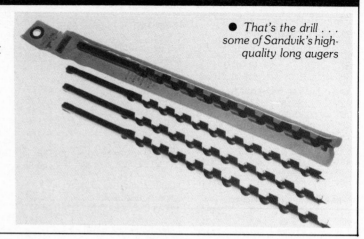

WOODWORKING WHEEZE *of the* **month**

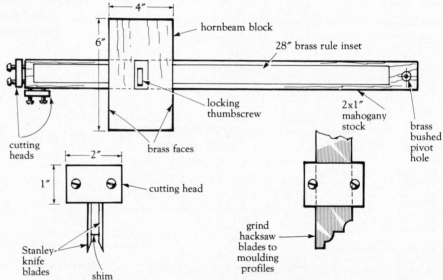

hornbeam block

6" 4"

28" brass rule inset

locking thumbscrew

cutting heads

brass faces

2" 1"

1" cutting head

2x1" mahogany stock

brass bushed pivot hole

Stanley-knife blades

shim

grind hacksaw blades to moulding profiles

Sandvik winner

Multi-gauge

I'm a beginner to woodworking, but decided to make a tool to cut inlay, banding, grooves, etc. The 'head' is a 6x4in block of hornbeam with a central mortise lined with steel to keep it true; the 'stock' is 2x1in mahogany with a brass rule inset in a routed groove. Steel plates at the end of the stock are screwed into threaded inserts set in the end; they sandwich the cutters securely. The block screws down to the stock with a thumbscrew from an old plane.

The end cutting head carries two Stanley blades, shimmed apart to a maximum of 10mm, with a hagstooth behind to lift waste. The edge cutting head carries steel scribe pins for marking; at the other end of the stock is a brass-bushed hole for pivoting, to draw — and cut — circles up to rather more than 56in diameter. Both faces of the block are lined with $\frac{1}{16}$in brass. Using the tool like a scratch-stock I can mark, cut veneers, inlay, crossband and create inlay patterns; I can also use it as a T-square, ruler, mortise gauge, compass cutter, straight-edge — and of course, a scratch-stock! I have made a number of different cutters and hagstooths. It cost me 80p and took a few hours to make.

Graham Smith, Port Talbot

Silicone saw

Give your handsaw-blades a spray of silicone furniture polish to keep the damp off and make them cut a real treat.

W. Lane, Axminster

Dust catcher

Drilling holes in walls where you want to minimise dust and clearing-up, tape an open envelope to the wall below where you drill. It won't catch it all, but it will take care of those nasty little piles and the spread of fine dust.

L. A. Ford, Prescot

Saw sharpener

Not the teeth, but the vertical back end of the blade underneath the handle. Sharpen it up and you always have an edge to use for your pencils, wedges, whatever — close to hand.

P. R. Lay, Saltburn

Hand-tool tenons

A good way of ensuring uniform tenon thickness and flatness across the face if you don't use power tools or machinery is to cut all the pieces 1-1½in overlength, and mark and cut to depth the shoulder line and the line at the far end of the tenon. Make a couple of saw-cuts to depth between the shoulder line and the far line, then clamp all the pieces together on the bench with the shoulder lines lined up and work across them with a hand router. The uncut waste at the far end supports the outside edge of the router.

Peter Tonks, Bromsgrove

Tyre holdall

An ideal (and cheap!) holdall for carpenter's tools, drills, bits and pieces can be made by cutting an oval section out of an old inner-tube from a car tyre. The natural curve of the tube means you don't have to worry about shaping, and you can cut handle holes as well. It's as strong as an ox.

Jim Rodwell, Elgin

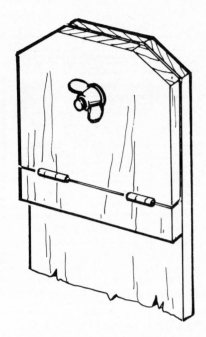

HOW TO DO IT

We want to publish as many wheezes as possible, so we must use only the barest bones of the ideas. Be as precise and brief as possible; type your words if you can, double-spaced on one side of an A4 sheet; make drawings, if any, as few and as clear as you can, and annotate them clearly.

Saw-blade vice

To hold circular saw-blades easily when you're sharpening or dressing them, hinge a piece of board — ply, softwood, blockboard, anything will do — to a batten fixed to a backboard of the same material. The corners of both should be cut off so as not to impede the circumference of the blade. Drill for the wing-nut and bolt to hold the blade and boards together; the hole should be about 1in less than the blade radius down from the top — ie, drill 4in down if you use 10in blades. Clamp it all up and hold it in your bench vice.

Ian Knapper (14yrs), Stoke

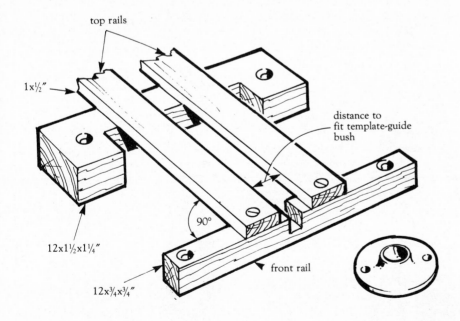

Housing jig

This simple router jig is very good for housing joints, used in conjunction with a router and template guide. Set the top rails apart just enough to let the template guide slide closely between them, and screw them to the bottom rails so the bookcase uprights

(or whatever your job is) will fit closely between them. Pass the cutter through the front rail so you can line up your marks accurately with the line of cut. The bottom rails are screwed to the bench, and the job itself should also be clamped down.

D. G. Farr, Usk, Gwent

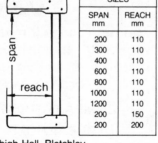

TRICKS OF THE TRADE FROM THE EXPERTS

Use Nitromors Varnish Remover. Its special formula "crystallises" varnish, makes less mess and lessens the danger of scraping damage.

Remove the varnish with a nylon pot scourer – which works better on rounded surfaces and is kind to your wood.

Get a smooth finish by wiping down with a fine gauge wire wool soaked in methylated spirit. You can re-varnish or french polish almost immediately.

VARNISH REMOVAL.

NITROMORS®
PREPARE FOR THE PERFECT FINISH.

The Turning Point

A new centre in the South East for all your
WOODTURNING SUPPLIES

We stock:
Lathes by TYME MACHINES together with accessories.
A comprehensive range of quality tools from HENRY TAYLOR TOOLS and ROBERT SORBY LTD.
A wide selection of products from CRAFT SUPPLIES LTD.
And a choice of nearly 50 different timbers from low-cost beginners wood to exotic types.

WOODTURNING DEMONSTRATIONS are held periodically; call us on the number below for details.

BRITISH GATES & TIMBER LTD., BIDDENDEN, NR. ASHFORD, KENT TN27 8DD. 0580 291555

Introductory OFFER - SS20" Scroll/Jigsaw

COMPLETE WITH LEG STAND
Value for Money features include:
- 20" throat, 23" x 14" cast alloy table.
- Left & right 45° tilt.
- 2-speeds for correct cutting of wood, plastic and non-ferrous metal.
- Fully adjustable arm takes almost any length of blade inc. fret and copping.
- Cast-iron supports for cast alloy arms.

£242
incl. carriage
UK mainland

To order: post cheque or telephone with Access or Visa Card number.

asles
VINEYARD RD., WELLINGTON, TELFORD, SHROPS.
0952 — 48054
Open Mon.-Fri. 8.30-5.30
Sat. 8.30-3.30

CREATIVE WOODCRAFTS LTD.
EVERYTHING FOR THE CRAFTSMAN UNDER ONE ROOF

Telephone: Langley Mill (0773) 760129

PRICES FROM
£1795 + VAT

- -

PLEASE SEND DETAILS ON:
VAMAC

NAME ....

ADDRESS ....

....

.... POST CODE ....

To: VAMAC (UK) Ltd., Stanley Works, Eyam, Nr. Sheffield S30 1QX. Tel: (0433) 31888

NORMAL OPENING: Monday-Friday 9-5.30. Saturday 9-4.00.

VAMAC

The new fantastic value for money wood-working machines. Compare these features, then compare the prices and the only answer is VAMAC.

COMPARE THESE FEATURES
- ★ FOUR MOTORS
- ★ 1500mm LONG PLANER TABLES FOR STRAIGHTENING TIMBER
- ★ 3 KNIFE PLANER BLOCK FOR BETTER FINISH.
- ★ MACHINE SPLITS IN TWO HALVES TO GO THROUGH 2'6" WIDE DOOR
- ★ HANDWHEEL RISE & FALL & TILT ON SAW
- ★ PRICE INCLUDES SLIDING TABLE
- ★ ALL CAST TABLES

NEW FEATURES
- ★ CAST IRON SPINDLE GUARD
- ★ CAST IRON PLANER FENCE
- ★ MULTIPOSITION SAW FENCE

12" PLANER MODEL FROM **£2,290** + VAT

10" PLANER MODEL FROM **£1,795** + VAT

Question box

Our panel of experts solve your woodworking problems

We will try to answer any questions you can throw at us, but the ones we publish are the ones of most general interest to readers.

Please type your question double-spaced with generous margins, and include a stamped self-addressed envelope. Send it to: Question Box, Woodworker, 1 Golden Sq., London W1R 3AB.

Laying parquet flooring

Q *I want to lay a floor of strip T&G chestnut parquet on a concrete sub-floor. Can you advise me on secret nailing, clamping and the spacing of the battens? The flooring is in pieces 0.6-1m long, and all 70x24mm, tongued and grooved.*

J. F. Quail, Dordogne, France

A Your battens should be, say, 50x50 mm, rather than 25x50mm, and be spaced at about 450mm centres. The extra 25mm will allow for greater ventilation, which is paramount under a wood floor. Also, I would suggest a PVC membrane (500 gauge) — or a thick coat of bitumen — to cover the whole area, with the battens or bearers laid and fixed on it. As the flooring strips are tongued and grooved all round, cross-bearers aren't necessary; they would impede ventilation anyway. And the cross joints can of course come anywhere; they don't have to line up.

Once you've laid the membrane and bearers, think about the service-lines you'll need (gas, electricity or water). Lifting a T&G board, secretly-nailed, is by no means a pleasant job; the tongues have to be sawn through — that's if all the nails are well driven home!

Ordinary T&G flooring can be cramped in, say, groups of five boards at a time, and then nailed along the tongue edge through the surface (fig. 1). Secret-nailed boards can't be cramped; they are nailed singly (fig. 2). If a board is distorted, it can be chisel-cramped (fig. 3). The last board or two can be cramped off the wall.

It used to be practice to leave an 18mm or so clearance along each side of the floor, to allow for expansion; the skirtings would then cover the gap. But the merits were doubtful; if the outer boards are going to 'slide' this distance, what's happening to the nailing!

Setting-out is merely a matter of positioning the bearers; just start at one side of the room, and work through. If the final spacing is greater than the 450mm, just slip in an extra bearer.

Stan Thomas

● Stan Thomas is a joiner of vast experience who holds live 'Question box' and 'tool hospital' at Woodworker Shows.

Pie-crust edging

Q *I'd like to make an 18th century pie-crust table and intend to glue the edging blanks to the flat table before working the edge. How should I go about it?*

R. Robinson, Beeston, Nottingham

A Visit the nearest museum of furniture and get to see 18th century piecrust tables in general, and little tray-top tripod tables in particular. Make a series of well-detailed pencil sketches. Note how although tables of this period have all manner of scoop- and scallop-edge profiles, most of them are quartered and then set out, so that there are a total of eight edge hollows or 'bites'.

Once you appreciate all the tool, technique and material implications of the project, settle on the form and size of the table top — easiest to go for a small mahogany disc top about 12in diameter. Check your blank for faults; it needs to be free from splits, knots and stains. Screw a waster to the lathe face-plate and screw-mount the blank to the waster. Lower and waste the centre of the disc until you are left with a thin level central area and a thickish rim.

Once you have turned off a small disc-like tray, start setting out the pie-crust profile. Decide on the size and character of the edge repeat, and make a card template. Once you've worked the template to fit, go round the edge of the turned tray with a pencil, and establish the various 'ins' and 'outs'. Take a coping saw and clear away the main areas of waste.

You should now have a tray with eight equally-spaced bites taken out of the edge. Take a pencil and establish the beautiful and characteristic parallel-edge beads — you could use a scratch-stock or even a pencil-and-block. When you've set out the edging, take your gouges and start shaping the hollows. There's no easy way to carve the edge profile, just try to relate to the grain wherever possible, meaning work both with, and across the grain until you've achieved a good beaded and mitred moulding. Finally rub the work down with graded glasspaper and polish or varnish to a good finish.

Alan Bridgewater

● Alan Bridgewater is a multi-skilled craftsman and author.

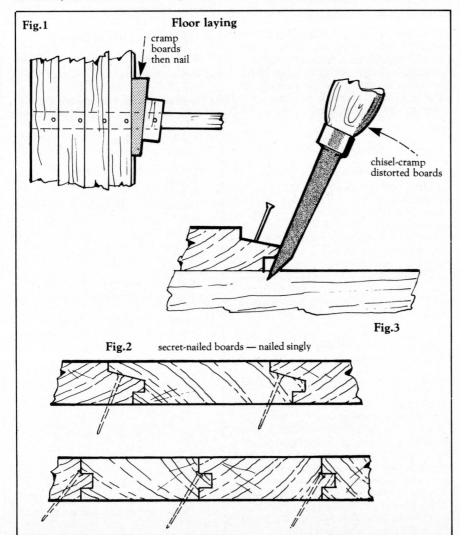

Fig.1 Floor laying

cramp boards then nail

chisel-cramp distorted boards

Fig.3

Fig.2 secret-nailed boards — nailed singly

Guild notes

Guild of WOODWORKERS

The Guild was set up by *Woodworker* to create a meeting ground for all those involved in working wood, whether professional, amateur, or enthusiastic beginner. Guild members get:

- Access to Guild courses and events
- Free publicity in *Woodworker*
- Specially arranged tool insurance at low rates
- 15% off Woodworker Show entry
- A free display area and meeting point at the Show
- 15% discount off *Woodworker* plans
- Inclusion in our register of members' skills and services

For details, please send an sae to the Guild of Woodworkers, 1 Golden Sq, London W1R 3AB.

Country chairmaking with Jack Hill

26-29 May, Dartington, Devon, £141 inc. VAT.
A fully residential course (three nights' accommodation, all meals and light refreshments) introducing traditional chairmaking.
● Full details direct from Rick James, The Old Postern, Dartington, Totnes, Devon, TQ9 6EA, quoting ref. NC3 — **not from the Guild.**

Power Routing — Roy Sutton

13th June, 10-5, Herne Bay, Kent, £25+ VAT.
Roy is an expert on this subject. Starting from first principles, he covers housing, grooving, rebating, straight and circular moulding, tenoning, mortising, and rule-joint and template work; he also deals with designing and setting up your own jigs.

Rudiments of restoration — Barry Honeyborne

2-3 July, Leominster, Herefordshire, £54.
Bring along your antique and learn how to restore it. From initial cleaning to repairs and final polishing, Barry will show you all the steps — he has been 25 years in the trade. This two day course is an introduction to every aspect of restoration, plus a chance to make a start on your own piece under expert supervision.

GUILD COURSES

● Only Guild members are eligible to go on these courses. You must book in advance, and we must have a cheque for the full cost of the course at the time of booking. If you cancel less than four weeks before the advertised date you will forfeit 50% of the cost, unless there are exceptional circumstances.

French polishing — Ian Hosker

18-19 July, 10-5, Chester, £50.
One of our most popular course subjects, led by Ian, a teacher and a practising professional. It covers preparation of old and new pieces, staining and colouring techniques, grain filling, shellac finishes, fadding, bodying in, spiriting off and giving new life to existing polished surfaces. The fee includes course materials. Ian will make up a polishing kit to take away at £9.50 if you order in advance.

Decorative techniques — Ian Hosker

12-13 September, 10-5, Chester, £55.
Another chance to learn all sorts of wonderful decorative techniques, including dragging, lining, sponging, rag-rolling, marbling, spattering and tortoiseshelling. The fee includes materials, but bring a few paintbrushes and jam-jars.

French polishing — Charles Cliffe

17-18 September, Bexleyheath, £45.
These courses by expert Charles Cliffe are among the most popular run by the Guild, so book early to avoid disappointment. You'll learn about preparation, staining and techniques of french polishing itself, with ample hands-on experience under Charles' eye. You'll learn the correct way to sharpen a cabinet scraper, so bring yours along, and he's willing to offer advice on any small piece of furniture you want to refinish.

Basic woodcarving — Eric Ingham

NEW

19-20 September, 9.30-5.30, Lytham St Annes, £50.
We're pleased to be able to offer this introduction to woodcarving. On this course you'll learn about use of tools and sharpening, types of wood, design and finishing. Eric's been carving for 15 years and will give you a good start. Wood is provided and you're free to carve whatever you want. Bring carving tools if you have them. There's plenty of accommodation in this resort area and your spouse might enjoy the sea air while you learn.

NEW   NEW   NEW
Green wood working — Mike Abbot and Jack Hill

30 July-2 August, Forest of Dean, £90. Learn and practise some traditional woodland crafts in a woodland setting in the Forest of Dean, Glos. Cleaving, shaving and turning with and without machinery; chair bodging, stool making, steam bending, seat weaving; rake making, stick making, spoon carving, etc. You've seen Mike and Jack at Woodworker Shows — they're at Bristol too — and if you've fancied having a go, now's your chance.

Group accommodation is being arranged at a very reasonable price, though you can make your own arrangements if you wish. Think about bringing your spouse, for there's lots to do in this delightful scenic area.

The course begins with an introductory session in the evening of 30 July, followed by three full workshop days; a small individual charge will be made for materials used.

BOOKING FORM

I wish to book for the following course(s).

☐ **Power routing** 13 June, £25+VAT = £28.75

☐ **Rudiments of restoration** 2-3 July, £54; make cheque payable to Barry Honeyborne

☐ **French polishing** 18-19 July, £50; make cheque payable to Ian Hosker.

☐ **Green wood working** 30 July-2 August, £90; make cheque payable to Jack Hill

☐ **Decorative techniques** 12-13 September, £55; make cheque payable to Ian Hosker

☐ **French polishing** 17-18 September, £45; make cheque payable to Charles Cliffe

☐ **Basic woodcarving** 19-20 September, £50; make cheque payable to Eric Ingham

Please make cheques payable to 'The Guild of Woodworkers/ASP Ltd' unless otherwise stated.

Name...

Address...

....

....

Guild no..
Send to: The Guild of Woodworkers, 1 Golden Square, London, W1R 3AB.
The Guild reserves the right to cancel any course.

The carver of York

Woodcarver Trevor Rooney, who cut his artistic teeth on the timber and stone of York's great Minster, will be demonstrating at the Bristol Woodworker Show. Here's his wife Jayne's introduction

For the inhabitants of York, the Minster is a familiar and much loved sight. So familiar, in fact, that it's possible to forget just what an awe-inspiring structure it is, and what an abundance of superb craftsmanship it displays. Like most York people, Trevor Rooney had rather taken the Minster for granted, until he started his apprenticeship as a stone and woodcarver there in 1974. The restoration and maintenance work is almost continual, and of course since the fire in the South Transept in July 1984, there has been great scope for craft carvers with an artistic flair.

● **Above**, *a predatory owl with its mouse prey – in stained lime;* **below**, *wrens in springtime, carved in English walnut*

● **Left**, *a limestone grotesque, carved by Trevor during his time at York Minster*

After a month cutting back lumps of oak and stone to straight lines, Trevor realised he truly had the carving bug. His five-year apprenticeship over, he stayed on in the Minster stoneyard for another three years; his first 'proper' piece was a stone cherub playing a flute. Other demands made on a carver in such historical work include recreating in fine detail a boss or gargoyle from an original whose features have been all but obscured by centuries of weather and wear. Trevor also got the chance to use his own imagination, producing gargoyles and grotesques with a degree of personal 'artistic licence.' He has carved a number of stone tributes to friends and benefactors of the Minster, whose lifelike busts now adorn a 60ft pinnacle on a buttress of the Chapter House. Trevor specialised in bosses, many of which perished in the 1984 fire; he also did decorative scroll work and lettering — including the 'Push' and 'Pull' signs on the great West doors. There was not as much woodcarving as stonework during Trevor's years — he left before the 1984 fire to start a photographic business — but he maintains that the principles for the two materials are basically the same, and that it's only the grain in the wood that makes the difference.

These days, apart from running the photographic business, Trevor sculpts, teaches and exhibits from his modest York studio, working to private commissions and displaying at Craft Shows. He particularly likes animals and birds, which he carves using taxidermist's specimens as reference. He has energy and confidence, and there are some of us who believe he also has a great future! ■

● Trevor Rooney, 21 Wolfe Ave, Heworth, York YO3 0SF, (0904) 426767.

THE WOODWORK BUSI

The nitty gritty to anyone's living in woodwork —
what will you charge? Hugh O'Neill looks at some
of the ideas, Michael Whitford delivers a
(foolproof?) formula

The combination approach – Hugh O'Neill

Why do you work at woodwork? To many of you it will be a wholly absorbing hobby, and to others a means of supplementing a pension or adding to other income. For a substantial number, of course, it will be a primary source of income. Of course those who regard woodwork as a hobby will also want to make a little money from it, selling at least some of what you make to offset against the rising costs of timbers and tools. We all always want more tools and machines, costs which are often difficult to justify if they have to be taken out of the household budget. Even as a total amateur, once in a while you are going to be asked if you would sell one or other of your pieces. So sooner or later, we're all going to be faced with the same very basic question: 'How do you fix price?'

Broadly there are three approaches: Rationally: Randomly: or by Research. It's only a very small proportion of the sale price of a piece of woodwork that actually ends up in the maker's pocket. The very fact that so many craftspeople say they'd be better off in employment indicates that something might be wrong with their marketing or with the quantity/quality of their work. The root cause of the problem is often one of pricing.

The rational approach

Do you consider your craft skills are greater or lesser than the car fixing skills of an average garage mechanic? If you think they're comparable, the rational approach would be to price your output on the basis of materials costs (at retail prices) plus the cost of your time at £20 per hour. This is the London price every time you take your car into even the humblest garage (it may come down to £10 per hour in the less affluent parts of the country). But you meet craftspeople who stand aghast at the idea. 'What! £20 an hour? That's at least £100 per day — over £20,000 a year. You must be joking!'

It's no joke. By the time you have paid for heat, rates, energy, tools, machinery depreciation, telephone, stationery, invoicing, the thousand and one 'petty cash' items, and paid National Insurance and other essentials, there isn't going to be a lot left for a living wage. And you haven't yet paid VAT or income tax!

That figure of £20,000 is also based on the assumption that for at least five hours a day, on most of the days of the year, you have actually been making things you will sell or doing work you'll get paid for. It's taken for granted you will be doing your book-keeping and administration in the evenings and that you will be going out doing your selling after that — certainly most weekends.

What happens is that when we first start we invest time in achieving highest quality. We look at the finished product with pride and work out that it has taken us 16 hours. We know that the market price for a similar

● *Some of Hugh's work; bowls in zebrano. 'Spectacular grain raises the price'*

item would allow about £80 for the labour element, so we price it accordingly — and charge for only four hours. Later we try to justify this with talk of 'Building up a reputation', but the reputation you're most likely to achieve is the one you get from the bankruptcy court. The other reputation you get is for doing 'a really good job at an incredibly low price'. You do get work this way, often a lot of work, but it's not business; it's philanthropy.

Cutting prices, or not pricing a realistic figure for your labour, can only come out of your own pocket. All the overheads remain the same. OK, this way there's less tax to pay, but only because you have made less — a lot less.

Think of any item you make and jot down the materials costs — don't forget glue and screws. How many hours did it take? (If you don't know, you should. Time it next time.) Multiply the hours by £20, as a starting point. Should that spinning wheel actually be priced at £540, that small rosewood dish at £40, that kitchen cabinet at £285? If that's what your calculation has led to, then OK. But if your conclusion is that the figure is unrealistic, you must work out how you can make the article in much less time next time.

Sometimes it's easy both to price rationally, and to sell at that price. Builders' joinery, domestic carpentry and the like can be priced on a 'cost-plus' basis, with sometimes even a margin for adding an extra per cent or two. Perhaps you need more that £20 per hour. But there is another side to the equation. The less significant the aspect of aesthetics — design, finish, and so on — the more important the question of competition becomes. There's little point in trying to charge £275 for an ordinary window frame, even if it is hand made, when an equivalent factory-made unit is available in the area for £198.

It's at this stage that some craftspeople pay too much heed to the competition, and decide that 'people buy on price alone'. They put their product in at a lower price and immediately enter the downward spiral syndrome; more and more work, frequent ulcers, less and less profit. Looking at what the competition is charging is 'research'; pricing solely on the basis of the findings is not 'rational'! Neither is it SELLING. But it is 'rational' to put your price above that of the competition and then positively 'sell' the fact that the goods are higher priced, because they're hand crafted, better quality, or any other distinction you can claim for them.

Research or random?

The true 'research' approach to pricing is first to find out what the buying public is prepared to pay, and then set out to produce to that price and quality, but with the margin you need. Random price fixing is really little more than grabbing a figure out of the air. We look at the finished item and

think: 'Mmm . . . I think I'll charge X for that. This can be fine if you're at the 'arty' end of the business where there's an added aesthetic ingredient. Take that away and you're in for disaster — not covering costs if too low, not selling anything at all if too high.

Actually it's never totally 'random'. The X figure is based on a notion of what went into making the item; a knowledge of what the competition is charging for similar goods; an idea of the margin you require; your own experience of previous sales; and your own feeling for the finished piece. It would be impudent to suggest that John Makepeace's or Ray Key's pricing policies were 'random', but they certainly don't have a wholly rational 'cost-plus' base. Probably, a sensible blend of rational, research and random is the best idea, as long as your work is produced with much the same techniques and time taken for each job is comparatively easy to predict.

A 'test run'

When faced with pricing for my first craft fair I mounted my display 'stand' in my dining room. A number of friends were invited in to help me 'price'. The group included two who regularly visit craft centres, fairs and demonstrations, who also make the occasional purchase. There was a young lady of taste who is setting up a home but who has cash constraints, there was a

craftsman from another field, and a friend who is a works accountant for a small production company. My wife completed the panel. The members came at different times for convenience. Each was given a number of small pieces of paper, on which they wrote what they thought each item should be priced at. The implication was of a secret ballot. If I was asked I told them a little about the rarity and value of a particular piece of raw material.

Then I compared all the prices. I had a fairly clear idea of who had written which slip and I gave weighted credence to what the regular craft viewers had said. (I paid least heed to the over-generous 'statements of support' from my wife!) In deciding on an actual figure I increased some prices and decreased others according to what I felt about the piece — it's quality, design, and the materials value. After all, it would be me who was actually selling them.

What was most interesting was that on some of the items, there was less than 5% variation between all the prices — some times the whole range was higher than I would have fixed myself, even allowing for the 'aesthetic' element. On others there was a huge variation. One piece was valued by the craft viewer wife at £9 while her husband had suggested £35. Items where prices were closest were those of the highest quality finish, larger, and of orthodox design (although aesthetically satisfying).

The discrepancies came where the prices were 'different' and where some natural feature was emphasised — knots, bark, natural edges — where there was some 'character', in other words.

When all was completed it was clear that except for some small pieces, the prices suggested had been higher than I would have reached working on a strictly rational 'cost-plus' basis. But then I had set out to aim at the upper end of the market, deliberately pricing myself above what some of the competition charges in my area.

This left the question of what to do about the small pieces. Should they be put in at cost-plus, or at the recommended panel figures? Some people adopt the idea of 'loss leaders', having a few lower-priced items for the casual and less affluent buyer. Others feel that this actually loses your a few sales of slightly higher-priced items. I tend towards the latter view, particularly as I was trying to present a higher priced, quality image. The final figure for the smalls was nearer to, but not quite, cost-plus. This I justified on the basis that most of the materials involved were scraps and that in future I would work out how to make these items more quickly.

When I get the figures back from the accountant I will know just how rational my 'three-in-one' approach really was!

● Hugh O'Neill is a professional business consultant and craftsman woodturner.

Nailing down the cost — Michael Whitford

Fine-quality workmanship, combined with a high volume of sales or commissions, doesn't necessarily ensure solvency when you translate your craft into a woodworking business. In fact, failure can stem directly from apparent success. The key to this paradox lies in effective cost analysis and planning during the pre-production phase of your project. Care at this stage can turn a losing venture into a profitable business.

A couple of years ago, I had a plum commission for a suspended wall unit which consisted of five vertical slats of ½in perspex with a wall interface of machined lengths of black walnut. The shelves were ¼in plate glass supported by ⅜in perspex dowels let into the verticals. The thing was about 6ft high and close to the Golden Mean in front elevation. The problem was, it weighed a ton. I did all the shear calculations on the suspension screws and applied a safety factor of three. No way was this going to fall down. The fact that the client was into Ming porcelain and other goodies made me double check my calculations: 25 lead wall-inserts with 2½x12 screws into the concrete wall of the apartment building would be more than adequate. The holes in the rails were even counterbored to accept walnut modesty plugs after finishing. A

● A stained pine dresser by Michael lends itself well to batch production

final assembly check on my own garage wall proved the system, and it looked absolutely fabulous.

They say if everything seems to be going your way, you're probably in the wrong lane. I lived at the time in Canada, about 150 miles from the Toronto waterfront apartment that was to house the beast, so naturally, I only wanted to go there once. I planned everything with military precision, even down to two brand-new tungsten carbide drills for the concrete wall, in case I broke one. I also enlisted the help of a local

heavy for the day, as I could forsee lifting problems at the other end, and set off. He was to cost me $120; the entire exercise $800, not including my own labour.

To cut a long and painful story short, we finally managed to elevate all this hardware up to the 16th floor, despite parking problems and the rejection of our plea for use of the priority lift. The lounge that awaited us was like something out of *Architectural Digest*; a fountain played onto a 4ft rock pile, the resulting stream disappearing under the bar. The target wall,

THE WOODWORK BUSINESS

which was finished in $100-a-yard covering, turned out to be good old Gyproc plasterboard on 16in centred studs. The vital concrete wall lay beyond and un-questionably out of reach — contractually out of scope, so to speak. The verticals in the wall unit were conveniently spaced, according to Murphy's Law, at 29in. Thank God the client was on vacation.

I still have 80% of that wall unit; one cannibalised vertical made my wife a fine (but almost invisible) coffee table with a glass, circular top. Many of our friends have walked into it since that abortive mission, but that's another story. What I'm stressing is the need for meticulous planning and its associated cost analysis. One can assume nothing. I had assumed the friend who rode shotgun would do it because he liked me. I had also assumed that the interior designer who gave me the job knew what he was talking about structurally. Luckily I hadn't asked for money up front — which one should always do, by the way; had I done so, I would have been obliged to somehow recess the wall back to the concrete, install the piece and make good the interior finish. And go quietly broke.

Most of my cabinetmaking assignments have not been this harrowing, but I use this example to illustrate how important hidden costs can be when one is trying to make a living in the business. With a less complex assignment, a trestle table, for example, the hidden costs are different, but nevertheless they're still there. You don't actually use all the purchased timber for a piece; a fair amount ends up as sawdust, offcuts and the odd mistake, or as shrapnel from a badly adjusted spindle moulder. The small amount of sealer you needed for that stubborn endgrain would, had you measured it, amounted to quarter of a can. Then there's all that up-front design work, perhaps even a jig or a fixture to make. All these bits and pieces tend to be overlooked if you're in a hurry to deliver. Last but not least, who pays for the workshop electricity, the rent, or that super new gizmo that's been high on your 'wish list' for as long as you can remember?

The baseline

Let's start at the beginning. Over the next 12 months you need to earn a certain number of £ to survive as a human being; forget the workshop at this point. Being human, you may feel that 40 hours in the workshop is enough for anyone with a rudimentary commitment to wife and family. You also need an annual holiday; be generous and allow four weeks, spread whenever. This means you actually work 48x40 hours per year, a paltry 1920. If you divide this into the above value of X, your certain number of £, you end up with your hourly rate, H. If you're some sort of masochist, you could stretch this to 48x60=2880 hours a year, or 52x60=3120 — 60 hours a week every week without a holiday, it's up to you.

The above exercise results in a baseline hourly rate which only *contributes* to the price you ask for your pieces. It is, in fact, your own private money for clothes, food and other delights, nothing whatever to do with your business. The way you take care of your shop is tied up in the following formula:

$$(Mw+Lb) P=S$$

where:

M = Cost of Material
w = Wastage Factor
P = Profit Multiplier
b = 'Burden', or Overhead factor
L = Cost of Labour
S = Selling Price

Cost of Material — M This is the total amount you pay for all the different materials you use to make *one* of your pieces. Wood, adhesives, finishing materials should all be included. Stock consumables, such as glue and stain, are best estimated by monitoring use over several pieces; a £3 tin of glue that makes 20 pieces, for example, has a material cost contribution of 15p per piece. 19½ft of pine at 34p per ft contributes £6.63. And so on. Adding all these individual costs gives the total, M, which should be what it costs you, in materials only, to make one piece.

Wastage Factor — w This factor is introduced to inflate the value of M you have just calculated so you won't lose money through wastage or damage to your materials.

Cabinetmaking entails a large quantity of deliberate and accidental waste; deliberate in such tasks as the selection of grain matches or sizing and jointing stock, and accidental in unplanned events that are aptly termed 'cock-ups'. It varies widely depending on the type of woodworking involved, but this wastage will have to be averaged out over a number of pieces. Factor w can be anything from 1.1 to 1.35, depending on the nature of your product. So increase M by factor w to account for this loss.

Cost of Labour — L In the formula, this is the hourly rate you think you are worth, multiplied by the time it takes to make one piece. In other words, H times to produce. As mentioned earlier, this part ends up in your pocket, ready for the Inland Revenue.

Burden, or Overhead Factor — b Industry calls this little number 'burden', which is a nice way of saying you have to live with it. Getting a handle on this factor is extremely important to the success of your workshop, so the calculation should be done with great care.

Overheads are what you have to spend in order to stay in business. This includes rent, equipment, bank interest, coffee, telephone, heating, insurance and so on. Make a detailed list of all your projected expenditures for the year and divide the total by your value of H discussed earlier. The following simplified example illustrates the point:

Shop rental	£4800
Telephone	£400
Insurance	£150
Heating	£150
Heating	£250
3-year loan (equipment)	£1000
TOTAL	£6600

Hours planned for year = 1920, therefore overheads per hr = divided by 1920 = £3.44.

If you work out of your garage, most of this goes away, or is substantially reduced by apportionment from your home expenditures. There will still be craft-specific items, however, that can't be shared. If you aren't sure what can be included as overheads, simply log all your expenditures for a couple of months then spend some time with your accountant. This professional will clarify all the costs which can legally be classed as overheads for the essential running of your shop.

Based on the above example, you now have an hourly overheads figure. This means that every hour you work, or had planned to work, you spend £3.44 just keeping your operation going without even lifting a mallet. With this sobering thought in mind, b can be calculated as the ratio of your hourly rate H plus the hourly overheads, divided by your hourly rate. Thus, if you wanted to earn £15.00 an hour clear, b = 15+3.44 divided by 15 = 1.23.

This makes the product Lb in the formula £15x1.23 which equals £18.44; just as we inflated M by w, labour has now been inflated to cover overheads.

Factor b never changes, unless, of course, your overheads increase or you decide you need more £ per hour. In that case, calculate a new value. If your mathematics is a disaster, the verbal ratio statement in the previous paragraph should get you out of trouble.

Profit Multiplier — P If this multiplier is not greater than one, all you will do is break even having covered your overheads, material and labour. You *must* make a profit, not only so your business can grow, but if you have an emergency or a drop in sales, you will have funds to weather the storm. You need profit to buy new tools and materials for speculative projects or for the impulsive acquisition of bargains. Since your material and overheads per piece are separately covered by the formula, you should aim for a profit of 30-50%. In other words, P should be between 1.3 and 1.5.

Selling Price — S This is the magic number! If you have used the formula correctly, then the answer is a price you can be confident with, and one that you can later reduce for special sales and still make a profit.

Example

Let's use the formula to analyse a typical workshop with overheads of £5000 and a wastage factor w of 1.3. The Artisan works 2000 hours, wants only £10 per hour, but decides to make a profit of 50%. Here's how the selling price **S** shapes up on a large pine mirror which needs £20 in materials **M** and takes 2 hours and 15 minutes to make:

(Mw+Lb) P=S — the costing formula
Mw = £20.00x1.3
    = £26.00 inflated material cost
Overheads per hour = £5000 over
    2000hrs = £2.50 per hour
 b = £10.00 + £2.50 over £10.00
    = 1.25 overhead factor
Lb = (£10.00x2.25hrs)x1.25
    = £28.13 (rounded-up) inflated
      labour cost
(Mw+Lb) = £26.00 + £28.13
        = £54.13 'break-even' selling
          price

This is the rock-bottom selling price. Let's multiply this by **P** to arrive at a selling price **S** with a built-in profit of 50%.
S = (Mw+Lb)P
  = £54.13x1.5 times profit multiplier
  = **£81.20** (rounded-up)

Which is a normal sort of price for a well-made mirror. Your gross profit can be calculated by subtracting **(Mw+Lb)** from **S**. In the above example, this equates to £27.07; a margin which gives plenty of room for haggling, or a price reduction later in a special 'sale'.

The chart shows a convenient form which I developed for use in my own shop. Notice that the labour part has several lines in which to itemise the time spent on various operational steps such as jointing, assembly, finishing and so on. Time each identifiable step in the manufacturing process; if you are running a batch, average the times taken for each of these steps over the total number of pieces.

Contingencies

Once you have calculated a price using the formula, all bases should be covered and you can confidently look the client in the eye and say, 'This is the price I need for this.'

Or is it? What do you do about covering a bad debt? They do crop up now and again. Or what about that piece that ran way over your quoted price, but that you proudly finished with your usual care? No problem. You build such losses into your formula.

Four years ago in Toronto, I had a commission to build an entrance door within a large apartment (Yes, here we go again; I'm a sucker for high-rise views). This time, the subject was Honduras mahogany with etched, bevelled glass lights double-hung in a lighted, fixed frame; seven windows in all. Brass fittings; the thing oozed wealth. Unfortunately, I had a tight deadline and was forced to buy some stock which turned out to be not quite 'dead'. One of the door stiles warped, so I had to make another. I also cracked one of the bevelled panels during assembly; I forgot that glass doesn't bend. At $1.00 per perimeter inch for bevelling and polishing, the replacement

added a further $96.00 to my growing sense of doom. By the time I collected my cheque from my delighted client, I was $450.00 out of pocket. Luckily, I was costing to formula by then and running a **b** factor of 1.27. By adding the $450.00 to my $9200 overheads for 12 months the following happened:

Although my total overheads rose by 4.9%, my **b** factor only went up to 1.28. You can check this by feeding in 1920 hours at $18.00 per hour into the earlier part of this article. Also, take the figures you have worked out for your own shop and try feeding in various imaginary disasters; the results will please you.

The next piece I made, which was a reproduction Shaker dresser for a restaurant, consumed 22½ hours. Instead of my **Lb** being $514.34, the new **b** factor made it $518.40; hardly noticeable, but after 12 months, that entrance door became a fond memory instead of a recurring horror show in my subconscious. You can

do the same with a bad debt. Write it off over the next 12 months or, if you've caught a really bad cold, over two years.

Labours of love can be dealt with in the same way. There are times when you want to put that little bit extra into a piece and you know it's outside the client's budget. If you're on top of your costing, do it anyway; you'll feel great for indulging your artistic license and the client will become excellent word-of-mouth advertising. ■

● Michael Whitford lives in Cornwall. His book, 'Craft Survival' is available from Magdala House Publications, 38, Albert Rd, Saltash, Cornwall, PL12 4EB (6.95 inclusive). In addition to cost analysis, the guide covers breaking-even, product promotion and analyses consignment sales, with some case histories.
● We are grateful to *Fine Woodworking*, 63 South Main St, Newtown, Ct 06470, USA, for permission to use Michael's article. It appeared in *FWW* May 1985.

COST ANALYSIS

PROJECT:		DATE:
CUSTOMER:		

ITEM	MATERIALS	COST/BATCH	COST/UNIT

ANALYSIS BASED ON S=P(MW+LB)

| | (M) TOTAL MATERIAL COST | ① ▶ | |
| | ① X WASTAGE FACTOR (W) = | ② ▶ | |

STEP	LABOUR	TIME/BATCH	COST/BATCH	COST/UNIT

	(L) TOTAL LABOUR COST/UNIT	③ ▶	
SELL PRICE (S) = PROFIT FACTOR (P) X ⑤	③ X BURDEN/OVERHEAD (B) =	④ ▶	
© MAGDALA HOUSE LTD =	ADD ② AND ④ =	⑤ ▶	

PMH04/86

Vacuum-bag press

Veneers and laminates often come in awkward shapes and need vacuum-pressing. But don't fork out on an expensive machine: you can make your own cheaply and easily

The vacuum-bag press is a method for laying veneers and making laminations using atmospheric pressure at approximately 14lbs p.s.i. Though available commercially, it's quite an expensive piece of equipment and any way you can put one together reasonably cheaply and easily yourself.

First of all you need a compressor; use a small portable machine such as those for tyre-inflation or paint-spraying. It must operate by piston, not fan, and can have an integral motor or be mounted on a board with, say, a ¼hp motor. You can often get one secondhand from firms advertising air-tools in the local press, or Yellow Pages. You must be able to transfer the hose from the output to the input of the compressor. The air-pressure gauge can be replaced cheaply by a vacuum gauge, but you can work without one. An air filter somewhere in the line can be useful, but again you can work successfully without it, by making sure that only clean material is put into the bag.

Airline hose and the necessary fittings are available from local garage-tool and equipment dealers. Talk to them to see what's in stock and suitable for your requirements.

The bag itself is constructed from black sheet-rubber; ⅛in for individual use but for a communal workshop ¼in might be better. Size depends on your needs but for a start, try 4x3ft. A larger or smaller bag can be added later. You can buy it from local agricultural engineers or from Portmerc Rubber Co. Ltd, Victoria St, Northan, Southampton SO1 1QX, (0703) 223628.

Buy two pieces of 4ft from a 3ft roll and the smallest tin of standard rubber solution. Assemble on a large table or a sheet of chipboard. Apply the solution to three edges of each piece and allow to dry (leave one 3ft edge untreated on both). Put the pieces together, separated by two pieces of paper which overlap in the middle. Weight down or cramp one half, exactly in position, and slide the paper from the other half. Press the joints firmly together, then hammer using a wood block, or run over heavily with a paperhanger's seam-roller. When it's secure, slide out the other paper and repeat.

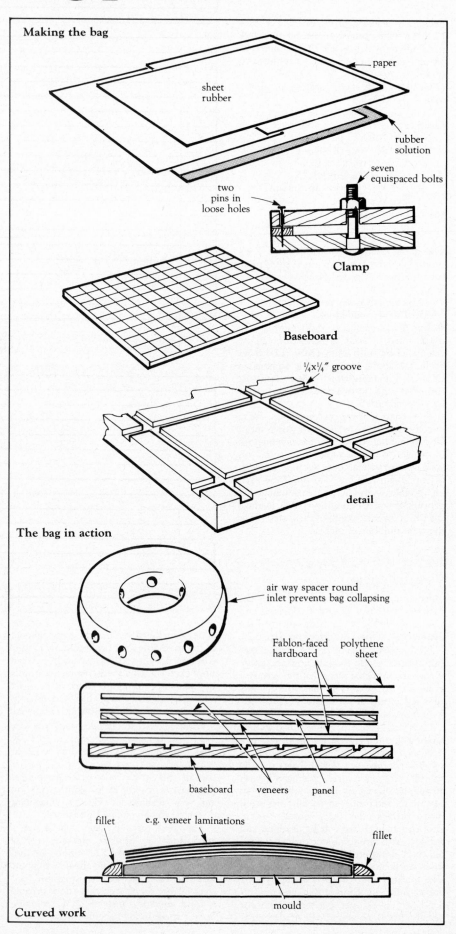

Making the bag

paper

sheet rubber

rubber solution

two pins in loose holes

seven equispaced bolts

Clamp

Baseboard

¼x¼" groove

detail

The bag in action

air way spacer round inlet prevents bag collapsing

Fablon-faced hardboard

polythene sheet

baseboard   veneers   panel

fillet   e.g. veneer laminations   fillet

Curved work

mould

The hose can be joined to the bag in one of two ways. Try rubber patches, inside and out, with solution and put the hole through the lot. Suitable metal fittings can be bought or adapted; saucer-shaped washers are more effective than flat ones. Alternatively, attach a short length of rubber hose with one of the super-strong glues. Check carefully that it's recommended for use with rubber. Drill through the sheet after fixing. A tapered-coupling adaptor allows the main hose to be disconnected when you want.

Fittings

● Use a stud fitting to connect 8mm nylon tubing to the compressor, or one that accepts rubber airline hose. Do the same for the other end. You need a female adaptor to join to the coupler (fitted to the bag). Where an air filter is incorporated, two further stud fittings are needed. You'll also want a screwdown stop tap.
● The bag can be closed by two wood battens and a number of G-cramps — or make your own closing cramp.
● A grooved baseboard about 6in less than the bag's length and width is also needed: use ¾in blockboard. Divide it roughly into 3in squares by grooves routed out at ¼x¼in. The corners of the board should be comfortably rounded.

● Make a square or round spacing-washer to go under the air outlet to prevent the bag from closing up around it in use. Again the corners should be well rounded.
● An assortment of hardwood boards covered with Fablon or similar will come in handy (glue won't stick to them).

Adhesives

Scotch glue is impracticable, it chills too quickly. PVA begins to set before preparations are complete and pressure is obtained which prevents the squeezing-out of surplus glue, or the proper bedding-down of the veneer, and generally needs too great an operating speed.

Cascamite has proved to be the most successful but if it's applied thickly it oozes through the pores, giving a glazed finish almost impossible to remove.

Veneering a ply panel

Lay the grooved board on a sheet of polythene the width of the board and twice the board length. Place hardboard sheet on to the board Fablon side up.

Glue both sides of the ply panel and lay the veneers on both sides of it; fix with four tabs of masking tape. A very quick rub-over with a rubber roller may help to stabilise the veneer. Remember that the glue should be spread very thinly either with a serrated

plastic spreader or better still, a rubber roller. Place this sandwich centrally on the hardboard sheet, put the second hardboard on top and then pull the polythene sheet over the lot.

The entire assembly is slid into the bag press and the spacer positioned below the airpipe. The mouth of the bag is closed and the compressor switched on. Extraction continues until a vacuum of about 14lbs psi is reached or until the bag feels very tight, and the shape of the panel and the grooved board can clearly be seen. You'll hear the note of the compressor change as this stage approaches. Close the stop tap, switch off and wait for the recommended time.

Sharp edges are dangerous so all corners must be rounded. Angled fillets are pinned round thicker shapes. Larger laminations will require a considerable amount of this preparation to avoid damage to the bag.

It's important at all stages to take every care to prevent exuded glue from coming into contact with the bag.

If the bag doesn't hold the vacuum, close the mouth and inflate it very slightly, using little pressure. Moisten all the seams with a strong solution of washing-up liquid and search for bubbles. When it's dry, insert more rubber solution. There's no strain on the seams as the nature of the vacuum is to pull them together. ∎

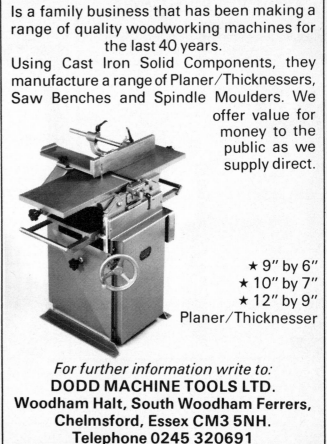

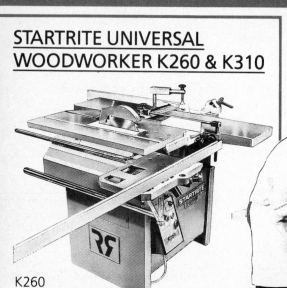

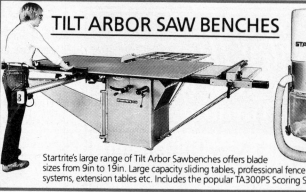

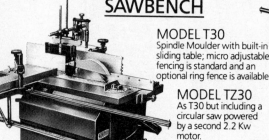

TRICKS OF THE TRADE FROM THE EXPERTS

INTRICATE PAINT REMOVAL.

Use Nitromors Original Paint Remover in the yellow can.

It flows freely into crevices and is transparent so you can see what you're doing.

Use a combination shavehook with flat and contoured edges to scrape off the paint. Try a nylon toothbrush in very intricate areas.

After scraping, wash down with fine gauge wire wool soaked in white spirit.

Nitromors Original won't raise the grain or spoil the surface of your fine wood.

NITROMORS®
PREPARE FOR THE PERFECT FINISH.

---

triton

SEE THE AMAZING MK3 WORKCENTRE DEMONSTRATED AT THE FOLLOWING VENUES

CUTWELL TOOLS; Creech Heathfield, Taunton, Somerset. Tel: (0823) 443766 — **May 22nd & 23rd.**

WIMBOURNE TIMBER CO. Wimbourne, Dorset. Tel: (0202) 881331 — **May 30th**

WALKER & ANDERSON LTD. Windsor Road, Kings Lyn, Norfolk. Tel: (0553) 2443 — **June 5th**

Send for details of forthcoming demonstrations to:
TRITON WORKCENTRES (UK), FREEPOST, P.O. Box 128, Bexhill-on-Sea, Sussex. Tel: (0424) 216897

Arundel QUALITY BRITISH LATHES

For details of our lathes and FREE accessories OFFER send to:

TREEBRIDGE LTD.
Mills Drive, Farndon Road, Newark, Notts. NG24 4SN.
Telephone: Newark (0636) 702382

"Home of Woodturning"

Everything for the woodturner, woodturning tools, machinery, accessories, wood blanks, all by mail order.

Precision Combination chuck, the proven answer to all work holding problems on lathes. New robust boxing can incorporate a variety of optional accessories.

Craft Supplies
The Mill, Millers Dale, 123
Buxton, Derbyshire SK17 8SN.
Telephone: (0298) 871636.

The world leaders in woodturning CRAFT SUPPLIES

Over 10,000 satisfied customers! Send £1.50 for a Colour Catalogue

---

BETTER THAN A BANDSAW!

THE NEW BT250
*Other patents applied for

For fast and accurate cutting of WOOD, METAL, PLASTICS, SLATE, TILES etc.

- Takes standard coping-saw, fretsaw or tungsten blades
- Works off standard 13amp household socket
- Cutting depth 7.3cm. Throat length 48cm
- Speed infinitely variable 0-4000 cuts a minute
- Blade tilts 45deg. for slanting cuts
- Foot switch leaves both hands free
- Superbly made for sustained operation
- Dimension: 36cm wide × 87cm long.
- Ring for details of our financial package which means you can buy a machine for £4.93 + VAT per week (ownership guaranteed)

£465 + VAT

BRI-TON TOOLS LTD
26 The Square, Dobcross, Oldham, Lancs OL3 5AA. Tel: 04577-70127 04577-3045

AS SEEN AT THE WEMBLEY EXHIBITION 1987

Salvage showpiece

Michael Evans used demolition pitch pine to make this attractive dresser with more than a hint of the rustic

I got interested in using pitch pine, with its beautiful grain, when I obtained some old beams from a local church. I made a coffee table, staining it with 2:1 mahogany and dark oak to enhance the grain and give it a lovely warm colour.

I designed this wall unit to match the coffee table, and after some difficulty discovered a source of old beams from a firm of demolition experts; they cut up the beams into one inch planks and had them planed. I found the boards varied from 5-5¾in wide, so I've avoided giving exact measurements for this unit, though if you're buying new timber you could get 5¾in finished boards.

I must thank my wife for her patience; I used the lounge to make this unit, and you can imagine the dust (even though my orbital sander has a collection bag) and the shavings underfoot!

The unit is assembled in stages, and I sanded all the components for each stage before gluing up, since it's easier with the pieces laid flat. I scalloped with a spokeshave all facing edges, cupboard doors and so on.

Base section

Start by making up the sides. I sawed lengths off the boards, retaining the left-over portions and marking them so they could be used for the sides of the top, with the grain pattern appearing continuous. I cut them slightly oversize to allow surplus for squaring up the ends along the full width of the joined panels. I planed each of the four boards for each end to a good square edge, and then joined them using a loose tongue, ¾x¼in, cutting the groove with a combination plane.

I made up the back of the unit in the same way, but chamfered each board ⅛x⅛in along the joining edges; on reflection I realised that ½in ply would be quite suitable, since the back doesn't show. I glued the back up in three pieces (two of four boards, one of five) before finally gluing the three sections together.

I planed one long edge of the sides straight and square as the datum edge, marking top and bottom from this, cutting and planing before finishing the opposite long edge to form a rectangle. I cut a half-thickness rebate at the back of each side, the full depth of the back, and also cut the cut-out for the fascia/footboard at the front bottom corners.

Then I prepared the division pieces; these are to be butt-jointed to the back. Note that the cut-out for the fascia/footboard is higher with these division pieces, since the

● *Plain lines, sturdy proportions . . . see overleaf in glorious technicolour*

top horizontal section of the footboard, which acts as a front support for the bottom shelves, is butted up to them, while it is dovetailed in at each end.

Then I cut the fascia and its bottom front shelf support, cutting the dovetails in the support. The rear shelf support and four base support rails are rebated ⅛x½in for the bottom shelves. I also cut cross rails, making tenons at their ends and mortising them into the base support rails. I half-lapped the rear base support rail to receive the base rails which fit each side of the division pieces.

Base assembly

I started assembling the base by gluing and screwing through the back into the sides, into the top back rail (you could slot-screw here), and into the rear shelf support rail. I offered the division pieces up to the back and marked and cut the cut-outs for the top, the shelf support rails and the base top front rail. I marked out and cut mortises for the drawer division rails, and cut tenons on these rails to match.

After gluing and cramping the drawer division rails to the division pieces and checking for squareness, I let this section dry before gluing and screwing it into place, with screws going through the back into the division pieces. I screwed the top back rail sections between the divisions, and the bottom front shelf support to the division pieces. Then I glued and screwed the fascia to the bottom front shelf support, setting the screws in the rebate so they would be covered by the bottom shelves. I used glue blocks to fasten the fascia to the division pieces and the ends.

After gluing and cramping the side base

supports and the base cross-rails together, I glued and screwed these components into the half-lap cut-outs in the bottom front shelf support. I also glued and screwed the rear base support rails into the ends and the division pieces.

Turning attention to the top section of the base, I cut dovetails on the ends of the top front rail and the ends; after fastening these together I glued and screwed corner block strengtheners and division piece strengtheners into place.

Then I prepared boards to make up the front top surface of the base, behind which the top section sits. This overlaps the front of the unit by 1in, and the ends by ½in, and is rebated underneath at the back. I glued and screwed it from beneath into position. I cut and fit the bottom shelves, which are ⅛in ply.

Cupboard doors and drawers

I selected the wood for the doors and drawers carefully before joining the boards together as I did for the ends. The three drawer fronts can be made up as one, then cut into three pieces, to get the grain continuous.

To fit the doors, I lined the face edge up with the outer edge of the unit, with a ⅛in gap between the top of the door and the underside of the top front surface. I trimmed the lower edge level with the bottom of the underside fascia; the final vertical edge finishes 1/16in to one side of the centre of the division piece.

For the drawer-fronts I left the made-up boards in one piece until I had made the drawers, planing one long edge to work from. Once the drawers were completed I cut the fronts, leaving a gap of ⅛in between each drawer, and 1/16in between the drawer sides and the cupboard doors.

Top section

Make up panels for the ends, top, division pieces, base, centre shelf and top back. When the glue has set on the back piece, plane the bottom edge straight and square, and cut to the same length as the base back.

The base matches up with the top front surface section of the base, so plane it to width, and rebate the front edge to match the rebate on the top front surface (screws through the rebates will hold the sections together later). Cut the base to the same length as the back.

Plane the ends to the same width as the top's base, but cut them ⅜in longer than the back; the bottom edge of this piece rests on the top of the lower end piece and should be cut exactly to fit. Cut the three rebates on the top and bottom edges and the rear long edge.

Then I planed the division pieces; these are the widths of the ends less the thickness of the back, and are butt jointed to the back. Prepare the top middle rail, and cut mortises and tenons for the rail and division pieces. The centre shelf is the same width as

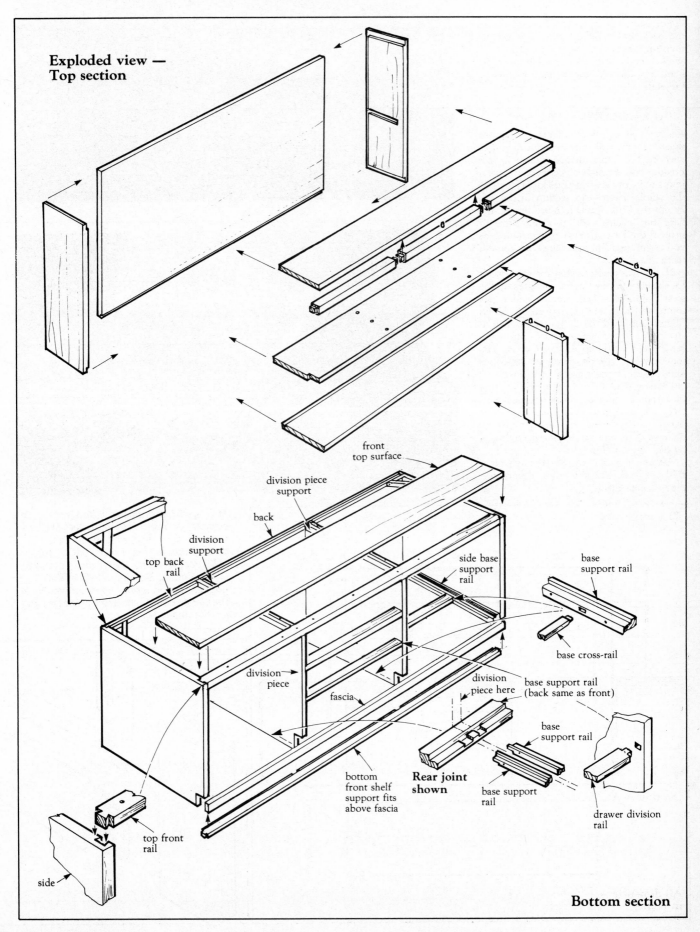

**Exploded view —
Top section**

front
top surface

division piece
support

back

division
support

top back
rail

side base
support
rail

base
support rail

division
piece

base cross-rail

fascia

division
piece here

base support rail
(back same as front)

base
support rail

**Rear joint
shown**

base support
rail

bottom
front shelf
support fits
above fascia

drawer division
rail

top front
rail

side

Bottom section

Salvage showpiece

the division pieces, and the same length as the back. Prepare the top, and dowel the division pieces into the top and the centre shelf. Mortise and tenon the left and right hand top rails into the division pieces and the ends.

Top assembly

Assemble all pieces dry first so you can see where cramps will have to go; once you've checked the joints, dismantle and have a practice run through, since there are many joints to be put together quickly. I glued up the whole of the top section in one go, except the back, doing it in position on the base, but placing a sheet of newspaper to protect the base. Check for squareness as you cramp up. Once the glue is set you can fit the back.

Now I was ready to start the framework for the glass doors; these are rebated for the glass, with haunched mortise and tenon joints and with the glass fixed by mitred fillets. I finished the doors with $\frac{1}{4}$in lead strip, applied in diagonals, starting from the centre and working out both ways. The inner shelves are also made of glass, but with the front edges ground for safety.

I had used my orbital sander at each stage of assembly, and now hand-sanded with finer and finer grades, finishing with flour paper. I stained with a mixture of two parts mahogany to one part dark oak, followed by high gloss polyurethane.

Although I used recovered pitch pine, this unit could as easily be made from new pine or a hardwood. ∎

Dimensions

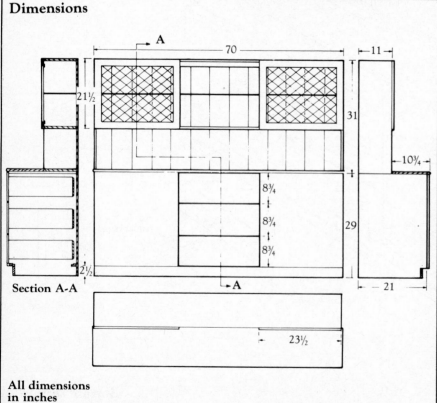

Section A-A

All dimensions in inches

● **Top**, *front drawer-rail, top front surface, corner blocks and steel drawer-runners all in view;* **above**, *straight comb-joints for the drawer backs, the sides recessed into the fronts. Note the vertical grain.* **Below**, *details of the haunched tenons and rebated members in the upper doors, and the mitred beading for the heavy leaded panes*

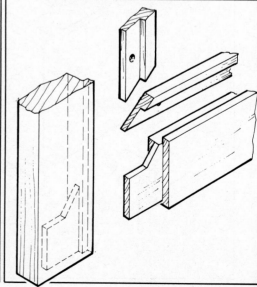

Cutting list

For this unit I ordered 250ft of 6x1in rough sawn, cut to 26 at 5ft and 20 at 6ft. All ¾in finished unless specified.

Base

Back	1	70in x	29in x	
Sides	2	29	21	
Top surface	1	71	10¾	
Divisions	2	19¾	24¾	
Doors	2	23	26	
Fascia	1	70	3	
Front shelf support	1	70	2½	
Rear shelf support	1	68½	1¼	1
Side shelf supports	4	20¼	1¼	1
Top front rail	1	69¼	2	
Top rear rail	1	68½	1¼	1
Corner supports	1	36	1¼	1
Shelf support cross rails	2	22	1¼	⅞
Drawer division rails	2	25	2	
Drawer fronts	3	23½	8¾	
sides	6	19	6	
backs	3	23½	5½	
bases	3	23½	19	⅛ ply
base rails		23½	⅝	⅝
		19	⅝	⅝
Bottom shelves	2	19	22½	⅛ ply
Internal shelves	2	17	22½	

Top

Back	1	70	31	
Sides	2	31	11	
Top	1	70	11	
Base	1	69¾	11	
Divisions	2	20¼	10¼	
Cornice	3	24	1¾	
Centre shelf	1	69¾	10¼	
Door frames	4	23½	2½	
	4	21½	2½	
Fillets	8	21	¾	⅝

● *Hand tools all the way; rebating the bottom 'shelf' of the top unit in the comfort of the lounge workshop. Thanks are due, says Michael, to the tolerance and patience of his wife . . .*

● *Traditional jointing of boards on the re-clad breast of the buck.* **Top right**, *an early tinted photograph of the mill, c1897.* **Right**, *the buck jacked up for trestle restoration*

Trouble at t'mill

Conserving Britain's
historic landmarks is
lengthy and exacting work
as Peter Casebow found

For nearly 200 years the sails of the old wooden post mill at High Salvington, just north of Worthing, were turned by the South Downs breezes. It stopped grinding corn in 1897, but the idle mill remained a local landmark, standing 320ft above sea level, with Beachy Head and the Isle of Wight visible from the roof.

Extensive work to the body, or buck, of the mill was carried out after Worthing Borough Council bought the mill in 1959, but an inspection in 1976 revealed that the trestle supporting the buck of the mill was seriously weakened by rot and death watch beetle, and the whole mill was in danger of collapse. A trust was set up to completely restore the mill, but progress was slow until a group of friends got together and decided to tackle the restoration themselves.

Our first task was to build a new 10ft diameter brake wheel; the old one was crumbling with age and decay. Building the replacement was far more difficult than we originally envisaged, but we were fortunate to be able to use facilities at the local College of Design.

The main construction of the wheel took three years, but we've only recently installed it and completed profiling the gear

● **Top left**, *the old brake wheel.* **Top right**, *hauling the new brake wheel into position.* **Above**, *routing ⅜in from the circumference to increase roof clearance.* **Above right**, *the new sprattle-beam end was fitted after the wheel was in place.* **Right**, *repair work to curved rafters during re-cladding of the buck*

teeth — eight years from starting the project.

We took great care to ensure that the new wheel was exactly like the old one in every respect. We made the rim from 16 pieces of elm in two staggered layers of eight segments to get maximum rigidity. We used oak for the clasp arms, and the 136 gear

teeth are applewood, traditionally used for this specific purpose.

The elm took two years to dry out enough to work on; we occasionally planed the surfaces flat, which also removed the layer of mould affecting the elm. When the wood was stable we cut out the 16 pieces, using carefully made templates, and jointed

them together. Our biggest problem was ensuring that the mortises for the gear teeth would be accurately positioned around the rim of the wheel; to solve this we made an accurate template showing the centre line of each mortise with the outside dimensions of the mortises cut through.

We marked the mortises from the template on to the upper eight segments of the wheel, with the centre lines scribed radially into the wheel surface; these centre lines later proved invaluable when we were profiling the teeth *in situ*, for they gave us datum lines to work from.

The mortises themselves were time-consuming and exacting to cut, since the tenon of each tooth was tapered in two planes — so the tooth could be inserted without pressure most of the way and then finally driven home with a heavy mallet.

● **Left**, *post-mill brake wheels are not as rough and ready as you might think. Note the two-part wheel, the double-tapered tenons of the teeth, and their offset mortises to avoid the effect of wear on the tenons. The teeth are set into the face of the wheel, not the rim edge*

Fig. 1   Sections through a tooth and wheel

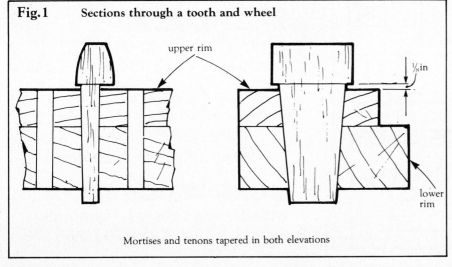

upper rim

⅛in

lower rim

Mortises and tenons tapered in both elevations

continued

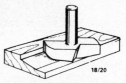
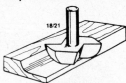
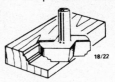
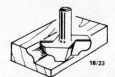

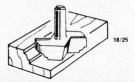

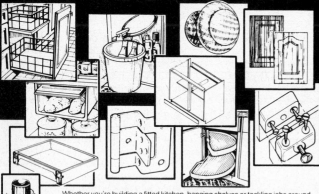

Trouble at t'mill

WOODWORKER JUNE 1987

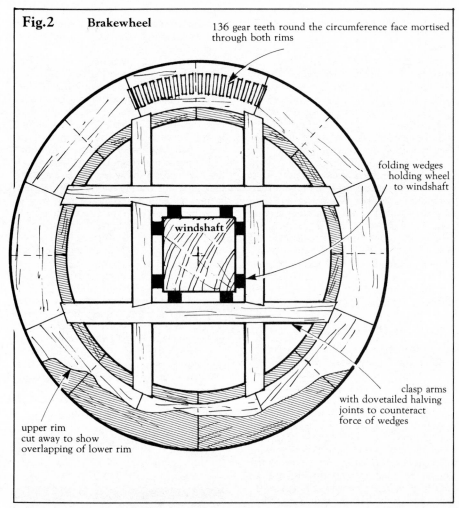

Fig.2   **Brakewheel**

136 gear teeth round the circumference face mortised through both rims

folding wedges holding wheel to windshaft

windshaft

clasp arms with dovetailed halving joints to counteract force of wedges

upper rim cut away to show overlapping of lower rim

We made the apple teeth, with their long tapered tenons, but left the ends to be shaped to the gear tooth profiles once they were in place. We carefully fitted each tenon through its mortise through the 2¾in upper layer of the wheel. To get a good fit, we rubbed coloured wax crayon on the tenons, removing high spots from the mortises with a chisel. We fitted the teeth leaving ⅛in clearance between the tenon shoulder and the rim, so we could drive it home later with a mallet (fig. 1).

After cutting the mortises in the upper rim, we bolted the lower rim in place and marked the bottom of the mortises through. Then we separated the rims again and roughed out the mortises in the 5in thick lower rim before fine chiselling for a tight fit. It took about 90 minutes to fit one tooth through both parts of the rim, even after we had roughed out the mortise. With the teeth fitted we assembled the wheel fully for the first time, and were delighted to find it was circular to within 3/32 in.

Next we made and fitted the eight large oak clasp arms which hold the wheel on to the windshaft of the mill. These were notched into the rim and bolted in position. We followed the traditional technique of a dovetailed halving joint to prevent splitting (fig. 2).

After completing the wheel we dismantled the pieces, treated each with preservative, and transported them to a barn lent

● **Below**, the old brake wheel and crowntree

Trouble at t'mill

● *The final, careful trimming of the teeth with mallet and chisel*

by Worthing Museum where it was re-assembled, awaiting installation. That didn't happen for another four years.

Fitting the brakewheel

When the time came to install the wheel we found the steel bolts holding the oak clamp arms to the elm wheel had rusted, and needed to be driven out. We split the wheel into two halves by removing four of the clasp arms and 36 teeth with two sections of the upper rim; the other clasp arms acted as ties, holding the heavy rim together. We moved the sections on a farm trailer and had eight strong men to move each half-tonne section into place at the mill, using chain hoists and removing part of the stone floor.

Assembling the two halves round the windshaft was difficult, since there was little room to work and the large sprattle beam, holding the end of the drive shaft to the millstones, was in the way; this beam was rotten at one end, so we removed it with a chainsaw for repair and replacement later.

We used two chain hoists to get the two halves in position. Then we discovered how close the wheel was to the roof, missing it by less than ½in at one place. It was only later when replacing another piece of machinery that we realised that the roof replaced in the 1960 reconstruction was four inches lower than the original, and how fortunate we had been in getting the wheel in position.

Once the wheel was in place, it took nearly three months of exasperating work to centralise it and secure it to the windshaft using folding wedges. We managed to get it true to within ⅛in in circumference and ³⁄₁₆in on wind; we decided this leeway was acceptable, since elm is notorious for moving, and we could get closer tolerances when profiling the teeth. We scarfed a new end on to the sprattle beam and replaced it, a handy anchor for our router jig when shaping the teeth.

Profiling the teeth

We marked the inner and outer ends of the teeth by turning the wheel while holding a pencil against the top of the teeth. Then we removed each tooth and trimmed it on a bandsaw, before replacing and driving it home with a heavy mallet until the shoulders were flush to the rim. We fitted a large industrial router to a home-made jig (fig. 3) which was clamped to the sprattle beam with the router positioned against the face of the wheel. Then we slowly turned the wheel, so the router machined the top of each tooth. We transferred the centre lines from the mortises to both inner and outer faces of the teeth. We made separate profile templates for the inner and outer faces of the teeth.

We had already noticed in studying the old wheel that the teeth were offset relative to their tenons (fig. 4); this meant that as the teeth became worn in use, the tenons weren't weakened by being worn as well. This observation confirmed the direction of rotation of the windshaft.

We marked an offset centre line on the teeth templates so we would copy this technique, having one side of each tooth wider than the other. Using the profiles and lining up the marks we drew an accurate profile in sharp pencil at either end of each tooth. This careful marking up, using the centre lines scribed on the wheel rim as a datum, ovecame any inaccuracies in cutting and fitting the teeth to the mortises, as well as the winding error on the face of the wheel.

The actual profiling was fairly straightforward. We set the router on the guide bars of the jig at the require angle and cut each tooth in turn (fig. 5), repeating the process for various angles approximate to the profile. A plywood pointer (fig. 3) pointed to the centre line of the tooth to help with indexing. Once most surplus material was removed, we used a chisel and mallet to produce the final profile.

Since there was so little clearance between the rim and the mill roof, we set the router up and took a further ³⁄₈in off the edge of the wheel all round. We did this in several stages, rotating the wheel slowly and moving the router across the 8in thickness. The extra clearance would be handy when we started on our next job, fitting a wooden band brake . . . ■

● *Fitting clasp arms to the underside of the wheel, carefully following the pattern of the old one in the background*

● *Adzing a dovetail on the tailbeam – traditional tools for traditional constructions*

● *The new tail beam, ready to fit with its massive dovetail*

Fig.4 **Tooth**

tooth profile
offset to allow
wear without
weakening joint

Fig.3 **Teeth profiling jig**

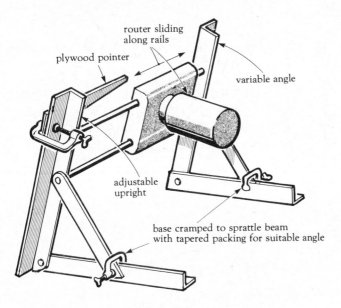

router sliding
along rails

plywood pointer

variable angle

adjustable
upright

base cramped to sprattle beam
with tapered packing for suitable angle

Fig.5
Profiling the teeth

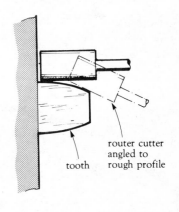

router cutter
angled to
rough profile

tooth

● *A sail blew off the mill in a storm in 1976*

● *The main post and trestle, with new
quarter bars holding up the post*

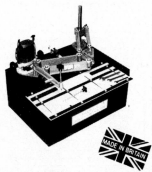

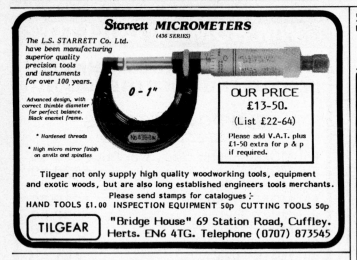

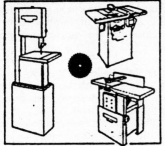

Lattice lectern

Photo Tim Imrie

James Gray's extravagant pitch pine lectern, with its myriad turned components, was a Gold Medal winner at the '86 London Woodworker Show

This open lattice design of church lectern avoids obscuring the person using it, and the turnings also make a pretty sight as sunlight streams through it from a nearby window. The book rest is a latticed frame resting on two sloping rails which are supported on two pillars branching off from each side of the main support pillar. Reading height is adjustable, locking into one of three positions.

I recommend that you read right through the operation schedule at least twice so you get a clear idea of what work is involved before you start.

Many of the holes can be drilled to slightly different sizes according to your collection of drill bits, but bear in mind that the strength of the supporting frame is paramount.

Feet

Prepare the wood to the rectangular section (fig. 1) and draw in all the centres and shapes before drilling carefully through the holes (on a drill press if possible) at a slow feed speed with a sharp drill but to avoid break-out. Cut out the curves, blending them gently into the drilled holes, cut out the half-lapped joints and clean up before gluing the two halves together.

Bottom brackets

Mark out the four brackets (fig. 3), cut the curves and clean them up; this is easier if you've made the curves the same diameter as the pulley on a belt sander, or alternatively you could cover a wooden cylinder with sandpaper and mount it on a lathe. Cutting the square sides accurately will make assembly straightforward.

Main pillar

This is a large turning, so you may have to borrow a friend's lathe if yours doesn't have the capacity. Start by squaring the material to 93mm (fig. 2), and reduce the top 230mm down to 66mm square. Drill four holes as shown at this end, including one into the end which you can use as a centre on the lathe. Don't cut out the double notches at the bottom end until you've finished the turning. Because this is a large chunk of wood, keep the lathe at a lowish speed, taking small cuts with a sharp bevelled chisel at the square-to-round transitions.

While the wood is still on the lathe, aply base coat or sealer, allowing it to dry hard before smoothing off with fine paper while running the lathe at a low speed, again being careful at the squared areas.

If you follow the same procedure as you finish each turning you'll save a great deal of hard work before applying any finishing coats.

Finials

The finial (fig. 4), which fits on the top of the main pillar, is a simple turning between centres; the only critical dimension is the 22mm diameter pin which should fit snugly into the hole at the top of the main pillar.

Lateral pillars

Prepare the 60mm square wood (fig. 5), then reduce the bottom 160mm of each piece down to 43mm square. Before you start turning, drill the 22mm holes exactly 90mm apart, leaving the twin tenons at the top end uncut as you'll need the centre for turning. After turning, flatten the sharp edges of the holes back equally, so the overall dimension is exactly 47mm; this ensures the shoulders on the lateral support fits neatly against the turning.

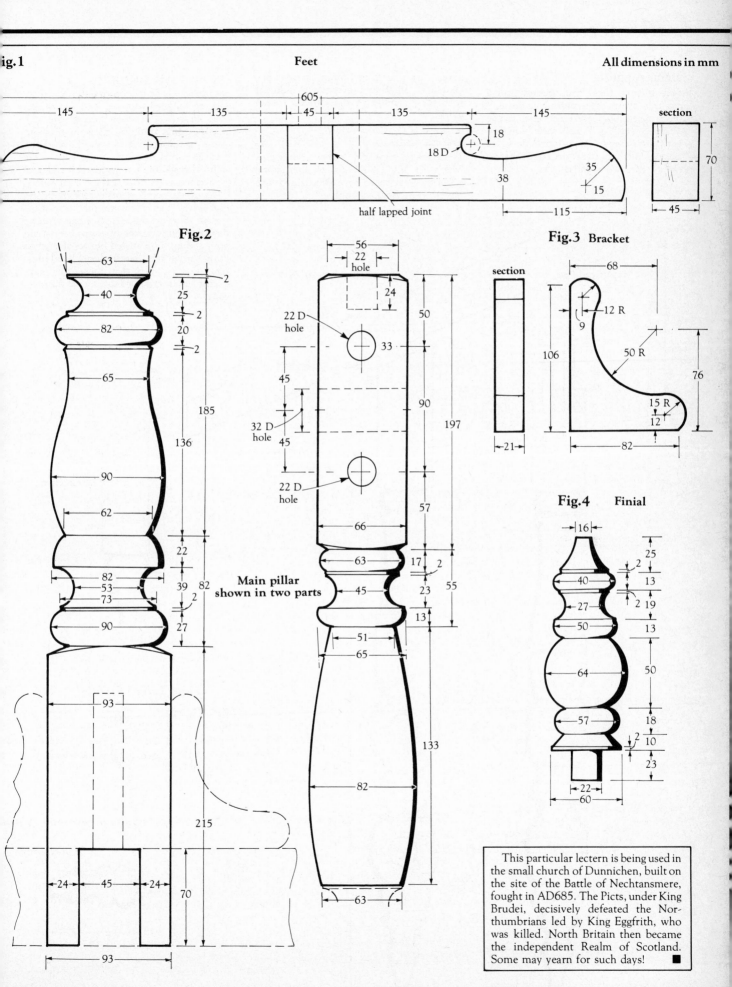

Fig.1

Fig.1 Feet All dimensions in mm

605

145 · 135 · 45 · 135 · 145

section

18

18 D

35

38

15

70

half lapped joint

115

45

Fig.2

63

40

82

65

90

62

82
53
73

90

2

25

2

20

2

185

136

22

39 · 82

2

27

93

215

24 · 45 · 24

70

93

**Main pillar
shown in two parts**

56

22
hole

24

22 D
hole

33

45

32 D
hole · 45

22 D
hole

66

63

45

51

65

82

63

50

90

197

57

17 · 2

23 · 55

13

133

Fig.3 Bracket

section

68

12 R

9

106

50 R

76

15 R

12

21

82

Fig.4 Finial

16

25

2

40

13

27

2 · 19

50

13

64

50

57

18

2 · 10

23

22

60

This particular lectern is being used in the small church of Dunnichen, built on the site of the Battle of Nechtansmere, fought in AD685. The Picts, under King Brudei, decisively defeated the Northumbrians led by King Eggfrith, who was killed. North Britain then became the independent Realm of Scotland. Some may yearn for such days! ■

Lattice lectern

Lateral supports

Before turning these four pieces, drill a 9mm hole 20mm deep centrally in one end of each piece. Fit these holed ends to the tailstock centre (fig. 6), turn the 22mm pins at each end so they are a push fit in the holes at the top end of the main pillar and the twin holes of the lateral pillars. As you turn, make sure you keep 86mm between the shoulders, vital to prevent misalignment with the openings of the latticed framework.

Lateral caps

These lateral caps (fig. 7) have 9mm pins which fit into the ends of the lateral supports after these have been glued into place on the final assembly.

Inclined rest and drops

Prepare wood for the front and rear drops, and the inclined rest, marking out the six twin mortise-and-tenon joints (fig. 5). Leaving some waste on the four drops to use as turning centres, cut out the mortises. Cut the mortises on the underside of the inclined rests, the tenons at each end, and the tenons at the top of the lateral pillars. Clean up the components before gluing and assembling the drops to the rest, using angled blocks made of scrap timber clamped lightly to the drops to keep them from sliding. Use angled blocks also when gluing the lateral pillars to the inclined rests. You must ensure that these two sub-assemblies are cramped together at the same angle.

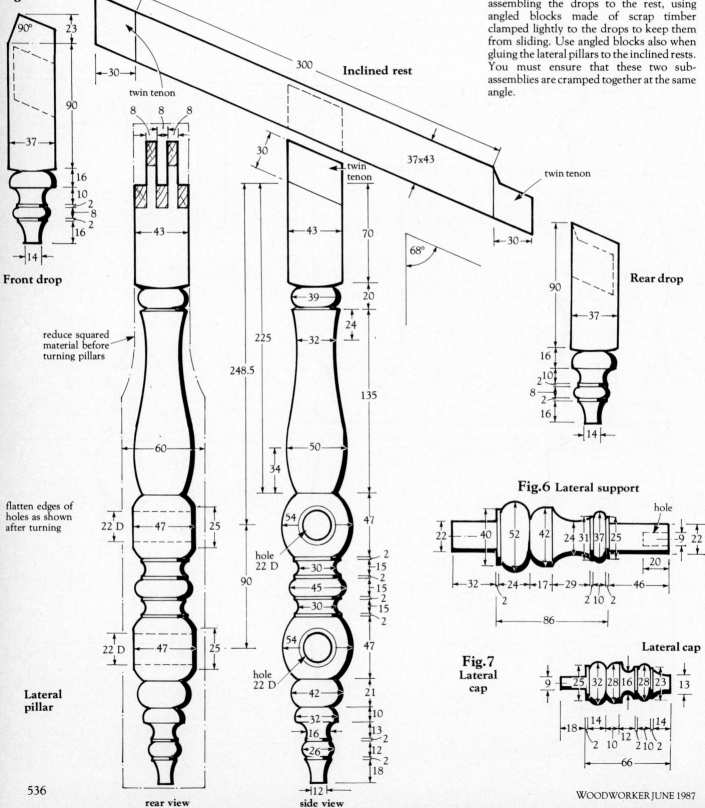

Fig.5

Front drop

reduce squared material before turning pillars

flatten edges of holes as shown after turning

Lateral pillar

rear view

Inclined rest

twin tenon

37x43

twin tenon

side view

Rear drop

Fig.6 Lateral support

Fig.7 Lateral cap

Lateral cap

Front and rear turnings

Turn the prepared wood for the front turning (fig. 8) between centres, making sure the 32mm pin fits firmly into the hole at the front of the main pillar.

Square up the wood for the rear turning before drawing in the position of the holes and centres. Drill the 35mm-diameter angled hole first; for safety and accuracy clamp the component to a scrap block angled at 12°, preferably of the same thickness as the component. Then drill an 18mm-diameter hole on the lathe from the rear end clean through to meet the angled hole; this end hole houses the rear turning pin, along with the two collars and the spring. Finally turn the wood to shape.

For the collars prepare the squared material and drill out with a 12mm bit; then turn to an external diameter which fits smoothly into the 18mm hole of the rear turning. Cut two collars 20mm long from this wood.

To complete the components for this sub-assembly, turn the 12mm pin on the rear turning pin, so it fits tightly inside the collars. Taking one of the collars, ease the inside so it slides freely on the pin. Place this collar on the pin, fit a 20mm length of weak coiled spring next to it, then glue the inside of the second collar and push it up to meet the coil spring without compressing it at all; this should leave about 14mm of the pin projecting past the second collar. Leave the glue to harden; if you don't trust the glue, put a small nail through the collar and the pin to secure.

Once the glue has set, coat the outer surface of the collar nearest the shaped end with wax and push the assembly into the 18mm hole of the rear turning, as shown.

Lattice rails

Make these components from defect-free material, since they form the top of the lectern and will be most prominent to the user. Cut overlength (fig. 9). Apply a spot of glue to the ends of each so you can clamp them together and cut the notches at one cut. After completing the notches trim off the glued waste and round the ends before final sanding and assembly.

After shaping the book stop (fig. 12) use three small locating dowels and glue to secure this to the bottom rail of the latticed frame.

Before securing the hinge blocks (fig. 10) decide on your hinges. I used modified cranked brass hinges, shaped on the edge to repeat the curved line at the square to the turned section of the two front drops (fig. 11). Glue the hinge blocks into the third space in from the end at the top of the latticed frame.

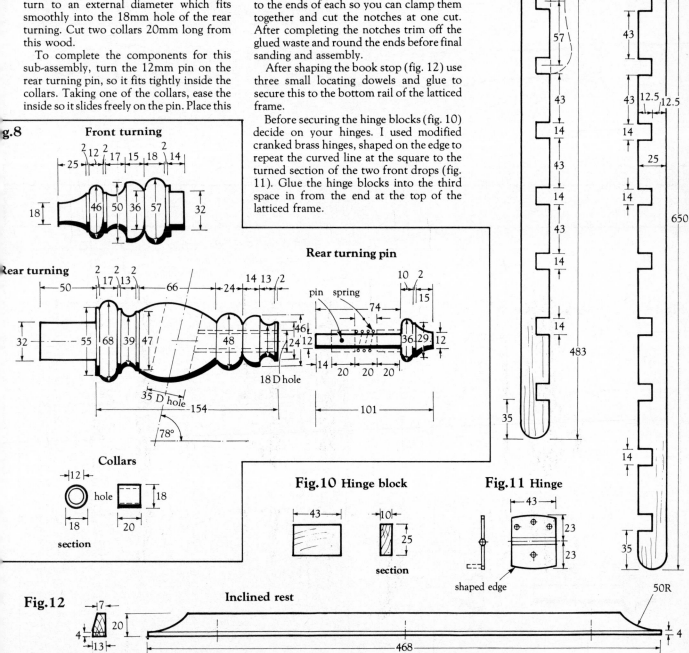

Fig.9 Lattice rails

Fig.8 Front turning

Rear turning

Rear turning pin

Collars

Fig.10 Hinge block

Fig.11 Hinge

Fig.12 Inclined rest

Lattice lectern

Drilled turning

Prepare the wood to 34mm square before marking the positions of the three angled holes. Angle a piece of scrap wood to 22° as shown (fig. 13) as a rest when drilling the holes, which are 12mm diameter and 15mm deep. Don't drill out the 12mm holes at the top end at this stage; you can determine the position best as you finally hinge the latticed top.

Complete the turning to the dimensions, using light cuts with small sharp chisels. Sandpaper and basecoat as usual.

Holed brackets

You need two holed brackets (fig. 15); I made them by laminating the pitch pine together for extra strength, but you wouldn't need to do this if you used a timber like oak.

Glue the holed brackets 35mm apart at the bottom of the underside of the latticed frame, as shown in fig. 9.

The dowel and dowel cap (fig. 16) connects the holed brackets to the top end of the drilled turning; glue the cap on after final assembly. ∎

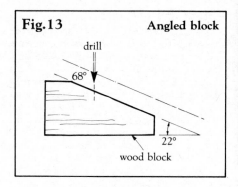

Fig.13   Angled block

Fig.14

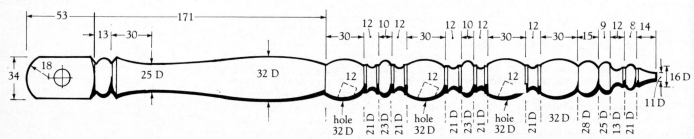

Drilled turning

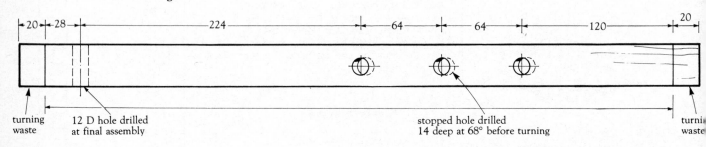

turning waste

12 D hole drilled at final assembly

stopped hole drilled 14 deep at 68° before turning

turning waste

Fig.15   Holed bracket

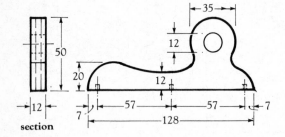

section

Fig.16   Dowel and dowel cap

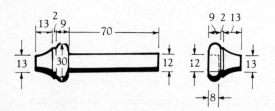

Cutting list

Feet	2	70mm x 45mm x 605mm
Brackets	4	85 21 110
Main pillar	1	93 93 917
Finial	1	68 68 200
Lateral pillars	2	60 60 500
Lateral supports	4	56 56 180
Lateral caps	4	36 36 100
Inclined rests	2	37 43 400
Front drops	2	37 43 180
Rear drops	2	37 43 180
Front turning	1	60 60 140
Rear turning	1	72 72 220
Rear turning pin	1	40 40 110
Collars	2	25 25 80
Lattice rails A	8	25 14 650
Lattice rails B	11	25 14 483
Book stop	1	20 13 468
Hinge blocks	2	25 10 43
Holed brackets	2	50 12 128
Drilled turning	1	34 34 530
Dowel	1	34 34 100
Dowel cap	1	34 34 60

Pair of suitable brass hinges, 40-42mm wide
Spring, 12mm internal diameter, 15mm external

Letters

Angle wrangling

I READ BOB WEARING'S Workshop (*WW/Feb*) about constructing angles with interest. There is nothing 'rough and ready' about stepping a radius round a circle to define a hexagon. This is exactly how geometricians (I prefer 'geometer') would do it — but they would use a pair of compasses rather than a compass, which would be more use to a navigator!

Even simpler than stepping round the circle is this method. Draw a diameter — any straight line through the centre of the circle) to intersect the circumference at X and Y. Put the point of the compasses on X and swing an arc of the same radius as the circle to cut the circle at A and B. Do the same at Y to give points C and D. Easy!

However, I have a rough and ready method for marking out the end of a small square section before reducing it to an octagon for turning. I draw one diagonal, and then use a steel rule as a marking guide, as shown (the rule must have similar markings down each edge, either inches or mm). With the saw table tilted at 45° it is then a simple matter to set the fence so that the line I have drawn across one corner comes up against the saw blade. The setting is then correct for the other three corners. This method will obviously work fully only with small-section material, but in practice it can be used with any size material since all you need is a short line to set the saw blade against.

W. Geoffrey Heath, Stockport

Hexagonal shaping

Octagonal shaping

line up edges
of rule against
diagonal divide

draw line
here

Jumping switch

RE MR G. A. HOLLIDAY'S letter about his starter switch (*WW/March*), I suspect that the no-volt/overload release is faulty and this ought to be adjustable. However, he should be able to obtain a suitable replacement (possibly not identical) from the switch manufacturers: M.E.M. Ltd, Reddings Lane, Tyseley, Birmingham B11 3EZ, (021) 706 3300.

T. D. Walshaw, Kendal

Pooling our resources

PICK UP ANY NEWSPAPER or switch on the radio, and you'll encounter **confrontation** — even our government is founded upon such a philosophy. While those who adopt this attitude may be taking a long hard look at themselves, we can turn away from this worst of all bad habits, and press ahead with co-operation.

Two organisations have caught my attention recently: The Woodland Trust and the National Hardwood Campaign. While I await confirmation of the aims of the latter, I suggest that, whatever they are, those of both organisations needn't necessarily be mutually exclusive.

I sometimes wonder if I ought to leave a bob or two so that someone can plant a tree on my behalf. 'Any old tree?' Certainly not! 'For posterity?' Not at all.

It seems to me that there's opportunity here for a large-scale tie-in between many organisations who want 'to grow trees'. Pushing out a donation into the great blue yonder or leaving a legacy seems to be 'only half a story'.

'A tree with your name on' is nothing new, but I'd like to see it made into a countrywide professional thing of ever-enduring scope.

It will be clear that I write in almost complete ignorance of what's going on. It will also be clear that I am not alone in this.

The 'green' organisations and the hardwood industry (not to mention the government) should get together over this. And the sooner the better — I imagine.

H. H. Bridge, Southport, Merseyside

Miniature lathe

I AM ALWAYS GLAD to see improvisations and expedients, but I hope Robert Cutler ('Small is beautiful', *WW/March*) will not mind a few improvements!

First, the motor shaft will soon get burred up if setscrews are used, and I think he should have suggested filing a flat or flats on the shaft to take the screw pads — the ends, of course, should be rounded, not pointed.

Second, his sketches show two setscrews in most of the chucks. It is a standard rule that if two such screws (or even keys) are used then they should be at an angle to each other, not diametrically opposite. On a

small shaft like this, I would set them at 120°; though 90° would be dynamically correct for this application the two flats might run into each other in this small size.

Next, chuck mounting. The Jacobs drillchuck socket is not a 'Morse' taper but the Jacobs in-house standard. I wouldn't care to rely on the truth of the minor diameter of the thread inside a threaded socket type chuck; this dimension is not bored to limits and could well be burred during the threading process. The method I've used for similar applications is to buy a Morse taper chuck arbor, No. 1 or No. 2 MT at one end, Jacobs taper the other. These are not hardened and are easily machined. Set the arbor in the lathe headstock socket; drill fairly deep, about 15-29 thou. below reaming size, true the hole with a tiny boring tool and then ream. The un-needed part of the morse taper shank can then be sawn off, and the result will be a dead true mounting.

Finally, I would suggest putting some ventilation holes in the base of the motor casing as well as at the top of the sides. These little motors are not too efficient, and one of ⅛hp could be throwing out as much heat as a 100watt lamp. Good circulation of air is important, and though the motor may have an integral fan, this will tend to re-circulate the air inside the box in the arrangement shown.

By the way, don't forget to earth the motor and the switch if it is a metal one as shown in the photo!

Tubal Cain, Kendal

shopguide

AVON

BATH Tel. Bath 64513
JOHN HALL TOOLS ★
RAILWAY STREET

Open: Monday-Saturday
9.00 a.m.5.30 p.m.
H.P.W.WM.D.A.BC.

BRISTOL Tel. (0272) 741510
JOHN HALL TOOLS LIMITED ★
CLIFTON DOWN SHOPPING CENTRE
WHITELADIES ROAD
Open: Monday-Saturday
9.00 a.m.-5.30 p.m.
H.P.W.WM.D.A.BC.

BRISTOL Tel. (0272) 629092
TRYMWOOD SERVICES
2a DOWNS PARK EAST, (off North View)
WESTBURY PARK
Open: 8.30 a.m.-5.30 p.m. Mon. to Fri.
Closed for lunch 1.00-2.00 p.m.
P.W.WM.D.T.A.BC.

Read Model Engineer for a new angle on construction & design

BRISTOL Tel. (0272) 667013
WILLIS
157 WEST STREET
BEDMINSTER
Open Mon.-Fri. 8.30 a.m.-5.00 p.m.
Sat. 9 a.m.-4 p.m.
P.W.WM.D.CS.A.BC.

BERKSHIRE

READING Tel. Littlewick Green
DAVID HUNT (TOOL 2743
MERCHANTS) LTD ★
KNOWL HILL, NR. READING
Open: Monday-Saturday
9.00 a.m.-5.30 p.m.
H.P.W.D.A.BC.

READING Tel. Reading 661511
WOKINGHAM TOOL CO. LTD.
99 WOKINGHAM ROAD

Open: Mon-Sat 9.00 a.m.-5.30 p.m.
Closed 1.00-2.00 p.m. for lunch
H.P.W.WM.D.CS.A.BC.

BUCKINGHAMSHIRE

MILTON KEYNES Tel. (0908)
POLLARD WOODWORKING 641366
CENTRE ★
51 AYLESBURY ST., BLETCHLEY
Open: Mon.-Fri. 8.30-5.30
Saturday 9.00-5.00
H.P.W.WM.D.CS.A.BC.

SLOUGH Tel: (06286) 5125
BRAYWOOD ESTATES LTD. ★
158 BURNHAM LANE
Open: 9.00am-5.30pm.
Monday-Saturday.
H.P.W.WM.D.CS.A.

BUCKINGHAMSHIRE

HIGH WYCOMBE Tel. (0494)
ISAAC LORD LTD. 22221
185 DESBOROUGH ROAD KE

Open: Mon.-Fri. 8.00 a.m.-5.00 p.m.
Saturday 9.00 a.m.-5.00 p.m.
H.P.W.D.A.

HIGH WYCOMBE Tel. (0494)
SCOTT SAWS LTD. 24201/33788
14 BRIDGE STREET ★

Mon.-Sat. 8.30 a.m.-6.00 p.m.

H.P.W.WM.D.T.CS.MF.A.BC.

CAMBRIDGESHIRE

CAMBRIDGE Tel: (0223) 63132
D. MACKAY LTD. ★
BRITANNIA WORKS, EAST ROAD

Open: Mon.-Fri. 8.30 a.m.-1 p.m./2.00-
5.00 p.m. Sat. 8.30 a.m.-1.00 p.m.
H.P.W.D.T.CS.MF.A.BC.

CAMBRIDGE Tel. (0223) 247386
H. B. WOODWORKING K
105 CHERRY HINTON ROAD
Open: 8.30 a.m.-5.30 p.m.
Monday-Friday
8.30 a.m.-1.00 p.m. Sat.
H.P.W.WM.D.CS.A.MF.BC.

PETERBOROUGH Tel. (0733)
WILLIAMS DISTRIBUTORS 64252
(TOOLS) LIMITED K
108-110 BURGHLEY ROAD
Open: Monday to Friday
8.30 a.m.-5.30 p.m.
H.P.A.W.D.WH.BC.

CHESHIRE

NANTWICH Tel. Crewe 67010
ALAN HOLTHAM K★
THE OLD STORES TURNERY
WISTASON ROAD, WILLASTON
Open: Tues.-Sat. 9.00 a.m.-5.30 p.m.
Closed Monday
P.W.WM.D.T.C.CS.A.BC.

WIDNES Tel: 051 424 4545/7965
THE POWER TOOL CENTRE ★
54/58 VICTORIA ROAD, WA8 7RJ
Mon.-Fri. 8.30am-5pm
Sat. 8.30am-4pm.

H.P.W.WM.D.CS.A.BC.

CLEVELAND

MIDDLESBROUGH Tel. (0642)
CLEVELAND WOODCRAFT 813103
(M'BRO), 38-42 CRESCENT ROAD K

Open: Mon-Sat 9.15 a.m.-5.30 p.m.

H.P.T.A.BC.W.WM.CS.D.

CORNWALL

SOUTH WEST Power Tools
CORNWALL Tel: Helston (03265) 4961
HELSTON AND LAUNCESTON Launceston
(0566) 4781
H.P.W.WM.D.CS.A. K

CUMBRIA

CARLISLE Tel: (0228) 36391
W. M. PLANT
ALLENBROOK ROAD
ROSEHILL, CA1 2UT
Open: Mon.-Fri. 8.00 a.m.-5.15 p.m.
Sat. 8.00 a.m.-12.30 noon
P.W.WM.D.CS.A.

DEVON

BRIXHAM Tel. (08045) 4900
WOODCRAFT SUPPLIES E★
4 HORSE POOL STREET

Open: Mon.-Sat. 9.00 a.m.-6.00 p.m.

H.P.W.A.D.MF.CS.BC.

PLYMOUTH Tel. (0752) 330303
WESTWARD BUILDING SERVICES ★
LTD., LISTER CLOSE, NEWNHAM
INDUSTRIAL ESTATE, PLYMPTON
Open: Mon-Fri 8.00 a.m.-5.30 p.m.
Sat. 8.30 a.m.-12.30 p.m.
H.P.W.WM.D.A.BC.

PLYMOUTH Tel: (0752) 665363
F.T.B. LAWSON LTD.
71 NEW GEORGE STREET
PLYMOUTH PL1 1RB
Open: Mon.-Sat. 8.30 am-5.30 pm.
H.P.W.CS.MF.A.

DORSET

WEYMOUTH Tel. (0305) 770303
WEYMOUTH HIRE & SALES LTD. K
5 KENT CLOSE
GRANBY INDUSTRIAL ESTATE
Open 7.30 a.m. - 5.30 p.m. Mon.-Fri.
Sat. 8 a.m. - 1 p.m.
H.P.W.WM.D.CS.A.K.

ESSEX

LEIGH ON SEA Tel. (0702)
MARSHAL & PARSONS LTD. 710404
1111 LONDON ROAD EK

Open: 8.30 a.m.-5.30 p.m. Mon-Fri
9.00 a.m.-5.00 p.m. Sat.
H.P.W.WM.D.CS.A.

ILFORD Tel: 597 7461
CUTWELL WOODWORKING ★
776 HIGH ROAD
GOODMAYES IG3 8SY
H.P.W.WM.D.CS.A.

GLOUCESTER

Advertise here to capture both local + national markets

HAMPSHIRE

ALDERSHOT **SOUTHAMPTON**
(0252) 334422 (0703) 332288
BIRCH & HILLS POWER TOOL CENTRES
374 HIGH ST. 7 BELVIDERE RD.
Open Mon.-Fri. 8.30-5.30. Sat. 8.30-12.30
Closed for Lunch 1.00-2.00
H.P.W.WM.D.CS.MF.BC.K.★

HERTFORDSHIRE

WARE Tel: (0920) 870 230
HEATH SAWS 870 636
6 LEESIDE WORKS K★
STANSTEAD ABBOTTS (near Ware) HERTS.
SG12 8DL
Open: Mon.-Fri. 8.30am-5.30pm
Sat. 8.30am-1pm. Sunday by appointment.
P.W.WM.D.CS.A.

ENFIELD Tel: 01-363 2935
GILL & HOXBY LTD.
131-137 ST. MARKS ROAD ADJ.
BUSH HILL PARK STATION, EN1 1BA
Mon.-Sat. 8-5.30
Early closing Wed. 1 p.m.
H.P.A.M.MC.T.S.W.

HUMBERSIDE

GRIMSBY Tel. Grimsby (0472)
58741 Hull (0482) 26999
J. E. SIDDLE LTD. (Tool Specialists) ★
83 VICTORIA STREET
Open: Mon-Fri 8.30 a.m.-5.30 p.m.
Sat. 8.30 a.m.-12.45 p.m. & 2 p.m.-5 p.m.
H.P.A.BC.W.WMD.

HULL
HUMBERSIDE FACTORING/H.F.C.
SAW SERVICING LTD.
MAIN STREET
Open: Mon.-Fri. 8am-5pm.
Saturday 8am-12.00pm.
H.P.W.WM.D.CS.A.BC.K.

KENT

**01-437 0699
= RESULTS**

GLOUCESTER

TEWKESBURY Tel. (0684)
TEWKESBURY SAW CO. LTD. 293092
TRADING ESTATE, NEWTOWN K.

Open: Mon-Fri 8.00 a.m.-5.00 p.m.
Saturday 9.30 a.m.-12.00 p.m.
P.W.WM.D.CS.

shop guide

WOOD SUPPLIERS

Classified Advertisements

All classified advertisements under £30.00 must be pre-paid: Cheques/PO made payable to A.S.P. Ltd. (WW).
Rates: Lineage: 52p per word (VAT inclusive) minimum £7.80. **Semi-display:** £8.60 + VAT per single column centimetre (minimum 2.5 x 1). **Copy to Classified Dept. (W.W.), A.S.P. Ltd., 1 Golden Square, London W1.**
All advertisements are inserted in the first available issue. There are no re-imbursements for cancellations.

Telephone 01-437-0699 ext. 290

FOR SALE

THE FINEST SELECTION ON DISPLAY IN SCOTLAND!
WOODWORKING & METALWORKING MACHINERY POWER TOOLS HAND TOOLS

THE SAW CENTRE

LARGE STOCKS COMPETITIVE PRICES. PHONE AND TRY US NOW!

Eglinton Toll, Glasgow G5 9RP Tel: 041-429-4444

38 Haymarket Edinburgh EH12 5J2 Tel: 031-337-5555

OPEN Mon - Fri 8am - 5pm Sat 9am - 1pm

WOODCARVING tools

LARGEST STOCK IN EUROPE

Henry Taylor
Arkansas Bench & Slip Stones
Strops & Strop Paste
Bench Screws, Carvers' Vices

WOODTURNING tools
Complete range of Henry Taylor handled or unhandled

send 40p in stamps for illustrated catalogue

ALEC TIRANTI LTD
70 High St, Theale, Reading, Berks RG7 5AR
27 Warren Street, London W1.

CONTENTS of 3 school workshops, engineering and woodworking machines and various tools. For detailed list write to: Warners Machinery Centre, Unit 10, Finedon Road, Irthlingborough, Northants.

QUALITY MOVEMENTS FOR QUALITY CASES
Eight Day Long case clock movements hand made of traditional design and very high quality, suitable for fitting in reproduction clock cases. These should appeal to the craftsman who requires the quality of the original Long Case movements. Dials and hands available made to your requirements. Brassware for clock cases including, capitals, escutcheons, etc. available.
Catalogue on castings + parts U.K. £1.25. Overseas £2.50.
RICHARDS OF BURTON
Woodhouse Clockworks
Swadlincote Road, Woodville
Burton-on-Trent   Tel: (0283) 219155

BANKRUPT STOCK
Sandvik circular saw blades tungsten tipped.
5", 5½", 6", 6¼" **£4.00** each
Any bore up to 30mm.
P&P £1 extra per order.
Tel: 643 0244
Hannett, 11 Lind Road, Sutton, Surrey.

BLADES
Spindle tooling, circular saw blades, dado sets, planer blades, router cutters and router accessories, machinery of particular merit, Forstener bits, mortise chisels, profile cutter blocks, radial arm saw accessories, etc.
Send £1 (refunded on first order) for your copy of our brochure.
Blades, Dept. WWM. Freepost, Petersfield, Hampshire. GU32 2BR *(no stamp required)*

STARTRITE SAW 12" Sliding table £850, Coronet lathe, Saw and planer attachment £385. Gloucestershire, Nailsworth 4674.

CORONET MAJOR (Blue) with saw, planer/thicknesser, bowl turning rest, many extras, tools and bench, £650. Plymouth 892669.

STANLEY (USA) No. 55 Rebate and moulding plane. All cutters — tilting fence — fine adjustments. In mahogany presentation box £250. Tel: 01-998 0628.

KITY 10" planer thicknesser Spindle Moulder & slot cutter. Table mounted 1½ h.p. motor. Offers. Tel: Bath (0225) 27598.

WOODWORKER MAGAZINES: from 1937 to 1984, 94 copies 1970, 71, 72 complete, 1969 and 1973 eleven copies. Offers. Mr. Morton, Letchworth (0462) 685483.

MINIMAX T90 lathe copier stand plus accessories, excellent condition, good value £770. Tel: 0884 33892.

WINDSOR CHAIRS
Full size bends. 50 × 1⅜ × 1⅛" in Ash £6.95.
Childs Windsor Chair bends in Ash 36 × 1⅛ × ⅞" £4.95.
All prices include p&p.
Please send cheque/P.O. with order to:
**P. Stuffin, Spurn View, North End Road, Tetney, Grimby DN36 5NA.
Tel: (0472) 812576
(Afternoons)**

CONTENTS OF TECH COLLEGE woodwork, engineering and sheet metal machines, some 240 volt approx 70 items. For list send s.a.e. Write only to "Trade", 155 High Street, Irthlingborough, Northants.

THE WHISTON CATALOGUE
Nuts, bolts, screws, washers, bar materials. In brass, alloy, steel, stainless steel, P.T.F.E., nylon, Tufnol, sheet material, electrical and mechanical items. We could go on and on! Better to send for free catalogue No. 114 and see for yourself.
K. R. Whiston Ltd., Dept. WW, New Mills, Stockport, Cheshire. Phone: 0663 42028.

LATHES Coronet, Myford, Arundle from £220. Also Coronet Imp Bandsaw, Multico 12" Sawbench. All 240v. Phone 0902 743675.

SERVICES

TOOL/SAW SHARPENING
DYFED SAWS
CAN OFFER A FAST, EFFICIENT, RESHARPENING SERVICE BY RETURN POST.
ALSO...
NEW T.C.T. SAWS WITH UP TO 25% OFF LIST.
Phone or write for price list.
"BWLCH-Y-FFIN", RHYDLEWIS, LLANDYSUL, DYFED, WEST WALES
RHYDLEWIS (023975) 510

RESTORATION

Furniture Restoration Materials
Everything you need to give your furniture that professional restoration look. Waxes, cleaners, french polishes, traditional upholstery supplies and many more items.
Send sae for full price list:—
Furniture Restoration Supplies,
42 Acacia Avenue, Hale,
Cheshire WA15 8QY. Tel: 061-928 3903.

CRAFT/ANTIQUE/ SECONDHAND TOOLS

Brunel Curios for collectors and craftsman tools.
Large stocks. Most trades bought, sold, sharpened.
**29 Catherine Street, Frome, Somerset BA11 1DB.
Tel: 0373 63226**

QUALITY TOOLS for craftsmen and collectors, order list £1. All types of woodwork tools wanted, particular paring chisels, pre-war carving tools, wooden planes. The Old Tool Store, Kirkby Fenside, East Kirkby, Spilsby, Lincs. PE23 3DD. Phone 07903 372.

SECONDHAND/TRADITIONAL tools — bought & sold. Norris, Spiers, Preston, Stanley, Record, Addis, etc., and our own. List £1. Bristol Design, 14 Perry Road, Bristol. Tel: (0272) 291740.

HANDTOOLS & MACHINERY. Antique and modern. Wood and metalworking. Bought and sold. The Tool Box, Craft Centre, Umbourne Bridge, Colyton, Devon. (0297) 52868.

ANTIQUE and modern woodworking tools bought and sold at Woodworkers World, 77 Shakespear Street, Derby. Tel: Derby (0332) 761779.

OLD WOODWORKING TOOLS AND BOOKS bought, exchanged and sold. Paul Rougetel, 77 Watergate Row, Chester. Tel: 0244 — 318782.

THE TOOL SHOP, BOSHAM WALK, Bosham, Chichester, Sussex. For collectors and second hand tools. Tel: 0243 572937/572475.

WORKWEAR

WORKWEAR
Smocks to protect clothing in washable polyester/cotton twill. Unisex fitting size range. For leaflet and colour swatch send S.A.E. to:
Geinine Brown (Styled Garments)
8 Belmont Road, Malvern, Worcs. WR14 1PL.

FILL THIS SPACE!
01-437 0699

MARQUETRY

MARQUETRY stars, shells and fans, made to order inlays for restoration and reproductions. Send design and colour scheme for quote to: S. Rockwood, 13-15 Seel Street, The Courtyard, Liverpool L1 4AU or Telephone 051-708 8961. Send large S.A.E. for details.

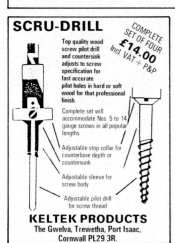

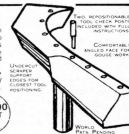

LONDON BOROUGH OF REDBRIDGE PERSONAL SERVICES DIRECTORATE - SOCIAL SERVICES

DESIGNER/TECHNICIAN FOR DISABLED PEOPLE
(Based at Barkingside)

Salary: £8,619 inclusive to £9,378 inclusive

This post is based at Oakside Industrial Rehabilitation Unit, Fullwell Cross, Barkingside, Essex. The Unit is concerned with training disabled people to gain employment.

The Designer/Technician will be enthusiastic, flexible and able to initiate ideas and resolve problems in a practical sense to help disabled people overcome their problems in everyday living in the community.

The successful applicant is likely to be a craftsman carpenter holding appropriate qualifications and have some design flair/experience, able to take up the challenge of making furniture and equipment for handicapped people.

Working hour arrangements allow for one days paid leave per month in addition to the annual 21 days leave entitlement.

The successful applicant will be required to carry tools and goods to clients homes therefore an appropriate car allowance will be paid.

Applicants are invited to contact Oakside Manager, Sam Small, on 01-500 8772 to arrange an informal visit to the Unit for more information. Copies of job description and application forms are available from:
Director of Social Services, Personal Services Directorate, 17/23 Clements Road, Ilford, Essex.
Or telephone our answering service on 01-478 3020 extension 4147.
Please quote reference number: 916
Closing date: 29-5-87

Woodworkers, Joiners & Carpenters
YOU CAN'T CHANGE THE WORLD.
But you **can** make a world of difference.

Skills taken for granted in this country are vital to members of poorer Third World communities.

In a world which by and large does nothing about poverty and injustice (let alone hunger), VSO volunteers work directly with those seeking to become more self-reliant:

No one can change the world. But as a VSO volunteer, you could make a world of difference.

We are now receiving requests for January '88 departure. The jobs include instructing young people, mostly school leavers, in basic woodworking skills to help them get jobs or set up their own businesses. Most of the work will be using locally available wood and hand tools. Some jobs will be training people in the building and construction trades. If you like working with people and have the necessary qualifications and skills for these jobs, please apply now.

You should be without dependants and willing to work for the local rate of pay. Postings are for two years – although many choose to stay longer – and most U.K. employers should be prepared to grant leave of absence.

For more information please complete and return.

VSO Charity no. 313757.

I'm interested.
I have the following training/experience:
_____
Name_____
Address_____

VSO SUPPORTS WALK FOR THE WORLD MAY 9 – JUNE 6

Post to: **Enquiries Unit, Voluntary Service Overseas, 9 Belgrave Square, London SW1X 8PW.** (24p S.A.E. appreciated).   W/6/87

Woodworker

CONTENTS

design . . . craft . . . and the love of wood

July 1987
Vol. 91
No. 7

FEATURES

WOODWORKER

VOL. LVI. No. 701. APRIL 1952 ONE SHILLING

GARDEN SEAT
(See pages 61-63)

Other features in this issue:
BRUSH MAKING : REFRIGERATOR CABINET : PICTORIAL MARQUETRY
WOOD TURNING FOR THE BEGINNER : WARDROBE
MEASURED DRAWING — SERPENTINE-FRONT SIDEBOARD

PROJECTS

REGULARS

On the cover: *John Storrs in his workshop – see p568. Photo David Walker, CoSIRA.* **Above:** *the way it was then. Make the garden seat from p609*

Editor Aidan Walker
Deputy editor John Hemsley
Assistant editor Kerry Fowler
Advertisement manager Trevor Pryer
Advertisement production Laura Champion
Graphics Jeff Hamblin / ASP Design Studio
Technical illustrator Peter Holland
Guild of Woodworkers John Hemsley, Kerry Fowler

Unfortunately we cannot accept responsibility for loss of or damage to unsolicited material. We reserve the right to refuse or suspend advertisements, and regret we cannot guarantee the bone fides of advertisers.
Published every third Friday

Editorial, advertisements and Guild of Woodworkers
1 Golden Square, London W1R 3AB; telephone 01-437 0626

ABC
UK circulation
Jan-Dec 86
32,849

Back issues and subscriptions Infonet Ltd, 10-13 Times House, 179 Marlowes, Hemel Hempstead, Herts HP1 1BB; telephone Hemel Hempstead (0442) 48434

Subscriptions per year UK £16.90; overseas outside USA (accelerated surface post) £21.00, USA (accelerated surface post) £28, airmail £48

UK trade SM Distribution Ltd, 16-18 Trinity Gardens, London SW9 8DX; telephone 01-274 8611

North American trade Bill Dean Books Ltd, 151-49 7th Avenue, PO Box 69, Whitestone, New York 11357; tel. 1-718-767-6632

Printed by Chase Web, Plymouth
Mono origination Multiform Photosetting Ltd, Cardiff
Colour origination Derek Croxson Ltd, Chesham, Bucks
© Argus Specialist Publications Ltd 1987
ISSN 0043 776X

Argus Specialist Publications Ltd

1 Golden Square, London W1R 3AB; 01-437 0626

This month

Hitching a LIFS Student furniture at the London International Furniture Show, as uncompromising as ever; surprising co-winner was Julienne Dolphin — Wilding's 'rope chair' (**far left**); another of her marine-inspired pieces **left**. **Below**, Christopher Lyons and Nicholas O'Flynn of the LCF worked their CNC equipment hard to get this table and chair set; **bottom**, D. Livingstone of Cornwall College's answer to the variable height problem. **Right**, Rycotewood's Philip Chandler made this walnut side table, and **far right**, Jayne Muir of Newcastle on Tyne Polytechnic the shelf/storage unit in bird's-eye maple and ash

NEWS DIGEST

Design in Furniture is a new high-design furniture show from Philbeach Events, the creators of LIFS and the 'Style' series, to be held at Olympia 2 from **25-28 October**. Show organiser Jacqui Wheeler quotes their research into the demand for an autumn furniture show, 'which made it evident that the furniture industry was looking for a high-design exhibition.' The Henley Centre's findings point to a growing consumer and retail interest in contemporary furniture, and potential for huge growth in the 'high design' sector. Applications for space will be accepted subject to approval of the products to be shown, and there may be a limit on stand size to get as many exhibitors as possible in. Write to Philbeach Events, Earls Court Exhibition Centre, London SW5 9TA, 01-385 1200.

The Model Horse-Drawn Vehicles Club is holding a **show of models** at College Farm, 45 Fitzalan Rd, London N3 on **19 July**. Details from R. Bates, 169 Middleham Rd, London N18 2RY, 01-807 7745. The Club invites any maker to display models, but you must let them know what you want to bring.

The New Spirit: innovation in British Craft and Design. New approaches to furniture are brought together in this Crafts Council exhibition, which shows work by makers who have been attracting international acclaim and media coverage; including sculptural metal by Andre Dubreuil, John Webb

and Tom Dixon; a rough hewn timber table by Daniel Reynolds; and ornate collaged mirrors by Sue Golden.

● 24 June-6 September, Crafts Council Gallery, 12 Waterloo Place, London SW1Y 4AU.

Also, the **International Turned Object Show**, whose leading light is Albert LeCoff, is a juried/invitational **exhibition of world-class turnings**; sculpture, furniture, bowls, vessels, you name it. ITOS is expected to tour for two years in the US, Canada, UK, Australia, Japan and New Zealand; LeCoff, who started woodturning seminars in the US in 1975 and is organising a Woodturning Centre for promotion of the craft/art, will be speaking at the Loughborough Seminar. For further details of ITOS, write to

ITOS, American Association of Woodturners, PO Box 982, San Marcos, TX 78667, USA.

Appreciating Wood, the Australian third national **Wood Conference** in Canberra, will include presentations by turner Mick O'Donnell, furniture maker Richard La Trobe Bateman, and carver Susan Wraight. Dates are **27-30 November**, and there are post-conference workshops. Details from Woodcraft Guild ACT Inc., PO Box 1411, Woden, ACT, Australia 2902.

Open Day: Midland School of French Polishing are holding their second annual open day on **Saturday 18 July**. Come for a chat and discuss your traditional-finishing problems; 18a Mansfield Rd, Eastwood, Notts NG16 3AQ, (0773) 715911.

Chris Simpson, leader of the Furniture Design course at Rycotewood College, is leaving the world of academia and setting up as an independent furniture designer/maker, specialising in replicas of classics by giants such as Van Der Rohe, Gaudi, Thonet, Gimson, Mackintosh . . . 54 High St, Thame, Oxon OX9 3AH, (084 421) 2500.

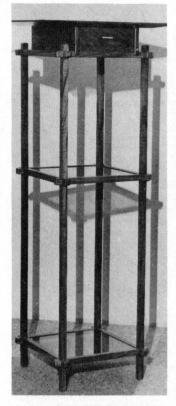

Trend Award The delicious de luxe specially-made cabinet full of £300 of Trend TCT and HSS router cutters — and that's only first prize! Second is another identical cabinet with £150 worth of cutters. Make sure you enter the Trend Award at the **London Woodworker Show** if you're a routerist — details in 'This Month', WW/June or your Show entry form

Router lathe

Peter Skilton's article 'Plant on top' in our 'routing special' section of May's WOODWORKER says imports of the Sears-Craftsman router lathe have 'apparently dried up'. We are happy to say that the tool is available from **A-Z Tool Sales**, Kettlebrook Rd, Tamworth, Staffs, (0827) 56767, and from **Steerdawn Ltd**, PO Box 404, Rednal B45 9HS, 021-453 6633. We are sorry to those companies for any inconvenience this may have caused.

NEW PRODUCTS

Complete range of TCT **sawblades** from Royalsaw for portable and lightweight saws — including the 'revolutionary "Chip Devil"'.

Aaronson Bros, who make Contiboard and Contiplas, announce 'the first of many new ideas you'll be seeing' — the Conti Job Mate, a set of **clamps, markers and spacers** for putting carcases together from their board products; £6.99 retail from most stores.

Footprint are now doing a **Precision Honing Guide**, manufactured under licence from Lee Valley Tools of Ottawa. It's in two parts, a pentangle setting gauge and a honer with a 'bridge' type construction. You can grind then hone without re-setting the blade in the guide, which takes all kinds of chisel and plane irons. £13.65+VAT.

Trend are now doing a one-metre long version of their **tracking fence**, which will allow you to make yet longer perfectly straight cuts with your hand-held router. It's available with a universal base plate for use with any portable router, and costs £42.70+VAT.

Woodworker 1986 Indexes now available; £1.25 inc. p&p from Reader Services, 9 Hall Rd, Mayland Wood Estate, Hemel Hempstead, Herts HP2 7BH.

● Royalsaw, Midhage Associates, 2 Poplar Grove, Bollington, Macclesfield, Cheshire SK10 5LS, (0625) 74123: Aaronson Bros PLC, Aro House, 18-19 Long Lane, London EC1A 9NT, 01-606 8050: Footprint Tools Ltd, PO Box 19, Hollis Croft, Sheffield S1 3HY, (0742) 753200: Trend, Unit N, Penfold Works, Imperial Way, Watford, Herts WD2 4YY, (0923) 49911.

A WOODWORKER SPECIAL

Amid escalating concern about growing crime rates and the safety and security of your home, WOODWORKER has done the decent thing — produced a special guide for the sake of your peace of mind. The WOODWORKER GUIDE TO HOME SECURITY gives detailed information on the products you can buy and the ways to fit and use them — locks for doors and windows, viewers, safes, child-proofing, lighting, alarms, fire doors . . . it's all there. Don't be without the information you need to make the marauder's life a misery!

£1.50 from newsagents or £2 inc. p&p from Infonet, 10-13 Times House, 179 Marlowes, Hemel Hempstead, Herts HP1 1BB

AXMINSTER POWER TOOL CENTRE

HORIZONTAL WETSTONE GRINDERS (OUR PRICE INC. VAT)

JAPANESE Wetstone grinder £129.00
180G stone for above £40.00
1000G stone for above £40.00
6000G stone for above £43.00
PRECISION grinding jig £43.00

SHARPENSET Wetstone grinder £240.00
SHARPENSET 150G stone £18.40
SHARPENSET 280G stone £20.41
SHARPENSET Green stone (TCT) ... £18.40
10" Planer Knife grinding jig £65.00
15" Planer Knife grinding jig £78.00
CHISEL grinding jig £67.00

VERTICAL WETSTONE GRINDERS

SCANGRIND 150 6" wetstone £77.95
SCANGRIND 200 8" wetstone £99.00
SCANTOOL COMBI WET AND DRY STONES
COMBI SC150 6" wet & dry £89.00
COMBI SC200 8" wet & dry £112.00
LUNA KIRUNA 11" wet & 4" dry .. £125.00
LUNA KIRUNA 14" wet & 5" dry .. £195.00

BENCH GRINDERS

ELU EDS163 6" 360W £73.95
ELU EDS164 7" 390W £77.95
ELU MWA149 6" Honer grinder £90.95
LEROY SOMER 5" 180W £33.00
LEROY SOMER 6" 250W £44.00
LEROY SOMER 6" with chuck £49.00
WARCO 5" 180W (European) £33.00
WARCO 6" 380W (European) £43.00
WARCO 8" 570W (European) £69.00

GRIND STONES (state bore size)

	5"	6"	7"
COARSE 36G	£6.60	£7.90	£11.40
FINE 60G	£6.60	£7.90	£11.40
WHITE 60G	£7.20	£8.50	£13.50
GREEN (TCT)	£7.20	£8.50	£13.50

JIGSAWS (Light Duty)

Bosch PST50 Single Speed £29.95
Bosch PST50E Var. Speed £38.50
Bosch PST55PE Var. Speed Pend ... £68.50
Hitachi FJ50SB Single speed £29.50
Hitachi FJ50VA Var. speed £37.95
Hitachi FCJ55V Var. Speed Pend. Act £61.95

JIGSAWS (Heavy Duty)

Elu ST142 2 speed £101.95
Elu ST142E Var. speed £110.95
Elu ST152 2 Speed £98.95
Elu ST152E Var. speed £106.95
Cases for above Jigsaws £10.00
Hitachi CJ65 2 speed £100.95
Hitachi CJ65VA Var. speed £104.95
Hitachi CJ65V Var. speed £104.95
Bosch 1581.7 Var. speed £108.95

DISC AND BELT SANDERS

Picador 10" Disc Sander £219.00
Warco BDS460 6" Disc 4" Belt £86.00
Warco BDS690 9" Disc 6" Belt £179.00
Holmes 6" 2HP £399.00
Luna Favourite 4" £285.00
Luna De-Lux Sander 4" £599.00
Luna YKV Pad Sander £647.00
Luna YK1500 Pad Sander 1PH .. £1564.00
Luna YK1500 Pad Sander 3PH .. £1509.00
Picador Unmotorised 3" Belt £49.00
Picador Unmotorised 3" Belt £65.00
Holmes 4" Belt Sander £94.00
Holmes 6" Belt Sander £120.00

CIRCULAR SAWS

HITACHI FC5SA 6" TCT 710W £42.95
BOSCH PKS46 6" TCT 600W £53.50
BOSCH PKS66 7⅞ TCT 1200W £90.95
HITACHI PSU6 6" 1050W HSS £79.95
HITACHI PSU7 7" 1600W HSS £103.95
HITACHI PSU9 9" 1759W HSS £133.95
HITACHI PSM7 7" 1200W TCT £151.50
HITACHI PSM9 9" 1600W TCT £160.50
ELU MH151 6" 850W TCT £90.95
ELU MH65 7" 1200W TCT £131.95
ELU MH85 9" 1600W TCT £177.95
ELU MH182 8" 1400W TCT £148.95
ELU 550 COMBI (for MH182) £130.00
ELU555 Snip saw (for 182) £179.00
WOLF 9" CIRCULAR SAW £135.00

FINISHING SANDERS

(DB Dust Bag)

BOSCH PSS230 1/3rd Sheet £29.95
HITACHI FS10SA 1/3rd Sheet £27.95
HITACHI FSV12 Sheet DB £53.50
BOSCH PS280A ½ Sheet DB £59.95
B&D P6303 ½ Sheet £59.95
ELU MVS156 1/3rd Sheet DB £73.95
ELU MVS156E Var. Speed DB £85.95
ELU MVS 94 ½ Sheet DB £111.95
ELU MVS47 ½ Sheet £123.95
HITACHI SV12 ½ Sheet £116.95
HITACHI SOD110 ½ Sheet DB £94.50
HITACHI SO110 ½ Sheet £86.95
BOSCH 1288 9½ Sheet DB £99.95
WOLF ½ Sheet DB £96.00

POWER TOOL WORK BENCHES

Post/Delivery £5.00

TRITON £159.00
Stand £29.00
Router/Jigsaw Base £39.00
Wheel Kit £9.50
DUNLOP POWER BASE £119.95
Extension Table £21.50
Additional sole plates £8.65
WOLFCRAFT VARIOTEC £59.50
BOSCH MT92 Saw Table £109.95

POWER PLANES (Light Duty) (OUR PRICE INC. VAT)

BLACK & DECKER DN710 ...... £29.95
BOSCH PHO100 82mm 450W £47.95
HITACHI FP20SA 82mm 320W £41.50

HEAVY DUTY

ELU MFF80 82mm 850W £109.95
ELU MFF80K (in kit box) £127.95
ELU MFF40 82mm 1000W £189.95
INVERSION Std. for MFF80 ...... £20.95
INVERSION Std. for MFF40 ...... £29.00
HITACHI P20SA 82mm 720W £100.95
HITACHI FU20 82mm 620W £97.50
HITACHI F30A 92mm 900W £143.50

BELT SANDERS

ELU MHB 157 3" 600W £106.95
ELU MHB 157E 3" var. speed £119.95
ELU 157 FRAME £35.00
ELU 157 inversion stand £28.00
ABRASIVE BELTS FOR MHB 157/pkt. 3
40G, 60G, 80G, 100G, 120G, 150G £3.00
BOSCH PBS75 3" 620W £71.95
ELU MHB 90 4" 850W £193.95
ELU MHB 90K With frame £234.95
HITACHI SB75 3" 950W £117.95
HITACHI SB10T 4" 950W £141.95
HITACHI SB10V 4" var. speed £148.50
MAKITA 9401 4" 1040W £169.00
MAKITA 9924DB 3" 950W £117.00

BISCUIT JOINTER

ELU DS140 Biscuit Jointer £197.95
No. 20 Biscuits (1000 off) £19.95
No. 10 Biscuits (1000 off) £19.50
No. 0 Biscuits (1000 off) £18.63
Mixed Box 0, 10, 20 (500 off) £12.50
DS140 saw blade 12T Std. £29.95
DS140 saw blade 30T Fine £29.50
DS140 Dust Tube adaptor £5.95
BOSCH Biscuit Jointer £124.95

★ ★ ★ **SPECIAL OFFERS** ★ ★ ★

WOODSCREWS

Twin Fast Zinc Plated GKN 1600 Woodscrews from 1" × 6 to 2" × 10" with Free Screwdriver. (State slotted or pozidrive).
ONLY £19.99 inc. VAT and P&P

RIDGWAY DRILL MORTICER

c/w Free Hitachi Drill ½" Chuck and ¼" Chisel and Bit
£186.00 inc. VAT and P&P

MARTEK DRILL SHARPENER

Excellent for Sharpening all Drill Bits
ONLY **£24.95** inc. VAT and P&P

POWER BREAKERS

Avoid electric shocks when using power tools. A must for all power tools at **£19.95** inc. VAT and P&P

S.D.S. POWER DRILLS

Hitachi DH16v £119.95
Hitachi VRV16 ...... £182.95
B&D PB020 ...... £112.95
B&D P8020T (c/w 110v Transformer) £185.95

DRILL/BREAKERS

Hitachi DH28Y £291.50
Hitachi DH50SA £478.50
HAMMERS
H55 SA £418.50
H90 SA £780.00

POWER DRILLS (K-Kit box)

NEW ELU POWER DRILLS
ECD304K 420W V/S 10mm Compact £73.95
EMD400K 600W 2 Speed 13mm £81.95
ESD705K 320W V/S & Rev. 10mm £102.95
EMD403K 500W V/S/R Ham. 13mm £90.95
EMD405K 500W V/S/R Ham. 13mm £114.95
EMD406K 550W V/S Hammer 13mm £106.95

B&D 2162 KM V/S RW 450v £63.95
B&D P2264K 13mm 2 Speed 550W £74.95
B&D P2266K 13mm V/S Rev. 480W £69.95

BOSCH 400-2 10mm 440W £29.95
BOSCH 500RLE 13mm 500W V/S Rev. £49.95
BOSCH 7002E 13mm 700W £79.95
BOSCH 850RLT 13mm 850W V/S Re £111.95

HITACHI FV12VA 13mm 420W V/S £40.50
HITACHI FDV16V 13mm 600W V/S/R £61.95
HITACHI FDV20VA 13mm 710W V/S/R £82.95
HITACHI VTP13K 13mm 2 Speed 460W £86.00
HITACHI VTP16AK 2 Spd. 800W . £118.50

ANGLE GRINDERS

HITACHI PDP100C 4" £44.85
HITACHI G13SB 5" 750W £66.81
HITACHI G23SC 9" 2000W £89.00

PALM GRIP SANDERS

(DB Dust Bag)

ELU MVS500 1/6th Sheet 135W DB £60.95
ELU MVS501 1/4 Sheet 135W DB £60.95
B&D P6301 1/6th Sheet 136W DB £51.50
B&D P6302 1/4 Sheet 135W DB £51.50
HITACHI SV12SA 1/4 Sheet 180W £51.50
MAKITA BO45 10 1/4 Sheet £43.95

LIBERON WAXES

Waxes Sealers Stains Polishes Etc.
All Your Requirements in One
Send for Free Price List

GLUE POT ...... £23.00 inc. P&P
470 FLUTED DOWELS 6mm 8mm 10mm ...... £5.75 inc. P&P

HITACHI 10mm CORDLESS DRILL-SCREWDRIVERS (OUR PRICE inc. VAT)

DTC 10 6 cell 2 spd. & rev. £79.95
DRC10 as above torque adjustable . £98.50
DTC10K 6 cell 2 spd. & rev. in case £86.50
D10DB 6 cell variable spd. & rev. ... £88.50
D10DD 8 cell 2 spd. & rev. £90.00
D10D as above torque adjustable £111.00
DV10D 8 cell 2 spd. & rev. hammer £115.95

MAKITA 10mm CORDLESS DRILL SCREWDRIVERS

6012DWK 6 cell 2 spd. & rev. in case £92.95
6012HDW 8 cell 2 spd. torque adj. £111.95
8400DW 8 cell 1 spd. & rev. hammer £119.95
MAGNETIC Screwdriver kit 7 piece .. £5.95
REPLACEMENT BITS (state type) £0.50

CORDLESS TOOLS (OUR PRICE INC. VAT)

HITACHI CK12D Knife cutter £103.85
HITACHI C6DA 6" Circular saw ... £143.95
MAKITA 5600DW 6" circular saw £179.95
MAKITA 4300DW Jig saw £119.95
B&D INDUSTRIAL Jig saw £110.95
BOSCH INDUSTRIAL PAINTS STRIPPER £82.95
BELLE ELECTRIC CEMENT MIXER £135.00

MISCELLANEOUS POWER TOOLS

KEW HOBBY PRESSURE WASHER £239.00
DREMEL D576 FRETSAW £69.95
BOSCH WET 'n' DRY Vacuum cleaner £110
BOSCH 520 HOT AIR paint stripper £27.00
BOSCH 560 HOT AIR paint stripper £39.00
NEW ELU DUST EXTRACTORS
EVE 938 ...... £275 EVE 948 ...... £395

SASH CRAMPS (P&P £2.00 per order) may be mixed for quantity

RECORD 135-24" 1 off .. £18 5 off .. £17.50
135-36" 1 off .... £20 5 off £19
135-48" 1 off £22.50 5 off £19.50
135-48" 1 off .... £21 5 off £20

DRAPER 18" 1 off ...... £14 5 off £12
30" 1 off ...... £17 5 off £15
42" 1 off ...... £19 5 off £17
T bar 42" 1 off ...... £30 5 off £28

RECORD CRAMP HEADS M130
1 off £10.40 5 off £10.00 (P&P £1.50)

PARAMO CRAMP HEADS
1 off £10.00 5 off £9.00 (P&P £1.50)

G CRAMPS (P&P £1.50 per order) may be mixed for quantity

RECORD 120-3" 1 off .. £5.20 5 off .. £4.80
120-4" 1 off .. £5.50 5 off .. £4.90
120-6" 1 off .. £7.50 5 off .. £6.90
120-8" 1 off £11.00 5 off £9.80
120-10" 1 off £18.00 5 off £17.00
RECORD DEEP THROAT 4" 1 off ... £13.27

PARAMO 3" 1 off .... £5.30 5 off £4.60
4" 1 off .... £5.55 5 off £4.78
6" 1 off .... £7.76 5 off £6.60
8" 1 off ... £11.41 5 off £9.50
10" 1 off . £16.90 5 off . £15.77
PARAMO DEEP THROAT 4" 1 off ... £12.45

KLEMSIA QUICK CLAMPS

(P&P £1.50)

SPAN	REACH	1 off
200mm	110mm	£3.70
300mm	110mm	£4.00
400mm	110mm	£4.40
600mm	110mm	£5.20
800mm	110mm	£6.00
1000mm	110mm	£7.10
200mm	150mm	£6.70
200mm	200mm	£6.10

★ ★ ★ ★ ★ ★ ★ ★ ★ ★ ★ ★ ★ ★ ★ ★

Taunton Press
Fine Woodworking Books
All titles ex stock
£7.95 inc. P&P

★ ★ ★ ★ ★ ★ ★ ★ ★ ★ ★ ★ ★ ★ ★ ★

RECORD HAND PLANES

(P&P £1.50/Order)

03 Smoothing 240 × 45mm . £19.50
04 Smoothing 245 × 50mm . £17.99
041/2 Smoothing 260 × 60mm . £18.99
05 Jack 355 × 50mm £21.99
051/2 Jack 380 × 60mm £29.50
06 Jointer 455 × 60mm £33.99
07 Jointer 560 × 60mm £39.75
778 Rebate 215 × 38mm £30.80
010 Rebate 330 × 44mm £39.50
020C Circular Plane £69.50
0601/2 Block Plane £16.50
073 Shoulder Rebate £42.50
CLIFTON 420 Rebate Plane £57.00
CLIFTON Multi-Plane £189.00
CLIFTON Cap Iron 2" or 2⅜" £5.00

STANLEY HAND PLANES

(P&P £1.50/Order)

3 Smoothing 240 × 45mm . £23.60
4 Smoothing 245 × 50mm . £20.00
41/2 Smoothing 260 × 60mm . £21.60
5 Jack 355 × 50mm £27.00
51/2 Jack 380 × 60mm £28.00
6 Fore 455 × 60mm £37.80
7 Jointer 560 × 60mm £39.40
78 Duplex Rebate £18.50
10 Rebate 330 × 44mm £33.00
80 Scraper £9.50
601/2 Block Plane £21.00
92 Rebate Plane £22.50
CLIFTON 3 in 1 Rebate Plane £67.00
RECORD 3 in 1 Plane £39.00

WOODWORKING VICES (P&P £4.50)

RECORD 52½E 9" Quick Release ... £44.00
52½ED 9" Quick Release £47.00
53E 10" Quick Release ... £69.00

DRILL BIT SETS

	Lip & Spur	HSS Std.
1/16"-½" × 64ths	—	£21.00
1/16"-½" × 32nds	£42.00	£17.00
1-13mm × 0.5mm	£54.00	£19.00

JAPANESE WATER STONES (P&P £1.00)

KING BRAND 800G WETSTONE £8.00
KING BRAND 1200G WETSTONE £8.00
SUPER FINISHING STONE 6000G £8.90
COMBINATION WATER STONE £10.80

MISCELLANEOUS HAND TOOLS (P&P £1.50 PER ORDER)

RECORD Dowel Jig £34.00
140 Corner Cramps £12.00
145 Hold Fast £12.90
Floorboard Cramp .. £56.95
18" Extension Rods . £4.95
141 Corner Cramps £19.40
146 Hold Fast £14.70
169 Bench Stop £7.50
Drill Bushes £1.90
Spare Collars £3.20
Priory Bench Stop ... £2.95
STANLEY Web Clamp £7.99
Stanley Yankee Screwdrivers 13" ...... £12.86 20" ...... £14.17 27" £18.50

HANDSAWS (P&P £1.50)

DISSTON D8 26" 6pt ...... £27 RIDGWAY SPEED SAW 22" or 26" £19
ROBERTS & LEE 10" DOVETAIL BRASS BACK £21 ROBERTS & LEE DORCHESTER 10" £27

SANDERSON KAYSER "PAX" HANDSAWS (P&P £1.50)

BRASS BACK TENNON SAWS 8" £18.50 10" £19 12" £19.50 14" £20 D/Tail £25
HANDSAWS 20" × 10pt £21 22" × 8pt £22 24" × 7pt £23 6" × 6pt £24 26" × Rip £24

CHISEL SETS (State bevel edge or firmer P&P £1.00/Order)

MARPLES CARVERS ASH 4 piece .. £13.60
MARPLES SPLITPROOF 4 piece .. £24.50
MARPLES BOXWOOD 5 piece .. £38.50
PARAMO ROSEWOOD 4 piece .. £29.50
STANLEY 5001 6 piece .. £33.39
MARPLES BLUE CHIP 4 piece .. £17.42
MARPLES BLUE CHIP 5 piece .. £23.00
SORBY BOXWOOD 5 piece .. £26.00
PARAMO ROSEWOOD 6 piece .. £42.50
STANLEY 5002 5 piece .. £23.68

WOODTURNING CHISEL SETS (P&P £1.80)

HENRY TAYLOR Carbon Steel Sets, 3 Piece ...... £17 5 Piece ...... £29 8 Piece £46
SORBY Carbon Steel Sets 5 Piece (51c) ...... £26 6 Piece (61c) .... £45 8 Piece (82c) £63
SORBY High Speed Sets 5 Piece (51h) .... £40 6 Piece (61h) .... £81 8 Piece (82h) £107
LUNA Swedish Steel Sets GOOD VALUE 3 Piece ...... £14 4 Piece ...... £27 5 Piece £37
MINIATURE SETS SORBY HSS set of 5 ...... £28 HENRY TAYLOR SUPER FIVE £18

ABRASIVES (West German top quality P&P £1.00/Order)

SANDING BELTS resin bonded aluminium oxide cloth belts (price each)

Size (length width)	M/C	40G	60G	80G	100G	120G
75 × 480mm — 3" × 19"	(Elu)	£1.11	£1.08	£0.99	£1.05	£1.02
75 × 510mm — 3" × 20"	(B&D)	£1.14	£1.12	£1.03	£1.07	£1.04
75 × 533mm — 3" × 21"	(Bosch Hit)	£1.28	£1.17	£1.07	£1.09	£1.05
100 × 560mm 4" × 22"	(Elu 90)	£1.58	£1.43	£1.40	£1.37	£1.32
100 × 610mm 4" × 24"	(Wolf Hit)	£1.67	£1.53	£1.48	£1.43	£1.38
100 × 915mm — 4" × 36"	(Coronet)	£2.22	£1.99	£1.88	£1.85	£1.81
150 × 1090mm — 6" × 42"	(Coronet)	£4.20	£3.80	£3.55	£3.45	£3.40

★ ★ OTHER SIZES AVAILABLE ON REQUEST MANY IN STOCK ★ ★

ABRASIVE SHEETS (P&P £0.50 PER ORDER) state grit when ordering 100G and finer

Type	Description	60G/10	60G/50	80G/10	80G/50	100G+/10	100G+/50
PGF	GARNET FINISHING	£2.13	£8.90	£1.85	£7.70	£1.67	£6.94
GCAB	GARNET CABINET	£3.02	£12.59	£2.61	£10.90	£2.35	£9.82
PSF	SILICON FINISHING	£3.16	£13.17	£2.73	£11.40	£2.46	£10.27
WS	WET 'n' DRY	£6.19	£25.81	£5.28	£22.03	£3.59	£14.99

★**SPECIAL OFFER**★ 50 Sheets of asstd. Abrasives **£5.99** inc. P&P Garnet-Glass-W/Dry

WIRE WOOL

	0000 Fine	00/0 Medium	1/2 Coarse	3/4 V Coarse
1 KG ROLLS	£4.73	£4.35	£4.25	£4.13
250g ROLLS	£1.50	£1.45	£1.42	£1.38

SAVE 20% ON ALL HAND TOOLS SEND NOW FOR NEW HAND TOOL CATALOGUE £1.50 (REFUNDABLE ON 1st ORDER

0297 33656 24 hour answerphone **CHARD STREET AXMINSTER DEVON** 6.30-9pm **34836** BARCLAYCARD VISA

The grand furniture saga

Thomas Chippendale, 18th-century master craftsman, needs no introduction. But his contemporary reputation owed much to his entrepreneurial and marketing talents, as Vic Taylor explains

The 18th century, often described as the 'Golden Age of Cabinet Making' was dominated by the personalities of Thomas Chippendale Snr, George Hepplewhite, and Thomas Sheraton.

England was at last at peace with Europe after the Peninsular Wars, and had gained footholds all over the world by the Treaty of Utrecht in 1713. The religious strife which had bedevilled the Tudor and Stuart periods had been settled for ever, and trade with both the East and West could now develop — the Hudson's Bay Company had actually been granted a charter in 1670, but trading rights weren't recognised by the French until 1713.

Probably the largest stimulus for trade came with the emergence of a new class — that of the landed gentry. The old 'open field' system of peasant farming was recognised as wasteful of land and time, and incapable of improvement or experiment. In the 18th century the system of Enclosure Acts forced the peasants to sell their strips of land to any person rich enough to bid for them; in the reign of George II a quarter of a million acres were enclosed and more than six million under George III when the change was at its height.

There were plenty of buyers for enclosed land. Many men had grown rich in the industrial towns, but they were still social nonentities unless they had acquired land, which not only gave them status, but more importantly, the right to take part in local and national government.

Members of this social class bought Josiah Wedgwood's pottery ware and made him a fortune, and, along with the aristocracy, became the target of Chippendale's *The Gentleman and Cabinet Maker's Director*, first published in 1754. An enlarged edition was published in weekly parts between 1759 and 1762.

Thomas Chippendale Snr was born at Otley, Yorkshire in 1718, the son of the village carpenter, although N. I. Bienenstock, editor of the American *The Furniture World* points out 'others believe that he [Chippendale] was born in London and that his father, also a cabinetmaker, was already well known for his skill.'

The confusion arises because the earliest records tell of his marriage to Catherine Redshaw in London in 1748. He lived at Conduit Court in Long Acre from 1749 to 1752, then Somerset Court, Strand, and finally at 60-61 St Martin's Lane, at the Sign of the Chair, until he died from tuberculosis in 1779. A plaque near the junction of St Martin's Lane and Long Acre marks the site of the workshop.

In 1754 he took James Rannie into partnership until Rannie's death in 1766; in 1772 Thomas Haig (Rannie's book-keeper) became the new partner and survived Chippendale until he himself died in 1796. There was also a third partner, Henry Ferguson, about whom little is known.

Chippendale and Rannie were known as cabinetmakers and upholsterers — or upholders — and therein lay the secret of their success. *The London Tradesman* (1747) details an upholder's skills: 'This tradesman's genius must be universal in every branch of furniture . . . He employs journeymen in his own proper calling, cabinet makers, glass grinders, looking-glass frame carvers, carvers for chairs, testers, and post of beds, the woollen draper, the mercer, the linen draper, several species of smiths, and a vast many tradesmen of other mechanic branches'. And the book goes on to say 'A master cabinet maker is a very profitable trade; especially if he works for and serves the quality himself; but if he must serve them through the channel of the upholder, his profits are not very considerable.' No doubt every cabinetmaker's ambition was to become an upholder!

● *Formal day-bed by Giles Grendey, 1730. Made in beech, japanned in red with silver and gilt decoration*

The trade card of Strickland and Jenkins, cabinet-makers and upholsterers, in business circa 1773–93. Reproduced by courtesy of the Trustees of the British Museum.

The popular image of Chippendale as a lonely craftsman lovingly creating masterpieces in his dusty workshop is almost as far from the truth as you can get. Ralph Edwards says in his *Shorter Dictionary of English Furniture* 'Chippendale's accounts and correspondence prove that for most of his career he was not a working cabinetmaker, but the organiser of a highly successful firm which furnished and decorated important houses.' A report in the *Gentleman's Magazine* (April 1755) tells how a fire at his workshop destroyed 22 workmen's benches, and his establishment was much smaller than that of George Seddon, (1727-1801) who employed 80 cabinetmakers in 1768 and over 400 craftsmen of all kinds by 1786.

Such facts emphasise that many of Chippendale's well-known contemporaries were not craftsmen struggling to make a living, but entrepreneurs with aspirations to the status of gentleman. (Chippendale himself was a member of the Society of Arts which was founded in 1754, as was his son). Perhaps the best example was John Cobb (died 1768) who, with his partner William Vile, was a neighbour of Chippendale's at 72 St Martin's Lane (*WW/Jul '86*). They supplied furniture to the Royal Family, notably George III both as Prince of Wales and as King, and the King's mother. Cobb was described as a 'singularly haughty character' and left £20,000 in his will 'to support ye name of Cobb as a private gentleman.' John Gloag's *Short Dictionary of Furniture* tells of how Cobb was with George III in the library at Buckingham House when the King asked him to pass a book from a shelf. Such a menial task was beneath the mighty Cobb who said to a workman — 'Fellow, give me that book!' The King asked what the workman's name was and received the reply, 'Jenkins, Your Majesty.'

'Then,' said the King 'Jenkins, you shall hand me the book.' And the story has a happy ending as Jenkins took over the business when Cobb died and continued it in partnership with Vile's nephew, William Strickland.

There must have been many cabinetmakers and 'upholders' working in London during Chippendale's time but in most cases the only records are a trade card, a label, or one or two invoices. There were several, however, who contributed directly, or indirectly and without acknowledgement, to *The Director*. Two such were Henry Copland and Matthias Lock, described as 'Chippendale's ghosts' by R. W. Symonds in his book *Chippendale Furniture Designs*. Copland was in business as early as 1738, although it was not until 1752 that he collaborated with Lock, a master carver and designer, to produce *A New Book of Ornaments*. Lock produced many designs for the embellishment of tables, sconces and mirrors; and an original portfolio of many of his drawings is in the Victoria and Albert Museum, London.

● *Magnificent delicacy and sureness of design – a Chippendale-style riband-back settee*

Photos Victoria & Albert Museum

Several pieces which were originally ascribed to Chippendale (particularly the Chinese bed from Badminton House) have been found to be the work of John Linnel who died in 1796. He was a carver, designer, and cabinetmaker at 28 Berkeley Square, London, considered 'in the first line of his profession'. Much of his work is at Shardeloes, near Amersham, Buckinghamshire, and also at Dyrham House in Gloucestershire. The V&A also has a collection of his drawings.

Another contemporary London firm which had connections with Chippendale was Ince and Mayhew (the names are frequently transposed). The *Public Advertiser* of January 1759 announced the formation of the partnership in a house opposite Broad Street, Carnaby Market; between 1759 and 1762 they brought out the *Universal System of Household Furniture*. Ince was among the subscribers to Chippendale's *Director* on which he based the *Universal System*, but used fewer designs. Sheraton didn't think much of it and described it as 'a book of merit in its day, though much inferior to Chippendale's.'

There are three other craftsmen of the period whose work is becoming increasingly valued. Giles Grendey, exporter of furniture on a large scale, made his speciality japanned work. There is a magnificent day-bed of his in beech, japanned red, with silver and gilt decoration, in the V&A.

Another was Thomas Shearer, who contributed 17 out of the 20 illustrations in the *Cabinet-Maker's London Book of Prices* 1788. The dates of his birth and death, and the

address from which he worked are unknown, and no bills survive. A delicate and attractive breakfront bookcase of his in the Shearer style is at Dyrham House. The other craftsman was John Channon, again about whom little is known other than his workshop was on the west side of London's St Martin's Lane. Pieces that have been ascribed to him, mainly bookcases, desks, chest-of-drawers, and chairs, are all of the highest quality.

The firm of Gillows of Lancaster, founded in 1695 by Robert Gillow, a joiner from Kirkham, Yorkshire, definitely deserves a mention. It is unique among English furniture manufacturers in that cost-books and records still exist. They date back to 1731, when the firm appears to have been engaged mainly in building and surveying — indeed, Robert's son Richard trained as an architect. About 1760 the company, which then consisted of the father and his three sons, Thomas, Robert, and Richard, opened a branch at 176 Oxford Street (then known as Tyburn Street) in London, although all the furniture was continued to be made at Lancaster. This later became the well-known store of Waring and Gillow. From the early 1790's the firm occasionally stamped its products, and from 1820 almost all were stamped 'Gillows' or 'Gillows, Lancaster.' They were considered reputable cabinetmakers, using good timber and workmanship, although lacking in originality — a criticism which seems hardly fair if you recall that they developed the Davenport writing desk and also patented an extension system for a dining table. ∎

THE WOODWORK BUS

Finding money

If you don't need it, it's easy to get; if you're desperate for it, it can be hard. But there are exceptions; Hugh O'Neill maps the route to getting your hands on the cash you need

The time had come for me to go it alone, and I needed start-up money. I automatically thought of that docile little man in my bedroom cupboard — the bank manager. Wrong.

I phoned the manager, made an appointment, and went in to ask for a loan to purchase some equipment, and for overdraft cover to patch over some probable holes in the cash-flow. The manager wanted to see my order book: I produced the envelope-backs; a set of accounts — my pocket note book — and my cash-flow projection for the next twelve months. Here the best I could produce was a stack of unpaid bills.

Obviously my management systems didn't generate much confidence. He offered a small loan — I'd been a steady customer for 21 years — but it was nowhere near what I wanted and it was 5½% above bank rate. The manager said: 'If you want any more, you'll have to put up your house as collateral, and on the basis of this evidence' — his hand swept across the papers — 'I don't think you'll want to risk that.'

I should have started with another telephone call: Dial the operator and ask for FREEPHONE ENTERPRISE. This will connect you with the Local Enterprise Agency from whom you will obtain all the advice that you need — free! They will tell you:
● What financial assistance is available
● What is available nationally
● What there is specific to your region
● Anything of a special nature exclusive to development zones.
They will also:
● Advise whether you should remain a sole trader or form a limited company
● Direct you to various sources of aid
● Tell you the various things you should think about
● Help you prepare a persuasive case to take to the bank manager (they even have a quiet word with him on the old boy network)

● Certainly help take much of the heartache and soul-searching out of producing cash flow forecasts.

Only on the third visit do they start to charge for their services; and even then it's only a nominal amount.

There are over 250 Local Enterprise Agencies in the UK. Most are at least part-funded by the local authority, but don't be put off by this, they aren't quangos or beaurocrats. They are staffed by people who have worked in, or run, small businesses and who understand the real problems. In my experience, their advisers have been helpful, discreet, sharp-thinking and sound.

One thing they can't do is give you any money. They don't offer any grants or loans, but they will know all the sources and most of the avenues.

Free money

The first direction they're likely to point you is towards the Enterprise Allowance Scheme operated by the Manpower Services Commission. This is one of the best sorts of free money there is. Making sure that you will meet the qualification requirements should be one of your first actions, and it's all explained in the first of the series in March's WOODWORKER.

The 'awareness day' you attend, and making an application, brings subtle benefits: a cursory assessment is made of whether or not your business is likely to succeed, but much more important, you will meet specialist advisers who can often nudge you in the right direction. There is free consultancy and advice on other sources of assistance.

In some parts of the UK, particularly the designated development areas, your business may qualify for some support under schemes operated by the Department of Trade and Industry, the Department of Employment, the Local Authority and/or the Small Firms Service.

Broadly speaking you may find that 'seed corn' start-up money is sometimes available as grants. or low-cost loans; frequently workshop space can be obtained at special rates (even rent-free in some areas). There are also grants available towards paying the wages of assistants and even more towards the wages of bona-fide trainees.

The Enterprise Allowance scheme requires you to have £1000 capital of your own to invest in the business, and it's at this stage you may turn to the bank. But this can be a major problem; to qualify for the Allowance you mustn't have started the business, and if you haven't started it, you have little to show to a bank manager. When you really need money, it's not always easy to get it. So again use the Local

Enterprise Agency — let them grill you, let them poke, probe and pry; don't be defensive — encourage them. They're trying to be helpful. Get them to help you to produce a cashflow forecast for the bank manager.

The bank and loans

An earlier visit to the bank can be useful. Most have a bundle of free literature; some of the booklets just outline the bank's services, but some go much further and are very good guides to setting up and managing finances. NatWest, for instance, include very helpful materials on planning, forecasting, cashflows and book keeping.

Banks make money by lending money and charging an interest on it. They take calculated gambles, but the bigger the risk, the greater the return they seek. Their overall risk tolerance is, however, low; and that of some local branch managers almost zero!

You are considered a good risk if:
1 You have been a client for many years.
2 Your account has been generally 'well-managed', i.e. considerably more black than red.
3 You have demonstrated an ability to cope with the world, a career and finances.
4 You now have a watertight plan for quickly making a million or two.
5 You can put up a substantial amount of security.
6 You have clearly thought through your proposed business in precise and minute detail.

The guarantee of loan success rests upon the quality of your business plan and the detail of your cash-flow forecasts, and, even better, on a full order book. The better prepared you are in this sense, the less of a risk you are seen to be.

A word of warning here. It's sometimes easier to get money from a bank as a private individual than it is as a limited liability company. If a company defaults, the bank can only come back to the level of your liability, but if you are just an individual, they can call in everything you've got.

Putting up some form of security reduces the risk to the bank. Putting up 'the business' isn't viewed too favourably, but if you have a house that isn't already fully mortgaged up to its present-day market value, you'll get a good hearing. Other securities, shares, insurance policies with a surrender value and the like are acceptable; a favourable mention in the will of an ageing aunt isn't.

In broad terms the banks will help in a small way without security. They'll be a little more forthcoming if you are known and reliable, and they will be much more helpful if you cover the loan with some security. Fortunately, thanks to government intervention through the Business Loan Guarantee Scheme, they can also be helpful even when you have absolutely no collateral.

Straight overdrafts are best. You agree

with the manager how far your account can go into the red and then you pay interest on the overdraft only. The rates are negotiable, but are usually in the order of 2-3% above the current bank rate.

There are then various types of Business Loan. Usually you have the option of fixed or variable-interest loans. Variable-interest loans are a gamble. They become a better bet when interest rates are high and substantial drops are expected. The interest per cent over the current bank rate is likely to be higher with base-rate linked loans than the per cent charged when you enter a fixed-rate agreement — the banks too expect interest rates to fall.

Business loans span anything from £2000 to a million (or more) and repayment periods from one to 30 years. It's normal that the repayment period would not exceed the useful life of any asset the loan is intended to purchase. Various repayment options are available, ranging from monthly to annual, some with a suspended initial payment. Banks pressurise small businesses to cover the loan with repayment insurance and for loans of over 10 years, substantial security is usually required.

At least one bank now offers a repayment plan based on endowment assurance, which greatly reduces the total cost of a long-term loan. For instance, a fixed-interest loan of £50,000 over 20 years would cost £121,570, whereas on an endowment scheme the net cost would be only £68,060.

Currently fixed-interest loans are set at between 12.5% and 15%, and within this bracket, the rates *are negotiable*. Some people either fear or scorn their bank manager. Don't! Treat him/her like any other salesperson, and negotiate. Although most of the major clearing banks offer similar facilities, there is still some variation between them. If you're an established customer you may get slightly preferential treatment, but it can work the other way. There is now healthy competition, and by shopping around (with a well prepared case) you may be able to obtain better terms. The way that terms are 'better' is usually seen in the interest charges that you are asked to pay. But even if you don't shop around, your own bank manager often works within a 2-4% discretion band, so don't bite his hand off with his first offer.

The Small Firms Loan Guarantee Scheme is operated by the banks and is basically available to anyone who has no personal collateral to put up; usually this means they don't have a house. Seventy per cent of the loan made by the bank is guaranteed by the government, making it a relatively low risk to the bank. The maximum loan available is £75,000 and the rate charged is 1¾% above bank base rate. However, the Department of Trade also levies an arrangement fee and an annual premium.

The Guaranteed Loan is probably the toughest to obtain. the requirements are strict in that the applicant must have already put up all personal assets to obtain conventional funding. The business assets then have to be put up as security on the guaranteed loan. The bank will ask for very detailed plans, objectives, marketing assessments, current and projected financial figures; and they will require that your accounts and management information systems conform to the bank's own format.

Banks can also offer other financial assistance, including arranging leasing and hire purchase to cover plant, machinery and vehicles; and of factoring trade accounts and debts. If the proposed business is large, the High Street bank may not be the best bet. You could be looking for venture capital or a special deal with a merchant bank. Some banks will nudge you in this direction.

Crafty money

It's unlikely that you'll think about starting a craft-based business if you aren't an established craftsperson. There will be craftsmen who have worked for an employer, others who over years of part-time have built up considerable skills; and there will be students who have recently graduated from college: but no complete novices. Which means anyone setting up a business will be likely to have some finished work to show. If that work is of good enough quality, it could qualify you for further financial assistance. The more successful you have been, the more likely you are to qualify.

So let's look at some of the specifically craft-related grants and loans from the Crafts Council and various regional crafts associations.

The Crafts Council has a grant of £2m a year to fund its activities in promoting craft work. One form of promotion is giving grants and loans.

Some regard the Crafts Council as elitist. They do have a clear remit to encourage innovative work, so their grants aren't the easiest to obtain. In almost all cases, the process starts with a submission of slides of your work (and both the slides and the work have to be of the highest professional standard). If you pass this entry test, you're invited to attend an interview and take some samples of your work (hard luck if you make four-poster beds). Your application is vetted by a panel of professional craftspeople.

On offer are:
● Setting-up Grants, as Equipment Grants and Maintenance Grants
● Workshop Assistance Grants
● Advanced Training Grants
● Loan Schemes
● Bursary Scheme

At any time during your first two years of operation you may qualify for a start-up grant in one or both of two forms. The Equipment Grant can cover up to 50% of the cost of workshop equipment, and the Maintenance Grant, to a maximum of £2120, is intended to contribute towards

● *A flight of fancy – bowls in burr elm using figure to best advantage*

continued

the first year's running costs. Although these are 'start-up' grants, the qualifying standards are so high that you will already have completed some years of training or sound experience.

If you've been in business for two or more years, other Crafts Council finance is available. 'Loan Scheme A' offers £5000 towards improving the workshop or its equipment. Repayment is over five years and the interest rate is 10%. 'Loan Scheme B' provides up to £1000 for the purchase of bulk materials, or will cover the cost of attendance at a trade fair, and the repayment period is one year.

There are other grants. The Workshop Assistance Grant, of up to £2120 contributes towards a 'living wage' for a trainee for one year. You yourself may also obtain a grant towards your own advanced training in another workshop. Again the sum is £2120, and in both cases the duration is for up to one year. A Bursary Scheme is operated (every second year) to enable craftspeople who have been working for seven years or more to take a sabbatical to reassess their work, or to undertake a special project.

All Crafts Council grants do carry very distinct advantages. They are prestigious; they also mean that officers of the Council visit the workshop and provide advice; and it can mean that your work is exhibited both at home and abroad in Council displays.

Craftspeople in the regions have other facilities as well as the Crafts Council. The Welsh Arts Council offer a Special Projects Scheme, Special Awards, a Commission Aid Scheme, and a Craft Residency Programme to craftsmen prepared to set up their workshops in selected secondary schools and other public institutions. The Regional Arts Association in Wales further promotes projects and exhibitions with their Craftsmen at Work, Moving Pictures and Exhibition Aid schemes.

Emigrating?

No, not to Australia or Alaska, but to Mid Wales or the Highlands of Scotland. There's gold in them there hills. Many inducements are offered to the person interested in setting up business outside London. Indeed, the further you move away from London, the more prompt, efficient and helpful are the official organisations; the more ready they are with loans; the greater the range of incentives offered; and the more likelihood there is of free money.

So by the time you get to Mid Wales, you find items such as the Craft Shop Improvement Scheme, which will give up to £5000 for the improvement of craft shop buildings and fixed display equipment. The Highlands and Islands Development Board go one better. Under their Relocation Grant, if you take your existing business up there, you may be eligible for 80% reim-

bursement of travel and accommodation expenses; dismantling, removal and reinstallation of workshop plant; relocation of stocks; even redundancy payment of those employees left behind!

Regional organisations cover the various parts of the UK. All have a broadly similar function — that of helping business start and grow. Some are concerned only with small businesses, such as CoSIRA (Council for Small Industries in Rural Areas) which covers England; and the Welsh Development Agency (Small Business Division) and the Scottish Development Agency (Small Business Division). There are then agencies with a specific regional focus such as the Mid Wales Development Board, the Highlands and Islands Development Board, the Local Enterprise Development Unit (LEDU) in Belfast, and others; all of whom are interested in businesses of any size.

All agencies offer business advice. This can cover management, marketing, finance and accounting, production management, and technical. Most provide at least two free consultations (usually a half-day each) and some thereafter charge in the region of £15 per half-day. Most offer training courses across the same range of subject areas, and again many of these are free. CoSIRA has a very wide range of courses of the very highest quality. If you want to be a thatcher, for instance, this is one of the few places where you can learn the trade.

All these agencies, throughout the UK, provide loan facilities at rates well below normal commercial level and often 2-3% below the best the banks will do. The loan periods are typically up to 20 years for buildings, 5-10 years for plant and equipment, and up to 10 years for working capital. According to where you are and the type of loan sought, sums of between £1000 and £75,000 are available. Where larger sums are needed the agencies will put you in touch with sources of venture capital. Most of the agencies also offer grants towards the conversion of old or redundant buildings to workshops, which can be anything from a one-quarter contribution (as with CoSIRA in England) through 35% in Mid Wales, to (in a few special cases) cover of the full conversion costs.

The special incentives offered in the development areas are almost open-ended. Mention has already been made of the Relocation Grant available for a move to the Highlands and Islands region. As an example, to typify the rest, let's take the Mid Wales Development scheme and list some of their main offers and facilities of interest to the craftsman.

- Regional Development Grant of 15% of capital expenditure, or £3000 per job created
- Regional Selective Assistance with grants towards fixed and working capital costs, plus 40% of training costs, and loans of up to £½ million
- Mid Wales Development Grants direct

to some businesses, plus grants to Local Authorities for the provision of serviced industrial sites
- Development of Rural Initiative, Venture and Enterprise (DRIVE) Grants of up to 50% for fixed assets, land, buildings, plant and machinery for projects that increase the number of jobs or improve the environment. Crafts are one of the nominated subject areas.
- Investment Funds for large projects.
- Small Business Low-Interest Loans in Rural Areas. Loans for the purchase of buildings, equipment or working capital of £1000-£7000 at 3% below commercial lending rates.
- Factories and workshops: purpose-built units at between £1.50 and £2 per sq ft, with rates at 65p per sq ft. In some cases the units are rent- and even rates-free for an initial period (up to two years).
- Building Conversion Grants covering 35% of fees and costs in converting buildings (old farm buildings, empty schools, redundant chapels, disused railway stations, etc) to workshops.
- Housing: modern housing for rent convenient to the factory or workshop.
- The New Workers Scheme provides payment to employers who take on young people: One year's grant of £50 per week for an under 20, and £65 per week for an older person.
- In addition the Board provides special support for projects in Agriculture, Social Development, Tourism and Forestry, together with a range of training programmes in business management.

Plenty of money

So if you have an established business and want to move it to the other end of the country, it's easy. You may even get paid to do it. If you are starting up, most areas will be glad to have you and will offer different incentives. Even if you want to stay where you are there are several sources of finance, support and assistance.

Again, if you're established, reasonably successful, and wish to raise money, there's no difficulty. Even if you aren't so successful, but have collateral, there's little problem.

The new starter should take advantage of the Enterprise Allowance and then raise whatever other money is needed, first through one of the special agencies listed below and/or through a bank. The Crafts Council grants are based solely upon the quality of the work you present — they make no assessment of the viability of your business. The Enterprise Allowance is given on the basis of a broad assessment of viability, but this isn't very stringent. Everybody else gives you a grilling! Development Boards, Small Firms Agencies, all will have to be convinced you have a viable proposition — banks are the toughest, special development area boards less so.

There are, of course, two problems. One we have referred to in an earlier article; no point going to the Outer Hebrides just because you can get grants if your business is aiming at a commuter-belt market.

The other is that although there may be little or no difficulty in obtaining money, some of it at least still has to be paid for. Every piece you make or item you sell has to carry the raw materials or buying-in costs, the overheads, the production costs or mark-up, your wages or profits, plus the interest charges on the money you have borrowed for your premises, your equipment, your working capital, your raw materials stocks, and everything else. Many people go out of business (including some well known names in the woodwork field) because every penny they make goes to pay off bank and other interest charges. ∎

● Hugh O'Neill is a professional management consultant and craftsman woodturner.

● Dial 100 and ask for FREEPHONE ENTERPRISE. This will put you in touch with your Local Enterprise Agency and the **Small Firms Service**. Advice and details of available local finance plus the addresses

of **Regional and Local Development Boards**.

● Your local **Job Centre** will start you on the road to the **Enterprise Allowance.**

● **Crafts Council**, 12 Waterloo Place, London SW1Y 4AU, 01-930 4811. Crafts grants and loans for skilled craftspeople.

● **Welsh Arts Council**, Craft & Design Dept., Museum Place, Cardiff, CF1 3NX, (0222) 394711. Grants and Residency programme.

● **Regional Arts Associations:**
   North Wales Arts Association, 10 Wellfield House, Bangor, Gwynedd, (0248) 353248
   South-East Wales Arts Association, Victoria Street, Cwmbrân, Gwent NP44 3ZYT, (0633) 75075
   West Wales Arts, Red Street, Carmarthen, Dyfed, (0267) 234248
   For Craftspeople at Work and Residency Programmes.

● **Council for Small Industries in Rural Areas** (CoSIRA), 141 Castle Street, Salisbury SP1 3TP, (0722) 336255. For loans and addresses of local CoSIRA offices.

● **Welsh Development Agency** (Small Business Division), Treforest Industrial Estate, Pontypridd CF37 5UT, (044-385) 266. For Welsh aid.

● **Development Board for Rural Wales** and **Mid Wales Development Board**, Ladywell House, Park Street, Newtown, Powys SY16 1JB, (0686) 26965). For grants, loans and incentives.

● **Scottish Development Agency** (Small Business Division), Rosebery House, Haymarket Terrace, Edinburgh EH12 5EZ, 031-337 9595.

● **Highlands & Islands Development Board**, Bridge House, 27 Bank Street, Inverness IV1 1QR, (0463) 234171. For grants, loans and incentives.

● **Local Enterprise Development Unit** (LEDU), LEDU Business Centre, 17-19 Linenhall Street, Belfast BT2 8AB, (0232) 242582. For grants, loans and incentives.

● **National Federation of Self-employed & Small Businesses**, Yorkshire Bank Chambers, 32 St Anne's Road West, Lytham St Anne's, Lancs, (0253) 720911. A pressure group and for small commercial mortgages.

The Old Music Masters

The distinctive, ringing tones of the harpsichord are finding a growing following among music lovers — players and listeners both. We visit two makers of Baroque musical instruments who employ enormously different styles

● John Storrs made this highly decorated double manual harpsichord in his high-tech workshop

Photo John Morris

● A Mike Johnson concert double manual harpsichord – handmade for the maestro

Mike Johnson

Nicky Ashford spent some time in the two-man workshop of a modern craftsman with a traditional approach to excellence

If you're a lover of harpsichord music you almost certainly listen to the instruments of Mike Johnson. Considered one of the handful of foremost international makers in Britain by the big names in Baroque music, Mike makes around five instruments a year to the most demanding standards. The German master Gustav Leonhardt will be using two Johnsons at one of his recitals later this year — a 16th century and an 18th century model, two because of the different styles of music he will be playing during the performance.

John Toll of London Baroque, a respected group of performers in this specialised field, plays Johnson's instruments and owns two himself. But Mike is reluctant to blow his reputation's own trumpet. 'I make tools of the trade for musicians. I got into instrument making because I'm a redundant musician, basically. I knew I would never make the grade as a concert pianist, so I got a job with a small London firm restoring pianos, then moved to an apprenticeship at John Broadwood and Sons. I moved into tuning and restoring pianos in this part of the country (Mike's workshop is now in Bedchester in Dorset), via contact with Julian Bream, who had built a workshop for David Rubio to make his guitars for him. I worked there with José Romanillos, a fantastic guitar maker and cabinetmaker. I learnt an enormous amount from him. José says: "Johnson, you're a very good woodworker, but you'll never make a cabinetmaker"!'

By 1969 Mike was 'pretty fed up with restoring other people's work. You can only be as good as the intrument you're working on — you can't interfere if you find something the original maker got wrong. You have to put it back wrong, as it were. That's why I won't restore now.'

As Mike's reputation as a piano restorer grew, he found a developing taste for harpsichords, with their pure, delicate sound. He started to make them himself, and admits his first two instruments were 'terrible', but by now had found his forte, and spent time in Edinburgh, studying a Goermans/Taskin in the Russell Collection in St Cecilia's Hall. It is a double manual, and has been the base for one of the three designs Mike produces.

Discussing the subject of reproducing and 'copying' instruments is illuminating as a key to one of Mike's main themes. 'I'm not a copier — I never have been a copier —

Photo John Morris

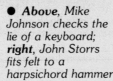

● **Above**, Mike
Johnson checks the
lie of a keyboard;
right, John Storrs
fits felt to a
harpsichord hammer

Photo David Walker, CoSIRA

but I'm a great respecter of the designs and craftsmen of a particular period. They had years of experience. To ignore that would be a great mistake. The first instrument of a new design I make will be as near as I can get to the original without being pedantic about it, so I can understand what the maker was trying to achieve. Then I develop it the way I feel it should be developed.' His sense of tradition is strong; not for him the misguided arrogance that can come with 20th century technology, nor indeed the desire he sees among numbers of younger craftsmen to copy every instrument in sight, leaping from one to another, giving themselves no time to learn about the design. If you stay with a model some time, you really learn, then you can develop what you know about it.' The 18th century French double manual instrument he studied in Edinburgh in 1971 has since been redrawn five times. Mike also makes a single manual harpsichord based on a design from the Ruckers family — 'the grandfathers of harpsichord making' — who worked in Antwerp all through the 16th century. French makers in the 18th century developed and embellished on Ruckers work, and before the Flemish, in the 16th century, there were the Italian instruments often made by luthiers, with cases as thin as 4mm. Strung, such an instrument would be taking about a ton strain; 'but they've survived incredibly well,' says Mike. 'That wonderful eggshell design, the curved case, you see. Fantastic strength.' Mike's version of the Italian-style harpsichord comes from an anonymous instrument in the Smithsonian Institute in Washington DC. 'It's dated 1698, so I'm starting with what was obviously already a copy.' Along with Romanillos, Mike sits on the Crafts Council Advisory committee for musical instrument making, and is emphatic that young craftsmen should find an instrument that really inspires them and 'stick with it. Then they can learn both the tradition, and the original craftsman's thinking.'

The craftsman as student; the encouraging and familiar discovery of yet another maker at the top of his craft who

insists that he is continuing to learn, and will never cease. The same theme comes up when Mike begins to talk about his timber, the way he uses and dries it. Lime, poplar, cedar; he buys the tree in the round, and air dries it for two or three years before cutting it — usually through and through to ¾ or 1in for cases and keyboards, quartered to 8 or 9mm for soundboards. It's kept in stick outside for two to two-and-a-half years, or at least a winter. 'I like timber to winter outside at least one year. I just cover the top of the pile, let the winter weather right through the timber. That way you let all the tensions and stresses out naturally, and get that lovely buttery quality for working. Hand thicknessing to get just the right tone, you've got to be sure the timber will work well. That's what's different about an instrument maker from a furniture maker — most of our work is lacquered so we're not really concerned with weather staining or appearance. It's quality and stability we go for. There's no way you could kiln-dry timber for a soundboard, there'd be just too many stresses in it. No tonal quality, either. Then we know the tree, you see, working with it right through from the round. I get many instruments from one tree, so I get to know the wood intimately from the sound point of view; for instance, just now I think we've got too much wood in the casework. We'll be going down from 17 to 16mm thickness — no worries about strength, we're way over the top with that anyway, when you consider what the Italians did with 4mm thicknesses. I just have a feeling we can get more resonance from the instrument with a slightly thinner case; and working with Charlie (his cabinetmaker came to him 10 years ago straight from Poole Grammar School) is great, because any decision I make like that can go straight into the making.' Mike is enthusiastic about

the working relationship he has with Charlie Gellett; 'I didn't want to take him on at first — I couldn't afford him. but he pestered me, and I'm glad he did. He wanted to be a cabinetmaker from the musical instrument point of view, and we work really well together. A harpsichord maker isn't necessarily a cabinetmaker!' Charlie does the casework, turnings, and most of the other woodwork, while Mike takes care of the keyboards, actions and soundboards. They also make all their bits and pieces in the workshop; brasswork, everything. Not a component is 'put out'. The trees he works are almost like companions themselves; he quotes a poplar whose first cut produced 140cu ft, and a cedar of Lebanon that yielded 200. 'I'll be dead before I use all that. One tree, you might work with it for five years. You really get to know it, to know how it'll sound, how it works. We made a keyboard up out of lime, but the tree had grown slightly on the twist, so the stresses kept it moving. So you say, we can't use that for keyboards — need something a bit more placid. Working with a whole tree like this is a bit of a luxury, one not many people can afford. But I allow myself that, and anyway it's more economical over a long period.'

Mike also enjoys a good relationship with his timber supplier, Chris Ridley of Ridley Sawmills in Ansty, Wiltshire, where logs are cut under Mike's direction. Chris looks out for trees for him when the firm is out felling. 'He'll ring me up and say, I've got a lovely tree, do you want it? If I can't afford it, he'll curse at me and put it in the back of the yard until I can . . . I'm very lucky with Chris.' Mike buys ebony and some other imports from North Heigham Sawmills ('they're very good'), but most of the bulk timbers come from Ridley's.

Finishing? 'Yes, well I suppose you would

The Old Music Masters

call them highly decorated. The basic finish is lacquer with gold leaf banding — both Charlie and I do the lacquering. We sometimes do marbling with art oil colours, then seven or eight coats of oil varnish; for the lacquers we use J. T. Keep's coach paints, another oil-based finish. The varnish is Keep's 'Victovar'. The soundboards (on which the whole tone of the instrument depends) aren't treated at all; except we give them a coat of the whites of two eggs. It brings the colour out marvellously, and it's a good protectection that allows the movement you must have with a soundboard. Seal it and it'll surely split.' Mostly soundboards are decorated by an artist with birds, flowers, butterflies in tempera — water-colour pigments ground in egg yolks — and the 'white of egg' seal is an ideal basis for that. 'It's a natural size for the work; otherwise the colours would just bleed into the grain of the spruce.'

Four or five handmade harpsichords a year, built to antique designs and developed by an internationally renowned maker with as much feel for the music as for the timbers. No, they can't be cheap — a

● **Above**, soundboard decoration in tempera; **right**, a frame being worked on in the Johnson workshop

Johnson Concert double manual might cost £14,500 — but for a master of Baroque music, as for any master, the tools of the trade must be the best. That's why Mike Johnson has a three-year order book and a lifetime's worth of timber; a continually growing understanding of the instruments he makes, and above all, the hallmark of a truly committed craftsman — the conviction that there's an unlimited amount to learn, and that he'll keep learning till his dying day.

John Storrs

At the other end of the scale, ex-structural engineer John Storrs is refining computer-controlled woodworking to new heights — and he makes clavichords, harpsichords and spinets

John and Charlotte Storrs and their three colleagues make early keyboard instruments. From their workshop, tucked away down a country footpath in North Mundham, near Chichester, they produce clavichords, spinets, harpsichords, music stools, and music stands — in kit form and complete. They export about 75% of their production and have distributors in a number of European countries and Japan. The Storrs' approach to the work is essentially precision engineering in wood, and for some years now they have successfully applied micro-electronics in production as well as general business management.

John trained as a structural engineer at Cambridge, going on to work with several firms of consulting engineers. He quotes as the high point of his structural engineering career his responsibility for the analysis of the National Westminster Bank tower in the City of London. In 1972 he took the plunge and started on his own, first of all as a structural engineer; he had been developing a strong interest in early keyboard instrument making and playing since university, and began at this time to design several instruments for production in kit form. This was at a time when interest in early music, stimulated in large part by David Munrow, was increasing rapidly. A few advertisements in a musical journal and a small stand in the first London Early

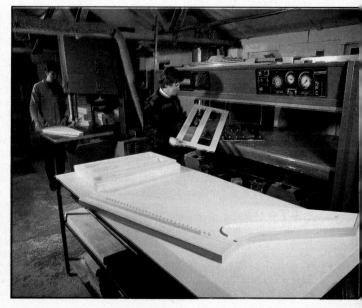

Musical Instrument exhibition saw the present business established, and orders began to flood in. They set up a workshop in the double garage near the house, installed three craftsmen, and began to send clavichord and spinet kits all over Britain and overseas, from Greenland to Japan. Despite strong opposition from the local planners (overcome with much effort and expense) the workshop was transferred to the present buildings in 1975. At an exhibition in Frankfurt, with valuable assistance from the British Overseas Trade Board, the Storrs found a number of distributors in Europe, and the firm is now well known and respected for design and craftsmanship internationally.

The instruments, based on historic prototypes, belong to the modern 'authentic' school, although they are not 'just reproductions'. They are made from first-quality solid timber, most of it home-grown, and display a striking design feature in the glued panel construction of lids and bases. Traditional loose panelling has been brought up to date, with the help of modern adhesives and careful drying. The result is very pleasing to the eye, dimensionally stable, and easy to produce as well. The kits are designed for easy glued assembly, using the traditional wooden joiner's cramps which are supplied. All the components are shaped and drilled to a high standard of accuracy and finish, and the critical parts, including the carefully thicknessed soundboard and the bridges, are pre-assembled in the workshop.

The standard timber used for the instrument's casework is black Italian poplar, which has a long tradition of use in harpsichord making and has very good acoustical properties. John also uses sweet chestnut, English walnut and cherry, all with excellent results. The wrestplanks, which carry the tuning pins, are beech. Soundboards are of first quality quarter-sawn European spruce, while lime is used for key levers, with ebony or bone key coverings and arcades. The jacks have beech bodies and holly tongues, and jack guides are machined from solid beech.

The Storrs take very great care with selection and drying of their timber. They buy logs sawn to a particular specification which maximises the amount of near quarter-sawn material, but doesn't increase the cost. A large slab, up to 250mm thick, is cut first; this is put aside while the rest of the log is sawn through and through, until you reach a similar slab on the other side. Both slabs are then 'turned down' and sawn through and through at right angles to the first sawn face. The workshop has its own timber-drying kiln, a dehumidifier type with a maximum capacity of 500cu ft. Drying and

● **Far left**, *the Storrs computer-controlled drill; millions of holes in the service of music.* **Left**, *loading the panel sander – note the jig*

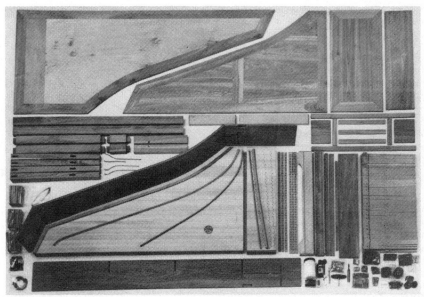

● *This is what you get from John Storrs when you buy a single manual harpsichord kit*

conditioning cycles can vary from three to six weeks, depending on species, thickness, and other factors.

John Storrs' workshop is well equipped with a range of conventional medium-sized woodworking machines; bandsaw, sliding-table panel saw, panel sander, planer, spindle moulder, router, lathe and a hot platen press. John and his colleagues have developed many interesting techniques with these machines over the years; the way the panelled instrument lids and bases are machined and glued, for example. The inner panels are tongued, the frame pieces grooved; the external frame pieces are mitred and grooved where they meet, and a loose tongue glued in later to give strength to the joint. Where there is a curve, as with the harpsichord, the inner panel curve must mate properly with the corresponding frame piece. They do this by shaping the parts, including the tongue and the groove, on a spindle moulder fitted with a ring fence, using special cutters and templates. Because the inner panels are machined on all edges, it would be clumsy to use cramps to hold the workpiece and template together, plus it would need a special machine table, so the Storrs' workshop uses vacuum cramping. The templates are made of densified beech ply, designed for this sort of purpose; it's stable and durable, and can easily be worked with woodworking tools. The lid and base templates are exactly the same size as the components they are used for, so it isn't too difficult to produce a matching set of templates. If the templates fit together properly, so should the components.

Once the machining is done, the lids and bases are glued up straight away before the parts change shape or size. This is done in a jig on the hot platen press, which is run at about 80-90°C. The jigs consist of an aluminium sheet fitted with many soft rubber blocks, a few millimetres higher than the work. The parts are glued, assembled, and fitted snugly between the rubber blocks; when the press is closed, the blocks compress and expand sideways, exerting substantial force on the work. When the press is fully closed the work is under pressure in two planes, downwards and inwards. The glue they use sets in a few minutes at the temperature of the press, and John can get a cycle time of about 10 minutes.

Although the workshop is well equipped conventionally, John gives pride of place at the moment to a large-bed computer-controlled drill, developed at the workshop four years ago, which has drilled several million holes in the service of music! This is about to be eclipsed as a much more ambitious computer-controlled woodworking machine begins to come on line, which in its final form will be able to saw, mill, or drill. A parallel project, using the same technology, will automate the use of the panel sanding machine, allowing a whole table-full of components to be sanded to thickness, working in multiple passes under the sanding head. The development of this higly sophisticated machinery is supported by the Department of Trade and Industry as part of their Microelectronics Application Project.

The computer-controlled drill is basically an X-Y plotter over a 72x30in bed, operating a gantry-mounted air-operated self-feed drill head. The bed of the machine is three hollow aluminium castings, mounted on a welded frame base; they function both as stiff structural elements and as vacuum tanks. The top of the bed is grooved, and has location pins for the jig sheets which define the positions of the workpieces. Jigs and work are held by vacuum, and quick-action valves allow the air to move from beneath the work to the

The Old Music Masters

vacuum tanks rapidly enough to get an initial seal. The programmes for drill control are stored on disk on the main workshop microcomputer system, and downloaded to the drill controller (a small microcomputer) as they're needed. The appropriate drill is fitted, depth-stops adjusted, and the machine is ready for work. It takes about three minutes to change from one task to another, and the drill then runs for between five minutes and three hours without attention, depending on the task. The longer the better, in fact, as it allows people to get on with other jobs without disturbance.

The super-high-tech general-purpose machine under construction is based on the same general principles as the drill, but it's much larger. It's an application of a modular machine system which will allow a range of different gantry-type machines to be constructed from standard cast aluminium components, and when it's completed, will boast a 3200x1600mm bed. The head will have full five-axis control with automatic tool changing. The Storrs will use the same vacuum chucking system as on the drill, with modular jig sheets to configure the machine for a particular task. They will be able to fit saw-blades up to 300mm diameter, spindle blocks, router and milling cutters, drills, and even non-rotating tools such as chisels! It will certainly revolutionise the work-shop's approach to design and production. But all this takes time, and the first incarnation of this new system will be a three-axis router — an extremely useful workshop machine. Foundry patterns for the new machine's castings have (of course) been made in the workshop, while the actual machining work has been done in the Midlands. After extensive testing the Storrs intend to arrange for the system to be produced and marketed commercially.

The sander automation project is attacking a significant consumer of work-shop time. Because planer cutters tear such woods as poplar, and because of high planer noise levels, thicknessing is done in the Storrs workshop on the panel sander with a very coarse belt. The machine can only remove quite a small amount at a time, so the work must be passed through many times to reach a final dimension; if a travel-ling table could be loaded with work and reciprocated beneath the belt, rising by the correct amount with each pass, many workshop hours would be saved. Two computer-controlled support tables designed for this have been made, and will be coupled to the sander shortly.

In anticipation of the contribution these latest workshop developments will make to productivity and efficiency, expanding capacity as they will, John and his team are already designing more fine products in wood, under the common title theme of 'support for creativity'. Music continues to be prominent; music stands, both single and duet (for chamber-music playing), and

cabinets for organised music storage will be ready for production shortly.

● All of which, in John and Charlotte Storrs' own unassuming language, adds up to a most extraordinary marriage of advanced high technology, woodworking expertise, and love for old music and the instruments on which to play it. Very mystifying, until you remember John is an engineer, and music is a very mathematical discipline — particularly Baroque music. If Johann Sebastian Bach and his forebears had got their hands on a computer-controlled synthesiser . . .   ∎

● John Storrs' instruments range from . £480 for a poplar clavichord kit (£1360

finished) to £4820 for a decorated double-manual harpsichord (£1620 kit). John also runs early keyboard-instrument making courses at Bishop Otter College in Chichester, by the end of which you could have a playing clavichord or spinet, or have made considerable progress on a harpsichord, from Storrs' kits. There is advice, guidance, talks, 'music making and other diversions'. The course this year is 24 July-3 August. The John Storrs workshop open day is an annual event, which this year ties in with the Chichester festivities; 11 and 12 July.

John Storrs, Hunston, Chichester, W. Sussex PO20 6NR, (0243) 776263.

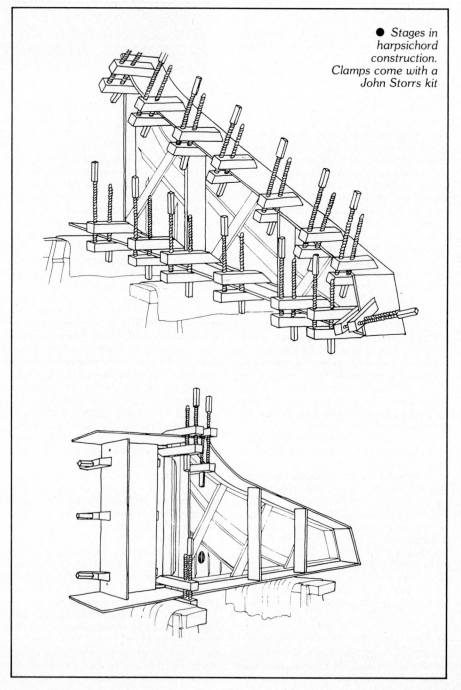

● *Stages in harpsichord construction. Clamps come with a John Storrs kit*

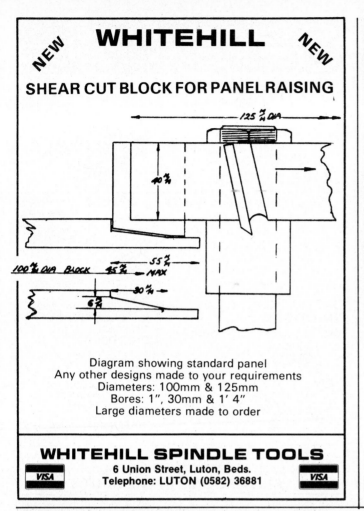

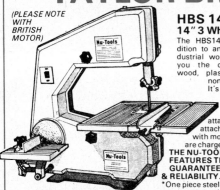

● **Left**, offcuts of tree-trunks litter the site as log cabins are constructed in traditional fashion. **Right**, DIY cabins from standard machined log-components

● **Right**, fibreglass insulation is placed between the logs during construction to prevent draughts. **Below**, a miniature log-cabin children's playhouse

Lapp-joint log homes

Photographer Tony Deane found himself in the traditional log cabins of northern Finland — and took a look at the DIY kit versions

L ooking out of the window, I had to remind myself of the date; 25th August. There had been a sharp frost during the night which left the forest glistening and shimmering in the hard morning light. A spectacular rehearsal for Christmas. The thermometer stuck on the outside of the window read —4°C.

Three hundred and fifty miles north of the Arctic Circle, amid the endless forests of Finnish Lapland, autumn frosts come early. Another four weeks and the first snows would herald the beginning of nearly six months of dusk and temperatures as low as —40°C. I snuggled back under my duvet and looked round my log cabin.

Bed was a kind of shelf that spanned the 18ft or so of the room. A single tree trunk stretched across the room 4ft from the wall and 3ft off the stone floor, its ends housed in the opposite walls. Wooden slats filled the gap between wall and log. A double bed with a difference — feet to feet, head to head, head to feet, the choice was yours. The pine logs, stripped of bark, that the Lapps had used to make the cabin, looked reassuringly weatherproof and sturdy. Here and there the gnarled surface had been etched by wood-boring beetles, leaving a fascinating display of hieroglyphics and modern art. The room, despite the temperature outside, was beautifully warm and draughtproof. Heating came from thermostatically controlled electric panels.

Nothing, surely, epitomises better the

ancient relationship between human and tree than a home fashioned out of rough-hewn wood. Over the Arctic regions of the world, in the vast coniferous forests that stretch from horizon to horizon, people have perfected the arts and skills necessary to construct a durable, snug home in the harshest of climates.

The insistent buzz of a chainsaw led me, ankle deep through moss and lichen, to a building site where a couple of Lapps were cutting and trimming logs to make a typical house. Offcuts of tree-trunks, up to 18in in diameter, littered the site. Balanced on partially built walls, the two men, one with a small chainsaw, nibbled away at a semi-circular notch that would form a large housing joint with the previous log, already fixed in position. They had already cut a V-slot along the length of the log, which solves the problem of having two roundish surfaces abutting. No measurement or line was used to do this part of the job. The man with the saw just straddled the log and walked backwards cutting an angled kerf. Retracing his steps, he chopped out the 'V' with another angled cut. As one log is laid on the other, a strip of fibreglass insulation is placed between the logs in the groove, which stops the inevitable draught whistling through the walls. Once upon a time, the Lapps used moss and lichen to insulate their homes. Log by log, criss-crossing one way and then the other, the

walls rose rapidly. The stub ends on the logs at the corners were left to the end of the construction stage. If a particular log had an unusual feature, it was left to add character to the building, otherwise the stubs were cut level. Gaps for doors and windows appeared under the chainsaw. Positioned near right-angles in the building, the doors don't leave walls weakened.

In a clearing about a mile away from the builders, I came across their 'timber yard'. Huge piles of trees were stacked according to diameter. Trees had been chosen for their straightness, and only trees that had died *in situ* have been felled for cabins.

The Finnish people are passionately fond of outdoor pursuits, and are drawn by the mystical lure of the forests and lakes that cover most of their country. At the last count they reckoned there were some 63,000 lakes in Finland — and with a small population, everyone can get away from town to your own patch of water.

Come the summer, most Finns migrate to a small cottage on some remote lake shore. These cottages are cherished, and rarely is one allowed to go to rack and ruin. To meet the increasing demand for small log cabins, thriving businesses have sprung up for factory-made cabins, which can be bought ex-catalogue and delivered on site for the

ambitious DIY weekender. This is Dad's Lego. Green wood is used in the construction; trees of about 150mm diameter are fed through huge proforming machines that turn out perfectly shaped and sized logs, with a neat semi-circular groove that ensures accurate butting between them. Holes are drilled vertically through the logs so dowels can help to keep the walls upright. Instead of the marvellously chaotic scene of odds and ends that you get in the forest, this is a very sterile situation. Nevertheless it must be satisfying to put up your own house, on your own lake, backing on to your own bit of forest.

The supplied joinery inside the house is as you would expect in a Scandinavian country — superb. 'Functional without frills' probably sums up the current designs. Birch, the other common tree of the tundra, is used to relieve the overall impression of pine. Door panels are faced with birch ply, and small artefacts like sauna buckets are made from the same wood.

Despite the liberal use of polyurethane varnish, the packaged log-cabin complements the traditional forest home, and blends well into Sibelius' idyllic landscape.

I couldn't help musing that a similar industry might be created in this country, particularly in the regions of plantations and high unemployment — but the Brits would need some re-education in log cabin living first! ■

Biting the cherry

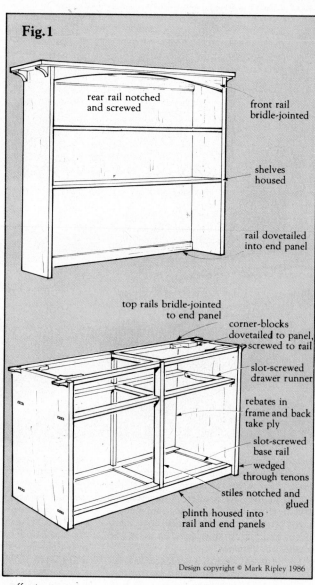

Fig. 1

rear rail notched and screwed

front rail bridle-jointed

shelves housed

rail dovetailed into end panel

top rails bridle-jointed to end panel

corner-blocks dovetailed to panel, screwed to rail

slot-screwed drawer runner

rebates in frame and back take ply

slot-screwed base rail

wedged through tenons

stiles notched and glued

plinth housed into rail and end panels

Design copyright © Mark Ripley 1986

● *The warmth of cherry, the subtle curves and details . . . a pleasing effect*

Mark Ripley's sensitive combination of hand-tool technique and machining ingenuity contribute to the individuality of this delightful cherry dresser

I recently fitted a kitchen in American cherry, a timber with a lovely rich colour and a fine grain — and it works quite easily. During one or two gaps in the proceedings I took the opportunity to make this dresser which I had been planning as a speculative piece, and I found I could use some excess cherry stock for it.

Apart from the chance to develop some ideas without the constraints of a brief, it was an opportunity to put a new planer/thicknesser through its paces. The only

other machines I used were a bandsaw and linisher, plus a portable belt sander and router.

The dresser is small — 64¾in overall height by 40in wide — in keeping with the room sizes of modern houses. All the corners are rounded over, especially on the top section; I find this is safer, and of course round corners wear considerably better than sharp ones. I went for some subtle visual effects, notably tapering the solid, jointed-up vertical side members in thickness right through from bottom to top; at the base of the lower unit they are 1⅛in finished, at the top of the upper unit they finish at ⅝in. I have not given a full cutting list because I would expect your own design considerations to operate should you make something like this, and of course there are also limitations of materials. You will see from the photo and drawings that I also echoed the faintly Oriental theme by

scalloping the top surface of the base to give it upturned ends — interesting visually and technically, though it loses a lot of wood! — and a further detail that carried the idea is the shaping of the top rails of both units, which come through the solid, jointed-up sides.

Construction
Timber selection

At the outset, prepare a full cutting list's worth of stock, slightly oversize to allow for final thicknessing and dimensioning. Store it in a warm dry place ready for use. This is particularly important for the drawer sides and the timber for the boarded back. As far as possible, select straight-grained timber for the framework, especially the door frames. The door panels are 1in stock sawn through to ½in, and the back of the upper unit is out of 1¼in stock sawn through twice to get ⅜in boards. At this stage it's a good idea to sort out the pieces for the end panels

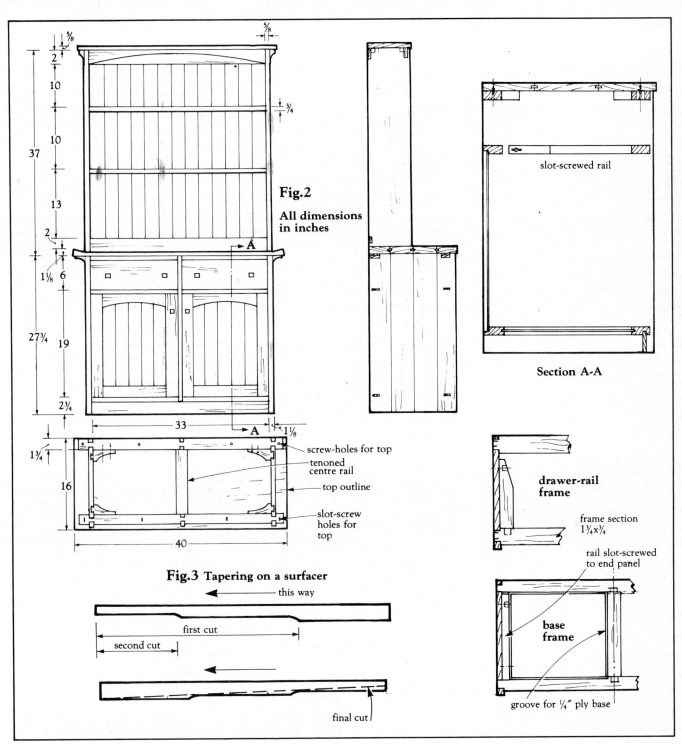

Fig.2

**All dimensions
in inches**

Section A-A

screw-holes for top

tenoned
centre rail

top outline

slot-screw
holes for
top

**drawer-rail
frame**

frame section
1¾ x ¾

rail slot-screwed
to end panel

**base
frame**

groove for ¼" ply base

Fig.3 Tapering on a surfacer

this way

first cut

second cut

final cut

for both base and top units, ensuring that the grain runs in the same direction along the finished board, and also that the effects of cupping are cancelled out. If possible, use quarter-sawn stock for the end panels of the top unit.

Base unit end panels

These are jointed with splined edge-butt joints, the splines in this case of ¼in ply. Remember to slightly offset the grooves for the ply to allow for the taper in thickness. I got a chance to try tapering on my surface planer, though it would be possible to use

2in stock and cut the boards to shape with a bandsaw. Even more wasteful! If you opt for the planer method, produce two stopped cuts in one direction, and finish the job by surfacing once to form a flat surface (fig. 3). The panels should be finally surfaced by hand planing diagonally across the board with a fine sharp smoothing plane to ensure flatness.

Base framework

This is a standard format and may be made with either dowelled or mortised joints. It's best to do the base and middle frames first,

which includes fitting the ply base panels into grooves in the base frame. Note from the drawings (figs 1 and 2) that the side rails that go up to the solid sides are slot-screwed into the solid across the grain; in the base frame they are half-lapped on to the front and back rails, and in the drawer-rail frame they are tenoned in at the front and stop short of the back rail.

Dry assemble the frames, and once the mortises are routed and squared in the end panels and the rebates cut in the frames for the back, you can go to final assembly of the end panels and first two frames. It is important to check for squareness to ease

continued

Biting the cherry

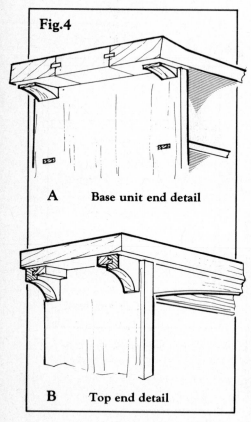

Fig.4

A   Base unit end detail

B   Top end detail

the later drawer fitting. The top frame in the base is fitted with bridle joints for the projecting rails, and the corner-blocks are screwed to the rails and lap-dovetailed into the tops of the side panels. The scalloped rail ends were done with a bandsaw and finished on the linisher before assembly, and the slots in them to screw through to the top surface are also done at this stage. A front plinth may either be housed in place or fitted to blocks, and the vertical stiles, notched in front and back, complete the framework.

Top unit

This is a simple structure, with the ends tapered in the same way as the base panels. The bottom rail is dovetailed into bottom back edges of the uprights, the top rear rail is notched in, and the front rail, with its bandsawn curve, is bridle jointed. A rebate is worked in rails and end panels to take the back; mark this when it's in dry assembly to get an accurate position for the stopped rebates on the ends. Housings are cut for the shelves.

The top is a flat board buttoned to the top rails. The buttons are fitted into grooves which run all the way along the rails, and are open where the rails project through the end boards. The end buttons are fitted outside the boards and so are visible from the side of the dresser (fig. 4B). The curve in the top rail is cut and sanded before final assembly. I routed shoulders to the ends of the shelves to give a clean joint in their housings; use a modest amount of glue fixing them, and clean any excess off with a sharp chisel when it has gone off.

The back is matchboarded, and although the rebates are best machined (fig 5A), the final surfacing and chamfering were done with a sharp plane. When you get a good fit for the back, pin it in place.

Base top

As with the end panels, this piece is splined and edge-butted, but this time the through splines are solid timber, again offset from centre to allow for scalloping (fig. 4A).

The stock may be removed in a variety of ways, but if you use a radial-arm saw, make sure the work is well secured to the table, because the removal of all that waste releases a lot of tension in the wood, and you may get some bowing. Using a router is a long and not particularly pleasant job but it does follow the surface. If you use a portable router, the top will need accurate surfacing before you start, and the ends must be cut square. The end curves are cut in a series of steps, running the router fence along the ends of the board; the rest is removed free hand at a constant depth setting, in bands of about 3in. Leave raised strips at intervals to support the router base — also at the ends, of course, where you are cutting the upward curves. The proud strips are removed with a plane. I finished the ends with the round end of a portable belt sander, and sanded the whole top by hand with glasspaper. I also cut two grooves 6mm wide and 8mm deep on the underside of the top to help restore the balance in the piece. It is mounted to the base, screwed at the back and slot-screwed at the front.

Doors

These are a straightforward haunched mortise-and-tenon construction, fitted with 10mm panels which are joined with loose 4mm tongues (fig. 5B). Again the panels may be hand surfaced to match the back. The top rails have a curve in them to pick up the curve in the upper unit top rail.

Drawers

There is no quick way of making drawers, though if you use ply bottoms fitted into grooves in the drawer sides and back, you avoid the need for drawer-slips. If you're unfamiliar with drawer construction, it's worth reading up on the subject, but dry timber, dry weather, sharp tools and plenty of time are the order of the day.

I used ¾in cherry (cut from a single piece so the grain runs on) for the fronts, and good, dry, straight-grained ½in mahogany for the sides and back. The sides are half-lap dovetailed into the front, and through-dovetailed into the back; all regular drawer practice. There is a groove in front and sides for the 4mm ply bottom — make sure you cut it at the right height to come out of the ends of the fronts through the dovetail socket, so it won't show on the endgrain; and the backs, also as normal practice, are cut short so they finish above the drawer-bottom, which is screwed upwards into them. Make the drawers to full size of the front opening, and plane carefully to fit; whether you taper them narrower to the back is up to you, and all a matter of personal preference and much debate. They are 14in long outside to outside.

Fitting and finish

Ball catches and brass butt hinges are probably the most suitable fittings for this job with the oil finish I used. If books are to be stored in the piece, a polyurethane or lacquer finish would be more appropriate. The handles are hand-worked from cherry and screwed through from the backs of door stiles and drawer-fronts.

I hope you enjoy making and using this piece; I must say I did. I feel the design suits the warm golden flavour of cherry admirably, but of course you can try any timber; I have a notion it would be fine in Douglas fir or first-quality pine. ■

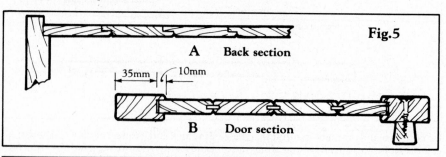

Fig.5

A   Back section

35mm   10mm

B   Door section

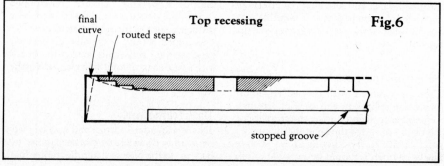

Fig.6

final curve   routed steps

Top recessing

stopped groove

Hands on

WOODWORKING WHEEZE of the month

Sandvik winner

Infinitely adjustable dowel sizer

Turning a dowel using calipers to check size at the end of a workpiece can be tedious; you can drill an appropriate hole in a piece of flat steel bar with a slot cut and filed (fig. 1), and force this on to the revolving workpiece to produce a standard if somewhat rough dowel. I modified it to produce an acceptable tool (fig. 2) but got fed up with making new dowel sizers for all the diameters I needed.

So cannibalising an old Footprint adjustable spanner, I ground back the upper jaw and added a locking screw to produce a reliable dowel sizer to suit any dimension I wanted (fig. 3). I've used it now for more than 16 years and it has needed sharpening or re-grinding about 10 times.

Fig. 1

Fig. 2

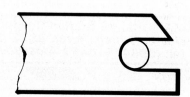

Fig. 3

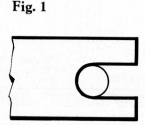

Fig. 4

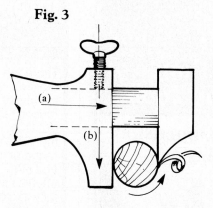

To use this sizer, you need to offer the lower jaw against the revolving dowel, and then push it slowly but firmly downwards, keeping pressure in the (a) direction all the time until the cutting is completed.

I find the tool works even better if you grind the cutting edge with a curve, or angled both sides (fig. 4); this gives a slight skew action which can be increased by twisting the sizer a little and moving it along the workpiece.

For best results turn the dowel down to within ¹⁄₁₆in of the required size, then use the sizer. It will produce dowels down to ¼in diameter, and as large as the adjustment allows, mostly without needing to move the tool rest. I adjust it against the drill I bored the socket with, generally a Forstner or lip-and-spur. The locking screw tends to close the gap so you may have to fiddle around a little to get the size accurate.

R. D. Clements, Wootton Bassett

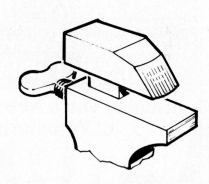

Squaring round mouldings

It's time-consuming to square round moulded timber sections such as ovolo sash with ordinary tools, but here's a gadget that speeds it up. You need two pieces of ⅜in or ½in ply, 3x6in or whatever size comes to hand; the ends must be planed dead square,

and the edges should be parallel. Butt-joint them, using glue and screws or 1in panel pins. Draw along the ends to get a square round a moulding. The device can also be used to square a line by placing it in a rebate, as shown.

M. J. Farman, Church Stretton

Stocking filter

I use a nylon stocking as an air filter on my router to prevent the cooling system clogging up; dust and chippings are easily blown off after use.

C. F. Mullan, Thorpeness

Truly square on a radial-arm

You don't need a known accurate square to cut true and square with a radial-arm saw. With the table level, no free play anywhere, and a TCT blade fitted, pin a piece of hardboard or plywood (white if possible) to the table, and cut across it about 1mm deep for a reference cut.

Now take another piece of hardboard or plywood about 300mm square, marking the corners A, B, C and D clockwise. Trim edge AB with the saw, then place the edge AB against the fence and trim edge BC. Keep turning anti-clockwise and trim until you've cut all four edges. Now place edge DA, the final cut, against the fence and align edge AB with the reference cut; any discrepancy between AB and the reference cut is four times the difference between the angle of cut and 90°, so it shows up quite clearly. If the gap is near the fence the cut is less than 90°, if it's the other end of the board from the fence it's greater than 90°.

Adjust the angle of the arm, move the backing board and make a new reference cut. Then cut the square again. Continue this process until you're satisfied.

N. K. Milne, Margate

Easy kerfing

To solve the problem of knowing how many kerfs to cut and how far apart if you want to bend wood this way, draw out your radius on a piece of ply or white hardboard, and strike an arc. Take your board to be bent and cut a single kerf with a fine blade to within 1/8-3/16in of the face. Position the board along the radius, the single kerf on the centre point, and bend it to close the cut. The distance the board has moved down the arc — A-B — is the distance apart your kerfs should be. Cut all the kerfs, rub glue into them, bend the board round the arc, and hold it with a string cramp or

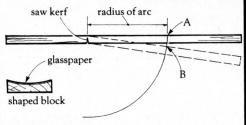

blocks until it's set. You can improve the finish by making up a curved sanding block to fit the arc and rubbing down with that.

N. K. Collins, Maidstone

'Shadow' mitre

For a quick way of cutting mitres for architraves, skirtings and so on, you don't need to mark out or use a mitre box. Just use the reflection or 'shadow' from the stock you're cutting in your (shiny) tenon-saw blade. Make your cut once the reflection in the blade makes a right angle with the stock. You may need to touch up with a block plane, but it's accurate enough for fixing work. It's possible with a crosscut saw too.

Rod Grimshaw, Keswick

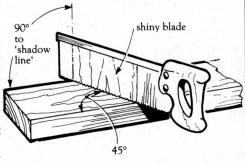

Non-stick dovetail slides

When I make routing tables and jigs with dovetail sliders for guides, I find it's not easy to get a really tight fit with a clean sliding action, and lubricant such as linseed oil or wax polish tends to pick up dust and cause jamming.

I overcame this problem by cutting the dovetails slightly loose and then inserting small 1/4in-diameter brass inserts along one edge. I press-fitted them and then carefully filed them for a perfect fit and slide; the frictional surface area is much reduced.

Roy Benfield, Walton-on-Thames

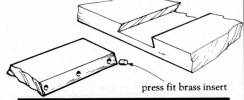

press fit brass insert

Miniature filling knife

I recommend an artist's tool you can buy from any artist's materials shop, a tiny trowel with a good length handle and a flexible steel blade. It's ideal for filling small holes with plaster or wood filler, doesn't damage the wood and places the filler precisely where you want it. Cheap, too!

G. G. Haigh, Newbury

HOW TO DO IT

We want to publish as many wheezes as possible, so we must use only the barest bones of the ideas. Be as precise and brief as possible; type your words if you can, double-spaced on one side of an A4 sheet; make drawings, if any, as few and as clear as you can, and annotate them clearly.

586

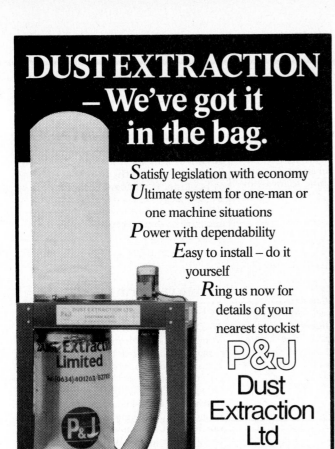
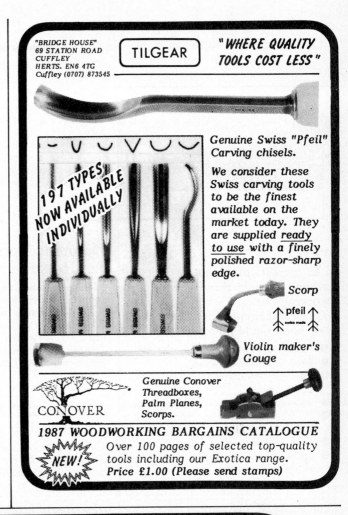

Guild notes

WOODWORKERS

The Guild was set up by *Woodworker* to create a meeting ground for all those involved in working wood, whether professional, amateur, or enthusiastic beginner. Guild members get:

● Access to Guild courses and events
● Free publicity in *Woodworker*
● Specially arranged tool insurance at low rates
● 15% off Woodworker Show entry
● A free display area and meeting point at the Show
● 15% discount off *Woodworker* plans
● Inclusion in our register of members' skills and services

For details, please send an sae to the Guild of Woodworkers, 1 Golden Sq, London W1R 3AB.

Rudiments of restoration — Barry Honeyborne

2-3 July, Leominster, Herefordshire, £54. Bring along your antique and learn how to restore it. From initial cleaning to repairs and final polishing, Barry will show you all the steps — he has been 25 years in the trade. This two day course is an introduction to every aspect of restoration, plus a chance to make a start on your own piece under expert supervision.

French polishing — Ian Hosker

18-19 July, Chester, £50.
One of our most popular course subjects, led by Ian, a teacher and a practising professional. It covers preparation of old and new pieces, staining and colouring techniques, grain filling, shellac finishes, fadding, bodying in, spiriting off and giving new life to existing polished surfaces. The fee includes course materials. Ian will make up a polishing kit to take away at £9.50 if you order in advance.

Green wood working — Mike Abbott and Jack Hill

30 July-2 August, Forest of Dean, £90. Traditional woodland crafts in a woodland setting — cleaving, shaving, and turning with and without machinery; chair bodging, stool making, steam bending, seat weaving; rake making, stick making, spoon carving.
Group accommodation arranged if you wish — why not bring your spouse? Course begins in evening of 30 July, followed by three full working days; small individual charge for materials used.

Decorative techniques — Ian Hosker

12-13 September, 10-5, Chester, £55.
Another chance to learn all sorts of wonderful decorative techniques, including dragging, lining, sponging, rag-rolling, marbling, spattering and tortoiseshelling. The fee includes materials, but bring a few paintbrushes and jam-jars.

French polishing — Charles Cliffe

17-18 September, Bexleyheath, £45.
These courses by expert Charles Cliffe are among the most popular run by the Guild, so book early to avoid disappointment. You'll learn about preparation, staining and techniques of french polishing itself, with ample hands-on experience under Charles' eye. You'll learn the correct way to sharpen a cabinet scraper, so bring yours along, and he's willing to offer advice on any small piece of furniture you want to refinish.

Basic woodcarving — Eric Ingham

19-20 September, 9.30-5.30, Lytham St Annes, £50.
We're pleased to be able to offer this introduction to woodcarving. On this course you'll learn about use of tools and sharpening, types of wood, design and finishing. Eric's been carving for 15 years and will give you a good start. Wood is provided and you're free to carve whatever you want. Bring carving tools if you have them. There's plenty of accommodation in this resort area and your spouse might enjoy the sea air while you learn.

Design and workshop drawing — Bob Grant

26 September, 9.30-5, Oxford, £25VAT
If putting your design on paper doesn't come easy, here's the course to learn how. Bob will help you gain confidence in freehand sketching, show you how to use grid paper and drawing boards, and lots more.

Hand veneering — Bob Grant

10 October, 9.30-5, Oxford, £35VAT
Veneering is much more than the art of disguising chipboard. It's a skill with a long history, and can create some beautiful effects — and it saves fine and expensive wood! You'll be laying a panel with veneer, mitring a cross-banding, inlaying lines round it, and applying a balancer veneer on the back. If you have a veneer hammer, bring it; but materials will be provided.

BOOKING FORM

I wish to book for the following course(s).

☐ **Rudiments of restoration** 2-3 July, £54; make cheque payable to Barry Honeyborne

☐ **French polishing** 18-19 July, £50; make cheque payable to Ian Hosker.

☐ **Green wood working** 30 July-2 August, £90; make cheque payable to Jack Hill

☐ **Decorative techniques** 12-13 September, £55; make cheque payable to Ian Hosker

☐ **French polishing** 17-18 September, £45; make cheque payable to Charles Cliffe

☐ **Basic woodcarving** 19-20 September, £50; make cheque payable to Eric Ingham

☐ **Design and workshop drawing** 26 September, £25VAT = £28.75

☐ **Hand veneering** 10 October, £35 VAT = £40.25

Please make cheques payable to 'The Guild of Woodworkers/ASP Ltd' unless otherwise stated.

Name..

Address..

....

....

Guild no..
Send to: The Guild of Woodworkers, 1 Golden Square, London, W1R 3AB.
The Guild reserves the right to cancel any course.

Guild rep appeal

We received the following comments and appeal from Hertfordshire rep John Waigh:
It's now just over a year since fellow rep Mike Cripps complained in these pages (March 1986) about the negative response from members. He also put forward some interesting ideas for getting members together but nothing appears to have been done to help the situation.

I now have to make the same complaint. The basic idea is good but lacks communication. We've heard about success of some groups but how have the rest fared? What about the reps getting together? Since we are, geographically speaking, far apart, it has its problems. So what about meeting at the next Woodworker Show? That shouldn't make a dent in Guild funds. Better once a year than never.

Referring to the lack of response, perhaps there's some reticence because it's thought special skills are needed to contribute or some members feel their involvement in woodwork is too limited. On the other hand, maybe you're hiding your light under a bushel. If you are, please don't. I'm sure we can learn from each other. In any case, just talking woodwork is enjoyable.

I have a well equipped workshop, dozens of books on many aspects of the craft, and eight years' collection of WOODWORKER and similar magazines. I simply like woodwork and want to keep learning. I read with some envy about various courses open to us, but time (and money) doesn't allow me — and I'm sure many others — to indulge.

Whatever we have by way of a workshop, be it a bench in the garage or garden shed; whatever our skill; whatever our ages (I'm 57) — we must be kindred spirits to have joined the Guild in the first place.

So let's be hearing from you budding woodworkers and make this basically good idea work. If you live in Hertfordshire, please ring me on (05827) 62039.

John Waigh

Opportunity knocks — 1

Cherry Trees Organic Farm, Rickmansworth, Herts, is seeking traditional craftspeople to help create a rural village atmosphere of interest to visiting school and college parties. The 35 acre farm set in the Hertfordshire Chilterns offers 'the perfect working environment in idyllic surroundings', initially on a weekend basis but with something more permanent likely to ensue.
● Mrs. Mary Bell, Cherry Tree Farm, Olliberrie Lane, Belsize, Sarratt, Rickmansworth, Herts.

Opportunity knocks — 2

A new mail order catalogue specialising in craft work is being compiled. Organisers of 'The Craft Collection' say they want to produce a catalogue of high quality items made in the UK by craftsmen and women, aimed at potential customers who don't generally attend craft fairs or other retail outlets. The emphasis will be on quality and originality, especially traditional craft methods, and the collection aims to have items that are not available in shops.

The catalogue will be advertised in such magazines as *Country living* and *Homes & Gardens* and sent out free on request. The annual fee for appearing in the catalogue will be about £80. This is a commercial venture, but the organiser wants it to be a service to British craftspeople.
● Mrs Pam Johnson, The Craft Collection, 1 The Holt, Hare Hatch, Upper Wargrave, Berks RG10 9TG.

Guild address change

All enquiries about membership and subscription renewals are now being dealt with at Guild of Woodworkers, 9 Hall Rd, Maylands Wood Est, Hemel Hempstead, Herts HP2 7BH, (0442) 211882.

Guild courses and overall Guild administration continue to be dealt with at 1 Golden Sq, London W1R 3AB, 01-437 0626.

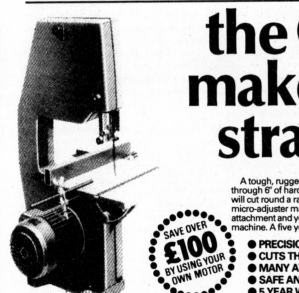

Question box

Our panel of experts solve your woodworking problems

We will try to answer any questions you can throw at us, but the ones we publish are the ones of most general interest to readers.

Please type your question double-spaced with generous margins, and include a stamped self-addressed envelope. Send it to: Question Box, Woodworker, 1 Golden Sq., London W1R 3AB.

Strip slip

Q *I used Nitromors Original to strip part of a coffee table, and applied a two-part lacquer, Essar AC Malamine. The finish will not dry on the parts I stripped.*

Stephen Hague, Malton, N. Yorks

A This problem is common with chemical stripping compounds; they must be used correctly, following the manufacturer's instructions. Also modern finishing materials such as Acid Hardened Lacquers (AC) need a sterile substrate; the slightest trace of methylene chloride or ammonia or even old polish/silicones/gunge will react with the surface coating.

Here's the procedure you should have followed before you refinished:

1 Apply chemical stripper (Nitromors) and leave for 15-20 minutes.
2 Scrape off soft gunge with cabinet scraper, used end on.
3 Apply more stripper, scrubbing into the gunge using No. 4 steel wool.
4 Wipe off all deposit using waste wool.
5 Wash down using cellulose thinners and waste wool and dry off.
6 Sand down using 80-grit garnet paper.
7 Wash again with cellulose thinners and waste wool, or alternatively white spirit at this stage, and dry off.
8 Sand with 100-grit garnet paper.
9 Wipe down with clean water without soaking the wood, and dry off.
10 Sand with 240-grit garnet paper.

Now the substrate is ready for refinishing. Don't use oil stains, oil fillers or chemical stains under an AC lacquer. When mixing lacquer, follow the instructions carefully: too little acid delays curing, too much encourages a brittle film.

Noel Leach

Discolouring oak

Q *I built an oak cabinet with 4mm bookmatched oak plywood panels. Before finishing it I brought it into the house to acclimatise, but after two weeks dark stains began to appear in the open parts of the grain. I've discovered this was caused by glue percolation in the plywood. Two weeks later the discolouration had become very prominent and extended to about 80% of the panel area.*

I intended to finish the cabinet in light oak to match existing furniture, and would be grateful for any suggestions to rectify the discolouration.

Other woodworkers using decorative plywood – store it in a warm room for at least two weeks before use!

Leslie Duff, Linlithgow, West Lothian

A Oak has high levels of tannic acid in the fibres. This acid reacts with many other chemicals including alkalis and other acids, with a tendency to darken the wood either by liquid contact or by the fumes. After studying your letter I conclude your problem has been caused by one or more of the following factors:

1 Damp storage conditions.
2 Presence of lime, salts, plaster, cement or farm chemicals stored nearby.
3 Industrial fumes.
4 The plywood manufacturers may have used a PVA glue containing ammonia, an alkali that reacts with tannic acid.
5 Storage near where animals are kept.

You won't be able to get the light oak effect you wanted, but you may be able to rectify the discolouration. Try experimenting first on an offcut of the ply, since nothing is certain when you're dealing with chemical reactions. Here's the procedure:

1 Lightly sponge down both sides of the ply with clean water, but don't soak.
2 Apply with a sponge a weak solution of oxalic acid (50% water), leave on the substrate for 5-10 minutes. Oxalic acid is a very mild bleach.
3 Wash off with clean water and dry it with paper towels.
4 Leave two to three days to dry out.
5 Sand down with 240-grit garnet paper.
6 Apply one coat of dewaxed sanding (shellac) sealer, which is a clear finish.
7 When it's dry, sand again using 320 grit 'Lubrisil' abrasive paper.

The substrate is now ready for any finishing surface coating. You'll find more information on bleaching in my book *The Woodworker Book of Wood Finishing*, published by Argus Books.

Noel Leach

Mahogany fireplace

Q *I've made a wooden mantle for an Adam style fireplace and would like to know the best way of fitting wood resin motifs on to it. Is cellulose stain, sealer and lacquer suitable for this kind of work?*

J. Bainbridge, Kidsgrove, Staffs

A Mahogany is fine, close-grained, solid, workable wood, value for its stability and natural colour; imported into this country in 1680, it became very popular with cabinetmakers and joiners. Brazilian mahogany is one of the newer species.

● Don't on any account use cellulose-based products near any source of heat, such as a fireplace, or you'd create a potential fire-hazard. I suggest a safe organic finish like shellac-based french polish.

● Damp down the wood to pre-raise the grain with clean water. When it's dry, sand down using 240-grit garnet paper.

● Mix a strong solution of bichromate of potash in warm water — it's best to use rainwater for all water-stain mixing — apply to the timber with a rag, fad or sponge and allow to dry out. This will give a lovely authentic brown colour because of the chemical reaction with the natural structure of the wood.

● Don't sand down at this point, but apply several coatings of button polish by mop or rubber. If a darker shade is needed use an AC garnet de-waxed french polish. Allow to dry for 12 hours at approximately 65°F.

● Use 0000 steel wool and a good furniture-wax polish and rub into the french-polished surface film to produce a fine smooth antique finish.

● When your polishing and waxing is completed, fix the resin motifs using brass veneer pins instead of glue. You may need to colour the motifs by using a spirit-based stain with a little french polish applied with a No. 2 mop.

Noel Leach

● Noel Leach is a professional wood finisher and lecturer.

What the ekki?

Q *Can you give me some information on a wood called ekki, and answer these specific questions. Can I use a stain preservative such as Sadolin? Can it be finished in undercoat and gloss paint and would I need a sealer first? Which glue do you recommend? Will the timber distort after air drying? Do the splinters turn wounds septic as with green hart, as I understand the woods are similar?*

R. F. Wellman, Portsmouth

A Ekki is indigenous to West Africa and dark red/brown. The grain is usually interlocked with a coarse and uneven texture. The wood is very hard and heavy, weighing 1000kg per cu m. at 12% moisture content. It is hard to work with both machine and hand tools.

1 Stain preservatives are unnecessary since the heartwood is very durable; only the sapwood, if used, would benefit.
2 The wood could be finished in undercoat and gloss paint and should require no sealer. It's not usual to paint dense hardwoods, most people preferring a colourless transparent finish.
3 Any urea or phenol formaldehyde adhesive should be satisfactory. The wood is reported to have varying gluing characteristics, but there should be few problems if joints are properly constructed and well fitting.
4 Possible distortion after adequate air drying depends on the final air dried moisture content and the conditions of use. Material air dried to, say, 18% MC would be highly likely to distort if placed in a centrally heated room. If the ekki is very thick (350mm or more) air drying will take a long time, and it would be very difficult to dry satisfactorily.

5 No information is available on whether splinter wounds may become septic. Many hardwoods have this characteristic, so you should handle ekki with care.

Ron Hooks

Tulip tree wood

Q *I have a tulip tree which is dying. I understand the wood is quite sought after for inlays and marquetry. When is the best time to fell it, and roughly how much might it fetch per cubic foot?*

Claire Faron, Salisbury

A I assume your tree is *Liriodendron tulipifera*, indigenous to North America but widely grown in Europe. Generally the forest-grown material from America is of better quality than that grown here, where most trees are free-growing parkland specimens. In the USA the pale brown heart wood is used as a lightweight utility wood and for plywood.

Unfortunately it's unlikely that your one tree, particularly when it's dying, would be saleable other than for low-grade purposes. You could enquire from Henry Venables Ltd, Doxey Road, Stafford, (0787) 59131, who specialise in home-grown timbers.

Ron Hooks

● Ron Hooks is a professional timber consultant.

Purpleheart

Q *I have some purpleheart timber which is a very deep purple on the outside and reddy brown on the inside. Could you please tell me what finish to apply to bring out the purple colour?*

R. Flynn, London E.7.

A The colours of purpleheart range from brownish red to a beautiful purple when freshly cut, but will blacken with age. Any stain applied to the wood to restore some of the purple colour can only be effective for a short time, after which the natural darkening of the wood will bring about a further colour change.

Purpleheart polishes well and should be finished by polishing with transparent-white french polish which will have the least effect on changing the colour.

Charles Cliffe

● Charles Cliffe is a professional polisher, author and teacher.

Sticking drawers

Q *The drawers of an old wooden writing bureau have become very loose, with a lot of movement both vertically and horizontally. What's the best way to tighten them up?*

J. H. C. Hicks, Woking

A Restoration means building up the worn parts. Start by checking that the drawer-front is still a good fit in its recess. The front itself is unlikely to have worn, but if it is a sloppy fit then it's possible the bureau carcase has sprung and you must fix this first.

If only the drawer sides are worn, I advise you to eliminate the vertical sloppiness first as this may cure the horizontal problem as well; a small amount of sideways movement is desirable to prevent the drawer binding. If the sideways sloppiness is too bad to be ignored, allow extra thickness on the repair piece and later plane the side face to fit.

Drawers wear in a characteristic way, as indicated in the sketch; remedial action involves starting from a new datum line and gluing a piece on.

If the dovetail joints aren't sound it's best to knock the whole drawer to pieces, do the repairs and then re-assemble. The work is more awkward if you don't want to disturb the existing joints, as you'll have to scarf new pieces on to the bottom edges; top edges are less prone to wear, but if they are also bad the procedure is similar.

Scribe a datum line to remove the worn area, as shown. Cut back to this line using a bullnose plane and a chisel for the last bit to the front; if the drawer is dismantled you can run a plane the whole length of the side. If the datum line is short of the groove holding the drawer bottom, glue on a new piece allowing enough extra width and thickness for planing the drawer to fit the opening; if wear is really bad and into the groove holding the bottom, work a small rebate into the new piece so the original width of the groove is maintained.

The new timber should match the original if you want to faithfully restore the piece. You'll get a better repair, though, by fitting strips made from quarter-sawn oak or beech, because they are hard wearing. A little candle grease rubbed into the running surfaces helps to lubricate the drawer.

Charles Hayward's book, *Antique Furniture Repairs*, published by Evans, is an excellent reference work.

Bob Grant

● Bob Grant is an all-round wood craftsman and tutors courses for the Guild of Woodworkers.

Repairing drawers

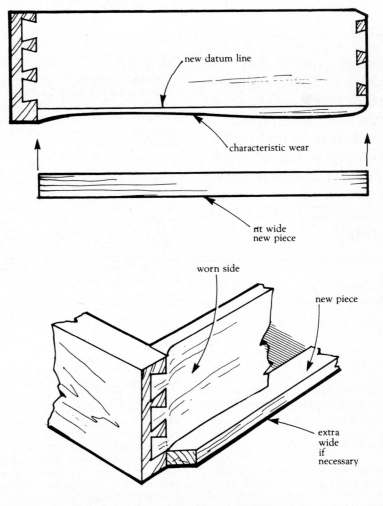

new datum line

characteristic wear

rit wide
new piece

worn side

new piece

extra
wide
if
necessary

Nouveau for old

● *Pretty, yes. But is a chair in this state really worth restoring?*

Auctions, junk shops, jumbles — there's hidden furniture treasure out there. When Sterling Roncraft offered to help us bring a piece back to life, we found an oak Art Nouveau carver and gave it to professional restorer Philip Bailey to do the magic

Restoring old furniture is a great national pastime — the thrill of finding a bargain and the challenge of problem-solving can become almost addictive — but unless you want a house littered with half-completed projects, you'll need to know how to avoid a number of pitfalls. Our project, an Art Nouveau oak armchair in need of upholstery, joint and finishing work, highlights what you should look for if you want to restore furniture to its former glory.

First impressions

No matter how strong your initial attraction is to what you see in the junk shop or the skip next door, take a second look. Most restoration will try your patience along the way and it will have to be your strong attachment to the item that sees you through. Our chair could be a single, functional piece of furniture or part of a growing collection of this style of design. It has elegant lines typical of the period and interesting inlays to the cresting rail and back splat — instantly appealing to Art Nouveau enthusiasts.

Time and effort

Spare time has a price and if the restoration proves boring, messy and unresponsive to your efforts, you'll end up asking 'Why did I ever start this job?'

Chairs in general (and ours in particular) provide good guidelines in assessing whether or not you can cope with the restoration.

● Construction: some chairs have complex designs and cramping up loose joints will present special problems. Cabriole legs, curved seat rails and elaborate detailing require specific tools and making complex cramping blocks. Check all the joints very thoroughly: if they're loose, ensure you can cope with the work required to secure them. Don't be afraid to give the chair a detailed test for joints before you buy. In our example, there was slight movement in the stretcher joints; but you can see that the joints are simple with good right-angles where cramps can be applied easily to give pressure when re-gluing. Note that the arms are curved: if these had been loose at the joints with the rear uprights, appropriate blocks would have to be made for cramping up.

● Upholstery: if you have to attend to seat-rail joints, upholstery may have to be removed if the seat is 'stuffed-over'. If you're not attempting the re-upholstery yourself, keep in mind the cost of professional upholstering.

Our chair with a drop-in seat didn't present this problem; access to the joints was easy and the cost of re-upholstery less than half of that for a stuff-over seat.

● Finish: try to imagine all the component parts of the chair laid flat on a surface. This gives you an idea of the surface area, and time it will take to strip the finish by hand and apply a new finish. Chairs have a surprising surface area and the surfaces aren't always wasy to get at. Some finishes can be difficult to remove and may require several attempts at stripping. All of this should be considered before you buy.

Our chair could be expected to take four to six hours to strip overall, and may take a good deal longer if the finish is stubborn. Only experience will allow you to determine the resistance of a finish or distinguish french polish from varnish — so ask someone who does know. Here we had a readily removable varnish, thick in places, but worn sufficiently on the inside back and arms during years of use to reveal an attractive mellow colour of the oak beneath the dark varnish.

Not all finishes need to be stripped. Grime, old wax and grease can sometimes be cleaned away (Colron Restorer/Cleaner) to reveal the original finish.

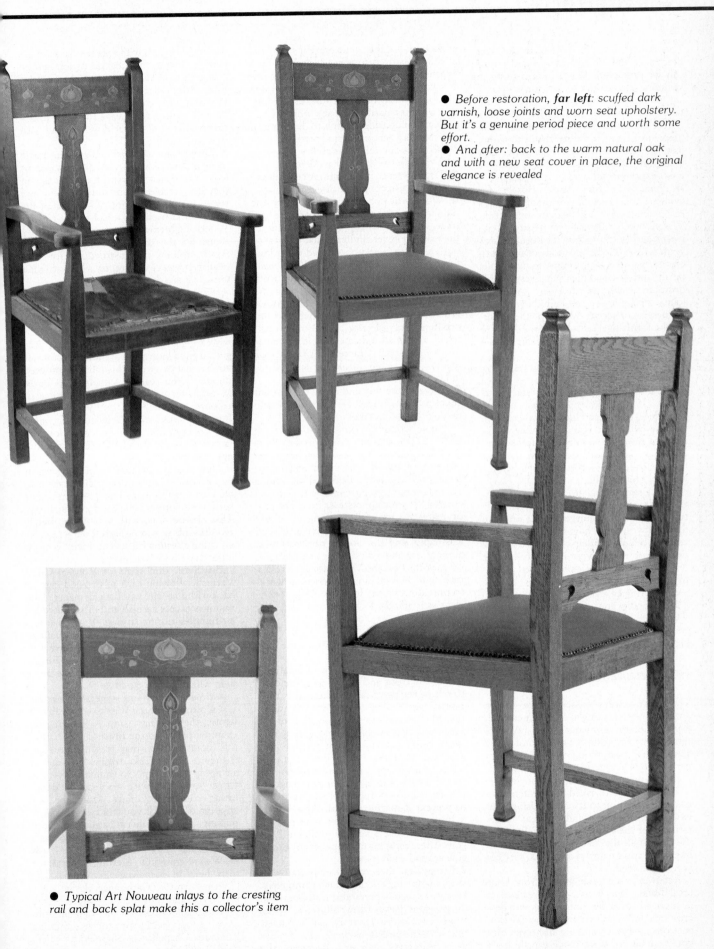

● *Before restoration, **far left**: scuffed dark varnish, loose joints and worn seat upholstery. But it's a genuine period piece and worth some effort.*

● *And after: back to the warm natural oak and with a new seat cover in place, the original elegance is revealed*

● *Typical Art Nouveau inlays to the cresting rail and back splat make this a collector's item*

continued

Nouveau for old

This is where the value of many antiques lies, especially where the acquired patina can be preserved. Don't be too hasty in stripping — if in doubt, ask for advice.

One further warning: rosewood doesn't take kindly to stripping and may turn a dark purple colour; fading in this timber takes place in the polish rather than the wood, just as with walnut and mahogany. Our chair has the advantage of being oak — a good experimental wood for beginners.

● **Previous repairs:** look closely for evidence of previous restoration. If it's badly done, you could be in for extra work. Watch out for damage caused by woodworm, and be sure to treat it before it infests your house (Colron Woodworm Fluid). Chairs can take 10-16 hours to dismantle, repair and re-assemble, and irresponsible 'restorers' will use shortcuts to secure joints. Bodged jobs can be hidden behind the hessian or scrim covering on the underneath of stuff-over seats, so ask the dealer to remove at least part of the scrim from a sample chair.

Look closely for worm holes, large corner blocks badly fitted, screws driven into rails at the joints, nails and metal straps. If the dealer declines, he has something to hide, so look elsewhere. You can also detect bad repairs from the visible parts of the chair: a joint may feel secure, but make sure it hasn't been screwed together and the traces covered with a wooden plug or filler.

Our example had no previous repairs, and was made in oak, a hardwood generally resistant to worm damage. Make a list of all the work you might have to do — either by yourself or with the help of a trusted professional — to restore your item to full use or decoration. The oak chair yielded a relatively short list:

a securing of stretcher joints
b stripping and re-finishing the frame
c re-upholstery of the drop-in seat

Once you have your list you're better prepared to answer the next question.

Is the restoration worth doing?

There are two ways of assessing this — from a purely monetary angle, or from personal, non-monetary considerations. Always remembering that the satisfaction of doing such a job is great, though not great enough perhaps to risk domestic disruption, we will concentrate on the commercial angle.

The price you're asked for the item may bear little relation to its value. Using your work list, make an independent value-estimate of the piece as it stands. Estimate the cost of all the materials you'll need to buy, then add on any professional services you might need.

Refer to trade price guides from your local library which use prices realised at auction, and provide photographs with descriptions. Judge by your own experiences at auctions, or from searching in shops. Once you've an idea of what the piece might fetch

at auction — either in its present state or as a fully restored piece — deduct your expenses figure from your auction estimate. If it works out below the price asked, you're in a position to haggle; it may take a little time and persuasion, but it's worth it.

Our first consideration is to determine if our chair is a genuine period piece and not a cheap reproduction. This ability will come with time but follow our guidelines:

● Use reference books and price guides to confirm the appropriate design.

● Worn seat upholstery tells a story: the number of tack holes in the seat frame, and traces of previous top covers underneath the existing cover, indicate that the seat of our chair has been upholstered on at least three occasions. Allowing for 20-25 years between each re-upholstery, we can work back to circa 1900.

● The chair's mortise-and-tenon joints, generous use of oak throughout, and fine detailing and selection of wood for the inlaid motifs all indicate that it was made before cheaper, faster reproduction methods came in. Look for such detail indicators.

● Wear to the feet and arms; that on our chair indicates at least 80 years' use — and that's not easy to fake!

In good condition our chair might fetch £180-£220 at auction. You'd need to allow £20-£25 each to have the stretcher joints and upholstery (in soft cover and braid) done professionally. Brass-nailing and a stained leather top cover adds to the cost, so check with your upholsterer first. The cost of materials for the finishing — cheap brushes, wire wool, protective gloves, glasspaper, and the Colron products — is about £10, and you'll have materials left over for the next job. Allow for £60-£80 in cash outlays including professional work, so providing we pay less than £100 for the chair as it stands, we're in front.

Step-by-step restoration

1 Secure stretcher joints: we were able to spread the front and back legs sufficiently to release the two side stretchers from their mortise joints. The tenons at each end of the stretchers and the mortise joints on the legs were cleaned of the old glue with a sharp chisel, using a scraping action. We applied animal glue to the joints and used sash-cramps to apply pressure through each joint from front to back, along the length of the stretchers — soft pine blocks were used to prevent damaging the oak show-wood.

If you don't have a hot glue pot for animal glue, use a readily available PVA glue. After cramping up, wipe off any excess glue around each joint.

2 Stripping: there was no alternative to stripping the ugly dark varnish completely. Prepare a space — preferably outdoors or in the garage and away from children and pets. Brush on Colron Hard Finish Remover, following the directions on the can. Always use protective gloves. Remove the

dissolved varnish with coarse wire wool. Be patient, let the chemical do its job and be prepared to go over the entire chair several times. Neutralise the stripper traces left in the oak with clean white spirit, applied liberally with a rag. Leave the chair to dry thoroughly, and rub it down overall with fine wire wool.

3 Finishing: as chairs are often made using offcuts of wood from different parent logs, and because of stains from hands, you may have to bleach out some staining and try to match the colour of sections of the show-wood frame. We had to use Colron Wood Lightener to remove the patchy stains on the chair arms after stripping. Again, follow the instructions for best results. If you're unsure, try a little at a time until you see the desired result.

Now choose a basic colour to stain the frame. You can see what a purely natural finish would look like after sealing with a clear varnish, by applying methylated spirit with a rag over sections of the frame. This gives a good indication of the final colour. If you're happy with this shade, proceed direct to the sealing. Otherwise, Colron Wood Dyes are available in a wide range of colours: from light oak and yellow pine to Burmese teak and Peruvian mahogany. They're easy to apply — just follow the instructions and do a little area first before applying overall.

Our example revealed a pleasing warm natural oak colour under all the varnish, so we were ready for sealing. The purpose of sealing is to protect the wood from staining. This can be done with wax alone, but it requires lots of wax — and elbow grease. By applying a sealing varnish correctly, a more attractive finish is achieved.

Brush on thin coats of Ronseal Clear Varnish, allowing each to dry and cutting back with fine wire wool or glasspaper. This removes excess varnish and nibs caused by air-bubbles during drying. Varnish often gets a bad name, not because of its qualities as a finish, but because of the clumsy way it's applied. The essence of good finishing is the cutting back after each coat. Care taken here will reap rich rewards.

A final and satisfying stage is the waxing. Use Colron Finishing Wax to achieve a soft lustre, the the first step in creating an eventual patina to the finish.

Decorative inlays may present a problem if they're lifting. Take special care during stripping not to apply too much pressure or to get strands of wire wool caught under lifting corners of inlays. Don't be disappointed should you find some inlays missing. You can either fill again using your own inlays, or Colron Hard Wax; or seek professional help. ■

● We are grateful to Sterling Roncraft for their help in preparing this article. The Colron Furniture Care range, designed for the careful and enthusiastic — and even the professional! — restorer, is available from most good hardware stores: Sterling Roncraft, Chapeltown, Sheffield S30 4YP, (0742) 467171.

Three for the garden

Lounging, sitting, dining; try any or all of Anthony Hontoir's straightforward designs for solid, traditional, summery outdoor furniture

This folding garden chair, built in 'Director's Chair' style, is useful because the design allows assembly with detachable bolts for the hinges, enabling the sides to be removed so you get a handy stool. You can use conventional steel rivets, of course, to ensure the hinges remain permanently fixed. This would keep the construction as a seat with arms and backrest. Use a good quality hardwood such as sapele or utile, and cut and prepare it perfectly straight.

The chair is made in three parts, two rigid side frames and a collapsible centre stool, hinged in two places to each of the upright legs. As both sides are identical in almost every respect, the method of construction is the same for both. You can 'double up' on components as you go, but I shall describe how one frame is made.

The frame

Cut two legs to length, remembering to allow for the tenon at the top, and mark in the position of the mortises for the rail (fig. 1). Chop them out (fig. 3a), then measure and cut the four-shouldered tenons on the rail (fig. 3b). Check the joints fit snugly.

Mark in the two mortise positions in the underside of the armrest (fig. 1) and chop these out, then cut corresponding tenons at the top of both legs (fig. 3b). Fit the frame together temporarily, and measure up for the backrest, which requires a specially-angled mortise as shown in fig. 2. Note that

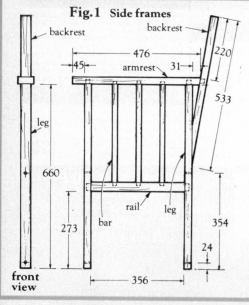

Fig. 1 Side frames

backrest · backrest · 476 · 45 · 220 · armrest · 31 · 533 · leg · 660 · rail · bar · leg · leg · 273 · 354 · 24

front view

356

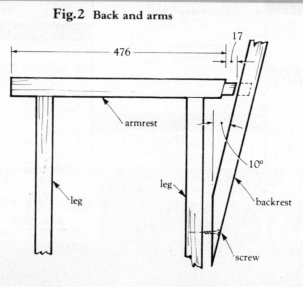

Fig. 2 Back and arms

476 · 17 · armrest · leg · leg · 10° · backrest · screw

● Direct
the three
assemble
for cover

● *Relax with a drink, deckchair and picnic table – but no fur coats, please.* **Below**, *the 'Director's' chair*

...hair – ...es ...dy

Three for the garden

the tenon cut at the rear end of the armrest must be similarly angled to make for a perfect fit. Then measure and cut a wedge-shaped slice from the bottom of the backrest, marking the correct angle when the frame is dry-assembled. Fit three lengths of 16mm dowelling between the armrest and the rail, spaced at equal intervals in holes 9mm deep.

Round off the front edge of the armrest and the top edge of the backrest with a coping saw, rasp and glasspaper. At this stage, the joints are only fixed together loosely. Don't glue them yet.

The stool

This is made in two parts, with a slight difference in the placing of the legs to permit both halves to be hinged. Mark two mortises on each stool seat rail and chop these out, then cut tenons at the top of each stool leg. Repeat this operation for the second half of the stool, putting the mortises in their complementary positions as shown in fig. 4.

The next step is to drill 4mm rivet holes in each of the four frame upright legs and each of the four stool legs. Copy the pattern of holes given in figs 1 and 4. Also drill

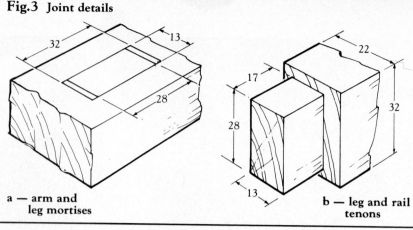

Fig.3 Joint details

a — arm and leg mortises

b — leg and rail tenons

16mm holes in the stool legs to take lengths of dowelling for the stretcher rails.

Clean up and round off the edges of the component pieces lightly with a plane, and rub down thoroughly with medium and then fine-grade glasspaper. Treat the wood with preservative, applying several coats, and leave for at least two days to dry completely.

The chair is now ready for assembly. I recommend you glue and screw the joints for maximum rigidity, using waterproof wood glue and 1in x 6 screws. If you screw the joints, do it from inside the chair, leaving the outside surfaces perfect. You can also draw-bore the mortises and tenons with dowels, of course: either way the hole in the tenon should be fractionally nearer the shoulder than the corresponding position through the mortise cheeks.

Hinging

You have the option of making detachable hinges from nuts and bolts, or permanent hinges with rivets. For the permanent arrangement, the rivets are made from 100x4mm mild steel flat-headed nails. Each nail is turned into a simple rivet by sawing it to length, allowing for plain washers and large rubber washers to act as spacers, then tapping the sawn end with a rivet-punch and a hammer to squash it out (fig. 5).

Two circular wooden spacer blocks, 28mm diameter by 22mm thick, are fitted between two of the stool legs and their corresponding upright legs. Finally, metal brackets are cut according to the pattern in fig. 5, using any suitable metal strip not less than 2mm thick. They are also fixed in place with bolts or rivets.

The chair should now be painted or

THE PICNIC TABLE

A portable picnic table is ideal for family days out. Its folding legs tuck away neatly into the frame, making it easy to get into the back of a car. It can also be used as a spare table at home, for children's rooms or the lounge, if it's well polished. The top surface is slatted to reduce weight.

The top is a straightforward frame, two side members and two crosspieces in 32x16mm hardwood, into which six 48x16mm slats are fitted (fig. 6). The wood should be durable and have an attractive grain, such as African iroko, Brazilian mahogany or Japanese oak. The legs are also 32x16mm section.

Top

All the joints in the top are mortises and tenons. Cut the two side members over-length to prevent the wood from splitting as the mortises are cut. An overhang of 25mm is retained anyway at each end as part of the design, but measure a 50mm excess initially.

Chop out the mortises in the side members and cut matching four-shouldered tenons at both ends of the two crosspieces (fig. 7a). Make sure the joints all fit, and draw-bore them for screws or dowels as for the Director's Chair.

Prepare the six slats, and mark the mortises on the crosspieces (fig. 7c). You can determine your own intervals if you

like, but you must remember to leave room for the leg assemblies to be hinged between the side members and the two outermost slats, with space to tighten the wing-nuts that hold the legs in position. Cut the bare-faced tenons at both ends of each slat with three shoulders, and check that all twelve joints fit easily together (fig. 7b).

Legs

Before cutting the four legs to length, mark in and drill each 4mm hinge hole 16mm from the top, centrally positioned (fig. 8). At the same time, drill corresponding holes through the side members.

The legs are best angled outwards for stability. When each leg has been drilled and sawn to length, the top edge that would otherwise bear against the crosspiece must be rounded off by light planing, to allow it to fold up (fig. 8).

Mark out and cut the halved joints to attach the crossbars to each pair of legs (fig. 9). The bar is set 50mm from the bottom of the legs.

Assemble the table top by gluing the six

slats to the two crosspieces, cramping up the assembly with the side members set on dry to keep everything square. When the glue is set hard, remove the cramps and fit the two side members to the crosspieces, gluing the joints and draw-boring if you wish with 19mm screws. Cut back the projecting ends of the side members to the required 25mm overhang.

Drill small holes for the halved joints of the leg assemblies, and glue and screw them.

When everything is dry, rub down with medium- then fine-grade glasspaper, and treat all the surfaces with a wood dye. Our example is stained dark oak. When this is completely dry, apply teak oil or poly-urethane varnish, depending on your preference. If you choose oil, finish off with a good wax polish.

Slide the leg assemblies inside the table framework and hinge them with galvanised 38x4mm bolts, washers and wing-nuts.

The picnic table is an easy and inexpensive project, and you'll find it is as useful in the home as it is on a daytrip or a camping holiday. Perhaps more so!

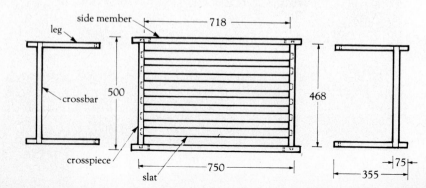

Fig.6 Basic construction

side member

leg

crossbar

crosspiece

slat

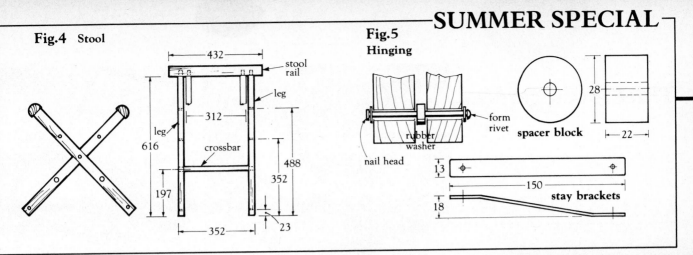

Fig.4 Stool

Fig.5 Hinging

varnished, paint giving a much brighter finish. The material for the seat and backrest is canvas. Plain cloth is preferable to the striped variety; sunblind fabric is eminently suitable, with its wide range of colours. Measure the chair to determine exactly how much fabric you will need, allowing for a 12mm hem to be stitched all around, and tack it with round-headed brass tacks.

Used either as a stool or a proper seat, this garden chair should prove a comfortable and versatile way of relaxing through the summer months.

Cutting list: Director's chair
Finished sizes including tenons where applicable

Legs	4	677mm x	35mm x	22mm
Armrests	2	493	45	22
Backrests	2	533	35	22
Rails	2	390	32	22
Stool legs	4	633	32	16
Stool rails	2	432	35	25
Side bars	6	380	16 dia.	
Short stool stretcher	1	312	16 dia.	
Long stool stretcher	1	352	16 dia.	

● *Bracket and simple 'nail-rivets' ready for cutting and punching*

Cutting list: Picnic table
Finished sizes including tenons

Side members	2	800mm x	32mm x	16mm
Crosspieces	2	492	32	16
Slats	6	734	48	16
Legs	4	355	32	16
Crossbars	2	465	32	16

● *Right, drilling 9mm holes in side members for the leg hinge bolts. Below right, the leg hinge showing rounding-over and wing-nut*

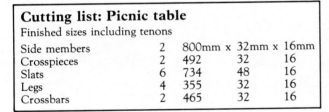

Fig.7

Joint details

a — crosspiece tenons

b — slat tenons

c — crosspiece mortises

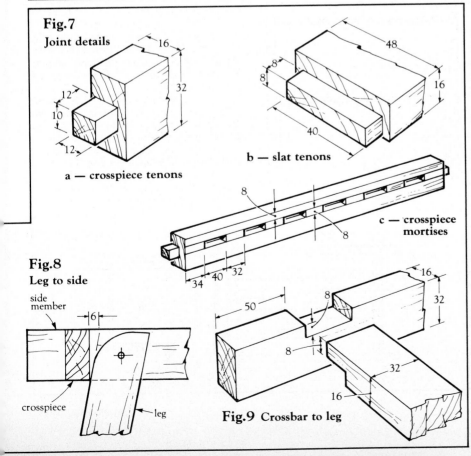

Fig.8

Leg to side

side member

crosspiece

leg

Fig.9 Crossbar to leg

continued

Three for the garden

THE DECKCHAIR

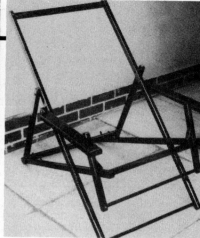

● *The traditional ease of a deckchair, complete with canopy and leg-rest.* **Right**, *the basic frame, finished and ready to cover*

You don't have to go on a world cruise to appreciate the lazy comfort of a deckchair, especially if it has the added advantage of arms, a leg-rest and sunshade canopy for maximum ease. The frame is hardwood, and the bright striped fabric is an acrylic fibre woven into strong seating material.

Select a suitable durable hardwood such as iroko or sapele. Remember that the chair has to fold flat, which will only be possible if you select and machine very carefully, or if you are buying prepared, check your wood carefully before paying for it.

The chair

Concentrate first on the basic chair minus arms and canopy. Check the drawings and cutting list, and see how it is made up of three separate assemblies hinged together into the stable triangular configuration. I have marked all the components with key letters. The narrowest part forms the lower seat support, the middle section is the upper seat support, and the widest part is the securing frame which also serves as the variable height adjuster. All the wood for these parts is 32x22mm section. The three sections are hinged to each other by rivets, and the gap between each is as small as 2mm; hence the need for straight wood!

Start with the lower seat support. Select two lengths of material for the long side members C and cut them to size. Do the same for the rail D, noting the allowance for the 16mm tenons. The second rail P, shaded black in the diagrams, is cut from 16mm dowelling and doesn't require a mortise and tenon.

Taking the two side members, measure and cut the mortises, which are set in 25mm from the end. Measure and mark where the dowelling is to go at the other ends, the centre also 25mm from the ends. Bore the flat-bottomed holes with a 16mm centre bit. Now measure for the tenons at either end of the front rail, and saw them to size. Check all the joints for fit. Measure and cut the dowelling and push it into place. Loosely assembled, this completes the main construction of the lower seat support, though one task remains; measure and drill holes to take the six pegs used to hold the height adjuster bar in its various positions, three to each side member. You can if you wish cut sloped notches in the side members, but I prefer the pegs for structural strength. The holes should be spaced 100mm apart, commencing 100mm from the rear end. Each hole is 9mm diameter, drilled to about 19mm deep.

Set the lower seat assembly aside, and

Fig.10 Folded frames

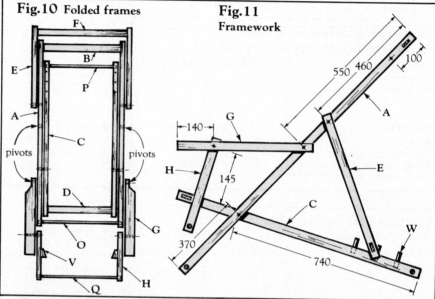

Fig.11 Framework

Fig.12 Canopy struts

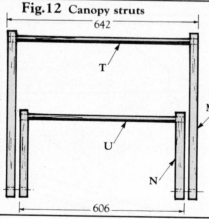

repeat the process for the upper seat support, remembering that this must fit around the lower support to permit folding flat. Take care with measurements, allowing that vital 2mm clearance on either side. Apart from being wider, the upper support has longer side members A, and of course no pegs are required.

The third assembly is the height-adjuster frame, also mortised and tenoned. No dowelling is needed, because the top end hinges to the upper seat support frame.

Next, measure and drill all the 9mm rivet holes in the side members (fig. 11). Note that where the holes emerge on the outer face of the inner member, they are recessed

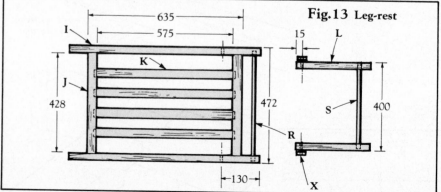

Fig.13 Leg-rest

● *Fix the leg-rest to the main frame with hooks and eyes*

slightly with a 19mm centre bit to permit the tapped part of the rivet to lie flush with the surface.

Using 9mm-diameter 100mm mild steel nails, temporarily assemble the chair to check that it stands well. Then dismantle all the joints and treat the wood with preservative. When it's dry, cut six 50mm pegs from 9mm dowel to form the six height-adjuster stops, bevel the tops slightly by giving them a twist in a pencil sharpener, and glue them into the drilled holes.

Arms

Saw the arms G to length and shape them according to the plan on fig. 10. Two 9mm holes are drilled through the sides of each one in the positions shown. Make the arm-stays — out of 32x22mm material for the uprights and 16mm dowel for the rail Q. Cut two wooden wedges V, and attach them to each upright with glue and screws, getting the position for them to bear on the lower seat frame from the assembled chair. The upright arm-stays H are drilled at the top for riveting to the arms. Once again, attach these temporarily with nails.

Canopy

The canopy framework consists of two U-shaped sections made from 28x16mm material (fig. 12). This time the holes for the dowel can be drilled right through, as they will be covered by fabric later. One part of the framework fits inside the other, and the whole completed frame attaches to the top of the chair with 70x6mm bolts, plain washers, rubber washers and wing-nuts to tighten up.

Leg-rest

Finally, the leg-rest is a straightforward frame built from 32x22mm material with mortise and tenon joints, allowing an overhang of 63mm at both ends of each side member (fig. 13). Into this frame fit four slats K, cut from 32x16mm material and slotted home with 6mm-deep mortise and tenon joints. A dowel rail R is added at one end for decoration, and a folding leg arrangement constructed along similar lines to the arm-stays, fitted in place with bolts and wing-nuts. Wooden spacer blocks lend an attractive finishing touch. The leg-rest

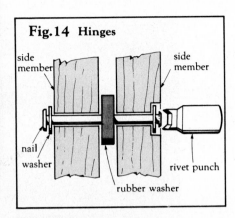

Fig.14 Hinges

side member
side member
nail
washer
rivet punch
rubber washer

can be attached simply to the chair with hooks and screw-eyes.

All the components now have their edges lightly planed to round them off. Use a chisel to pare a bevelled finish to the front end of the arms and a curve at the extremities of all the side members, finishing off the job with sandpaper.

Assemble the joints with glue and screws, using a strong waterproof wood glue and 25mm brass screws.

Hinging

All the chair's hinges are formed with rivets, made from mild steel nails. Place each nail in position, using plain washers and a hard rubber washer to act as spacers, then mark the appropriate rivet length and hacksaw off the end. Tap the sawn end with

a hammer and rivet punch to squash out the end of the nail within the drilled recess, taking care not to damage the adjacent wood (fig. 14).

Brush on a dark stain, and when this is completely dry, finish with an application of teak oil and polish for the best result. You can use any finish you like in fact, as long as it will have 'weatherability'. See the feature 'Wood in the weather' for details.

The fabric for the seat, canopy and headrest is an acrylic fibre made in a variety of bright colours and stripes, often for exterior sunblinds. Cut the material to 1370x470mm, stitch a 12mm hem all round and tack into place. As it's being fitted, make sure the chair folds completely flat without straining the material.

The canopy is harder to make, as the side pelmet panels are stitched on separately and then tucked in at the corners and sewn up. Your household may require a division of labour here — the woodworker might not be the best seamster, but don't fight over it! The completed canopy is tacked on to the frame at each of the four corners.

The headrest is simply a small rectangular bag containing a foam pad, with loops for attaching it to the chair. The bag is turned inside-out after stitching, to keep hems out of sight for a neater finish.

The result is a comfortable and traditional chair suitable for the garden or conservatory from where you can relax, put your feet up — and dream about that world cruise you always meant to go on! ■

Cutting list: Deckchair

Finished sizes including tenons

A	Upper seat side members	2	1220mm x	32mm x	22mm
B	Upper seat rail	1	565	32	22
C	Lower seat side members	2	1040	32	22
D	Lower seat rail	1	515	32	22
E	Height-adjuster side members	2	560	32	22
F	Height-adjuster rail	1	610	32	22
G	Arms	2	508	57	22
H	Arm-stays	2	330	32	22
I	Leg-rest side members	2	760	32	22
J	Leg-rest rails	2	464	32	22
K	Leg-rest slats	4	587	32	22
L	Leg-rest legs	2	305	32	22
M	Long canopy struts	2	534	28	16
N	Short canopy struts	2	330	28	16
O	Upper seat dowel rail	1	565	16 dia.	
P	Lower seat dowel rail	1	515	16 dia.	
Q	Arm-stay dowel rail	1	565	16 dia.	
R	Leg-rest dowel rail	1	464	16 dia.	
S	Leg-rest leg rail	1	394	16 dia.	
T	Long canopy rail	1	642	16 dia.	
U	Short canopy rail	1	606	16 dia.	
V	Arm-stay wedges	2	50	32	22
W	Height-adjuster pegs	6	50	9 dia.	
X	Spacer blocks	2		32 dia.	9

● The 'Director's' Garden Chair and the Picnic Table appear in *The Practical Woodwork Book* by Anthony Hontoir, published by John Murray Ltd, 50 Albemarle St, London W1X 4BD. We are grateful for permission to use the plans.

Power of the press

Solid and simple in concept, Chris Coupe's flower press design has a couple of challenging features to get right before you flatten the flourishing flora

● *This sturdy press can flatten a surprising number of flowers at one go if you layer them between sheets of plywood and blotting paper*

If, like me, you live in an area where there is an abundance of wild flowers, you may be interested in making this simple-but-strong flower press — for your own enjoyment, or perhaps to give the kids an unfair advantage in Nature Study!

All the information you need is in the drawings; construction is really quite straightforward. Make the platens first, from pieces of 16mm chipboard laminated together, with ply inserts set into routed grooves for strength.

Cut a recess in the centre of the top, or moving platen — it is 4mm smaller in width than the base platen, note — for a piece of 3mm mild steel plate which will take the bottom of the threaded rod and washers which provide the rise-and-fall. The detail on the drawing shows how they fit together.

Then assemble the cross-beam and the nut-retaining piece, which is counterbored to take an M16 nut, glued in with epoxy. I cut the recess with a router. Once the nut is well fixed in its recess, glue the support piece to what will be the underside of the beam. Use your piece of M16 studding, threaded through a 16mm hole in the centre of the cross-beam and the nut-support piece, to make sure the holes line up accurately when you are gluing. It is best to leave them oversize until you have fixed the two pieces together.

The cross-bar is set into full-size mortises in the tops of the sides, and the base platen is fixed to the bottom inner edges of the sides with a 6x12mm ply tongue, plus glue and screws.

I used iroko for the cross-bar, nut-retaining piece, handwheel and sides, but any dense and stable hardwood would do. Turn the round components to the sizes indicated, and screw the handle to the wheel through an oversize full-depth hole. The washer and split-pin arrangement at the bottom of the studding is straightforward once you have turned the studding down at the end, but where the studding goes into the handwheel at the top you need to make sure you won't suffer from 'drift'. I got round this by cutting a recess for the M16 nut in the centre of the wheel, screwing the nut on to the studding, then 'lockwiring' them together by drilling a 3mm hole through both and pushing a piece of wire through. Then I glued the nut and studding into the recess with epoxy. 'Loctite' adhesive alone without the wire may be enough, but if you want to make doubly

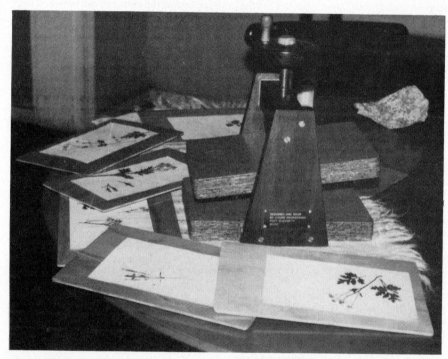

sure I think the lockwire is a good belt-and-braces solution.

I finished all the surfaces with linseed oil, except for the pressing surfaces of the platens, which I varnished to prevent sticking. You can press quite a quantity of flowers at one time by sandwiching them between sheets of 3mm ply and blotting paper; go in the order: ply, blotting paper, flowers, blotting paper, ply, blotting paper, flowers, blotting paper, ply and so on. Depending on how many flowers you use, you can get a drying time as short as three days.

Now all that remains is for you to be out and about in the summer hedgerows . . .■

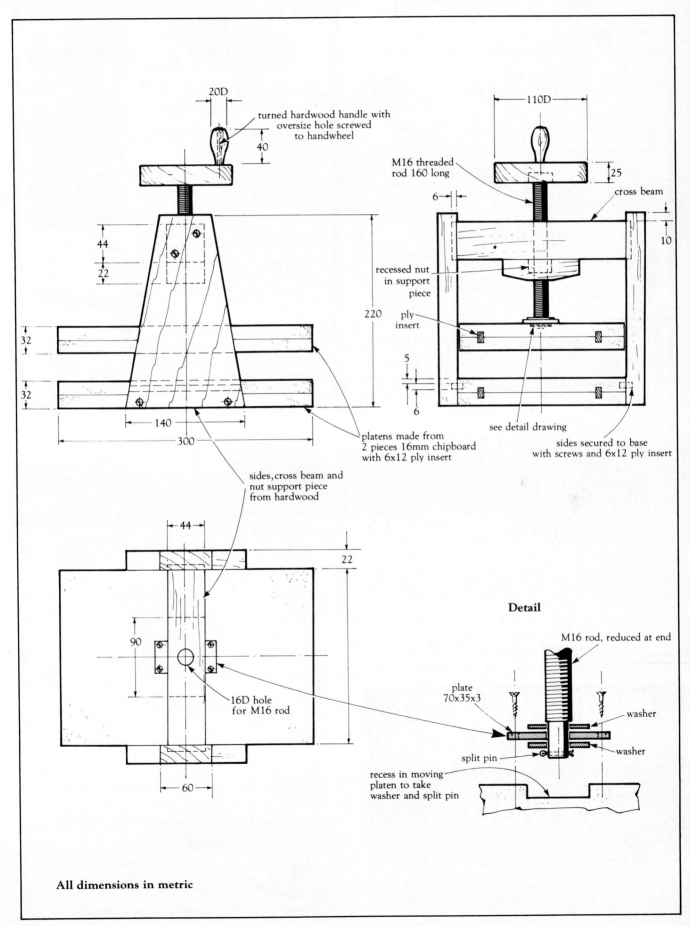

20D

turned hardwood handle with
oversize hole screwed
to handwheel

40

110D

M16 threaded
rod 160 long

25

cross beam

6

44

22

recessed nut
in support
piece

10

ply
insert

220

32

5

32

6

140

see detail drawing

300

platens made from
2 pieces 16mm chipboard
with 6x12 ply insert

sides secured to base
with screws and 6x12 ply insert

sides, cross beam and
nut support piece
from hardwood

44

22

Detail

90

M16 rod, reduced at end

plate
70x35x3

washer

16D hole
for M16 rod

60

split pin

washer

recess in moving
platen to take
washer and split pin

All dimensions in metric

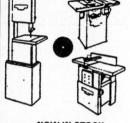

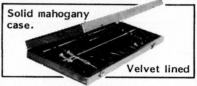

Wood in the weather

Tough to think about winter, but now's the time you should be busy on your exterior woodwork, making sure it will survive the next onslaught. We look in detail at timber preservatives and microporous finishes

Wood is a dynamic material, a living one — which is maybe why we like it so much. Most of us prefer it in a natural finish in fine furniture and interior fittings, and it's also fair to assume that WOODWORKER readers generally will go for natural timber outside as well — garden furniture, sheds, summerhouses, pergolas, fences. There's nothing like the warmth of natural wood.

There are obvious disadvantages, of course, to this wonderful living material. It's good food for all manner of bugs and fungi — fine in the forest where nature demands that old material must decay and break down to make room for new growth, but distinctly undesirable where we have taken over and made our own wooden artefacts, which naturally enough we want to keep. Mould, decay and wood-eaters don't just spoil the looks of timber — they spoil its structure.

So if you don't want to put your foot through the summerhouse floor next summer, this summer's the time to do something about it — use a preservative.

Wood preservatives

These fall into three categories, depending on their base:

- **Tar oil based** — mainly the familiar creosote. Notoriously poisonous to plants and animals, especially when wet, tar-oil based preservers are widespread because of product familiarity. Newer treatments are gaining ground.

- **Water-borne preservers** such as Cuprinol's Garden Timber Care, say the manufacturers, provide the modern alternative to creosote. 'Kind to plants and animals' — we've all seen the advertising campaigns. Very little smell, easy to apply, easy to wash clothes and brushes, greater coverage than creosote, and won't harm plants, even in direct contact. But water-based preservers aren't designed to work on wood in ground contact, and many of them

● *Top, a stained wood siding on an American house – timber as an attractive cladding.* **Middle**, *solvent-based Exterior Wood Preserver on garden gates and pergolas;* **bottom**, *Cuprinol green in the attic. Photos from* The Enemies of Timber *by E. Austin Hilditch, published by Cuprinol*

continued

Wood in the weather

carry more pigment, which means there is a thicker colour in the finish. Fence panels above the ground are suggested as surfaces you can treat with these.

● **Organic solvent based** — the kind ready-made joinery manufacturers use; solutions of fungicides and insecticides in a petroleum distillate solvent similar to white spirit, organic-solvent preservatives dry relatively quickly, don't raise the grain as do the water-based ones and some of them can be painted over — or varnished or polished, for that matter. The organic solvent base means they penetrate far better than the other types — around 10 times deeper than water-based, say Cuprinol — and they're good for timber in ground contact. They can be compatible with mastics and glues and non-corrosive to metal fittings; all of which make them popular with the industry. Cuprinol's 'Exterior Wood Preserver' is a solvent-based product.

Application

All three types can be applied by immersion, brush or spray. Industrial methods for solvent-based products include total immersion and double vacuum/pressure cycles, using sophisticated equipment; not much use for us, unless we want to be sure the made-up joinery we're buying is treated to a certain specification. The double vacuum process is now included in British Standard BS5589, 'Code of Practice for Preservation of Timber'.

Preservers — coverage and application

Green, clear, dark/light oak: for these Cuprinol products, dip small timbers like roof trusses, joinery, floorboards or horticultural structural components for three minutes, or brush or spray three uniform coats. Minimum level of treatment is 1 litre per 8sq m for two coats. For outdoor or larger timbers not in ground contact, dip for 10 minutes or brush/spray three coats; you'll need 1 litre per 4sq m for three coats. For small timbers in ground contact, soak for at least an hour, reckoning on 40 litres per cu m; for large timbers in ground contact, soak for at least 24 hours, using the same level of 40 litres per cu m.

Exterior wood preserver: for outdoor timber not in ground contact, say Cuprinol, dip for 10 minutes or brush/spray two or three coats, reckoning to use 1 litre per 4-8sq m for two coats. For small timber in ground contact, soak at least an hour and use 40 litres per cu m; for large timber in ground contact, soak for at least 24 hours, using the same treatment level.

Red cedar: Cuprinol suggest you brush two uniform coats on planed timber, allowing 1 litre per 6sq m for two coats; for rough timber, use one heavy brush coat and reckon on 1 litre for 3sq m.

Garden timber care: Brush one or two uniform coats on light timbers not in ground contact, such as fence panels, allowing 1 litre for up to 12sq m per coat.

● *Microporous woodstain goes well on house timbers; sheen or matt according to preference and function*

Microporous finishes

It's a finish buzzword of the 80s, microporous; 'let the wood breathe'. Most major paint and finish manufacturers now have their ranges of microporous paints and stains. They really do offer advantages for exterior applications, in that unlike a traditional gloss paint which seals the wood completely — moisture in as well as out — they allow moisture in the wood to escape as vapour. They are impervious, though, to water in droplet form. Apart from Berger Cuprinol's Gloss Wood Paint, most microporous paints and stains can be applied to bare wood without a primer, and re-treatment usually only means you have to clean it off and rub it down a little. Low maintenance, high performance.

The most important factors in how an exterior finish behaves are: adhesion, flexibility, vapour permeability, water repellency, resistance to ultra-violet light, mould and algae resistance, and overall durability. Exterior finishes need to respond to wood's natural movement, so there needs to be a good balance between adhesion and flexibility. The ideal as far as water resistance is concerned is to minimise absorption but allow it to escape where it enters via open joints, cracks, bad glazing and so on. UV resistance is a product of the amount of pigment in the finish — colour, in other words — while resins which carry the pigments solidify and bind them to the surface. The more pigment, the more opaque the colour; the more resin, the higher the 'build', or greater film thickness.

'Varnishes', a catch-all term used these days for clear finishes of almost any sort, have lower durability than paints and stains, because they have no pigments; unless you are able to maintain an exterior varnish regularly, it's wise to consider one of the new microporous stains, which carry the sunlight-resistant pigments as well as resins. Local authorities and builders have certainly discovered the advantages of

microporous woodstains, and much of the newly-built and refurbished housing stock is being treated with these products now. The cost benefits are attractive on that sort of scale — preparation and maintenance are both minimised.

Berger Cuprinol microporous wood paints and stains are both 'solvent-borne' and water-borne; the solvent-borne varieties are based on modern elastic alkyd resins, while the water-borne finishes use new acrylic co-polymer technology for water resistance and adhesion in wet conditions. They are formulated more for flexibility, while the solvent-borne products aim to provide an optimum balance of all the key properties — coming down on durability as an overall priority. Thus the higher-build (more resins) paints move less but are harder, and so more suitable for joinery, where good dimensional stability is expected anyway. Berger Cuprinol Wood Paint Matt is a medium-build finish, good for timbers where stability is neither so important or so likely; cladding, soffits, fascias and fencing. This is a self-priming water-borne finish. Their Wood Paints Gloss and Sheen are higher build, more for joinery; the gloss is water-

● *'Timber Care', water-based for timber not in ground contact*

borne and used with a special primer, the sheen is self-priming and solvent-borne.

Likewise the stains come in both medium and high-build formulations. The higher-build products ('Sheen', in Cuprinol's case) are good for structures where dimensional stability is critical; joinery again. Berger Cuprinol's Wood Stain Natural has a lower resin content, and is thus classed as medium-build; useful for an exterior finish on timbers without critical dimensional stability considerations, such as cladding, soffits, fascias and fencing — and, depending on how complicated it was to make, that garden seat!

Finally, even though microporous finishes may be said to provide the answer to exterior woodwork problems, there is always the fact that any finish is only as good as the preparation. Don't skimp the sanding and cleaning down; don't apply any finish when the wood's wet, or when the weather is cold and wet. Also bear in mind that some timbers weather better than others; however good a clear finish is, if it's on mahogany sooner or later that colour is going to fade. ■

● Our thanks to Cuprinol for their help in preparing this article. For further information please write to them at Adderwell, Frome, Somerset BA11 1NL, (0373) 65151.

DRY YOUR OWN TIMBER.
WATCH YOUR WOOD COSTS FALL.

If it goes against the grain to keep on paying through the nose for dried wood, why not do something about it? An Ebac wood dryer costs less than you think and will boost your quality and your profitability overnight.

CUT COSTS – INCREASE PROFITS

Even after allowing for modest running costs you can cut your timber costs by usually a half or more by buying green wood and drying it yourself. Within just a few months you could recover your outlay and start making big savings that go straight into your pocket.

BROADEN YOUR BUYING OPTIONS

Owning your own Ebac wood dryer gives you total independence. You can buy wood wherever and whenever the price is right – even in less expensive log form. Your Ebac dryer will even dry mixed loads of different species and thicknesses simultaneously.

IMPROVE QUALITY – ENHANCE YOUR REPUTATION

With an Ebac dryer you have total control over the moisture content of the wood you use. No need to rely on a supplier – and no more risk of bowed table tops, loose joints or badly fitting doors.
What's more, by improving quality, you

improve your customer relations. The word will spread and your reputation will grow stronger.

EASY TO OPERATE

Even if you have no previous experience of wood drying, you can't go wrong with an Ebac dryer. Operation is virtually automatic and controls have been designed for simplicity.

WHY STOP AT DRYING YOUR OWN WOOD?

Instead of suffering from the high cost of dried wood you can actually turn it to your own advantage. Use your Ebac dryer to dry timber for resale and you can charge the premium price you once had to pay yourself! How's that for a simple, effective way to generate extra turnover?

For more information on Ebac wood dryers, and details of our no-obligation feasibility study offer, please complete the coupon below and post it (no stamp required) to **Ebac "Freepost," St Helen Trading Est., Bishop Auckland, Co. Durham, DL14 9BS.**

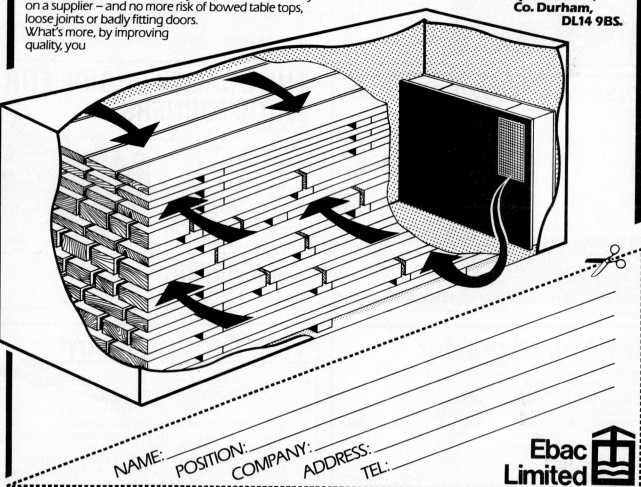

NAME: _____ POSITION: _____ COMPANY: _____ ADDRESS: _____ TEL: _____

Ebac Limited

Ebac, Number One For Drying.

THIS REPRINT FROM DAYS OF
OLD SHOWS A CLASSIC PIECE
OF GARDEN FURNITURE WHICH
WILL REMAIN TIMELESS

SUMMER
SPECIAL

Vol. 56   No. 701

WOODWORKER

APRIL, 1952

STURDY GARDEN SEAT
USEFUL AND ORNAMENTAL GARDEN FEATURE

This design will appeal to those who want a dignified seat which is both comfortable and durable. It is carried out in English oak left in the white, and has a protective coat of clear preservative which will be repeated occasionally. It is obvious from the photograph that stout timbers have been used, this being essentially part of its character. This makes it somewhat expensive, however, and readers are advised to ascertain the cost from the timber suppliers before beginning. Apart from the thickness, the shaped parts cut into a great deal of wood, which again raises the cost. An alternative readers may like to consider is that of cutting down certain of the thicknesses, as this would reduce the cost appreciably

WHEN making an item of this kind which has several shaped parts and members set at an angle, it is always advisable to draw out the end elevation in full size. In the long run it is a saving in there is an advantage in this since the squared edge of the wood forms the portion opposite the seat rails, and is bound to be accurate. Plane the surface of the wood, make one edge square, and thickness it.

FIG. I. ATTRAC-
TIVE SEAT WHICH
SHOULD LAST
FOR YEARS. MADE
IN OAK THROUGH-
OUT. ALL JOINTS
ARE PEGGED

A seat of this kind
could be used equally
well in a small garden
or in a public position.
Length 4 ft. 3 in.

time since it enables exact shoulder sizes and angles to be obtained, and allows shapes to be drawn in exactly. A front elevation is not needed because all shoulders of back and front rails are square, and are easily calculated.

Legs.—Taking first the back legs, two pieces of oak, 6¾ in. by 3 in. in section, are needed. If wide stuff is available, and one has access to a bandsaw, it is possible to economise by plotting one shape within the other, but otherwise two separate pieces are needed. In some ways

The shape is best marked by cutting a template in card or thin hardboard. The shape can be plotted from Fig. 2 in which the squares represent 1 in. each. Use this on both sides of the wood, taking care to hold it level with the same side. This marking from both sides is always an advantage when working thick stuff, and saves time in the long run, especially when the wasting-away method of working has to be followed. In this, cuts are made with the saw across the grain of the waste

APRIL, 1952

WELL-MADE JOINTS ARE ESSENTIAL IN A SEAT OF THIS KIND

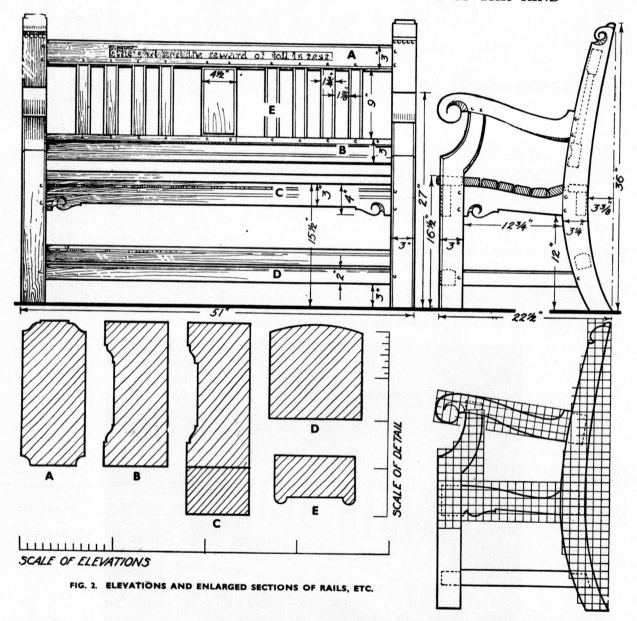

FIG. 2. ELEVATIONS AND ENLARGED SECTIONS OF RAILS, ETC.

portions, and the latter part chopped away with chisel and mallet. It is finished with spokeshave and plane, followed by scraper. Those who have no access to a machine bandsaw will find this a simpler method of working than attempting to cut with the betty saw or large bow saw. If the latter is used the slightest degree out of square, the wood may be badly undercut.

The front legs are marked out similarly, but, although the shaped part may have to be wasted away, the straight portion should be sawn, as it leaves as waste a quite useful piece of timber.

Mortising.—Positions of the mortises can be taken from Fig. 2. In most cases they are ¾ in. wide, and a heavy chisel is desirable. Most of the waste can be bored away, a ½ in. bit being used. If an electric drill is available this will save much hard work, though it may

be necessary to use a ⅜ in. bit, as ½ in. may offer too much resistance in hardwood. Whatever the method used, put a depth gauge on the bit to prevent its going in too far. At seat level, and in the case of the front stretcher, mortises can meet in the thickness of the wood.

Have the wood over a solid part of the bench when chopping, and cut as true as possible because the strength of the job depends upon the mechanical fit of the joints rather than upon any adhesive used. Take special care with the mortise ends, holding the chisel upright so that the ends really are true.

In the case of the mortises in the back legs to hold the back rails, these follow the general curve. The only upright rail is that at seat level. Those to hold the side rails are cut so that the direction of the tenon is followed. For instance, the stretcher is horizontal (Fig. 2), and,

WHERE POSSIBLE CUT JOINTS BEFORE WORKING THE SHAPES

assuming the mortising to be done on the bench, the chisel is held upright. Put a square on the bench alongside as a guide. The seat rail mortise also is square, whilst that for the arms inclines somewhat. Either a saddle is needed when chopping the seat rail mortises, or the wood will have to be held in the vice with a waste piece beneath to prevent the screw from bruising the underside.

Side Rails.—The two ends are put together independently as complete units. The preparation of the rails is therefore the next job. The seat rails are shaped to take the seat slats, and require stuff 4 in. wide. Having squared up the wood, mark out the shape of the top and bottom edges (see squared portion in Fig. 2). The tenon positions are obvious from the full-size drawing already prepared. At the front the tenon occupies the entire rail width, but is necessarily reduced at the back owing to the shaping. The dotted lines in Fig. 2 make this clear. The shoulders should be set out before the shaping is cut as this enables the lines to be put in with the square.

In the case of the stretcher rails, the tenon is straight although it enters the leg at an angle. This means that the shoulder has to be at an angle. Here both the angle and the shoulder length can be obtained from the full-size drawing. Note that the leg should be planed flat where the stretcher joins it so that the shoulder beds down properly. The ends of all tenons of rails which are on a level with other rails should be cut at an angle to form a sort of mitre so that they have maximum length.

Arms.—The arms should be marked out on both sides with a card template similarly to the legs (see squared lines in Fig. 2). Arrange a flat portion on the underside where the front legs meet them. Chop the mortise for this and cut the back tenon before working the shapes. Most of the last-named should be completed before assembling, but the carved scrolls can be left until afterwards; also the various chamfers. Parts which cannot be reached later must be cleaned up first, but joints which finish flush must be levelled after assembling.

All joints are draw-bored, and this necessitates boring all dowel holes through the mortises, and making a trial assembly so that the positions of the holes in the tenons can be marked with the point of the bit. The tenon holes are then bored about $\frac{1}{16}$ in. nearer the shoulders. Make sure that the parts go together free from winding before finally assembling. For an outdoor job of this kind ordinary Scotch glue is of no use. Thick paint is frequently used, but care must be taken not to leave it on surfaces which are exposed. Even though it may be wiped off, it is liable to be left in the grain where it will look unsightly. Synthetic resin glue is most satisfactory in every way, but is considerably more expensive.

Back and Front Rails.—These are all straightforward. The tops of the tenons are set in slightly, and all are draw-bored. After jointing, the various mouldings

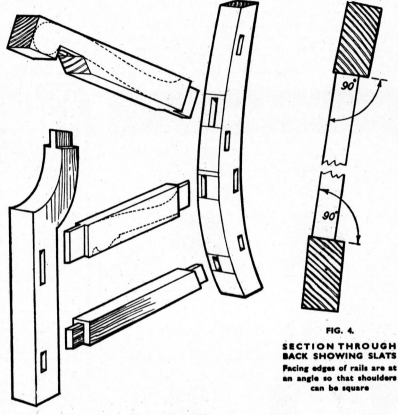

FIG. 3. DETAILS OF END JOINTS

FIG. 4.

SECTION THROUGH BACK SHOWING SLATS

Facing edges of rails are at an angle so that shoulders can be square

are worked. It is advisable to do the latter before sawing the shoulders as it enables the ends to be finished cleanly. In the case of the channelling the main groove should be formed first, and the mouldings scratched afterwards. As the groove is fairly wide it is as well to use a cutter of just over half the width and run it through twice with the fence reset. In the case of the front seat rail, it is a good plan to complete the whole moulding before working the bottom shape, as this enables the scratch stock to be used from both edges. The advantage of this is that the cutter is set to work the moulding on the far side. Then, should there be any tendency to drift from the edge, no harm is done since the cutter pulls away from the moulding. The other moulding is worked with the fence bearing against the opposite edge.

Back Slats.—These are all stub-tenoned in, and a little thought shows that there is a slight complication in that the two horizontal rails are not in the same plane, since each follows the curve of the back uprights. There is no difficulty, however. All that happens is that the facing edges of the horizontal rails are planed at a slight angle so that they are parallel with each other, as shown in Fig. 4. The tenons are cut straight in line with the slats, but the mortises are set at an angle—they are, in fact, square with the angle at which the edges are planed. As a guide when chopping, a piece of card or ply can be cut to the required angle and placed on the bench beside the wood. The chisel can then be kept parallel with it.

The carving in the top rail adds considerably to the

interest and appearance but is not essential. If it is to be included it should be completed before the whole is assembled. The quotation is from *James Beattie*, and reads: " The end and the reward of toil is rest." Few tools are needed. The background is recessed, and the surface of the letters is slightly hollowed. It is advisable to use a small router to ensure that the background is recessed to the same depth throughout.

When assembling, put the slats into their rails first. The whole can then be regarded as a single unit. When all is together add a centre rail running from back to front. Its top edge follows the shape of the side rails, and it is slot-dovetailed in position. All the seat rails are fixed with brass screws, and it adds to the appearance if these are fitted with cups. All sharp edges are planed off, and the ends are slightly rounded.

It is advisable to give the whole thing a coat of preservative such as clear *Cuprinol*, paying special attention to end grain, joints, etc. If for use on the grass it should stand on bricks or concrete footings, as in Fig. 1.

CUTTING LIST

	Long ft.	Long in.	Wide in.	Thick in.
2 Back Legs	3	$\frac{1}{2}$	$6\frac{3}{4}$	3
2 Front Legs	2	2	6	3
3 Back Rails (A), (B) and Seat	4	1	$3\frac{1}{4}$	$1\frac{3}{8}$
1 Front Rail (C)	4	1	$4\frac{1}{4}$	$1\frac{3}{8}$
2 Stretchers (D)	4	1	$2\frac{1}{4}$	2
2 Arms	1	$7\frac{1}{2}$	$4\frac{1}{4}$	3
2 Side Rails	1	6	$4\frac{1}{4}$	$1\frac{3}{8}$
2 Stretchers	1	$7\frac{1}{2}$	$2\frac{1}{4}$	2
1 Middle Rail	1	6	$3\frac{1}{4}$	$1\frac{3}{8}$
1 Panel		11	$4\frac{5}{8}$	1
8 Slats		11	2	1
1 Seat Slat	3	10	4	1
6 ,, ,,	4	$4\frac{1}{2}$	$2\frac{1}{4}$	1
1 ,, ,,	3	10	$2\frac{3}{4}$	1

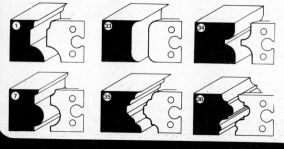

Happy returns

● The flight not of the humble bee, but of the boomerang – WOODWORKER style

No-one to frisbee with in the still summer evenings? Or perhaps you fancy knocking off the odd kangaroo. Rik Middleton has been developing the art of making and flying boomerangs, and presents his findings

The boomerang is probably one of the world's oldest wooden toys. But it originated as a weapon of war and hunting — not a plaything. The killing boomerang is too heavy to return, and who would want it to? I like to think the return-boomerang came into being by accident when a father made a harmless lightweight model of his favourite weapon for his son to play with; but I wonder whether the son ever got to play with it after its unusual homing behaviour had been discovered.

Australian aboriginal men have used return-boomerangs as toys and in flying competitions since the early ages. These boomerangs can bring down a few flocking birds, but they bounce off kangaroos.

The hunting boomerang of the Australian aborigine (and incidentally the Ancient Egyptian) was a stick sharpened at the leading edge of its flat blade, with shaped extremities and a distinct bend in the middle. This bend meant it could be thrown, spinning without falling about its long axis. The axis of spin was at right angles to the blades and when the weapon was thrown forward, spinning in a horizontal plane, curvature and twists in the structure gave it lift to counteract its weight; so it could fly at a fairly constant height for a considerable distance.

Australian aboriginals are said to have decapitated kangaroos at a range of around 100yds — if you imagine 5lb of well-sharpened hardwood doing 60mph and 200rpm you can see how. In the genuine aboriginal boomerang the bend is the

● A 8oz 'war' boomerang with an easy 125yd range. Can you throw half-a-pound of ply 125 yards?

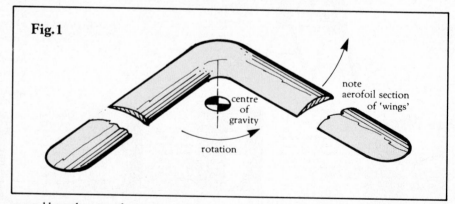

Fig. 1

centre of gravity

note aerofoil section of 'wings'

rotation

natural branch point of a tree. I've never got round to trying this, I just use plywood.

Standard exterior grade plywood isn't strong enough to take the knocks. Birch ply is suitable — seven-layered ⅜in is about right — but best of all is the type with dark red-brown glue layers. The stuff with colourless glue isn't as strong or convenient during construction.

A boomerang is basically a propeller with two or more blades, which are aerofoil sections with a small positive uptilt or 'angle of attack'. When it's thrown forward with spin, both aerofoils meet the air front-edge first. The traditional boomerang (fig. 1) is therefore a low-attack-angle propeller, with one blade missing, but this doesn't affect flight or return; a large model-aircraft propeller with three blades will return if it's thrown correctly.

The return effect is caused by the gyroscopic properties imparted by the spin. Forward motion, along with the spin, means that one wing (the one going forward at any given moment) has a higher airspeed than the one going backwards. This makes the entire gyroscopically-spinning projectile move in a strangely distorted manner known as 'precession'.

Precession will take place if you take a bike wheel in two hands, by the ends of its spindle, and spin it hard. Now try to push it into a horizontal position so your right hand is above your left. It'll move all right, but definitely not where you're telling it to. A very weird experience when you try it for the first time.

Enough of the physics; quite simply, when a boomerang is thrown correctly it flies a gradually decreasing spiral path. The trick is to adjust the throw so the end of the first spiral occurs at ground level and the boomerang falls at your feet or, when you're more ambitious, at a catchable height.

Making a boomerang

I cut my boomerangs out of ⅜in ply with a jigsaw. The blades have to be shaped to low-angle aerofoils like aircraft wings. Draw a large seven-layer sandwich in the proportions of your wing (2in wide is recommended). Draw your own idea of an aerofoil section on it and project the points where your section meets the glue lines in the plywood up to the surface. Connect these all to a single point above the section and find the level where this makes the whole section 2in wide. Measure off where the glue lines should come and you have drawn a contour map of your aerofoil (fig. 2).

I use a Cintride coarse disc to remove material down to the approximate shape. This rips stuff off very brutally and you might find that a rasp or Surform, or even a spokeshave, allows more control and time for your first considered actions. The convex surface of a Cintride is ideal for the slightly concave aerofoil underside. You can easily judge the shape you're creating with the recommended plywood type, as the glue lines stand out clearly like countours on a map.

The shape you cut out can vary enormously. But from past good (and bad) results I've learnt that the wings should be about 2in wide and 9-12in long. The optimal internal angle at 12in long is about 120° or just under; this comes down to roughly 90° at 9in long. Too large an internal angle gives the boomerang a rapid rate of sink, and it inevitably hits the ground before completing one spiral path. My best traditional-style boomerang has 12in blades with an internal angle of 115°, weighs 4½oz (125g) and is 7mm thick at the thickest point. This returns easily in still air, but heavier models and those with shorter

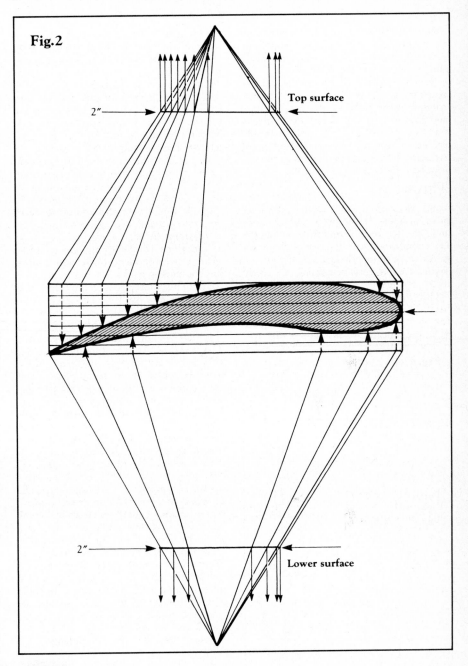

Fig.2

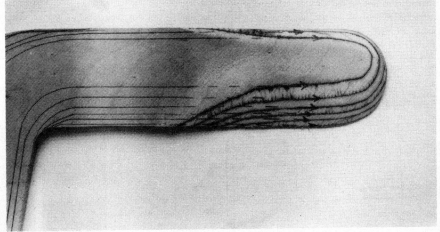

● *Cutting the profile; check it corresponds to the drawn contours*

continued

wings will only return wind-assisted or with more throwing power. Three- and four-armed boomerangs return even more easily and are recommended for children.

When you've shaped and sanded the boomerang to a smooth and regular contour, treat it against water penetration and abrasion — I have used polyurethane, but two-part plastic coating is better. My earliest models had a smeared-on coating of Araldite, thickest on the exposed points — it must have been cheaper then.

Throwing it

You really need 100yds clear in all directions for safety. Never throw in a high wind; and I strongly recommend that you wait for flat calm conditions at least until you've gained a few hours 'flying time'. If there is a slight breeze it must be coming in directly from your left.

Grip the boomerang firmly in your right hand. You need to throw it hard and spin it fast with a wrist movement. It should pass your head nearly vertical for a first try.

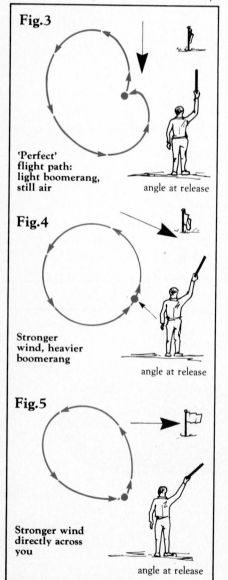

Fig.3

'Perfect' flight path: light boomerang, still air

angle at release

Fig.4

Stronger wind, heavier boomerang

angle at release

Fig.5

Stronger wind directly across you

angle at release

Throw it at an imaginary point 20yds in front of you, head-height. It will bank away left. If it climbs and accelerates towards you from a great height, you didn't have it near enough to vertical. If it banks left but drifts down to hit the ground away to your left, you should lay it over further from the vertical as you throw, and/or throw it harder. If it keeps hitting the ground to your left, the internal angle is too large.

A word for the left-handed among you. Left-handed boomerangs are mirror images of right-handed ones so you probably won't be able to throw those illustrated. Go through this article and transpose every 'left' into a 'right', and vice-versa, and view all diagrams through a mirror.

Variations of flight-path are possible. What I call a 'perfect' flight-path is when the boomerang banks left and maintains a constant height as it goes round behind you and comes in at you from about 45° front-right. This usually only works with a light but long-wing boomerang in still air (fig. 3).

If there is some wind, this flight-path gets distorted downwind and you'll have a long walk if you try to get a full throw. Wind from the left needs an 'incomplete' flight-path so the wind foreshortens the first half of the spiral path and carries it back to you. You'll need lighter throws, further off the vertical for light long-wing types. Shorter and heavier boomerangs are easier to control in this situation (figs 4 and 5).

Remember that although the boomerang only weighs 4oz or so, the advancing wing-tip of a boomerang can have a ground speed in excess of 100mph. I don't recommend trying to catch it until you have had many hours of flying time, and even then wear a glove. Remember also your responsibility to local property and the spectators you're likely to attract. If a crowd of children gathers around your heels, the only safe thing is to pack up and go home. In some parks you may fall foul of model aircraft bye-laws; please check. WOODWORKER and I can accept no responsibility for damage caused by your boomerangs!

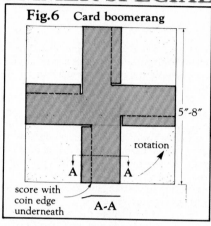

Fig.6 Card boomerang

5"-8"

rotation

A   A

score with coin edge underneath

A-A

The indoor model

This is made from card; the sort used for exercise book covers is ideal. Paper plates are a good alternative. Cut a square as shown (fig. 6) and then mark and cut the cruciform shape. This model relies for lift on ailerons (hinged flaps), scored with a coin edge and turned down.

Throw from thumb and forefinger, giving lots of spin from the vertical plane.

Experimental models

Distribution of weight can markedly influence the flight-path of a boomerang. You can re-distribute weight by drilling a series of $\frac{3}{8}$ or $\frac{1}{2}$in holes through the wing. This makes the boomerang a bit less robust, but you could make the wings a little thicker in the first place. Weight the holes with fishing lead weights and seal up the top and bottom smoothly with wide sticky-tape. Try moving the weights from the centre to the two wing ends, and watch the flight-path change.

I've failed to come up with a design for a joint at the junction of the wings which would allow the internal wing-angle to be changed from one throw to the next — and withstand the considerable torque stress of the throwing movement. On safety grounds, I've rejected anything that uses wing-nuts. A challenge for WOODWORKER joint specialists? ∎

● *A three-arm model. The ends were left uncut then shaved off for wingtip weight adjustments*

Lathe stand

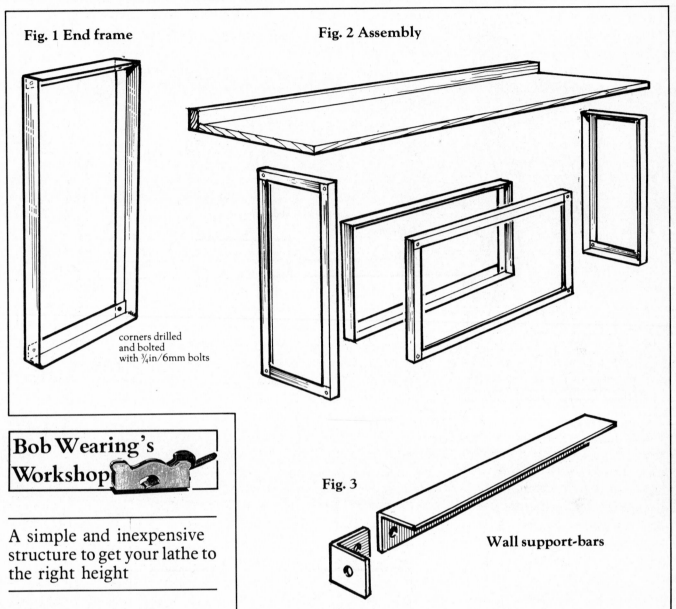

Fig. 1 End frame

corners drilled
and bolted
with ¾in/6mm bolts

Fig. 2 Assembly

Fig. 3

Wall support-bars

Bob Wearing's Workshop

A simple and inexpensive structure to get your lathe to the right height

Most woodturning lathes seem now to be sold without a stand. Stands supplied by the makers are often overpriced and in one case were obviously designed for dwarfs. There's no need to go to extra expense when a satisfactory stand can be custom-made at no great cost.

This design uses salvaged bed irons, available from most scrapyards though scrap dealers tend to overvalue them, probably because of the steady demand. The steel in them is of good quality; they are thin enough to give easy hacksawing, drilling and filing while remaining amply strong. Common dimensions are 1½ x 1½ x ⅛in. The stand is demountable so you can easily get it in and out of a small restricted workshop.

You can choose your own centre height. Fred Pain in his book *The Practical Woodturner* advises elbow height when the forearm is horizontal. I find bowl turning benefits from a higher centre, spindle turning from a lower.

When you've decided on height, saw material for the two end frames (fig. 1). Drill the corners and bolt them together using ¾in or 6mm bolts. Make up the front and back frames similarly to fit neatly into the end frames. You can drill holes in the bottom rails of the end frames to screw or bolt to the floor.

Now the bolted frames can be welded, with no chance of the welder getting it wrong. Many garages will undertake this in the absence of a welding service, but whoever does it should check the diagonals and for twist. You can now remove the bolts as they serve no useful purpose. Clean up the frames, drill holes to join them and then bolt them together (fig. 2). Unbolt, paint the frames and re-assemble.

You can make a good top board by gluing together two pieces of ¾in (19mm) block-board, adjusting the width to suit the space available. Fix a small back strip to stop small articles rolling down behind the lathe. Then bolt the top to the end frames and the lathe itself in place.

If possible fasten the end frames to the floor, using Rawlbolts for a big lathe, coachbolts or large woodscrews in Rawlplugs for lighter lathes. You could fit two chipboard shelves.

The end frames should also be secured to the wall. I used bed iron to make two bars with a small offcut bolted to the wall end (fig. 3); these may also be used to support the top board.

Lathes are generally fitted against the wall, satisfactory for lathes with a revolving headstock, such as the Coronets. But when there are outward turning facilities the lathe must be far enough from the wall to allow a right-handed turner to work unhampered.

You can increase stability further by storing turning blocks and other heavy material on the shelves. ∎

Trusty steed

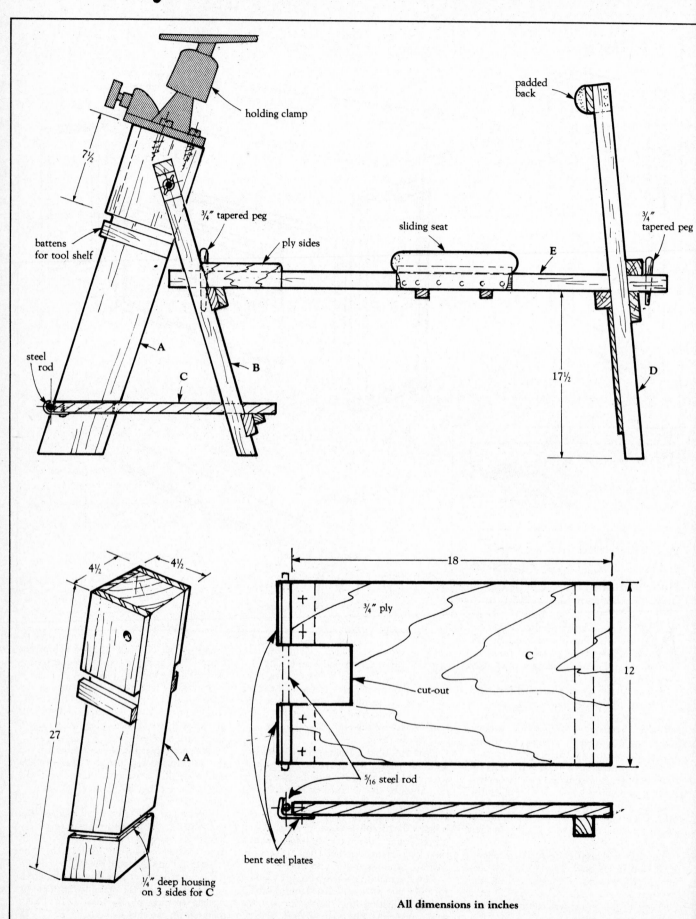

holding clamp

7½

battens
for tool shelf

¾" tapered peg

ply sides

sliding seat

padded
back

¾"
tapered peg

E

17½

steel
rod

A

B

C

D

4½

4½

27

A

¼" deep housing
on 3 sides for C

18

¾" ply

C

12

cut-out

+

+

5/16 steel rod

bent steel plates

All dimensions in inches

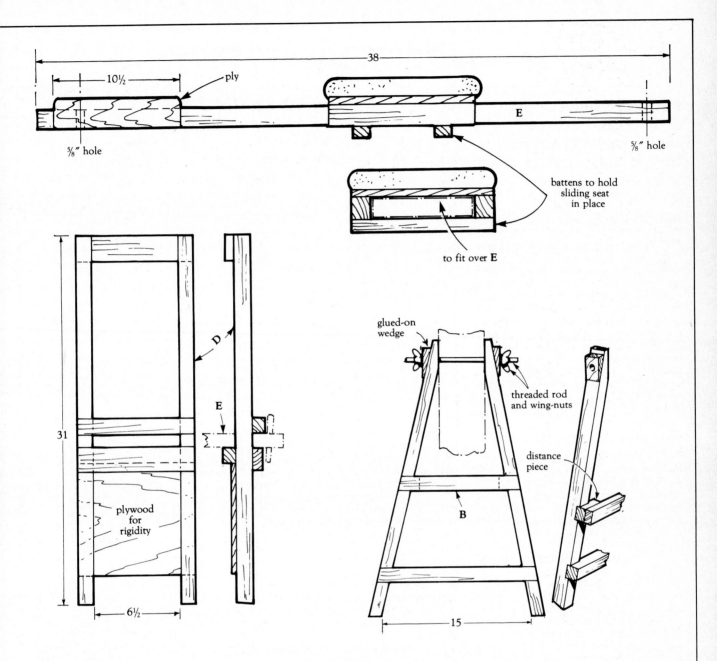

38

10½ — ply

⅝" hole

E

⅝" hole

battens to hold
sliding seat
in place

to fit over **E**

D

E

31

glued-on
wedge

threaded rod
and wing-nuts

distance
piece

B

plywood
for
rigidity

6½

15

If you were impressed by Maurice Lund's unique carving horse at the Woodworker Shows, here's how to make your own

This carving horse was basically knocked together from timber I had lying around, but it's extremely strong and effective if you have one of those useful universal carver's holding clamps.

The horse consists of a solid block **A**, on which the clamp is bolted, a folding leg mechanism for portability and a sliding seat with padded back for sitting on while you

carve. If you don't need to sit and carve, you can just make **A** and hold it upright in a bench vice.

The block **A** must be hefty, no less than 4½x4½in to hold the bolts of the clamp; I used 4x4in made up to size at the top. A ¼in housing on three sides holds **C**, a piece of ¾in plywood, with a cut-out at one end, together with bent steel plates; this piece is held in place with a ⁵⁄₁₆in steel rod which slides through the bent steel plates, gripping behind **A**. The legs **B** are secured to **A** with a threaded rod and wingnuts (the distance piece on **B** is there simply to allow the tripod to close up neatly for transporting).

You'll find that the legs **B** tend to spread while you're putting the tripod up; avoid this by tightening the wing-nuts, inserting **C** in place, and then slip the steel rod through

the bent steel plates. Now pull the legs firmly open and the two battens, one on **C** and one on **B**, will lock together.

The seating board **E** is just one board, 38x6½x1¼in, with a ⅝in hole near each end to hold the tapered pegs. You can stick pieces of ply on the sides near the business end so you get a rim to stop tools rolling off.

You could make a proper plywood tool tray to fit round **A**, which would slip into position and be held by battens; but make sure the sides are high enough to prevent tools jumping over.

I glued and screwed all the joints.

To erect the horse, fix **C** in place to hold **A** and **B** open. Rest one end of **E** on **B**, and insert a ¾in tapered peg. Slide **D** over the other end of **E** and peg similarly.

I hope you'll find the carving horse as useful as I do. ∎

Trouble-free curving

JOINERY CLASSICS

For those amongst us daunted and defeated by sophisticated geometry, Stan Thomas has no-sweat solutions to curved stairbuilding and handrailing

There seems to be a traditional anti-pathy to the word 'curved' in connection with stairbuilding. Call it a 'geometrical' stair if you will, but they certainly weren't geometrical in the workshops of my apprenticeship days; the men I worked with didn't know of the *existence* of geometry. But I and my peers sweated blood over it, for even though no full-sized curved stair was ever made by geometry in the bread-and-butter workshops, it was a regular City & Guilds subject, and if you wanted your 'Final', you just had to get down to it.

The non-geometrical stair

Back in the sixties I had a shop to fit out, including a stair up to the first floor. It was an ideal situation for a curved stair, but the economics wouldn't go to that, so I figured out a compromise; an open-tread curved stair on straight strings (!),and very nice it looked too. It was quite non-technical to construct.

The first move was to mark the area of the first-floor landing out on the ground floor (fig. 1). From this, at points corresponding to the width of the stairs (36in), I struck two arcs of radius 12 and 15ft respectively. The total rise was divided into 14, which gave a riser height of 7¾in, and applying the 2R + T = 24in (twice riser height plus tread width should always equal 24in) formula at the walking line, I got the requisite tread width; 13 at 8½in.

Next, lines were struck from the 'focal' point, intersecting on the tread points of the walking-line arc, and terminating on the outer arc. This determined the outline of each tread. Then the strings were marked in, the outer one with the outer faces of its extreme ends intersecting the arc on nosing 1 and the back edge of tread 13, forming a chord. The inner string was drawn parallel to this with the centre of its length on the inner face touching the inner arc, forming a tangent.

For geometrical reasons — note the tread cuts vary for each step — the strings couldn't be set out with a pitch-board. Each string was given its top and bottom cut, and placed in its 'working' position; the rise cuts were then picked up by plumb-bob off the floor plan (fig. 2). It will be seen from fig 1

that treads 1 and 13 overhang the inner string by about 10in, and that this measurement decreases as the centre of stairs is reached to about 2in. The reverse occurs on the outer string. It may also be seen that the vertical cuts — 'riser' cuts — of the strings are, at rise 7, square to the face of the timber, and that this angle of 90° varies as you go down and up from obtuse to acute. With the full-size setting-out, there is of course no problem in finding these angles. And since there was so much of the string cut away — they were 11x2in — 1½x¼in mild steel reinforcing strips were screwed to the bottom edge of each string.

The handrailing for a stair of such a 'slow' curve was quite simple. In this stair they terminated as shown in fig. 3. They could have run into an ordinary newel, of course.

So there is an attractive, bona fide, curved stair of simple non-geometrical construction, ideal, I would say, for any domestic situation. DIY 'Geometrical stair-building' if you like!

Non-geometrical handrailing

What makes handrailing so difficult is the fact that besides having to be curved, it has to be twisted, so its top surface anywhere is horizontal along any radius line of the curve in section (fig. 4). This is the basis of hand-railing by 'normal sections'. However, a simple way of surmounting this little problem is to make the handrail circular in section — 'mopstick'. Such a rail can look very attractive, and we are not now bothered by this tiresome 'twist', or 'twist

Fig.1 Setting out

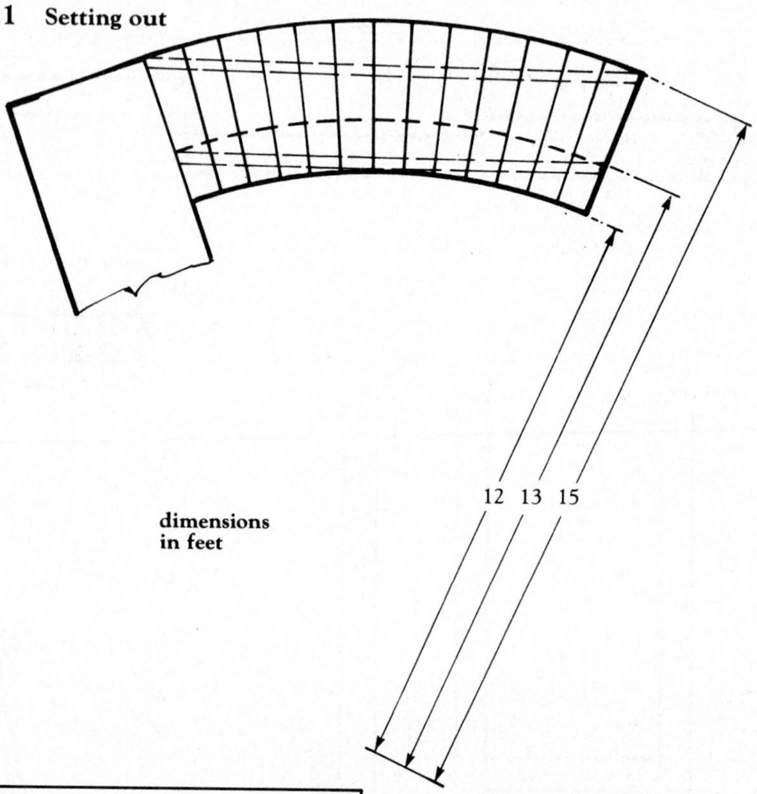

12 13 15

dimensions in feet

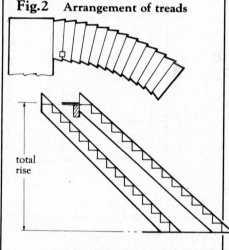

Fig.2 Arrangement of treads

total rise

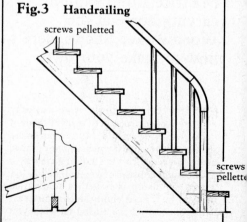

Fig.3 Handrailing

screws pelletted

screws pellette

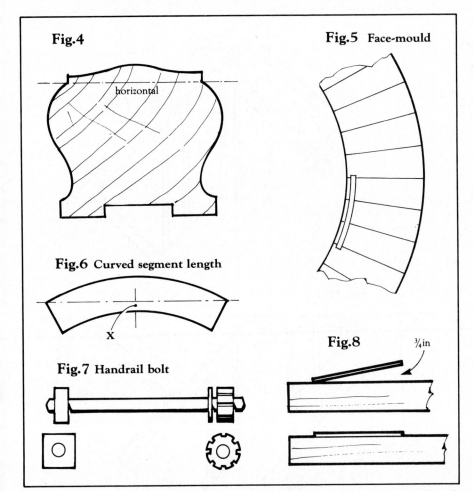

Fig.4

horizontal

Fig.6 Curved segment length

X

Fig.7 Handrail bolt

Fig.5 Face-mould

Fig.8   ¾in

from fig. 9 that if we cut our material to finished rail width (3in), we aren't going to have enough width for twist, so our segments will have to be 3in wide plus measurement **Y** — say ¼in (fig. 9). Half this measurement is added to each side of our pattern. So we need segments of 3¼x2⅜in section, plus again, a little working allowance. Technically on the centre of their length, the segments could be 3x2in dead, for the twist (half top and bottom) neutralises here, the template lying flat on the nosing. But the work is simplified by ignoring this, and cutting the segments parallel in width and thickness. Having done this, each sement must now be spoke-shaved on its underside to fit on the plane of the nosings; we have now achieved on our rail what we had by pressing down on our pattern. It's now a relatively simple job to square along the edges off this bottom face (fig. 10), and similarly with the top face, then finish up with a calipers to get even width and thickness. We now have the rail

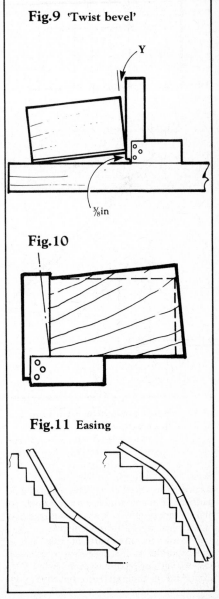

Fig.9 'Twist bevel'

Y

⅜in

Fig.10

Fig.11 Easing

bevels'. All we now need is a 'face-mould', and this is produced by the simple process of cutting a segment of ply or hardboard to rest upon the nosings; in the case of a closed-string stair, this template can be fitted to the top edge of the string (fig. 5). Say now that the rail has to be 2in section; our face-mould should be 2⅛in wide, and the required number of segments cut out of 2⅛in material — the ⅛in being 'working allowance'. These segments can now be rounded off to approximately the finished section. Their lengths will depend on the radius of the curve; as a guide to length of segment, see fig. 6. Let measurement **X** be about a third of segment width, so only about half the short grain 'runs out' inside the curve. For a stair of, say, 12ft radius in plan, the segments would be about 4-6in long; but as this would require 7in-wide material, they can be shortened if preferred, and to advantage.

The classic method of jointing up is by handrail bolt, and this rail would need to be fixed with handrail brackets. But it would be a most difficult job to locate and tighten the live nuts, working underneath the assembled rail with the rail lying on its brackets. So turn the segments upside down, lay it on the stair nosings vertically beneath the rail's finished location, assemble, glue, and tighten the live nuts (fig. 7). The rail can now be fitted and finished with glasspaper.

So much for the simple 'mop-stick' rail, which depends on side walls and brackets for its fixing. But for a stair that has no side walls, the rail has to be supported on balusters ('sticks'), and for this a flat under-surface is required — which will have to be helical (twisted) Here come those dreadful 'twist bevels'; in handrailing geometry, they are applied to each end of the rail section, but we aren't using geometry.

So we start as before with cutting face-moulds of ply, as in fig. 5. The mould should be of rail width, say 3in, and of segment length as mentioned. Now if this face-mould or pattern is rested on the stair nosings directly beneath the finished location of the rail, it will be seen that while at one end — say the bottom — it will lie flat on the nosing, its upper end will be inclined. Being thin material, it can be pressed down so it lies flat at top and bottom, which gives our helical surface to which the rail has to be shaped. but it wouldn't be possible to press our rail segments into shape, so in cutting out our segments this time, unlike the mop-stick, allowance must be made for 'twist'.

Let's assume that with our pattern laid on the nosings, its top end 'kicks up' ¾in (fig. 8). Our rail is to be 3x1in section, so our 'thickness of plank' will be 2in plus *half* the kick-up, ie 2⅜in. Half because the pattern can be tilted to give equal tilt top and bottom — ⅜in (fig. 9). Now it can be seen

continued

Trouble-free curving

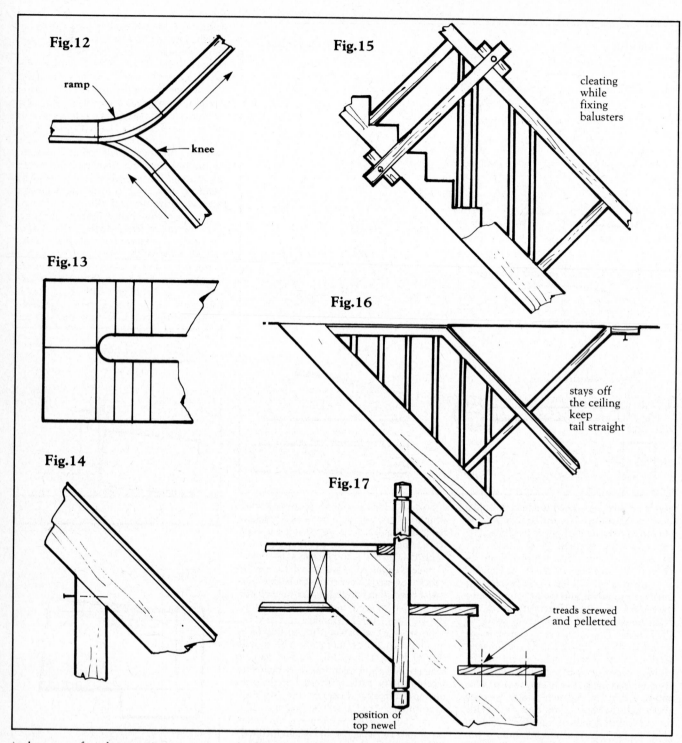

Fig.12

ramp

knee

Fig.13

Fig.14

Fig.15

cleating
while
fixing
balusters

Fig.16

stays off
the ceiling
keep
tail straight

Fig.17

treads screwed
and pelletted

position of
top newel

in the square; from here on it's just a matter of moulding to the required section.

This is the principle of *practical* handrailing. The same methods apply to a small-diameter wreath, but here of course the twist may be far more pronounced, according to whether we have a landing or winders. If in any doubt, it's a good plan to make a mock-up of softwood — no need to mould, just up to 'in the square'.

A kink in any part of the rail is unacceptable, so it's necessary to connect any two varying pitches with an 'easing' (fig. 11). And if the rail runs on to a half-

landing, the wreath here should be in a flat plane, connected by a ramp and a knee (fig. 12). But should there be a single riser, making two quarter-landings as in fig. 13, the rail should rise continuously.

The balusters can be dowelled or dovetailed at their bottom ends, according to location. In the 'cut and mitred/bracketed' stairs, they were dovetailed into the tread ends, and this jointing was then concealed by the return nosings. But for 'open plan', the newels have to be kept rather too far from the tread ends for this, so they can be fixed with dowels. Don't be tempted to

screw up through the treads; screws are useless in endgrain. The tops are usually fixed with a pin (fig. 14). But the tapping of each pin will tend to bend the rail upwards, so your balusters will get too short and the rail will look like a banana. Guard against this by cleating as in fig. 15, or by stays off the ceiling (fig. 16). With straight-string stairs, the rails, instead of terminating into the usual newel or scroll, can run right down to the floor (figs 17 and 3). ■

● **Note:** In any stair work, be sure to check up on current rules and regulations regarding pitch, clearances, etc.

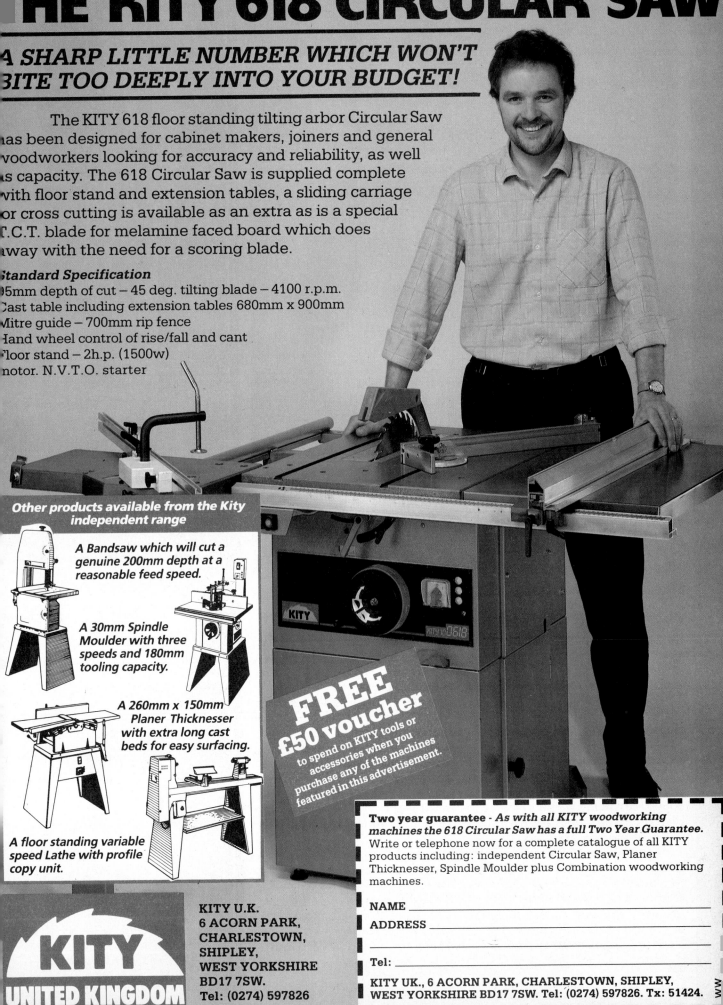

Top left, an imposing post-modern-inspired side table by Gareth Hale. Its bold MDF structure is offset with pretty pastels and marbling. Above, geometrics and glass – Katherine Scott's cleverly devised Skyscraper table. Fascination grows as the marbled MDF blocks change perspective from every angle. Below, for the discerning Lilliputian: left, a model of Sidney Barnsley's dining table by Carl Allen and Adam Barwell; centre, an 8in oak coffer by Andrew Gillmore from a Gimson original; right, a miniature Peter Waals bookcase in solid Macassar ebony by Peter Jackson.

38 Create

Big dreams, high craft and grand designs are recognisably Rycotewood. Thirty eight final-year students from the Oxfordshire college displayed their work at last month's aptly named '38 Create' exhibition in Henley, where innovation and sellable style were seen in equal proportions.

And there were some strong contenders to join the growing ranks of furniture designer makers who actually earn a living from their craft. These students are aiming straight at the demand-and-supply commissioned furniture market; the designs are exciting — not shocking — useable, and in harmony with modern taste.

As well as the original pieces, chunkier than last year but showing the same preference for pastel shades, the reproduction copies confirmed Rycotewood's commitment to highest quality craftsmanship, delicate use of expensive timbers, and finish as an integral part of the piece.

Post-modernism seemed a popular source of inspiration, but it's good to see nostalgia taking a bashing with designs emerging that can be appreciated here and now. These 38 won't have to wait a couple of decades for the laughter to die down, or hang on for an '80's revival' before they receive the fruits of their labours. They organised the exhibition independently, at the Henley Exhibition Centre — signs of an entrepreneurial flavour to all that high craft?

Top right, streamlined seating –
David Hunt's fine cantilevered chair
in maple and brown oak has warm
sophistication. Below right, a chair
with character and post-modern
manners by Nicolas Richardson.
Striking geometric forms in MDF
and steel tubing, with carefully har-
monised hues: an interesting place
to put your feet up.

All photos Royston Carrs

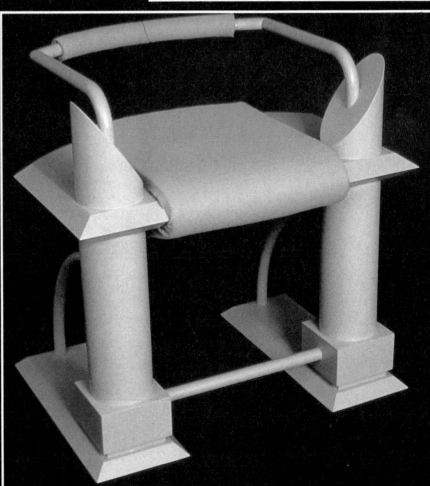

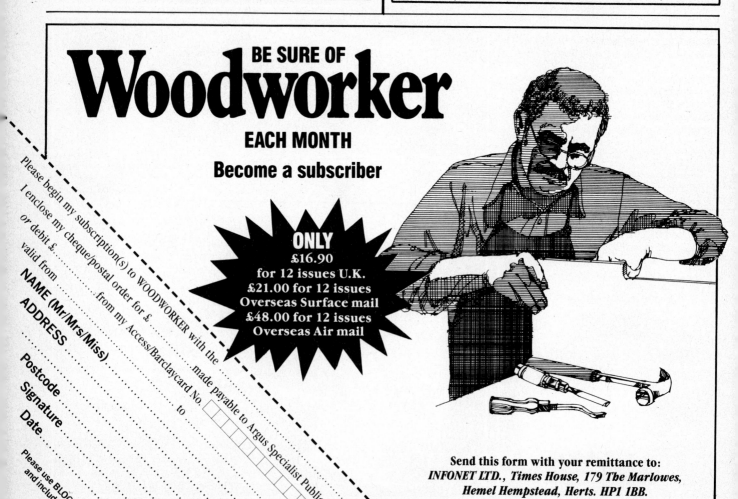

Books galore

Eric Stephenson
Spindle moulder handbook
Stobart & Son, £10.95 softback
Reviewed by David Bailie

The spindle moulder is without doubt the most fascinating, absorbing and technically demanding of woodworking machines. It can also be fairly awesome, and demands constant respect if it is to be used safely. It is the machine I'd choose to work with above all others — and I'd also want a copy of Eric Stephenson's *Spindle moulder handbook*.

It contains a wealth of no-nonsense detail on virtually every aspect of set-up and use — even, or maybe especially, for the experienced hand. Indeed, the beginner would need an additional guide to the machine's less adventurous applications. It is primarily a handbook which focuses on thorough technical information, but keeps in mind the safe application of the recommended techniques.

The illustrations (by the author himself) are excellent. He has obviously suffered in the past trying to decipher smudged or fussy line-drawings, and has set out to ensure that the reader can pick out the salient points quickly.

I was going to quibble that the book was a little dry in style, but thinking about it, if the information had been more elaborate, the book would have become a tome, and lost its clarity.

The book has taken its place on my workshop bookshelf under 'essential reading'.
● David Bailie is a partner in a specialist cabinetmaking and joinery firm.

V. J. Taylor and H. A. Babb
**Making and Repairing
Wooden Clock Cases**
David & Charles, £14.95
Reviewed by Bill Watts

When I first began to make clock cases several years ago, the many reference books mostly concentrated on historical and mechanical aspects of clocks. There was little guidance to aspiring case makers, so I resorted to the so-called 'fumble factor', seeing as many examples as possible in museums throughout the country to discover the old techniques. Unfortunately you need a trained eye to pick out subtleties of method since so much of the applied skills would have been hidden; veneers may be laid with great artistry, but they cover carcase work which might have been nailed or jointed for all you can see of them.

Probably all the answers for the case maker are contained in this quite excellent book. The 10 chapters each cover a particular aspect: repairs to doors; joints and panels; repairs to mouldings, and so on. The illustrations are large and clear and the narrative is in simple language — a welcome change from many 'learned' authors. The way the historical background is covered stimulates you to further study and research.

The authors make a clear distinction between restoration and conservation and set out related aspects of clock-case making and repair in appendices, which include further reading and useful addresses. The index is thorough and comprehensive.

I have just two tiny criticisms. The authors assume some prior experience; I'd still like to know an easier way to mould the curve of the arch. I would also like to know how to select and mount brasswork such as locks, capitals, hinges, spandrels — what did the craftsmen of old use before there was Superglue?

A quite superb and beautifully produced book which will give a lot of pleasure to its readers.
● Bill Watts is a professional clock maker in Gloucestershire.

Bruce Boulter
Woodturning projects and techniques
Argus Books, £13.95 softback
Reviewed by John Buckley-Golder

After I'd read Bruce Boulter's book, I sought the reactions of five of the people at whom it is aimed — the inexperienced. Their comments included: 'bitty', 'hotchpotch' and 'no flow through the book'.

My comments are that the printing of photographs leaves much to be desired; the constant use of the word 'stuff' (when the English language has so many alternatives) could lead overseas readers astray; and I noticed one inaccuracy, where the text refers to a $\frac{1}{4}$in skew, and the photograph depicts a $\frac{1}{4}$in parting tool.

This book doesn't do the author justice. He has written many good articles for magazines and developed a following with their readers. My advice to the inexperienced: 'look elsewhere, this isn't for you'.
● John Buckley-Golder is a professional woodturner, demonstrator and teacher.

John Sainsbury
Turning Miniatures in Wood
Guild of Master Craftsmen Publications, £8.50 +£1.00 p&p
Reviewed by Nicholas Perrin

Here at last is a comprehensive and clearly set out volume on miniature turning.

John Sainsbury always treats his subject thoroughly. The early pages deal with the standard topics, including types of lathes, tools and their sharpening, and choice of timbers relevant to miniature turning.

We then reach the techniques of miniature turning. John deals in great detail with the many different ways of holding these tiny works of art in the making; a variety of multichucks is appraised, and we are also shown much cheaper ways of making our own wooden chucks.

Care has been taken in choosing the projects described in the book; they've been selected to show a wide variety of techniques. Each project is fully described and is accompanied by clear photographs.

Then follows the illustrated work of a number of highly talented contemporary turners. The lace bobbins of David Francis and Ken Smith combine artistry with practical design: so many lace bobbins made today are unusable. The miniature work of Graham Spalding, David Wadsley and others must give inspiration to readers. Marsh Dawes shows imaginative use of the wood at his disposal, while Del Stubbs brings a new dimension to turning with his miniature goblets just over $\frac{1}{8}$in tall. Most of these experts make and use their own tools and there is an excellent appendix on this.

The book is a reasonably priced and worthwhile addition to any turner's library.
● Nick Perrin is a professional lace-bobbin maker.

Ian Norbury
Projects for Creative Woodcarving
Stobart & Sons Ltd, £15.00 hardback
Reviewed by Hugh O'Neill

The craftsman's life has four stages of development. First there are basic skills to learn — at this stage our whole concern is with the how to. So we seek teachers who show us. In our second age, as skills start to firm up, we are still very conscious of 'how to' problems, but we begin to think more on the what to — what to make; what alternative approaches there are; what styles to adopt; what schools to follow. We search and experiment, but eventually seek out the master and sit at his feet.

When skills have become second nature, we cease to worry about the how. Our creative instincts take over and ideas and originality begin to emerge. We now consort with other craftsmen who further stimulate our thinking.

The fourth stage, reached by relatively few, is that of Master where we become our craft and our craft becomes us.

Ian Norbury is a master, and in this book he shares some of his 'mastership'. His main aim however is to provide a feast of ideas in the 'what to' area. Many 'what to' books still contain reams of regurgitated material on basic skills — what tools to use, how to sharpen them, basic tool handling, etc, etc. Ian does not, and this lifts this book apart.

We are presented with 49 detailed projects, ranging from simple, lily-shaped candle holders to the intricate Pied Piper and a dynamic horse and jockey in full gallop. Squared plan and section drawings are expanded with detail sketches; and while the accompanying notes may suggest suitable timbers and give a few specific tips on the 'how', they are more insights into Ian's thinking and ideas generation.

The developing carver may follow the designs slavishly — and those just moving out of the skills-learning stage will. But you won't have worked very far through the projects before ideas of your own will be stimulated. This book will be a valuable asset whether you are still at the copyist end, or have already moved well down the path towards originality.
● Hugh O'Neill is a woodturner and novice carver. He writes on 'how to'.

continued

Books galore

Noel Johnson Leach
The Woodworker Book of Wood Finishing
Argus Books, £9.95 softback
Reviewed by Ian Hosker

The reason for the recent flurry of publishing activity in the wood finishing area is, quite clearly, that there's a market as yet unsaturated — perhaps expanding. The reasons, I suggest, are mainly based on a heightened awareness of the importance of the surface looks and textures of wooden objects, and also confusion about the bewildering array of products now available to the home finisher.

The advertising tells us that this book is primarily aimed at the student, professional restorer and home craftsman. Certainly, in terms of the breadth of materials and techniques covered, the student can glean much basic information. The technicalities of modern finishes are covered very well and I particularly liked the early chapters on Health and Safety, and tools and materials. However, the book is a Guide, not a textbook. It contains nothing that a professional restorer should not already know. As for the home craftsman, I have generally found that he or she wants to be able to use a book almost as a manual, kept nearby and referred to as work progresses. The application of each finish is presented in schedule form, making this possible. The advantages and disadvantages of the chosen finish are also in schedule format, which makes it easier to decide which is best.

Wood finishing is a contentious area and much emphasis must be placed upon experience; what works for one can be less successful for another. I felt the book was a little pedantic in one or two places, but then a good book should warn about possible problems. The real test is the chapter on french polishing, which is 7½ pages long. The description of materials, 'tools' and the various finishing methods is good and accounts for most of the chapter. Alas, only half a page is devoted to a schedule of its application to a surface. I agree with Noel when he says that the correct 'feel' of a rubber is impossible to communicate on paper, but a few line drawings showing how the fad and rubber are used (and made) would have been useful.

Indeed, there are instances elsewhere in the book where drawings would have brought about a better understanding of the text. The photographs illustrating the different types of spraygun are useful, but the one of a compressor is not. There are three photographs showing different finishes, but the difference between them is too small to justify their inclusion. One photograph appears twice — not a problem in itself, except that they illustrate different things (one of using steel wool to denib a surface, the other of using a reviver). There are many poorly focused photographs which are too similar. It would have been

better to exclude them and create more space for other forms of illustration or even an expansion of the text in places where it's a little too brief.

The text is easy to follow and understand; there isn't that terrible feeling of knowing that you have to plough through pages of extended prose to acquire the simplest piece of knowledge. The information is concisely presented (a bit too much so in places) and while there are a couple of contradictions, there is nothing of substance that might be misleading.

The book gives a very thorough account of modern finishes, and places great emphasis on safe working practices and thorough preparation of surfaces. There is even an important chapter on Flatting (maintaining a perfectly smooth surface between coats), something which many other books tend to skate round. I feel it weakens on the traditional finishes; some of the techniques are inadequately explained and there are one or two occasions where the book assumes a certain prior knowledge — a 'pounce bag' is mentioned, but not how to make it. Oil polishing is practically ignored and waxing isn't really treated thoroughly. There are many woodworkers who are unclear of the order of working when finishing or refinishing a job, so a flowchart or similar showing the sequence of events would have been of great value. The chapter on grainfilling did not really explain whether this came before or after staining.

For its strength on modern finishes alone, however, if you are interested in venturing into that area (or want to improve your results) the The Woodworker Book of Wood Finishing is worth serious consideration when it comes to updating your library.
● Ian Hosker is a professional wood finisher, antique restorer and lecturer.

David Swindells
Restoring Period Timber-framed Houses
David & Charles, £14.95 hardback
Reviewed by David Ouvry

David Swindells' book aims not so much to tell owners of timber-framed buildings how to go about repairing or replacing damaged structures — although it often does just that — as to give them informed knowledge to help them discuss with builder or surveyor how best to put things right, and how to maintain their property in good condition.

This is an excellent book which always leans towards sensible conservation of buildings in traditional forms; the author applauds the use of thatch, tile and hung-tile where traditionally used, and he recommends the unpainted, unstained finish to exterior oak, so the natural silvery appearance can be appreciated for what it is.

Here you may learn the secrets of making daub for wattle, applying limewash, and how to make or repair the many joints devised by our ancestors; what to do with

obstinate chimneys, wet rot, dry rot, and the depredations of armies of beetles, from 'Death-watch' to 'Church-yard'.

Most of the author's remedies are traditional, but it may surprise some to find that epoxy resin is recommended for repairing rotted joints. Purists may shake their heads, but at times there can be no other method, short of total dismantling.

The author is a surveyor of many years' experience of ancient timber-frame buildings, and has enough confidence to live in one himself. His book abounds with the jargon of the trade: bressumers, trenails, table scarf joints, crown posts, stylobates ... The jargon is as well explained as it is necessary, which makes it odd that drawbore pins are described simply in one case as 'metal holding pins'. In general, if the author's advice is followed, the restorer shouldn't go far wrong, for he rightly insists that building traditions and methods should be understood before repairs are carried out.

The illustrations, both sketch and photograph are generally admirable, though some may not care for the heavy delineation of the drawings, which emphasise the weightiness and density of the structures portrayed.

One or two puzzles remain. How, for example, were the elaborate mouldings of the 14th-16th centuries worked? The appearance can only suggest the use of moulding planes, and not the simple scratch-stocks that W. L. Goodman in British Plane Makers Since 1700 suggests were used at the time.

A useful list of organisations connected with historic houses and a glossary of technical terms are provided in the appendices. Since the author details the history of timber-frame dwellings, the book is of extra interest to those wishing to explore the way this kind of building construction developed. Mr Swindells' work will be welcomed by any owner of a timber-frame house who values it beyond mere domestic convenience (or inconvenience!); and it should be required reading by builders who may have to repair such houses with little previous experience.
● David Ouvry's account of his restoration (and re-location!) of a timber-frame house appeared in WOODWORKER January.

In brief

The Furniture Makers: a history of trade unionism in the furniture trade, 1868-1972 (Hew Reid: Malthouse Press, £15.95 hardback)
A fascinating account for anyone who worked in the industry and engrossing bedtime reading for all interested in the 'bad old days'. Jam-packed with facts, enlivened with human interest material. Borrow it if you can't buy it.

The Technique Of Furniture Making
(Ernest Joyce, revised by Alan Peters: Batsford, £19.95 hardback)
A serious book for the committed craftsman, professional or enthusiastic amateur; Joyce's standard work of reference has been a Bible since 1970, but was beginning to look a bit long in the tooth. Who better to revise and update it than Alan Peters, whose own Cotswold School heritage (his apprenticeship was with Edward Barnsley) admirably qualifies him to add and alter all that's necessary, yet keep the distinctive, authoritative style. Materials, tools and equipment, basic and advanced furniture techniques, hardware, business, design, restoration, finishes; if you really want to know furniture making and can only afford one book, this has to be it. Lots more photos, some in colour, especially of work by designer/makers whose names will be familiar to regular WOODWORKER readers; pity that the new black and white pictures reproduce so poorly compared to the old. The breed of designer/maker has grown enormously since Joyce's book first appeared, and this timely revision cannot but play an important part in its increasing health and strength.

Reader's Digest New DIY Manual
(Reader's Digest Association: £19.95, ringbound, plastic covers)
No, not another revision but a completely new edition of the grand-daddy of all the DIY Manuals. These books are becoming increasingly expensively produced and designed; more than 500 full-colour pages, all loose-leaf, a hard plastic back — and it even comes with a little plastic folder so you can take a page with you on the job or down the builder's merchants. The blurb quotes £3½ million a year being spent on tools and materials by enthusiastic DIYers, and Reader's Digest are clearly aiming at a good chunk of that money. Have they thought of everything? Well, if there's something new they can always publish a new page and you can slot it in . . . a whole section is devoted to 'ideas for the home' — kitchens, bathrooms, bedrooms, kids' rooms, work areas; 'techniques, tools and materials' covers painting, woodwork, plumbing, heating, electrics, the garden, roofs, staircases, soft furnishings, brickwork . . . the list is (almost) endless, and it's a beautiful production. If you can't find it in here you have a problem.

Fun-to-Make Wooden Toys *(Terry Forde: David & Charles, £8.95 hardback)*
Dozens of attractive ideas for easy-to-make toys in the author's second book. He's a birch plywood man, relying on wizard work with paint for eye appeal. Some of these toys could be hazardous for young children — he recommends panel pins (screws are safer, dowels best) and, unbelievably, he suggests bent dressmaking pins for hinges!

Das Werkzeug des Zimmermans *(The Tools of the Carpenter (Schadwinkel, Heine & Gerner: Verlag Th. Schafer, Hanover, 148 DM, hardback)*
German text, but this book fills a glaring gap in woodworking history. Until relatively recently carpenters constructed most buildings, bridges, cranes and other machinery, with special tools for the job, here recorded comprehensively. A large chunk, 58 pages, is devoted to what used to be the most important woodworking tool — the axe. Expensive, but of high quality and there's nothing comparable in English. Obtainable from Roy Arnold, 77 High Street, Needham Market, Suffolk at £54.
Philip Walker

Machine and Power Tools for Woodwork *(Gordon Stokes: Bell & Hyman, £10.95 softback)*
A very lightweight contribution to the field, regrettably. This book is neither comprehensive enough for the first-time buyer deciding his or her priorities or detailed enough for the person equipping a power workshop. Gordon Stokes may know a great deal about power machinery, but in this book he does not communicate it.

Sculpting Wood – contemporary tools and techniques *(Mark Lindquist: Lewis Books, £26.40 hardback. Available only from the publisher, 2 Blagdon Rd, New Malden, Surrey KT3 4AD, 01-949 4699)*
Turners particularly will be familiar with the work of artist, sculptor, carver and woodturner Lindquist, a major figure in the American 'Woodturning as Art' movement which has enthused a number of notable British turners. The book has a warm, personal tone, a fascinating section on Lindquist's own search for direction, a beautiful but lamentably small section of colour pictures of the work of Lindquist and other artists — including his father, Melvin — all of which is sandwiched between exhaustive information on timber, its growth, behaviour, cutting and drying, some carving projects, and more practical information, with projects, on unusual approaches to turning. Much of the practical timber stuff differs in language and practice from the UK. Definitely for carvers and turners, at least something for most wood lovers; not everyone will get £26 worth out of it, but it looks set to become important reference and inspiration.

Repairing and Restoring Antique Furniture *(John Rodd: David & Charles, £12.95 hardback)*
This book is intended for the serious restorer and not for the DIY step-by-step enthusiast. John Rodd is a cabinetmaker by trade and has spent much of his life restoring antique furniture.

The instructions are detailed and clear, but the prose is rather dry and set across the whole width of the page; you'll probably need to read a chapter through first, and then go back to it when you start work.

It describes the process of restoration in six steps and goes on to specific work like carcase and drawer repair, veneering and marquetry. The illustrations are very simple, which works for some techniques; others could have done with more detail.

Interest is stepped up in the later chapters which tackle myriad methods and problems, from worm-eaten wood to renewing the leather on bellows and coromandel screens. The 'examples of jobs' section covers some of the typically varied pieces that a restorer comes across (rope handles for sea-chests and Regency toilet mirrors); it's just a shame that all the photography is in black and white.

Interesting advice from someone who obviously knows his stuff.

Craftsman's Guides; Decorative Paint Finishes *(Belinda Hunt)*; **Picture Framing Techniques** *(Mark Lister: Ebury Press, both £5.95 hardback)*
If you're hung-over on Habitat or listless with Laura Ashley, Belinda Hunt's book on alternative paint-finishes could lend some individuality to your home. From marbling and graining to stippling and stencilling, this neat little book gives straightforward instructions on re-vamping your walls and furniture. It's attractively laid out and makes you want to partake in this young and outwardly individualist pastime (even if it does cover the now *passé* rag-rolling).

Less trendy but just as popular, picture framing is a skill made open to all in Mark Lister's book. It details the equipment you'll need, how to cut and join a frame, and explains projects for different subject matter: family snaps, oil-paintings, tapestry and dried flowers.

The books are identical in format, show good use of colour and illustrations, and are easy to follow, but they would have been just as handy and not so grim pocket-wise if they'd been softback.

Dining & Bedroom Chairs & Stools *(R. J. McDonald: Batsford, £7.95 hardback*
This is the first in a series of four books on the techniques of upholstery, and covers traditional and modern methods. Whether your chairs are upholstered in foam or stuffed, sprung and stitched, there's solid advice on preparation, technique and the best materials to use.

A lot of the photographs (all black and white) are blurred, which rather detracts from their usefulness and you'll need good eyesight for the measurements on the illustrations. It's a small, bound volume, with fairly condensed text so you may have problems using it as a working reference.

If you're a keen collector of waif-and-stray chairs, you'll find this book informative but rather lacking in aesthetics.

Turning it up

When Tobias Kaye's ambitions for large bowl-turning outgrew his equipment, he acquired and modified a heavy capstan lathe. Here's what he did with it

Some time ago I got the chance to acquire a heavy cast-iron floor-standing toolrest, and I was quick to take it up. The photo shows the stand and an extra long bowl gouge I had made, with a standard to show comparison. Long having been dissatisfied with the limitations on bowl size imposed by my Harrison Graduate, I had already extended its capacity by lowering and spacing out the bolt-on outbed for left-hand turning (*WW/June '85*).

The floor-standing toolrest offered immediate expansion and unseen limitations. I was soon struggling with blanks weighing more than 1cwt, turning out bowls deeper than ever before at 11 and 12in, up to 26in diameter. But I began to suspect that as these pieces weighed at least twice what the Graduate was designed to take, it mightn't be wise to continue abusing it in this way. What I needed was something with bigger bearings.

The answer soon appeared in a local ex-engineering works clearout. A 'Herbert' Capstan lathe, built about 1950, with bearings about 3½in diameter and 3-4in long; phosphor-bronze shells, continuously splash-oiled. 'That', I thought, 'should be man enough for anything.' Other advantages of this machine were a large chuck in which to hold faceplates and accessories, eight forward speeds 30-511rpm, the same eight reverse speeds, a 3hp motor; and the cost — £30 delivered.

But the Herbert only had a 6in swing over the bed, and was cluttered with tooling

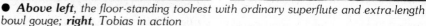

● **Above left**, *the floor-standing toolrest with ordinary superflute and extra-length bowl gouge;* **right**, *Tobias in action*

devices. It needed some refinements. To wit: unbolt and throw away the capstan, the cross-slide with tool posts, the gearbox and power train. Unbolt, remove with a winch, and place to one side the headstock/gearbox assembly, then measure out and drill five new ⅝in holes in the bed to re-fit the headstock in its new position, with the chuck outboard instead of over the bed.

This was a lengthy process. Drilling ⅝in holes through 1in or more of cast iron is no joke, especially when absolute accuracy is essential. I managed it by clamping my floor-standing drill-press on to the side of the lathe tray, removing all but one of the bed mounting-bolts, and pivoting the bed and the drill head until I got precise alignment. Several trips of the headstock/gearbox unit by winch and pinch-bar across the workshop floor were necessary before all the holes were correct and aligned, and once

the headstock was finally back on, bits of bedrail had to be ground away for the bolts to slide up to the head in the new holes.

Now, of course, the motor wouldn't fit where it was before, and a new carriage had to be made for that at the neighbouring forge, and fixed to the bed. I drilled through this and dowelled it into the bed with nails, as it tended to slop around under belt pressure. Also a nut welded onto the frame allows use of a bolt and spacers to tension the belts.

The motor that came with the lathe had a very small belt pulley on it, to give a pulley speed of 500rpm into the headstock/gearbox. I wanted to increase this, to get final drive speeds of two or two-and-a-half times those on the plate. My first attempt to this end was in the shape of a smaller pulley on

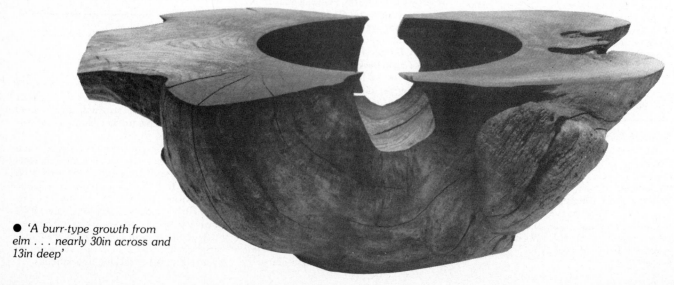

● *'A burr-type growth from elm . . . nearly 30in across and 13in deep'*

the gearbox. The result was just belt slip — and it also showed that the gearbox used so much power that 3hp wasn't enough to get that extra speed. I managed to get a 5hp motor with a larger pulley than the three-horse one, so I put the original big pulley back on the gearbox, and calculated from the diameters that the speed was almost exactly doubled.

Now it was going, I found the centre height too low for the toolrest, so I raised it up on two bits of 3x5in channel iron, bolting them into the floor and the lathe on to them.

Soon I had bigger bits than ever swinging — a burr-type growth from elm, for instance, nearly 30in across and 13in deep; and then (struggle, struggle!) a beech bowl 40in diameter and again about a foot deep that must have weighed at least 5cwt when it first went up. This was turned, not on the biggest faceplate I had, which is aluminium, but on the strongest, which is only 5in diameter. This meant I had to be a bit careful truing up the bottom and re-siting the faceplate to obtain true running for the hollowing. This massive piece tended to make the faceplate, screwed on to a shaft held in the chuck, walk out of the chuck, so I had an extra-large chuck key made. Putting all my weight on it held the shaft in.

This weighty piece also tested some of the clutches in the gearbox, of which there are four altogether: two on the forward/reverse lever, two on the high range/low range lever. The first two are small-diameter steel cone clutches, and they slip quite badly until they get hot. I don't know how long they're going to last — maybe soon all this will have been in vain.

Photos David Spires

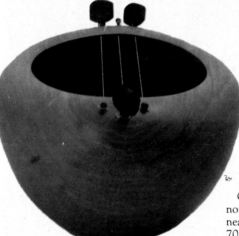

● *Two of Tobias' revolutionary 'Sounding bowls': 13in-diameter apple with holly, ebony and copper fittings, and 9in apple with padauk fittings. See below to know how they sound*

Other disadvantages of my new set-up; noise — working with it in a high gear is nearly as bad as sitting in a Mini Van at 70mph. It also sprays Hypoy gear oil round at high speeds, and drips it at low ones, using about a pint in 20 hours' working. Worse than the cost of Hypoy is the smell, which is a major nuisance.

All in all the big Herbert is worth the trouble I put into it at least ten times over, and it only cost me about £100. If it packs up I plan to experiment with a heavy half-shaft from a lorry or tractor with a donkey engine, as the variable speed from a power source like that would solve a lot of problems. Maybe I'll even set a car gearbox in between — a local friend powers his potter's wheel through a Volvo unit.

One thing I wouldn't dispense with is the large chuck. It's an extremely versatile holding device, and presents the least of many dangers involved with turning ridiculously large bowls! ∎

● Tobias' turning ingenuity has expanded into realms musical — he has developed the 'Sound bowl', examples of which you see here, with a special acoustic shape and delicately undercut rims. He has also recorded a tape of **Bowl Music**, sonorous and meditative, an unusual treat for the ear and mind. It is available at £4.45+50p p&p from Magpie Music, Whites Cross, Buckfastleigh, Devon TQ11 0LS.

● *The final version of the lathe with a 40x12in beech bowl that 'must have weighed at least 5cwt when it first went up'*

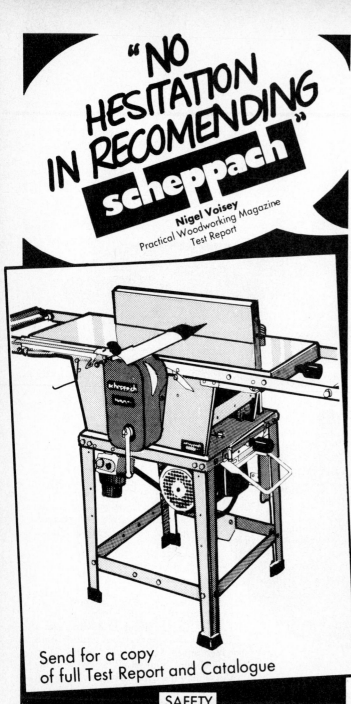

Letters

Rod, pole or perch

IT WASN'T UNTIL AFTER I'd measured up the interior of our c1385 weavers' house-cum-workshop for modern installations and removed the ceiling of a first-floor room, that the significance of this mysterious dimension, once found on the back of all school exercise-books, suddenly dawned.

One rod, pole or perch, was 5½yds and four made a cricket pitch; the East Anglian rod (pole or perch in other parts of the country) was the basic measurement on all allotments. Now I recognised it as the standard proportion for mediaeval, prefabricated buildings: length = 1 rod; width = ¾ rod; storey height = ½ rod; length of rafters = 1 rod; length of collars ¼ rod.

The carpenter took his measuring rod into the woodland, offered it up to the coppice-grown oak poles, and immediately knew what would be available from each in terms of cills, plates and so on. They'd be felled with an axe, cut to length with a frame-saw, squared with a side-axe and carted to the framing yard. There the necessary mortises and tenons, scarfs and dovetails would be cut and holes bored for the dowel pins: after temporary assembly the various parts would be marked and taken to the site. Earlier and smaller buildings would be reassembled in part before erection with the assistance of a team of neighbours, like in quite recent American barn-raising parties.

Revd Canon John Griffin, Hadleigh, Suffolk

Extremely aware

HAVING READ YOUR ARTICLE 'Who is AWARE?' in WOODWORKER March, I don't think Mr Cox can see the wood for the trees.

I'm almost too scared to write on my piece of re-cycled paper. Surely the AWARE logo will have to be advertised, but on what? Slate, magnetic tape, television, re-cycled paper? I hope Mr Cox doesn't smoke! Unfortunately I'm addicted to tobacco and have a love-hate relationship with cigarettes — rolled in some paper, made from some wood.

But according to Mr Cox, it's okay to carry on the carbon cycle; didn't I learn in school that trees use carbon-dioxide and replenish oxygen? So if we're cutting down all those trees and burning the trees in oxygen to produce more carbon-dioxide, we must be using oxygen to produce carbon-dioxide, and must be a great ally to the tree, and the tree to us.

So why do we pollute our skies with dust and ash, and our lungs with smoke when we could be busy planting trees to give us more oxygen to enable our brains to think more clearly. We need warmth and relaxation; why then don't we burn the legislation, mostly written on paper, to save the trees that can become a cabinet in iroko (tropical hardwood) to keep our books in?

No, my small contribution will be to buy more re-cycled toilet paper; desperately try to give up smoking; use pound coins instead of notes to pay for my hardwood; make laminated wooden-bowls which I'd sell for five pound coins; press my woodshavings into fuel blocks; stop buying garbage newspapers and cut down on plastic glues and chemical finishes which breed nasty chemical plants — but I'm not sure about cow-bone for glue, my vegetarian brother would object.

I will use both sides of my writing paper, cut down on documents, drawing, computer-stationery, letters, stamps, leaflets, cheques and ticker-tape; the War Cry, pornographic magazines, wrappers, fags and matches.

And invest coins in real food, fresh air, trees and clean water. Renewable treasures are great, but why differentiate between trees and coal, gas and oil. Coal comes from compressed trees, so do gas and oil; so why don't we have a campaign like plant a tree in '73. (I planted two apples.)

I'm sure if Mr Cox looked around he could find some nice wood. I haven't bought a piece of hardwood in about three years and I'm making a living out of it, I must be if I can afford to smoke. What's wrong with driftwood, old wood and gash timber, most of which is burnt to keep us warm. I see it all the time and if it's not used it'll compost down to replenish the fauna or eco-structure.

C. J. Paine, Barry, S. Glamorgan

Re-vid

I FEEL I MUST REPLY to Ken Cooper's review of the 'Dennis White Teaches Woodturning' video (*WW/Mar*). We intend to pass on in this series all the knowledge and experience Dennis has gained in his 65 years of turning.

'Frequent cooling in water is advocated, but not shown.' Do we really want to waste valuable time showing every cooling moment?

'Novice woodturners could be forgiven for wondering what the . . . basic concepts are.' In the first 3½ minutes Dennis says: 'I am going to teach you how to turn the bead, the fillet and the hollow. Once you have mastered these, you will be able to turn anything at all between centres.' Dennis then goes on for half an hour doing just that — turning beads, fillets and hollows — the basic concepts of turning between centres.

'Deals repetitively with trivia, but ignores important things.' Parts of the tape are repetitive; I make no apologies for that. We go to great lengths to show the viewer just what to practice — the very basis of learning to turn is practice, practice.

I feel that Mr Cooper didn't really watch the tape when he says 'the last part of the programme has no commentary.' The last 20 minutes is taken with turning a 10in salt mill, and has commentary throughout.

To say our tape is unlikely to improve anyone's theoretical understanding or practical skill leaves me speechless. I maintain that just watching the oldest and finest professional woodturner alive today, working at his lathe, is enough to make even a competent turner into a better one. I feel Mr Cooper's review is one-sided and ill-considered, and would give a totally wrong impression of our product. The people who have bought it so far have expressed their pleasure with it.

Kevin Baxendale, Director,
Knowhow Productions Ltd

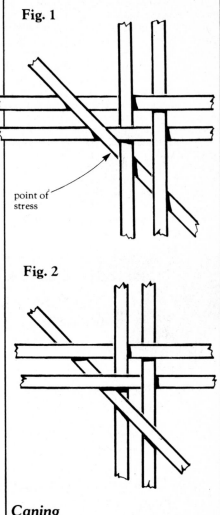

Fig. 1

point of stress

Fig. 2

Caning

I WOULD LIKE to comment on Ronald Snell's article on Rattan pattern caning (*WW/Apr*) where, in step 5, he states that the diagonal weave should go over the horizontal and under the vertical as in fig. 1.

I refer to two books: *Chair caning method for frames of all types* by J. Dunwell and M. Kindon, and *The Illustrated handbook of furniture restoration* by George Buchanan — where both show the diagonal woven so that it can slip between the horizontal and vertical (fig. 2).

Surely it's preferable to have it slide between as in fig. 2 to avoid a point of friction and possible fracture of the cane.

W. Ford, Uckfield, E. Sussex

continued

Letters

Sex bias

HURRAY FOR NICKI GREAVES' letter decrying sexism in January WOOD-WORKER. Not wishing to wimp or whine too much, I nevertheless must agree whole-heartedly with her.

I started in this trade four years ago with a TOPS course during which I suffered terrible ribbing from the instructor! I emerged shaken but not deterred. All my fellow male students (one or two of whom may have actually been a bit worse than myself) immediately got jobs.

I made two dozen or so applications and was laughed at, ignored, and excused out — 'Oh it'll be too heavy for you dear' — or just had the phone put down on me. I went self-employed!

After two years, my confidence had increased somewhat and I applied for another job and got it — because the employer was absolutely desperate.

During the last nine months I have been slave-driven, badly underpaid (£2.20 per hour self-employed), sexually harassed, insulted and shown up in front of my fellow workers. But I did learn how to use machinery — albeit without training.

My confidence has survived somehow and I still love my trade. But please, oh please, men out there give us a chance. Some of us are average, some of us are poor, some of us are good. But to be in this trade we must be keen, we must wish to learn — so give us a break.

Sarah Caswell, Stalham, Norwich

Honing

WHEN I READ the question and answer on honing in April WOODWORKER the infrequently remembered wooden hone came to mind. A small flat piece of fine-grained hardwood coated with some fine abrasive offers a low-tech, superb surface for that final touch to edge tools.

I use a 5x7in piece of flat-sawn rock maple, and previously the mud from an 8000-grit Japanese finishing stone as abrasive. However, I find I am now happier with green rouge. The surface needs only be recharged on loss of efficacy. It is used dry, with the edge of the tool being pulled along the abrasive surface and not pushed into it.

Using the hone seems to break down the abrasive grit to a smaller size and give an even finer polishing surface. This, and the 'hard' surface which does not round-over the cutting edge are two advantages over leather. I know of a carver who swears by a piece of partly mineralised cherry as his hone.

R. Hayward, New South Wales, Australia

AVON

BATH   Tel. Bath 64513
JOHN HALL TOOLS   ★
RAILWAY STREET

Open: Monday-Saturday
9.00 a.m.5.30 p.m.
H.P.W.WM.D.A.BC.

BRISTOL   Tel. (0272) 741510
JOHN HALL TOOLS LIMITED   ★
CLIFTON DOWN SHOPPING CENTRE
WHITELADIES ROAD
Open: Monday-Saturday
9.00 a.m.-5.30 p.m.
H.P.W.WM.D.A.BC.

BRISTOL   Tel. (0272) 750045
TRYMWOOD SERVICES
2a DOWNS PARK EAST (off North View)
WESTBURY PARK
Open: 8.30 a.m.-5.30 p.m. Mon. to Fri.
Closed for lunch 1.00-2.00 p.m.
P.W.WM.T.A.BC.

**Read Model Engineer
for a new angle on
construction & design**

BRISTOL   Tel. (0272) 667013
WILLIS
157 WEST STREET
BEDMINSTER
Open Mon.-Fri. 8.30 a.m.-5.00 p.m.
P.W.WM.D.CS.A.BC.

BERKSHIRE

READING   Tel. Littlewick Green
DAVID HUNT (TOOL   2743
MERCHANTS) LTD   ★
KNOWL HILL, NR. READING
Open: Monday-Saturday
9.00 a.m.-5.30 p.m.
H.P.W.D.A.BC.

READING   Tel. Reading 661511
WOKINGHAM TOOL CO. LTD.
99 WOKINGHAM ROAD

Open: Mon-Sat 9.00 a.m.-5.30 p.m.
Closed 1.00-2.00 p.m. for lunch
H.P.W.WM.D.CS.A.BC.

SLOUGH   Tel: (06286) 5125
BRAYWOOD ESTATES LTD.   ★
158 BURNHAM LANE
Open: 9.00am-5.30pm.
Monday-Saturday.
H.P.W.WM.CS.A.

BUCKINGHAMSHIRE

MILTON KEYNES   Tel. (0908)
POLLARD WOODWORKING   641366
CENTRE   ★
51 AYLESBURY ST., BLETCHLEY
Open: Mon.-Fri. 8.30-5.30
Saturday 9.00-5.00
H.P.W.WM.D.CS.A.BC.   **INCA**

BUCKINGHAMSHIRE

HIGH WYCOMBE   Tel. (0494)
ISAAC LORD LTD.   22221
185 DESBOROUGH ROAD   KE
Open: Mon.-Fri. 8.00 a.m. to 5.30 p.m.
Saturday 8.30 a.m. to 5.00 p.m.
H.P.W.D.A.WM.MF.

HIGH WYCOMBE   Tel. (0494)
SCOTT SAWS LTD.   24201/33788
14 BRIDGE STREET   ★
Mon.-Sat. 8.30 a.m.-6.00 p.m.
H.P.W.WM.D.T.CS.MF.A.BC.

CAMBRIDGESHIRE

CAMBRIDGE   Tel: (0223) 63132
D. MACKAY LTD.   ★
BRITANNIA WORKS, EAST ROAD
Open: Mon.-Fri. 8.30 a.m.-1 p.m./2.00-
5.00 p.m. Sat. 8.30 a.m.-1.00 p.m.
H.P.W.D.T.CS.MF.A.BC.

CAMBRIDGE   Tel. (0223) 247386
H. B. WOODWORKING   K
105 CHERRY HINTON ROAD
Open: 8.30 a.m.-5.30 p.m.
Monday-Friday
8.30 a.m.-1.00 p.m. Sat.
H.P.W.WM.D.CS.A.MF.BC.

PETERBOROUGH   Tel. (0733)
WILLIAMS DISTRIBUTORS   64252
(TOOLS) LIMITED   K
108-110 BURGHLEY ROAD
Open: Monday to Friday
8.30 a.m.-5.30 p.m.
H.P.A.W.D.WH.BC.

CHESHIRE

NANTWICH   Tel. Crewe 67010
ALAN HOLTHAM   K★
THE OLD STORES TURNERY
WISTASON ROAD, WILLASTON
Open: Tues.-Fri. 9.00 a.m.-5.30 p.m.
Sat. 9.00 a.m.-5.00 p.m. Closed Monday.
P.W.WM.D.T.C.CS.A.BC.

WIDNES   Tel: 051 424 4545/7965
THE POWER TOOL CENTRE   ★
54/58 VICTORIA ROAD, WA8 7RJ
Mon.-Fri. 8.30am-5pm.
Sat. 8.30am-4pm.

H.P.W.WM.D.CS.A.BC.

CLEVELAND

MIDDLESBROUGH   Tel. (0642)
CLEVELAND WOODCRAFT   813103
(M'BRO), 38-42 CRESCENT ROAD   K

Open: Mon.-Sat. 9.15 a.m.-5.30 p.m.

H.P.A.BC.W.WM.CS.D.

CORNWALL

SOUTH WEST Power Tools
CORNWALL   Tel: Helston (03265) 4961
HELSTON AND LAUNCESTON   Launceston
(0566) 4781
H.P.W.WM.D.CS.A.   K

CUMBRIA

CARLISLE   Tel: (0228) 36391
W. M. PLANT
ALLENBROOK ROAD
ROSEHILL, CA1 2UT
Open: Mon.-Fri. 8.00 a.m.-5.15 p.m.
Sat. 8.00 a.m.-12.30 noon
P.W.WM.D.CS.A.

DEVON

BRIXHAM   Tel. (08045) 4900
WOODCRAFT SUPPLIES   E★
4 HORSE POOL STREET
Open: Mon.-Sat. 9.00 a.m.-6.00 p.m.
H.P.W.A.D.MF.CS.BC.

PLYMOUTH   Tel. (0752) 330303
WESTWARD BUILDING SERVICES   ★
LTD., LISTER CLOSE, NEWNHAM
INDUSTRIAL ESTATE, PLYMPTON
Open: Mon-Fri 8.00 a.m.-5.30 p.m.
Sat. 8.30 a.m.-12.30 p.m.
H.P.W.WM.D.A.BC.

PLYMOUTH   Tel. (0752) 665363
F.T.B. LAWSON LTD.
71 NEW GEORGE STREET
PLYMOUTH PL1 1RB
Open: Mon.-Sat. 8.30 am-5.30 pm.
H.P.W.CS.MF.A.

DORSET

WEYMOUTH   Tel. (0305) 770303
WEYMOUTH HIRE & SALES LTD.   K
5 KENT CLOSE
GRANBY INDUSTRIAL ESTATE
Open 7.30 a.m. - 5.30 p.m. Mon.-Fri.
Sat. 8 a.m. - 1 p.m.
H.P.W.WM.D.CS.A.K.

ESSEX

LEIGH ON SEA   Tel. (0702)
MARSHAL & PARSONS LTD.   710404
1111 LONDON ROAD   EK
Open: 8.30 a.m.-5.30 p.m. Mon-Fri
9.00 a.m.-5.00 p.m. Sat.
H.P.W.WM.D.CS.A.

ILFORD   Tel: 597 7461
CUTWELL WOODWORKING   ★
776 HIGH ROAD
GOODMAYES IG3 8SY
H.P.W.WM.D.CS.A.

GLOUCESTER

**Advertise here to
capture both local
+ national markets**

HAMPSHIRE

ALDERSHOT   SOUTHAMPTON
(0252) 334422   (0703) 332288
BURCH & HILLS POWER TOOL CENTRES
374 HIGH ST.   7 BELVIDERE RD.
Open Mon.-Fri. 8.30-5.30. Sat. 8.30-12.00
Closed for Lunch 1.00-2.00
H.P.W.WM.D.CS.MF.BC.K.★

HERTFORDSHIRE

01-437 0699
= RESULTS

ENFIELD   Tel: 01-363 2935
GILL & HOXBY LTD.
131-137 ST. MARKS ROAD ADJ.
BUSH HILL PARK STATION, EN1 1BA
Mon.-Sat. 8-5.30
Early closing Wed. 1 p.m.
H.P.A.M.MC.T.S.W.

WARE   Tel: (0920) 870 230
HEATH SAWS   870 636
6 LEESIDE WORKS   K★
STANSTEAD ABBOTTS (near Ware) HERTS.
SG12 8DL.
Open: Mon.-Fri. 8.30 a.m.-5.30 p.m.
Sat. 8.30 a.m.-1 p.m. Sunday by appointment.
H.P.W.WM.D.T.CS.MF.A.BC.★K

HUMBERSIDE

GRIMSBY   Tel. Grimsby (0472)
58741 Hull (0482) 26999
J. E. SIDDLE LTD. (Tool Specialists)   ★
83 VICTORIA STREET
Open: Mon-Fri 8.30 a.m.-5.30 p.m.
Sat. 8.30 a.m.-12.45 p.m. & 2 p.m.-5 p.m.
H.P.A.BC.W.WMD.

HULL
HUMBERSIDE FACTORING/H.F.C.
SAW SERVICING LTD.
MAIN STREET
Open: Mon.-Fri. 8am-5pm.
Saturday 8am-12.00pm.
H.P.W.WM.D.CS.A.BC.K.

shopguide

KENT

MAIDSTONE Tel. (0622) 50177
SOUTH EASTERN SAWS (Ind.) LTD. ★
COLDRED ROAD
PARKWOOD INDUSTRIAL ESTATE
Open: Mon.-Fri. 8.00 a.m.-5.00 p.m.
Sat. 9.00 a.m.-12.00 a.m.
B.C.W.CS.WM.PH.

MAIDSTONE Tel. (0622) 44350
HENSON AND PLATT
TOKE PLACE
LINTON
Open Mon.-Fri. 8.00 a.m.-5.00 p.m.
Saturday 8.00 a.m.-1.00 p.m.
H.P.W.T.CS.A.

LANCASHIRE

PRESTON Tel. (0772) 52951
SPEEDWELL TOOL COMPANY E★
62-68 MEADOW STREET PR1 1SU
Open: Mon.-Fri. 8.30 a.m.-5.30 p.m.
Sat. 8.30 a.m.-12.30 p.m.
H.P.W.WM.CS.A.MF.BC.

ROCHDALE Tel. (0706) 342123/
C.S.M. TOOLS 342322
4-6 HEYWOOD ROAD E★
CASTLETON
Open: Mon-Sat 9.00 a.m.-6.00 p.m.
Sundays by appointment
W.D.CS.A.BC.

LANCASTER Tel. (0524) 32886
LILE TOOL SHOP K
43/45 NORTH ROAD
Open: Monday to Saturday
9.00 a.m.-5.30 p.m.
Wed. 9.00 a.m.-12.30 p.m.
H.P.W.D.A.

All shops with an
asterisk *
have a Mail Order
Service

BLACKPOOL Tel. (0253) 28262
FYLDE WOODTURNING SUPPLIES ★
255 CHURCH STREET, FY1 3PB
Open: 9.30-5.30 Monday to Friday.
9.30-4.30 Saturday. Closed Wednesday.
H.T.W.WM.A.MF.BC.D.

LONDON

ACTON Tel. (01-992) 4835
A. MILLS (ACTON) LTD. ★
32/36 CHURCHFIELD ROAD W3 6ED
Open: Mon.-Fri. 8.32 a.m.-5.30 p.m.
Saturdays 9.00 a.m.-1.00 p.m.
H.P.W.WM.

LONDON Tel. 01-723 2295-6-7
LANGHAM TOOLS LIMITED
13 NORFOLK PLACE
LONDON W2 1QJ

LONDON

FULHAM Tel: (01-636) 6109
I. GRIZARD LTD. E
84a-b-c LILLIE ROAD, SW6 1TL
Open: Mon.-Sat. 9.00-5.30 p.m.
Half day Thursday
H.P.A.BC.W.CS.WM.D.

**Read Model Engineer
for a new angle on
construction & design**

**Use this space
for your
Summer Plans**

MANCHESTER

MANCHESTER Tel. (061 789)
TIMMS TOOLS 0909
102-104 LIVERPOOL ROAD ★
PATRICROFT M30 0WZ
Weekdays 9.00 a.m.-5.30 p.m.
Sat. 9.00 a.m.-1.00 p.m.
H.P.A.W.

MANCHESTER Tel: 061 834 0714
TILL AND WHITEHEAD ★
ELLESMERE STREET, M15 4JX
Open: Mon.-Fri. 8.00 a.m.-5.00 p.m.
H.P.W.A.BC.

MERSEYSIDE

LIVERPOOL Tel. (051-207) 2967
TAYLOR BROS (LIVERPOOL) LTD K
195-199 LONDON ROAD
LIVERPOOL L3 8JG
Open: Monday to Friday
8.30 a.m.-5.30 p.m.
H.P.W.WM.D.A.BC.

MIDDLESEX

RUISLIP Tel. (08956) 74126
ALLMODELS ENGINEERING LTD. E★
91 MANOR WAY
Open: Mon-Sat 9.00 a.m.-5.30 p.m.
H.P.W.A.D.CS.MF.BC.

NORFOLK

NORWICH Tel. (0603) 898695
NORFOLK SAW SERVICES
DOG LANE, HORSFORD
Open: Monday to Friday
8.00 a.m.-5.00 p.m.
Saturday 8.00 a.m.-12.00 p.m.
H.P.W.WM.D.CS.A.

KINGS LYNN Tel. (0553) 772443
WALKER & ANDERSON (Kings Lynn) LTD.
WINDSOR ROAD, KINGS LYNN
Open: Monday to Saturday
7.45 a.m.-5.15 p.m.
H.P.W.WM.D.CS.A.

NORFOLK

NORWICH Tel. (0603) 400933
WESTGATES WOODWORKING Tx
61 HURRICANE WAY, 975412
NORWICH AIRPORT INDUSTRIAL ESTATE
Open: 9.00 a.m.-5.00 p.m. weekdays
9.00 a.m.-12.30 Sat.
P.W.WM.D.BC. K

KINGS LYNN Tel. 07605 674
NORFOLK WOODTURNING CENTRE ★
UNIT A, HILL FARM WORKSHOPS
GREAT DUNHAM (Nr. Swaffham)
Tues.-Sat. 9.00am-5.30pm
H.P.W.D.T.MF.A.BC.

NORTHAMPTONSHIRE

RUSHDEN Tel. (0933) 56424
PETER CRISP OF RUSHDEN ★
7-11 HIGH STREET
Mon.-Fri. 8.30-12.30/1.30-5.30
Thurs. 8.30-1.00. Sat all day.
H.P.W.WM.D.M.F.A.K.

NOTTINGHAMSHIRE

NOTTINGHAM Tel. (0602) 225979
POOLEWOOD and 227064/5
EQUIPMENT LTD. (06077) 2421 after hrs
5a HOLLY LANE, CHILLWELL
Open: Mon-Fri 9.00 a.m.-5.30 p.m.
Sat. 9.00 a.m. to 12.30 p.m.
P.W.WM.D.CS.A.BC.

OXON

WITNEY Tel. (0993) 76431
TARGET TOOLS (SALES, OXON
TARGET HIRE & REPAIRS) ★
TOOLS SWAIN COURT
STATION INDUSTRIAL ESTATE
Open: Mon.-Sat. 8.00 a.m.-5.00 p.m.
24 hour Answerphone
BC.W.M.A.

SHROPSHIRE

TELFORD Tel. Telford (0952)
ASLES LTD 48054
VINEYARD ROAD, WELLINGTON EK★
Open: Mon. Fri. 8.30 a.m.-5.30 p.m.
Saturday 8.30 a.m.-4.00 p.m.
H.P.W WM.D.CS.BC.A.

SOMERSET

TAUNTON Tel. (0823) 335431
JOHN HALL TOOLS ★
6 HIGH STREET
Open Monday-Saturday
9.00 a.m.-5.30 p.m.
H.P.W.WM.D.CS.A.

**Read 'Model
Engineer' for a
new angle on
construction & design**

STAFFORDSHIRE

TAMWORTH Tel. (0827) 56188
MATTHEWS BROTHERS LTD. K★
KETTLEBROOK ROAD
Open: Mon.-Sat. 8.30-5.30 p.m.
Demonstrations Sunday mornings by
appointment only
H.P.WM.D.T.CS.A.BC.K.

SUFFOLK

**All shops with an
asterisk ★
have a Mail Order
Service**

IPSWICH Tel. (0473) 40456
FOX WOODWORKING 463884
142-144 BRAMFORD LANE ★
Open: Tues.-Fri. 9 a.m.-5.30 p.m.
Sat. 9 a.m.-5 p.m.
W.WM.D.T.CS.MF.A.BC.K.*

SUSSEX

WORTHING Tel. (0903) 38739
W. HOSKING LTD (TOOLS & KE★
MACHINERY)
28 PORTLAND RD, BN11 1QN
Open: Mon.-Sat. 8.30 a.m.-5.30 p.m.
Closed Wednesday
H.P.W.WM.D.CS.A.BC.

TYNE & WEAR

NEWCASTLE-UPON-TYNE ★
J. W. HOYLE LTD
CLARENCE STREET
NEWCASTLE-UPON-TYNE
TYNE & WEAR
NE2 17J
H.P.W.WM.D.CS.A.BC.K.

W. MIDLANDS

WOLVERHAMPTON Tel. (0902)
MANSAW SERVICES 58759
WARD STREET, HORSELEY FIELDS K★
WOLVERHAMPTON, WEST MIDLANDS
Open Mon.-Fri. 9.00am-5.00pm
Sat. 8am-3pm
H.P.W.WM.A.D.CS.

YORKSHIRE

THIRSK Tel. (0845) 22770
THE WOOD SHOP ★
TRESKE SAWMILLS LTD.
STATION WORKS
Open: Seven days a week 9.00-5.00
T.H.MF.BC.H.

SHEFFIELD Tel. (0742) 441012
GREGORY & TAYLOR LTD KE
WORKSOP ROAD
Open: 8.30 a.m.-5.30 p.m.
Monday-Friday
8.30 a.m.-12.30 p.m. Sat.
H.P.W.WM.D.

HARROGATE Tel. (0423) 505328/
MULTI-TOOLS 66245
158 KINGS ROAD K★
Open: Monday to Saturday
8.30 a.m.-6.00 p.m.
H.P.W.WM.D.A.BC.

HOLME UPON Tel. (0696) 60612
SPALDING MOOR
CRAFT TOOLS AND TACKLE LTD.
HOLME INDUSTRIAL ESTATE
Open: Mon.-Fri. 9.00 am-5.30 p.m.
Saturday & Bank Holiday 9.00 am-4.30 pm
H.P.W.D.T.CS.MF.A.BC.

WOOD SUPPLIERS

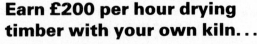

Classified Advertisements

FOR SALE

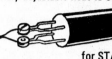

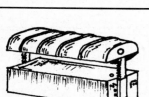

MIDLANDS SCHOOL OF FRENCH POLISHING

LEARN THE TRADE
5 days or longer courses.
OPEN DAY Saturday July 18th, 10am until 4pm.
Everyone welcome.

SAE to:
Mr. A. V. Fry DLC, LCG, M CollP
**18A Mansfield Road,
Eastwood, Notts.
(0773) 715911** after 5pm

TAKE A BREAK
from the noise and dust of your workshop.
Green-Woodwork Courses
using pole-lathes, shaving-horses and hand tools. Courses this summer working in the woods.
MIKE ABBOTT
159 Cotswold Road, Windmill Hill, Bristol BS3 4PH or phone (0272) 636244

EXPERT TUITION

Peter Hibbard's creative woodcarving, woodturning and sculpture courses.
SAE for brochure.
Old School Arts Workshop, Middleham, Leyburn, North Yorkshire DL8 4QG or Phone: Wensleydale (0969) 23056

MERSEYSIDE'S COMPLETE WORLD OF WOODTURNING

Two day courses by Ray Jones demonstrator of Tyme lathes £25 per day, 3 students or for locals evening tuition 7-10. £3 per hour. Shop open for Tyme lathes and accessories. Sorby tools turning blanks and sundries plus gifts. For details ring **051-420-3379** or write to: **Dept. WW, The Baluster, 102 High Street, Wavertree, Liverpool 15.** *Free Saturday tuition with every lathe sold.*

WOODTURNING COURSES

2 Day courses, mid-week or weekend. Expert personal tuition in modern well equipped workshop. Comfortable accommodation available in pleasant surroundings.
SAE for details to
Cliff Willetts, Gables, Frisby On The Wreake, Melton Mowbray, Leics.
Tel: Rotherby (066 475) 246

WOODWORKER = RESULTS

WOODTURNING IN NORTH WALES
Courses, Beginner/Intermediate, weekdays/weekends ● Turning blanks in natural/exotic finishing materials. Tyme lathes & accessories.
Keith Lawrence, Old Stables Turnery, Tri Thy Centre, Coed Talon, Nr. Mold, Clwyd. Tel: 0352 771771.

Creative Woodcarving
Courses in Cornwall.
Beautiful Helford River Area.
Experienced Instructor & Craftsman offers short courses ideal for beginners in carving. Tuition limited to three students per course and each receives a detailed 50 page carving manual. Beautiful Helford River area.
Details from: **Jeremy Williams,** Sycamore Cottage, Trabae, St. Martin, Helston, Cornwall TR12 6EA.
Tel: 032-623-609

CRAFT WOODTURNING
A two-day residential woodturning course for beginners in a fully modernised 17th century Devon coaching inn. Teaching limited to two students per course, accommodation for families if required.
S.A.E. for brochure to:
Oliver Plant, Hartford Barton, Gittisham, Honiton, Devon, EX14 0AW or **Phone Honiton 44155.**

WOODTURNING COURSES
One and two day Woodturning Courses in a fully equipped studio, under the expert tuition of:
ALLAN BATTY
Maximum of 2 students
Please write or phone for details.
Allan McNair Woodturning Studio
St. James Sq. Boroughbridge N. Yorks YO5 9AR
Telephone (09012) 4064

JOHN GOLDER
Woodturning courses day/evening.
Personal tuition with Registered Professional Turner in fully equipped workshop.
**76 Burntwood Road, Norton, Canes, Cannock, Staffs.
Telephone (0543) 79137**
On the register of the Worshipful Company of Turners.
Demonstrator for Liberon Waxes.

NEED TO IMPROVE YOUR SKILL in cabinet making, Antique restoration or Polishing? Come on one of my courses and benefit from 25 years trade experience. Details: Barry Honeyborne, Whyle Cottage, Pudleston, Leominster, Herefordshire.

GORDON STOKES
Author of six books on woodturning, international demonstrator, and long established instructor, offers two day, one day, or hourly tuition for beginners. Maximum three students. No previous knowledge required. Benefit from forty years practical experience. More than two thousand satisfied students. Ring us on BATH (0225) 22617, or send S.A.E. (A4 size) for full details to:
202 THE HOLLOW, BATH, AVON BA2 1NG.
Act today – start a creative and lucrative hobby.

FULL TIME COURSES
IN FINE CABINET MAKING
David Savage FURNITURE MAKER
Two places exist for a one year course, leading to work of exhibition quality
FOR PROSPECTUS APPLY TO:
DAVID SAVAGE CABINET MAKING
21 WESTCOMBE, BIDEFORD, DEVON EX39 3JQ

KINDLY MENTION THE MARKET LEADER "WOODWORKER" WHEN REPLYING TO ADVERTISEMENTS

Woodworker

Lineage 52p per word (inc. VAT). Minimum £7.80. Semi-display £8.60 per single column + VAT. Minimum 2.5 x 1. No reimbursements for cancellations. All ads must be pre-paid.
Write your advert in BLOCK CAPITALS in the grid below, ticking the section you wish it to appear under, INCLUDING YOUR NAME AND ADDRESS IN THE WORD COUNT and send it to: 'WOODWORKER', ASP ADVERTISEMENT DEPARTMENT, No. 1 GOLDEN SQUARE, LONDON W1R 3AB.

☐ W/S/E	☐ FOR SALE	☐ MATERIALS & FINISHES	☐ WOOD SUPPLIES	☐ COURSES	☐ PLEASE STATE

CLASSIFIED COUPON

ALL CLASSIFIED ADVERTISEMENTS MUST BE PRE-PAID. THERE ARE NO REIMBURSEMENTS FOR CANCELLATIONS.

I enclose my Cheque/Postal Order* for £.............. for .... insertions, made payable to Argus Specialist Publications. (*Delate as necessary) or
Please debit my Access/Barclaycard No.

Expiry Date

£ .... for .... insertions.

Name ....
Address ....
.... Post Code ....
Day Time Tel. No. ....
Signature .... Date ....

IF YOU DO NOT WISH TO CUT YOUR MAGAZINE, PHOTOCOPY THIS FORM

Woodworker

CONTENTS

design . . . craft . . . and the love of wood

August 1987
Vol. 91
No. 8

FEATURES

PROJECTS

REGULARS

*On the cover: delights from the Bristol Show – see p666.
Above: a classic design by Carl Malmsten, founder of the 'Swedish School' – p654*

Editor Aidan Walker
Deputy editor John Hemsley
Assistant editor Kerry Fowler
Advertisement manager Trevor Pryer
Advertisement production Laura Champion
Graphics Jeff Hamblin/ASP Design Studio
Technical illustrator Peter Holland
Guild of Woodworkers John Hemsley, Kerry Fowler

Unfortunately we cannot accept responsibility for loss of or damage to unsolicited material. We reserve the right to refuse or suspend advertisements, and regret we cannot guarantee the bone fides of advertisers.
Published every third Friday

Editorial, advertisements and Guild of Woodworkers
1 Golden Square, London W1R 3AB, telephone 01-437 0626

ABC
UK circulation
Jan-Dec 86
32,849

Back issues and subscriptions Infonet Ltd, 10-13 Times House, 179 Marlowes, Hemel Hempstead, Herts HP1 1BB; telephone Hemel Hempstead (0442) 48434

Subscriptions per year UK £16.90; overseas outside USA (accelerated surface post) £21.00, USA (accelerated surface post) $28, airmail £48

UK trade SM Distribution Ltd, 16-18 Trinity Gardens, London SW9 8DX; telephone 01-274 8611

North American trade Bill Dean Books Ltd, 151-49 7th Avenue, PO Box 69, Whitestone, New York 11357; tel. 1-718-767-6632
Printed by Chase Web, Plymouth
Mono origination Multiform Photosetting Ltd, Cardiff
Colour origination Derek Croxson Ltd, Chesham, Bucks
© Argus Specialist Publications Ltd 1987
ISSN 0043 776X

Application to mail at Second Class rates is pending at Rahway N.J., USA. Postmaster: send address corrections to Woodworker, c/o Mercury Airfreight International Ltd Inc, 10B Englehard Ave, Avenel, NJ 07001.

Argus Specialist Publications Ltd

1 Golden Square, London W1R 3AB; 01-437 0626

This month

New Spirit in Craft and Design —
yes, it's here, love it or hate it.
People like Daniel Reynolds,
whose work appears **above**,
apparently see a sturdy, textural
approach as more important than
joints that fit like a glove. Multi-
discipline Crafts Council
exhibition until 6 September, 12
Waterloo Place, London SW1, 01-
930 4811

Visual function Winners of the WOODWORKER Award
for Products in Wood at the Direct Design Show, **Imperial
Woodworks'** outrageous, extreme, delicate, decorated
pieces . . . selection for November's show 01-587 0256

NEWS

Mixed reception for the **London International Furniture
Show** from exhibitors . . . business was up, attendance slightly
down, and the experimental 'public days' were also popular
with some traders, unpopular with others — staying the extra
days didn't seem worth the business to all. All nine Production/Management students on
the **London College of Furniture**'s stand have been
offered jobs on the strength of their work . . .

The CBI and MSC commissioned a **survey** among more
than 1000 industrial companies, and 61% of furniture manufacturers polled said that **skill
shortage** was limiting their output. **Carpenters and
joiners** are at the top of the 'wanted' list . . . Compared to
1984 and 1985 the shortage is no worse, but the demand is now
greater.

Which may or may not be relevant to the **Skill Olympics**,
international apprentices competition to be held at the
National Exhibition Centre in Birmingham in September
1989. Skill-UK aims to improve the quality of skills training in
this country; drawing its team from national skills competitions, this co-ordinating body
works with Britain's industrial training boards and other bodies
to select and train the entrants. More details from the Director,
Skill-UK, 2 Beverley Gdns, Westbury-on-Trym, Bristol
BS9 3PR, (0272) 683604.

After you've read 'Eastenders' in this issue, the story of two energetic young firms in London's
embattled **East End furniture industry**, hie yourself to the
Geffrye Museum in Kingsland Rd, London E2, to view the
delights of 'The East London Furniture Trade 1830s-1980s'
an **exhibition** about just that. Drawing on the museum's
reserve collections and loans from local people, the exhibition
uses specific pieces to illustrate the chequered story; garret and
alley workshops in Bethnal Green, aircraft manufacture in
the First World War, Utility furniture in the second, right
through to the young designers of today. 01-739 9893.

Brave Son of Thor, 80-year old Viking-style boat, is the centre-
piece of York's 'Viking Ships' exhibition, St. Saviour's Centre.
(0904) 643211

Swanning in Sweden

John Green, winner of last year's Sjöberg 'Workbench of the future' competition, reports on his prize trip to Sweden and Sjöberg-land:

Sjöberg invited not just me but my wife and two children, all expenses paid, to stay in an excellent country hotel in Sweden — what an interesting and pleasant trip we had. The executives from Sjöberg were very kind and not only showed us round the factory but the local towns, countryside, and tourist attractions.

The Sjöberg complex is in the small village of Stockaryd, quite near to Huskvarna of chain-saw fame. Mr Weine Karlsson and Mr Olle Ringefelt looked after us, and the whole family went round the plant, in the board-room — everywhere. Indeed, Olle Ringefelt described Sjöbergs' 60-strong workforce as a family rather than employees. Mr Sjöberg himself lives only five minutes from the factory and Weine and Olle are neighbours in Vrigstad. That's the way it is in Sweden.

We examined the complete range of Sjöberg benches in the showroom, including the model I use at home, which of course was the other part of the competition prize. The quality and attention to detail were impressive everywhere we went. The rings in the timber Sjöberg use were so close together you could hardly see them, such is the quality. During the laminating operation to make the bench tops, a special humidifier machine keeps the environment at the optimum for gluing, double-checked every hour by a technician. The bench reminded me of one of the 'Workbench of the future' ideas, and I realised that maybe Sjöberg are already there, so to speak.

Sjöberg have been supplying the Swedish schools' wood and workbench requirements for decades and from the age of seven, youngsters are taught good practice using specially made small workbenches. We were shown the complete range of Wolfcraft tools that Sjöberg market which are all compatible for use with the workbenches.

Weine took us to see local craftspeople — woodworkers, potters, glass-makers and knitters — at work in a craft village where the atmosphere was friendly and relaxed. Sjöberg employ some mentally handicapped people and one day we dropped in for lunch at their residence, Loevängen. Weine said he and his colleagues often eat there and it inspired me how these busy men cared for their community.

Too soon it was time to go home to England. Our travel arrangements worked like clockwork, thanks to Geoff Brown of Brimarc and his careful planning and advice. Weine and Olle told us that the competition had been valuable to them — and of the high opinion they have for WOODWORKER and its English readers.

As a Cornishman, I say thank you one and all for a unique trip combining the best of a business, education and holiday into a wonderful experience.

Diary

Guild courses are shown by an asterisk(*); for further details see Guild pages

July
18-19 **French Polishing** Ian Hosker*
18 **Open Day, Midland School of French Polishing**, Eastwood, Notts. (0773) 715911
19 **Model Horse-drawn Vehicle Club Show**, College Farm, 45 Fitzalan Rd, Finchley, London N3
22-13 Sept **Alvar Aalto Exhibition**, Victoria & Albert Museum, London SW7

30-2 Aug **Green Wood Working** Jack Hill, Mike Abbot*

August
2-5 **BFM Furniture Show**, G-MEX Centre, Manchester, contact 01-724 0854
3-5 Sept **Cubic Metre Furniture Exhibition**, Design Centre, 29 Haymarket, London SW1, 01-839 8000
16-19 **Scottish Furniture Exhibition**, Scottish Exhibition Centre, Glasgow, (041) 5541317
31 **Islwyn Craft Fair 87**, Waunfawr Pk, Crosskeys, Gwent (0495) 226622, Ext. 2367

30-30 Sept **The Working Woodland Exhibition**, Parnham House, Beaminster, Dorset DT8 3NA (0308) 862204

September
12-13 **Decorative Techniques** Ian Hosker*
17-18 **French Polishing** Charles Cliffe*
19-20 **Basic Carving** Eric Ingham*
26 **Design and workshop drawing** Bob Grant*

October
2-4 **Festival of Ecclesiastical Crafts**, Salisbury Cathedral, exhibitors' en-quiries: J. Davis, Yew Tree Lodge, Minchington, Blandford, Dorset OT11 8DH
2-4 **Heart of England Craft Market**, Sports Centre, University of Keele, Stoke-on-Trent (0920) 870040
21 **Style for Living 87**, furniture show, Earls Court, London 01-385 1200
22-25 **London Woodworker Show**, Alexandra Pavilion, London N22
21-25 **Modern Home 87**, trade and public furniture show, 3f Prince Rupert Hse, 64 Queens St, London EC4R 1AD
25-28 **Design in Furniture**, Olympia, London (trade only)

Shoptalk

NEW PRODUCTS

Dunlop release 'Fast Bond' **Wood Glue**, which they claim reaches high bond strength 15 minutes after application . . . dries clear, suitable for all types of wood.

Zoë Gertner is running five- or six-day **carving courses** in picturesque Somerset; beginners welcome, weekend courses for the more experienced. £90 for the six-day, £75 for the five-day, £30 for the weekend version, including lunches.

Detail Master **pyrographs**, 'used by 70% of decorative decoy duck carvers in the USA', now available — the trick is there's no transformer. £122 introductory price includes two handpieces; suppliers Pintail Decoy Supplies also have a decorative decoy carver's range of equipment, catalogue £1.

Anthony Dew, **rocking-horse** maker and writer, featured in WOODWORKER May 1986, has been putting together attractive **plan packs** for would-be rocking-horse creators; he also has a range of accessories you need — eyes, saddles, tails and other pieces of non-timber-based anatomy. Further, plans for bowed psaltery, hammered dulcimer, and carver's chops. Toddler's rocking-horse plan £4.49 plus £1 p&p, small carved traditional rocking-horse plan £5.99 plus £1 p&p; they have drawings, full colour pix of the finished item, and some colour pix of the step-by-step too.

● Dunlop Adhesives, Chester Rd, Birmingham B35 7AL, 021-373 8101: Zoë Gertner, Deans Cottage, Bagley, Wedmore, Somerset, (0934) 712679: Pintail Decoy Supplies, 20 Sheppenhall Grove, Aston Heath, Nantwich, Cheshire CW5 8DF, (0270) 780056: Anthony Dew, the Rocking Horse Shop, Holme upon Spalding Moor, York YO44AB, (0696) 60563.

Dust extraction for the big Elu routers is here (**above left**): this is a prototype plate, the real thing is transparent. Kit £29+VAT. Elu, West Point, The Grove, Slough SL1 1QQ, (0753) 74277. See 'Suck it and see' in this issue. **Above right**, production turning, all sorts of marvels with Hapfo automatic **copying lathes** from Pollards, 51 Aylesbury St, Bletchley, Milton Keynes MK2 2BQ, (0908) 641492

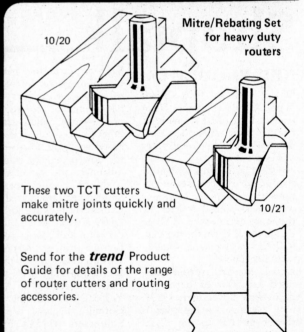

The Swedish School

Carl Malmsten is one of the greatest names in Swedish furniture, a designer whose influence is subtle and widespread. Philip Livsey saw an exhibition of work by students from the School of Fine Woodworking that bears his name

The Nordiska Museet, in Stockholm, Sweden, which displays the social and cultural activities of the Swedes, last year put on an exhibition by the Carl Malmsten School of Fine Woodworking. Among the 18 items on show were renovated furniture and musical instruments, but I shall concentrate on the cabinetmakers.

All the items were so-called journeyman's testpieces, made during the last period of the students' two-year course at the school. The testpiece is regulated by the Ministry of Education in co-operation with the Small Craftsmen's Association, and points are awarded for difficulty in execution, nicety in workmanship, finish and time taken. The students have a nominally free hand in deciding what they are going to make, and from what, but the way they tackle it is interesting.

Olle Pira, the Principal, told me: 'In this school we want the products to come from the feeling in the hands, the ability of the hand to form, and the flair of the student. We don't want them to draft hard, flat furniture. What they produce must come from their imagination and sensitiveness to the wood, using it as the initial source of inspiration. So when they have made a few sketches, decided more or less what they want to make and have talked about it amongst themselves and with their instructors, the first real bit of spadework is started — making a small-scale model. Here they can see the volumes, correct them and find the right form. We don't have the capacity or time in two years to teach them how to draw furniture and get it right from there, but we have the capacity to make it.'

▲ Traditional writing table

Jonas Grundell copied a writing table with a built-on writing case, originally made by a Swedish court cabinetmaker around 1760. Jonas got plenty of experience with curves and veneering, but on the other hand, he didn't have to think up a design of his own. Unfortunately, he lost quite a few marks because it took him too long. This is probably a bit unfair, since to be fast on veneering one has to be a real 'pro' with years of experience, and of course there is a lot more pure hand work in it.

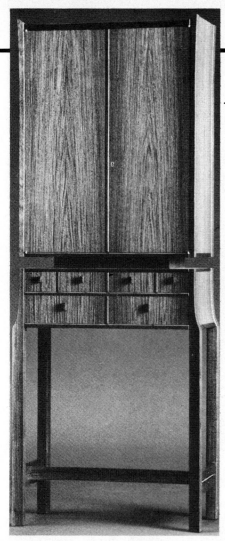

◀ Modern cabinet

Olof Salmonsson designed his own cabinet. The concavely curved sides and front of the upper unit are reminiscent of Krenov (also once a pupil at the school) and in this case they bring it alive and take away its massiveness. On its plinth above the lower unit it has a life of its own, its own personality. Putting it on a stand illustrates how difficult it can be to get forms to harmonise — maybe it's because the curves on the upper unit have no counterpart in the lower.

'Stockholm' cabinet ▶

Leif Burman didn't go too far away from Malmsten with his cabinet in mahogany and jacaranda, although the curved sides and straight legs give it a very different feel. The inlaying makes this a showpiece, giving the viewer glimpses of 'The Queen of Lake Malaren' (Stockholm) in her fair summer robes. Surprisingly, Leif doesn't profess to be much of an artist. 'I went around town and took a lot of pictures. Then I copied them on to paper and finally made up a composition. What I enjoy is sawing out the figures, matching the woods from the veneers I have collected and the practical side of it generally. Of course, it would be better if I could draw a design myself.'

◀ Malmsten cabinet

Olaf Paulsson copied one of Carl Malmsten's cabinets, which gives a good idea of Malmsten's admirable sense of proportion. Of course, this is a 'classic'; one can hardly call the design spectacular, but related to the products of the 30s and 40s it must have made a big impact on furniture architecture. The inlaying is very attractive and well cut in this case, but with its bold 'Argentina' motif in sharply contrasting woods (also designed by Malmsten) it has a tendency to dominate its surroundings. The doors and joints, as well as the gentle sigh each drawer gives as it's pushed in, all contributed to the impression of near perfection.

Oak tool cupboard ▶

This beautifully made Japanese oak cupboard is by Frode-Björn Henriksson. Not only did he make the cupboard, he also made a set of hand-tools (excluding the irons) to put in it: put your hands round one of his planes, and it feels just right. This is a living-room piece: one couldn't possibly condemn such a handsome piece of furniture to be knocked about in the workshop.

▲ Writing desk

Karl-Gustav Jönsson started off by being fascinated with a Japanese joint while browsing over some of the literature at the school, after a seminar on Japanese woodwork. He decided to base his writing table on this joint, which he wanted to show off. Square timber had to be used for it to function. One thing is certain — he didn't make the joints by hand! They were done on the bandsaw — enough of a job in itself, especially when you share it with about 16 other people.

Using this joint in the basic structure of his writing table caused a few problems. One of these was how to fix up the nests of drawers, when each rail of the quite open structure goes straight into the one it's mating with. The idea was to have the drawers directly on top of each other, giving a solid façade and filling in the sides as well. Instead of guiding the drawers in the usual manner with their bottom edges against strips on the frame, there is a rebate on the carrying member which mates with an L-shaped strip on the outside of the drawer.

Display cabinet ▶

This cabinet by Jacob Zeilon in Japanese oak is a typical example of modern design (his own) at its best — solid wood, good proportions, nicely executed and with open joints forming a part of the pleasing appearance. This is a piece of furniture that needs to stand alone. Any other wooden furniture near it will lose its own individuality — unless it's a companion piece. The idea of the cabinet suspended in its frame will require a lot of thought in designing something to match it.

Wall cupboard

Britt Möllerud's wall cupboard, with a bow front and outwardly sloping sides in amarant and pearwood was the most popular item with visitors. The asymmetrical doors were a novel feature, as was the absence of a lock. Her own carefully carved finger grips (they could hardly be called handles) helped, together with a well-cut ivy leaf inlay, give life and character to the front. The reason for the big door is really quite simple — behind it there is a nest of drawers, and of course there is only the need to open one door to get at them.

She got the urge to be a woodworker over six years ago, when she took a summer course at a sister school to the Malmsten School. She says: 'After three weeks there I found that working with wood is exciting. There is such a lot you can do with wood, and there are so many varieties of it!'

One of the problems with her cupboard when she got started on it was that it wasn't difficult enough — a serious matter if you want to get high marks for your test piece (you can't get a bronze medal unless it's classed as 'difficult'). 'I started off having the doors flat, then I had them angled and then I tried them bowed. Happily for me this gave them the most graceful look, especially when I rounded them off at the sides as well. As I've got no supporting stand to give the judges a bit more to go on I was pleased that they looked better when they were more complicated.'

◀ Corner cupboard

Eva Risinger's corner cupboard was my favourite. This is made in maple and padauk to her own design. Partly because of the light maple and the angling of the doors, a photo of it makes it look rather like a bulky Swedish tiled oven. Getting a proper impression of the different volumes (upper cupboard, space, lower cupboard and feet) is very difficult when they are only seen in two dimensions. In this case the model and the mock-up must have been invaluable in getting the proportions exactly right. One only gets this feeling of rightness when standing in front of the finished product.

continued

Eva's background casts some light on her obvious ability to realise an original concept, and also illustrates some of the opportunities available to school 'drop-outs' — Eva's school didn't point her in a direction to take advantage of her individual talent. 'In school I spent most of the time in handicrafts at sewing, when we had woodwork I didn't do enough, just a bookshelf or two, and I didn't work up any interest during these classes. After school I got interested in pottery and went to a school for further adult education for two years and then a bit more at university and then a job in a pottery. Six other girls and I decided we could get no further in courses so we started our own pottery business.

After a while I realised that the other girls, who were older than I, had other trades to fall back on. This made me want a trade of my own too, so I applied to the job centre for a one-year (with wages!) industrial woodworking course.

'We learnt practically nothing about using hand-tools, and later this was rather a handicap for me. Afterwards I got a job in a big shopfitting firm. I was there for two years and learnt a tremendous amount. Then I heard about two girls who had started their own workshop and I thought this was great so I met them and they rented workspace to me. This went on for about six months, but although I was getting enough jobs of my own, the organisation

side of it was a bother, so I said goodbye to them and moved back to southern Sweden, and I had my own workshop for two years.

'I made just enough money to get by on. I took anything that came my way and I was really enjoying myself. I wasn't very good at getting the right shapes, so I did what the customer wanted, and in that way I could see afterwards when it wasn't right, even if it was what the customer wanted.

'I came to Malmsten's for the professional experience. I tried when I finished the trade course, but they wouldn't have me. After I'd had my own firm for two years I had quite a few references and things I could show them, so I got in.' ∎

---

better a woodworker on earth than a shadow in Hades

● **Left**, Malmsten's early work, the 1916 cabinet for Stockholm City Hall.
Right, beauty, grace and comfort in this 1961 Malmsten armchair

Krenov's mentor

He said of himself that he was 'a wood-working apprentice renegading from the upper class'. Born in 1888 of well-situated cosmopolitan parents, Carl Malmsten was a talented student struggling against becoming a professional man when he took his *studentexamen* (A levels) in 1908. After national service and a course in national economics he decided he would 'rather be a woodworker on earth than a shadow in Hades', and became apprenticed to master carpenter Pelle Jönsson in 1910. His breakthrough came with a first and second prize in a competition for writing chairs and desks to be used in Stockholm City Hall, then under construction.

After supplying furniture and designs to public buildings, industries, hotels and exhibitions, both domestic and international, he was awarded a professorship in 1936. In spite of his other activities, or perhaps because of them, he found time and energy to ensure the education and training of people making furniture based on his own ideals. His workshop school started in 1930, and in 1950, after various moves, reorganisation and changes in funding, it moved to its present home as the state-

Carl Malmsten

supported Carl Malmsten School of Fine Woodworking, in a newly erected building for manual trades in Stockholm.

Right up to his death in 1972, he was deeply engaged in promoting his revival and refinement of the art of furniture making, where he neither copied nor broke with tradition, while keeping his furniture to a large extent compatible with the requirements of factory production. Especially after the 30s, it isn't possible to escape the individuality of his particular form language; in the words of an outstanding contemporary: 'Before the eruptive force invested by Malmsten in the forms he created according to his own ideas, all other "isms" and theories of fashion become disrupted. He was his own "ism" from decade to decade.'

In his earliest work, for example the cabinet (still under the Jugend influence) in the Cultural Commissioner's office at the City Hall, to the revolutionary simple furniture of the 40s that was designed for the everyday apartment, he lived up to his motto: 'Beauty and grace are one's lifesblood if one is a true member of human society.'

he was his own 'ism' from decade to decade

Turner's tiff

● *Art, craft or semi-functional sculpture? Mike Darlow's label-defying piece, The Russian Caravan Teapot, sold for £1200*

Controversial woodturner and author Mike Darlow has some contentious views on themes raised by August's woodturning seminar 'From Craft to Art'. We asked organiser Ray Key and co-sponsor Nick Davidson of Craft Supplies and Sorby to reply

The British Woodturning seminar to be held in August has been announced even in the Australian craft press. The seminar is entitled 'From Craft to Art'. I support a rise in the status of woodturning and in the prices which it would therefore command; I support the design and technical innovation implicit in such a title; and I support a freeing of turning from the undesirable tentacles of its trade heritage. But I have doubts about whether the vision conjured up by the theme is particularly relevant, or well-founded.

I doubt whether woodturning is a practice which lends itself to the creation of a significant body of significant art. How many turners in Britain produce pieces which are perceived by non-woodturners as art rather than craft? How many in Australia? How many in America? I suggest that the total could be comfortably accommodated on the fingers of one hand. And this despite the numbers of artists who turn wood and the large production of 'artistic woodturning' by turners who care enough to put in the extra effort.

Some readers may be familiar with a spurious academic timewaster known as 'the arts/crafts debate'. To summarise: artists and their proponents say that craft is intrinsically inferior; craftspeople retort that their work is of no less merit, but that the craft label recalls associations which lower the status and accordingly the price of their work. We could learn from jewellery which refuses to join either camp, calls itself jewellery, and suffers neither status nor image problems as a result. We could simply call woodturning woodturning.

The goal of 'art woodturning' implicit in the Seminar's title will be, I have suggested, unattainable by virtually all attending. Perhaps therefore the Seminar might also consider the present state of British woodturning and its future, of concern to turners and the industry which has grown to supply and inform them. Interestingly, this industry appears much more influential in Britain than in other countries. It also appears to have been very successful, but I wonder if the approaches which have apparently been so fruitful to date may not paradoxically be sowing the seeds of decline.

Let me admit my self-interest. As the author of a woodturning book I am obviously concerned about the long-term health of amateur woodturning. Nevertheless, as one whose hobby and main interest outside work and family is woodturning, the future vigour of the craft is important to me for other than purely material reasons, even though I am resident in Australia.

Woodturning is apparently riding high. Yet from America I learn that sales of all woodturning books are slow, and that after almost two years the American Association of Woodturners has less than 2,000 members (less than one in 150 of the subscribers to the major American woodworking magazine). I have no knowledge of British trends, but wonder whether the surge in popularity may be waning. A reading of relevant British books, magazines and catalogues seems to reveal some worrying trends. A few examples:

Lathes There seems to be an ever-increasing number of hobby lathes on the market. However, with the exception of the Harrison Graduate which appears unchanged even after 30 years, there are apparently not any lathes being produced for the serious hobbyist, let alone professional.

There is little appreciation of the importance of an outboard facility, even for small bowls. Manufacturers, who are surely aware of the vibration-damping properties of cast iron, persist in promoting steel beds, no doubt to cut costs.

Tools HSS tools have been in use by commercial turners in Australia, America and no doubt Britain for decades. Why did the

● **Above**, *wafer-thin burr oak turning by Anthony Bryant.* **Below**, *Cecil Jordan's oval box*

major British turning tool manufacturers take so long to introduce them? Surely it was not ignorance; HSS was discovered in 1868 yet even now, when HSS is the norm and cross-sectional geometry is approaching its pre-World War II soundness, the blades are too short and too weak. So slender now are the gouges that manufacturers dare not grind the flute more than a third of the way along the blade!

Chucks A wide range of excellent quality chucks is now available, but as I shall describe later, the philosophy supporting the introduction of some of them is flawed.

Writing Britain led the English-speaking world in woodturning writing. This lead was further strengthened by Pain in 1956 and Child in 1971. Thereafter British woodturning authors have pitched their writing firmly at an audience they assume to be unskilled, miserably equipped and likely to remain so, uneducated, undiscerning, and without ambition to progress. The average British woodturner may be a beginner in his or her fifties, but it does not therefore follow that he or she has no thirst for knowledge, no wish to rise above mediocrity. Not until Richard Raffan's book (published in America in 1985) has there been an exception. Many may disagree: I suggest they push for a comparative review of all the woodturning books in print.

It's good that an increasing number of amateurs and professionals are reaching for their pens, but the audience assumptions that I have described are just as prevalent in magazine writings and editorial policies. I was recently asked to produce an article for a British magazine (not this one). It was rejected for being too technical. It contained some simple trigonometry and a graph. Yet I must admit some sympathy with the editor; many of the questions that readers send in to magazines appear again and again and could be answered by five minutes' reading in any public library. One wonders how many even experienced practitioners have bothered to acquire the most rudimentary reference library. Think how much better woodwork magazines would be if editors could assume that their readers were familiar with even two or three standard texts.

Bowl turning There is an undue emphasis on this speciality. No British woodworking magazine seems complete without yet another article on turning waney-edged bowls. I will not argue against bowl-turning's fascination, but in the absence of fresh material could not the more fertile pastures of spindle and cup-chuck turning receive more attention? This imbalance stems in part from a misunderstanding of the role of woodturning, and is reinforced by the ability of just a few to make a living from this speciality. Areas deserving of stronger emphasis vis-à-vis bowl turning are the remainder of treen and woodware and the amateur equivalent of professional woodturning's major role as a service trade. Components for building, furniture, boats; interior design items, replacements and

● *Elm salad bowl and servers by Stephen Marchant*

patterns. Look around, most households would appreciate tens of turned items and items incorporating turning, but how many of them would be bowls?

Quality Judgements on design are inevitably in part subjective, but I submit that many of the designs illustrated in books and magazines are harmful influences. Proper leadership in technical excellence is also wanting. For example, since the advent of the two-bearing headstock 400 years ago, the only excuse for not fully turning-off the bottoms of bowls has been that one was content to produce the second rate. No matter how neatly you plug your screwholes, fix your felt, or turn the recess or shoulder demanded by your new chuck, you have allowed your method or equipment to dictate your design. Yet such practices are repeatedly recommended without qualification.

Quality is also dependent on intent, and it is this that is largely lacking. I believe that only truly excellent craft hand-turnings should be offered to the public. Anything less degrades woodturning further. Yet the

● *Machine and nature in harmony. Mike Scott's elm burr with burnt bark, 23in diameter, 6in high*

overwhelming proportion of woodturning offered is second-rate or worse; produced by ignorant or non-caring turners. Those who have the knowledge to criticise such work look aside; they are understandably reluctant to incur the opposition that forth-rightness would guarantee.

I am conscious that I have not named names. It would be unfair to single out a few and irrelevant to my argument, a vital plank of which is my allegation that writers, manufacturers, and others have (perhaps unconsciously) a low opinion of their consumers. Their opinion is now without foundation, but it ignores the hardy perennials of cause and effect, supply and demand, and the vicious circle. Let me elaborate:

1 Few who own lathes have the skills which woodturners should have. Few will submit to the discipline of learning and practising to correctly turn a bead and a hollow. These cuts are complicated in their theory and among the most difficult in woodturning to master, yet in only one book

continued

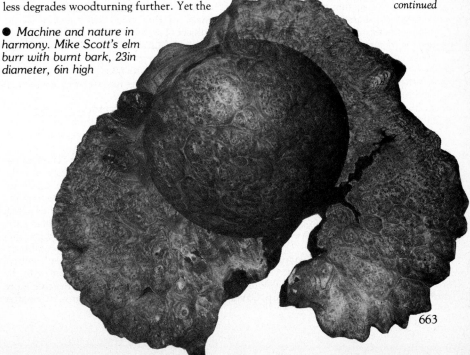

Turner's tiff

are they described in full detail. Elsewhere they are treated superficially, either because of the author's ignorance or so as not to scare the reader.

2 It's sad but true that the better your equipment the greater your potential in woodturning. Obviously most of us have a limited budget, but is it really as limited as seems to be assumed? Inferior equipment is, I suggest, often purchased out of ignorance, because it is all that is on show or because it is advertised as being 'for the professional'.

3 Obviously there is a range of education and discernment levels amongst lathe owners. Should the focus be on the lowest common denominator or on the average? I believe neither. I believe that we should try and encourage, perhaps even demand, that those less well endowed lift their game. My experience is that many of them will.

4 Many who buy lathes have limited ambitions for their turning. Woodturning leaders should be trying to enlarge those ambitions. It is in everyone's interests. Turners of limited ambition soon cease to buy books, magazines and equipment, cease to take lessons or attend seminars. But ambition is not just turning bigger items or trying to produce art, its main thrust must be quality.

Does the above illustrate a movement which has reached maturity? One in which the cosy afterglow of Pain and Child obscures the loss of Britain's pre-eminence in woodturning in the English speaking world? I suggest that if woodturning writers and manufacturers continue to pander to the largely uncritical mass market, then long-term vigour will be stifled by a multiplication of mediocrity. The seminar will undoubtedly be a success, but the glamorous chimera of transforming woodturning 'from craft into art' is not a substitute for striving for excellence.

Ray Key replies:

As organiser of this year's Woodturning Seminar I shall confine most of my comments to this area of Mike's pontification. With much of the rest of his comments about lathes and so on I find myself in total agreement.

What I find difficult to accept is that he berates everything from 13,000 miles away without being in full possession of the facts. For instance, he has not been in touch for details of our Seminar. So the views he expresses are from a preconceived position taken from what he has seen in the press. The event's full title is 'British Seminar on Woodturning 1987 — From Craft to Art'; the latter part of the title was bestowed by myself to reflect what the Lecturers/ Demonstrators will illustrate in their presentations, and the content of the selected exhibition.

A recap on the names of our presenters, I submit, ably supports our title. Stephen Marchant, Jim Partridge, Mick O'Donnell, Al LeCoff, Ray Key, Ed Moulthrop, David

Ellsworth. With this line-up, craftsmanship, innovation, and art will be fully dealt with, but most important of all will be their willingness to impart freely what each has learnt over the years, and encourage all to greater things.

The assertion that few pieces of work produced are seen as art rather than craft by non-woodturners is probably well founded at this time. But surely even Mike would have to agree David Ellsworth must be one of those he counts as an artist, once again giving substance to our title. The negative, doubting, carping attitude Mike displays would ensure woodturning never scaled the heights many other crafts have done. We, Mick O'Donnell, Margaret Lester, and myself have taken a positive attitude to put on an event that we trust will create and stimulate a much greater creative awareness and encourage all to strive for excellence in the practice of their craft and art.

As to 'the arts/crafts debate' this is perpetrated by and large by those with narrow views in both camps, by artists who haven't mastered their craft, and by craftsmen who have little artistic ability.

Yes, it would be nice just to call woodturning woodturning, but you can't put the clock back, too many people have a preconceived idea of what a woodturner does. The prefixes 'artist', 'creative', 'studio', 'production', 'reproduction', etc, are attempts to make it clear to the public the area of work in which a turner specialises — it would be almost impossible to reverse this now. The title 'Woodturner' many bestow upon themselves is so ill-founded, many workers try to extricate themselves with a prefix to indicate a certain expertise.

Mike says he worries about the long-term health of amateur woodturning and wonders if the influence of the industry is sowing the seeds of decline. Well if it is, I think the Seminar may well have a halting effect.

It's our intention to launch an association at the Seminar that will address itself to many of the points Mike makes on the subject of suppliers of turner's needs, training and education. To exhibit work only of the highest quality, but at the same time encourage all to take pride in what they produce; these are just a few of our aims, and there are many more.

Only when woodturners produce work consistently of the highest quality and excellence will it achieve the status many of us feel it should reach.

Mike's final comment, that 'The seminar will undoubtedly be a success, but the glamorous chimera of transforming woodturning "from craft into art" is no substitute for striving for excellence', demands a final comment. The Seminar, we are also sure, will be a success. Mike seems to suggest that you can't have art and excellence combined. I would have thought the best would always combine the two, and as we will be displaying some of the best, the title more than stands. Perhaps a question mark after

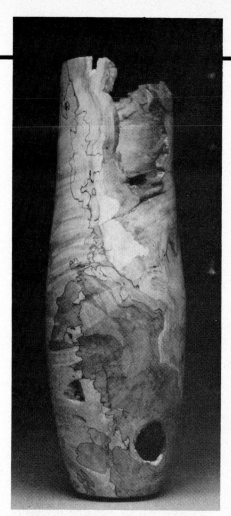

● **Above**, wooden vessel by David Ellsworth in spalted sugar maple. **Below**, Ray Key's use of spalted beech, 7in diameter

'Art' would have placated him?

My dictionary defines 'Artist' as one who makes his or her craft a fine art. I rest my case, in my bunker, tin hat on, thousands of British woodturners on stand-by!

Nick Davidson replies:

Mike Darlow seems to be confusing the obvious. He is indeed an academic, and I believe he thinks the world is full of people who think like him. My experience is otherwise. I won't enter the 'art vs craft' argument, but I believe there is sufficient scope to strive for excellence. I have demontrated in England, the US, France and Germany, and I am sufficiently encouraged to know there is a world market for artistic talent in woodturning.

What really amazes me about Mike Darlow's letter is his lack of accuracy on matters he should know better. I understand Mike is a well-qualified and successful engineer, so it surprises me when he describes tools so inaccurately. I can only speak for Robert Sorby (whose tools are most readily available in Australia). Mike leads us to believe only one-third is fluted; in actual fact, when a typical bowl gouge is put into a handle, two-thirds of the steel showing is fluted and available for use. The tool is fully hardened all the length of the flute and then the hardness tapers off into the handle. If it was fully hardened into the handle there would be a high risk of breakage from brittle fracture when the tool is subjected to too much shock. Hardening high-speed steel is a difficult process.

Mike also has a go at us manufacturers for being late at getting into high-speed steel. I have personally been promoting HSS for more than eight years. Woodturning is a very traditional craft, old traditions die hard, and in my experience it has been the manufacturer who has encouraged the distributor to take high-speed steel. Manufacturers, leading turners and the magazines

have been responsible for getting the message over to the woodturner — it's not a case of the manufacturer reluctantly changing to suit the needs of the user. An example close to Mike's home — a new Australian distributor placed a big order with Sorby for carbon steel turning tools in May. Sorby telexed him back advising him to consider HSS, informing him of its merits and sales potential in Australia. He resisted changing, saying he was testing out his market, which he considered more traditional and he might venture into HSS later. Mike, you have a crusade in Australia yet to complete.

I'm gratified the progress we have made in chucking has not gone unnoticed by Mike Darlow — but since there are now nearly 20,000 users of the Precision Combination Chuck, it's not that surprising.

I do, however, share some of Mike Darlow's reservations about lathe manufacturers. There are many very poor lathes on the market, designed to sell and not for performance, but I believe there is a reasonable chance available to the potential user who is prepared to shop around. We must consider the market; woodturning is an expanding market, and there are many first-time buyers who cannot afford or do not wish to spend £1000 on a hobby, not knowing if they will enjoy it. A £200 lathe may be the only way to get those customers'

interest. Lathe makers — please consider very carefully the woodturners' needs when designing a lathe, whether it's for £200 or £2000.

To sum up, I believe Mike Darlow has a distorted view of woodturning matters. If Mike's opinions stimulate some sensible thought then his efforts are not totally in vain, but I — perhaps sceptically — think we will return to where we started! Beware all 'spurious academic timewasters'!

PLEASE NOTE — THE SEMINAR IS NOW FULLY BOOKED AND IS ONLY OPEN TO THOSE WHO HAVE BOOKED AND PAID!

Semi seminar

For those in North Wales who can't get to Loughborough on the weekend of 15-16 August, professional turner **Keith Lawrence** is organising a **'Woodturning Show'** to further the interests of turners generally and get hobbyist turners together. Keith will be demonstrating, there'll be bowl-turning videos showing, it'll be a good chance for a hob-nob, and there's a restaurant on the same craft centre site as Keith's workshop. Details from Keith at the Old Stables Turnery, Tri Thy Centre, Coed talon, Mold, Clwyd, (0352) 771771.

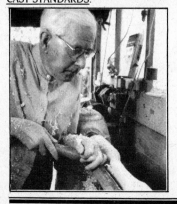

Photos Ed Davis

BRISTOL SHOW SPECIAL

May's Bristol Woodworker Show is getting bigger, better and bolder — it's only natural. Editor Aidan Walker was there in both official and unofficial guise

The Bristol Woodworker Show is getting well into gear, of that there is no doubt. Its first incarnation in 1985 was a testing of the water, and now it can honestly be said: 'Come on in, the water's lovely.' The increasing strength and individual flavour of the 1986 and 1987 Shows make it obvious that Bristol was the right place; it's a natural focus for the busy Midlands, and even more for the west country, where for some unaccountable reason large numbers of craft workers in all materials seem to be based. Perhaps it's the air, perhaps it's the strength of the traditions — whatever it is, there's a lot going on in that part of the country for woodworkers, and the Bristol Show is taking from and adding to that phenomenon. Some of the exhibitors, it's true, get as far as London, but as a local outlet for those craftspeople who don't orient themselves towards the Big Smoke, Bristol is paying off.

The exhibits

There were many entries in the carving and turning categories, almost all of a high technical standard; but remember it's not always sheer technical excellence the judges look for. A note to the enthusiastic amateur — as an opportunity to display your work that you never thought to see outside your home, the Woodworker Shows have just got to be a good idea. Don't worry about the prizes, though of course it would be nice if you got a gold award; nothing is turned away, and who knows what may happen? You could at least be sure you'd get constructive criticism from some of the best craftspeople in the country. What other venue offers the double attraction of the finished work to see alongside the tools and equipment to buy — the inspiration, the education, and the gear to bring your ideas to fruition?

Which is a preamble to a slight sense of disappointment that there were a mere five entries in the cabinetmaking class. No disappointment about the standards the makers work to, however — in one case, more a question of downright awe. David Lilburn, an ex-hotelier from the Lake District who moved to Stroud two-and-a-half years ago, stunned and amazed every beholder with his outstanding curved folding screen in cherry. It doesn't just fold, it turns into a column; with its leaded glass lights, it is an undoubted design-and-make *tour de force*, one of the best things we've seen at any show anywhere.

'I started off with an interest in leaded glass, really,' says David — 'but I realised there was a lot of potential in combining glass and wood. I love wood, anyway — it's living, it's got such warmth.' Not the first person to make either of those discoveries, perhaps — but David could honestly say he

● **Top left**, *this relief carving of oak leaves on a plate won a silver medal for Mr P. Biles.* **Above**, *Gerald Jones' 18th-century style mahogany child's chair also got silver*

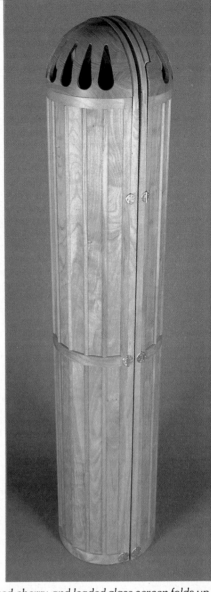

● **Above**, *David Lilburn's magnificent curved cherry and leaded glass screen folds up to a compact column – a well-deserved gold.* **Below**, *Pete Reay's walnut and yew coffee table (bronze medal) was the subject of much discussion*

hadn't been searching through art history books for the design inspiration. 'No, it's not consciously Art Nouveau, I don't study things like that. I'm entirely self-taught, anyway; WOODWORKER has taught me all I know, really.' Inspired, entrant of the future?

Wanting to get away from 'the usual flat form of a screen when it's folded', David developed the sphere/column idea himself — giving himself enormous technical problems in the process. It's all in solid cherry; the panels are ¼in thick, easy to produce with his 'very old' Coronet Minorette. He is by no means well equipped — an Elu router was the only other power tool he quoted, bar a Myford metalworking lathe. Just goes to show what resourcefulness and imagination can do. 'I was working on the limits of the capacity of my equipment all the time' — this with a glint in the eye, a man to whom overcoming the challenge is three-quarters of the fun. The top dome is slightly less than a perfect hemisphere, in that a section is cut out to allow for the flat-folded thickness; the hand-carved overlap detail where the dome joins when the screen is folded is a joy to behold.

continued

David jigsawed out semicircles and glued them together to rough the dome out, their ends overlapping within the waste allowance that would be lost on assembly. Then he turned it on the Coronet — which he had to modify with new pulley gear to reduce the speed. The tear-shaped openings were also jigsawed freehand, then finished with the router and template-follower in a curved (to follow the dome) metal template he made (of course) himself. It took him 400 hours — work, we hope, with which he was well pleased, carrying away his gold medal. We didn't get to ask David about his Northumbrian bagpipes, which took a gold in the musical instrument section . . .

Gerald Jones' 18th-century-style child's chair, nicely and functionally finished in Danish Oil, was worth silver, in the judges' opinion — fractionally ahead of Pete Reay's imposing walnut and yew coffee table, with an ash frame and an unusual 'big dovetail' treatment of the top perimeter joints. A fine effort technically, though the mixture of strongly coloured and figured timbers was definitely 'love it or hate it' in aesthetic terms; we could find no evidence of allowing for possible movement in that jointed-up flush top, Mr Reay.

It was a turner's show in many ways, both from the point of view of equipment, and of work on display. As usual, the turning category was encouragingly highly subscribed, and much of the work drew appreciative comments from luminaries Ray Key, Bert Marsh and Nigel Voisey. John Kelly, a Scot who lives in Ireland (he drove from Co. Clare to Bristol, to relations in Scotland, to Bristol, in one weekend!) romped away with golds for his beautifully proportioned and profiled ash bowl — though the glued-on base had begun to separate from the top by Sunday afternoon — and his extraordinary endgrain-turned yew 'box'. There could hardly be a less descriptive word for this elegant vase-like lidded shape, carefully worked so the whitewood of the yew formed a 'flash' on one side; a rod fixed into the lid carries another lidded container deep inside the base, something like an apple. 'It was inspired by a tabernacle I made for a private offertory in a convent,' explained John. 'The idea of the box inside is so you can keep things in it and get them out without having to drop half your handful because the neck's too narrow.' John has been turning for four years, and professionally for only 12 months; all sorts of work come his way in rural Ireland, in which spindle work for turned-component bar stools seems to figure largely. He uses an old Denford Viceroy ('Probably older than I am') and a Kity 664, doing most of his faceplate work on the spigot version of a Craft Supplies Precision Combination Chuck. The base of the box is hollowed out, friction-held and reverse-chucked, with a Swedish hook tool; 'It was an excuse to try it for hollowing. It takes a bit of a knack, but

it's great once you get used to it — much smoother than a scraper. No snagging.'

Chris Stott was the other half of the seemingly unbeatable turning pair, and indeed there were similarities between his experience and John Kelly's, though not of the work displayed. Chris has been turning for not much longer than John, and professionally for four years; he had to be content with silver for his beautiful deep-turned burr ash piece. 'If I hadn't been a professional I would have tried to go deeper,' said Chris with a deadpan twinkle. It looked quite deep enough to us. Chris' presence at the Show, with his wife Kathy, was notable in that he was behind his own stand, selling a delicious array of lidded decorative boxes, natural-edged and large fruit and salad bowls in most timbers you could think of, both exotic and home-grown. His favourite? Burr elm, sadly scarce. Despite the range, all Chris' work showed an individual style, and he is definitely a businessman. He produces 3000 pieces a year, selling them at agricultural shows and craft fairs; unusual and encouraging to see a turner actually selling his work at a Woodworker Show. No, he didn't find a lot of his time spent on trying not to give hints on technique, skating uncomfortably close to hard-won secrets; though 'woodturners are

● **Right**, John Kelly's yew 'box' (gold) and ash bowl, **bottom**; Ron Packman's long-tailed tits (silver), Martha Price's burr oak bowl, Ron Packman's otter and fish, Chris Stott's burr ash bowl

the most critical audience in the country', he was pleased with the commercial result, particularly Sunday's take. He has a 50-year old Harrison Jubilee and a home-built lathe, doing almost exclusively faceplate work with a Craft Supplies Precision Combination Chuck and two six-in-ones, both home-made, one of them by himself. We examined some of his fumed acacia bowls, light and pretty; 'Yes, there's a story behind them. I rough-turn them then kiln them dry and finish them, and I had a roughed-out load waiting for the kiln. They were next to the goats (the Stotts have a smallholding) for a good while, and when they came out of the kiln the heartwood had that deep green colour.' Strong ammonia from goats. 'Some of them even got nibbled by the damn goats.'

Mention of other turners' work must be made; Fred Marks' segmented gold-medal winning vase with a lid in cherry and mahogany, Roger Holley's witty 'Holley Brolly', a piece of whimsy in English ash with a segmented hook handle and a wafer-thin shade in a delicate shade of green. It could have used a better switch than cheap black plastic, surely? That took a silver, as did John Shepherd's olive ash 'compots', a pair of pedestal bowls which went very well as a group with Maurice Price's cakestand in bubinga. Maurice's sister Martha won a silver medal for her natural-form carved oak burr bowl in the Juniors — a wood-working family, and a creative one at that.

● **Top**, cakestand (bronze) and compots (silver) by Maurice Price and John Shepherd.
Above, John Kelly's box opens thus, as does Fred Marks' 'vase with lid' (gold).
Left, Roger Holley's 'Holley Brolly' table lamp amused and amazed

Carving was as well subscribed as turning, if not better; but it's always invidious, judging carvings. Here is the section where the 'art *vs* craft' debate comes on strong; personal tastes necessarily come into it. It's the class above all others where inspiration, a 'genuine' feel and an appreciation of line and form — all the province of the artist — should be considered as equal in importance to technique. We liked Colin Whitehead's lime Crucifixion for its particular purity in this respect, exuding clarity and calm, an honestly spiritual rendition. Gordon Anderson's 'Potter', however, topped the class with gold; the Crucifixion was given silver. Ron Packman's pair of long-tailed tits in cherry had sweetness, and we were also attracted

continued

BRISTOL SHOW SPECIAL

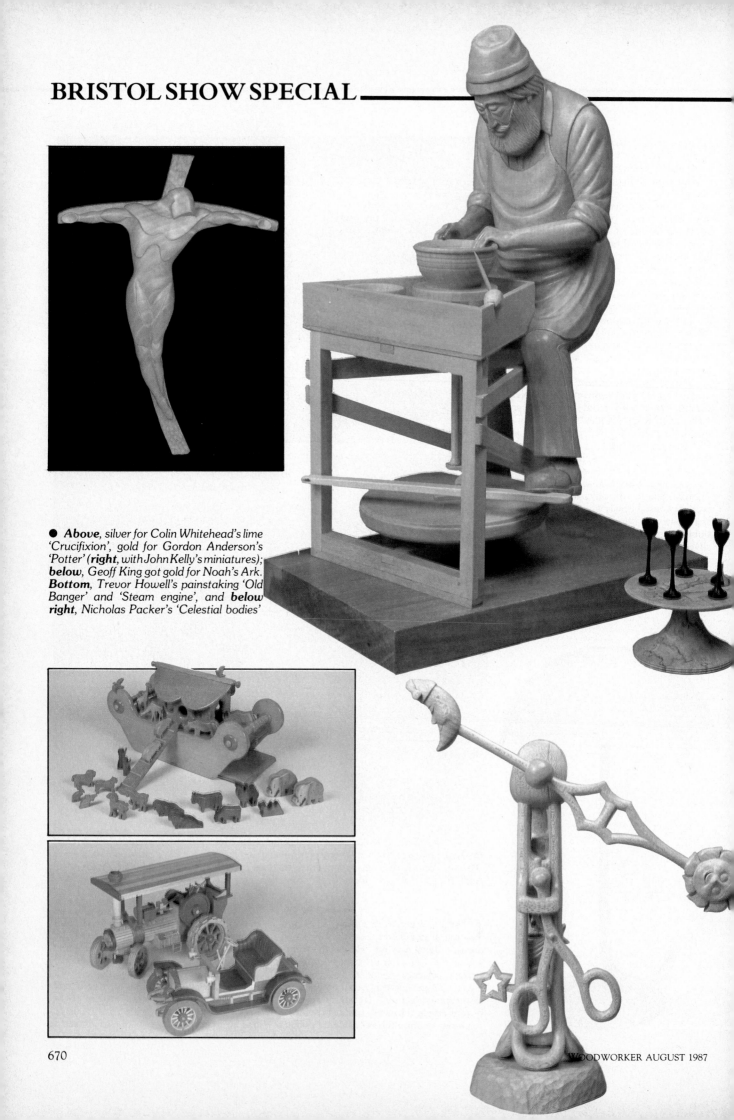

● **Above**, silver for Colin Whitehead's lime 'Crucifixion', gold for Gordon Anderson's 'Potter' (**right**, with John Kelly's miniatures); **below**, Geoff King got gold for Noah's Ark. **Bottom**, Trevor Howell's painstaking 'Old Banger' and 'Steam engine', and **below right**, Nicholas Packer's 'Celestial bodies'

670

by the humour and invention in Nicholas Packer's 'Celestial Bodies', carved in lacewood-like sycamore to commemorate the passage of Halley's Comet. It was another piece informed with a strong idea, and a good helping of mechanical ingenuity to boot — the various celestial bodies orbited when you cranked the handle. Sculpture restorer Julian Cox's great fish in yellow pine — a 'bearded' carp and a hunting tarpon — were unplaced; sadly perhaps, because in our view they showed a vitality, a sureness and definition that made the unsophisticated technique unimportant. Perhaps Julian doesn't aim for highly developed technique anyway?

No doubt in anyone's mind about the gold-medal winner of the toys. There are toymakers who make staggering efforts to achieve ever-higher flights of painstakingly detailed precision work; remarkable display pieces like Trevor Howell's 'Old Banger' and 'Steam Engine' are a case in point. Definitely for the older child, if not the adult! Then there are toymakers who make toys for children to play with, in whose work a love of children and play is highly evident. Such a man is Geoff King; his Noah's Ark is well and stoutly made, no sharp edges, no poisonous finishes (he uses non-toxic wax), no small or breakable bits and pieces — and perhaps most important of all, he goes for a subject to delight and stimulate a child's imagination, something that will go on and on while the Zoids and Little Ponies meet their fate on the infant

● *Julian Cox's carp and tarpon – a 'genuine feel'*

scrapheap. Geoff won a gold in London last year with a beech whale, its belly filled with interlocking brightly coloured fish; this year the animals came, in two by two and all sorts of woods, every piece from salvage or from trees that had died a natural death. Yew elephants and rhinos, olive ash doves and pelicans, sycamore pigs, walnut camels and walruses, oak lions and horses . . . and Mr and Mrs Noah in afrormosia.

People and products

The Craft demonstration section was peopled with some familiar faces and one new one; green wood working and country crafts must owe much of their revival to Jack Hill, and more recently, Bristol-based Mike Abbott, both of whose work has been featured in WOODWORKER — and both of whose courses are available through the Guild of Woodworkers. Zach Taylor and Stan Thomas were there, dispensing

wisdom and good humour in equally large portions on the several subjects of instruments, music, and everything you ever wanted to know about joinery but didn't know how to ask; and as for showmen, newcomer Trevor Rooney, the carver of York (*WW/June*) is set fair to bid for the title. His uninhibited extrovert manner and deft carving skills attracted a constant crowd, and if there weren't enough people around Trevor was to be seen striding up and down the aisles announcing his next demo without the benefit of amplification. 'It was an eye-opener for us,' he says; 'we (he and his wife Jayne) are used to handling large crowds and entertaining them, becuase we run 'Ghost Tours' for tourists in York — but it's different with woodworkers, where you have to produce the goods at the same time as you entertain — not let the people get bored. Could have been embarrassing if a chisel had slipped —

● *Top left, explaining the Masterchuck for the umpteenth time;* **left,** *Mike Abbott turns his umpteenth green wood leg.* **Above, Jeff Ottey** *(left) of* **Tyme Machines** *and* **Paul Merry** *(right) of* **Triton Workcentres** *dip in for the winners of the free draw. All smiles for Messrs* **Owens** *and* **Cooper** *who struck lucky*

continued

BRISTOL SHOW SPECIAL

hard work, but great fun.' Trevor and Jayne will be there in force at the Alexandra Pavilion in October.

Of the new bits of kit to catch your eye and tug at your pocket, there was a goodly selection, the most interesting undoubtedly for turners. **Craft Supplies**, generous sponsors of the woodturning prizes for the London Show this year, had their new and much-acclaimed oval skew on the stand, along with their ring gouge and the new Precision Collet chuck; Roy Child on the **Henry Taylor Tools** stand had no escape, it seemed, from the barrage of questions and cheques flying over the counter as he demonstrated and explained his new design of chuck — the Masterchuck, definitely a product to watch. The jaws open or close at the twist of a wrist, without need to dismantle or fit new bits and pieces for the different operations; there is a wide range of accessories allowing great variation in workpiece size, and a locking facility so you can turn your own jaw blank, split it, and have adjustable jaws sized to the job in hand.

Specialist handtool manufacturers **Clico** are increasing their presence in the market, as have **Coronet** with their revitalised lathes and new ranges of tools and accessories; they were also showing the new **Wm Ridgway** mortiser, a handsome bit of British engineering for around £600. Clico have ist opened a new factory with forging and iand-grinding skills to increase their range of woodborers, and were showing some giant augers. They have recently taken an order from a Naval dockyard for four 1¼in-diameter augers a mere 42in long; their current fave, the Clifton 410 shoulder plane, has recently been in the hands of cabinetmaker, author and show judge **David Savage**, who has this to say:

'VERY SIMILAR in form to the other planes of Clico's Clifton family, the 410 is really a little gem. The beauty is the size of it. For cabinetmaking, you seldom need a big shoulder plane — most of the work is on quite small rebates or shoulders. Delicately trimming this, shaving that, one shave at a time, for a really good fit. A big plane is cumbersome, awkward and inappropriate. The ⅝in width of cut of the 410 will do 80% of all shoulder-plane jobs in furniture making. The sole is only 5½in long, and it weighs just about 1lb. The body is comfortable to hold, many of the edges having been properly deburred for once. The sole of the tool I had was reasonably but not quite flat, and acceptably square to the sides; the adjustment mechanism worked well, the knurling to the adjustment having been improved over previous Clico planes.

'It's very good to be able to say nice things about a British toolmaker — but Mr Clico, when do we get laminated steel cutting irons back again? The 410 Shoulder Rebate Plane costs £52.50+VAT; more information on stockists from Clico Tools Ltd in Sheffield.'

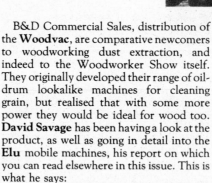

● *From right: the view from* **Chris Stott's** *woodturning sales stand;* **Trevor Rooney** *demonstrates;* **Jack Hill** *and junior woodturner; putting the Woodvac's extraction capacity to the test*

B&D Commercial Sales, distribution of the **Woodvac**, are comparative newcomers to woodworking dust extraction, and indeed to the Woodworker Show itself. They originally developed their range of oildrum lookalike machines for cleaning grain, but realised that with some more power they would be ideal for wood too. **David Savage** has been having a look at the product, as well as going in detail into the **Elu** mobile machines, his report on which you can read elsewhere in this issue. This is what he says:

'ONE OF THE BEST portable dust extractors I have seen lately is the Woodvac, from B&D Commercial Sales of York. This is a very efficient 'low tech' product. The collector unit is a painted-up heavy-duty 200 litre oil drum, mounted on a trolley — the lid of the drum forms an explosion relief panel. Power is from three independently switched 1hp single-phase motors; each has 7in impellors, giving an airflow of 16,500cu ft per minute, or so they say. All I can say is that the thing does suck a lot, provided the filters are kept clear. Ignore them and performance falls off dramatically. There are two types of filter, a canvas bag in the main drum and paper filters over each power unit, which give final filtration down to 0.5 microns. This is an easily portable machine, ideal for dust rather than chipping extraction. Chippings will go down the 4in hole, of course, like anything else, but there are other cheaper extractors that do this job. For getting rid of sanding dust and sawdust, using a portable extractor with H&SE-approved explosion relief, this has got to be a good product to look at. The big Woodvac 200-litre standard package, including 3.75 metres of 110 mm hosing, costs £480+VAT, and the heavy-duty tooling kit £120+VAT.'

There's also a smaller version of the Woodvac, made specially by B&D for AEG, which has two 1hp motors and costs £325+VAT. They both look good, but there's no way round the fact you have to tip those drums up to empty them . . . the whole lid, on which the motors are mounted, comes off, of course.

Two directly competitive products in small-scale sanding were being enthusiastically demonstrated, upstairs and downstairs — flexibly mounted sanding discs, the **Langton 'Flexi disc'** and the **Wolfcraft 'Fixoflex'**, represented at Bristol by **Steerdawn**. The designs differ somewhat, but the effect is the same and the price identical,

£9.99 for genuinely scratch-free disc sanding. Don't disbelieve it, try them for yourself — we did, and the claims are true. The flexible mounting absorbs the shocks that cause scratches, they're at pains to explain; not to sand round corners.

Warren Machine Tools, who market the Eumenia radial-arm saw in the UK (*WW/June*), are very proud of their 'Melamine' TCT blade, and justifiably so. An unbelievably clean finish on both sides of the cut on melamine-faced board, notoriously chippable with even fine-toothed blades. Generally the only way out is a scoring saw, but samples cut with their blade looked as if they had been cut with exactly that. Impossible for people who use a lot of this stuff in kitchen cabinet work, for instance, to ignore. And it's all a matter of cutting angle, they say. One hitch, though — the blade is only available to fit the Eumenia at the moment. Do it for more machines, we said, and you'll be rich.

We haven't mentioned everyone, we haven't mentioned everything — but then how could we? The Bristol Show is firmly established, growing healthier every year with the strong blood of west-country craftsmanship flowing in its veins. If you didn't enter your work this year, be sure to do it next year — or consider the next opportunity; the undoubted leader of the field, our own **London Woodworker Show** is at the **Alexandra Pavilion, London N22**, from **22-25 October**. Do it, see it, be there — you just can't afford to miss it. ∎

Prizewinners

Cabinetmaking Gold medal: David Lilburn, cherry folding screen with leaded glass

Figure carving Gold medal: Gordon Anderson, 'The Potter'

Relief carving Silver medal: P. Biles, Oak-leaf carving on a plate

Woodturning Small — Silver medal: John Kelly, miniature goblets; Segmented — Gold mdeal: Fred Marks, cherry and mahogany lidded vase; Endgrain — Gold medal: John Kelly, yew 'box'; Faceplate — Gold medal: John Kelly, ash bowl

Musical instruments Gold medal: David Lilburn, Northumbrian bagpipes

Marquetry and inlay Gold medal: David Evans, 'Nature's Way'

Toys Gold medal: Geoff King, Noah's Ark

Carpentry and joinery Silver medal: J. Shapiro, garden seat

Miniatures Silver medals: J. Watt, miniature library table; K. Gould, collection of utensils

Juniors Silver medals: M. Price, burr oak bowl; S. Knight, rocking chair

LONDON WOODWORKER SHOW GOODIES GALORE

Enter your work in the Show and apart from prestige, publicity and accolades you can win something from this marvellous collection of desirables — it's from 22-25 October, Alexandra Pavilion, London N22

● *The AEG Trophy*

CABINETMAKING
The AEG/WOODWORKER Pre-Professional Award

Open to any furniture college student in their last year, the award gives you the chance to win an **AEG MAXI 26 Universal woodworking machine**, a commemorative trophy, and all the publicity you can handle — we send your details to consumer and trade publications, and follow your fortunes through the year. Jointly sponsored by AEG Woodworking, WOODWORKER magazine and Argus Specialist Exhibitions. Make your entry on the form for cabinetmaking (WA) and be sure to notify that you want to be considered for the Pre-Professional Award.

WOODTURNING
Spindle turning — The Robert Sorby Awards

Two categories in spindle turning; the overall winner gets **£100 worth of Sorby HSS tools**, the winner in the other category and one overall runner-up each get £50 worth of Sorby HSS tools, and there's a further £50 worth of tools for more runners-up.

Faceplate turning — the Craft Supplies Awards

£100 worth of Craft Supplies' Precision Combination Chuck and/or accessories for the overall winner, three sets of £50 worth of Craft Supplies' chucking equipment for three runners-up, and another £100 worth of tools to be won for the best amongst the other entries.

WOODCARVING
The Ashley Iles Carving Awards

First prize, for the overall best work in all the categories; an 18-piece tool set based on the Ashley Iles 'Westminster' set, but specially selected, hand forged and polished; second prize, the same treatment for the 12-piece 'Canterbury' set, and third prize, specials based on the 6-piece 'York' tool set.

ROUTING
The Trend Routing Award

Open to any entrant in any class who has made extensive use of the router, Trend Cutting Tools' special prize consists of **£300 worth of TCT and HSS cutters** for the overall winner, presented in a specially made cabinet — plus Trend director Jim Phillips' book *Techniques of Routing*. The runner-up wins £150 worth of cutters, again TCT and HSS, again in a special cabinet. Judges will be looking for number of profiles, quality of finish, aesthetic appearance obtained through extensive use of the router in conjunction with wood grain and selection, best use of the router for high quality construction, innovative or subtle use of jigs, clamps and guides, and the quality of presentation of drawings and photographs submitted in support of the entry. Enter in the class you wish on the normal form, but be sure to say you wish to be considered for the Trend Award, and submit those photos and drawings when you send or bring your work to the Show itself — **not before.**

WOOD FINISHING
The Henry Flack Awards

Open to any entrant in any category, J. W. Bollom Ltd, makers of the famous Briwax, are looking for the best finish in the show — it doesn't matter what you use. All types of finish will be considered; and just in case you don't use Briwax (horror!), the prizes are designed to cover the whole range of products. First prize is **£150 worth of J. W. Bollom products**, second is £100 worth, and third is £50 worth.

YOUNG PROFESSIONALS
Roger's Award

First prize in this category, donated by Roger's the specialist tool supplier, goes to the gold medal winner; a set of **10 handsome Japanese chisels.**

JUNIORS
Roger's Award

To encourage the young 'uns, Roger is also giving a total of **£100 worth of tool vouchers** to the winners in the various categories.

STICKMAKING
The Theo Fossel Trophy

First awarded last year, this prize, donated by Theo Fossel, founder member of the British Stickmaker's Guild, is a beautiful glass goblet, engraved with your name — yours to keep.

Further, there's the **Robbins Rose Bowl** from Robbins of Bristol for cabinetmaking; **Woodworker Challenge Cups** in many classes; the **Richard Blizzard Cup** for toymakers, the **World of Wood Cup** for marquetarians, donated by the Art Veneers Company; the **Stuart King Award** for miniaturists, and the **John Thompson Trophy** for model horse-drawn vehicle makers.

GET YOUR ENTRY FORMS FROM ARGUS SPECIALIST EXHIBITIONS, WOLSEY HOUSE, WOLSEY RD, HEMEL HEMPSTEAD HP2 4SS, (0442) 41221

LONDON WOODWORKER SHOW

22ND — 25TH OCTOBER 1987
ALEXANDRA PALACE & PARK, WOOD GREEN, LONDON N22 4AY

OPENING TIMES
22nd — 24th   10.00am-6.00pm
25th   10.00am-5.00pm

ADMISSION PRICES
Adults   £3.50
Senior Citizens   £2.25
Children   £1.50

How to get there — free shuttle service.
Travel by British Rail to Alexandra Palace station and then by free shuttle service or W3 bus.

By road: follow the AA sign posts. Free car parking.

Further information available from:
Argus Specialist Exhibitions Ltd., PO Box 35, Wolsey House, Wolsey Road, Hemel Hempstead, Herts HP2 4SS Tel: 0442 41221

The London Woodworker Show is organised by Argus Specialist Exhibitions and sponsored by Woodworker Magazine.

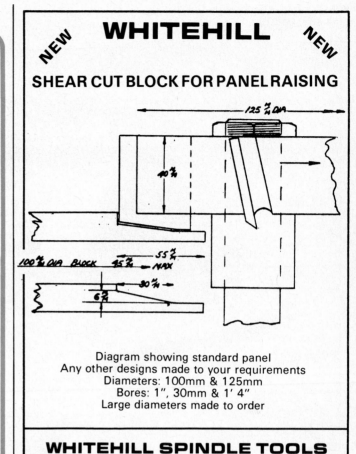

Patterns of tradition

Tunbridge ware is mosaic marquetry with a difference. David Springett reveals its secrets and tells you how to decorate a box with your own designs

I have always been fascinated by Tunbridge ware; that is by its unique method of production, rather than the finished items. The technique of gluing square-section sticks together to form an endgrain mosaic pattern was developed in Tunbridge Wells, a small town south-east of London. It developed as a famous spa resort in the 1600s and for centuries gentry visited to take the waters and improve their health.

The local craftsmen were well known for their turnery and marquetry and traded on the influx of visitors by producing various woodware souvenirs. One type of turned wood peculiar to Tunbridge Wells was 'stickware', whereby several various coloured woods were glued together in a geometric pattern and turned, producing an interesting effect. It didn't take long to work out that the endgrain pattern created by these blocks could be used to form a mosaic, but exactly when the discovery was made isn't known. The fact that an endgrain picture could be made, and that each section sawn off the block produced an identical picture, was a superb production technique, not to be missed. At the height of their skills the craftsmen produced the most marvellous range of mosaics, some

containing up to 13000 individual pieces covering every imaginable subject.

I began making Tunbridge ware by cheating a little. A veneer catalogue was offering $\frac{1}{16}$in sections in boxwood, rosewood, blue, green and black, so I didn't have to cut my own pieces.

The sticks came in 36in lengths which I bundled together, wrapping them with masking tape at 4in intervals — four inch lengths would be more than long enough for me to handle. The masking tape helped stop the wood chipping and breaking while it was being crosscut.

Now I could draw out the pattern on squared paper, making the best of the colours I had. In a small book on embroidery I found a delightful butterfly already squared-out for counted thread work, also some amazing Berlinwork and alphabets, but decided they were for when I had more expertise. The drawn-out butterfly filled a rectangle 29 squares long by 33 wide — which meant just under 1000 pieces in all.

I made a listing of the lines and the colours they contained; for example, line 4: 3 boxwood, 2 rosewood, 1 green, 2 rosewood, 4 boxwood, 2 black and 19 boxwood. I added 2 extra box, one front one

back, to cope with any inaccuracy or slippage when gluing.

This gave me my method of working. I'd realised that each line would need to be glued up separately, allowed to dry, and then when all 29 lines were finished, they would be glued to form the block.

I spent days devising jigs for holding these 33 pieces, each $\frac{1}{16}$in sq and 4in long, and finally decided on a simple baseboard, with two side pieces and an end piece screwed to it. To stop the pieces gluing themselves to the baseboard, I cut polythene oversize enough to loosen the screws on the side and end pieces, slip it underneath and screw down again, clamping the polythene in place.

I used folding wedges with an extra piece to fit against the square lines for the clamping, and waxed all the edges of the jig and wedges touching a glued surface to avoid problems. Once I'd selected the pieces for the first line I laid them aside.

Now up until then I'd considered myself as a traditionalist — the smell of hot animal-glue bubbling away, carefully applying the glue with a brush dripping with that hot stuff — but when I thought of applying it to such tiny pieces with the glue chilling, hot glue scorching my fingers, bits of stringing sticking everywhere, all these romantic visions dropped away. I settled for off-the-shelf white PVA glue.

Applying the glue from a glue bottle would be tedious, so I squeezed a small puddle on a scrap of wood through which I pulled each piece.

I laid the first piece dry on the polythene, up against the side; the second and subsequent ones I pulled through the glue, laid each alongside the piece in the jig, and with a small stick, pushed it up tight and pressed it down for alignment, squeezing out excess glue. The glue had a good grip and held firm. Any excess glue on the surface was cleaned as work progressed.

When I came to awkward pieces which wouldn't hold together and others which were slightly warped, I stopped applying the folding wedges until the piece had settled, then continued. To my delight the pieces held firmly by themselves as I went along. I concluded that when the original Tunbridge craftsmen worked with hot animal glue they must have used plain paper, not polythene, as the base — the animal glue gripped firmly and the paper prevented the glue from sticking to any surface other than the neighbouring piece of wood. The paper would later be scraped off.

I carefully numbered each layer as I had finished it, peeled off the polythene, then

● **Far left**, the butterfly design made up of 957 pieces, assembled, sliced and finally glued to the box. To the right is an antique folding crib board decorated in Tunbridge ware

● **Right** and **below right**, gluing the individual sections and wedging them firmly in the jig

● **Below**, close-up of the decorated box, showing the mosaic of tiny squares in the design

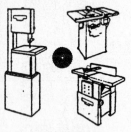

laid it aside in order. Each layer needed careful scraping to level and remove excess glue. All that remained was to lay the pieces in order, double-check everything, separate, apply glue and cramp all the layers together with scrap blocks between four G-clamps.

The mosaic was complete — like a stick of rock with the picture running through it. It wasn't truly square, but some careful planing squared it up. Cutting off the first piece was a little worrying. I marked off a little under ⅛in leaving enough to give it strength and began by handsawing; after two blocks I decided to use the bandsaw for speed. I discovered that if masking tape was applied to the area to be cut, it supported the outer edge and stopped breakout.

(And then I noticed all the sawdust — after I'd put so much work in, I wasn't going to lose that hand-crafted stuff. It's now in a jar on a shelf in my workshop. I don't know what to do with it, I'm certainly not going to throw it away. Any suggestions?)

I got very excited with all those Tunbridge butterflies and rushed them round to a friend for him to admire. He did all the right things and when my ego was well and truly inflated, he said 'Do you want to know how it was really done?' His woodwork teacher had told him back in the 1940s about the original practice.

● **Right**, cutting a mitre on the banding

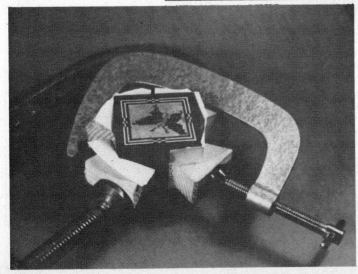

● **Left** corner blocks used for cramping up

A sheet of newsprint or cartridge paper was laid down and then liberally coated with bill-stickers' paste. The lengths of wood were laid in order, tight together on the glued surface, but no glue between them — like a tambour. It was laid aside for about a day to dry and other layers prepared.

When it had dried, it was lifted and the paper backing was flexed, opening the joints between each strip. Hot animal glue was applied to fill the joints. The fan of wood was then released, allowing the joints to close, and a piece of paper placed on top, clamped tight between two wooden blocks. All that remained was to clean off the paper, and glue the layers together to form the complete block. I tried this method and it is faster to begin with, but more tedious with all the scraping required towards the end.

If you do decide to prepare your own sections they must be exact — any inaccuracies add up, causing misalignment in the overall design. The hawk-eyed might spot one or two in mine, but don't they add a sort of homespun charm?

● Beware if you prepare from veneer. Although all veneers appear to be the same thickness they vary slightly, enough to cause problems.

● Some of the workers in Tunbridge Wells had problems with grey staining in their holly. They overcame this by boiling it in water.

● **Above**, traditional gluing method for Tunbridge ware

Making the box

When I'd sliced off a piece of mosaic I supported it by gluing and cramping it to a piece of ply. It looked a little stark so I sorted through various veneers and bandings, and came up with a banding — no doubt produced in a similar manner in blocks then sliced off — which looked good and sufficiently subdued not to distract from the mosaic pattern.

I discovered that if a length of the banding was laid on each side of the mosaic, fixed firmly with masking tape, I could cut the mitre on the corners by slicing through the two thicknesses of the banding with a very sharp modelling knife. The cut was made across the intersection of the two pieces, forming a perfect mitre.

The masking tape still in position acted as a hinge while I glued them in place; each piece was lifted and glue squeezed beneath then fixed down again, extra masking tape securing the corners. When the whole piece was dry, I sanded it flat.

The box I made was of a simple construction, as they were traditionally: a rebated edge, top and bottom, with the corners mitred — mine cut on a mitre guillotine. The first time I glued the box together I used six G-clamps, two each side and two across top and bottom. Every time one was tightened a mitre joint slipped, so I tightened the opposite one and the base popped out of the rebate. It was like handling a bag of eels. Anyway, I won — but after 33 minutes of struggling I decided there must be an easier way. I made some corner-blocks, and with only two G-clamps and careful adjustment and pressure top and bottom, the job can be glued in three minutes. The lid can then be cut off and the box lined or the lid hinged. ■

Mallets

Bob Wearing's Workshop

Not as unsubtle as you might think — there's a mallet for every occasion. Learn how to make the right one for the right job

Most toolboxes boast a whole range of hammers — but only one mallet. Consider the different amounts of force needed to mortise a gate and chop fine drawer dovetails, and this seems rather strange. I've outlined the dimensions and makings of six mallets (three this month; three next) so you can choose the ones you're likely to need.

You can use any good dense non-splitting hardwood — beech is generally used for British-manufactured mallets. Lignum vitae is the deluxe option but it's expensive and hard to come by; some turned mallets can be made from lignum bowling-green woods. Fruit woods are good, as are oak, elm, ash and walnut. Remember that within a given specie there's a wide range of hardness, so check blocks individually.

Traditional carpenter's mallet

This model (fig. 1) is for the dyed-in-the-wool traditionalist. The only problem in making it is cutting the long, deep, tapered mortise. Accurate marking out is essential before you attempt shaping the block. The ends of the mortise must be well cut and straight; after use any hollowness may force the short grain material into the hollow, resulting in a very hollow striking-face or a split head (fig. 2).

Find the angle of the faces by using your elbow as the pivot-point from where the necessary lines can be drawn (I'm not at all sure that we swing only from the elbow, but it is a good enough theory). For those not wishing to do this research, the drawings give quite a satisfactory face angle.

The handles are usually manufactured from beech, but straight-grained or cleft ash would be better. Saw out the handle oversize and gradually plane down, testing frequently to get the right fit. Finally shape the handle to suit.

German pattern mallet

While British mallets are traditionally bench-made, German craftsmen use a lathe and apply the same method for hammer and mallet heads, by fixing a round stem into a bored hole with a wedge (fig. 3). This simplifies the problem considerably. Using a brace and bit, put through a small pilot-hole about 1/8in, starting from both sides, then bore the main hole. Now shape the head.

Turn the handle from a cleft piece of rectangular-section ash. Thread a small piece of thin plywood which has been bored with the same bit on to the lathe tailstock. Try this regularly to make sure of a really tight fit and shape the rest of the handle to personal preference. This rectangular shape gives a better grip than a fully turned handle by reducing the tendency to twist in the hand. Traditional British handles taper away from the head. Far better, is a handle which thickens where it's gripped. If you want a fully turned handle, turn from rectangular stock, leaving some flat on the two wide faces.

The average manufactured handle is far too long for all but the heaviest work. Try a shorter one and I am sure you'll prefer it, particularly for light bench-work, such as chopping dovetails or clearing housings. Driving a wedge into a circular hole does little to improve the grip; it just compresses the handle. So before driving in the wedge, open out the hole to a slight ellipse.

Laminated mallet

The dimensions for this mallet (fig. 4) can also be used for the traditional model. This method is particularly suitable for heavier mallets which otherwise require very thick, dry material.

Make full-size ply or cardboard patterns and cut out the five components from accurately-thicknessed stock. Offcuts of walnut and cherry are particularly successful and attractive; use a synthetic resin glue (Cascamite or Aerolite). I usually glue the two small blocks to a larger one, putting in four fine moulding pins to stop them slipping. Next day the fourth block is added. Another way to prevent the pieces sliding, is to cramp up with the handle in place, then knock it out when the cramps are firmly on; you'll need four G-cramps. Clean out the surplus wet glue from the mortise right away.

I like to thicken the handle at the grip end, so I secure the head with two wedges which swell out the handle to fit the tapered mortise. A disc sander makes quick work of cleaning up the striking faces and curved top, but with freshly sharpened tools this is still not the slog one imagines.

● *More mallets next month*

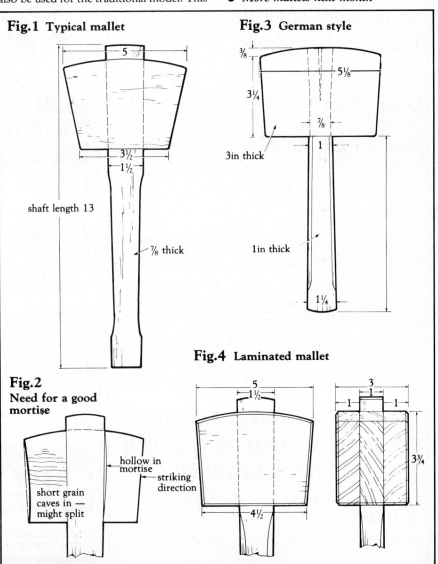

Fig.1 Typical mallet
5
3½
1½
shaft length 13
⅞ thick

Fig.2 Need for a good mortise
hollow in mortise
striking direction
short grain caves in — might split

Fig.3 German style
⅜
5⅛
3¼
⅞
1
3in thick
1in thick
1¼

Fig.4 Laminated mallet
5
1½
3
1
1
1
4½
3¾

683

The grand furniture saga

Passion for European and Chinese style in the 18th century gave Chippendale the excuse to revel in the florid and exotic. Vic Taylor examines the combined impact of Rococo, Gothic and Chinoiserie on British furniture making

● *Chippendale library table decorated in carved solid mahogany with lion-motifs in the 'tern' style (three of each). Housed at Nostell Priory, Yorkshire*

Rococo style came to London in the late 1730s via the work of goldsmiths and silversmiths, and was soon in demand for architecture and furniture, from a clientele tired of the strictly formal Palladianism of William Kent. English woodcarvers and plasterers had to learn the new techniques from immigrant Italian craftsmen (*stuccatori*), although the more exotic and exaggerated Continental examples never took off in Britain.

Matthias, or Matthew Lock was one of the first exponents of the new style, and in 1740 he published *A New Drawing Book of Ornaments, Shields, Compartments, Masks, etc.*; he was also a practical woodcarver of the highest rank. A large mirror with matching console table made by Locke is now in the Victoria and Albert Museum.

Another was Thomas Johnson, a woodcarver who published a set of engraved plates entitled *Twelve Girandoles* in 1755. Between 1755 and 1763 he was in business at Queen Street, Seven Dials, London, and later at the 'Golden Boy' in Grafton Street, Soho. In 1758 he published *The Book of the Carver*, and *One Hundred and Fifty New Designs*, published in monthly parts between 1756 and 1758. Johnson was particularly influenced by Francis Barlow's illustrations for the book of Aesop's Fables (1687); he became adept at translating the animals and scenery into motifs for carving. Ince and Mayhew were great admirers of Johnson's style and many of the Rococo designs in their *Universal System of Household Furniture* (1759-1762) obviously owe a great deal to him.

Girandoles (status-symbol wall-lighting comprising a bracket fitted with candle-holders), mirrors, and *torchères* (candle-stands) were the main vehicles for Rococo as they were purely decorative and not load-bearing. Tables and chairs, which needed constructional strength, were not so well suited.

Chippendale, who was as much an entrepreneur as a designer cabinet-maker, popularised the Rococo style probably more than any other English designer. Although his early Rococo chairs generally had cabriole legs, his later models favoured French-style scroll feet, often with the 'tern' design. In Chippendale's *Director*, the upholstered armchairs are referred to as

'French'; such chairs were better known in France than in England, and Chippendale was strongly attracted to French fashions. In 1768 he visited Paris (possibly Portugal too) and in 1769 he fell foul of Customs and Exise who fined him for under-declaring the value of 60 French chairs.

The main differences between 'Chippendale Rococo' and the French equivalent was that his designs were made in mahogany and lacked the metal mounts used by the French. Chippendale's designs were often over-enthusiastic in the use of Rococo ornament, and it's doubtful if the more exuberant examples were ever made up without modification. Indeed, he had critics who said the designs couldn't be made up at all (particularly the Gothic and Chinese), and he was stung to retort 'Upon the whole, I have here (the *Director, 1762*) given no Design but what may be executed with Advantage by the Hands of a skilful Workman, though some of the Profession have been diligent enough to represent them . . . as so many specious Drawings, impossible to be worked off by an Mechanick whatsoever. I will not scruple to attribute this to Malice, Ignorance, and Inability . . .'

Despite his liking for Rococo, Chippendale's larger furniture such as library bookcases, tables, and desks still retained the massive and monumental appearance of the Palladian style, although the effect was softened by the use of Rococo-inspired carved ornament. Much of this kind of furniture can now be seen at Temple Newsam House, near Leeds, and Nostell Priory, near Wakefield, Yorkshire; originally such dignified library furniture was sold to the *nouveau riche* landowners and gentlemen of means.

Strictly speaking, 'commode' refers to a low chest containing two or three

drawers. In France, commodes were either used in the bedroom or, suitably enriched with marquetry, ormolu, marble or scagliola tops, and shaped bombè-fronts, they graced reception rooms and salons. The English commodes were more restrained in design than the French, both in the type of ornamentation and the amount it was used. There are several chest-commode designs in the *Director* as well as some for commode tables. It's a pity that the word 'commode' was applied in the 19th century to chests or cupboards designed to accommodate chamber-pots — and an even greater pity that the term has persisted.

The *Director* also contains some designs for Buroe Dressing tables ('buroe' was the contemporary spelling for bureau), and there's an interesting historical side-light here. Chippendale's designs were eagerly taken up and reproduced in the eastern states of America; the *Connoiseur Encyclopaedia of Antiques* says 'In America, ever since the 18th century, the word bureau means a chest of drawers, with or without a mirror, and regularly used in the bedroom'. The four designs given by Chippendale have an assortment of shaped tops, and they all have knee-holes. His 'desk-bookcases' correspond to today's bureau-bookcases.

The success of the *Director* was undoubtedly due to its wide coverage of the variety of artefacts used by its contemporary upholders. There were drawings for organ cases, basin stands, shaving tables, candle-stands, lanterns, clockcases, chimney-pieces, wall-brackets, terms, beds and their hangings, breakfast tables, tea caddies, picture frames, mirrors, fretwork, brass handles, stove-grates, and borders for wall-hangings. There were two conspicuous absentees: large dining tables, which Chippendale never dealt with, and sideboards with cupboards which were a later

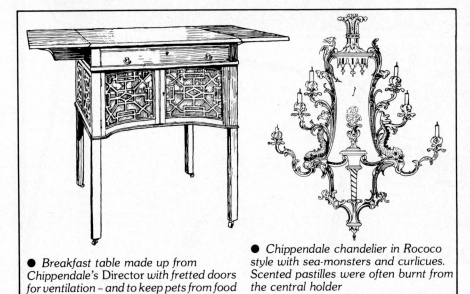

● Breakfast table made up from Chippendale's *Director* with fretted doors for ventilation – and to keep pets from food

● *Chippendale chandelier in Rococo style with sea-monsters and curlicues. Scented pastilles were often burnt from the central holder*

development, although he does include sideboard tables.

There were two more or less concurrent styles which became fashionable round the middle years of the century. One was Chinoiserie, which was the name given to furniture, furnishings and related artefacts rendered in the Chinese style; the other was the Gothick genre, spelt with a 'k' to differentiate it from the medieval Gothic.

The desire for all things Oriental was not new in the 18th century; it had appeared and re-appeared intermittently for about 100 years prior to 1750. John Evelyn enumerated a list of books about China and the Orient in 1662, and Pepys was full of praise for 'a most excellent book with rare cuts' about China which he bought from Martin the bookseller in 1668.

The freedom of expression associated with Rococo designs allowed Chinese motifs to be incorporated quite happily, and the style became all the rage. William Whitehead, a contemporary writer, noted 'According to the present prevailing whim, everything is Chinese, or in the Chinese taste; or . . . partly after the Chinese manner. Chairs, tables, chimney-pieces, frames for looking-glasses, and even our most vulgar utensils, are all reduced to this new-fangled standard: and without doors [out-of-doors], so universally has it spread that every gate to a cow-yard is in Ts and Zs, and every hovel for cows has bells hanging at the corners.' (*The World, 1753*).

One principal instigator of the craze was Sir William Chambers, an architect who designed the famous pagoda for Kew Gardens in 1762. In his youth he had made several trade voyages to China under the aegis of the Swedish East India Company, and in 1757 he published a book of plates entitled *Designs for Chinese Buildings, Furniture, Dresses, Machines, and Utensils*. It was a huge success; but not to the delight of its author, who complained of 'the extravagant fancies that daily appear under the name of Chinese', and who came to wish that he had had nothing to do with the subject.

Chippendale, in his role as a hard-headed Yorkshire entrepreneur, knew a good thing when he saw it and joyfully included some pretty outrageous designs in the *Director*, with dragons, herons, trailing moss, bells, unearthly flowers and grasses, plus the obligatory Chinese peasants. Ince and Mayhew had Chinese designs for cases, shelves, chairs, and stands in their *Universal System of Household Furniture* (1759-1762), as did Robert Manwaring for chairs in his *The Cabinet and Chair-maker's Real Friend and Companion* (1765). The best examples of this style are found in the Chinese room at Claydon House, Buckinghamshire and in Saltram House, Devonshire.

By 1780 the craze had burned itself out; there was a brief revival when the Prince Regent commissioned Henry Holland to design the Marine Pavilion in Brighton in 1786 '*à la Chinois*', but he was persuaded to adopt a Hindu rather than a Chinese style for most of the building.

The Gothic medieval style had never died out completely and was used architecturally by Wren, Vanburgh and Kent, but not to any great extent despite several books on the subject written by architect Batty Langley (1696-1751). Horace Walpole, who had an acid tongue, said at the time that 'All that his books achieved, has been to teach carpenters to massacre that venerable species . . . [Gothic styles].'

It was the same Walpole (1717-1797) who singlehandedly invented the Gothick style, often called 'Strawberry Hill Gothick' after the house he had at Strawberry Hill in London. It was a modest early Georgian building which Walpole determined to enlarge and decorate in his interpretation of the medieval period. It took him 30 years, and his success was signalled by the guided tours of sightseers (conducted by himself) which had to be limited to one tour a day.

The Gothic style had no real academic basis; the architecture and furniture employed any motif which had a remote association with medievalism. In architecture, this included fan-vaulted ceilings, pinnacles, arches, pierced columns, quatrefoils, and even rose-windows; in furniture, the lancet arch was the dominant motif, accompanied by turrets, pinnacles, tracery, and cluster-column legs (whether these were based on the clustered columns seen in churches, or representations of bundles of bamboo, is a moot point, especially as the Gothic and the Chinese fashions often appear on the same piece).

It's generally agreed that the style succeeded in a light-hearted way and at all events it seems to have caught the public's fancy. It survived well into the 19th century, when the romanticism engendered by Sir Walter Scott's novels changed it into a more serious and ponderous expression of nostalgia for past grandeur. ■

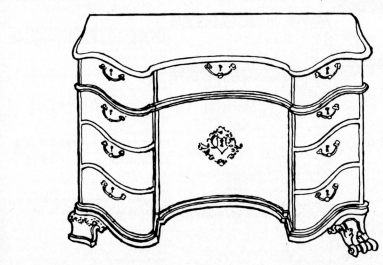

● An ancestor of today's American bureau: a Buroe Dressing table from a *Director* design

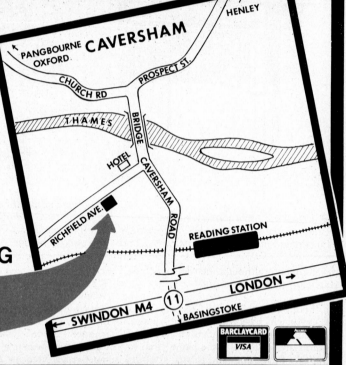

THE WOODWORK BUSINESS

Books and records

The traditional hate of woodworkers everywhere — and indeed most craftspeople — 'doing the books' is undeniably crucial to your business survival. Hugh O'Neill goes through the basics, Chris Yonge expands on using a microcomputer for a small workshop-based business

The books — Hugh O'Neill

Salesmen hate them, craftsmen grudgingly do them on the backs of envelopes, businessmen thrive on them, accountants revel in them, the taxman demands them. Books and records are the bane of most people running a small business. It's worse if we have a business loan from any source: the lenders will have added to the burden of records. We can all feel weighed down by these requirements.

If this is our view, it's likely to be reflected in our behaviour. There will be a carrier bag full of invoices; we pay bills only on final demand; we make one oversight, end up in the county court and acquire an everlasting negative credit record; we never know whether we have any money to spend — then the unexpected tax demand arrives and we know we haven't. Our costings are 'by guess and by God'; and at the end of the year we either have to take ten days off production to get the books ready, or hand the whole lot over to an accountant and incur another enormous bill.

There is another view. 'Books' tell us what is going on. They give us confidence (or tell us when drastic action is required). They help us control stocks and complete orders on time. The Cash-flow Forecast tells us that we can actually afford that new machine now. (It even allows us to plan and take holidays!) Book-keeping should be viewed as a positive, helpful activity — but only if we take the medicine regularly.

Certainly the greater the discipline, the better run will be the business, and the more likely it is to succeed. Most business failures (and many more fail than succeed) can be traced to poor record-keeping and inadequate knowledge of what's really going on.

So you need to design your records with two separate requirements in mind.
● To be able to produce the financial data required by the VAT office, the Inland Revenue, and any loan agencies.
● To provide you with a clear picture of what is going on in all aspects of the business: Bills, Payments, Sales, Costs of sales, Sales/markets analysis, Invoices, Receipts, Stocks, Production costs, Orders and progress, Client activity, etc.
Often, a good set of books that meets the second requirement will, with minimum addition, also provide most of the material for the first.

For Official Use

The accounts/tax element records, supports, justifies and balances all the monies that the business pays out against all the income. VAT records take this one step further by separately identifying the VAT element and show what you owe the Customs and Excise for the tax that you have collected on their behalf, reduced by the amount of VAT that you can reclaim as a business expense on the goods and services that you buy in. (As an aside, VAT registration can be beneficial under certain circumstances even if you are just below the threshold.)

What the basic tax and VAT records do not do is to show the real connection between costs and returns. They are totally inadequate for business control purposes.

Control records provide breakdowns of material usage and costs and relate this to the total selling price of items. They help to identify where all the money really goes and where you have to make changes and savings. Fundamentally they show whether your pricing, production and selling methods are right.

Cash-flow forecasts extrapolate what you expect the costs (outgoings) are going to be for a given period in the future, and offset against this the sales or income you expect. They will be required by any agency you approach for a loan; but much more, they provide an advanced warning of areas of business activity that might need attention. They aren't easy to produce as it is very difficult to foretell the future, particularly in a new venture. But if you can't produce a forecast, it probably means that you have no strategy or plans. The business is living from hand to mouth, drifting in whatever direction the wind blows — inevitably, the rocks! Profits are possible when the forecast indicates a positive flow and the business might survive. A negative flow indicates that the rocks are now hard by. It's not quite that simple, but not a bad basis to start working on.

You will need to agree with your tax inspector, and *separately* with your VAT office, the records, breakdowns and allowances that they require/will allow. Their requirements are very different.

You will find that the Tax Inspector will allow a percentage of the costs of running a private car and will make an allowance against the purchase price. VAT will be allowed on running costs but not at all on the purchase price. Both agencies may allow a similar percentage against private use of the car, but may offer differing figures on, say, the telephone. Both parties have some areas of discretion, both interpret facts differently, and bargaining is always possible.

Neither party can make you use an accountant. Accountants can be expensive and the more you ask them to do, the bigger the bill. However they can be useful if you have no idea where to start. (Don't forget the free advice from the Enterprise and Small Business agencies).

On the plus side, accountants can:
● Design you a set of books/records
● Guide you on the tax concessions available to the business, and get you rebates that you may not know about
● Argue your case with the tax office, (and Tax Inspectors believe them!)
● Do all your book-keeping if you wish.
Choose a suitable level of involvement. You may find that with the free advice you can design your own books, agree the adequacy of these with the Inland Revenue, and produce your own end-of-year trading statements. Only at this stage may you decide to employ an accountant to check your calculations and put them into an appropriate form for the tax assessment. Certainly let the accountant fight your battles with the Inland Revenue — they usually save you more than they cost.

VAT records are a pain, particularly if you have a large number of sales of small items, you make daily sales, and some are in cash. The craftsman producing only a dozen or two high-priced items a year is lucky. Talk over your business with the VAT office and explain the level of activity you anticipate. They will suggest the best form for the records and will probably suggest how the VAT requirement can be integrated with your purchase and sales records. Alternatively they may suggest a pre-printed account book, such as the Simplex VAT Record Book. This is straightforward to use as all the column headings and analysis pages are laid out, and examples are included. If you are considering using software on your micro, the VAT office has to approve the system.

For your own use

Your own records are more important. These provide you with the data so you can:

- Accurately cost the production of each item
- Assess the viability of different materials and production methods
- Account for and control all stocks and raw materials (and ensure that you don't run out)
- When you are bigger, identify where orders and materials are in the production process.
- Trace the path of raw materials into the finished product and identify areas of wastage and potential use/costs improvements
- Identify which products, design and materials variations sell best and make the most profit
- Probably most important, identify which products to drop. (I can't understand why anybody makes pepper mills!)

We use the business records and the overall financial accounts to determine strategy. Here we look at the global figures for such items as cost of production, cost of sales, cost of delivery, and so on. These can provide some nasty shocks. For instance; you have always known that a lot of expense is incurred in selling through, say, craft fairs. When you see at the end of the year that your cost of sales consumes 41% of your gross sales income, then you may realise it would be cheaper to have your own retail outlet. It certainly caused me to re-think after my first year.

Fortunately, record-keeping is not addictive (although some aspects of computer analysis are), so you're unlikely to keep too many records. It is however sometimes tempting to extend the breakdown of figures too far. The year-end accounts will show 'Costs of delivery'. In the purchases ledger we may well wish to identify separately: vehicle repairs, petrol/oil/incidentals, and courier/package/postal charges. But is there any value in breaking these down further and, say, having a separate column for petrol and another for oil? Keep in mind that the purpose of breakdown is to provide you with the ability to be able to spot costly problem areas (e.g. when the van needs replacing) and to compare alternative ways of undertaking activities.

The simplest set of basic records for a small business probably consists of:

1 Financial Accounts These are year-end figures laid out on a balance-sheet basis, the summaey provided to the Inland Revenue. And, alternative 'A' for irregular or one-off sales:

2 A Purchase Ledger (Purchases Day Book) which records all the purchases made including services; rent, rates, telephone, insurance, etc. These are entered in date order (invoice date) and are then allocated to costing headings.

3 A Sales Ledger (Sales Day Book). Sales are entered in date order and again may be broken down into product categories.

Or, Alternative 'B' for daily sales:

2 & 3 Cash book Again Simplex do an excellent pre-printed book — the 'D' Cash Book. This provides a near-complete system for the small trader. It records sales, purchases and bank reconciliation. It provides a crude breakdown of expenses into global headings, but has no sales analysis provision.

Plus:

4 A separate VAT register. (This may be incorporated into the Purchase and Sales ledgers but it does take up valuable analysis columns.)

If not using pre-printed books then the Cathedral (and other) Analysis Books are useful. These can be obtained with various numbers of pre-drawn columns. I find I need the 21-column book for purchases analysis and 16 for sales.

Of course there are other records that are useful: client lists and contact addresses are obvious. If you make repeated sales to the

---

'Extended credit is the way most small businesses fail . . . '

---

same few clients, you might consider an alternative to the Sales Day Book and have a Sales Ledger which has a page per client and shows the current account and or re-ordering status for each purchaser. If you work on the Sales Day book principle *and* have repeat business clients, than you might consider a client card index which shows current status. A breakdown of this nature shows you which accounts need chasing, who should be chased for an order, and who is due a bottle of whisky at Christmas.

Certainly the more clients you service, the more necessary it becomes to have a mechanism for regularly identifying who owes you money. Taking extended credit is the way that some major organisations now finance their business — and allowing extended credit is the way that most small businesses fail.

A list of suppliers' names, addresses, telephone numbers, and the names of key contacts is essential — it saves so much time. A card index is probably the best (but make sure that you can't remove and then lose any card).

Some will think 'computers', and they are certainly useful; excellent software is available for some machines. Some lower-priced programmes are however a little like pre-printed accounts books and don't permit you to do just the sort of analysis you need. Better business accounting software costs too much, and tailor-made programmes run to ICI-level money.

Computers are also fascinating (addictive) and the means can easily overtake the ends. You can become so interested in playing with databases and in analysing everything in sight, you have no time left to spend upon production.

To me a word processor (with a spelling checker) is essential. It produces good-looking business letters, mail-outs, sales literature, and clean businesslike invoices. (The businesslike ones get paid quicker). It acts as my filing system; I take risks, and don't keep 'hard copy' back-ups unless it is a contract or invoice.

A database and spreadsheet programme has given me the opportunity of making detailed assessments of the type of item (woodturning) that sells best, of the most popular sizes, price ranges, materials, etc. I know what items and at what prices are going to be successful in London, the suburbs, commuter belt, the Midlands, the North, and so on. I know what markets and which craft fair organisers to avoid; not only by name, but on the basis of a number of identifiable parameters. I know that, subject to specific and clear exceptions, there is little point in bothering with craft fairs before July or in the month of September. I know what to take to shops in Bournemouth and what to take to High Wycombe (it's substantially different) and I can anticipate the changes between July and the Christmas trade. Above all it has shown me with overwhelming evidence, that competing on price, undercutting, offering reduced or 'sale' prices, reduces profit *and* gross sales for the year. Even further, it suggests that at least some craft work is in no way price sensitive. But then, I have wasted a lot of potential woodturning time playing with the computer.

On balance I find the computer a great help. If the business had four or five people, there would be no doubt that all the 'books' would be put on to it, and if I were buying again it would probably be Amstrad.

Whether you computerise or not, one thing is clear. Seeing record-keeping as an undesirable chore is counterproductive. Seeing records and analysis as contributing to efficiency, confidence and profitability is more than justified.

Details of Main Books and Records

1 FINANCIAL ACCOUNTS: two facing pages — 'double entry'.

Left hand page shows income summary. For a few accounts you may itemise by client, or for a few products you may summarise by product.

To meet the tax requirements you may give a single total figure provided that this can be supported by a Sales Ledger or a Sales Day Book, copies of invoices and bank paying-in books and statements.

Right-hand page shows the expenditure for the year under various categories. A typical set of headings might include:

Capital equipment depreciation
Buildings and maintenance
Equipment leasing or hire costs
Wages

Tools and repairs
Timber and raw materials
Sundries, fittings and finishes
Publicity and advertisements
Travel and delivery
Printing, stationery and office
   supplies
Display, exhibitions and shows
Postage and telephone
National Insurance
Insurance
Rent and Rates
Heat, power and light
Bank and interest charges

At the foot of the right-hand page
it's useful to record the written
down value of all capital equipment (including new purchases),
but in the above only show the depreciation or allowances claimable.
Where, during the year, a piece of
equipment has been sold the difference between the selling price
and the book (depreciated) value is
shown as income or expenditure,
whichever is appropriate.
The expenditure is sub-totalled and
the difference between this and the
income represents the profit,
shown as 'Profit for the Year . . . '
(or 'Loss . . . '!)

2 PURCHASES DAY BOOK
An analysis book with columns to
break down the purchases. The headings may be as above or be extended,
i.e. 'Travel and delivery' may have
'Motor repairs and maintenance';
'Running expenses'; 'Accommodation'; 'Carters'.
Books with up to 32 analysis columns
are available, but most find about 20
satisfactory.
Normally entries are made in date order
and each is given a folio number to
cross-refer to filed bills. (You may have
to produce these for up to seven years).
The entry will show date; name of supplier; folio number; the cost (distributed under the appropriate headings);
the total cost.
At the end of each month the columns
are added and are cross-checked against
the sum of the total costs.
At the end of the year the figures for
each month are listed to produce the
year-end figures for transfer to the
Financial Accounts.
3 SALES DAY BOOK
Again a multi-column analysis book
with the column headings showing
either main products, or sales outlets.
Totals produced at the month end and
year end as above.
If VAT records are incorporated you
will need columns to show: date and
number of invoice; customer name;
gross invoice total; value of sale (at
standard and positive rates); zero,
exempt and export sale values; VAT
output tax payable.

Three-dimensional drawing programs allow you to see new designs from all sides...

and combine them in the same drawing.

A computer is probably not the first
thing you think of when listing the
essentials for setting up a small
workshop. Over the past 18 months,
however, I've found that, properly used, a
computer can make previously boring
administrative jobs enjoyable as well as
handling information more quickly and in
greater detail that traditional methods.
They can be a good investment if you deal
with the bookwork yourself. If you aren't
familiar with the various machines
available, however, it's easy to make expensive mistakes or end up with a system
that can't grow as your business expands.
   Since I'm not a computer specialist I can't
compare different makes, but can only
write from my own experience and
situation. If you want further information
on the range of computers around and,
equally important, the business programmes available for each, then your best
start is to buy or borrow a selection of
computer magazines, and to talk to other
business users. Avoid the games-playing
enthusiasts, though: they tend to be
fascinated more by the technical specifications of their machines than their
usefulness and reliability in a busy office.
   You should also analyse what you want
the computer and its programmes to do. It
may well be that your paperwork is not
sufficient to justify the expense, that you
can hire someone to handle the administration, or that your clients and jobs are
such that the presence of a computer would
detract from a traditional image.
   I will concentrate on woodworking business similar to my own: small, expanding,
taking on subcontract as well as individually commissioned and batch-produced
pieces, and aiming for maximum efficiency
and quality in a limited equipment budget.
My experience in this situation is that one
of the current small office computers is well
worth the effort and expense.
   Before spending what may turn out to be
a great deal of money it's essential to talk to

● **Above** and **below**, working out how
shelf units in grey and natural ash will
look . . . the prototypes are pre-batch
production

someone who already owns and uses as
close a system as you can find to the one
you're considering buying. Not only can
you experience the machine and some of its
programmes in a non-commercial environment, you should also get impartial advice
about the equipment's good and bad
points, and be able to call for help later,
during the setting-up. You can also discuss

continued

your programme library, and share users' journals containing reviews of equipment and software.

I started off with a secondhand BBC B computer, with 'View' word-processing and spreadsheet chips installed to maximise the working memory. Both of these are attractive and convenient programmes to use, but I found the BBC's limited memory (32k) an irritating restriction when writing or modelling the workshop's financial structure. The logical next step in the BBC family (which would have allowed me to continue using my existing files and programmes) was the Master series, but I felt these were uncompetitively priced for the features offered. A friend's enthusiasm for his Atari 520 computer led me to examine and finally buy one. It has proved to be ideally suited to my current needs while offering the potential for affordable expansion to a full multi-user office system. Its main use is for word processing and letter writing; less for graphic work and three-dimensional design because of the limitations of my original budget 9-pin Epson LX-80 printer (good value in its reliability and features).

A micro can help a woodworking business in several ways:

Word processing: mailing shots/writing articles and books/desktop publishing of business newsletters

Accounting: cash flow forecasting and analysis/record keeping/invoicing

Graphics: computer-aided design/drafting and sketches/creating forms

Utility programmes: wood optimising/information storage and retrieval/address files

Teaching programmes: touch typing/accounts and record keeping.

Software

Don't buy any programmes without either trying them out on a friend or supplier's machine or, if you buy from the cheaper mail-order firms, reading at least one review. Nine times out of ten you will not be able to send back programs which don't turn out to be what you want because the supplier will inevitably (and reasonably) suspect you of simply copying it. Copy protection on the cheaper business programs is becoming rare, allowing users to make backups for their own use, but has the drawback that they are not returnable.

Unless you have unlimited time and patience, don't expect to write your own programs or modify commercial ones. Modern business software is so complex and relatively cheap that it's not worth the effort unless you're a real enthusiast.

You will require at least half a dozen programs to use your computer's capabilities to the full, and should budget for purchasing them as soon as possible. These include:

Word processing for letters, articles, leaflets, and record keeping; the better ones allow for inserting pictures and special typefaces into the text

Graphics/3D Design for sketching and making pictures or special headings

Mailing for circulating potential and present clients with standard letters

Accounting and spreadsheet for accounts keeping and financial forecasting

Printer/Plotter drivers to print out your writing and drawings exactly as they appear on the screen

Database to record names, addresses, etc for the mailing program.

Some of these may be supplied together; for the Atari the word processing program *First Word Plus* includes a selection of drivers for most current makes of printers, plus a mailing program which is available separately — don't make the mistake of buying something twice! *First Word Plus* also includes a 40,000 word dictionary; even if you're the best speller in the world this facility will pick up most of those irritating typing mistakes that can slip through to ruin the effect of a carefully composed letter. It's a good idea to make sure as many of your programs as possible come from the same software house, so you can be sure they will work together and exchange information easily.

In my opinion small workshops simply don't have the volume or complexity of sales to make computer invoicing and accounts worth while. This is not only because of the time taken to edit the accounts file and its back-up copy every time you buy another batch of supplies: I find the ability to instantly compare one month with another too useful to lose by computerising, and still do my accounts and invoicing in traditional fashion on a day-to-day basis. This also removes the slight risk of losing essential data. As work increases you may have to look again at computerised accounting, however, and should keep such a requirement in mind when choosing your machine.

Computer-aided design is an attractive idea, but in practice is still too complex and expensive for most small businesses to set up. Furniture's three-dimensional and intricately detailed shapes make it unlikely that the necessary combination of programs and technical drawing machines will be economic for a few years yet. Currently affordable programs such as *CAD-3D* for the Atari range are useful for sketching designs and for seeing how a projected design will appear from all sides, but cannot support volumetric or stress analysis. I find a good graphics program essential for brightening up letters, however, as well as taking a lot of the spadework out of producing a monthly newsletter for a designers' group I belong to.

Whether you want to buy teaching programs is a matter of personal taste: I learnt to touch-type on a BBC machine, a skill that had previously eluded me, and found this form of learning fast and enjoyable. The advantage of such methods with a well produced program is that the difficulty of the exercises keeps pace with your improvement, concentrating automatically upon weak points and the elimination of bad habits as you work — effectively the same as having a teacher looking over your shoulder the whole time. If a group of people buy such a program together and pass it round as they learn (and this is the only time such a practice is justified) the modest cost is further reduced.

Budgeting

A computer can be expensive to set up, but not to maintain. My own setting up costs were:

	Price in £ (ex VAT)
500k Atari ST, mono monitor, 1mb disc drive	550.00
Epson LX-80 printer, paper handling accessories like cut-sheet feeder, and cables	300.00
Blank discs	25.00
Appropriate software and manuals	200.00
Tractor fed paper and labels	25.00
Total	£1100.00

Don't count on the computer having any secondhand value if you keep it longer than a couple of years. Technology is advancing and prices falling, so a four or five-year old machine, though otherwise in perfect order, will fetch little more than scrap prices. In this situation you're better advised holding on to it as a backup or home machine, and should take into account when buying how likely you are to find a compatible system in five years' time.

Remember that changing to a computer-based system will have implications for your stationery requirements, and make sure that the size and thickness of paper you favour will feed through the printer. Some machines will not take anything heavier than 80gsm paper in other than hand-fed sheets, for example, so if you want to use a sheet feeder which automatically supplies paper to the printer for batches of letters, you may have to have your headed paper reprinted. Computerised labelling of letters is not always a good idea (even the best examples often look like junk mail) and I recommend using window envelopes, which offer the advantage of making it impossible to put the wrong letter inside.

If you want to produce mailing lists, storing personal information on your computer, even of names, addresses, and occupations, you will have to register under the new Data Protection Act (ask at your local Post Office) and be prepared to supply a copy of your file entry about any individual to them if they request it. You must balance your need for such a facility against the cost and time needed to register.

Peripheral devices are generally to do with feeding information into the machine, storing it, and getting it back in an understandable form. The most common peripherals (and certainly the most essential) are data storage devices such as tape and disc drives. After these come printers, of which the most sensible buy for a small business would be as high-quality a dot matrix machine as you could afford; used with one of the latest generation of word processing programs, these are capable of producing graphics integrated with letter-quality printing. Matrix printers are faster and cheaper than daisywheel machines, which produce text of slightly higher printed quality, but more slowly, and without a graphics capability.

An essential addition to the system, and one which I see as another peripheral device in its own right, is a good quality photocopying machine (preferably A3 size). This will save you money on printer ribbons as well as speeding up bulk mailings of information. You should also buy as large capacity and reliable a disc drive as you can — at least 1 megabyte — and preferably two, to speed the backup copying files.

Don't expect the computer to be totally reliable; nothing is. The current generation of micros is generally very good, but still vulnerable to peaks and interruptions in the power supply common in the rural areas where so many small woodworking busi-

nesses such as mine are situated. A basic power cleaning unit to remove the worst voltage peaks will cost around £30, and is a good investment, particularly if you're spending a lot of time with complex programs and data files.

Computers are notoriously susceptible to dust, damp, vibration, and power fluctuations — exactly the kind of conditions found in many small workshops. Keep them well apart, or you'll have problems. The same applies to wet hands and dusty clothes. There are several other ways of minimising both the chance and the effects of any loss of information in the machine and its disc records.

The first is simply to make sure that you have at least two copies of every program and file, and to keep your discs well away from any sources of magnetism, including the screen and the computer itself (which often contains a small but powerful speaker). Even driving around with them in a car or van can erase vital information and expensive programs; wrap in aluminium foil or place the discs in a (clean) metal biscuit tin when transporting them. The second is to keep draft printouts of important letters, articles, financial records, and other information; this really requires you to have a good dot matrix printer for speed and legibility. Finally, keep traditional

methods as emergency backup; your old portable typewriter and pocket calculator in a cupboard, for example, so you never end up being unable to send out invoices or do the books.

It may be argued that computers have no place in the smaller craft-based workshop, and that they interfere with the essential human contact that makes for successful work. All I can say is that the use of a computer in my own business has added greatly to my understanding and enjoyment of its running, and has allowed me to offer my clients more and better information rather than less. It's only another machine, after all. Like the dimension saw or the router, how you use it is up to you. It should also be said the Atari 520 is a personal choice — not a recommendation! ■

Eastenders

The great cabinetmaking traditions of London's East End have been sorely eroded in recent years — but there's more than enough room for hope. Alan Smith has been managing the Joint Furniture Project and meeting a number of spirited small firms

● *Davenport by JPM Furniture*

Cheap and plentiful labour, refreshed by regular waves of immigration from Europe, and timber imports to local docks kept furniture making alive and well in London's East End until the 1960s. But the last 25 years have seen a general trek from London to green field sites in Essex and Kent.

Despite this trend, East London remains home to a stubborn, skilful remnant of this previously thriving industry. Georgian reproduction furniture making now tends to dominate, usually in small workshops employing from 2 to 20 people, though some larger companies make other types of household and office furniture.

A legacy from the past is the array of specialist supply and service firms: veneer and timber merchants, tool suppliers, saw doctors, woodcarvers, turners, and wholesalers of fittings — if you're searching for out-of-the-ordinary materials you should look in this part of town.

Local conditions encouraged a fragmented approach; many firms send work out for veneering and polishing, and door-barring and drawer dovetailing may be done by specialised workshops. The system helps tiny workshops turn over work faster, capitalising on their assembly skills.

But while firms survive, they have faced increasing odds in inner London in the 1980s. Rents have risen through competition for space; large tracts of previously industrial land have been taken over for housing. At the same time, small firms have found it hard to get skilled labour; many of the most skilled workers are coming up for retirement, and the firms lack resources to train new entries.

Earlier this year the London College of Furniture was asked by two local authorities, Tower Hamlets and Hackney, to collaborate in a programme of practical help for local furniture makers. The aim was to see whether manufacturers would benefit from exposure to new customers and new product ideas. The Joint Furniture Project which emerged is still running, funded and encouraged by the boroughs.

While managing this project, I contacted many local companies, all of which have impressed me in some way. Two in particular stand out as typical of businesses in a part of London I know and love.

JPM Furniture

JPM Furniture opened in September 1986, with a working capital of £12,000, mostly bank loans, topped up by a grant of £1000 from the local council-backed Hackney Enterprise Board. The grant was used to form a registered co-operative, and for some initial advertising in the trade press.

At first there were three directors, but financial worries led to the resignation of one in April 1987. The two who remain, Mike Hogan and Phillip McCann, are determined to continue with the business into which they have put so much.

Mike and Phillip have years of experience in the furniture trade. Mike was sales director of another furniture company, and Phillip is a skilled cabinetmaker. Both are energetic, practical men, as they need to be to work a 60-or 70-hour week alongside their three staff, all cabinetmakers made redundant by other local firms.

Bad luck for JPM started almost as soon as they moved into Unit 13 in a purpose-built workshop block in Cremer St, Hackney. Wiring work was more expensive than they expected, and they had to meet the full cost of this themselves. Buying machines left them short of working capital, a problem which still dogs them.

They have around 500sq ft, pretty cramped and dusty when they are all working. The workshop houses a table sander, panel saw, router, and other small machines, and furniture is stacked up in every spare corner.

Mike and Phillip started the business during a spell of unemployment, with the idea of providing work and independence for themselves. They are proud of the contribution they have made by providing a few jobs for local people.

Unlike some other types of business, they have been unable to obtain a rent grant from the borough. This is mainly because they form part of the very competitive reproduction furniture sector. Hackney is reluctant to grant-aid reproduction furniture firms, since money for one would allow unfair competition with other's, making no net gain for local business as a whole.

Mike and Phil are both bitter about the elusiveness of government support for small firms, since they don't seem to qualify for the available schemes.

JPM make Georgian-style reproduction furniture, mostly assembled from lipped and veneered chipboard panels. They make a davenport (desk) style hi-fi unit, open bookcases, and a number of other small items. Everything is clearly in the 'mahogany repro' style, but they have an individual approach, and few similar products are manufactured by anyone else. From time to time they have made other items, drum cases, advertising props, and display units. Despite the pressure to cut corners they maintain a good standard of craftsmanship.

A typical JPM product starts as a collection of sawn chipboard panels, lipped with strips of Brazilian mahogany, then transported to a local veneerer who lays mahogany or yew veneers on to them. When the panels come back they are sanded and trimmed to finished size, then jointed together to make the finished items. Mouldings and other decorative parts are glued and pinned in place, and finally doors and drawers are fitted, together with the brassware. Most of their production is sold 'in the white', although they can arrange polishing at another workshop if necessary.

Like many other small workshops around East London they sell to factors, middlemen who pay in cash and then sell goods on to retailers. Most factors also arrange polishing and transport, and prosper mainly because of their speedy payment system. Rapid payment for work is essential to JPM to keep afloat. Chasing slow payers has been a constant headache with other sales, and at one time they had to put their workers on to a three-day week as a direct result of this problem. This tight cash-flow cost them the opportunity to supply a big retail chain whose buyers were impressed by their work. The problem is made worse because it's difficult for JPM to get credit themselves — they have to pay cash for everything. This is typical of the fast-moving, cynical world of London manufacturing, and no reflection on the firm.

Talking to Mike and Phil, the overriding impression is one of determination. Despite their many worries, they are fighting through the early days, convinced they can win and become flourishing suppliers of quality furniture.

Certainly the way they have maintained their quality despite the pressure to 'make it cheap' suggests they will succeed. One thing that would help would be for a furniture polisher to open up in the empty unit next door.

● Discussing the fine detail at JPM Furniture

DKM Designs

Dek Messecar's DKM Designs is in Chance St, a narrow alley in Bethnal Green. The old factory, around 5000sq ft, seems at once both cramped and spacious, a warren of staircases and odd-shaped rooms. DKM moved in during September 1985, and have four staff plus Steve, a cabinetmaking student from the London College of Furniture who helps out two days a week. Like all local furniture firms, Dek finds obtaining skilled staff a problem, and he is currently looking for an all-round machinist/maker. As well as manufacturing, DKM run a small timber yard, selling 17 varieties of English hardwoods.

Tower Hamlets Council, DKM's local authority, have given the company a rent grant, which helped to offset start-up costs. Dek appreciates the support given by their Economic Development Unit. The high design content of DKM products helped persuade the council to back the company.

Dek Messecar is a shrewd, amiable Canadian. A professional musician for 15 years, he gave up the stage in 1980, and pursuing a lifelong interest in tools and craftsmanship, trained as a boat-builder at Lowestoft. He also gained experience in coachbuilding, and designing and making domestic fitted furniture and accessories.

Dek makes a 'bread-and-butter' range of white-painted bedroom furniture, as well as a couple of smart 'own design' cabinet pieces. Generally, the company makes a broader range of goods than JPM, and sells some of it at higher prices. Very little work is sold to middlemen, which gives DKM a bigger margin but slower payment.

The more spacious factory means they can do their own veneering and polishing, so furniture leaves the plant ready for installation. One advantage of this is that Dek has more control over the work flow, and can experiment with new products more easily.

DKM use a lot of modern materials. A typical piece of furniture will be made from panels of MDF, which needs no lippings; the rest of the structure is made from selected hardwoods. As a dealer Dek can pick the best timber for the job. A sprayed finish is the norm for DKM products, and the company has developed some attractive two-colour crackle finishes as well as more ordinary work.

An interesting combination of traditional style re-worked in the modern idiom is their half-round glazed cabinet. The job is based on an old design, made in East London since the 1920s, but it looks modern enough to be exhibited in the design-conscious Independent Designer's Federation showroom in Camden Town.

Dek's plans include moving the workshop to larger premises in a nearby improvement area, which will give space for 10 staff; he will also be able to let space out to other small firms.

There are also plans to go over to contract furniture, the factory producing directly for architects and interior designers. Recent successful efforts in this field — a run of over 500 bedroom units for an Oxbridge college — have convinced DKM that this is where the future lies. Dek will be attending a projected meeting at the LCF in November, where contract buyers can meet new suppliers face to face. His varied experience, and the skill and enthusiasm of his staff, are good reasons for confidence in the face of problems that may lie ahead. ■

● China cabinet by Dek Messecar

● **Joint Furniture Project**
Ring Alan Smith on 01-247 1953, or write to London College of Furniture, 41-71 Commercial Rd, London E1, or contact Hackney or Tower Hamlets Council Economic Development Units.

● **JPM Repro** Ring Mike Hogan on 01-729 3141.
● **DKM Design** Ring Dek Messecar on 01-729 5736.
● Alan Smith is lecturer in Craftsmanship at the London College of Furniture. Research by Ramsey Pattison.

Hands on

WOODWORKING WHEEZE *of the* month

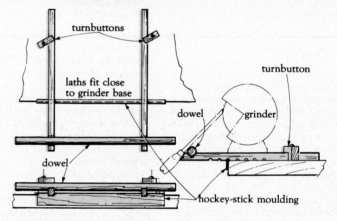

turnbuttons

laths fit close to grinder base

turnbutton

dowel · grinder

dowel

hockey-stick moulding

Sandvik winner

Adjustable grinding guide

This simple tool-grinding guide has solved the problem of multi-faceted bevel grinding on my turning tools.

Mark along the centre of a 12x2x½in bit of hardwood (dimensions not critical), and drill holes at ½-¾in intervals of a diameter to match (or be slightly smaller than) the radius of any available 'hockey-stick' edging. Rip along the gauge line to produce two laths with equally spaced notches.

Clamp the laths cheek to cheek with the notches aligned, and cut a V-shaped notch on the other edges about 1½in from the ends to take a piece of, say, 1in dowel. It should be longer than the spindle length of your grinder by about 4in at each end.

Glue and pin the dowel into the notches, the laths set far enough apart to give a sliding fit against the ends of the grinder base. Fix a strip of hockey stick to the edge of the bench to engage in the notches on the underside of the laths and screw turnbut-

tons to the bench to keep a firm grip on the inner end of the laths, yet allow them to be slid in and out. Number the notches from 1 upwards with a marking pen, choose the notch which gives you the grinding angle you need on each gouge or chisel, and mark the tool with the right notch number.

Result: faultless grinding angles every time, no matter how many times you take the tool away to dip it in water.

J. Narey, Bingley

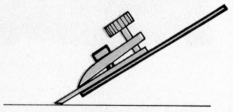

Spokeshave-blade sharpener

I find my adjustable spokeshave blade quite difficult to hold when sharpening, so I made up the metal extension piece shown in the sketch. The lever cap from the spokeshave can be used to clamp the blade firmly to the plate and the whole thing then put in the plane blade section of a honing guide.

R. J. Prosser, Sidmouth

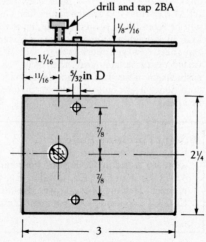

drill and tap 2BA

⅛-1/16

1 1/16

11/16 5/32in D

⅞

2¼

⅞

3

Router dowelling jig

This is designed to be used with any plunge router to which drilling bushes can be fitted. It consists of two parts, the alignment bar and drill plate, both of which can be made of wood or any other suitable material. It can be designed to drill any number of holes on any pitch and, because it's so simple to make, you can quickly make one for any new requirement.

The design is shown in fig. 1. The alignment bar is L-shaped and the two inner faces are used to align the jig to one end and one face of the workpieces. Its dimensions must therefore be in keeping with the task in hand. The drill plate must be large enough to provide a stable base on which to mount the router and the same thickness or more than the height of the bush. Drill the appropriate number of holes of a diameter to match the bush on the router. The alignment bar is fitted to it to provide the required relationship between the two inner faces and the row of holes. It is retained by one or more screws, and 0.125in-diameter dowel holes are drilled through both parts. The two parts are thus positioned by the dowels, preferably 0.125in silver steel, and retained by the screws.

The operation of the jig is illustrated in figs. 2 and 3. Fig. 2 shows holes being drilled in the end of the first workpiece, and fig. 3 on the face of the second. In between the two drilling operations, the alignment bar is replaced on the opposite side of the drill plate as shown in the drawing.

Any inaccuracies in producing the holes in the drill plate will be repeated precisely in both workpieces, and so are of no consequence.

It's important that the screw(s) securing the two parts must be flush with the surface of the drill plate, otherwise they will foul the router base.

Robin Anderson, Harpenden

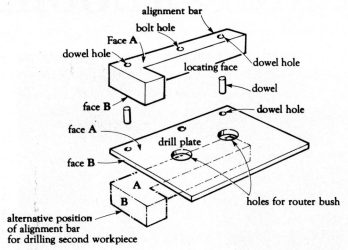

Fig.1 Dowelling jig: exploded view

alignment bar
bolt hole
Face A
dowel hole
locating face
dowel hole
dowel
face B
face A
face B
drill plate
dowel hole
A
B
holes for router bush
alternative position of alignment bar for drilling second workpiece

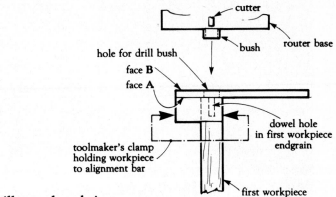

Fig.2 To drill first workpiece

cutter
router base
bush
hole for drill bush
face B
face A
toolmaker's clamp holding workpiece to alignment bar
dowel hole in first workpiece endgrain
first workpiece

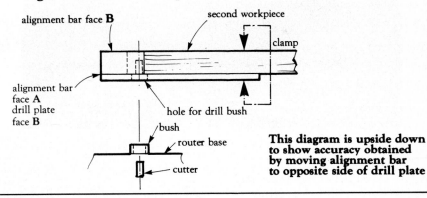

Fig.3 To drill second workpiece

alignment bar face **B**
second workpiece
clamp
alignment bar face A
drill plate
face B
hole for drill bush
bush
router base
cutter

This diagram is upside down to show accuracy obtained by moving alignment bar to opposite side of drill plate

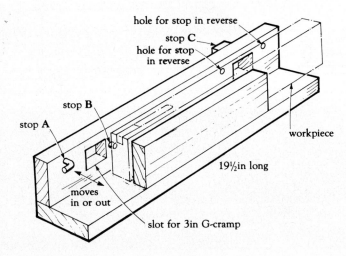

hole for stop in reverse
stop C
hole for stop in reverse
stop B
stop A
moves in or out
slot for 3in G-cramp
workpiece
19½in long

Router mortise jig

I have used this jig to make hundreds of joints with my Elu MOF96 plunge router.

Set the workpiece up in the jig as shown and hold it with three G-clamps. The router's own fence gives you the lateral position of the mortise. Stops **A** and **C** control router movement along the length; stop **A** is ¼in steel rod, stop **C** a small offcut pinned where you need it. Cut the deepest part of the mortise using the router's depth stops; pull stop **A** inwards, then machine the haunch with the router on a second depth stop. It's important to machine all your stiles from one face only for accuracy, so do them all one end only then re-set your stops in the alternative holes and do them all at the other end.

Peter Bonnett, Chester

The mill's a boon

The medieval concept of trades guilds was a bond between practitioners of a given craft; it was also the model later used by the trade union movement for the renowned institution the 'closed shop'. (One function of a guild was to restrict the number of widgit makers in a given area, to a level the local market would bear.) However, a concept turned to malice and individual gain can be turned to serve mutual advancement, education and the common good.

Guilds were, and are, a valuable source of co-operative support; they can further the interests of a group of skilled people more effectively than the individual. Guilds have had tremendous power and wealth, and played a valuable part in the development of our commerce and culture. But the great guilds have had their heyday, and their passing is mourned by some as a part of a decay in standards. They leave us their history and the great shells which were once their focus, the Guild Halls.

Many of today's more serious guilds are well-intentioned, if not well-run, exhibition or marketing agencies for their members' work. Often the more successful the guild, the more difficult it is to become a member. As a newly elected member to the Devon Guild of Craftsmen, I know that having your work judged by more experienced craftsmen can be a humbling and worrying experience. The Devon Guild, formed in 1955 by furniture maker Edward Baly, is now well served by woodworkers, and furniture makers in particular.

● *Left, and **below**, the delightful Riverside Mill. An ideal setting for mixing pleasure with business*

With co-operative funding and spirit, the craftsmen of the Devon Guild have turned a glorious old mill into a profitable crafts showcase. Novice member David Savage has seen the Guild achieve what others dream . . .

There are two ways to look at craftsmen's guilds. The first recognises that they support and encourage the ideals of fellowship, sustained high standards, mutual help, and education. The second agrees with Groucho Marx; any club that would consider you for membership isn't worth joining.

696

Recently the Guild has got its act together and spend £220,000 on a beautiful stone mill-house in Bovey Tracey, a market town on the edge of Dartmoor. The feeling was that the Guild had been staging the annual exhibition in school halls for too long: it either had to find a home or risk stagnation and possible closure. With its own base it could grow and flourish.

Riverside Mill was to be auctioned in May 1986 and Guild members had only weeks to make up their minds and raise the money. A syndicate of members agreed to loan to the Guild sums ranging from £1000 to £50,000 — and the go-ahead was given. On this basis, bank loans of £85,000 and overdraft facilities were raised and a viable scheme proposed to the local authority.

From where we sit today, this was a courageous and dynamic decision for any business to take, let alone a loosely-knit collective of craftspeople.

The mill was bought in May, converted into a shop, gallery and restaurant and open to the public, all within eight weeks. The result is a first rate venue, ideally sited for tourists driven off the moors and the beaches by summer rain. The restaurant is an attraction in its own right, the shop has a typical selection of pottery and widgets; and the gallery has a changing display of touring exhibitions and members' individual and collective shows.

This is the Guild concept really working for the good of the group; it provides a market-place for members' work, which sells with surprising ease.'

The ground floor is coming to the end of its first year in use. The first floor has yet to be opened to the public; it is planned to house a crafts museum there, although quite when is uncertain. Discussion and argument about the way forward is at an emotional high, which is only to be expected from an organisation of creative individuals.

In less than 12 months, the members have covered an incredible distance. It's difficult to comprehend the courage and determination necessary to initiate such a move, from a once-a-year exhibition society to gallery owner, shopkeeper and restaurateur.

The future is now full of plans — artistic directors, education programmes, craft archives, video displays — yet without that initial group spirit, nothing would have been possible. ∎

● *Guild members' work harmonises beautifully with the simple stone interiors of the mill.* **Top**, *Ian Weller's oak cabinet;* **centre**, *a chunky rural dining-set by Guy Martin.* **Right**, *the picturesque central courtyard of Riverside Mill*

Photos Ian Wellens

Curves in the bathroom

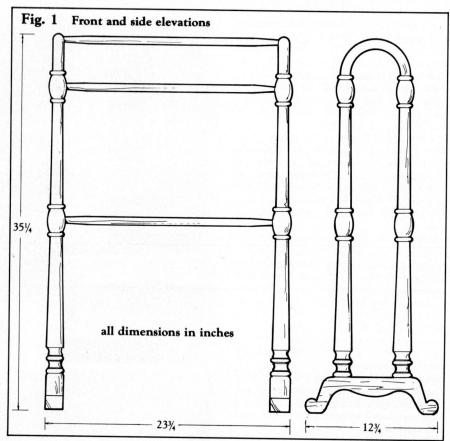

Fig. 1 Front and side elevations

35¼

all dimensions in inches

23¾   12¾

Jim Robinson re-created
an early Victorian towel rail
to suit his period home

This design of towel rail is typical of
those made around 1860, when our
house was built. Obviously everything cannot fit in with this period —
otherwise we wouldn't have a bathroom at

all. In those days a towel rail would be in the
bedroom.

I have used iroko for the construction,
chiefly because I already had a large well
seasoned piece. You could use ash or beech
and, if you are lucky enough to be able to
obtain suitable pieces, yew could be a
preference as this turns well, polishes easily
and mellows to a particularly attractive
colour. If you use iroko then inspect it carefully for calcareous deposits which
sometimes occur as laminations in the
timber; these quickly blunt saw-blades and
turning tools. It's also advisable to wear a
dust mask when sanding or machining, as
the dust can be unpleasant, even harmful to
some people with a tendency to allergy. The
wood finishes well with an attractive colour
and appearance.

The photographs of the complete rail and
fig. 1 reveal the construction. Each end
consists of two uprights mounted on a base
with two feet. The two uprights are then
joined at the top with a semi-circular ring
and these two ends are joined by five rails.

Bases

Draw the side view to full size, using the
square grid on fig. 2. If you are only making
one towel rail don't bother to make a
template but transfer the shape to suitable
2in thick wood with pencil and carbon
paper — or glue paper with the outline on
to the wood using a thin smear of contact
adhesive (useful with dark wood); this can
be easily removed with a cabinet scraper

when cleaning up. Make two holes in the
top of the base, ¾in diameter and 1in deep;
drilled before shaping to ensure that the
uprights will be at right angles. Use a flat-
bottomed bit. Next cut the two bases to
shape using a bandsaw with a narrow blade
or a coping saw, though this is more
difficult with 2in wood. Smooth by filing
and sanding where a scraper can't be used,
and carefully put a small radius on all the
edges with a file before sanding smooth.

Uprights

Make the uprights from four pieces of
31x2x2in timber. Square the ends and
centre for mounting in the lathe between
centres. Turn to rough shape using a fairly
large gouge, then a large skew chisel for
most of the final shaping and finishing, with
a smaller skew or beading chisel for the
beads. If your lathe has only a short bed you
may need to turn each of the uprights in two
pieces, joining them in the middle as shown
in fig. 3 with a 1½in long pin of ½in
diameter, glued into a suitable hole. If the
join is made at this position it will be virtually invisible (if you add one or two drops
of gravy browning when mixing the glue the
lines hardly show). Cut a small groove into
the pin to let air and surplus glue escape.

Semi-circular rings

This is the interesting stage and shouldn't
be too difficult. The semi-circular ring is
made by turning a single ring and then

Fig. 2

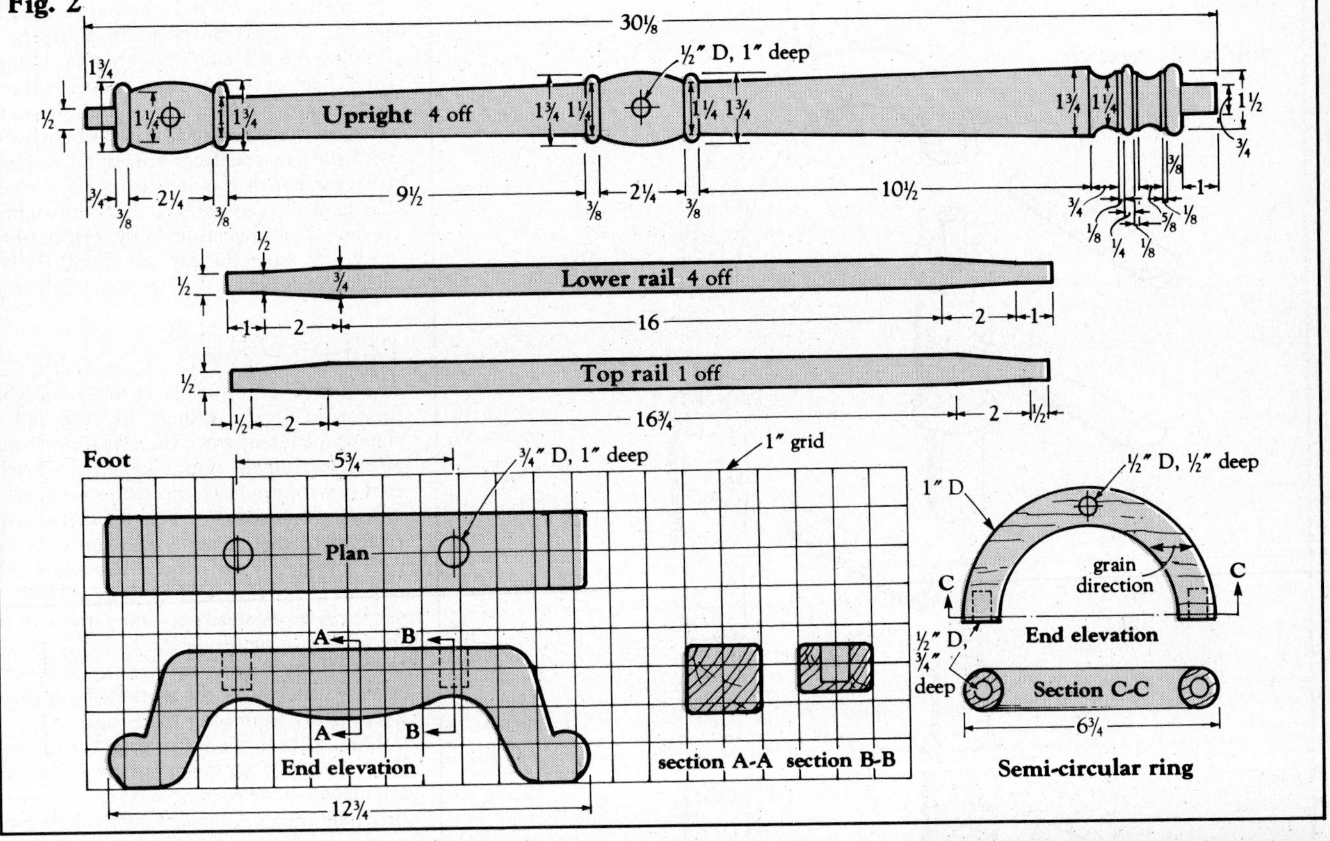
30⅛
½″ D, 1″ deep
1¾
½
1¼
1¾
Upright 4 off
1¾ 1¼
1¼ 1¾
1¾ 1¼
1½
¾
¾ 2¼ 9½ 2¼ 10½
⅜ ⅜ ⅜ ⅜
⅜ 1
¾ ⅝ ⅛
⅛ ¼ ⅛
½
½
¾
Lower rail 4 off
1 2 16 2 1
½
Top rail 1 off
½ 2 16¾ 2 ½
Foot
5¾
¾″ D, 1″ deep
1″ grid
Plan
A A B B
End elevation
12¾
section A-A section B-B
1″ D
½″ D, ½″ deep
grain direction
C C
End elevation
½″ D, ¾″ deep
Section C-C
6¾
Semi-circular ring

Fig. 3 Spigot joint for uprights

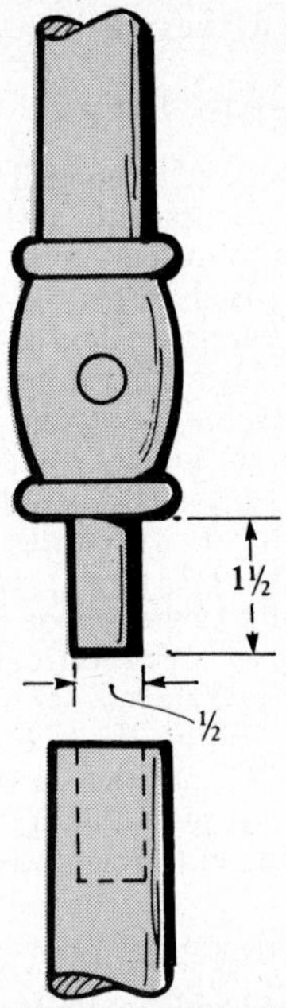
1½
½

Fig. 4 Turning inner face of ring with scraper

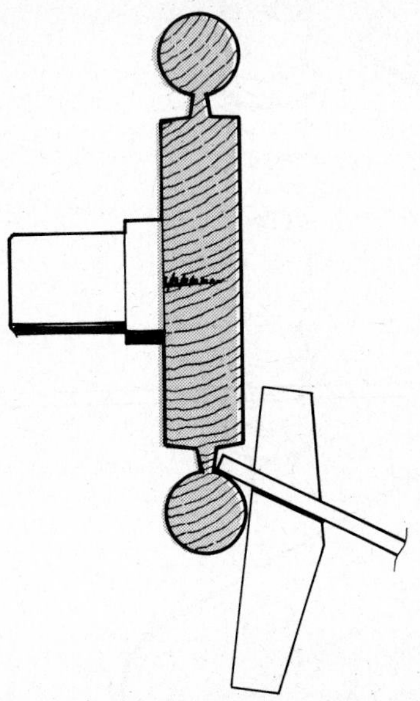

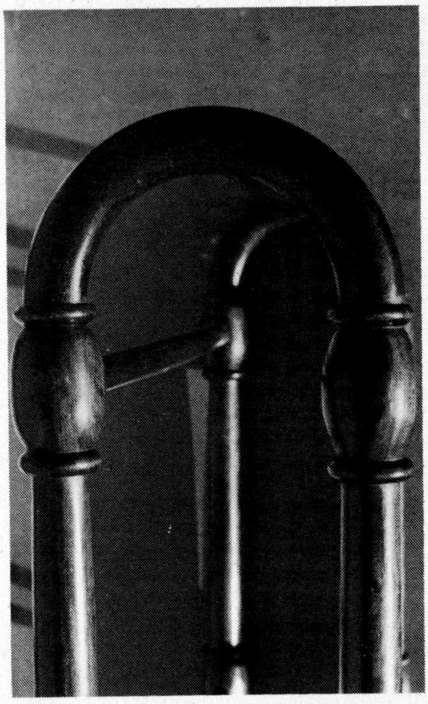

● *Turn the semi-circular end pieces from a single ring and then cut in half*

cutting it in half to form the two end pieces. Select a piece of wood about 7in square and a little over 1in thick to produce a ring of 1in cross-section and 6¾in outside diameter. Cut to a circle using a bandsaw or whatever you have. Find the centre, drill a pilot hole, then mount it on a small screw chuck. I turned the outside of the ring using a bowl gouge on its side to give a slicing action and the inner side of the ring using a flat scraper to the section as shown in fig. 4; you could do all the turning with a scraper, but light cuts will be necessary to avoid tearing out the grain. Sand in the lathe. If you have to turn the wood over in the screw chuck drill the pilot hole completely through the thickness of the wood, preferably on a bench drill to ensure it is perpendicular and you have accurate centring from each side. After sanding, you could carry on scraping until the ring is free, but it is less nerve-racking to cut off the thin section with a coping saw.

Clean up the inside with a file, sanding to

continued

Curves in the bathroom

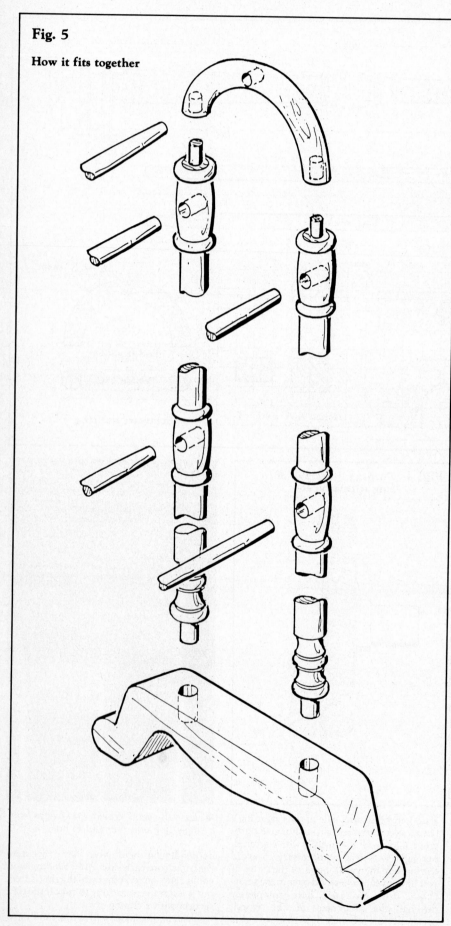

Fig. 5

How it fits together

make it uniformly circular in cross-section. Then carefully saw in half along the grain as in fig. 2. Flatten the ends squarely by holding the half ring upright and rubbing it on a sheet of 80-grit garnet paper laid on a flat surface. Then drill the ½in holes in the ends, putting the half ring in the bench vice, with the sawn surfaces horizontal and level with the bench top and using a brace with the drill aligned in each direction with a square. The single hole in the centre of the curve, to take the top towel rail, is best drilled in a bench drill with a depth stop.

Rails

The design of the rails is fairly straightforward (fig. 2), though the top rail is slightly different from the remaining four. When turning the rails, take only very light cuts to avoid building up ridges because of vibration caused by their slenderness in relation to their length. You can turn the rails completely with a gouge and sand, or if care is taken they can be finished with a skew chisel. A steady for the lathe will be useful if you have one but I usually steady the work by placing the fingers of my left hand at the rear of the work being turned, keeping my thumb on the gouge.

Drill holes in the four uprights to accept the remaining four lower rails after the rails are made, so they can be used to assist with drill alignment. After drilling the first hole perpendicular to the centre-line of the upright, place a rail in the hole and line up a hand brace in one direction with the rail and a square in the other.

Assembly

I first glued and assembled both ends, using a single cramp with a shaped softwood block cut to the curvature of the top semicircle. I used carpet underlay to avoid marking the iroko and applied only light pressure. Then I glued into position, again using softwood blocks and felt. If you can't insert the rails easily you could release the pressure on the end cramps to enable the uprights to be twisted slightly to bring the holes for the rails in the correct alignment. I glued it all together in one operation, but it can be rather tricky and it might be easier to allow the two ends to set before gluing the rails into position. If you do this, then insert the rails dry into the uprights in case it's necessary to twist the uprights to get the holes facing in the right direction.

Finishing

Wax finish would look all right but I think a little more protection is needed — the woodwork can be splashed with wet hands when you reach for a towel. I used one coat of Colron Oil Reviver, followed by two coats of Colron Antique Oil which I've found very durable in a bathroom.

Having completed the towel rail all that remains is to get the usual request from the offspring — 'Make me one, Dad'. ∎

WORLDWIDE TOOLS AND MACHINERY

Scott & Sargeant

PREMIUM QUALITY TCT SAW BLADES

Diameter	6″		7″				8″				9″			
No. of Teeth	24	36	18	30	42	56	20	36	48	64	24	40	54	72
Price £	21	24	19	23	26	30	21	28	31	34	23	29	35	39

PLEASE STATE BORE SIZE WHEN ORDERING

Diameter	10″				12″				14″			16″		
No. of Teeth	24	42	60	80	32	48	72	96	36	54	84	40	72	96
Price £	24	26	38	42	30	38	45	50	42	52	63	57	64	71

TCT GROOVING CUTTERS

¼″ .. £46.77 | ⅝ ... £66.78 | 6″ Diam.
⅜ ... £50.92 | ¾ ... £74.81 | 6 Teeth
½ ... £58.48 | 1 .... £86.62 | P&P £2.00

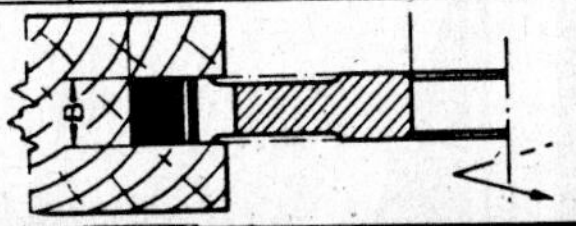

SAWBENCHES

Scheppach TKU 12″ 3HP Sitesaw ... £229
Elu TGS171 Flip Oversaw 10″ ... £401
Elu TGS172 Flip Oversaw 10″ ... £495
Startrite TA145 9″ Saw ... £768
*Startrite TA300PS 1PH ... £1283
*Sliding Table 48″ Return ... £306
*Startrite TA275DS 12″ 1PH ... £1364
Multico NTA300 12″ 3HP ... £1099
Sliding Table 48″ Return ... £316
Sedgwick LK 16″ 1PH ... £1236
*Wadkin AGS250/300 3HP 1PH ... £1129
*Sliding Table 39″ Return ... £432
*Wadkin AGSP Scoring Saw 3PH ... £1245
*Wadkin SP12 48″ Return ... £2336
*Wadkin CP12 48″ 2 Motors ... £3245
*Wadkin CP25 96″ 2 Motors ... £3857
*Wadkin CP32 10′ Panel Saw ... £4301

BANDSAWS

DW100 4″ with Disc ... £149
DW3401 6″ 2 Speed ... £273
DW3501 6″ Var. Speed ... £281
Sumaco TBS350 Bandsaw ... £299
Startrite 301 6″ ¾HP ... £429
Startrite 351 8″ 1HP ... £525
Startrite 352 11″ 1HP ... £749
Startrite 502 2HP ... £1259
Griggio Snal 440E ... £845
Griggio Snal 440 ... £1121
Griggio Snal 540 ... £1316
Griggio Snal 640 ... £1552
Wadkin C5 ... £1355
Wadkin C6 ... £1516
Wadkin C9 880mm throat ... £2639
Wadkin PBR 10HP Rip Saw ... £4043
Wadkin PBR HD 15HP Resaw ... £5458

HAKANSEN SWEDISH STEEL INDUSTRIAL BANDSAW BLADES

	3/16″	¼″	⅜″	½″	⅝″	¾″
Burgess 57″	4.42	4.42	4.51	4.67	5.99	5.62
Bed 59.5″	4.42	4.42	4.51	4.67	5.99	6.62
Coronet 67.5″	4.42	4.42	4.51	4.67	5.99	6.62
Inca 73″	4.42	4.42	4.51	4.67	5.99	6.62
DW3401 82.5″	4.42	4.42	4.51	4.67	5.99	6.62
Kity 612 83.5″	4.42	4.42	4.51	4.67	5.99	6.62
Minimax P32 85.5″	4.42	4.42	4.51	4.67	5.99	6.62
Startrite 301 88″	4.42	4.42	4.51	4.67	5.99	6.62
Startrite 351 102″	4.74	4.74	4.83	5.02	6.45	7.14
Startrite 352 112″	5.04	5.04	5.15	6.62	6.82	7.66

Guaranteed Weld. P&P £1.50
Any size blade made to order.

COMBINATIONS

Startrite K260 1PH. ... £2390
Startrite K260 3PH. ... £2350
Startrite K310 1PH. ... £3890
Startrite K310 3PH. ... £3599
Luna W59 Master 3HPX3 C/W SL. T £2599
Ask about our easy purcahse plans.

MORTICERS

Multico HM 9/16 Cap ... £369
Multico HMT 9/16″ Cap ... £495
Multico M/1 1″ Cap 1.5HP ... £625
Sedgwick 571 1″ Cap 1HP ... £619
Wadkin EDA 1″ Cap ... £627
Ridgway 1″ 1HP C/W Chisel ... £579
*Dominion BAA Chain Mortiser ... £2333

FINANCE

THERE'S A WIDE RANGE OF OPTIONS AND EASY PURCHASE PLANS ON ALL MACHINES — CALL FOR ADVICE AND INFORMATION — NOW.

RADIAL ARM SAWS

DW1201 10″ 1HP ... £249
DW1251 10″ 1.5HP c/w Legs ... £420
DW1501 10″ 1.5HP c/w Legs ... £496
DW8001 12″ 2HP c/w Legs ... £616
DW1751 10″ 1.5HP 24″ XCUT ... £571
DW8101 12″ 2HP 24″ XCUT ... £699
DW1600S 4HP 24″ XCUT ... £999
DW1875 4HP 34″ XCUT ... £1150
Wadkin BRA MOD2 4HP ... £1500
*Wadkin BRA MOD 1 ... £1502
*Wadkin BRA MOD 3 ... £1249
* Wadkin BRA MOD 4 ... £1137

SPINDLE MOULDERS

Scheppach HF33 ... £499
Startrite T30 1PH ... £1099
Startrite T230 1PH ... £1359
Sedgwick GW 1PH 2HP ... £1081
Wilson FM 5.5HP ... £1751
Wilson FX 7.5HP ... £2211
*Wadkin BEL 4SP 5.5HP ... £1980
Wadkin BEX 5.5HP ... £2300
Griggio T1000 ... £2300
Griggio TPL2000 2.5mm Tables ... £3737
Griggio T45 Tilting Spindle ... £5744

TENONERS

Multico TM/3 ... £1399
Multico TM/1 ... £1579
*Sedgwick TE/3 c/w Tooling ... £1560
*Sedgwick TE/1 c/w Tooling ... £1695
*Wadkin JET/2 ... £4483
*Wadkin JET/3 ... £5549

TOOLING

Spindle Moulder Handbook ... £10.95
Whitehill 100mm Panel raising block ... £83
Whitehill 124mm Panel raising block ... £96
Whitehill Panel raising cutters ... £16
T.C.T. Vari Angle Block ... £189
50 × 12 × 1.5 TCT Tips per 10 ... £18
Tigerhead Block ... £51
Cutters Per Pair ... £12.65
Blanks ... £7.50
Rebate Blocks TCT 244 125 × 50 ... £119
200mm TCT Wobblesaw ... £90
TCT Rebate Block 100 × 50 ... £89
Whitehill Block 4⅞″ × 15/16″ ... £51
Whitehill Block 4⅞″ × 1¼″ ... £78
Phone for details of other tooling.
Full range of Whitehill in stock.

PANEL RAISING CUTTERS

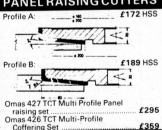

Profile A: ... £172 HSS

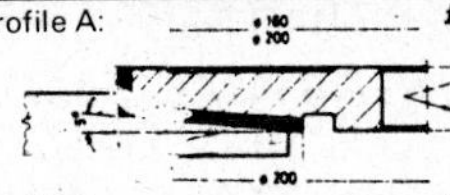

Profile B: ... £189 HSS

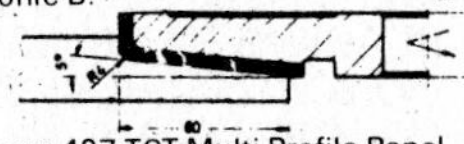

Omas 427 TCT Multi Profile Panel raising set ... £295
Omas 426 TCT Multi-Profile Coffering Set ... £359

BOOKS

£1.50 P&P
The Spindle Moulder Handbook ... £10.95
Techniques of Routing ... £7.95
DeWalt Handbook ... £7.20
Cabinet Making — Alan Peters ... £17.50
Manual of Wood Veneering ... £15.95

LATHES

Coronet No. 1 2ft. ... 239
Coronet No. 1 3ft. ... £259
Coronet No. 1 4ft. ... £285
Coronet Elf ... £379
Coronet Major ... £590
Tyme Cub 30″ ... £299
Tyme Cub 39″ ... £309
Tyme Avon 36″ ... £409
Tyme Avon 48″ ... £419
Killinger KM5000S, KM1400 MM BTC P.O.A.
Killinger KM5000SM with motorised feed ... P.O.A.
Plus Fittings, Wire Wool, Combination Chucks
Ask about our low cost finance packages.

TURNING CENTRES

ADD £1.50 P&P	1M	2M
4 Prong drive ctr. 1″ dia.	£7.94	£8.17
4 Prong drive ctr. ⅜″ dia.	£7.48	£7.71
2 Prong drive ctr. ¾″ dia.	£7.19	£7.42
2 Pront drive ctr. ⅜″ dia.	£6.44	£6.67
Jacobs Drill chuck ½″ dia.	£15.35	£15.64
Jacobs Drill Chuck ¾″ dia.	£32.78	£33.35

Sorby Precision Combination Chuck £56.00.

	1M	2M
Revolving ctr.	£18.00	£18.00
Lace Bobbin Drive	£7.76	£7.99
Deluxe Rev. ctr.	£28.41	£29.56
Cup Centre	£4.03	£5.06

DUST EXTRACTORS

DeWalt DW60 ... £264
Sumaco ... £199
P+J Mite ... £207
P+J Mini 635 cfm ... £322
P+J Junior 900 cfm ... £473
P+J Super Junior 1200 cfm ... £506
P+J One 2100 cfm ... £647
P+J Two 2600 cfm ... £806
Startrite Cyclair 55 ... £409
Startrite Cyclair 75 ... £529

PLANERS + THICKNESSERS

Ryobi AP10 Portable 10 × 5 ... £399
DeWalt DW1151 10 × 6 ... £489
Scheppach Combi ... £599
Startrite PT260 10 × 7 1PH ... £875
Startrite SD310 12 × 9 1PH ... £1499
Sedgwick PT 10 × 7 1PH ... £1098
Sedgwick MB 12 × 9 ... £1776
Multico CPT 310/230 ... £1699
Griggio FS430 16 × 9 ... £3852
Griggio FS530 ... £4772
PF430 2.75mm Table ... £3214
PSA520 20 × 10 Power R+F ... £4249
*Wadkin S400 16″ Surfacer ... £3089
*Wadkin T500 20″ Thicknesser ... £4146
*Wadkin BTS630 24 × 9 O/U ... £7342

TCT PLANING KNIVES

L × H × W	Machine	each £
150 × 20 × 2.5	Kity	£24
200 × 20 × 2.5	Kity	£32
210 × 20 × 2.5	Lurem	£33
210 × 25 × 2.5	Lurem	£33
210 × 30 × 3	Emco	£43
260 × 18 × 3	Scheppach	£45
260 × 20 × 2.5	Lurem, Kity	£45
260 × 20 × 3	Emco	£45
260 × 25 × 3	DeWalt	£45
262 × 25 × 2.5	Inca	£46
262 × 25 × 3	Inca	£46
312 × 25 × 3	Startrite	£54
12¼ × 1 × ⅛	Sedgwick	£50
12¼ × 1 9/16 × ⅛	Wadkin	£53
12¼ × 1¼ × ⅛	Cooksley	£53

Other sizes available.

GLUE-JOINT CUTTER

Diameter 120mm T.C.T. 2 teeth.
Profile and counter-profile can be cut with the same cutter.

B mm	Wood Thickness	Height of Profile	TCT each £	HSS each £
50	45	15.4	189	129
60	55	23	POA	159

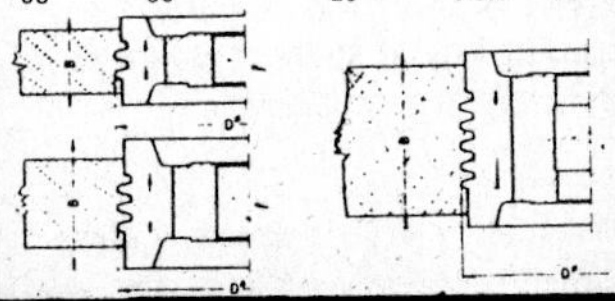

ROUTERS

Elu MOF96 600w ¼″ ... £99
Elu MOF96E 750w ¼″ ... £119
Elu MOF177 1600w ¼″ + ½″ ... £194
Elu MOF177E 1850w ¼″ × ½″ ... £219
Elu MOF11/2 ½″ 2000W c/w base £337.33
RYOBI R150 ¼″ 730W ... £75.95
Bosch POF52 ¼″ 520W ... £55.00
Bosch 1604 Fixed base 1300W ... £163.95

ACCESSORIES

Elu Dovetail Kit TCT cutter ... £74.00
Elu MOF96 Accessory kit ... £74.00
Elu Router Combi Bench ... £123.00
Elu Router Brkt. for DeWalt ... £39.00
Elu 96 Dust extraction kit ... £36.00
Elu MOF96 Height adjuster ... £3.95
Elu Tracking Set ... £35.00
Stair Jig ... £109.00
Elu 12 piece Guide bush set ... £35.00
Elu MOF98, 31, 177 Height adjuster £16.95
Elu 96 177 side fence adjuster ... £6.90

PROFILE + SCRIBER SETS

PR-SC/4 Ogee Profile Scriber Set £114.95
PR-SC/5 Ogee Profile Scriber Set £114.95
PR-SC/5 Ogee Profile Scriber Set £114.95
PR-SC/6 Ogee Profile Scriber Set £114.95
PR-SC/7 Classic Profile Scriber Set £114.95
PR-SC/8 Ovolo Profile Scriber Set £114.95
PR-SC/9 Round Profile Scriber Set £114.95
PR-SC/10 Raised Panel Profile Scriber Set ... £114.95
P&P £1.50

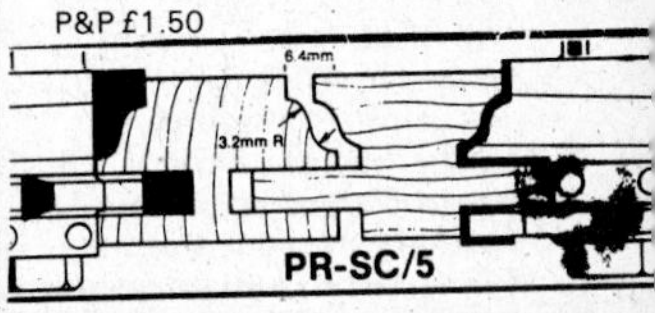

BELT SANDERS

Elu MHB157 3″ 600W ... £106.95
Elu MHB175E 3″ var. speed ... £119.95
Elu 157 Frame ... £35.00
Elu 157 inversion stand ... £28.00
Elu MHB 90 4″ 850W ... £193.95
Elu MHB 90K With frame ... £234.95
Hitachi SB75 3″ 950W ... £116.95
Hitachi SB110T 4″ 950W ... £129.00

PLANERS

Elu MFF80 82mm 850W ... £109.95
Elu MFF80K (in kit box) ... £127.95
Elu MFF40 82mm 1000W ... £189.95
Inversion Std. for MFF80 ... £20.95
Inversion Std. for MFF40 ... £29.00

CIRCULAR SAWS

Bosch PKS66 7⅞ TCT 1200W ... £90.95
Elu MH151 6″ 850W TCT ... £90.95
Elu MH65 7″ 1200W TCT ... £131.95
Elu MH85 9″ 1600W TCT ... £177.95
Elu MH182 8″ 1400W TCT ... £148.95
Elu 550 Combi (for MH182) ... £130.00
Elu 555 Snip saw (for 182) ... £179.00
Elu DS140 Biscuit Jointer ... £197.95

KILLINGER

UNIVERSAL COPYING LATHE KM5000S

The right machine for economical copy turning in one pass — and for hand turning.

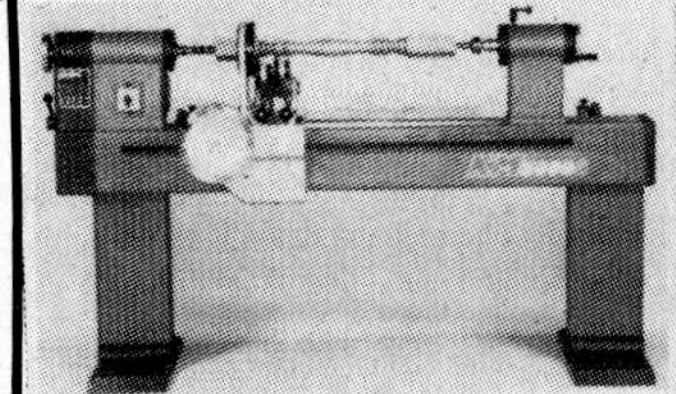

★ *EXCELLENT PERFORMANCE*
★ FIRST-CLASS WORKMANSHIP
★ ELEGANCE OF DESIGN
★ GOOD PRICE

are the specific advantages of KILLINGER lathes. As specialists for turning lathes we have a wide range of products to offer — *ask* for detailed brochures.

Scott & Sargeant

ALL PRICES INCLUDE VAT UNLESS ASTERISKED. PHONE FIRST TO CONFIRM AVAILABILITY. EXPORT ENQUIRIES WELCOMED.

IF YOU DON'T SEE IT - JUST ASK

PHONE TODAY
OFFER LIMITED PERIOD.

SHOP TALK SPECIAL

Suck it and see

Elu's pair of new mobile extractors are an interesting development in the war against dust. David Savage has been using the larger one in everyday workshop conditions

I hate dust. It's workshop-pervasive, getting into every corner, on to every surface, into every cupboard. If you leave them long enough, rows of tools, jars of pigments, acquire little pale-brown furry hats — dust. And two modern developments for the cabinetmaking shop have made this problem even more acute; that wonderful tool the router, and, of course, MDF — medium-density fibreboard. We all know about the advantages of routers. With the appropriate jigs and tooling a good router can have a set of 14 Sheraton side chairs zizzed before morning coffee entirely without human help. All you do is switch it on and point it in the direction of a pile of mahogany. (I think I hate routers too.) MDF is like 'user-friendly' chipboard. It doesn't dull your tools, it saws, planes and routs very cleanly, with great style, and great dust.

Combine this superb material with a router and billions of tiny dust particles are blown into the air — not like sawdust or planer shavings, these are specks less than one micron in size. It's a problem, for both material and machine are very convenient. How dangerous is this dust? I don't know more than the next man, but my instinct is not to get anywhere near it without either good dust extraction or a face-mask. So the prospect of the health-conscious woodworker, going into battle kitted out with ear-defenders, face-mask and respiratory system, is not quite as silly as it seems.

Into the dust storm step Elu, with their new 'Ultimate Extraction Machines'. These are developments of wet and dry vacuum cleaners, to meet the needs of woodworkers in the workshop or on site. And to go with the extractors, they have developed adaptors for a number of Elu hand-held power tools. The obvious efforts of the manufacturers made me think the products were worthy of a serious workshop test. Elu, confident that the extractors could withstand critical examination, agreed, and for the past three months we have had a good long 'suck and see'.

● *Getting what you pay for — quality extractors for power tools, at a price*

The machines

The extractors come in two sizes, the EVE 938 and the EVE 948. Both models feature the same rate of extraction having identical 1000w motors and filtration specifications. Where they differ is in their collection capacity and chassis arrangement. The smaller EVE 938 will collect up to 30 litres of dust before you have to empty it. The motor is mounted on a plastic container, and there are castors for mobility. At 14kg empty, it's light enough to carry on site.

The larger EVE 948 was the one we tested. This collects up to 40 litres in a stainless steel container, the drum mounted on a chassis with wheels and brakes for stationary positioning. There is also a pram-handle arrangement to help manoeuvring. Both units have a three-pin UK socket built into their switch panel, so power tools up to 1850w can draw power via the vacuum extractor, automatically switching the extractor on and off at the same time. We found this is an extremely useful facility, as — for instance — routing sessions can be intermittent, especially when the job is being set up. The extractor also has a second switch position for manual operation, when dust is being drawn from two tools at the same time.

The extraction is via the quite powerful motor to a replaceable cartridge filter in the drum. This can be swept clear of dust in a trice by raising and lowering an external plunger, but for it to operate effectively you must do this regularly while you work. Any serious build-up of dust isn't effectively cleared by the brushing system, so it's important to heed the warning light which flashes when there's an obstruction in the suction line.

The machines are supplied with a good length of rubber three-core cable, which gives a working distance from a power point of 10 metres. The suction hose is 28mm-diameter and a decent 3.5m long.

It's also possible to fit a disposable dust collection bag in the collection drum. These make dust collection convenient, but they aren't essential for many applications. The dust bags aren't re-usable and they reduce the collection capacity considerably. The filtration of the extractor is rated at 0.5 microns, lower than many industrial dust extractors — essential for the collection of MDF dust. The machine is claimed to have a motor with brushes capable of 600 hours' use without attention.

In general the EVE 948 is well constructed and nicely finished, but the construction could be criticised as being on the light side for industrial applications. Catches connecting the bin to the motor might suffer misuse at the hands of a careless operative. The cover to the three-pin socket fell off in the first few days, and I have doubts about the strength of the system that cleans the filter. Nothing wrong that careful use won't allow for, but these machines are often dragged round at the end of a day when everyone is tired and less than careful.

The applications

The other end of the system is the power tool. Manufacturers fit hand-held power tools with dust bags, but Elu themselves admit they have 'only limited effectiveness'; perhaps a polite way of saying they don't work very well. Especially on belt sanders, they fill up very quickly and filter only the worst dust. But until now it was all there was, and better than nowt.

continued

703

Suck it and see

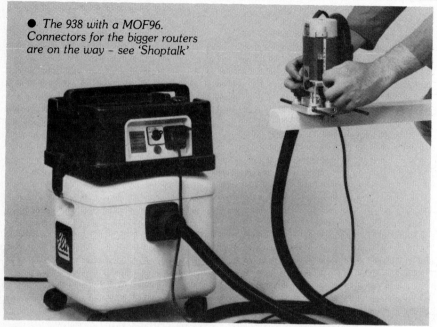

● *The 938 with a MOF96. Connectors for the bigger routers are on the way – see 'Shoptalk'*

The connectors are often very simple tube fittings. Some machines have connectors already available, others will be in the shops by the time this article appears. I tested the MHB90 4in belt sander, the MFF80 portable planer, the DS 140 biscuit jointer, and (an old friend) the MOF 96 Router.

The adaptor for the router is particularly well designed, very effective — and it must be said, quite expensive. But given the difficulty of effectively extracting dust from a portable plunge router, I must say these few bits of plastic and hosepipe are worth the money. All our routers but one are MOF96's, and most are now sporting these 'turbo-charger' bolt-on goodies.

Using the extraction with a router is not without difficulty. The hose needs to be hung above the work area to improve the balance of the tool and keep itself out of the way. It's often difficult to set the job up with the extraction in place, as the view of the cutter is restricted. The cowling round the cutter is clear plastic for visibility and the size of the opening can be enlarged by removing a ring of plastic, but in use this plastic will soon be scratched by chippings. The cowling is held in place by the rods that attach the fence to the router base. What do we do, Mr Elu, when we're using the router without side fence and rods? Working with jigs or templates almost always involves this problem. The answer we found was two short lengths of rod that didn't protrude beyond the router base, and these would be a sensible addition to the adaptor kit.

The adaptor for the DS140 biscuit jointer made this useful tool all the more pleasant to use. It's also commonly used in board material, kicking dust out nicely up to mouth level — until now. The extraction was almost 100% effective.

The MHB90 4in belt sander was also effectively voided by the extraction system, as was the MFF80 planer. I wouldn't recommend using the dust bag with the planer; planer chippings — indeed, any

plane shavings — fill it up very quickly. Working with dust, the standard hose that comes with the extractor was fine. It choked up very easily, though, if given a mouth full of hand-plane shavings.

A much more effective larger-diameter hose is available as an optional extra, as are all kind of gadgets for sweeping floors and walls. Our sweeping-up in the workshop is generally shared by Neil our young apprentice, and a local schoolboy affectionately known as 'Beastly'. Both Neil and Beastly gave the extractor their qualified approval; Neil gave it a name and drags it round the bench shop like a dog on a lead, but Beastly was less pleased when EVE 948 gobbled up his school tie.

I wasn't able to test the extractor with the TGS171 flip-over saw or the PS 174 pull-over saw. I would expect that the small extractor that fits beneath the saw table would be a good means of working on site without making a mess. For joiners and kitchen fitters working in people's homes, this facility has to be worth quite a lot. ('They did such a good job and didn't make any mess'.)

Conclusion

Without doubt, the development of dust extraction facilities for power tools is a considerable aid in the small workshop. Work is more comfortable, cleaner, more efficient and safer. Beyond that there is the long-term question of personal health; the incidence of nasal cancer in the furniture industry is high. Any means that can economically and easily control dust makes sense to me. So first points to Elu; without their intervention we would have no option but to suck dust. The connections to the power tools that I have seen all work well with this level of powerful extraction.

The extractor is effective and well designed, and once the dustbag is removed it's even more effective. Two routers plunging in stereo didn't give it any problem at all. The cut-off switch that enables you to

turn the extractor on and off automatically with the power tool is very useful.

The paper filter clogs relatively quickly, but it has a filtration capacity down to 0.5 microns. There are dust extractors capable of taking out airborne dust, and there are so-called dust extractors that are not. Most woodworkers are familiar with common dust extractors, the type with a large polythene collection bag beneath a felt-lined or canvas top bag. These machines are wizard for clearing up planer chippings, spindle-moulder chippings and (to a lesser extent) sawdust extraction. But they will not generally filter out airborne dust from sanders, and certainly won't filter out the fine dust of MDF.

As you can see from the list prices given below, the extractors and connections aren't cheap. Even with the discount of 30% on list which seems to be generally available, I doubt if I could say the EVE 948 is good value, but it does the job very well. Cut-off switches and any noise reduction (the EVE 948 is quiet to operate) are valuable; but are they that valuable?

The connections to enable you to extract dust from your power tools are good news. They work, and to date Elu are the only people giving us the choice of sucking or not sucking dust. Given that I already have several Elu power tools, I'm delighted to have that choice, and perhaps pay the price for the dust-free working environment I want. The EVE 948 is a more difficult judgement to make. It should be cheaper, Mr Elu, but thank you for making it all the same. ■

Prices excluding VAT	
Elu EVE 938	£332
Elu EVE 948	£477
Connector spouts	
For MHB90 belt sander	£6.38
For MH65 circular saw	£4.10
For MH85/182 saws	£4.20
For DS140 biscuit jointer	£5.60
For MFF80 planer	£3.75
For MOF96 router	£32.45
For TGS171/2 flip-over saw (two points)	£25.50
For PS174 pull-over saw (two points)	£11.55
Inlet connector for second power tool (simultaneous extraction)	£6.50
Y-junction for second power tool	£11.50
4m suction hose, 36mm internal diameter	£35
Pack of 5 disposable filter dustbags	£15
Replacement cartridge filter	£15

A range of other accessories are available. Discounts: you should get an EVE 938 for around £275 and a 948 for around £395, both inc. VAT.

● Elu Power Tools, West Point, The Grove, Slough, Berks SL1 1QQ, (0753) 74277

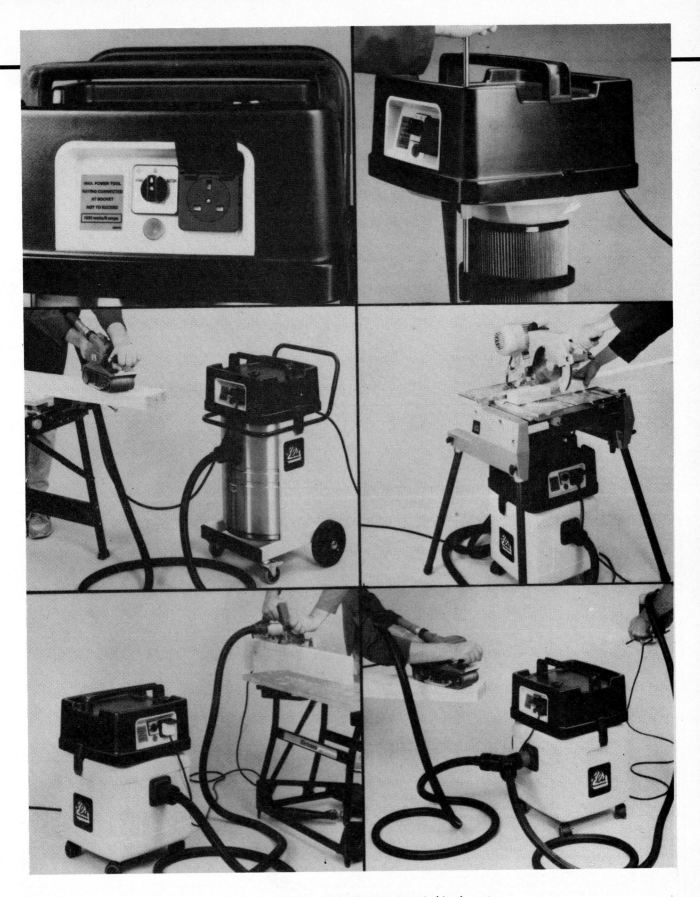

● **Clockwise from top left**: plug-in auto switching for extractor via the tool if you want it; the plunger needs quite a lot of plunging. 938 fits neatly under the flip-over saw table; 938 with sander and router, at the same time. 938 with planer – larger hose is a better choice; 948 with belt sander – a welcome end to inefficient bags

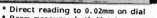

706 WOODWORKER AUGUST 1987

Question box

Our panel of experts solve your woodworking problems

We will try to answer any questions you can throw at us, but the ones we publish are the ones of most general interest to readers.

Please type your question double-spaced with generous margins, and include a stamped self-addressed envelope. Send it to: Question Box, Woodworker, 1 Golden Sq., London W1R 3AB.

Split resistance

Q *Can you suggest a comprehensive book which explains how to make small timber buildings, such as car porches? I would welcome your comments on my sketches (figs A and B) – there seems to be little information available on the split-resistance of timber.*

J. W. Towell, Ferndown, Dorset

A I don't know of a book which deals exclusively with this subject — your library's 'building construction' section should help.

The beam-end in your fig. A is notched up to the centre-line of depth; in fact it shouldn't be more than ⅓ depth. It's far better to let the un-notched end of the beam rest on a runner (fig. 1). Your sketch suggests using a wall-plate, so you could apply the method in fig. 2. You don't have to halve the purlins; a positioning-notch of about ½in will do the job (fig. 3).

In fig. B the bottom-edge of the beam is notched, again up to half-way, with the purlins to be screwed upwards. On a loaded beam the top edge is in compression, while the under edge is in tension. Try a simple experiment: take a piece of two by one about 2ft long, and put a saw-cut down to half-way (fig. 4). Insert a cabinet scraper into the cut and support the timber at each end (fig. 4). Now apply pressure and you'll see that the timber isn't weakened at all by the saw-cut. Turn the timber over and lightly apply pressure; first the scraper will fall out and then the timber will fail. So on no account cut the under edge of a beam.

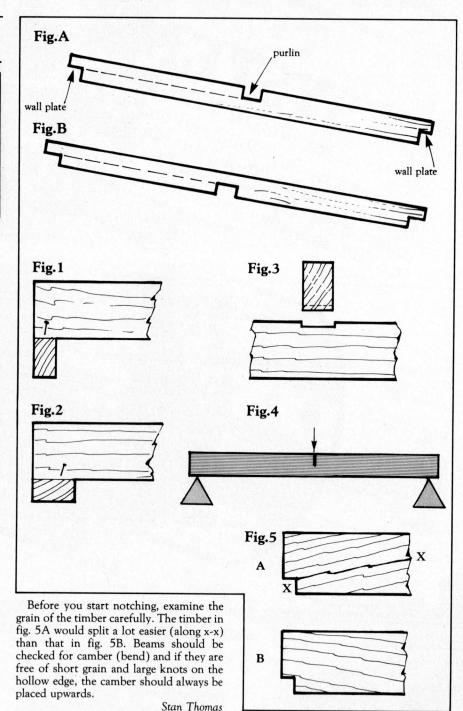

Before you start notching, examine the grain of the timber carefully. The timber in fig. 5A would split a lot easier (along x-x) than that in fig. 5B. Beams should be checked for camber (bend) and if they are free of short grain and large knots on the hollow edge, the camber should always be placed upwards.

Stan Thomas

Backyard surface

Q *I want to resurface an area 15x15ft sq, between the kitchen and garage, with wooden planks. I've been quoted £2000 for oak planks – what cheaper wood can I use which will be as serviceable?*

Should it be finished or left sawn, and what problems am I likely to have in freezing or wet weather? Is it best to build on brick piers or on cross-beams?

Pat Heery, London SW15

A Presumably your yard is open to the weather, so the best solution would be concrete or flagstones. But as you're stuck on wood, you could see if you can find a farm which might have any cheap unseasoned oak for sale — the sort that's used for fencing posts. It would be rough-sawn, but a blow-lamp and a wire brush would produce an acceptable surface. Iroko would be a good alternative hardwood, but almost as expensive; and I wouldn't advise any of the mahoganies for an outdoor job like this. As for softwoods, well-treated deal is often used for verandah planking and wears very well. Whatever timber you choose, all the nails used must be galvanised; this especially applies to oak.

Freezing will have no effect upon the timber, but rain will. All joints (except end-to-end) should be 'open' to allow for swell. This gap depends upon board width — 6in boards, ⅛in gap between each.

Brick piers or cross-beams? It would have to be both; the cross-beams (say 4x4in at 3ft centres) rest on the piers, which should be 3ft centres, both ways. If height is restricted, the area can be excavated down to about 3in, and levelled up with ¾in chippings. The crossbeams, which can now be smaller, say 2x2in, can rest on the chippings, which are to provide drainage. If water is going to collect, then a soak-away should be dug about 18x18x36in deep, and filled with chippings.

Stan Thomas

● Stan Thomas is a joiner of vast experience who holds a live 'Question box' and 'tool hospital' at Woodworker shows.

Staining MDF

Q *I built a computer desk in MDF and intended to fill the endgrain, stain, and finish with a dull-sheen polyurethane for hard wear.*

The MDF wouldn't take up the Colron stain evenly and is left with a flecked appearance. How can I overcome this and what is the best way to finish MDF?

I'd also welcome your advice on turning MDF on the lathe.

F. J. Rice, Godalming

A My commiserations! After all your careful work I'm sure the finish is a disappointment. On your behalf, I carried out a number of experiments on MDF with various stains and dyes and was rewarded with the same, messy, flecked result. Obviously MDF isn't suited to this type of finish; it's structural board intended to be faced with decorative veneer, wood foils, or an opaque finish such as coloured melamine or paint — and for these purposes it makes an excellent ground.

It's made of fine wood chippings, usually willow, and a bonding agent, and it is the varying, random densities of the chippings that affects the penetrating power of the stain: different absorbency rates produce the unsightly flecked effect. There appears to be no remedy, except to cover the surface in one of the opaque finishes mentioned.

The same applies to turning MDF. It cuts well with the conventional turning tools but it's a very dusty business. Once the case-hardened skin is turned off, you're left with a comparatively soft core and the same problem of stain absorbency arises. My advice is to use a paint which has to be applied off the lathe.

Bob Grant

● Bob Grant is an all-round wood craftsman and teaches courses for the Guild of Woodworkers.

Snooker cues

Q *I've already made two-piece snooker cues with the threaded joint turned on a metalworkers' lathe from aluminium rod, and am now attempting to make a cue with a wooden screw-joint.*

I believe the thread can be cut with a screw-box – can you tell me what this is and how it's used? How do I line up the two sections of the cue so they finish true?

F. R. Williams, Southport, Lancs

A When you buy a screw-box, it comes with a matching tool for cutting internal threads. They are the equivalent of the engineers' taps and dies and can be bought, mail-order, complete with instructions. As you've already used taps and dies

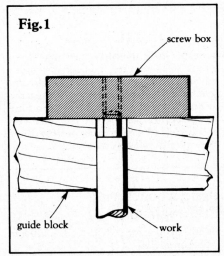

Fig. 1

screw box

guide block   work

on metal, you shouldn't have any problems. The question of alignment depends on whether you turn or plane the two sections of the cue.

Turning: If you have a three-jaw chuck, and the workpiece will go through the hollow mandrel of the lathe, you can turn each half parallel between centres, preparing the spigot for the male thread on the butt half. Now you can hold each in turn close into the chuck to cut the threads. Bore and cut the internal thread using a chuck in the tailstock — accuracy should be OK.

The external thread is more difficult. Back-up and support the screw-box with the tailstock of the lathe — with care you should be able to keep it square with the axis of the work and produce an accurate thread. Each half will have to be remounted between centres and turned to the required taper; it might be necessary to insert an accurately centred 'plug' in the half with the internal thread. The plug must be close-fitting but not necessarily threaded.

It's unlikely that the hollow mandrel of your lathe will take the size of your work and you'll probably have to cut the threads with the work off the lathe. The male thread is made by drawing the workpiece into the box through a guide block with a hole bored through it, vertical to its face (fig. 1). Cutting the female thread doesn't lend itself to any simple guiding method, but it is easier to sight the tap accurately.

Planing: This is a slightly more difficult method, but once the sections are made, it's easier to achieve good alignment, at least when the threads are closed. Turn down the spigot for the male thread on the lathe. Then proceed as before, except that the hole in your guide block will have to be square and you'll have to rotate the screw-box rather than the workpiece.

When the threads are cut, join the two sections and plane the whole piece to a square taper. This is then placed to an octagonal taper and finally rounded. I do much of the final rounding by holding the cue in my hand and using a block-plane.

John Prince

● John Prince is a designer craftsman who works in Bournemouth.

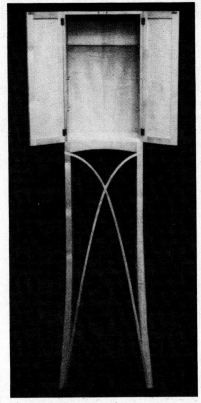

Guild notes

WOODWORKERS

The Guild was set up by *Woodworker* to create a meeting ground for all those involved in working wood, whether professional, amateur, or enthusiastic beginner. Guild members get:

- Access to Guild courses and events
- Free publicity in *Woodworker*
- Specially arranged tool insurance at low rates
- 15% off Woodworker Show entry
- A free display area and meeting point at the Show
- 15% discount off *Woodworker* plans
- Inclusion in our register of members' skills and services

For details, please send an sae to the Guild of Woodworkers, 1 Golden Sq, London W1R 3AB.

Decorative techniques — Ian Hosker

12-13 September, 10-5, Chester, £55.
Another chance to learn all sorts of wonderful decorative techniques, including dragging, lining, sponging, rag-rolling, marbling, spattering and tortoiseshelling. The fee includes materials, but bring a few paintbrushes and jam-jars.

Rudiments of restoration — Barry Honeyborne

17-18 September, Leominster, Herefordshire, £54.
Bring along your antique and learn how to restore it. From initial cleaning to repairs and final polishing, Barry will show you all the steps — he has been 25 years in the trade. This two day course is an introduction to every aspect of restoration, plus a chance to make a start on your own piece under expert supervision.

French polishing — Charles Cliffe

17-18 September, Bexleyheath, £45.
These courses by expert Charles Cliffe are among the most popular run by the Guild, so book early to avoid disappointment. You'll learn about preparation, staining and techniques of french polishing itself, with ample hands-on experience under Charles' eye. You'll learn the correct way to sharpen a cabinet scraper, so bring yours along, and he's willing to offer advice on any small piece of furniture you want to refinish.

GUILD COURSES

- **Only Guild members are eligible to go on these courses. You must book in advance, and we must have a cheque for the full cost of the course at the time of booking. If you cancel less than four weeks before the advertised date you will forfeit 50% of the cost, unless there are exceptional circumstances.**

Basic woodcarving — Eric Ingham

19-20 September, 9.30-5.30, Lytham St Annes, £50.
We're pleased to be able to offer this introduction to woodcarving. On this course you'll learn about use of tools and sharpening, types of wood, design and finishing. Eric's been carving for 15 years and will give you a good start. Wood is provided and you're free to carve whatever you want. Bring carving tools if you have them. There's plenty of accommodation in this resort area and your spouse might enjoy the sea air while you learn.

Design and workshop drawing — Bob Grant

26 September, 9.30-5, Oxford, £25 + VAT
If putting your design on paper doesn't come easy, here's the course to learn how. Bob will help you gain confidence in freehand sketching, show you how to use grid paper and drawing boards, and lots more.

Hand veneering — Bob Grant

10 October, 9.30-5, Oxford, £35 + VAT
Veneering is much more than the art of disguising chipboard. It's a skill with a long history, and can create some beautiful effects — and it saves fine and expensive wood! You'll be laying a panel with veneer, mitring a cross-banding, inlaying lines round it, and applying a balancer veneer on the back. If you have a veneer hammer, bring it; but materials will be provided.

Routing — Roy Sutton

14 November, 10-5, Herne Bay, Kent, £25 + VAT.
Another chance to learn the full potential of this versatile tool. Roy's courses are very popular, so book early. Starting from first principles, he covers housing, grooving, rebating, straight and circular moulding, tenoning, mortising, and rule joint and template work; he also deals with designing and setting up your own jigs.

Course congrats

A letter from Roger Watt of Bolton: I thought I should let you know how much I enjoyed the course in cabinetmaking run before Easter at the Manchester College. I came to know of the course via your magazine, having previously passed by the college building many times without realising what went on inside it.

We worked hard and the college tutors gave freely of their time and skills. I would certainly recommend the course highly. Not only did we all learn a lot but came away with a fine table. In my case as I was a little slower than others on the course I did not quite complete it, but have now done so. I shall now have to attend a course in wood finishing skills!

And another from Mr R. W. Hayward of Northwich: After attending the Manchester course on modern wood finishing I must write to congratulate Richard Hill and Eric Lyons, the course tutor, on what was a very enjoyable and interesting five days. I would advise any professional woodworker considering a course that they should contact the Manpower Services Commission; if you can convince them the course would be beneficial, you can claim daily expenses.

BOOKING FORM

I wish to book for the following course(s).

☐ **Decorative techniques** 12-13 September, £55; make cheque payable to Ian Hosker

☐ **Rudiments of restoration** 17-18 September, £54; make cheque payable to Barry Honeyborne

☐ **French polishing** 17-18 September, £45; make cheque payable to Charles Cliffe

☐ **Basic woodcarving** 19-20 September, £50; make cheque payable to Eric Ingham

☐ **Design and workshop drawing** 26 September, £25 + VAT = £28.75

☐ **Hand veneering** 10 October. £35 + VAT = £40.25

☐ **Routing** 14 November £25 + VAT = £28.75

Please make cheques payable to 'The Guild of Woodworkers/ASP Ltd' unless otherwise stated.

Name...

Address..

....

....

Guild no..

Send to: The Guild of Woodworkers, 1 Golden Square, London, W1R 3AB. The Guild reserves the right to cancel any course.

Local Meets

The West Sussex Group of the Guild held its third meeting in May. They now have a system of taking it in turns to meet in each other's houses, the host member acting as chairman and producing the minutes of the meeting. Co-ordinator Clive Green says the meetings are lively, and the group is now trying to arrange a visit to the Barnsley Trust.

The West Midlands Branch were having a special session on routing techniques and cutters in June. This branch is offering a new service to local members; it will circulate details of equipment, machines, tools and so on offered by its members. Now that's a good idea which could stimulate other local Guild representatives.

Craft stalls

Camden Lock, one of London's best markets attracting about 80,000 visitors each weekend, is keen to have more genuine craft, fine art and design items on the stands. Usually stands are available on a lottery basis to new traders, with demand outstripping supply. To encourage more crafts, they are now offering regular stands at a rent of £12 a day. On these stands the majority of items must be made by the applicant and not goods bought in for resale. Application forms from Camden Lock, 39 Camden Lock Place, London NW1 8AF, 01-485 4457, 482 2323.

Local reps

Edgar Lawrance, who was our West Yorkshire rep before moving to Devon 12 months ago has now found his feet in the West Country and has volunteered his services as Devon rep. Contact him at 42 Bolton St, Brixham, TQ5 9DH.

And offering to be liaison person in West Yorkshire is Neil Rymer, of Merlin Traditional Furniture. Why not write to him at 4 Churchill Grove, Heckmondwike, West Yorkshire WF16 0BW.

Show case

Morrison Thomas, Surrey Guild member, will have work on show at a major Festival of Ecclesiastical Crafts at Salisbury Cathedral in October. Other wood craftsmen represented there include Allardus van den Bosch, who specialises in inlaying fruit woods into a precious ground wood, and Milbourne Port Dorset designers Illingworth & Partridge. The Festival also includes work by stone/wood carving and lettering designers, silversmiths, stained glass, textiles and bookbinding.
● Festival of Ecclesiastical Crafts, Salisbury Cathedral, 2-4 October, 10-6, admission £1.

Courses

The Parnham Trust, home of John Makepeace's Furniture Workshops and The School for Craftsmen in Wood, has a plethora of summer courses, each running from Sunday evenings to mid-day the following Saturday. Fees include lunch and dinner (not accommodation), basic material and instruction, and range from £180 to £230. Subjects include woodturning, making furniture, decorative decoy carving and gilding.
● The Parnham Trust, Parnham House, Beaminster, Dorset DT8 3NA, (0308) 862204.

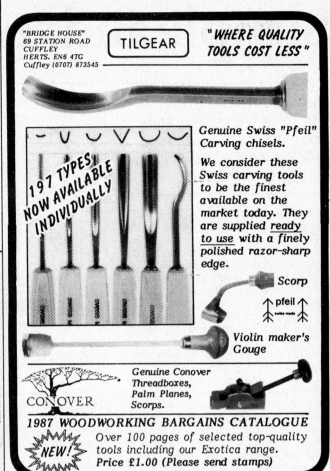

Simple and suite

Unconventional it may be, but John Merry worked from first principles to produce this sturdy elm dining suite

When our original dining table and chairs were giving up the ghost after 15 years' use from new, I noticed that conventional middle price-range dining room furniture hadn't changed much, and still had many of the same shortcomings. Why not have a go at making my own?

I wanted to produce something functional and sturdy — and durable enough to survive family use for a good deal longer than 15 years. In trying to meet these requirements I used unorthodox methods and an unconventional design, the outcome of which was predictably odd-looking. The unorthodox methods used in some instances produced effective but clumsy results and I skip over these for obvious reasons. On the other hand the design was unconventional for what I think were sound motives and the aim of this article is to explain why.

The table

To my mind a functional table is one around which any number of people (up to the intended maximum) may be seated without table legs, chair legs and human legs becoming uncomfortably mixed up. One person should be able to move it easily and when it has been moved there should be no unsightly dent-marks on the carpet or scratches on a polished wooden floor.

My table will seat eight people. I rate it as sturdy because if those people should choose to sit on the table instead of around it no damage would be caused. Our last table would have collapsed!

It seemed to me that the simplest way of meeting these objectives was to fashion the top from solid $1\frac{3}{8}$in timber — two boards joined down the middle — and put a leg at each corner. There would need to be enough distance between the legs to accommodate three chairs each side and enough overhang at each end for a person to sit without knees colliding. Siting the legs near the sides of the table-top meant it would be difficult to fix them firmly without resorting to the usual side and end rail arrangement, which I didn't want because the top was strong enough without them. In the end I decided to make the pair of legs at each end a separate and very strong sub-assembly and bolt the top to them.

You'll see from fig. 1 that the legs were joined top and bottom to form a more or less square structure. The top cross-member is wider than the lower one so the joint between it and each leg can be made good and solid — also to allow the fixing

Fig. 1. Table underview

bolts sunk into table top

leg assembly

spreader

bolts to be well spaced, and so spread the loads on them, most importantly the endways 'wobbling' loads. Finally I fixed a long 'kick bar' between the centres of each lower cross member to provide added strength against the endways loads.

I used $1\frac{3}{8}$in elm for all the parts of the leg assemblies and what looked sound on paper turned out to be extremely rigid in the finished article. The other reason for joining the legs at their feet was to distribute the weight of the table over a much larger area than conventional feet to avoid marking carpets and to make the table easy to push around — which it does.

The chairs

For me a functional chair has a backrest against which backs may be rested and not a beam, however shaped and padded, which catches the occupant neatly and uncomfortably in the kidneys. It also would not leave marks on the carpet. Finally it would be robust enough to allow the Billy Bunters of this world, should they want, to tilt back and balance on the chairs' back legs without the risk of structural failure.

From the seat up the chairs are more or less conventional and I could have supported them on the usual arrangement of legs, stretchers and spreaders. Properly made I'm sure it would have worked fine but my woodworking expertise wasn't up to it and so I had to devise some other way. I knew the foot-to-side member joint had to be exceedingly robust, which is why the bridle joint is so large. I gave up trying to make it look nice. Before starting the production line I made a prototype joint and then tested it to destruction. It took a massive amount of punishment and got a definite thumbs-up.

The 45° brace from each side member to the underside of the seat was an afterthought: it's not elegant but it gives the necessary sideways strength. The first batch of chairs had three equally spaced spills as the backrest because I thought it looked nice but I had failed to take into account that most people's backbones are more comfortable leaning against two broader

Fig. 2. Chair side view

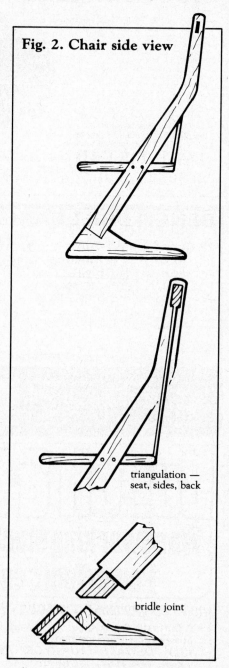

triangulation — seat, sides, back

bridle joint

spills, so later chairs have two. I would have liked to have shaped the solid seat but the timber wasn't thick enough and I'd no idea how to go about it: my wife has agreed to make suitable cushions.

Finish

I wanted an oiled finish but not knowing the technique and time being very short (I work overseas for most of the year) my 'holding' solution was to sand all surfaces as assiduously as time allowed, to anoint liberally with linseed oil and rub furiously with a suitable pad. It looked rather nice but was unpleasantly rough to the touch. Never mind, I thought, next time home more oil and glasspapering should fix it. Wrong: the result was lots of clogged glasspaper and no improvement to the surface.

The only sensible thing to do was to take

● *Strong enough for Desperate Dan! Eight people could sit on this tough table and the chairs can take any amount of punishment. Bring on the cow pie . . .*

all the gunge off with wire wool and finish with matt polyurethane varnish, the do-it-yourselfer's ultimate solution. While rubbing with kitchen wire wool I observed the surface of the wood becoming quite smooth. What about wire wool and linseed together, I wondered? It looked promising. The local wire wool merchant said there were several grades, which did I want? One thing led to another and I found that lots of wire wool, linseed and elbow grease produced a beautiful silky finish — really lovely. The table and chairs are all finished that way.

Timber

Why choose elm? Because it was there. Eight years ago it was cheap and plentiful and I bought a large trailer-load of 1½in sawn boards thinking it might come in hand one day. I know it has a mind of its own and is sometimes difficult to predict but it's a tough, longlasting timber which seems to

take an oil finish nicely. Anyone wanting toolmaker's accuracy in his furniture please move along to the manmade board department.

Reflections

Thinking about the project took more than a year, of which the greatest proportion was spent pondering the chairs. A recent article in WOODWORKER pointed out that making chairs isn't easy — I agree wholeheartedly. Another writer expressed strong views about furniture being fit for purpose and not simply a means of demonstrating the maker's expertise — he has my vote.

At the time the table and half the chairs were finished I hadn't even heard of WOODWORKER, let alone read it, and that was about two years ago. Having discovered the magazine, I have read every page of every issue since and have learnt a great deal — in particular how much I didn't know when I started! ∎

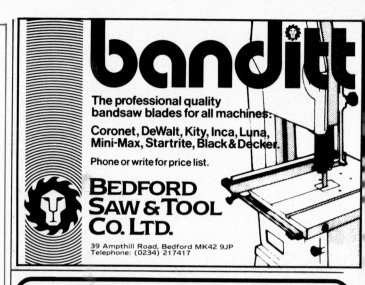
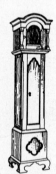

● A place for
everything, and
everything in its place

the timber, but I found this uncommon wood compared favourably with Scots pine and finished sharp and clean. It is almost knot-free, straight-grained and differently toned from red deal, being paler in the sapwood and deeper red in the heart.

Now I'd always wanted to own a bureau-cum-bookcase — shelves for books above, and storage below in drawers or cupboards; I wanted space for writing and draughting materials, camera, business files, woodworking magazines and catalogues, and a space large enough to hold my portable typewriter and briefcase. The straight-grained wood seemed appropriate for something with straight edges and a clean cut appearance, so I went ahead.

I looked at books on antique furniture and photographs of comtemporary designs to develop my ideas. I wanted something visually interesting and thoroughly useful. Then I measured the items I wanted to store and got out some drawing paper.

Proportion

Proportion and the way I wanted the piece to feel were my starting point. I wanted something that felt solid without looking bulky, unmistakably contemporary yet retaining the storage capacity of traditional designs. What I was after was a clean-cut welterweight of a bureau/bookcase.

The timber dimensions gave me a lead: a one-metre width and two-metre height seemed to make the most efficient use of the eight boards.

I wanted the bookcase to be at least 230mm deep to suit wide hardbacks, and I soon worked out the optimum depth of the desk. Using a simple 45° slope and a writing surface height of 750mm, I drew up the shape to scale and found the appropriate depth to be about 500mm. These rough measurements combined with my design aims gave me plenty to chew on, and I slowly found my way towards deciding where to store what. I discovered all the sketches I made used symmetry, although I hadn't consciously decided that the front should look symmetrical. Was I playing it safe, or had I tapped into intuitive feelings of rightness? I'll probably never know the answer, but the design from the start was a controlled exercise in balance.

Bookcase

This balance wasn't just about left/right symmetry, but also about the top/bottom balance. To prevent it looking top-heavy, I shortened the bookcase, incorporating a row of drawers immediately under the bookshelves. To avoid the bookcase looking fat and heavy I decided to emphasise the vertical lines. I played around with several ideas, but eventually arrived at having two pairs of doors, and a central partition. This gave me six short shelves which could be individually adjusted for different sizes of books, each shelf with natural 'ends' for the books to lean against and keep upright; the opened doors didn't extend beyond the front of the closed desk, so they were unlikely to be walked into; aesthetically, four simple framed doors seemed more in keeping with my aims than if I used doors with glazing bars.

Pine with poise

From a bargain lot of yellow pine and an individual brief, Phil Townsend developed this custom design for a bureau/bookcase

Four boards of yellow pine, 14ftx8inx 2in, acquired at a knock-down price, were the starting point for my bureau/bookcase. I had them sawn into 8x1in boards by a local sawmill owner, who complained that the heavy, hard, resinous wood had blunted his fresh bandsaw blade. This made me apprehensive about working

● **Above**, the chamfered V-groove on the long drawer locates the drawing board, the angle of which is altered by moving the drawer in or out. **Right**, spacer bar with twin dowels through desk top to act as stop for the flap support drawer, shown removed to the right, with its secret compartment and false back

I turned my attention to the top of the bookcase; I didn't want any sort of cornice, but it needed something to cap it off, so I ran a 50mm wide batten under the top before the doors begin. It works visually, but restricts access to the top bookshelves.

I also decided to incorporate a light source built into the unit to cast light on the desk. That's why the central drawer is double width, so it has a 12in striplight with independent switch incorporated; it works reasonably well, but an angled reflector would make it better.

Bureau

I wanted knee-space and set my sights on a knee-hole desk style, where you can get to knee-hole desk style, where you can get to the drawers without pulling out your chair; this led me to split the storage into three with two vertical partitions. Deep filing drawers at the bottom kept the weight low and were wide enough for files while leaving knee-room. Drawers above would hold a camera and accessories.

To accommodate a drawer large enough to take an A2 drawing board I decided to cut the partitions short with their top ends fixed to a rail spanning across, giving me a long slim drawer.

How to support the top flap? Traditionally simple wooden battens or 'lopers' at either side are pulled out before lowering the flap. I decided to use two long narrow drawers instead, giving extra storage and more positive support for the sloping front than battens on edge. The vertical framing bars between these drawers and the long central drawer fall midway between the ends and the partition — symmetry again.

Now I was left with finding a home for the portable typewriter and briefcase. The only possible place was the knee-hole space I had wanted to leave. Would I have to abandon this idea? Thinking a bit more, I realised that even a shallow knee-hole gaining 2-3in of room was preferable to having one's shins bang the front, so I

started playing with the idea of a breakfront.

I decided on a cupboard front, since there were plenty of drawers elsewhere. The framed double doors would bring in more vertical lines, and echo the bookcase doors. The file drawers have a similar construction, and the vertical panelling is used again on the outside of the fall flap and the backing of the bookcase; the one central framing member of the flap is picked up by the door frames above and below.

Profile

So far, so good . . . but then I sketched the whole thing as it would appear from the side and was subdued by its lack of interest. The character of the wood helped me forward; one of the four original planks had a strongly contrasting dark red heartwood, and I decided to use this feature in the bookcase and bureau sides, livening up the side interest.

It was still rather flatfooted, though. I sketched out various ideas to alter the profile, and finally hit on the device of taking a long angled cut from under the long drawer right down to the ground; the profile immediately took on a 'poised' feeling, which I consider the most distinguishing feature of the whole design, and one I have re-used on other furniture since.

That was the overall design sorted out, but inevitably ideas occurred as I was

putting it together. The most important was to plane a deep chamfer on the long slim drawer and drawer front, a V-groove which supports the lower edge of the draughting board so I can use it while seated at the bureau. A strip of felt glued to the back of the drawing board's top edge prevents scratching of the closed flap. I can adjust the angle of the board simply by moving the drawer in or out, and use the narrow supporting drawers each side for holding pencils and drawing equipment. The built-in light source is ideally placed.

Also, when fitting the narrow support drawer it was seen as desirable to incorporate some simple stop so they couldn't be pulled out beyond the edge of the lowered flap. As I had made the drawers full depth, I realised that several inches at the rear of the drawer wouldn't be accessible if 'stopped'. This dead area was therefore readily made into a secret compartment by fitting a false back. Access is gained by removing the lower drawer from inside the desk compartment above and then lifting out the small spacer bar (this allows the lower drawers to clear the flap hinge-knuckles when pulled out). The spacer bar has two short dowels glued into its underside and these are a slightly loose fit into two holes in the desk top. They protrude through just enough to act as a stop to the back of the support drawers, while the false back is made shorter and so clears them.

continued

Pine with poise

Improvements

If I were to build another bureau/bookcase I would make a few changes from this initial design. Light frameworks between the inner and outer 'gables' of the bureau would simplify fitting the drawers and prevent them knocking against the front edges of the gables through side play when opening and closing. This would mean widening the bureau 100mm or so, and this would have increased the bureau's versatility; I found it a squeeze putting in the typewriter, and I'd like the narrow drawers a bit wider.

I would also include a partition piece between the upper and lower side drawers within the desk; I hadn't thought about this in advance, couldn't work out how to fit one afterwards, and ended up with the curious hinged flap on top of the lower drawer so its contents aren't on view.

I would also opt for rectangular door and drawer handles, as the round knobs seems out of place.

Notes on construction

You may not be impressed by the way I constructed the lower half, but you must remember I had a very limited amount of wood to work with. I wanted the sides to be free from signs of fixing, so I relied heavily on accurately routed dadoes and the holding power of the glue. It was sufficient, but I realise I would have gained greater rigidity if I had cut dovetailed slots for both the writing surface ends and those of the baseboard (I made up the baseboard and the partitions from white deal edged with yellow pine to economise, by the way).

I've mentioned the desirability of using light frameworks between the gables. In fact, I did use battens screwed to either side of the central cupboard to facilitate the cutting in of hinges. It might have been

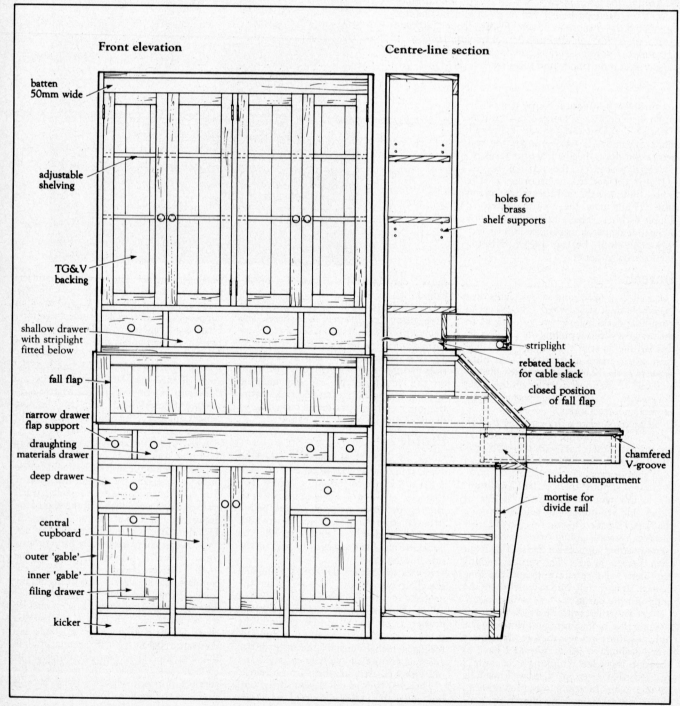

Front elevation

batten 50mm wide

adjustable shelving

TG&V backing

shallow drawer with striplight fitted below

fall flap

narrow drawer
flap support

draughting materials drawer

deep drawer

central cupboard

outer 'gable'

inner 'gable'

filing drawer

kicker

Centre-line section

holes for brass shelf supports

striplight

rebated back for cable slack

closed position of fall flap

chamfered V-groove

hidden compartment

mortise for divide rail

better to have made a frame for the doors and dowelled this to the bookshelf carcase.

I used the straightest grain boards for backing the bookcase, for the top of the bureau and the door panelling, making 100x10mm TG&V sheeting, but used plywood for backing the lower half.

Solid brass butts were used for the doors, with brass ball catches unobtrusively pushed into holes bored in their top edges. I dowelled the door frames, and machine-dovetailed the drawers, which run on central runners made of iroko.

I wasn't very happy about the finish I used. I gave component parts three coats of satin precatalysed lacquer, sprayed on before assembly; this required considerable masking off and was rather long-winded. Brushed-on coats of polyurethane would have been simpler and maybe more durable.

These construction notes are minimal because you've got to have a reasonable level of ability to tackle this project, and you'll likely come up with better ways of putting it together. ∎

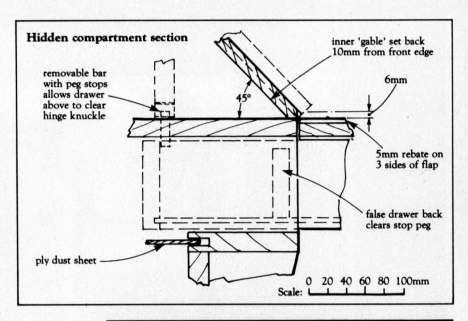

Hidden compartment section

inner 'gable' set back 10mm from front edge

removable bar with peg stops allows drawer above to clear hinge knuckle

45°

6mm

5mm rebate on 3 sides of flap

false drawer back clears stop peg

ply dust sheet

Scale: 0 20 40 60 80 100mm

Half-plan of desk

Scale: 0 100 200 300 400 500mm

interior compartment screwed to inner 'gable'

removable peg stop bar

rebated finger pull

Cutting list

All timber 19mm thick unless specified

Bookcase

Gables	2	1000mm	x 260mm
Top/bottom	2	985	260
Horizontal divider	1	985	250
Shelves	4	475	230
Vertical divider	1	825	250
Drawer dividers	2	150	250
Top batten	1	975	50
Door stiles	8	755	40
Door rails	8	160	40
Drawer fronts	2	225	130
Drawer front	1	480	130

Bureau

Outer gables	2	1000	560
Inner gables	2	610	400
Inner desk surface	1	1005	510
Top	1	1005	280
Base	1	1005	430
Long rail	1	1005	110
Kicker	1	1005	75
Vertical drawer dividers	2	110	510
Horizontal drawer dividers	2	280	50
Fall flap stiles	3	360	50
Fall flap rails	2	910	50
Centre cupboard door stiles	4	500	50
Centre cupboard door rails	4	120	50
Filing drawer front stiles	4	330	50
Filing drawer front rails	4	190	50
Narrow drawer fronts	2	120	100
Long drawer front	1	700	100
Deep drawer fronts	2	270	150

Bureau interior

Drawer dividers	2	140	140
Drawer fronts	4	125	100
Paper/envelope tray from	1	1700	250
Angled interior gables from	1	250	750

Angled offcuts from the outer gables can be used to face the front edges of the inner gables. This list does not include material for drawer sides and bases or the ply backing and dustsheet. In addition about 200 metres of TG&V board, 100x10mm, is needed to back the bookcase, the top part of the bureau, and the panels of all doors and fall flap.

Photo Tim Imrie

Clear through to the wood

● *Above*, *an opulent ripple sycamore desk and chair by John Makepeace, and* **below**, *John Coleman's contrastingly severe dining/conference chair in black stained ash*

A current exhibition in Cambridge puts the work of leading furniture makers together with some exciting contemporary glassware

Work from leading British furniture makers and glass makers is on show at a major exhibition in Cambridge's Fitzwilliam Museum, one of the oldest and most remarkable in the country. The Twentieth Century Gallery is filled with light, form and texture in a show that is primarily intended to provoke public interest in glass — more than 30 glass makers are showing new work, ranging from tableware to major pieces of sculptural art.

Many of the pieces of furniture have been designed as foils for the glassware, in some cases to house it. It's an opportunity to see work by such different furniture makers as John Coleman, Martin Grierson, John Makepeace, Alan Peters and Danny Lane under one roof.

Work for the exhibition has been selected by Henry Rothschild, who is best known for his many exhibitions of contemporary pottery. His last exhibition at the Fitzwilliam on leading English and eight foreign potters attracted more than 25000 people and focused attention of collectors on contemporary work. Now he hopes to encourage a similar sustained interest for glassware, and obviously considers that furniture and glass go well together.

● **Clear through to the wood**, Fitzwilliam Museum, Cambridge, 12 July-9 August, Tuesdays to Sundays

● **Above left**, Martin Grierson's 'Orient' chairs in rock maple, either stained or natural, are designed for batch production. **Above right**, Alan Peters explores the oriental theme with a three-way mitre on a white sycamore writing table. **Below**, Danny Lane's outrageous – but finely crafted – glass chair, and **below left**, glass forms by Stephen Proctor and (bottom) Ray Flavell

Knock on wood

Jamie Linwood's magnificent marimba won a Gold medal at the London Woodworker Show last year; here's how he designed and made it

I had started making African percussion instruments — drums, thumb pianos and so on — as a hobby when I heard the sound of marimbas about three years ago at a concert by a Ghanaian marimba player. I decided to make a marimba, but thought I needed to devote time to this more demanding project, so I started the part-time 'craft related to musical instruments' course at The London College of Furniture in September 1985.

I chose a marimba as opposed to a xylophone because I prefer the marimba's characteristic mellow tone to the crisp thin sound of the European xylophone.

I wanted to make a marimba that was not just functional, but a finely sculpted piece of art, like the Indonesian Gamelan instruments. I became aware of the sculpture of the Makonde people of Mozambique and Tanzania. Their *Shetani* sculpture is an imaginative interpretation of the creatures involved in old myths; their artistic integrity is widely respected as their sculpture is largely free from the commercial pressures of the tourist trade. There are many different kinds of *Shetani* (or spirits), and the figures on my marimba are similar to a type known as *beer shetani*, which appear as though they have been disturbed and are staring out at the onlooker, while still retaining movement to give life to the piece.

Having made sketches of how I wanted the frame to look I thought about the layout of the bars, soundboards, and resonators around which the frame would be built. Since this was the first marimba I had made

● *Startling* Shetani *sculpture echoes the marimba's African origins*

● *Variations on a musical theme: exquisitely carved Gambang by one of Java's most reputed Gamelan makers*

Photo courtesy Bate Collection, Oxford

I had little idea of the construction methods. I started going to libraries, reading all the information I could find and studying instruments at museums. This is how I came across the marimbas of the Chopi people of Mozambique. They are renowned for their sophisticated music and instruments; their orchestras of up to 30 marimbas range from double bass to treble instruments and together cover just over four octaves. On my marimba I used the Chopi method of supporting and securing the bars and also their backbone or soundboard of the instrument.

I chose western tuning and so needed two soundboards to permit the layout of the chromatic scale. I decided to make an instrument with a range of two octaves, G to G# (196Hz to 784Hz).

Before I could go any further with the design I had to make all the resonating bars so I knew the dimensions for the frame.

Construction of bars

I bought a plank of very old Laviuna rosewood from a local timber merchant for the bars. Marimba bars are shaped quite differently from xylophone bars, each being made to produce their own distinctive sounds. The bars of the marimba are wider and have a deeper arch cut on the underside (figs 1a, 1b), giving a fuller, richer sound with many harmonics. The principle behind this is quite simple: a slat of wood without any arch produces one note only, the fundamental. When an arch is cut this produces harmonics, and it follows that the deeper the arch the greater the number of harmonics. To achieve the desired sound the bars in the bass register can be as little as ¼in thick at the centre. This very much weakens the fundamental note, and to overcome this the bars are 3-4in wide in the bass, far wider than those of the xylophone.

I cut all the bars to size, and then drilled a hole at one of the nodal points through which the locating string passes (fig. 1a). These nodal points are places of least vibration and are approximately 0.224 of the length of the bar at either end.

I tuned each note by hollowing out the arch on the underside of the bar until the note fell to the desired pitch. If too much wood is removed you can raise the pitch by carving the ends (fig. 1c).

Soundboard

Once I had assembled all the finely tuned notes I made a full-scale plan of the marimba (fig. 3). I made the soundboards and straining bars of teak. One straining bar lies between every two notes and each one has two holes drilled through it, which the supporting string passes through. A leather thong passes through the hole in the resonating bar and under the supporting string, securing the bar to the string (fig. 2a). At the other nodal point the thong simply passes over the bar and under the supporting string (fig. 2b). I drilled a 1in-diameter hole through the soundboard. The resonators are attached directly beneath each hole.

Resonators

Having assembled the tuned notes on the soundboard I could now tune the resonators. I had wanted to use gourds as resonators but could only find the ornamental type from Covent Garden flower market; these went mouldy when I tried drying them out! My next idea was coconuts with a small hole made in the top and the fruit scraped out; these worked very well but I couldn't get them small enough for the treble notes. I also tried balloons covered in hessian which had been dipped in plaster, and even pomegranates! Eventually I opted for bamboo as being most suitable.

I used resonators closed at one end because these only have to be half the length of an open resonator. The tuning of the resonators depends on a number of factors: density of medium (air) which varies with temperature; length of resonator; area of opening of resonator; and velocity of sound in the medium.

There is a formula to which these factors can be applied when working out the dimensions of a trough resonator. But I found it easier to cut a piece of bamboo to length and see to which note it roughly corresponded. I made fine adjustments by pouring water into the resonator (raising the pitch) and then shortening the bamboo by an equivalent amount, on a disc sander. Another way to raise the pitch of the resonator is to increase the area of the opening, i.e. the hole in the soundboard. (You can lower the pitch by reducing the

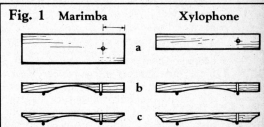

Fig. 1 Marimba   Xylophone

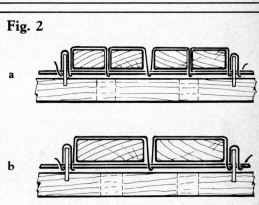

Fig. 2

aperture.) Next I degreased the teak soundboard with methylated spirits and glued the bamboo resonators on with Araldite.

Frame

I could then decide on the height of the frame which was governed by the length of the longest resonator. I went back to my sketches of the figures and made final designs for the frame. This took a long time; the drawing of each figure is not in itself difficult, but making each one fit into a certain area dictated to by the previous figure can be trying — especially when shuffling them around to fit in the last one!

Having arrived at the final design I decided to use ¾in birch plywood for the panels of the frame, avoiding the problem of short grain in solid timber. I traced the designs and then transferred them to the plywood before using a large floor-standing jigsaw to cut out the figures. Next I roughly cut away the layers of plywood with a flat chisel to make the figures appear three-dimensional. I had intended to carve the figures using gouges, but met the inherent problem with plywood: its inconsistency. Some layers are good, hard birch whilst

continued

Knock on wood

others are almost like balsa. So I used riffler rasps to shape the bodies and finished off with glasspaper. I had to carve the faces, and the eyes caused great problems with their tendency to split off. The teeth were impossible to carve in the plywood so I whittled them out of ebony and then glued them in position.

I made the soundboards detachable from the frame by using thumbscrews; this meant the instrument could be taken apart quickly and easily for transporting. I made the thumbscrews by turning the blanks on the lathe and then cut the threads with a screw-box. I attached two supporting blocks for the soundboards on both end panels of the frame; these had two threads cut in them for the screws.

Finishing

I ebonised each panel before assembling the frame, first staining the wood with black shoe dye, and then applying seven or eight coats of blackboard paint, before burnishing with very fine wire wool. At all four corners of the frame I attached battens the full height of the frame which were screwed and glued to increase strength and rigidity. I filled the countersunk holes for the screws with fine, ready mixed Tetrion, sanded down and then ebonised. Finally I polished the whole frame with one thin application of Briwax to get rid of the grey colour left by the wire wool.

Beaters

These must be of the correct hardness to bring out the tone of a marimba. A blow on a bar must immediately evoke the fundamental note by setting the wood in vibration. If the beater is too hard, only the shorter wavelengths are evoked and the fundamental note may remain dead. If the beater is too soft it will not sound the high notes well. For this reason a marimba needs two types of beater; the harder held in the right hand and the softer in the left (for a right-handed player). I made my beaters out of ¾in ramin dowelling tapered at one end, with strips of soft bicycle inner tube wrapped round the end. The harder beater is wrapped more tightly.

Afterword

I didn't originally apply any finish to the rosewood bars for fear of slightly deadening their resonance. I then noticed a rise in the pitch of the instrument, especially of the lower notes, because the wood was drying out. I re-tuned the bars and then applied one coat of Danish Oil to lessen the change in moisture content. This finish appears to make no difference to the quality of tone.

Most rosewoods produce a very good tone but the heavier Dalbergias like *D. stevensonnii* (Honduras) are superior. I have tried using a variety of other woods, and have found padauk and wengé produce a very good tone; even mahogany can produce a surprisingly bright note. ∎

Fig. 3 Plan: without resonating bars

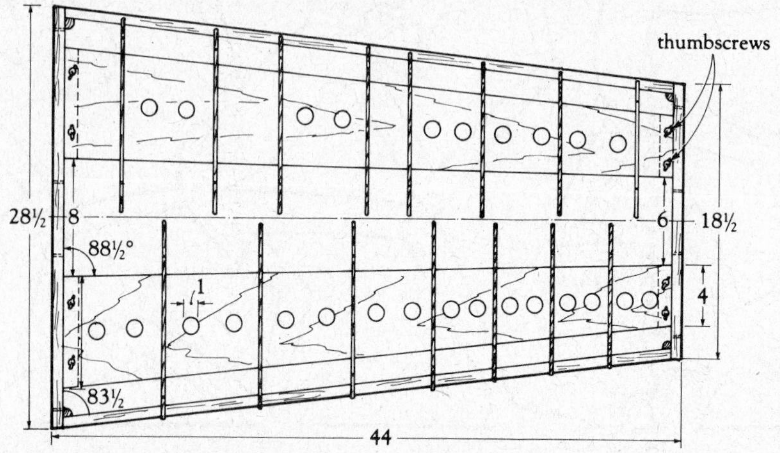

thumbscrews

28½   8   88½°   83½   6   18½   4   1   44

Fig. 4 Section   All dimensions in inches

1   2¼   15

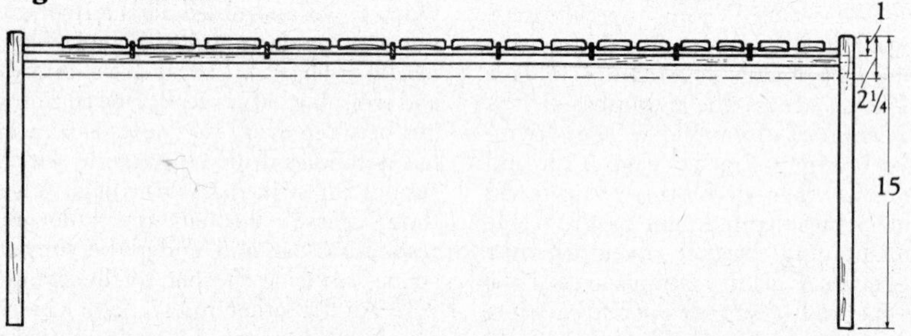

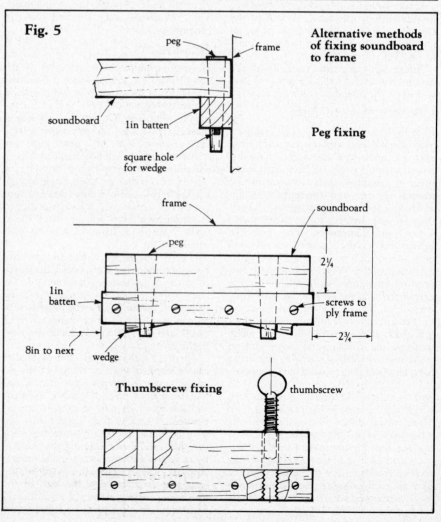

Fig. 5   **Alternative methods of fixing soundboard to frame**

peg   frame

soundboard   1in batten

square hole for wedge

Peg fixing

frame   soundboard

peg   2¼

1in batten   screws to ply frame

8in to next   wedge   2¾

Thumbscrew fixing   thumbscrew

WOODWORKING MACHINERY

Nu-Tools
5 speed woodturning lathe NWL37. This superb brand new wood lathe is fitted with many features found on machines twice its price, finished to the highest standards giving strength and stability.
¾ H.P. Motor
5 Speed
Turning Capacity (length) 941mm
Turning Capacity (diameter) 305mm
Supplied with face plate, drive centre, revolving centre.
9" & 6" tool rests.
Headstock
Spindle protrudes to accept left hand face plate for outboard turning. Also headstock is bored through for deep hole boring.

PRICE £139 inc. VAT/Del.

Accessories: 4 jaw chuck £45
9" Sanding Plate £15
9" Sanding Plate £15
Sanding Table £15
8 Piece Woodturning Chisel Set £29

Nu-Tools
Heavy Duty Scroll Jigsaw
20" throat
Cast alloy surface
Adjustable arm
Two speeds
Professional machine
Supplied with many standard accessories
500mm throat
¼ HP Motor
45° Tilting Table
Price £249 inc. VAT/Delivery

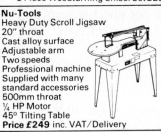

Nu-Tools
14" 3-wheeled Bench Bandsaw
Multipurpose, light industrial with a range of accessories to meet almost every type of bandsawing operation.
3 speeds
Sealed bearings
⅓ HP British Motor
Supplied with circle cutter, rip & mitre fences, sanding belt & disc.
Cutting capacity 360mm
Cutting depth 145mm
Table tilting 0-45 degrees
Size of table 400mm × 400mm

PRICE £164 incl. VAT/Delivery

Nu-Tools
10" Hobby Table Saw
Lightweight, powerful, compact sawbench, cast alloy table, 2 HP motor, rise and fall, tilting arbor, depth of cut 80mm.
PRICE £154 incl. VAT/Delivery

Nu-Tools
Heavy duty 12 speed bench drill
⅝" capacity
¾ HP motor
2 m/t chuck
Rack & pinion
Free mortising attachment with this unit
PRICE £199 incl. VAT/Delivery

*Send SAE for colour brochures.
Many other woodworking machines available.*

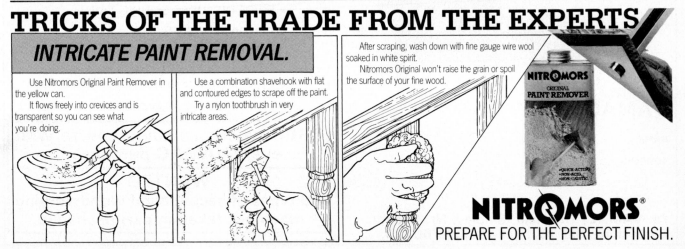

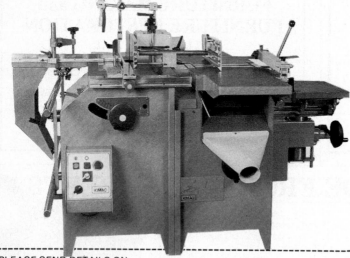

shopguide

AVON

BATH Tel. Bath 64513
JOHN HALL TOOLS
RAILWAY STREET ★
Open: Monday-Saturday
9.00 a.m. 5.30 p.m.
H.P.W.WM.D.A.BC.

BUCKINGHAMSHIRE

HIGH WYCOMBE Tel. (0494)
ISAAC LORD LTD. 22221
185 DESBOROUGH ROAD **K**
Open: Mon.-Fri. 8.00 a.m. to 5.30 p.m.
Saturday 8.30 a.m. to 5.00 p.m.

H.P.W.D.A.WM.MF.

CORNWALL

SOUTH WEST Power Tools
CORNWALL Tel: Helston (03265) 4961
HELSTON AND LAUNCESTON Launceston
(0566) 4781
H.P.W.WM.D.CS.A. **K**

BRISTOL Tel. (0272) 741510
JOHN HALL TOOLS LIMITED
CLIFTON DOWN SHOPPING CENTRE
WHITELADIES ROAD ★
Open: Monday-Saturday
9.00 a.m.-5.30 p.m.
H.P.W.WM.D.A.BC.

HIGH WYCOMBE Tel. (0494)
SCOTT SAWS LTD. 24201/33788
14 BRIDGE STREET **T★**
Mon.-Sat. 8.30 a.m.-6.00 p.m.

H.P.W.WM.D.T.CS.MF.A.BC.

CUMBRIA

CARLISLE Tel. (0228) 36391
W. M. PLANT **T**
ALLENBROOK ROAD
ROSEHILL, CA1 2UT
Open: Mon.-Fri. 8.00 a.m.-5.15 p.m.
Sat. 8.00 a.m.-12.30 noon
P.W.WM.D.CS.A.

GLOUCESTER

TEWKESBURY Tel. (0684)
TEWKESBURY SAW CO. LTD. 293092
TRADE ESTATE, NEWTOWN **K**
Telex No. 43382
Open: Mon-Fri 8.00 a.m.-5.00 p.m.
Saturday 9.30 a.m.-12.00 p.m.
P.W.WM.D.CS.

BRISTOL Tel. (0272) 750045
TRYMWOOD SERVICES
2a DOWNS PARK EAST (off North View)
WESTBURY PARK
Open: 8.30 a.m.-5.30 p.m. Mon. to Fri.
Closed for lunch 1.00-2.00 p.m.
P.W.WM.T.A.BC.

CAMBRIDGESHIRE

CAMBRIDGE Tel: (0223) 63132
D. MACKAY LTD. ★
BRITANNIA WORKS, EAST ROAD
Open: Mon.-Fri. 8.30 a.m.-1 p.m./2.00-
5.00 p.m. Sat. 8.30 a.m.-1.00 p.m.
H.P.W.D.T.CS.MF.A.BC.

DEVON

BRIXHAM Tel. (08045) 4900
WOODCRAFT SUPPLIES ★
4 HORSE POOL STREET
Open: Mon.-Sat. 9.00 a.m.-6.00 p.m.
H.P.W.A.D.MF.CS.BC.

HAMPSHIRE

ALDERSHOT   SOUTHAMPTON
(0252) 334422   (0703) 332288
BURCH & HILLS POWER TOOL CENTRES
374 HIGH ST.   7 BELVIDERE RD.
Open Mon.-Fri. 8.30-5.30. Sat. 8.30-12.00
Closed for Lunch 1.00-2.00
H.P.W.WM.D.C.S.MF.BC.K.* **T**

01-437 0699 = RESULTS

BRISTOL Tel. (0272) 667013
WILLIS **T**
157 WEST STREET
BEDMINSTER
Open Mon.-Fri. 8.30 a.m.-5.00 p.m.
P.W.WM.D.CS.A.BC.

CAMBRIDGE Tel. (0223) 247386
H. B. WOODWORKING **TK**
105 CHERRY HINTON ROAD
Open: 8.30 a.m.-5.30 p.m.
Monday-Friday
8.30 a.m.-1.00 p.m. Sat.
H.P.W.WM.D.CS.A.MF.BC.

PLYMOUTH Tel. (0752) 330303
WESTWARD BUILDING SERVICES ★
LTD., LISTER CLOSE, NEWNHAM
INDUSTRIAL ESTATE, PLYMPTON
Open: Mon-Fri 8.00 a.m.-5.30 p.m.
Sat. 8.30 a.m.-12.30 p.m.
H.P.W.WM.D.A.BC.

Read Model Engineer for a new angle on construction and design.

BERKSHIRE

READING Tel. Littlewick Green
DAVID HUNT (TOOL 2743
MERCHANTS) LTD ★
KNOWL HILL, NR. READING
Open: Monday-Saturday
9.00 a.m.-5.30 p.m.
H.P.W.D.A.BC.

PETERBOROUGH Tel. (0733)
WILLIAMS DISTRIBUTORS 64252
(TOOLS) LIMITED **TK**
108-110 BURGHLEY ROAD
Open: Monday to Friday
8.30 a.m.-5.30 p.m.
H.P.A.W.D.WH.BC.

PLYMOUTH Tel. (0752) 665363
F.T.B. LAWSON LTD. **T**
71 NEW GEORGE STREET
PLYMOUTH PL1 1RB
Open: Mon.-Sat. 8.30 a.m.-5.30 p.m.
H.P.W.CS.MF.A.

HERTFORDSHIRE

WARE Tel: (0920) 870 230
HEATH SAWS 870 636
6 LEESIDE WORKS **K★**
STANSTEAD ABBOTTS (near Ware) HERTS.
SG12 8DL.
Open: Mon.-Fri. 8.30 a.m.-5.30 p.m.
Sat. 8.30 a.m.-1 p.m. Sunday by appointment.
H.P.W.WM.D.T.CS.MF.A.BC.*K.

CHESHIRE

READING Tel. Reading 661511
WOKINGHAM TOOL CO. LTD. **T**
99 WOKINGHAM ROAD
Open: Mon-Sat 9.00 a.m.-5.30 p.m.
Closed 1.00-2.00 p.m. for lunch
H.P.W.WM.D.CS.A.BC.

NANTWICH Tel. Crewe 67010
ALAN HOLTHAM **TK★**
THE OLD STORES TURNERY
WISTASON ROAD, WILLASTON
Open: Tues.-Fri. 9.00 a.m.-5.30 p.m.
Sat. 9.00 a.m.-5.00 p.m. Closed Monday.
P.W.WM.D.T.C.CS.A.BC.

DORSET

WEYMOUTH Tel. (0305) 770303
WEYMOUTH HIRE & SALES LTD. **TK**
5 KENT CLOSE
GRANBY INDUSTRIAL ESTATE
Open 7.30 a.m.-5.30 p.m. Mon.-Fri.
Sat. 8 a.m.-1 p.m.
H.P.W.WM.D.CS.A.K.

HUMBERSIDE

GRIMSBY Tel. Grimsby (0472)
58741 Hull (0482) 26999
J. E. SIDDLE LTD. (Tool Specialists) **T★**
83 VICTORIA STREET
Open: Mon-Fri 8.30 a.m.-5.30 p.m.
Sat. 8.30 a.m.-12.45 p.m. & 2 p.m.-5 p.m.
H.P.A.BC.W.WM.D.

BUCKINGHAMSHIRE

MILTON KEYNES Tel. (0908)
POLLARD WOODWORKING 641366
CENTRE **T★**
51 AYLESBURY ST., BLETCHLEY
Open: Mon.-Fri. 8.30-5.30
Saturday 9.00-5.00
H.P.W.WM.D.CS.A.BC. **INCA**

WIDNES Tel: 051 424 4545/7965
THE POWER TOOL CENTRE ★
54/58 VICTORIA ROAD, WA8 7RJ
Mon.-Fri. 8.30am-5pm
Sat. 8.30am-4pm.
H.P.W.WM.D.CS.A.BC.

ESSEX

LEIGH ON SEA Tel. (0702)
MARSHAL & PARSONS LTD. 710404
1111 LONDON ROAD **K**
Open: 8.30 a.m.-5.30 p.m. Mon.-Fri.
9.00 a.m.-5.00 p.m. Sat.
H.P.W.WM.D.CS.A.

HULL
HUMBERSIDE FACTORING/H.F.C.
SAW SERVICING LTD.
MAIN STREET
Open: Mon.-Fri. 8am-5pm.
Saturday 8am-12.00pm.
H.P.W.WM.D.CS.A.BC.K.

CLEVELAND

MIDDLESBROUGH Tel. (0642)
CLEVELAND WOODCRAFT 813103
(M'BRO), 38-42 CRESCENT ROAD **TK**
Open: Mon.-Sat. 9.15 a.m.-5.30 p.m.
H.P.A.BC.W.WM.CS.D.

KENT

SLOUGH Tel: (06286) 5125
BRAYWOOD ESTATES LTD. ★
158 BURNHAM LANE
Open: 9.00am-5.30pm.
Monday-Saturday.
H.P.W.WM.CS.A.

ILFORD Tel. 597 7461
CUTWELL WOODWORKING **T★**
776 HIGH ROAD
GOODMAYES IG3 8SY
H.P.W.WM.D.CS.A.

MAIDSTONE Tel: (0622) 44350
HENSON AND PLATT
TOKE PLACE
LINTON
Open Mon.-Fri. 8.00 a.m.-5.00 p.m.
Saturday 8.00 a.m.-1.00 p.m.
H.P.W.T.CS.A.

shopguide

LONDON

FULHAM   Tel. (01-636) 6109
I. GRIZARD LTD.
84a-b-c. LILLIE ROAD, SW6 1TL
Open: Mon.-Sat. 9.00-5.30 p.m.
Half day Thursday

H.P.A.BC.W.CS.WM.D.

**Advertise here to
capture both local
+ national markets**

KENT

MAIDSTONE   Tel. (0622) 50177
SOUTH EASTERN SAWS (Ind.) LTD.   ★
COLDRED ROAD
PARKWOOD INDUSTRIAL ESTATE
Open: Mon.-Fri. 8.00 a.m.-5.00 p.m.
Sat. 9.00 a.m.-12.00 a.m.
B.C.W.CS.WM.PH.

LANCASHIRE

PRESTON   Tel. (0772) 52951
SPEEDWELL TOOL COMPANY   ★
62-68 MEADOW STREET PR1 1SU
Open: Mon.-Fri. 8.30 a.m.-5.30 p.m.
Sat. 8.30 a.m.-12.30 p.m.

H.P.W.WM.CS.A.MF.BC.

ROCHDALE   Tel. (0706) 342123/
C.S.M. TOOLS   342322
4-6 HEYWOOD ROAD   T★
CASTLETON
Open: Mon-Sat 9.00 a.m.-6.00 p.m.
Sundays by appointment
W.D.CS.A.BC.

LANCASTER   Tel: (0524) 32886
LILE TOOL SHOP   K
43/45 NORTH ROAD
Open: Monday to Saturday
9.00 a.m.-5.30 p.m.
Wed. 9.00 a.m.-12.30 p.m.
H.P.W.D.A.

**Read Model Engineer
for a new angle on
construction & design**

BLACKPOOL   Tel. (0253) 28262
FYLDE WOODTURNING SUPPLIES   ★
255 CHURCH STREET, FY1 3PB
Open: 9.30-5.30 Monday to Friday.
9.30-4.30 Saturday. Closed Wednesday.
H.T.W.WM.A.MF.BC.D.

LONDON

ACTON   Tel. (01-992) 4835
A. MILLS (ACTON) LTD.   ★
32/36 CHURCHFIELD ROAD W3 6ED
Open: Mon.-Fri. 8.32 a.m.-5.30 p.m.
Saturdays 9.00 a.m.-1.00 p.m.

H.P.W.WM.

LONDON   Tel. 01-723 2295-6-7
LANGHAM TOOLS LIMITED
13 NORFOLK PLACE
LONDON W2 1QJ

LONDON

FULHAM   Tel. (01-636) 6109
I. GRIZARD LTD.
84a-b-c. LILLIE ROAD, SW6 1TL
Open: Mon.-Sat. 9.00-5.30 p.m.
Half day Thursday

H.P.A.BC.W.CS.WM.D.

**Use this space
for your
Summer Plans**

MANCHESTER

MANCHESTER   Tel. (061 789)
TIMMS TOOLS   0909
102-104 LIVERPOOL ROAD   ★
PATRICROFT M30 0WZ
Weekdays 9.00 a.m.-5.30 p.m.
Sat. 9.00 a.m.-1.00 p.m.
H.P.A.W.

MANCHESTER   Tel: 061 834 0714
TILL AND WHITEHEAD   ★
ELLESMERE STREET, M15 4JX

Open: Mon.-Fri. 8.00 a.m.-5.00 p.m.

H.P.W.A.BC.

MERSEYSIDE

LIVERPOOL   Tel. (051-207) 2967
TAYLOR BROS (LIVERPOOL) LTD.   TK
195-199 LONDON ROAD
LIVERPOOL L3 8JG
Open: Monday to Friday
8.30 a.m.-5.30 p.m.
H.P.W.WM.D.A.BC.

MIDDLESEX

ENFIELD   Tel. 01-363 2935
GILL & HOXBY LTD.   T
131-137 ST. MARKS ROAD ADJ.
BUSH HILL PARK STATION, EN1 1BA
Mon.-Sat. 8-5.30
Early closing Wed. 1 p.m.
H.P.A.M.MC.T.S.W.

RUISLIP   Tel. (08956) 74126
ALLMODELS ENGINEERING LTD.   ★
91 MANOR WAY

Open: Mon.-Sat. 9.00 a.m.-5.30 p.m.

H.P.W.A.D.CS.MF.BC.

NORFOLK

NORWICH   Tel. (0603) 898695
NORFOLK SAW SERVICES
DOG LANE, HORSFORD
Open: Monday to Friday
8.00 a.m.-5.00 p.m.
Saturday 8.00 a.m.-12.00 p.m.
H.P.W.WM.D.CS.A.

KINGS LYNN   Tel. (0553) 772443
WALKER & ANDERSON (Kings Lynn) LTD.   T
WINDSOR ROAD, KINGS LYNN
Open: Monday to Saturday
7.45 a.m.-5.15 p.m.

H.P.W.WM.D.CS.A.

NORFOLK

NORWICH   Tel. (0603) 400933
WESTGATES WOODWORKING   Tx
61 HURRICANE WAY,   975412
NORWICH AIRPORT INDUSTRIAL ESTATE
Open: 9.00 a.m.-5.00 p.m. weekdays
9.00 a.m.-12.30 Sat.
P.W.WM.D.BC.   K

KINGS LYNN   Tel: 07605 674
NORFOLK WOODTURNING CENTRE   ★
UNIT A, HILL FARM WORKSHOPS
GREAT DUNHAM (Nr. Swaffham)
Tues.-Sat. 9.00am-5.30pm

H.P.W.D.T.MF.A.BC.

NORTHAMPTONSHIRE

RUSHDEN   Tel. (0933) 56424
PETER CRISP OF RUSHDEN   ★
7-11 HIGH STREET
Mon.-Fri. 8.30-12.30/1.30-5.30
Thurs. 8.30-1.00. Sat all day.
H.P.W.WM.D.M.F.A.K.

NOTTINGHAMSHIRE

NOTTINGHAM   Tel: (0602) 225979
POOLEWOOD   and 227064/5
EQUIPMENT LTD.   (06077) 2421 after hrs
5a HOLLY LANE, CHILLWELL
Open: Mon-Fri 9.00 a.m.-5.30 p.m.
Sat. 9.00 a.m. to 12.30 p.m.
P.W.WM.D.CS.A.BC.

OXON

WITNEY   Tel. (0993) 76431
TARGET TOOLS (SALES,   OXON
TARGET HIRE & REPAIRS)   T★
TOOLS SWAIN COURT
STATION INDUSTRIAL ESTATE
Open: Mon.-Sat. 8.00 a.m.-5.00 p.m.
24 hour Answerphone
BC.W.M.A.

SHROPSHIRE

TELFORD   Tel. Telford (0952)
ASLES LTD.   48054
VINEYARD ROAD, WELLINGTON   K★

Open: Mon.-Fri. 8.30 a.m.-5.30 p.m.
Saturday 8.30 a.m.-4.00 p.m.
H.P.W.WM.D.CS.BC.A.

SOMERSET

TAUNTON   Tel. (0823) 335431
JOHN HALL TOOLS
6 HIGH STREET

Open Monday-Saturday
9.00 a.m.-5.30 p.m.
H.P.W.WM.D.CS.A.

SUFFOLK

IPSWICH   Tel. (0473) 40456
FOX WOODWORKING   463884
142-144 BRAMFORD LANE   T★
Open: Tues.-Fri. 9 a.m.-5.30 p.m.
Sat. 9 a.m.-5 p.m.
W.WM.D.T.CS.MF.A.BC.K.★

**All shops with an
asterisk ★
have a Mail Order
Service**

SURREY

GUILDFORD   Tel. (0483) 61125
MESSINGERS FOR TOOLS
14-18 CHERTSEY ST.
(TOP OF NORTH ST.)
Open: Tues.-Sat. 8.30 a.m.-5.30 p.m.

H.P.W.CS.MF.A.BC.K.

**Read Model Engineer
for a new angle on
construction & design**

SUSSEX

WORTHING   Tel. (0903) 38739
W. HOSKING LTD. (TOOLS &   KT★
MACHINERY)
28 PORTLAND RD, BN11 1QN
Open: Mon.-Sat. 8.30 a.m.-5.30 p.m.
Closed Wednesday
H.P.W.WM.D.CS.A.BC.

TYNE & WEAR

NEWCASTLE-UPON-TYNE   ★
J. W. HOYLE LTD
CLARENCE STREET
NEWCASTLE-UPON-TYNE
TYNE & WEAR
NE2 17J
H.P.W.WM.D.CS.A.BC.K.

W. MIDLANDS

WOLVERHAMPTON   Tel. (0902)
MANSAW SERVICES   58759
WARD STREET, HORSELEY FIELDS   TK★
WOLVERHAMPTON, WEST MIDLANDS
Open Mon.-Fri. 9.00 a.m.-5.00 p.m.
Saturday 8 a.m.-3 p.m.
H.P.W.WM.A.D.CS.

YORKSHIRE

THIRSK   Tel. (0845) 22770
THE WOOD SHOP   ★
TRESKE SAWMILLS LTD.
STATION WORKS
Open: Seven days a week 9.00-5.00

T.H.MF.BC.H.

SHEFFIELD   Tel. (0742) 441012
GREGORY & TAYLOR LTD.   K
WORKSOP ROAD
Open: 8.30 a.m.-5.30 p.m.
Monday-Friday
8.30 a.m.-12.30 p.m. Saturday
H.P.W.WM.D.

HARROGATE   Tel. (0423) 505328/
MULTI-TOOLS   66245
158 KINGS ROAD   K★

Open: Monday to Saturday
8.30 a.m.-6.00 p.m.

H.P.W.WM.D.A.BC.

HOLME UPON   Tel. (0696) 60612
SPALDING MOOR
CRAFT TOOLS AND TACKLE LTD.
HOLME INDUSTRIAL ESTATE
Open: Mon.-Fri. 9.00 am-5.30 pm.
Saturday & Bank Holiday 9.00 am-4.30 pm
H.P.W.D.T.CS.MF.A.BC.

WOOD SUPPLIERS

WOOD SUPPLIERS

736

Classified Advertisements

FOR SALE

THE FINEST SELECTION ON DISPLAY IN SCOTLAND!

WOODWORKING & METALWORKING MACHINERY POWER TOOLS HAND TOOLS

THE SAW CENTRE

LARGE STOCKS COMPETITIVE PRICES. PHONE AND TRY US NOW!

OPEN Mon - Fri 8am - 5pm Sat 9am - 1pm

Eglinton Toll, Glasgow G5 9RP Tel: 041-429-4444

38 Haymarket Edinburgh EH12 5J2 Tel: 031-337-5555

WOODCARVING tools

LARGEST STOCK IN EUROPE

Henry Taylor
Arkansas Bench & Slip Stones
Strops & Strop Paste
Bench Screws, Carvers' Vices

WOODTURNING tools

Complete range of Henry Taylor handled or unhandled

send 40p in stamps for illustrated catalogue

ALEC TIRANTI LTD
70 High St, Theale, Reading, Berks RG7 5AR
27 Warren Street, London W1.

QUALITY MOVEMENTS FOR QUALITY CASES

Eight Day Long case clock movements hand made of traditional design and very high quality, suitable for fitting in reproduction clock cases. These should appeal to the craftsman who requires the quality of the original Long Case movements. Dials and hands available made to your requirements. Brassware for clock cases including, capitals, escutcheons, etc. available.

Catalogue on castings + parts U.K. £1.25. Overseas £2.50.

RICHARDS OF BURTON
Woodhouse Clockworks
Swadlincote Road, Woodville
Burton-on-Trent   Tel: (0283) 219155

Yorkwire (Leeds) Ltd.

BRASS WIRE, ROD, STRIP & TUBE

Suitable for Miniature furniture, Clock Pendulums, Inlay work and many other Crafts.

SAE for Price List to:
Yorkwire (Leeds) Ltd.
34 Lupton Street,
Leeds LS10 2QW.
Tel: 0532 777472

J. Lajevardi
20A Lower Park Row
Bristol · BS1 5BN
England
Tel: (0272) 273874

Fast and efficient mail order service

For your catalogue send £1 and a large S.A.E.
(Redeemable with your first order).

OLDER TOOLS

Very wide range in stock at Shop.
Mail Order Catalogue £1 or 6 issues £5.
Tyzack 1908 Tool Cat. Reprint £7.50

BRISTOL DESIGN
14 Perry Rd, Bristol BS1 5BG
Tel: (0272) 291740

INCA EURO 260 motorised bandsaw	£390.00
ESCO Type 530 battery tacker	£165.00
MAKITA 6092 DWK driver drill	£121.00
A-Z 1 dust extractor	£200.00

Prices include VAT & carriage. Write NOW with your requirements for a competitive quotation. Also our wood working tooling catalogue (price £1.00) refunded on first order.

BLADES, Freepost, Petersfield, Hampshire GU32 2BR (no stamp required).

BUSINESS OPPORTUNITIES

YORKSHIRE DALES

An excellent and unique opportunity exists for a number of craftsmen in an established workshop in North Yorkshire. Successful applicants will have full use of a comprehensively equipped machine shop and individual bench space. In addition full reception, administration and marketing back-up will be provided. In short a complete business package geared towards the individual trading craftsman and a superb opportunity for craftsmen to start in their own business. Places available for Cabinet makers, furniture makers, timber machinists, woodturners.

Phone (0423) 780901

BUSINESS FOR SALE

SMALL WORKSHOP suitable for joinery and furniture manufacture. New machinery. Emigration forces sale. Serious enquiries only. South East London location. Offers over £12,000 considered. Enquiries to: Woodworker Classified Dept., Box No. WW127, No. 1 Golden Square, London W1R 3AB.

SMALL fully equipped workshop. Beds/Bucks borders. Long lease for full details ring Leighton Buzzard 372719.

SITUATIONS VACANT

 CABINET-MAKER

THE POST WOULD SUIT A MAKER WITH WIDE EXPERIENCE OF WORK DONE TO THE VERY HIGHEST STANDARDS. A UNIQUE OPPORTUNITY TO JOIN THIS HAPPY AND CREATIVE WORKSHOP.

FOR DETAILS SEND LARGE SAE TO:
DAVID SAVAGE FURNITURE,
21 Westcombe, Bideford EX39 3JQ

LOCAL Fretsaw owner wanted for 60 hours sub-contract work Hegner/Diamond required Storrington 4920 W. Sussex.

Advertisers please note: Rates are subject to review from October issue.

CONTENTS of 3 school workshops, engineering and woodworking machines and various tools. For detailed list write to: Warners Machinery Centre, Unit 10, Finedon Road, Irthlingborough, Northants.

UNIVERSAL, M1A6 (Luna Z40) 6½" Saw, 6". Planer/Thicknesser Morticer, Spindle moulder, complete with instructions, accessories, cost new £700, £450 ono. Tel. 0272 848180 daytime, 0272 842866 evenings.

GOOD used 3-phase Woodworking Machines, very reasonable prices. SAE list. Western Joinery, Heylesbury, Wilts. Tel. 0985 40686.

UNUSED Elu Router, planer, sander + accessories. Hegner Multicut 2 Universal saw. Fantastic prices. Tel: 0228 60985.

SMALL three-phase spindle moulder £170. Large 3-phase bandsaw, good condition. Tel. (0594) 60084.

THE WHISTON CATALOGUE

Nuts, bolts, screws, washers, bar materials. In brass, alloy, steel, stainless steel, P.T.F.E., nylon, Tufnol, sheet material, electrical and mechanical items. We could go on and on! Better to send for free catalogue and see for yourself.
K. R. Whiston Ltd., Dept. WW, New Mills, Stockport, Cheshire. Phone: 0663 42028.

SUPERB QUALITY Grandfather/Grandmother/Mantle Clocks triple chime movements with exclusive dials at bargain prices — limited quantity only large s.a.e. to M. R. Pemberton, 9 Marlborough Avenue, Weston Park Estate, Stafford ST16 3SG. Phone Stafford 47737.

DeWALT RADIAL ARM SAW Model 1875, 900mm reach, 3 phase with TCT blade. Bargain £400. Ring 0926 832428.

UNUSED EBAC mini timber seasoner with custom drying cabinet £500 or offers. Further details Huddersfield 852 887.

CONTENTS OF TECH COLLEGE woodwork, engineering and sheet metal machines, some 240 volt approx 70 items. For list send s.a.e. Write only to "Trade", 155 High Street, Irthlingborough, Northants.

EBAC Dehumidifier/Control Panel/Protoimeter for wood kilning processes. Also powerful larger dehumidifier all excellent condition, open to offers. Tel: Stafford 47737 after 6pm.

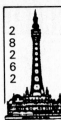

WOODWORKER AUGUST 1987

739

Letters

Design?

I HAVE MADE MY fair share of criticism of WOODWORKER over the years but I am pleased to say that the March issue was in my view the best for a very long time, with an enormous number of projects, virtually every one of interest — at least to me.

I write particularly, however, to ask why you continue to give space to the so-called designers some of whose chairs you chose to feature ... you are surely in a very small minority in thinking that Susi Janus' maple chair was 'well balanced and neat to look at'. I can't recall a more inharmonious chair design and the distance by which the bottom point of the near 'leg' stands in from the tip of the heavily raked back must make it hazardous to use. You made your own comments on its comfort ...

Again and again and I see the examples of work by students/young designers which you show from time to time, I find myself wondering what their lecturers have to say for themselves.

Putting aside Ms Janus' obvious skill in making her chair to the high standards you mention, the project was surely a complete failure, and since your intent appeared not to be to ridicule, I have to wonder why you chose to feature such an item ... I could wish you would pay more attention to merit and less to difference.

H. Jackson, Bristol

Bias in bowls

RE THE LETTER from Mr E. T. Haddock (*WW*/*April*) about hand-turning crown green bowls, our company has been associated with making bowls since 1830 and our skilled turners still face the problems he does in producing bias. We use shaping templates to guide the turners, but a lot is down to experience and 'eye'. We run bowls down a test table 30ft long and 6ft wide, comparing the new bowl to a 'standard,' and making any small final adjustments to the running sole with fine-grade sandpaper.

We renovate several thousand sets of lignum vitae crown green bowls each year, but composition bowls are steadily gaining ground. We now use computer-controlled lathes to give standard shaping for both composition and lignum vitae bowls to ensure accuracy.

Peter Clare, Director,
E. A. Clare & Son, Liverpool

Rainforest – the view from Oz

I AM A PARTNER in a small milling business which makes timber products that replace rainforest products, and I was very pleased to read Chris Cox's article, 'Who is Aware?' (*WW*/*March 1987*).

We as consumers must start changing consumption patterns as it is plain that there would not be a tree left before the established timber industry took action. Like Chris I have been a joiner and faced the same dilemma, except that for me the timbers I was using were coming from the rainforest just up the road. My solution was to start my business, which utilises local regrowth non-rainforest species to produce cabinet and joinery stocks.

I believe very strongly that even though the cabinet and joinery trade is a proportionately small timber consumer, it is nevertheless the primary area where changes in timber usage can have the greatest effect on the general consciousness. When the more widely acclaimed timber artists and the more exclusive furniture makers refuse to use rainforest timbers, the public sit up and take notice.

As Chris notes, the replacements for rainforest timbers are generally more expensive, because they include the cost of sustainable management, and this means that the acceptance of replacements is slow. People must make a conscious decision not to use rainforest timbers and then pay for that decision. However, I have been surprised at the number of people in my area who are prepared to pay.

I cannot resist replying to the comments from the timber industry.

Firstly, contrary to Dan Kemp's statement that Malaysia, Burma and Java balance harvesting with regrowth, large areas of Sarawak and Borneo rainforest (from where most of our meranti comes) are entirely denuded and the major timber companies there are planning to shift to Papua New Guinea soon.

The primary source of forest degradation in South-East Asia is logging by foreign timber companies who notoriously do little for the local economy, use foreign capital and have no vested interest in the continuance of their resource base. Nearly all the timber produced by these countries is exported to countries such as England and Australia. Thus to suggest that by continuing to buy from these sources we are pressurising countries to harvest sustainably borders on delinquency.

It is true, as Chris Holmes-Smith says, that the timber trade must accept the use of timbers which are little known, as long as they do the job. The main problem is finding durable, stable species for house joinery, the greatest user of rainforest joinery timber. Unfortunately the species which naturally colonise cleared rainforest are seldom durable and stable.

Nearly half Australia's forest output is produced and exported by Japanese companies in the form of woodchips for paper. From first-hand knowledge I can tell Dr Peter Hansom, who believes that responsible management comes when the local economy is prosperous, of the effect of a foreign country exporting unprocessed products; a tiny local workforce and widespread forest mismanagement as the Government scrambles for a small export income despite pressure from a sophisticated domestic conservation lobby.

Timber exporting countries can multilaterally lift forest royalty rates to cover reforestation costs and enforce minimum levels of processing prior to export. This would have the effect supposedly sought by the timber industry, increased employment and export earnings. Timber importing countries can impose taxes on timber, and particularly paper, to finance their own much-needed reforestation programmes.

In short, we are not effectively managing the forests that have been logged because we are not prepared to pay for good management. There is no justification to log more virgin forest unless we can show that we do effectively manage what we have logged.

All sections of the timber consumption cycle can respond to the forest crisis in their own way. I fully support Chris Cox's initiative. It is vital that timber consumers are aware of where their timber comes from and also that producers respond to the increasing number of people who wish to actively support the sustainability of our forests.

David Wood, Bellingen, NSW, Australia

Nail stain hazard

IN THE APRIL ISSUE, Charles Cliffe gave the method for preparing a chemical stain suitable for use on oak which I demonstrate and recommend for certain cases — soaking iron rails in vinegar. However, an incident involving this method was brought to my attention by one of the students on the Guild of Woodworkers' polishing course in Chester.

To my horror, he reported to me that his mixture exploded after having been stored for some weeks in a sealed container. The nails were still soaking. I have never heard of this happening before or since but the moral of that story is: prepare in an open vessel and remove the nails before storing in sealed bottles. The reason for this is that the action of acids, however weak (and vinegar contains acetic acid), on metals produces hydrogen gas. The quantity of gas evolved in the 'rusty' nail stain is normally too small to be considered a hazard but clearly it would build up, and pressurise, under the conditions outlined above. At least enough to send splinters of glass all over a workshop. Thank God he wasn't in it at the time.

Ian Hosker (Guild Course Tutor), Chester

Misuse of tools

MORTISE CHISELS, although robust and designed for levering, should not be encouraged for use as described in fig. 3 of the 'Question Box' answers in WOODWORKER June 1987, on laying parquet flooring. The same effect can be achieved by using the block and wedge as shown in fig. 1, or a purpose-made flooring cramp which straddles the joist and pushes the boarding tight. Although perhaps too expensive to buy for just one job, such cramps can be hired from a good tool hire company. The questioner Mr J. F. Quail, may raise a few eyebrows if he tries to find a source in the Dordogne!

C. D. Rosekilly, Crowthorne

continued

Letters

Trouble at t'mill

I WAS INTERESTED to read about the restoration of the post mill in June WOOD-WORKER; I'm involved in a similar project at Herne, but ours is a Kentish Smock Mill and apparently in better condition.

We found on profiling the teeth that they soon wear to shape and then settle for a long run. We also found that a gap of about ⅜in between the teeth when meshed with the wallower was ideal — in a post mill this could possibly be less as the brake wheel does not have to turn relative to the wallower as well as revolve, as in a smock mill.

The accuracy with which the brake wheel was set on the windshaft does them credit, but it will need resetting after a running-in period, especially if any load (the stones) is placed on the gearing. Most gear trains in a mill are pretty sloppy as the movement of the body timbers and framing must always be allowed for. Our mill is pretty stiff but she still moves very slight in a blow!

But that picture on page 528 of the adzing — with those shoes? The first time I used an adze 45 years ago I was very aware of the need for a stout pair of boots! Anyway, I would have used a good stout firmer chisel for that job.

However, I wish them the best of luck in

● *Trainers – good footwear for adzers? Picture from June WOODWORKER*

their efforts. There are far too few mills left around today and in particular post mills. Once the work is finished and they are open to the public they will find the appreciation will make it all worthwhile.

D. J. Bean, Chairman, Friends of Herne Mill

CONTENTS

Woodworker

design . . . craft . . . and the love of wood

September 1987
Vol. 91
No. 9

FEATURES

On the cover: 'Star table' by Malcolm Temple, co-judge at the Direct Design Show. Read his comments on p762ff. Above: Clare Green of Kingston Polytechnic made this fanciful set of storage boxes – more on p772

PROJECTS

REGULARS

Editor Aidan Walker
Deputy editor John Hemsley
Assistant editor Kerry Fowler
Advertisement manager Trevor Pryer
Advertisement production Laura Champion
Graphics Jeff Hamblin/ASP Design Studio
Technical illustrator Peter Holland
Guild of Woodworkers John Hemsley, Kerry Fowler

Unfortunately we cannot accept responsibility for loss of or damage to unsolicited material. We reserve the right to refuse or suspend advertisements, and regret we cannot guarantee the bone fides of advertisers.
Published every third Friday

Editorial, advertisements and Guild of Woodworkers 1 Golden Square, London W1R 3AB, telephone 01-437 0626

ABC
UK circulation
Jan-Dec 86
32,849

Back issues and subscriptions Infonet Ltd, 10-13 Times House, 179 Marlowes, Hemel Hempstead, Herts HP1 1BB; telephone Hemel Hempstead (0442) 48434

Subscriptions per year UK £16.90; overseas outside USA (accelerated surface post) £21.00, USA (accelerated surface post) $28, airmail £48

UK trade SM Distribution Ltd, 16-18 Trinity Gardens, London SW9 8DX; telephone 01-274 8611

North American trade Bill Dean Books Ltd, 151-49 7th Avenue, PO Box 69, Whitestone, New York 11357; tel. 1-718-767-6632

Printed by Chase Web, Plymouth
Mono origination Multiform Photosetting Ltd, Cardiff
Colour origination Derek Croxson Ltd, Chesham, Bucks
© Argus Specialist Publications Ltd 1987
ISSN 0043 776X

Application to mail at Second Class rates is pending at Rahway N.J., USA. Postmaster: send address corrections to Woodworker, c/o Mercury Airfreight International Ltd Inc, 10B Englehard Ave, Avenel, NJ 07001.

ARGUS PRESS GROUP

Argus Specialist Publications Ltd

1 Golden Square, London W1R 3AB; 01-437 0626

This month

Preserve us . . .

Simultaneously with the announcement of the formation of the **Creosote Council** for independent manufacturers, packers and industrial users of 'Britain's best-known garden wood preservative' comes the news that the Council has complained to the Independent Broadcasting Authority about **Sterling Roncraft's** claims for its water-based 'Fencelife' preserver (*WW/July*). Creosote chairman Dr Howard Pearce pours scorn on the Roncraft claim that Fencelife is 'a really effective longer lasting wood preservative' in a direct comparison with Creosote: 'Fencelife may be a nice decorative finish', says the doctor, 'but we challenge them to prove it works as a real wood preservative . . . effective against the insects, fungus and organisms which destroy wood . . . Creosote was patented . . . 151 years ago and timbers treated with it in the last century are still going strong. How on earth can they prove their comparison?'

In response, Sterling Roncraft are in contact with the Independent Broadcasting Authority and the Independent Television Companies Association to confirm all the relevant facts and establish that the Creosote Council's claims 'can be refuted outright'. The company interprets the Creosote Council's release as a clear attack on its integrity, and is looking into the legal aspects of the matter.

Tradeswomen

Carpentry is by far the most popular trade of respondents to a survey of tradeswomen by the organisation Women and Manual Trades (WAMT). Almost half are chippies, with painting and decorating the next in line. The organisation has 600 tradeswomen on their list, some of them self-employed. Women replying to the section on training had complaints about centres. One woman said 'The "boys" are mostly a pain. They do not believe we have completed work — they think the tutors do it for us. A typical comment was: "Did you sleep with Mr X to get such high marks?" I answered, "No, did you?".'

A woman carpenter said: 'The first day of my TOPS course I was told carpentry wasn't a woman's job and I wouldn't need to know how to grind a plane-iron!'

Although physical sex harassment was infrequent, verbal harassment happened almost every week for two out of three women. Most women react to men's sexist comments by telling them to stop. The harassment is bad enough, say WAMT, to make 30% seriously consider getting out of the manual trades.

BRIEFING

LIFS '88 Next year's London International Furniture Show will be trade only. Public attendance in 1987 was significantly down on previous years. The organisers are planning to expand the show over the next three years, and in 1989 it will extend into a new hall being constructed at Earls Court. The show will run for five days from Sunday 24 April.

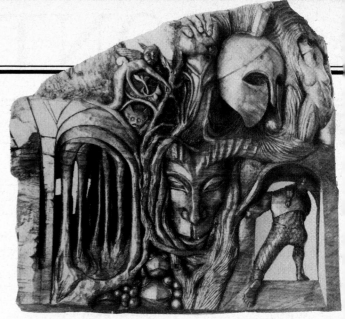

Twenty five pieces by carver **Ian Norbury** will be on show at Eastington Hall, a Tudor manor house near Upton upon Severn, Worcestershire, from Monday 31 August to Saturday 5 September. Stately surroundings for the prolific work of a carver of renown. Most of the work — prepared over two years for this exhibition — is studies of the human figure, from the powerful form of the gladiator to the grace and beauty of Salome. **Above** you see 'Midsummer Night's Dream', carved in walnut. The exhibition moves to the Bury Walk Gallery, 15 Bury Walk, London SW3, from 16 September-3 October.

Makers The newly launched Furniture Makers' Association (originally the National Association of Furniture Makers) is urgently seeking extra members to help get it off the ground. The association was formed to promote small-batch and hand-made furniture producers. Chairman Chris Simpson says the association needs 100 members to make it worthwhile, has got 45 companies interested, and is currently mailing about 300 potential recruits.

Wood Turning Center Philadelphia, USA, is to have a Wood Turning Center — archives, museum, classrooms and woodturning shop — with Albert LeCoff as executive director. A fund-raising campaign is currently under way for this non-profit making venture. Donate $25 and you'll become a Founding Member, receive 250 decoratively turned Japanese toothpicks and invitations to exhibition openings. Give large sums and you'll receive extra gifts and benefits. Wood Turning Center, P.O. Box 25706, Philadelphia, PA 19144, USA.

Dust hazard New legislation is to crack down on dust levels in woodworking factories next June in a bid to reduce health risks from nasal cancer, asthma and skin problems. The new laws will make mandatory advice in a leaflet called *Wood Dust: hazards and precautions*, issued by the Woodworking National Industry Group of the Health and Safety Executive. Between now and next June every workshop with employees will have to examine its dust problems and ensure their filter/extraction systems meet the standards required.

Toy test More than 50 South-west England schools competed to win a **Startrite 352 Bandsaw** by designing and making a wooden toy. Winner was the Upper Avon School, Durrington, with a model of a working roundabout by 13-year old Colin Hughes. The competition was run by **Willis (Profectus)** of Bristol, in conjunction with the West Wiltshire consortium for purchasing and distribution, and **Startrite** themselves.

Old Stores Open day — 'Woodturning extravaganza' at Alan Holtham's Old Stores Turnery, 25-26 September, will include demonstrations, videos, equipment, techniques, bargains . . . 9.30-5. The Old Stores Turnery, Wistaston Rd, Willaston, Nantwich, Cheshire CW5 6QJ, (0270) 67010.

Old Stores Open days — 'Woodturning extravaganza' at Alan Holtham's Old Stores Turnery, 25-26 September, will include demonstrations, videos, equipment, techniques, bargains — open from 9.30-5. The Old Stores Turnery, Wistaston Rd, Willaston, Nantwich, Cheshire CW5 6QJ, (0270) 67010.

Happy handshakers Above left, Idwal Owens, winner of the **Triton Workcentre** in the Bristol Show prize draw, shakes hands with Paul Merry (left) of Triton; above right, Roy Cooper, who won the **Tyme Lathe,** gets a grip on Roy Sealey (right) of Tyme Machines of Bristol. Many thanks to Triton and Tyme for their generosity, and also to **Sarjents of Reading** for the lavish hospitality in their impressive new premises.

Shoptalk

NEW PRODUCTS

The **Out of Print Book Service** will try to find any book that's been eluding you on the second-hand stalls. There's no search fee, but the minimum cost for a paperback is £5.00; if they find the book, they inform you of the cost first, and you then decide whether to buy or not. Send an SAE to: Out of Print Book Service, 17 Fairwater Grove East, Cardiff CF5 2JS.

WOODWORKER **Plans Handbook** — new edition now available, hundreds of plans to choose including furniture, toys, musical instruments, clockcases, model horse-drawn vehicles, miniatures, spinning wheels, looms . . . £1.60 inc. p&p for the catalogue from Woodworker Plans Service, 9 Hall Rd, Maylands Wood Est, Hemel Hempstead, Herts HP2 7BH.

Excel Machine Tools have moved to Brindley Rd North, Bayton Rd Industrial Est, Exhall, Coventry CV7 9EP. Phone number remains the same — (0203) 365255.

Quick wedge screw-holding **screwdriver** for slot-head screws is now available to the smaller user; splits blade wedges apart and locks with a sleeve to hold any size screw slot. 'One screwdriver drives many sizes of screws'. Prices range from £4.35+VAT for 4in blade, $\frac{3}{16}$in blade diameter, .031in tip ('small'), to £6.05+VAT for 'heavy duty' 6in blade, $\frac{1}{4}$in blade diameter, .042in tip. The range starts smaller and goes bigger. Longs Ltd, Hanworth Lane Trading Est, Chertsey, Surrey KT16 9LZ, (0923 28) 61241.

Gilding courses The Binningtons, featured in their own words in WW/Sep '86, announce week-long courses in oil and water gilding for mirror frames, furniture and restoration. This autumn sees a new course in gilding for porcelain and glass. Frances Binnington, 65 St John's Hill, London SW11 1SX, 01-223 9192.

Board saw Sandvik's specialist 24in saw for cutting large-section timber and manufactured board. It has normal teeth at the toe and then a set of special 'group' toothing for fast, clean cutting. £14.77+VAT; Sandvik, Manor Way, Halesowen, W. Mid B62 8QZ, 021-550 4700.

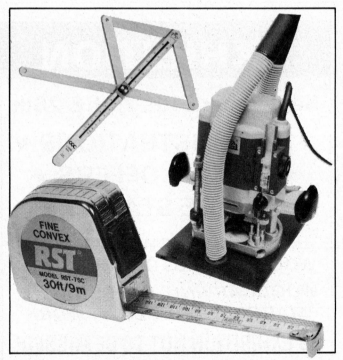

Top left Swedish **'Tool for all Angles'** measures, checks and sets internal or external angles; parallelogram action means you set one angle and can read off half that as well. £27.03 inc VAT; Alan Hughes Distributors, Unit G, Wallows Industrial Estate, Brierley Hill, W. Mid DY5 1QA, (0384) 265333. **Above right,** we showed you this **dust extractor** for heavy Elu routers last month and said it was made by Elu; sorry, it's actually a **Trend** design. £29+VAT; Unit N, Penfold Works, Imperial Way, Watford WD2 4YY, (0923) 24991. **Above,** Rollins 30ft/9m **tape** with 25mm-wide convex blade extends up to 10ft without bending; £7.68. Rollins House, Mimram Rd, Hertford SG14 1NW, (0992) 587555.

Diary

Guild courses are shown by an asterisk(*); for further details see Guild pages

August
30-30 Sept **The Working Woodland Exhibition**, Parnham House, Beaminster, Dorset DT8 3NA (0308) 862204
31 **Islwyn Craft Fair 87**, Waunfawr Pk, Crosskeys, Gwent (0495) 22662, Ext. 2367

September
5-1 Oct **Peter Chatwin and Pamela Martin Exhibition**, boxes, bowls and plates, Crafts Council Shop, Victoria and Albert Museum
9-31 Oct **Rupert Williamson Exhibition**, Contemporary Textile Gallery, 10 Golden Sq, London W1R 3AF 01-439 9070
12-13 **Decorative Techniques** Ian Hosker*
17-18 **French Polishing** Charles Cliffe*
19-20 **Basic Carving** Eric Ingham*
23-25 **Southern Counties Craft Market**, The Maltings, Farnham, Surrey, Contact (0920) 870040
26 **Design and Workshop Drawing** Bob Grant*

October
2-4 **Festival of Ecclesiastical Crafts**, Salisbury Cathedral, exhibitors' enquiries: J. Davies, Yew Tree Lodge, Minchington, Blandford, Dorset OT11 8DH
2-4 **Heart of England Craft Market**, Sports Centre, University of Keele, Stoke-on-Trent (0920) 870040
3-4 **Irish Woodturners Guild 6th Annual 2-day Seminar**, Riverchapel, Courtown, Co. Wexford, application forms: T. Dunlop, Shanbough Upper, Via New Ross, Co. Kilkenny
4-28 **Mainly Wood Exhibition**, Parnham Hse, Beaminster, Dorset DT8 3NA
20-30 **Annual International Creative Marquetry Show**, Virginia, USA, application forms: S. Cartwright, 63 Church Lane, Sproughton, Ipswich IP8 3AY
21 **Style for Living 87**, furniture show, Earls Court, London 01-395 1200
22-25 **London Woodworker Show**, Alexandra Pavilion, London N22
21-25 **Modern Home 87**, trade and public furniture show, 3f Prince Rupert Hse, 64 Queens St, London EC4R 1AD
25-26 **Woodturning Extravaganza**, The Old Stores Turnery, Wistaston Rd, Willaston, Nantwich, Cheshire CW5 6JQ (0270) 67010
25-28 **Design in Furniture**, Olympia, London (trade only)

Woodturning Extravaganza

A two day woodturning extravaganza gives you an opportunity to see and talk to Alan Holtham in his unique Woodturning Store.

This promises to be the best show ever featuring the latest turning equipment and techniques, with demonstrations and displays.

There will be many exciting surprises 'in store'.

Apollo, Coronet and Tyme lathes with chuck 'new boys' Henry Taylor and their Masterchuck, the latest chuck system.

There will be discounts on lots of small blanks from a vast range of exotic woods.

We look forward to seeing you at The Old Stores Turnery on 25th/26th September 1987 between 9.30 a.m. until 5.00 p.m.

Visitors to the show will have a chance to win a woodturning prize in a free-entry quiz.

Alan Holtham

THE OLD STORES TURNERY,
Wistaston Road, Willaston, Nantwich, Cheshire CW5 6QJ.
Telephone: Crewe (0270) 67010.

Ashley Iles
woodcarving & turning tools
made in the old tradition

All carving tools supplied honed ready for use. See the full range of Ashley Iles Carving and Turning Tools including the range of: All Black HSS Turning Tools.

Send for our new enlarged colour catalogue (16 pages) showing the full range of carving and turning tools. Callers and trade enquiries welcome.

Ashley Iles (Edge Tools) Ltd.,
East Kirkby, Spilsby,
Lincolnshire PE23 4DD.
Telephone (07903) 372

EXHIBITION

September 24th, 25th & 26th

★ **DEMONSTRATIONS** ★
★ **SPECIAL OFFERS** ★
★ **TRADE STANDS** ★

SEE ROLF HARRIS WOODCARVING ON THURSDAY

WOODCARVING, PYROGRAPHY, MARQUETRY, CABINET WORK

AN EXHIBITION NOT TO BE MISSED!
REFRESHMENTS AVAILABLE

10.00 a.m.-5.00 p.m. Thurs. & Sat. 10.00 a.m.-7.00 p.m. Fri.

CHARLTONS TIMBER CENTRE
FROME ROAD, RADSTOCK, NR. BATH.
TEL: 0761 36229

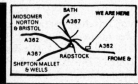

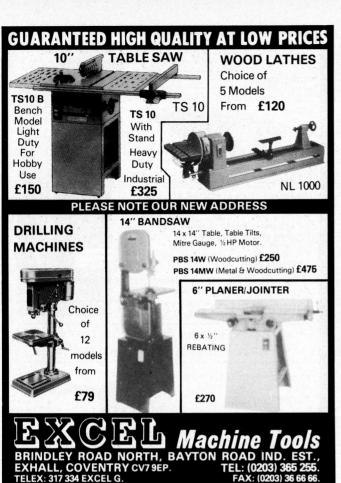

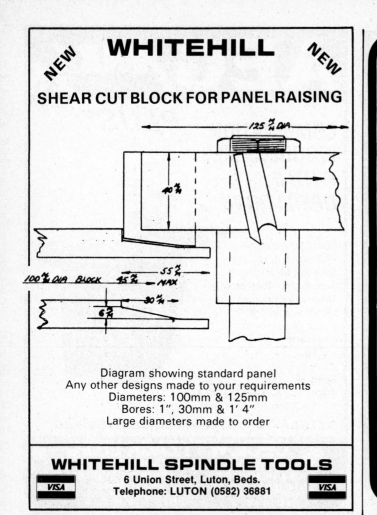
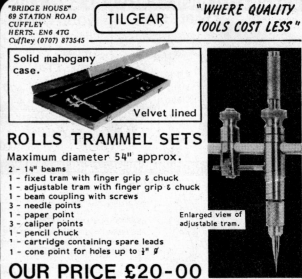

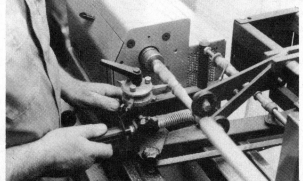 

Chess master

If you enjoy chess you'll love playing with this elegant board, designed and made by Colin Murdoch

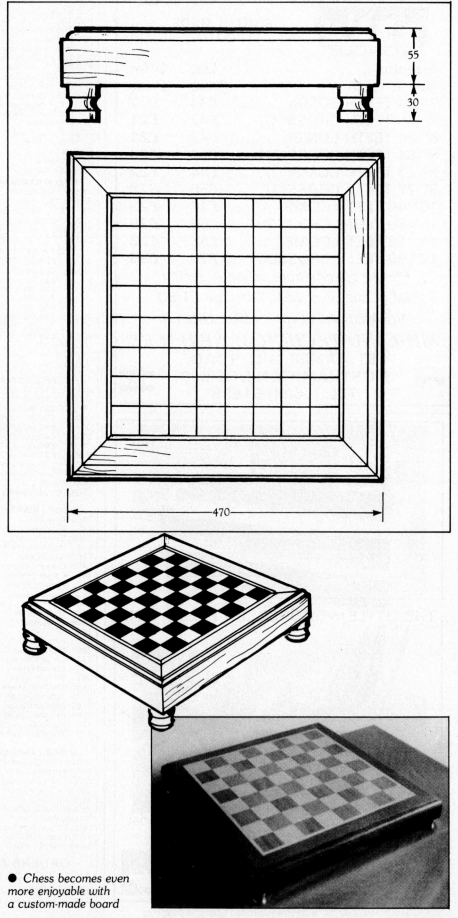

There is a vast and varying array of chessboards available today, in many different materials and designs, but a quality wooden chessboard is still expensive and difficult to find. I find playing chess and inviting others to play is far more enjoyable when using a hand-made and sizeable board. This one is versatile, as it has an unobtrusive compartment beneath to hold draughts; chess pieces can be displayed while the draught pieces are neatly hidden away. It's extremely simple in design, but has an elegant appearance with its attractive moulded edges, banding and brass legs; these brass fixtures are easy to make if you have a three jaw chuck so don't let this worry you. I used mahogany and jelutong because they are lovely timbers to work with and they contrast beautifully with each other.

Start with the checkered section. First cut four pieces of jelutong and four pieces of mahogany 460x48x12mm. Take a shaving carefully from the edges with a smoothing plane. Apply PVA glue to joining edges (fig. 1) and cramp the pieces together with sash-cramps.

When the glue is dry trim the end square and cut eight strips 48mm wide. Turn over every second piece before gluing (fig. 2). Then glue the entire checkered section to a piece of multi-ply (fig. 3) and trim to size.

I made the frame from four pieces of mahogany 500x45x45mm. Rebate the edges 7x7mm for the banding (fig. 4). Glue an 8x8mm piece of jelutong into place (fig. 5), then square up with a smoothing plane, before mitring the four pieces to fit round the checkered section. Do this carefully so you get a good quality finish. Then glue the frame together (fig. 6), using blocks of wood under the checkered section to give support while the sash-cramps pull the frame together. Once this has dried, clean up the board with a plane before using a router or moulding plane to shape the edges.

The storage department is underneath the top, with 20x10mm mahogany fillets glued in place (fig. 7). Make the door to fit from mahogany ply with solid wood edging which will be fitted with hinges.

Shape the brass legs from a 250mm length of 25mm-diameter solid brass bar, which you can get from any metal wholesaler. Cut the brass into four pieces 60mm long, and mount them one by one in the three-jaw chuck (fig. 8). I used an old file, ground down to roughly the same

● Chess becomes even more enjoyable with a custom-made board

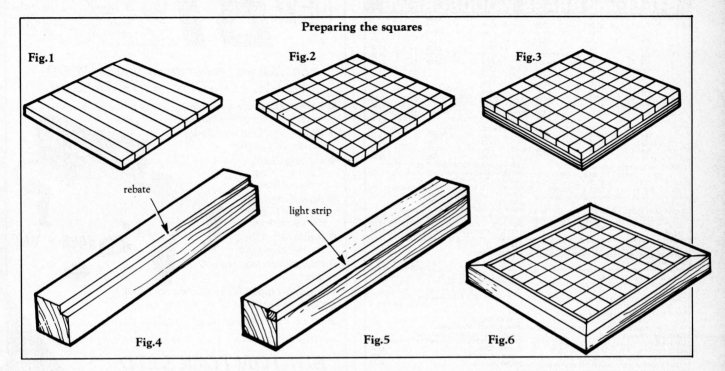

Preparing the squares

Fig.1

Fig.2

Fig.3

rebate

light strip

Fig.4

Fig.5

Fig.6

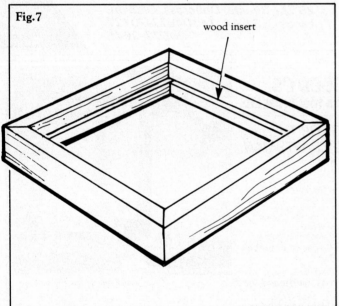

Fig.7

wood insert

Cutting list

Checkered section, jelutong	4	460mm x	48mm x	12mm
Checkered section, mahogany	4	460	48	12
Frame, mahogany	4	510	45	45
Inlay, jelutong	4	510	7	7
Insert, mahogany	4	400	20	10
Base, multiply	1	400	400	12
Door, mahogany ply	1	400	400	12
Door edging, mahogany	4	400	20	12

You'll also need two hinges, a handle, a brass turn catch, 250mm
of 25mm diameter brass bar, and some felt.

shape as a scraper, to turn the brass to size.
Set the lathe to an intermediate speed and
slowly turn the brass pins to 10mm
diameter (fig. 8a). Then reverse the brass
legs (fig. 8b) and shape them as in the three-
dimensional drawing. Drill holes under the
chessboard at the corners and glue in the
legs, using epoxy resin. Fit the door, a
suitable catch and handles.

Finally sand the entire board and apply
four coats of polyurethane varnish, flatting
down with wet-and-dry between coats.
Tone down the final finish with wax and
steel wool to leave a fine, satin finish, and
line the compartment with felt.

The result is an individual, elegant board.
I hope you enjoy using and making this
board as much as I have, checkmates! ■

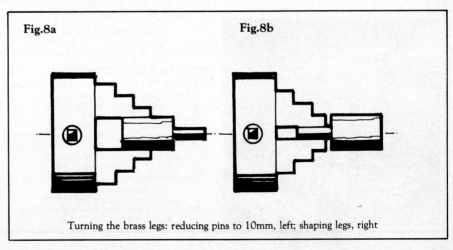

Fig.8a

Fig.8b

Turning the brass legs: reducing pins to 10mm, left; shaping legs, right

Here's some versatile new holding devices at enticing prices

Hold on!

Crab grab

A clamp for those awkward holding jobs that defeat traditional G-clamps. The Crab clamp will secure cylindrical, tapered and bevelled workpieces as well as flat sections. Strongly made of steel, with a tough plastic finish, the clamp has plug-in nylon jaw pads to prevent marking your work. The fine pitch thread, guaranteed for 20 years, gives sensitive but powerful clamping action through a cantilever, with up to 400psi pressure. We can also supply a Third Leg, a screw-threaded ancillary that fits into the clamp to produce side pressure for securing lippings and other difficult holding operations. Crab clamps come in two sizes, 4½in capacity and 6½in capacity, and you can order them singly or in pairs.

Drill clamp

A simple-to-use versatile device that holds your power drill securely by the collar, with many applications:

● clamp your drill horizontally to use flexible drive, polishing mop, wire brush, drum sander and so on,
● clamp drill vertically to use a rigid disc sander or drum sander in conjunction with a table,
● fit it into suitable drill stand to mill holes vertically (or use a router in it if the collar fits),
● and when you're not using it, fasten it next to your bench as a handy drill holder.

The Wolfcraft 4800 Universal drill clamp fits on a bench or table up to 2½in thick; the collar mounting (takes 43mm drill collars) fits horizontally or vertically, swivels around 360°, and is quickly locked into position. A device you'll soon find lots of uses for, and at a considerable saving.

The Drill Clamp usually retails at £13.99: we can get it to your door for **£11.95!**

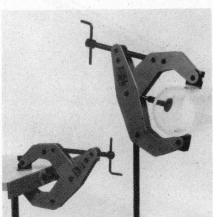

ASP Reader Services, 9 Hall Rd, Maylands Wood Est, Hemel Hempstead, Herts HP2 7BH, (0442) 41221

Two-tool test

Tobias Kaye tries out the
oval skew chisel and a new
ring gouge, both from
Robert Sorby

The skew

The Robert Sorby 'oval' skew chisel,
designed for easier skew control,
seems to be taking off. Everyone I
spoke to who has used it has liked it. It is
oval in section round the bottom and sides,
but the top is square cornered as with other
skews (fig. 1). I've been trying out the ¾in
oval, and I really recommend it, particularly
for beginners.

The oval base means firm continuous
contact on the rest as you slide it along or
twist it to produce a complex curve, instead
of putting all the tool's weight and all your
trust on a corner. The continually changing
radius gives a remarkably 'soft' feel in use,
compared with the slightly brittle 'fine line'
feel of an ordinary skew. I found I could
even wiggle it about a bit during a cut
without it kicking or snatching, an obvious
advantage over a square-based skew.

A much greater area of the tool is in
regular contact with the rest, as revealed
when I examined how much of the original
lacquer coating was worn or chipped away
after a bit of use (fig. 2). A square skew
would show wear at the base and corners.

This large contact area also means that
much more of the cutting edge is safe to use. I
found myself using three-quarters of the cutting edge quite safely and without kicking
compared to a little over half on a conventional skew. The oval skew seemed to give a
perceptible flutter before getting out of control, warning me to adjust the cut.

It was a pleasure to handle for long cuts,
smooth curves and straight lines. It was also
good for beading, since the curved bottom
makes the tool roll along the rest slightly as
you roll it over the top and down the side of
the bead. This rolling movement became a
slight disadvantage when making very small
beads, ⅛in wide or less, when the movement becomes greater than you want,
making a catch more likely — but a ¾in tool
is a bit large for ⅛in beads anyway!

I found it did not shine in heavy work; for
roughing out or removing large quantities off
a shoulder, I found it less steady to handle
than a square tool. But you may have another
skew suitable for this.

It's a shame the manufacturers didn't

remove the arrises as part of finishing the
tool; although with these skews the sharp
arrises are only at the top, there are
situations in which I want to use the long
corner. The blending where the curves of
the oval have been cut is not perfect either, a
minor point perhaps, but I like to see well-
finished tools.

Sharpening

I had imagined that the round sides would
make the oval more difficult to sharpen
than an ordinary skew, but in practice it
wasn't. I use an adjustable grinder-rest
about 2in wide and 4in long, and I rested
the tool on this and slid it across the wheel
with my thumb and forefinger gripping the
sides to stop it rocking on its curves. I don't
hone skew chisels myself, finding it no
advantage; a second bevel, however slight,
always seems to sacrifice in control what's
gained in edge.

I found the oval skew a very good tool.
I'm pleased to have one among my other
skews, and it will probably soon become
my favourite. Its increased flexibility and
forgiving characteristics make it an ideal
beginner's tool and well worth having for
anyone finding problems with skew work.

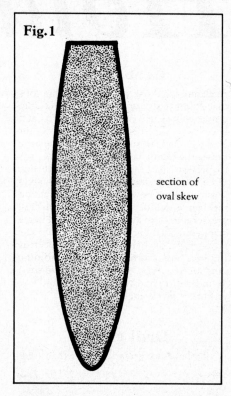

Fig.1

section of
oval skew

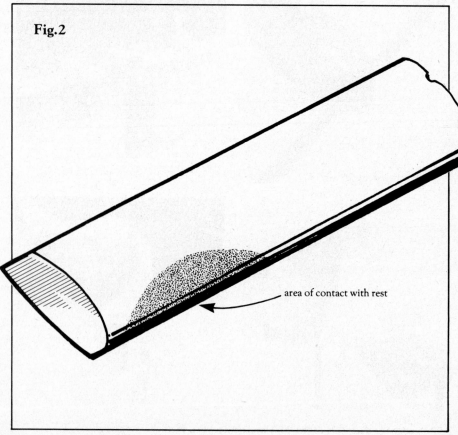

Fig.2

area of contact with rest

● *Left, the oval base of the skew gives
continuous contact with the tool rest*

Ring tool

Sorby have also introduced a ring gouge, a
type of tool that has recently been shown a
growing amount of interest. In the turning
world, giant bowl-turner Ed Moulthrop's
techniques — and tools — have caused
quite a stir (*WW/June '86*); for his huge,
endgrain-turned, slow-speed work, he
adapts traditional treadle-turner's tools for
hollowing, massive things with a finger-like
hook which cuts on both side and end.
Moulthrop's tools, plus Australian
versions of the ring gouge, Swedish hook
tools, and the traditional ones are all
bevelled on the inside, which means they
can't be ground, only honed.

Sorby's ring tool is bevelled and
sharpened on the outside, but they also
recommend honing only, not grinding. I
asked them why bevel the outside and they
said it makes it easier to sharpen. The
Australian ring tool uses a conical stone,
drill-mounted, to sharpen the inside bevel.
'Too complex,' said Sorby. 'We wanted to
produce a tool that needed no gadgetry to
sharpen . . . but we are experimenting with a

● *Left, hollowing with the ring tool;
above, grinding the ring tool requires a
steady hand*

continued

Two-tool test

grit-impregnated rubber cone with which to sharpen the inside of our gouge.' Which makes me wonder; if you sharpen the inside of a gouge with an outside bevel, surely you reduce your cutting angle? More on sharpening later.

To look at, the tool is not the most elegant, a piece of HSS tubing mortise-and-tenon brazed to the end of a rod. The ring is bevelled round the top edge as well so the cutting edge lies in planes perpendicular to the top rim. Ungainly it may be, but strong. It certainly stood some pretty rough mis-handling from me, and I imagine most of these tools will take a beating initially because of the extremely unfamiliar cutting action. There's bound to be a few snags before the technique is mastered.

As a hollowing tool, as which of course the ring gouge is specifically designed, it has no equal on endgrain. It simply gives a clean cut here, which no other tool I've ever tried does. But when you get across the bottom endgrain and get to the sidewall of the work, beware. You're told to use it bevel rubbing, which you can do really effectively on the endgrain; but a bevel-rubbing cut needs leverage to control it, and the only control you have over the tool when it gets to the sidewall is to twist the handle. So if you try to cut with the bevel rubbing, the tool twists and digs in. By all means use the bevel rubbing across the bottom of the pot, box, goblet or whatever, where it cuts beautifully; but when you get to the wall, swivel it round and scrape with it (fig. 3).

Once you've mastered the knack of changing from rubbing to scraping this way, the tool is certainly very useful for hollowing, doing a better job quicker than any other tool. To obtain the best advantage from it, one really ought to have pivot pins in the toolrest to get the most leverage for a heavy cut. However, you now come across a significant disadvantage of bevelling the outside ring. After a certain depth, the angle at which you have to hold the tool so that the bevel allows the cutting edge to contact the base surface causes the shaft to rub the edge or rim of the work (fig. 4). Try and go deeper and you won't be able to cut; the bevel heel, only, will rub the bottom, pre-venting the cutting edge from reaching the wood.

With the tool I had, a vessel 3½in dia-meter could be made 4in deep at a push. Obviously if the bevel were on the inside this problem wouldn't arise. You could extend the depth you can reach by lengthening the bevel, but that means grinding, and here we come up against sharpening questions again. If you are going to confine yourself to honing as Sorby suggest, you will have to be careful not to round over the bevel at all. If you find that difficult on a gouge, it is far more dif-ficult on this tool, whose cutting edge is transverse to rather than in line with the rest of the tool. Even if you are expert at honing you will probably want to grind this tool sooner or later; if you aren't expert it will be sooner, and now you will have to be expert at grinding. Holding the tool at a constant angle

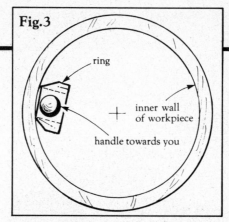

Fig.3
ring
inner wall of workpiece
handle towards you

while watching what you are doing and rotat-ing the tool through a 300° arc is no joke. It will not yield satisfactory results unless you are experienced, patient and possessing a very steady hand.

Sorby recommend purchasing a honing stick for doing inside the ring, but some fine aluminium oxide or silicone carbide paper wrapped round a dowel does the job well, if the paper is tight against the dowel and doesn't round over the inside of the ring. This inside surface is the one Sorby are plan-ning to make an abrasive-laden rubber cone to sharpen. This is obviously going to create a second bevel on the cutting edge, effec-tively reducing the cutting angle. I haven't tried a ring tool so treated, but I have experi-mented with applying the same inside bevel to a fluted gouge, and it adversely affected its cutting ability quite seriously.

All in all this seems an idiosyncratic tool of limited use, even to a turner doing a lot of hollow work. It excels at shallow hollow work, but it won't go any deeper than the diameter of your hollow, so it seems rather a small area of work for which to invest in a special tool. ∎

Comments from Nick Davidson, chairman of Robert Sorby Ltd

Oval skew We recommend that the 1in oval skew is more suitable for heavier cuts — and we shall endeavour to improve the finish in future.

Ring tool This is an entirely new concept from Robert Sorby and since production started we have made various modifications to improve its performance. We're investi-gating means of simplifying sharpening and, like Tobias Kaye, I found wrapping a bit of wet and dry abrasive on a dowel a satis-factory way of honing the inside.

We have already solved the problem of cutting deeper bowls, by pivoting the ring on the end of the shaft, to enable the tool to cut with the shaft perpendicular to the bowl base. The drawback is that two tools would be required to complete some difficult shapes. The same problem arises when producing deep shapes with a bowl gouge.

We have found the ring tool exceptionally useful for turning cherry logs, into massive goblets. The problems normally en-countered with endgrain work, including splitting when drying and poor finish inside the bowl, were overcome with ease.

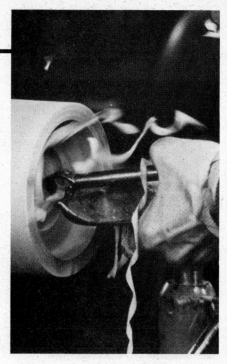
● **Above,** hollowing end grain holly

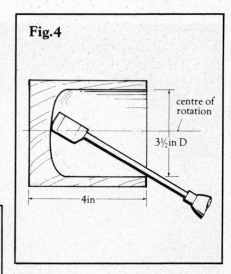
Fig.4
centre of rotation
3½in D
4in

Prices
Including VAT and handles

Oval skew	½in	£11.04
	¾in	£12.25
	1in	£14.50
	1¼in	£18.29
Ring gouge	½in	£13.29
	1in	£17.60

● Instructions and hints for using the ring tool are available if you send a SAE to Tony Walker, Robert Sorby Ltd, Athol Road, Sheffield S8 0PA, (0742) 554231

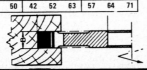
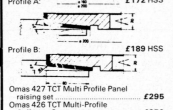

AXMINSTER POWER TOOL CENTRE

WOODTURNING LATHES — *OUR PRICE INC. VAT*

TYME STUDENT 10" swing 30" centres (With accessory voucher £20) **£199**
CORONET HOBBY 10" swing 39" centres 1MT ½HP 3 speed **£179**
CORONET No. 1 12" swing 3 Speed 24" ctrs **£229** 36" ctrs **£249** 48" ctrs **£289**
CORONET No. 1 22" Bowl Rest Assbly **£39** 48" Bed Extension for existing 24" lathe **£59**
ELU DB180 39" centres 15" swing 1½HP motor 3 speed **£299**
TYME CUB 30" centres (With accessory voucher £32) **£319**
TYME AVON 36" centres (With accessory voucher £44) **£437**
MYFORD ML8B 36" centres 9" Rear turning **£459** ML8C 42" centres **£499**
KITY 663 3 Speed Lathe 1.0M Centres **£554** 1.5M Centres **£576**
KITY 664 Var. Spd. Lathe 1.0M Centres **£649** 1.5M Centres **£669**
MINIMAX Centre lathes T90 **£462** T100 **£534** T120 **£564** Legs **£75**
MINIMAX COPIERS for above lathes CT90 **£519** CT100 **£551** CT120 **£599**
LUNA SPKA 900 COPIER medium duty copier for all lathes **£256**
CORONET CMB600 33" Centres 23" bowl cap **£589** Bowl rest **£49.95**
HARRISON GRADUATE 30" Centres **£1250** 42" Centres **£1299** Shortbed **£1037**

WOODTURNING FITMENTS & ACCESSORIES (State m/c)

Coronet collet chuck sets (state m/c) **£69**
Coronet collet bodies only **£29**
Collets ⅝", ¾", 1" each **£11**
Expanding Jaws 3", 2", 1" each **£24**
Spigots ⅝", ¾", 1" each **£13**
Speedaneez polish std/wht **£20**
Coronet planer blades 4½" **£20** 7" **£23**
Multistar Duplex Chuck 45mm Jaws **£65**
Multistar Duplex Chuck 60mm Jaws **£66**
Multistar Duplex Chuck 75mm Jaws **£68**
Screwchuck Set (for above) **£22**
Faceplate Ring 60mm **£7**
Pinchucks (State size) **£8**
Revolving centres 1MT or 2MT **£18**
Craft supplies chuck **£56**
0-½" Drill chuck 1MT or 2MT **£15**
Long hole boring kit ⁵⁄₁₆" **£32**
2½" Woodscrew chuck **£22**
Sorby sizing tool **£7**
Carnuba wax turning stick **£1.80**
Henry Taylor Master Chuck **£56.95**
Henry Taylor 3" Ext. Jaws **£16.50**
Henry Taylor 1¼" Ext. Jaws **£13.50**
Henry Taylor Wood Jaw Plates **£4.60**
Henry Taylor Pin Chuck **£4.60**
Janik Pyrographer **£48.00**

CORONET SPARES

Drive Belts (State M/C Type) **£3.90**
Bronze Bearing Major **£21** Elf **£18**
Bronze Bearing Consort **£23** Minor **£23**
Ball Race Bearing Major/12 Others **£9.60**
Main Spindle Consort/Minor **£44**
Main Spindle Major c/w ⅞" or ¾" **£59**
Major Poly-Vee Conversion Kit **£98.00**
¾HP Motor for CMB500 (speeds 500-2000) **£92.00**
Locking Rings (Major or Elf) **£6.50**
Drive Centres 4 Prong ⅞" **£7.00**
Lace Bobbin Drives 1MT or 2MT **£7.00**

WOODTURNERS "AT LAST PERFECTION"

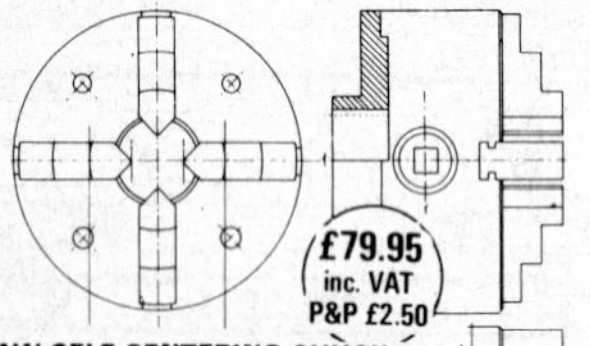

£79.95 inc. VAT P&P £2.50

4 JAW SELF CENTERING CHUCK
AVAILABLE IN THREAD SIZES FOR MOST LATHES.
SPECIFICATION: GRIPPING CAPACITY ⅛"-4" DIAMETER 4" WEIGHT 2KG. SUPPLIED READY THREADED (LH OR RH) WITH TWO SETS OF PRECISION JAWS (INTERNAL & EXTERNAL).
5" 4 Jaw S/C **£99.95**
4" 3 Jaw S/C **£69.95**

HENRY TAYLOR HSS CHISELS

GOUGES
HS1 Superflute **£26**
HS3 ¾" D/Fte **£18**
HS4 1½" D/Fte **£27**
HS5 ½" Spindle **£6**
HS6 ⅜" Spindle **£5**
HS7 ½" Spindle **£11**

PARTING TOOLS
HS2 Fluted **£17**
HS11 ¼" Std. **£6**
HS12 ⅜" Std. **£8**
HS13 ¾" × ½" **£11**
HS33 Diamond **£15**
HS32 ½" × ⅛" **£7**

CHISELS
HS8 ½" Skew **£8**
HS21 ¾" Skew **£8**
HS22 1" Skew **£10**
HS91 1" Skew **£16**
HS23 ½" Square **£8**
HS24 ¾" Sqre **£9**
HS25 1" Sqre **£11**
HS10 1¼" Sqre **£17**

SCRAPERS
HS26 ½" Rnd **£8**
HS38 ¾" Rnd **£8**
HS27 1" Rnd **£11**
HS28 ½" Sq **£8**
HS29 ¾" Sq. **£8**
HS30 1" Sq. **£10**
HS15 HD Round **£22**
HS16 HD Domed **£22**

CORONET HSS CHISELS

GOUGES
600 ½" Bowl **£22**
100 ¾" Roughing **£15**
120 1¼" Roughing **£21**
200 ¼" Spindle **£6**
210 ⅜" Spindle **£8**
220 ½" Spindle **£11**

CHISELS
300 ½" Skew **£8**
310 ¾" Skew **£8**
320 1" Skew **£11**
330 1¼" Skew **£15**
400 ½" Square **£8**
410 ¾" Square **£8**

PARTING TOOLS
420 1" Square **£11**
430 1¼" Square **£15**
500 ⅛" Parting **£9**
520 ¾" Parting & Beading **£8**

SCRAPERS
700 ½" Domed **£8**
701 ¾" Domed **£9**
702 1" Domed **£10**
800 HD Straight **£21**
810 Round **£21**
840 Skew (LH or RH) **£21**

BANDSAWS (Send for Free Bandsaw Blade List)

BURGESS BK111+ 45° 3" cut jigsaw freisaw (inc. P&P) **£115**
7" Sanding attachment for Burgess **£23.50** Mitre fence **£8.50** Rip fence **£7.50**
DeWALT DW100 45° tilt 4" cut c/w sanding table (P&P £2.50) **£149**
DeWALT 6" cut 14" throat 45° DW3401 **£269** DW3501 **£279**
MINIMAX P32 45° tilt 6" cut 14" throat cast iron table **£425**
KITY 513 8" cut Large table 1½HP (+ £57.50 Kity Accessory Voucher) **£427**
MINIMAX S45 45° tilt 10" cut 14" throat **£676**
STARTRITE 301B 45° Tilt 6" cut Bench Mtg. **£329**
STARTRITE 301 6" Floor Standing c/w mitre & rip fence **£419**
STARTRITE 351 45° tilt 8" cut c/w rip & mitre fence floor standing **£519**
STARTRITE 352 45° tilt 10" cut c/w rip & mitre fence floor standing **£739**
STARTRITE 502 14" cut 20" throat **£1259** 3PH **£1170**
METAL BLADE GUIDES for DeWalt DW100, 1310, 3401, 3501, Luna & Minimax **£5.20**

RADIAL SAWS — DeWALT Radial Saw Handbook **£6.00** inc. P&P

EUMENIA 9" blade 1¾HP 15" C/cut **£339** 24" C/cut **£399**
EUMENIA Stand **£112** Router Bracket **£76** Wobble Washers **£14.50**
DeWALT 1201 Portable 10" TCT Folding Radial Saw 1½ HP **£255**
DeWALT DW1251 10" TCT blade 1½ HP 16" C/cut **£420** Stand **£25**
DeWALT DW1501 10" TCT blade 1½ HP 18" C/cut **£476**
DeWALT DW1751 10" TCT blade 1½ HP 24" C/cut **£570**
DeWALT DW8001 12" TCT blade 2HP 18" C/cut floor standing **£559**
DeWALT DW8101 12" TCT blade 2HP 24" C/cut floor standing **£695**
DeWALT DW1600S 14" TCT blade 24" C/cut 1PH **£993** 3PH **£956**

PORTABLE AND WORKSHOP SAWBENCHES

MAKITA 2708 8" arbor tilt bench saw **£229**
ELEKTRA 12" Sawbench floor standing TCT blade 3HP **£189**
SCHEPPACH TKU 12" Sawbench floor standing TCT blade 3HP **£229**
Elektra & Scheppach Sliding Table **£90** Panel Cutting Extension **£75**
ELU TGS Sawbench/Mitre Saws c/w TCT blade TGS 172 **£496** TGS 171 **£399**
KITY 618 10" tilt arbor sawbench (+ £57.50 Kity Accessory Voucher) **£591**
MULTICO NTA300 3HP 12" **£1099** Sliding table 48" cap. **£316**
WADKIN AGS250/300 3HP 1PH **£1299** Sliding table 35" cap. **£496**
STARTRITE Scoring Saw 1PH **£1476** Sliding table 30" cap. **£352**
LUNA L18 12" 3HP 1PH **£950** Sliding table 24" cap. **£170**
SEDGWICK LK 16" Saw Bench 3PH **£899** 1PH **£1143**

ROLLER SUPPORT STANDS (P&P £3.00)

LUNA 10" support roller adjustable height sturdy construction **£29.95**
LUNA 16" combined roller support adjustable height **£42.00**

PREMIUM QUALITY INDUSTRIAL SAWBLADES
THE BEST IN QUALITY T.C.T. SAWBLADES LEITZ & SPEAR & JACKSON

BLADE DIAMETER	6"				7"-7¼"				8"				9"-9¼"			
No. OF TEETH	16	24	36	48	18	30	42	56	20	36	48	64	24	40	54	72
SPEARTIP	£16	£17	£20	£26	£16	£20	£22	£26	£20	£23	£24	£29	£26	£29	£32	£36
LEITZ						£37	£43	£49		£41	£51					

BLADE DIAMETER	10"				12"				14"				16"			
No. OF TEETH	24	40	60	80	32	48	72	96	36	60	84	108	28	36	60	96
SPEARTIP	£23	£26	£35	£38	£28	£36	£42	£48	£34	£42	£50	£57	£39	£44	£54	£63
Leitz	£39	£43	£51	£59	£42	£52	£61	£70	£48	£61	£70	£81	£54	£59	£70	£92

PLEASE STATE BORE SIZE WHEN ORDERING

MORTICING MACHINES — *OUR PRICE INC. VAT*

SMITHS BCM 75 bench morticer c/w lateral table ¾" cap. **£422**
SMITHS CM75 floor standing morticer dual table movement ¾" cap **£528**
MULTICO HM bench morticer ⅝" capacity precision morticer **£356**
MULTICO HMT bench morticer dual table movement **£499**
MULTICO M floor standing 1" capacity dual table movement 1PH **£625**
WADKIN EDA-2 floor standing 1" capacity dual table **£626**
RIDGWAY MORTICER 1" cap. 1HP Full Table Movements **£540**
RYOBI portable chain morticer **£365** Portable chisel morticer **£395**
RIDGWAY mortice/drill stand (requires ½" power drill) **£165**
SEDGWICK 571 Floor standing 1½HP 1" Cap **£599**

MORTICE CHISELS & BITS

JAPANESE ¼" **£20** ⅜" **£21** ½" **£25** ⅝" **£32** ¾" **£48** 1" **£59**
8mm **£21** 10mm **£24** 12mm **£25** 16mm **£29** 20mm **£44**
RIDGEWAY ¼" **£19** ⅜" **£23** ½" **£24** ⅝" **£35** ¾" **£37** 1" **£45**
6mm **£21** 8mm **£22** 10mm **£25** 12mm **£26** 16mm **£31** 20mm **£46**
CHISEL BITS ONLY ¼" **£6** ⅜" **£7** ½" **£8** ⅝" **£10** ¾" **£14** 1" **£18**
MORTICE CHISEL SHARPENING SETS set 1 (¼"-½") **£23** Set 2 (⅜"-¾") **£28**

DUST EXTRACTORS

LUNA W178 975m/hr excellent general purpose extractor c/w hose **£324**
LUNA NF243 1500m/hr mobile 5" hose ideal for high volume waste **£429**
LUNA NF259 2000m/hr heavy duty suitable for up to 3 machines **£599**
LUNA 4" × 3m hose **£19** 5" × 4m hose **£28** LUNA dust bags (per 10) **£3**
MULTICO DEA 960m/hr mobile extractor 4" hose **£335**
DeWALT DW60 500m/hr 5" hose **£265** ELEKTRA 1000m/hr 4" hose **£199**
STARTRITE CYCLAIR 55 960m/hr 4" **£409** CYCLAIR 75 1800m/hr 6" **£529**

MITRE CUTTERS & MITRE SAWS

ELU PS174 8" Portable mitre crosscut saw 8" crosscut **£298**
DeWALT DW250 Portable mitre saw 1¼HP 10" Blade **£179**
HITACHI CF10A 10" Portable precision mitre saw **£259**
ORTEGUILLE MITRE CUTTERS ORC55 **£238** ORC80 **£299** ORC100 **£439**
LION MITRE TRIMMER Excellent for clean cuts and mitres **£249**
NOBEX 202 PRO Hand Mitre saw **£72.95** NOBEX 303 **£44** (P&P £2.50)
NOBEX 202 Replacement Blades 12T, 18T or 24T **£4.30** each

PLANER THICKNESSERS

DeWALT DW1151 10" × 6" 2HP 2 speed power feed **SPECIAL PRICE**
Stand for DW1150 **£30** Slot Morticer **£69.95** HSS knives **£18.90**
ELECKTRA 10" × 6" floor standing power feed **£490**
SCHEPPACH HMO SOLO 10" × 6" 2HP floor standing Adjustable fence **£490**
KITY 7136 10" × 6" (+ £50.00 Kity Accessory Voucher) **£585**
STARTRITE PT260 10" × 7" floor standing ⅝" rebate capacity **£869**
STARTRITE SD310 12" × 9" 3 cutter block 1PH **£1399** 3PH **£1360**
LUNA 3HP Planers 10" × 9" **£1428** 12" × 9" **£1690** 16" × 9" **£2399**
MULTICO NS300 surfacer 3 cutter block 2HP 1PH **£1388** 3PH **£1271**
MULTICO THA300 12" × 10" thicknesser only 1PH **£1399** 3PH **£1299**
MULTICO CPT 12" × 8" Combined planer/thicknesser ¾" rebate 1PH **£1749** 3PH **£1649**

DRILLING MACHINES

WARCO HOBBY ½" 5 speed rack and pinion table bench mounting **£139**
WARCO ⅝" cap 2MT 12 speed 2B12 bench mounting **£189** 2F12 floor standing **£222**
FOBCO STAR ½" precision drill bench mounting **£359** 2F12 floor standing **£411**
STARTRITE SP250 ½" 5 speed bench mounting **£379** floor standing **£428**
Morticing attachments Warco 2B/2F **£24** Fobco **£61** Startrite **£110**

SPINDLE MOULDERS AND TENNONERS

SCHEPPACH HF33 3HP 30mm 3 speed with adjustable fences **£499**
SEDGWICK GW Spindle 30mm **£999**
KITY 623 2HP 3 speed C/W sliding table (+ £57.50 Kity Accessory Voucher) **£776**
STARTRITE T30 30mm C/W sliding table 1PH **£1089** 3PH 3HP **£1049**
LUNA L28 30mm 3 speed 3HP Heavy duty 1PH 3HP **£999** 3PH 3HP **£988**
MULTICO TENNONER TM1 240v twin motors (with tooling) **£1579**

SPINDLE MOULDER TOOLING (State bore size P&P £1.50)

OMAS "TIGER" BLOCKS 392 **£50** BLOCK in wooden case with stone etc. **£59**
OMAS cutter profiles **£12** CUTTER BLANKS **£7** SAW SEGMENTS **£17**
KITY PROFILE Door set **£99** OMAS ART 176D1 DOOR SET complete **£139**
WHITEHILL BLOCKS 4⅞" × ¹⁵⁄₁₆" **£50** 5⅜" × ⁹⁄₁₆" **£69** Panel Raising Block **£92**
LEITZ 488 Cutter block 100mm **£59** 40mm blanks ea. **£6.95**
TUNGSTEN REBATE BLOCKS 125mm × 50mm **£98** 6" Wobble saw 3-21mm **£89**
T.C.T. GROOVERS 6" 6 WING ¼" **£44** ⁵⁄₁₆" **£46** ⅜" **£48** ½" **£54** ⅝" **£62**
LUNA MINI POWER FEED 2 speeds **£329**
SEND FOR FREE SPINDLE TOOLING CATALOGUE.

COMBINATION MACHINES (Carriage £10.00 UK Mainland)

STARTRITE K260 saw spindle planer etc. FREE TIGER HEAD SET **£2390**
STARTRITE TZ30 saw spindle only FREE TIGER HEAD SET **£1359**
SPECIAL OFFER LUNA W59 2HP 240v c/w sliding table slot morticer **£2399**
LUNA MASTER COMBINATIONS 240v W64 **£3100** W69 **£3899**
AEG MAXI COMBINATION 5 function **£1604**
STARTRITE K310 12" Planer 12" Saw **£3850**

★★★★★★ KITY COMBINATION MACHINES ★★★★★★

K5 COMBINATION COMBI STAR CK26 TABLE COMBINATION K704 DIRECT DRIVE AND ACCESSORIES ALL AT SPECIAL PRICES SEND FOR LATEST PRICE LIST.

BORING BITS

CLICO SAW TOOTH & FORSTNER BITS (State type) 6" long ½" shank ⅜" **£8.10** ½" **£8.35**
⅝" **£9.20** ¾" **£10.00** ⅞" **£10.50** 1" **£11.55** 1⅛" **£13.55** 1¼" **£16.50**
1⅜" **£17.20** 1½" **£18.15** 1⅝" **£20.90** 1¾" **£23.75** 1⅞" **£26.30** 2" **£27.80**
2¼" **£34.95** 2½" **£46.35**
CLICO PLUG CUTTERS ⅜" **£22** ½" **£24** ⅝" **£28** ¾" **£30** 1" **£36** 1⅛ **£40.00**
CLICO SAW TOOTH set ½", ¾", 1" **£28** ECONOMY 5 piece set ½"-1½" × ¼" **£58**
RIDGEWAY ADJUSTABLE FORSTNERS WR10/½"-1¾" **£16** WR10/3⅝"-3" **£18**
RIDGEWAY ADJUSTABLE FORSTER (h/duty) WR20/2⅞"-2" **£29** WR20/3 1⅜"-3" **£34**

ROUTERS

ELU MOF96 ¼" 600W **£98.00**
ELU MOF31 ¼", ⅜", ½" 1200W **£152.50**
ELU MOF177 ¼", ½" 1600W **£193.50**
HITACHI TR8 ¼" 730W **£79.95**
RYOBI R150 ¼" 730W **£75.95**
HITACHI FM ¼" 550W **£46.95**
MAKITA 3600B ¼", ½" 1500W **£168.95**
ELU MOF96E ¼" Var. speed **£119.50**
ELU MOF11/2 ½" 2000W c/w base **£337.33**
ELU MOF177E ½" Var. speed **£218.50**
HITACHI TR12 ¼", ½" 1300W **£137.95**
RYOBI R500 R500 ¼", ½" 1500W **£124.95**
BOSCH POF52 ½" 520W **£52.00**
MAKITA 3612BR ½" 1600W **£175.95**

ROUTER ACCESSORIES

ELU DOVETAIL KIT TCT cutter **£69.95**
ELU MOF96 Accessory kit **£69.95**
STAIR JIG (General duty) **£69.00**
ELU ROUTER BRKT. for DeWalt **£38.00**
ELU 96 Dust extraction kit **£36.00**
ELU MOF96 Height adjuster **£3.95**
ELU TRACKING SET **£35.00**
TREND STAIR JIG **£112.00**
TREND OVERHEAD ROUTER Bench Mtg. **£687.00**
TREND OVERHEAD ROUTER Fl. Stdg. **£1200.00**
ELU 1½ ROUTER for above stands **£181.00**
TREND POST FORM JIG **£434.00**
RYOBI Dovetail jig fits above **£99.95**
ELU ROUTER COMBI BENCH **£118.00**
STAIR JIG (heavy duty) **£160.00**
ELU 12 piece Guide bush set **£35.00**
ELU MOF98, 31, 177 Height adjuster **£16.95**
ELU 96 177 side fence adjuster **£5.30**
ELU ROUTING VIDEO **£12.00**

★★★★ SPECIAL OFFER ★★★★
ROUTER PROFILE SCRIBER SETS ⅜" or ½" Shank only **£110.00** inc. P&P
★★★★★★★★★★★★★★★★★

HSS ROUTER BIT SETS (inc. P&P)

SAVE 30% ON HSS ROUTER BIT SETS AND GET A FREE ROUTER BIT CASE.
13 PIECE SET **£59.95**
8 PIECE SET **£37.95**
5 PIECE SET **£21.95**
ROUTER BIT CUTTER BOX ONLY **£4**

ROUTER CUTTERS
20-25% OFF LEADING BRANDS EXCELLENT STOCKS OF HSS & TCT ROUTER CUTTERS OVER 500 PROFILES IN STOCK. SEND NOW FOR FREE CUTTER CHART:- TECHNIQUES OF ROUTING £7.95 (inc. P&P)

IMMEDIATE DESPATCH ON CREDIT CARD PHONED ORDERS — CREDIT TERMS AVAILABLE OVER £120

0297 33656 CHARD STREET AXMINSTER DEVON EX13 5DZ POST OFFICE C.O.D. VISA CONNECT BARCLAYCARD VISA

AXMINSTER POWER TOOL CENTRE

HORIZONTAL WETSTONE GRINDERS
OUR PRICE INC. VAT

JAPANESE Wetstone grinder £129.00
180G stone for above £40.00
1000G stone for above £40.00
6000G stone for above £43.00
PRECISION grinding jig £43.00
SHARPENSET Wetstone grinder £240.00
SHARPENSET 80g stone £20.00
SHARPENSET 150G stone £18.40
SHARPENSET 280G stone £20.41
SHARPENSET Green stone (TCT) ... £18.40
10" Planer Knife grinding jig £65.00
15" Planer Knife grinding jig £78.00
CHISEL grinding jig £67.00

VERTICAL WETSTONE GRINDERS
SCANGRIND 150 6" wetstone £69.00
SCANGRIND 200 8" wetstone £88.00
SCANTOOL COMBI WET AND DRY STONES
COMBI SC150 6" wet & dry £89.00
COMBI SC200 8" wet & dry £112.00
LUNA KIRUNA 11" wet & 4" dry .. £118.00
LUNA KIRUNA 14" wet & 5" dry .. £184.00

BENCH GRINDERS
ELU EDS163 6" 360W £73.00
ELU EDS164 7" 390W £77.00
ELU MWA149 6" Honer grinder £90.95
LEROY SOMER 5" 180W £33.00
LEROY SOMER 6" 250W £44.00
LEROY SOMER 6" with chuck £49.00
WARCO 5" 180W (European) £33.00
WARCO 6" 380W (European) £43.00
WARCO 8" 570W (European) £69.00

GRIND STONES (state bore size)

	5"	6"	7"
COARSE 36G	£6.60	£7.90	£11.40
FINE 60G	£6.60	£7.90	£11.40
WHITE 60G	£7.20	£8.50	£13.50
GREEN (TCT)	£7.20	£8.50	£13.50

JIGSAWS (Light Duty)
Bosch PST50 Single Speed £29.95
Bosch PST50E Var. Speed £38.50
Bosch PST55PE Var. Speed Pend ... £65.00
Hitachi FJ50SB Single speed £29.50
Hitachi FJ50VA Var. speed £37.95
Hitachi FCJ55V Var. Speed Pend. Act £61.95

JIGSAWS (Heavy Duty)
Elu ST142 2 speed £101.00
Elu ST142E Var. speed £110.00
Elu ST152 2 Speed £98.00
Elu ST152E Var. speed £106.00
Cases for above Jigsaws £10.00
Hitachi CJ65 2 speed £100.95
Hitachi CJ65VA Var. speed £104.95
Hitachi CJ65V Var. speed £104.95
Bosch 1581.7 Var. speed £108.95

DISC AND BELT SANDERS
Picador 10" Disc Sander £219.00
Warco BDS460 6" Disc 4" Belt £86.00
Warco BDS690 9" Disc 6" Belt £179.00
Holmes 6" 2HP £399.00
Luna Favourite 4" £285.00
Luna De-Lux Sander 4" £599.00
Luna YKV Pad Sander £647.00
Luna YK1500 Pad Sander 1PH .. £1564.00
Luna YK1500 Pad Sander 3PH .. £1509.00
Picador Unmotorised 3" Belt £49.00
Picador Unmotorised 3" Belt £65.00
Holmes 4" Belt Sander £94.00
Holmes 6" Belt Sander £120.00

CIRCULAR SAWS
HITACHI FC5SA 6" TCT 710W £42.95
BOSCH PKS46 6" TCT 600W £53.50
BOSCH PKS66 7⅝ TCT 1200W £86.00
HITACHI PSU6 6" 1050W HSS £79.95
HITACHI PSU7 7" 1600W HSS £103.95
HITACHI PSU9 9" 1759W HSS £133.95
HITACHI PSM7 7" 1200W TCT £151.50
HITACHI PSM9 9" 1600W TCT £160.50
ELU MH151 6" 850W TCT £90.95
ELU MH65 7" 1200W TCT £131.95
ELU MH85 9" 1600W TCT £177.95
ELU MH182 8" 1400W TCT £148.00
ELU 550 COMBI (for MH182) £130.00
ELU555 Snip saw (for 182) £179.00
WOLF 9" CIRCULAR SAW £135.00

FINISHING SANDERS
(DB Dust Bag)
BOSCH PSS230 1/3rd Sheet £29.95
HITACHI FS10SA 1/3rd Sheet £27.95
HITACHI FSV12 Sheet DB £53.50
BOSCH PS280A ½ Sheet DB £59.95
B&D P6303 ½ Sheet £59.95
ELU MVS156 1/3rd Sheet DB £73.00
ELU MVS156E Var. Speed DB £85.95
ELU MVS 94 ½ Sheet DB £111.00
ELU MVS47 ½ Sheet £123.00
HITACHI SV12 ½ Sheet £116.95
HITACHI SOD110 ½ Sheet DB £94.50
HITACHI SO110 ½ Sheet £86.95
BOSCH 1288 9½ Sheet DB £99.95
WOLF ½ Sheet DB £96.00

POWER TOOL WORK BENCHES
Post/Delivery £5.00
TRITON £159.00
Stand £29.00
Router/Jigsaw Base £39.00
Wheel Kit £9.50
DUNLOP POWER BASE £119.95
Extension Table £21.50
Additional sole plates £8.65
WOLFCRAFT VARIOTEC £59.50
BOSCH MT92 Saw Table £109.95

OUR PRICE INC. VAT

POWER PLANES (Light Duty)
BLACK & DECKER DN710 ...... £29.95
BOSCH PHO100 82mm 450W £46.95
HITACHI FP20SA 82mm 320W £41.50

HEAVY DUTY
ELU MFF80 82mm 850W £109.95
ELU MFF80K (in kit box) £127.95
ELU MFF40 82mm 1000W £189.95
INVERSION Std. for MFF80 ...... £20.95
INVERSION Std. for MFF40 ...... £29.00
HITACHI P20SA 82mm 720W £100.95
HITACHI FU20 82mm 620W £97.50
HITACHI F30A 92mm 900W £143.50

BELT SANDERS
ELU MHB 157 3" 600W £106.95
ELU MHB 157E 3" var. speed £119.00
ELU 157 FRAME £35.00
ELU 157 inversion stand £28.00
ABRASIVE BELTS FOR MHB 157/pkt. 3
40G, 60G, 80G, 100G, 120G, 150G £3.00
BOSCH PBS75 3" 620W £71.95
ELU MHB 90 4" 850W £193.95
ELU MHB 90K With frame £234.00
HITACHI SB75 3" 950W £117.95
HITACHI SB10T 4" 950W £141.95
HITACHI SB10V 4" var. speed £148.50
MAKITA 9401 4" 1040W £169.00
MAKITA 9924DB 3" 950W £117.00

BISCUIT JOINTER
ELU DS140 Biscuit Jointer £197.00
No. 20 Biscuits (1000 off) £19.95
No. 10 Biscuits (1000 off) £19.50
No. 0 Biscuits (1000 off) £18.63
Mixed Box 0, 10, 20 (500 off) £12.50
DS140 saw blade 12T Std. £29.95
DS140 saw blade 30T Fine £29.50
DS140 Dust Tube adaptor £5.95
BOSCH Biscuit Jointer £124.95

★ ★ ★ ★ SPECIAL OFFERS ★ ★ ★ ★
WOODSCREWS
Twin Fast Zinc Plated GKN 1600 Woodscrews from 1" × 6 to 2" × 10" with Free Screwdriver. (State slotted or pozidrive).
ONLY £19.99 inc. VAT and P&P

RIDGWAY DRILL MORTICER
c/w Free Hitachi Drill ½" Chuck and ¼" Chisel and Bit
£186.00 inc. VAT and P&P

MARTEK DRILL SHARPENER
Excellent for Sharpening all Drill Bits
ONLY **£24.95** inc. VAT and P&P

POWER BREAKERS
Avoid electric shocks when using power tools. A must for all power tools at **£19.95** inc. VAT and P&P

★ ★ ★ ★ ★ ★ ★ ★ ★ ★ ★ ★ ★ ★ ★ ★ ★ ★ ★ ★

POWER DRILLS (K-Kit box)
NEW ELU POWER DRILLS
ECD304K 420W V/S 10mm Compact £73.95
EMD400K 600W 2 Speed 13mm ... £81.95
ESD705K 320W V/S & Rev. 10mm £102.95
EMD403K 500W V/S/R Ham. 13mm £90.95
EMD405K 500W V/S/R Ham. 13mm £114.95
EMD406K 550W V/S Hammer 13mm £106.95
BOSCH 400-2 10mm 440W £29.95
BOSCH 500RLE 13mm 500W V/S Rev. £49.95
BOSCH 7002E 13mm 700W £79.95
BOSCH 850RLT 13mm 850W V/S Re £111.95
HITACHI FV12VA 13mm 420W V/S £40.50
HITACHI FDV16V 13mm 600W V/S/R £61.95
HITACHI FDV20VA 13mm 710W V/S/R £82.95
HITACHI VTP13K 13mm 2 Speed 460W £86.00
HITACHI VTP16AK 2 Spd. 800W .. £118.50

PALM GRIP SANDERS
(DB Dust Bag)
ELU MVS500 1/6th Sheet 135W DB £60.95
ELU MVS501 1/4 Sheet 135W DB £60.95
B&D P6301 1/6th Sheet 136W DB £51.50
B&D P6302 1/4 Sheet 135W DB ... £51.50
HITACHI SV12SA 1/4 Sheet 180W £51.50
MAKITA B045 10 1/4 Sheet £48.95

SWEDISH STEEL INDUSTRIAL BANDSAW BLADES

		3/16"	1/4"	3/8"	1/2"	5/8"	3/4"
BURGESS	57"	—	£3.20	£3.30	£3.45	—	—
DeWALT	59.5"	—	£3.20	£3.30	£3.45	—	—
CORONET	67.5"	—	£3.43	£3.50	£3.70	—	—
WARCO	70"	—	£3.60	£3.70	£3.80	—	—
INCA	73"	£3.91	£3.70	£3.80	£3.90	£4.80	—
BIRCH	81"	—	£4.25	£4.35	£4.52	—	—
DeWALT	82.5"	£4.75	£3.95	£4.10	£4.20	£5.11	£5.69
MINIMAX	86"	£4.10	£3.95	£4.10	£4.20	£5.11	£5.69
STARTRITE	88"	£4.10	£3.95	£4.10	£4.20	£5.11	£5.69
KITY	90.5"	£4.42	£4.14	£4.25	£4.42	£5.40	£5.90
STARTRITE	102"	£5.41	£4.66	£4.71	£4.86	—	£5.99
EVENWOOD	104"	£5.41	£4.66	£4.71	£4.86	—	£5.99
STARTRITE	112"	£5.06	£4.80	£4.90	£5.10	£6.30	£7.02
MINIMAX	144"	£6.46	£5.29	£5.46	£6.46	£7.13	£7.99

10% DISCOUNT WHEN ORDERING 10 OR MORE BLADES
POST PAID ON ORDERS £5.00 & OVER.

LIBERON WAXES
Waxes Sealers Stains Polishes Etc.
All Your Requirements in One
Send for Free Price List
GLUE POT ...... £23.00 inc. P&P

CORDLESS DRILLS HITACHI 10mm
OUR PRICE inc. VAT

DTC 10 6 cell 2 spd. & rev. £79.95
DRC10 as above torque adjustable . £98.50
DTC10K 6 cell 2 spd. & rev. in case £86.50
D10DB 6 cell variable spd. & rev. ... £88.50
D10DD 8 cell 2 spd. & rev. £90.00
D10D as above torque adjustable £111.00
DV10D 8 cell 2 spd. & rev. hammer £115.95

MAKITA 10mm
6012DWK 6 cell 2 spd. & rev. in case £92.95
6012HDW 8 cell 2 spd. torque adj. £111.95
8400DW 8 cell 1 spd. & rev. hammer £119.95
MAGNETIC Screwdriver kit 7 piece .. £5.95
REPLACEMENT BITS (state type) £0.50

MISCELLANEOUS POWER TOOLS
KEW HOBBY PRESSURE WASHER £239.00
DREMEL D576 FRETSAW £69.95
BOSCH WET 'n' DRY Vacuum cleaner £110
BOSCH 560 HOT AIR paint stripper £39.00
Steam Wallpaper stripper £125.00
NEW ELU DUST EXTRACTORS
EVE 938 ...... £275 EVE 948 ...... £395
BOSCH INDUSTRIAL PAINT STRIPPER £82.95
BELLE ELECTRIC CEMENT MIXER £135.00

KLEMSIA QUICK CLAMPS

SPAN	REACH	
200mm	110mm	£3.70
300mm	110mm	£4.00
400mm	110mm	£4.40
600mm	110mm	£5.20 (P&P £1.50)
800mm	110mm	£6.00
1000mm	110mm	£7.10
200mm	150mm	£6.70

RECORD CRAMP HEADS M130
1 off **£10.40** 5 off **£10.00** (P&P £1.50)

DRILL BIT SETS
OUR PRICE INC. VAT

	Lip & Spur	HSS Std.
1/16"-1/2" × 64ths	—	£21.00
1/16"-1/2" × 32nds	£42.00	£17.00
1-13mm × 0.5mm	£54.00	£19.00
1-10mm × 0.5mm	£39.00	£11.00
1/8"-1/4" × 64ths	—	£4.50
1/16"-1/4" × 1/16ths		£2.00

WOODWORKING VICES (P&P £4.50)
RECORD 52½E 9" Quick Release ... £50.00
52½ED 9" Quick Release ... £54.00
53E 10" Quick Release £69.00
V150 6" Woodcraft £11.50 (p&p £1.50)
V175 7" Woodcraft ...... £12.95 (P&P £2.00)

CLIFTON HAND PLANES
CLIFTON 3 in 1 Rebate Plane £67.00
CLIFTON 410 Shoulder £49.95
CLIFTON 420 Rebate Plane £57.00
CLIFTON Multi-Plane £189.00

WOODWORKING BOOKS inc. P&P
MAKING WOODEN TOYS THAT MOVE £7.95
TRADITIONAL CABINETMAKING £9.95
WOOD FINISHING £9.95
FINISHING AND POLISHING £2.50
WOODWORKER GUIDE TO TURNING £9.95
TURNING PROJECTS (BOLTER) £13.95
Fine Woodworking Series
BENDING WOOD £7.95
SPINDLE TURNING £7.95
MARQUETRY & VENEER £7.95
THINGS TO MAKE £7.95
Many other titles available
FINE WOODWORKING TECHS (state vol.) £15.95

PARAMO CRAMP HEADS
1 off **£10.00** 5 off **£9.00** (P&P £1.50)

G CRAMPS (P&P £1.50 per order) may be mixed for quantity
RECORD 120-3" 1 off .. £5.20 5 off .. £4.80
120-4" 1 off .. £5.50 5 off .. £4.90
120-6" 1 off .. £7.50 5 off .. £6.90
120-8" 1 off £11.00 5 off £9.80
120-10" 1 off £18.00 5 off £17.00
RECORD DEEP THROAT 4" 1 off £13.27

PARAMO 3" 1 off .... £5.30 5 off £4.60
4" 1 off .... £5.55 5 off £4.78
6" 1 off .... £7.76 5 off £6.60
8" 1 off ... £11.41 5 off ... £9.50
10" 1 off . £16.90 5 off . £15.77
PARAMO DEEP THROAT 4" 1 off .. £12.45

SASH CRAMPS (P&P £2.00 per order) may be mixed for quantity
RECORD 135-18" 1 off .... £18 5 off £17
135-24" 1 off .. £18 5 off .. £17.50
135-36" 1 off .... £20 5 off £19
135-42" 1 off .... £21 5 off £20
135-48" 1 off .... £22 5 off £21

RECORD 42" 1 off .... £35 5 off £32
T bar 48" 1 off .... £36 5 off £34
54" 1 off .... £37 5 off £35
66" 1 off .... £40 5 off £38
78" 1 off .... £47 5 off £45.00

JAPANESE WATER STONES (P&P £1.00)
KING BRAND 800G WETSTONE £8.00
KING BRAND 1200G WETSTONE £8.00
Super Delux Finishing 8000G £29
Slipstones 100 × 50 × 12 1 or 4000G £5.40
SUPER FINISHING STONE 6000G ... £8.90
COMBINATION WATER STONE £10.80
SORBY Diamond honing system (state Med. fine or Ex fine) £14.00

STANLEY HAND PLANES
(P&P £1.50/Order)

3	Smoothing 240 × 45mm	£23.60
4	Smoothing 245 × 50mm	£20.00
41/2	Smoothing 260 × 60mm	£21.60
5	Jack 355 × 50mm	£27.00
51/2	Jack 380 × 60mm	£28.00
6	Fore 455 × 60mm	£37.80
7	Jointer 560 × 60mm	£39.40
78	Duplex Rebate	£18.50
10	Rebate 330 × 44mm	£33.00
80	Scraper	£9.50
601/2	Block Plane	£21.00
92	Rebate Plane	£22.50

CLIFTON Cap Iron 2" or 2⅜" £5.00

RECORD HAND PLANES (P&P £1.50/Order)

03	Smoothing 240 × 45mm	£19.50
04	Smoothing 245 × 50mm	£17.99
041/2	Smoothing 260 × 60mm	£18.99
05	Jack 355 × 50mm	£21.99
051/2	Jack 380 × 60mm	£29.50
06	Jointer 455 × 60mm	£33.99
07	Jointer 560 × 60mm	£39.75
778	Rebate 215 × 38mm	£30.80
010	Rebate 330 × 44mm	£39.50
020C	Circular Plane	£69.50
0601/2	Block Plane	£16.50
073	Shoulder Rebate	£42.50

RECORD 3 in 1 Plane £39.00

MISCELLANEOUS HAND TOOLS (P&P £1.50 PER ORDER)
RECORD Dowel Jig £34.00 | 18" Extension Rods . £4.95 | Drill Bushes £1.90
140 Corner Cramps £12.00 | 141 Corner Cramps £19.40 | Spare Collars £3.20
145 Hold Fast ...... £12.90 | 146 Hold Fast ...... £14.70 | Priory Bench Stop £2.95
Floorboard Cramp .. £56.95 | 169 Bench Stop ...... £7.50 | STANLEY Web Clamp £7.99
Stanley Yankee Screwdrivers 13" ...... £12.86 20" ...... £14.17 27" £18.50

HARDPOINT HANDSAWS (P&P £1.50)
SANDVIK 250 22" 1 off ..... £10.60 5 off ..... £9.90 24" 1 off ..... £11.59 5 off £10.90
SANDVIK 251 22" 1 off .... £14.23 5 off .... £13.00 24" 1 off .... £15.59 5 off £14.50
LUNA 22" 1 off ...... £6.62 5 off ...... £5.90 24" 1 off ...... £6.68 5 off £6.32

HANDSAWS
DISSTON D8 20" × 10pt .. £23 D8 22" × 10pt .. £24 D8 24" × 7pt .. £26 D8 26" × 6pt .. £27
SPEAR & JACKSON PROFESSIONAL 22" × 10pt .... £27 24" × 8 .... £28 26" × 6pt £30
TENON SAWS S&J PROFF 8" × 20pt ...... £23 10" × 15pt ...... £22 12" × 15 ...... £23
Roberts and Lee Dorchester Dovetail Saw ...... £27 RIDGWAY SPEEDSAW £19

SANDERSON KAYSER "PAX" HANDSAWS (P&P £1.50)
BRASS BACK TENNON SAWS 8" £18.50 10" £19 12" £19.50 14" £20 D/Tail £25
HANDSAWS 20" × 10pt £21 22" × 6pt £22 22" × 8pt £22 22" × 10pt £22 24" × 6 £22
24" × 7pt .... £23 24" × 8pt .... £?? 26" × 6pt .... £23 26" × 8pt .... £23 26" × 51/2pt £23

ABRASIVES (West German top quality P&P £1.00/Order)
SANDING BELTS resin bonded aluminium oxide cloth belts (price each)

Size (length width)	M/C	40G	60G	80G	100G	120G
75 × 480mm — 3" × 19"	(Elu)	£1.11	£1.08	£0.99	£1.05	£1.02
75 × 510mm — 3" × 20"	(B&D)	£1.14	£1.12	£1.03	£1.07	£1.02
75 × 533mm — 3" × 21"	(Bosch Hit)	£1.28	£1.17	£1.07	£1.09	£1.05
100 × 560mm 4" × 22"	(Elu 90)	£1.58	£1.43	£1.40	£1.37	£1.32
100 × 610mm 4" × 24"	(Wolf Hit)	£1.67	£1.53	£1.48	£1.43	£1.38
100 × 915mm — 4" × 36"	(Coronet)	£2.22	£1.99	£1.88	£1.85	£1.81
150 × 1090mm — 6" × 42"	(Coronet)	£4.20	£3.80	£3.65	£3.45	£3.40

★ ★ OTHER SIZES AVAILABLE ON REQUEST MANY IN STOCK ★ ★
★ ★ NEW ABRASIVES CATALOGUE/PRICE LIST OUT NOW ★ ★
Send for your free copy covers all belts discs sheets Etc.

WIRE WOOL

	0000 Fine	00/0 Medium	1/2 Coarse	3/4 V Coarse
1 KG ROLLS	£4.73	£4.35	£4.25	£4.13
250g ROLLS	£1.50	£1.45	£1.42	£1.38

ABRASIVE SHEETS (P&P £0.50 PER ORDER) state grit when ordering 100G and finer

Type	Description	60G/10	60G/50	80G/10	80G/50	100G+/10	100G+/50
PGF	GARNET FINISHING	£2.13	£8.90	£1.85	£7.70	£1.67	£6.94
GCAB	GARNET CABINET	£3.02	£12.59	£2.61	£10.90	£2.35	£9.82
PSF	SILICON FINISHING	£3.16	£13.17	£2.73	£11.40	£2.46	£10.27
WS	WET 'n' DRY	£6.19	£25.81	£5.28	£22.03	£3.59	£14.99

★SPECIAL OFFER★ 50 Sheets of asstd. Abrasives £5.99 inc. P&P Garnet-Glass-W/Dry

SAVE 20% ON ALL HAND TOOLS SEND NOW FOR NEW HAND TOOL CATALOGUE £1.50 (REFUNDABLE ON 1st ORDER

0297 33656 5 Lines 24 Hour **CHARD STREET AXMINSTER DEVON** 6.30-9pm **34836**

BARCLAYCARD VISA

FUNCTION

Decor as

'There is a radical change', announces Joe Tibbetts from the rostrum at the Direct Design Show, 'in public and professional perception. There is a radical change in the way the British perceive British talents.' The rostrum takes on a hint of the hustings as Joe, the show's creator and organiser, bemoans the lateness of the British awakening to the British Designer-Maker Movement. Did you know there was a British Designer-Maker Movement? After the first Direct Design Show, claims the first sentence of the first page of the catalogue, a buyer from Saks Fifth Avenue 'said that the British designer-maker movement was the most exciting thing in the world at the moment.'

Natural hyperbole. But Joe's tone of voice takes on an edge as his discourse develops; he considers the traditional (British) craftsperson's approach to business. 'Trade is vulgar, profit anathema, and marketing a four-letter word.' But, he emphasises, 'marketing is an essential skill which the designer must acquire.' Poor design colleges, how little sense of foreboding they must have had as they blithely binned the show's pre-event publicity mailouts. Three hundred colleges were mailed, two applied for students' work to be selected, and so they come in for Joe's big stick. 'How little do students know or care about marketing? Go to any college degree show, and ask yourself — where are the students?'

From an administration and marketing background at the Design Council (representing it at product fairs and shows in the UK and Europe), Joe has conceived, brought forth and nurtured — to the point of force-feeding — his brainchild, which in influence and media coverage now challenges the Chelsea Crafts Fair. The first Direct Design Show was just a year ago. 'Function and decor' is the theme; nothing that wouldn't get used or appreciated in the home. Designer makers, and the growing sector of the buying public who will pay over the odds for originality and craftsmanship, are latching on to it in a big way, and it has already grown out of its Kensington venue; it moves to the Royal Horticultural Halls in November. A case of the representation of the scene creating the scene itself? Certainly, the DDS has an interest in promoting the phenomenon of the designer maker, and such two-way fertilisation is a recognisable dynamic in media-conscious events of this kind; show promotes itself by promoting designer makers, designer makers grow in numbers and confidence as they see their identity defined — and their products sold.

To see the growth of such a breed and such a wealth of British vitality, energy and talent is exciting, inspiring, encouraging. There are excesses, of course, but there's quality too — and, horror of horrors, the two are not necessarily mutually exclusive. In both innovation and craftsmanship there's a liveliness, a pushiness even, that is finding a commercial ally in the Direct Design Show.

Being design- and business-headed, Joe rides the hobby-horse of the designer maker's relationship with the market. Which, regular readers may have noticed, is also one of WOODWORKER's own themes, and which is why we got involved with the show in the first place.

The WOODWORKER Award for products in wood, we decided, should this time round be for imaginative, sensitive, skilled use of colour in the designing and making of wooden products. There's a current colour explosion in furniture; either because it's a specially rich vein to tap for ideas, inspiration and experiment, or because it's something that's easy to deal with if your notions for forms and structures are thin on the ground.

Touring the stands at the DDS, it hits you in the eye. Nearly everyone is using colour somehow or other; on flat surfaces, where the decoration is 99% of the job; on pieces displayed alongside strong well-crafted shapes in natural timbers (Stephen Down); or in timbers themselves chosen for colour and used as structural, 'integral' decoration (Nick Dyson). But it wasn't only in the work we were judging we saw the colour, we felt it in the atmosphere as well. The third Direct Design Show had greater glow, greater enthusiasm than the last. If these are British designers, they are leaving behind British restraint, that familiar basic element of our visual sense. We need, it may be argued, to go well over the top at times, and it's evident that this is one of those times.

There were furniture makers exhibiting, and there were also artists working on furniture, which meant that in much of the work the marriage between function and decoration was faintly unhappy. We gave the Award to **The Imperial Woodworks** because they are uncompromising; their work has an entirely visual function. It is decorative, and that's that. They have developed a highly personal style that pays the absolute minimum of lip service to the practical usefulness of furniture, concentrating on the sculptural form, the beautifying effect. Yes, you can sit on the chair — but wouldn't you rather sit on another one and look at that one?

Brian James and David Davies (the Imperial Woodworks partners) get by on minimal woodwork skills, putting almost all their efforts into their finishing techniques, in which they are true craftsmen — painstaking, patient, hard to satisfy. They use oil paints, shellac, copal and dammar varnishes, bronze powders in japan gold size, french polish; coating and rubbing down many times over, working tirelessly to get the effect they want.

Their work is grotesque, outlandish, bizarre, characterised by a 'contrived eccentricity' (their phrase); and I personally believe it has a place amongst the classics of English furniture. It isn't re-hash, it isn't derivative, it isn't fashionable, it isn't even modern, but it's startlingly innovative. Much of their reference and inspiration is found in ancient cultures and styles; they look to cave paintings, burial sculptures, mythical animals, heraldry, Harlequin — and put it all together without taking it or themselves too seriously. Yes, of course, now you may hate it. But it performs its visual function outstandingly, and it's honest.

In just a year, London's Direct Design Show has filled an important gap in 'designer-maker product awareness'. Aidan Walker took the pulse and helped decide where the *Woodworker* Award went

● **Left**, exotic and outlandish – Imperial Woodwork's winning table-and-chair team

● **Top**, Stephen Down's giant portable tray table and turned bowl, decorated with batik technique of wax resist and stains

● **Above**, solid and stylish cantilevered stool with foot-rest, by Giles Charlton

FUNCTION
Decor as

Painter, sculptor, designer, textile artist and joiner and decorator's son Malcolm Temple is a member of the Show's selection panel and a co-judge of the *Woodworker* Award. Here's the view through his eyes.

A show like Direct Design is a welcome relief from the precious shop or gallery where these exhibitors usually sell. Sometimes it's the first showcase for their work, and it's also valuable because it allows prospective clients to meet them. Discussing motives and methods opens their eyes to the wonder of some of their work, while diminishing what they feel for other of their pieces. The makers become sellers, and thus learn a lot about their work. They realise that a well-placed 'can I help you?' is sometimes the difference between a sale or no-sale.

As an artist, I found it an auspicious role-reversal to be judge, rather than judged, at WOODWORKER's 'Surface Decoration on Wood' award. *Decoration* should spring instinctively from the heart of the object, intrinsically linked with its spirit and not applied randomly — the term 'Applied Art' seemed more appropriate to me. This year's winners, the Imperial Woodworks, make furniture which displays a visual language independent of its undoubted influences — despite the odd addition of carbuncular animal forms for handles, inappropriate to such slender, poised structures. Egyptian and Etruscan Art shaking hands with Rennie Mackintosh and Bugatti. A refreshingly confident vision that both surprised and delighted.

● **Above**, beautiful lines and classic overtones characterise the work of Francesca Graham and Lucy McCann. **Below**, gorgeously rich painted chest from Peter Milne.

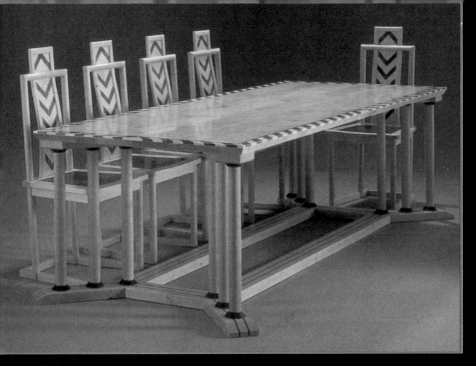

● **Above**, imposing dining table and chairs in sycamore and American walnut by Nicholas Dyson. **Below**, Tony Isseyegh's table and chair, decorated in strong monochrome lines with primary highlights

What I'd been looking for were bal statements, effective restraint, passior even honest vulgarity, and not necessaril beauty. The shock of the new rather tha the comfort of the familiar. Great dexterity like great learning, can inhibit the adven turous spirit. There's nothing amiss with well-placed 6in nail for a joint; an inspired stroke will outshine and sometimes outlas the perfect dovetail. Concentrating or detail can drain the essence from an idea.

Walking round the show maybe 20 times, I was struck by the familiarity o most work, not because I'd seen it before but because of the distinct categories rep resented. There was furniture whos structural sense was camouflaged by confusion of patterning; there were dolls house mansions masquerading as cup boards and tables — toys for grown-ups There were bland ideas beautifully made and interesting innovations glibly applied to forms which were boring when they wer fashionable 20 years ago.

For me the most frustrating groups present constituted the 'let's-get-back-to the-18th-century' movement. This is furniture Jane Austen would have come home to after a spin round the shires beautifully-crafted with just enough ornamentation to tease the weary eyes Bookcases for the Flora and Fauna of the British Isles, tables round which would chime effortlessly the frivolous conver sations of the well-heeled. Furniture for a polite, 'naice' dream-world, a worlc untroubled by inner-city blight and pun music, where only the barest trace of colou or texture invades.

This is design devoid of any concern fo social enhancement; it's furniture for the new gentry and echoes a crisis of confi dence, the abandonment of radicalism What's important nowadays is to be likec bought and asked out to dinner by clients the Arts, just a pleasing backdrop to well manicured lifestyles. Ultra-modern caree people return at night to their Regenc homes — a dispiriting trend considering the wealth of untapped creative talent ir Britain.

Students, before the art school system homogenizes them, are vibrant, passionate crude, unformed. Tutors should encourag these qualities, not the 'please employ me attitude seeping from colleges today. Those who survive this process intact go abroad for success or bloody-mindedly engage in a difficult existence back home, struggling against peer-group taste and people's fear o visual confrontation.

The real growth area is individualism and November's Direct Design Show will, hope, be alive with it.

● Malcolm Temple's decorated table is featured on the front cover

The next Direct Design Show is at the Royal Horticultural Halls, London SW1, 27-29 November. The selection panel is at work in early September; information from the Jardine Llewellyn Partnership, 1 Lawn Lane, London SW8 1UD, 01-587 0256

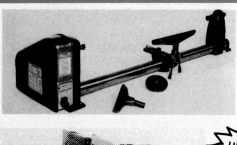

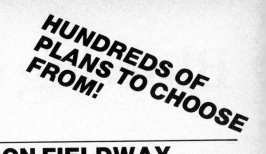

Blowing in the wind

Douglas Rae has been
interviewing bellows-maker
John Jones at his workshop,
Hangover Hall, Wilts

● *Big bellows, nearly a foot across, and baby bellows – John Jones makes them all.*
***Below**, a pair of bellows boards*

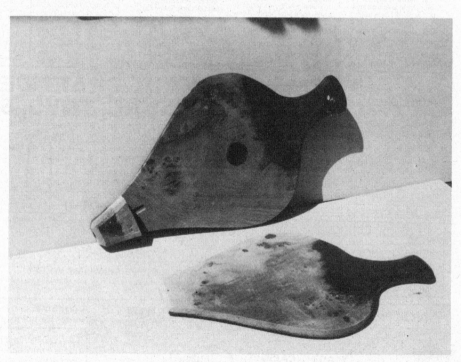

Hot air is the stuff of life for John
Jones. For the last nine years, since
he retired from running a nearby
pub, he's been eking out his pension by
making and repairing bellows. He now
makes 200 a year and repairs many more.

The bellows he makes range from
miniatures 3½in wide to monsters nearly a
foot across. The baby bellows may look
suitable only for blowing out candles on a
birthday cake, but they actually produce
more puff than me or you. The big fellows,
which deliver much more air, require a
blacksmith's muscles to operate.

Bellows as we know them today probably
haven't changed much since medieval
times, when the shape was invented. The
elaborate carving of mother-and-child on
the bellows John recently repaired looks to
me as though it comes from the 17th
century, or even earlier.

The principle of the bellows was known
back in ancient Egypt, where it was used to
generate white heat in a fire for metal
working. Before that time a ring of slaves
would stand around the fire, blowing
through long pipes in ordered sequence like
bell-ringers.

A bellows has three vital parts: an air-
chamber which can be expanded and compressed alternately; a large air-intake hole
which is open in the expansion stroke and
closed by a valve in the compression; and a
nozzle to carry the forced air in the direction
you want.

John Jones mostly uses ¾in elm for the
two compression board-cum-handles, but
you could also use oak, ash and yew if you
are careful to avoid splitting when you drive
the numerous upholstery nails into the

edges. The upper board in the picture
carries the air-intake hole, and a drilled
block in which a brass nozzle is to be fitted.
The other board is of matching shape, but
cut short to butt against the nozzle block; he
makes this block from the piece cut off the
second board. Shape of these boards is not
critical, provided there is a smoothly
curved periphery around which the leather
forming the air-chamber can be stretched
and nailed. The second shorter board is
'hinged' to the block with a piece of leather
nailed to each.

John Jones uses 1.5mm cowhide,
smooth, supple and strong, costing around
£3 per square foot. Like wood, leather has a
'grain' which makes it more flexible in one
direction than at 90° to that direction. But
unlike wood, you can't see the grain; you
have to finger it and find how it flexes.

The air-chamber leather, the long elliptical shape in the picture at right, must be cut
so the grain allows for flexing across the
major axis of the ellipse as the bellows
opens and shuts. You also need to get the
grain orientation right for the leather hinge

on the nozzle block. The length of the air-chamber leather is determined by the length of the board periphery, and the width by the distance the boards will separate at the handle end, plus an allowance for nailing and trimming. The other pieces of leather in the picture include strips for reinforcing the air-chamber leather along the board edges, to ensure an absolutely air-tight chamber.

Also in the leather picture is a square piece of ply which acts as the flap-valve; it is glued to a slightly larger rectangle of leather, the overlapping end of which is nailed to board on the handle side of the hole. The airstream to the nozzle hold the valve closed when you compress the air-chamber.

The quality bellows made by John Jones all have a pair of willow canes inside to act as springs, returning the bellows to the expanded shape after compression — you won't find these in cheap bellows. Because they hold the leather apart when not in use, they prevent the leather developing permanent creases. The canes are nailed temporarily in place until the leather is fastened.

The leather is soaked in water before fastening, so it shrinks as it dries out, and is held taut by the canes. John uses ½in-long domed upholstery nails (with ¾in or ½in heads) wherever the nails will be visible. When there's a double thickness of leather to nail through, he tacks down the lower leather with gimp pins.

To complete the bellows you'll need a metal nozzle, which prevents the wooden end being charred by fire embers. John's nozzles are turned from brass to his own design, pinned into place with a nail through nozzle-block and nozzle. You could design and turn your own, or settle for a piece of plain brass tube rounded off with

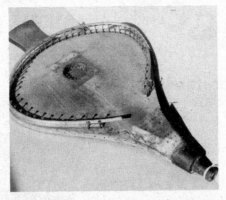

● **Above**, canes being formed on an old board. **Right**, mother-and-child carving on antique bellows. **Below**, John Jones at his workshop door – the origin of the name is a long story!

file and emery paper at one end. An internal hole diameter of ¼in is suitable for most sizes of bellows.

If you fancy making your own bellows, you'll have to work out some of the detailed procedures for yourself — just as John Jones did when he started. ■

● **Below**, John Jones in his workshop

● **Below**, all the leather you need for an average pair of bellows

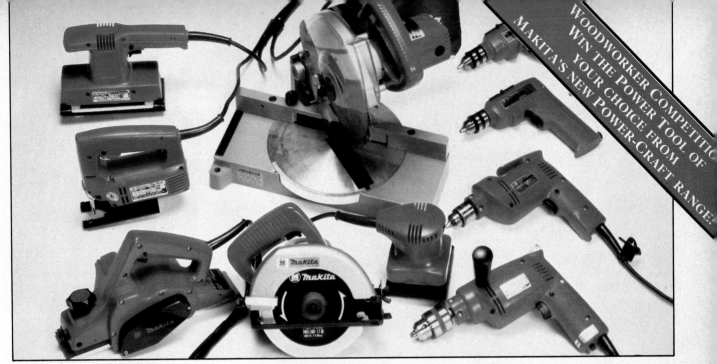

Enter this super competition from **Woodworker**, the UK's best woodwork journal, and **MAKITA**, the world's leading power-tool specialists. Ten readers can choose a power tool of their choice from Makita's new Power-Craft range.

Makita is well known as the brand leader in the UK industrial power tools market. Their tools are built to industrial specifications and have a reputation for power and reliability. They are also well ahead in cordless tools, as our June supplement, 'Mobile Power', showed. Now Makita have introduced a brand-new range of power tools — of the same industrial quality, but priced at an affordable level. The new range is called **Power-Craft,** and we're pleased to offer 10 of you the power tool of your choice from 12 models.

Each tool in the Power-Craft range is strong and sturdy, with ball-bearing construction and safety design features. Each is supplied with Makita's full service back-up and a ONE YEAR GUARANTEE — no more than one would expect from such a company.

Power-Craft is available from Makita stockists nationwide and comes complete with a full range of accessories. For your nearest Makita stockist contact Makita's Customer Service Department, 8 Finway, Dallow Road, Luton, Beds LU1 1TR, (0582) 455777.

You can choose any one from the following 12 Power-Craft models:

Drills

M802 13mm Variable Speed Hammer Drill This power-packed but lightweight (1.7kg) hammer drill, with a 430w motor, has a useful reverse action facility, and a capacity of 13mm in metal and concrete, 18mm in wood. RRP £72+VAT.

M602 10mm Rotary Drill This 305w drill is capable of drilling 10mm in steel or 15mm in wood. It weighs only 1.5kg. RRP £52 + VAT.

Saws

M432 Variable-Speed Jigsaw This powerful jigsaw (350w motor) offers a speed of 0-3300spm with 18mm stroke length. Cutting capacity up to 50mm in wood and 6mm in steel. Built-in blower for easy cutting lines; clear plastic shield for safety. RRP £77.39+VAT.

M511 160mm Circular Saw This tough saw has a no-load speed of 4000 rpm and is input-rated at 800 watts. 160mm TCT blade, hole diameter

15.8mm; maximum cutting capacity 55mm at 90° and 36mm at 45%. RRP £88.69+VAT.

M241 210mm Mitre Saw High performance 800w mitre saw with 210mm TCT blade operates safely and efficiently at 5000rpm. It is light (5.3kg) and totally portable. Electric brake trigger release and operator guard for safety. RRP £178+VAT.

Power Planer

M102 82mm Power Planer A well-balanced 580w durable machine with 1600rpm maximum cutting-speed. Planing depth 1mm and width 82mm. RRP £89.47+VAT.

Sanders

M902 ⅓ Sheet Finishing Sander Robust 160w finishing sander, with a no-load speed of 10,000opm. Lock-on trigger for continuous use, specially designed handle for comfortable one-handed operation. RRP £52+VAT.

M904 ¼ Sheet Palm Sander A highly manoeuvrable 160w tool with 12,000opm. Pad size 110x100mm. RRP £52+VAT.

Cordless

M001W 10mm Reversible Cordless Drill/Driver Overload protector to prevent motor burn-out. Built-in chuck key holder; reverse action. No-load speed of 600rpm in wood, metal or plastic to capacity of 10mm. RRP £65.04+VAT.

M003W 10mm Variable Speed Cordless Screwdriver/Drill Electric brake for precision screwdriving, overload protector; 0-600rpm drive in 10mm steel and wood. Integral spirit level for level drilling, built-in storage for screwdriver bit and chuck-key holder. Reverse action. RRP £75.56+VAT.

Both these cordless drills have an integral 7.2v 6-cell nickel cadmium battery, and are supplied complete with three-hour charger.

And two brand new models (not in the photo)

M992 76mm Belt Sander High performance 740w, well balanced, lightweight sander has a belt speed of 380m/min. Efficient dust-extraction system with dust bag. RRP £118+VAT.

M362 ⅜in Plunge Router Lightweight and portable with a no-load speed of 24,000rpm, 860w, 35mm plunge capacity. RRP £98+VAT.

HOW TO ENTER OUR POWER-CRAFT COMPETITION

To win the Power-Craft tool of your choice just answer our three questions below. Two are very easy (you don't have to look much further than this page for the answers!), while the third requires a spot of research in the rest of the magazine. Don't worry, the answer's there somewhere.

Just fill in the coupon below and send to WOODWORKER Power-Craft competition, WOODWORKER, 1 Golden Square, London W1R 3AB, by **Wednesday 30 September 1987.** The first 10 correct entries we draw out of the 'hat' will each win a Power-Craft model of their choice.

Questions

1 What is the maximum cutting speed of the Makita Power-Craft power planer M102?

2 Which Power-Craft model has a lock-on trigger for continuous operation?

3 Name one of the woodworking partnership who won the WOODWORKER Award for Products in Wood at the Direct Design Show in June.

RULES OF ENTRY

1 The competition is open to everyone over 18 years other than employees or relatives of employees of Makita Electric (UK) Ltd. and Argus Specialist Publications Ltd.

2 The entry form must be completed in ink and sent to WOODWORKER, 1 Golden Square, London W1, by Wednesday 30th September 1987.

3 Prizewinners will be notified separately by post. (A list of winning entries will be published in the December issue of WOODWORKER.)

WOODWORKER/MAKITA Power-Craft Competition, September 1987

Answers

1 ....

2 ....

3 ....

Name ....

Address ....

....

Telephone No. ....

Please state here which Power-Craft model you would like ....

▲ Middlesex: *Triumphant arcs in laminated beech form Sam Chan's curvilinear chair, all radii similar so only one former needed*

Fresh ideas, brilliant colours, careful workmanship, exciting innovation. Britain's furniture students delight us year after year with their verve and skill. We can only show a small selection here, but there'll be more next month . . .

Norwich: *Modern antique marquetry circular breakfast table by Simon Robinson, crossbanded in satinwood and rosewood*

Bright Young Things

▲Edinburgh: *Beam-me-up-Scottie coffee table by Jane Cameron, made from sprayed timber and glass with the yuppie alien in mind*

continued
773

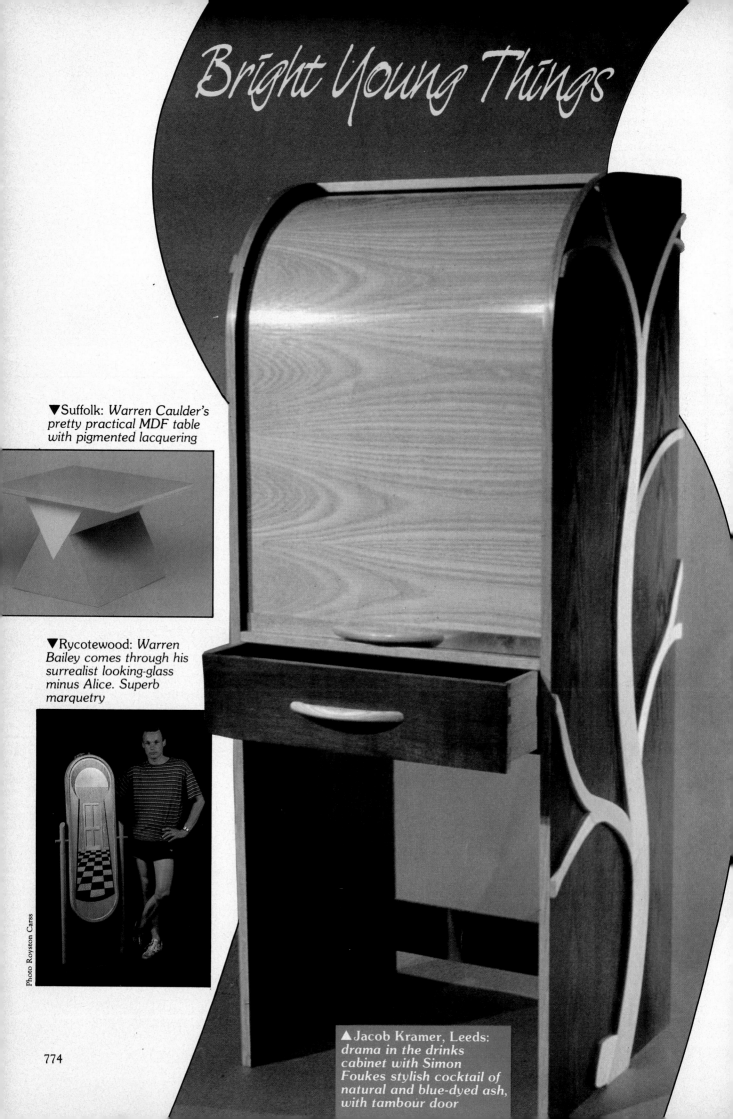

Bright Young Things

▼Suffolk: *Warren Caulder's pretty practical MDF table with pigmented lacquering*

▼Rycotewood: *Warren Bailey comes through his surrealist looking-glass minus Alice. Superb marquetry*

Photo Royston Carss

▲Jacob Kramer, Leeds: *drama in the drinks cabinet with Simon Foukes stylish cocktail of natural and blue-dyed ash, with tambour door*

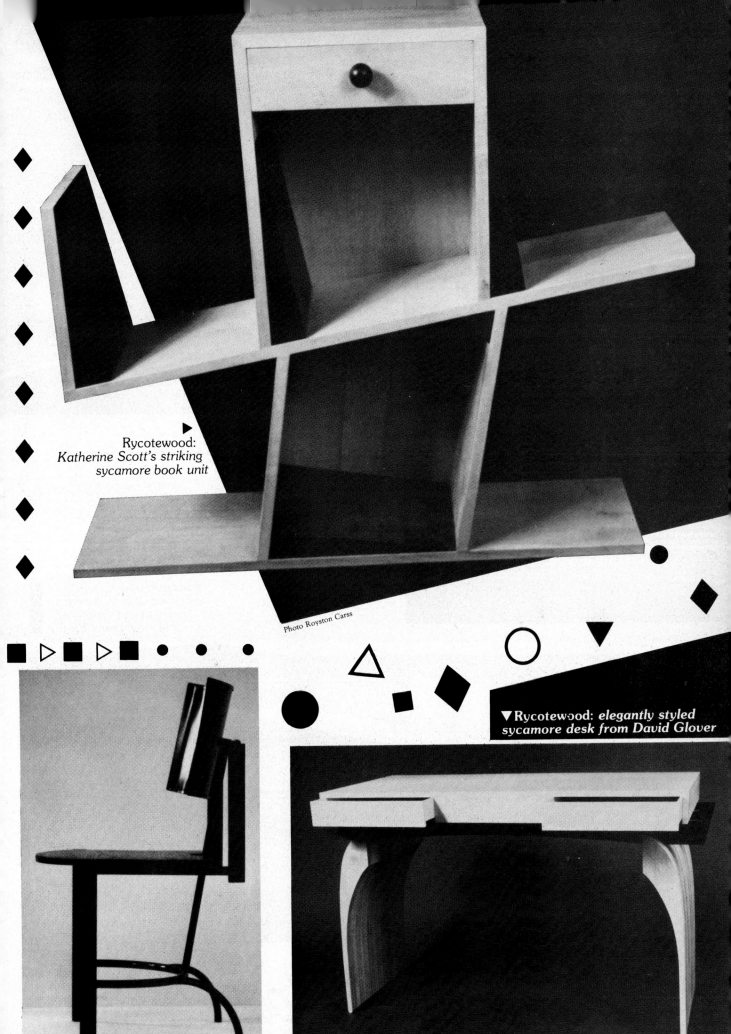

▶Rycotewood:
*Katherine Scott's striking
sycamore book unit*

Photo Royston Carss

▼Rycotewood: *elegantly styled
sycamore desk from David Glover*

▲Middlesex: *Friedbert Meinert's marriage
of high-tech and trad in black ash*

Photo Royston Car

continue

▲Suffolk: *catering for the artist's palette, Austin Neves' fun furniture 'pencil desk' in ash*

◀Rycotewood: *high art is back with Brian Fowler's stunning chair*

Photo Royston Carss

▼Rycotewood: *Carl Allen's executive desk in American cherry would satisfy even the most select Filofax*

Photo Royston Carss

Bright Young Things

▼Norwich: *Ian Newson's classic antique mahogany cabinet, with satinwood crossbanding*

▼Edinburgh: *Sally Rotarides' bold dressing table in sycamore with stainless steel mesh trim*

◄Rycotewood: *James Harrington's dining chairs strike up a witty conversation*

Don't need no doctor

Be your own physician;
Bob Wearing prescribes
treatment for ailing saws
in this step-by-step guide to
sharp teeth with long life

S aws which need sharpening generally
fall into one of four categories: the
new saw that has not previously been
resharpened; the well-maintained saw; the
poorly-sharpened saw; and the saw with
broken teeth.

Each of these needs its own special treatment, though some processes are common
to all. Most steps will be covered by considering a saw which has previously been
poorly sharpened.

There are two main families of saw, the
ripping saws and the crosscutting saws. The
former consists of the ripsaw, the half
ripsaw, the dovetail saw, bowsaw, padsaw,
coping saw and, as described later, the
rip/tenon saw. Crosscuts include the handsaw, panel saw and tenon saw.

The ripsaw family is filed across at right
angles to give teeth like small chisels (fig. 1).
You can see the cutting action if you use a
⅛in chisel to simulate one tooth: along the
grain you can cut a clean groove rapidly and
easily; working across the grain produces a
poor groove with very splintered sides.

The crosscuts are filed at an angle, giving
teeth like little knives (fig. 2). To simulate
this action, two heavy knife lines must be
made across the grain and the waste chipped

out with something smaller and less
efficient than the ⅛in chisel.

The practical effect is that the ripsaw cuts
easily, quickly and cleanly along the grain
but makes a rough job with rather hard
work across the grain. On the other hand,
the crosscut cuts quickly, smoothly and
easily across the grain but while it will
produce a clean cut along the grain it is
slower and harder work.

Saw vice

You need a saw vice before you can start
work on a saw. As this costs £25 or more
and will be used infrequently by the
amateur and small business craftsman, I
suggest you make the model illustrated in
fig.3, or something like it, and spend the
money on some other item which you can't
make yourself.

The vice consists basically of two hinged
plywood jaws with spacing strips top and
bottom to accept the thickness of a saw
handle. The jaws can be about 10in long (or
the length of the bench vice jaws) with two
rounded strips on the outside to take the
pressure of the bench vice. The inside
capacity of the saw vice should be such that
your widest handsaw will fit in. You may
prefer to make a smaller vice simply for
tenon saws. Line the jaws with leather or
rubber (pieces from an old car inner tube
are quite suitable) to reduce the unpleasant
noise often associated with saw sharpening.
You may need to cut away one end of the
saw vice jaws to accept the handles of small
saws. You could fit an opening spring (fig.
4) made from piano wire.

continued

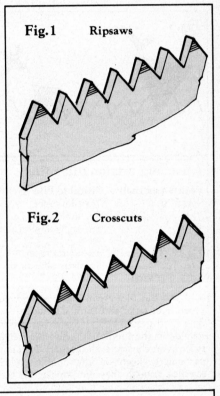

Fig.1   Ripsaws

Fig.2   Crosscuts

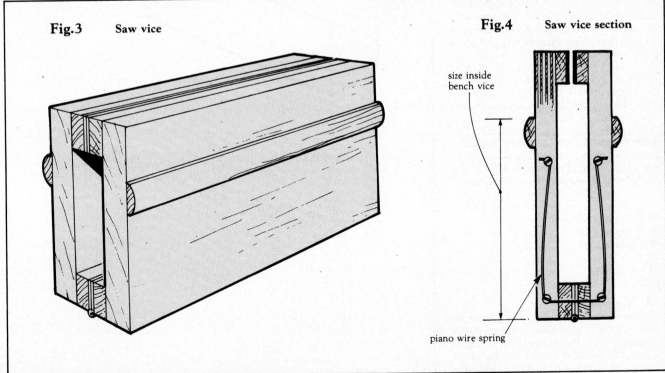

Fig.3   Saw vice

Fig.4   Saw vice section

size inside
bench vice

piano wire spring

Don't need no doctor

Files

The first file you need is a 10in second cut mill file. This shouldn't be used for rough work; keep it carefully stored in a plastic sleeve or cloth (you can also use it to sharpen scrapers and scraper plane blades).

Choose the triangular files with care, for their life, when used on the best saws, is not very long. It's important that the working face of the file should be slightly over twice the saw tooth depth (fig. 5), otherwise a

Fig.5

Choosing a triangular file

Points per inch	Suitable File
4½, 5, 6,	7in slim taper
7, 8,	6in slim taper
9, 10,	5in or 5½in slim taper
11, 12, 13, 14, 15,	4½in slim taper
over 16,	4in extra slim taper
extra fine saws	needle file

4, 5 and 6in files are available as regular taper, slim taper and extra slim taper.

strip down the middle of the file will receive twice as much wear as the corners. I am not particularly keen on the double ended sawfiles, though they are popular for the larger saws. The table may help you select the right file for the job. Points per inch are counted inclusively (fig. 6). Too large a file creates too rounded a gullet. Roll sawfiles in a cloth; don't leave them rattling about in a box damaging themselves.

If you've got poor eyesight, are working under poor lighting conditions or liable to be interrupted, I recommend engineer's blue marking fluid (people used to run the saw through a smokey candle flame to blacken the teeth to show which teeth had been filed). Those old reading spectacles come in handy for fine saws, worn on the top of the others; they magnify well but you do have to come rather close. Commercial clip-on magnifiers are available at a price.

A saw which has been poorly sharpened in the past requires four operations:
● Topping (sometimes called jointing)
● Shaping
● Setting
● Sharpening

1 Topping

The teeth may be of different heights or the edge may have been sharpened hollow (or round) or both. Fix the saw in the vice, hold a mill file (without its handle) along the blade and square to it, then run it along the

length of the saw. Avoid rocking the file since this will round over the teeth. You can prevent this hazard by holding the file in a grooved block (fig. 7); for this the saw must be raised well above the vice jaws.

Topping produces a 'shiner' on the top of each tooth (fig. 8); make sure that each tooth has one (a wipe of the blue marking fluid is helpful here). When the height of the teeth varies a lot, you could top the saw relatively lightly, missing the low teeth, to avoid cutting away too much of the saw.

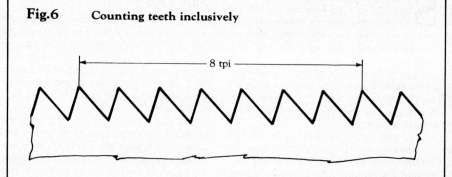

Fig.6   **Counting teeth inclusively**

8 tpi

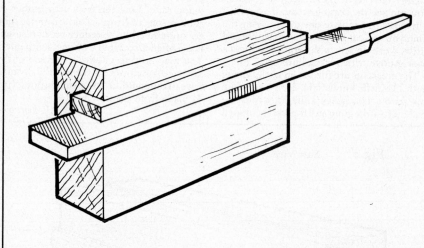

Fig.7   **File in grooved block to avoid rocking**

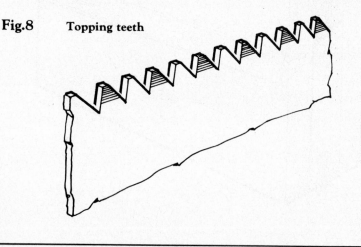

Fig.8   **Topping teeth**

2 Shaping

Select an appropriate triangular file, and hold it horizontally at right angles to the saw, and twisted to an angle of 14° to the vertical for crosscut saws and 3° for ripsaws (fig. 9). Some people prefer less than 14° but the angle should be substantial. These are the theoretical angles and your saw may have been cut slightly differently; you can see the angle from the unused teeth by the handle and you could slowly alter the angle over a number of sharpenings.

File half of a shiner with the file in one gullet, then the remainder with the file in the next. Once these shiners are filed away, top again until every tooth gets a shiner; this method prevents the spacing being lost and ensures teeth of equal height. A useful aid is a part-used sawfile which has had the teeth ground off one side (fig. 10): this permits a bad tooth to be filed without danger to a good one.

It's not particularly difficult to keep the 90° angle constant but you may find the angle of 3° or 14° difficult: the wrist gets quickly tired by rigidly holding that angle and of course if work is interrupted it is difficult to exactly pick up the angle again.

There are three devices which may help. The first is a commercial British saw filer which appears attractive and works well, but requires special tangless files which are not commonly stocked; also the file is large, thus making work on fine tenon saws impossible. I prefer a simple American tool which adjusts to any angle and accepts any standard file; this takes out all the risk, ache and concentration, and seems to me to be the perfect answer for the occasional, non-professional sharpener.

You could make the third aid yourself (fig. 11). Turn or whittle a decent handle and fit it with a tight metal ferrule. Make a second ferrule to fit over this and rotate it. Solder a threaded nut or block to this outer ferrule and continue the thread through. A 4in rod with a screwdriver slot screws into this and clamps on the inner ferrule. To use, settle the file firmly in a good gullet, swing the rod horizontal or vertical according to preference and lock there. You'll find it's much easier to maintain the angle using this rod as a guide or sight.

Shaping is complete when all the teeth have lost their shiners and the gullets are all the same depth.

3 Setting

Teeth are bent to alternate sides, so the saw doesn't bind in the kerf; the method goes back to the Romans. Setting should be arranged so that the kerf will be no more

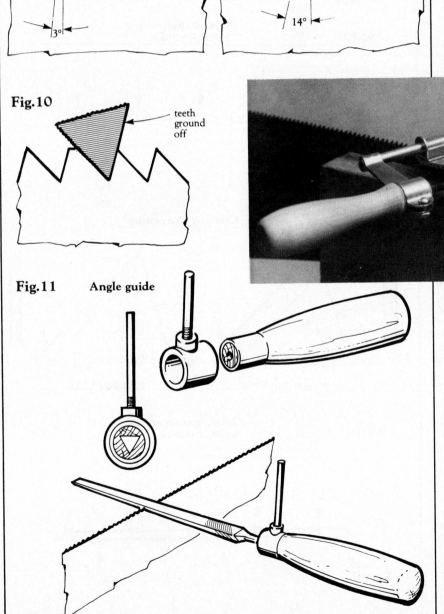

• American saw filer

than 1½ times the sawblade thickness. Softwoods require greater set than hardwoods and wet wood more still. Taper-ground handsaws require very little set. It is vital that each tooth be given exactly the same set; if not the saw will want to run out of line, a fault often incorrectly attributed to teeth not holding their edge. Only the top half of a tooth should be set. Never attempt to reset teeth to the opposite side: this will cause cracking and loss of teeth, as will trying to bend over the whole tooth. The most common fault in home maintained saws is oversetting.

For most of us the professional way of setting using a fine crosspein hammer on a special anvil is just not on: the skill takes too long to acquire. The pliers-type sawset offers the best service to the amateur. Several patterns are on the market but examine them carefully before buying. One make will cope with only below 12 teeth per inch; another can be dismantled and filed to do smaller work. The Stanley 42SS, made

Fig.9   Shaping teeth

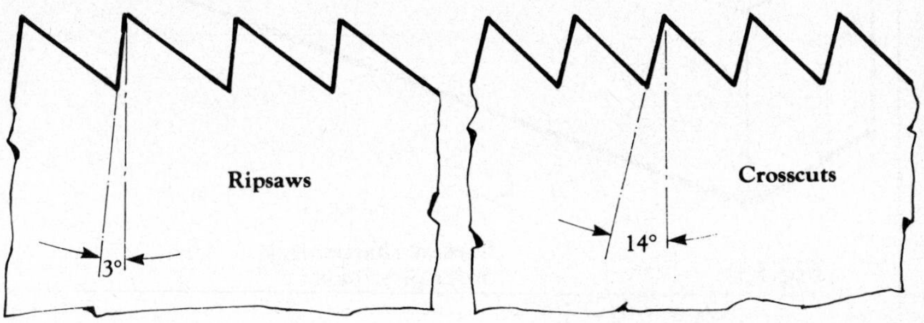

Ripsaws

3°

Crosscuts

14°

Fig.10

teeth ground off

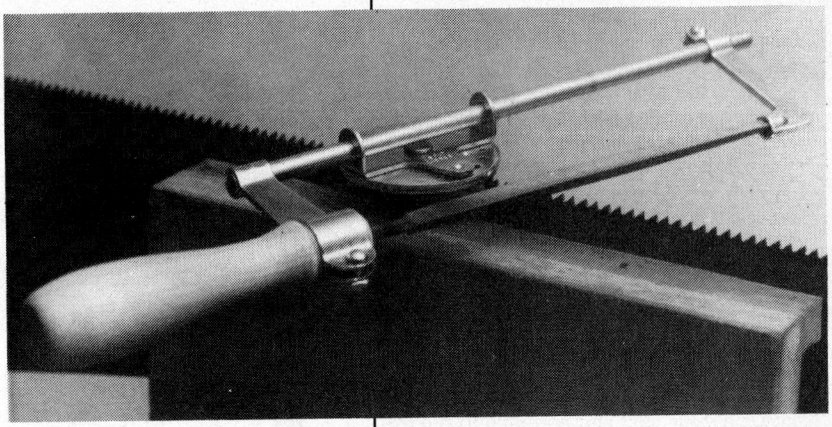

Fig.11   Angle guide

Don't need no doctor

in the USA, sets between 4 and 16 tpi and is one of the best currently available. The Disston No. 28 does 4 to 10 tpi while the No. 280 sets 10 to 16 tpi.

If you can't buy a suitable sawset or want to set even finer teeth I recommend the following method (fig. 12). Carefully plane a short length of 2in thick hardwood on one endgrain, and grip it in the vice. Secure the saw to it with two woodscrews and large washers. The set is put on alternate teeth using a fine punch, preferably brass, giving two or three light blows with a small hammer. The saw is turned over and the process repeated.

After setting, place the saw flat on the bench and lightly run an oilstone along the teeth; turn over and repeat. This corrects the odd tooth which may be too prominent, thus preventing a jump when sawing.

4 Sharpening

Different methods are used for sharpening saws of the ripsaw and crosscut families.

Ripsaws are sharpened at 90°, in the same manner the teeth were reshaped. Fix the saw in the vice with the handle to the right. Top the saw again, very lightly putting a very small shiner on each tooth. Now blue the teeth if you like that idea. File at right angles to the saw and horizontal, starting on the front edge of the first tooth set towards you and continue on alternate teeth (fig. 13). Two or three steady push strokes should be enough to take off half of the shiner. You'll see it's the front edge of the tooth towards you that gets the filing; this puts any 'rag' or roughness on the tooth to the inside, where it has no effect and is lost in work. The blueing helps, particularly with small saws, to make sure that you don't get out of step and file two adjacent teeth. At the end, reverse the saw and sawvice also if preferred (handle now on your left) and continue to file the front edge of the tooth set towards you. Using a saw filing tool the angle of 3° will be reversed for this second side. You won't save time by filing every tooth at 90° from the same side: it makes the saw run to one side.

Crosscut saws are sharpened at an angle, not at 90°, giving bevelled teeth producing knife-like edges. A long, thin bevel on a tooth (fig. 14a) cuts well for a time, particularly on dry hardwoods, but quickly wears, so a shorter bevel (fig. 14b) is more suitable for general use.

Again fix the saw in the vice, projecting about ¼in (or the minimum required for a filing aid) with the handle at the right and lightly top all the teeth. Blue them at this stage. Begin filing on the front edge of the first tooth set towards you (fig. 15), with a filing aid set to the crosscut position, if you use one. Working freehand, the file handle is moved to the left to make an angle of 65° to 75° depending on preference and the type of timber expected to be worked: softwoods take a thinner bevel, hardwoods a stouter one. Maintain this angle, filing alternate teeth and removing half of the shiner. It may be found helpful to mark this

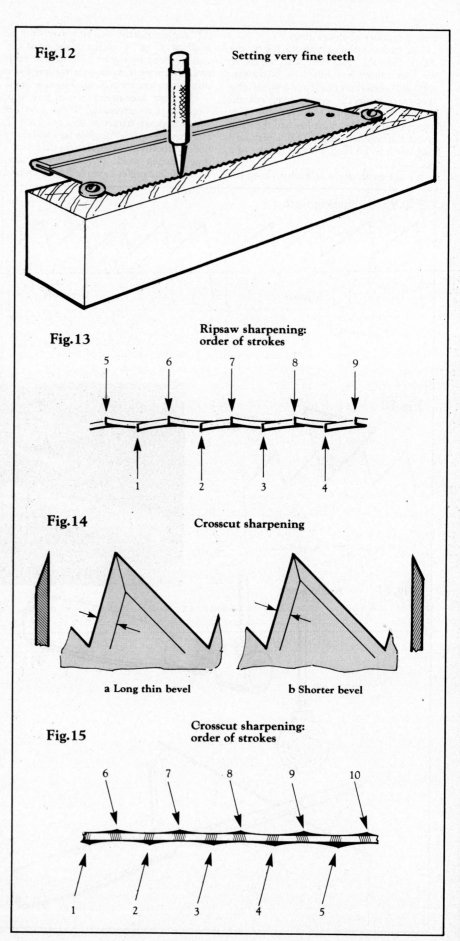

Fig.12 Setting very fine teeth

Fig.13 Ripsaw sharpening: order of strokes

Fig.14 Crosscut sharpening

a Long thin bevel   b Shorter bevel

Fig.15 Crosscut sharpening: order of strokes

angle in pencil on the top of the saw-vice jaws. On reaching the end, reverse the saw (handle to left), reverse the angle of the filing aid and repeat, removing the remaining half of the shiner, keeping the file horizontal at all times.

Angles

If you're experienced, then angles become a matter of personal preference. The angles I have stated are about 14° front angle for a crosscut saw and about 3° for a rip. These are the angles which Spear & Jackson say they put on their saws; their tenon saw, being a crosscut, is given 16°. Disstons claim to put on 15° for a crosscut saw and 8° for a ripsaw. When the angle to the front of the tooth is appreciably more than recommended it is described as having too much 'hook' or pitch and may 'hang up' or jolt suddenly in the cut which could cause a kink in the blade.

When filing aids reach the end of the saw, guidance is lost yet still a few teeth need to be filed. I've found it helpful to fit in the vice a thin piece of metal at about tooth height to continue to give guidance (fig. 16). Two small holes through the vice jaws and the metal, fitted with thin pins, hold this in place.

Fine dovetail saws have such small teeth that if filed front and back at say 70°, there would be no tooth left. So you should sharpen them with a needle file at 90° as a ripsaw. As most of their work is with the grain this is no disadvantage.

Rip tenon saws

For sawing through a 2½in board you'd use a ripsaw of probably 4½tpi, the saw built for the job. For sawing the cheeks of a 2½in wide tenon, most people use a tenon saw of 15tpi whose teeth have been specifically filed for crosscutting. It really doesn't make sense to me, so I recommend making a rip tenon saw.

Obtain a second tenon saw with sufficient depth of blade left to cope with the average tenon. You'll also need an old power hacksaw blade of 10tpi or so. With the mill file, file off the teeth from the tenon blade. Cramp the hacksaw blade and your tenon saw together in the saw vice and, using the hacksaw blade as a guide, file the new teeth until the hacksaw blade stops further filing; this is a bit rough on the file

● *Cutting rip teeth in tenon saw*

but it only happens once. Having got the teeth well marked proceed exactly as for topping and shaping; then set and sharpen. This saw will cut tenons more accurately and rapidly than the standard crosscut tenon saw, for the longer the saw runs in the kerf the easier it is to get off line.

Broken teeth

When one or more teeth are completely missing you face quite a lengthy job. Top the saw strongly giving quite large shiners. Then shape, bringing the teeth to points. Give a touch to the gullets on each side of the broken tooth so that they remain the same depth as the others. Continue topping and shaping for a number of times until the new teeth emerge and are the same height as the others. The standard routine is then followed.

New saws

Well maintained and new saws require the minimum of topping, just sufficient to reveal that no tooth has been damaged by perhaps being caught on some metal. If all is well the shaping process may be omitted for a few treatments and the sharpening proceeded with right away. Few people appreciate how little set is required, so frequently two or three light sharpenings can be carried out without resetting. A little and often can be regarded as a sound maxim for saw care.

Maintenance

A sharp saw should be well protected when not in use. Either hang it up or use a teeth guard as in fig. 17, held in place with two strong rubber bands. Most damage occurs to saws left lying in the well of the bench where they meet cramps, hammers and other metal agents.

The blade should be kept very lightly oiled. A carpet oil pad (a rectangle of carpet glued to a wooden block) is the most convenient way to do this. This used to be the common practice but now you can use an aerosol silicon spray which is equally successful on plane soles and the tables of sawbenches and planers.

The requirements for good saw sharpening are:
● Sharp files
● A firm vice
● Good lighting
● Good eyesight (or good spectacles)
● Plenty of time
● And don't talk or if possible, don't allow interruptions

Go on — have a go. At the very worst only the teeth are spoilt, not the saw. ∎

● The saw filer illustrated can be obtained from Bob Wearing at 3 Chapel St, Wem, Shropshire SY4 5ER; it accepts any standard files, including needle files, and costs £10.50, including file and postage in the UK and Ireland.

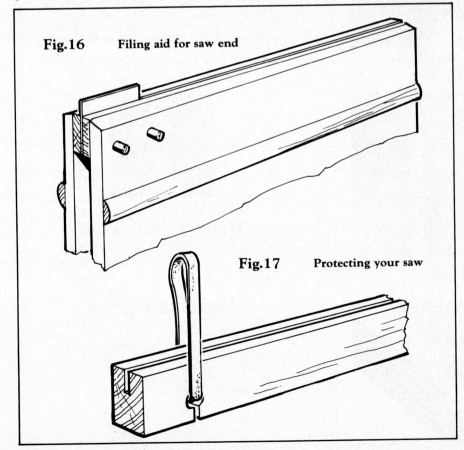

Fig. 16 **Filing aid for saw end**

Fig. 17 **Protecting your saw**

NEXT MONTH

he October 1987 issue of Britain's oldest and biggest-selling woodwork journal is an important one indeed. Accustomed as you are to being informed, entertained, inspired — and challenged — by what we serve up every month, next month you'll really be riveted. Not just by the fantastic **FREE GIFT** we've arranged for you — no less than a **3mm centre-point wood-boring drill bit**, precision ground for accurate centring and split-free cutting; not even by the unbeatable **READER OFFER** we've got in conjunction with the makers of your gift, who are giving you the chance to get a full metric or imperial set of these excellent drills at a silly price.

You won't just be riveted by the superb presentation of a selection of major **American Woodworkers'** work, such as Garry Knox Bennett's pugnacious 'Nail cabinet', shown here; not even, perhaps, by more comprehensive pictorial coverage of **College Degree Shows**. Nor will our usual selection of **designs for all skill levels** — build a teak desk or a Gothic chest, among others — be the only things that hold your gaze.

What we're giving you next month, apart from all these and more delicious items, is a WOODWORKER with a new look. Featuring as we do the very best in design and making from all spheres of this wonderful craft, we decided it was about time we gave the magazine a new graphic style to support and reflect that breadth and quality. We've been working out how to make WOODWORKER easier to read and use, how to make it more flexible, how to use colour pictures better; how to improve, in other words, what we hope and believe is already a first-quality product. And we hope you'll agree that October's WOODWORKER looks better than ever, and gives you better value than ever. We say it every month, because every month it's true; but next month — a very special issue — is really the one you just **cannot afford to miss**. Be sure!

● **Above,** Garry Knox Bennett caused a furore amongst American woodworkers when he made this superb cabinet, then banged a 4in nail into it – as much to say 'Don't get trapped in tour-de-force craftsmanship and lose vitality and ideas'; **left,** get a free sample of these excellent BBW centre-point drills, then buy a set at a tempting price

---

ON SALE 18 SEPTEMBER

Guild notes

The Guild was set up by *Woodworker* to create a meeting ground for all those involved in working wood, whether professional, amateur, or enthusiastic beginner. Guild members get:

● Access to Guild courses and events
● Free publicity in *Woodworker*
● Specially arranged tool insurance at low rates
● 15% off Woodworker Show entry
● A free display area and meeting point at the Show
● 15% discount off *Woodworker* plans
● Inclusion in our register of members' skills and services

For details, please send an sae to the Guild of Woodworkers, 1 Golden Sq, London W1R 3AB.

Decorative techniques — Ian Hosker

12-13 September, 10-5, Chester, £55.
Another chance to learn all sorts of wonderful decorative techniques, including dragging, lining, sponging, rag-rolling, marbling, spattering and tortoiseshelling. The fee includes materials, but bring a few paintbrushes and jam-jars.

Rudiments of restoration — Barry Honeyborne

17-18 September, Leominster, Herefordshire, £54.
Bring along your antique and learn how to restore it. From initial cleaning to repairs and final polishing, Barry will show you all the steps — he has been 25 years in the trade. This two day course is an introduction to every aspect of restoration, plus a chance to make a start on your own piece under expert supervision.

French polishing — Charles Cliffe

17-18 September, Bexleyheath, £45.
These courses by expert Charles Cliffe are among the most popular run by the Guild, so book early to avoid disappointment. You'll learn about preparation, staining and techniques of french polishing itself, with ample hands-on experience under Charles' eye. You'll learn the correct way to sharpen a cabinet scraper, so bring yours along, and he's willing to offer advice on any small piece of furniture you want to refinish.

French polishing — Ian Hosker

14-15 November, Chester, £50.
One of our most popular course subjects, led by Ian, a teacher and a practising professional. It covers preparation of old and new pieces, staining and colouring techniques, grain filling, shellac finishes, fadding, bodying in, spiriting off and giving new life to existing polished surfaces. The fee includes course materials. Ian will make up a polishing kit to take away at £9.50 if you order in advance.

Basic woodcarving — Eric Ingham

19-20 September, 9.30-5.30, Lytham St Annes, £50.
We're pleased to be able to offer this introduction to woodcarving. On this course you'll learn about use of tools and sharpening, types of wood, design and finishing. Eric's been carving for 15 years and will give you a good start. Wood is provided and you're free to carve whatever you want. Bring carving tools if you have them. There's plenty of accommodation in this resort area and your spouse might enjoy the sea air while you learn.

Design and workshop drawing — Bob Grant

26 September, 9.30-5, Oxford, £25 VAT
If putting your design on paper doesn't come easy, here's the course to learn how. Bob will help you gain confidence in free-hand sketching, show you how to use grid paper and drawing boards, and lots more.

Hand veneering — Bob Grant

10 October, 9.30-5, Oxford, £35 + VAT
Veneering is much more than the art of disguising chipboard. It's a skill with a long history, and can create some beautiful effects — and it saves fine and expensive wood! You'll be laying a panel with veneer, mitring a cross-banding, inlaying lines round it, and applying a balancer veneer on the back. If you have a veneer hammer, bring it; but materials will be provided.

Routing — Roy Sutton

14 November, 10-5, Herne Bay, Kent, £25+VAT.
Another chance to learn the full potential of this versatile tool. Roy's courses are very popular, so book early. Starting from first principles, he covers housing, grooving, rebating, straight and circular moulding, tenoning, mortising, and rule joint and template work; he also deals with designing and setting up your own jigs.

GUILD COURSES

● Only Guild members are eligible to go on these courses. You must book in advance, and we must have a cheque for the full cost of the course at the time of booking. If you cancel less than four weeks before the advertised date you will forfeit 50% of the cost, unless there are exceptional circumstances.

Busy branch

More than 30 Guild members from the West Midlands area enjoyed a practical demonstration of routing techniques and cutters by Trend Machinery and Cutting Tools Ltd in June. The demonstration was given by John Tigg and Dave Ivory, who work for Trend. Bill Ferguson reports it was an easy to follow practical session, with a busy question-time. He was interested to see what great strides had been made in dust extractors for routers, one of the traditionally 'dirty' machines.

If you live in the area and haven't yet made contact, write to Bill Ferguson at 40 Quinton Lane, Quinton, Birmingham B32 2TS.

BOOKING FORM

I wish to book for the following course(s).

☐ **Decorative techniques** 12-13 September, £55; make cheque payable to Ian Hosker

☐ **Rudiments of restoration** 17-18 September, £54; make cheque payable to Barry Honeyborne

☐ **French polishing** 17-18 September, £45; make cheque payable to Charles Cliffe

☐ **Basic woodcarving** 19-20 September, £50; make cheque payable to Eric Ingham

☐ **Design and workshop drawing** 26 September, £25+VAT = £28.75

☐ **Hand veneering** 10 October. £35+ VAT = £40.25

☐ **Routing** 14 November £25+VAT = £28.75

☐ **French polishing** 14-15 November, £50; make cheque payable to Ian Hosker

Please make cheques payable to 'The Guild of Woodworkers/ASP Ltd' unless otherwise stated.

Name...

Address..

....

....

Guild no..
Send to: The Guild of Woodworkers, 1 Golden Square, London, W1R 3AB. The Guild reserves the right to cancel any course.

Hands on

WOODWORKING WHEEZE
of the
month

Joint Sandvik winner

Clothes peg edging clamp

When you're short of edging clamps, try combining a cheap G-clamp and open sprung clothes pegs to apply pressure.
David Hodge, Leytonstone

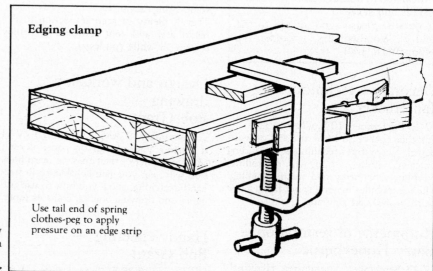

Edging clamp

Use tail end of spring clothes-peg to apply pressure on an edge strip

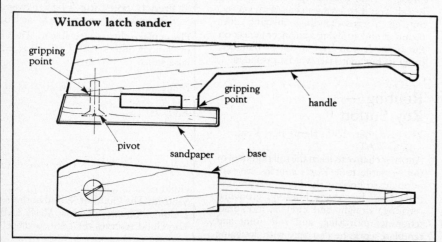

Window latch sander

gripping point

gripping point

handle

pivot

sandpaper

base

Joint Sandvik winner

A latch is a key

I discovered an old unwanted window latch consisting of two pivoting sections, tightened together with a screw. I loosened the screw, inserted a piece of sandpaper under the flat base and tucked the ends at two natural gripping points before tightening the screw. I had a handy little device for sanding small or thin areas, with square edges useful for rebates and tenons. I call it my handysander and use it a great deal.
Bob Shenton, aged 16, Little Haywood

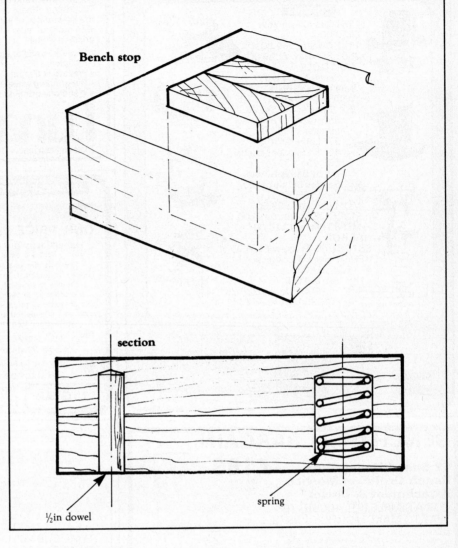

Bench stop

This wooden bench stop has no parts that can be lost and is easily adjusted. Cut two pieces of beech about 5in long which together are a push fit in the bench-stop hole. Mark both for blind holes 1in from the end and large enough diameter to take a strong compression spring; I used an old valve spring about ¾in diameter. The hole should be deep enough so the spring can be completely compressed when the two pieces are squeezed together in the vice.

Try the assembly in the bench-stop hole; it should be a good fit, requiring a light mallet blow to remove it. Then put the assembly in the vice and bore a ½in hole ½in from the bottom end for a dowel which prevents relative movement.

Use the stop with the join in the direction of the plane stroke.

Glyn Condick, Birmingham

Bowl-turning chuck

File one side off the heads of three or four countersunk set-screws (preferably 8mm or more diameter) and drill faceplate holes the same size, using concentric holes. File flats on the other ends of the set-screws.

Turn a recess in the wood blank and undercut to suit the taper on the screw-head. Mount the blank over the filed screwheads, then turn the screw via the flats to engage on the taper, finally locking into position with nuts. Aim for a tight fit on the wood taper and take the usual safety precautions with the rotating screws behind the faceplate.

E. Wilkinson, Sheffield

Extraction cheap and cheerful

I converted an old upright domestic vacuum cleaner to provide an effective extraction unit for a small workshop. It's the kind to which you can attach a suction tube, which in this case goes to the machine you're extracting. I took off the handle and cut away about half the dust collection bag, retaining the rest to act as a filter. I made an outlet tube from a 2.5 litre paint tin with the bottom cut away — leaving aboue ¼in round the circumference to stop it collapsing. The cut end of the dust collection bag is glued and taped round the top rim of the tin, and it now acts as a filter; for a collection bag I use plastic dustbin liners, secured to the tin with an elastic luggage strap. The attachment hose fits to the connector on my Eumenia radial-arm saw, and the motor/fan unit is fixed to the wall with strip metal tags and self-tapping screws into the body of the cleaner. The head of the cleaner is upwards, the old dustbag that now acts as a filter bag below that, then the paint tin tube, then the collection bag.

John Hardaker, Stockport

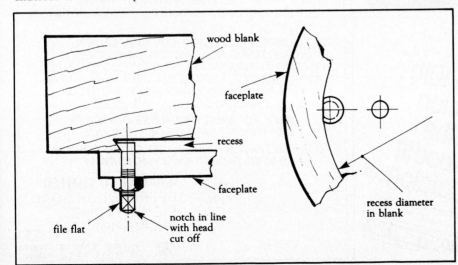

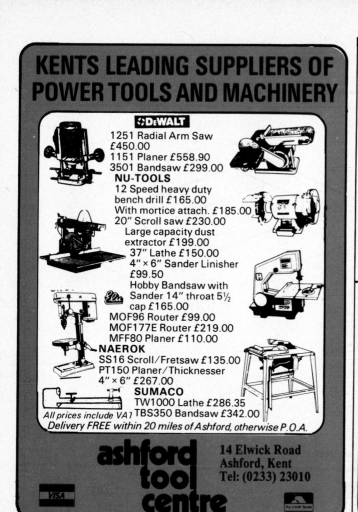

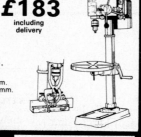
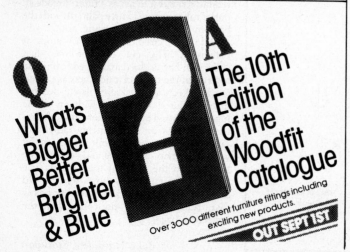

Mallets

More mallets for you to make, shape and knock on the head

Light carver's mallet

These mallets (fig. 1) are very popular amongst cabinetmakers, particularly for fine dovetailing. They are manufactured from boxwood and beech, but fruitwoods are equally acceptable. Assess the wood you've got to hand for suitability. Turned mallets are made with the grain running horizontally or vertically; it doesn't seem to matter either way. Probably most common is with the grain running at right angles to the handle.

Drill the handle hole then saw the block roughly circular. The head can be turned as a tight fit on the partly turned handle, or better still, on a separate, very slightly tapered mandrel. These mallets are often embellished with a couple of incised rings on the top, and similar, or burnt-in, rings on the handle. Open the hole to a slight ellipse and wedge.

Heavier carver's mallet

Here the method is the same but the dimensions are increased and the handle thickened (fig. 2). The heavier models are generally made to a more bulbous shape as shown; 6in diameter is fairly large by woodworking standards, but masonry and sculpting mallets are even bigger.

Endgrain mallet

The continuous endgrain is achieved by laminating. You could use tiny offcuts, but to avoid tedious planing of such small pieces it's better to cut from previously thicknessed stock. Three layers of 1in stock will do the job. Make ply or cardboard triangle templates with a 60° angle and an arc opposite that angle, using a radius of 2¾in (fig. 3). Position the templates on the wood so the grain runs from the angle to the arc. You'll need 18 sectors to make three layers.

Gently skim the jointing faces and glue together six pairs. Push them together by hand into a 120° jig (fig.4) with a piece of waxed paper or polythene under them; after a couple of minutes, slide them gently out and put aside to dry. The next day you can add a third piece (fig. 5). When the jointing faces are dry, skim them with a sharp plane and join the six sectors together.

After the surfaces have been skimmed, the three layers can be glued together, well cramped. The joints should be staggered like brickwork. From then on the method is as already described. I find a very sharp high-speed steel scraper is best for finishing all the endgrain.

Whatever sort of mallet you make, it will need a finish — I prefer to use several coats of linseed oil, with a maintenance coat at Christmas and birthday, but you could use polyurethane or shellac.

Remember that the only proper uses for mallets are striking gouges and chisels (except those with iron rings on) and driving dowels through dowel plates. Mallets shouldn't be used for knocking up joints; the striking-area of a mallet may be 12sq in, that of a hammer, 1sq in, so the hammer, used with a wood block, will strike with much greater precision. ∎

● Note that all the models described must have the sharp edges rounded over, chamfered, to prevent splitting out.

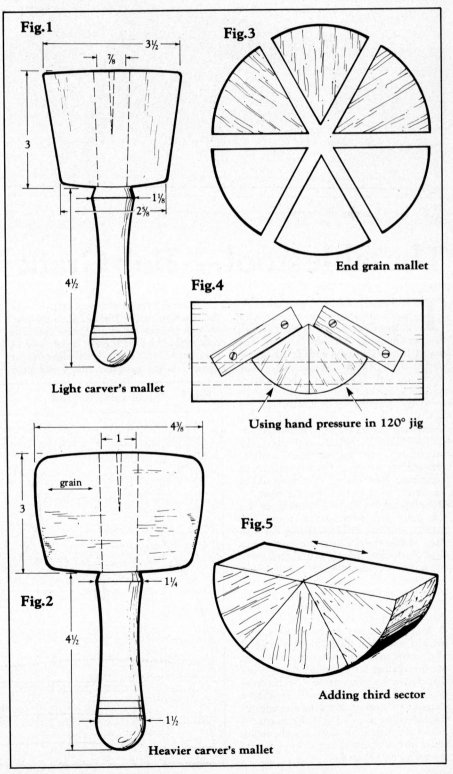

Fig.1

3½

⅞

3

1⅛

2⅝

4½

Light carver's mallet

Fig.3

End grain mallet

Fig.4

Using hand pressure in 120° jig

Fig.2

4⅜

1

grain

3

1¼

4½

1½

Heavier carver's mallet

Fig.5

Adding third sector

Stool times table

Is it a stool or is it a table?
Here are two simple designs
to make and use either way

The table stool — Bob Grant

This handy occasional table is loosely based on a style popular from Tudor times onwards, and would look well in a traditionally furnished house. The design features splayed ends and a curved tie-rail fixed with wedges, and is ideally made in oak. Originally, the securing wedges at the end of the tie-rail could be removed, and the table dismantled, but now they are just for cosmetic effect. The tenons and wedges are glued in and the side rails are housed, screwed and glued on. The procedure for making the table is straightforward but there are a few points that need explaining. Note that no shaping should be cut until you've marked out the joints.

● **Splay angles** for the housings on the side rails and stretcher-rail tenons are marked out by setting a sliding bevel to $81\frac{1}{2}°$. Make the housings as a handed pair first, fit the legs into them and then mark the position of the stretcher rail shoulderline length by laying the rail on the assembled structure at 4in from the floor. The angled shoulder line can now be marked off on the stretcher rail.

● **Mortise, tenon and elbow** are all marked out when the rail is still straight. The curve can be marked out in pencil later, using a springy lath; it mustn't rise more than $\frac{3}{8}$in in the centre or the effect becomes exaggerated. The $\frac{1}{2}$in mortises need to be gauged and squared from the face edge of the legs; bear in mind that the mortise is driven through at an angle and the tenon slides through parallel to the floor, despite the ends being sloped.

Be careful when you're punching through the tenon to receive the wedge, as the protruding piece of tenon may break out. The holes should be set slightly under flush of the mortise outer face so the wedge can bear tightly; during assembly, the wedge only

needs to be pushed home, not driven, and held by glue.

● **Tops and bottoms of the legs** need to be bevelled away at assembly stage so the tops sit level and the foot ends sit square on the floor. A slight relieving curve should be

Fig. 1   **Shaping for end**

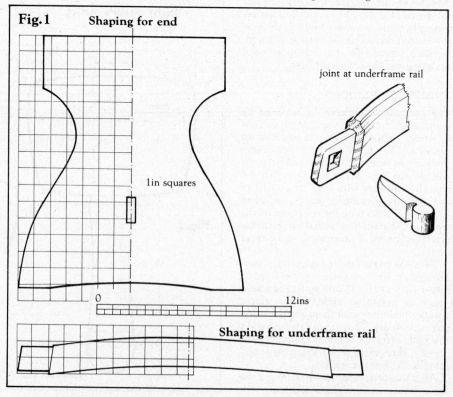

1in squares

0   12ins

joint at underframe rail

Shaping for underframe rail

worked across the bottoms to make the four feet.
- **Fixing screws** on the side rails can be hidden by pelleting the holes or, as the picture shows, by inlaying a lozenge-shaped piece which you get by chopping out the hole with a hollow chisel-mortiser.
- **Cavetto moulding** around the top and the stretcher rail was worked with a portable router fitted with a pilot-guided coving bit, but you could use a simple scratchstock.
- **The top** can be fixed with six slotted-steel table-plates or traditional wood buttons.
- **Any finish** sympathetic to the wood you've chosen can be used (oak used to be waxed or oiled and sometimes left without any finish applied at all).

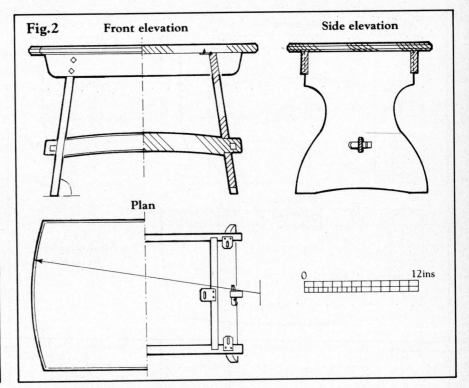

Fig.2 Front elevation   Side elevation

Plan

0   12ins

Cutting list

Finished sizes

Top	1	24in	x	15⅜in x	⅝in
Side rails	2	14¾		14	¾
Ends	2	20½		2¼	¾
Stretcher rail	1	21½		1¾	¾
Wedges	2	2¾		¾	¾

The stool table — Alan Thomas

This was very much a Saturday afternoon, Sunday morning job, to a succinct brief. 'What we need', I was told firmly, 'is a good solid stool — the sort that is meant to be stood on. No fancy finish; just a good solid thing with four legs.' Which at least decided the basics.

And the result, I think, looks good too.

Overall dimensions were settled on the 'does that seem about right?' principle, and several years of hard usage have shown that while the height is generally convenient the top is large enough for feet to shuffle about a bit without slipping over the edge. The

rounded edges and corners have proved their worth by not chipping ankles that have come into contact with them, and the structure as a whole has proved to be fault-free and remains solid and uncreaking. In an unplanned-for testimonial the stool has also proved a favourite seat for small children. A useful addition to the domestic furnishings all round, in fact.

Enough of the reasons why; now to the how. First, the wood. Mine is softwood, simply because there were enough pieces of convenient size lying about in the shed. The legs are nominal 2x2in, the rails and top nominal 1in — nominal, because the stuff was left over from a planed-all-round lot purchased for some building job or other. Something a little classier would be nice, and buying enough oak, for example, would not break the bank.

Start with the legs. Cut a card template for the curve and mark out all the front faces. (fig. 2); if the shapes are to be cut with a handsaw, mark out the backs of the shapes too. If you are going to use a turning saw then work from both sides of each cut. In that way not only will splintering be reduced to vanishing point, but the proper shape can be maintained easily. Mine were cut on a small bandsaw, which was ideal. My Bosch jigsaw wouldn't do it unless the 2in dimension is nominal to the extent of being more like 1¾in. In any case, so little effort is needed to cut the legs by hand that the only real advantage in favour of a power

continued

Stool times table

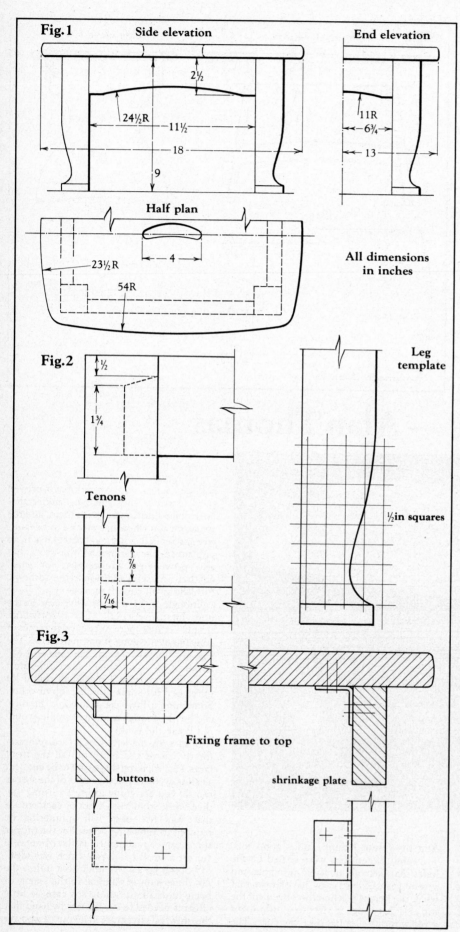

Fig. 1

Side elevation

End elevation

2½

24½R — 11½ —

18

9

11R

6¾

13

Half plan

23½R

54R

4

All dimensions
in inches

Fig. 2

½

1¾

Leg
template

½in squares

Tenons

⅞

⁷⁄₁₆

Fig. 3

Fixing frame to top

buttons

shrinkage plate

saw is that it may reduce the amount of finishing needed.

The four rails, two short, two long, are simple profiles, and by using a half template for each one it is easy enough to get them quite uniform — lopsided curves would look horrid. As always with mortises and tenons it pays to get the slots clean and accurately at right angles with the surfaces. Make the tenons a good fit into the bargain (fig. 2). When they all go together properly, free from winding, and the four feet will stand on a level surface without rocking, glue up the joints of the two long sides and their legs. Using white glue, this lot will be hard enough in a couple of hours for the short rails to be put into place. Use proper sash cramps if you have them, or cramp-heads on a plank (as I do), or even a Spanish windlass tourniquet (protect corners against bruising).

With the basic frame complete and hardening, turn to the top. It's another simple profiling job, and rubbed joints for the separate pieces would do perfectly well. I chose to tongue and groove them before gluing because I have a suitable pair of tongue and groove planes. I drew out the curved sides with improvised trammels — two nails hammered part-through a batten. Make the handhold any shape you like, but the banana looked better than a cigar: we thought so, anyway.

The textbook way of uniting top and frame would be by wooden buttons screwed to the underside of the top and locating in mortises cut in the end rails — a detail is shown in fig. 3. Instead I used some offcuts of light alloy sheet, about 1/16in thick, and bent up the brackets which are also shown. By simply drilling the screwholes a little oversize for the screw shanks there was more than enough allowance for the stool top to expand and contract, and there is no sign of strain or splitting in the original.

Before finally putting the top in place give everything a really good sanding, taking particular care to get rid of all the across-the-grain ridges that sawing will have left. The more care you take the better the final result will be. Break all the sharp corners with a generous radius; there will then be less tendency in after-life for them to show all the knocks and kicks that will undoubtedly come their way.

Apply the finish you want while the stool is still in two parts. Shiny varnish would look out of place in such a utilitarian piece, but a couple of coats of matt polyurethane should be all right. Ours has never had more than an occasional rub with ordinary furniture polish. Inadvertently leaving it out in the rain on a couple of occasions produced that greyish colouring character-istic of old stripped pine in 'antique' shops, and indeed it does look rather nicer than the original hue.

Finally, screw on the top, using round-head screws long enough but no longer, and there it is, ready for a lifetime of hard work, being trodden underfoot. ∎

The grand furniture saga

Colonial America was the New World but its fashions and styles were echoes from the mother countries. Vic Taylor explains how American furniture slowly adapted to its new environment

By 1650 the American colonies were settling down and establishing their own varied ways of life and culture. As well as the founding Pilgrim Fathers and their descendants, there were many Dutch, German, and Swedish settlers, who had their own enclaves strung along the eastern seaboard.

Life for the early settlers had been too rough and tough to allow any indulgence in the niceties of furniture design, and each settlement adapted the styles from the mother country. Only the favoured few could import furniture from Europe and anyway it was a notoriously difficult cargo.

The first native American furniture which had any pretensions to design appeared between 1650 and 1670 and was based on the English Jacobean style. Home-grown woods such as American oak, pine, cherry and maple were used, and the range of designs included court cupboards, press cupboards and gate-leg and trestle tables. Painted chests were popular, with the tulip and sunflower as favourite motifs. One of the best-known furniture painters was Thomas Child, an Englishman who emigrated to Boston about 1688; Nicholas Disbrowe, the joiner, was famed for what are known as 'Connecticut chests.'

Thomas Dennis left Portsmouth for America in the 1660s and became a renowned chairmaker. He was originally a joiner and specialised in ponderous 'wainscot' armchairs which were heavily carved and had large bulbous turned legs. Other chairs which developed during this period were the Brewster, the Carver, the Crosswicks, the slat-back (our 'ladder-back'), and the high-backed cane-seat chair, with bold scroll and carved work after the style of the English Charles II chair. The Brewster chair is probably named after William Brewster, one of the Pilgrim Fathers, and is reputed to have been modelled on an original *Mayflower* chair. The Carver, a simpler version of the Brewster, is so called after the first Governor of Plymouth Colony. Crosswicks was an early settlement near Burlington, New Jersey; the chair was Cromwellian-style with spiral barley-twist legs and was made principally by two English-

trained joiners, Matthew Robinson and Robert Rhea. The slat-back Colonial armchair was a New England design and its unique feature was mushroom-shaped knobs on the upper ends of the front legs.

The sheer number of Dutch settlers, and the adoption of Dutch styles in England after the accession of William and Mary of Orange in 1689, had a strong influence on American furniture design over the following years. Both British and Dutch settlers approved of the new styles, when they reached them, about 10 years late, by the end of the 17th century. The designs lingered on until the second half of the 18th century, when they were superseded by those of the ubiquitous Thomas Chippendale.

The Americans developed their own versions of William and Mary and Queen Anne styles, but never departed far from the originals. Some purely American designs evolved as the highboy, the lowboy, the 'bonnet-top' and the 'block-front' chest. The highboy (or 'tallboy') was a set of five or six tiers of drawers mounted on a stand high enough so you could open the drawers without stooping. The early models had six legs — four at the front — joined by diagonal stretchers, and adorned with the inverted trumpet-shaped turning typical of William and Mary furniture. The two central front legs were actually redundant and were soon done away with, although their vestiges were kept in the form of turned pendant knobs or finials.

● *Fine mahogany highboy with bonnet-top made in Philadelphia circa 1770*

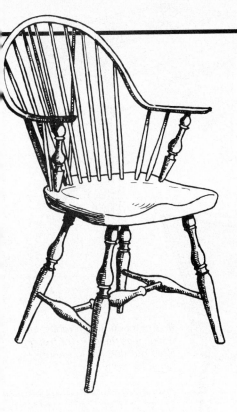

● *American Windsor chair with brace-back (our 'tail seat'). It has a grace and simplicity all of its own*

During the 18th century the turned legs were replaced by the new cabriole style, and the stretchers disappeared. The lowboy was its smaller counterpart for ladies; it went through the same metamorphoses as its larger brother ending with cabriole legs.

Americans have always been fond of bureaux and bureau-bookcases which they now call 'desks' or 'secretaries', and 'secretary-bookcases' respectively; in the 18th century they were 'escritoires' or 'scrutoires'. What the Americans call 'bureau' is a chest of drawers with or without a mirror and is used exclusively in the bedroom. A 'bonnet-top' was a swan-necked pediment often fitted to the top of a secretary-bookcase; whereas this kind of pediment on an English piece was purely a façade, the top of the carcase behind a bonnet-top was covered with a shaped coving following the line of the swan-neck.

The 'block-front' technique applied to chest of drawers, desks, and secretaries was a wholly American invention. It involved making the drawer fronts extra-thick to stand forward of the main carcase frame by about ⅜in, so the chests looked massive and luxurious. The backs of the drawer fronts were scooped out by the same amount as they stood forward to prevent them looking clumsy. The idea is said to have been originated in the mid-1760s by John Goddard, a master cabinetmaker working in Newport, Rhode Island, although it may well have been the brainchild of the Townsend family of cabinetmakers in the same town (Goddard married one of the Townsend daughters).

By the 1760s Chippendale fashions had become overwhelmingly popular, and his designs were being made by such craftsmen as Thomas Affleck, Thomas Elfe, John Fisher, John Folwell, Peter Hall, William Savery, John Goddard and the Townsend family. The number of cabinetmakers in the 18th century is surprisingly large; there were nearly 200 cabinetmakers, chair-makers, joiners, and upholsterers in the Boston area between 1725 and 1760; and 239 furniture businesses were recorded in Charleston between 1700 and 1825. These two towns, with the addition of Jamestown, Newport, New York, and Philadelphia were the main centres of furniture production.

Colonists and their descendants are noted for their sturdy independence, and although the spirit of Chippendale's furniture designs was widely and enthusiastically accepted, its interpretation in America was less ostentatious and grandiose — particularly in the New England states where the Pilgrim Fathers had left a legacy of austerity. So while Americans did adopt cabriole legs, ball and claw feet, shell carving, bracket feet, the Cupid's bow top rail on chairs and the interlaced riband splats, they didn't indulge in the wilder flights of Rococo or Chinoiserie. American furniture of the period tended to be slimmer, smaller, and more restrained in decoration than its English counterparts.

There was also a range of country or folk furniture used by the settlers outside the cities. Wood was the most abundant raw material and the settlers used it for everything imaginable, including maple-sap buckets, water buckets, water benches, dry sinks, dough trays and boot jacks. The most essential household item was the chest. They were made by the man of the house or the local carpenter, and painted by travelling painters using motifs from the mother country.

The centre of the settler's home was the kitchen. It was by far the largest room and the only one which was warm in the long cold winters; often the fire and ovens occupied the whole of one wall. Many kitchens included a sleeping area; if there were any upstairs-rooms they were set aside for meetings of various kinds — there's nothing like a bitterly cold room to cut short a meeting!

Kitchens always had at least one large dresser; several tables including the favourite gate-leg, a dry sink, and a complement of chairs. Along with the Colonial slat-back there would have been Windsor chairs, which achieved a lightness and grace

● *Massachusetts block-front desk in mahogany made about 1770 in the Philadelphia style*

continued

The grand furniture saga

in America never surpassed elsewhere. The settlers utilised every scrap of available material, which was apparent in their 'splint' and 'taped' seats. The splint seat was made of hickory splints or thin interwoven slats; the taped seat was woven from long strips of material from worn-out clothing.

Another essential item was the 'pie safe', the equivalent of the British meat safe. The door of the pie safe was fitted with a panel of pierced tin plate (the British used perforated zinc) and the holes were arranged in patterns of stars, roses, Grecian keys and so on. All these designs are now eagerly collected.

By about 1785 the Chippendale influence began to wane. In 1775 the War of Independence broke out and lasted until 1783; Anglo-American trade wasn't resumed until 1784. This period of almost 10 years was enough to prevent the Adam style of furniture and architecture having an effect upon the new United States; the next English influences to reach America were those of Hepplewhite and Sheraton. ■

● For those interested in Americana, a visit to the American Museum is a 'must'. It is at Claverton Manor, Bath, Avon BA2 7BD, (0225) 60503, and offers a fascinating insight into all aspects of American history and their furniture styles.

● *Farm-settler's water bench in yellow pine*

● *American dough table – the dough was mixed in the trough, lifted out and left in a warm place to prove*

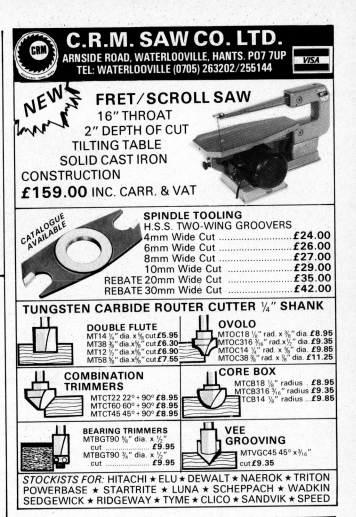

Question box

Our panel of experts solve your woodworking problems

We will try to answer any questions you can throw at us, but the ones we publish are the ones of most general interest to readers.

Please type your question double-spaced with generous margins, and include a stamped self-addressed envelope. Send it to: Question Box, Woodworker, 1 Golden Sq., London W1R 3AB.

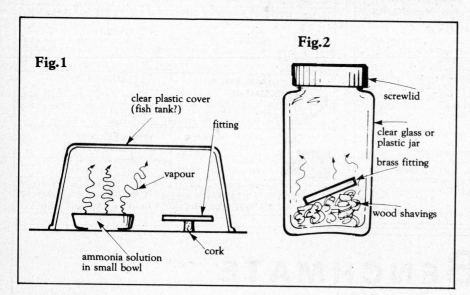

Fig.1
clear plastic cover (fish tank?)
fitting
vapour
ammonia solution in small bowl
cork

Fig.2
screwlid
clear glass or plastic jar
brass fitting
wood shavings

Ageing brass

Q *I repair antiques and sometimes have to replace a missing brass fitting. The new fitting stands out rather brazenly from its more mature fellows, and I wonder whether there is a proper method to age brass.*

R. R. Biggs, Carshalton Beeches, Surrey

A Modern brass fittings are supplied with a protective lacquer coat to prevent tarnishing. This must be removed with a paint-stripper before distressing. Make a thorough job of this, otherwise the distressing will be patchy (bright polished areas will remain where the lacquer hasn't been removed).

The easiest and quickest way to age brass is with ammonia. Buy 0.880 ammonia from your chemist and fume the fittings as shown in fig. 1. But take care, this strength of ammonia can be distressing to you as well as brass (particularly if you have respiratory problems or sensitive skin). Wear protective clothing and, if possible, a mask fitted with a gas filter. Watch the progress of the distressing and stop when satisfied.

The effect is to create an even, overall tarnish. If you want a blotchy effect with a background of normal dull tarnish and areas of very dark discolouration adopt the method shown in fig. 2. Some crushed wood shavings are placed in the bottom of

the jar and a little ammonia poured over to moisten, not saturate, them. Insert the fitting, screw the lid on, and shake the jar quickly. Where the moist shavings contact the brass will be the discoloured areas.

This is a pretty fast process, so don't overdo it. Remove the fitting when you're satisfied. If the effect is overdone, the staining can be removed with fine wire wool and the process repeated. Do not use a metal polish with the wool as this provides an unwanted protective layer.

Ian Hosker

Colourfast wood

Q *I have a collection of over 500 different woods from all over the world, and very beautiful they are – until they fade or darken. Is there a list of coloured woods which don't fade?*

Frank Nunn, Sheffield

A This question poses a fascinating problem for many woodworkers who prefer to leave their work in the natural colours of the timber. I'm afraid that there's no simple answer because of the nature of the natural chemicals which cause the colour. Many natural colours are 'fugitive', that is they aren't permanent and are easily destroyed under a given set of circum-

stances. The chemicals are usually complex organic compounds and colour changes are caused by chemical reactions which alter the compounds. This process is difficult to stop, but it can be retarded.

When a piece of wood is worked, new surfaces are exposed to the atmosphere and light and it's the combined action of light and oxygen that brings about the degradation of these compounds. Practically, there's little you can do about it. The Victorians were well aware of the problem and used heavy drapes to exclude bright light. I've had to restore colour to exposed furniture which has turned grey; grey mahogany is not attractive, and under these circumstances it's a nuisance.

The only way of combating the problem is to exclude the agents causing the change — light and air, plus pollutants. Hard-surface finishes will certainly exclude the air and should slow down the process, remembering that a little air will be trapped beneath the polish. Unfortunately the applied finish does impart a certain colour-cast of its own and will probably undergo its own colour change through long term exposure to the elements.

Ian Hosker

Golden oldies

Q *Can you tell me how to achieve 'gold' and 'antique' finishes like those used by pine furniture manufacturers? I'd like the final finish on my pine to be varnish or polyurethane rather that wax.*

I. R. Giles, Wick, Caithness

A The structure of pine makes it a difficult wood to stain evenly. One approach is to apply a brush coat of linseed oil thinned with turps (1 part oil to 3 parts turps), allow to dry overnight and then stain with an oil stain (Colron, Blackfriars). However, the 'antique' effect of commercially-produced furniture is reached by using pigments rather than dyes. These finishes contrive to simulate the effect of age; they have a dusty, almost dirty look about them which you can achieve with the following method.

You intend to use polyurethane which can be used as the base for your 'stain'. You'll need a tin of matt varnish, white spirit and tubes of artist's oil-colours in earth tones like sienna, umber and ochre. For the gold colour, you'll need raw sienna and burnt umber with, perhaps, a little burnt sienna; it's really a matter of experiment. Prepare the colour by thinning it with white spirit to a liquid. They can be intermixed to achieve the final colour. The varnish needs to be thinned with 50% white spirit and the colour gradually stirred in. Trial and error will create the right shade; experiment by brushing it on to scrap pieces of the timber. It takes some sense of colour to get it right and the other problem is density of colour. Pigments act like paint, actually masking the wood texture, so don't make it too thick or dense.

When you're satisfied, carefully brush the stain over the work ensuring even coverage and colour tone. Allow to dry overnight. Don't sand the work before applying full-strength polyurethane.

I can't over-emphasise the need for careful experimentation. Also, always keep the stain well stirred during application as the pigments tend to settle out. The overall effect of the pigment should create a dusty, mellow look.

Ian Hosker

● Ian Hosker is a professional finisher and Guild course tutor.

Splined mitres

Q *Peter Howlett referred to splining long mitre joints in his article on box-making (WW/Mar) using a 1.5mm cross-grained tongue. I find it very difficult to prepare cross-grained material of this thickness in strips 10mm wide or less, and would welcome your advice.*

A. E. Ely, Loughton

A The simple solution is to buy some 1.5mm veneer from your stockist and cut it with a knife. Mahogany, oak and ash are all commonly supplied in this thickness.

I resaw at 2mm with one face planed, and then reduce to 1.5mm using a false bed on the thicknesser. A swage saw-blade in a table saw is the traditional method but a carbide-tipped blade, 60-80 teeth (on a 250mm blade) would give a suitable finish straight from the saw. Again, knife these into strips. Then cut them using length stops on a radial-arm saw with a veneer-cutting blade.

Peter Howlett

● Peter Howlett is a professional box maker.

Garden furniture

Q *Can you suggest an alternative timber to elm for use in garden furniture? Would sweet chestnut be a good substitute?*
E. Wardman, Halifax

A Traditionally, elm has been used for garden furniture because it was readily available, and one of the cheapest hardwoods. From a technical standpoint, it won't check or split on exposure, but distortion may be considerable (particularly if the timber comes from hedgerow trees) and also, elm isn't naturally durable.

So, provided that the furniture is properly constructed, and protected when not in use, almost any homegrown hardwood would be a suitable substitute. Sweet chestnut would offer grain and colour similar to elm and so would English oak. Apart from walnut, British hardwoods like ash, beech, hornbeam, and sycamore, which vary from white to pale brown in

colour, are all suitable for the occasional external exposure garden furniture receives.

Ron Hooks

● Ron Hooks is a professional timber consultant.

Preventing cracks

Q *I have two pieces of elm, cut down two years ago, which have been indoors for the past two months. The modular rays are starting to open as cracks – is there anything I can do to stop them getting worse?*

R. J. Moore, Liskeard, Cornwall

A It's apparent that the cracking started with the change of environment, and from the date of your letter, it would seem you took the elm inside around March, when it was fairly cold and very wet. I wouldn't have thought that moving the logs into an unheated garage or workshop would have changed the atmospheric conditions to any great degree, so perhaps you took them into some part of the house which was much warmer, with a much reduced moisture content. This would have been enough to accelerate the drying.

I don't think you need bother unduly. The high initial moisture content will have been reduced considerably during two years, and end-checking is almost inevitable at some stage. Keep a close watch on the situation; if the cracks worsen to any alarming degree, place the logs outside in a shaded position, thoroughly soaking the affected ends with water, which will help stabilise the drying. I'm fairly certain that the checking won't increase too much, and that you'll soon be able to proceed with your work.

Next time you take timber inside for final drying, do it in the summer months, when atmospheric conditions are most likely to be the same indoors as out. If you need to convert the log, cut all dimensions full-to-size prior to storing, rather than taking round wood inside. This gives the blanks the opportunity of drying equally on all faces, and over the same period of time.

Graham James

● Graham James is an ex-timber merchant of long experience who specialised in home-grown hardwoods.

Wood in a cold climate

Q *I'm making a slatted shelf unit for storage in a shop cold-room, using deal, brass screws and polyurethane-varnish finish. I intend using draw-dowelled mortises and tenons in the framework, relying on the firm fixing of the slats to keep it rigid – do you think diagonal braces at the rear are necessary?*

What effect will the prolonged exposure to temperatures of $-2°$ to $+10°$ have on the timber, PVA adhesive and the finish?

R. C. Langley, Helston, Cornwall

A Glues and adhesives will react varyingly under these conditions; either contact individual manufacturers or the British Adhesives and Sealants Association, Stafford (0785) 817885 for advice.

If the goods are stored in boxes, I would leave the wood untreated and clean it periodically. As you're using such small tenons, they'd be better wedged than draw-dowelled. You should use diagonal braces at the rear to strengthen the framework; they can be of quite thin aluminium strip as they'll be under tension. As you suggest, brass, or plate, screws must be used to fix the slats.

I would do without varnish finish as any moisture that gets under the endgrain will freeze, swell and split the varnish skin. If you're intent on using it, contact the manufacturers for their comments first.

Bob Wearing

● Bob Wearing is a woodwork lecturer of vast experience and a regular contributor to WOODWORKER.

Antique oak-finish

Q *I am reproducing 16th and 17th century furniture using Scottish oak. Can you tell me how to create the dark finish characteristic of this period? Linseed oil is a solution, but a long and time-consuming method.*

James Gatherer, Dalmuir, Clydebank

A It could take years to achieve the right colour if you use linseed oil to darken and polish oak. There are several water stains which will produce a good Jacobean shade but before applying them, raise the grain by sponging over the surface with warm water. When the piece has thoroughly dried, cut down the raised grain fibres with fine abrasive paper and then brush on the stain.

A more satisfactory solution is to buy a litre of Jacobean Oak oil stain and apply it evenly with a clean rag. A second application will darken the oak further.

The oil stain won't raise the grain and should be allowed to dry for at least 24 hours. Then brush on a coat of white french polish and after two or three hours, when it's hard, glasspaper it smooth, dust off and give it another coat. When the third coat has hardened, smooth it lightly and then wax polish several times to give it that depth of finish typical of antique furniture. A black antique wax will pick out the open pores of the grain and help to give an appearance of age.

The Woodworker Manual of Finishing and Polishing, price £2.50 from Argus Books Ltd, Freepost, Hemel Hempstead, Herts HP2 4SS, contains a great deal of valuable information on finishing oak furniture, as well as stains for oak and other woods.

Charles Cliffe

● Charles Cliffe is a professional polisher, author and teacher.

THE WOODWORK BUSINESS

Advice — where and how to get it

Hugh O'Neill takes a general look at how to find out what you need to know, while CoSIRA press officer Paul Eastaugh explains his agency's work in detail

'Don't do it!' That's the advice you're likely to hear when you say you're setting up in business on your own. If you have more drive than sense you'll probably ignore it. And it's not the advice I would give you, although in an earlier article I did say 'Think it through.'

Think very hard and long whether setting up is for you. Does it meet your needs for independence? Can you live on uncertainty and through periods of feast and famine? Could you survive an accident or a long period of illness?

These are the questions you'll hear time and again from almost all the agencies you approach for assistance — finance or just advice. You'll get sick of hearing them. But don't close your ears; try to answer each question as though it were the first time you've heard it — it may just give you some useful new insight.

Most of the people who ask these things will have asked the same questions a thousand times. They know the problems; they have seen scores of hopefuls, and picked up the pieces of dozens of failures. But always remember one thing: THEY are not working for themselves. Some may have tried to go it alone and have themselves failed; many will never have even tried. A few will have run their own business successfully, and some of these will be doing so still, putting in a few hours a week with the agency to help hopefuls like you.

So you may find two sorts of advice. Both will be sound. But one may be slightly tinged with envy; you have the courage to do what they themselves haven't dared — or have done and failed. The other will be fatherly and caring. Both could be equally practical.

There's one piece of advice they may not give you, so I will. You must have the 150% support of your spouse (and family). This is almost more important than your own personal commitment. So it's essential that you sit down together and jointly explore the worst possible failure scenarios and make sure that you all understand the implications. Is your family really prepared to risk losing their home? Do they realise they may have to change their lifestyle when there is no longer a pay packet coming in? Are they really prepared for the lean years that will inevitably precede the (possibly) good?

Some people think that even considering the possibility of failure is being 'negative' and is programming for disaster. In practice, those who fully realise the implications of failure are spurred on to succeed. They know they *have* to!

What kinds of specialist advice can you obtain? Broadly they fall into three areas: financial; managerial/administrative; and technical (the first two overlap). Some agencies, notably CoSIRA, offer all three. Trade and research organisations specialise in technical advice (lists below). Most of the organisations that offer finance are also ready to give advice on business organisation and administration. Finally there are the agencies who don't offer direct financing, but who do advise on sources and on most aspects of business management. There are also various consultancies who may be useful.

A lot of advice is available free, especially at the moment when the government is trying to promote the development of new businesses. Government-sponsored agencies such as the Small Businesses Service, CoSIRA, and the Development Agencies in the regions will provide or find for you free advice on almost anything. The position varies but the general rule is that the first two or three visits are free and thereafter a small charge is levied.

The Local Enterprise Agencies are mostly local authority sponsored. They give some free advice, and fees, when charged, are also reasonable. Banks and other organisations giving grants or making business loans are a very useful source of advice on business and systems matters. Consultants cost money. Some are even worth what you have to pay! In the main the new business is unlikely to wish to make much use of consultancy except, occasionally, for something very special such as design, public relations promotion or similar. There are schemes where a consultant can be employed for up to 15 days and their fees will be met by PERA (listed below), but this applies mainly with quality and production control).

Some of the agencies will push you on to an appropriate professional as soon as they can, most frequently an accountant or, as required, a lawyer. This is where you can start to spend big money. Many accountancies have charge-out rates of £50-£60 per hour.

Choosing the right accountant is vital. Find a good one (not just the cheapest) and make sure they are used to dealing with small businesses and that they have a good standing with the local tax office. Avoid friends who will do your books and tax returns in their spare time: they can actually cost you money!

Having found someone you think you can work with, ask them to tell you how to set up your books and what records they wish you to keep. Do as much of the actual book-keeping yourself as you possibly can. Agree with the accountant that you will only want them to do the tax computation for you and to deal with the tax office on

your behalf. Say you would like the work to be done by one of their assistants (and not a partner) at an appropriate charge-out rate. Resist being pushed into fully audited books and accounts — that really is expensive! This way you get good advice, pay less, and, by having chosen a good firm, will find that their word is accepted by the tax office and may well save you money.

As a consultant myself, the question I'm most asked by self-employed and small business managers is where to get advice on:
● Ideas for products
● Design
● Sales and marketing.

The simple answer is that you can't get advice in these areas. If you need it — particularly in the first two — then you shouldn't be in business on your own. There are consultants who specialise in marketing and promotion, and they can be worth their corn.

You'll find advice on how to sell in sales training courses or books. Don't spurn these: selling is part of your business. I'll be looking more specifically at this subject next month.

The reference section of your area central library is a starting point for most sources of advice, and a good librarian is a mine of information (my first contact with the local Enterprise Agency came from a talk with the librarian). The library will have lists of contact addresses, can often provide a wad of leaflets on particular advice agencies and services, and will certainly have shelves full of trade directories, street directories, telephone directories, maps, electoral rolls — all the data that good salesmen need before they start to canvas an area. Your reference library can be the source of a lifetime's worth of business contacts. It can also be the source of leads to most of your business inputs. It is certainly the first stop on the route to finding any supplies that you might need.

There is an art to obtaining advice. First, you have to actually ask for it! Many people adopt a British stiff upper-lip attitude when they have a problem. They suffer in silence: it really is stupid — other people actually like to help.

Here are some practical pointers on getting advice:
● Invite people to help — not just to give you some small fact, or whatever. Tell people what your problem is and ask them for their ideas rather than tell them precisely what you (think you) want. Involving people in problem-solving generates support and commitment.
● Ask several people and get a range of ideas. Even better get a group of people together; two and two makes five as ideas spark off each other.
● Even when you have got past the idea-generation stage, it still helps to state your problem before you ask for precisely what you want. It can often be the trigger which changes the sullen 'No, we don't have anything like that' answer to the helpful: 'Sorry we can't help you there, but have you tried . . .'
● Never spurn the non-expert. It can be the naïve child that comes up with that new, breakthrough idea.
● If they are an expert acknowledge it. 'Bill, you are the expert, what do you think about . . . ' A little genuine flattery buys an awful lot of goodwill and help.
● Remember, time costs money. If your professional advisor has a high charge-out rate get straight to specifics. Work out in advance precisely what it is you want, then make contact and say: 'Can I have 10 minutes of your time, I have a specific problem that I would like a couple of pointers on.' When you do meet, set the tone straight away: 'Thank you for seeing me; this will only take a few minutes . . . ' and then go straight in. (This is a polite way of saying 'let's cut out all that small talk about the weather, the journey, the family and the holiday, that we both find difficult and that you charge me for in any case.')

When you've got what you want, of course you smile and say thank you. Sometimes it is even worth going back to report on your success. You never know when you might need some **real** help.

Business and financial advice sources

Council for Small Industries in Rural Areas, (CoSIRA), 141 Castle St, Salisbury, Wilts. SP1 3TP.

Crafts Council, 12 Waterloo Place, London SW1Y 4AU, 01-930 4811.

Development Board for Rural Wales, Ladywell Hse, Park St, Newton, Powys SY16 1JB, (0686) 26965.

Highlands & Islands Development Board, Bridge Hse, 27 Bank St, Inverness IV1 1QR, (0463) 234171.

Local Enterprises Agencies through the telephone operator asking for FREEPHONE ENTERPRISE.

Local Enterprise Development Unit, LEDU Business Centre, 17-19 Linenhall St, Belfast BT2 8AD, N. Ireland, (0232) 242582.

National Federation of Self-Employed & Small Businesses, Yorkshire Bank Chambers, 32 St. Anne's Rd, Lytham St Annes, Lancs, (0253) 720911.

Production Engineering and Research Association, (PERA), Nottingham Rd, Melton Mowbray, Leics, (0664) 64133.

Scottish Development Agency (Small Business Division), Rosebery Hse, Haymarket Tce, Edinburgh, EH12 5EZ, (031) 337 9595.

Small Firms Service, Ebury Bridge Hse, 2-18 Ebury Bridge Rd, London, SW1W 8QD, 01-730 8451.

Welsh Development Agency (Small Business Division), Treforest Industrial Est, Pontypridd, South Wales, CF37 5UT, (044) 385 266.

Northern Ireland Local Enterprise Development Unit, Lamont Hse, Purdys Lne, Mewtonnbreda, Belfast 8, (0232) 242582.

Key Directories & Reference Books

Craftsmans Directory — Stephen & Jean Lance.
Listings of craft fairs and fair organisers plus guilds and craft societies.

Craft Workshops — AA/CoSIRA joint publication.
Joint AA and CoSIRA publication listing craft workshop outlets.

Decorators Directory — Benn Publishing.
Suppliers of decorators materials.

Directory to the Furnishing Trade —Benn Publishing.
Suppliers of tools and materials used in the furnishing trade.

Hardware and DIY Buyers Guide — Benn Publishing.
Sources of supply of DIY based hardware.

Hardware & Ironmongery Manufacturers & Distributors
London & South & Midlands & North.
Two (massive) volumes cover the two halves of the country. (£88). A listing of ironmongers.

Kompass Register of British Industry & Commerce — Kompass Publishers Ltd.
Comprehensive listing of British manufacturers and contractors and the products and services they supply.

Machinery Buyers Guide
Comprehensive listing of suppliers of machinery and machine tools with an engineering predominance.

Showmans Directory Stephen & Jean Lance.
Lists of major shows (mainly 'agricultural') and of show promoters and contractors.

Specialist Information Resources Directory — P. Marcan.
A guide to special information sources and specialist directories.

Trade Associations & Professional Bodies — Patricia Millard. Complete listing of all trade associations, institutes and professional bodies.

Willings Press Guide — Thomas Skinner Directories.
Full lists of magazines including professional and trade.

Woodworker Directory — Argus Specialist Publications, out October '87.
Complete listing of sources of supply for all the woodworker's requirements.

Technical & Professional Bodies

Fellowship of Makers & Researchers of Historical Instruments, Faculty of Music, St Aldates, Oxford, OX1 1DB.

Furniture Industry Research Assn, Maxwell Rd, Stevenage, Herts, SG1 2EW, (0438) 3433.

Institute of Musical Instrument Technology, 20 Disraeli Rd, London, W5 5HP.

Institute of Wood Sciences, Premier Hse, 150 Southampton Row, London, SC1B 5AL, 01-837 8219.

Royal Forestry Society of England & Wales, 102 High St, Tring, Herts. HP23 4AH, (044282) 2028.

Timber Research & Devpmnt Assn, Stocking Lne, Hughenden Vy, High Wycombe, Bucks HP14 4ND, (024024) 3091.

THE WOODWORK BUSINESS

CoSIRA — easing the strain

Paul Eastaugh introduces the services of small businesses' favourite agency

One of the more unexpected problems of being self-employed, is loneliness. Working for yourself can often mean working *by* yourself, and whether your business involves working with wood or selling encyclopaedias, you'll encounter many problems that could take you by surprise.

The idea of a little workshop in the country is the attainable dream of many craftspeople, but in the relative quiet of the workshop, where there's nobody else to turn to, even the most trivial doubts and difficulties can remain a nagging distraction. If you live in the country however, help is only a phone call away.

Since it was founded in 1923, the Council for Small Industries in Rural Areas (CoSIRA) has been providing help and guidance on the whole gamut of problems which affect woodworkers and other rural businesses. Today it provides a very wide range of carefully tailored services to some 20,000 non-agricultural businesses in the countryside and small towns of England.

CoSIRA is the main agency of the Development Commission for Rural England, and was created to help communities in the English countryside prosper. It does this through its network of 32 offices from which Small Industries Organisers act

as the link between the client firm and CoSIRA's repertoire of services. The Organisers grow to understand the problems and aspirations of the firm by being available to give help and advice when it's needed.

The smaller the business, the greater the demands placed on the person running it. You may be a skilled woodworker, but you'll also have to become accountant, marketing director, chief buyer, works manager and personnel director, all rolled into one. And while you're juggling these jobs, you'll still have to remain productive in your main area of work.

But instead of wasting time away from the bench in a battle to understand the labour laws, you could call the CoSIRA Organiser. With his broad experience he's likely to have the answer at his fingertips, saving you hours of unproductive research. If the Organiser doesn't know the answer to a problem, he'll be able to spend the time finding out, leaving you free to get on with your job.

When the problems become more specialised, the Organiser has a team of experts to call on for help. CoSIRA's Management Accountants are always busy advising firms on their financial planning, helping them to set up accounting systems

● *Furniture makers Jill and Tony Ingham had their workshop at Stoke sub Hamden near Yeovil converted from a farm building with CoSIRA's advice*

Photos: CoSIRA

● *Ted Doulton of CoSIRA demonstrates woodturning techniques at a training workshop*

and giving a service which usually goes beyond that of ordinary accountants. There are also Marketing Consultants to advise on the best way of selling a product; publicity experts who can promote the business; and Building Officers who can help with the construction of a new office or factory.

Certain parts of England have been designated as Rural Development Areas by the Development Commission. In these areas CoSIRA administers a 25% grant scheme for anyone wishing to convert a redundant rural building into workshop premises. Many joinery shops in England have had their premises built with the help of such a grant and even more have taken advantage of the range of services which CoSIRA offer the woodwork industry.

Training is a major element of these services and CoSIRA runs a number of courses designed to help people working in wood acquire profitable new skills. The courses are either held at CoSIRA's well-equipped training workshops in Salisbury or, when circumstances permit, at a firm's

own premises. They range from general training in furniture and furniture restoration, to short courses in specialised topics like veneering and polishing, paint and lacquer spraying, restoration painting and gilding, turning and carving. All the subjects are taught to be commercially practicable; they're short enough for students to attend without their business suffering, but long enough to teach a new skill which can start earning them extra right away.

All of CoSIRA's courses exist to meet a demand. The revival of interest in carriage driving boosted the need for skilled wheelwrights and CoSIRA now offers training for improved methods and standards in the craft. Recently four young men trained by CoSIRA obtained the first wheelwrighting City and Guilds certificates issued for at least 20 years.

George Nunn, head of CoSIRA's Crafts and Building Section, readily admits to his love of craftsmanship but, if there are techniques which enable the same job to be done more quickly, his instructors will teach them. 'Students on our woodcarving courses will be shown working methods which eliminate the need for time-consuming marking up,' he explains. 'Similarly, woodturners are taught how to achieve a quality finish without a final sanding-down of the workpiece. At CoSIRA we believe in teaching craftsmanship which is productive and which makes the best use of the craftsman's time'.

Efficiency is the cornerstone of all CoSIRA's services, and there are specialists

to advise on workshop layout and selection and use of power tools; there's also an inspection and vetting service for second-hand machinery. Courses are run to teach safe and efficient use of equipment and to help you decide which machines would be of most value to your business. Client firms can call on advisors to examine the best way of machining a new project and a special Projects Section helps develop simple automated systems to help boost output. Many small joinery businesses are using reliable, low-cost hydraulic clamping systems designed and built specifically for their needs by the special Projects Section at Salisbury and at a cost far lower than they would expect to pay elsewhere.

The cost of all CoSIRA services is carefully controlled to keep them within the reach of even the youngest firm. The advice of its Small Industries Organisers is always free, while its specialist consultants provide their services to new firms at a flat rate of £15 per half-day and £30 for a full-day. It's policy that a firm shouldn't suffer because it's in a remote rural location, so the client is never charged for the travelling time involved. ■

● CoSIRA's aim is to provide a prompt and helpful service — if you wish to take advantage of it for your small rurally-based business, contact their local office (their number is in the telephone directory) or CoSIRA headquarters in Salisbury: CoSIRA (Headquarters) 141 Castle St, Salisbury, Wilts SP1 3TP, (0772) 336255

sumaco
multico

sumaco
multico

multico

multico
MACHINERY LIMITED

NOW SERVING HOME USERS AND PROFESSIONAL USERS

From 1st July, Multico and Sumaco announced the formation of a new company - MULTICO MACHINERY LTD Bringing together 40 years experience, producing quality British Woodworking Machines and selected complimentary products from some of the worlds most conscientious manufacturers. Multico can now offer a full range of light, medium and heavy duty machines.

MULTICO MACHINERY LTD
HEAD OFFICE: Brighton Rd., Salfords, Redhill, Surrey RH1 5ER Tel: (0293) 820250
NORTHERN OFFICE: Huddersfield Rd., Elland, W. Yorks. HX5 9AA Tel: (0422) 79811

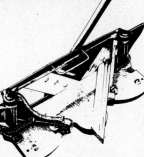
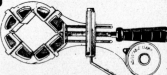

WOODWORKER
BRINGS
YOU
THE
BEST.
QUALITY
AND
QUANTITY
NOW
MORE
THAN
EVER.
WE'VE
GOT
PLANS
FOR
... YOU ...

Light fantastic

Fig. 1

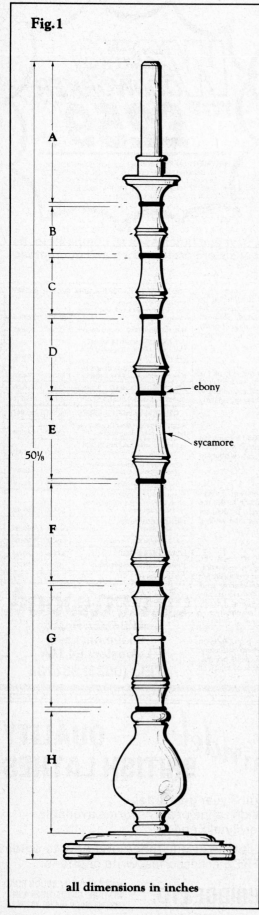

50⅛

ebony

sycamore

all dimensions in inches

Inspired by the elegant simplicity of Art Deco, Jim Robinson used sycamore and ebony to create a bamboo-effect standard lamp

I was influenced by the Art Deco style in designing this standard lamp. The requirements were that it shouldn't be out of place with 1930's style of furniture in a house built around 1920, and it shouldn't occupy too much floor space. The Art Deco style takes its name from the exhibition held in Paris in 1925, *'L'Exposition Internationale des Arts Decoratifs et Industriels Modernes'*, when oriental styles and exotic woods were in favour. That's why I used ebony and sycamore, shaped rather like bamboo. With the limited amount of floor space available I kept the base diameter relatively small and also kept the centre of gravity low to increase stability.

I had to purchase a piece of sycamore for the base but the remainder was taken from a neighbour's tree, converted by splitting convenient lengths into quarters with wedges; I dipped the ends in wax before seasoning the pieces for about four years. This project is a useful way of using timber of this type because with limited equipment it isn't easy to convert into boards.

Fig. 2

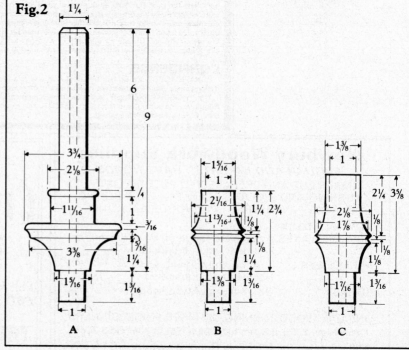

A   B   C

Cylinders

First I turned pieces of the sycamore into cylinders slightly larger than the maximum diameter of pieces **A-H** shown in fig. 2, best done with a large gouge. Next I drilled all the cylinders using a ⁵⁄₁₆in-diameter long hole-boring tool. When using long hole-borers, I find it best to drill half way from one end before reversing the timber and locating the hole that has just been bored on to the ⁵⁄₁₆in pilot of a 1in-diameter counterboring tool, which will act as a four-prong driving centre. The work can then be drilled until the two holes meet around the centre of the cylinder. Proceed slowly, removing the auger after about each 1½in of penetration to remove the debris.

I mounted the cylinders in the lathe using

tighten the work, so the counterbore cutters could then be used as a driving centre. I turned each section to the shape shown in the drawings, chiefly with a gouge and a small chisel for the decorations, and turned the lower end of each section down to 1in diameter to locate in the holes already drilled. In section **F** and **G** this pin is 1¼in long and **H** 1in long, while the remainder are 1³⁄₁₆in long (fig. 1) to allow for the ebony discs. Before removing each piece from the lathe I sanded it down to 320 grit before finishing with a wax polish.

Base and feet

I turned the base from a disc of sycamore mounted on a faceplate with screws to the underside. First I turned the outside edge of

Fig.3 — Section of base

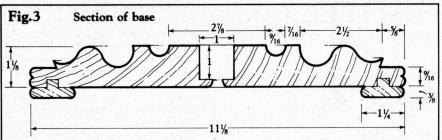

the counterbore tool as the drive centre located in the ⁵⁄₁₆in-diameter hole at the tailstock end. If you use a fixed centre you'll probably have to locate the centre in a plug turned to fit the ⁵⁄₁₆in hole. I drilled the 1in hole at the top end of each section a little over 1in deep, by holding the workpiece firmly in the hand and feeding slowly, by the tailstock, on to the cutters of the counterbore tool using the pilot rod as a guide. When the hole was deep enough, I stopped the lathe and used the tailstock to

the disc to a circular shape using a well-sharpened bowl gouge on its side, giving a light slicing action to avoid tearing out the grain, and sharp scrapers with a very light cut for the rest. Then I drilled a ⁵⁄₁₆in-diameter hole through the centre of the base; I used this to locate the ⁵⁄₁₆in pin on the counterbore mounted on the tailstock, which was used to drill the 1x1in hole to take the pin turned on section **H**. You could also make this hole with a small scraper. After waxing, I removed the base from the

faceplate, rounding the underside of the ⁵⁄₁₆in-diameter central hole to avoid possible damage to the flex by chafing. To complete the base I drilled four ³⁄₈in-diameter holes ¼in deep at equidistant positions round the base, with the centres ⁵⁄₈in from the outer edge, for the feet pins.

I turned the four feet in one operation from a piece of sycamore mounted between centres (fig. 4), almost separating each one with the parting tool, then removing the piece from the lathe and sawing through by

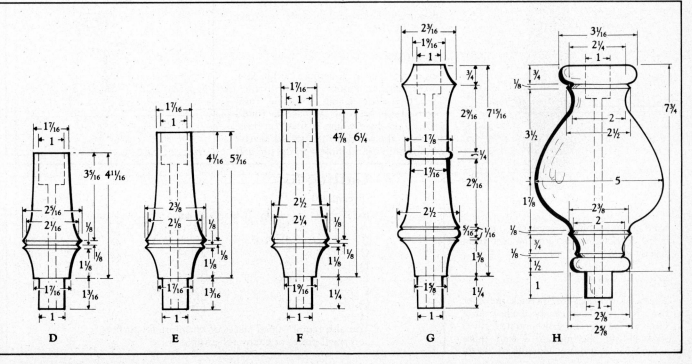

D   E   F   G   H

Light fantastic _____

Fig.4   Turning feet

Fig.5   Turning ebony rings

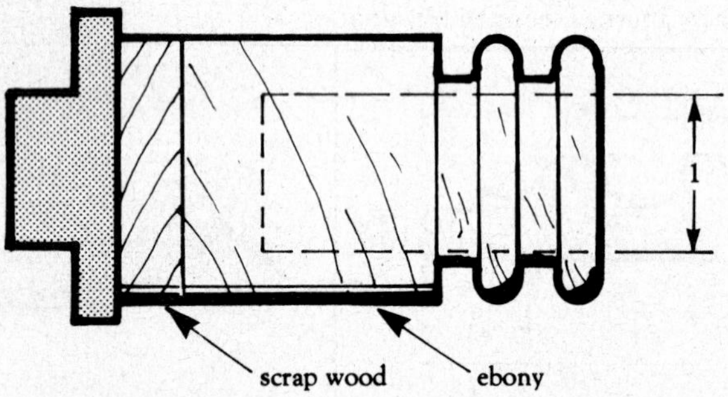

scrap wood   ebony

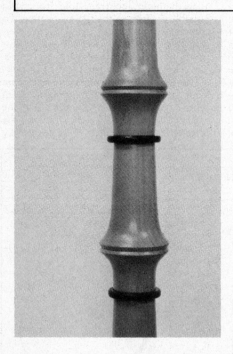

threaded to fit the lamp holder and the lower half threaded with a coarser thread to screw into a $\frac{5}{16}$in hole drilled in the wood. The nipple can sometimes be successfully screwed into the wood using a tang of a file as a screwdriver to avoid damaging the fine thread by gripping with pliers; there's much less likelihood of the wood splitting on the relatively small section of the top if a $\frac{3}{8}$in BSW metal tap is first used to cut a thread on the inside of the wooden hole before screwing the nipple in place.

I used a gap-filling glue such as Cascamite for the assembly of the lamp. First glue the four feet to the base, locating the pins turned on the feet in the holes drilled in the base. You can see in fig. 6 how the ebony rings are positioned on the pins turned on the sycamore. Glue section **H** to the base and then thread the flex through before each section is added. If the flex is threaded through after gluing up, you may find its passage is impeded by hardened glue squeezed out into the central hole at the joints. Also remember that the two $\frac{1}{4}$in thick ebony rings separate **F/G** and **G/H** and the remaining rings are $\frac{3}{16}$in. All that remains now is to complete the wiring up, remembering to fit a 2amp fuse in the 13amp plug used and to find a suitable shade.

Then you can switch on and enjoy your new lamp.   ■

timber is to fix the ebony to scrap wood fixed to a faceplate using a hot metal glue gun (fig. 5). I first drilled a 1in-diameter hole in the centre of the ebony; if you use a screw-chuck, scrape a 1in-diameter hole leaving a central pillar containing the screw, otherwise you'll waste precious material. Complete rings using a parting tool and small beading chisel. The outside diameter of the rings is such that the upper five rings project by $\frac{3}{16}$in all round from the adjoining sycamore and the lower two rings project by $\frac{1}{4}$in.

Assembly

Before assembling you must decide how you're going to mount the lamp holder. Two types are readily available from electrical supply shops; one has a flat round plate at the base which is fixed by three screws to the wooden top, but the neatest method is to use a nipple with the top half

Fig.6

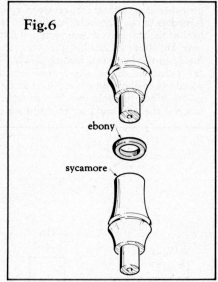

ebony

sycamore

hand before sanding to complete (it may be more economical to turn the feet from several scrap pieces).

Ebony rings

The two lower rings are $\frac{1}{4}$in thick, the other five are $\frac{3}{16}$in. They can be made from a piece of wood endgrain-mounted on a screw-chuck; the method I find more convenient and least wasteful of costly

Cutting list

(Sycamore)

Base	$11\frac{1}{4}$in	x	$11\frac{1}{4}$in	x	$1\frac{1}{4}$in
A	$10\frac{3}{8}$		$3\frac{7}{8}$		$3\frac{7}{8}$
B	$4\frac{1}{8}$		$2\frac{1}{4}$		$2\frac{1}{4}$
C	5		$2\frac{1}{4}$		$2\frac{1}{4}$
D	6		$2\frac{1}{2}$		$2\frac{1}{2}$
E	$6\frac{3}{4}$		$2\frac{1}{2}$		$2\frac{1}{2}$
F	$7\frac{5}{8}$		$2\frac{5}{8}$		$2\frac{5}{8}$
G	$8\frac{3}{8}$		$2\frac{5}{8}$		$2\frac{5}{8}$
H	$8\frac{7}{8}$		$5\frac{1}{8}$		$5\frac{1}{8}$

You also require small pieces of sycamore for turning feet and small pieces of ebony for turning discs.

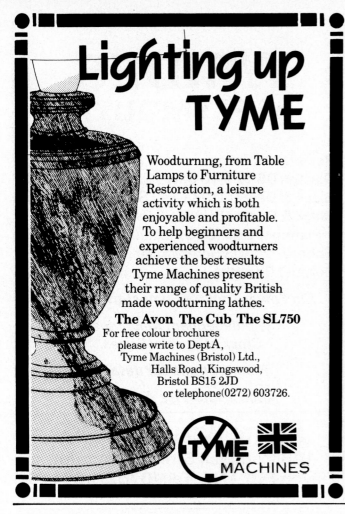
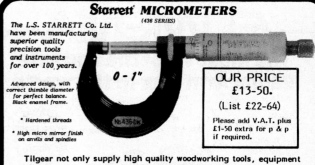

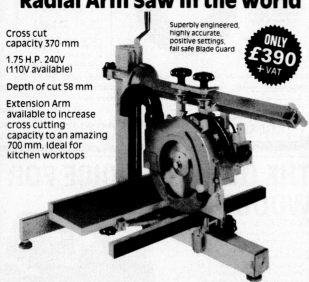
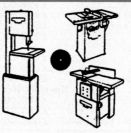

BUCKS
Fizz

Speaking of college work, Andrew Ball designed and made this elegant tall cocktail cabinet at Buckinghamshire College last year

I began this design with the vague idea of a drinks cabinet supported on a tall stand; at first, I had no specific plans for an X-frame support, bow-shaped front or even curves. All I wanted to achieve was a very stark yet elegant piece of work. I started with many sketches, then models and eventually a full-size working drawing, having my overall idea in mind, but no clear picture of what the end product was going to be like. I wanted the legs to be as slender as possible, and this was the biggest problem: how to support a cabinet which would contain glasses and bottles, maintaining fine proportions and equally fine leg supports, but still be sturdy and well balanced? This is where the complex arch supports came in; something I never really wanted, but a happy compromise.

Once I had designed the stand, I felt the need to repeat the curves on the cabinet. I achieved his by making the doors concave and by selecting a veneer that would enhance the curve of the doors — some beautifully figured fiddleback sycamore. I made the two curved panels with a mould, and fitted them using traditional frame-and-panel construction.

The second curving problem was forming the underframe arches; I needed six identical formed shapes. The obvious answer was laminating but laminated ply would have spoilt the visual effect. So, I steam-bent each piece, making a mould for the shape and a strap for bending. I carefully selected straight-grained sycamore with no knots or splits and began the tedious process of trial-and-error bending. With steam-bending, the shape tends to move after it's removed from its strap; so I did

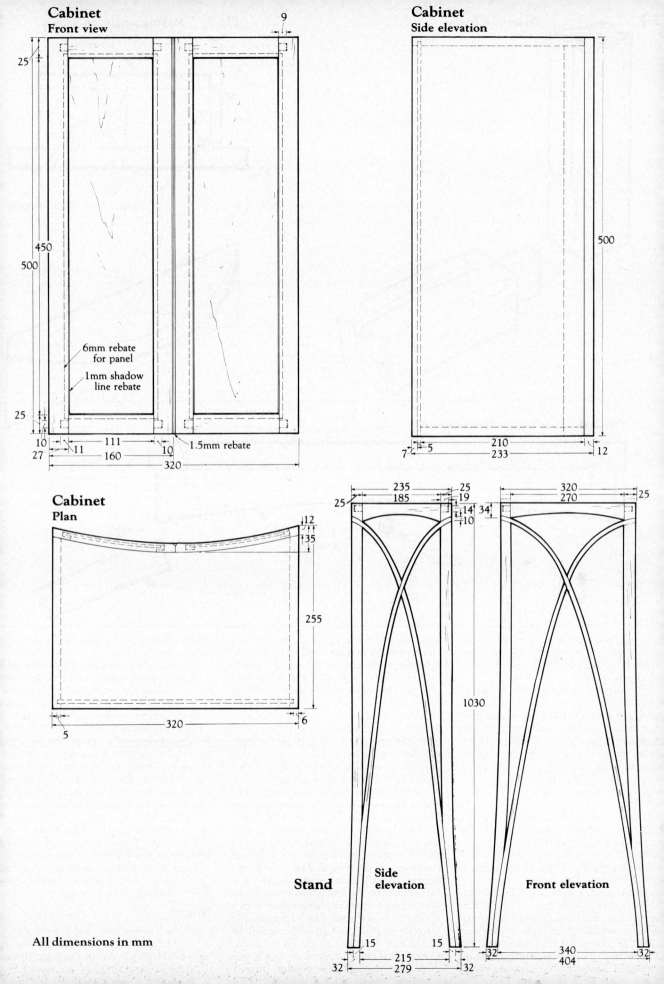

Cabinet
Front view

9

25

450

500

6mm rebate
for panel

1mm shadow
line rebate

25

10
27   11   111   10
      160   1.5mm rebate
   320

Cabinet
Side elevation

500

7 5   210   12
      233

Cabinet
Plan

12
35

255

5   320   6

Cabinet
Side elevation

25

235
185   25
      19
      14
      10

320
270   25

34

1030

15   15   32   340   32
32   215   32   404
   279

Stand   Side
            elevation   Front elevation

All dimensions in mm

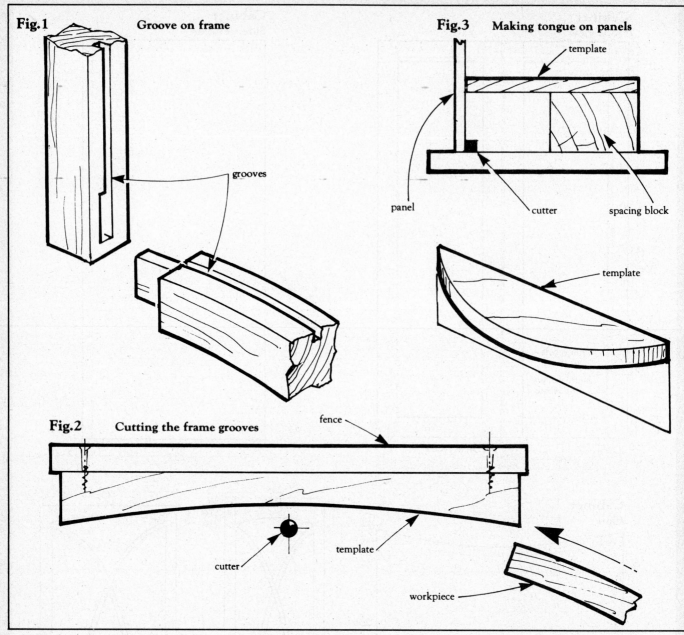

Fig.1 Groove on frame

grooves

Fig.3 Making tongue on panels

template

panel

cutter

spacing block

template

Fig.2 Cutting the frame grooves

fence

cutter

template

workpiece

movement and allowed for it on the mould. An article on steam-bending in April 1985's WOODWORKER gave me the basic techniques.

After shaping each piece with a spokeshave, I fitted them individually to the four legs which were also shaped to a fine taper. Then came positioning and fixing of the two together; not so easy, as I had to get the whole thing to stand straight and be balanced equally.

Cabinet

The cabinet carcase is lipped and veneered chipboard. I made mitre joints on the dimension saw, strengthened by biscuit-joints. I had to complete the two doors before shaping the front of the cabinet; both featured a laminated panel which would dictate the front shape of the cabinet.

I made a template of the door panels from the full-size working drawing in 10mm plywood, which I used with an overhead router to construct the mould for the formed panels. All the panels are identical in shape. I laminated the complete shape, then split it in two to fit the two doors. The

laminate was made up of three pieces of constructional veneer and a piece of sycamore fiddleback on either side. I used a hydraulic bag press for the laminating process, although the panel could possibly be formed using male and female moulds. The glue ('Cascamite') had fully cured after four hours in the press. Removing the panel from the mould, I used it as the new template for the front of the carcase. I used a bandsaw to rough it out, finishing with a spokeshave and then gluing it up.

I then constructed the door frames into which the panels would fit, using hand-cut mortise and tenons, before bandsawing the laminated panels into two separate pieces and planing to finished sizes. Using a hand router, I made a grove on the inside face of each frame of the door and an accompanying tongue on the two panels (fig. 1). For the grooves on the curved members of the door frame I set up the hand router with a table (like a spindle moulder). I then made a template the reverse shape of the piece to be routed and fixed this to the fence on the router. Each curved piece (four in all) was then passed over the cutter, firmly supported against the template (fig. 2). I

simply passed the straight pieces over the cutter, using a fence.

For making the tongue on the panels I used a router and table again, but with a different set-up. Taking the original template for the door I pinned it to a piece of 2x2in which was then G-clamped to the router table. Then I passed the curved panels over the cutter, holding them firmly against the template (fig. 3). I made the tongues slightly oversize in depth, I wanted a shadow line round each panel when the door was assembled. I glued the doors together, making four angled blocks for cramping aids when the whole thing was sash-cramped (fig. 4). To keep a shadow line between the edge of the frame and the panel; I inserted veneer all the way round the edges during cramping up (fig. 5).

Then I hung the doors on the carcase using ³⁄₄in brass flap hinges, leaving a gap of 2mm down the centre for movement.

Stand

Once the cabinet was made, I set about constructing the stand on to which it would be fixed (Making the cabinet first and fitting the stand to it is easier than vice versa.)

The four legs which make up the stand

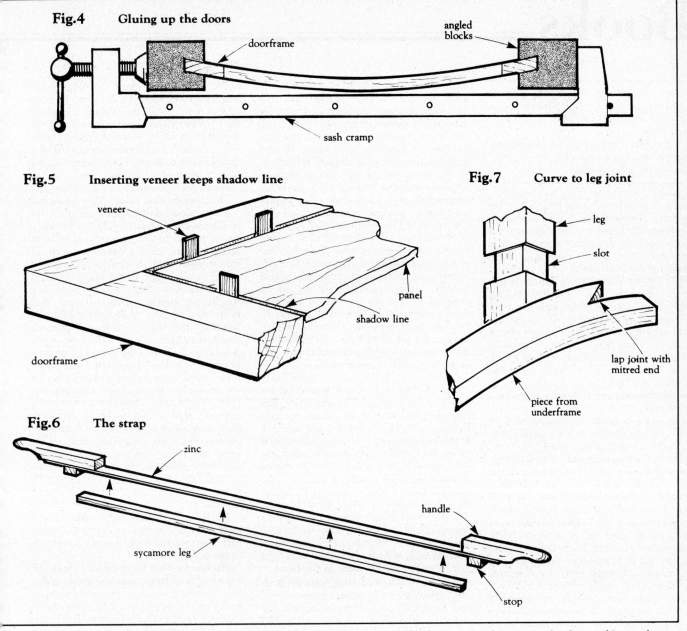

Fig.4   Gluing up the doors

doorframe

angled blocks

sash cramp

Fig.5   Inserting veneer keeps shadow line

veneer

panel

shadow line

doorframe

Fig.7   Curve to leg joint

leg

slot

lap joint with mitred end

piece from underframe

Fig.6   The strap

zinc

handle

sycamore leg

stop

feature a taper on both front and side. I prepared two templates from the full-size drawings, then did the initial roughing-out of the shapes of the solid pieces with a bandsaw. I finished that stage with spokeshave and cabinet scraper. For the mortises on the connecting pieces of the stand I used a mortiser, but cut the tenons by hand; the setting-up time for a tenoner wouldn't have been justified by the number of tenons to be cut. I dry-jointed the whole assembly and started the underframe.

Underframe

I chose steam-bending, to shape each component of the underframe; laminating may have been easier and more reliable, but I didn't want the unsightly cross ply to be visible. I needed another mould, so I made a plywood template from my working drawings of the inside shape of each curved component and then used it with the overhead router to make the mould from chipboard. Then I had to make a strap which keeps the bent wood in shape on the mould. This was basically a piece of zinc over the length of the piece and wide enough to accommodate two pieces. Shaped beech

handles were attached with nuts and bolts at the ends, together with two beech stops into which the pieces of sycamore would fit (fig. 6).

After wood that has been bent is removed from a mould it tends to 'spring back' or move. So I did a trial piece to assess the amount of 'springback' and alter the mould appropriately. My procedure was to take two pieces of carefully selected sycamore and steam them for about 30-35 mins. Removing them from the case, I fitted them to the strap, bent it round the mould and firmly cramped it on. The pieces were then left to dry in a workshop atmosphere for two days. I went on to bend all six pieces like this. In retrospect I can see it would have been easier to bend one fairly wide piece of sycamore with an appropriately sized strap and mould and then simply bandsaw all the pieces out of it; this way all the pieces would be identical.

I then put a fine taper on each piece with spokeshave and cabinet scraper. I dry-jointed the underframe pieces and the legs, cramped them into position and marked off where each piece crossed the other. I cut simple halving joints where the curved

members met each other, and I cut a slot on each leg, then a simple lap joint on the end of each curved piece, before mitring (fig. 7).

Then I glued and assembled the whole underframe, making a jig to keep the stand in position on its base. This was simply a piece of chipboard with four beech blocks screwed to it in the correct positions (taken from the plan on the working drawing). This jig held the whole assembly firmly and in the correct position whilst gluing up.

When the underframe was assembled I fixed the cabinet on top with brass mirror hooks let horizontally into slots in the top of the stand. I finally chose a level surface (circular saw-table or planer table) and placed the stand on top, using a plumbline to determine whether the unit was standing straight and taking shavings off the legs to make the assembly stand correctly.

I finished the cabinet with a coat of pre-catalysed sealer and pre-catalysed satin sealer, de-nibbed lightly after each coat, before waxing with fine wire wool and buffing to a high finish.

The fine details and proportions may not be immediately apparent, but I believe they gradually become appreciated in time. ∎

Books

Wood Machining: *A complete guide to effective and safe working practices*
Stobart & Son, £10.95 softback
Nigel Voisey
Woodworker Book of Wood-machining
Argus Books, £9.95 softback
Reviewed by Mike Rossage

At last! How nice to have two readable books on wood machining and their safety aspects. These two books certainly comprise 'the finger grabber's guide to the galaxy' of woodworking machines. The only thing they lack is the words 'don't panic' on the front cover.

The books appear to be aimed at different markets: the WOODWORKER publication more suitable for the beginner or someone who is thinking of moving into the world of machining; Mr Voisey's book a more comprehensive and detailed volume, of greater value to someone with some experience and certainly providing excellent reference throughout the years for anyone, however much they know or think they know.

Mr Voisey's book commences with an excellent introduction to the general safety of wood machining which is well illustrated, using very clear line drawings. This technique is carried on throughout the book as it moves on to individual machines, a chapter being devoted to each main group of machines. Each chapter starts with a very clear exploded diagram of the machine, pointing out relevant safety features and guarding. The spindle moulder section is exceptionally thorough and illustrated with some very nice diagrams, and deals very clearly with such topics as cutter projection, which is generally difficult to grasp. It is probably worth buying this book just for this chapter alone since recent publications on this machine have been so complex and badly written as to be incomprehensible, making one wonder if the best approach was simply to press the button and duck. Mr Voisey also deals nicely with the radial-arm saw, leaving out all the irrelevant ancillary operations while concentrating on its main sawing operation, referring readers to other publications.

The book in general is extremely readable and Mr Voisey's 'hands on' experience comes across admirably. I read the chapter on the lathe with great interest as I have never used one of these machines and soon found myself itching to be let loose with a lump of spinning wood. At the end of the book he devotes a few shorter chapters to some of the more exotic machinery, such as tenoners and overhead routers, with a rather nice section on universals, culminating with a section on waste extraction.

The approach of the WOODWORKER book is substantially different — a more visual book making good use a wide range of photographs. It too is divided into sections on the various machines with an initial chapter on general safety. It devotes most of its attention to the more commonly used machines. The chapter on the planer/thicknesser and bandsaw I felt were particularly thorough and well illustrated. If you were looking to purchase a machine for the first time this book would be very useful in deciding what use one is likely to get out of a given machine and also how to set about using it. No chapter on the lathe, surprisingly, and I found that the chapter on power sanding seemed rather incongruous in a book which would appear to be aimed more at the beginner. The section on the radial-arm saw, while thorough and avoiding entanglement in some of the more bizarre and wondrous attachments available (which if the manufacturers are to be believed will enable you to do anything from building York Minster to peeling an avocado pear), did seem to be rather thin on the ground for a machine which is one of the more commonly purchased saws — not even a reference to other publications.

In general both books were very pleasurable to read, which is unusual for technical publications. The section on dust extraction in both books should perhaps have come first as waste is a major nuisance of power machinery. My second criticism is of the WOODWORKER book's radial arm chapter in which in one picture they show a demonstration of cutting a mitre on the crosscut using a fence substantially higher than the workpiece. While not dangerous, this effectively showers the operator with a stream of high velocity sawdust the minute the blade passes through the fence — it acts as a deflector, as most of the sawdust cannot exit through the kerf mark in the fence.

All in all if you are feeling rich then both books are worthy of purchase. For myself if I had to opt for one I would suggest Mr Voisey's, although this must be qualified by one's experience. The WOODWORKER book is more suitable for the beginner.
● Mike Rossage is a woodworker and machinist who has been restoring his period home for the last three years.

Walter Rose
The Village Carpenter
A & C Black, £6.95 softback
Reviewed by John Hemsley

Walter Rose was the third generation in a family of Buckinghamshire master carpenters. This book, first published in 1937, lovingly describes the craft in Victorian times, when the village carpenter built windmills and farmgates, cribs and coffins, and faced the drudgery of the saw-pit and preparing floorboards by hand. This is a beautifully written book that arouses nostalgia and should be on every woodworker's bedside table.

I found most intriguing and inspiring the final chapter on the prospects for hand woodworking skills, written in the '30s but still relevant today. Mr Rose observed that traditional crafts, such as wheelwrighting, had almost vanished as the car replaced the horse, while the work of the village tailor and boomaker had been absorbed by mass production. Was the village carpenter likely to be driven out in the same way? He thought not, for though many items of old-time carpentry lent themselves to mass production, the complete craft covered such a wide variety that demand for a skilled versatile local workman would remain.

He observed that villages were becoming less agriculture-centred but more attractive as homes for people working in towns, a return to nature that he approved of. This ingress would mean a continued demand for carpentry skills, but he queried whether young people would be well enough trained to give the new village dwellers what they sought, 'the subtle quality of work that bears the impress of the artist's mind'. Learning the skills and the craftsman's touch was a lifetime's work. Already in one generation he'd seen the period of apprenticeship cut from seven years to four, and he found there was 'a general disinclination for any apprenticeship at all and a sad misconception as to the amount that has to be learned'. New woodworkers should look back at the work of the previous century to observe 'the artist mind that prompted the hands, the perception that had grasped the principles of design, the certain knowledge in its decisive finish: there is the secret of its permanent inspiration, its power to soothe and charm'.

Mr Rose welcomed the introduction of machinery to ease the drudgery, but urged carpenters not to become merely the servant of the machine.

His chief reason for optimism about the future of woodcrafts was 'the growing dislike of the monotony of the machine-made and a greater appreciation for that which, made by hand, bears the impress of the individual craftsman'. Half a century later we still have his confidence.

In brief

The Woodworker's Manual (Gosta Vass; Macdonald Orbis, £11.95 hardback)
Not so much a manual, more a collection of 30 step-by-step projects, ranging from a simple bread board to a writing desk. Each step is clearly illustrated. Leaf through it if you get the chance, for the Scandinavian design sense is refreshing.

Make Your Own Wooden Toys (Jeff Burke, Fiona Nevile, Ron Fuller, Dik Garrood, Windward, £7.95 hardback)
Everything a toymaking book should be. Simple, fun, imaginative designs which will bring pleasure to the maker and the player alike, and with 20 chunky toys to choose from — puffa trains and bulldozers, to cradles and go-karts — they could end up being one and the same person. Wonderful colour pages with clear instructions and easy-to-follow exploded diagrams — quite the best toymaking guide around.

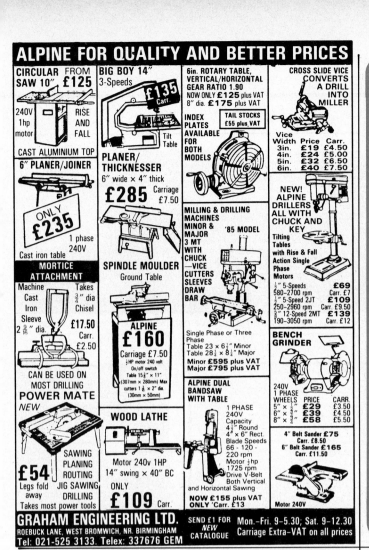

819

Pen friend

Bill Walker re-discovers
the traditional writing slope
— a quaint but popular
design which demands
some deft detailing

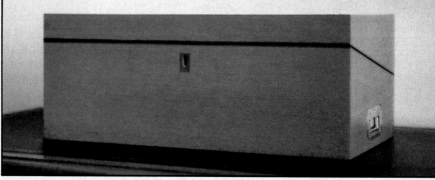

● *The hinged writing slope becomes an attractive compact box when not in use*

Thousands of these writing boxes were made during the 19th century, many in choice woods, lavishly decorated and internally fitted out. Cheaper boxes were made of pine veneered with walnut or mahogany. They turn up in sales and antique shops from time to time but it's rare to find one that has not been broken inside, probably from impatient or clumsy attempts to find the secret drawer or compartment which the better boxes often featured. I made this box as a present and I found it an interesting piece of cabinet work both to design and make. You can vary the way the box is fitted out to suit your own requirements; this one actually has two concealed compartments, but I have not included them in the drawings.

Before starting this project I experimented a little with the theory of proportion — some rectangles are visually more satisfying than others. I had decided the box would be 178mm high, and using the 'Golden Mean' rectangle gave an end elevation of 178 × 295mm, a bit too wide. So I tried a Fibonacci series rectangle (fig. 1): this gave an end elevation in the ratio 2:3, front elevation 2:5 and plan 3:5 — box dimensions 178x267x445mm which seemed more like it. I drew these rectangles full size but the proportions were still not comfortable to my eye, so I altered them to 178x254x458mm. This looked more satisfying to me. It's purely subjective of course, but try it yourself. The dimensions also had to be considered bearing in mind the internal fitting-out of the box (fig. 2)

I used Brazilian mahogany for the main carcase, good quality 9mm plywood for the top and bottom, darker Cuban mahogany for the interior parts, and crown cut Honduras mahogany veneer for the top.

continued

Fig.1

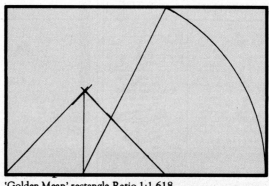

'Golden Mean' rectangle Ratio 1:1.618

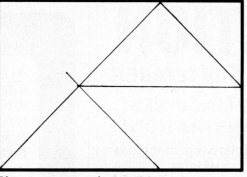

Fibonacci series rectangle. Ratio 2:3

● *Fit for the finest vellum and wax-sealing stamps – even writing the bills could be a pleasure!*

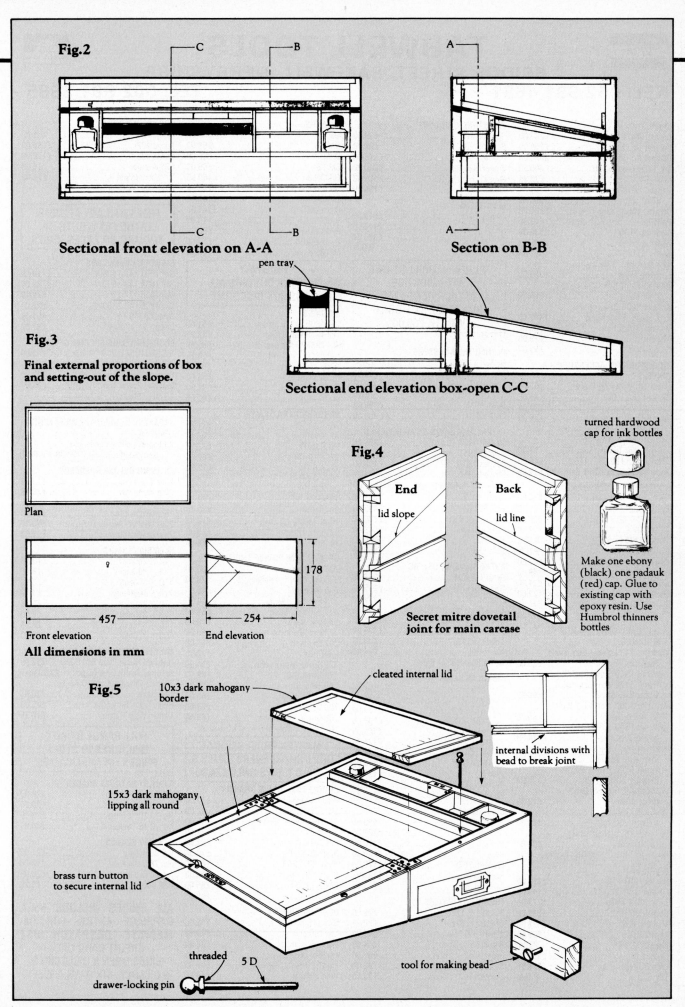

Fig.2

Sectional front elevation on A-A

Section on B-B

pen tray

Fig.3

Final external proportions of box
and setting-out of the slope.

Plan

Sectional end elevation box-open C-C

Front elevation

End elevation

457

254

178

All dimensions in mm

Fig.4

End

lid slope

Back

lid line

**Secret mitre dovetail
joint for main carcase**

turned hardwood
cap for ink bottles

Make one ebony
(black) one padauk
(red) cap. Glue to
existing cap with
epoxy resin. Use
Humbrol thinners
bottles

Fig.5

10x3 dark mahogany
border

cleated internal lid

internal divisions with
bead to break joint

15x3 dark mahogany
lipping all round

brass turn button
to secure internal lid

threaded

5 D

drawer-locking pin

tool for making bead

Construction

1 Prepare the front, back and two ends from one length of board so the grain will follow around the box when it is assembled, except for one corner which can be at the back. If the timber isn't quarter-sawn, make sure the heart side will be outside.

2 Mark out the rebates, groove and lid cut-off lines. The corner joints are secret mitre dovetails; you could use other joints but they must be strong because the lid section will be heavy and part of one end is cut away to provide the drawer opening.

3 Make top, bottom and horizontal divisions from plywood, veneered both sides for balance. Solid wood was used in the old boxes but often split because of shrinkage.

4 After cutting the corner joints, rebates and grooves, clean up and polish the internal parts. I used clear shellac polish applied with a rubber. Keep the polish away from joints and rebates by masking them out if necessary.

5 Assemble the carcase with the grooved-horizontal division in place and cramp up dry to test for squareness. Before gluing up, saw about 50mm along the sloping lid line on both end pieces; this makes things a lot easier when separating the lid from the box later.

6 When the main carcase has set, you can fit the top and bottom veneered plywood pieces and glue them into their respective rebates.

7 Cut the drawer opening from one end of the box. Use a padsaw to cut inside the marked line, and trim the opening square with a paring chisel. If it's carefully cut out, the piece removed can be used as the drawer-front, but a cock bead will be needed to make up for the wood lost in sawing it from the opening. I rejected this method and cut a drawer front from another piece with near matching grain (don't tell anyone!).

8 Use a fine-toothed tenon or dove-tail saw to cut along the lid line to separate the lid section from the box; watch the angle of slope. This is where having started the cut on the ends beforehand pays off. Plane the edges true so that both parts fit together neatly all round. Mitre and glue a lipping 3mm thick around the meeting edges; this allows for the thickness of the leather writing surface and the hinges.

9 Fit the divisions for ink bottles and pen tray in their respective positions with housing joints. A small bead line worked round the interior edges acts as a break joint between the divisions and the

carcase. I used a no.10 csk wood screw in a hardwood block to score this bead (fig. 5).

10 The internal lids or flaps which provide the writing surface are made from solid wood with tongued and grooved cleats each end. Mitre a 3mm thick border around to provide a protective edging for the leather. Using solid wood is better than ply in this case because it can be planed true and flat.

11 The drawer is of conventional construction with lap dovetail joints at the front and through dovetails at the back. The drawer can be subdivided for pencils, crayons or other items but I made a separate pencil box and tray which can be taken out of the drawer in use.

Hardware

The old boxes were often broken at the hinges because the lid is quite heavy. I cut a pair of brass back-flaps into L-shapes to fit on the corners. This gives a broader knuckle which should be stronger than narrow box hinges. One slight disadvantage is that the internal lids cannot be opened through 180° and laid back flat; but this is seldom necessary. The restriction avoids creasing the leather too much along the joint.

I used a turned brass pin to secure the drawer when the box is locked; this is inserted into a hole drilled down the end and part way into the top edge of the drawer front. The lock is a conventional brass box lock. You should make a small brass turn button to secure the internal lid so that it doesn't flap open when the box is opened.

I chose military-chest type handles, one at each end of the box; that is, one let into the drawer front and one at the other end. Take care when cutting them in as a lot of material is removed.

Polishing

I had finished all the internal parts of the box before gluing up. All parts were french polished with transparent shellac (Special Pale) polish to a full-bodied finish, allowing plenty of time for drying between applications and very little white oil to lubricate the rubber. I didn't use a grain filler because the Brazilian mahogany used for the main carcase is very light in colour, almost salmon pink, and this contrasts very well with the darker mahogany used for lippings and the interior divisions. Apart from this contrast the case when closed is devoid of decoration except for the natural grain and colour of the wood used.

Fixing the leather

I purchased the dark green leather tooled with gold border to my specification from the Art Veneers Co. Ltd. in Mildenhall. It arrived on time (14 days after ordering), carefully packed and of excellent quality.

With the box in its open position, glue a piece of brown or green linen over the whole writing surface with scotch glue or one of the 'Clam' adhesives. Make sure that it is well glued down with no bubbles or creases; allow the glue to dry hard. This type of adhesive is best if it's coloured to match the leather or the wood of the box, because it shows along the lid joint when the box is closed. Cut the leather slightly oversize, glue it down on to the linen covered surface and smooth out bubbles from the centre with a cloth pad, but try not to stretch the leather. Cover the surface with polythene, a board and some weights until the glue has dried. Finally trim the edge neatly into the border with knife and straight-edge.

Hey presto, there's your writing slope. ∎

Cutting list (finished sizes)

Front and back	2	500mm x	185mm x	15mm	Brazilian mahogany
Ends	2	300	185	15	Brazilian mahogany
Top	1	500	300	9	Veneered plywood
Middle surface	1	500	300	6	Veneered plywood
Bottom	1	500	300	9	Veneered plywood
Drawer front	1	250	50	15	Brazilian mahogany
Drawer sides	2	450	50	9	Brazilian mahogany
Drawer back	1	250	50	9	Brazilian mahogany
Drawer bottom	1	450	250	4	Plywood
Internal lids	1	800	250	9	Brazilian mahogany
Cleats	1	800	50	9	Cut 4, Brazilian mahogany
Internal divisions	1	450	80	9	Utile (or darker mahogany)
Internal divisions	1	450	80	5	Cut for intermediate parts
Pen tray	1	200	50	20	Utile
Lippings and borders	8	460	15	3	Utile

1 pair solid drawn brass back-flap hinges 1½in wide
1 2in cut box lock
1 pair 2½in brass military chest handles
2 square glass bottles with screw tops
Green leather skiver with gold tooling all four edges, to size of writing surface

LONDON WOODWORKER SHOW

22ND — 25TH OCTOBER 1987
ALEXANDRA PALACE & PARK, WOOD GREEN, LONDON N22 4AY

OPENING TIMES
22nd — 24th   10.00am-6.00pm
25th   10.00am-5.00pm

ADMISSION PRICES
Adults	£3.50
Senior Citizens	£2.25
Children	£1.50

How to get there — free shuttle service.

Travel by British Rail to Alexandra Palace station and then by free shuttle service or W3 bus.

By road: follow the AA sign posts. Free car parking.

Further information available from:
Argus Specialist Exhibitions Ltd., PO Box 35, Wolsey House, Wolsey Road, Hemel Hempstead, Herts HP2 4SS Tel: 0442 41221

The London Woodworker Show is organised by Argus Specialist Exhibitions and sponsored by Woodworker Magazine.

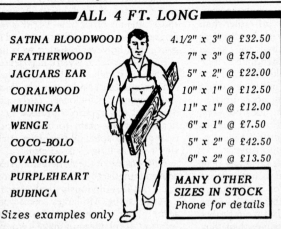

Letters

Carpenter v Joiner

TODAY WE REFER to the man who does our woodwork as a joiner, but the term did not emerge until the 16th century, with the development of panelling work. Disputes between the Guild of Carpenters and the newly-formed Guild of Joiners led to the following definitions:

Carpentry. The art of framing timber for structural work, both temporary and permanent, mainly on-site.

Joinery. Non-structural work, including doors, windows, panelling, skirting and architraves, where appearance not strength is the prime consideration. May be carried out on site or in a workshop.

Today many craftsmen carry out both operations on site and are know as joiners. This is because woodwork on site is divided into first fixing (structural woodwork such as floors, roofs and partitions) and second fixing. So the term first-fixing joiner has replaced carpenter.

Alex Moorehead, Carpentry and Joinery
Lecturer, N. Ireland

Raising the roof: 1

AS A REGULAR READER of WOOD-WORKER since 1946 and a retired carpenter/general forman, may I say how pleased I was to read the article on the steel square in the May issue.

I have used the square for very many roofs and stairs but may I point out that the final item of the roofing table 'purlin cross cut' should read 'blade gives cut', not 'tongue' as printed. The readings for jack rafter and purlin cross cuts differ; one uses the tongue and the other uses the blade.

R. W. Leavett, Maldon

Raising the roof: 2

INSTEAD OF BUYING a roofing square to erect one roof it would be better to buy a roofing ready reckoner from a good bookshop — cheaper and easier to use. The rule of 12 method used is prone to accumulation errors; any inaccuracy in setting the fence or marking the timber will soon alter the length of the roof member.

R. E. James, Basingstoke

● Mr James has devised a computer listing for all the lengths and angles of a normal roof. Please write to us, enclosing sae.

Skittle balls

RE THE QUESTION BOX answer on skittle balls in May's WOODWORKER, I disagree about the woods suggested. White poplar and willow, particularly willow, are two of the softest 'soft hardwoods' grown in this country. Anyone with an elementary knowledge of cricket will know the damage which occurs to the blade of the bat, almost every time it strikes the leather ball, and it has got to be true to say that indentations keep occurring until the bat is really played in, or played out. A skittle ball must be produced from a timber with equal, if not greater, density — or 'weight for weight' to the skittle, otherwise we have a hypothetical situation of bowling a balloon to a table leg — it will bounce off rather than bend the leg. This is obviously a ridiculous comparison, but if skittle balls were made of either of the species mentioned, then they would be virtually useless because they would tend to bounce, not only when running up the alley, but upon impact, rather than hitting the pin and following through. My guess is that neither species would last more than a month on an alley where games were played most nights.

Wych elm would have no advantage over red elm, and in my opinion would be more likely to split. My choice for an alternative would be oak. If elm or this species were used, free of heart centre, but from timber of as curly a grain as possible, then they would be next suitable to lignum vitae in my opinion. The correspondent should not worry unduly over the balls 'breaking up' unless he is experiencing actual splits, because all show dents, ovalling after age, which is accepted by players in general.

Finally, in my opinion it is wrong to recommend oiling the balls. When hardwood dries, it becomes not only harder to work, but harder in itself, and to add oil must, in the same way as water, increase the liquid content. This only serves to soften the surface again to some degree. When the pins are made, they are then treated with coats of the hardest lacquer or varnish available, which not only preserves the original surface, but helps to absorb the immediate impact of the ball. It follows therefore that a number of coats to the actual balls will have the same effect.

G. James, Bridgwater

Tobias Kaye replies:

Some of the points Mr James makes about my suggestions for treating wood for skittle-ball making (*WW/May*) are most interesting. Some are based on a misunderstanding of certain properties of wood.

My interpretation of the original question was that flaking was the problem and I think if wood with heart or pith had been used, major cracking would also have occurred with elm.

Elm was not a bad choice as I said, not the best but better than most. On the question of willow or oak, I think Mr James is a little confused. Hardness and resistance to splitting are two completely different things. As most people will know, if you make a carving mallet, baseball bat — or any item receiving shocks — from oak, it quickly flakes off and ceases to be much use (apart from transmitting shock to the hands).

Willow and white poplar are well known for their resistance to splitting, be it with an axe, as clogs for feet or with a cricket ball. However, Mr James' point about weight bears consideration. Apart from his balloon and table leg fantasy I can appreciate that residual momentum from a glancing blow to the first pin is important for knocking down further pins, plus the momentum transmitted from the ball to any pins knocked down is useful when those pins hit other pins. For this reason I can see choosing a lightweight wood is not a good idea, however resistant to splitting.

In my experience wych elm is denser than English or Dutch elm (I've never heard of red elm and can't find it in my book of trees and timbers). Obviously curly grain is desirable: any type of interlock or densification of the grain formation increases resistance to splitting but even curly oak won't last as long as good elm.

It is because of the difficulty and expense of obtaining large sections of lignum vitae that I put this obviously ideal wood in last.

As to oiling, Mr James seems confused again about hardness and resistance to splitting. If oil does not make a wood more flexible and resistant to splitting why do cricketers oil their bats and why did carvers and carpenters of old stand their mallets in pots of oil?

Fast service!

IN REMOVING THE BARS on my Tyme Cub lathe to fit longer ones, I damaged the studs which hold the bar. I attended the Woodworker Show at Bristol on the Saturday, and spoke to the young man on the Tyme Machines stand to see if he would have a spare stud. He said, unfortunately no, but if I would leave my name and address he would post one on. I thought, I have heard that before, but on the Tuesday following two studs arrived in the post. I call that really something.

In these days of 'couldn't care less' attitudes I thought that was a very fine gesture on the part of Tyme Machines of Bristol.

H. Laycock, Barnstaple

Wheeze errata

SOME OMISSIONS and 'misinterpretations' found their way into the reproduction of Graham Smith's 'Woodworking Wheeze of the Month' in the June issue.

The blades of the Multi-gauge's cutting head were shown as if they were held side-on to the end of the stock. Of course they are pinched between plates and stock-end on their flat faces. The moveable hornbeam block (the 'head') is 6x4x3in; the hag's tooth is fixed to the side of the end of the stock, sitting behind and slightly below the cutting edges of the blades to lift the work, with two 2BA screws into threaded inserts. It is a piece of mild steel shaped into a dog's leg. And if you wondered how you could cut an adjustable-diameter circle, it's because the pin on the bottom of the 'head' was not shown; it is a small brass BA screw stripped of head and thread, ground to a point, and push-fitted into a bush Araldited into the bottom face of the 'head'. It can be used as a pivot for the cutters, or as a cutter (or marker) itself, with the pivot hole

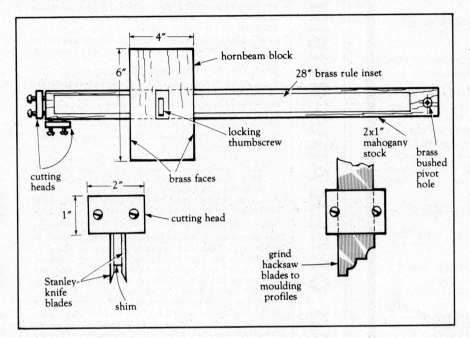

Diagram labels:
- 4″
- 6″
- hornbeam block
- 28″ brass rule inset
- locking thumbscrew
- 2x1″ mahogany stock
- brass bushed pivot hole
- brass faces
- cutting heads
- 2″
- 1″
- cutting head
- Stanley-knife blades
- shim
- grind hacksaw blades to moulding profiles

bushed in at one end of the stock operating as the centre of the circle. It is all made from materials which Graham had or was given — and the cost is a genuine 80p. We're sorry for embarrassment this may have caused Graham, or inconvenience to readers.

Exploitation

FOLLOWING THE COMMENTS in your excellent column 'The Woodwork Business' (*WW*/June) saying that fancy grain commands a higher price, I must make these observations.

Articles have appeared in your magazine about the disappearing rainforests, about over-use of some popular species of timber and non-use of others, which in turn leads to burning of vast quantities of excellent timber *in situ* due to commercial non-viability. Other articles have described how species we value as 'exotic', such as ebony and some rosewoods, are being made virtually extinct. These articles appear to have been generally appreciated and are of great value to the future of woodworking, but so long as people look no further than the ends of their noses, and buy, process and sell for a quick profit, pretty-looking timbers from foreign climes, they are as guilty as anybody of exploiting the world's timber resources.

Considering the timbers available in this country, I think it behoves us to ask whether we can select aspects of the world socio-economic process to support, and other to boycott.

As consumers, it is up to us to select timber in such a way that we do not cause or encourage unnecessary exploitation of the world's resources. There are many beautiful timbers grown in Britain.
Tobias Kaye, Buckfastleigh, Devon

● **Wheeze errata:** *check corrections if you intend making the useful multi-gauge featured in* Hands On/June

Realistic advice?

COULD THIS BE the long-awaited realistic advice I have not yet seen written I asked myself when I spotted 'The Woodwork Business — The Price' (*WW*/June)?

Hugh O'Neill started off all right at first but blew it all in the second and subsequent paragraphs. He talks of random price-fixing. I would accuse him of random figure fixing! A woodworker earning £20,000 a year for working five days a week, for only five hours a day! I wasn't surprised to read at the end of his article that he is not a professional woodworker.

You can't compare the average woodworker with a garage who are charging £20 per hour for repair work: the mechanic won't be getting that amount, at least half of it will be taken up in overheads and the garage has employees — so it's a completely different ball-game.

As for Mike Whitford's article, it certainly looked impressive — all those figures and formulas, not to mention 'burden factors' and 'profit multipliers'. I haven't got any of these, perhaps that's what I need — do Startrite make them?

I have been a furniture maker for many years and only recently have I been able to consider holidays or charging anywhere near £20 per hour. The only way to put yourself in this position is to build up a reputation for producing good quality work are reasonable prices.

Most of the amateurs I know, are amateurs because they couldn't earn a living as a professional woodworker; very few professionals are making a decent living. Those who are employ staff and are into things like kitchens and shopfitting work. A

classic example is a cabinetmaker who, to look at his publicity literature, is a second John Makepeace. In fact he employs several people who mass-produce kitchen fitments to fund his commissioned work which, when it comes down to it, is nothing more than a hobby.

What I'm saying is that the hand-made market is not as easy as it's made out. Just because something is hand-made does not necessarily mean that it's better than a mass-produced item. Unfortunately, the opposite is often the case; because you're doing something you enjoy doing, you can't expect people to pay over the odds for it. The 'handmade in solid wood' tag is in danger of getting a bad name. So my advice to a would-be professional woodworker is to stand back and look at what you are producing. Is it worth £20 per hour? Would you pay the same for a comparative piece in clay, made by a potter of similar skill and experience as yourself?

Don't forget you are doing something you enjoy and gives you great personal satisfaction; where does this come into Michael Whitford's formula? Costings are important but they must be realistic — overcharging can be just as damaging as undercharging.

Stephen Edgar, Salisbury

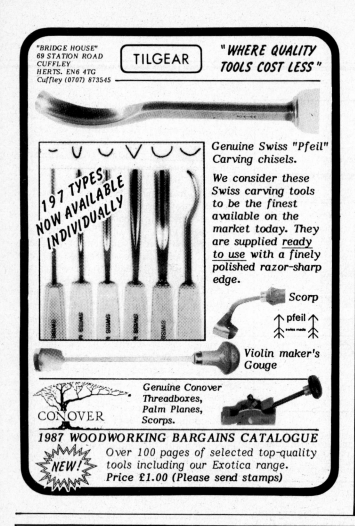

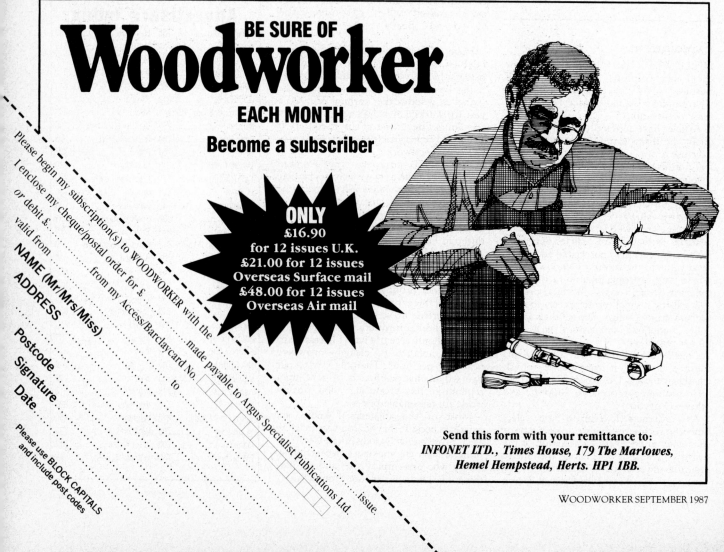

WOODWORKER SEPTEMBER 1987

shopguide

AVON

BATH   Tel. Bath 64513
JOHN HALL TOOLS   ★
RAILWAY STREET
Open: Monday-Saturday
9.00 a.m.5.30 p.m.
H.P.W.WM.D.A.BC.

BRISTOL   Tel. (0272) 741510
JOHN HALL TOOLS LIMITED   ★
CLIFTON DOWN SHOPPING CENTRE
WHITELADIES ROAD
Open: Monday-Saturday
9.00 a.m.-5.30 p.m.
H.P.W.WM.D.A.BC.

BRISTOL   Tel. (0272) 667013
WILLIS   T
157 WEST STREET
BEDMINSTER
Open Mon.-Fri. 8.30 a.m.-5.00 p.m.
P.W.WM.CS.A.BC.

BERKSHIRE

READING   Tel. Littlewick Green
DAVID HUNT (TOOL   2743
MERCHANTS) LTD   ★
KNOWL HILL, NR. READING
Open: Monday-Saturday
9.00 a.m.-5.30 p.m.
H.P.W.D.A.BC.

READING   Tel. Reading 661511
WOKINGHAM TOOL CO. LTD.   T
99 WOKINGHAM ROAD
Open: Mon-Sat 9.00 a.m.-5.30 p.m.
Closed 1.00-2.00 p.m. for lunch
H.P.W.WM.D.CS.A.BC.

BUCKINGHAMSHIRE

MILTON KEYNES   Tel. (0908)
POLLARD WOODWORKING   641366
CENTRE   T★
51 AYLESBURY ST., BLETCHLEY
Open: Mon.-Fri. 8.30-5.30
Saturday 9.00-5.00
H.P.W.WM.D.CS.A.BC.   **INCA**

SLOUGH   Tel: (06286) 5125
BRAYWOOD ESTATES LTD.   ★
158 BURNHAM LANE
Open: 9.00am-5.30pm.
Monday-Saturday.
H.P.W.WM.CS.A.

HIGH WYCOMBE   Tel. (0494)
ISAAC LORD LTD.   22221
185 DESBOROUGH ROAD   K
Open: Mon.-Fri. 8.00 a.m. to 5.30 p.m.
Saturday 8.30 a.m. to 5.00 p.m.
H.P.W.D.A.WM.MF.

Advertise here to
capture both local
+ national markets

CAMBRIDGESHIRE

CAMBRIDGE   Tel: (0223) 63132
D. MACKAY LTD.   ★
BRITANNIA WORKS, EAST ROAD
Open: Mon.-Fri. 8.30 a.m.-1 p.m./2.00-
5.00 p.m. Sat. 8.30 a.m.-1.00 p.m.
H.P.W.D.T.CS.MF.A.BC.

CAMBRIDGE   Tel. (0223) 247386
H. B. WOODWORKING   TK
105 CHERRY HINTON ROAD
Open: 8.30 a.m.-5.30 p.m.
Monday-Friday
8.30 a.m.-1.00 p.m. Sat.
H.P.W.WM.D.CS.A.MF.BC.

CHESHIRE

NANTWICH   Tel. Crewe 67010
ALAN HOLTHAM   TK★
THE OLD STORES TURNERY
WISTASON ROAD, WILLASTON
Open: Tues.-Fri. 9.00 a.m.-5.30 p.m.
Sat. 9.00 a.m.-5.00 p.m. Closed Monday.
P.W.WM.D.T.C.CS.A.BC.

WIDNESS   Tel: 051 424 4545/7965
THE POWER TOOL CENTRE   T★
54/58 VICTORIA ROAD, WA8 7PJ
Mon.-Fri. 8.30am-5pm
Sat. 8.30am-4pm.
H.P.W.WM.D.CS.A.BC.

CLEVELAND

MIDDLESBROUGH   Tel. (0642)
CLEVELAND WOODCRAFT   813103
(M'BRO), 38-42 CRESCENT ROAD   TK
Open: Mon.-Sat. 9.15 a.m.-5.30 p.m.
H.P.A.BC.W.WM.CS.D.

CORNWALL

SOUTH WEST Power Tools
CORNWALL   Tel: Helston (03265) 4961
HELSTON AND LAUNCESTON   Launceston
(0566) 4781
H.P.W.WM.D.CS.A.   TK

CUMBRIA

CARLISLE   Tel. (0228) 36391
W. M. PLANT   T
ALLENBROOK ROAD
ROSEHILL, CA1 2UT
Open: Mon.-Fri. 8.00 a.m.-5.15 p.m.
Sat. 8.00 a.m.-12.30 noon
P.W.WM.D.CS.A.

DEVON

PLYMOUTH   Tel. (0752) 330303
WESTWARD BUILDING SERVICES   ★
LTD., LISTER CLOSE, NEWNHAM
INDUSTRIAL ESTATE, PLYMPTON
Open: Mon-Fri 8.00 a.m.-5.30 p.m.
Sat. 8.30 a.m.-12.30 p.m.
H.P.W.WM.D.A.BC.

DEVON

PLYMOUTH   Tel. (0752) 665363
F.T.B. LAWSON LTD.   T
71 NEW GEORGE STREET
PLYMOUTH PL1 1RB
Open: Mon.-Sat. 8.30 a.m.-5.30 p.m.
H.P.W.CS.MF.A.

DORSET

WEYMOUTH   Tel. (0305) 770303
WEYMOUTH HIRE & SALES LTD.   TK
5 KENT CLOSE
GRANBY INDUSTRIAL ESTATE
Open 7.30 a.m.-5.30 p.m. Mon.-Fri.
Sat. 8 a.m.-1 p.m.
H.P.W.WM.D.CS.A.K.

ESSEX

LEIGH ON SEA   Tel. (0702)
MARSHAL & PARSONS LTD.   710404
1111 LONDON ROAD   K
Open: 8.30 a.m.-5.30 p.m. Mon.-Fri.
9.00 a.m.-5.00 p.m. Sat.
H.P.W.WM.D.CS.A.

ILFORD   Tel. 597 7461
CUTWELL WOODWORKING   T★
776 HIGH ROAD
GOODMAYES IG3 8SY
H.P.W.WM.D.CS.A.

GLOUCESTER

TEWKESBURY   Tel. (0684)
TEWKESBURY SAW CO. LTD.   293092
TRADE. ESTATE, NEWTOWN   K
Telex No. 43382
Open: Mon-Fri 8.00 a.m.-5.00 p.m.
Saturday 9.30 a.m.-12.00 p.m.
P.W.WM.D.CS.

HAMPSHIRE

ALDERSHOT   **SOUTHAMPTON**
(0252) 334422   (0703) 332288
BURCH & HILLS POWER TOOL CENTRES
374 HIGH ST.   7 BELVIDERE RD.
Open Mon.-Fri. 8.30-5.30. Sat. 8.30-12.00
Closed for Lunch 1.00-2.00
H.P.W.WM.D.CS.MF.BC.K.★   T

HEREFORDSHIRE

HEREFORD   Tel. (0432) 271366
WOODWORKING CENTRE
100 WIDEMARSH ST., HR4 9HG
Open: Mon.-Sat. 8 a.m.-5.30 p.m.
H.P.W.WM.D.CS.MF.A.T.

HERTFORDSHIRE

WARE   Tel: (0920) 870 230
HEATH SAWS   870 636
6 LEESIDE WORKS   K★
STANSTEAD ABBOTTS (near Ware) HERTS.
SG12 8DL.
Open: Mon.-Fri. 8.30 a.m.-5.30 p.m.
Sat. 8.30 a.m.-1 p.m. Sunday by appointment.
H.P.W.WM.D.T.CS.MF.A.BC.★K.

HUMBERSIDE

HULL
HUMBERSIDE FACTORING/H.F.C.
SAW SERVICING LTD.
MAIN STREET
Open: Mon.-Fri. 8am-5pm.
Saturday 8am-12.00pm.
H.P.W.WM.D.CS.A.BC.K.

KENT

MAIDSTONE   Tel: (0622) 44350
HENSON AND PLATT
TOKE PLACE
LINTON
Open Mon.-Fri. 8.00 a.m.-5.00 p.m.
Saturday 8.00 a.m.-1.00 p.m.
H.P.W.T.CS.A.

MAIDSTONE   Tel. (0622) 50177
SOUTH EASTERN SAWS (Ind.) LTD.   ★
COLORED ROAD
PARKWOOD INDUSTRIAL ESTATE
Open: Mon.-Fri. 8.00 a.m.-5.00 p.m.
Sat. 9.00 a.m.-12.00 a.m.
B.C.W.CS.WM.PH.

LANCASHIRE

PRESTON   Tel. (0772) 52951
SPEEDWELL TOOL COMPANY   ★
62-68 MEADOW STREET PR1 1SU
Open: Mon.-Fri. 8.30 a.m.-5.30 p.m.
Sat. 8.30 a.m.-12.30 p.m.
H.P.W.WM.CS.A.MF.BC.

ROCHDALE   Tel. (0706) 342123/
C.S.M. TOOLS   342322
4-6 HEYWOOD ROAD   T★
CASTLETON
Open: Mon-Sat 9.00 a.m.-6.00 p.m.
Sundays by appointment
W.D.CS.A.BC.

LANCASTER   Tel. (0524) 32886
LILE TOOL SHOP   K
43/45 NORTH ROAD
Open: Monday to Saturday
9.00 a.m.-5.30 p.m.
Wed. 9.00 a.m.-12.30 p.m.
H.P.W.D.A

Read Model Engineer for a new angle on construction & design

BLACKPOOL   Tel. (0253) 28262
FYLDE WOODTURNING SUPPLIES   ★
255 CHURCH STREET, FY1 3PB
Open: 9.30-5.30 Monday to Friday.
9.30-4.30 Saturday. Closed Wednesday.
H.T.W.WM.A.MF.BC.D.

shopguide

LONDON

ACTON   Tel. (01-992) 4835
A. MILLS (ACTON) LTD.
32/36 CHURCHFIELD ROAD W3 6ED
Open: Mon.-Fri. 8.32 a.m.-5.30 p.m.
Saturdays 9.00 a.m.-1.00 p.m.
H.P.W.WM.

LONDON   Tel. 01-723 2295-6-7
LANGHAM TOOLS LIMITED
13 NORFOLK PLACE
LONDON W2 1QJ

FULHAM   Tel. (01-636) 6109
I. GRIZARD LTD.
84a-b.c. LILLIE ROAD, SW6 1TL
Open: Mon.-Sat. 9.00-5.30 p.m.
Half day Thursday

H.P.A.BC.W.CS.WM.D.

MANCHESTER

MANCHESTER   Tel. (061 789)
TIMMS TOOLS   0909
102-104 LIVERPOOL ROAD   ★
PATRICROFT M30 0WZ
Weekdays 9.00 a.m.-5.30 p.m.
Sat. 9.00 a.m.-1.00 p.m.
H.P.A.W.

MANCHESTER   Tel: 061 834 0714
TILL AND WHITEHEAD   ★
ELLESMERE STREET, M15 4JX

Open: Mon.-Fri. 8.00 a.m.-5.00 p.m.

H.P.W.A.BC.

MERSEYSIDE

LIVERPOOL   Tel. (051-207) 2967
TAYLOR BROS (LIVERPOOL) LTD.   TK
195-199 LONDON ROAD
LIVERPOOL L3 8JG
Open: Monday to Friday
8.30 a.m.-5.30 p.m.
H.P.W.WM.D.A.BC.

MIDDLESEX

ENFIELD   Tel. 01-363 2935
GILL & HOXBY LTD.   T
131-137 ST. MARKS ROAD ADJ.
BUSH HILL PARK STATION, EN1 1BA
Mon.-Sat. 8-5.30
Early closing Wed. 1 p.m.
H.P.A.M.MC.T.S.W.

RUISLIP   Tel. (08956) 74126
ALLMODELS ENGINEERING LTD.   ★
91 MANOR WAY

Open: Mon.-Sat. 9.00 a.m.-5.30 p.m.

H.P.W.A.D.CS.MF.BC.

NORFOLK

NORWICH   Tel. (0603) 898695
NORFOLK SAW SERVICES
DOG LANE, HORSFORD
Open: Monday to Friday
8.00 a.m.-5.00 p.m.
Saturday 8.00 a.m.-12.00 p.m.
H.P.W.WM.D.CS.A.

NORFOLK

KINGS LYNN   Tel. (0553) 772443
WALKER & ANDERSON (Kings Lynn) LTD.   T
WINDSOR ROAD, KINGS LYNN
Open: Monday to Saturday
7.45 a.m.-5.15 p.m.

H.P.W.WM.D.CS.A.

NORWICH   Tel. (0603) 400933
WESTGATES WOODWORKING   Tx
61 HURRICANE WAY,   975412
NORWICH AIRPORT INDUSTRIAL ESTATE
Open: 9.00 a.m.-5.00 p.m. weekdays
9.00 a.m.-12.30 Sat.
P.W.WM.D.BC.   K

KINGS LYNN   Tel. 07605 674
NORFOLK WOODTURNING CENTRE   ★
UNIT A, HILL FARM WORKSHOPS
GREAT DUNHAM (Nr. Swaffham)
Tues.-Sat. 9.00am-5.30pm

H.P.W.D.T.MF.A.BC.

NORTHAMPTONSHIRE

RUSHDEN   Tel: (0933) 56424
PETER CRISP OF RUSHDEN   T★
7-11 HIGH STREET
Mon.-Fri. 8.30-12.30/1.30-5.30
Thurs. 8.30-1.00. Sat. all day.
H.P.W.WM.D.M.F.A.K.

NOTTINGHAMSHIRE

NOTTINGHAM   Tel: (0602) 225979
POOLEWOOD   and 227064/5
EQUIPMENT LTD.   (06077) 2421 after hrs
5a HOLLY LANE, CHILLWELL
Open: Mon-Fri 9.00 a.m.-5.30 p.m.
Sat. 9.00 a.m. to 12.30 p.m.
P.W.WM.D.CS.A.BC.

OXON

WITNEY   Tel. (0993) 76431
TARGET TOOLS (SALES,   OXON
TARGET TOOLS HIRE & REPAIRS)   T★
SWAIN COURT
STATION INDUSTRIAL ESTATE
Open: Mon.-Sat. 8.00 a.m.-5.00 p.m.
24 hour Answerphone
BC.W.M.A.

SHROPSHIRE

TELFORD   Tel. Telford (0952)
ASLES LTD.   48054
VINEYARD ROAD, WELLINGTON   K★

Open: Mon.-Fri. 8.30 a.m.-5.30 p.m.
Saturday 8.30 a.m.-4.00 p.m.
H.P.W.WM.D.CS.BC.A.

SOMERSET

TAUNTON   Tel. (0823) 335431
JOHN HALL TOOLS   ★
6 HIGH STREET

Open Monday-Saturday
9.00 a.m.-5.30 p.m.
H.P.W.WM.D.CS.A.

SUFFOLK

IPSWICH   Tel. (0473) 40456
FOX WOODWORKING   463884
142-144 BRAMFORD LANE   T★
Open: Tues.-Fri. 9 a.m.-5.30 p.m.
Sat. 9 a.m.-5 p.m.
W.WM.D.T.CS.MF.A.BC.K.*

STAFFORDSHIRE

TAMWORTH   Tel: (0827) 56188
MATTHEWS BROTHERS LTD.   TK★
KETTLEBROOK ROAD
Open: Mon.-Sat. 8.30 a.m.-5.30 p.m.
Demonstrations Sunday mornings by
appointment only
H.P.WM.D.T.CS.A.BC.K.

SURREY

GUILDFORD   Tel. (0483) 61125
MESSINGERS FOR TOOLS   T
18-18 CHERTSEY ST.
(TOP OF NORTH ST.)
Open: Tues.-Sat. 8.30 a.m.-5.30 p.m.
H.P.W.CS.MF.A.BC.K.

**Read Model Engineer
for a new angle on
construction and
design.**

SUSSEX

WORTHING   Tel. (0903) 38739
W. HOSKING LTD. (TOOLS &   KT★
MACHINERY)
28 PORTLAND RD, BN11 1QN
Open: Mon.-Sat. 8.30 a.m.-5.30 p.m.
Closed Wednesday
H.P.W.WM.D.CS.A.BC.

TYNE & WEAR

NEWCASTLE-UPON-TYNE   ★
J. W. HOYLE LTD
CLARENCE STREET
NEWCASTLE-UPON-TYNE
TYNE & WEAR
NE2 17J
H.P.W.WM.D.CS.A.BC.K.

W. MIDLANDS

WOLVERHAMPTON   Tel: (0902)
MANSAW SERVICES   58759
WARD STREET, HORSELEY FIELDS   TK★
WOLVERHAMPTON, WEST MIDLANDS
Open: Mon.-Fri. 8.00 a.m.-6.00 p.m.
Saturday 8 a.m.-3 p.m.
H.P.W.WM.A.D.CS.

YORKSHIRE

THIRSK   Tel. (0845) 22770
THE WOOD SHOP   ★
TRESKE SAWMILLS LTD.
STATION WORKS
Open: Seven days a week 9.00-5.00

T.H.MF.BC.H.

SHEFFIELD   Tel. (0742) 441012
GREGORY & TAYLOR LTD.   K
WORKSOP ROAD
Open: 8.30 a.m.-5.30 p.m.
Monday-Friday
8.30 a.m.-12.30 p.m. Saturday
H.P.W.WM.D.

HARROGATE   Tel. (0423) 505328/
MULTI-TOOLS   66245
158 KINGS ROAD   K★

Open: Monday to Saturday
8.30 a.m.-6.00 p.m.
H.P.W.WM.D.A.BC.

YORKSHIRE

HOLME UPON   Tel. (0696) 60612
SPALDING MOOR
CRAFT TOOLS AND TACKLE LTD.
HOLME INDUSTRIAL ESTATE
Open: Mon.-Fri. 9.00 am-5.30 pm.
Saturday & Bank Holiday 9.00 am-4.30 pm
H.P.W.D.T.CS.MF.A.BC.

LEEDS   Tel. (0532) 574736
D. B. KEIGHLEY MACHINERY LTD.   ★
VICKERS PLACE, STANNINGLEY
PUDSEY LS2 86LZ
Mon.-Fri. 9.00 a.m.-5.00 p.m.
Sat. 9.00 a.m.-1.00 p.m.
P.A.W.WM.CS.BC.

CLECKHEATON   Tel. (0274)
SKILLED CRAFTS LTD.   872861
34 BRADFORD ROAD   ★

Open: 9.00 a.m.-5.00 p.m. Monday
Saturday Lunch 12.00 a.m.-1.00 p.m.
H.P.A.W.CS.WM.D.

SCOTLAND

PERTH   Tel. (0738) 26173
WILLIAM HUME & CO.   TK
ST. JOHN'S PLACE
Open: Monday to Saturday
8.00 a.m.-5.30 p.m.
8.00 a.m.-1.00 p.m. Wednesday
H.P.A.BC.W.CS.WM.D.

EDINBURGH   Tel. 031-337-5555
THE SAW CENTRE   T
38 HAYMARKET TERRACE
EDINBURGH EH12 5JZ
Mon.-Fri. 8.30 a.m.-5.30 p.m.
Saturday 9.00 a.m.-1.00 p.m.
H.P.W.WM.D.CS.A.

PERTH   Tel: (0738) 36777
WORKMASTER POWER TOOLS LTD.   T★
8 SHORE ROAD, PH2 8BW
Mon.-Fri. 8.30 a.m.-5 p.m.
Sat. 9.00 a.m.-4 p.m.
Other times by appointment
H.P.W.WM.D.CS.A.

GLASGOW   Tel. 041-429-4444/
THE SAW CENTRE   4374 Telex: 777886
650 EGLINTON STREET   T★
GLASGOW G5 9RP
Mon.-Fri. 8.00 a.m.-5.00 p.m.
Sat. 9.00 a.m.-1.00 p.m.
H.P.W.WM.D.CS.A.

IRELAND

NEWTOWNARDS   Tel: 0247 819800
NORLYN MACHINERY   or 812506
UNIT 10, MALCOLMSON IND. EST.
80 BANGOR ROAD, CO. DOWN
Open: Mon.-Fri. 9.30am-5.30pm
(Closed 1-2pm for lunch)
Any other time by request.
H.W.WM.D.T.MF.A.   24 Hour Service.K

PORTADOWN   Tel. (0762) 332546
LOCKE TOOLS   ★
50 WEST STREET BT62 3JQ
Mon.-Sat. 9 a.m.-5.30 p.m.
Any other time by request.
H.D.W.WM.D.CS.A.BC.

shop guide

WOOD SUPPLIERS

WOOD SUPPLIERS

NEXT DEADLINE
9th September
November issue

Classified Advertisements

All classified advertisements under £30.00 must be pre-paid: Cheques/PO made payable to A.S.P. Ltd. (WW).
Rates: Lineage: 58p per word (VAT inclusive) minimum £8.70. **Semi-display:** £9.65 + VAT per single column centimetre (minimum 2.5 × 1). **Copy to Classified Dept. (W.W.), A.S.P. Ltd., 1 Golden Square, London W1.** All advertisements are inserted in the first available issue. There are no re-imbursements for cancellations.

Telephone 01-437-0699 ext. 293

FOR SALE

THE FINEST SELECTION ON DISPLAY IN SCOTLAND!

THE SAW CENTRE

WOODWORKING & METALWORKING MACHINERY POWER TOOLS HAND TOOLS

NEW! Coronet and Triton stockist. Glasgow in-store demo — Sept. 3/4/5.

LARGE STOCKS - COMPETITIVE PRICES. PHONE AND TRY US *NOW!*

Eglinton Toll, Glasgow
G5 9RP
Tel: 041-429-4444

38 Haymarket
Edinburgh
EH12 5J2
Tel: 031-337-5555

OPEN
Mon - Fri
8am - 5pm
Sat 9am - 1pm

WOODCARVING tools

LARGEST STOCK IN EUROPE

Henry Taylor
Arkansas Bench & Slip Stones
Strops & Strop Paste
Bench Screws, Carvers' Vices

WOODTURNING tools
Complete range of
Henry Taylor
handled or unhandled

send 40p in stamps for illustrated catalogue

ALEC TIRANTI LTD
70 High St, Theale, Reading, Berks RG7 5AR
27 Warren Street, London W1.

CONTENTS of 3 school workshops, engineering and woodworking machines and various tools. For detailed list write to: Warners Machinery Centre, Unit 10, Finedon Road, Irthlingborough, Northants.

BLADES — also for machinery!

INCA Euro 260 Popular Bandsaw	**£390.00**
NAEROK PT150 Planer/Thicknesser	**£250.00**
A-Z1 Dust Extractor	**£179.00**
RYOBI R500 Plunge Router ½"	**£150.00**

Prices include VAT & carriage UK mainland. Send a foolscap SAE for more details and our new price list of planer knives, router cutters, moulding heads, and circular saw blades to: BLADES, Dept. WW, PO Box 27, Petersfield, Hants. GU32 2NB.

STANLEY VICTOR COMPASS PLANE £45.
Stanley Traut - Skew - Cutters, Plow and Fillet-ster £65. Tel: 0208 863585.

BANKRUPT STOCK

Sandvik circular saw blades tungsten tipped
Hurry! Last few remaining
5", 5½", 6" **£4.00** each.
Any bore up to 30mm.
8¼" **£6.00** each.
Any bore up to 35mm.
P&P £1 extra per order.
Tel: 643 0244
Hannett, 11 Lind Road,
Sutton, Surrey.

Yorkwire (Leeds) Ltd.
BRASS WIRE, ROD, STRIP & TUBE

Suitable for Miniature furniture, Clock Pendulums, Inlay work and many other Crafts.

SAE for Price List to:
Yorkwire (Leeds) Ltd.
34 Lupton Street,
Leeds LS10 2QW.
Tel: 0532 777472

CONTENTS OF TECH COLLEGE woodwork, engineering and sheet metal machines, some 240 volt approx 70 items. For list send s.a.e. Write only to "Trade", 155 High Street, Irthlingborough, Northants.

CORONET LATHE saw/planer attachment £495. Hampshire. Alton 63374.

THE WHISTON CATALOGUE

Nuts, bolts, screws, washers, bar materials. In brass, alloy, steel, stainless steel, P.T.F.E., nylon, Tufnol, sheet material, electrical and mechanical items. We could go on and on! Better to send for free catalogue and see for yourself.
K. R. Whiston Ltd., Dept. WW, New Mills, Stockport, Cheshire. Phone: 0663 42028.

SITUATIONS VACANT

ANTIQUE RESTORERS

Needed for English and Continental furniture, porcelain, carvers and gilders for high level antique restoration business in North America.
Must be intelligent and of highest calibre. Qualifications: Graduate of an intensive hands-on recognised school of antique objects restoration with at least 3 years job experience, or a more mature applicant with an apprenticeship and 10 years job experience. Return our flight and immediate accommodation, assistance with long-term housing and work permits offered in return for a minimum of 2 years commitment to the growth of the most unique antique restoration business today. Exciting long term position available to only the best willing to expand their horizons into teaching and management.

Successful retail and restoration antiques
business owners

Seeking an opportunity to expand into a most lucrative market are encouraged to respond. The company seeking applicants is showing tremendous growth and potential and will welcome all contacts.
References, short explanation of expectations for future and CV's including full U.K. Tel. No. to:
For U.K. interview in September.
Box No. WW128, Woodworker Classified, ASP Ltd., 1 Golden Square, London W1R 3AB.

Cabinet Maker/Joiner Wanted

Good opportunity for intelligent, hard working, adaptable, reliable and experienced woodworker.
If you are interested telephone 0258 72717 and see if you fit the bill or write to:
Poisedale Ltd., The Workshop, Hinton, St. Mary, Sturminster, Newton, Dorset DT10 1NA.

BUSINESS OPPORTUNITIES

YORKSHIRE DALES

An excellent and unique opportunity exists for a number of craftsmen in an established workshop in North Yorkshire. Successful applicants will have full use of a comprehensively equipped machine shop and individual bench space. In addition full reception, administration and marketing back-up will be provided. In short a complete business package geared towards the individual trading craftsman and a superb opportunity for craftsmen to start in their own business. Places available for Cabinet makers, furniture makers, timber machinists, woodturners.

Phone (0423) 780901

To advertise ring
01-437 0699

BUSINESS FOR SALE

SMALL fully equipped workshop. Beds/Bucks borders. Long lease for full details ring Leighton Buzzard 372719.

WANTED

Skilled and experienced foreman joiner wanted

to join small team producing custom-built conservatories and quality joinery. Please write for details to:
Cowlie and Roberts,
Unit 17,
Ddole Road Industrial Estate, Llandrindod Wells, Powys.
LD1 6DF.

David Savage FURNITURE MAKER — CABINET-MAKER

THE POST WOULD SUIT A MAKER WITH WIDE EXPERIENCE OF WORK DONE TO THE VERY HIGHEST STANDARDS. A UNIQUE OPPORTUNITY TO JOIN THIS HAPPY AND CREATIVE WORKSHOP.

FOR DETAILS SEND LARGE SAE TO:
DAVID SAVAGE FURNITURE, 21 Westcombe, Bideford EX39 3JQ.

WALL PANELLING

COMPLETE, individual traditionally styled hardwood and veneer wall panels. Removable, unique fixing system, easy to install. Send S.A.E. for information or £3.85 for full details and set of finished panel inserts to: Pardale Panelling, Glasfryn, Ponterwyd, Aberystwyth, Dyfed, SY23 3JU. Tel: 0970 5154.

Kindly mention 'Woodworker' when replying to advertisements

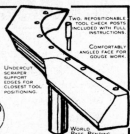

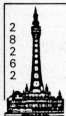

FYLDE WOODTURNING SUPPLIES

2
8
2
6
2

VISIT OUR NEW SHOWROOM AND SEE OUR RANGE OF WOODTURNERS, TOOLS, LATHES, BANDSAWS, DUST EXTRACTORS, BAROMETER ETC, FINISHING MATERIALS, CERAMIC TILES & CLOCK FACES, QUARTZ MOVEMENTS, FINGERS, ETC. ALSO SELECTION OF EXOTIC & ENGLISH HARDWOODS. *S.A.E. FOR PRICE LIST. MAIL ORDER A PLEASURE.*

255 CHURCH STREET, BLACKPOOL FY1 3PB

Eric Tomkinson Woodturner

Woodturning Supplies by mail order or over the counter. Our mail order department was established in 1973 and has a reputation second to none for speed of delivery and quality of merchandise. Why not visit our shop where friendly advice and help is always available. Shop hours 9-5 Mon.-Fri., Sat. 9-4pm. Most major credit cards accepted. Please send s.a.e. for list.
**ERIC TOMKINSON, 86 Stockport Road, Cheadle, Cheshire SK8 2AT.
Tel: 061-491-1726**

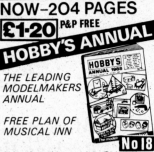

NOW–204 PAGES
£1·20 P&P FREE

HOBBY'S ANNUAL

THE LEADING MODELMAKERS ANNUAL

FREE PLAN OF MUSICAL INN

No 18

New plans, kits, models. Ships, giant crane, cab with trailer. Match-craft fire engines, masks, 3D cutout pictures. Musical and clock movements. Tools, fretsaw machines. Doll's house fittings and furniture. Unlimited ideas.
From W.H. Smith, Menzies and leading newsagents or direct.

W. Hobby Ltd. (Dept. W) Knight's Hill Square, London SE27 0HH. 01-761 4244.

Caranda Crafts

Cross Lane, Alkborough, Nr. Scunthorpe, S. Humberside. Tel: (0724) 720614
Shop Open Mondays to Fridays 10 a.m. to 5 p.m. Sundays 2 p.m. to 5 p.m.
Other times by appointment.
Mail Order Service available.
Send Now for our 25 page catalogue (50p + SAE). Fast friendly service; very competitive prices.
We supply a complete range of woodturners supplies including attractive, unusual lamp glasses from £1.80 each inc. VAT. Clock movement, faces, barometer insertions, & lots, lots, more.

TUDORCRAFT WOODTURNERS SUPPLIES

We are pleased to announce that we now have new premises offering the best in craft supplies and timbers, which includes exotic and homegrown. We are open from 9.30am to 5pm Monday to Friday.

Please note our new address:
Tudorcraft, Unit 34a Birchbrook Industrial Estate, Off Lynn Lane, Shenstone, Nr. Sutton Coldfield, Staffs. WS14 0DS. Tel: 0543 481515
Please send 50p for our mail order catalogue or call and collect one free.

GUITAR KITS

For under £35 you can make your own classical guitar with our comprehensive kit. Mahogany veneered back and ribs, solid rosewood fingerboard — a quality product with superb tone. Compares with factory made guitars costing many times this price. For full details write or phone:
The Early Music Shop
28 Sunbridge Rd, Bradford, W. Yorks. BD1 2AE
Tel: 0274 393753

MINIATURA

THE SHOWCASE FOR DOLLSHOUSE CRAFTS

in one-twelfth and related scales
AT THE PAVILION SUITE, COUNTY CRICKET GROUND, EDGBASTON ROAD, BIRMINGHAM.
– FREE PARKING –

Saturday, September 26th, 1987
10.30am-5.00pm

Adults £1.75; Children 50p (accompanied)

41 EASTBOURNE AVENUE, BIRMINGHAM B34 6AR.

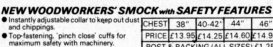

NEW WOODWORKERS' SMOCK with SAFETY FEATURES

● Instantly adjustable collar to keep out dust and chippings.
● Top-fastening, 'pinch close' cuffs for maximum safety with machinery.
● Large, **rear** hip pockets to avoid collecting machine waste.
● 'Clean', uncluttered front with no flaps etc. to snag on work projections.
● Close weave, hard wearing **cotton** drill keeps dirt out but lets you breathe.
● Available in BROWN, NAVY or D. GREEN.

CHEST	38"	40-42"	44"	46"
PRICE	£13.95	£14.25	£14.60	£14.95
POST & PACKING (ALL SIZES) £1.25				

P. LOVELL (WORKWEAR)
3, HEOL ESGYN, CYNCOED, CARDIFF. CF2 6JT
TEL:
(0222) 753014

QUARTER SIZE GRANDFATHER CLOCK KIT

Traditionally styled in solid **mahogany throughout**. Deep etched, **solid brass** break arch dial, with tempus fugit. Easily assembled from our complete D-I-Y kit. Ideal gift at £19.95 + £2 p&p, or send. Just £2.50 for full scale drawing and all details. (Refundable on first order).

CRAFTWOODS WALES
Gwalia Works, Dulais Road, Portardulais, Swansea SA4 1RH Wales. Tel: 0792 884456

THE ONE THE PROFESSIONALS USE

Pyrography TOOL

Burns decoration on Wood, Leather, Cork, etc.
* Takes wire points & solid shaped points
* Light & precise. Quick & easy to use
* Finely adjustable heat to over 1000 C

* Handle stays cool & comfortable

Send £44.50 for STARTER OUTFIT
or send SAE for free brochure

MADE IN UK BY
PETER CHILD
The Old Hyde, Little Yeldham, Essex CO9 4QT.

0787 237291

PYROGRAPHS AND CRAFT SUPPLES

Janik

The biggest range of pyrographic equipment on the market.
The biggest sellers world wide.
Single and duel outlet. Solid point or hotwire. Brands, lettering, numbers etc. Full heat control.
Double insulated. Versatile and reliable. Also a wide range of craft supplies, all wood related.
Craft kits, design books and over 100 white wood articles for various crafts.

Send 50p (stamps) refundable for catalogue and price list to:
**Janik Enterprises (WW),
Brickfield Lane, Ruthin,
Clwyd, North Wales.
Tel: (08242) 2096**

WOODWORKER = RESULTS

"PGS" BALL BEARING PLANER UNITS

Build your own Planer using these superb units, independent housing to allow for thicknessing if required. Rebate to a depth of ½". Planers up to 8". Free drawing of planer with every enquiry. SAE to:
P. SERGENT *Precision Engineer,*
6 Gurney Close, Costessey, Norwich.
Tel: (0603) 747782 Prestel No. 603 747 782

Hobbies
1987 EDITION!
SEND 75p STAMP
POSTAGE INCLUDED (No Cheques please)

FOR LEISURE, PLEASURE AND PROFIT!
Make Wheeled Toys, Dolls Houses, Forts, Garages, Clocks, Musical Novelties etc. A host of spare-time ideas on model making and fretwork. Plus catalogue of Hobbies Plans and sets of fittings for above with
details of fretwork outfits, machines and Hobbies tools.
7 free plans incl.

HOBBIES
1987
HANDBOOK

HOBBIES (DEREHAM) LIMITED
20 ELVIN ROAD
DEREHAM
NORFOLK
NR19 2DX

CONTENTS

October 1987   Vol. 91   No. 10

Woodworker

FACE & EDGE

Look what came out of Woodworker!

The latest commission for furniture designer and maker Martin Grierson came after a feature in this magazine (WW/Dec '86). Nigel Tibbles of Bartholomew Investments, Hove, Sussex, who reads the magazine, says the company had a problem finding a suitable designer/maker for their new boardroom furniture. 'We went to look at the Crafts Council Index. The work of Martin Grierson had the distinction and style that we were seeking. I had seen his work depicted in WOODWORKER, and we arranged a meeting.' In the picture, Robin Furlong is sanding the top of the boardroom sideboard for Bartholomew Investments.

In the other picture Martin Grierson himself is seen assessing the work of Gordon Russell, a student on the new Furniture Craft and Management Diploma course at Buckinghamshire College of Higher Education. The course embraces both furniture design/making and setting up a craft workshop. Martin Grierson is external assessor for the students.

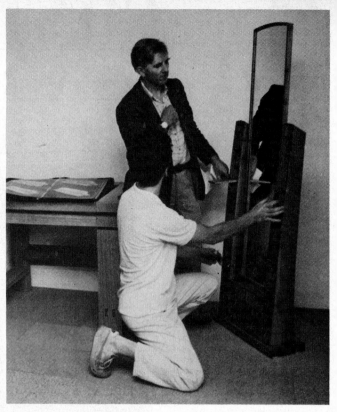

New look

The new WOODWORKER? Well, it looks new — but of course, we're still the same.

One of the crafts you have to master when you deal with words and pictures on a page is how to make that page both informative and attractive. You the reader have to want to read the page, and you have to be able to read it easily.

For some time we've been thinking about how to improve the overall design of WOODWORKER itself; we've felt we need a style to reflect the fine classical traditions of craftsmanship and a modern consciousness of design, both of which it's our job to promote. We have felt that features and projects should have slightly different treatments, and our 'regulars' should be even more immediately recognisable; we have gone for more visual variety, with a coherent scheme at the same time; and, of course, a new set of news and contents pages.

It's a change I believe we needed to make, so we could continue to grow. I hope you like it; I hope you find it easier to read and use, and what's more good to look at. I'm confident you will.

Aidan Walker, Editor

Postform jig

Ever-inventive Trend Machinery introduce a jig to enable you to cut accurate butt and scribed joints on postformed worktops from 600-1000mm wide, 30-40mm thick. It needs a 1200w router with 2in plunge, plus guide bushes and special Trend cutters; buy the jig and use your own router, or get a complete set. Jig with templates costs £378+VAT; 1000mm version £458+VAT. Trend, Unit N, Penfold Works, Imperial Way, Watford, Herts WD2 4YY, (0923) 249911.

Screw gifts

Here we are in July (writing this) announcing Xmas boxes from European Industrial Services (the screw makers Nettlefolds, of course — who else?). The Nettlefolds Handi-box gives you 170 Supascrews, 30 Supaplugs, 30 Supatops and a Supadriv screwdriver for £4.99; the Handi-pack is smaller, for £2.99. Just the thing for the family's stockings. Nettlefolds, Woden Rd, Kings Hill, Wednesbury, W. Mid WS10 7TT, 021-1556 1991.

Forest Action Plan

A Conference in Italy between leaders of 25 developing countries and international agency heads has called for world leaders to support global action and policy reforms to save disappearing tropical forests.

Involving local communities and the private sector in conservation, forest management and reforestation; deforestation monitoring; and strengthening research are among the conference's recommendations. International action all to be pulled together in the framework of the Tropical Forestry Action Plan, which was conceived by the World Resources Institute, the World Bank and the UN Development Program in 1985.

Friends of the Earth welcome the move, but claim there are flaws in the plan itself; it doesn't account for the fact that much deforestation, they say, is the product of schemes funded by institutions like the World Bank itself. Nor does it allocate enough cash, or address the problem of deforestation caused by local subsistence agriculture.

Hole gauge

Solid brass drill and dowel gauge, made to within a thou by master toolmaker Richard Kell, ranges from 1/8-1/2in diameter in nine steps. Fix it on your key ring; give it as an Xmas present. Good tool stores or £3.50 inc. VAT, p&p from Richard Kell, 67 Newbiggin Rd, Ashington, Northumberland NE63 0TB (0670) 351909.

Skill Olympians

Congratulations to Michael Hanson, Gerald Crittenden, Matthew Rohan and Warren Handley, who are in the Skill Olympics UK team for Australia Feb 1988, in cabinetmaking, carpentry, joinery and machine woodworking.

Lignum vitae goblets won Paul Coker of Rothwell, Northants, £200 first prize in the Worshipful Company of Turners' competition.

New price

Sorry, we've had to raise the price of your WOODWORKER to £1.30. Rising costs are as usual to blame, particularly paper; but we're trying harder than ever to give you better value than ever, and not just with another winning series of useful and valuable free gifts. Our insatiable desire to bring you the best projects, the best features, the best writing and the best photographs in the business spurs us ever on. It's the same in magazines as it is in the rich craft of woodwork — you can always improve. We don't intend to stop.

DIARY

Guild courses are shown by an asterisk (*); for further details see **Guild** pages

September

12-7 Nov Castles in the Air, David West woodcarving and paintings exhibition, Cliffe Castle Museum, Spring Gdns Lane, Keighley, W. Yorks, (0535) 664184, open 10-5 Tues-Sun

16-3 Jan Craft and Design for the Home, Crafts Council, 12 Waterloo Pl, London SW1, 01-930 4811

1-3 Jan Furnishing the World: East London Furniture Trade 1830-1980, Geffrye Museum, Kingsland Rd, London E2 8EA, 01-739 8368

23-25 Southern Counties Craft Market, The Maltings, Farnham, Surrey, contact: (0920) 870040

26 Design and Workshop Drawing Bob Grant*

October

2-4 Festival of Ecclesiastical Crafts, Salisbury Cathedral, exhibitors' enquiries: J. Davies, Yew Tree Lodge, Minchington, Blandford, Dorset OT11 8DH

2-4 Heart of England Craft Market, Sports Centre, University of Keele, Stoke-on-Trent, (0920) 870040

3-4 Irish Woodturners Guild 6th Annual 2-day Seminar, Riverchapel, Courtown, Co. Wexford, application forms: T. Dunlop, Shanbough Upper, Via New Ross, Co. Kilkenny

4-28 Mainly Wood Exhibition, Parnham Hse, Beaminster, Dorset DT8 3NA, (0308) 862204

12-24 Chelsea Crafts Fair, Old Town Hall, London SW3

20-30 Annual International Creative Marquetry Show, Virginia, USA, application forms: S. Cartwright, 63 Church Lane, Sproughton, Ipswich IP8 3AY.

21 Style for Living 87, trade and public furniture show, 3f Prince Rupert Hse, 64 Queens St, London EC4R 1AD

22-25 London Woodworker Show, Alexandra Pavilion, London N22

25-26 Woodturning Extravaganza, The Old Stores Turnery, Wistaston Rd, Willaston, Nantwich, Cheshire CW5 6JQ, (0270) 67010

25-28 Design in Furniture Exhibition, Olympia, London (trade only)

November

14 Power Routing Roy Sutton*

14-15 French Polishing Ian Hosker*

13-15 Eastern Counties Craft Market, Rhodes Ctre, Bishops Stortford, Herts, contact: (0920) 870040

17-19 Northern Interior Design Exhibition, G-MEX, Manchester, contact: 01-868 4499

20 Woodland Ecology Debate, Parnham Hse, Beaminster, Dorset, (0308) 862204

22-28 Interbuild 87, building and construction exhibition, NEC, Birmingham, contact: 01-486 1951

New launches

Accessories available for Dunlop Powerbase, including sole plates, bench clamps and router guard kit. Dunlop Powerbase, 140 Fielden St, Glasgow G40 3TX, (041 554) 3811.
Makita Power-Craft ⅜in plunge router M362, £98+VAT, one of the prizes in the WOODWORKER/ Makita power tool competition (WW/ Sept).
AEG's latest Maxi 26 Plus universal woodworking machine, £1,549+VAT: AEG Power Tools, 217 Bath Road, Slough, Berks SL1 4AW, (0753) 812101.

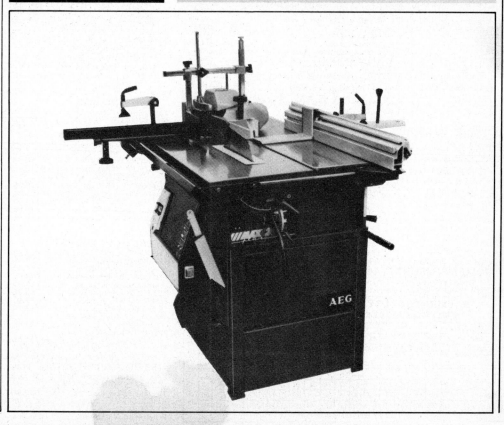

AXMINSTER POWER TOOL CENTRE

WOODTURNING LATHES — *OUR PRICE INC. VAT*

TYME STUDENT 10" swing 30" centres (With accessory voucher £20) ... **£199**
CORONET HOBBY 10" swing 39" centres 1MT ½HP 3 speed ... **£179**
CORONET No. 1 12" swing 3 Speed 24" ctrs ... **£259** 36" ctrs ... **£279** 48" ctrs ... **£309**
CORONET No. 1 22" Bowl Rest Assbly .. **£39** 48" Bed Extension for existing 24" lathe .. **£59**
ELU DB180 39" centres 15" swing 1½HP motor 3 speed ... **£299**
TYME CUB 30" centres (With accessory voucher £32) ... **£319**
TYME AVON 36" centres (With accessory voucher £44) ... **£437**
MYFORD ML8B 36" centres 9" Rear turning ... **£459** ML8C 42" centres ... **£499**
KITY 663 3 Speed Lathe 1.0M Centres ... **£554** 1.5M Centres ... **£576**
KITY 664 Var. Spd. Lathe 1.0M Centres ... **£649** 1.5M Centres ... **£669**
MINIMAX Centre lathes T90 ... **£462** T100 ... **£534** T120 ... **£564** Legs ... **£75**
MINIMAX COPIERS for above lathes CT90 ... **£519** CT100 ... **£551** CT120 ... **£599**
LUNA SPKA 900 COPIER medium duty copier for all lathes ... **£256**
CORONET CMB600 33" Centres 23" bowl cap ... **£589** Bowl rest ... **£49.95**
HARRISON GRADUATE 30" Centres ... **£1250** 42" Centres ... **£1299** Shortbed ... **£1037**

WOODTURNING FITMENTS & ACCESSORIES (State m/c)

Coronet collet chuck sets (state m/c) ... **£69**
Coronet collet bodies ... only **£29**
Collets ⅝", ¾", 1" ... each **£11**
Expanding Jaws 3", 2", 1" ... each **£24**
Spigots ⅝", ¾", 1" ... each **£13**
Speedaneez polish std/wht ... **£5**
Coronet planer blades 4½" .. **£20** 7" .. **£23**
Multistar Duplex Chuck 45mm Jaws ... **£65**
Multistar Duplex Chuck 60mm Jaws ... **£66**
Multistar Duplex Chuck 75mm Jaws ... **£68**
Screwchuck Set (for above) ... **£22**
Faceplate Ring 60mm ... **£7**
Pinchucks (State size) ... **£8**
Revolving centres 1MT or 2MT ... **£18**
0-½" Drill chuck 1MT or 2MT ... **£15**
Craft supplies chuck ... **£56**
Long hole boring kit 5/16" ... **£32**
2½" Woodscrew chuck ... **£22**
Sorby sizing tool ... **£8**
Carnuba wax turning stick ... **£1.80**
Henry Taylor Master Chuck ... **£56.95**
Henry Taylor 3" Ext. Jaws ... **£16.50**
Henry Taylor 1¼" Ext. Jaws ... **£13.50**
Henry Taylor Wood Jaw Plates ... **£4.60**
Henry Taylor Pin Chuck ... **£4.60**
Janik Pyrographer ... **£48.00**

CORONET SPARES

Drive Belts (State M/C Type) ... **£3.90**
Bronze Bearing Major ... **£21** Elf ... **£18**
Bronze Bearing Consort **£23** Minor **£23**
Ball Race Bearing Major **£12** Others **£9.60**
Main Spindle Consort/Minor ... **£44**
Main Spindle Major c/w ⅞" or ¾" ... **£59**
Major Poly-Vee Conversion Kit ... **£98.00**
¾HP Motor for CMB500 (speeds 500-2000) ... **£92.00**
Locking Rings (Major or Elf) ... **£6.50**
Drive Centres 4 Prong ⅞" ... **£7.00**
Lace Bobbin Drives 1MT or 2MT ... **£7.00**

HENRY TAYLOR HSS CHISELS

GOUGES		PARTING TOOLS	
HS1 Superflute	£24	HS2 Fluted	£14
HS3 ¾" D/Fte	£13	HS11 ¼" Std.	£5
HS4 1½" D/Fte	£24	HS12 ⅜" Std.	£7
HS5 ¼" Spindle	£5	HS13 ¾" × ½"	£9
HS6 ⅜" Spindle	£7	HS33 Diamond	£13
HS7 ½" Spindle	£11	HS32 ½" × ⅛"	£6
CHISELS		**SCRAPERS**	
HS8 ½" Skew	£7	HS26 ½" Rnd	£7
HS21 ¾" Skew	£8	HS38 ¾" Rnd	£8
HS22 1" Skew	£9	HS27 1" Rnd	£9
HS9 1¼" Skew	£14	HS28 ½" Sq	£7
HS23 ½" Squar	£7	HS29 ¾" Sq.	£8
HS24 ¾" Sqre	£8	HS30 1" Sq.	£9
HS25 1" Sqre	£9	HS15 HD Round	£19
HS10 1¼" Sqre	£14	HS16 HD Domed	£19

WOODTURNERS "AT LAST PERFECTION"

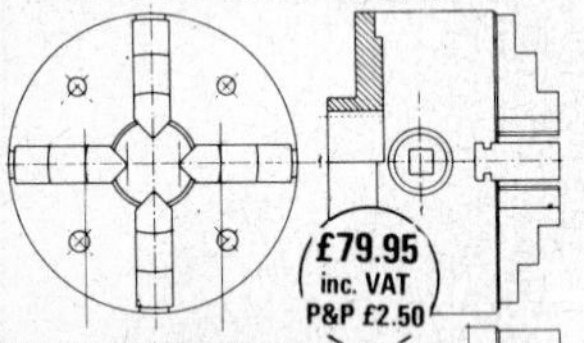

4 JAW SELF CENTERING CHUCK
AVAILABLE IN THREAD SIZES FOR MOST LATHES.
SPECIFICATION: GRIPPING CAPACITY ⅛"-4" DIAMETER 4" WEIGHT 2KG. SUPPLIED READY THREADED (LH OR RH) WITH TWO SETS OF PRECISION JAWS (INTERNAL & EXTERNAL).
5" 4 Jaw S/C ... **£99.95**
4" 3 Jaw S/C ... **£69.95**

CORONET HSS CHISELS

GOUGES		CHISELS	
600 ½" Bowl	£22	420 1" Square	£11
100 ¾" Roughing	£15	430 1¼" Square	£15
120 1¼" Roughing	£21	**PARTING TOOLS**	
200 ¼" Spindle	£6	500 ⅛" Parting	£9
210 ⅜" Spindle	£8	520 ⅜" Parting & Beading	£8
220 ½" Spindle	£11		
CHISELS		**SCRAPERS**	
300 ½" Skew	£8	700 ½" Domed	£8
310 ¾" Skew	£9	701 ¾" Domed	£9
320 1" Skew	£11	702 1" Domed	£10
330 1¼" Skew	£15	800 HD Straight	£21
400 ½" Square	£8	810 Round	£21
410 ¾" Square	£9	840 Skew	£21

BANDSAWS (Send for Free Bandsaw Blade List)

BURGESS BK111+ 45° 3" cut jigsaw fretsaw ... (inc. P&P) **£115**
7" Sanding attachment for Burgess ... **£23.50** Mitre fence ... **£8.50** Rip fence ... **£7.50**
DeWALT DW100 45° tilt 4" cut c/w sanding table ... (P&P £2.50) **£149**
DeWALT 6" cut 14" throat 45° DW3401 ... **£269** DW3501 ... **£279**
MINIMAX P32 45° tilt 6" cut 14" throat cast iron table ... **£425**
KITY 513 8" cut Large table 1½HP (+ £57.50 Kity Accessory Voucher) ... **£427**
MINIMAX S45 45° tilt 10" cut 17" throat ... **£676**
STARTRITE 301B 45° Tilt 6" cut Bench Mtg. c/w Mitre Fence ... **£329**
STARTRITE 301 6" Floor Standing c/w mitre & rip fence ... **£419**
STARTRITE 351 45° tilt 8" cut c/w rip & mitre fence floor standing ... **£519**
STARTRITE 352 45° tilt 10" cut c/w rip & mitre fence floor standing ... **£739**
STARTRITE 502 14" cut 20" throat 1PH ... **£1259** 3PH ... **£1170**
METAL BLADE GUIDES for DeWalt DW100, 1310, 3401, 3501, Luna & Minimax ... **£5.20**

RADIAL SAWS

DeWALT Radial Saw Handbook ... **£6.00** inc. P&P
EUMENIA 9" blade 1¾HP 15" C/cut ... **£339** 24" C/cut ... **£399**
EUMENIA Stand ... **£112** Router Bracket ... **£76** Wobble Washers ... **£14.50**
DeWALT 1201 Portable 10" TCT Folding Radial Saw 1½ HP ... **£255**
DeWALT DW1251 10" TCT blade 1½ HP 16" C/cut ... **£420** Stand ... **£25**
DeWALT DW1501 10" TCT blade 1½ HP 18" C/cut ... **£476**
DeWALT DW1751 10" TCT blade 1½ HP 24" C/cut ... **£570**
DeWALT DW8001 12" TCT blade 2HP 18" C/cut floor standing ... **£559**
DeWALT DW8101 12" TCT blade 2HP 24" C/cut floor standing ... **£695**
DeWALT DW1600S 14" TCT blade 24" C/cut 1PH ... **£993** 3PH ... **£956**

PORTABLE AND WORKSHOP SAWBENCHES

MAKITA 2708 8" Portable tilt arbor bench saw ... **£229**
ELEKTRA 12" Sawbench floor standing TCT blade 3HP ... **£189**
SCHEPPACH TKU 12" Sawbench floor standing TCT blade 3HP ... **£229**
Elektra & Scheppach Sliding Table ... **£90** Panel Cutting Extension ... **£75**
ELU TGS Sawbench/Mitre Saws c/w TCT blade TGS 172 ... **£496** TGS 171 ... **£399**
KITY 618 10" tilt arbor sawbench (+ £57.50 Kity Accessory Voucher) ... **£591**
MULTICO TS1/314" Tilt Arbor Saw ... **£1339** Sliding Table 48" cap. ... **£336**
WADKIN AGS250/300 3HP 1PH ... **£1299** Sliding table 35" cap. ... **£496**
STARTRITE Scoring Saw 1PH ... **£1476** Sliding table 48" cap. ... **£352**
LUNA L18 12" 3HP 1PH ... **£950** Sliding table 24" cap. ... **£170**
SEDGWICK LK 16" Saw Bench 3PH ... **£899** 1PH ... **£1143** Sliding Table ... **£279**

ROLLER SUPPORT STANDS (P&P £3.00)

LUNA 10" support roller adjustable height sturdy construction ... **£29.95**
LUNA 16" combined roller support adjustable height ... **£42.00**

PREMIUM QUALITY INDUSTRIAL SAWBLADES

THE BEST IN QUALITY T.C.T. SAWBLADES LEITZ & SPEAR & JACKSON

BLADE DIAMETER	6"				7"-7¼"				8"				9"-9¼"			
No. OF TEETH	16	24	36	48	18	30	42	56	20	36	48	64	24	40	54	72
SPEARTIP	£16	£17	£20	£26	£16	£20	£23	£26	£20	£26	£28	£32	£24	£26	£29	£36
LEITZ	—	—	—	—	—	—	—	—	—	£37	£43	£49	—	£41	£51	—

BLADE DIAMETER	10"				12"				14"				16"			
No. OF TEETH	24	40	60	80	32	48	72	96	36	60	84	108	28	36	60	96
SPEARTIP	£23	£26	£35	£38	£28	£36	£42	£48	£34	£42	£50	£57	£39	£44	£54	£63
LEITZ	£39	£43	£51	£59	£42	£52	£61	£70	£48	£57	£70	£81	£54	£59	£70	£92

PLEASE STATE BORE SIZE WHEN ORDERING.

MORTICING MACHINES — *OUR PRICE INC. VAT*

SMITHS BCM 75 bench morticer c/w lateral table ¾" cap. ... **£422**
SMITHS CM75 floor standing morticer dual table movement ¾" cap ... **£528**
MULTICO HM bench morticer ⅝" capacity precision morticer ... **£356**
MULTICO HMT bench morticer dual table movement ... **£499**
MULTICO M floor standing 1" capacity dual table movement 1PH ... **£625**
WADKIN EDA-2 floor standing 1" capacity dual table ... **£626**
RIDGWAY MORTICER 1" cap. 1HP Full Table Movements ... **£540**
RYOBI portable chain morticer ... **£365** Portable chisel morticer ... **£395**
RIDGEWAY mortice/drill stand (requires ½" power drill) ... **£165**
SEDGWICK 571 Floor standing 1½HP 1" Cap ... **£599**

MORTICE CHISELS & BITS

JAPANESE ¼" ... **£20** ⅜" ... **£21** ½" ... **£25** ⅝" ... **£32** ¾" ... **£48** 1" ... **£59**
8mm ... **£21** 10mm ... **£24** 12mm ... **£25** 16mm ... **£29** 20mm ... **£44**
RIDGEWAY ¼" ... **£19** ⅜" ... **£23** ½" ... **£24** ⅝" ... **£35** ¾" ... **£37** 1" ... **£45**
6mm .. **£21** 8mm .. **£22** 10mm .. **£25** 12mm .. **£26** 16mm .. **£31** 20mm .. **£46**
CHISEL BITS ONLY ¼" ... **£6** ⅜" ... **£7** ½" ... **£8** ⅝" ... **£10** ¾" ... **£14** 1" ... **£18**
MORTICE CHISEL SHARPENING SETS set 1 (¼"-½") ... **£23** Set 2 (⅜"-¾") ... **£28**

DUST EXTRACTORS

LUNA W178 975m/hr excellent general purpose extractor c/w hose ... **£324**
LUNA NF243 1500m/hr mobile 5" hose ideal for high volume waste ... **£429**
LUNA NF259 2000m/hr heavy duty suitable for up to 3 machines ... **£599**
LUNA 4" × 3m hose ... **£19** 5" × 4m hose ... **£38** LUNA dust bags (per 10) ... **£3**
DeWALT DW60 500m/hr 5" hose ... **£265** ELEKTRA 1000m/hr 4" hose ... **£199**
STARTRITE CYCLAIR 55 960m/hr 4" ... **£409** CYCLAIR 75 1800m/hr 6" ... **£529**

MITRE CUTTERS & MITRE SAWS

ELU PS174 8" Portable mitre crosscut saw 10" crosscut ... **£298**
DeWALT DW250 Portable mitre saw 1¼HP 10" Blade ... **£179**
HITACHI CF10A 10" Portable precision mitre saw ... **£259**
ORTEGUILLE MITRE CUTTERS ORC55 ... **£238** ORC80 ... **£299** ORC100 ... **£439**
LION MITRE TRIMMER Excellent for clean cuts and mitres SPECIAL OFFER ... **£199**
NOBEX 202 PRO Hand Mitre saw ... **£72.95** NOBEX 303 ... **£44** (P&P £2.50)
NOBEX 202 Replacement Blades 12T, 18T or 24T ... **£4.30** each

PLANER THICKNESSERS

DeWALT DW1151 10" × 6" 2HP 2 speed power feed ... **SPECIAL PRICE**
Stand for DW1150 ... **£30** Slot Morticer ... **£69.95** HSS knives ... **£18.90**
ELECKTRA 10" × 6" floor standing power feed ... **£490**
SCHEPPACH HMO SOLO 10" × 6" 2HP floor standing Adjustable fence ... **£490**
KITY 7136 10" × 6" (+ £50.00 Kity Accessory Voucher) ... **£585**
STARTRITE PT260 10" × 7" floor standing ⅝" rebate capacity ... **£869**
STARTRITE SD310 12" × 9" 3 cutter block 1PH ... **£1399** 3PH ... **£1360**
LUNA 3HP Planers 10" × 9" ... **£1428** 12" × 9" ... **£1690** 16" × 9" ... **£2399**
MULTICO NS300 surfacer 3 cutter block 2HP 1PH ... **£1388** 3PH ... **£1271**
MULTICO THA300 12" × 10" thicknesser only 1PH ... **£1399** 3PH ... **£1299**
MULTICO CPT 12" × 8" Combined planer/thicknesser ¾" rebate 1PH . **£1749** 3PH . **£1649**

DRILLING MACHINES

WARCO HOBBY ½" 5 speed rack and pinion table bench mounting ... **£139**
WARCO ⅝" cap 2MT 12 speed 2B12 bench mounting ... **£179** 2F12 floor standing ... **£222**
FOBCO STAR ½" precision drill bench mounting ... **£359** floor standing ... **£411**
STARTRITE SP250 ½" 5 speed bench mounting ... **£379** floor standing ... **£428**
Morticing attachments Warco 2B/2F ... **£24** Fobco ... **£61** Startrite ... **£110**

SPINDLE MOULDERS AND TENNONERS

SCHEPPACH HF33 3HP 30mm 3 speed with adjustable fences ... **£499**
SEDGWICK GW Spindle 30mm ... **£999**
KITY 623 2HP 3 speed C/W sliding table (+ £57.50 Kity Accessory Voucher) ... **£776**
STARTRITE T30 30mm C/W sliding table 1PH 2HP ... **£1089** 3PH 3HP ... **£1049**
LUNA L28 30mm 3 speed 3HP Heavy duty 1PH 3HP ... **£999** 3PH 3HP ... **£988**
MULTICO TENNONER TM1 240v twin motors (with tooling) ... **£1579**

SPINDLE MOULDER TOOLING (State bore size P&P £1.50)

OMAS "TIGER" BLOCKS 392 ... **£50** BLOCK in wooden case with stone etc. ... **£59**
OMAS cutter profiles ... **£12** CUTTER BLANKS ... **£7** SAW SEGMENTS ... **£17**
KITY PROFILE Door set ... **£99** OMAS ART 176D1 DOOR SET complete ... **£139**
WHITEHILL BLOCKS 4⅞ × 15/16 ... **£50** 5⅜" × 15/16" ... **£69** Panel Raising Block ... **£92**
LEITZ 488 Cutter block 100mm ... **£59** 40mm blanks ... **£3** 60mm ... ea. **£5**
TUNGSTEN REBATE BLOCKS 125mm × 50mm ... **£98** 6" Wobble saw 3-21mm ... **£89**
T.C.T. GROOVERS 6" 6 WING ¼" ... **£44** 5/16" ... **£46** ⅜" ... **£48** ½" ... **£54** ⅝" ... **£62**
LUNA MINI POWER FEED 2 speeds ... **£329**
SEND FOR FREE SPINDLE TOOLING CATALOGUE.

COMBINATION MACHINES (Carriage £10.00 UK Mainland)

STARTRITE K260 saw spindle planer etc. FREE TIGER HEAD SET ... **£2390**
STARTRITE TZ30 saw spindle only FREE TIGER HEAD only ... **£1359**
SPECIAL OFFER LUNA W59 240v c/w sliding table ... **£2399**
LUNA MASTER COMBINATIONS 240v W64 ... **£3100** W69 ... **£3899**
AEG MAXI COMBINATION 5 function ... **£1604**
STARTRITE K310 12" Planer 12" Saw ... **£3850**

★★★★★★★★ KITY COMBINATION MACHINES ★★★★★★★★

K5 COMBINATION COMBI STAR CK26 TABLE COMBINATION K704 DIRECT DRIVE AND ACCESSORIES ALL AT SPECIAL PRICES SEND FOR LATEST PRICE LIST.
★★★★★★★★★★★★★★★★★★★★★★★★★★

BORING BITS

CLICO SAW TOOTH & FORSTNER BITS (State type) 6" long ½" shank ⅜" .. **£8.10** ½" .. **£8.35** ⅝" .. **£9.20** ¾" .. **£10.00** ⅞" .. **£10.50** 1" .. **£11.55** 1⅛" .. **£13.55** 1¼" .. **£16.50** 1⅜" .. **£17.20** 1½" .. **£18.15** 1⅝" .. **£20.90** 1¾" .. **£23.75** 1⅞" .. **£26.30** 2" .. **£27.80** 2¼" .. **£34.95** 2½" .. **£46.35**
CLICO PLUG CUTTERS ⅜" .. **£22** ½" .. **£24** ⅝" **£28** ¾" **£30** 1" **£36** 1½ .. **£40.00**
CLICO SAW TOOTH set ½", ¾", 1" ... **£28** ECONOMY 5 piece set ½"-1½" × ¼" ... **£58**
RIDGEWAY ADJUSTABLE FORSTNERS WR10/2½"-1¾" ... **£16** WR10/3⅞"-3" ... **£18**
RIDGEWAY ADJUSTABLE FORSTNER (h/duty) WR20/2⅞"-2" **£29** WR20/3 1⅜"-3" **£34**

ROUTERS

ELU MOF96 ¼" 600W ... **£98.00**
ELU MOF31 ¼, ⅜, ½" 1200W ... **£152.50**
ELU MOF177 ¼, ½" 1600W ... **£193.50**
HITACHI TR8 ¼" 730W ... **£79.95**
RYOBI R150 ¼" 730W ... **£75.95**
HITACHI FM ¼" 550W ... **£46.95**
MAKITA 3600B ¼, ½" 1500W ... **£168.95**
ELU MOF96E ¼" Var. speed ... **£119.50**
ELU MOF11/2 ½" 2000W c/w base **£337.33**
ELU MOF177E ½" Var. speed ... **£218.50**
HITACHI TR12 ¼, ½" 1300W ... **£137.95**
RYOBI R500 R500 ¼, ½" 1500W ... **£124.95**
BOSCH POF52 ¼" 520W ... **£52.00**
MAKITA 3612BR ½" 1600W ... **£175.95**

ROUTER ACCESSORIES

ELU DOVETAIL KIT TCT cutter ... **£69.95**
ELU MOF96 Accessory kit ... **£69.95**
STAIR JIG (General duty) ... **£69.00**
ELU ROUTER BRKT. for DeWalt ... **£38.00**
ELU 96 Dust extraction kit ... **£36.00**
ELU MOF96 Height adjuster ... **£3.95**
ELU TRACKING SET ... **£35.00**
TREND STAIR JIG ... **£112.00**
TREND OVERHEAD ROUTER Bench Mtg. ... **£687.00**
TREND OVERHEAD ROUTER Fl. Stdg. ... **£1200.00**
ELU 11/2 ROUTER for above stands **£181.00**
TREND POST FORM JIG ... **£434.00**
RYOBI Dovetail jig fits above ... **£99.95**
ELU ROUTER COMBI BENCH ... **£118.00**
STAIR JIG (heavy duty) ... **£160.00**
ELU 12 piece Guide bush set ... **£35.00**
ELU MOF98, 31, 177 Height adjuster **£16.95**
ELU 96 177 side fence adjuster ... **£5.30**
ELU ROUTING VIDEO ... **£12.00**

★★★★ SPECIAL OFFER ★★★★

ROUTER PROFILE SCRIBER SETS
⅜" or ½" Shank
only **£110.00 inc. P&P**
★★★★★★★★★★★★★★★★★★

HSS ROUTER BIT SETS (inc. P&P)

SAVE 30% ON HSS ROUTER BIT SETS AND GET A FREE ROUTER BIT CASE.
13 PIECE SET ... **£59.95**
8 PIECE SET ... **£37.95**
5 PIECE SET ... **£21.95**
ROUTER BIT CUTTER BOX ... ONLY **£4**

ROUTER CUTTERS

20-25% OFF LEADING BRANDS EXCELLENT STOCKS OF HSS & TCT ROUTER CUTTERS OVER 500 PROFILES IN STOCK. SEND NOW FOR FREE CUTTER CHART:- TECHNIQUES OF ROUTING £7.95 (inc. P&P)

IMMEDIATE DESPATCH ON CREDIT CARD PHONED ORDERS — CREDIT TERMS AVAILABLE OVER £120

0297 33656 CHARD STREET AXMINSTER DEVON EX13 5DZ POST OFFICE C.O.D. **34836** BARCLAYCARD VISA

AXMINSTER POWER TOOL CENTRE

HORIZONTAL WETSTONE GRINDERS
OUR PRICE INC. VAT

JAPANESE Wetstone grinder £129.00
180G stone for above £40.00
1000G stone for above £40.00
6000G stone for above £43.00
PRECISION grinding jig £43.00
SHARPENSET Wetstone grinder £240.00
SHARPENSET 80g stone £20.00
SHARPENSET 150G stone £18.40
SHARPENSET 280G stone £20.41
SHARPENSET Green stone (TCT) ... £18.40
10" Planer Knife grinding jig £65.00
15" Planer Knife grinding jig £78.00
CHISEL grinding jig £67.00

VERTICAL WETSTONE GRINDERS
SCANGRIND 150 6" wetstone £69.00
SCANGRIND 200 8" wetstone £88.00
COMBI SC150 6" wet & dry £89.00
COMBI SC200 8" wet & dry £112.00
LUNA KIRUNA 11" wet & 4" dry .. £118.00
LUNA KIRUNA 14" wet & 5" dry .. £184.00

BENCH GRINDERS
ELU EDS163 6" 360W £73.00
ELU EDS164 7" 390W £77.00
ELU MWA149 6" Honer grinder £90.95
LEROY SOMER 5" 180W £33.00
LEROY SOMER 6" 250W £44.00
LEROY SOMER 6" with chuck £49.00
WARCO 5" 180W (European) £33.00
WARCO 6" 380W (European) £43.00
WARCO 8" 570W (European) £69.00

GRIND STONES (state bore size)

	5"	6"	7"
COARSE 36G	£6.60	£7.90	£11.40
FINE 60G	£6.60	£7.90	£11.40
WHITE 60G	£7.20	£8.50	£13.50
GREEN (TCT)	£7.20	£8.50	£13.50

JIGSAWS (Light Duty)
Bosch PST50 Single Speed £29.95
Bosch PST50E Var. Speed £38.50
Bosch PST60PEA Var. Speed Pend. £65.00
Hitachi FJ50SB Single speed £29.50
Hitachi FJ50VA Var. speed £37.95
Hitachi FCJ55V Var. Speed Pend. Act £61.95

JIGSAWS (Heavy Duty)
Elu ST142 2 speed £101.00
Elu ST142E Var. speed £110.00
Elu ST152 2 Speed £98.00
Elu ST152E Var. speed £106.00
Cases for above Jigsaws £10.00
Hitachi CJ65 2 speed £100.95
Hitachi CJ65VA Var. speed £104.95
Hitachi CJ65V Var. speed £104.95
Bosch 1581.7 Var. speed £108.95

DISC AND BELT SANDERS
Picador 10" Disc Sander £219.00
Warco BDS460 6" Disc 4" Belt £86.00
Warco BDS690 9" Disc 6" Belt £179.00
Luna Favourite 4" £285.00
Luna De-Lux Sander 4" £599.00
Luna YKV Pad Sander £647.00
Luna YK1500 Pad Sander 1PH .. £1564.00
Luna YK1500 Pad Sander 3PH .. £1509.00

CIRCULAR SAWS
HITACHI FC5SA 6" TCT 710W £42.95
BOSCH PKS46 6" TCT 600W £53.50
BOSCH PKS66 7⅞ TCT 1200W £86.00
HITACHI PSU6 6" 1050W HSS £79.95
HITACHI PSU7 7" 1600W HSS £103.95
HITACHI PSU9 9" 1759W HSS £133.95
HITACHI PSM7 7" 1200W TCT £151.50
HITACHI PSM9 9" 1600W TCT £160.50
ELU MH151 6" 850W TCT £90.95
ELU MH65 7" 1200W TCT £131.95
ELU MH85 9" 1600W TCT £177.95
ELU MH182 8" 1400W TCT £148.00
ELU 550 COMBI (for MH182) £130.00
ELU555 Snip saw (for 182) £179.00

FINISHING SANDERS
(DB Dust Bag)
BOSCH PSS230 1/3rd Sheet £29.95
HITACHI FS10SA 1/3rd Sheet £27.95
HITACHI FSV12 Sheet DB £53.50
BOSCH PS280A ½ Sheet DB £59.95
ELU MVS156 1/3rd Sheet DB £73.00
ELU MVS156E Var. Speed DB £85.95
ELU MVS 94 ½ Sheet DB £111.00
ELU MVS47 ½ Sheet £123.00
HITACHI SV12 ½ Sheet £116.95
HITACHI SOD110 ½ Sheet DB £94.50
HITACHI SO110 ½ Sheet £86.95
BOSCH 1288 9½ Sheet DB £99.95

DRILL STANDS
BOSCH S7 ...... £21.00
BOSCH S2 ...... £52.00
BOSCH S8 ...... £25.00
WOLFCRAFT 3403 ...... £29.00
WOLFCRAFT 5120 ...... £59.00

POWER TOOL WORK BENCHES
Post/Delivery £5.00
TRITON £159.00
Extension Tables £69.00
Stand £29.00
Router/Jigsaw Base £39.00
Wheel Kit £9.50
DUNLOP POWER BASE £119.95
Extension Table £21.50
Additional sole plates £8.65
WOLFCRAFT VARIOTEC £45.00
BOSCH MT92 Saw Table £109.95

OUR PRICE INC. VAT

POWER PLANES (Light Duty)
BLACK & DECKER DN710 ...... £29.95
BOSCH PHO100 82mm 450W £46.95
HITACHI FP20SA 82mm 320W £41.50

HEAVY DUTY

ELU MFF80 82mm 850W £109.95
ELU MFF80K (in kit box) £127.95
ELU MFF40 82mm 1000W £189.95
INVERSION Std. for MFF80 ...... £20.95
INVERSION Std. for MFF40 ...... £29.00
HITACHI P20SA 82mm 720W £100.95
HITACHI F30A 92mm 900W £143.50

BELT SANDERS
ELU MHB 157 3" 600W £106.95
ELU MHB 157E 3" var. speed £119.00
ELU 157 FRAME £35.00
ELU 157 inversion stand £28.00
ABRASIVE BELTS FOR MHB 157/pkt. 3
40G, 60G, 80G, 100G, 120G, 150G £3.00
BOSCH PBS75 3" 620W £71.95
ELU MHB 90 4" 850W £193.95
ELU MHB 90K With frame £234.00
HITACHI SB75 3" 950W £117.95
HITACHI SB10T 4" 950W £141.95
HITACHI SB10V 4" var. speed £148.50
MAKITA 9401 4" 1040W £169.00

BISCUIT JOINTER
ELU DS140 Biscuit Jointer £197.00
No. 20 Biscuits (1000 off) £19.95
No. 10 Biscuits (1000 off) £19.50
No. 0 Biscuits (1000 off) £18.63
Mixed Box 0, 10, 20 (500 off) £12.50
DS140 saw blade 12T Std. £29.95
DS140 saw blade 30T Fine £29.50
DS140 Dust Tube adaptor £5.95
BOSCH Biscuit Jointer £124.95

★ ★ ★ **SPECIAL OFFERS** ★ ★ ★

HITACHI TR12 ROUTER
Powerful 1300w ½" Router in Metal Carrying Case £129.95 inc. VAT & P&P

RIDGWAY DRILL MORTICER
c/w Free Hitachi Drill ½" Chuck and ¼" Chisel and Bit
£186.00 inc. VAT and P&P

MARTEK DRILL SHARPENER
Excellent for Sharpening all Drill Bits ONLY £23.95 inc. VAT and P&P

★ ★ **CHAINSAW OWNERS POWER BREAKERS** ★ ★
25% off OREGAN SAW CHAINS
All chain Ex Stock By Return Post
State Type of Saw and Number of Links

POWER DRILLS (K-Kit box)
NEW ELU POWER DRILLS
ECD304K 420W V/S 10mm Compact £73.95
EMD400K 600W 2 Speed 13mm £81.95
ESD705K 320W V/S & Rev. 10mm £102.95
EMD403K 500W V/S/R Ham. 13mm £90.95
EMD405K 500W V/S/R Ham. 13mm £114.95
EMD406K 550W V/S Hammer 13mm £106.95
BOSCH 400-2 10mm 440W £29.95
BOSCH 500RLE 13mm 500W V/S Rev. £49.95
BOSCH 7002E 13mm 700W £79.95
BOSCH 850RLT 13mm 850W V/S Re £111.95
HITACHI FV12VA 13mm 420W V/S £40.50
HITACHI FDV16V 13mm 600W V/S/R £61.95
HITACHI FDV20VA 13mm 710W V/S/R £82.95
HITACHI VTP13K 13mm 2 Speed 460W £86.00
HITACHI VTP16AK 2 Spd. 800W . £118.50

PALM GRIP SANDERS
(DB Dust Bag)
ELU MVS500 1/6th Sheet 135W DB £60.95
ELU MVS501 1/4 Sheet 135W DB £60.95
B&D P6301 1/6th Sheet 136W DB £51.50
B&D P6302 1/4 Sheet 135W DB £51.50
HITACHI SV12SA 1/4 Sheet 180W £51.50
MAKITA B045 10 1/4 Sheet £48.95

SWEDISH STEEL INDUSTRIAL BANDSAW BLADES

		3/16"	1/4"	3/8"	1/2"	5/8"	3/4"
BURGESS	57"	—	£3.20	£3.30	£3.45	—	—
DeWALT	59.5"	—	£3.20	£3.30	£3.45	—	—
CORONET	67.5"	—	£3.43	£3.50	£3.70	—	—
WARCO	70"	—	£3.60	£3.70	£3.80	—	—
INCA	73"	£3.91	£3.70	£3.80	£3.90	£4.80	—
BIRCH	81"	—	£4.25	£4.35	£4.52	—	—
DeWALT	82.5"	£4.75	£3.95	£4.10	£4.20	£5.11	£5.69
MINIMAX	86"	£4.10	£3.95	£4.10	£4.20	£5.11	£5.69
STARTRITE	88"	£4.10	£3.95	£4.10	£4.20	£5.11	£5.69
KITY	90.5"	£4.42	£4.14	£4.25	£4.42	£5.40	£5.90
STARTRITE	102"	£5.41	£4.66	£4.71	£4.86	—	£5.99
EVENWOOD	104"	£5.41	£4.66	£4.71	£4.86	—	£5.99
STARTRITE	112"	£5.06	£4.80	£4.90	£5.10	£6.30	£7.02
MINIMAX	144"	£6.46	£5.29	£5.46	£6.46	£7.13	£7.99

10% DISCOUNT WHEN ORDERING 10 OR MORE BLADES
POST PAID ON ORDERS £5.00 & OVER.

LIBERON WAXES
Waxes Sealers Stains Polishes Etc.
All Your Requirements in One
Send for Free Price List
GLUE POT ...... £23.00 inc. P&P

CORDLESS DRILLS HITACHI 10mm
OUR PRICE inc. VAT

DTC 10 6 cell 2 spd. & rev. £79.95
DRC10 as above torque adjustable . £98.50
DTC10K 6 cell 2 spd. & rev. in case £86.50
D10DB 6 cell variable spd. & rev. ... £88.50
D10DD 8 cell 2 spd. & rev. £90.00
D10D as above torque adjustable £111.00
DV10D 8 cell 2 spd. & rev. hammer £115.95

MAKITA 10mm
6012DWK 6 cell 2 spd. & rev. in case £92.95
6012HDW 8 cell 2 spd. torque adj. £111.95
8400DW 8 cell 1 spd. & rev. hammer £119.95
MAGNETIC Screwdriver kit 7 piece .. £5.95
REPLACEMENT BITS (state type) £0.50

MISCELLANEOUS POWER TOOLS
KEW HOBBY PRESSURE WASHER £239.00
DREMEL D576 FRETSAW £69.95
BOSCH WET 'n' DRY Vacuum cleaner £110
BOSCH 560 HOT AIR paint stripper £39.00
Steam Wallpaper stripper £125.00
NEW ELU DUST EXTRACTORS
EVE 938 ...... £229 EVE 948 ...... £395
BOSCH INDUSTRIAL PAINT STRIPPER £82.95
BELLE ELECTRIC CEMENT MIXER £135.00

KLEMSIA QUICK CLAMPS

SPAN	REACH		
200mm	110mm	£3.70	
300mm	110mm	£4.00	
400mm	110mm	£4.40	
600mm	110mm	£5.20	(P&P £1.50)
800mm	110mm	£6.00	
1000mm	110mm	£7.10	
200mm	150mm	£6.70	

RECORD CRAMP HEADS M130
1 off £10.40 5 off £10.00 (P&P £1.50)

DRILL BIT SETS
OUR PRICE INC. VAT

	Lip & Spur	HSS Std.
1/16"-1/2" × 64ths	—	£21.00
1/16"-1/2" × 32nds	£42.00	£17.00
1-13mm × 0.5mm	£54.00	£19.00
1-10mm × 0.5mm	£39.00	£11.00
1/8"-1/4" × 64ths	—	£4.50
1/16"-1/4" × 1/16ths		£2.00

WOODWORKING VICES (P&P £4.50)
RECORD 52½E 9" Quick Release ... £50.00
52½ED 9" Quick Release £54.00
53E 10" Quick Release ... £69.00
V150 6" Woodcraft £11.50 (p&p £1.50)
V175 7" Woodcraft .... £12.95 (P&P £2.00)

CLIFTON HAND PLANES
CLIFTON 3 in 1 Rebate Plane £67.00
CLIFTON 410 Shoulder £49.95
CLIFTON 420 Rebate Plane £57.00
CLIFTON Multi-Plane £189.00

WOODWORKING BOOKS inc. P&P
MAKING WOODEN TOYS THAT MOVE £7.95
TRADITIONAL CABINETMAKING £9.95
WOOD FINISHING £9.95
FINISHING AND POLISHING £2.50
WOODWORKER GUIDE TO TURNING £9.95
TURNING PROJECTS (BOLTER) £13.95
Fine Woodworking Series
BENDING WOOD £7.95
SPINDLE TURNING £7.95
MARQUETRY & VENEER £7.95
THINGS TO MAKE £7.95
Many other titles available
FINE WOODWORKING TECHS (state vol.) £15.95

PARAMO CRAMP HEADS
1 off £10.00 5 off £9.00 (P&P £1.50)

G CRAMPS (P&P £1.50 per order) may be mixed for quantity
RECORD 120-3" 1 off .. £5.20 5 off .. £4.80
120-4" 1 off .. £5.50 5 off .. £4.90
120-6" 1 off .. £7.50 5 off .. £6.90
120-8" 1 off £11.00 5 off £9.80
120-10" 1 off £18.00 5 off £17.00
RECORD DEEP THROAT 4" 1 off £13.27

PARAMO 3" 1 off .... £5.30 5 off £4.60
4" 1 off .... £5.55 5 off £4.78
6" 1 off .... £7.76 5 off £6.60
8" 1 off .... £11.41 5 off £9.50
10" 1 off .. £16.90 5 off .. £15.77
PARAMO DEEP THROAT 4" 1 off .. £12.45

SASH CRAMPS (P&P £2.00 per order) may be mixed for quantity
RECORD 135-18" 1 off .... £18 5 off £17
135-24" 1 off .. £18 5 off .. £17.50
135-36" 1 off ... £20 5 off £19
135-42" 1 off ... £21 5 off £20
135-48" 1 off ... £22 5 off £21

RECORD 42" 1 off .... £35 5 off £32
T bar 48" 1 off .... £36 5 off £34
54" 1 off .... £37 5 off £35
66" 1 off .... £40 5 off £38
78" 1 off .... £47 5 off £45.00

JAPANESE WATER STONES (P&P £1.00)
KING BRAND 800G WETSTONE £8.00
KING BRAND 1200G WETSTONE £8.00
Super Delux Finishing 8000G £29
Slipstones 100 × 50 × 12 1 or 4000G £5.40
SUPER FINISHING STONE 6000G ... £8.90
COMBINATION WATER STONE £10.80
SORBY Diamond honing system (state Med. fine or Ex fine) £14.00

STANLEY HAND PLANES
(P&P £1.50/Order)

3	Smoothing 240 × 45mm	£23.60
4	Smoothing 245 × 50mm	£20.00
41/2	Smoothing 260 × 60mm	£21.60
5	Jack 355 × 50mm	£27.00
51/2	Jack 380 × 60mm	£28.00
6	Fore 455 × 60mm	£37.80
7	Jointer 560 × 60mm	£39.40
78	Duplex Rebate	£18.50
10	Rebate 330 × 44mm	£33.00
80	Scraper	£9.50
601/2	Block Plane	£21.00
92	Rebate Plane	£22.50

CLIFTON Cap Iron 2" or 2⅜" £5.00

RECORD HAND PLANES
(P&P £1.50/Order)

03	Smoothing 240 × 45mm	£19.50
04	Smoothing 245 × 50mm	£17.99
041/2	Smoothing 260 × 60mm	£18.99
05	Jack 355 × 50mm	£21.99
051/2	Jack 380 × 60mm	£29.50
06	Jointer 455 × 60mm	£33.99
07	Jointer 560 × 60mm	£39.75
778	Rebate 215 × 38mm	£30.80
010	Rebate 330 × 44mm	£39.50
020C	Circular Plane	£69.50
0601/2	Block Plane	£16.50
073	Shoulder Rebate	£42.50

RECORD 3 in 1 Plane £39.00

MISCELLANEOUS HAND TOOLS (P&P £1.50 PER ORDER)
RECORD Dowel Jig £34.00
140 Corner Cramps £12.00
145 Hold Fast £12.90
Floorboard Cramp £56.95
18" Extension Rods .. £4.95
141 Corner Cramps £19.40
146 Hold Fast £14.70
169 Bench Stop £7.50
Drill Bushes £1.90
Spare Collars £3.20
Priory Bench Stop £2.95
STANLEY Web Clamp £7.99
Stanley Yankee Screwdrivers 13" ...... £12.86 20" ...... £14.17 27" £18.50

HARDPOINT HANDSAWS (P&P £1.50)
SANDVIK 250 22" 1 off ..... £10.60 5 off ..... £9.90 24" 1 off ..... £11.59 5 off £10.90
SANDVIK 251 22" 1 off ..... £14.23 5 off ..... £13.00 24" 1 off ..... £15.59 5 off £14.50
LUNA 22" 1 off ..... £6.62 5 off ..... £5.90 24" 1 off ..... £6.68 5 off £6.32

HANDSAWS
DISSTON D8 20" × 10pt .. £23 D8 22" × 10pt .. £24 D8 24" × 7pt .. £26 D8 26" × 6pt .. £27
SPEAR & JACKSON PROFESSIONAL 22" × 10pt ..... £27 24" × 8 .... £28 26" × 6pt £30
TENON SAWS S&J PROFF 8" × 20pt ...... £23 10" × 15pt ...... £22 12" × 15 ...... £23
Roberts and Lee Dorchester Dovetail Saw ...... £27 RIDGWAY SPEEDSAW £19

SANDERSON KAYSER "PAX" HANDSAWS (P&P £1.50)
BRASS BACK TENNON SAWS 8" £18.50 10" £19 12" £19.50 14" £20 D/Tail £25
HANDSAWS 20" × 10pt £21 22" × 6pt £22 22" × 8pt £22 22" × 10pt £22 24" × 6 £22
24" × 7pt ... £23 24" × 8pt ... £?? 26" × 6pt ... £23 26" × 8pt ... £23 26" × 5½pt ... £23

ABRASIVES (West German top quality P&P £1.00/Order)
SANDING BELTS resin bonded aluminium oxide cloth belts (price each)

Size (length width)	M/C	40G	60G	80G	100G	120G
75 × 480mm — 3" × 19"	(Elu)	£1.11	£1.08	£0.99	£1.05	£1.02
75 × 510mm — 3" × 20"	(B&D)	£1.14	£1.12	£1.03	£1.07	£1.02
75 × 533mm — 3" × 21"	(Bosch Hit)	£1.28	£1.17	£1.07	£1.09	£1.05
100 × 560mm 4" × 22"	(Elu 90)	£1.58	£1.43	£1.40	£1.37	£1.32
100 × 610mm 4" × 24"	(Wolf Hit)	£1.67	£1.53	£1.48	£1.43	£1.38
100 × 915mm — 4" × 36"	(Coronet)	£2.22	£1.99	£1.88	£1.85	£1.81
150 × 1090mm — 6" × 42"	(Coronet)	£4.20	£3.80	£3.45	£3.27	£3.40

★ ★ OTHER SIZES AVAILABLE ON REQUEST MANY IN STOCK ★ ★
★ ★ NEW ABRASIVES CATALOGUE/PRICE LIST OUT NOW ★ ★
Send for your free copy covers all belts discs sheets Etc.

WIRE WOOL

	0000 Fine	00/0 Medium	1/2 Coarse	3/4 V Coarse
1 KG ROLLS	£4.73	£4.35	£4.25	£4.13
250g ROLLS	£1.50	£1.45	£1.42	£1.38

ABRASIVE SHEETS (P&P £0.50 PER ORDER) state grit when ordering 100G and finer

Type	Description	60G/10	60G/50	80G/10	80G/50	100G+/10	100G+/50
PGF	GARNET FINISHING	£2.13	£8.90	£1.85	£7.70	£1.67	£6.94
GCAB	GARNET CABINET	£3.02	£12.59	£2.61	£10.90	£2.35	£9.82
PSF	SILICON FINISHING	£3.16	£13.17	£2.73	£11.40	£2.46	£10.27
WS	WET 'n' DRY	£6.19	£25.81	£5.28	£22.03	£3.59	£14.99

★SPECIAL OFFER★ 50 Sheets of asstd. Abrasives £5.99 inc. P&P Garnet-Glass-W/Dry

SAVE 20% ON ALL HAND TOOLS SEND NOW FOR NEW HAND TOOL CATALOGUE £1.50 (REFUNDABLE ON 1st ORDER

0297 33656 5 Lines 24 Hour CHARD STREET AXMINSTER DEVON 6.30-9pm 34836

BARCLAYCARD VISA

AFTER THE SUN SET

The French Regency period and Madame de Pompadour brought fresh, feminine ideas to furniture design. Baroque was out; Rococo was in, and a new elite of furniture makers was born. Vic Taylor explains the details

In 1715 the 'Sun King', Louis XIV of France, died and was succeeded by his five-year old son, Louis XV. Philippe, Duke of Orleans, was appointed as Regent until Louis was crowned in 1723; but for the point of furniture history, the French Regency period spanned from the last years of the reign of Louis XIV, about 1700, until 1735.

The Regent was fond of a life of luxury and leisure, and during his regency French furniture fashions switched from the masculine, rather pompous Baroque to the feminine and more light-hearted Rococo style.

The reign of Louis XV, which ended with his death in 1774, saw many new designs of furniture. Most of them were aimed at women rather than men, probably as a result of the influence of Madame la Marquise de Pompadour. Many of the styles were adopted by English designers and are now in common parlance here (see column opposite).

Madame la Marquise de Pompadour (1721-1764), became the King's mistress in 1745. She was born Jeanne Antoinette Poisson; her father was a small-time financier of rather doubtful reputation and her mother's morals were equally suspect; at the age of nine she was told by a fortune teller that she would become the king's mistress and was called *la reinette* (the little queen) by her family. Brought up in close social contact with many wealthy Parisian families, she was taught all of the graces considered essential to young ladies, and her accomplishments were many and varied.

She had a passion for architecture, and encouraged the development of furniture design and interior decoration. She succeeded in her ambition to surround the King with an ambience of elegance and culture in which craftsmen of all kinds could flourish. The King himself became an accomplished woodturner and designed several pieces of furniture, notably the adjustable height *table volant*.

There was great disparity in character between la Marquise and the Queen, the Polish Marie Lesczynska. The Queen was excessively pious; it's said that the King was excluded from her bed on the feast days of the major saints — the uncharitable said that as she grew older, the number of saints increased.

It was almost certainly the Queen who commissioned two magnificent bureaux, which are probably the finest pieces of furniture ever made. One was for her husband, the other for her father. The King's bureau is known as the *Bureau du Roi Louis XV,* and her father's as the *Bureau du Roi Stanislas.* The first was begun by J. F. Oeben in 1760 and completed by J. H. Riesener in 1769; the second was by Riesener (or Riesner). Both bureaux are now in the Wallace Collection, London. The period produced a veritable catalogue of extremely fine craftsmen:

Jean Francois Oeben (c1720-1763) was born in Essen, Germany, the son of the local postmaster. It's not known when he arrived in Paris, but in 1751 he began working for Charles Joseph Boulle, the youngest surviving son of the illustrious Andre-Charles. Oeben was free to work on his own behalf and soon attracted the attention of Madame la Marquise de Pompadour, who became one of his best and most reliable patrons. In 1761 he became a *maître-ébéniste,* and specialised in elaborate pieces with concealed accessories such as secret drawers and compartments, and complicated locks. On his death, his widow took over the business and continued to use his guild stamp until 1767, when she married Riesener.

Jean Henri Riesener (1734-1806) was born at Gladbeck near Essen, Germany, and joined Oeben's workshop about 1754. He was made *ébéniste ordinaire du Roi* in 1774, and some of his work is in the Wallace Collection and the Victoria and Albert Museum. There's also a beautiful little writing table he made for Queen Marie Antoinette at Scone Palace, near Perth, Scotland.

Charles Cressent (1685-1758) was the son of a sculptor, and he followed the craft until his father's death, when he adopted his grandfather's profession of cabinetmaking. He is said to be the originator of the typical Louis XV *bombé commode,* and specialised in designing and casting his own ormolu mounts (which annoyed the Guilds — who retaliated by seizing his work on several occasions).

In 1748 his lavish use of wildly expensive gilded bronze ormolu mounts got him into financial trouble and so he substituted it with floral marquetry.

Antoine-Robert Gaudreau (c1680-1751) who worked for the King from 1726, was a competitor of Cressent; he produced a sumptuous commode (now in the Wallace Collection) for the King's bedroom.

Juste-Aurele Meissonier (c1693-1750) and **Nicolas Pineau** (1684-1754) were the principal originators of the style known as *genre pittoresque,* which was a more flamboyant development of the Rococo style; it rejected any kind of formal restrictions and embraced fantasies of flowers, rocks, shells, dripping water, cascades, C-scrolls, Chinamen, putti, and pagodas. Meissonier worked more as a silversmith than a furniture maker and published a series of designs for complete interiors, with special emphasis on metal work.

Pineau was born in Paris but worked in Russia from 1716-1726 as an interior decorator for Peter the Great at the Peterhof, and on his return to Paris undertook a series of grand furnishing schemes for wealthy Parisian patrons.

The family **Risenburgh** consisted of three cabinet makers, all called Bernard, referred to as Bernard I, II, and III. Bernard II (c1700-1765) is the best-known; his work is characterised by inset *Sevres* porcelain plaques, and *vernis Martin.*

Vernis Martin was developed by the four Martin brothers (Guillaume, Etiènne-Simon, Julien, and Robert) and the formula has never been divulged. It is known that it consisted of copal varnish applied over many layers of colour, and that garlic was one of the essential ingredients; gold or silver dust was then applied either in striations or as an overall powdering.

Robert Martin was the outstanding practitioner and enjoyed the patronage of Madame la Marquise de Pompadour; in 1744 the brothers were granted a monopoly on its production and soon had at least three factories in Paris, producing the varnish for use on *papier-mâché,* panels for sedan chairs and coaches, and furniture. ∎

Above, an ornate Louis XV bureau; below, a typical *bergère* chair, c1730, a *fauteuil en cabriolet*, c1760, a *bonheur-du-jour*, and a *bureau-de-dame* in *vernis Martin* to imitate Chinese lacquer

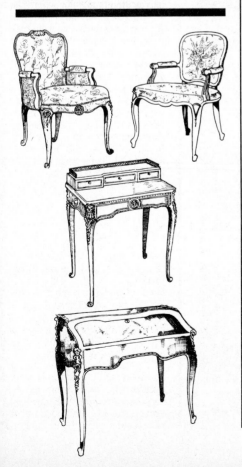

Furniture of 18th Century France

Bergère — an armchair with closed arms and a loose cushion; entirely different from the English 'bergere', 'burjair', or 'bergier', a tub-like chair with caned back and sides and a loose cushion

Bergère voyeuse — similar to above, with a padded arm-rest across the top of the back so the occupant could sit astride and watch card-playing or gambling

Bonheur-du-jour — small writing table for ladies, fitted with drawers and trays for toilet accessories, with a small cabinet mounted across the back of the top fitted with drawers or cupboards for jewellery

Bureau-a-cylindre — roll-top desk

Bureau-de-dame — small desk with a sloping fall-front

Bureau plat — alternative, lighter version of the *bureau Mazarin* of Louis XIV's reign; a table on four cabriole legs, with drawers in the frieze

Canapé — sofas or settee. The popular *canapé-a-confident,* was slightly curved so two persons people seated on it half-faced each other; also known as a *causeuse,* a *téte-a-téte,* or (in England) a 'love seat'

Cartonnier — small low cabinet with an upper stage of open shelves often incorporating a clock

Duchesse — two *bergères* with an upholstered stool between them, or one *bergère* with a footstool

Encoignure — corner cupboard, usually with shelves above, and often including a clock

Fauteuil — armchair with open arms but no loose seat cushion

Fauteuil en confessional — wing chair with a high back, adjusted with a ratchet movement

Guéridon — small stand with a circular top, used to support a candelabrum. First made in 17th century Italy and named after a black slave folk-hero. The term is still used in Britain for any small stands for *bibelots* or *objets d'art*

Marquise — straight-fronted *canapé* or settee for two

Secrétaire à abattant — small bureau with a fall front and open shelves in the lower section, enclosed at the back

Secrétaire à capucin — when closed, a small table with an extraordinarily deep frieze; when the fold-over top is lifted forwards, a bank of drawers springs up into position

Sieges courants — types of small chairs; one type with a straight back, *la reine,* the other with concave-back called *en cabriolet*

Siege meublant — sofa positioned against a wall, not intended to be moved

Veilleuse — development of a *chaise longue*, with the head and end all upholstered

Vitrine — glass-fronted display cabinet

UNDERNEATH THE ARCHES

O ur house has a gothic archway either side of the front facade, but the wood had all but rotted away, so I decided to make new doors and arch frames. Having removed the festering remains, I made some measurements, transposing them on to ¼in ply; the difficult part was to work out the centres from which the arcs were struck (there are several different styles of gothic arch). Finally I had a full size drawing of the arch on a sheet of ply, and I designed the door and frame to suit.

I made the two doors some months apart, the first of prime hemlock, the second of Douglas fir, as I thought it would be interesting to compare how durable the timbers were. The only difference in construction was that on the first I used traditional bridles at the spring of the door arch, but as these were time-consuming, I used multiple key-jointing for all the curved members of the second. To cut the curved members I used router and trammel bar; if I had made both at once I would have made a template and cut them on a spindle moulder. In both cases I used Cascophen glue — gap-filling, totally waterproof and plenty of workability. I treated them with preservative before priming with two coats of lead primer (it was almost a crime to paint the second door as the Douglas fir figuring looked so handsome).

Door

I first prepared the timber from 12x4in cross-section material in 3m lengths; I find these both cheaper and more convenient, since I can do the conversions to minimise waste. I cross-cut the timber for the doors, ripped the boards on the bandsaw, then planed and thicknessed. Next I dimensioned each set of components before marking out. I opted for 16mm mortises, so I used bare faced tenons on the middle rail and the lower muntin/lower rail joint to maximise strength and give the necessary offset for the boarding.

I cut the mortises, using haunched mortises on the bottom rail (my Sedgwick mortiser doesn't have a haunching attachment, but by simple machining I adapted the depth slide to incorporate a two position depth stop).

Then I cut the tenons, setting the machine up on some scrap first. Three height changes were

Mike Rossage faced a challenging renovation problem when he made replacement gothic doors

necessary to allow for the 44mm bottom rail, the 25mm barefaced middle rail and the muntins with normal centralised tenons. I cut the lower muntin 1mm over-length, preferring to trim down shoulders rather than risk having a rail a fraction too short. I tenoned only the lower end of the upper muntin at this stage, as the top end was to be comb-jointed to match up with the loose keys of the top of the arch, and in any case the shoulders have to be marked out once the arch is made. I haunched the tenons, cut out the waste in the double tenons, and then trimmed them to fit the mortises. Then I test-assembled the door frame components to check the measurements were correct and the angles true.

I used the spindle moulder for the boarding profile, with one pair of cutters producing the bead, another the tongue and V-groove, and a rebate head to cut the lower part of the tongue. I machined the bead a little lower than the final board thickness so later sanding wouldn't flatten the beads.

Now I was ready to tackle the arch part of the door; this was already drawn up full size on a sheet of ply, with the arch divided into quadrants to show where the separate components would fall. After cutting to rough shape with a jigsaw, I stuck the pieces of wood in place on the ply one at a time with double-sided tape. I screwed a 44mm block over the centre point of the arc in each case, and obtained an accurate centre for the radius using a marking out trammel from two divergent points on the arc back to the block, so the lines intersected. I drilled a small pilot hole here and located a screw into it.

For cutting I used a long piece of ply as a trammel, with the router at one end, having previously plunged the router through the ply to locate the cutter accurately. For cutting I used a long reach ½in shank 18mm cutter, and worked to my markings of outer edge trim, inner edge trim and rebate. After cutting the arc on one piece, I substituted the other component, cutting it from the back and turning it over later to form the opposite side of the arch.

I marked the cut-off points on the wood from the drawing below, removing the wood from the ply and then trimming the ends by eye on the De Walt radial arm saw; for the sake of four cuts on ▶

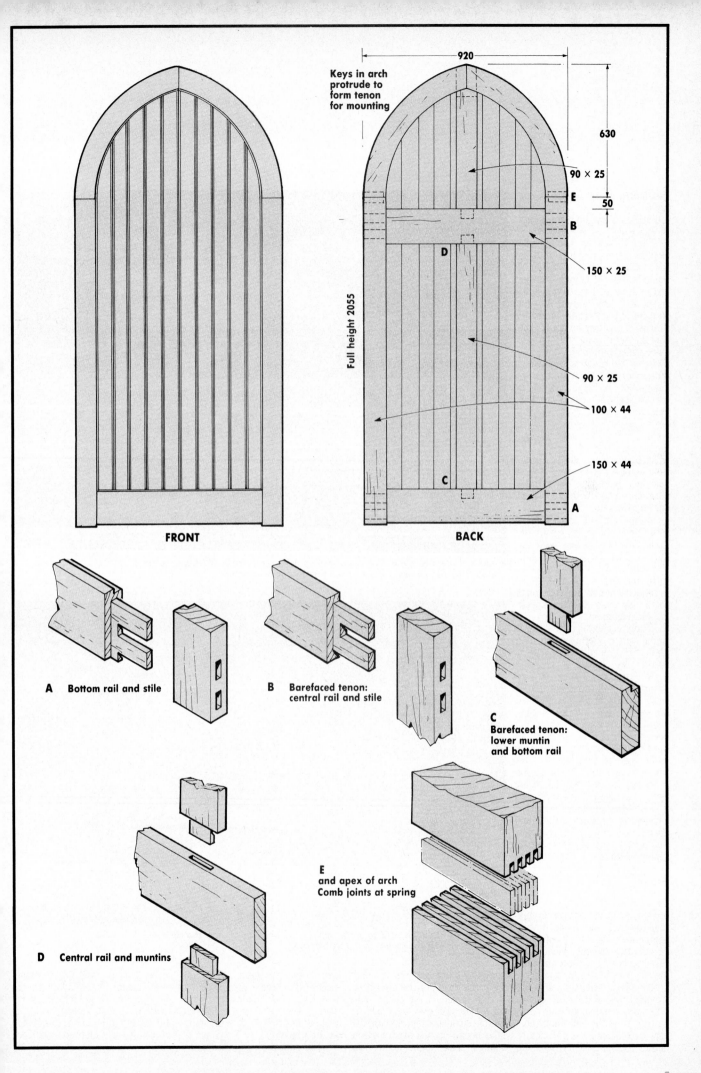

FRONT

Keys in arch protrude to form tenon for mounting

920

630

90 × 25

E

50

B

150 × 25

D

Full height 2055

90 × 25

100 × 44

150 × 44

C

A

BACK

A Bottom rail and stile

B Barefaced tenon: central rail and stile

C Barefaced tenon: lower muntin and bottom rail

D Central rail and muntins

E and apex of arch Comb joints at spring

one door it wasn't worth making jigs to get the exact dimensions and angles. I used a plane to get an exact fit.

Then I set up the spindle moulder with a 6mm grooving saw, after marking where I wanted to cut the keyways on one end of a piece. I set the spindle on the first one, and made a cut on each of the joint faces before altering the cutter height for the next keyway, using the spindle fence as a depth guide. The cuts have to be done sequentially, remembering the cuts in the top muntin, for precise realignment is very difficult. You could use multiple wing cutters if the spacing can be adjusted to suit; it makes for extremely fast jointing, but there was a degree of break-out, which I later filled before painting. Bear in mind the accuracy of your machine; I found inadequate support on mine, with a risk of altering the cut.

I then cut the keys to size from 6mm mahogany, with the grain direction in line with the joint. I glued the apex joint with the two lower keys protruding to form the tenon for the upper muntin, clamping the arch joints to the ply board to allow checking for alignment.

Then I glued up the lower frame, left it overnight and then glued the arch and upper muntin to the lower frame.

With the door frame complete, I marked out the boarding and cut to fit, with a bead in the centre line of the apex, before nailing them in position. They should be secret-nailed, but the shape of the arch doesn't allow for the boards to be slid into place so that was out of the question. If you decide to varnish the door you'd probably use some kind of back screwing.

With the door fully assembled I cleaned it up, finish sanded, and then treated with preservative and a coat of lead primer before finish painting.

Frame

The frame the door fits in was made in a similar fashion, except that the arch was made in four segments. Each segment comprised two pieces glued and screwed together, automatically forming the rebate for the door. I shaped the pieces using the trammel-mounted router just as I did the framing for the door, cutting to size on the radial arm saw and planing to fit, before cutting the comb joints. To clamp

Range of cutters for producing the boarding, with replaceable TCT-blade safety rebate block (left) and the block which takes your own cutters

The trammel has been used to mark radii on the baseboard; now the centre is raised to transfer the curves to the timber itself.

the pieces together when gluing I cut the shape of the arch from a large piece of ply; good joint alignment was easy to obtain by simple hand pressure, with the glue taking up any slack. If you wanted really tight joints you would have to glue blocks on either side of the joints and clamp the blocks. I made the keys slightly shorter than the slots to prevent any risk of the joint being pushed apart.

The door took quite a time to make. I have several more planned — unfortunately all different dimensions — and I intend trying laminating next time. It will be interesting to compare durability of the different methods over the next few years. ∎

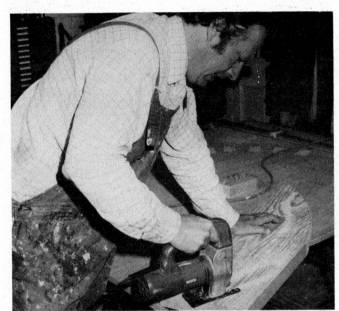

Cutting the rough outline of the curved pieces with the jigsaw

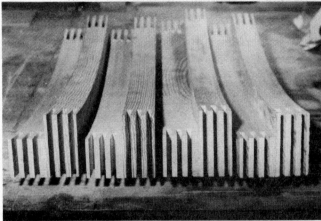

A clear view of the curved members for the frame, showing the multiple keyways. Four two-piece segments makes eight pieces. . .

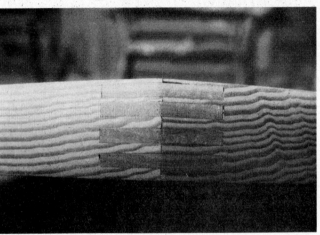

Apex joint of the door itself. Neat and strong, a nice job for the machine-crazy

No toy, this router. A shop-made 'router trammel' gives a perfectly accurate curve and a good finish to boot

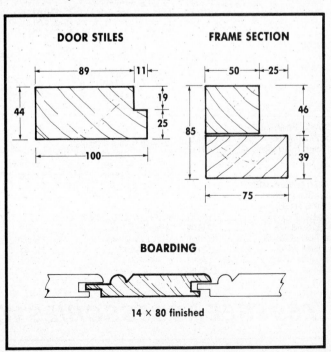

DOOR STILES **FRAME SECTION**

BOARDING

14 × 80 finished

Cutting list

Door

Boarding	11	1850mm x	80mm x	14mm
Middle rail	1	960	150	25
Lower rail	1	960	150	44
Upper muntin	1	800	90	25
Lower muntin	1	1200	90	25
Side pieces	2	1500	100	44
Arch sides	2	820	240	44

Frame

Arch sides	4	500	125	39
Rebate arch sides	4	500	90	46
Side pieces	2	1600	85	75

LONDON WOODWORKER SHOW

22ND — 25TH OCTOBER 1987
ALEXANDRA PALACE & PARK, WOOD GREEN, LONDON N22 4AY

OPENING TIMES
22nd — 24th 10.00am-6.00pm
25th   10.00am-5.00pm

ADMISSION PRICES
Adults	£3.50
Senior Citizens	£2.25
Children	£1.50

 How to get there — free shuttle service.
Travel by British Rail to Alexandra Palace station and then by free shuttle service or W3 bus.

By road: follow the AA sign posts. Free car parking.

Further information available from:
Argus Specialist Exhibitions Ltd., PO Box 35, Wolsey House, Wolsey Road, Hemel Hempstead, Herts HP2 4SS Tel: 0442 41221

 The London Woodworker Show is organised by Argus Specialist Exhibitions and sponsored by Woodworker Magazine.

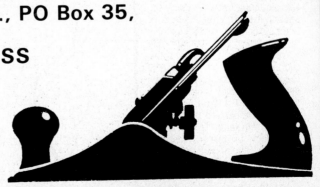

INTO THE RING

Originally I designed this towel ring to complement the towel rail featured in WOODWORKER August, but it has enough charm and character to be a single accessory for your bathroom. I used iroko to match the towel rail, but home-grown hardwoods, in particular yew or sycamore, are just as suitable. I prefer yew because it turns and polishes so well and mellows to a handsome colour. If you use iroko wear a dust mask during sanding and turning, as the dust can be unpleasant. Avoid iroko with calcareous deposits which appear as laminations in the timber.

If you're careful both rings can be turned from one piece of wood, so you'll only need two pieces for the entire construction. The main body is turned between centres to a finished size of 12⅜in long by 2¼in diameter, (fig. 1). After squaring the ends and mounting, turn the body to a cylinder shape using a fairly large gouge. A large skew chisel does the rest of the work with a smaller skew or beading chisel for the three beads and a smaller gouge for the two hollows. You could use a gouge instead of the large skew but it'll probably mean more sanding.

It's a good idea to sand the body to a final finish at this stage, working down to a 320-grit paper before removing from the lathe, although you'll have to sand again at the hand-shaping stage. When you've taken your work off the lathe hold it carefully in the bench vice using padded jaws to avoid damaging the surface of the wood (carpet underlay offcuts are ideal).

The next stage is to produce two flats on opposite sides of the body. The first which provides a surface for a stable mounting to the wall or door should be about 1in wide; don't make it too wide, or the lower ball shape will touch the mounting surface. Plane the second flat on the opposite face, taking great care that it's parallel to the first. The finished size across the flat should be 1¼in, the same as the finished size of the maximum cross-section of the smaller ring which is oval in cross section. (fig. 1 F-F). Ensure that the flat surfaces are in a parallel plane by removing a little at a time and check by placing strips of wood held across each flat at right angles to the main body axis.

When you've completed this stage the body should have a cross-section as shown in section A-A, C-C and E-E in fig. 1, but the remaining cross-section, B-B and D-D, won't be correct until you've hand shaped it later.

Drill two holes through the body at right angles to the planed surface at sections A-A and C-C for a screw fixing which will attach the small holding ring to the body. I used 1½in x no.6 screws and drilled the holes leaving a clearance hole for the screw shaft and for the head of the screw part of the way through the body, so the screw projects into the holding ring by about ⅝in.

The construction of the two rings may appear daunting but it can really be quite interesting. The large towel ring is 7¼in outside diameter with a cross-section of 1¼in diameter (fig. 2). The smaller holding ring is made by cutting a segment off a complete ring (fig. 1). It is oval in section F-F with the same width of 1¼in as the larger ring but with an outside diameter of 3⅜in and an inside diameter of 1⅜in. You can turn both rings from a single piece of wood, a little over 1¼in thick and about 7½in square, for a maximum finished size of 1¼in

A towel ring should look good and hold its own. Jim Robinson tells you how to make this bathroom classic

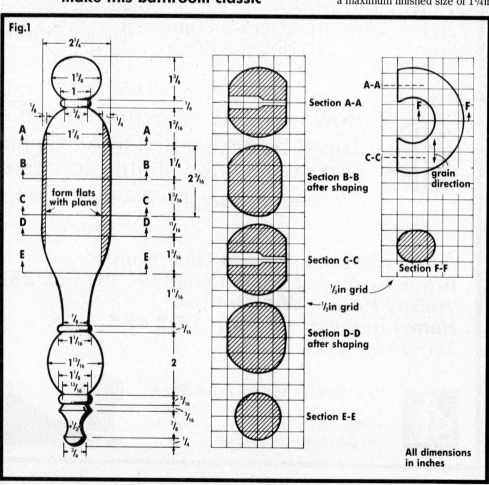

Fig.1

Section A-A

Section B-B after shaping

Section C-C

Section D-D after shaping

Section E-E

form flats with plane

½in grid

A-A

F   F

C-C

grain direction

Section F-F

All dimensions in inches

x 7¼in diameter.

Cut the wood to a circular disc with a bandsaw or to a rough circle by other means. Find the centre of the disc and drill a small pilot hole so the disc can be firmly mounted on a screw chuck. The pilot hole allows you to reverse the disc on the screw chuck and achieve a true centre; use a bench drill for the hole as it's important that it's perpendicular to the face. You should be able to turn both faces of the large diameter ring without reversing the disc on the screw chuck on most lathes, but you will have to reverse it for turning the small ring (see fig. 3). Alternatively, you could turn the large ring mounted on the screw chuck and then turn the small ring between centres, again the pilot hole will allow accurate centring.

A good way to turn the outside of the ring to the circular cross-section is with a bowl gouge on its side to give a slicing action; use a flat scraper for the inner side (fig. 3). You could use a scraper for all the turning but make light cuts to avoid tearing the grain.

When you've turned the large ring to the stage in fig. 3, it saves a lot of work later if you sand it as much as possible now. If your nerves are steady, carry on turning until you break through and separate the ring; or you can saw through the waste by hand with a coping saw. Either way you'll have to do some sanding and shaping, but rather more if you've used the latter method or if you've accidentally dented the surface against the rest when breaking through.

Repeat the process to produce the small holding ring. If you use the screw chuck, one side will have to be completed before reversing the mounting to complete the other side. If you mount the smaller ring between centres, however, you can complete it in one operation. Saw the small ring through to give a segment (fig. 1). I found the best method to ensure that both surfaces were flat and in the same plane was to place a sheet of 80-grit garnet or similar paper on a flat surface, then rub the faces smooth taking care to hold the ring perpendicular to this flat surface. You'll need to slightly round the edge of these flat surfaces so the large towel ring fits in the smaller centre space of the holding ring (fig. 1). Note the grain direction because of the reduced holding capacity of screws into endgrain.

For the remaining shaping work you'll have to assemble the project dry. Place the holding ring in its correct position and mark the screw position through the clearance holes in the body. Drill pilot holes in the face of the small ring to take the screws, by holding the ring in the vice with its cut faces in line with the surface of the bench and carefully aligning the drill with a square in both directions before drilling. Screw the holding ring to the body and pencil-mark round the point of contact with the body before removing. You should now have two almost circular rings marked on the flat surface of the body. Using a file and abrasive paper to shape, remove the sharp edge between the flat and the turned part of the body, allowing the body to flow slightly towards the holding ring (fig. 1 D-D). Remove part of the body to allow free movement of the towel ring within the holding ring (fig. 1 B-B). When you're satisfied with the line of the curves and the free

▶

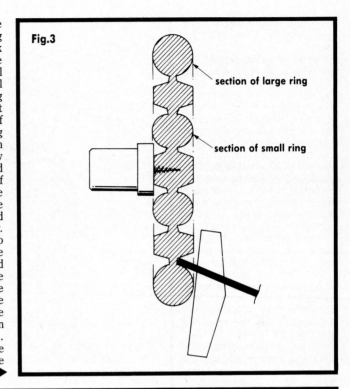

Fig.3

section of large ring

section of small ring

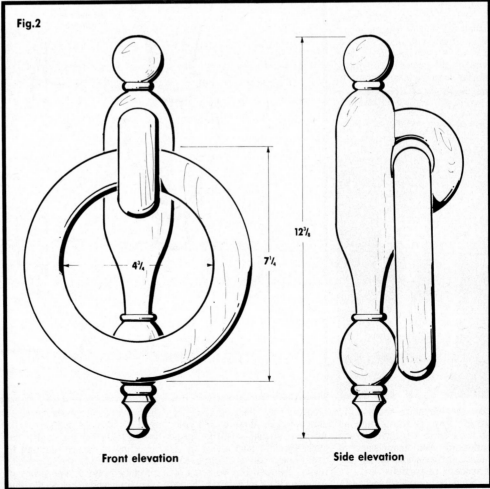

Fig.2

4³⁄₄   7¹⁄₄   12³⁄₈

Front elevation   **Side elevation**

movement of the towel ring, the project can be taken apart for finishing.

Before finishing, prepare the mounting surface for fixing the completed towel ring. A good method is to use a technique similar to the slot screw system of jointing boards edge to edge. Fig. 4 shows how the slot screw fixings are located to be clear of the screws used for assembly. One slot screw would support the weight of the ring and towel but it's better to use two positioned in a vertical line, to prevent the unit rotating if the towel is removed by pulling sideways .

Undercut the slot to take the screw head; remove a slot with an ⅛in wide chisel and pare the sides. The size of the fixing depends on the size of the screw, but I find a no.8 screw ideal. Screw the fixing screw into the wall or door until the towel ring can just be easily slid into position, if the screws are inserted a further half-turn, the unit can be gently tapped home with a fist to produce a good secure fixing.

My doors are solid pine panelled, if you're using a hollow ply or hardboard door you may have to fix a thin base to the door with gravity toggles or something similar to provide a support to

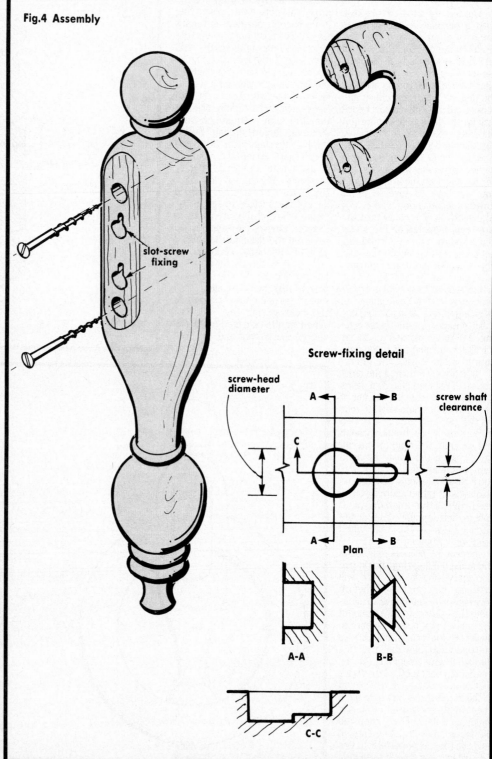

Fig.4 Assembly

slot-screw fixing

Screw-fixing detail

screw-head diameter

screw shaft clearance

A B

C C

A B

Plan

A-A   **B-B**

C-C

take the mounting screws. My towel ring is of generous proportions to suit my door and bathroom; you may want to reduce all dimensions by say 10% if space is restricted.

Sand the completed parts with progressively finer grades of abrasive paper down to 320-grit. All parts should have the finish applied before final assembly. I used one coat of Colron Oil reviver followed by two coats of Antique Oil — take care to keep the finish away from the surfaces to be glued. Glue and screw the holding ring to the body, not forgetting to insert the ring to hold the towel. I used Cascamite and added one or two drops of gravy browning to colour the glue to match the iroko, although if it's well made you should hardly see the glued joint.

When I'd finished I received the wry comment from my offspring 'Is that to tie your boat to when you are in the bath Dad?' ■

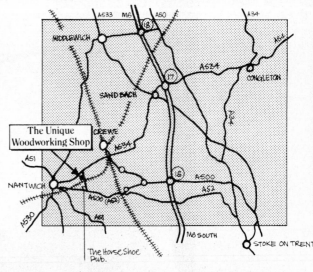

TREND BENDERS
USA

Esherick's cherry and hickory library ladder with steps tenoned into the centre post and dovetailed to the legs

With roots in the Arts and Crafts Movement, an exciting craft revival has been taking place in America since the 1960s. A recent book, *Contemporary American Woodworkers,* looks at leading personalities in the movement.

Wharton Esherick, the oldest of the group (born 1887, died 1970), was an inspiration in the early days of the revival. George Nakashima, Tage Frid, Sam Maloof, Arthur Espenet Carpenter and James Krenov, all born in the first 20 years of this century, are now elders of the movement. Wendell Castle, Garry Knox Bennett and Jere Osgood are among the first generation of woodworkers spawned by the revival itself.

Just as the Arts and Crafts Movement was a reaction to the mass production of Victorian ornament, so the crafts revival can be interpreted as a protest against the colour and gloss of the fashionable pop and high-tech styles of the 1960s and 1970s.

This is an extract from *Contemporary American Woodworkers* by Michael A. Stone, published by Gibbs M. Smith at £25 hardback. We are grateful to Michael himself, to the editor of *Fine Woodworking* magazine, to Esto Photographics and to the publishers for their help in compiling this article.

Wharton Esherick

This artist turned craftsman was among the first Americans to apply the aesthetics of contemporary art and design to the woodworking craft. When Esherick began to make furniture in the early 1920s, mass production was unchallenged and most pieces of furniture were nostalgic reproductions or European imports. Yet Esherick stubbornly adhered to the ideals of individuality and craftsmanship left over from the recently faded Arts and Crafts Movement. Art nouveau, cubism and art deco were among the movements Esherick incorporated into his designs, elevating furniture to a level of artistic expression then unknown in the USA. Gradually Esherick developed his own style of fluid, organic forms inspired by the wood itself. This reliance on the material for ideas characterised his work throughout his long career. 'Trees were the very life of Wharton', said Louis Kahn, the Philadelphia architect. 'He had a love affair with them; a sense of oneness with the very wood itself . . .'

Many of the country's leading designer craftsmen recognise their debt to him. Wendell Castle, for example, has said he first came to realise that furniture could be art when he saw Esherick's work. 'Esherick taught me that the making of furniture could be a form of sculpture; Esherick caused me to come to appreciate inherent tree characteristics in the utilisation of wood; and finally he demonstrated the importance of the entire sculptural environment.'

Arthur Espenet Carpenter, whose innovative designs and independent life-style have influenced many young craftsmen in San Francisco's Bay area, claims that Esherick's designs dared him to escape the limitations of traditional furniture forms: 'It was in the mid-50s when I first saw Esherick's work and began to see the possibilities of sculpting the edges of my furniture and eventually making it asymmetric.'

Sam Maloof, whose career began about 25 years after Esherick's, dubbed him 'the dean of American craftsmen,' and remembers the encouragement Esherick offered him when they first met in 1957, a time when furniture makers who created their own designs were few and far between.

George Nakashima

More than anyone else, George Nakashima embodies a movement in contemporary woodworking in which the craftsman allows the wood to dictate the form and function of the object. To Nakashima, wood is sublime and design is relegated to the mostly technical process of engineering. Nakashima's genius is his ability to determine the most appropriate use for the magnificent timber he acquires from around the world. 'Each log, each board, each plank can have only one ideal use,' he says. 'The woodworker, applying a thousand skills, must find that ideal use and then shape the wood to realise its true potential.' Nakashima harbours no interest in self-expression, preferring to 'create beauty not art,' a goal he sees lacking in most American crafts. His self-appointed mission is to preserve the splendour held within great hardwood trees by using them to create practical objects.

A disciple of the Hindu leader Sri Aurobindo, Nakashima chose woodworking as his *Karma Yogin* — his 'yoga of action'. He describes the relationship between his personal philosophy and profession in his book, *The Soul of a Tree:* 'We work with boards from the trees, to fulfill their yearning for a second life, to release their richness and beauty. From the planks we fashion objects useful to man, and if nature wills, things of beauty. In any case, these objects harmonise the rhythms of nature to fulfull the tree's destiny and ours.'

To Nakashima, furniture is most successful when the design is unobtrusive and the craftsman's ego does not intrude upon the natural beauty of the wood. Sculptural wood furniture he dismisses as 'better suited to plastic.' Nakashima's workshop produces about 75 stock designs that he has created and adapted over the years, including tables and chairs, benches and beds, cabinets and wall cases, chests and desks and lamps. Elements of both Early American and Japanese styles, the two major traditions in his background, are evident in his work. The lines in his designs are simple and precise, and Nakashima's masterful sense of proportion gives his work a classic look.

▲
Nakashima's side table with burr top. Frid's walnut and redwood grandmother clock betrays his Danish background ▶

Tage Frid

Tage Frid stands for the principle that furniture design must be based on a firm understanding of established techniques. 'Design around construction' is the underlying theme of his lectures, articles and books. Frid represents the single greatest influence on American woodworking education today.

The American Craft Council recruited Frid from his native Denmark in 1948 to help establish the wood department of its School for American Craftsmen at Alfred University in New York — the country's first college-level programme for training designers and craftsmen in wood.

The product of a typical Danish craft education, which included a traditional apprenticeship and modern university education, Frid brought to America his wealth of experience, an infectious enthusiasm for his craft and a subtle approach to design. For Frid believes that wood's innate beauty requires sensitivity and restraint, distinguishing it from other media, which force the craftsman to impose himself on the material. 'It is not like metal,' he has said, 'A piece of metal by itself is very cold and has to be hammered, shaped and polished before people will even look at it. A piece of clay, which is really dirt, must be shaped, fired and glazed. But take a piece of wood — plane, sand and oil it, and you will find it is a beautiful thing. The more you do to it from then on, the more chance that you will make it worse. Working with a material of such natural beauty, I feel that we have to design very quietly and use simple forms.'

Woodworkers, he stresses, should design with a sensitivity toward their clients' needs. 'Furniture should be in proportion to the size of the buyer and reflect his or her personality. I don't think that anything can make a small person look more ridiculous — and perhaps make him feel smaller — than disappearing into an over-sized upholstered chair.' ▶

Sam Maloof

As one of American woodworking's eminent practitioners. Sam Maloof has proven that a furniture maker can succeed simply by producing fine work without resorting to novelty or mass production. Instead of feeling compelled to introduce new forms, Maloof concentrates on refining and improving his existing designs. And there is no mistaking the Maloof style — simple, rounded parts that flow together, reflecting his concern and involvement with every detail of his work — it pervades everything he makes. 'People ask me why I do not go off on a tangent and work in different directions. My answer is that I have not really perfected what I am doing now. I do not think I ever will.'

Ninety-five per cent of Maloof's work is made of black walnut — he likes the way it works and feels its rich colour and grain complements his designs. 'Some woodworkers like to work in a wide variety of woods, but my palette is quite small. Furthermore, I do not mix my woods and do not use metal hardware of any kind or other materials for embellishment.' By selecting timber with knotholes, he obtains wood with more interesting grain than the expensive grades. Whenever possible, he accentuates the contrast between the walnut's honey-coloured sapwood and its dark heartwood. He finishes his furniture with a mixture of varnish, boiled linseed oil, raw tung oil and beeswax, although he adds thinner and varnish for tabletops to make them water resistant.

Arthur Espenet Carpenter

Carpenter's work can best be defined by the five criteria he considers when designing furniture: function, durability, simplicity, sensuality and practicality of construction. Function is the starting point for all his work. 'When I sit down with my clipboard in my lap fiddling over a new design, I shut out all references to furniture I've seen and concentrate on the functional requirements of the piece. First I draw the points or lines or angles that satisfy these specifications. Then I attempt to arrange the form and joinery in an unclichéd and aesthetically pleasing manner.' As a maker of utilitarian objects, Carpenter insists his furniture withstands everyday wear. If a piece breaks under normal use, he repairs it without charge — even years later.

Recently, his compulsion to investigate new areas has involved applying colour and materials such as plastic, steel and enamel to his work. In his Mondrian chest, Carpenter faced the drawers with brightly coloured plastic panels separated by black horizontal and vertical lines, mimicking the style of Dutch painter Piet Mondrian. Some experiments seem playful, such as when Carpenter paints a leg of his walnut music stand emerald green, while others like the Mondrian chest, reveal a serious interest in exploring new approaches to colour and form.

◀ Maloof's cradle hutch designed to save mothers bending over to lift up their babies — with pull-out shelf for nappy-changing.

One in a series of Carpenter's chests inspired by the abstract paintings of Piet Mondrian. The case is walnut and the drawer fronts are madrone▼

James Krenov

James Krenov is America's most fervent voice for craftsmen who resist the economic and stylistic pressures of the marketplace to create their own deceptively simple, well-crafted furniture. His ardent love of the material and his passionate defence of hand tools over more 'efficient' machine methods have earned him a wide following both in America and abroad, especially among the growing ranks of serious amateur craftsmen.

He is best known for the four books and many articles he has written, which articulate his philosophy on the craft and present his work in numerous illustrations. Amid the plethora of dry how-to books on furniture-making, Krenov's deeply personal style strikes such a responsive chord among readers that hundreds have written to express their appreciation for the inspiration and support he has lent them.

Instead of working from precise drawings, most of Krenov's furniture evolves as he works. 'I am not much for drawing... My pieces are composed around an idea, a feeling — and a chosen piece of wood. All the little details, the way things add up, are unpredictable — or nearly so. It is a *fingertip adventure*.'

In contrast to many craftsmen who take pride in their speed and production, Krenov has rarely made more than six to eight major pieces a year. 'Where did we get the idea that fine things are made quickly?' he asks. In direct conflict with the dominant trends of modern craft, which seek to 'elevate' woodworking to an art form, Krenov advocates a return to the values traditionally associated with cabinetmaking, such as integrity, durability and independence. He personalises each facet of his craft: every board he selects, every joint he cuts, every detail he creates is performed in a way to immerse himself in the process of making. The result is a craftsman totally inseparable from his work and secure in knowing he has done his best and done it by himself. ▶

◀
Known as the Pagoda cabinet, this creation of cherry with Lebanon-cedar drawers is among Krenov's favourite works

Wendell Castle

At the forefront of today's art-furniture movement, he has redefined and expanded American attitudes toward art and furniture. His early, laminated pieces ignited the imaginations of woodworkers across the country and horrified many traditional craftsmen who saw their cherished techniques and conventional forms swept aside. He has been through several divergent styles since, and in his most recent work, he continues to implement his philosophy that furniture can transcend its utilitarian role and communicate a message.

As an artist, as well as a craftsman, Castle believes his primary obligation is to fulfil an aesthetic need, and his furniture reflects this. This is not to say that his furniture does not meet minimum functional requirements — it does. For as Castle says, 'I don't start with the function, I take that for granted. A chair has to be suitable and a table has to be able to support something or it wouldn't be a table. Now in some cases...they won't hold very much, but they will hold something.' Castle's ▶

Top: Castle's Brazilian rosewood *demilune* table. **Centre:** Bennett's Checkerboard bench. **Bottom:** Osgood's Brazilian rosewood and ash desk with double-tapered lamination in the legs and bent-stave lamination in the case

Top: Castle's Chippendale chairs and a squashed hat, all derived from Swiss pearwood. Centre: cantilever English walnut table and Conoid chair in Nakashima's house. Bottom: Castle's lacquered jewellery box in Carpathian elm

chairs are, in fact, more comfortable than those of many craftsmen.

In the tradition of the great cabinetmakers, Castle steadfastly refuses to compromise his high standards of quality, but fine craftsmanship is not enough for Castle. 'Craftsmanship is a means, not an end,' he says. As an artist, he feels compelled to continously break new ground. His latest work, a series of long-case clocks, attempts to merge his two recent interests: the eloquence of art deco and the boldness of architecture. To Castle, clocks are poetic images representing the passage of time and how people spend their lives. His series consists of 13 variations of long-case clocks, which Castle uses as surrogates for the human figure. 'Long-case clocks are a way to present the human figure, which, according to the classic and poetic ideal, is the perfect image. They have a face, hands and a body of roughly the same proportions as the human body. Some even have feet.' The clocks were designed to be shown as a group. All employ exotic materials, including precious metals, and involve geometric forms, especially pyramids and triangles.

Garry Knox Bennett

Because he came to the craft via a convoluted route of sculpture and metalworking, Bennett holds no preconceived notions of how furniture is made or what it should look like. He breaks all the rules. His use of form, colour, texture and materials is freer than that of most American woodworkers. His irreverence for traditional woodworking borders on hostility. Although he works predominately in wood, he prefers to think of himself as a furniture maker rather than a woodworker. To him, wood is merely a 'convenient medium for making large objects.'

Bennett's designs are a panoply of vibrant colours and bold shapes. He creates them piece by piece, which accounts for their feeling of spontaneity. He sketches directly on the wood out of an impatience to create. 'I put pieces together in my head — what a table leg should look like or where a drawer should go,' he says. 'I work most of my designs out at night instead of counting sheep. Then I come into the shop the next day and start sawing.' Yet Bennett never allows his impulsiveness to run wild — he maintains complete control, balancing contrasting elements so they accentuate each other.

In 1979, Bennett rebelled against what he saw as a growing emphasis on technique among craftsmen by pounding a 6in nail into the front of a 6ft tall, solid padauk display cabinet that he built. With its finely dovetailed carcase, graceful curved front and secret latches, the case might otherwise have earned the admiration of cabinetmakers everywhere. 'I thought people were getting a little too goddamn precious with their technique,' he says. 'I think tricky joinery is just to show, in most instances, you can do tricky joinery.' To complete the irony, Bennett constructed the cabinet using several intricate woodworking methods including compound mitres and curved laminations. Dozens of outraged woodworkers wrote angry letters denouncing the 'desecration'.

Jere Osgood

Jere Osgood is most widely known for his expressive yet subtle use of such modern woodworking techniques as tapered lamination and compound bending. Most pieces of Osgood's furniture resemble their conventional counterparts — chests look like chests, chairs look like chairs. But Osgood gives them a contemporary twist. The sides of an otherwise plain cabinet bulge slightly for an air of understated elegance, or the legs of a desk swerve sharply to one side, creating a sense of tension and motion. Says Osgood, 'The techniques grew out of a searching in the design stage for new forms that would be strong and have a sense of freedom.'

Despite Osgood's interest in manipulating wood, he is committed to natural, tree-like forms. But instead of incorporating slabs or branches into his furniture, he suggests these images through his elaborate techniques. Osgood defends his methods as consistent with the nature of the material: 'I feel that lamination the way I use it follows the growth patterns in a tree better than can be achieved with traditional joinery techniques using square milled-to-thickness timber. I place more emphasis on pre-planning than shaping. The form comes from bending the wood into a light shell instead of removing stock. I'd rather spend my time drawing and drafting and making jigs than chopping away lumber.'

Osgood's methods lend themselves to limited production runs. Although the time required to make a single piece is the same whether you carve solid stock to create the form or bend thin layers of wood, with lamination the craftsman is left with moulds and jigs that can be used to create an identical piece in a fraction of the original time.

Osgood represents the new generation of university-trained woodworkers and the application of modern techniques at their best. Rather than allow himself to be carried away by the new ability to force wood into previously unattainable forms, he uses it to support his design ideas. Despite his innovative methods, Osgood is reluctant to embrace some of the new trends in the craft, like painting furniture or using other materials. 'I'm a long way from exhausting the potential of wood,' he says. ∎

Left: the shell of Osgood's walnut desk forms a perfect ellipse. The legs were his first use of tapered laminations. Below: Bennett's controversial Nail cabinet elicited the outraged reaction he sought

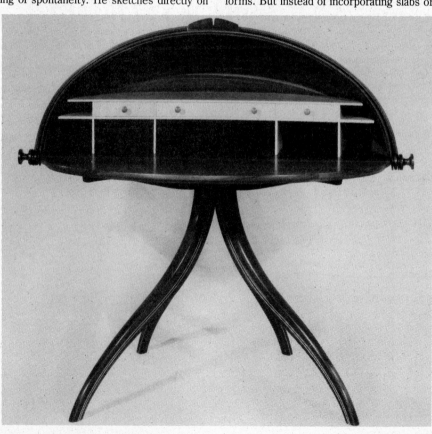

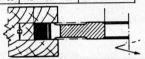
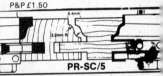
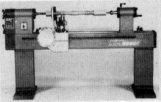

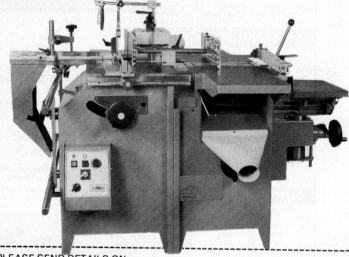

DRILLORAMA

Quality wood drilling bit sets in metric or imperial sizes at powerful savings

These sets of metric or imperial woodworking drill bits are brothers and sisters to the free drill on the cover, and we are offering them at more than £4.50 off the recommended shop price.

These top quality bits are not roll forged, but ground from solid metal, giving greater precision for really accurate drilling of shallow or deep holes.

The tips are unusual, ground to the European specification 'E'. This means they have two outer rounded cutting spurs as well as a centre point. The spurs score the surface of the wood before the main body, ensuring a splinter-free entry and exit while drilling. The centre point, standing proud of the cutting spurs, gives pinpoint accuracy when starting the hole.

Yet another feature of these drills is that they are ground again cylindrically, so they produce precise diameter holes but don't jam.

The drills are recommended for use with a power drill for hardboard, plywood, chipboard, MDF and all soft and hard woods. Optimum drillings speeds are 1800rpm for the $5mm/\frac{3}{16}$ in drill bits, 1000rpm for the $8mm/\frac{5}{16}$ in, and 750rpm for the $12mm/\frac{1}{2}$in.

The WOODWORKER offer is of either an eight piece metric set or a seven piece imperial set — but feel free to buy both! Each comes complete in a sturdy storage case so they don't get mislaid around the workshop.

The metric set contains the following diameter drills: 3mm, 4,5,6,7,8,9,10. Recommended retail price, including VAT, is £14.61. Our special offer price, including VAT, p&p, is £9.95, so you save **£4.66**.

The imperial set contains: $\frac{1}{8}$, $\frac{3}{16}$, $\frac{1}{4}$, $\frac{5}{16}$, $\frac{3}{8}$, $\frac{7}{16}$, and $\frac{1}{2}$in bits. Recommended retail price is £18.62, but we offer them to you for just £12.95, including p&p — a saving of **£5.67**.

AN EIGHT LEGGED FRIEND

Four pairs of legs and lime-wedged through tenons add a distinctive elegance to Lindon's ideal desk

M y aim was to make a writing table different from anything I'd ever seen and one that had none of the faults I'd come across during my long career as a teacher. Often I've ended up with injured knees when I'd forgotten about the large drawers on either side of the desk, which, in any case, invariably become convenient waste-bins to scoot all the clutter into. So many painful experiences and the literal waste-space of the drawers led me to envisage a writing table with plenty of leg room and which would be a pleasure to use.

The design objective

As a teacher of Art and Design, I tend to associate fine furniture makers Alan Peters and James Krenov with sculptors such as

Knee-snagging desks were the bane of Lindon Shepperd's life. His solution was to design and make an unusual hardwood writing table

Henry Moore and Barbara Hepworth; they've all created beautiful forms in wood and have had to work out a design before starting on their projects — even if it changes as work progresses. My criterion were that the desk was pleasant to look at and could be made with hand tools.

I was lucky enough to acquire a long teak worktop which had been used for at least 50 years. My table was for writing and drawing and I wanted the top to be free of adornment so the grain wouldn't be hidden at all and the teak shown off to the full. I decided to dispense with top rails altogether to get a different look. I'd use mortises and tenons, perhaps wedged to make the joints really secure.

If I was leaving out the drawers, I'd need something else to add to the design. What about eight legs instead of four? This

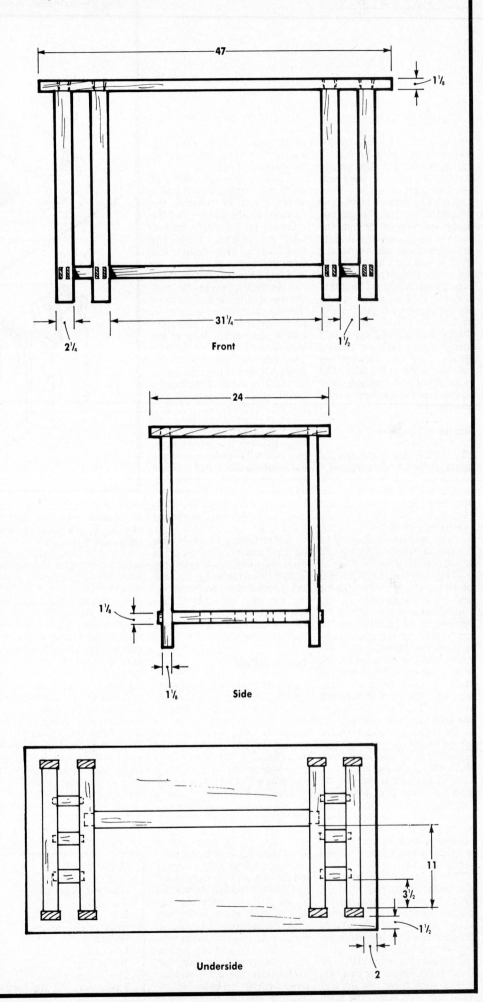

Fig. 1 – Elevations

all dimensions in inches

47

1⅛

31¼

Front

2¼

1½

24

1⅛

1⅛

Side

11

3½

1½

2

Underside

would add to stability without obstructing the underside. Each saw-cut and every joint would have to be near-perfect; the legs obviously had to be equal length to rest level on the floor. I would need some rails to make the construction strong, but they could be jointed into the legs across the width, just 2-3in above the floor. The rails on each side of the table would also have to be joined to prevent any sideways movement, and the two sets of rails linked with short pieces of teak with stopped mortises and tenons. I opted for three short pieces of teak with stopped mortises and tenons on each side. The legs would be about 2in apart, and the linking pieces could be the same, perhaps slightly more as the rails wouldn't be the same width as the legs. I decided to use lime for the wedges of the through tenons at the table top to contrast with the brown teak, and install a footrest set back from the centre.

Timber preparation

My workshop is tiny, 10x7ft, so I use a Workmate as my carpentry bench and am limited to using hand tools, and electric drill and a jigsaw. If you have a bandsaw or circular saw, the long sections of timber can be cut easily; I worked entirely with handsaws and didn't find it too difficult. I cut the legs with an old ripsaw with a good cutting edge and it was a joy to hear it singing as I cut down the length of teak. The rest of the work was done with crosscut and tenon saws.

My piece of wood had a few blemishes so I took off just under ⅛in from the surface with a hand-electric planer, and planed off the ridges with a smoothing plane. I could now admire the fine surface of the teak.

Dimensions

The width of the desk top was determined by the original 26in work top but it had been badly dented, so it ended up at 24in. Deciding the length of the top was no problem: eight legs plus the desk top had to be cut from the original 7ft length, so I cut the top 48in long leaving a 36in length for the legs.

The width of the table legs was all important. By making rough drawings and visualising the final piece of furniture, I worked ▶

out the width of the legs and the distance they had to be apart. I cut the wood 2½in wide, planing it down to 2¼in; the space between each set of legs was 1½in.

I sat at a number of desks to determine the right height and finally decided on 28½in, the same as my classroom desk. I cut the legs from the remaining 36x26in teak but I hadn't accounted for the joins in the timber, so I completed the leg rails and footrest with an extra piece of wood. My ripsaw went through the teak easily and I took great care cutting each leg to 2½in wide. I then crosscut each leg giving a length of 28¾in, allowing ¼in over the height of the table. The extra ¼in could be cut away after I'd glued and wedged the tenons into the top.

Joints

I took great care in marking the tenons at the top of the legs: each tenon's length had to be the thickness of the top which was 1⅛in after being planed, plus an extra ¼in. It took a while to cut the tenons which had to fit perfectly into the mortises and would be the special feature on the top with wonderful end grain.

The leg nearest to each corner of the top was to be 2in from the end, 1½in from the side. By now I had almost worked out all the dimensions so I marked out the top to take the tenons, top surface and underneath. As I was using lime wedges to fix the tenons in place, the underside had to be the width and depth of the leg, while the top of this mortise needed to be longer. My wedges would be ¼in thick at the top end, so the rectangle which I marked for the mortises on the top of the table had to be ½in longer than the width of the leg tenon.

I chopped each mortise out with a mortise chisel and mallet, keeping within the lines that I marked on the top, working towards a tight fit on each leg. I numbered each leg and its corresponding mortise as I worked around the top.

The footrest would determine the height of the rails from the floor; I opted for 3in from the bottom of each leg to the bottom of the rails, with the rails through-tenoned into each leg. Since the legs were 2¼in wide after planing, I planed the rails and footrest down to 2in, before marking twin tenons at each end. As the legs were 21in apart across the width

of the table, I cut my rails 21¼in long so that ⅛in would project on the outside of each leg.

You'll see from the plan that each rail needed considerable work; I had to consider the mortises for the spacers, and the mortises on the inside rails to take the footrest. I cut the spacers from 1¾in timber, 11in from the front legs.

I looked at the overall design and decided to wedge the rails into the legs in the same way as the top, with three spacers on each side underneath the table; light wedges at the base of the legs would have taken the eye away from the top. I made the through tenons of the rails to project slightly, bevelled each tenon before knocking it through into the leg mortises.

The spacers divided the rails by 1½in, so I cut each one 3¼in long, allowing ¾in tenons to go into each rail. The footrest was a link between one set of rails and the other, as well as a footrest, so I glued a 1¼in-long tenon into the inside rails. I cut the joints very carefully and everything fitted well.

Before setting the whole table up dry, I sawed the full length of each leg tenon to take the wedges. With two wedges in each leg, I sawed down to the shoulder ¼in from the ends of each tenon. I also bevelled the ends of the tenon to ensure a clean entry into the table top.

Construction

I was now ready to join the parts together, starting with the rails and spacers, connecting the footrest to the rails, knocking the rail tenons into the legs and finally placing the table top on to the underframe. A few of the joints were slightly too tight so I took a shaving off with a paring chisel.

I applied PVA to the tenons of the spacers to connect the rails and then cramped each set of rails with two sash-cramps on each set. After wiping away excess glue, I allowed them to set overnight. The following day I connected the rails with the footrest and the third day the legs were stuck to the rails, checking the legs were at right angles to the rails while cramping up. I could now connect the table top to the legs.

For the wedges I cut the lime across the grain 1¼in wide, ⅛in thicker than the table, and the same as the thickness of the tenon at the top of the leg. I

Fig. 2 — Exploded view of wedged joints

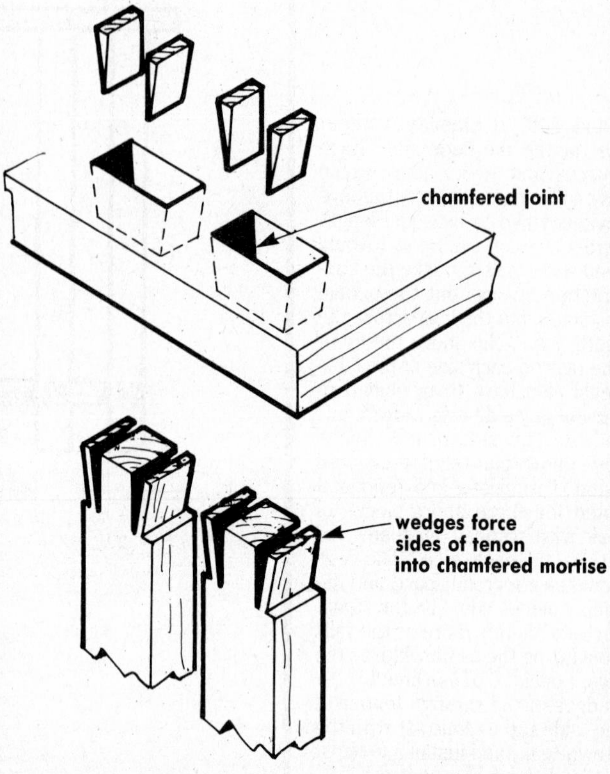

chamfered joint

wedges force sides of tenon into chamfered mortise

marked off the first wedge cutting at an angle from just over ¼in sloping off to a point to make a right-angled triangle.

When I'd applied glue to all the tenons I dropped the table top into place and wedged each joint, knocking the wedges into place with a hammer and a small piece of wood the same width and length as the top of the wedge. Each wedged tenon was approximately ⅛in proud of the top of the table after gluing. The table was left for 24 hours so that the glue could harden off.

I had to be particularly careful in cutting the excess away from the tenons to bring them level with the table top. I tried using a mallet and paring chisel but this was too dangerous as the wood could easily chip off below the level of the joint. I used a fine toothed hacksaw blade, and left about $\frac{1}{32}$in protruding, then sanded them level with the top, using a medium grade paper and finishing off with fine glasspaper.

Finish

Time for a final rubbing down with fine glasspaper before polishing. I applied teak oil, allowing it to soak in well before rubbing off with a dry cloth. The first two coats of oil soaked straight into the teak but the third coat gave me the finish that I wanted: a high sheen would have detracted from the natural beauty in the grain of the wood. Every month or two I'll give the table an extra application of teak oil until it thoroughly penetrates the wood.

There's a certain anti-climax when a creative process is completed, whether it's sculpture or cabinet-making. But even so I experienced a great satisfaction when I stood back and looked at the writing table. I had achieved my ambition in producing something of a unique design, produced from start to finish by me. ∎

Cutting list

(finished sizes)

Top	1	47in	x 24in	x 1⅛in
Legs	8	28½	2¼	1⅛
Rails	4	21¼	2	1⅛
Spacers	6	3¼	1⅝	1⅛
Footrest	1	33¼	2	1⅛
Wedges	16	1¼	1	¼

I used teak but any hardwood will suit.

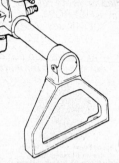

Guild of WOODWORKERS

The Guild was set up by **WOODWORKER** to create a meeting ground for all those involved in working wood — professional, amateur, and enthusiastic beginner.

For details, please send an sae to the Guild of Woodworkers, 9 Hall Road, Maylands Wood Est, Hemel Hempstead, Herts HP2 7BH, (0442) 41221.

Hand veneering — Bob Grant

10 October, 9.30-5, Oxford, £35 + VAT. Veneering is much more than the art of disguising chipboard. It's a skill with a long history, and can create some beautiful effects — and it saves fine and expensive wood! You'll be laying a panel with veneer, mitring a cross-banding, inlaying lines round it, and applying a balancer veneer on the back. If you have a veneer hammer, bring it; but materials will be provided.

Routing — Roy Sutton

14 November, 10-5, Herne Bay, Kent, £25 + VAT.
Another chance to learn the full potential of this versatile tool. Roy's courses are very popular, so book early. Starting from first principles, he covers housing, grooving, rebating, mortising, and rule joint and template work; he also deals with designing and setting up your own jigs.

French polishing — Ian Hosker

14-15 November, Chester, £50. One of our most popular course subjects, led by Ian, a teacher and a practising professional. It covers preparation of old and new pieces, staining and colouring techniques, grain filling, shellac finishes, fadding, bodying in, spiriting off and giving new life to existing polished surfaces. The fee includes course materials. Ian will make up a polishing kit to take away at £9.50 if you order in advance.

Attention Yorks carvers

Anyone interested in woodcarving and living in West Workshire is welcome to attend meetings of Keighley Carving Club on Thursday evenings, 7-9 pm, at Keighley Technical College, or telephone Mr Park at Keighley 603401.

Guild courses

Only Guild members are eligible to go on these courses. Use the booking form, enclosing cheque for the full cost. If you cancel less than four weeks before the course date, you will forfeit 50% of the cost, unless there are exceptional circumstances.

London Gallery

You have your chance to put your work on public display at the London Woodworker Show (Alexandra Pavilion, 22-25 October). As in previous years, we'll have some room on the WOODWORKER stand to display Guild members' work. We like to have as large a variety as possible — carvings, turnings, small pieces of furniture, but nothing too substantial.

Send photos of your work, limiting yourself to two or three items at most, so we can select those most suitable to make an attractive display. Send your pictures to London Gallery, Woodworker editorial, 1 Golden Square, London W1R 3AB.

BOOKING FORM

I wish to book for the following course(s)

☐ **Hand veneering** 10 October, £35+VAT = £40.25.

☐ **Routing** 14 November £25+VAT = £28.75

☐ **French Polishing**, 14-15 November, £50: make cheque payable to Ian Hosker

Please make cheques payable to 'The Guild of Woodworkers/ASP Ltd' unless otherwise stated.

Name . . . .

Address . . . .

. . . .

. . . .

Guild no . . . .
Send to: The Guild of Woodworkers, 1 Golden Square, London, W1R 3AB. The Guild reserves the right to cancel any course.

Choose Your Perfect Bench

No. 602 with cupboards

Shoulder vice on No's 610/611

As Europe's leading specialist bench manufacturers (serving the needs of craftsmen for over 90 years) we can offer you unrivalled work units to give free rein to your creative efforts. Lervad benches are sound, practical and tested designs which make good woodwork less effort and more pleasure. Look at the choices we can offer.

★ Two or three workholding points on every bench. Tail vice plus optional extra front vice or full width tail vice plus built in shoulder vice. Additionally all models have surface clamping system full length of top, single or double row according to model.

★ Rectangular tops in 1500mm (with tool well) or 1200mm (flush top) or Scandinavian patterns in 1800mm, 1500mm and 980mm (with wells).

★ Built in cupboards or open centre rail underframes to take hang on tool racks.

★ All sturdily built of solid prime Danish beech, kiln dried and oil treated.

Send now for detailed colour brochure and choose a Lervad bench for a lifetime's use and satisfaction.

Full width tail vice

Fold away models

Surface clamping

Scandinavian pattern No. 611

Woodworker PLANS SERVICE

GRANDMOTHER/GRANDFATHER CLOCK CASES
Long Case (Grandmother) Clock Case WW/104
An imposing design 6ft. 9in. tall 1ft. 7in. width. Glazed front with facility for moon phase dial. **Price £4.00.**
Grandfather Clock Case WW/111
A classical design with shaped Chippendale style bracket feet. Finished with brass ball capitals and finials 8ft. 6in. high, 1ft. 6in. width. **Price £3.25.**
Grandfather Clock Case II WW/112
A truly grand clock, 7ft. 6in. tall and 1ft. 6in. width. Authentic fretwork panel and cross banding with veneered panels. **Price £3.25.**
Grandmother Clock Case WW/113
A dignified design for a smaller clock, turned swell columns, moulded arches and base panel — 5ft. 10in. tall. **Price £3.25.**

CLOCK MOVEMENT DRAWINGS
Weight Driven Regulator Timepiece G.7
Claude B Reeve design, 2 sheets of detailed drawings for the mechanism. **Price £6.25.**
M.E. Jubilee Electric Clock G.8
An Edgar T. Westbury design modified by John Wilding. Two sheets. **Price £5.50.**
English Dial Clock G.12. Price £5.50.
Crystal Skeleton Clock G.13. Price £5.50.
Frame Template for the above. Price £1.00.
Model Engineer Musical Clock G.10
Complete set of 5 sheets of drawings including case details. **Price £10.60.**

WALL CLOCKS
Vienna Regulator WW/102
A 19th Century design pendulum clock. 3ft. 9in. high, 12in. width **Price £4.00.**
Hooded Wall Clock WW/105
A Dutch design, popular on the Continent takes an 8 day movement. Case 22in. × 14in. **Price £3.25.**
Deborah Vienna Clock WW/117
An attractive variation of the Vienna regulator. **Price £3.25.**
Grandmother Wall Clock WW/114
Early style of clock dating back to the reign of James II. 28in. high by 15in. width. **Price £3.25.**
Grandfather Wall Clock WW/115
An imposing wall clock with arched top and fluted columns. 33½in. high, 16¾in. wide. **Price £3.25.**
English Dial Clock ADW 130
Handsome design with enclosed pendulum visible through glazed panel. **Price £4.25.**

CLOCKS
18th Century Balloon Clock ADW 132
Attractive pedestal mounted clock by Ashley Design Workshop. **Price £4.25.**
19th Century Lancet Clock ADW 131
Another design from Ashley Design Workshop. **Price £4.25.**
Bracket Clock WW/103
Classical dignity with inverted bell top 14in. high by 10in. width. **Price £2.50.**
Georgian Bracket Clock WW/109
Glazed side apertures and brass embellishments with ogee shaped facet. 19½in. high by 12¼in. width. **Price £3.25.**
Queen Anne Bracket Clock WW/116
A popular style of clock case with bracket top and glazed sides 13¾in. high, 12in. wide. **Price £3.25.**

Argus Specialist Publications, 9 Hall Road, Maylands Wood Estate, Hemel Hempstead, Herts. HP2 7BH. Delivery 21 days

BORN TO TOIL

Bill Gates designed this sturdy woodworking bench with some special features

You can't do good work without good tools and a good bench. The basic requirements of a bench are rigidity, a true flat working surface, a vice and a bench stop. It mut also be sufficiently heavy to prevent it moving in use. This design is very stable and suitable for a small workshop where you're doing cabinet work or joinery. The two top boards are quarter-sawn beech: this timber is dense, close-grained and excellent for this purpose. I used redwood for the legs and the rails, drawers, aprons and the centre board; blockboard for the bottom and the division; I cut the back and the two end panels from plywood, and finished them with white paint before assembling. Storage for tools is provided by the drawers and the cupboard space.

Construction

Work out your dimensions and prepare a full-size rod for marking out the timber (fig. 1); the rod can be either a thin board, a good quality lining paper or plywood. Although the example shows the detail all together this is not

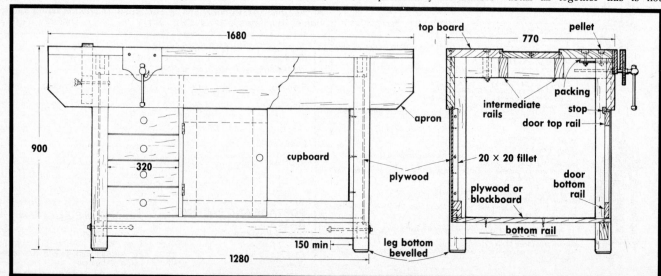

always practical and both sides of the board may have to be used, or a combination of paper and plywood depending on the area.

The legs for the end frames are slot-mortised at the top and mortised for the bottom rails at their lower ends. Mortise-and-tenons are also used for the front and the back rails. The front rail is secured with a long bolt and a nut inset into the rail (fig. 2). A hardwood fillet is tongued to the front edge of the blockboard bottom (fig. 3) and the division. The bottom is fixed with screws to the front, end and back rail. The two intermediate rails are dovetail-housed to the ends (fig. 4); these rails support the top and the centre board. The top of the leg is reduced in width and fits into the housing in the apron; I cut the legs before assembling the ends on my Inca bandsaw.

Assembly

Glue up the two ends of the carcase and assemble with the plywood panels; cramp and wedge the bottom rails, and drill and pin the top rails. Now finish the division to size, place this on the rod and mark the position of the drawer runners on the edge. Put the end frame and the division together into their relative positions and transfer the marks for the drawer runners. Cut the runners to length and drill them for screw holes. The runners are set back from the face of the leg and form the stop for the drawers: set a marking gauge to this measurement and mark this on the leg and the division. Now screw the runners into position (fig. 5). Clean up the end frames before proceeding.

Fit the bottom rails; place the intermediate rails in their position on the end frames, mark, cut and fit the dovetails and then number to identify their location. Cut and fit the bottom, as this is assembled with the rails (it can't be dropped in afterwards because of the different level of the back rail).

When you're satisfied that these parts fit correctly, glue and assemble the bottom rails to one end, place the bottom in position, apply adhesive to the other end frame and put this together with the rails. Add the intermediate rails and drive home. You'll need a cramp for the bottom rail at the back. The joints of the front rail are pulled up by the bolts, so check the diagonal distances of the front and adjust these if they ▶

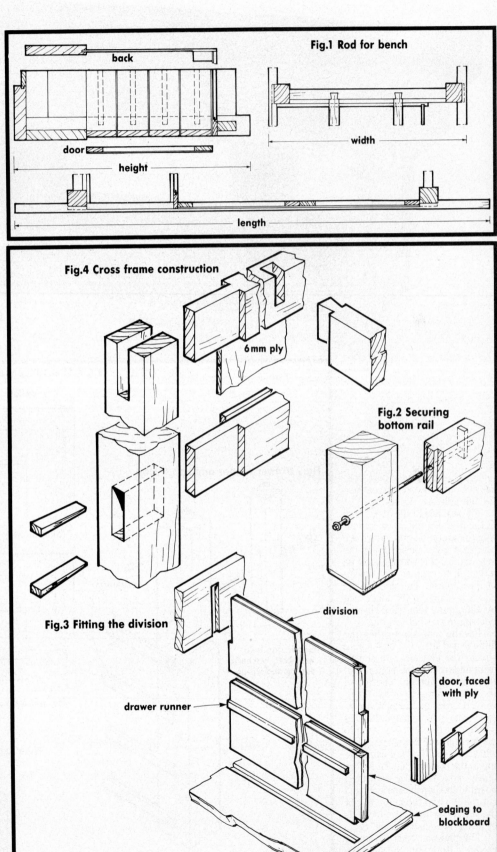

Fig.1 Rod for bench

back

door

height

width

length

Fig.4 Cross frame construction

6mm ply

Fig.2 Securing bottom rail

Fig.3 Fitting the division

division

drawer runner

door, faced with ply

edging to blockboard

are not equal. Leave the carcase for the adhesive to set.

Prepare and fit the bench stop to the front leg (fig. 5), before fitting the apron boards, which are prepared and housed to fit the legs (fig. 6); this housing must be a tight fit to maintain the rigidity of the carcase. The division fits into a housing on the inner face of the apron and also in the housing in the bottom (fig. 3).

Fix the rear apron, then the division and lastly the front apron; secure the division with screws from underneath the bottom and through the aprons. The top of the bench consists of two hardwood boards and the sunk centre piece; the selection and the preparation of the boards is vital to preserve a true flat surface. I've shown two methods of fixing the top to the carcase (fig. 7). Before finally attaching the top front board to the bench, mark out and cut the top and the apron to suit the vice being fitted; two methods of fitting are shown in fig. 8.

The plywood back fits into a groove in the apron, the sides are screwed to the fillets attached to the legs and the bottom edge is fixed to the bottom rail.

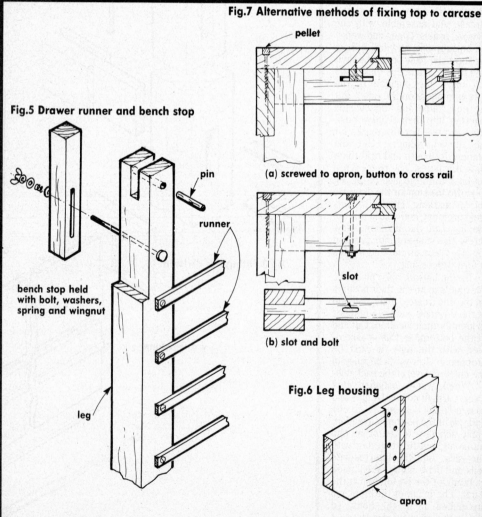

Fig.7 Alternative methods of fixing top to carcase

pellet

(a) screwed to apron, button to cross rail

slot

(b) slot and bolt

Fig.5 Drawer runner and bench stop

pin

runner

bench stop held with bolt, washers, spring and wingnut

leg

Fig.6 Leg housing

apron

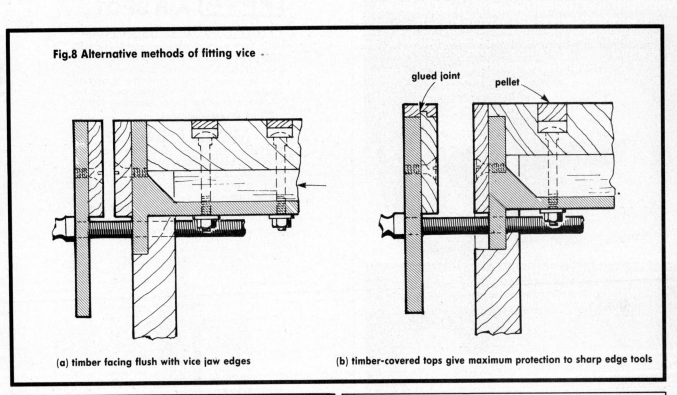

Fig.8 Alternative methods of fitting vice

glued joint

pellet

(a) timber facing flush with vice jaw edges

(b) timber-covered tops give maximum protection to sharp edge tools

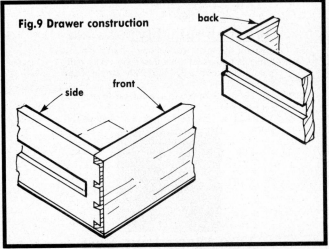

Fig.9 Drawer construction

back

side

front

Cutting list

Carcase

Legs	4	900mm x	70mm x	70mm	
End rails, top	2	750	90	38	
End rails, bottom	2	750	70	38	
Front rail	1	1300	70	38	
Back rail	1	1300	70	38	
Intermediate rails	2	1300	90	38	
Aprons	2	1700	230	35	
End panels	2	670	620	6	plywood
Back	1	1160	520	6	,,
Fillets	2	420	20	20	
Door stop	1	800	30	20	
Bench stop	1	270	50	50	beech
Division	1	570	680	19	blockboard
Fillet division	1	570	40	19	hardwood
Bottom	1	1220	680	19	blockboard
Fillet bottom	1	1220	40	19	hardwood
Top boards	2	1700	250	45	beech
Centre board	1	1700	290	22	

Drawers

Fronts	4	340	115	22	
Sides	8	540	115	14	
Backs	4	340	115	14	
Bottoms	4	340	540	6	plywood
Runners	8	660	25	8	hardwood
Centre support runner	1	700	60	19	softwood

Doors

Stiles	4	490	60	20	softwood
Top rails	2	400	60	20	,,
Bottom rails	2	400	70	20	,,
Facing	2	490	400	6	plywood

All redwood except where indicated

Sundries

Vice, bolts, hinges, lock, screws, adhesive, knobs

Drawers

The side and the front are constructed with dovetails (fig. 9); the back fits into a housing in the side. Glue and screw the plywood bottom to the frame to provide the maximum strength and depth to the inside of the drawer. Groove the sides to suit the runner, stopping the groove at the front end to correspond with the distance the runner is set back; this measurement is critical because it controls the position of the drawer when it is closed.

Doors

The stiles and the rails are slot-mortised and tenoned together, and then covered with plywood. I glued the plywood to the frames, then placed the two doors face to face and held them under pressure with G-cramps; place a sheet of newspaper between the plywood so the face sides will separate without damage. Fix a rebated fillet to the inside of the apron to form a stop for the doors. I fixed two bolts and a cupboard lock to keep the doors closed, and fitted turned hardwood knobs to the doors and the drawers.

To keep the surface clean I applied a light spray coating of clear cellulose laquer to the bench, except for the painted panels and the working surfaces of the top. ∎

Our panel of experts solve your woodworking problems

We will try to answer any questions you can throw at us, but the ones we publish are the ones of most general interest to readers.

Please type your questions double-spaced with generous margins, and include an SAE. Send to: Question Box, WOODWORKER, I Golden Sq, London WIR 3AB.

Un-twisting timber

Q A mahogany drop leaf, measuring 42x20x¾in, from a late Georgian table, has curved slightly in two directions. I tried to straighten it, by slightly moistening one side and putting it under stress, but it didn't work. What can you recommend?
Stanley Clark, Salterton

A Unfortunately to straighten boards such as you describe is a task with only a limited chance of complete success. The board has taken a long time to reach this state, probably under quite adverse conditions. These conditions can't be reversed (i.e. excessive dampness countered by excessive dryness), nor can a long time be devoted to the process.

An early method was to groove the board, say every 2in on a circular saw, in the manner of a traditional drawing board. The weakened board is then pulled flat either by the table framework or by battens. The grooves are stopped just short of the ends. Nowadays a small router cutter would be used. The job is made neater by filling the grooves with strips of matching timber.

More recently, wider grooves are routed, say ⅜in or ½in, the depth being dependent on the amount of bow. The board is cramped flat and carefully planed strips are glued in. Naturally a very tight fit will bow the board away from the strip while a looser fit will allow it to curl towards the strip.

A bow in length is more difficult to correct. The above treatment, vigorously done, may help. As the bow is along the rule joint, increasing rule-joint hinges should improve matters.

As a last resort, additionally groove and fill across the grain. Do not go too deep or a series of flat facets will be visible from the top.
Bob Wearing
● Bob Wearing is a woodwork lecturer of vast experience and a regular contributor to WOODWORKER.

Finishing oak

Q I am unhappy with the finish I applied to a plain oak grandfather clock-case. The oil stain I used penetrated poorly, leaving a muddy finish with very stripey darker grain. The two layers of shellac I then applied failed to stop one or two patches of the stain being removed by waxing.

What can I use to strip or bleach away the wax, shellac and oil stain? Would a water stain penetrate the oak any better if traces of the oil stain remain? I want to produce an antique finish to match the 200-year-old movement.
Stephen Clarke, Chester

A It would seem that the two applications of shellac didn't provide enough coverage to prevent the white spirit in the wax polish from acting on the oil stain which most probably has a white spirit base. This would be the cause of the stain being removed in small patches when waxing.

Wax polish can be removed by wiping over the case with a rag moistened with white spirit. A meths-soaked rag will clean off the shellac. The remaining oil stain, which did not penetrate deeply, can be lightened by rubbing all over with steel wool.

Having cleaned up the case, sponge it all over with warm water to raise the grain before staining it with bichromate of potash. Let the stain dry thoroughly, lightly glasspaper and then brush on two coats of white french polish. When this has hardened give several applications of wax polish.

The different processes are fully described in the *Woodworker Manual of Finishing and Polishing*, price £2.50 from Argus Books Ltd. Freepost, Hemel Hempstead, Herts. HP2 4SS.

Regular waxing will produce a patina comparable to that found on well cared-for antique furniture. Be sure to buy all your polishing materials from a trade house. In this way you will obtain best quality materials and there will be no silicones in the wax polish. I do not know a trade supplier in your area but the following two firms will supply all necessary stains and polishes by post: Henry Flack (1860) Ltd, PO Box 78, Beckenham, Kent, BR3 4BL; James Jackson & Co (London) Ltd, 76-89 Alscot Road, London SEI 5SX.
Charles Cliffe
● Charles Cliffe is a professional polisher, author and teacher.

NEXT MONTH

November's WOODWORKER is crammed, as usual, with a stunning variety of information and entertainment — all that puts the country's best-selling woodwork journal at the very top of the tree.

Before you even open it, you'll be intrigued by what's on the front cover; a **FREE SAMPLE** of **Sandvik Sandplate**, the revolutionary new flexible steel abrasive material. We've made sure the bit you get is big enough to use; and there's a money-off coupon inside so you can get two Sandplate tools at a bargain price.

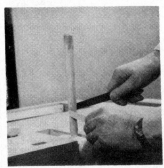

Cut it, bend it, use it with Sandvik's tools or devise your own. . . get a free sample of SANDPLATE next month and try your hand

The November issue is traditionally the WOODWORKER SHOW preview issue; it's on sale well before the show starts on 22 October, so you can read up on organiser Mary White's introduction, and work out what you want to see when you visit the show.

We have a report, with lots of colour pictures, on Britain's **first Woodturning Seminar** for six years — 'From Craft to Art' was held in Loughborough in August, and we were there. We have previews, news and reviews of **marquetry**, the **Chelsea Crafts Fair**, a **carving exhibition**, and for you to make we have one of WOODWORKER'S most ambitious projects yet — a single-hand replica **Black Forest Clock**, made entirely in wood. A magnificent piece, and a real challenge. There's also a **toy bulldozer** and two **folding tables**. Plus a **totem-pole maker** who'll be demonstrating at the Show, and an introduction to a traditional **basket maker**; we'd like to tell you all of it, but we just can't cram it in here. Just make sure you don't miss it — Britain's brightest and best woodworking monthly. The quality one!

ON SALE 16 OCTOBER

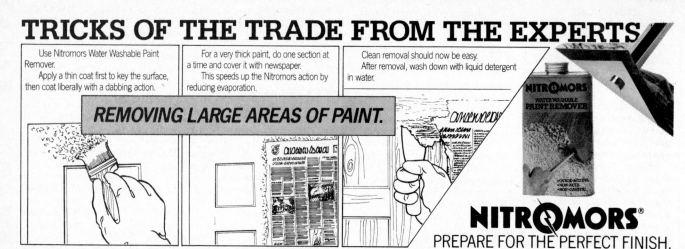

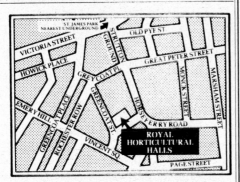

CLINCHING THE SALE

Worried about selling? Hugh O'Neill shows how to succeed at the sharp end

Without sales, your business is dead. But sales aren't just some happy accident made in heaven to put money into your pocket. They have to be thought about, prepared for, and worked at.

The best place to learn what selling is all about is a competitive situation; at a crafts fair, for instance, you're in competition with some others selling similar work, and ultimately you're working against every other stall holder who is after the same pound in the punter's pocket. Even a stroll round a crafts fair, studying the actions of the stall holders and the public, will give you an insight into how, and how not, to sell.

The selling process starts long before you stand in front of a customer: the roots are in marketing and in market research. You have to know what interests the public, and what sector of the public you're aiming at; how to price your work appropriately for each outlet and know what kind of work will sell there; you'll have to learn about display and pre-

sentation — catching the buyer's initial interest and holding it.

Of course there are differences between selling fancy bowls at crafts fairs and finding clients for custom-made architectural woodwork and joinery. Selling from your studio or workshop is different from selling in the client's home/workplace or on neutral territory like a crafts fair or exhibition.

But wherever and whatever you are selling, the process remains essentially the same. Your job is to satisfy the four questions which are going through the potential customer's mind:

- Why buy this product?
- Why buy from this organisation or company?
- Why buy from this person?
- Why buy now?

At a crafts fair these four questions start going through a visitor's mind the moment

they pass your stall, run their eyes over your display and get hooked on a particular item. Sometimes a person can fall for a piece so heavily that you have to do virtually no work to get the sale.

But it doesn't often happen that way. Customers may have settled in their minds that they would like to buy the piece, but they'll be affected by the nature of the event and venue, the kudos of buying direct from the maker, and by you as a person (talk enthusiastically, tell them about your training, show you care about wood, smile).

The 'why buy now?' is the most complex area and the point on which most sales are lost. Sales training is extremely useful here; it teaches you how to clinch a sale and, just as important, how not to take it personally if you get a rejection. Remember, the customer who doesn't buy is turning down your offer to sell, not you personally. You will get rejections, of course, but you won't get sales unless you ask

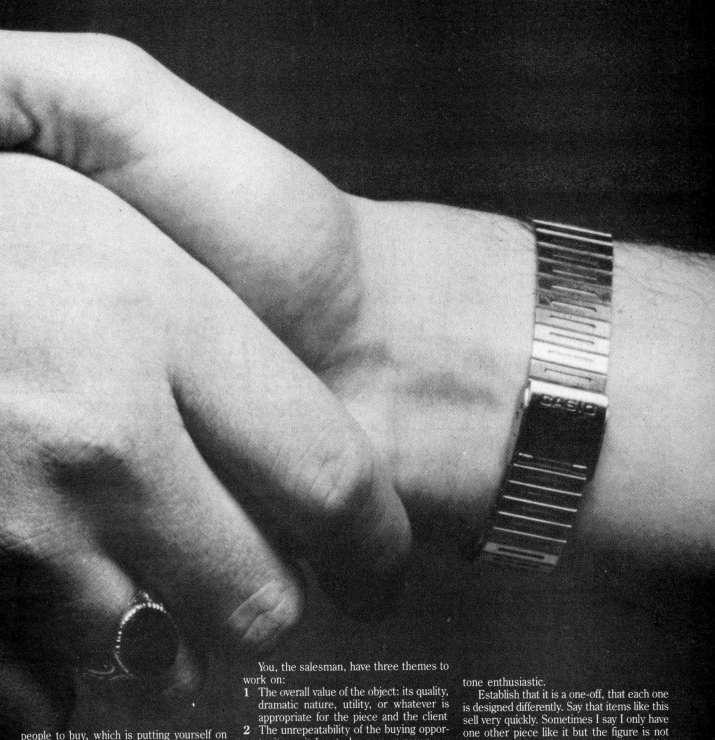

people to buy, which is putting yourself on the line.

You may hate being on the receiving end of 'high pressure salesmanship' yourself. Fair enough. But in my experience, very few people volunteer to buy — they need some encouragement, an invitation to buy. I reckon two-thirds of my sales would never have occurred if I had just sat there and waited for the customer to push money into my hands.

The golden rule of selling is to try and make the sale now. The potential customer who says 'I'll think it over and come back' rarely does (though some do).

So picture the scene. The customer wants to buy, likes the look of the venue and of you. What holds the customer back at this stage is not the price, but whether they can justify spending money at that moment or whether they should put off making the decision till later.

That's where you come in — helping them make their minds up that they do indeed want to buy now.

You, the salesman, have three themes to work on:
1 The overall value of the object: its quality, dramatic nature, utility, or whatever is appropriate for the piece and the client
2 The unrepeatability of the buying opportunity — it has to be now or never
3 The relatively little hurt and/or the convenience of making the purchase now. Handle this very carefully, it can backfire on you...

Whatever you say about the overall value you must be specific to the item and the particular client. Don't talk about the utility of the item to someone clearly interested in the design. As I once heard: 'Look how deep the drawers are — just think of the amount of clothing you could keep in that,' — describing a uniquely designed chest whose potential buyers were considering making it a feature in the main living room!

Talk about the materials and the construction — relate this to what the client has already told you of their interest in the object. Highlight features of the design, the texture, the figure. Weave in messages that will impinge upon the uniqueness and unrepeatability — the rarity of the particular figure; the scarcity of the timber and so on. Keep your tone enthusiastic.

Establish that it is a one-off, that each one is designed differently. Say that items like this sell very quickly. Sometimes I say I only have one other piece like it but the figure is not so dramatic — and I show them an item which is a very pale shadow of the one the buyer is interested in. They never even look at the price of the second!

Perhaps they are still not convinced, and you get the 'do you come here often' type of question. Try to appear helpful and interested in their conversation, but steer them back to the sale.

You may be able to answer their question: 'Yes it is oiled and waterproof and may be used for salads.' Or 'It has been treated with a sealant but you should not put damp earth in it.' Alternatively it may be something you cannot answer — whether it will fit at the top of the stairs.

Asking 'Is there any particular information that you need in order to help you make a decision?' can often clear away a simple block (and I have called at the house on the way back from a fair to see if a piece did fit).

There are two ways of dealing with the price ▶

barrier. Which you choose will be a matter of personal style. Some people believe that price cutting is the way of achieving sales. I don't. If you're happy with it, however, then build a bargaining element into your price structure, and use it if you have to (you will probably learn that you have been under-pricing as you'll still sell as much at the inflated price).

They are wavering — you think it is a price problem so you say: 'You've clearly fallen for that piece. I don't blame you, it really is..., and I would like you to have it. How about if I said £...? To make this work you need to do it in a confidential manner and offer a minimum of 10% and preferably 25% off the marked price. Sometimes it works. Often it clears their mind for them and they say 'No!'

The main alternative to price cutting is to push the waverer by a gentle: 'I can take Visa or Access, if you don't wish to pay that amount immediately. At least that way you will be sure of having it; I can't guarantee that I'll ever have another piece of wood just like it.'

Certainly the most effective way of dealing with the waverer is to dwell on the un-repeatability, the 'one-off' nature of the work. All the time the message that you are pre-senting is that 'if you don't buy it now there will never be another chance. This is unique and there will never be another one like it.'

Of course there will always be some people who are really taken by a piece of work. They are desperate to have it, but it really is beyond their means. I think you do them little favour by offering to cut the price. We appreciate most those things that it has hurt us to buy. You have to decide whether you are going to push them into a purchase that you guess they can't readily afford but which will give them a lifetime's pleasure. If you decide to push the sale, you can be sympathetic and understanding and prompt them to spoil themselves with the purchase of this lovely item that will give them so much pleasure. If you know that it really has hurt them, when they are making out the cheque (and not before), say 'Oh, make it for £...' Rounding it down by quite a small amount will make them feel really good about their pur-chase and about you as a person, and will often prevent any later feeling of guilt or recrimination. For both parties!

If they are beginning to harden their resolve against the possible extravagance, this is the time to sell down. 'I'm afraid that one is expensive,' (and this is the only time you use the word), 'but I do have another example.' (Note you do not say 'smaller' or 'cheaper'). You now put into their hands a lower priced alternative with: 'Now isn't that exquisite?' Sometimes they will buy the new offering because their means are not elastic, but frequently they will say: 'No! It's the bigger one that I like. I'll take it!' and the decision has been made.

'I'll think it over' is not always a death

knell. In 99% of the cases it's where they actually leave the studio or the location. This is why the skilful sales person develops ways of dealing with the problem. They immedi-ately come back with. 'Fine, I understand; tell me, precisely what is it that you want to think over, is it...?' and they restate all the sales points they have already made.

At crafts fairs there is a different scenario. I rarely expect to make a major sale to the person as they make the first visit to my stall. People frequently say: 'I would like to think about it, and look at the rest of the fair first.' This never worries me if the other signs have been right — particularly where they have been having difficulty choosing between two or three pieces. Such customers I don't push too hard, even on the second indecisive visit.

Not all the four basic questions have to receive totally satisfactory answers and certainly not all are considered consciously. In broad terms the more significant the pur-chase the more fully the questions are considered.

So what about the studio or studio/workshop? Here there is no immediate competition. We still get a lot of rubber-neckers but there is a higher chance of converting some to buyers.

People visit studios for one of three reasons:

1 They are genuinely interested in the subject and might buy
2 They are specifically looking for something or for a gift or a collection
3 They are practitioners (usually hobbyists), and have come to pick up a few tips or to be critical of your 'commercial' standards.

We still have to 'sell', and use all the approaches already discussed. Maybe we don't have to push quite so much. This is just as well. If our studio is open every day and we have to become personally involved and positively sell every time a visitor enters; then we aren't going to get much production done.

I saw this handled well in one rural studio, with a notice which read: 'If you want details about how the item you have now purchased was made, please ask. I will be delighted to

come through to talk with you. If you are a fellow carver and want lessons, then these can be arranged at a fee!' It was signed by the craftsman.

While all the above points relate to any selling activity, there are additional elements when we move away from the luxury and impulse-sale areas towards essentials such as architec-tural woodwork and joinery.

The four questions remain. The mistake is to assume that you know or can anticipate the precise form of answer the buyer will reach.

You make contact with the building con-tractor, make an appointment, go in and start by telling him what you do. 'I make doors, windows and frames. They are all hand-made to customers' specificiations using only the finest timber. Now what can I do for you sir?'

'Not much' comes the reply, 'you see we have our own shop and make everything ourselves.'

The key to this type of selling is to first find the buyer's needs. Then and only then can you show how you might meet the specific and identified needs.

'Good morning Mr Jerry Build. I am Brad Iron, a local jobbing joiner. I'd like to see if we might do some business at some time. Could you tell me something about your joinery needs — what do you use, how much, where do you get it at present, any problems, things you find difficult to obtain, what sort of quality, what do you pay...?' Now you are ready to tell him what you do, how your quality, service, price or whatever might be an advantage to him.

Most buyers in this field talk price. Some sales people believe that price is the only factor of any real influence. Sometimes the answer to why buy from this company is 'because it offers me exactly what I want (i.e. of a quality comparable to other suppliers) at a cheaper price'. Or the answer to the 'why buy now?' question might be 'because I am being offered a genuine sale price which I know will not be available tomorrow'.

The quality of the product, the appro-priateness of the price to the quality, the apparent competence of the producer in manufacture, the soundness of the producer as a businessman, the apparent ability to be able to deal with unexpected problems, the back-up after-sales service, the general acceptability of the individual salesman that the buyer meets — these and similar all pro-vide answers to different questions and all of those questions are there in the buyer's mind.

Show (by telling them) that this is what they are getting when they buy from you. Tailor each statement to something that your questioning has revealed as a need or area of special interest, and you won't have to ask for the order — they will ask you to supply; and may even be prepared to pay you for the privilege. ∎

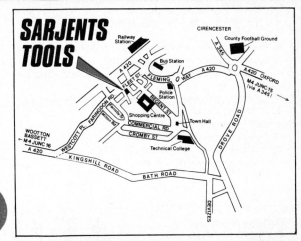

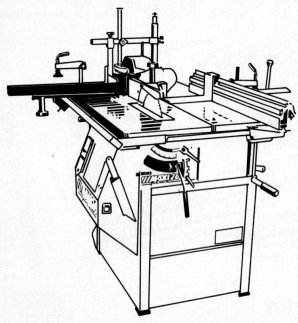

Bob Wearing's
WORKSHOP
ROUTER HINGING

A simple jig for dead-accurate hinge recessing

This device will successfully cut the hinge sockets for doors when half the hinge is let into the door and half into the frame or carcase. It doesn't cope with the sloping sockets needed in the best cabinet-making where the whole thickness of the hinge is let into the door. It is particularly useful in joinery when you have a number of similar large doors to be hung.

Glue up the top frame **A** (fig. 1), leaving enough gap to accept the thickest doors. Attach to this a wide fence **B** which must project beyond the top frame at both ends. One end of the top frame acts as a stop; the other end is fitted with the sliding stop **C**.

All sizes are but suggestions. Those given permit a Bosch router with a ½in cutter to deal with hinges up to 3in. With other makes, draw the top view out full size with the router in place at each end and with the chosen cutter fitted — allow say, ¼in. This will be the maximum distance from the fixed to the moving fence, as shown in fig. 2.

In use, set up and cramp to the previously marked door, fig. 3. Remove the waste, preferably with a rough cut followed by a fine finishing cut. Before removing for a trial with a hinge, knife in a reference mark across both the top frame and the job. This enables the device to be accurately re-positioned if necessary for a further cut. The mark on the top frame can be re-used for any other cut using the same router, cutter and hinge size.

The top frame is invariably cut into, but this is no disadvantage since it helps to set up for the next cut. The normal router fence controls the width of the hinge socket. The rounded corners need to be trimmed square. ■

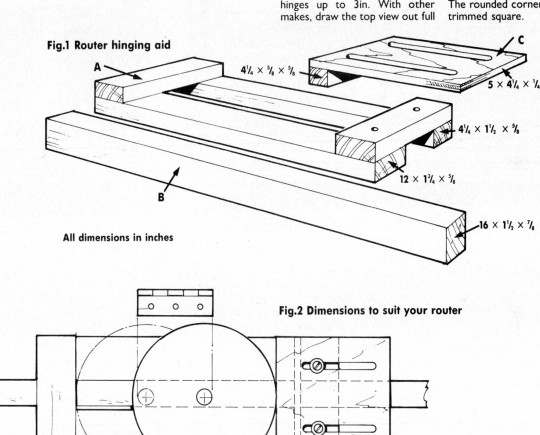

Fig.1 Router hinging aid

A — $4\frac{1}{4} \times \frac{5}{8} \times \frac{5}{8}$

C

$5 \times 4\frac{1}{4} \times \frac{1}{4}$

$4\frac{1}{4} \times 1\frac{1}{2} \times \frac{5}{8}$

$12 \times 1\frac{3}{4} \times \frac{5}{8}$

B

$16 \times 1\frac{1}{2} \times \frac{7}{8}$

All dimensions in inches

Fig.2 Dimensions to suit your router

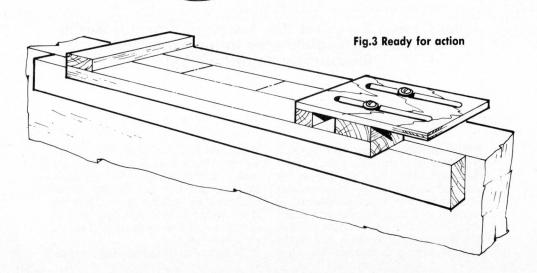

Fig.3 Ready for action

OUT OF FLANDERS

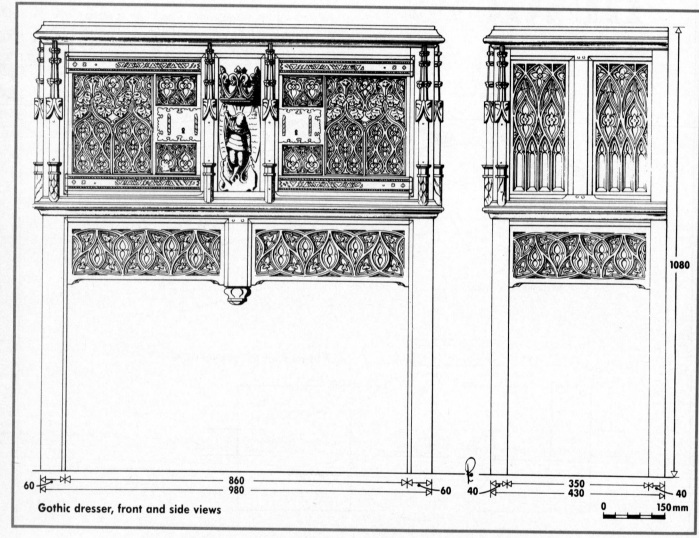

Gothic dresser, front and side views

60   860 / 980   60   40   350 / 430   40   1080   0   150mm

Rene Coolen describes the design of a grand Gothic dresser and explains the influence of stone-masonry in its decoration

This late-Gothic dresser was designed in Flanders in the 15th century and is made entirely from oak. The carving has a French character (the displaced Court of Burgundy had a strong influence in Flanders) evident in the diamond-shaped fillings on the open fields of tracery. Taken from stone-masonry decoration, the tracery is formed mainly by circle-arches. The centre panel, which is damaged, depicts the Archangel Michael overpowering Satan; the crown has remained intact but the angel's arm, leg and face are missing. These mutilations are probably the result of the icononclastic riots which swept over the Low Countries in 1566, when the faces of statues were struck off.

As with all Gothic pieces, the construc- ▶

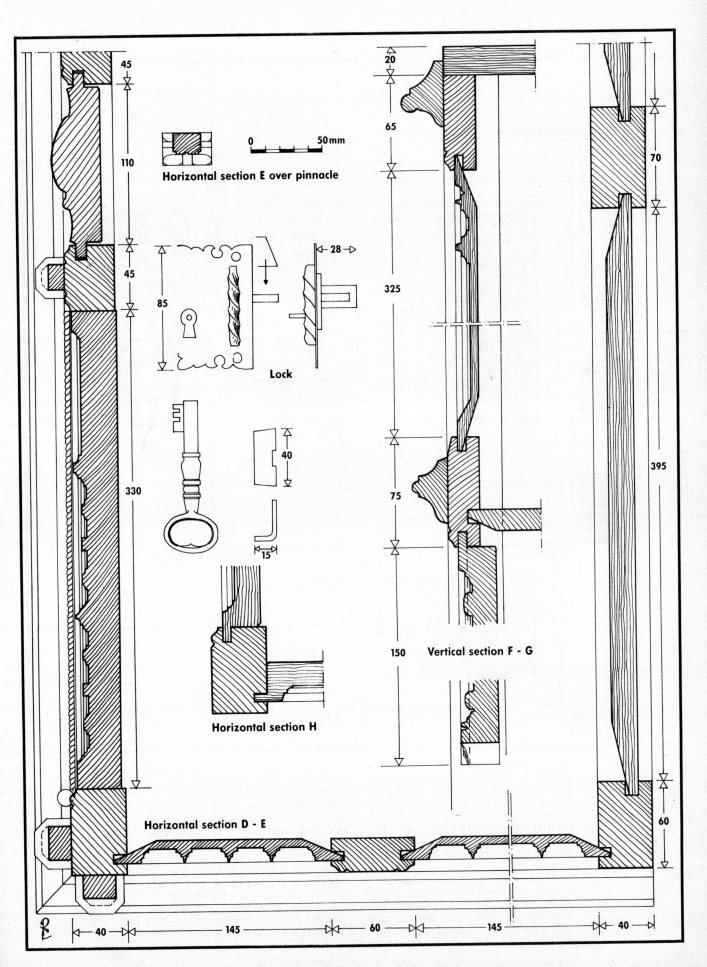

Horizontal section E over pinnacle

0   50mm

Lock

28

85

Horizontal section H

Vertical section F - G

Horizontal section D - E

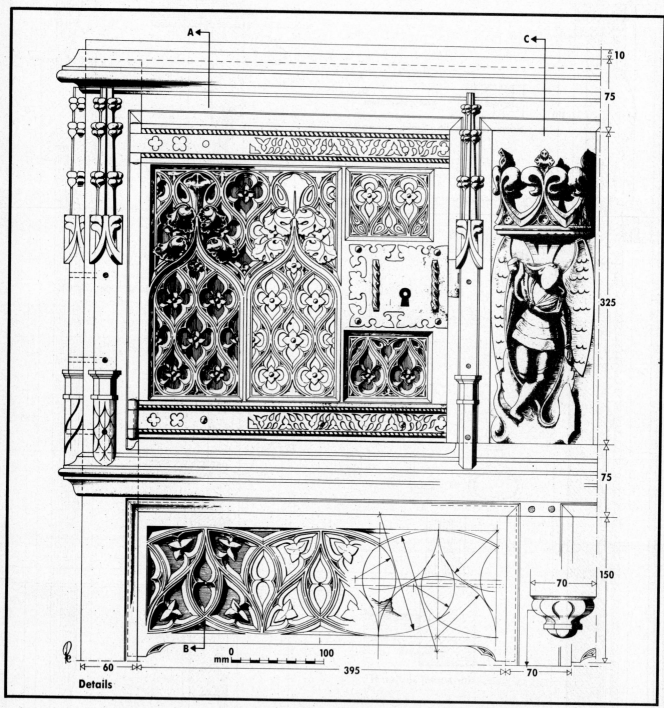

A ←

C ←

10

75

325

75

150

70

Details

60

0   100
mm

395

70

B ←

tion is simple: a straightforward unglued framework, with mortise-and-tenon joints fixed with wooden pegs. The striking difference between the plain construction and the elaborate carving on the panels is due to the demarcation of jobs by the guilds. Furniture was built by cabinetmakers and coffermakers, but decorated by wood or figure carvers.

The doors are made from a single piece of wood, and as with the carving on the side panels, there's an obvious influence from stone-masonry. The tracery has a slanting edge at the bottom, which was the 'waterline' used on stone work to allow any moisture to run off. The pilasters on the front and sides of the cabinet are fixed with wooden pegs and are also ornaments of stone-masonry.

The Gothic dresser usually had an under-leaf at the base — the proportions of this cabinet indicate the same — but the base was often so damaged that it was simply sawn off.

The term 'dresser' comes from the French verb *dresser* (to dress) but this cabinet was probably used in a church because of the iconoclastic damage. Much of the remaining Gothic furniture is in bad repair and a good way to see how they look originally is to study paintings and sculpture of the same period. ■

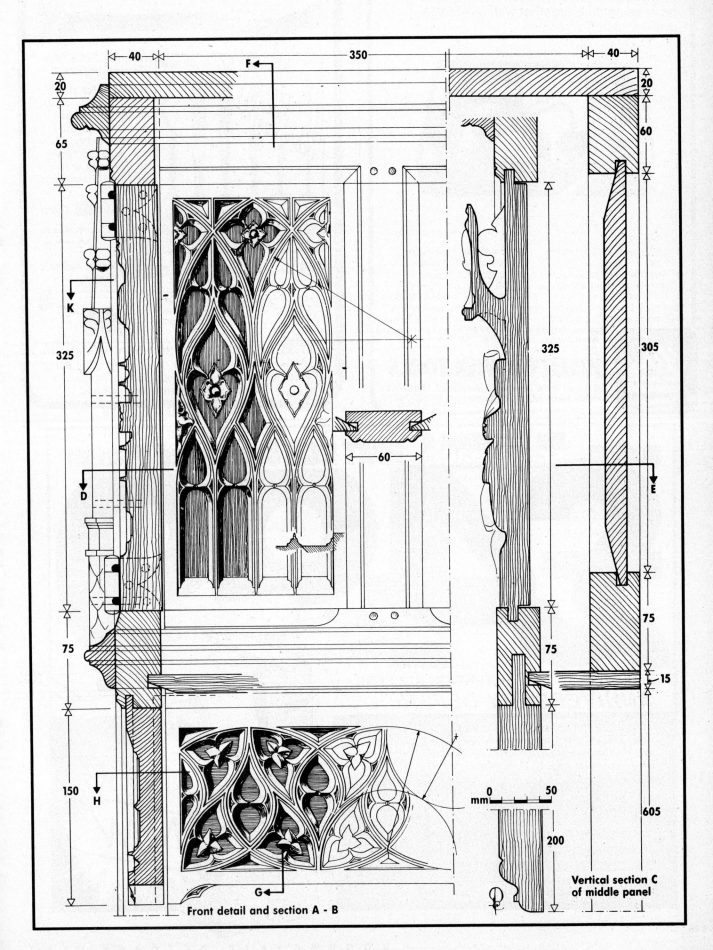

40　**350**　**40**

F

20　　　　　　　　　　　　　　　　　**20**

60

65

K

325　　　　　　　　　　　　**325**　　　**305**

D　　　　　　　　　　　　　　　　　　E

60

75

15

75　　　　　　　　　　　　　**75**

H

0　　　50
mm

150

605

200

G

Front detail and section A - B

**Vertical section C
of middle panel**

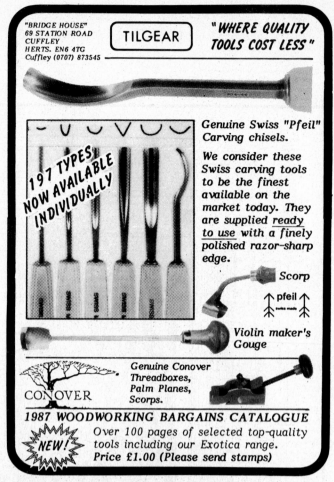

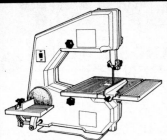

How to enter

We want to publish as many wheezes as possible, so we must use only the barest bones of the ideas. Be as precise as possible; type your words if you can, double-spaced on one side of an A4 sheet; make drawings, if any, as few and as clear as you can, and annotate them clearly.

WOOD WORKING WHEEZE OF THE MONTH

Each month, the best Woodworking wheeze — the neatest, cleverest idea that makes any sort of woodwork quicker, easier, more precise, more productive, more enjoyable, more efficient, more profitable — will win £60 worth of tools from Sandvik's enormous range.

Send your ideas to:

Hands on, WOODWORKER, 1 Golden Square, London WIR 3AB. If we print any wheeze you send in on these pages, you get a small fee — so write today!

Glue kettle

I use a 5in-diameter galvanised paint kettle inside a 7in paint kettle for melting scotch glue; it holds more water so the glue keeps hotter, and is far cheaper than buying a glue kettle. Drill three 3/16in holes in the inner kettle, thread one end of bent 4in galvanised nails, and bolt them in so they rest on top of the outer kettle.

E. D. Pritchard, Bromley

Win £60 worth of Sandvik tools!

Sandvik winner

Spare hand

If you can obtain an old estate agent's board, you can cut strips of the Correx cellular extrusion to make this really useful device for a radial-arm saw. You must weld or braze the end leaf of the hinge to the pin. The device is self-locking, infinitely adjustable and costs nothing.

Philip Oughtred, Rowlands Gill

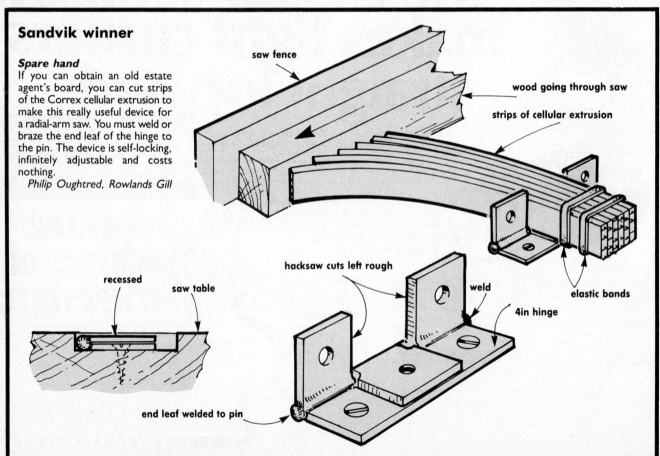

saw fence

wood going through saw

strips of cellular extrusion

elastic bands

recessed

saw table

hacksaw cuts left rough

weld

4in hinge

end leaf welded to pin

Anti-spelch

I put a blob of plasticine over a fine picture-frame moulding when cutting on a circular saw, cutting through plasticine and all. The plasticine should be at least ¼in thick and pressed firmly on for 1in either side of the cut. Most of the plasticine can be collected and re-used.

Bob End, Farnborough

Tooth protector

I use plastic spines from stationers' (used for holding together sheafs of papers) to protect tenon-saw teeth.

D. J. Ogborne, Bristol

Fluted dowels

Make your own fluted dowels by cutting rod to length, chamfer the ends, then hammer it through a pair of combination pliers.

Peter Nolan, Stanley

Magnetic solution

Fed up with losing wire wool among the lathe shavings and having it ruined, I fixed a magnet over the bench to which the wire wool sticks.

Frederick Brooks, Huntingdon

Removing screws

Old screws can be difficult to remove, and I use a series of methods. First I use an old screwdriver and hammer to remove any paint or dirt in the slot; this tapping sometimes loosens the screw sufficiently. Second attempt is either twisting the screwdriver while tapping with a hammer, or tightening the screw further and twisting back and forth.

If the screw still won't budge, I give it the heat treatment. I place a steel plate with a hole the size of the screw-head over the screw and heat with a blow lamp; to protect a finished surface I heat a metal rod and place that on the screw-head. After leaving the screw to cool, I find it comes out easily.

Sometimes the screw-head shears off. Drill a hole each side of the shank in line with the grain, tap sideways to loosen and remove with snipe-nosed pliers. Then glue in a small sliver of timber with grain in the same direction, ready for the new screw.

Peter Casebow, Worthing

Adjustable wooden cramp

Sash-cramps are expensive and often I find I need an extra one or two to glue up a project effectively.

This adjustable wooden cramp can be made easily and for very little cost. The approximate dimensions are given in the sketch. In use the wedge is driven in with a hammer and the cross-block pivots on the bolt and takes up the correct angle.

M. J. Varnam, Lincoln

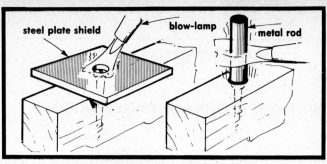

steel plate shield · blow-lamp · metal rod

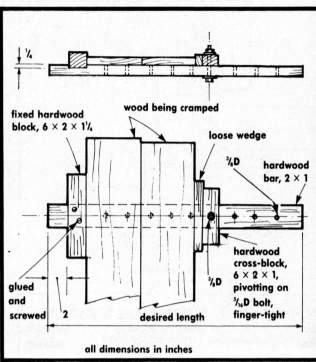

fixed hardwood block, 6 × 2 × 1¼ · wood being cramped · loose wedge · ³⁄₈D · hardwood bar, 2 × 1 · hardwood cross-block, 6 × 2 × 1, pivotting on ⁵⁄₁₆D bolt, finger-tight · ³⁄₈D · glued and screwed · 2 · desired length · ¼

all dimensions in inches

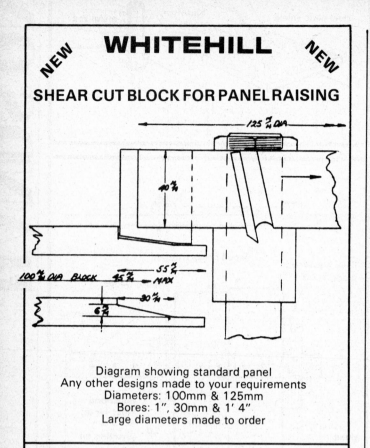
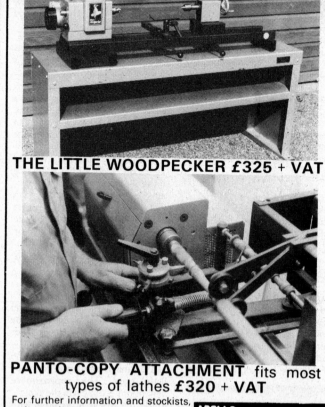
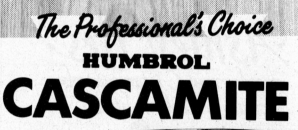

2

**More stunning
designs from this
season's college
shows**

Royal College of Art: bold and brassy
free-standing cabinet in hand-sprayed
MDF by Jiouxleigh Jacobs

Parnham: full of Eastern style — sublime jewellery box in laminated holly and 5000-year-old bog oak by Ewan Welsh ▶

Shrewsbury: beautifully-grained ash escritoire from Chris Parker. The side frames are steam-bent from solid timber ▼

Shrewsbury: Chris Ayres delicately fresh drinks-cabinet in solid sycamore and yew with coopered ends ▶

Kingston: resplendent storage box for precious objects by Clare Green ▶

Kingston: Tony O'Neill's imperious Gothic chair

Lancashire: solid cherry musical-instrument cabinet with silver inlay by Alison Joyce

al College of Art: bedroom furniture with a bent — valet stool in wood laminate with sycamore veneer by Philip ren

al College of Art: Skip Timmin's triangular storage units mirror; the drawers open to reveal through daylight ►

nham: playful children's stools in blue and yellow eers by Haege Kranstad

Bright Young Things

Manchester Central College School of Furniture: John Astley's low, low table and chair, mainly in ash and padauk, influenced by Mackintosh and Japanese furniture ▲

Parnham: dining table in wild English cherry with wrought iron trestles, by Patrick Stronach, winner of a Smallpiece Award ▼

◄*Parnham:* dining chair in wild English cherry by Patrick Stronach

London College of Furniture: ▶
Brian Bart's reproduction writing bureau with mahogany curl veneers

THE MIND'S EYE

Ideas for woodcarving come from the most unexpected quarters — in fact everything around us is a potential subject. Most of my inspiration springs from the animal world (I used to be a zoo-keeper); not just living creatures — remains of animals, bones and shells, provide a treasure-house of evocative thoughts.

When I was a professional diver, I carried out a particularly unpleasant job in North dock, Sunderland. Save for the occasional flash of phosphorescence from rotting vegetation, there was no relief to the blackness as I groped my way through the man-made underwater rubbish tip. Suddenly a white shape, inches from my mask, made me start: it was the guts of a fish. On the dockside, a shapeless mess; suspended vertically in the water, free from the crush of gravity, it was an unforgettable sight of bulbous beauty, its loops and whirls highlighted by the darkness. Curvaceous and exciting, it made a fantastic abstract shape for woodcarving.

A painter is classically inspired by a beautiful sunset, subtle blends of colour; a meeting of light and dark. A carver's starting-point is line and form. It is the shape that inspires, classically, the female torso or a jumping dolphin. Carvers have a distinct advantage over other creative artists: the medium can give its own direction by its very shape or the flow and movement of the grain. I've yet to meet a painter who's been inspired by a tube of paint or a writer by a blank sheet of paper.

A friend of mine was trekking through broad-leafed woodland when he spotted a gnarled and twisted projection from a beech tree. A wolf's snarling head stared down at him. Up the tree he went, axe in hand, and minutes later he and the hitherto arboreal canine were back on the ground. It took only a morning's work to complete the transformation: two eyes, the line of the mouth cut a little deeper, and the nose helped on a shade by the addition of nostrils. Set on a polished plinth and christened 'Timber wolf' it became a most effective (and cost-effective) carving.

However, it's rarely that easy. Last year I entered the Ashley Iles Award at the Woodworker Show in the Alexandra Pavilion, London. The subject was 'industry' and I spent many a long hour seeking inspiration, but in my mind's eye, all I could see were sweating workmen toiling over forges and anvils. Just when I despaired at my lack of imagination, I looked up 'industry' in all the dictionaries I could lay my hands on. 'Industrious; diligent; *beaver like*'. So obvious, why hadn't I thought of it before? Seek and ye shall find.

After several thousand wood chips had parted company from an extremely obstinate piece of English oak, I began to lose my bottle. I'd wake up in the night with a vision of the competition judge saying to his assistant 'Ay yon beaver is in t'wrong class, this year's soobject is industry'. All my fears were unfounded: the judges awarded me second place and two boxed-sets of the coveted Ashley Iles woodcarving chisels.

The Pope's lantern in the photograph was inspired by the mouth parts of a sea-urchin; each of the five segments were separate mandibles on the actual animal and each one of different wood (sycamore, walnut, boxwood...) on the carving. Apart from being 10 times larger than life, it's pretty close

Photos Applied Photographics

Imagination and vision are essential to good carving. David Saunders opens your eyes to a wealth of inspiration

to the original. I find animal bones are also a good source of inspiration. Skulls with their lovely curves and Henry Moore type holes translate into abstract carvings aching to be picked up and felt with the fingertips. Look at the fox-skull and you'll see the relationship between the source material and the carving.

When I started the fox-skull, I envisaged the carving just like the original, only in wood with all the lines and planes as nature intended. But then I thought, what was the point of a straight replica? After all I could paint the skull to look like wood, and even put in a grain-effect. So I changed course half-way and interpreted the skull in my own fashion. I used African boxwood, a close-grained light-brown to yellow wood, which readily accepts detail and polishes up a treat. A walk in the

country will turn up any amount of animal bones, usually rabbit, but mice-skulls are often discarded under trees used by owls. Bird skulls are common and their long tapering beaks broadening into spheres make marvellous shapes — imagine them six times larger, set perpendicularly on a highly polished base.

There's a lot to be said for abstract carving, it's designing an original, a piece of work no-one has ever done before. The knack is not to be limited in your choice of subject — open your eyes to what's around you, play with ideas and mould them into your own creations. The late Professor Jacob Bronowski described the hand as the 'cutting-edge of the mind'. Our hands may be limited, not so our minds. Inspired? I hope so. ∎

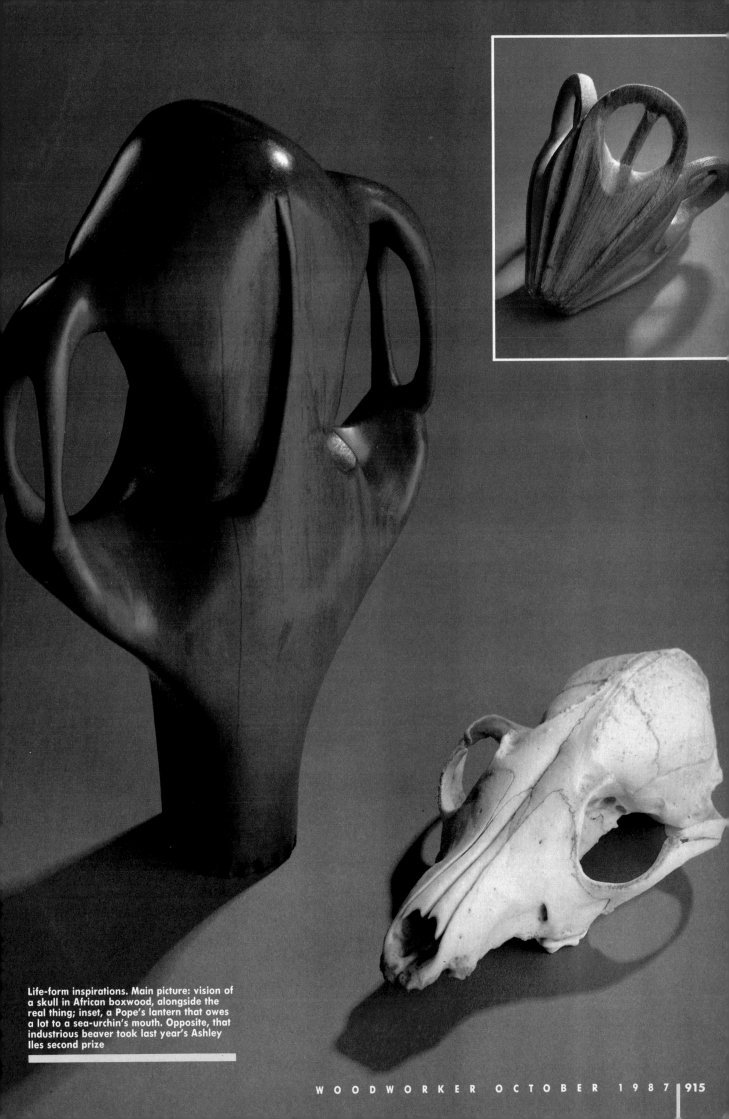

Life-form inspirations. Main picture: vision of a skull in African boxwood, alongside the real thing; inset, a Pope's lantern that owes a lot to a sea-urchin's mouth. Opposite, that industrious beaver took last year's Ashley Iles second prize

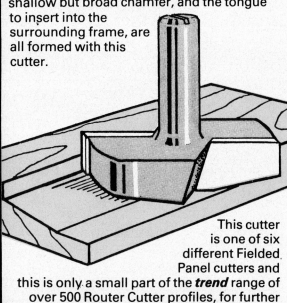

Jonna Behrens, 1-5 Chance St, London E1 6JT, 01-729 5736

BIG SCREEN SUCCESS

Jonna Behrens shaped his design for a curved screen into a commercial product. Peter Howlett explains how

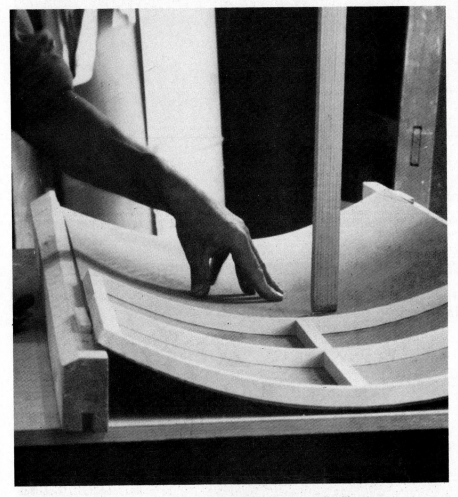

Left: decoration with curves...a doubly attractive idea, and the market likes it too. Above, ribs are hot-glued to the curved panels, held in shape in a jig with a shore to the roof

The idea for Jonna Behrens' screen design grew out of one of those slack periods common to self-employed furniture makers. He'd just finished making a cupboard with curved doors, and the possibility of curved screens — self-supporting when fully-open with endless variations of shape, yet still inherently stable, began to take hold.

Using ply offcuts, he bandsawed curved ribs to shape with a circular cutting-jig and notched them to take five stringers — much in the same way as the early aircraft wings were made. This framework was then skinned with 1.5mm laminating ply, using contact adhesive applied sparingly to both surfaces. (The new non-toxic, non-sniffable water-based contact adhesives can be put on with a brush, so they're ideal for this sort of application.)

This first attempt went together well but because laminating ply was used (only normally available as 60x60in) each panel had a joint half-way down which had to be disguised by filling and painting. Jonna's painter brother, Tim, designed a landscape on the first prototype, and although the result was exciting, the labour-intensive costs of manufacture and decoration meant the screens couldn't be marketed through even

the 'highest' of high street stores.

He changed the production methods radically: hardboard, thicknessed to 2mm through the speed-sander, replaced the ply, and he built a bending jig to shape the curves. The cost was cut by two-thirds. Instead of notched ribs and stringers, each panel was made separating the curved ribs with a straight spacer down each side and one in the centre. With the rough reverse of the hardboard removed by sanding, the ribs were efficiently glued in place with a hot melt glue-gun and a shore was propped against a roof-beam to hold the curve on the panels. The concave surface was then fixed with the shore and contact adhesive.

Jonna found that the paravent hinges he was using on the panels knocked the surface of the centre panel in the closed position, because the hinge knuckles projected beyond the frame. So he made the centre panel slightly wider to give clearance (fig. 1). His final prototype was remarkably elegant in simplicity — especially as it was put together with a glue-gun and contact adhesive.

With all the headaches and cursings swept up in the sawdust, Jonna was confident that he had a product to sell and approached the Conran Shop in the Fulham Road, London. Conran relies on small companies to produce limited editions and small batches and are receptive to new, commercial ideas. They expressed an interest not only in colour-sprayed screens but also a veneered version. However, it soon became obvious that the method of manufacturing the prototype wouldn't suit Conran's volume needs.

Following a suggestion by Richard Entwhistle of Conran Design Group, a

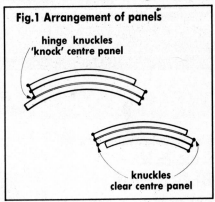

Fig.1 Arrangement of panels

hinge knuckles 'knock' centre panel

knuckles clear centre panel

Midlands firm was contracted to mould the screens using the same construction as internal flush doors. Conran's chose kevasing (a fancy trade-name for crowncut bubinga), aspen and ash, dispensing with the original idea of sprayed finishes. They specified ball feet to protect the lower edges of each screen — which tend to weaken the purity of the design. Jonna undertook to finish and assemble the screens which was a long job but a satisfying conclusion to nearly two years' development work.

Jonna's success proves that you don't have to be formally trained (he wasn't) or a big name to have your work accepted by high street stores. (It does help to be in the right place at the right time: Jonna met one of Conran's buyers at a party.)

He has now learnt the importance of meeting delivery times and how vital it is to have moral and physical support at the end of project like his. I left Jonna packing the screens for delivery, him at one end of a plank, his wife at the other. It was early afternoon; I wondered whether it was going to be a long night... ■

COMPUTER CONSOLATION

Struggling to get your computer equipment into efficient order? Here's three ideas to choose from

Box it in — Bob Grant

This piece was designed to carry the BBC Micro unit, comprising keyboard, VDU, disc drive and/or tape recorder, with a shallow drawer underneath for spare tapes and discs. The keyboard unit is set at the right height to use with a standard chair.

The construction is straightforward, with stopped housings for the carcase (a power router with a guide will be a great help), mortise and tenons for the stretcher rail and dovetails for the drawer. The carcase is made from ¾in veneered blockboard; it's worth seeking out a matching decorative veneer on both sides. Ideally, all the carcase components should be cut from one sheet for continuity of grain and colour.

Start by cutting out the ends as a handed pair. Mark and cut the housings at one-third depth, noting that they are stopped at different widths for the top shelf

Photo Ray Clayton

▲ A Rolls-Royce of computer desks: Whitehead and Lightfoot's design in grey bolivar veneer with banded lippings and ebony details boasts a touch-button rising table for the VDU, a hideaway keyboard, and — among other things — a drinks cabinet. . . .

◄ At a less ambitious level, Bob Grant's no-frills design for a veneered cabinet would be just the thing for a small study or office.

and lower shelf drawer-stop. The housings run out at the back and, apart from the top shelf, are later covered by the vanity panel which is set into a rebate that exactly matches the housing depth.

Hold the three pieces together in a vice and mark out the lengths along the ends. The shelves vary in width, and the top and bottom shelves, which don't come flush to the front, must be lipped before final assembly of the carcase. At the rear the top shelf is rebated, while the middle shelf is reduced in width by the thickness of the back and butts against it when assembled.

The stretcher rail also has a ¼x¼in rebate at the back to carry the vanity panel. Tenons at either end fit into ¼in mortises set in about ½in deep. The rail is set flush to the back. The tenons are dowelled through the back edge of the carcase and the front edges are worked with a decorative cavetto moulding.

The feet bars are held in a ¼in groove worked on the bottoms of the sides and will prevent the face veneers splitting as the piece is moved. The bottom edges of the bars are slightly relieved with a spokeshave to provide a 'four foot' bearing on the floor. The carcase ends should be polished before gluing the feet on, otherwise it will be difficult to get an even finish.

The vanity panel acts to firm up the entire construction. It's screwed, not glued, at intervals around the edge and is only fixed after the drawer has been made and fitted, so that you can check the fit on the back of the drawer.

When you assemble the carcase for gluing, the drawer bearers must be screwed into position; it will be a tight operation if you have to do it afterwards.

When you've cut all the joints: lip the top and lower shelves; seal and polish all the carcase components; fix the drawer bearers; and glue up, making the usual checks for square and winding. Dowel the stretcher-bar tenons and flush off the front edges. Fix the (previously polished) feet — you'll need substantial cramp bars to span the cut-off corners at the top front edges. Then apply the veneer lippings in one length each side from the front foot to the top back. You can buy iron-on edgings, but it's no great problem to cut slightly over-width strips of veneer, fix them with an impact adhesive and trim them with a sharp knife afterwards. Polish the lippings when fixed. The back edges remain in their raw state and are best stained and polished to match the rest of the piece.

The drawer has standard lap dovetails at the front, and through dovetails at the back, with the sides and front grooved on their inner faces to take the ¼in ply bottom. A central divider, housed at the back and front, serves as a muntin with the bottom screwed up to it, and also screwed at intervals along the underneath of the back.

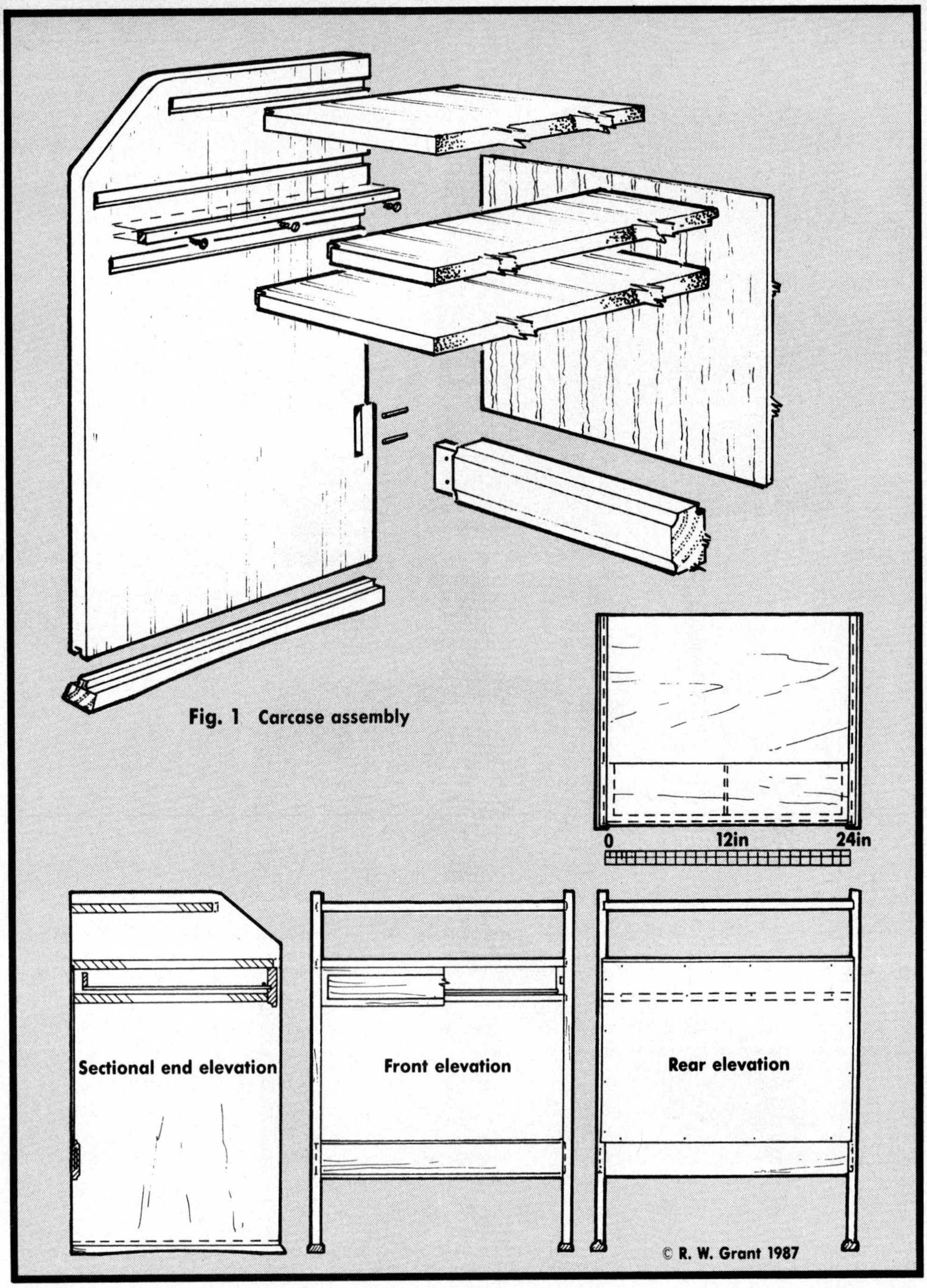

Fig. 1 Carcase assembly

Sectional end elevation

Front elevation

Rear elevation

© R. W. Grant 1987

The drawer front, which is set back under the middle shelf by ¼in, is also made to cover the front edge of the lower shelf. The shelf acts a drawer-stop and a cavetto finger-grip is worked on the inner under-edge of the front. The drawer back is set down about ¼in lower than the sides, preventing crumpled paper or whatever from jamming the drawer. That's why the back vanity panel is made so it can be removed. With the drawer glued up, work the grooves on the sides to fit the bearer bars on the carcase (a power router will help at this stage) and the final squaring of the end at the front can be cleaned out with a chisel. Rub some candle wax in the grooves to help the smooth running of the drawer. The ⅛in ebony inlay lines are positioned $1\frac{1}{16}$in in from the drawer edges and are mitred in to prepared scratchstock grooves. After they're glued in, clean and polish the whole drawer-front.

As the console was built for the home, not the office, I finished it with two coats of sanding sealer and then wax-polished it. Presanded faced blockboards will take most finishes, but avoid oversanding — the decorative facing veneers are paper-thin and bare patches 'grinning through' won't look very attractive. ▶

Cutting list

Carcase

Ends	2	33¾in x	20in x	¾in	sapele faced board
Top shelf	1	24	14	¾	,,
Middle shelf	1	24	20	¾	,,
Lower shelf	1	24	19	¾	,,
Stretcher rail	1	23½	3½	¾	solid sapele
Vanity panel	1	18½	24	¼	sapele faced ply
Drawer bearers	2	18	½	$\frac{3}{16}$	solid beech
Lippings	all front edges	¾			sapele veneer
Feet	2	20¼	1⅛	¾	solid sapele

Drawer

Drawer front	1	23½	3½	⅞	solid sapele
Drawer back	1	23½	2	⅜	,,
Drawer sides	2	18	2¾	⅜	,,
Drawer divider	1	18	2	⅜	,,
Inlay lines	to 'frame'				ebony or black
	drawer		⅛	$\frac{1}{16}$	stained lines
Drawer bottom	1	23	18	¼	ply

Photo Ray Clayton

Pile it up —
Bob Grant

This piece of equipment is designed to accommodate home computing hardware based on the popular makes of micro-computers — the computer and its keyboard; a disc drive or tape recorder unit; a printer; and a portable television (or VDU). Before embarking on the project check the sizes of equipment and make modifications as necessary. The work station heights (chair seat to middle shelf and operator's eye level to screen), are based on the average human sizes. At 6ft 3in I'm above average so these sizes would be too small for me.

The structure is simple, based on mortise and tenon frameworks. The drawings show the necessary details and you can check against the cutting list for finished sizes.

I used pine, but any straight-grained wood is suitable. Make the two end frames first; glue up the cross rails first, with the leg ends dry-fitted into the foot bars. Shape the foot bars underneath with a spokeshave to provide four bearing points before gluing. Check for square and wind before leaving the cramped structure to dry. The tenons on the front ends of the frame rails (fig. 2) are modified to allow for the meeting with the shelf support rail tenons, which are slightly offset to gain a longer length.

Flush off the frames when the glue is dry and mark and cut the mortises for the middle shelf support-rails and the stretcher bar tenons.

Now you can glue the whole structure together; shoot the two shelves to dead length and then button or bracket them on. Wedge the stretcher-bar through tenons from the outsides.

Apply what finish you like, avoiding high-gloss slippery polish to the shelf surfaces.

Cutting list
(includes 1½in tenons)

Front legs	2	27¼in	x	2⅛in	x	⅞in
Back legs	2	35½		2⅛		⅞
Top brackets	2	8½		2½		⅞
End rails	2	9½		2½		⅞
Foot bars	2	20		2½		⅞
Top shelf	1	33¼		9		⅞
Middle shelf	1	33¼		10½		⅞
Middle shelf support rails	2	34¼		1¼		⅞
Stretcher bar	1	35		3½		⅞

Fig. 2   Joint details

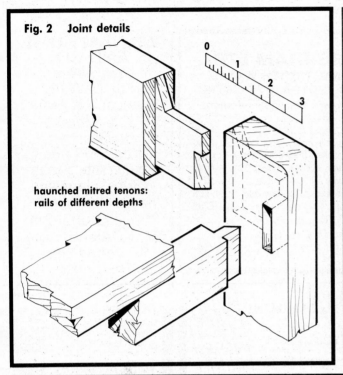

haunched mitred tenons: rails of different depths

Spread it out — Alan Cranston

The vital element for housing your computer equipment is a sturdy worktop — long, wide and thick. It needs to be long to carry all the different pieces of equipment; I recommend a length of 12ft, a depth of about 27in, and 1½in thick so you need fewer supports underneath.

On the left-hand side of the top I've added an extra piece I call an 'elbow board', on which you can rest your forearms; computer keyboards are easier to use if they are set back about 9in from the front edge. This board is also handy for holding copy paper, pens and pencils and to use the 'mouse'. My board is 4ft long, 9in wide and 1⅜in thick, adjoins the front edge of the worktop and is fixed by two or three 2x1in battens screwed under the worktop and extending them forward about 8in.

This is how I've laid out equipment on my worktop: computer, disc drive, monitor and keyboard clustered around the elbow board; dot matrix printer and tape drive to the left; daisy wheel printer to the right with a couple of video recorders further to the right. With this amount of equipment I've got three 13 amp double socket outlets lined up on the wall at the back of the worktop about 3in above the surface.

You could also use trestles, pedestals or a purpose-made fitment to support the worktop. You could use a piece of furniture to support one end and an adjustable tripod at the other. Keep the height about 31in, with a batten along the wall to support the back. Keep it simple and flexible, for computers are an ever-changing scene.

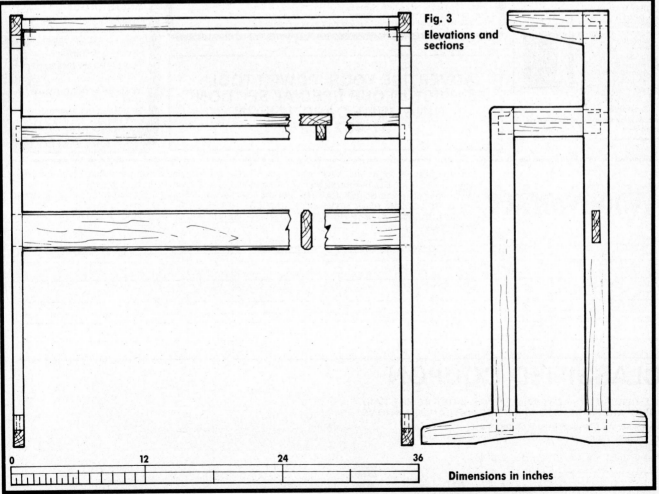

Fig. 3
Elevations and sections

Dimensions in inches

Woodworker

Lineage 58p per word (inc. VAT). Minimum £8.70. Semi-display £9.65 per single column + VAT. Minimum 2.5 x 1. No reimbursements for cancellations. All ads must be pre-paid.

Write your advert in BLOCK CAPITALS in the grid below, ticking the section you wish it to appear under, INCLUDING YOUR NAME AND ADDRESS IN THE WORD COUNT and send it to: 'WOODWORKER', ASP ADVERTISEMENT DEPARTMENT, No. 1 GOLDEN SQUARE, LONDON W1R 3AB.

☐ W/S/E	☐ FOR SALE	☐ MATERIALS & FINISHES	☐ WOOD SUPPLIES	☐ COURSES	☐ PLEASE STATE

CLASSIFIED COUPON

ALL CLASSIFIED ADVERTISEMENTS MUST BE PRE-PAID. THERE ARE NO REIMBURSEMENTS FOR CANCELLATIONS.

I enclose my Cheque/Postal Order* for £.............. for .... insertions, made payable to Argus Specialist Publications. (*Delate as necessary) or
Please debit my Access/Barclaycard No.

☐☐☐☐☐☐☐☐☐☐☐☐☐☐☐☐ Expiry Date

£ .... for .... insertions.

Name ....
Address ....
.... Post Code ....
Day Time Tel. No. ....
Signature .... Date ....

IF YOU DO NOT WISH TO CUT YOUR MAGAZINE, PHOTOCOPY THIS FORM

AVON

BATH Tel. Bath 64513
JOHN HALL TOOLS ★
RAILWAY STREET

Open: Monday-Saturday
9.00 a.m.5.30 p.m.
H.P.W.WM.D.A.BC.

BRISTOL Tel. (0272) 741510
JOHN HALL TOOLS LIMITED ★
CLIFTON DOWN SHOPPING CENTRE
WHITELADIES ROAD
Open: Monday-Saturday
9.00 a.m.-5.30 p.m.
H.P.W.WM.D.A.BC.

BRISTOL Tel. (0272) 667013
WILLIS T
157 WEST STREET
BEDMINSTER
Open Mon.-Fri. 8.30 a.m.-5.00 p.m.

P.W.WM.D.CS.A.BC.

BERKSHIRE

READING Tel. Littlewick Green
DAVID HUNT (TOOL 2743
MERCHANTS) LTD ★
KNOWL HILL, NR. READING
Open: Monday-Saturday
9.00 a.m.-5.30 p.m.
H.P.W.D.A.BC.

READING Tel. Reading 661511
WOKINGHAM TOOL CO. LTD. T
99 WOKINGHAM ROAD
Open: Mon-Sat 9.00 a.m.-5.30 p.m.
Closed 1.00-2.00 p.m. for lunch

H.P.W.WM.D.CS.A.BC.

SLOUGH Tel: (06286) 5125
BRAYWOOD ESTATES LTD. ★
158 BURNHAM LANE
Open: 9.00am-5.30pm.
Monday-Saturday.

H.P.W.WM.CS.A.

BUCKINGHAMSHIRE

MILTON KEYNES Tel. (0908)
POLLARD WOODWORKING 641366
CENTRE T★
51 AYLESBURY ST., BLETCHLEY
Open: Mon-Fri. 8.30-5.30
Saturday 9.00-5.00
H.P.W.WM.D.CS.A.BC. **INCA**

HIGH WYCOMBE Tel. (0494)
ISAAC LORD LTD. 22221
185 DESBOROUGH ROAD K
Open: Mon.-Fri. 8.00 a.m. to 5.30 p.m.
Saturday 8.30 a.m. to 5.00 p.m.

H.P.W.D.A.WM.MF.

CAMBRIDGESHIRE

CAMBRIDGE Tel: (0223) 63132
D. MACKAY LTD. ★
BRITANNIA WORKS, EAST ROAD

Open: Mon.-Fri. 8.30 a.m.-1 p.m./2.00-
5.00 p.m. Sat. 8.30 a.m.-1.00 p.m.
H.P.W.D.T.CS.MF.A.BC.

CAMBRIDGE Tel. (0223) 247386
H. B. WOODWORKING TK
105 CHERRY HINTON ROAD
Open: 8.30 a.m.-5.30 p.m.
Monday-Friday
8.30 a.m.-1.00 p.m. Sat.
H.P.W.WM.D.CS.A.MF.BC.

CHESHIRE

NANTWICH Tel. Crewe 67010
ALAN HOLTHAM TK★
THE OLD STORES TURNERY
WISTASON ROAD, WILLASTON
Open: Tues.-Fri. 9.00 a.m.-5.30 p.m.
Sat. 9.00 a.m.-5.00 p.m. Closed Monday.
P.W.WM.D.T.C.CS.A.BC.

WIDNESS Tel: 051 424 4545/7965
THE POWER TOOL CENTRE T★
54/58 VICTORIA ROAD, WA8 7PJ
Mon.-Fri. 8.30am-5pm
Sat. 8.30am-4pm.

H.P.W.WM.D.CS.A.BC.

CLEVELAND

MIDDLESBROUGH Tel. (0642)
CLEVELAND WOODCRAFT 813103
(M'BRO), 38-42 CRESCENT ROAD TK

Open: Mon.-Sat. 9.15 a.m.-5.30 p.m.

H.P.A.BC.W.WM.CS.D.

CORNWALL

SOUTH WEST Power Tools

CORNWALL Tel: Helston (03265) 4961
HELSTON AND LAUNCESTON Launceston
(0566) 4781
TK
H.P.W.WM.D.CS.A.

CUMBRIA

CARLISLE Tel. (0228) 36391
W. M. PLANT T
ALLENBROOK ROAD
ROSEHILL, CA1 2UT
Open: Mon.-Fri. 8.00 a.m.-5.15 p.m.
Sat. 8.00 a.m.-12.30 noon
P.W.WM.D.CS.A.

DEVON

PLYMOUTH Tel. (0752) 330303
WESTWARD BUILDING SERVICES ★
LTD., LISTER CLOSE, NEWNHAM
INDUSTRIAL ESTATE, PLYMPTON
Open: Mon-Fri 8.00 a.m.-5.30 p.m.
Sat. 8.30 a.m.-12.30 p.m.
H.P.W.WM.D.A.BC.

DEVON

PLYMOUTH Tel. (0752) 665363
F.T.B. LAWSON LTD. T
71 NEW GEORGE STREET
PLYMOUTH PL1 1RB
Open: Mon.-Sat. 8.30 a.m.-5.30 p.m.

H.P.W.CS.MF.A.

DORSET

WEYMOUTH Tel. (0305) 770303
WEYMOUTH HIRE & SALES LTD. TK
5 KENT CLOSE
GRANBY INDUSTRIAL ESTATE
Open 7.30 a.m.-5.30 p.m. Mon.-Fri.
Sat. 8 a.m.-1 p.m.
H.P.W.WM.D.CS.A.K.

ESSEX

LEIGH ON SEA Tel. (0702)
MARSHAL & PARSONS LTD. 710404
1111 LONDON ROAD K

Open: 8.30 a.m.-5.30 p.m. Mon.-Fri.
9.00 a.m.-5.00 p.m. Sat.
H.P.W.WM.D.CS.A.

ILFORD Tel. 597 7461
CUTWELL WOODWORKING T★
776 HIGH ROAD
GOODMAYES IG3 8SY

H.P.W.WM.D.CS.A.

GLOUCESTER

TEWKESBURY Tel. (0684)
TEWKESBURY SAW CO. LTD. 293092
TRADE ESTATE, NEWTOWN K
Telex No. 43382
Open: Mon-Fri 8.00 a.m.-5.00 p.m.
Saturday 9.30 a.m.-12.00 p.m.
P.W.WM.D.CS.

HAMPSHIRE

ALDERSHOT SOUTHAMPTON
(0252) 334422 (0703) 332288
BURCH & HILLS POWER TOOL CENTRES
374 HIGH ST. 7 BELVIDERE RD.
Open Mon.-Fri. 8.30-5.30. Sat. 8.30-12.00
Closed for Lunch 1.00-2.00
H.P.W.WM.D.C.S.MF.BC.K.* T

HEREFORDSHIRE

HEREFORD Tel. (0432) 271366
WOODWORKING CENTRE
100 WIDEMARSH ST., HR4 9HG

Open: Mon.-Sat. 8 a.m.-5.30 p.m.

H.P.W.WM.D.CS.MF.A.T.

HERTFORDSHIRE

WARE Tel: (0920) 870 230
HEATH SAWS 870 636
6 LEESIDE WORKS K★
STANSTEAD ABBOTTS (near Ware) HERTS.
SG12 8DL.
Open: Mon.-Fri. 8.30 a.m.-5.30 p.m.
Sat. 8.30 a.m.-1 p.m. Sunday by appointment.
H.P.W.WM.D.T.CS.MF.A.BC.*.K.

HUMBERSIDE

HULL
HUMBERSIDE FACTORING/H.F.C.
SAW SERVICING LTD.
MAIN STREET
Open: Mon.-Fri. 8am-5pm.
Saturday 8am-12.00pm.
H.P.W.WM.D.CS.A.BC.K.

KENT

MAIDSTONE Tel: (0622) 44350
HENSON AND PLATT
TOKE PLACE
LINTON
Open Mon.-Fri. 8.00 a.m.-5.00 p.m.
Saturday 8.00 a.m.-1.00 p.m.
H.P.W.T.CS.A.

MAIDSTONE Tel. (0622) 50177
SOUTH EASTERN SAWS (Ind.) LTD. ★
COLDRED ROAD
PARKWOOD INDUSTRIAL ESTATE
Open: Mon.-Fri. 8.00 a.m.-5.00 p.m.
Sat. 9.00 a.m.-12.00 a.m.
B.C.W.CS.WM.PH.

LANCASHIRE

PRESTON Tel. (0772) 52951
SPEEDWELL TOOL COMPANY ★
62-68 MEADOW STREET PR1 1SU
Open: Mon.-Fri. 8.30 a.m.-5.30 p.m.
Sat. 8.30 a.m.-12.30 p.m.

H.P.W.WM.CS.A.MF.BC.

ROCHDALE Tel. (0706) 342123/
C.S.M. TOOLS 342322
4-6 HEYWOOD ROAD T★
CASTLETON
Open: Mon-Sat 9.00 a.m.-6.00 p.m.
Sundays by appointment
W.D.CS.A.BC.

LANCASTER Tel: (0524) 32886
LILE TOOL SHOP K
43/45 NORTH ROAD
Open: Monday to Saturday
9.00 a.m.-5.30 p.m.
Wed. 9.00 a.m.-12.30 p.m.
H.P.W.D.A.

shopguide

LONDON

ACTON   Tel: (01-992) 4835
A. MILLS (ACTON) LTD.   ★
32/36 CHURCHFIELD ROAD W3 6ED
Open: Mon.-Fri. 8.32 a.m-5.30 p.m.
Saturdays 9.00 a.m.-1.00 p.m.
H.P.W.WM.

LONDON   Tel: 01-723 2295-6-7
LANGHAM TOOLS LIMITED
13 NORFOLK PLACE
LONDON W2 1QJ

FULHAM   Tel: (01-636) 6109
I. GRIZARD LTD.
84a-b-c. LILLIE ROAD, SW6 1TL
Open: Mon.-Sat. 9.00-5.30 p.m.
Half day Thursday

H.P.A.BC.W.CS.WM.D.

MANCHESTER

MANCHESTER   Tel: (061 789)
TIMMS TOOLS   0909
102-104 LIVERPOOL ROAD
PATRICROFT M30 0WZ   ★
Weekdays 9.00 a.m.-5.30 p.m.
Sat. 9.00 a.m.-1.00 p.m.
H.P.A.W.

MANCHESTER   Tel: 061 834 0714
TILL AND WHITEHEAD   ★
ELLESMERE STREET, M15 4JX

Open: Mon.-Fri. 8.00 a.m.-5.00 p.m.

H.P.W.A.BC.

MERSEYSIDE

LIVERPOOL   Tel: (051-207) 2967
TAYLOR BROS (LIVERPOOL) LTD.   TK
195-199 LONDON ROAD
LIVERPOOL L3 8JG
Open: Monday to Friday
8.30 a.m.-5.30 p.m.
H.P.W.WM.D.A.BC.

MIDDLESEX

ENFIELD   Tel: 01-363 2935
GILL & HOXBY LTD.   T
131-137 ST. MARKS ROAD ADJ.
BUSH HILL PARK STATION, EN1 1BA
Mon.-Sat. 8-5.30
Early closing Wed. 1 p.m.
H.P.A.M.MC.T.S.W.

RUISLIP   Tel: (08956) 74126
ALLMODELS ENGINEERING LTD.   ★
91 MANOR WAY

Open: Mon.-Sat. 9.00 a.m.-5.30 p.m.

H.P.W.A.D.CS.MF.BC.

NORFOLK

NORWICH   Tel: (0603) 898695
NORFOLK SAW SERVICES
DOG LANE, HORSFORD
Open: Monday to Friday
8.00 a.m.-5.00 p.m.
Saturday 8.00 a.m.-12.00 p.m.
H.P.W.WM.D.CS.A.

NORFOLK

KINGS LYNN   Tel: (0553) 772443
WALKER & ANDERSON (Kings Lynn) LTD.   T
WINDSOR ROAD, KINGS LYNN
Open: Monday to Saturday
7.45 a.m.-5.15 p.m.

H.P.W.WM.D.CS.A.

NORWICH   Tel: (0603) 400933
WESTGATES WOODWORKING   Tx
61 HURRICANE WAY,   975412
NORWICH AIRPORT INDUSTRIAL ESTATE
Open: 9.00 a.m.-5.00 p.m. weekdays
9.00 a.m.-12.30 Sat.
P.W.WM.D.BC.   K

KINGS LYNN   Tel: 07605 674
NORFOLK WOODTURNING CENTRE
UNIT A, HILL FARM WORKSHOPS   ★
GREAT DUNHAM (Nr. Swaffham)
Tues.-Sat. 9.00am-5.30pm

H.P.W.D.T.MF.A.BC.

NORTHAMPTONSHIRE

RUSHDEN   Tel: (0933) 56424
PETER CRISP OF RUSHDEN   T★
7-11 HIGH STREET
Mon.-Fri. 8.30-12.30/1.30-5.30
Thurs. 8.30-1.00. Sat. all day.
H.P.W.WM.D.M.F.A.K.

NOTTINGHAMSHIRE

NOTTINGHAM   Tel: (0602) 225979
POOLEWOOD   and 227064/5
EQUIPMENT LTD.   (06077) 2421 after hrs
5a HOLLY LANE, CHILLWELL
Open: Mon-Fri 9.00 a.m.-5.30 p.m.
Sat. 9.00 a.m. to 12.30 p.m.
P.W.WM.D.CS.A.BC.

OXON

WITNEY   Tel: (0993) 76431
TARGET TOOLS (SALES,   OXON
TARGET HIRE & REPAIRS)   T★
TOOLS SWAIN COURT
STATION INDUSTRIAL ESTATE
Open: Mon.-Sat. 8.00 a.m.-5.00 p.m.
24 hour Answerphone
BC.W.M.A.

SHROPSHIRE

TELFORD   Tel. Telford (0952)
ASLES LTD.   48054
VINEYARD ROAD, WELLINGTON   K★

Open: Mon.-Fri. 8.30 a.m.-5.30 p.m.
Saturday 8.30 a.m.-4.00 p.m.
H.P.W.WM.D.CS.BC.A.

SOMERSET

TAUNTON   Tel: (0823) 335431
JOHN HALL TOOLS   ★
6 HIGH STREET

Open Monday-Saturday
9.00 a.m.-5.30 p.m.
H.P.W.WM.CS.A.

SUFFOLK

IPSWICH   Tel: (0473) 40456
FOX WOODWORKING   463884
142-144 BRAMFORD LANE   T★
Open: Tues.-Fri. 9 a.m.-5.30 p.m.
Sat. 9 a.m.-5 p.m.
W.WM.D.T.CS.MF.A.BC.K.*

SURREY

GUILDFORD   Tel. (0483) 61125
MESSINGERS FOR TOOLS   T
18-18 CHERTSEY ST.
(TOP OF NORTH ST.)
Open: Tues.-Sat. 8.30 a.m.-5.30 p.m.
H.P.W.CS.MF.A.BC.K.T.

**Read Model Engineer
for a new angle on
construction and
design.**

SUSSEX

WORTHING   Tel. (0903) 38739
W. HOSKING LTD. (TOOLS &   KT★
MACHINERY)
28 PORTLAND RD, BN11 1QN
Open: Mon.-Sat. 8.30 a.m.-5.30 p.m.
Closed Wednesday
H.P.W.WM.D.CS.A.BC.

TYNE & WEAR

NEWCASTLE-UPON-TYNE   ★
J. W. HOYLE LTD
CLARENCE STREET
NEWCASTLE-UPON-TYNE
TYNE & WEAR
NE2 17J
H.P.W.WM.D.CS.A.BC.K.

W. MIDLANDS

WOLVERHAMPTON   Tel: (0902)
MANSAW SERVICES   58759
WARD STREET, HORSELEY FIELDS   TK★
WOLVERHAMPTON, WEST MIDLANDS
Open: Mon.-Fri. 8.00 a.m.-6.00 p.m.
Saturday 8 a.m.-3 p.m.
H.P.W.WM.A.D.CS.

**All shops with an
asterisk ★
have a Mail Order
Service**

YORKSHIRE

THIRSK   Tel. (0845) 22770
THE WOOD SHOP   ★
TRESKE SAWMILLS LTD.   ↓
STATION WORKS
Open: Seven days a week 9.00-5.00

T.H.MF.BC.H.

SHEFFIELD   Tel. (0742) 441012
GREGORY & TAYLOR LTD.   K
WORKSOP ROAD
Open: 8.30 a.m.-5.30 p.m.
Monday-Friday
8.30 a.m.-12.30 p.m. Saturday
H.P.W.WM.D.

HARROGATE   Tel. (0423) 505328/
MULTI-TOOLS   66245
158 KINGS ROAD   K★

Open: Monday to Saturday
8.30 a.m.-6.00 p.m.
H.P.W.WM.D.A.BC.

YORKSHIRE

HOLME UPON   Tel. (0696) 60612
SPALDING MOOR
CRAFT TOOLS AND TACKLE LTD.
HOLME INDUSTRIAL ESTATE
Open: Mon.-Fri. 9.00 am-5.30 pm.
Saturday & Bank Holiday 9.00 am-4.30 pm
H.P.W.D.T.CS.MF.A.BC.

LEEDS   Tel. (0532) 574736
D. B. KEIGHLEY MACHINERY LTD.   ★
VICKERS PLACE, STANNINGLEY
PUDSEY LS2 86LZ
Mon.-Fri. 9.00 a.m.-5.00 p.m.
Sat. 9.00 a.m.-1.00 p.m.
P.A.W.WM.CS.BC.

CLECKHEATON   Tel. (0274)
SKILLED CRAFTS LTD.   872861
34 BRADFORD ROAD   ★

Open: 9.00 a.m.-5.00 p.m. Monday
Saturday Lunch 12.00 a.m.-1.00 p.m.
H.P.A.W.CS.WM.D.

SCOTLAND

PERTH   Tel. (0738) 26173
WILLIAM HUME & CO.   TK
ST. JOHN'S PLACE
Open: Monday to Saturday
8.00 a.m.-5.30 p.m.
8.00 a.m.-1.00 p.m. Wednesday
H.P.A.BC.W.CS.WM.D.

EDINBURGH   Tel. 031-337-5555
THE SAW CENTRE   T
38 HAYMARKET TERRACE
EDINBURGH EH12 5JZ
Mon.-Fri. 8.30 a.m.-5.30 p.m.
Saturday 9.00 a.m.-1.00 p.m.
H.P.W.WM.D.CS.A.

PERTH   Tel: (0738) 36777
WORKMASTER POWER TOOLS LTD.   T★
8 SHORE ROAD, PH2 8BW
Mon.-Fri. 8.30 a.m.-5 p.m.
Sat. 9.00 a.m.-4 p.m.
Other times by appointment
H.P.W.WM.D.CS.A.

GLASGOW   Tel. 041-429-4444/
THE SAW CENTRE   4374 Telex: 777886
650 EGLINTON STREET   T★
GLASGOW G5 9RP
Mon.-Fri. 8.00 a.m.-5.00 p.m.
Sat. 9.00 a.m.-1.00 p.m.
H.P.W.WM.D.CS.A.

IRELAND

NEWTOWNARDS   Tel: 0247 819800
NORLYN MACHINERY   or 812506
UNIT 10, MALCOLMSON IND. EST.
80 BANGOR ROAD, CO. DOWN
Open: Mon.-Fri. 9.30am-5.30pm
(Closed 1-2pm for lunch)
Any other time by request.
H.W.WM.D.T.MF.A.   24 Hour Service K

PORTADOWN   Tel. (0762) 332546
LOCKE TOOLS   ★
50 WEST STREET BT62 3JQ
Mon.-Sat. 9 a.m.-5.30 p.m.
Any other time by request.
H.D.W.WM.D.CS.A.BC.

WOODWORKER OCTOBER 1987   927

WOOD SUPPLIERS

WOOD SUPPLIERS

Classified Advertisements

All classified advertisements under £30.00 must be pre-paid: Cheques/PO made payable to A.S.P. Ltd. (WW).
Rates: Lineage: 58p per word (VAT inclusive) minimum £8.70. **Semi-display:** £9.65 + VAT per single column centimetre (minimum 2.5 × 1). **Copy to Classified Dept. (W.W.), A.S.P. Ltd., 1 Golden Square, London W1.**
All advertisements are inserted in the first available issue. There are no re-imbursements for cancellations.

Telephone 01-437-0699 ext. 291

FOR SALE

Yorkwire [Leeds] Ltd.
BRASS WIRE, ROD, STRIP & TUBE

Suitable for Miniature furniture, Clock Pendulums, Inlay work and many other Crafts.

SAE for Price List to:
**Yorkwire (Leeds) Ltd.
34 Lupton Street,
Leeds LS10 2QW.
Tel: 0532 777472**

BANKRUPT STOCK
Sandvik circular saw blades tungsten tipped
Hurry! Last few remaining
5", 5½", 6" **£4.00** each.
Any bore up to 30mm.
8¼" **£6.00** each.
Any bore up to 35mm.
P&P £1 extra per order.
Tel: 643 0244
Hannett, 11 Lind Road, Sutton, Surrey.

**Sell your woodworking equipment and machine – Double Quick with 'WOODWORKER' – Ring Julie Capstick
01-437 0626, ext. 291**

CORONET MAJOR
Maroon with 10" Saw-table, 4½" Planer/Thicknesser Slot Morticer 4½" Belt Sander, assorted chucks, many estras £1,100 ono. Deliver max. 150 miles.

**C. H. MARTIN
11 LINCOLN ROAD, OXFORD
Tel: (0865) 726383 after 6 p.m.**

STARTRITE Cyclair 75 extractor, coupling kit, S.M. 1045, 3-phase. New condition, price £375. Telephone Portsmouth 0705-371897 anytime.

Bargains Galore
Grand sale of end of lines and surplus stock from our Mail Order catalogue. Hand tools, finishes, turning tools, plans etc., all at trade prices.
For details send S.A.E. but hurry they are selling fast!
**CORBETT TOOLS
111 St. Johns Avenue, Kidderminster, Worcs. DY11 6AX**

THE FINEST SELECTION ON DISPLAY IN SCOTLAND!

NEW!
Coronet and Triton Stockist.

WOODWORKING & METALWORKING MACHINERY POWER TOOLS HAND TOOLS

THE SAW CENTRE

Edinburgh Open Day November 12/13/14

LARGE STOCKS - COMPETITIVE PRICES. PHONE AND TRY US *NOW!*

**Eglinton Toll, Glasgow G5 9EP
Tel 041-429-4444**

**38 Haymarket Edinburgh EH12 5J2
Tel: 031-337-5555**

OPEN
Mon - Fri 8am - 5pm
Sat 9am - 1pm

CONTENTS OF TECH COLLEGE woodwork, engineering and sheet metal machines, some 240 volt approx 70 items. For list send s.a.e. Write only to "Trade", 155 High Street, Irthlingborough, Northants.

BANDSAW: Startrite 352, single phase, very good condition, £500. Tel: Ludlow 5385.

DENFORD Woodturning Lathe 36in. between centres. Complete with tailstock, face-plates, chucks and tool rests £600 ono. Tel: 0308 862204 (Dorset).

STARTRITE K260 single phase Universal, with Tiger head, 4 months old, as new £1,650. Tel: (Bonington) 043-885554.

MOTORS, 240v, ½h.p. with speed controller, 100 to 1500r.p.m. Ideal machinery £80 complete. Dorking (0306) 880590.

BLADES — also for machinery!
INCA Euro 260 Popular Bandsaw   £390.00
NAEROK PT150 Planer/Thicknesser £250.00
A-Z1 Dust Extractor   £179.00
RYOBI R500 Plunge Router ½"   £150.00
Prices include VAT & carriage UK mainland.
Send a foolscap SAE for more details and our new price list of planer knives, router cutters, moulding heads, and circular saw blades to:
BLADES, Dept. WW,
PO Box 27, Petersfield, Hants. GU32 2NB.

WOODCARVING tools

LARGEST STOCK IN EUROPE

**Henry Taylor
Arkansas Bench & Slip Stones
Strops & Strop Paste
Bench Screws, Carvers' Vices**

WOODTURNING tools
Complete range of
Henry Taylor
handled or unhandled

send 40p in stamps for illustrated catalogue
ALEC TIRANTI LTD
70 High St, Theale, Reading, Berks RG7 5AR
27 Warren Street, London W1.

GUILLOTINE. Interwood 56" blade, £390 + VAT. Collect from London E3. 01-980 0018.

THE WHISTON CATALOGUE
Nuts, bolts, screws, washers, bar materials. In brass, alloy, steel, stainless steel, P.T.F.E., nylon, Tufnol, sheet material, electrical and mechanical items. We could go on and on! Better to send for free catalogue and see for yourself.
K. R. Whiston Ltd., Dept. WW, New Mills, Stockport, Cheshire. Phone: 0663 42028.

QUALITY MOVEMENTS FOR QUALITY CASES
Eight Day Long case clock movements hand made of traditional design and very high quality, suitable for fitting in reproduction clock cases. These should appeal to the craftsman who requires the quality of the original Long Case movements. Dials and hands available made to your requirements. Brassware for clock cases including, capitals, escutcheons, etc. available.
Catalogue on castings + parts U.K. £1.25.
Overseas £2.50.
RICHARDS OF BURTON
Woodhouse Clockworks
Swadlincote Road, Woodville
Burton-on-Trent   Tel: (0283) 219155

CONTENTS of 3 school workshops, engineering and woodworking machines and various tools. For detailed list write to: Warners Machinery Centre, Unit 10, Finedon Road, Irthlingborough, Northants.

BELT DRIVEN 3 speed turning lathe on 9ft. bed £200 o.n.o. V. Reynolds Ltd, Prospect Works, Chesham.

OLDER TOOLS
Very wide range in stock at Shop.
Mail Order Catalogue £1 or 6 issues £5.
Tyzack 1908 Tool Cat. Reprint **£7.50**
BRISTOL DESIGN
14 Perry Rd, Bristol BS1 5BG
Tel: (0272) 291740

WOODWORKER ADVERTISING = RESULTS

BOOKS & PUBLICATIONS

BENCHBOOKS FOR WOODWORKERS Send 50p stamps for the latest bumper catalogue of Mansard publications – thousands of ideas, including Master Woodcarver's Manual £6.50; Profitable Woodcarving and Sculpture £7.30; Hints on Chip Carving by Eleanor Rower (reprint) £7.50; Viking Woodcarving £6.50; Woodcarving and Design by Lynn Miller (reprint) 2 vols £13; Graining and Marbling by W. L. Savage (reprint) £7.25; Painting and Decorating Furniture £6.50; The Lacquer Manual £6.50; Wood Finishing by Paul Hasluck (reprint) £8.00; Money From Wooden Toy Making £5; Woodturner's Handybook by Paul Hasluck (reprint) £8; Woodcarving and Crafts Ideas by Bill Perry £6.50; Possibilities of Small Lathes by James Lukin (reprint) £9.50. Post free. 24-hour Access/Visa ordering service on 01-579 7527. Mansard Press Ltd. WW, 15 Princes Road, Ealing, London W13 9AS.

WOODCRAFT BOOKS: We can offer new out of print, secondhand and antiquarian books on every aspect of woodworking — for catalogues send 50p stamp to: Woodcraft Books, P.O. Box 58, Worcester WR8 0EL.

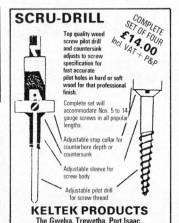

LETTERS

The seven stages of wood

Herewith a little story of the transitory life of some timber used originally for pallets. The pallets were 6ft long, of low-grade parana pine battens 4x1in and were dismantled and timber salvaged.

They started life as pallets; the battens were then used as walkways across newly-laid loose crazy-paving; they formed cantilever brackets and scaffolding on the exterior of my workshop; were assembled to form panels 6x1½ft for shuttering to a low concrete wall; each panel was then divided crossways and reassembled into a box about 5x3x4ft in the rear of my Land Rover to transport rubble; reassembled again in the garden to make a large box 20in high to contain compost; when the timber rotted it made a good bonfire on Guy Fawkes night for my grandchildren and the next day the ash was spread over a small area of garden as fertiliser. There endeth the tale.
Mr Pritchard, Bromley, Kent

Not for children

Two comments on Mr Tony Deane's article 'Lapp-joint log homes' *(WW/July)*.

One: 350 miles north of the Arctic Circle is in the Northern Atlantic. The most northern point of Finland is only 245 miles north of the Arctic Circle.

Two: the picture on page 576 is not a children's play-house. It's called *'nili'* and is a small storehouse, mostly for dry foodstuff. It's built on one or several poles to be out of reach of animals.
Atte Kyllonen, Oulu, Finland

A good caning

I am grateful for Mr Ford's comments *(WW/July)* on my article on chair caning about the positioning of the diagonals. It's now many years since I took up caning and I no longer have a reference of where I learnt the technique. However, I do remember the insistence on 'over and under' for the diagonals and I certainly have not had a problem with the two chairs in my possession caned some years ago. Nevertheless, Mr Ford's point is a very good one and a hard-worked chair could well fail with constant friction. Perhaps readers of my article would like to bear this point in mind and use the alternative approach.
R. S. Snell, Warrington, Cheshire

Carving clubs

I'd like to know more about any woodcarving clubs in the UK. Unlike the USA where such clubs abound, there never seems to any mention of any in this country. I am sure they must exist and maybe some mutual benefit could be had from an exchange of information between them.

We are a thriving society of some 60 members which has been an overseas member of the National Wood Carvers Association of America for some years and amongst our numbers we have both national and regional open competition winners, in addition to woodcarving teachers who conduct classes within our county.

We also have a regular programme of exhibitions and demonstrations during the spring and summer season and are frequently asked by visitors where contact can be made with similar clubs in their home vicinity.

Perhaps it would be possible to compile some sort of register and I would welcome contact from any interested parties.
A. Swift, West Notts. Society of Wood Carvers, 3 Rowan Ave, Ravenshead, Notts NG15 9GA.

Bolt up right

Recent sketches of handrail bolts show bolts of uniform thickness throughout their length. Traditionally handrail bolts had a swelling at the middle of the bolt. The holes were bored to give a tight fit at the centre and some clearance at the ends. This made the bolts easy to enter and when pulled up, held the parts firmly together as well as preventing sideways movement.
James Leisper, Grampian, Scotland

WOODWORKER, published every third Friday by **Argus Specialist Publications Ltd**
Editorial, Advertising; I Golden Sq, London WIR 3AB, 01-437 0626
Editor Aidan Walker **Deputy editor** John Hemsley **Assistant editor** Kerry Fowler
Advertisement manager Trevor Pryer **Advertisement production** Laura Champion
Design ASP Art Studio **Technical illustrator** Peter Holland **Guild of Woodworkers**
John Hemsley, Kerry Fowler

Subscriptions per year UK £16.90; overseas outside USA (accelerated surface post) £21; USA (accelerated surface post) $28, airmail £48
UK Trade SM Distribution Ltd, 16-18 Trinity Gdns, London SW9 8DX, 01-274 8611
North American Trade Bill Dean Books Ltd, 151-49 7th Ave, PO Box 69, Whitestone, NY 11357, phone 1-718-767 6632
Printed by Chase Web, Plymouth **Typesetting** Project 3, Whitstable **Colour origination** Derek Croxson Ltd, Chesham, Bucks

ARGUS PRESS GROUP

CONTENTS

November 1987   Vol. 91   No. 11

Woodworker

Amused in the workshop: Stephen Marchant, demonstrator at the Loughborough woodturning seminar, likes nothing better than a bit of spindle turning. See p964

Lesley Taylor's set of boxes in pau rosa and hornbeam: Kerry Fowler saw her work, which you can do on p1018

This confident 'boat bowl' by Terry Holland caught the eye at the Loughborough turning seminar: see p964

On the cover: *on a background of a very unusual laminated ply bowl by Richard Hooper stands the stark shape of Jan Van Tol's black-stained African mahogany vase; more top turning on p964*

Many a claim is made about new wonder-tools: the book whose cover you see below has every right, we believe, to be called the 'essential' tool for all woodworkers. Who amongst us has never experienced that frustrating search for the right fitting, the right machine, the right supplier — and the right price?

The WOODWORKER Directory 1988 is here to change those exasperating moments into happy ones. Hundreds of products, services and information sources are listed, many in tables so you can compare at a glance; the answer to the searcher's dream. Pick up a copy at the Show or order direct from 'Woodworker Directory', 1 Golden Sq, London W1R 3AB. £12.95 inc. p&p.

£12.95

THE Woodworker Directory

Manufacturers & U.K. importers
Product specifications
Prices
Brand Names
Services
Timber suppliers
Local suppliers
Courses
Further sources of information

The essential tool for all woodworkers

AN ARGUS SPECIALIST PUBLICATION

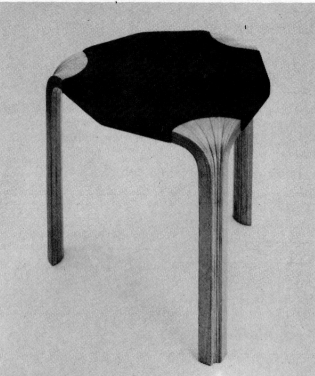

Top: 'Garret master hawking a sideboard to a furniture dealer', about 1860. Print from 'Furnishing the World', the exhibition of the East London furniture trade at the Geffrye Museum, London E8, until 3 Jan. See 'Diary'.

Above: Alvar Aalto, 'foremost exponent of modern Scandinavian design', conceived this stool in 1954. He was a master of lamination; choosing to create 'modernist' forms in wood rather than the metal or glass favoured by his contemporaries, he always retained a 'human warmth' that much of the stark Bauhaus furniture lacks. From a recent exhibition at the V&A.

Emotional harvest

Recent London Hardwood Club meetings have seen traders' feelings run high against the Friends of the Earth, reports *Timber Trades Journal* (15, 22 August). President Stuart Lindsay is quoted: 'There's no point in putting our heads in the sand and hoping the problem will go away. We have an obligation to ourselves to explain to people why the tropical rainforest problem is not being caused by us. Each and every one of us has got to act as an ambassador for the timber trade and explain how we're using the forests.' Chairman of the 29 July meeting, Howard Baker of Global Wood Products, claimed FoE's renewed activities were aimed at attaching a 'stigma to those of us who deal in tropical hardwoods. And if they say it often enough, some people will tend to believe it.' At the August 12 meeting, LHC members expressed dissatisfaction with the rational approach the Timber Trades Federation has used in dealings with FoE. 'Those people,' said one member, 'have launched an emotional attack on the hardwood trade. We should not try to combat that with facts and figures.'

Another member went further, claiming the FoE could not be seen as 'reasonable people. We must change our tack and show them up for the idiots they are.' Yet another importer held the view that the trade should stress the 'emotional' side of the 'harvest' of the rainforests, to present the commercial aspect of the tropical hardwood trade in a new light to the public. (There is no further explanation of what he meant.)

Another voice was heard adding a different tone: 'The timber trade has a certain responsibility to recognise. A road into the forest means cutting down only a few trees, but our logging roads then allow locals to move in and start felling for fuel.'

DIARY

Guild courses are shown by an (*); for further details see Guild pages

October

Until 31 **Rupert Williamson** room setting, Contemporary Textile Gallery, Golden Sq, London W1

Until 7 Nov **Castles in the Air,** David West woodcarving and painting exhibition, Cliffe Castle Museum, Spring Gdns Lane, Keighley, W. Yorks, (0535) 664184 (Tues-Sun).

Until 3 Jan **Craft and Design for the Home,** Crafts Council, 12 Waterloo Place, London SW1, 01-930 4811.

Until 3 Jan **Furnishing the World:** East London Furniture Trade 1830-1980, Geffrye Museum, Kingsland Rd, London E2 8EA, 01-739 8368.

4-28 **Mainly Wood Exhibition,** Parnham Hse, Beaminster, Dorset DT8 3NA (0308) 862204.

12-24 **Chelsea Crafts Fair,** Old Town Hall, London SW3.

20-30 **Annual International Creative Marquetry Show,** Virginia, USA, application forms: S. Cartwright, 63 Church Lane, Sproughton, Ipswich IP8 3AY.

21 **Style for Living 87,** trade and public furniture show, 3f Prince Rupert Hse, 64 Queens St. London EC4R 1AD.

22-25 **London Woodworker Show,** Alexandra Pavilion, London N22

25-28 **Design in Furniture,** Olympia, London (trade only).

31-28 Nov **Jim Partridge** Exhibition turned and carved wood, Crafts Council shop, V&A Museum, London SW7 2RL.

November

14 **Power Routing** Roy Sutton*

14-15 **French Polishing** Ian Hosker*

13-15 **Eastern Counties Craft Market,** Rhodes Ctre, Bishops Stortford, Herts, contact: (0920) 870040.

17-19 **Northern Interior Design Exhibition,** G-MEX, Manchester, contact: 061-868 4499.

20 **Woodland Ecology Debate,** Parnham Hse. Beaminster, Dorset, (0308) 862204.

22-28 **Interbuild 87,** building and construction exhibition, NEC, Birmingham, contact: 021-486 1951.

28-17 Dec **Eleanor Glover** exhibition carved and painted wood, Crafts Council Shop, V&A Museum, London SW7 2RL.

Woodturner's Association

The woodturning seminar 'From Craft to Art' in August was significant in more ways than one; it was unanimously agreed there that **The Association of Woodturners of Great Britain** should be formed. Unanimously-elected chairman Ray Key and well-known turner Mick O'Donnell have long felt that turning is held in greater esteem in countries where there are such associations; so now the UK has one too, with our own Hugh O'Neill as Hon. Secretary.

Membership is open to all interested in turning — full or part-time professionals, amateur or hobbyist — and there are no grades or differentiations in membership. The first year's subscription is £10.

The aims of the Association, says the release, can be broadly stated as 'to promote the image of the turner's art and craft in the mind of the general public, and to encourage all practictioners to aim for high quality turnery.' The idea is the Association will provide a forum for the exchange of ideas — a regular newsletter is one of the first aims — and arrange exhibitions and seminars. Development of training and educational facilities is also on the agenda, including the prompting of members to run their own local teaching workshops.

Write to: The Hon Secretary, Association of Woodturners of Great Britain, 5 Kent Gardens, Eastcote, Middx HA4 8RX.
● See 'The Great Turn-on' in this issue.

More drills

Peugeot Power Tools are 'consolidating' their range of drills for the UK, replacing two models with a medium-to-heavy duty range of three. The PC 771 single-speed, 500w, 13mm percussion drill costs £55 + VAT; the PC 793 has 580w, five speeds, variable speed control, 13mm chuck, and percussion for £63.50 + VAT; and the top-of-the-range PC 795 RC has 500w, ½in chuck, five reversible speeds, and electronic torque control for £70 + VAT. They also do a cordless screwdriver drill for £65 + VAT. 6 Churchbridge, Oldbury, W. Mid. B69 2AP, 021-552 4580.

Top-class craft

Woodworking book specialists Stobarts have commissioned Betty Norbury, journalist and craftspeople's PR and marketing consultant, to compile and write *British Craftsmanship in Wood*. The book will be a gallery, say Stobarts, a 'potential showcase to all those seeking appreciation of the state of the art or to those looking to commission new work.' Naturally it will be highly illustrated with 'the best possible illustrations/photographs of current and "classic" past work.'

But Betty doesn't just want the best-known people in the country, she tells us; she is intent on gathering a fine selection of excellent craftsmanship, and feels the book should feature people who haven't yet gained public prominence. If you know someone who you think should be included, or reckon you should be in it yourself, contact Betty Norbury at the White Knight Gallery, 28 Painswick Road, Cheltenham, Glos.

College award

Design in Furniture, the 'UK's first contemporary furniture exhibition', announces that among the attractions at Olympia (25-28 October) will be the display of work from colleges who have entered for the Design and Industries' Association/Gordon Russell Award. The award will go to the college with the best four pieces of furniture from the current academic year; so far a dozen colleges have applied.

Design in Furniture gives UK colleges, says show organiser Jacqui Wheeler, 'a remarkable opportunity to meet manufacturers, retailers and designers by offering them space to display . . . their work. (It) gives them a chance to forge links with the British furniture design industry and encourages a healthy relationship between today's manufacturers and tomorrow's designers.'

For further information contact Amelia Martinez/Dominic Lyle, Cameron Choat, 126-8 Cromwell Rd, London SW7, 01-373 4537.

Dust puller

We've seen one or two gadgets for sucking the dust away from a hole you're drilling in a wall or ceiling recently, but Trend's looks like it's ready to take the biscuit. Their 'Drill-Vac' connects to an ordinary domestic or industrial-rated vacuum cleaner — the three-metre hose has a stepped universal bayonet fitting for different diameters — and the plate has a soft neoprene-lined base which will take up the contours of uneven surfaces for a dust-tight seal. You position the plate over the mark (there is a combined sighting and drill-bit aperture, plus a graduated measure along the edge), the plate is held on by suction, and then it's just a matter of drilling. Not only convenient and clean, but safe too. £19.80 + VAT from Trend (or stockists), Unit N, Penfold Works, Imperial Way, Watford, Herts WD2 4YY, (0923) 249911.

Finishing tuition

Colin Campbell's 'International School of French Polishing' (he has students from as far afield as Turkey and the USA) runs four-day courses on french polishing or spray finishing, or a double-length one for both. Restoration, materials, advice; Colin's teaching is very business oriented, and he says that·he includes advice about starting your own business, pricing, customer relations, and — very important — a free back-up service of support and advice when you're out on your own. He can also do one-to-one courses between March and November, tailored to individual requirements, and he has french polishing and spraying videos for sale at £35 each or £55 for the two. A four-day course costs £275 including all materials and course notes (and the back-up), but not accommodation. International School of French Polishing, Sunnythwaite, Penton, Carlisle, CA6 5RZ, (0228 77) 262.

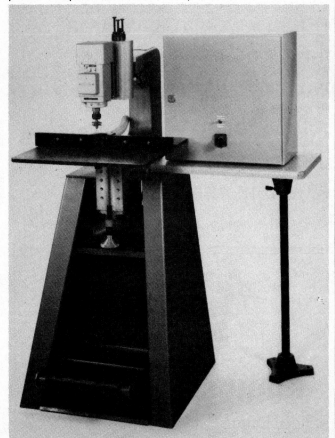

Trend's floor-mounted overhead copy router, with electronic controls, retains high torque under continuous load. Infinitely variable motor speed 6-18,000 rpm. Trend, Unit N, Penfold Works, Imperial Way, Watford WD2 4YF, (0923) 49911.

THE BIG'UN

Don't miss the 1987 London Woodworker Show, previewed by Show organiser Mary White

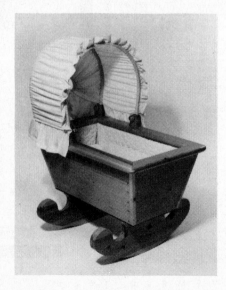

The UK's premier show for all that's best in the woodworking field will take place once again at the Alexandra Pavilion, Wood Green, London N22 from Thursday-Sunday, 22-25 October 1987.

All 169 stands at this year's show will be jam-packed with everything you can possibly wish to see and buy, from small hand tools, veneers and polishes to large machinery.

The centrepiece of this year's exhibition will once again be the competition entries covering the many classes from cabinet-making to marquetry. With over 200 entries you can't help but be amazed at the many inspirational ideas that craftsmen have. You never know — perhaps you'll go away thinking you can do as well and next year it could be your work there on display.

All your favourite craftsmen will be there to give you help and advice on the many different aspects of woodworking. Learn how to re-cane a chair, or perhaps make a musical instrument. New to the London Show will be Trevor Rooney, carver extraordinaire; Trevor was at at the Bristol Show in May and caused a great deal of interest with the visitors. Also new to the show is Paul Noon who, would you believe, carves totem poles! See Trevor's article on his carvings ('Show me a rose'), and Paul's on his work ('Totem Chester') in this issue.

Colleges, societies and institutes will be displaying the work of students and fellow craftsmen. Perhaps you would like to attend a course or just share your experiences with eager listeners.

Whatever your interest in woodwork you can be sure that someone or something will delight and inspire you. So don't miss this year's London Woodworker Show, a meeting place for one and all! ■

Mike Abbott's enthusiasm for the pole lathe is infectious

Cradle by Mr P. Allan of Shoreham, in pine

An unusual chamfer plane by G. Gardiner, to be seen on the Tool and Trades History Stand

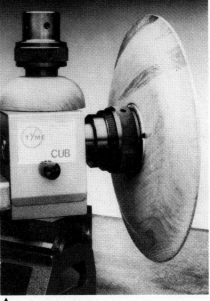

Turners: win one of these Craft Supplies chucks

London Woodworker Show, Alexandra Pavilion, London N22, Thursday 22 October to Sunday 25 October; open 10-6 daily (till 5 on Sunday). Admission £3.50, senior citizens £2.25, children £1.50. Reductions for party bookings and Guild of Woodworkers members. Further information, competition entry forms and advance tickets available from: Argus Specialist Exhibitions Ltd, Wolsey House, Wolsey Rd, Hemel Hempstead, Herts HP2 4SS, (0442) 41221.

Competition prizes

Cabinetmaking: *The AEG/Woodworker Pre-Professional Award.*
Open to final-year furniture college students, with a chance to win an AEG Maxi 26 Universal woodworking machine.
Spindle turning: *The Robert Sorby Awards.*
Beautiful Sorby HSS tools to be won.
Faceplate turning: *The Craft Supplies Awards.*
Precision Combination Chuck or accessories from Craft Supplies.
Woodcarving: *The Ashley Iles Carving Awards.*
Specially selected sets of tools.
Routing: *The Trend Routing Award.*
Valuable TCT and HSS cutters.
Wood finishing: *The Henry Flack Award.*
Open to any entrant in any category for the best finish at the Show, with prizes of J. W. Bollom (the Briwax people) products.
Young Professionals: *Roger's Award.*
A set of 10 Japanese chisels from the specialist tool supplier.
Juniors: *Roger's Award.*
Tool vouchers for young entries in various categories.
Stickmaking: *The Theo Fossel Trophy.*
A beautiful glass goblet, yours to keep.

Additionally, there's the **Robbins Rose Bowl** from Robbins of Bristol for cabinetmaking; **Woodworker Challenge Cups** in many classes; the **Richard Blizzard Cup** for toymakers; the **World of Wood Cup** for marquetarians, donated by the Art Veneers Company; the **Stuart King Award** for miniaturists; and the **John Thompson Trophy** for model horse-drawn vehicle makers.

How to get there:

By public transport. You can take either the British Rail service to Alexandra Palace, or the underground to Wood Green.
● **Main line:** service from King's Cross every half hour, alighting at Alexandra Palace station. Journey time is about 10 minutes, and you'll find a free bus service from the station to the Alexandra Pavilion and back.
● **Underground:** take the Piccadilly line from Piccadilly Circus or King's Cross to Wood Green station, journey time about 30 minutes. Free bus service from Wood Green underground station to Alexandra Pavilion and back.
By road. The M25 is the quickest route for most drivers, turning off at Junction 25. Alexandra Pavilion is just off the North Circular, and AA signs are being posted from the bottom of the M1. Ample car parking is available with a park-and-ride shuttle service to the Show, or an easy stroll if you prefer.

AEG Maxi, to be won by the best 'Pre-Professional':

Ashley Iles carving tools, prizes for top carvers

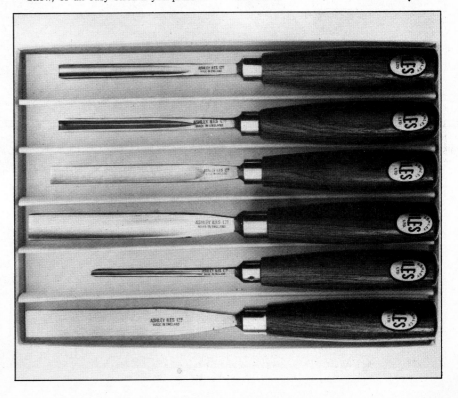

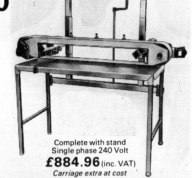

LOW PRICES UNBEATABLE SERVICE!

LOOK AT OUR PRICES ON JUST ONE OF THE MAJOR BRAND PRODUCT LISTS WE STOCK

KITY

	LIST PRICE £. p.	OUR PRICE £. p.
513 Bandsaw 8" cut. 12" throat 1 HP	554.93	**427.00**
613 Bandsaw 8" cut. 12" throat 1½ HP. stand, industrial spec.	700.01	**595.00**
623 Spindle Moulder. 30mm spindle 2 HP. 3 speeds	851.35	**668.75**
618 Saw. max 3¾" cut, tilt arbor to 45° 2 HP with table extensions	753.25	**591.70**
7636 10" × 6" planer thicknesser. 2 HP power feed. 2 year guarantee.	908.10	**585.00**

COMBINATION UNITS

Combi Star: Portable combination 8" saw complete with rise and fall tilt 1 HP 6" × 4" planer thickenesser. 2 year guarantee.	688.85	**645.00**
NEW Best Combi (replaces K5) NEW 8" saw, 2½" cut, tilts to 45° TCT blade 6" × 4" planer thicknesser, power feed, throwaway blades, 30mm spindle moulder	976.35	**775.00**
NEW Best Combi As above with Lever operated mortiser	1085.60	**875.00**
CK26 combination unit (replaces K704) 9" saw 3" cut, tilts to 45° rise and fall 10" × 6" planer/thicknesser, power feed 7000rpm. 30mm spindle moulder, 6200rpm. 2HP 240V, on stand and wheels.	1677.85	**1395.00**
CK26 As above, with mortiser unit.	1999.85	**1595.00**
704 DD Combination Unit capacities as CK26, but with push button machine changes, save moving belts.	2090.62	**1695.00**
704 DD with mortiser 20mm max bit size.	2459.77	**1995.00**

PLUS FREE TOOL VOUCHER WORTH £50 + V.A.T.

WHO ELSE CAN OFFER ALL THESE SERVICES?

- *3 retail stores, stocking and displaying over 20,000 lines*
- *Full mail order colour catalogue*
- *Hand tools, power tools, combination units, independent machines, books, finishes*
- *All major brands stocked, plus many "hard to find" hand tools*
- *Skilled staff in each store, trained to sort your woodworking tool problem*
- *Major credit cards accepted. H.P. terms available*
- *Delivery available nationwide*

OPEN 8.30 – 5.30 MONDAY TO SATURDAY
SEND £1.50 FOR CATALOGUE TO READING

SARJENTS TOOLS

14 RICHFIELD AVENUE
READING RG1 8NZ
(0734) 586522

62-64 FLEET STREET
SWINDON SN1 1RD
(0793) 31361

150 COWLEY ROAD
OXFORD OX4 1JJ
(0865) 245118

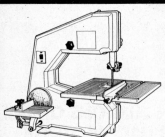
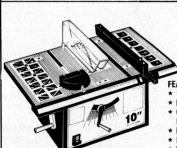

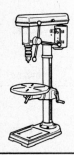

THE WOODWORKER GUIDE TO
ORNAMENTATION IN WOOD

Everything you need to know about decorating wood. From inlays to ornamental joints, turning to carved mouldings, this beautifully illustrated guide will teach you the trade secrets. Learn the intricacies of a decorative dovetail butterfly joint or the traditional art of Tunbridge ware...there are eight easy-to-follow projects plus a wealth of information on the techniques of decorative woodcraft. Go on — give that wood the treatment! In your shops on 30th October, price £1.50; or £2 inc. p&p from Infonet, 5 River Park Estate, Berkhamsted, Herts HP4 1HL, (04427) 76661-4.

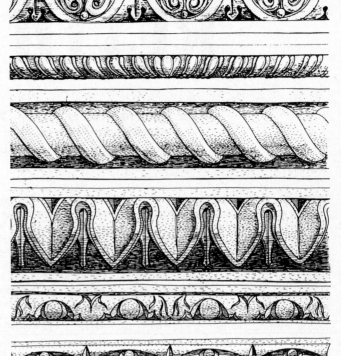

NEXT MONTH

December's issue of your top woodwork journal has, as usual, an array of attractions to tempt you — many of them, naturally enough, with a Christmassy feel.

First, before you even open the magazine you'll be the owner of a **Footprint Handiknife.** A quality retractable-blade knife useful for 1001 tasks in the workshop or at home, it's a first-class Christmas gift from WOODWORKER to its readers. Inside, we have features to entertain you and design for you to make. Everyone's thoughts turn to children at the time of giving, and what better than to give something you've made? Like the **Noah's Ark** in oak, with animals in various hardwoods, that won the gold medal for Geoff King at the Bristol Show this year? Or a **wooden seaplane,** modelled on the Supermarine race winner of the '30s, which is just tricky enough to give you a bit of a challenge? There's a **baby's rattle** to turn, and drawings for a dainty **hall chest;** there's an enthusiast's tale of the loving restoration of an old **horse-drawn tram.**

There's some very special gifts you can treat yourself to, on top of all this; a beautiful set of solid brass **marking and measuring tools,** at very special prices.

We've said it before, and we'll say it again; now more than ever, for the woodworking professional, the enthusiast, the amateur, or the beginner, WOODWORKER is the magazine of design, craft and making that you just cannot afford to miss. Make sure of yours — order a copy now!

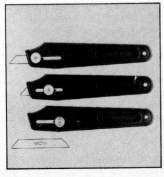

ON SALE 20 NOVEMBER

BEFORE THE REVOLUTION

After the demise of Louis XV, neo-classicism reigned strong in France. Vic Taylor outlines late 18th-century popular furniture and its makers

Ordinary household furniture in 18th-century France had its own provincial styles and functions, and was a far cry from the earlist Court or Crown designs. This folk furniture is known as *meubles régionaux* or *meubles provinciaux* (regional or provincial furniture) and each design should be judged on its own merits, as individual makers combined what little knowledge they had of the fashions of the *haut monde*, the materials at their disposal, and the customary furniture of the region — producing designs which were unrelated to any recognised style.

One of the most popular pieces was the *armoire-à-deux corps,* a two-stage cabinet with one small top cupboard mounted on a larger one. The *grande armoire* was a wardrobe of immense proportions, whilst the *petite armoire* or *bonnetière* was a small single-door wardrobe favoured in western districts to store the ladies wide-brimmed hats. Peculiar to these *armoires* were the loose-pin hinges which allowed the doors to be lifted off easily; perhaps this helped house removals to be trouble-free! Another storage piece was the *homme debout,* which was in three stages with a cupboard at the bottom, another smaller cupboard at the top, and drawers between the two. Buffets reminiscent of 17th-century English dressers were often over two metres long with a row of four or five cupboards with drawers above. Fitted with a set of shelves they were called *vaisseliers,* similar to our Welsh dresser.

Commodes were much in evidence and in this case, their makers strove to imitate Parisian styles, although they had to dispense with expensive accoutrements such as ormolu and veneer. So the commodes could not be made with *bombé* fronts or ends, as veneer is the only way to cover the underlying construction. Instead block fronts solved the problem and to compensate for the lack of ormolu and veneer, they were carved with Rococo ornament, in varying degrees of quality.

In 1774 Louis XV died and was succeeded by Louis XVI, who reigned until his execution in 1793 during the French Revolution. He happened to be an accomplished locksmith and clockmaker and it's said he was happier and more capable when indulging in these activities than when governing! His interests probably inspired the mechanical contrivances found in many items of furniture at the time.

During the last years of Louis XV's reign there was a growing reaction against the extravagances, both decorative and financial,

of making Rococo furniture. This, coupled with the natural desire for something new, ensured that Rococo was gradually replaced during Louis XVI's reign by the neo-classical style, which originated in Italy. Excavations of the site of Roman Pompeii and Herculaneum, from 1763 onwards, excited admiration for the restrained classical Roman architecture and decoration, contrasting with the exuberant and often frivolous Italian Rococo. The Rococo C-scrolls, sinuous curves, and florid adornments were superseded by geometrical motifs of squares, ellipses, rectangles, and circles. The cabriole leg also gradually disappeared and was replaced by turned and twisted, or square-tapered legs with bulbous or block feet. The Pompeiian style was interpreted more loosely than in the Roman original and included laurel wreaths, Vitruvian scrolls, urns, lions' masks, and classical columns, with the odd vestal virgin against a pseudo-Roman background thrown in for good measure.

Bombé shapes had enjoyed a good innings and gave way to rectilinear constructions for commodes, often incorporating a break-front. Boulle-work and marquetry were revived, and parquetry, inlaying differently coloured and grained pieces of wood to achieve a geometrical mosaic, became especially popular. The tops of the commodes were often covered with either solid marble or *pietre dure*, a mosaic of coloured stones.

THE NEO-CLASSICAL STYLE soon embraced the culture of classical Greece as well; this development was aptly known as the *goût grec*. One of the first to exploit the fashion

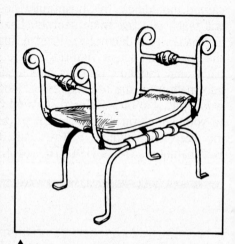

▲
Roman curule, a magistrates' seat which inspired many designs for Louis XV stools.

A country walnut commode: fittings and details are in Louis XV style, the rest from the Louis XVI era
◄

was Jean-François Neufforge (1714-1791) who not only chose Grecian female figures as ornaments, but also used Egyptian artefacts such as sphinxes, winged lions, and caryatids. Another innovator of the genre was Jean-Charles Delafosse (1734-1791) who published sets of engravings, all of Grecian inspiration with a profusion of key patterns and laurel wreaths.

The three leading exponents of French neo-classicism were: Adam Weisweiler (1750-1810); Jacques-Louis David (1748-1825); and J. H. Riesener. Weisweiler was one of the many German cabinetmakers who settled in Paris, attracted by the opportunity to make expensive furniture. His speciality was light, delicate pieces such as *semainiers,* a type of *chiffonière* consisting of a set of seven narrow shelves arranged vertically above each other, one for each day of the week. He also produced dwarf cabinets on diminutive feet; one of the distinguishing characteristics of his furniture was his use of cone-shaped turned and twisted feet. He seldom used marquetry and preferred plain mahogany combined with gleaming black lacquer; he frequently used bronze mounts and was known to have re-cycled boulle and *pietre dure* from older furniture. Despite these economies he was made bankrupt in 1788, and his ruin was completed by the Revolution in 1789.

David was an artist who visited Rome and

absorbed the antiquities at first hand. On his return he created designs more Roman or Grecian than any produced by his colleagues, and he was instrumental in translating the *klismos* chair and the *curule* into the contemporary idiom. His designs were made up for him by George Jacob (1739-1814), one of the finest chairmakers of the period who was made *maître* of the guild in 1765. (His trade mark was a carved marguerite on the seat rail). But the pre-eminent chair maker, and the one favoured by royalty, was Jean-Baptiste-Claude Sené (1748-1803). He supplied the chairs for Marie Antoinette's bedroom at Fontainebleau and was noted for his lyre-back chairs, which were free from gilding and made in mahogany. He became *maître* in 1769 and *fournisseur de la Couronne* (furnisher to the Crown) in 1785.

OTHER FINE CONTEMPORARY CRAFTSMEN included: Martin Carlin, who worked for the Royal family and Queen Marie Antoinette, and was noted for using Sèvres porcelain plaques on his furniture; René Dubois, who became a *maître-ébéniste* in 1754; heavily patronised by the Royal family and nobility, he eventually gave up making furniture in favour of selling it; and Jean François Leleu who learned his trade under J. F. Oeben (he hoped to marry Oeben's widow but the lady preferred Riesener and Leleu never really got over it), was made *maître-ébéniste* in 1764, and patronised by Queen Marie Antoinette, Madame du Barry and the Prince de Condeé.

David Roentgen (1743-1807) was a German from Frankfurt where his father, Abraham Roentgen, already had a flourishing workshop.

David took it over in 1772 and expanded it into an international business; eventually he had workshops and depots in Paris, Berlin, and Vienna. He also visited Italy, Flanders, and Russia, where he sold furniture to the Empress Catherine II. In 1774, on his first visit to Paris he supplied furniture to Queen Marie Antoinette and in 1780 he became a *maitre-ébéniste*. By 1791 he was court furnisher to Friedrich Wilhelm II in Berlin but the French Revolution dealt him a devastating blow when his depots in Paris and Neuwied were damaged by troops, and the goods confiscated.

Most of his furniture was made in Germany and sent abroad, as he preferred to work from Neuwied. He was a master of pictorial marquetry in the popular 'trophies', which were inlaid, marquetry, carved, or

A Louis XVI marquetry commode by J-F Leleu, reputed to have come from Versailles itself.

A 'Klismos' type chair, with characteristic sabre legs, from a design of Grecian devotee Thomas Hope (1807)

painted panels on pieces of furniture, depicting weapons, armour, musical instruments, or allegorical scenes with gods and goddesses. And, no doubt to the delight of Louis XVI, he also specialised in secret drawers and compartments, and all kinds of mechanical devices.

The cataclysmic events of the French Revolution created a watershed in French culture, and the *ancien régime* disappeared for good. Riesener, who regarded the Revolution as a minor event which would burn itself out, bought back pieces of his own at the Revolutionary sales, in the misguided belief that he could re-sell them at a profit when the troubles were over; both Weisweiler and Roentgen were ruined by the Revolution. David was anti-monarchist and survived the Revolution to go on to play a part in the creation of the new *Directoire* and Empire styles. He also helped his protégé chairmaker, Sené, through the troubles, and eventually Sené was employed making furniture for the new administration. ■

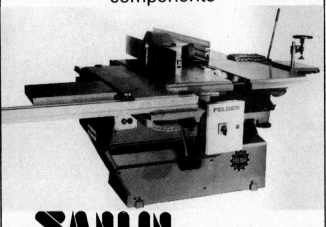

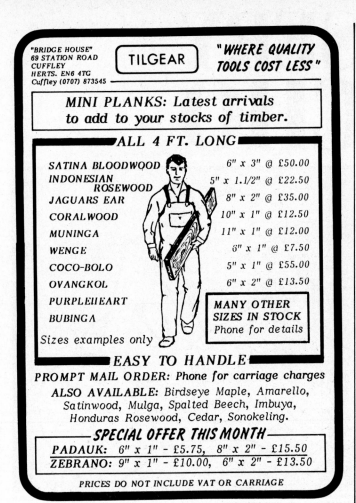
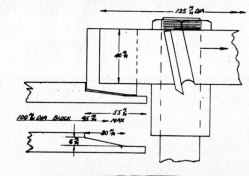

NURSERY MACHO

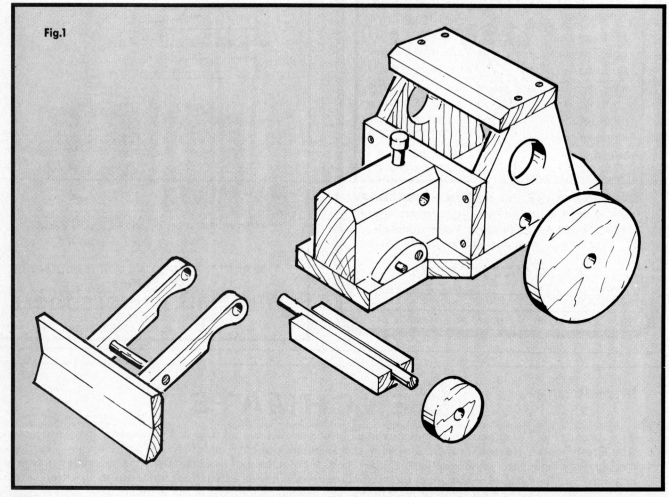

Fig.1

**James Wake designed this toy bulldozer
to avoid any dangers to children**

For me, safety is the paramount consideration in young children's toys. Here's a mechanical toy with a challenging solid wood, glued construction designed for safety and strength. No metal or plastic fittings are involved.

Beech is traditionally the favourite material, for strength, but cost and availability is a factor. You could use other hardwoods, carefully selected softwoods, plywood, laminated board and even chipboard, but the finish, painted or varnished, will be influenced by the choice of material. If painted, make sure you use non-toxic paint. I've found a clear polyurethane varnish, on carefully selected pine, produces a strong, hard-wearing and handsome result.

Joints

The strength of the toy relies upon glued and dowelled joints, which must be tight and well-fitting. It's essential that all structural parts are flat, exactly straight and square-edged, and clean and dust-free — particularly if you're using PVA glue. I strongly recommend using a sanding disc for end-grain. Mark out and pre-drill pilot holes in all the surface parts before assembly, preferably using a drilling machine or drill-stand. The joints rely upon tight fitting dowels, drilling the holes 0.5mm smaller than the dowels' diameter. Saw a groove in the sides of the dowel to provide an escape for air and surplus glue. If this saw-cut is made of sufficient depth, parallel with the surface grain, it provides some 'give', making a tight fitting joint without splitting. When ready for gluing, lay out all the parts, grip the first piece and the gluing jig in the bench vice (fig. 4). Check for accuracy, then holding the pre-drilled part firmly in position against the jig, and using the pilot holes as a guide, drill for the depth of the dowel. Apply glue, insert the dowel and drive into position. Still holding the pre-drilled part firmly, drill the next

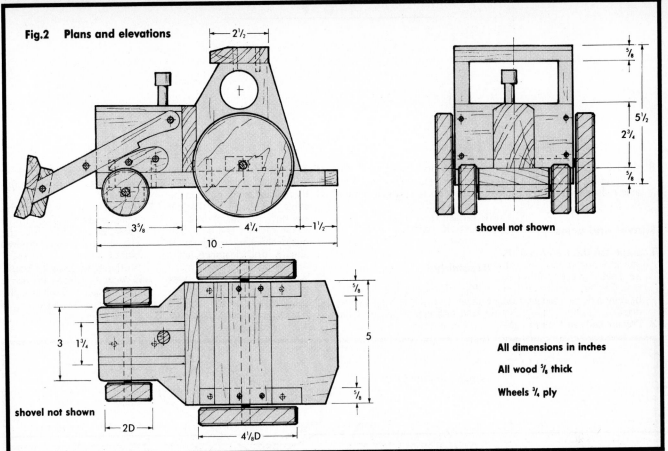

Fig.2 Plans and elevations

shovel not shown

shovel not shown

All dimensions in inches

All wood ⅝ thick

Wheels ¾ ply

hole and repeat the gluing process. Remove from the vice. Because of the tight fitting dowels it is possible, with care, to level off the protruding dowels immediately, and with some ingenuity, use the gluing jig fastened in the bench vice to complete the other corners. Remove all surplus glue.

Wheels and axles

Only wooden parts are used, all glued together. They are resilient to the hard knocks that toys are bound to receive and there are no small components which can be detached, picked up and swallowed.

The axles are hardwood dowels revolving in a grooved block of wood. Before fixing, a rub of candle wax along the dowels will ensure smooth running, but avoid waxing ends which have to be glued.

If a lathe is available, turn the wheels using ¾in plywood. Without a lathe, I've found the following method very successful:

● Saw wood into squares, slightly bigger than the wheel diameter. Mark the centre and draw the circular size. Drill the centre holes for the dowel axle, such as ⅜in diameter,
● Saw off the corners,
● Mount the wheel on the sanding disc wheel jig (figs 5/6),
● As the wheel is rotated, slide the jig backwards and forwards along the disc table. Remove the waste gradually until the wheel is finished to size.

The look and serviceability of the wheels is much improved if

the edges are bevelled. You can do this easily on the sanding disc by making another jig with the surface tilted to 30° or 45°.

Safety points:

● Don't allow fingers to touch the rotating disc,
● Don't apply too much pressure or the wood will overheat and scorch — not only wood but fingers,
● Sanding produces a lot of dust, so use a nose mask and eye protection.

Construction

1 Start by shaping the chassis base. Drill dowel pilot holes for fastening the cab and radiator.
2 Prepare and shape pieces for the cab. Hold the sides together and bore a hole for the side windows. Drill pilot holes in top and fascia.
3 Shape the radiator block and drill for exhaust pipe.
4 After cleaning and sanding all interior surfaces, use the gluing jig to assemble and glue the cab.
5 Glue and dowel the radiator to the chassis. Holding the cab firmly against the radiator, glue and dowel in position. When dry, clean up and sand the outside.
6 Glue the exhaust, and then varnish the whole assembly, except the underside of the chassis.
7 Prepare the wheels, dowel rod axles, and grooved axle retaining blocks. ▶

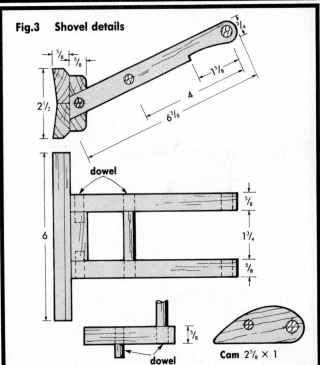

Fig.3 Shovel details

dowel

dowel

Cam 2⅝ × 1

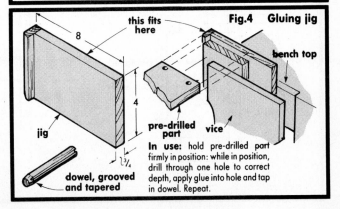

Fig.4 Gluing jig

this fits here

bench top

jig

pre-drilled part   vice

dowel, grooved and tapered

In use: hold pre-drilled part firmly in position: while in position, drill through one hole to correct depth, apply glue into hole and tap in dowel. Repeat.

8 Varnish the inside surfaces edges of the wheels. Wax the axle rods, except the ends to be glued.

Shovel and arms

1 Shape the three shovel parts and glue together. They can be held together with thin moudling pins, which can then be removed when the glue has dried.

2 Prepare and pair the arms and cams. Drill holes for the dowels and glue together, except for the pivoting dowels in the radiator.

3 Varnish these parts.

4 Cut the pivoting dowels to length.

Assembly

1 Place the bulldozer body on its side. Check it is lying square and drill clearance holes for the rear axle.

2 Temporarily position all the wheels and axles.

3 By trial and error, position the cams and shovel, so that the pivoting positions of the holes in the radiator can be found.

4 Again checking the body is square, drill clearance holes for the pivoting dowels.

5 With the wheels and axles glued together, and resting in the groove, glue the grooved blocks, temporarily fastening with moulding pins.

6 Glue the shovel and cams to the ends of the pivoting dowels.

7 Remove surplus glue and give a final coats of varnish to the outsides of the wheels, chassis base and grooved blocks.

So there you have it. A safe, solid wood toy which can't hurt a child of any age, and can give play pleasure for many years. ∎

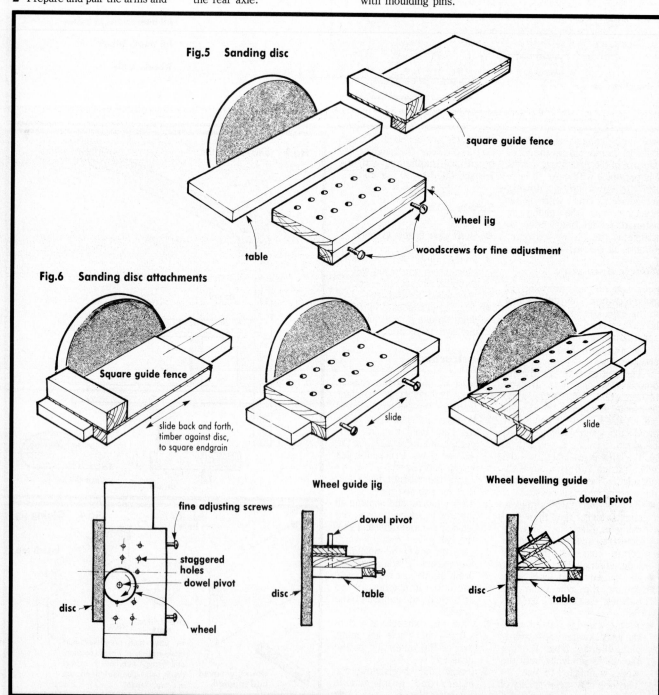

Fig.5 Sanding disc

square guide fence

wheel jig

table

woodscrews for fine adjustment

Fig.6 Sanding disc attachments

Square guide fence

slide back and forth, timber against disc, to square endgrain

slide

slide

fine adjusting screws

staggered holes

dowel pivot

disc

wheel

Wheel guide jig

dowel pivot

disc

table

Wheel bevelling guide

dowel pivot

disc

table

WOODWORKING MACHINERY

Huge range - Competitive prices - Fast service

SAWBENCHES

Scheppach TKU 12" 3HP Sitesaw ... £229
Elu TGS171 Flip Oversaw 10" ... £401
Elu TGS172 Flip Oversaw 10" ... £495
Startrite TA145 9" Saw ... POA
*Startrite TA300PS 1PH ... POA
*Sliding Table 48" Return ... £316
*Startrite TA275DS 12" 1PH ... POA
Multico NTA300 12" 3HP ... £1099
Sliding Table 48" Return ... £316
Sedgwick LK 16" 1PH ... £1236
*Wadkin AGS250/300 3HP 1PH ... £1129
*Sliding Table 39" Return ... £432
*Wadkin AGSP Scoring Saw 3PH ... £1245
*Wadkin SP12 48" Return ... £2336
*Wadkin CP12 48" 2 Motors ... £3245
*Wadkin CP25 96" 2 Motors ... £3857
*Wadkin CP32 10' Panel Saw ... £4301

RADIAL ARM SAWS

DW1201 10" 1HP + £48 free accs. ... £314
DW1251 10" 1.5HP + £82 free accs. ... £448
DW1501 10" 1.5HP ... £517
DW8001 12" 2HP ... £641
DW1751 10" 1.5HP 24" XCUT ... £596
DW8101 12" 2HP 24" XCUT ... £736
DW1600S 4HP 24" XCUT ... 1050
DW1875 4HP 34" XCUT ... £1150
Wadkin BRA MOD2 4HP ... £1500
*Wadkin BRA MOD 1 ... £1502
*Wadkin BRA MOD 3 ... £1249
* Wadkin BRA MOD 4 ... £1137

PREMIUM QUALITY TCT SAW BLADES

Diameter	6"		7"				8"				9"			
No. of Teeth	24	36	18	30	42	56	20	36	48	64	24	40	54	72
Price £	21	24	19	23	26	30	21	28	31	34	23	29	35	39

PLEASE STATE BORE SIZE WHEN ORDERING

Diameter	10"				12"				14"			16"		
No. of Teeth	24	42	60	80	32	48	72	96	36	54	84	40	72	96
Price £	24	26	38	42	30	38	45	50	42	52	63	57	64	71

TCT GROOVING CUTTERS

1/4" .. £46.77 — 5/8 ... £66.78 — 6" Diam.
3/8 ... £50.92 — 3/4 ... £74.81 — 6 Teeth
1/2 ... £58.48 — 1 .... £86.62 — P&P £2.00

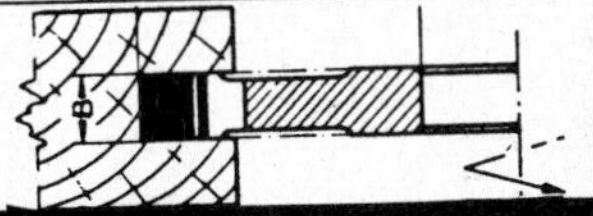

BANDSAWS

DW100 4" with Disc ... £158
DW3401 6" 2 Speed ... £289
DW3501 6" Var. Speed ... £298
Sumaco TBS350 Bandsaw ... £299
Startrite 301 6" 3/4HP ... POA
Startrite 351 8" 1HP ... POA
Startrite 352 11" 1HP ... POA
Startrite 502 2HP ... POA
Griggio Snal 440E ... £845
Griggio Snal 440 ... £1121
Griggio Snal 540 ... £1316
Griggio Snal 640 ... £1552
Wadkin C5 ... £1355
Wadkin C6 ... £1516
Wadkin C9 880mm throat ... £2639
Wadkin PBR 10HP Rip Saw ... £4043
Wadkin PBR HD 15HP Resaw ... £5458

HAKANSEN SWEDISH STEEL INDUSTRIAL BANDSAW BLADES

	3/16"	1/4"	3/8"	1/2"	5/8"	3/4"
Burgess 57"	4.42	4.42	4.51	4.67	5.99	5.62
Bed 59.5"	4.42	4.42	4.51	4.67	5.99	6.62
Coronet 67.5"	4.42	4.42	4.51	4.67	5.99	6.62
Inca 73"	4.42	4.42	4.51	4.67	5.99	6.62
DW3401 82.5"	4.42	4.42	4.51	4.67	5.99	6.62
Kity 612 83.5"	4.42	4.42	4.51	4.67	5.99	6.62
Minimax P32 85.5"	4.42	4.42	4.51	4.67	5.99	6.62
Startrite 301 88"	4.42	4.42	4.51	4.67	5.99	6.62
Startrite 351 102"	4.74	4.74	4.83	5.02	6.45	7.14
Startrite 352 112"	5.04	5.04	5.15	6.62	6.82	7.66

Guaranteed Weld. P&P £1.50
Any size blade made to order.

COMBINATIONS

Startrite K260 1PH. ... POA
Startrite K260 3PH. ... POA
Startrite K310 1PH. ... POA
Startrite K310 3PH. ... POA
Luna W59 Master 3HPX3 C/W SL. T £2599
Ask about our easy purcahse plans.

MORTICERS

Multico HM 9/16 Cap ... £369
Multico HMT 9/16" Cap ... £495
Multico M/1 1" Cap 1.5HP ... £660
Sedgwick 571 1" Cap 1HP ... £644
Wadkin EDA 1" Cap ... £627
Ridgway 1" 1HP C/W Chisel ... £579
*Dominion BAA Chain Mortiser ... £2333

FINANCE

THERE'S A WIDE RANGE OF OPTIONS AND EASY PURCHASE PLANS ON ALL MACHINES — CALL FOR ADVICE AND INFORMATION — NOW.

SPINDLE MOULDERS

Scheppach HF33 ... £499
Startrite T30 1PH ... POA
Startrite T230 1PH ... POA
Sedgwick GW 1PH 2HP ... 1081
Wilson FM 5.5HP ... 1751
Wilson FX 7.5HP ... 2211
*Wadkin BEL 4SP 5.5HP ... £1980
Wadkin BEX 5.5HP ... £2300
Griggio T1000 ... £2300
Griggio TPL2000 2.5mm Tables ... £3737
Griggio T45 Tilting Spindle ... £5744

TENONERS

Multico TM/3 ... £1399
Multico TM/1 ... £1579
*Sedgwick TE/3 c/w Tooling ... £1560
*Sedgwick TE/1 c/w Tooling ... £1695
*Wadkin JET/2 ... £4483
*Wadkin JET/3 ... £5549

TOOLING

Spindle Moulder Handbook ... £10.95
Whitehill 100mm Panel raising block ... £83
Whitehill 124mm Panel raising block ... £96
Whitehill Panel raising cutters ... £16
T.C.T. Vari Angle Block ... £189
50 × 12 × 1.5 TCT Tips per 10 ... £18
Tigerhead Block ... £51
Cutters Per Pair ... £12.65
Blanks ... £7.50
Rebate Blocks TCT 244 125 × 50 ... £119
200mm TCT Wobblesaw ... £90
TCT Rebate Block 100 × 50 ... £89
Whitehill Block 4 7/8" × 1 5/16" ... £51
Whitehill Block 4 7/8" × 1 1/4" ... £78
Phone for details of other tooling.
Full range of Whitehill in stock.

PANEL RAISING CUTTERS

Profile A: £172 HSS

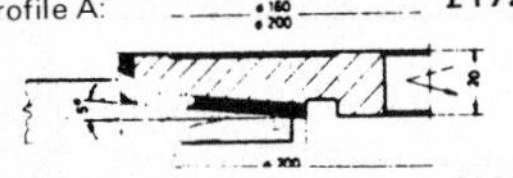

Profile B: £189 HSS

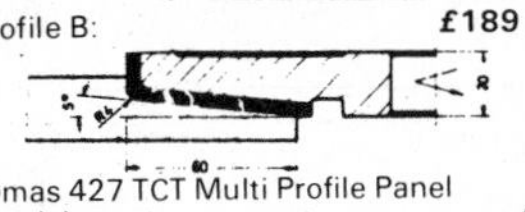

Omas 427 TCT Multi Profile Panel raising set ... £295
Omas 426 TCT Multi-Profile Coffering Set ... £359

BOOKS

£1.50 P&P
The Spindle Moulder Handbook ... £10.95
Techniques of Routing ... £7.95
DeWalt Handbook ... £7.20
Cabinet Making — Alan Peters ... £17.50
Manual of Wood Veneering ... £15.95

LATHES

Coronet No. 1 2ft. ... £269
Coronet No. 1 3ft. ... £289
Coronet No. 1 4ft. ... £319
Coronet Elf ... £379
Coronet Major ... £590
Tyme Cub 30" ... £299
Tyme Cub 39" ... £309
Tyme Avon 36" ... £409
Tyme Avon 48" ... £419
Killinger KM5000S, KM1400 MM BTC P.O.A.
Killinger KM5000SM with motorised feed ... P.O.A.
Plus Fittings, Wire Wool, Combination Chucks
Ask about our low cost finance packages.

TURNING CENTRES

ADD £1.50 P&P	1M	2M
4 Prong drive ctr. 1" dia.	£8.94	£9.00
4 Prong drive ctr. 3/8" dia.	£8.94	£9.00
2 Prong drive ctr. 3/4" dia.	£8.19	£8.47
2 Prong drive ctr. 3/8" dia.	£7.44	£7.67
Jacobs Drill chuck 1/2" dia.	£20.00	£20.00
Jacobs Drill Chuck 3/4" dia.	£36.00	£37.00
Sorby Precision Combination Chuck £56.00		
	1M	2M
Revolving ctr.	£18.00	£18.00
Lace Bobbin Drive	£7.76	£7.99
Deluxe Rev. ctr.	£28.41	£29.56
Cup Centre	£4.03	£5.06

DUST EXTRACTORS

DeWalt DW60 ... £273
Sumaco ... £199
P+J Mite ... £230
P+J Mini 635 cfm ... £345
P+J Junior 900 cfm ... £473
P+J Super Junior 1200 cfm ... £506
P+J One 2100 cfm ... £647
P+J Two 2600 cfm ... £806
Startrite Cyclair 55 ... Phone
Startrite Cyclair 75 ... POA

PLANERS + THICKNESSERS

Ryobi AP10 Portable 10 × 5 ... £399
DeWalt DW1151 10×6 + free DW600 ... £578.00
Scheppach Combi ... £599
Startrite PT260 10 × 7 1PH ... POA
Startrite SD310 12 × 9 1PH ... POA
Sedgwick PT 10 × 7 1PH ... £1098
Sedgwick MB 12 × 9 ... £1776
Multico CPT 310/230 ... £1699
Griggio FS430 16 × 9 ... £3852
Griggio FS530 ... £4772
PF430 2.75mm Table ... £3214
PSA520 20 × 10 Power R+F ... £4249
*Wadkin S400 16" Surfacer ... £3089
*Wadkin T500 20" Thicknesser ... £4146
*Wadkin BTS630 24 × 9 O/U ... £7342

TCT PLANING KNIVES

L × H × W	Machine	each £
150 × 20 × 2.5	Kity	£24
200 × 20 × 2.5	Kity	£32
210 × 20 × 2.5	Lurem	£33
210 × 25 × 2.5	Lurem	£33
210 × 30 × 3	Emco	£43
260 × 18 × 3	Scheppach	£45
260 × 20 × 2.5	Lurem, Kity	£45
260 × 20 × 3	Emco	£45
260 × 25 × 3	DeWalt	£45
262 × 25 × 2.5	Inca	£46
262 × 25 × 3	Inca	£46
312 × 25 × 3	Startrite	£54
12 1/4 × 1 × 1/8	Sedgwick	£50
12 1/4 × 1 9/16 × 1/8	Wadkin	£53
12 1/4 × 1 1/4 × 1/8	Cooksley	£53

Other sizes available.

GLUE-JOINT CUTTER

Diameter 120mm T.C.T. 2 teeth.
Profile and counter-profile can be cut with the same cutter.

B mm	Wood Thickness	Height of Profile	TCT each £	HSS each £
50	45	15.4	189	129
60	55	23	POA	159

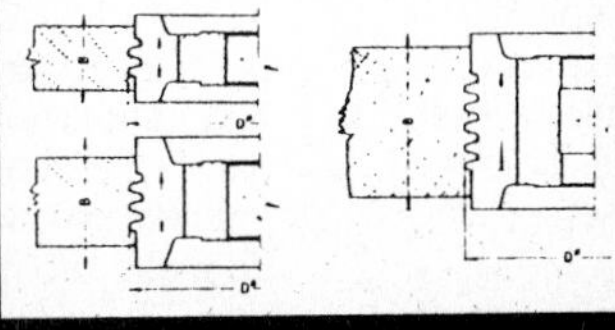

ROUTERS

Elu MOF96 600w 1/4" ... £99
Elu MOF96E 750w 1/4" ... £119
Elu MOF177 1600w 1/4" + 1/2" ... £194
Elu MOF177E 1850w 1/4" × 1/2" ... £219
Elu MOF11/2 1/2" 2000W c/w base £337.33
RYOBI R150 1/4" 730W ... £75.95
Bosch POF52 1/4" 520W ... £55.00
Bosch 1604 Fixed base 1300W ... £163.95

ACCESSORIES

Elu Dovetail Kit TCT cutter ... £74.00
Elu MOF96 Accessory kit ... £74.00
Elu Router Combi Bench ... £123.00
Elu Router Brkt. for DeWalt ... £39.00
Elu 96 Dust extraction kit ... £36.00
Elu MOF96 Height adjuster ... £3.95
Elu Tracking Set ... £35.00
Stair Jig ... £109.00
Elu 12 piece Guide bush set ... £35.00
Elu MOF98, 31, 177 Height adjuster £16.95
Elu 96 177 side fence adjuster ... £6.90

PROFILE + SCRIBER SETS

PR-SC/4 Ogee Profile Scriber Set £114.95
PR-SC/5 Ogee Profile Scriber Set £114.95
PR-SC/5 Ogee Profile Scriber Set £114.95
PR-SC/6 Ogee Profile Scriber Set £114.95
PR-SC/7 Classic Profile Scriber Set £114.95
PR-SC/8 Ovolo Profile Scriber Set £114.95
PR-SC/9 Round Profile Scriber Set £114.95
PR-SC/10 Raised Panel Profile Scriber Set ... £114.95
P&P £1.50

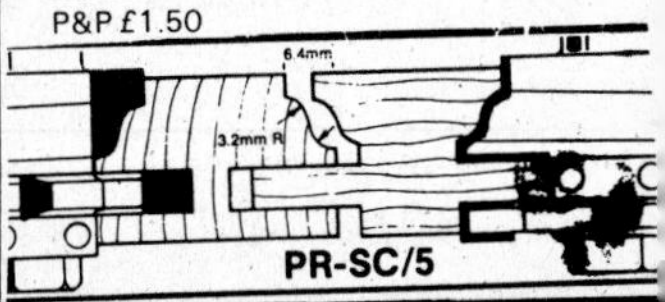

BELT SANDERS

Elu MHB157 3" 600W ... £106.95
Elu MHB175E 3" var. speed ... £119.95
Elu 157 Frame ... £35.00
Elu 157 inversion stand ... £28.00
Elu MHB 90 4" 850W ... £193.95
Elu MHB 90K With frame ... £234.95
Hitachi SB75 3" 950W ... £116.95
Hitachi SB110T 4" 950W ... £129.00

PLANERS

Elu MFF80 82mm 850W ... £109.95
Elu MFF80K (in kit box) ... £127.95
Elu MFF40 82mm 1000W ... £189.95
Inversion Std. for MFF80 ... £20.95
Inversion Std. for MFF40 ... £29.00

CIRCULAR SAWS

Bosch PKS66 7 7/8 TCT 1200W ... £90.95
Elu MH151 6" 850W TCT ... £90.95
Elu MH65 7" 1200W TCT ... £131.95
Elu MH85 9" 1600W TCT ... £177.95
Elu MH182 8" 1400W TCT ... £148.95
Elu 550 Combi (for MH182) ... £130.00
Elu 555 Snip saw (for 182) ... £179.00
Elu DS140 Biscuit Jointer ... £197.95

KILLINGER UNIVERSAL COPYING LATHE KM5000S

The right machine for economical copy turning in one pass — and for hand turning.

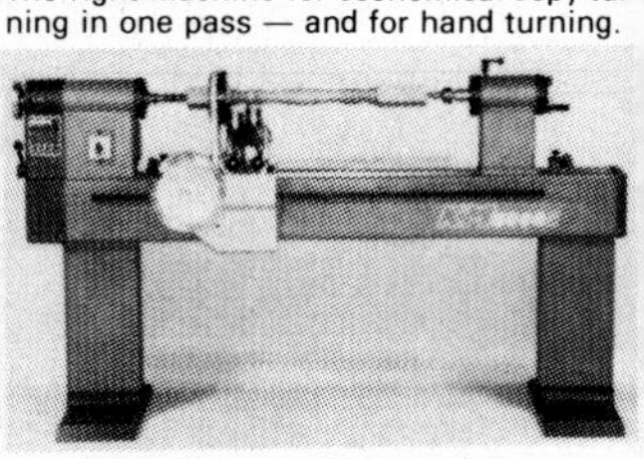

★ *EXCELLENT PERFORMANCE*
★ FIRST-CLASS WORKMANSHIP
★ ELEGANCE OF DESIGN
★ GOOD PRICE

are the specific advantages of KILLINGER lathes. As specialists for turning lathes we have a wide range of products to offer — *ask* for detailed brochures.

Scott & Sargeant

24-26 EAST STREET, HORSHAM, WEST SUSSEX
RH12 1HL (0403) 53761/65386 Telex: 878614

ALL PRICES INCLUDE VAT UNLESS ASTERISKED. PHONE FIRST TO CONFIRM AVAILABILITY. EXPORT ENQUIRIES WELCOMED.

IF YOU DON'T SEE IT - JUST ASK

PHONE TODAY
OFFER LIMITED PERIOD.

THE LAST LATH

Read how Mike Abbott tackled cleaving sweet chestnut for ceiling laths, then watch him in action at the Show

'I've been told you know how to cleave wood,' said a voice on the end of the phone. It belonged to Ian Phelps, a professional woodworker who had been offered an interesting contract. A 16th-century country house in South Wales was being restored, using, as far as possible, the authentic materials and methods. Ian's job was to supply and fix the ceiling laths, the strips of wood to which the plaster was applied. The architect had specified cleft chestnut laths, that is strips split along the grain from sweet chestnut logs. After a few enquiries he'd been given my name to get some advice on what the job would involve.

I suggested he should come along to the workshop where I was running green woodwork courses. It took me about two minutes to explain to him the theory of it.

You need four things:

1: **froe** a blade about 200mm long, either bent to form a ring at one end or welded to a section of tube. Into this ring is fitted a strong wooden handle about 400mm long.

2: **club** a very simple length of wood, thick at one end, tapering down to a handle at the other.

3: **cleaving brake** in its simplest form a large forked branch with its joined end propped about a metre high and its forked end supported by two crossed logs.

4: **log** to be cleft: quickly grown, straight-grained and without knots.
To make the laths you simply wedge the ▶

▲ **Mike Abbott cleaving older chestnut**
Geoff and Ian with the finished product ▶

log in the cleaving brake, and using the club against the back of the blade, drive the blade of the froe into one end. You then push down on the handle of the froe and the log splits in half down its length. You then split each half in half and so on until you are left with lots of thin strips. Easy!

We then had a go on a chestnut log that I had been using for chair legs. It had been coppice grown, that is grown from the stump of a tree after it had been cut down. Sweet chestnut is purpose grown in this way in south-east England to provide wood to be cleft for chestnut paling fences.

However, my log was a survivor from a plantation that had been felled and replanted with conifers. During its upbringing nobody had explained to it the theory of cleaving. Over the previous month, I had coaxed it into providing 2ft blanks for chair legs but when it came to providing 5ft ceiling laths, it just wasn't keen at all.

Undaunted by the experience and excited by the challenge, we undertook to provide 2000 metres of lath and set aside the second week in April. Ian had two more froes made up and I set about providing the wood. During this same period I had been looking hard for a woodland in which to run my next chair-making course. I had met a very helpful farmer, Brian Maggs, who had 70 acres of mixed woodland. Some of this was 30 year-old sweet chestnut growing on grade one land. Although much older than the usual coppice crop of about 15 years, they were probably the best looking sweet chestnuts west of Winchester. We agreed with Brian to start with these while Hayles and Howe (the firm carrying out the plastering) ordered some coppice wood from Kent.

The Monday arrived and we started on one of Brian's trees. It cleft perfectly into quarters using wedges and would have made excellent fence posts. However, when we started with the froes, it proved more brittle than I had hoped. The knack of successful cleaving lies in applying exactly the right pressure on to the log to direct the line along which it splits. Having spent some time last year with the oak-swill basket-makers in Lancashire, I had seen just how much control one can achieve. They used these methods to turn oak trees into bundles of strips which they then wove into delicate baskets.

We worked at it hard for three days and with the help of a few friends had produced about 800 metres of lath and a lot of kindling wood. We realised we still had room for improvement, when an old farmer came up to us for a chat. 'Oh ah,' he said. 'My uncle used to do that — half a crown a thousand he got.' We hoped for pearls of wisdom to gush forth. 'How did he go about it?' I hopefully asked. 'Never took much notice really,' was the reply from the old man. Cleaving laths from logs for him was no more unusual in his childhood than drilling holes with a power drill is to a child today.

By Thursday the wood arrived from Kent. Although by no means the best coppice wood I'd ever seen, it proved to be much more pliable. By the end of the week we were only 400m short of the initial target. The following week Ian nailed up the fruits of our labour. I made up some chairs and had a week's holiday.

When I came back, Ian had started on another 2000 metres with the help of a talented young turner called Geoff Urens. The woodland was now carpeted with bluebells and the sun shone down on us, a welcome

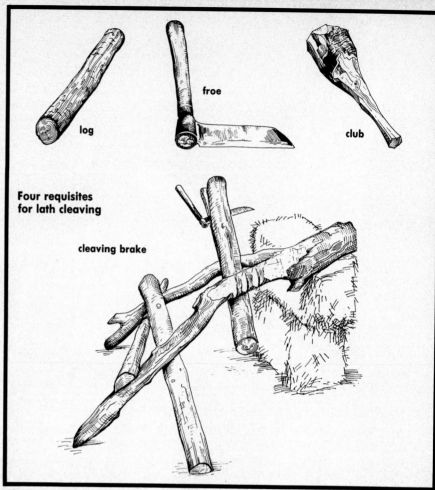

Four requisites for lath cleaving

log froe club

cleaving brake

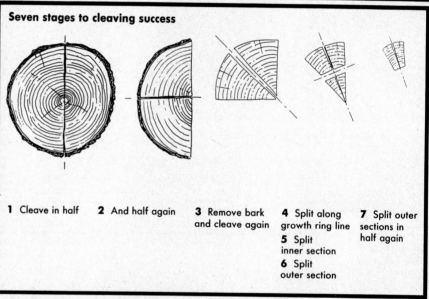

Seven stages to cleaving success

1 Cleave in half **2** And half again **3** Remove bark and cleave again **4** Split along growth ring line **7** Split outer sections in half again

5 Split inner section

6 Split outer section

break from the long cold winter. It was like working in a Walt Disney film set. Each time I looked up, nature was abounding: a dazzling cock pheasant strutting past, a robin eating up bread crumbs, a rabbit watching us through the greenery. The scent of the bluebells wafted past us on the warm breeze and we could hear the first cuckoos discussing foster parents for their future offspring.

Almost of secondary importance was the fact that we seemed to have got the hang of lath-making. Thirty metres an hour may not sound very fast but it is certainly efficient in terms of energy and capital. We were producing up to 50 laths from each log of 150mm diameter with no sawdust, very little waste and using only £20 worth of equipment. Because they are cleft, they are exceptionally strong and their rough finish gives a very

good key to the plaster. Above all, however, it provided a wonderful excuse to spend the first weeks of spring enjoying ourselves working in the fresh air in the woods.

If you want to try your hand, this is what I found to be the best approach. Start with a 150mm diameter log, cleave it in half, and then cleave it in half again. Remove the bark at this stage (it can be cut into strips to tie up the bundles), cleave it in half again, and then split it once along the line of the growth rings. The inner section can be split down the middle, and the outer section split in half and half again.

The resulting laths can be trimmed up with an axe or bill-hook if necessary. This gives (in theory) six laths from each eighth, a total of 48 laths. This must be adapted for smaller or larger logs. ∎

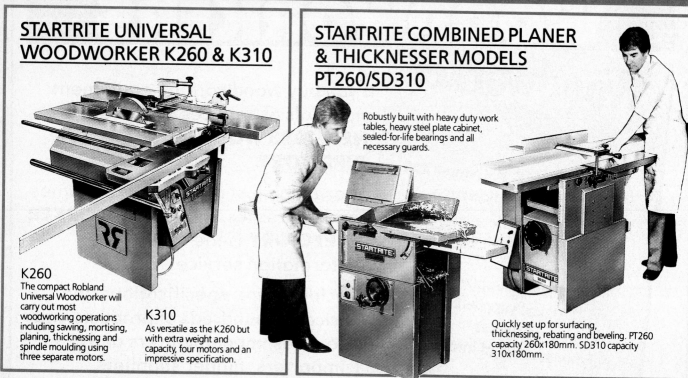

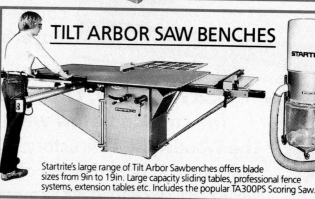
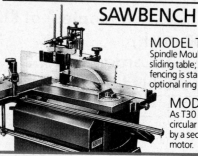

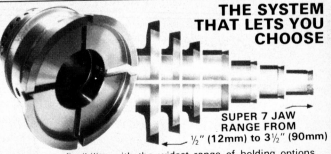

FROM CRAFT TO ART

SEMINAR ON

BRITISH WOODTURNING

LOUGHBOROUGH 1987

THE GREAT TURN-ON

The UK's first woodturning seminar for six years caused a stir before it happened, and now it's over it promises important consequences for the craft — and art? Hugh O'Neill took part

The first 'From Craft to Art' British Seminar on woodturning was an undoubted success. Although not all will have gone as far over the top in their enthusiasm for it as I did, it will only be the most blinkered or arrogant who won't have been affected in some way.

I arrived with interest and went away inspired. I brought with me questions, and took away answers; I came seeking a new direction and went away with an atlas of route maps . . . .

I must admit to some fairly heavy negative pre-conceived expectations; not necessarily about the event itself, but about my fellow delegates. I have come to believe that many woodturners are very introspective about their craft, traditional in their view of design and technique, and, above all, obsessed with seeking such perfection of finish that they take away all the real character of wood. So I thought that a gathering of 170 turners, professional, part-time and hobbyist, would prove to be an orgy of navel-examination in a rarefied atmosphere of self-congratulation; with a few of the less orthodox involved in esoteric discussion trying to make an art out of what is to many just a craft. How wrong I was. ▶

Colour photos Tim Imrie

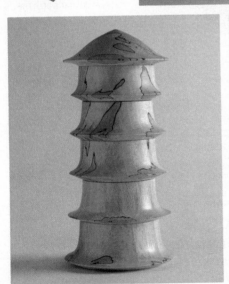

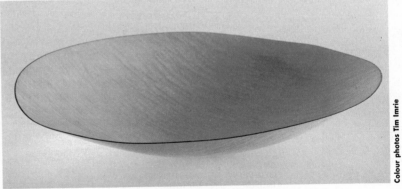

Left: Mike Scott's enormous burr oak commemorative plaque faced the entrance door. This page, clockwise from top: one of David Ellsworth's burr creations, about 6×9in; Liam O'Neill's pure form in spalted beech; wafer-thin bowl in figured sycamore by Anthony Bryant, 22×6in; Guy Martin's distinctive style — sycamore, 21in across; five-tier pagoda box in spalted beech by Ray Key, 6×3in

Perhaps we did represent a biased section of the fraternity. The very title 'From Craft to Art' may have drawn the 170 most inquisitive from the 20,000 or so woodturners there are in the country. Maybe the delegates from the Netherlands, Norway, France, New Zealand, Ireland, Belgium, and others also represented the more forward-thinking from those countries.

Certainly some of the more traditional and bigoted woodturners I know weren't present, but some were; and almost to a man, delegates left feeling 'we have all learnt a lot'; that 'there is much more to woodturning than we ever thought possible'; that 'you never stop learning'; and that 'we have a long way to go before we have fully explored all the possibilities of form, technique, design, function, — in fact, practically everything there is about woodturning'. The parting remark of one delegate summed it up. He said: 'I thought that I knew something about woodturning — now I realise how little I really know.'

THE FIRST OF THE PROBLEMS I had anticipated didn't arise. There were no discussions on the differences between, or the meanings of, 'art' and 'craft'. One speaker did make one provocative statement, that 'Craft is functional; art is not' — but even this wasn't taken up. It had been taken for granted by the organisers and many of the delegates that there is indeed an art element within the compass of 'woodturning'. I was sorry, however, that there weren't some organised discussions on how we could break out from the 'it must be functional' mantle that most of our customers place upon us, and that too many of our brethren too readily accept. It's all very well for us to think that woodturning can be an art form, but we still have to convince the art world and our customers in general.

As I think of it, I realise it was at the seminar that I myself wholly accepted the 'art form' idea for the first time. I'm not a traditionalist, at least I didn't think so. I look for different shapes; I make a feature of faults in the wood; I vary the finish as the piece and the particular wood demands; so one will be

Top: Stephen Marchant (cap and glasses) and delegates have an amusing idea for the oval skew; above, only ornamental turners cease to be amazed at ornamental turning. This is a standing cup and cover in ivory, 6½×2½in

near perfect, while another will be rough as old cobblers. Yet I like wood to 'look like wood'. I can't stand wooden objects so smooth and/or glossy that they look like plastic. Stains, varnishes, paints are anathema; and conventional segmented work, as far as I'm concerned, is just a nonentity.

The seminar has changed much of that. It has shown me that there is a place for (almost) anything; and just because I do (or did) not like it, it shouldn't be written off. We

were shown examples which more than challenged every one of my earlier prejudices — I may even try painting some items. Probably the problem has been that so much of the painted and segmented work I have seen in the past was too ordinary, totally without originality, and poorly executed — but that was before I had seen Jim Partridge's.

It was the presentations made by Al LeCoff that really disturbed the delegates' equilibrium. As Ray Key said in his introduction: 'Nobody who sits through one of Al's presentations could go away unchanged.' Al LeCoff is Curator for a number of collections and touring exhibitions in the States of the latest work in turning. He also acts as a go-between linking galleries and craftsmen.

In his first session, his slides took us from early Tudor times when woodturning was mainly concerned with the provision of decorative or functional elements in furniture, through to contemporary pieces where it was hard to conceive how they could have been produced on a lathe. He showed us bowls cut into segments and rejoined into new forms, vessels capped by space cities, lacquered work with a distinct flavour of oriental ceramics, wood sculptures with absolutely no utilitarian function, natural-edged work, thin work, solid work, plain wood, coloured wood, burnt wood, wood with metal and plastic, vases turned then steam-bent into unturnable new forms, miniatures with turned elements and a mind-blowing range beyond.

Once in a while Al's enthusiasm for the way-out caused a mild stirring of the 'here we go — into the "arty" bit' prejudice in me, but the feeling soon evaporated under the onslaught of originality. The visions he presented were of the unlimited potential out there to be explored.

It was however these same presentations that disturbed me in another way, directly connected with the Seminar's two exhibitions of work. One consisted of pieces by the principal speakers and demonstrators, and by invited craftsmen. The other was a display of work by the delegates themselves. Assuming that we were amongst the cream of innovative woodturners, the two exhibitions left much to be desired. I know this statement will cause howls of anguish from those that were present, because the quality was superb — but by and large, and particularly in the delegates' section, the work was very traditional, and, when compared with the American work Al had been showing, uninspired — my own included. But then as Stephen Marchant, one of the English speakers said: 'We are always 20 years behind the Americans.'

THE SEMINAR WAS FIRST conceived by Ray Key and Mick O'Donnell some two years ago when they were flying back from a woodturning convention in the States. Realising that the US and many other countries had federations or association of woodturners, they concluded that this was a contributory factor to the higher esteem in which turning is held by the general public in those countries. They thought we should have an association in this country, and that an international Seminar would be the ideal launching pad.

Gathering a small team of full and part-time turners and other helpers round them, they began to lay plans. One of the problems was, of course, money; until Denco offered to loan machines; Jack Clark of Rolston Timber to supply the wood; and the Crafts ►

Council and Nick Davidson of Craft Supplies and Sorby to underwrite the costs. This, plus the assistance of Loughborough College of Art and Design, meant that the fees could be kept down to a modest £140 to cover everything including accommodation.

Ray was the principal architect of the programme. In an introduction on the Friday night Ray set the scene for Ed Moulthrop (WW/June '86) to entertain with a slide presentation on the 'ABC of Giant Bowl Making.':

'A — you visualise the bowl in the tree'
'B — you get it out of the tree'
'C — you stand back and admire it!' And later: 'Bowls consist of only three things — outsides, insides and rims. Get those right and you've no problems!'

The mind boggled at the thought (and pictures) of Ed mounting (on a 9in - diameter face plate), and working on a tree trunk 4ft long by 3ft diameter. Later, in one of the workshops, he demonstrated, and allowed us to try, two of his 'only three tools'. Many delegates have gone away determined to make a 'lance' — the tool Ed uses for 'outsides and rims', and to talk the local blacksmith into making one of the 'hooks' — the tool used for 'insides' and endgrain work. Ed forged his hook himself from a 1¼in-diameter machine tap. Mounted on a 4ft long handle, it weighs some 60lbs, but cost 'only a little over a dollar'. The third tool looks like a winkle pin and is used for parting off.

The first full day, the Saturday, had been designed very cleverly. It built up successively in layers of excitement, reductions in formality, and increasing levels of participation. There were slide presentations all morning. Stephen Marchant focused on spindle work in 'Centre to Centre'; Jim Partridge set us thinking about breaking away from the round form polished with wax in 'Experiments with Shapes and Surfaces'. Who else would have thought of blue ink-stained talcum powder mixed with wax and rubbed into the grain of blow torch-scorched ash?

We were then hit with David Ellsworth's 'Craft — The Art of Risk'. Ray introduced him as an inspirational speaker, and he was quite right. David talked about the development of his thin-walled work, and showed us many magnificent examples; including one triumph of restoration on a huge sphere where he had inadvertently (distracted by a question from a young nephew) gone through the wall. As he talked we were rewarded with insights into his philosophy; not only of design, but of total living. One of his pieces gave me the sort of

Turners' moments: Jim Partridge (left) reflects on the relation of tool and dynamic timber, Ed Moulthrop (centre) emphasises a point, David Ellsworth finds one

thrill that opera lovers will know from the top 'C' in the aria of *Madame Butterfly*.

David also demonstrated and gave hands-on workshops. He too uses only two types of tool; external work he does with a deep-fluted gouge with the shoulders ground back over a 1½in-long curve. It's the interiors, however, that are his hallmark. An Ellsworth piece beggars description. Imagine a sphere 18in in diameter. The walls are an even ⅛in thick all the way round, top and bottom. The only way in is through a 1/16in diameter aperture. The tools are long — 4ft is the shortest. There is a long handle, then a long steel shaft, and slotted into the head a movable, tiny ¼in scraper. David judges where the tip is by keeping his head erect and dead over the centre line, and then just listening to the sound of the scraping to judge how thin the walls are becoming.

After the Ellsworth slide show we had the Al LeCoff presentation mentioned earlier, and it was still only lunchtime. Most delegates were bemused, and many of us were by then already looking towards a new world — of turning, not the one across the Atlantic.

The afternoon provided an opportunity for the maturing process to start. We thought about, talked about, watched, photographed, sketched, and then thought again about the things we'd seen on slide. We watched Ed tear the inside out of a large bowl mounted on a 4in-diameter endplate with no tailstock support. He was using a lathe Ray Key has had built for himself to Ed's own design.

David Ellsworth went thinner and thinner with a globe. The following day he produced a column 14x8in diameter, hollow, slightly angled, open top and bottom, with walls an even 1/16in thick. Mick O'Donnell (WW/Dec '86), who makes the most exquisite thin-walled bowls ('My favourite wood is the cheapest'), demonstrated his inimitable technique. His deep-fluted gouge is ground in the same way as David Ellsworth's, but he

uses it in a different way. In fact Mick uses all the tools in a different manner, and breaks most of the rules and conventions — and, next day, a thin-walled bowl he was working on!

Stephen Marchant took groups through working spindles big and small and revealed the secret of his superb finish. It's all done by scraping with bits of hacksaw blade. And Jim Partridge (and some of his audience) got his fingers stained with ink and his face covered in charcoal soot.

Sunday had a heavy workshop focus with Ray himself joining the demonstrators. Al LeCoff showed even more breathtaking pictures of work that he has been collecting for a major exhibition that is to tour the world for the next three years.

Just before lunch Ray saw the fulfilment of one of his (and many other woodturners') dreams. By a unanimous vote of the full assembly of delegates, **The The Association of Woodturners of Great Britain** was formed. Ray was appointed the first chairman; there are eight listed aims, but they all come down to one thing — to improve the awareness, image and quality of woodturning in the UK.

THE SEMINAR COULD WELL have marked a turning point (pun intended). It has inspired a number of turners, many in positions of influence, to think more highly of (and, we hope, charge more for) their work. Seeing that the prices commanded by some of the American superstars for a single piece equates directly with a whole year's income for some UK turners gave many of us food for thought. If turners can, at least occasionally, persuade the public that a wooden piece doesn't have to be functional, that there is an intrinsic value in the wood and the design, and that it really can grace an important position in their home, then the lessons can only benefit all of us.

Some delegates dashed home to try the things they had learnt. An awful lot of gouges are going to be re-ground .... Not for me, not yet. I'm going to sit and think a while. It's time to pause and see what the maturing process brings. Maybe it is time to go back to just two tools and a partner; to look again at techniques, finishes and design; to push the boundaries, if not of woodturning, then at least of my own ability, a bit further. ■

● **The Association of Woodturners of Great Britain**: write to The Secretary, 5 Kent Gardens, Eastcote, Ruislip, Middlesex HA4 8RX.

UNIVERSAL WOODWORKING CENTRE
AT CREATIVE WOODCRAFTS LIMITED
KITY UNIVERSALS — AT SPECIAL PRICES
Saw Blades, Planer Blades Spindle Blocks, Mortice Bits — all at discounted prices.

NEW from CREATIVE WOODCRAFTS (on Demonstration at The WOODWORKER SHOW)

CM 260 NORWOOD UNIVERSAL WOODWORKER

£1,595.00 inc. VAT

Planer/Thicknesser/Morticer/Spindle Moulder/Saw,
Compact Machine with Sliding Table, Cast Beds —
FANTASTIC VALUE FOR MONEY.

C260L/C300L UNIVERSAL WOODWORKER
* ★ 10" & 12" Planer Models.
* ★ 8" Thicknesser.   ★ 30mm Spindle Moulder.
* ★ 10" Circular Saw.   ★ Morticer.
* ★ Sliding Table.
* ★ Cast Machines Beds, Cast Planer & Saw Fences.
* ★ Cast Moulding Guard.
* ★ Machines split in HALF.
* ★ Complete with Tooling.

prices from £1,950.00 inc. VAT

STARTRITE K260 — AT VERY SPECIAL PRICES, COMPLETE WITH TOOLING.

VAMAC — K260 10" & K310 12" UNIVERSAL WOODWORKER

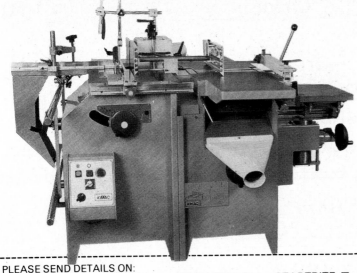

The new fantastic value for money woodworking machines. Compare these features, then compare the prices and the only answer is VAMAC.

COMPARE THESE FEATURES
* ★ FOUR MOTORS
* ★ 1500mm LONG PLANER TABLES FOR STRAIGHTENING TIMBER
* ★ 3 KNIFE PLANER BLOCK FOR BETTER FINISH
* ★ MACHINE SPLITS IN TWO HALVES TO GO THROUGH 2'6" WIDE DOOR
* ★ HANDWHEEL RISE & FALL & TILT ON SAW
* ★ PRICE INCLUDES SLIDING TABLE
* ★ ALL CAST TABLES

NEW FEATURES
* ★ CAST IRON SPINDLE GUARD
* ★ CAST PLANER FENCE
* ★ MULTIPOSITION SAW FENCE

PLEASE SEND DETAILS ON:

VAMAC VAMAC ☐   NORWOOD ☐   STARTRITE ☐
KITY ☐

NAME ....

ADDRESS ....

....

.... POST CODE ....

To: Creative Woodcrafts, The Field, Shipley, Nr. Heanor,
Derbyshire DE7 7JJ. Tel: (0773) 760129.

FREE woodmachining course with every VAMAC purchased.

WANTED
All types of secondhand woodworking machines taken in part exchange.

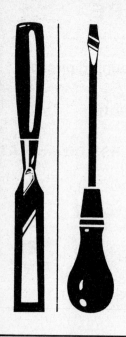

LONDON
WOODWORKER
SHOW

22ND — 25TH OCTOBER 1987
ALEXANDRA PALACE & PARK, WOOD GREEN, LONDON N22 4AY

OPENING TIMES
22nd — 24th 10.00am-6.00pm
25th 10.00am-5.00pm

ADMISSION PRICES
Adults £3.50
Senior Citizens £2.25
Children £1.50

How to get there — free shuttle service.
Travel by British Rail to Alexandra Palace station and then by free shuttle service or W3 bus.
By road: follow the AA sign posts. Free car parking.

Further information available from:
Argus Specialist Exhibitions Ltd., PO Box 35,
Wolsey House, Wolsey Road,
Hemel Hempstead, Herts HP2 4SS
Tel: 0442 41221

The London Woodworker Show is organised by Argus Specialist Exhibitions and sponsored by Woodworker Magazine.

SANDPLATE BARGAIN

£1.50 off!

As you will have discovered from your sizeable, useful free sample of Sandvik Sandplate on this month's cover, it has a genuine claim to be a real abrasive revolution. It's been developed from a new technological process that etches coarse, medium or fine sanding surfaces on to wafer-thin flexible steel sheet. Sandvik do a range of hand tools to stick the sheet to — and, as announced in 'Hands On' this month, we're also running a competition to see what ingenious devices or ways of using Sandplate you can come up with. Sandvik say their product removes material five times faster than sandpaper, and lasts 100 times longer — we've tried it, and we believe it.

The largest of the four tools you can buy is the **Professional**, which normally retails at £4.99. Then there's the rasp-type **Sandfile**, ideal for things like smoothing leading edges and inside angles; it's worth £4.99 retail. So buy them together for **£1.50 off the combined price**, and you've got a substantial saving. Use the coupon — but remember, it expires on 31 December, 1987.

Sandplate Stockists' Register direct line: phone 021-550 3133 for your nearest retailer

KITY UNITED KINGDOM

OLD TIMER

Peter Mantelow's one-handed replica Black Forest wooden clock is a superb test of your accuracy, patience and precision. As a clock, it's even simple to make! We present the project in two parts — and it's on display at the Woodworker Show

With an inbuilt passion for making things out of the ordinary, I usually revel in the challenge of the unknown; I recently put a long-felt desire to make a clock into reality. I hadn't the facilities for making an orthodox clock, so a clock made mostly from wood would be a nice change, I thought. Rather than try to emulate in wood, an 'ordinary' clock, I chose to work on the lines of an early wooden example: A Black Forest Balance Clock (*Fruhe Schwarzwalder Waaguhr*) would seem to be about the simplest clock for a first-timer to make, embodying weight drive and verge escapement. As this type of clock features only one hand, gearing would be at a minimum and accurate timekeeping wouldn't be taken too seriously. Before we go any further, study figs. 1 and 2 in detail and work out the way the whole thing — with named parts — fits together.

The clock described here is loosely based on the very early wooden balance clocks introduced into the Black Forest in the latter half of the 17th century and made, it is said, by farming people with little technical knowledge. The materials they used were all local, with wood, mainly beech, predominating. Metal (wire) was used for such things as pivots for the wheels, the 'leaves' for the lantern pinions, and also parts for the escapement which were subject to most wear.

Principles

In that every clock displays the time, this one does it with one hour hand against a circular dial. Because mechanical power is limited, it's an inherent requirement that maximum gain be derived, through gearing, for the longest possible time between attention. To achieve this in our weight-driven clock, the grooved pulley over which the drive rope passes, and from whose arbor the hour hand is driven, is controlled in its rate of revolution by a so-called 'escapement' mechanism. If the drive pulley was unimpeded under the influence of the drive weight, it would go round very rapidly indeed and *tempus* would indeed *fugit*! The escapement device is therefore introduced as a means of slowing down our clock in order to prolong the intervals between windings, and at the same time give the regulation needed for correct time display.

Loosely attached to the

grooved pulley, via a ratchet, is the largest wheel in the movement, the 'great wheel', whose purpose is to transmit, through step-up intermediate gearing, the motion to the escape wheel. It follows that the higher this gearing is, the faster will be the speed of the escape wheel in relation to the great wheel. Less power, therefore, will be placed upon the 'scape wheel, requiring the least effort to control its speed. To wind the clock, all that's necessary is to pull on the drive cord in the reverse direction to the drive to raise the drive weight. The ratchet, or 'click', connecting the grooved pulley to the great wheel will take care of this.

Checking or escapement devices have occupied the attention of clockmakers for centuries but we are only concerned here with what is probably the first of them all: the balance (or foliot) and verge. Our Black Forest clock has an escapement wheel which is checked by an oscillating crossbar which swings in a more or less determined period of time, and with each oscillation releases, or lets 'escape', one tooth of the escape wheel at a time. Regulation of the foliot is by two small

Fig.1

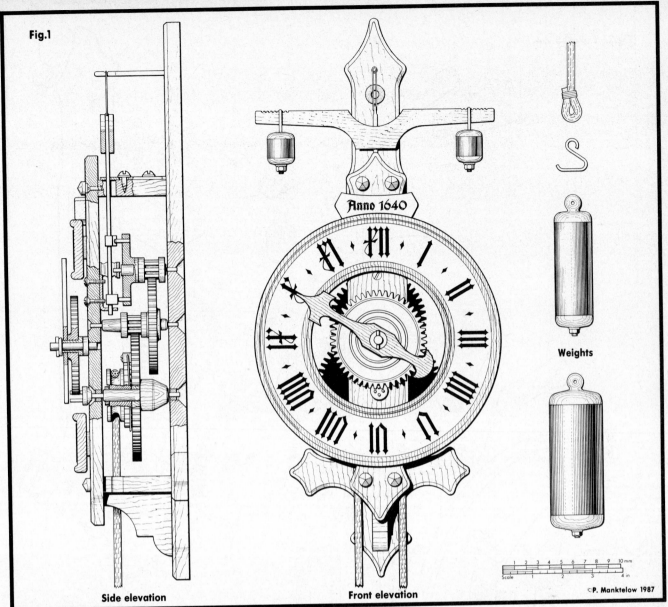

Side elevation

Anno 1640

Weights

Scale

©P. Manktelow 1987

Front elevation

weights suspended from the cross-bar, which can be moved either nearer or further from the centre, causing the foliot to oscillate quicker or slower as required. Whilst the foliot checks the speed of rotation of the great wheel through its inertia, it is at the same time being given a slight push by the pins on the 'scape wheel via the pallets, thus keeping up its momentum. Without this push the foliot would lose its impetus and the clock would stop. From the great wheel arbor a 'take-off' to the hour hand is effected, resulting in a revolution rate of once per 12 hours, no more and no less.

Conception and calculations

In the absence of decent data on the vital ingredients of wooden clocks, namely the 'works', I had to take myself back in time and ruminate on how they would have made clocks in the Black Forest all those years ago.

The heart of any mechanical clock is the gear train, and I knew that until I had devised a means of shaping the teeth of the 'wheels' there would be no point in taking the project further. I

didn't begin to consider shaping the teeth by hand; I could think of better ways of spending my valuable time. Had I owned metal turning facilities and indexing equipment, most of my problems would have taken on a different aspect, but I rate part of my enjoyment in such projects as overcoming obstacles with the minimum of outlay, so I thought I would see if I was equal to the task.

I now came to deciding the shape and size of the teeth of the wheels. I'm familiar with 'engineering' gearing, involute teeth and so forth, but I also knew that in clock work in general cycloidal profiles are used. The shape of my clock wheel teeth was arrived at by copying the wheels I had seen in a photograph of a wooden clock. The only reason, I surmised, why these teeth didn't conform to the traditional cycloidal profile of metal wheels was the need for extra strength at the root. I followed without experimentation, knowing that I would suffer a penalty in the form of engagement friction when the wheels were meshed with lantern pinions with circular 'leaves'. Ideally, meshing gears should roll

on their contacting surfaces and not slide as mine probably would. Then there was the matter of forming the cutting tool for shaping the teeth. With the simple tooth form envisaged this task would be a formality.

The centre line of contact between two mating gears, approximately in the middle of the teeth, is known as the 'pitch point' and circles passing through this point and concentric with each gear are known as their 'pitch circles' (see fig. 3, 'gear terms'). The rotational speeds of the gears are inversely proportional to the diameters of their pitch circles. So, in compounding sets of gears, one has to know the ratio between two sets and also their pitch circles to establish axle (arbor) centres. The distance between each tooth — the pitch — is measured on the pitch circle and is known as the circular pitch. Only gears of the same circular pitch will mesh together.

Although the size of gear teeth will have no bearing on the gear ratio (wheels of eight teeth and 16 teeth will have the same ratio as wheels of 10 and 20 teeth meshing together), tooth size will have to be considered in respect of

strength and available space. In my case it was also one of manufacture, for I had to choose a tooth size (pitch) that I could successfully cut with primitive equipment. I considered that eight 'leaves' was about the minimum that could be expected from an efficient lantern pinion as a driven element, so I drew one up to the minimum size I thought I could make with my limited range of tools. The circular pitch — distance between on the pitch circle diameter — came out at around 0.2in, and so this is how I settled my tooth pitch. The great wheel, attached to the rope pulley, I settled to revolve once every hour and a gearing of 1:12 from the arbor would give the hour hand the necessary 'revs'. The pinion on the great wheel arbor of most Black Forest clocks of the period had four teeth, or pins, and so the number of teeth on the hour hand was decided; needing 48 teeth for the required ratio of 1:12. That took care of the 'motion work'.

The method I used to arrive at the 'going' train, or movement, was somewhat unscientific, in that I couldn't calculate foliot oscillation as one would for pendulum rates. A pendulum has a natural fre-

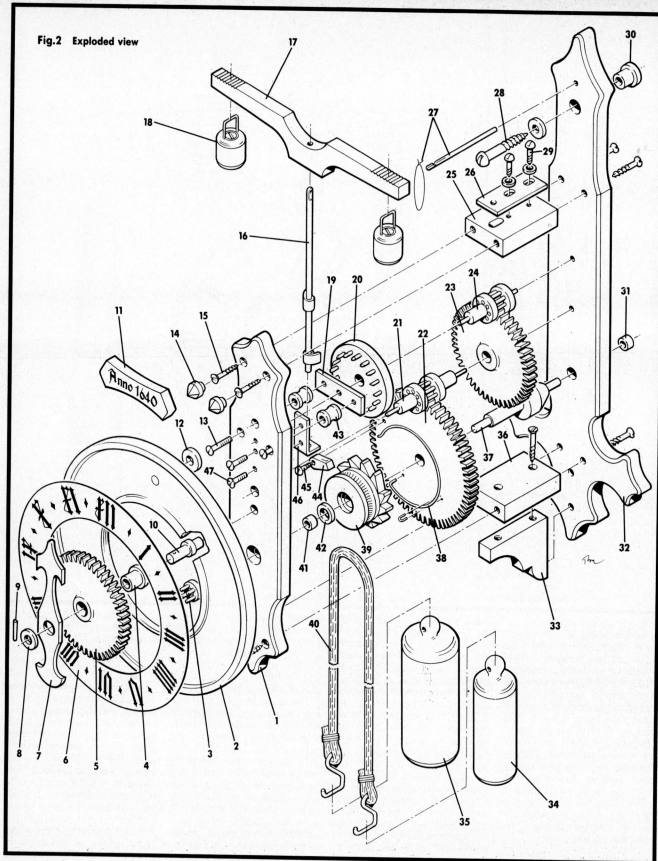

Fig.2 Exploded view

quency, unlike the balance in my clock, which must rely on the amount of energy imparted to it through the pallets. So I thought a nice slow two seconds' swing would look and sound about right and would keep the gearing from great wheel to 'scape wheel within bounds of two sets of gear ratio.

Learning that the wheel of a verge escapement must have an odd number of teeth for the mechanism to function, I set a figure of 19 teeth, or pins, as the maximum I could expect to fit on my 'scape wheel. Now for some simple, unavoidable sums:

One oscillation of a foliot carrying two pallets on the staff releases one tooth of the 'scape wheel one half pitch; thus we calculate one revolution of the 'scape wheel as passing 38 teeth. Thus 38x2 seconds oscillation = 76 seconds per revolution of the 'scape wheel. The great wheel takes 3600 seconds for one revo-

lution, so $\frac{3600}{76}$ = 47.36 is the ratio for the gearing. I decided on 48:1 as near enough.

As I already had one gear established with 48 teeth I would try to use another of this size to simplify manufacture. So with an eight-tooth pinion mating with a 48-tooth wheel, I had established one of the two ratios as 6:1. If I geared this ratio with one of 8:1 I would end up with my required 48:1 ratio. Thus wheels and pinions in the train are shown as:

$$\frac{\text{Wheels}}{\text{Pinions}} \frac{48 \times 64}{8 \times 8} = 48$$

If we want to be exact we divide 3600 by 48, giving us a figure of 75 seconds per revolution of the 'scape wheel. If we then divide 75 by 38 teeth per revolution of the 'scape wheel we get a figure of 1.97 as the swing rate of the foliot. Near enough to my original concept of two seconds rate.

To arrive at the diameters of the wheels and pinions, or their

Parts list

Item No.	Description	No. off	Remarks	Item No.	Description	No. off	Remarks
1	Front plate	1	Oak	25	Top spacer	1	Oak
2	Dial	1	Pine	26	Staff top bearing	1	Brass
3	1st motion pinion	1	Box, wire	27	Foliot suspension	1	Wire & cord
4	Hand pipe	1	Box	28	Fixing screw	1	5 x 35mm
5	12hr wheel	1	Pear	29	Wood screw	2	3 x 10mm
6	Chapter ring	1	Paper, art	30	Grommet, rubber	1	Optional
7	Hand	1	Wood, painted	31	Bearing rear	1	Brass or nylon
8	Retainer	1	Pear or box	32	Rear plate	1	Oak
9	Taper pin	1	Any hardwood	33	Stay	1	Oak
10	Spigot, 12hr wheel	1	Box	34	Compensating weight	1	
11	Motif	1	Oak	35	Going weight	1	
12	Spacer for dial	2	Pear	36	Bottom spacer	1	Oak
13	Screw csk hd	2	2 x 28mm	37	1st motion arbor	1	Box
14	Screw caps	4	Pear or lime	38	Click spring	1	Piano wire
15	Wood screw csk hd	12	3 x 25mm	39	Drive pulley	1	Box or pear
16	Staff	1	Steel	40	Drive rope	1	4 metres
17	Foliot	1	Oak	41	Bearing front	1	Brass or nylon
18	Foliot weight	2		42	Retainer	1	Pear
19	3rd motion bearing	1	Brass	43	Bearing spacer	2	Box
20	Escape wheel	1	Pear, wire	44	Click	1	Box or oak
21	2nd motion pinion	1	Box, wire	45	Wood screw	1	4 x 10mm
22	Great wheel	1	Lignum or pear	46	Staff lower bearing	1	Brass
23	2nd wheel	1	Lignum or pear	47	Screw csk hd	2	2 x 15mm
24	3rd motion pinion	1	Box, wire				

pitch circle diamater to be correct, was a simple matter of multiplying the number of teeth by 0.2in to arrive at the circumference. The resultant figure was then divided by Pi (3.142). Dividing the pitch circle diameter up into the number of teeth in the wheel gives, in truth, the distance between the teeth measured around the curve (circular pitch). On large diameters this difference is minimal but for my small pinions the difference would be magnified to give unsatisfactory meshing. I therefore slightly increased the pitch circle diameter of the pinions giving, in effect, a more truthful linear, or chordal pitch.

Having thus established the pitch circle diameters of the gears, the wheel and pinion centres could be used as a basis to lay out the side elevation of the clock on paper and establish the distance between the plates.

The tooth pitch, therefore, dictated all other dimensions to a great extent, although I did endeavour to keep the overall size of the clock to the minimum. I could now finish off the drawings with more confidence, secure in the knowledge that so long as I could make all the bits to a reasonable standard, the clock should 'go to time'. I had to ensure first, though, that whatever drive weight I applied, and whatever mass I arrived at for the foliot, this 1.97 seconds beat had to be maintained for the clock to keep correct time. From now on mathematics eluded me and I worked on instinct. Not worrying too much about the foliot mass at this stage, I decided I would build the clock and then, through trial and error apply or subtract weight where needed until I got the clock to time. The drive weight would be decided just by using the minimum weight

that would successfully drive the clock, with the compensating, or tension weight on the rope being the minimum that would prevent rope slip over the drive pulley. Once that had been established, the foliot movement and mass would be adjusted for correct timing of the clock.

Fig. 1 is the general arrangement of the clock whilst fig. 2 is an exploded drawing showing all the parts in order of disassembly. As I was treading an unknown path some adjustments to my original thoughts, were, in fact, carried out on my prototype as and when I hit a snag but it was surprising how few these were. I aimed to keep it as simple as possible using the minimum number of gears which turned out to be 15 hours. Thirty hours' duration is normally considered the minimum for a clock to run on one wind, as this allows daily attention once only. My clock needs attention once in the morning and again at night. If you must have your clock last at least 24 hours on one wind, the simplest way is to double the purchase of the drive rope, thus ensuring that the weight drops at half the rate of my single line. Of course the compensating weight must also be suspended likewise to prevent this contacting the clock prematurely and stopping it.

The tools

My pillar drill has a circular table that can be rotated, and rack-and-pinion table elevation — when I bought it, I had visions of a task coming my way where many holes had to be drilled on a circular pitch from a common centre. Although it wouldn't be accurate to index-table standards, it proved adequate for my clock. Using the drill table, with 'index'

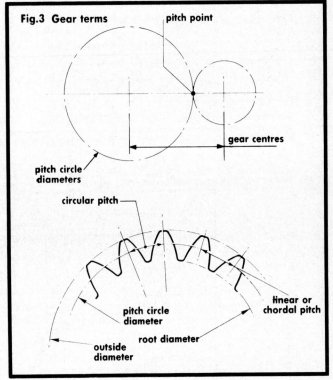

Fig.3 Gear terms — pitch point, gear centres, pitch circle diameters, circular pitch, pitch circle diameter, root diameter, outside diameter, linear or chordal pitch

markings around the periphery, an unlimited number of pitchings could be arranged for drilling on a circular pitch. The circumference of the drill table was used as a basis for the necessary scales made out of drafting film which, with the aid of a stationary pointer, were used as a guide for drilling the index-plate holes for wheel-teeth pitching and escape-wheel pins. You definitely need a lathe or some facility for turning wood.

I figured that the only feasible way to cut teeth without heavy outlay would be to use the fly-cutting technique, where the space between two adjacent teeth is cut by a single fly cutter, revolving at high speed and passing across the wheel disc or

blank. Having no suitable lathe for this task, nor wheel cutting engine, I had to use my pillar drill as the 'prime mover'. Thus the next few weeks were devoted to designing a tool which would enable me to successfully cut the teeth of the wheels of my clock. I made the fly cutter first, using a steel spigot from the scrap box and a piece of hardened silver steel dowel from tool-room leftovers. Mounting this in the drill chuck, I clamped various types of wood 5mm thick in the drill vice as test pieces and passed these across the cutter, cutting a rack of sorts. Along the grain of the wood was no problem but all the woods I tried split to some extent when cutting across the grain, as of course would happen if cutting ▶

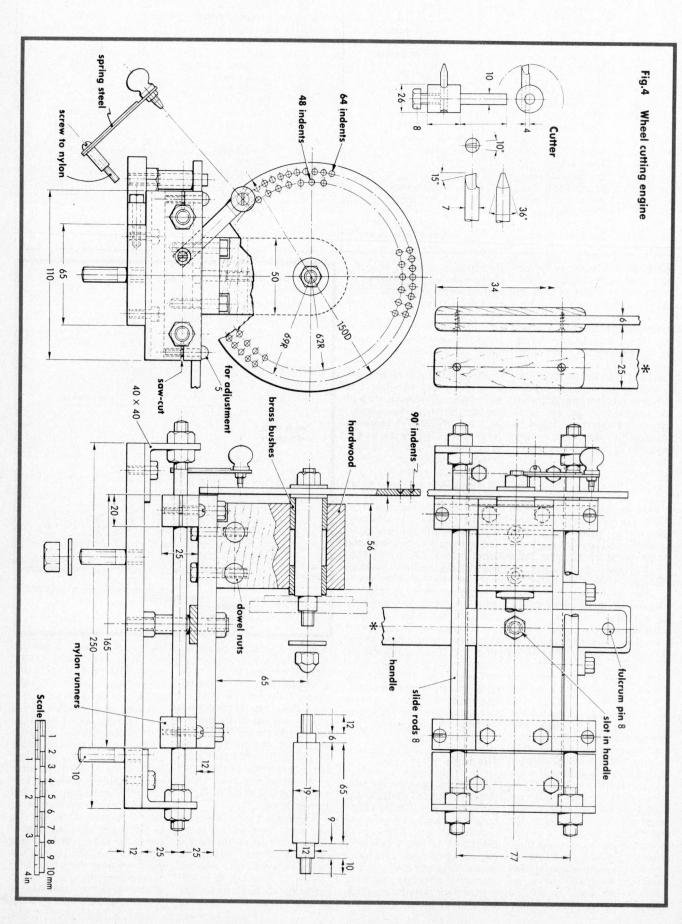

Fig.4   Wheel cutting engine

Cutter

spring steel

screw to nylon

48 indents

64 indents

saw-cut

for adjustment

40 × 40

brass bushes

hardwood

dowel nuts

90° indents

handle

slide rods 8

fulcrum pin 8

slot in handle

nylon runners

Scale

a circular disc of wood for a wheel. I did contemplate cutting two discs together and scrapping the backup one; or I could have constructed each wheel disc out of segments of wood with the grain running from the centre, entailing a lot of work in the process. A last resort if all else failed.

I turned up some blanks to get a more accurate assessment of the problem and cut some teeth around the periphery as accurately as I could just by clamping the disc again in the vice. I was getting better results in boxwood and beech, so I considered that by cutting the teeth on blanks thicker than I needed I could turn them down to the correct dimensions afterwards, hoping to remove traces of chipped teeth.

The wheel-cutting engine

So with somewhat dubious confidence, a start was made on the design of an 'engine' (fig. 4) designed with the knowledge that no metal-turning lathe was available. I'm sure other means of cutting teeth will present themselves to you, especially if you have a good lathe, or better still a Chronos engine. But I'm making do with what I have at the time and that, to me, is part of the fun of designing and building things — to a budget. Or so I keep telling myself!

I made an index plate out of a ⅛in alloy sheet, which I trepanned to a 6in disc using my pillar drill. The sheet was clamped to an arbor which was then chucked in the drill. A cutter was ground to shape from silver steel and this was clamped vertically in the bolted-down drill vice and held stationary at the correct radius. The workpiece was then rotated at the slowest speed of the drill and lowered on to the cutter. A noisy and slightly hairy operation — a lathe is far better. Without removing the article from the drill it was cleared of all burrs and given a nice 'turned' appearance with emery.

Three equidistant holes were drilled in the plate, which was then attached by woodscrews to a thick plywood disc. This assembly was clamped dead centre on the drill table, using a spigot in the drill chuck to check centre whilst slowly rotating the table. The table was then offset by an amount equal to the radius of the first set of 64 index holes for the

great wheel. I drew up an 'index' tape on drafting film, the length of which corresponded to the circumference of the drill table, carefully divided it up into 64 equal divisions, and stuck it to the drill table with double-sided adhesive tape. I set up a pointed from the drill base, and with the drill stop set to correct depth, drilled all the 64 holes. Then I released the drill table and set it over for the next circle of holes. A new index tape with 48 divisions was substituted, and the next set of holes was duly drilled. The whole thing was then polished and the result *looked* professional. If you don't have a pillar drill with a rotating table, you can make your own circular base with two ply discs; if everything is made and centred accurately, it should work well enough.

There are several ways in which to make up the divisional scales for the circular drill table, most of them based on the geometrical principles of triangular proportions. I made mine as follows (fig. 5). You will need a large surface to work on. The line **AB** represents the circumferential distance around the drill table. Line **AX** is drawn at any angle with **AB**. From A, any divisions representing the number of teeth in the wheel are stepped off along the line **AX**. From the last division along **AX** (say 48), join **B**. Parallels to this line are drawn from points along **AX** to cut **AB**. **AB** is the scale for the tape.

Another way, very easy when there is an even number of teeth in our wheels (divisions of 48 and 64, for instance) is as follows: an outline drawing of the tape is prepared, the length of which corresponds to the circumference of the drill table (diameter times 3.142). The scale along this tape is halved and halved again and so on until it gets down to 64 for the 64-division tape, and 16 for the 48-division tape. Dividing the 16s by three to get 48 divisions should then offer no problem. When finally wrapping the tape round the drill table rim, I make sure the two end divisions are lined up perfectly.

Whichever way you choose to draw out these scales, accuracy is of paramount importance as any error here will manifest itself in all further work on the wheels.

The rest of the construction of the 'engine' went straightforwardly enough and entailed, I hope, reasonble engineering practice.

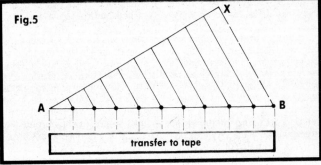

Fig.5

transfer to tape

Making the wheels

Cutting a wheel in mahogany proved very instructive, with chips and teeth flying everywhere. It was painfully obvious that this wasn't the wood to use. A talk with a member of the local bowling club produced a scrap 'wood' in lignum vitae, and it soon became apparent that I must now get down to serious business. Lignum vitae, I can tell you from my experience, can be very instructive indeed — or do I mean destructive! Centring this 'wood' at each end, and with a screw as a driver, I proceeded to partly turn it off into discs on my lathe, not knowing whether to treat the material as wood or metal. Whatever unorthodox method I was using at the time I can't remember, but I do recall getting out of my little workshop quicker than I thought was possible at my age. Next time I'll make sure my centres are drilled deep enough. After this explosive episode I bored the blessed wood right through and mounted it on an arbor, and ended up clamping the

thing in a vice and finishing off the parting with a bow-saw, feeling rather cowardly — as was to be expected.

Turning up the blanks for the wheels proved less hazardous than I had anticipated, considering my first acquaintance with lignum vitae. The discs, having already been bored ½in, were 'spotfaced' on both sides and then mounted, in turn, on an arbor chucked in the headstock. I found the blanks are better turned dead to size and finished both sides and to diameter. The turned fancy work on the front face of the wheels is best done at this stage too, to avoid the mischance of hitting the teeth. The turning of these blanks was done by trial and error, using any method I could devise that took off wood smoothly. A narrow, round-nosed scraping tool I found was the best implement to use, which gave a very polished finish, needing no further treatment except wax polishing. If you have a metal-turning lathe I recommend you use it rather than treat lignum vitae as wood.

▶

The fly cutter mounted in the drill chuck is used to mark tooth outlines

On my first attempt at making the definitive wheels, I cut all the teeth of the first wheel on a slightly oversize blank, hoping to finish off to size on the lathe afterwards and remove any traces of chipping on the outer surface. My first contact with the tool on the teeth removed most of them before I had a chance to get the wheel to size. You can imagine my choice of words; I was faced with the task of turning another blank and cutting another set of teeth.

The biggest challenge of all on this project was cutting the teeth of the three wheels. The outcome of this task, I knew, would determine the future activities of the project but by now I was full of confidence and very impatient to try out my 'engine'. The task of setting this up on the drill table was done with care, making sure that the stationary fly cutter, now chucked in the drill, was dead centre with the wheel arbor before all was clamped securely. I clamped, very tightly, the wheel blank on the engine arbor. I then adjusted the drill table in a sideways movement to bring the stationary cutter up to the blank to a trial position. Then, using a sharp pencil, I drew the outline of the cutter on the blank. By indexing to the next 'tooth' or two, a likewise outline was drawn enabling me to ascertain the correct depth of cut and final tooth form on the blank. This may seem a bit of a hit-and-miss affair but I found this approach worked quite well and allowed me to 'view' the teeth profile before committing myself to the actual cutting. Allowing plenty of time and trouble over this stage of the work pays dividends, of course.

The next step was to ensure that the travel, or stroke, of the blank passed the cutter with adequate clearance all round, otherwise I would have cut metal instead of wood. When I was satisfied that the cutter would effect a pass over the entire width of the wheel blank to form a parallel cut I clamped everything down really tight and was ready to go. I brought the stroke handle towards me to the stop making sure that the cutter (revolved by hand) missed the blank before cutting began. I set the drill speed to 3000rpm and switched on. Checking that I had the index pin in the appropriate range of holes in the index plate, I started cutting. The feed rate had to be very slow to avoid chipping the back side of the blank and the index pin checked to make sure it was truly home before commencing each cut. I had to ensure too that I fully completed each stroke to the stops to avoid the cutter hitting the blank whilst I turned the index plate for the next cut. Watching the chips fly and the teeth being miraculously formed is worth all the hard work and trepidation, believe me. That there is plenty of apprehension in the process of cutting the text I won't deny, for I've had the experience of getting to the 63rd tooth only to 'lose' the last one. If you lose a tooth whilst cutting your wheels and you can find it amongst the pile of shavings, glue it back on with epoxy resin! If the wood is sound you should have no trouble providing the tool is really sharp. If it's any consolation, I admit I used up all the spare blanks that I turned before arriving with a perfect set of wheels. Old bowling woods are notorious for having shakes in them and this is where any trouble is likely to occur when forming teeth.

Should you prefer to make your wheels in other woods I will explain my experience next month where events brought a change of preference in this area. There is nothing wrong in using lignum vitae if the wood is sound, and it's probably the most forgiving material to use because of its freedom from grain bias. Its self-lubricating properties also make it kind to cutting tools.

Making 'gear wheels' in wood is a fascinating, exacting business demanding probably as much accurate work than you are ever likely to contemplate. But equipped with the necessary tools and a fair amount of patience, good results can be achieved with surprising ease. What's more, the whole business can be one of experimentation if you are that way inclined, for methods, materials and means are not set by the established criteria that one associates with the making of metal gears. Even after making an acceptable set of wheels and pinions for my clock I continued to seek better methods, or more attractive results upon which to base my next project. ■

Wheels in motion; a gear wheel gets its teeth

Next month: Concluding Peter's clock, with more wooden parts, assembly, and alternative teething methods.

Make spare blanks so you can start again if you have to!

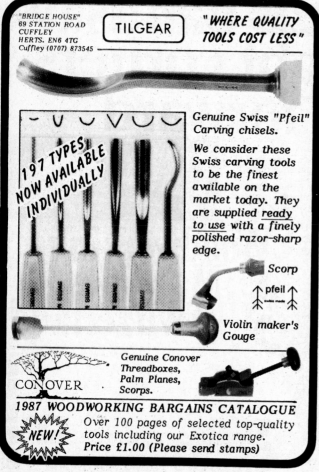

Guild of WOODWORKERS

A chest of five drawers in American cherry, along with a matching wardrobe, was a recent commission for new Guild member Alaric Miller, of Whitmore, Newcastle, Staffs.

Last month's Guild page featured more work by newly joined Guild members: a chair and plant stand by Mr V. Hart of Lytchett Matravers, Dorset, and a Montgomery-style Welsh dresser by Mr E. Elkington of Stoke Lacy, Herefordshire

The Guild was set up by WOODWORKER to create a meeting ground for all those involved in working wood — professional, amateur, and enthusiastic beginner.

For details, please send an sae to the Guild of Woodworkers, 9 Hall Road, Maylands Wood Est, Hemel Hempstead, Herts HP2 7BH, (0442) 41221.

Guild courses

Only Guild members are eligible to go on these courses. Use the booking form, enclosing cheque for the full cost. If you cancel less than four weeks before the course date, you will forfeit 50% of the cost, unless there are exceptional circumstances.

Guild network

The network of local Guild representatives continues to grow. Regular meetings, workshops, demonstrations, visits and seminars are all possible if you get involved locally.

So drop your local representative a line, explain what you're interested in, how you can contribute (meeting place, equipment, organisation energy) and any suggestions for developing your local group. The more people who get involved, the more everyone benefits.

Our network covers much of Britain; if there's no local rep in your area, why not volunteer to take on the role yourself: write to John Hemsley, Guild Administrator, 9 Hall Rd, Maylands Wood Est, Hemel Hempstead, Herts HP2 7BH.

Avon: I. Macdonald, 7 Pendock Rd, Winterborne, North Avon BS17 1EF
Bedfordshire: John Greenwell, 1 Plumtree Lane, Leighton Buzzard
Buckinghamshire: Jeff Trowe, Groveleigh, Langley Park Rd, Iver, Bucks SL0 0JG
Cheshire: Ian Hosker, 1 Spring Ave, Little Sutton, South Wirral L66 3SH; and G. M. Findlow, 12 Linnet Grove, Macclesfield, Cheshire
Cornwall: Mr Stoddern, 16 Woods Browning Est, Bodmin
Devon: Edgar Lawrance, 42 Bolton St, Brixham TQ5 9DH
Essex: Doug Woolgar, 49 Ascot Gdns, Hornchurch RM12 6ST
Hampshire: Robin Maddock, 25 Chessel Ave, Bittern, Southampton S02 4DY
Herefordshire: Paul Smith, Dinmaur, Hope under Dinmore, Leominster HR6 0PP
Hertfordshire: I. E. Waigh, 61 Roundwood Lane, Harpenden, Herts
Kent, East: Roy Sutton, 14 St George's Ave, Herne Bay
Kent, West: Bob Holman, Copley Dene, 8 Kippington Rd, Sevenoaks
London, South-east: M. J. Belcher, 30 Rusholme Grove, SE19 1HY
Merseyside, Central: Alan Hird, 25 Podium Rd, Liverpool L13
Merseyside, North: H. H. Bridge, 2 Ashley Rd, Southport PR9 0RB
Middlesex: Mike Cripps, 41 The Greenway, Ickenham UB10 8LS
Midlands, West: Bill Ferguson, 40 Quinton Lane, Quinton, Birmingham
Norfolk: Steven Hurrell, 25 Baxter Rd, Hingham, NR9 4HY
Northamptonshire: A. J. A. Jennings, 55 High St, Braunston, Daventry
Nottinghamshire: B. Hamer, West Bridgeford (Nottingham 815046).
Suffolk: S. Lloyd Jones, Varne, New St, Stradbroke, Eye
Surrey, North: George Netley, 19 Manor Way, Purley
Surrey, West: Morrison Thomas, 3 Oak Tree Close, Knap Hill, Woking GU21 2SA
Sussex, East: P. D. Wetherill, Glasfryn, Colebrook Rd, Southwick, Brighton BN4 4AL; and C. J. Allen, 3 Oakhurst Close, Hastings TN34 2SE
Sussex, West: Clive Green, The Lychgate, 20 Broadmark Lane, Rustington BN16 2HJ
Wilshire: David Ellis, Restorations Unlimited, Pinkney Park, Malmesbury
Yorkshire, South: Ken Davies, 27 Ennis Cres, Intake, Doncaster DN2 5LL; and Michael Judge, 8 Haden St, Sheffield S6 4LB
Yorkshire, West: Neil Rymer, 4 Churchill Grove, Heckmondwike WF16 0BW
Scotland: Peter St D. Boddy, Valdheim, Hatland, Carrutherstown DG1 4JX; and John Lochore, Tulachard, Fountain Rd, Golspie, Sutherland KW10 6TH

The 1988 Woodworker Directory

We are pleased to offer Guild members this unique Directory at a special price of £9.95 – saving £3. Please use the coupon on page 959 stating membership number.

Routing — Roy Sutton

14 November, 10-5, Herne Bay, Kent, £25 + VAT.
Another chance to learn the full potential of this versatile tool. Roy's courses are very popular, so book early. Starting from first principles, he covers housing, grooving, rebating, mortising, and rule joint and template work; he also deals with designing and setting up your own jigs.

French polishing — Ian Hosker

14-15 November, Chester, £50. One of our most popular course subjects, led by Ian, a teacher and a practising professional. It covers preparation of old and new pieces, staining and colouring techniques, grain filling, shellac finishes, fadding, bodying in, spiriting off and giving new life to existing polished surfaces. The fee includes course materials. Ian will make up a polishing kit to take away at £9.50 if you order in advance.

BOOKING FORM

I wish to book for the following course(s)

☐ **Routing** 14 November £25+VAT = £28.75
☐ **French Polishing,** 14-15 November, £50: make cheque payable to Ian Hosker

Please make cheques payable to 'The Guild of Woodworkers/ASP Ltd' unless otherwise stated.

Name . . . .

Address . . . .

. . . .

Guild no . . . .
Send to: The Guild of Woodworkers, 1 Golden Square, London, W1R 3AB. The Guild reserves the right to cancel any course.

AXMINSTER POWER TOOL CENTRE

WOODTURNING LATHES
OUR PRICE INC. VAT

TYME STUDENT 10" swing 30" centres (With accessory voucher £20)	£199
CORONET HOBBY 10" swing 39" centres 1MT ½HP 3 speed	£179
CORONET No.1 12" swing 3 Speed 24" ctrs £259 36" ctrs £279 48" ctrs	£309
CORONET No.1 22" Bowl Rest Assbly £39 48" Bed Extension for existing 24" lathe	£59
ELU DB180 39" centres 15" swing 1½HP motor 3 speed	£299
TYME CUB 30" centres (With accessory voucher £32)	£319
TYME AVON 36" centres (With accessory voucher £44)	£437
MYFORD ML8B 36" centres 9" Rear turning £459 ML8C 42" centres	£499
KITY 663 3 Speed Lathe 1.0M Centres £554 1.5M Centres	£576
KITY 664 Var. Spd. Lathe 1.0M Centres £649 1.5M Centres	£669
MINIMAX Centre lathes T90 £462 T100 £534 T120 £564 Legs	£75
MINIMAX COPIERS for above lathes CT90 £519 CT100 £551 CT120	£599
LUNA SPKA 900 COPIER medium duty copier for all lathes	£256
CORONET CMB600 33" Centres 23" bowl cap £589 Bowl rest	£49.95
HARRISON GRADUATE 30" Centres £1250 42" Centres £1299 Shortbed	£1037

WOODTURNING FITMENTS & ACCESSORIES (State m/c)

Coronet collet chuck sets (state m/c)	£69	Revolving centres 1MT or 2MT	£18
Coronet collet bodies only	£29	0-½" Drill chuck 1MT or 2MT	£15
Collets ⅝", ¾", 1" each	£11	Craft supplies chuck	£56
Expanding Jaws 3", 2", 1" each	£24	Long hole boring kit 5/16"	£32
Spigots ⅝", ¾", 1" each	£13	2½" Woodscrew chuck	£22
Speedaneez polish std/wht	£5	Sorby sizing tool	£9
Coronet planer blades 4½" £20 7"	£23	Carnuba wax turning stick	£1.80
Multistar Duplex Chuck 45mm Jaws	£65	Henry Taylor Master Chuck	£56.95
Multistar Duplex Chuck 60mm Jaws	£66	Henry Taylor 3" Ext. Jaws	£16.50
Multistar Duplex Chuck 75mm Jaws	£68	Henry Taylor 1¼" Ext. Jaws	£13.50
Screwchuck Set (for above)	£22	Henry Taylor Wood Jaw Plates	£4.60
Faceplate Ring 60mm	£7	Henry Taylor Pin Chuck	£4.60
Pinchucks (State size)	£8	Janik Pyrographer	£48.00

CORONET SPARES

Drive Belts (State M/C Type)	£3.90
Bronze Bearing Major £18 Elf	£18
Bronze Bearing Consort £23 Minor	£23
Ball Race Bearing Major £12 Others	£9.60
Main Spindle Consort/Minor	£44
Main Spindle Major c/w ⅞" or ¾"	£59
Major Poly-Vee Conversion Kit	£98.00
¾HP Motor for CMB500 (speeds 500-2000)	£92.00
Locking Rings (Major or Elf)	£6.50
Drive Centres 4 Prong ¾"	£7.00
Lace Bobbin Drives 1MT or 2MT	£7.00

HENRY TAYLOR HSS CHISELS

GOUGES		PARTING TOOLS	
HS1 Superflute	£24	HS2 Fluted	£14
HS3 ¾" D/Fte	£13	HS11 ¼" Std.	£5
HS4 1½" D/Fte	£24	HS12 ⅜" Std.	£7
HS5 ½" Spindle	£6	HS13 ¾" × ½"	£9
HS6 ⅜" Spindle	£7	HS33 Diamond	£13
HS7 ½" Spindle	£11	HS2 ½" × ⅛"	£6
CHISELS		**SCRAPERS**	
HS8 ½" Skew	£7	HS26 ½" Rnd	£7
HS21 ¾" Skew	£8	HS38 ¾" Rnd	£8
HS22 1" Skew	£9	HS27 1" Rnd	£9
HS9 1¼" Skew	£14	HS28 ½" Sq.	£7
HS23 ½" Squre	£7	HS29 ¾" Sq.	£8
HS24 ¾" Sqre	£8	HS30 1" Sq.	£9
HS25 1" Sqre	£9	HS15 HD Round	£19
HS10 1¼" Sqre	£14	HS16 HD Domed	£19

CORONET HSS CHISELS

GOUGES		CHISELS	
600 ½" Bowl	£22	420 1" Square	£11
100 ¾" Roughing	£15	430 1¼" Square	£15
120 ¼" Roughing	£21	**PARTING TOOLS**	
200 ½" Spindle	£6	500 ⅛" Parting	£9
210 ⅜" Spindle	£7	520 ¾" Parting &	
220 ½" Spindle	£11	Beading	£8
CHISELS		**SCRAPERS**	
300 ½" Skew	£8	700 ½" Domed	£8
310 ¾" Skew	£9	701 ¾" Domed	£9
320 1" Skew	£11	702 1" Domed	£10
330 1¼" Skew	£15	800 HD Straight	£21
400 ½" Square	£8	810 Round	£21
410 ¾" Square	£9	840 Skew	£21

WOODTURNERS "AT LAST PERFECTION"

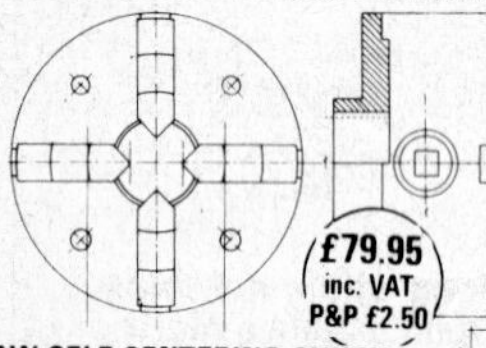

£79.95 inc. VAT P&P £2.50

4 JAW SELF CENTERING CHUCK
AVAILABLE IN THREAD SIZES FOR MOST LATHES.
SPECIFICATION: GRIPPING CAPACITY ⅛"-4" DIAMETER 4" WEIGHT 2KG. SUPPLIED READY THREADED (LH OR RH) WITH TWO SETS OF PRECISION JAWS (INTERNAL & EXTERNAL).

5" 4 Jaw S/C	£99.95
4" 3 Jaw S/C	£69.95

BANDSAWS (Send for Free Bandsaw Blade List)

BURGESS BK111+ 45° 3" cut jigsaw fretsaw	(inc. P&P) £115
7" Sanding attachment for Burgess £23.50 Mitre fence £8.50 Rip fence	£7.50
DeWALT DW100 45° tilt 4" cut c/w sanding table	(P&P £2.50) £158
DeWALT 6" cut 14" throat 45° DW3401 £289 DW3501	£279
MINIMAX P32 45° tilt 6" cut 14" throat cast iron table	£425
KITY 513 8" cut Large table 1HP (+ £57.50 Kity Accessory Voucher)	£427
MINIMAX S45 45° tilt 10" cut 17" throat	£676
STARTRITE 301B 45° Tilt 6" cut Bench Mtg.	£329
STARTRITE 301 6" Floor Standing 4½" throat & rip fence	£419
STARTRITE 351 45° tilt 8" cut c/w rip & mitre fence floor standing	£519
STARTRITE 352 45° tilt 10" cut c/w rip & mitre fence floor standing	£739
STARTRITE 502 14" cut 20" throat 1PH £1259 3PH	£1170
METAL BLADE GUIDES for DeWalt DW100, 1310, 3401, 3501, Luna & Minimax	£5.20

RADIAL SAWS

EUMENIA 9" blade 1¾HP 15" C/cut	£339 24" C/cut £399
EUMENIA Stand £112 Router Bracket £76 Wobble Washers	£14.50
DeWALT 1201 Portable 10" TCT Folding Radial Saw 1½ HP	£314
DeWALT DW1251 10" TCT blade 1½ HP 16" C/cut	£448 Stand £25
DeWALT DW1501 10" TCT blade 1½ HP 18" C/cut	£517
DeWALT DW1751 10" TCT blade 1½ HP 24" C/cut	£596
DeWALT DW8001 12" TCT blade 2HP 18" C/cut	£639
DeWALT DW8101 12" TCT blade 2HP 24" C/cut floor standing	£736
DeWALT DW1600S 14" TCT blade 24" C/cut 1PH £993 3PH	£956

DeWALT Radial Saw Handbook £6.00 inc. P&P

PORTABLE AND WORKSHOP SAWBENCHES

MAKITA 2708 8" Portable tilt arbor bench saw	£229
ELEKTRA 12" Sawbench floor standing TCT blade 3HP	£189
SCHEPPACH TKU 12" Sawbench floor standing TCT blade 3HP	£229
Elektra & Scheppach Sliding Table £90 Panel Cutting Extension	£75
ELU TGS Sawbench/Mitre Saws c/w TCT blade TGS 172 £496 TGS 171	£399
KITY 618 10" tilt arbor sawbench (+ £57.50 Kity Accessory Voucher)	£591
MULTICO TS1 3 1/4 Tilt Arbor Saw £1339 Sliding Table 48" cap.	£336
WADKIN AGS250/300 3HP 1PH £1299 Sliding Table 35" cap.	£496
STARTRITE Scoring Saw 1PH £1476 Sliding table 48" cap.	£352
LUNA L28 1.3HP 1PH £950 Sliding table 24" cap.	£170
SEDGWICK LK 16" Saw Bench 3PH £899 1PH £1143 Sliding Table	£279

ROLLER SUPPORT STANDS (P&P £3.00)

LUNA 10" support roller adjustable height sturdy construction	£29.95
LUNA 16" combined roller support adjustable height	£42.00

PREMIUM QUALITY INDUSTRIAL SAWBLADES
THE BEST IN QUALITY T.C.T. SAWBLADES LEITZ & SPEAR & JACKSON

BLADE DIAMETER	6"				7"-7¼"				8"					9"-9¼"			
No. OF TEETH	16	24	36	48	18	30	42	56	20	36	48	64	24	40	54	72
SPEARTIP	£16	£17	£20	£26	£18	£20	£23	£26	£20	£23	£24	£26	£23	£24	£29	£36
LEITZ	—	—	—	—	—	£37	£43	£49	—	£41	£51	—	—	—	—	—

BLADE DIAMETER	10"				12"				14"				16"			
No. OF TEETH	24	40	60	80	32	48	72	96	36	60	84	108	28	36	60	96
SPEARTIP	£23	£26	£35	£38	£28	£36	£42	£48	£34	£42	£50	£57	£39	£44	£54	£63
LEITZ	£39	£43	£61	£74	£42	£52	£67	£81	£54	£62	£70	£81	£54	£59	£70	£92

PLEASE STATE BORE SIZE WHEN ORDERING

MORTICING MACHINES
OUR PRICE INC. VAT

SMITHS BCM 75 bench morticer c/w lateral table ¾" cap.	£422
SMITHS CM75 floor standing morticer dual table movement ¾" cap.	£528
MULTICO HM bench mortiser ⅝" capacity precision morticer	£356
MULTICO HMT bench mortiser dual table movement	£499
MULTICO M floor standing 1" capacity dual table movement 1PH	£625
WADKIN EDA-2 floor standing 1" capacity dual table	£626
RIDGWAY MORTICER 1" cap. 1HP Full Table Movements	£540
RYOBI portable chain morticer £365 Portable chisel morticer	£395
RIDGEWAY mortice/drill stand (requires ½" power drill)	£165
SEDGWICK 571 Floor standing 1½HP 1" Cap	£599

MORTICE CHISELS & BITS

JAPANESE								
¼" £20 ½" £21 ½" £25 ⅝" £32 ¾" £48 1"								£59
8mm £21 10mm £24 12mm £25 16mm £29 20mm								£44
RIDGWAY ¼" £19 ⅜" £21 ½" £24 ⅝" £35 ¾" £37 1"								£45
6mm £21 8mm £22 10mm £25 12mm £26 16mm £31 20mm								£46
CHISEL BITS ONLY ¼" £6 ⅜" £7 ½" £8 ⅝" £10 ¾" £14 1"								£18
MORTICE CHISEL SHARPENING SETS set 1 (¼"-½") £23 Set 2 (⅜"-¾")								£28

DUST EXTRACTORS

LUNA W178 975m/hr excellent general purpose extractor c/w hose	£324
LUNA NF243 1500m/hr mobile 5" hose ideal for high volume waste	£429
LUNA NF259 2000m/hc heavy duty suitable for up to 3 machines	£599
LUNA 4" × 3m hose £19 5" × 4m hose £38 LUNA dust bags (per 10)	£3
DeWALT DW60 500m/hr 5" hose £265 ELEKTRA 1000m/hr 4" hose	£199
STARTRITE CYCLAIR 55 960m/hr 4" £409 CYCLAIR 75 1800m/hr 6"	£529

MITRE CUTTERS & MITRE SAWS

ELU PS174 8" Portable mitre crosscut saw 10" crosscut	£298
DeWALT DW250 Portable mitre saw 1¼HP 10" Blade	£189
HITACHI CF10A 10" Portable precision mitre saw	£259
ORTEGUILLE MITRE CUTTERS ORC55 £238 ORC80 £299 ORC100	£439
LION MITRE TRIMMER Excellent for clean cuts and mitres	£249
NOBEX 202 PRO Hand Mitre saw £72.95 NOBEX 303 £44 (P&P £2.50)	
NOBEX 202 Replacement Blades 12T, 18T or 24T	£4.30 each

PLANER THICKNESSERS

DeWALT DW1151 10" × 6" 2HP 2 speed power feed	**SPECIAL PRICE**
Stand for DW1150 £30 Slot Morticer £69.95 HSS knives	£18.90
ELECKTRA 10" × 6" floor standing power feed	£490
SCHEPPACH HMO SOLO 10" × 6" 2HP floor standing Adjustable fence	£490
KITY 7136 10" × 6" (+ £50.00 Kity Accessory Voucher)	£585
STARTRITE PT260 10" × 7" floor standing ⅝" rebate capacity	£869
STARTRITE SD310 12" × 9" 3 cutter block 1PH £1399 3PH	£1360
LUNA 3HP Planers 10" × 9" £1428 12" × 9" £1690 16" × 9"	£2399
MULTICO NS300 surfacer 3 cutter block 2HP 1PH £1388 3PH	£1271
MULTICO THA300 12" × 10" thicknesser only 1PH £1399 3PH	£1299
MULTICO CPT 12" × 8" Combined planer/thicknesser ¾" rebate 1PH £1749 3PH	£1649

DRILLING MACHINES

WARCO HOBBY ½" 5 speed rack and pinion table bench mounting	£139
WARCO ⅝" cap 2MT 12 speed bench mounting £179 2F12 floor standing	£222
FOBCO STAR ½" precision drill bench mounting £359 floor standing	£411
STARTRITE SP250 ½" 5 speed bench mounting £379 floor standing	£428
Morticing attachments Warco 2B/2F £24 Fobco £61 Startrite	£110

SPINDLE MOULDERS AND TENNONERS

SCHEPPACH HF33 3HP 30mm 3 speed with adjustable fences	£499
SEDGWICK GW Spindle 30mm	£999
KITY 623 2HP 3 speed C/W sliding table (+ £57.50 Kity Accessory Voucher)	£776
STARTRITE T30 30mm C/W sliding table 1PH 2HP £1089 3PH 3HP	£1049
LUNA L28 30mm 3 speed 3HP Heavy duty 1PH 3HP £999 3PH 3HP	£988
MULTICO TENNONER TM1 240v twin motors (with tooling)	£1579

SPINDLE MOULDER TOOLING (State bore size P&P £1.50)

OMAS "TIGER" BLOCKS 392 £50 BLOCK in wooden case with stone etc.	£59
OMAS cutter profiles £12 CUTTER BLANKS £7 SAW SEGMENTS	£17
KITY PROFILE Door set £99 OMAS ART 176D1 DOOR SET complete	£139
WHITEHILL BLOCKS 4¾" × 15/16" £50 5⅜" × 15/16" £69 Panel Raising Block	£92
LEITZ 488 Cutter block 100mm £59 40mm blanks £3 60mm ea.	£5
TUNGSTEN REBATE BLOCKS 125mm × 50mm £98 6" Wobble saw 3-21mm	£89
T.C.T. GROOVERS 6" 6 WING ¼" £44 5/16" £48 ½" £54 ⅝"	£62
LUNA MINI POWER FEED 2 speeds	£329

SEND FOR FREE SPINDLE TOOLING CATALOGUE.

COMBINATION MACHINES (Carriage £10.00 UK Mainland)

STARTRITE K260 saw spindle planer etc. FREE TIGER HEAD SET	£2390
STARTRITE TZ30 saw spindle only FREE TIGER HEAD only	£1359
SPECIAL OFFER LUNA W59 240v c/w sliding table	£2399
LUNA MASTER COMBINATIONS 240v W64 £3100 W69	£3899
AEG MAXI COMBINATION 5 function	£1604
STARTRITE K310 12" Planer 12" Saw	£3850

★ ★ ★ ★ ★ ★ KITY COMBINATION MACHINES ★ ★ ★ ★ ★ ★
K5 COMBINATION COMBI STAR CK26 TABLE COMBINATION K704 DIRECT DRIVE AND ACCESSORIES ALL AT SPECIAL PRICES SEND FOR LATEST PRICE LIST.

BORING BITS

CLICO SAW TOOTH & FORSTNER BITS (State type) 6" long ½" shank ⅜" £8.10 ½"	£8.35
⅝" £9.20 ¾" £10.00 ⅞" £10.50 1" £11.55 1⅛" £13.55 1¼"	£16.50
1⅜" £17.20 1½" £18.15 1⅝" £20.90 1¾" £23.75 1⅞" £26.30 2"	£27.80
2¼" £34.95 2½"	£46.35
CLICO PLUG CUTTERS ⅜" £22 ½" £24 ⅝" £28 ¾" £30 1" £36 1⅛"	£40.00
CLICO SAW TOOTH set ½", ¾", 1" £28 ECONOMY 5 piece set ½"-1½" × ¼"	£58
RIDGWAY ADJUSTABLE FORSTNERS WR10/2½"-1¾" £16 WR10/3⅞"-3"	£18
RIDGEWAY ADJUSTABLE FORSTNER (h/duty) WR20/2⅞"-2" £29 WR20/3 1⅜"-3"	£34

ROUTERS

ELU MOF96 ¼" 600W	£98.00	ELU MOF96E ¼" Var. speed	£119.50
ELU MOF31 ¼", ½" 1200W	£152.50	ELU MOF11/2 ½" 2000W c/w base	£337.33
ELU MOF177 ¼", ½" 1600W	£193.50	ELU MOF177E ½" Var. speed	£218.50
HITACHI TR8 ¼" 730W	£79.95	HITACHI TR12 ¼", ½" 1300W	£137.95
RYOBI R150 ¼" 730W	£75.95	RYOBI R500 R500 ¼", ½" 1500W	£124.95
HITACHI FM ¼" 550W	£46.95	BOSCH POF52 ¼" 520W	£52.00
MAKITA 3600B ¼", ½" 1500W	£168.95	MAKITA 3612BR ½" 1600W	£175.95

ROUTER ACCESSORIES

ELU DOVETAIL KIT TCT cutter	£69.95	RYOBI Dovetail jig fits above	£99.95
ELU MOF96 Accessory kit	£69.95	ELU ROUTER COMBI BENCH	£118.00
STAIR JIG (General duty)	£69.00	STAIR JIG (heavy duty)	£160.00
ELU ROUTER BRKT. for DeWalt	£38.00	ELU 12 piece Guide bush set	£35.00
ELU 96 Dust extraction kit	£36.00	ELU MOF98, 31, 177 Height adjuster	£16.95
ELU MOF96 Height adjuster	£3.95	ELU 96 177 side fence adjuster	£5.30
ELU TRACKING SET	£35.00	ELU ROUTING VIDEO	£12.00
TREND STAIR JIG	£112.00		

TREND OVERHEAD ROUTER Bench Mtg. £687.00
TREND OVERHEAD ROUTER Fl. Stdg. £1200.00
ELU 11/2 ROUTER for above stands £181.00
TREND POST FORM JIG £434.00

★ ★ ★ ★ SPECIAL OFFER ★ ★ ★ ★
ROUTER PROFILE SCRIBER SETS ⅜" or ½" Shank only £110.00 inc. P&P
★ ★ ★ ★ ★ ★ ★ ★ ★ ★ ★ ★ ★

HSS ROUTER BIT SETS (inc. P&P)
SAVE 30% ON HSS ROUTER BIT SETS AND GET A FREE ROUTER BIT CASE.

13 PIECE SET	£59.95
8 PIECE SET	£37.95
5 PIECE SET	£21.95
ROUTER BIT CUTTER BOX ONLY	£4

ROUTER CUTTERS
20-25% OFF LEADING BRANDS EXCELLENT STOCKS OF HSS & TCT ROUTER CUTTERS OVER 500 PROFILES IN STOCK. SEND NOW FOR FREE CUTTER CHART:- TECHNIQUES OF ROUTING £7.95 (inc. P&P)

IMMEDIATE DESPATCH ON CREDIT CARD PHONED ORDERS — CREDIT TERMS AVAILABLE OVER £120

0297 33656 CHARD STREET AXMINSTER DEVON EX13 5DZ POST OFFICE C.O.D. 34836

SIMPLY TRADITIONAL

Drop-leaf table

Two contrasting folding tables typical of country furniture in the Netherlands, described by Rene Coolen

Dating from the Middle Ages, the Gelderland folding table — named after a province of the Netherlands — is the oldest of the country style folding tables found in Holland. You'll see that the leaf of the oak table is fastened with a loose wooden peg which fits in the heavy wooden block to which the legs are fastened.

The drop-leaf table also comes from the Province of Gelderland, probably dating from the 18th century. As was usual with 'country' furniture, it was made completely from pine, and finished with paint to extend its life; this particular example was in plain red, with the leaves plain green, with a three inch band of red around the edges. In this design, two of the four legs are split down the middle, an ingenious approach to gate-legged construction. ■

Front elevation and vertical section at C

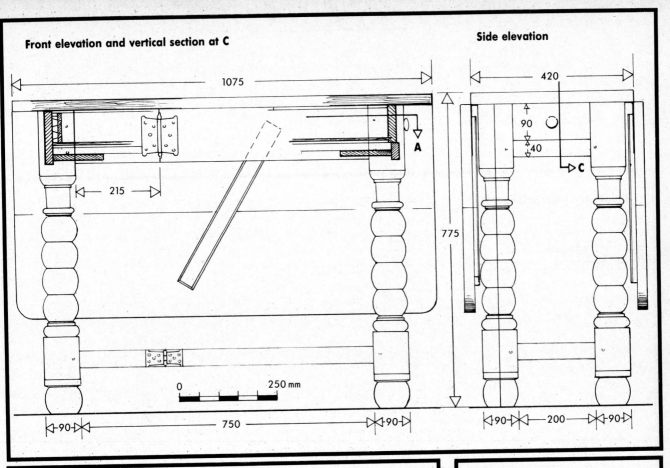

1075

215

775

0   250 mm

90   750   90

A

Side elevation

420

90

40

C

90   200   90

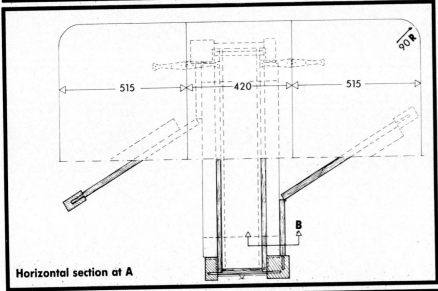

Horizontal section at A

90 R

515   420   515

B

Vertical section at B, enlarged

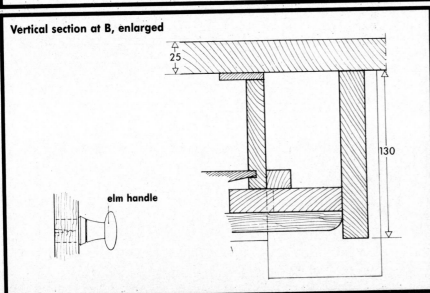

25

elm handle

130

Leg

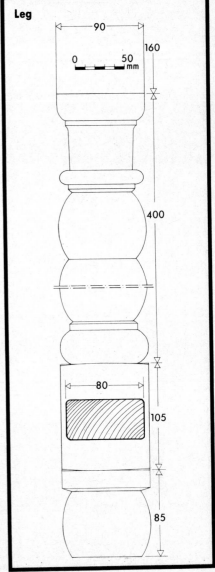

90

0   50   mm

160

400

80

105

85

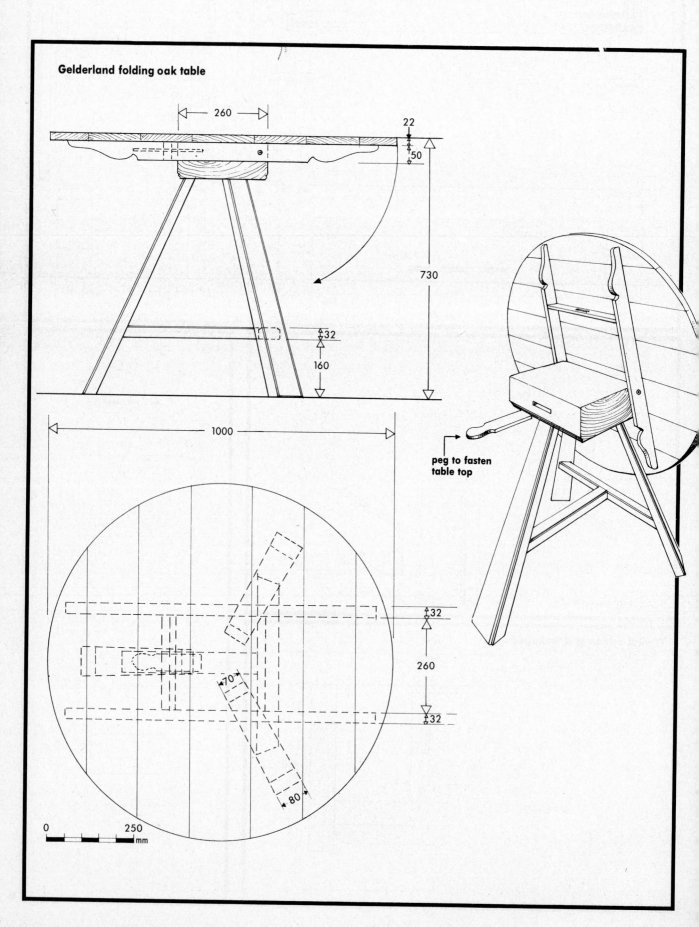

Gelderland folding oak table

260

22

50

730

32

160

1000

32

260

70

32

80

peg to fasten
table top

0   250
mm

WICKER'S WORLD

Osiery is the ancient craft of willow basket-making — and this century it almost breathed its last. Master craftsman John Taylor brought it new life and profitability with his Yorkshire business, as Leonard Markham discovered

Yorkshire's Wharfe Valley has been a home of traditional osiery since Viking times. One of its last surviving craftsmen is John Taylor of Ulleskelf, near York, whose basket-making ancestry goes back to the 16th century. But in the early 1950s bankruptcy loomed when industrial and agricultural demand for wicker products ceased. John was the only basket maker in Ulleskelf to survive the change to synthetic wares, by adapting his osiery production for the domestic and commercial display market — and expanding into cane-furniture manufacture.

The frequently flooded scrubland flanking the River Wharfe provides the four best types of willow for osiery, including the varieties Champion Rod and Black Mole, which are principally for basket-making. Blue Bud, a hardier, more resilient variety, is used for woven fencing; the fast-growing Longskin is preferred for hampers and mill-type skeps or baskets.

The willows are grown mainly on owned land which has been in the family for generations, spaced 18in apart in rows: competition for light promotes rapidly-growing straight stems that can reach 15ft in one season. No fertiliser is needed as regular flooding deposits a natural mulch, enriched with waste from the local brewery!

Cutting, with a traditional willow knife, begins in spring, before the sap rises. Stems ▶

▲ **Cutting rods in the spring with a traditional willow knife**

◀ **Myriad uses of willow, for furniture and screens as well as familiar baskets; inset, peeled 'white' and 'buff' willow ready for soaking**

Photos Hugh Mayfield

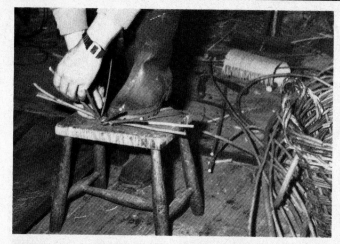

From the base grows the basket; crossed rods held in place with a foot, top left, as weaving starts in a circular pattern. Once the required diameter is reached, left, side rods are inserted, bent upright and held in place with a metal hoop as the sides are woven, above

are cut to within 6-8in of the ground to allow speedy regrowth the following season. Harvesting is usually annual, but some stems intended for more robust work are left for up to three years to thicken. The cut stems are bundled into 'bolts' and transported back to the workshops for sorting into lengths. A tractor with trailer attached is the usual conveyance, but John's cavernous estate car, which he backs into the marshes with alarming dash, is equally effective.

'White willow' is prepared when the stems are still sappy by immediate bark-stripping; this can be postponed until May by standing the bolts upright in wet hedge-bottoms or by frequent manual soaking. 'Buff willow', an attractive cinnamon-coloured alternative, results from boiling stems in hot water for three or four hours in a 10ft steel bath, raised above a brick wood-burning hearth. Boiling dissolves bark pigment, aids easy peeling and colours the stems. Some unskinned 'brown willow' is used just for its rustic appearance.

Before manufacture begins, often months after harvest, stem pliability is restored to all three types of willow by soaking in a water-filled vessel that looks like a horse-trough. White and buff willow are soaked up for up to four hours; the more impervious brown type is steeped for several days.

Baskets and a range of wicker goods are crafted in the ancient upper room of the former family cottage. Tools are traditional and simple: a knife and shears for cutting and trimming rods to length; a flat board and spike to hold and turn the work in place; a flat weave-compacting hammer; a pricking knife which delicately scores the rod to make it pliable; a bodkin, and a measuring stick. John's only concession to comfort is a tiny work stool.

BASE MAKING IS THE FIRST STEP in basketry. The radius of the base is made with sets of rods crossed at right angles and unceremoniously held in place on the stool with a foot. Weaving in a circular pattern, further rods are pulled alternatively over and under the radials — which are pushed apart to form spokes — until the required diameter is reached. The ends are trimmed and the base is pierced at its centre with a bodkin, and pushed on to the spike. The ends of thicker rods, which will form the uprights, are sharpened and rammed, at 1in-1½in spacings, horizontally into the rim. Once all the uprights are in place, each is scored where it enters the rim with the pricking knife, which enables the rods to be bent through 90° without splitting. The rods are bent upwards and held in place with a metal hoop and weaving of the basket sides can start.

Intended use and regional style have an influence on the choice of willow and weave. John uses the techniques of 'randing', 'slewing' and 'whaling'; ancient nefarious-sounding names that still arouse the suspicion of the village bobby. Randing is the simple process of weaving with single rods; slewing describes the use of three or four rods together, whilst whaling is alternate weaving of sets of three thick rods, then three thin rods, often in contrasting types of willow.

Perched on his stool with his legs holding the spiked board, John works quickly, alternately weaving, and tapping down the rods with his flat hammer. When the basket is the right height, John trims the ends and adds thick braided rims and handles. The whole process takes up to two hours, depending on size, and then the baskets are finished with two or three coats of clear varnish.

Basket manufacture is now very much on a small scale compared to pre-plastic days. John's other products — plant holders, screens, picnic hampers and fencing — are all based on basket-making techniques and keep his business viable. Another development crucial to his survival has been the expansion into cane-furniture making. Currently in vogue for the garden and the home, this furniture relies on imported canes (botanically either grasses or palms) from Malaysia and Indonesia. Three types of solid cane are bought in 50kg bundles of varying lengths. Strong Manau and Tahiti varieties are used for furniture whilst the more flexible Kaboo is used for basketry, and when split, as 'lapping' material for joints.

The frameworks for chairs and settees are made by bending the cane to shape in the vice (pre-steaming above the hot bath, or fanning with a hot-air gun or blow-lamp on the beds, is essential for elasticity). The cane loses shape within seconds if it isn't restrained in purpose-made formers, where it stays for 24 hours to assume its permanent shape.

Dousing with cold water speeds the process. The frames are fixed with heavy-duty 3in staples, fired from a compressed-air staple-gun — a rare concession to high-tech. The joints are bound tight with split Kaboo cane which gives added strength and improves the appearance. After varnishing, the furniture is fitted with loose cushions bought from a local manufacturer.

John's commitment to the ancient craft withstood the economic recession in Ulleskelf. Now with the increase in heritage-hungry tourists, particularly from nearby York, and a growing demand for practical wickerwork, he is proving that traditional basket-making can once more be a profitable business. ∎

Woodworker
PLANS SERVICE

NEW £1.25 + 35p P&P

MORRISON ORIGINALS

WOODCARVING PROJECT BOOKLETS

Trevor Rooney first experienced the world of carving in 1974, where at the York Minster he trained as a stone and woodcarver. During this time he was privileged to carve a number of the South Transept Bosses which were sadly destroyed in the recent fire. A lot of his work is still in existence in this magnificent building and will hopefully be admired for many years to come.

THE WREN

A 12 page booklet detailing the carving of this delightful bird of life size.
Plan No. TR1 Price £2.65

*Coming soon –
The Squirrel,
The Kingfisher*

STANDARD LAMP

Interesting modern design standing approx 6ft high. Fully detailed plans
£4.75 Plan MTC 5.

AUDIO CABINET RACK

A must for the woodworker who likes to take pride in his work, build this superb cabinet 1 sheet of explicit instructions and materials.
Price £4.00 MTC3 or in metric **MTC4 Price £4.00.**

NOW AVAILABLE WOODWORKER PLANS HANDBOOK
Hundreds of Plans to choose from

★ Ashby Design - full range illustrated
★ David Bryant - all his latest
★ More designs from Vic Taylor
★ **ORDER YOUR COPY NOW.**

ASHBY DESIGN WORKSHOP — TRADITIONAL FURNITURE FOR HOUSE & GARDEN

TAPA SYSTEM PLANPACKS

18th Century Gateleg Table

The convenience of the traditional gateleg table is admirably suited to the home of today. This design, which is based on an actual antique, features elegant turnings to a superbly designed profile. The original cable was built in brown oak, but any English hardwood or fruitwood would give a most satisfactory result.
ADW 103   Price £4.25

Workshop Accessories

Nineteen various tools & accessories are detailed on this drawing, including a plan for a saw horse. All the tools may be made with ease and economy and they will become valued additions to your workshop equipment.
ADW 109   Price £3.50

Lap or Table Desk

This compact item will be a favourite with all the family for letter writing & homework. The basic design offers good storage for papers, pens etc. Construction may be on a simple screw & glue basis or could incorporate dovetails or comb joints as desired. Build in solid wood or use plywood and veneers.
ADW 115   Price £4.75

Magazine Racks

This plan offers an open magazine rack and an alternative version with a table top. There is scope for decorative variations on both versions and suggestions are shown on the drawing. Construction incorporates simple housing joints.
ADW 116   Price £4.00

TAPA SYSTEM PLAN PACKS

Each Pack comprises:
A1 size Plan	2 Frameworks
3 A3 Plans	4 Chair designs
Full-size profiles	Cutting List
Joint details	Schedules

Featuring a series of modern furniture designs for the home, the TAPA system of plan-packs is a new concept in woodworking projects. Each plan-pack focusses on a specific object and explores many alternatives to the original model. The Dining Chair is the first in the series, featuring ideas based on the simple halving joint prototype.
Plan ADW401   Price £5.75

DAVID BRYANT CRAFT DESIGN PLANS
HOME & LEISURE, TOYS, SPINNING WEAVING

No. 59 SPINDLE WHEEL

An alternative to the Great Wheel No. 47, this non flyer wheel offers a smaller version with a 660mm (26")
diameter hoop rim wheel. This type of wheel was in common usage before the flyer type was invented, and the example here is a measured drawing of an original on display at Quarry Bank Mill, Styal (N.T.) and in daily use. Parts list and instructions.
DB 59   Price £7.13

No. 60 FRENCH SPINNING WHEEL

This design is of an unusual French spinning wheel. The original comes from the Loire valley, and is known to have been used in the last war when clothing was scarce. Wheel diameter 442mm (17⅜"). The triangular base is typical of French style wheels. The flyer has been slightly adapted to suit modern day useage. Parts list, instructions etc.
DB 60   Price £7.13

DRUM CARDER

Sooner or later spinners graduate to a drum carder. This design takes the toil out of hand carding. It uses a positive gear/sprocket drive which also reduces the drag which the belt drive alternative imposes. A little metalwork as well as woodwork involved. One sheet plan.
Plan No. DB54   Price £4.75

SLOPING STYLE SPINNING WHEEL

This design is a replica of an authentic spinning wheel doem olden days, having a 486mm (19 in.) diameter wheel with bent
wood rim. Plan is complete with mother-of-all, distaff, treadle operation etc. A feature of this wheel is its attractive turnings which make it a most decorative piece besides being functional. A design for the enthusiast woodturner. Two sheet plan.
Plan No. DB12   Price £7.13

UPRIGHT SPINNING WHEEL

In this vertical style spinning wheel the mother-of-all arrangement is situated above the main wheel. The latter is 460mm diameter and the rim is of segmented design. Simpler lines than the sloping wheel but nevertheless graceful in appearance and of course functional.
Plan No. DB13   Price £7.13

SPINNING STOOL

A spinning stool specially suited for use with the sloping bed wheel. Four legged arrangement, with richly carved seat and back. A good example of chip carving.
Plan No. DB20   Price £4.25

SPECIALIST WOODWORKING PLANS
From BOB GRANT

See Woodworker Plans Books for full lists

WRITING DESK

A handsome piece of furniture with top 30 × 18in., suitable for construction in any hardwood.
Plan No. BG/01   Price £3.25

GAZEBO

No garden should be without one! Full structural details for this Victoria style summer house – a practical proposition for the competent DIY enthusiast.
Plan No. BG/02   Price £3.25

**CREDIT CARD ORDERS WELCOME
TEL: 0442-41221**

SHOW ME A ROSE

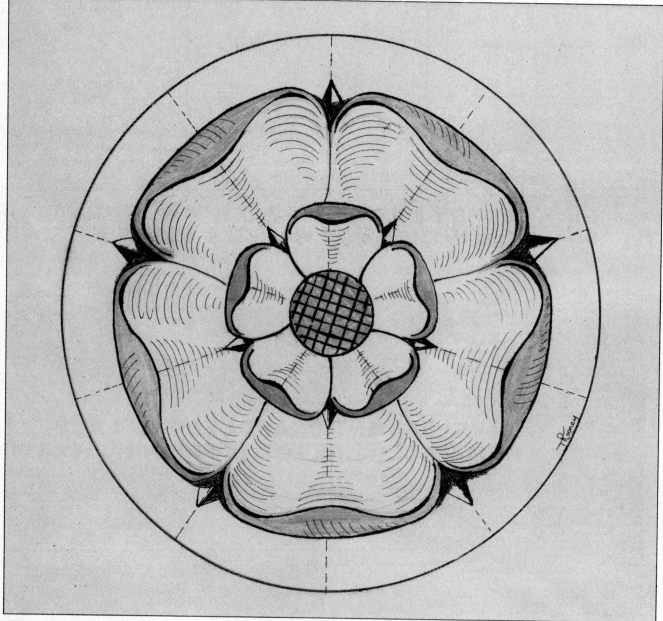

There are many variations of the Tudor Rose pattern — this one I intended to be cast and made into plaster ceiling-roses, but you can use it as a simple carving design for home-made furniture or turned bowls. The rose is formed from five overlapping petals creating a very attractive effect. The depth of your carving will depend on where you are using it; if you are adding the rose into the bottom of a turned bowl, leave a raised circle to a depth of ¼in to save having to relieve it away from the background.

Copy my ink drawing on to the wood, (thorns and branches are optional), making it smaller or

The symbol of the Tudor rose has been a hardy perennial down the centuries. Trevor Rooney — who will be demonstrating his carving prowess at London's WOODWORKER Show — shows how to relief-carve your own bloom

larger to suit (my rose measures 4¾in across, to give an idea of scale). Start by drawing a circle symbolising the outer edge of the petals and then describe the other circles in relative scale. Draw an extra circle about ½in around the outside of the design to act as your cutting line. Your cuts should end towards the outer petals of the rose and the depth of the final cuts will again depend on where the carving is to be made.

Carving the rose takes place in four stages:

Outlining: use a V-tool to outline the rose, always cutting in the direction of the grain to prevent the wood splitting **(A)**.

Setting in: make chamfered cuts

A

B

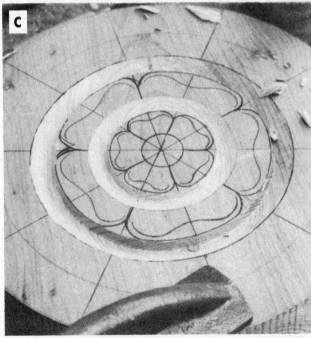

C

from the outer line to the rose. Be careful not to hit too hard or you'll break the edges of the petals **(B).** Repeat this process for the inner circle **(C).**

Grounding out: use a gouge suitable for cutting the petals and start work by shaping a petal overlapped on both sides **(D).** This saves having to cut divisions between all the petals. The overlapped petal should be given cuts to create the impression of folding away underneath the petals on its right and left. Try to develop flow and movement in the wood as you're cutting. Complete the remaining petals in the same way.

Modelling: Hollow out the petals leaving a raised wedge in the centre, wide at the outer edge and narrow on the inner **(E).** You can use your own style for the shaping, but try to keep it fluid in appearance. Make a shallow cut on the inner side of the arrowed area to leave a slight lip separating

▲
Outlining the rose, A, before setting in the outer, B, and inner circles, C ▶

Shaping the petals, D and E ▼

D

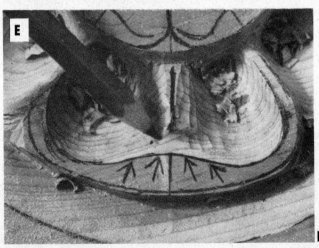

E

the outer side of the petals from the inner. I use a Minicraft Rotary Burr for this stage which cuts down on time considerably **(F)**. Repeat the procedure for the centre set area, but leave the bud raised **(G)**.

Round the bud over gently with a suitable chisel, riffler or small file, and smooth the surface with fine abrasive. Add the detail to the bud either with a punch **(H)** or by criss-crossing with a chisel — in fact you can use any design method that takes your fancy.

If you wish to add thorns to the design, refer to my drawing and cut them in when you've completed the rest of the rose. They are simply chamfered downwards from their centres using a flat chisel. The finished rose **(I)** should resemble mine — allowing for your own interpretation of style — and will make a decorative centre-piece for your bowl, chair or room. ■

▶
Shaping the outer petals, F, and inner, G, before rounding off bud and adding detail, H, to complete the rose, I ▼

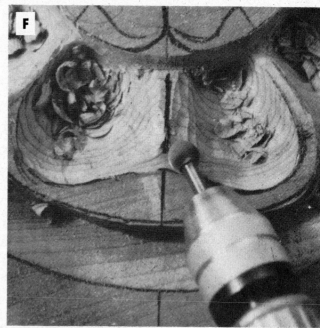

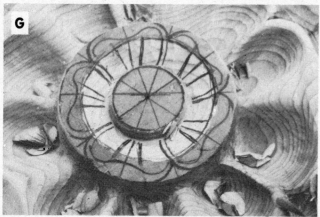

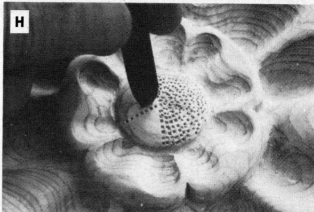

EUMENIA

FROM AUSTRIA

Cross cut capacity 700 mm.

1.75 H.P. 240V (110V available)

With this amazing machine you can add accessories to rout – plane – mortice – mould – groove – tenon

The Best Radial Arm Saw in the world

WE'LL PROVE IT ON STAND 59/62

- ● Unsurpassed for safety and accuracy.
- ● Extremely quiet in operation.
- ● Robust construction – Rigid over-arm.

WOOD PLANER

6″ Planer with rebating facility. Adjustable mitre fence. Robust cast iron construction with cabinet stand. Single phase.
£298

BELT SANDER

Table Length 32″. Belt width 6″. 1.5 HP. Variable tilt adjustment through 90° for Bevel and edge sanding. Supplied with Steel Cabinet Stand.
£412

BDS 690

Belt Disc Sander. 6″ Belt 9″ Disc. ½ HP. Single phase. Belt Horizontal/Vertical operation. Supplied with Steel cabinet stand.
£220

WOOD CUTTING VERTICAL BANDSAW

14″ Throat. Tilting table. **£272**

WETSTONE GRINDER

For a professional finish to chisels and planer blades **£19·70**

MORTICE ATTACHMENT

Well engineered - wide range of chisels **£147**

BDS 460

Belt Disc Sander. ⅓ HP. 4″ Belt 6″ Disc. Horizontal/Vertical Belt position. **£105**

314 BANDSAW

14″ Throat. 5″ Depth of Cut. 6″ Sanding Disc with tilting table and mitre gauge. Tilting Main table with mitre gauge. Circle cutting attachment and fence.
£170

BENCH AND FLOOR DRILLS

A Wide range from ⅜″ capacity to 1″ capacity, from **£88** please send for full details.

Visit our working showrooms.
Shere – Monday/Friday 8.45-5.15. Saturday 9.00-4.00.
Warrington – Monday/Friday 8.45-5.15.

Prices are subject to V.A.T. and carriage.

BARCLAYCARD VISA ACCESS

WARREN MACHINE TOOLS
Middle Street, Shere, Nr Guildford, Surrey GU5 9HF. Phone: 048 641 3434 Telex: 859455.
Adlington Court, Risley Industrial Estate, Birchwood, Warrington, Cheshire WA3 6PL. Phone: 0925 821616. Telex: 629397

HUMBROL CARPENTERS
ALIPHATIC RESIN
WOOD GLUE

- **Grabs fast and sets fast**
- **Stronger than wood itself**
- **Versatile, easy to use**

fix-it-fast

HUMBROL
MARFLEET, HULL, ENGLAND.

HUMBROL CARPENTERS' wood glue FAST GRAB MULTI-GLUE

Get it straight with DeWalt

DW1151 + DW600

The DW1151 is already the biggest-selling Planer thicknesser in U.K. but if you buy one now this special offer enables you, for about £20 + VAT extra (instead of around £65 + VAT otherwise), to buy the matching DW600 mortising attachment at the same time, thus adding an efficient, accurate slot-mortising facility to your DW1151.

DW1151
- 3mm planing depth/260mm wide
- 6–160mm thicknessing capacity/250mm wide
- Cast aluminium planing table over one metre long
- Cast iron thicknessing table 500mm long
- Quick and easy conversion from planing to thicknessing — no tools needed.

DW600
- Max. mortising length 130mm
- 80mm max. mortise depth
- 100mm worktable height adjustment
- Smooth, easy-action controls
- Can be used for tenoning also
- Complete with 4 mortising bit (6, 8, 10 and 10mm ∅)

* **SPECIAL OFFER** on this DeWalt multi-function woodworking machine

Buy a DW1151 Planer thicknesser plus its DW600 optional mortising attachment at the same time this winter and save £245 ! (compared with combined list price).

SPECIAL OFFER * around **£520.00** + VAT
Combined list price: £765 + VAT
OR Buy a DW1151 on its own for around £500 + VAT. (List price £675 + VAT)

The DeWalt DW1151 Planer thicknesser will put an end to inaccuracies in your workpieces. Whether you buy sawn, planed or reclaimed timber, this superb machine will enable you to prepare straight components with a consistent, uniform thickness — essential if your end product is to be as good as you want it to be!

Contact DeWalt at the address below for a colour leaflet and the address of your nearest participating dealer.
* Special offer subject to availability for a limited period from participating dealers.

PRECISION WOOD WORKING FROM...

◆ DeWALT ®

DeWalt Woodworking Machines, Dept. PLT., Westpoint, The Grove, Slough, Berkshire SL1 1QQ. Tel: 0753 74277

Bob Wearing's WORKSHOP

PICTURE CRAMPS

Here's three picture cramps: next month, the bespoke picture frame

Light wire cramp

This cramp is suitable for picture frames, small mitred boxes, circular mirror frames and the like. Tension is derived from wire and a guitar tuning peg (or machine); the latter are easily obtained from most music shops, either individually or as a fitting of three which you can cut up. Suitable wire would be twisted brass picture hanging wire (from hardware shops), or nylon-covered drawing board wire (from a drawing office supplier).

You'll need to prepare the small hardwood block to which the tuning peg is attached, as shown in the photograph: you could either mortise a solid block or laminate.

You'll also need four corner pieces to protect the work (fig. 2). I prefer angle iron, though wood could be used; old bed irons are ideal, since the material is thin and

Light picture cramp

This is probably the oldest frame cramping technique and certainly the simplest to make (fig. 1). You'll need four hardwood blocks for the corners, with holes through which is threaded the tensioning cord. You can make the blocks from the solid with a couple of sawcuts and some chiselling. Cut off the outside corners so it is easier to thread the wire through. Wax the inside surfaces well so the blocks don't stick to the frame.

You could use nylon cord for tensioning, passing a double thread through all the holes and tying it tightly. Apply tension with four small twisting sticks.

tension applied to frame with twisting sticks

double strings

Fig.1   Light picture cramp

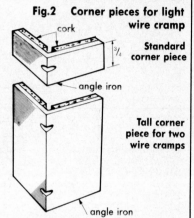

Fig.2   Corner pieces for light wire cramp

cork

Standard corner piece

angle iron

Tall corner piece for two wire cramps

angle iron

light, with an acurate inside 90° angle. File a well-rounded notch — two on longer pieces for joining small boxes — to reduce friction as the wire tightens over the corners. Line the blocks with thin cork (from a cork tile) or rubber, then cover with adhesive plastic such as Fablon to prevent glue adhesion.

You could fit either one or two tensioning devices to each cramp.

Stronger wire cramp

This cramp, though more work to make, is capable of larger and heavier work. The metal, being largely under tension, does not need to be particularly thick: 1.5mm is enough. You could get an offcut from your garage.

If you're making several, prepare a symmetrical card pattern (fig. 3). Blacken the metal surface with a thick felt marker then scratch round the outline. Mark the centres of the holes heavily with a centre punch. Saw out and file to shape, though great accuracy is not essential. Bend to shape round a piece of the metal to be used for the sliding block. Drill all the holes with a tighlty fitting wood block inside during the drilling. Countersink the small holes for the rivetting, and tap the hole in the centre of the bent section for 5/16 or 8mm screwed rod.

Prepare two pins with round tenons on the ends; if you haven't got a lathe, they can be filed in a vice, over a washer (fig. 4).

Drill and tap the sliding block

Fig.3   Stronger wire cramp

All dimensions in inches

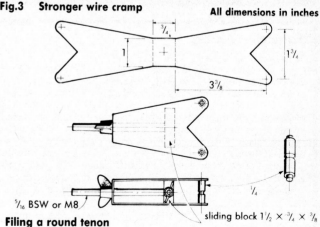

$\frac{3}{4}$ 1 $1\frac{3}{4}$ $3\frac{3}{8}$ $\frac{1}{4}$

$\frac{5}{16}$ BSW or M8

sliding block $1\frac{1}{2} \times \frac{3}{4} \times \frac{3}{8}$

Filing a round tenon

Fig.4

safe edge of file rests on washer

3/16in or 5mm. Screw two short lengths of screwed rod tightly into place each side, to hold the wire. Rivet a length of 5/16in or 8mm screwed rod into the block, passing it through the centre threaded hole in the body.

Fit the sliding block in position and rivet in the two pins. File a shallow central groove in each pin to gide the wire. Fit suitable washers and wing nuts for gripping the wire, or use round-head screws with washers, the block being tapped.

Make corner pieces as above except that one should be narrow enough to fit into the tensioner.

Each month, the best Woodworking wheeze — the neatest, cleverest idea that makes any sort of woodwork quicker, easier, more precise, more productive, more enjoyable, more efficient, more profitable — will win £60 worth of tools from Sandvik's enormous range.
Send your ideas to:
Hands on, WOODWORKER, I Golden Square, London WIR 3AB. If we print any wheeze you send in on these pages, you get a small fee — so write today!

How to enter

We want to publish as many wheezes as possible, so we must use only the barest bones of the ideas. Be as precise as possible; type your words if you can, double-spaced on one side of an A4 sheet; make drawings, if any, as few and as clear as you can, and annotate them clearly.

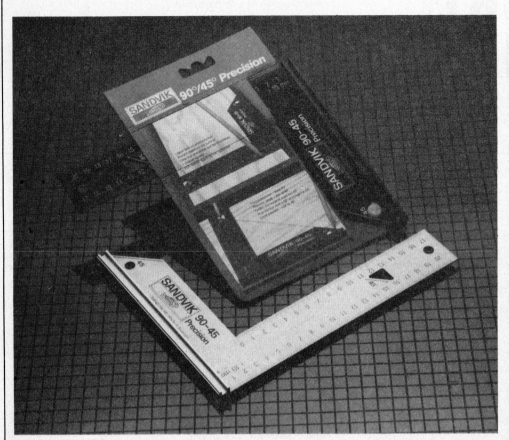

SANDPLATE COMPETITION

Every month in 'Hands on', woodworking wheezes of the month win £60 of Sandvik tools. Now you've got a free sample of Sandplate, and a money-off coupon to use with your purchase of the tools for it, why not enter the special **Sandplate Wheeze Competition?** This time there's **two prizes** of £50 worth of Sandvik tools to be won!

What you have to do: with your free sample — or more Sandplate if you've bought it — you will undoubtedly be trying out all sorts of different jobs; and you'll also be tempted to devise your own tools and gadgets to use it for specialised tasks. The prizes will be awarded to those entries which in our opinion are the most original and ingenious:
I Ways of using the material, or
2 Specially-designed tools for it.

Get your entries in, on one side of A4 sheets of paper, keeping drawings to the minimum and clearly annotated, by 30 NOVEMBER. Address your envelopes 'Sandplate Wheeze', WOODWORKER, I Golden Sq, London WIR 3AB. We will publish the winning entries in the March 1988 issue, along with a selection of the other ideas we receive.
Don't delay — abrade today!

Sandvik winner

Bargain sanding belts

Cut an old belt along the join, and allowing ½in extra for overlap make a template of the shape in glass. Pin two strips of wood slightly shorter than the overall length of the belt on a board so the template just fits snugly between them.

Cut a piece from a roll of abrasive, just longer than the template. Place it on the template and trim to width; then place between the two wooden strips and cut the ends. File the abrasive from the ½in overlap before joining with contact adhesive. Clamp the join tightly between two strips of hardwood until set.

A 50 metre roll of abrasive costs about £20, yielding about 100 belts at a bargain price.
Gerry Madden, Waterford

Magic with clay

To avoid adhesive, especially epoxy resins, clogging the thread when bonding nuts into work, I use my childrens' modelling clay to fill the interior of the nut; easy to clean off the clay afterwards.
Peter Clark, South Croydon

Coloured sawdust

I keep small pots of various types of sawdust (mahogany, oak etc) ready for making up with glue as filler; easier to match colours and to finish than some of the proprietary fillers.
R. Biggs, Carshalton Beeches

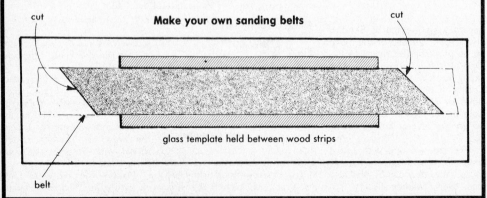

Make your own sanding belts

cut

cut

glass template held between wood strips

belt

Extra deep cramp

Sometimes you need a really deep cramp for such jobs as repairing lifted veneer in the centre of a table top. Here's an easily made device, the dimensions of which you can vary according to the depth of throat and the pressure you require for the job.

The two arms of the cramp and spacer block are held together by the two securing bolts and hardwood plates; this securing device should not be less than one inch from the end of the spacer block. At the other end of the top arm, a bolt goes through the timber and a recessed nut, with softening block to prevent damage to the work.

Roger Passmore, Worthing

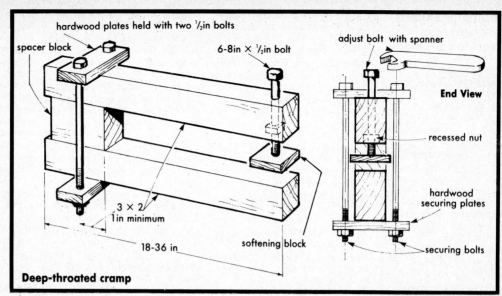

Deep-throated cramp

hardwood plates held with two ½in bolts

spacer block

6-8in × ½in bolt

adjust bolt with spanner

End View

recessed nut

hardwood securing plates

securing bolts

softening block

3 × 2
1in minimum

18-36 in

Jig for circles

This jig helps produce circular blanks for turning using a circular saw. For safety reasons the groove in the saw table is vital; please don't try to adapt the design for a plain table. Note that the steel strip rivetted to the top plate is off-centre so intermediate diameters are available if you reverse the plate or turn it through 180°.

The larger the piece of wood, the easier it is to grasp safely and the further your hands are from the saw blade, but I've found this device works satisfactorily with discs down to 6in diameter.

John Owen, Wadebridge

Circular saw cuts circles

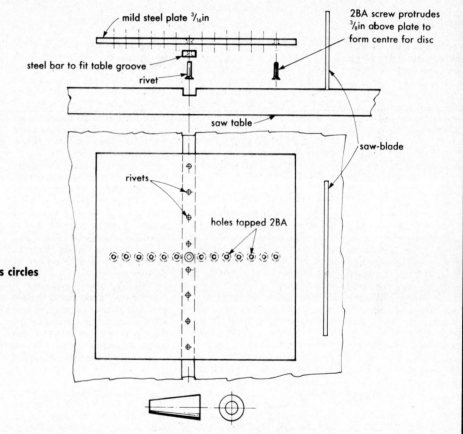

mild steel plate ³⁄₁₆in

2BA screw protrudes ³⁄₈in above plate to form centre for disc

steel bar to fit table groove

rivet

saw table

saw-blade

rivets

holes tapped 2BA

Multi-grooving lathe tool

I needed to make 12 evenly spaced grooves in some small spindles I was turning. To speed up the process, I made this cutting tool from a 1x4in strip of 1/16in steel. I drew a curve to a 3in radius at one end and filed to shape, then marked the curve off into 12 equal parts. I made radial cuts between each part about ⅛in long with a junior hacksaw, then used a small triangular file in the saw cuts from the underside to form a point on each section.

To use, I put the tool on the T-rest and press against the rotating spindle with a slight rolling action to enable the points to cut grooves one after the other.

D. G. Francis, Nottingham

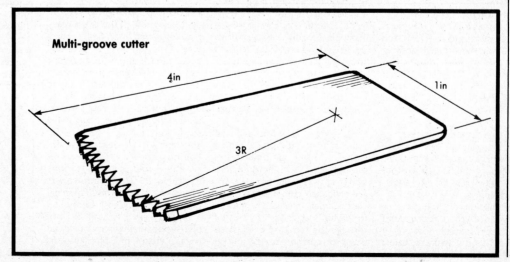

Multi-groove cutter

4in

1in

3R

Our panel of experts solve your woodworking problems

Oak preserver

Q A group of local craftsmen are making a large sign for the village green, with hand-carved oak panels and supported on an oak post. What is the best way to preserve it?

F. J. Watson, Blandford

A Unfortunately there's no finish I can recommend for exterior oak that won't require further attention.

The most durable finish would be a yacht varnish based on tung oil, such as Rustins. For maximum durability the panels should be varnished on both sides and edges to prevent water being absorbed, which would then cause the wood to expand and contract. It is the constant movement of timber, in external conditions, that usually causes finishes to fail. One coat on the reverse side of the panel should be sufficient to seal the wood, but the exposed sides should be given at least three coats of varnish.

Ronald Rustin

Jet finish

Q Can you recommend a durable, jet black gloss / semi-gloss finish for turned hardwood such as Brazilian mahogany? Ideally the grain filler and top finish would be applied at the lathe.

L. R. Parker, Great Easton

A There are two methods of ebonising timber — one where the grain can still be seen through the finish, the other where the grain is completely obliterated.

For the former, you can stain the wood with a penetrating ebony stain, either Colron or Rustin's. If you wish to use a grainfiller, it couldn't be applied on the lathe, unless you thinned the paste. I don't know of an ebony grainfiller, but you can mix Rustin's Ebony Wood Dye with their Dark Oak Grainfiller, which would make it nearer to an ebony colour. You should then finish the wood with black french polish.

If you wish to obliterate the grain, you could apply Rustin's Black Plastic Coating. But it can't be applied on the lathe, as it dries by a chemical reaction after mixing with the hardener. Drying time is about an hour. Three coats would probably be required to give a jet black finish and to obtain a high-gloss or semi-gloss finish, the surface would need burnishing, or rubbing with fine steel wool and wax polish. These processes can be carried out whilst the work is in the lathe.

Ronald Rustin

● Ronald Rustin is the director of Rustin's.

Ornamental cherry

Q I have an ornamental cherry tree in my garden — would the timber be suitable for turning or making furniture? What is the best way to prepare and treat it? It's about 30 years old and on its last legs.

R. G. Hunt, Oakham

A I have used this timber for turning and found it pleasing in appearance, easy to work and polish, and see no reason why it shouldn't produce attractive furniture. It's fairly soft however, and the surface dents and scratches rather easily.

From your description, the tree is almost dead, but if there was any leaf growth this there will still be some sap in the trunk — if so, delay felling until January. If, then, the bottom of the trunk is obviously very dry, there's been no sap movement, and you can start conversion.

If the wood has a large crack or is decayed, it's best used to make bowls (Ray Key's *Wood-turning and Design* has plenty of advice on the subject); if the wood is sound you could use it for a small piece of furniture. Estimate how many pieces, and what quantities you'll need by drawing up a cutting list. Arrange your conversion so each piece is cut to full size to allow for shrinkage; don't split the tree trunk down the middle or you'll loose any chance of quarter-sawn timber.

Splitting is unpredictable and can occur at any stage during drying, whether the timber is in the round or sawn. Small dimension stock sizes, such as chair legs, are produced commercially from green timber, and carefully stacked for drying. Many pieces are wasted through the resultant defects, so when you compile your cutting list make sure you have enough to produce a couple of extra pieces in each size.

Dry the blanks in a garage or shed for about 12 weeks, out of direct sunlight. Then take them indoors to the same environment that the finished article will occupy. I must stress that central heating reduces the moisture level, so this could be a crucial period. But as all your blanks have been cut almost to finished size, after six weeks any defects will have shown up — however, if in doubt wait a little longer.

Before you burn the remainder of the tree, look at the branches; if they're sound you could make use of them as table-lamps, bangles or a whole host of items.

Graham James

● Graham James is an ex-timber merchant of long experience who specialised in home-grown hardwoods.

Finishing touches

Q My first question is about a Pembroke table with a mahogany top, which responds well to polish reviver, and spiral stained beech legs, which are left a lurid orange colour after reviver treatment. How can I clean the legs to leave them matching the top?

Secondly, I have a sea-chest made from solid planks, which smells strongly of camphor. If it is camphorwood would french polish be a good way of finishing it (the outside is now blistered shellac)? Also can you tell me what species sandalwood is and where it comes from?

Finally, I'm restoring a clock-case and need some individual sheets of gold leaf for the quadrant mouldings. Can you tell me where I can get it from?

R. P. Ashley, Moseley

A The legs would appear to be 'barley twist' and before they can be coloured to match the table top they will need to be thoroughly cleaned. Washing them with warm water and toilet soap may be enough to remove the black grime. If the dirt is really ground in you may find rubbing carefully with 0000 grade steel wool is more effective. The table was probably french polished and if the polish on the legs is sound they can be re-polished with red french polish. This will bring up their colour to match the table top; you should then polish complete table with garnet polish. Polishing new work and re-polishing old pieces is fully explained in *The Woodworker Manual of Finishing and Polishing*, price £2.50 from Argus Books Ltd, I Golden Square, WIR 3AB. Camphorwood (*cinnamomum camphora*) is a native of China, Japan and Taiwan. It's moderately hard, reddish in colour, coarse-grained and is sometimes prettily marked — it is fragrant and durable on account of the large amount of camphor it contains. You can french polish it, but use a grain filler to choke the open pores of the grain before starting to polish. As the old finish is so badly perished you'll have to completely remove it before re-finishing. Sandalwood (*Santalum album*) grows in India, mainly in the south, and also in Malaysia.

Your local signwriters, listed in Yellow Pages, should be able to supply you with gold leaf.

Charles Cliffe

● Charles Cliffe is a professional polisher, author and teacher.

Green oak porch

Q I intend to use green oak to build a porch about 3ft square, with an oak frame of 4½x4½in timber, mortised and pegged. Do you think green oak is suitable for this use?

J. R. Oates, Craven Arms

A You don't say how 'green' the green oak is but I assume it's newly felled and therefore sap-saturated and very wet. I advise cutting oversize to rough lengths (for 4½x4½in cut at 5x5in) to allow for shrinkage. Then stack with sticks between for air circulation in a sheltered place, at least until the free water in the wood has dried out. In mainly dry weather conditions this would take several months. Even then the centre of a 5x5in would still be quite wet. However the oak can be worked (joints cut) before it is properly seasoned. This is how it was done traditionally, it's easier to work in this condition before it gets too hard. Joints should be left oversize to begin with then later trimmed to a tight fit. The porch could be assembled at this stage but shrinkage will still take place. If the porch faces south this may occur too quickly and cause some problems.

My advice is yes, you can use the oak available, choose knot-free pieces and proceed slowly. Give the wood time to 'settle down' — the old builders did.

Jack Hill

● Jack Hill is an expert in green woodworking and country chair-maker.

Since 1901 Question Box has had the answer

DONE TO A TURN

A workshop-made lathe demands solidity, simplicity — and accuracy. Vic Oliver presents his sturdy version

Simple and strong, this wooden lathe was originally designed with beech in mind as the material. Any good close-grained hardwood would do, as long as it is stable and dry. I also wanted to keep the metalwork to a minimum; no taps or dies, just accurate drilling with a stand, and a rivet or two. It's for light work — don't try and turn telegraph poles!

Bed and headstock

Cut the bed bars (fig. 1.1) to 48in. Mark and drill all the ¼in holes, then make the tongue tester (fig. 1.4), which uses masking tape to allow for the necessary clearance, and ensures that tongues on legs and upper assemblies are exactly the same. You will need two pieces, plus two bits of scrap wood which decide the distance of the bed bars apart.

Cut the two legs (fig. 1.2) and bases (fig. 1.3) to size. Cut tongues on the legs, and try them in the tester; they must be a good fit. Cut the headstock pillars (fig. 2.1), drill two $\frac{3}{16}$ in holes near the tongue shoulders, cut the tongues and test them too. Cut the distance piece fig. 2.2, clamp it between the headstock pillars at the tongue shoulders, transfer the $\frac{3}{16}$ in holes from the pillars to the distance piece, glue, and insert two 2BAx5¼in lengths of stud-

ding. This is extra length for a grindstone toolrest, which is bolted on to the studding — the distance piece isn't shown in the photos because I fitted it later.

Toolrest slide

Cut the main slide base (fig. 3.1) to size and drill the three ⅜in holes. Likewise, cut the outer guide (fig. 3.3) and drill for no. 8 woodscrews. Clamp it to the main base square with the end, and fix with 1in x 8 screws. Drill the centre of the tongue guide (fig. 3.2) for no. 8s, and also a ⅜in hole in the middle of the length. Stick two strips of masking tape on one of the 1¼in edges of the tongue guide, to give clearance in the bed bars; take an odd end of bed bar, lay it on the base hard to the outer guide, then clamp and screw the tongue guide hard to that. The toolrest should slide between the bed bars.

▲

Not the most graceful of machines; but functional is beautiful.

◀

The toolrest and slide: some metalwork, but nothing too daunting

Drill ³⁄₈in holes in the clamping plate (fig. 3.4), the tongue guide, and another in the main slide base. To assemble it all, lay the tool slide in the bed, insert a ³⁄₈x5in bolt into the clamping plate and up through the tongue guide of the tool slide into the main base, with washers top and bottom.

Tailstock

It's not a bad idea to do all the metalwork at one time, but I shall describe the pieces as you need them. You need a piece of ³⁄₄x³⁄₄x¹⁄₈in angle (fig. 4.7) to fit the notch in the toolrest support bar (fig. 4.6); also the two clamping plates (fig. 4.8), 2¹⁄₂x³⁄₄x¹⁄₈in mild steel, which should be drilled with ¹⁄₄in holes as shown. If

The headstock, with standard Picador pulleys, spindle and faceplate. Grindstone toolrest can also be fitted. ▼

you can't get angle iron for the piece to line the support bar notch — or indeed for the tailstock handle pivot mounts, shown in fig. 5.8 — you can simply bend pieces of flat bar by hammering them in a vice. Don't try for too sharp an angle, though, as the bar could crack.

The top and bottom sleeves (fig. 4.2) for the toolrest neck (fig. 4.3) are made from 1in pieces of ¹⁄₂in OD tube with a ³⁄₈in bore. Cut a 6in length of ³⁄₈in studding for the neck, and bend it by holding it in a piece of the tube in the vice. The tube should slip over the studding by 1in. Cut the two bits of tube to length and slide them over the studding at each end, and drill the rivet to fix them; at the base of the neck the tube should cover 1in and at the other end only ¹⁄₂in; you need to leave ¹⁄₂in of tube open for the Picador toolrest (fig. 4.1), which has a ³⁄₈in-diameter spigot.

Toolrest

The tailstock tube (fig. 5.6) is the main metal component of this assembly, in which the tailstock centre, drill chuck or what have you is mounted. Cut it to length,

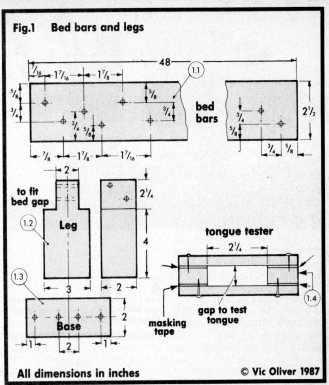

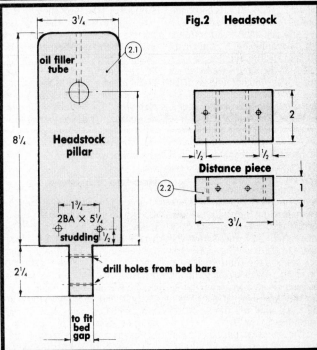

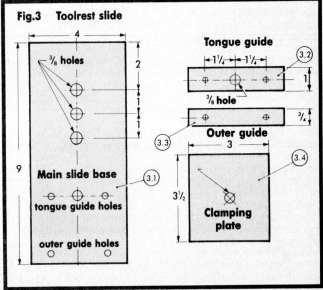

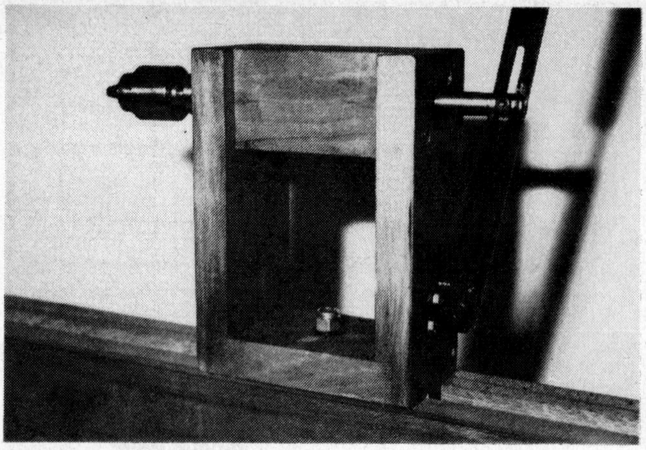

▲ **The tailstock, showing the handle and sliding spindle arrangement. Accuracy is everything . . .**

mark for a 1/8in hole to give the end of the slot, drill a series of holes and file the slot to size. Then drill a 3/16in hole at 90° to the slot, 3/8in from the end. Slide on a 1/2in (inside diameter) collar flush with the other end of the tube, drill through the tapped hole, open it out to 3/16in and debur it. Test the tube in a pair of 5/8in OD x 1/2in bore x 1 1/4in flanged bushes — it is supposed to slide in these, mounted in the tailstock pillars. If it is too tight, carefully ease the tube down with wet-and-dry until it slides freely. Cut the handle (fig. 5.7) and mark out and drill a number of 3/16in holes for the slot, which you can finish with small round and flat files. Drill the 1/4in hole at the end and remove all the burrs.

Make (or simply cut if you have got angle iron) and drill the pieces of angle iron (fig. 5.8) for the handle pivot mounts. You need both 3/16in and 1/4in holes as shown.

Cut and fit all the woodwork joints, but don't glue them. Mark the centre of the 2x2in spindle carrier (fig. 5.1) in the tailstock pillars (fig. 5.2) and screw the pillars to the base (fig. 5.3). Drill 1/8in holes in the centre marks on the pillars, and using each end, fix the spindle carrier temporarily. Cut the slots shown in the tongue (fig. 5.4), and drill the 3/16in and 3/8in holes as well.

The 5/8in through hole in the spindle carrier must be drilled dead accurately. It's as well to test your 5/8in drill and make sure it's running true. Disassemble the carrier from the pillars, drill the 3/8in hole through on the central screw-marks from each end, and insert one bush a little at a time. Slide the tube into the bush, checking to see it's exactly parallel to the outside of the carrier; if it isn't, ease the hole in the wood. Insert the second bush, testing as you go. If the bushes end up loose, take them out and Araldite them on the flanges only. Put it all together and insert the tube with a smear of oil on it to see if it still slides freely and parallel.

Screw the tongue through the slots to the centre of the tailstock base, so you can adjust the tailstock on the bars to get the tube sliding perfectly parallel to the bars. This is explained in fig. 5A. When you're satisfied, fix it to the base with a 2in x 8 screw at each end of the tongue, and drill up through the 3/8in hole.

The handle should be assembled first to the pivot mounts (fig. 5.8) before you fix them to the pillars; use a 1x1/4in bolt with a nyloc nut and washers each side. Slide the tube back in the carrier, lay the handle into the slot and bolt it up with a 2BA x 1in bolt and nut. Set the handle upright with the tube at the bottom of the slot, and position it dead centre of the tailstock pillars; clamp the pivot mounts, and drill and fix them to the pillars with 2BA x 1 1/4in bolts.

Headstock bushes

Mount a 3/8in twist drill in the tailstock tube and fix it with a collar screw. Remove just the top of the handle and slide the tailstock to the head pillars. With the drill just touching, revolve the tube to make an aligned centre for the head bush. Take the head out of the bed, and do a test with your 3/4in drill bit to make sure it's the accurate size. Drill the first hole, and insert one of the bushes (fig. 6.4), 5/8in bore x 1 1/4in flange, a little at a time. Check to see it's at 90° to the face of the pillar; if not, ease the hole a little. Repeat the process with the second bush, and Araldite them as you (perhaps) did with the tailstock, on the flanges only. The Picador spindle (fig. 6.1) should revolve; it may be a little tight but it will run in.

For the oil filler tubes to lubricate the spindle running in the bushes, mark on the top edges of the pillars at the centre of the bushes, and drill 1/32in right down into the bushes. Then open the hole out to 1/4in, down to the outside face of the bushes; clear the hole and insert the 1 1/2x1/4in OD copper tubes, which should stand no less than 1/2in above the edge of the pillars. You can turn the caps (fig. 6.9) when the lathe is running — but be sure to cover the tubes!

Fig.4 Toolrest

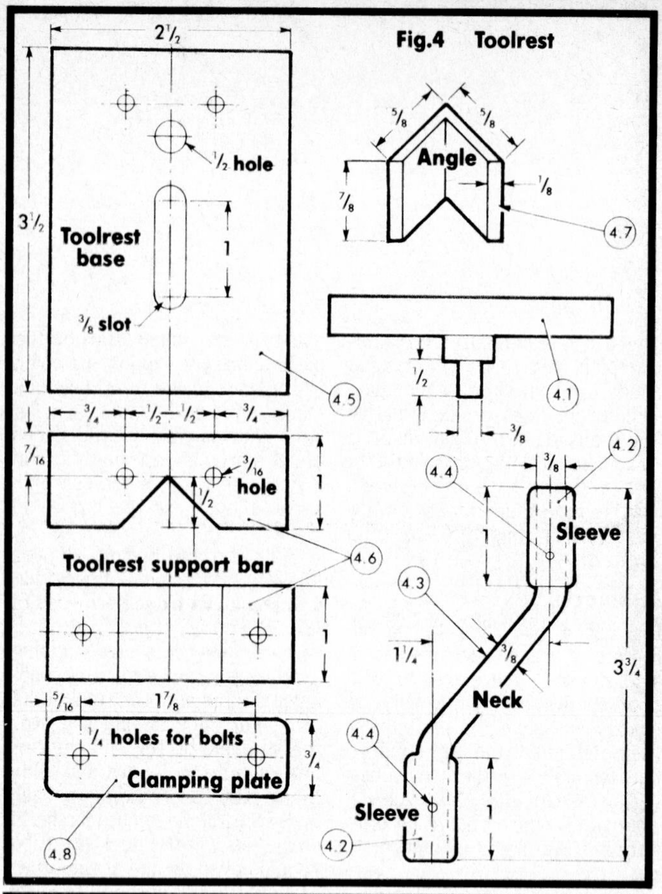

Fig.5 Tailstock

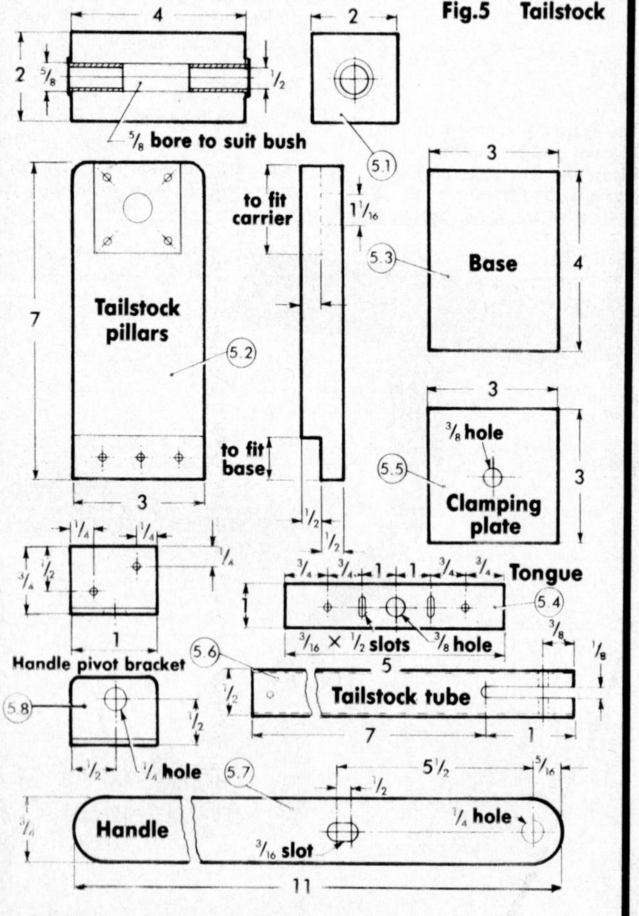

Fig.5A Tube parallel tester

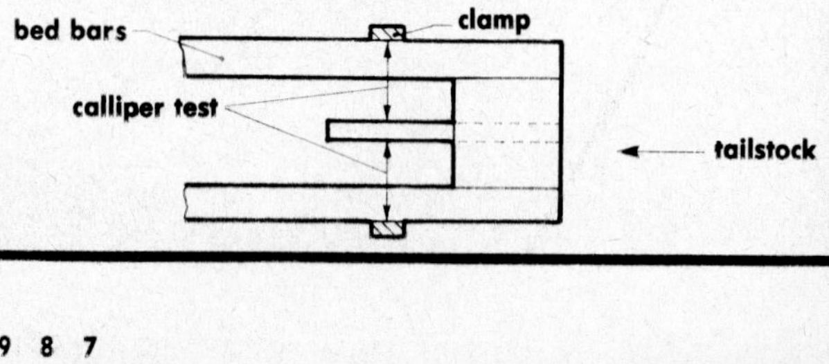

Parts list

All timber components finished sizes

Bed bars and legs

1.1	Bars	2	48in	x 2½in	x 1¼in	hardwood
1.2	Legs	2	6¼	3	2	hardwood
1.3	Bases	2	7	2	¾	hardwood
1.4	Tongue tester	from scrap				

8 off 4x¼in hex bolts, nuts and washers, 4 off 1½in x 8 csk screws

Headstock

2.1	Headstock pillars	2	10½	3¼	1¼	hardwood
2.2	Distance piece	1	3¼	$2\frac{1}{16}$	1	hardwood

Toolrest slide

3.1	Main base	1	9	4	1	hardwood
3.2	Tongue guide	1	4	1¼	1	hardwood
3.3	Outer guide	1	4	¾	½	hardwood
3.4	Clamping plate	1	3½	3	½	hardwood

1 off 5x⅜in hex bolt, 2 off 2in x 8 csk screws, 2 off 1in x 8 csk screws

Toolrest

4.1	Toolrest	Picador no. 702			
4.2	Sleeves	2	1	½	⅜ bore MS tube
4.3	Neck	1	6	⅜	MS studding
4.4	Rivets	2	½	⅛	
4.5	Base	1	3½	2½	½ hardwood
4.6	Support bar	1	2½	1	1 hardwood
4.7	Support bar liner	1	¾	¾	⅛ MS angle
4.8	Clamping plate	2	2½	¾	⅛ MS

2 off 2BA x 2in csk screws, nuts, washers; 2 off 2x¼in hex bolts, nuts, washers

Tailstock

5.1	Spindle carrier	1	4	2	2	hardwood
5.2	Tailstock pillars	2	7	3	1	hardwood
5.3	Base	1	4	3	1	hardwood
5.4	Tongue	1	5	1¼	1	hardwood
5.5	Clamping plate	1	3	3	½	hardwood
5.6	Tailstock tube	1	7	½		⅜ bore MS tube
5.7	Handle	1	11	¾	⅜	MS bright bar
5.8	Handle pivot mounts	2	1	1	⅛	MS angle

2 off ⅝in x ½in bore x 1¼in flanged bushes, 16 off 1¼in x 8 csk screws, 4 off 2in x 8 csk screws, 1 off 1x¼in bolt, locknut, washers, 1 off 2BA x 1in screw, locknut, washer, 4 off 2BA x 1¼in screws, locknuts, washers, 1 off 4½x⅜in bolt, nyloc nut, washers.

Headstock spindle

6.1	Spindle	1	Picador no. 705	
6.2	L/H nut for spindle	1		
6.3	Collar	1	½in bore	MS
6.4	Bush	2	⅝in bore 1¼in flange	
6.5	Pulleys	3	Picador 4in, 3in, 2in	
6.6	Collar	1	⅝in bore	MS
6.7	R/H nut for spindle	1		
6.8	Faceplate	1	Picador no. 735	
6.9	Oil caps	2	1 ¾ dia	hardwood
6.10	Oil filler tubes	2	1½ ¼	copper

Motor mount

7.1	Adjustable mount	1	8	8	½	plywood
7.2	Hex bolt, nuts, washer	1	4	⅜		long thread
7.3	Hinges	2	3			MS
7.4	Base top	1	8	8	½	plywood
7.5	Adjuster plate	1	8	1½	1½	hardwood
7.6	Legs	4	6½	2	2	hardwood
7.7	Base bottom	1	11	8	½	plywood

8 off 2BA x 1in csk screws, nuts, 3 off 2BA x 2in csk screws

Replace the headstock assembly in the bed, assemble the Picador pulleys (fig. 6.5), and screw the Picador faceplate (fig. 6.8) on to the spindle. Check to see how true it is.

Motor mount

Cut all the pieces to size and plane the chamfer on the adjuster plate (fig. 7.5). Assemble the base top (fig. 7.4) to the base legs (7.6) and base bottom (7.7) with glue and screws. Fix the hinges to the adjustable mount (fig. 7.1) with countersunk bolts and screw them down to the base top (fig. 7.4); drill $\frac{3}{16}$ in holes in the adjuster plate, and clamp, drill, glue and screw it to the base top, using 2BA x 2in bolts and nuts. Lay the adjustable mount down on the chamfer of the adjuster plate, and draw a line from the centre of the chamfer on to the edge of the mount. Square the line back across the top of the mount, and mark off the centre; it should be 4in from the edge. Mark 2½in out each side of the centre, and drill ⅜in holes on the marks for ⅜in bolts.

Lay the mount back down on the plate and mark through the ⅜in holes on to the chamfered surface. Remove the mount again and drill ½in holes on the marks, 1in deep to the point of the drill. Put two 4x⅜in bolts through the two holes in the mount and lock them up with two nuts underneath. This should give the motor belt enough adjustment for the various speeds.

Bits and pieces

All that remains are the oil caps, explained in the headstock section, and wooden linings for the handles, if you feel like the luxury touch. Turn a piece of (say) ash to 4¾x⅞in diameter, and saw it right down the middle. Mark and drill one half for two rivet holes, clamp it to the handle, and drill through the handle and into the other half of the lining. Don't forget to let the rivet below the surface. And good luck with your precision home-made lathe! ■

Vic Oliver is an amateur woodturner and maker of ancient musical instruments who lives in Hampshire.

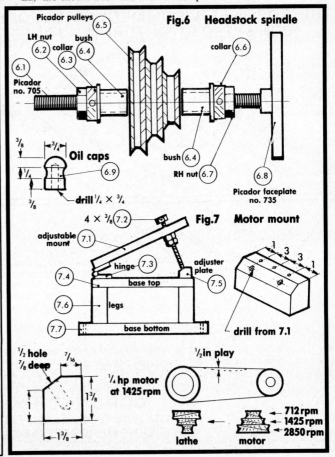

Fig.6 Headstock spindle

Fig.7 Motor mount

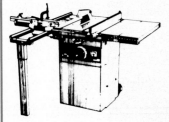

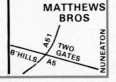
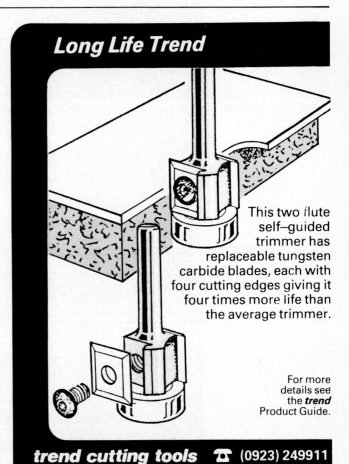

TOTEM CHESTER

Magnificent and powerful, the totem pole has a special kind of magic. Paul Noon, the organiser of an adventure playground, tells how he and the children brought Red Indian carving to the plains of Chester. See Paul at work at the Woodworker Show

Photos Paul Dickie

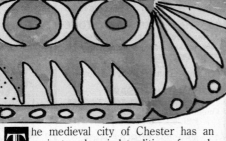

The medieval city of Chester has an ancient and varied tradition of wood-carving. But the huge totem poles which rise from the local adventure playground where I'm project organiser, are likely to be a first in its history.

Blacon Adventure Playground is on a housing estate two miles outside the city walls, attracting scores of youngsters every day. It is some of these young people, aged five upwards, who have helped prepare, construct, paint and carve the startling totem poles. You may think I've got Red Indian blood in me but I'm actually a self-taught carver from Liverpool and because the first carved poles, completed in December 1983, proved such a success with the children, I started to plan more projects. A campaign was launched to fund setting up a small workshop and tool store. Generous donations of tools from Ashley Iles and sponsorship from British Telecom enabled us to carve our tallest pole (32ft) in the summer of 1984. Since then carving has been a regular activity here and weekly woodwork and carving sessions have proved so popular that sadly we've had to limit the number of children who can participate. Over 50 children helped create the 'African' pole for our annual big-carving project and the end result, 25ft high with an outrageous pink elephant's head, was erected by British Telecom.

As we're a charity and work on a limited budget, we're always in need of funds and material donations in order to carry on. After talking to the manager of a local garden

Photographs of the Blacon Adventure Playground totem poles, with one of Paul Noon's original water colour illustrations, centre left

centre, we came up with the idea of a sponsored carve, which we held in the small play-area of the garden centre. We raised £250 for woodwork equipment and gained good publicity and prestige into the bargain.

Most of the wood I use is reclaimed timber, utility poles and the like, so it has to go through rigorous preparation, making sure that all the screws, nails and fastenings are removed. The next process — and here the children aren't involved — is planing the pole with a Black & Decker electric planer for a clean smooth finish to draw the design on to.

The designs are taken either from traditional ethnic and ancient carvings, or are simply flights of imagination. We use a small water-colour painting as the plan for the finished carving, which helps the children to visualise what they're making. The basic design is then drawn out on the pole, another step where the kids are involved. ▶

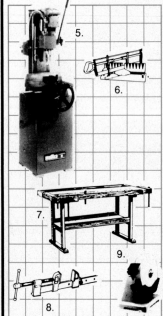
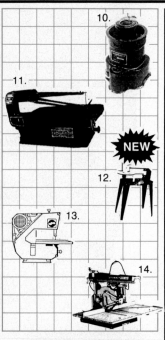

Adze made from brick hammer

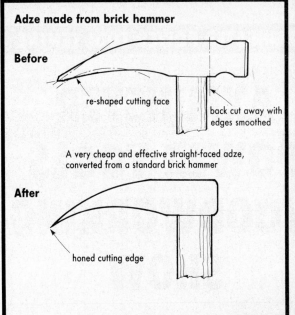

Before

re-shaped cutting face

back cut away with edges smoothed

A very cheap and effective straight-faced adze, converted from a standard brick hammer

After

honed cutting edge

Home-made traditional adze

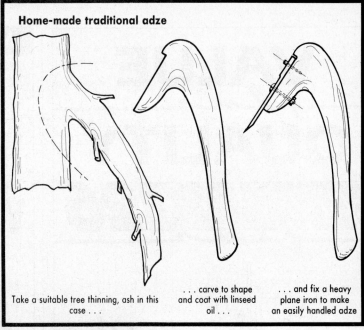

Take a suitable tree thinning, ash in this case . . .

. . . carve to shape and coat with linseed oil . . .

. . . and fix a heavy plane iron to make an easily handled adze

Other useful tools:

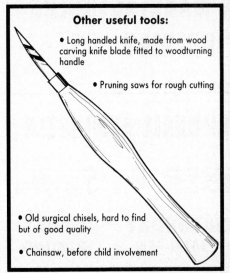

• Long handled knife, made from wood carving knife blade fitted to woodturning handle

• Pruning saws for rough cutting

• Old surgical chisels, hard to find but of good quality

• Chainsaw, before child involvement

Ingenious carving tools, with Paul Noon himself at the tiny workshop

MOST OF THE CARVING is roughed out using a variety of axes and adzes, both half-round and straight-faced. These tools are expensive but ingenuity came to the rescue once again; a few conversions to a standard brick hammer, and you've got a cheap and effective adze. A sturdy plane iron also makes an excellent adze head to fit on a custom-carve handle. This work is carried out by older children and spectators are kept at a safe distance.

For the serious detailed work, I use a range of chisels, and customise or shorten some for the smaller children to use. All the mallets are standard 4in beechwood carpenter's mallets which can also be adapted for a small grip. The main chisels we use are bevelled edge, of various sizes and lengths, which are easy for youngsters to sharpen when they use a honing guide, and are also cheap. Only children from nine upwards get involved at this stage, and the work is very strictly supervised; the actual number who participate depends on the length of the pole.

We're rather starved of good carving tools. All of the true carving chisels and knives are my own which I allow the most skilled and dedicated young carvers to use; it would be nice to afford a good selection of gouges just for the children.

The final carving is tackled with a selection of scrapers, rifflers, rasps and glasspaper. All the younger children join in and because there aren't any sharp tools involved, there's no limit on numbers. The final touches, ears, noses, tusks, horns and wings, are all jointed and glued into place using a synthetic resin glue like Cascamite. The pole is then given a coat of good quality primer and finished with several coats of high-gloss paint, donated by local decorators.

At the end of the summer-carving, when British Telecom pay us a visit and erect the pole, we usually have a big barbecue to mark the occasion and invite all the children who've helped. If we get a tree trunk with a large enough girth, then after this year's carving event a figure based on the stone giants of Easter Island will be taking its place of pride on the site. Many of the children who've taken part in the carving have gone on to complete some of their own pieces, using the facilities in our little workshop, and we hope to put on an exhibition of their work later this year.

I'm always on the look out for donations of small hand and power tools to improve our facilities and widen opportunities for the children. So if you have the odd chisel lying forgotten in a corner, then why not send it to us? It will be put to very good use. Also any books, diagrams, photographs, or anything you think will be suitable for starting a woodcarving library for children would be gratefully received. Send them to me, Paul Noon, Blacon Adventure Playground, Kipling Rd, Blacon, Chester (0244) 371129. ■

VALUE
plus
QUALITY
///MAXI 26
plus

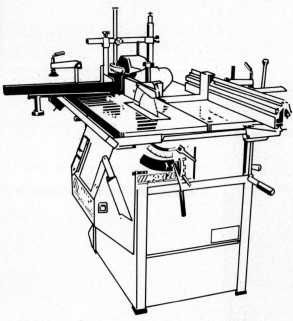

The ideal universal woodworking machine for the light professional and the keen hobbyist. Six functions – SAWING, THICKNESSING, TENONING, PLANING, MOULDING and MORTISING – all effortless, with flexibility, precision and safety, and driven by a powerful and reliable 2 HP motor.

The MAXI 26 Plus features

* Steel work tables for super finish and guaranteed long life.
* Planing guide in high-quality extruded aluminium: perfect square and bevel cutting.
* Mortiser has single-lever control for easy, accurate operation.
* Cast-iron thicknessing table for complete rigidity.
* Blade setting block and key.
* Castors and transport handle.

The Maxi 26 Plus offers the best value for money on the market today – and it is guaranteed for 2 years. Maxi 26 Plus – again the very best in craft woodworking from AEG.

Write or phone for descriptive leaflet, prices and the name of your nearest dealer.

AEG

AEG (UK) Limited
217 Bath Road, Slough, Berkshire
Telephone: Slough (0753) 872101

TAYLOR MADE

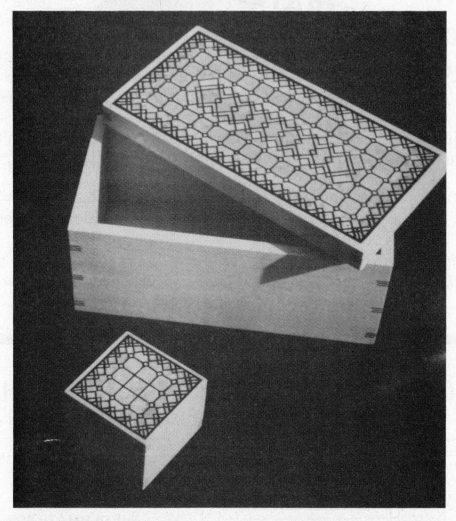

Lesley Taylor's talent and passion for making exquisite small boxes has made her a 'collectable' name among the cognoscenti. Kerry Fowler went to meet her

Lesley Taylor's craft merits rather more description than the 'decorative-box making' label she applies to it. Her tiny inlaid creations are made to a high standard of precision that's obviously appreciated by the exclusive galleries which sell her work, and the cabinetmakers who commission her to inlay prestige pieces of furniture.

She learnt her skill 10 years ago when she took a Wood, Metals and Plastics course at Wolverhampton, and now works from home in Horsham, Sussex, producing hardwood boxes with geometrical parquetry designs. 'I did have visions of going on to more traditional marquetry, using saws, but I never stopped enjoying clean, geometric lines'.

Instead of saws, she uses an old hacksaw blade sandwiched between two bits of wood, and a steel rule to do the work of cutting veneers. The inlay work is usually set in a recessed lid (side-panel inlays are too time-consuming) and Lesley draws out her pattern in pencil on the lid and then cuts the veneers correspondingly. Working from the centre of the design outwards, the tiny mosaics of veneer are glued with PVA to the base of the lid. Her eye for detail and accuracy is keenly developed — and it needs to be; most of her boxes are no bigger than 3in wide.

Her small workshop at the bottom of the garden houses all the veneers, hardwoods and tools, plus her essential lathe and bandsaw. The four basic shapes she uses — hectagonal, triangular, round and square — are cut to about 5mm thick with the bandsaw and the edges disc-sanded on the lathe. She then works in any mitred corners or finger joints. The lid is sawn off and a piece of wood set into it from the base. She is now so familiar with her patterns (although she varies each one slightly as a personal touch) that the inlay work takes just under an hour a box.

WHEN SHE LEFT COLLEGE, Lesley found a job with Bewdley Crafts Museum where she exhibited her skills to visiting parties of schoolchildren and the odd sceptical woodworker. 'When I said I was demonstrating woodwork they'd think, "Oh yes, it's not going to be very good, a bit amateurish". Attitudes change with experience and soon she had people bringing her gifts of wood and veneer. 'One man, who worked for a veneer company where they used to throw away offcuts, brought a huge pile of veneers, some of it 3ft long. I thought "This will do me for five years". I've been going seven and the pile's still almost as big.'

Lesley gets her base wood from the Timber Purchasing Pool, in 2x2 pieces and the total cost in materials per box is minimal. But Lesley's box-making is not primarily a business venture and she would hate to be forced into a mass-production routine. 'I could

Matching dice and card boxes in sycamore with bird's-eye maple and ebony inlay. Flip-top card box in pau rosa and hornbeam. Right-angled precision in padauk and sycamore. Stunning 3in mahogany boxes with shell-shaped lids in exotic hardwoods

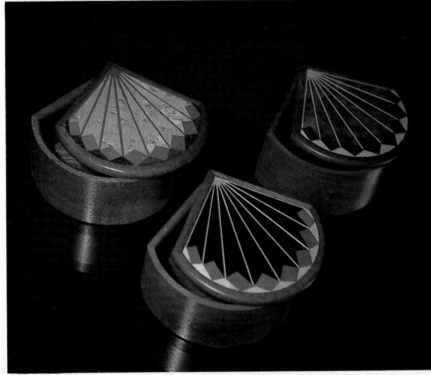

have made the transition, but I would have found it extremely boring.' Pride and pleasure are important facets of her work which keep gallery owners like Hugo Barclay of Brighton coming back for more. Her other main outlets, Lannards of Billingshurst and Ombersley Gallery in Worcestershire, have been warned that Lesley's box production may be intermittent over the next year, as she is expecting a baby.

Ante-natal classes have improved Lesley's social circle; she points out that her work isn't conducive to making friends. 'When you tell people what you do, they think "What a lovely life". They don't think about being alone all week.'

A box takes about eight hours to make, and it's then french polished and waxed. Lesley is now more meticulous about groundrules, such as boxes shouldn't be left in sunshine or exposed to temperature extremes which could warp and discolour them. When she was a student, she used to work against the tutor's instructions to prove that woodwork doesn't have to be hemmed in by rules. Now she admits there are rules, but she's learnt how to bend them. She's also convinced that when it comes to design, 'sometimes it's much better to be simple.'

When she's not making boxes she's planning new ones. The majority of the styles she sells have sliding removable lids, or swinghinge pivot tips, but the experimental boxes she showed me were extremely complex in their construction, with hidden compartments and interlocking lid-designs that opened up in a variety of patterns. They have remained experimental either because they're too costly to make, or because of minute flaws in the opening mechanisms. Her perfectionism, she explained, is necessary to match that of gallery owners and customers. Boxcollecting is a very British hobby and Lesley is now considered 'collectable'. Her sketchbook full of detailed drawings tackling engineering and design problems, is her insurance that there will always be something new of hers to buy.

Her favourite woods are paurosa and sycamore; she loves contrasting dark with light woods so it comes as no surprise that she also makes backgammon sets with parquetry work, to sell as presents. Her boxes range in price, a card box costs about £22, and mark-up by the gallery depends on whether it's on sale or return basis, and how steep local competition is — but it can be as much as 100%. 'It's a bit daunting thinking they can get a lot more money than you can for it sitting on a shelf.' Craft fairs are as far as she gets to selling direct, but they give her a chance to meet people and also get feedback about her work.

She plans to continue making and designing while her child grows up, but her one ideal would be 'to have a place in the country with a group of workshops. It's a nice atmosphere to work with fellow craftsmen around you because you share problems. But that's rather pie in the sky.' ■

Carving, canework, cabinetmaking, marquetry; we present a selection of work seen round the country, from recent or soon-to-come events and exhibitions

Photos Richard Davies

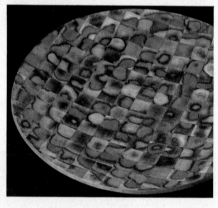

All at the Crafts Council shop Showcase, V&A Museum, London SW7; left, Eleanor Glover (28 Nov - 17 Dec), 'Woman with sacrificial bird'; top, Jim Partridge (31 Oct - 26 Nov), bowl in bleached burr oak, 6½in high; above, Peter Chatwin and Pamela Martin (5 Sep - 1 Oct), plate in laminated sycamore veneer, 17in across

Chelsea Crafts Fair, Chelsea Old Town Hall,
London SW3, 12-24 October; the fair this
year will include the work of John
Makepeace, among others. This is a basket
by Lois Walpole, who 'combines traditional
and non-traditional new and recycled
materials'

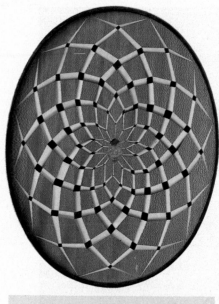

Fourth International Creative Marquetry Show, Norfolk, Virginia, USA, 20-30 Oct; the work above is from previous shows. Top, Ernie Ives' 'Controlled Air Space' took 1st at the 1986 show; middle, Richard Foote got an honourable mention in 1984 for 'Mondrian Box'; above, 'Pierced' by Barney Wander got an honourable mention in 1985. For details of how to apply for next year's show, send a large SAE to ICMS, 63 Church Lane, Sproughton, Ipswich IP8 3AY

'Woodsculptures', an exhibition by well-known carver Ian Norbury, was mounted in Eastington Hall, a beautiful Tudor manor house in Upton upon Severn, Worcs, 31 Aug - 5 Sep, then Bury Walk Gallery, London SW3, 16 Sep - 3 Oct. Main picture; 'Masai Warrior', American black walnut, 42in high; top inset, 'Salome' in Nutka cypress, 11in high; bottom inset, a host of allegories in 'Box of Delights', lime, 30in high. More information on (0242) 238582

PREVIEW

◄ The power of the good: detail from Ian Norbury's 'St George'

▲ A couple more from the London College of Furniture's summer show: above, Chris Ha's fascination with oriental joinery style and enclosures of space is clear from this 'stepped entry' box; left, Neville Sykes' ◄ expanding MDF table has created a lot of interest from a technical point of view

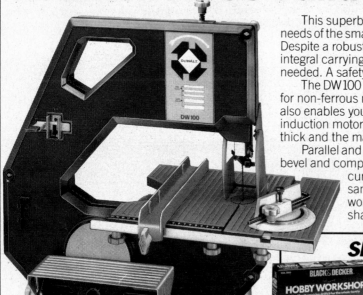

DESIGN
FOR PRODUCTION

A three-fold look at the problems and processes in designing for commercial makers. First: leave the world of one-offs behind and you encounter new problems, as John Barden of the Design Council explains

Smaller workshops abound — often under the direction of an increasing number of furniture designers and craftsmen intent on the batch-production of their own or other people's designs, instead of the making of individual or specially commissioned work.

Designing for production and general use exposes furniture to much wider scrutiny and assessment. However much you understand about basic furniture construction and costings, markets for batch-produced furniture are usually very price sensitive, particularly if retail shops are involved. Apart from hitting an appropriate price point the furniture really has to *attract the price*. This involves a lot more than just the cost of making and is where design in all its sense takes on extra meaning; you can create 'added value' or perceived value for your furniture. Scale, proportion, detailing, colour and other visual aspects, together with function, comfort and practical usage issues are some of the crucial issues concerned.

National product approval schemes, run by independent bodies and involving the expert assessment of products, can be of great assistance in determining the standard and success achieved. The Design Council's Design Centre Selection scheme is one such approval system and has a furniture Selection Committee comprising designers, retailers, manufacturers and others. They consider furniture agains the following criteria:

● **Performance** Does the product satisfy its performance specification and, if so, is the specification itself satisfactory; i.e. does the product do what it was designed to do?

● **Construction** Are the materials, finishes and assemblies such that the product will continue to perform reliably for its specified life span, or for what the user would expect to be a reasonable life span?

● **Ergonomics** Is the product easy to use and maintain? Are the instructions, if any, adequate in describing the use or maintenance of the product?

● **Aesthetics** Are the forms, colours, patterns and textures appropriate to the function of the product?

● **Value for money** Does the price of the product seem reasonable in relation to its characteristics as defined by the answers to the above questions and in relation to similar products on the market?

In addition the Design Council requires that products conform to relevant safety, mandatory and technical standards where ever appropriate. Remember once you sell to a wider audience you can be liable for failures and accidents that might occur in your furniture. Product testing and compliance with British Standards is therefore highly recommended.

Although there are some specific and important safety British Standards for furniture, notably BS5852 for ignitability of upholstery, most attention by the general furniture industry is given to what is broadly described as technical performance, where test-houses such as the Furniture Industry Research Association can rigorously test to a number of British Standards. Here are some of the details:

1 Structural tests (*Test Standards: BS4875 and BS5459*).

Furniture is not only used in the conventional sense but also moved around, knocked over, stood and leant on. The various types of activity to which the frame of a piece of furniture is subjected can be grouped into use, misuse and abuse. The standards used as a basis for the performance testing allow for use and reasonable misuse but not abuse.

As an illustration of this, a chair may not only be sat on many thousands of times during its life, but also occasionally knocked over, bumped into or stood on. It would be unrealistic to suppose that a chair is never subjected to these activities and so the performance standards are designed to simulate the highest loads which might reasonably be applied in such situations.

The standards for structural testing of desks, tables and storage furniture of all types operate within the same principles and to each item of furniture the following loads are applied:

(a) Fatigue, representing normal operational use. Loads representative of the human frame applied thousands of times, e.g. opening and closing doors and drawers, sitting down into chairs, leaning on desks.

(b) Static, representing the infrequent high loads applied during reasonable misuse, applied 10 times only, e.g. standing on tables and chairs, leaning on doors and drawers.

(c) Impact, representing furniture being knocked over, bumped into or stepped down on to. Applied 10 times only.

Slam open-and-shut tests on component parts and sustained load tests (long-term high loads on shelves, etc, to assess deflection over time) are also carried out.

The standards are graded according to the end use of the furniture tested but level 4, or its equivalent, representing normal contract use is frequently adopted.

2 Surface finish tests (*Test Standards: BS6250 and BS3900*).

These tests deal specifically with the top surface of cabinet furniture and some of the larger show-wood arms on chairs. On chipboard or wood substrates, the testing is representative of three main areas of possible damage:

(a) marking or staining by chemicals and household liquids, e.g. ink, nail varnish, alcohol.

(b) marking by wet or dry heat, e.g. a coffee cup.

(c) mechanical damage, e.g. scratching and lack of adhesion to the undersurface.

3 Upholstery (*Test Standards: BS2543 and BS5852*)

The range of upholstery fabrics available for the seating is often very extensive and it is often impractical to test many fabric and foam/fabric combinations — especially as 'special' orders to the customer's specification are common.

A common approach therefore is to test a limited number of standard combinations and concentrate on these in your marketing. The tests carried out on fabrics include procedures to determine tensile strength, tear strength, seam slippage, visible soiling and colour fastness.

A full list of British Standards for furniture is provided in a BSI Sectional List.

References

The Design Council, 28 Haymarket, London SW1Y 4SU.
The Consumers Association, 14 Buckingham St, London WC2.
British Standards Institution, 2 Park St, London W1A 2BS.
Furniture Industry Research Association, Maxwell Road, Stevenage, Herts SG1 2EW.

THE THREE STAGES OF DESIGN

Design is full of conflict. You want your product to 'look good', be capable of making at a sensible price, stand up to the kind of wear customers will give it . . . and also make clients fall in love with it.

So many different pressures. No wonder that as you're drawing up a design you suddenly stop and think: 'No, that won't be strong enough.' You rub it out and start again.

Yet as we now understand the creative process, you shouldn't be trying to cope with all these different pressures at one and the same time. First let the ideas flow, get something on paper. Only at a later stage should you switch to thinking about the strength, manufacturing, marketing and other considerations.

Letting the ideas flow, or 'brainstorming', is often used in business. Judgement on whether the ideas are practical is suspended until later.

The reason this approach works is that we use a different part of the brain when generating ideas from when we are evaluating and analysing them. Research shows the left hemisphere of the brain works in facts and details. The right side of the brain works in concepts, form and shape, not in words. So ideas are generated in the right hemisphere and are passed over to the left hemisphere to sort out the details.

Original design comes from having a free-reined right brain. If you don't use this side of your brain, your designs will be orthodox, wholly practical — but not inspiring.

Hugh O'Neill explains why you must get both sides of your brain working if you're going to achieve good design

You can encourage the right side of the brain by doodling during the initial design stage. Forget about practicality and problems of production. Just put down on paper in very quick rough sketches the ideas as they bubble up from your right brain.

Of course, what you put down on paper is influenced by all sorts of subtle factors. Originality doesn't occur in people who have little experience of what they're working on. New ideas come from people who have studied the work of others, who go to contemporary exhibitions and collections, browse in museums. These people feed the left side of their brains with dimensions, structures, details and embellishments; and at the same time are putting away into their right brains a store of shapes, forms and concepts to be drawn on later.

In my view the distinguishing feature of good design is the ability of the finished object to stand alone in its own space and sit comfortably in its own environment. Some chairs you just have to push under the table because it is 'their place.' Others you want to pull back and even display in different parts of the room because they each make a statement about themselves.

There are basically three stages in designing:

1 Decide, in the broadest terms, what is the primary function of the object you're designing. Don't think of it as 'a chair' but as 'a means of supporting a person while they sit to eat meals or work at a table'. The objective, and the end product should be very different if the chair is 'to support a person in comfort while they are relaxing'.

2 With the broad objective in mind, let your imagination run free and sketch what emerges — maybe you'll come up with a hammock and not a chair at all.

3 With half a dozen rough ideas sketched out, you can start to look at each and ask questions such as: How could this be made? What would have to be done to make this idea workable? Will it fit into the sort of environment in which it is likely to be placed by my sort of clientele? If not, what would I have to do to produce and market this idea?

Only when you've gone through this kind of process, coming up with ideas and testing them out, do we finally ask the harder-edged question: Is this design really viable? ▶

Oak chest and side table in the 'Ovolo'
range, part of a series Luke designed for
production by Birmingham manufacturers
Juckes. On the wall, a 'bull's-eye' mirror
framed in multi-colour Italian veneers

THE WORKING WOODWORKER

Luke Hughes takes the lid off his own experience since setting up in business

Some years ago a prison strike necessitated the use of the Army and a military encampment to supervise prisoners. More street-wise prisoners hoped to exploit the situation and made a point of objecting, thinking they might squeeze concessions out of their captors' inexperience of rules. Some went on hunger strike to draw attention to their cause, complaining that the rules of captivity were not being properly observed. An inspired sergant-major left them to get hungry for a couple of days and then pronounced 'sod the rules Corporal Jones! In the back of that Land Rover you'll find 50 rashers of bacon, a frying pan, and a primus. You will fry until two o'clock this afternoon'. The seductive waft of sizzling rashers proved too great; the hunger strike was called off at once. Moral: an attitude of 'sod the rules', an inspired idea, and knowing what people want — even though they might not know it themselves — is the key to making any business work, not least a woodwork business.

I have read more pages of helpful but irritating advice about how to start up or manage a business over the last seven years than I've had parking tickets when working on building sites in central London. I've given up both — reading the pages of verbiage, that is, and working in central London. You don't have to believe in Darwin to learn from your mistakes, though to judge from the hard-luck stories that are fashionable amongst woodworkers, it's amazing they have progressed beyond Neanderthal man. Reading about starting a business is like reading the car manual; being able to recite the words is no substitute for picking up a spanner and having a go. I don't intend to add any more 'Golden Rules', but briefly to look back at what we've done, and what lessons we have learned.

Although after university I trained as a solicitor, I kept gravitating back to wood. I had paid for much of my law course from the proceeds of repairing the woodwork on Morris Travellers, and school and college vacations had always been spent working for local builders. When I finally took the plunge and ditched the law, I worked for two years as a site carpenter fitting floors, stairs, kitchens and wardrobes using the back of my Morris, a Black & Decker Workmate, a radial-arm saw and a router as principal aids. The money was superb in central London if you were fast and punctual, and one quickly became the Master of the Artful, Tasteful Bodge. It may not have been great craftmanship, but I learned to solve structural and aesthetic problems.

I kept on thinking I should go on a course to learn about furniture, but no one was going to pay and there never quite seemed the time to organise going. So I bought Alf Martensons *Woodworkers' Bible* and devoured it page by page. I slipped into the V & A to see how they really made furniture (only to discover that most classic makers of the past were really bodgers at heart); I browsed round the museums in London, around country houses, and exhibition galleries and decided that this mystique about making furniture wasn't all it was cracked up to be.

What was needed was skill, machinery, and experience. Being nourished on 4in nails was no ground training for skill, but it was apparent that to acquire that skill I needed information and experience. Well, the information is all over the place. There are books, manuals, encyclopaedias and reference works crammed with more wise words, tips and shortcuts than any 100 craftsmen could have bottled up in all their careers. Stobarts have a splendid catalogue; WOODWORKER carries adverts constantly; shows and exhibitions have book stalls everywhere. Even the pages of WOODWORKER carry fascinating information. I am still building a library of such books, but as with reading a car manual, it's not much use without knowing how to pick up a spanner.

So where was one to get the experience? Well, by working of course . . . on as many varied woody jobs as could be fitted into the week. From fitting the shelf in the bathroom, to disguising the hi-fi cabinet, from mending the neighbour's chair to building the girlfriend's bed I very quickly learned what was fun, and what one did well, and what brought in enough cash to be worthwhile. From being versatile, one developed a local reputation; it became possible to be more selective; clients began to show more trust, and clearly liked the idea that they were in some way involved in helping you get started.

One client I picked up in the queue of the builders' merchants asked me to fix a shelf in his kitchen. I worked in his house for three months, and at the end of it he asked me to make the new archive library for the Grenadier Guards opposite Buckingham Palace (opened by the Duke of Edinburgh). Every year since he has bought something new. That was some kitchen shelf.

Gradually skill and experience was acquired. My work became faster, more accurate and confident and it was perfectly clear I needed someone else to hold the other end of the 8x4ft. Being rather ashamed of not having been properly trained, I was sorely inhibited from advertising, and persuaded Mark Adams to join me, a very old family friend who had been working in Oman fixing radar systems for Marconi for three years. He knew absolutely nothing about wood but he was great to work with, and we guessed that with a few more good ideas and the next chapter in the *Woodworkers' Bible* we might muddle through.

But I also knew that I stood a better chance of muddling through if I didn't have to waste time filling in VAT returns. An essential ingredient of the small business is economy of effort; why should one get upset doing something that raised the blood pressure when someones else might do it better, more efficiently, and more accurately. What was needed was a Fairy Godmother who would look after all the accounts, administration, correspondence, PAYE forms, troublesome customers, invoicing, ordering, selling . . . even finishing off the drawings that were late when I was really under pressure. Who believes in Fairy Godmothers? Well I do, and two years ago Mark and I were joined by Christian Jebb who has brought all her enthusiasm and energy — and magic spells — to the team.

Others worked for me on and off, but this year we were joined by Joss Skottowe, who having trained for three years at the London College of Furniture in antique restoration, was better qualified than any of us, even though he spent two years proofing sub-machine guns in the East End.

But how were we to afford the machines? I looked at all the grants and loans available but somehow their regulations were so complicated that we thought it quicker just to get on and earn the cash. So we made bookcases for lawyers who at the end of a profitable year need justifiable expenses to reduce their tax liability — they tend to update their law library, and a set of All England Law Reports is not much use without a tax deductible bookcase to fit the books in. We offered an overnight and weekend bookcase service and in six months earned enough to put a deposit down on a freehold workshop and to buy a few basic machines. The machines were the cheapest I could afford and I regretted many of the purchases immediately . . . and yet they did a job of a kind, and enabled me to buy bigger and better machines two years later.

The arrival of Christian coincided with a bigger plan, that of opening a shop. It was clear I needed to raise about £30,000. There seemed to be two ways to do it — a bank loan, or through Venture Capital. A bank loan was ▶

likely to cost up to 20% and would crucity me if the expansion failed. And yet Venture Capital Funds considered the sums involved too puny, and six Funds rejected the proposition; but one of them asked if we had considered raising the capital through the Business Expansion Scheme. The BES allows for higher tax rate payers to avoid income tax liability if they invest in an approved BES business, and allow them Capital Gains Tax exemption on any profit they make on their shareholding so long as they leave their investment in for five years. It is also provided that the company can get income tax relief on the interest of any loan needed to buy back its own shares from BES investors after that initial five year period.

The plan was simple; I needed six shareholders to put up £5,000 each, and to have one to represent the interests of the others on 'the Board' but who might also tell me something about how to run a business. This is exactly what happened. And now I retain the majority shareholding, I have a freehold workshop on one side of a backstreet in Covent Garden and a long, cheap lease on a shop on the other side of the same street; the benefit of professional financial advice for free, and a superb versatile team whose skills and aspirations complement each other. Together we have a lot of fun (another essential ingredient in the small business) and have even begun to to make a profit.

THROUGHOUT ALL THESE EARLY YEARS I was dogged by the notion that I wasn't really making the furniture I wanted; I was haunted by some of the short cuts we were forced to take to pay the mortgage and permanently depressed by feeling unable to reach the standards to which I aspired. I kept on trying to reassure myself by saying, 'Well, an old fashioned apprenticeship was seven years, you shouldn't expect to be perfect in four; your problems will really begin when you cease to aspire to get better'. To be fair to ourselves, during every job our standards became higher, and that fact, coupled with the experience of being able to judge exactly how far the contract price allowed a pursuit for perfection, gradually enabled us to make what we wanted, to be sure of selling it, and at a price that people could afford. I have firmly come to the belief that furniture has a 'right' price which is reflected in the design and manufacture, and that if you can't make it for that 'right' price, even if one or two barmy clients are prepared to pay a premium for it, then the design is wrong and you shouldn't be making it. Reputation is built up over years, and there is nothing like a reputation for fair pricing to develop a faithful client list.

That leads to my approach to design — slightly unorthodox, again for want of a disciplined training. This is seen by many as a distinct advantage. One of the driving forces of my decision to be a furniture maker was a passionate love for English furniture, particularly of the ages before 1750 when big architectural theories began to dominate. Before then, much of the design of furniture had evolved in local areas out of particular conditions to meet specific needs. The skills of the craftsmen and the shape of his tools were far more important than the 'correctness' of the classical proportion or the detail of the Empire swag. The freshness and wit of early English furniture is based on this direct involvement of the craftsman with the design; this was long before the ravages of the Industrial Revolution prompted the emergence of the Arts and Craft Movement. It appeared to me that the evolution of a tradition was continual process and the iconoclasm of much contemporary work has done little either to push frontiers on or to help that tradition develop. What I set out to do was to evaluate what were the essential ingredients of that English tradition, to play with them, and to use them to develop my own style. Todate it has been embryonic and cautious, but the chord it strikes in potential clients has surprised many people, not least me. But what of the practicalities?

About twice a year I have whims and make something which develops an idea, usually pretentious, which no one wants to buy. From those pieces other more practical ideas arise which become attractive to clients and useful to make. But mostly, my work is in response to a specific problem and I find most of the structural form and the subsequent detailing derives directly from the function the piece is to serve. In the part this happened by accident and frequently for want of my having a more original thought, but recently I have learned that this is a good way of solving design problems, and if you read the manuals, it's the only way. Defining exactly what a client wants is tricky; they usually don't know themselves. But with the right questions it is possible to reduce the options. Two watchwords are Compromise, and Aspiration. Compromise what you want to make with what he wants you to make; compromise with the limitations of the material and the price; compromise with aesthetics and function; compromise between always seeking to express a novel idea, and the reality of sacrificing sound, solid, and trusted solutions ... but aspire! Always aspire to get him to see it your way, to push the standards higher, to experiment with new techniques and materials, and to make a profit as well.

ONE OF THE MOST INTERESTING ASPECTS of our work has been designing for mass production, compromising all the limitations of a furniture factory, all the limitations of price and marketing potential, all the details of proportion with the reality of a commercial cutting list. The aspiration has been to take back into mass production many of the virtues of craftsmanship and an English tradition and to produce them economically for factory, retailer, and client alike. Our biggest success has been with the Ovolo collection of oak bedroom furniture which was launched nine months ago and is now selling in 40 shops across the country, as well as in Japan. Typical of the compromises made was the height of the wardrobe, carefully tailored to be no higher than the factory lift shaft. I cannot pretend the exercise of launching such products is easy: I have witnessed first-hand all the symptoms of a dying industry, an industry that desperately needs the talent that should be graduating (properly trained) from the art colleges. It is a world beset by interest rates, union legislation, broken-down delivery lorries, and the world going shopping on a Bank Holiday weekend down at the Arndale Centre. It is a far cry from the friendly screech of a router, the sweet odour of teak dust filling your lungs, and the joys of dropping your freshly honed chisels on the concrete floor. But there is hope, and for designers there are tremendous challenges.

Alan Peters has written more sense about the realities of running a workshop than most, extracts of which were quoted in the second article in this series (WW/April). The following seems so apt, and has been forgotten by so many at their peril: 'You will never succeed in the area of commissioned work unless you readily accept that you are providing a service to the public in return for work and your livelihood, and that simple fact must never be forgotten however successful you may become. If on the other hand you secretly consider yourself God's gift to the world of art and design and that it is an honour for anyone to possess your work you will not last long unless you really are brilliant'.

And that from a man who really is brilliant.

I feel that the most useful conclusion that might be drawn from my experience is that in the woodwork business there are no rules for the sergeant-major to abuse. In fact the so-called rules of marketing, design, or making may inhibit one from thinking of a fresh approach, let alone applying common sense. ∎

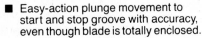
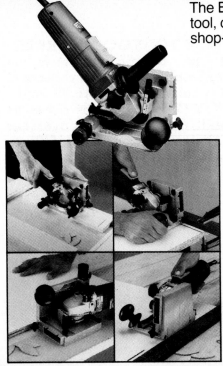

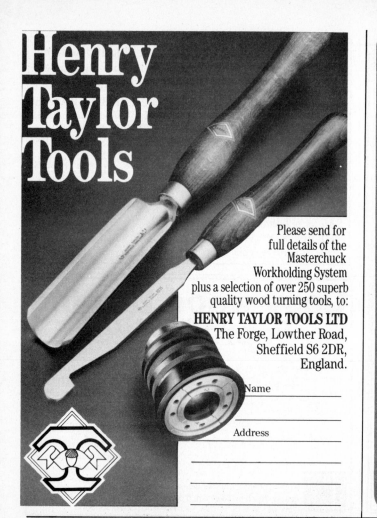

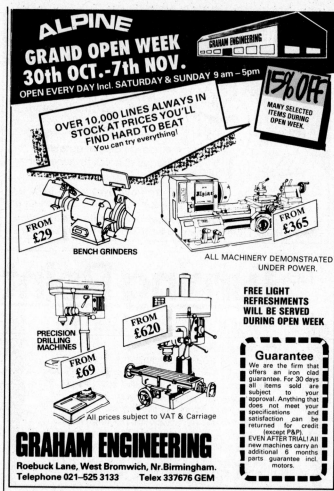

shopguide

AVON

BATH   Tel. Bath 64513
JOHN HALL TOOLS   ★
RAILWAY STREET

Open: Monday-Saturday
9.00 a.m.5.30 p.m.
H.P.W.WM.D.A.BC.

BRISTOL   Tel. (0272) 741510
JOHN HALL TOOLS LIMITED   ★
CLIFTON DOWN SHOPPING CENTRE
WHITELADIES ROAD
Open: Monday-Saturday
9.00 a.m.-5.30 p.m.
H.P.W.WM.D.A.BC.

BRISTOL   Tel. (0272) 667013
WILLIS   T
157 WEST STREET
BEDMINSTER
Open Mon.-Fri. 8.30 a.m.-5.00 p.m.

P.W.WM.D.CS.A.BC.

BERKSHIRE

READING   Tel. Littlewick Green
DAVID HUNT (TOOL   2743
MERCHANTS) LTD   ★
KNOWL HILL, NR. READING
Open: Monday-Saturday
9.00 a.m.-5.30 p.m.
H.P.W.D.A.BC.

READING   Tel. Reading 661511
WOKINGHAM TOOL CO. LTD.   T
99 WOKINGHAM ROAD
Open: Mon-Sat 9.00 a.m.-5.30 p.m.
Closed 1.00-2.00 p.m. for lunch

H.P.W.WM.D.CS.A.BC.

SLOUGH   Tel: (06286) 5125
BRAYWOOD ESTATES LTD.   ★
158 BURNHAM LANE
Open: 9.00am-5.30pm.
Monday-Saturday.
H.P.W.WM.CS.A.

BUCKINGHAMSHIRE

MILTON KEYNES   Tel. (0908)
POLLARD WOODWORKING   641366
CENTRE   T★
51 AYLESBURY ST., BLETCHLEY
Open: Mon.-Fri. 8.30-5.30
Saturday 9.00-5.00
H.P.W.WM.D.CS.A.BC.   **INCA**

HIGH WYCOMBE   Tel. (0494)
ISAAC LORD LTD.   22221
185 DESBOROUGH ROAD   K
Open: Mon.-Fri. 8.00 a.m. to 5.30 p.m.
Saturday 8.30 a.m. to 5.00 p.m.

H.P.W.D.A.WM.MF.

Advertise here to
capture both local
+ national markets

CAMBRIDGESHIRE

CAMBRIDGE   Tel: (0223) 63132
D. MACKAY LTD.   ★
BRITANNIA WORKS, EAST ROAD
Open: Mon.-Fri. 8.30 a.m.-1 p.m./2.00-
5.00 p.m. Sat. 8.30 a.m.-1.00 p.m.
H.P.W.D.T.CS.MF.A.BC.

CAMBRIDGE   Tel. (0223) 247386
H. B. WOODWORKING   TK
105 CHERRY HINTON ROAD
Open: 8.30 a.m.-5.30 p.m.
Monday-Friday
8.30 a.m.-1.00 p.m. Sat.
H.P.W.WM.D.CS.A.MF.BC.

CHESHIRE

NANTWICH   Tel. Crewe 67010
ALAN HOLTHAM   TK★
THE OLD STORES TURNERY
WISTASON ROAD, WILLASTON
Open: Tues.-Fri. 9.00 a.m.-5.30 p.m.
Sat. 9.00 a.m.-5.00 p.m. Closed Monday.
P.W.WM.D.T.C.CS.A.BC.

WIDNESS   Tel: 051 424 4545/7965
THE POWER TOOL CENTRE   T★
54/58 VICTORIA ROAD, WA8 7PJ
Mon.-Fri. 8.30am-5pm
Sat. 8.30am-4pm.

H.P.W.WM.D.CS.A.BC.

CLEVELAND

MIDDLESBROUGH   Tel. (0642)
CLEVELAND WOODCRAFT   813103
(M'BRO), 38-42 CRESCENT ROAD   TK

Open: Mon.-Sat. 9.15 a.m.-5.30 p.m.

H.P.A.BC.W.WM.CS.D.

CORNWALL

SOUTH WEST Power Tools

CORNWALL   Tel: Helston (03265) 4961
HELSTON AND LAUNCESTON   Launceston
  (0566) 4781
H.P.W.WM.D.CS.A.   TK

CUMBRIA

CARLISLE   Tel. (0228) 36391
W. M. PLANT   T
ALLENBROOK ROAD
ROSEHILL, CA1 2UT
Open: Mon.-Fri. 8.00 a.m.-5.15 p.m.
Sat. 8.00 a.m.-12.30 noon
P.W.WM.D.CS.A.

DEVON

PLYMOUTH   Tel. (0752) 330303
WESTWARD BUILDING SERVICES   ★
LTD., LISTER CLOSE, NEWNHAM
INDUSTRIAL ESTATE, PLYMPTON
Open: Mon-Fri 8.00 a.m.-5.30 p.m.
Sat. 8.30 a.m.-12.30 p.m.
H.P.W.WM.D.A.BC.

DEVON

PLYMOUTH   Tel. (0752) 665363
F.T.B. LAWSON LTD.   T
71 NEW GEORGE STREET
PLYMOUTH PL1 1RB
Open: Mon.-Sat. 8.30 a.m.-5.30 p.m.

H.P.W.CS.MF.A.

DORSET

WEYMOUTH   Tel. (0305) 770303
WEYMOUTH HIRE & SALES LTD.   TK
5 KENT CLOSE
GRANBY INDUSTRIAL ESTATE
Open 7.30 a.m.-5.30 p.m. Mon.-Fri.
Sat. 8 a.m.-1 p.m.
H.P.W.WM.D.CS.A.K.

ESSEX

LEIGH ON SEA   Tel. (0702)
MARSHAL & PARSONS LTD.   710404
1111 LONDON ROAD   K

Open: 8.30 a.m.-5.30 p.m. Mon.-Fri.
9.00 a.m.-5.00 p.m. Sat.
H.P.W.WM.D.CS.A.

ILFORD   Tel. 597 7461
CUTWELL WOODWORKING   T★
776 HIGH ROAD
GOODMAYES IG3 8SY

H.P.W.WM.D.CS.A.

GLOUCESTER

TEWKESBURY   Tel. (0684)
TEWKESBURY SAW CO. LTD.   293092
TRADE ESTATE, NEWTOWN   K
  Telex No. 43382
Open: Mon-Fri 8.00 a.m.-5.00 p.m.
Saturday 9.30 a.m.-12.00 p.m.
P.W.WM.D.CS.

HAMPSHIRE

ALDERSHOT   **SOUTHAMPTON**
(0252) 334422   (0703) 332288
BURCH & HILLS POWER TOOL CENTRES
374 HIGH ST.   7 BELVIDERE RD.
Open Mon.-Fri. 8.30-5.30. Sat. 8.30-12.00
Closed for Lunch 1.00-2.00
H.P.W.WM.D.CS.MF.BC.K.*   T

HEREFORDSHIRE

HEREFORD   Tel. (0432) 271366
WOODWORKING CENTRE
100 WIDEMARSH ST., HR4 9HG

Open: Mon.-Sat. 8 a.m.-5.30 p.m.

H.P.W.WM.D.CS.MF.A.T.

HERTFORDSHIRE

WARE   Tel: (0920) 870 230
HEATH SAWS   870 636
6 LEESIDE WORKS   K★
STANSTEAD ABBOTTS (near Ware) HERTS.
SG12 8DL.
Open: Mon.-Fri. 8.30 a.m.-5.30 p.m.
Sat. 8.30 a.m.-1 p.m. Sunday by appointment.
H.P.W.WM.D.T.CS.MF.A.BC.*K.

HUMBERSIDE

HULL
HUMBERSIDE FACTORING/H.F.C.
SAW SERVICING LTD.
MAIN STREET
Open: Mon.-Fri. 8am-5pm.
Saturday 8am-12.00pm.
H.P.W.WM.D.CS.A.BC.K.

KENT

MAIDSTONE   Tel: (0622) 44350
HENSON AND PLATT
TOKE PLACE
LINTON
Open Mon.-Fri. 8.00 a.m.-5.00 p.m.
Saturday 8.00 a.m.-1.00 p.m.
H.P.W.T.CS.A.

MAIDSTONE   Tel. (0622) 50177
SOUTH EASTERN SAWS (Ind.) LTD.   ★
COLDRED ROAD
PARKWOOD INDUSTRIAL ESTATE

Open: Mon.-Fri. 8.00 a.m.-5.00 p.m.
Sat. 9.00 a.m.-12.00 a.m.
B.C.W.CS.WM.PH.

BIDDENDEN   Tel. (0580) 291555
THE TURNING POINT
BRITISH GATES AND TIMBER LTD.
BIDDENDEN, NR. ASHFORD TN27 8DD
Open: Mon.-Fri. 7.30 a.m.-5.30 p.m.
Sat. 8.30 a.m.-12.00 a.m.
H.P.W.D.T.CS.MF.A.BC.

LANCASHIRE

PRESTON   Tel. (0772) 52951
SPEEDWELL TOOL COMPANY   ★
62-68 MEADOW STREET PR1 1SU
Open: Mon.-Fri. 8.30 a.m.-5.30 p.m.
Sat. 8.30 a.m.-12.30 p.m.

H.P.W.WM.CS.A.MF.BC.

ROCHDALE   Tel. (0706) 342123/
C.S.M. TOOLS   342322
4-6 HEYWOOD ROAD   T★
CASTLETON
Open: Mon-Sat 9.00 a.m.-6.00 p.m.
Sundays by appointment
W.D.CS.A.BC.

LANCASTER   Tel: (0524) 32886
LILE TOOL SHOP   K
43/45 NORTH ROAD
Open: Monday to Saturday
9.00 a.m.-5.30 p.m.
Wed. 9.00 a.m.-12.30 p.m.
H.P.W.D.A.

Read Model Engineer for a new angle on construction & design

shopguide

LONDON

ACTON   Tel. (01-992) 4835
A. MILLS (ACTON) LTD.   ★
32/36 CHURCHFIELD ROAD W3 6ED
Open: Mon.-Fri. 8.32 a.m.-5.30 p.m.
Saturdays 9.00 a.m.-1.00 p.m.
H.P.W.WM.

LONDON   Tel. 01-723 2295-6-7
LANGHAM TOOLS LIMITED
13 NORFOLK PLACE
LONDON W2 1QJ

FULHAM   Tel. (01-636) 6109
I. GRIZARD LTD.
84a-b.c. LILLIE ROAD, SW6 1TL
Open: Mon.-Sat. 9.00-5.30 p.m.
Half day Thursday

H.P.A.BC.W.CS.WM.D.

MANCHESTER

MANCHESTER   Tel. (061 789)
TIMMS TOOLS   0909
102-104 LIVERPOOL ROAD   ★
PATRICROFT M30 0WZ
Weekdays 9.00 a.m.-5.30 p.m.
Sat. 9.00 a.m.-1.00 p.m.
H.P.A.W.

**Read Model Engineer
for a new angle on
construction and
design.**

MERSEYSIDE

LIVERPOOL   Tel. (051-207) 2967
TAYLOR BROS (LIVERPOOL) LTD.   TK
195-199 LONDON ROAD
LIVERPOOL L3 8JG
Open: Monday to Friday
8.30 a.m.-5.30 p.m.
H.P.W.WM.D.A.BC.

MIDDLESEX

ENFIELD   Tel. 01-363 2935
GILL & HOXBY LTD.   T
131-137 ST. MARKS ROAD ADJ.
BUSH HILL PARK STATION, EN1 1BA
Mon.-Sat. 8-5.30
Early closing Wed. 1 p.m.
H.P.A.M.MC.T.S.W.

RUISLIP   Tel. (08956) 74126
ALLMODELS ENGINEERING LTD.   ★
91 MANOR WAY

Open: Mon.-Sat. 9.00 a.m.-5.30 p.m.

H.P.W.A.D.CS.MF.BC.

NORFOLK

NORWICH   Tel. (0603) 898695
NORFOLK SAW SERVICES
DOG LANE, HORSFORD
Open: Monday to Friday
8.00 a.m.-5.00 p.m.
Saturday 8.00 a.m.-12.00 p.m.
H.P.W.WM.D.CS.A.

NORFOLK

KINGS LYNN   Tel. (0553) 772443
WALKER & ANDERSON (Kings Lynn) LTD.   T
WINDSOR ROAD, KINGS LYNN
Open: Monday to Saturday
7.45 a.m.-5.15 p.m.

H.P.W.WM.D.CS.A.

NORWICH   Tel. (0603) 400933
WESTGATES WOODWORKING   Tx
61 HURRICANE WAY,   975412
NORWICH AIRPORT INDUSTRIAL ESTATE
Open: 9.00 a.m.-5.00 p.m. weekdays
9.00 a.m.-12.30 Sat.
P.W.WM.D.BC.   K

KINGS LYNN   Tel: 07605 674
NORFOLK WOODTURNING CENTRE   ★
UNIT A, HILL FARM WORKSHOPS
GREAT DUNHAM (Nr. Swaffham)
Tues.-Sat. 9.00am-5.30pm

H.P.W.D.T.MF.A.BC.

NORTHAMPTONSHIRE

RUSHDEN   Tel: (0933) 56424
PETER CRISP OF RUSHDEN   T★
7-11 HIGH STREET
Mon.-Fri. 8.30-12.30/1.30-5.30
Thurs. 8.30-1.00. Sat. all day.
H.P.W.WM.D.M.F.A.K.

NOTTINGHAMSHIRE

NOTTINGHAM   Tel: (0602) 225979
POOLEWOOD   and 227064/5
EQUIPMENT LTD.   (06077) 2421 after hrs
5a HOLLY LANE, CHILLWELL
Open: Mon-Fri 9.00 a.m.-5.30 p.m.
Sat. 9.00 a.m. to 12.30 p.m.
P.W.WM.D.CS.A.BC.

OXON

WITNEY   Tel. (0993) 76431
TARGET TOOLS (SALES,   OXON
HIRE & REPAIRS)   T★
SWAIN COURT
STATION INDUSTRIAL ESTATE
Open: Mon.-Sat. 8.00 a.m.-5.00 p.m.
24 hour Answerphone
BC.W.M.A.

SHROPSHIRE

TELFORD   Tel. Telford (0952)
ASLES LTD.   48054
VINEYARD ROAD, WELLINGTON   K★

Open: Mon.-Fri. 8.30 a.m.-5.30 p.m.
Saturday 8.30 a.m.-4.00 p.m.
H.P.W.WM.D.CS.BC.A.

SOMERSET

TAUNTON   Tel. (0823) 335431
JOHN HALL TOOLS   ★
6 HIGH STREET

Open Monday-Saturday
9.00 a.m.-5.00 p.m.
H.P.W.WM.D.CS.A.

SUFFOLK

IPSWICH   Tel. (0473) 40456
FOX WOODWORKING   463884
142-144 BRAMFORD LANE   T★
Open: Tues.-Fri. 9 a.m.-5.30 p.m.
Sat. 9 a.m.-5 p.m.
W.WM.D.T.CS.MF.A.BC.K.★

SURREY

GUILDFORD   Tel. (0483) 61125
MESSINGERS FOR TOOLS   T
18-18 CHERTSEY ST.)
(TOP OF NORTH ST.)
Open: Tues.-Sat. 8.30 a.m.-5.30 p.m.
H.P.W.CS.MF.A.BC.K.T.

STAFFORDSHIRE

TAMWORTH   Tel: (0827) 56188
MATTHEWS BROTHERS LTD.   TK★
KETTLEBROOKS ROAD
Open: Mon.-Sat. 8.30 a.m.-5.30 p.m.
Demonstrations Sunday mornings by
appointment only
H.P.WM.D.T.CS.A.BC.K.

SUSSEX

WORTHING   Tel. (0903) 38739
W. HOSKING LTD. (TOOLS &   KT★
MACHINERY)
28 PORTLAND RD, BN11 1QN
Open: Mon.-Sat. 8.30 a.m.-5.30 p.m.
Closed Wednesday
H.P.W.WM.D.CS.A.BC.

TYNE & WEAR

NEWCASTLE-UPON-TYNE   ★
J. W. HOYLE LTD
CLARENCE STREET
NEWCASTLE-UPON-TYNE
TYNE & WEAR
NE2 17J
H.P.W.WM.D.CS.A.BC.K.

W. MIDLANDS

WOLVERHAMPTON   Tel: (0902)
MANSAW SERVICES   58759
WARD STREET, HORSELEY FIELDS   TK★
WOLVERHAMPTON, WEST MIDLANDS
Open: Mon.-Fri. 8.00 a.m.-6.00 p.m.
Saturday 8 a.m.-3 p.m.
H.P.W.WM.A.D.CS.

**All shops with an
asterisk ★
have a Mail Order
Service**

YORKSHIRE

THIRSK   Tel. (0845) 22770
THE WOOD SHOP   ★
TRESKE SAWMILLS LTD.
STATION WORKS
Open: Seven days a week 9.00-5.00

T.H.MF.BC.H.

SHEFFIELD   Tel. (0742) 441012
GREGORY & TAYLOR LTD.   K
WORKSOP ROAD
Open: 8.30 a.m.-5.30 p.m.
Monday-Friday
8.30 a.m.-12.30 p.m. Saturday
H.P.W.WM.D.

HARROGATE   Tel. (0423) 505328/
MULTI-TOOLS   66245
158 KINGS ROAD   K★

Open: Monday to Saturday
8.30 a.m.-6.00 p.m.

H.P.W.WM.D.A.BC.

YORKSHIRE

HOLME UPON   Tel. (0696) 60612
SPALDING MOOR
CRAFT TOOLS AND TACKLE LTD.
HOLME INDUSTRIAL ESTATE
Open: Mon.-Fri. 9.00 am-5.30 pm.
Saturday & Bank Holiday 9.00 am-4.30 pm
H.P.W.D.T.CS.MF.A.BC.

LEEDS   Tel. (0532) 574736
D. B. KEIGHLEY MACHINERY LTD.   ★
VICKERS PLACE, STANNINGLEY
PUDSEY LS2 86LZ
Mon.-Fri. 9.00 a.m.-5.00 p.m.
Sat. 9.00 a.m.-1.00 p.m.
P.A.W.WM.CS.BC.

CLECKHEATON   Tel. (0274)
SKILLED CRAFTS LTD.   872861
34 BRADFORD ROAD   ★

Open: 9.00 a.m.-5.00 p.m. Monday
Saturday Lunch 12.00 a.m.-1.00 p.m.
H.P.A.W.CS.WM.D.

SCOTLAND

PERTH   Tel. (0738) 26173
WILLIAM HUME & CO.   TK
ST. JOHN'S PLACE
Open: Monday to Saturday
8.00 a.m.-5.30 p.m.
8.00 a.m.-1.00 p.m. Wednesday
H.P.A.BC.W.CS.WM.D.

EDINBURGH   Tel. 031-337-5555
THE SAW CENTRE   T
38 HAYMARKET TERRACE
EDINBURGH EH12 5JZ
Mon.-Fri. 8.30 a.m.-5.30 p.m.
Saturday 9.00 a.m.-1.00 p.m.
H.P.W.WM.D.CS.A.

PERTH   Tel: (0738) 36777
WORKMASTER POWER TOOLS LTD.   T★
8 SHORE ROAD, PH2 8BW
Mon.-Fri. 8.30 a.m.-5 p.m.
Sat. 9.00 a.m.-4 p.m.
Other times by appointment
H.P.W.WM.D.CS.A.

GLASGOW   Tel. 041-429-4444/
THE SAW CENTRE   4374 Telex: 777886
650 EGLINTON STREET   T★
GLASGOW G5 9RP
Mon.-Fri. 8.00 a.m.-5.00 p.m.
Sat. 9.00 a.m.-1.00 p.m.
H.P.W.WM.D.CS.A.

IRELAND

NEWTOWNARDS   Tel: 0247 819800
NORLYN MACHINERY   or 812506
UNIT 10, MALCOLMSON IND. EST.
80 BANGOR ROAD, CO. DOWN
Open: Mon.-Fri. 9.30am-5.30pm
(Closed 1-2pm for lunch)
Any other time by request.
H.W.WM.D.T.MF.A.   24 Hour Service K

PORTADOWN   Tel. (0762) 332546
LOCKE TOOLS   ★
50 WEST STREET BT62 3JQ
Mon.-Sat. 9 a.m.-5.30 p.m.
Any other time by request.
H.D.W.WM.D.CS.A.BC.

shop guide

WOOD SUPPLIERS

Classified Advertisements

FOR SALE

THE FINEST SELECTION ON DISPLAY IN SCOTLAND!

NEW!
Coronet and Triton Stockist.

WOODWORKING & METALWORKING MACHINERY POWER TOOLS HAND TOOLS

THE SAW CENTRE

Edinburgh Open Day November 12/13/14

LARGE STOCKS - COMPETITIVE PRICES. PHONE AND TRY US NOW!

OPEN
Mon - Fri
8am - 5pm
Sat 9am - 1pm

Eglinton Toll,
Glasgow G5 9EP
Tel 041-429-4444

38 Haymarket
Edinburgh
EH12 5J2
Tel: 031-337-5555

Woodturning Tools

A UNIQUE OPPORTUNITY TO ACQUIRE NEW, GOOD QUALITY TURNING TOOLS AT LOW PRICES
25% OFF LIST PRICE
WHILE STOCKS LAST
Send 13p stamp
for free brochure
ALEC TIRANTI LTD
70 High Street, Theale, Reading, Berks. RG7 5AR
Tel: Reading (0734) 302775

SALE

BOOKS & PUBLICATIONS

FURNITURE MAKERS FORUM

CoSIRA
Agency of the Development Commission

Devon Furniture Makers Forum.

Ted Doulton will be running a one day clinic for furniture restorers/makers at the Hartnoll Hotel, Tiverton on November 12.

Free consultations on any business/technical problems.

For further details contact:
CoSIRA, 27 Victoria Park Road, Exeter, Devon, EX2 4NT — Tel: 0392 52616

Yorkwire (Leeds) Ltd.
BRASS WIRE, ROD, STRIP & TUBE

Suitable for Miniature furniture, Clock Pendulums, Inlay work and many other Crafts.

SAE for Price List to:
Yorkwire (Leeds) Ltd.
34 Lupton Street,
Leeds LS10 2QW.
Tel: 0532 777472

MYFORD MLS LATHE, good condition 30" centres, rear turning 4", 8", 16" & 20" Rests. With Cabinate Stand. Some extras available. £500.

CORONET MAJOR wide range of accessories in good condition £725. Oakham 2055 evenings.

INCA 7" Compact saw, 9" planer, mortise attachment, mounted on stand with 1½ h.p. motor — £550. Tel: Skelmersdale (0695) 27608.

EBAC LD82 Wood Dryer and Universal controller, nice clean condition — £295.00. Tel: 070 — 681 — 7716 Daytime, West Yorkshire.

THE WHISTON CATALOGUE
Nuts, bolts, screws, washers, bar materials. In brass, alloy, steel, stainless steel, P.T.F.E., nylon, Tufnol, sheet material, electrical and mechanical items. We could go on and on! Better to send for free catalogue and see for yourself.
K. R. Whiston Ltd., Dept. WW, New Mills, Stockport, Cheshire. Phone: 0663 42028.

ADVERTISE YOUR ITEMS FOR SALE HERE – WE ACCEPT ACCESS/BARCLAYCARD BOOKINGS.

BLADES — also for machinery!
INCA Euro 260 Popular Bandsaw **£390.00**
NAEROK PT150 Planer/Thicknesser **£250.00**
A-Z1 Dust Extractor **£179.00**
RYOBI R500 Plunge Router ½" **£150.00**
Prices include VAT & carriage UK mainland. Send a foolscap SAE for more details and our new price list of planer knives, router cutters, moulding heads, and circular saw blades to: BLADES, Dept. WW, PO Box 27, Petersfield, Hants. GU32 2NB.

WOODWORKER = RESULTS. RING 01-437 0626

THREE MULTICO machines in excellent condition. 9" surface planer with sliding table. 12" thicknesser, 12" sawbench, Coronet Imp bandsaw, old morticer, Black Torrington (Devon) 386.

CIRCULAR SAWBENCH 10" Royal Mk3DL £350. Also quantity woodworking magazines and Kity combination table. Offers. Tel: Etwall 2987.

WORKSHOP, 600 square feet, Furniture Craft permission, with large detached bungalow in ⅔ acre. Four double bedrooms, 2 reception, large kitchen, bathroom, cloakroom, utility room, sun lounge, 5 miles from Hastings, £147,000. Tel: 0424/753166.

DECORATIVE DECOYS

WILDLIFE WOODCARVING SUPPLIES

J. LAJEVARDI
20A Lower Park Row
Bristol BS1 5BN, England
Tel: (0272) 273874

Fast and efficient mail order service
For your catalogue send £1 and a large S.A.E.
(Redeemable with your first order).

BENCHBOOKS FOR WOODWORKERS
Send 50p stamps for the latest bumper catalogue of Mansard publications – thousands of ideas, including Master Woodcarver's Manual £6.50; Profitable Woodcarving and Sculpture £7.30; Hints on Chip Carving by Eleanor Rower (reprint) £7.50; Viking Woodcarving £6.50; Woodcarving and Design by Lynn Miller (reprint) 2 vols £13; Graining and Marbling by W. L. Savage (reprint) £7.25; Painting and Decorating Furniture £6.50; The Lacquer Manual £6.50; Wood Finishing by Paul Hasluck (reprint) £8.00; Money From Wooden Toy Making £5; Woodturner's Handybook by Paul Hasluck (reprint) £8; Woodcarving and Crafts Ideas by Bill Perry £6.50; Possibilities of Small Lathes by James Lukin (reprint) £9.50. Post free. 24-hour Access/Visa ordering service on 01-579 7527. Mansard Press Ltd. WW, 15 Princes Road, Ealing, London W13 9AS.

WOODCRAFT BOOKS: We can offer new out of print, secondhand and antiquarian books on every aspect of woodworking — for catalogues send 50p stamp to: Woodcraft Books, P.O. Box 58, Worcester WR8 0EL.

WANTED

WANTED for Emco-Star woodworking machine, any spares and attachments, including lathe, planer, moulding accessories. J. Slater, Loganbank, Milton Bridge, Midlothian EH26 0NY. Tel: 0968 75668.

WANTED — Second hand spindle moulder and bandsaw and accessories. Single phase 240 volts — any offers. Tel: 0480 74791.

SPECIALIST TOOLS

UNIQUE SOLID BRASS TOOLS
Made by Richard Kell
Nine items in the range. All unique. Send for details:
67 Newbiggin Road, Ashington, Northumberland NE63 0TB.

RESTORATION

Furniture Restoration Materials
Everything you need to give your furniture that professional restoration look. Waxes, cleaners, french polishes, traditional upholstery supplies and many more items. Send sae for full price list:-
Furniture Restoration Supplies,
42 Acacia Avenue, Hale,
Cheshire WA15 8QY. Tel: 061-928 3903.

COPY DEADLINE:
January 1988 issue —
10th November

**MARKET YOUR EXPERTISE IN
WOODWORKER — RING JULIE
CAPSTICK ON 01-437 0699 FOR DETAILS.**

LETTERS

LETTERS TO THE EDITOR

If you are writing for publication, address your letter to 'Letters to the Editor', *Woodworker*, I Golden Sq, London WIR 3AB. We make every effort to keep the writer's individual tone intact, but reserve the right to edit and cut for brevity and clarity.

If you write to us for any other reason, we regret we cannot guarantee a reply if you do not enclose a stamped self-addressed envelope.

Skittle balls

Further to the discussion on the relative merits of timber for skittle balls ('Question box', WW/May, 'Letters', WW/Sep), hardness and resistance to splitting are indeed two different things. Carpenters' mallets and cricket bats are oiled because the shocks they take could cause them to split; skittle balls are subject to *wear* on the alley floor. The shock with which they hit the sycamore skittles is virtually negligible, in that the skittles are far lighter — a set of balls normally wears out two sets of pins. Thus splitting isn't the potential problem; the balls need to be as hard as possible, and oiling would make them softer. Timber tends to case harden, and skittle balls, after 'wearing in', do just that.

Red elm is, of course, English elm.

Graham James, Bridgwater

Courtesy

I visited the Arundel works recently with a slight vibration problem in my lathe motor. I was given first-class attention, the problem was solved and I departed a happy customer. They have also been most helpful in making additional items to my specifications. I consider they have a well-engineered lathe, made from good old cast iron castings, strong, vibration-free and one which reproduces quality work.

Name and address supplied

Pricing

Stephen Edgar of Salisbury has taken me up on my pricing figures (Letters, WW/Sep), but I think it is he who is missing the point.

Yes, it would be nice if on a five-day week of five-hour days we could put £20,000 into our pocket from any branch of woodworking; but just like the garage mechanic charged out at £20 an hour, the money does not go into our pocket. We too have overheads, dead time, travelling time and costs, materials to pay for (beyond those that we charge out), and other outgoings. If we don't think in terms of £20 an hour for when we are actually making the goods, then we had better give up now. Perhaps it is because too many woodworkers have thought of turnover as profit in the past, that our work is so often undervalued.

One well-known woodworker told me he calculates his time at £10 per hour when doing conventional work; but 45% of his time is spent on 'specials' where the price that the finished items can command makes his hourly rate anything between £20 and £100.

In a survey I am currently undertaking among a number of craftsmen, some woodworkers, I find a considerable number of the more successful work on a similar basis; they take the cost of materials and add their labour at £10 an hour for the time spent in actually making the item. They then multiply the resultant figure by 2½-3 times to get their selling price. Some go a stage further, judging what price the market might stand and selling at the higher of the two figures.

Mr Edgar may not like this 'random price fixing' approach, but if he also writes off Mike Whitford's excellent formulae, then where does he go? Certainly it won't be on holiday!

I would suggest he also looks very carefully at his pottery analogy, for it supports a number of my arguments. On a materials-plus-labour basis many pots make a fair return. A good potter spends relatively little time in total on each pot, and the materials are not expensive for the professional. In fact, very few woodturners are making as much 'profit' per piece as does a quite average potter. The trouble is that the potters' market is even more flooded than the turners', and therefore their gross sales and turnover are low, individually.

Finally, there is no such thing as 'overcharging,' except within a monopoly essential service. Overpricing, yes. But if a client is prepared to pay a price, however high it is, then you have not overcharged. I still contend that in this country the one-man operation has consistently undercharged for woodwork. I believe that's why wood and woodwork is less valued in this country than in many others.

Hugh O'Neill, Ruislip

Tunbridge ware

It was a pleasure to read David Springett's article (WW/Aug). If you want to know more, visit the Tunbridge Wells Municipal Museum where a whole room is devoted to the craft, with replica workshops, tools, original charts and instructions and work at all stages of production of the various kinds of ware: stick, half-square, mosaic, marquetry and so on, along with hundreds of fine finished originals.

If you can't get there, an illustrated book by the curator, Dr Margaret A. V. Gill, called *Tunbridge Ware*, Shire Album No. 130, at £1.25 is available; you can also buy it at the museum.

Robert Vale, Beccles

Snooker cues

Re the question on two-piece snooker cues, (WW/Aug), I think a wooden screw thread would have little strength and soon fail. I suggest Mr Williams buys studding, preferably brass, and drills and taps both ends of the billiard cue with a coarse thread tap. Araldite the studding in the base section. The only jig required would be a drill jig of two holes, one of the cue outside diameter, the other of the thread tapping size.

Terry Carter, Harpenden

WOODWORKER, published every third Friday by **Argus Specialist Publications Ltd**
Editorial, Advertising; I Golden Sq, London WIR 3AB, 01-437 0626
Editor Aidan Walker **Deputy editor** John Hemsley **Assistant editor** Kerry Fowler
Advertisement manager Trevor Pryer **Advertisement production** Andrew Selwood
Design ASP Art Studio **Technical illustrator** Peter Holland **Guild of Woodworkers** John Hemsley, Kerry Fowler

We cannot accept responsibility for loss of or damage to unsolicited material. We reserve the right to refuse or suspend advertisements, and regret we cannot guarantee the bona fides of advertisers.
ABC UK circulation Jan-Dec '86 **32,849**

Back issues and subscriptions Infonet Ltd, 5 River Park Estate, Berkhamsted, Herts HP4 IHL, (04427) 76661-4
Overseas sales, non-newstrade sales Magazine Sales Dept., I Golden Sq, London WIR 3AB, 01-437 0626

Subscriptions per year UK £16.90; overseas outside USA (accelerated surface post) £21; USA (air freight assisted) $28, airmail £48.
UK Trade SM Distribution Ltd, 16-18 Trinity Gdns, London SW9 8DX, 01-274 8611
North American Trade Bill Dean Books Ltd, 151-49 7th Ave, PO Box 69, Whitestone, NY 11357, phone 1-718-767 6632
Printed by Chase Web, Plymouth **Typesetting** Project 3, Whitstable **Colour origination** Derek Croxson Ltd, Chesham, Bucks

© Argus Specialist Publications Ltd, 1987
ISSN 0043 776X
Second class postage paid at Rahway, NJ, USA. Postmaster: send address corrections to Woodworker, c/o Mercury Airfreight International Inc., 10B Engelhard Ave, Avenel, NJ 07001

ARGUS PRESS GROUP

CONTENTS

December 1987   Vol. 91   No. 12

Woodworker

Full size magnificence: Vic Taylor examines the Adam style (p. 1056), here interpreted, almost certainly, by Chippendale.
Miniature magnificence: champion doll's house maker Den Young with his William and Mary mansion (p. 1108)

On the cover: William Hepper's 'phone cabinet allowed him to indulge his furniture-making fantasies; let yours loose, p1128. The tools are a selection of the enticing Xmas special offers this month: p1078

Slaving over a hot jigsaw

Three people who switched careers after having families and learnt woodwork at Bath Womens Workshop have formed 'Splinter Group', a team of professional women carpenters.

Jill Hiron, pictured below left, couldn't face going back to office work but never dreamt the course would be the start of a whole new career. Former teacher Maggie Fitzpatrick says:

'We believe there's a market for women carpenters. We minimise dust and disruption and leave the house as tidy as possible.

The group doesn't want to do major building work. 'You could say we're happier in the home,' says Maggie,' though now you won't find us slaving over a hot stove, but rather a hot jigsaw.'

Lynne Baker, below right, started her own business this year to design and make lounge and garden furniture. At the hub of her business, L&R Joinery, of

Keynsham, Bristol, is a Startrite K260 Universal Woodworker; she was introduced to the machine at a six month furniture making course run by Avon County Council, and choose to buy one for its versatility and accuracy.

Splinter Group, 4F New King St, Bath, (0225) 446642

L & R Joinery, The Lays Farm, Charlton Rd, Keynsham, Bristol (0272) 833210

Makita winners

Ten lucky people out of the bag on September 30 all got their easy-peasy questions right in our Win-a-Makita Powercraft power tool competition. Surprise — five of the 10 opted for the M102 power planer. They are Anthony Malyon of Cheltenham, F. Mackay of Rowlands Gill, R. Mortimer of Rotherham, J. Narey of Bingley, and B. Fripp of Bristol. Messrs R. Taylor of Harlow and A. Allwood of Vaynor Newtown in Powys went for the M802 variable-speed hammer drill; R. Passmore of Worthing chose the M432 jigsaw, J. Scott of Arbroath decided on the M241 mitre saw, and Ray Thompson of Chester-le-Street gets an M511 circular saw. Congratulations all, and commiserations to those who didn't get it.

Forest hopes

The tropical rainforest/conservation/hardwood debate goes on... A letter from the chairman of the National Hardwood Importers Section of the Timber Trades Federation to the *Timber Trades Journal* was by no means supportive of the London Hardwood Club's 'emotional outburst' against Friends of the Earth, reported in last month's WOOD-WORKER: the NHIS met with FoE and other conservationist groups

at the end of August to agree on a definition of 'sustainable sources'. They also aimed to plan a strategy to work together to get the UK government to financially support one of the International Tropical Timber Organisation's forest management projects. 'The hardwood trade', says a long letter from FoE rainforest campaigner Simon Counsell, published in *TTJ* 5 September, 'can either choose to bury its head in the sand and pretend that the resources upon which it depends are not doomed to imminent exhaustion; or it can seek ways in which to lead the world in creating a market for a sustainable commodity, thereby prolonging the life of the rainforests and the trade indefinitely.' There's no doubt a serious section of the trade agrees.

Furniture fashion

Two independent reports on the state of furniture manufacturing and retailing identify the need to make the public view furniture as renewable, as styles change. Mintel's 'Furniture Retailers' says: 'Retailers, aided by their suppliers, must find ways of stimulating British consumers to be more adventurous and fashion-conscious in their views of furniture,' while Marketing Strategies for Industry's three-fold furniture report claims

that 'the problem facing manufacturers is how to develop styles and designs that will establish fashions in furniture and encourage intending purchasers to replace their existing possessions quicker'. (*Cabinet Maker, 4 Sep 87*). New models for '88 — but will the staid British public see the need for change? A lot more marketing needed...

IDF goes bust

The Independent Designers' Federation, followed in WOOD-WORKER since October 1985, crashed amidst a financial brouhaha at the end of August. Originator and co-ordinator Bill Borland had left, and Joe Tibbetts (who organises the Direct Design Shows) took over; but he discovered incomplete files, 'naive' cash-flow forecasts, and that the co-op was effectively trading while insolvent. A bright idea, whose loss is to be lamented; but it seems a co-operative venture that demands a high level of commitment from members for not a lot of immediate return will anyway be dogged by administrative and management difficulties. Other ways of giving independent designer craftspeople more marketing and business clout by banding them together must be found...

Handiknife

Many thanks, FOOTPRINT, for supplying the excellent quality retractable blade knife on this month's cover — we don't need to go into pages of explanation about what to do with such a Handi little knife, do we? A gift you can really use, just like what we always try to bring you.

Devon Show

Axminster Power Tools are throwing open their premises for a three-day woodworking show, 4-6 December. Thirty five manufacturers will be represented; no hard sell, they promise. Chard St, Axminster, Devon EX13 5DZ, (0297) 33656.

Trevor Rooney

WOODWORKER and Argus Exhibitions would like to apologise for the absence of Trevor Rooney from the London Woodworker Show, although he was billed in both the magazine and the Show catalogue to appear. We are sorry if readers who were expecting to see him at the Show were disappointed; we only knew at the last minute that he was unable to come.

DIARY

Panel hand tools

Jaydee announce they're importing the Pollma hand-held edgebanding press, for applying both natural timber and synthetic pre-coated edgings, working up to 1mm thickness at 200-220°C. It costs £299; they're also doing Pollma's strip-cutting unit, another neat hand-held tool that will split plastic laminate edging to a maximum width of 80mm, thickness 1.5mm. It costs £62.50. Jaydee (Machine Sales) Ltd, The Old Exchange, New Pond Road, Holmer Green, Bucks HP15 6SU, (0494) 714448.

New Universal

Startrite are bringing out the TA 3200 panel saw — 400mm main blade, scoring saw, 10ft panel capacity, 5hp motor, three speeds; plus the Super 260 Universal, an up-rate of the K260 with larger table and saw-blade, more thicknessing capacity, longer spindle travel, increased mortiser stroke. Startrite, Waterside Works, Waterside Lane, Gads Hill, Gillingham, Kent ME7 2SF, (0634) 281281.

Double-sided sheet

Adhesive tape is one thing; double-sided adhesive sheet is quite another. 'Facilitate the assembly of wood constructions prior to dowelling, screwing, etc,' says the blurb; but there must be 1001 ways to use wide bits of double-sided adhesive film. JH Equipment even do one that is stickier one side than the other, for parts that will need offering up, marking and re-positioning. Three sheets of A4 film cost £2.50 post free. JH, 91 Redbrook Rd, Timperley, Trafford, Lancs, 061-904 9384.

New catalogue

Craft Supplies' new full-colour catalogue will be on sale at branches of WH Smith; you can also get it by post (it costs £2) from Craft Supplies, The Mill, Millers Dale, Derbys, (0298) 871636.

Kity has upgraded the K5 and relaunched it as the Bestcombi, top, with 30mm spindle moulder, 2½in saw cut, 6 × 4 planer/thicknesser and slot mortiser at about £750 inc. VAT.

Nearly 600 K5s have been sold in the UK since 1978. Rawdon Machinery Sales, 6 Acorn Pk, Charlestown, Shipley, W. Yorks, BD17 7SW, (0274) 597826

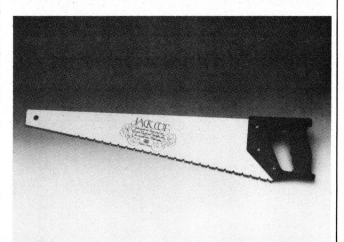

Jack, Danish saw makers, have launched a new saw, above, for cutting chipboard, coarse wood and firewood. It has fine teeth on the point of the blade for easy starting, with coarser teeth for fast cutting.

1053

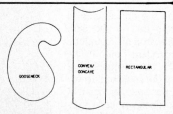

GRACE AND BEAUTY

Robert Adam, celebrated late-18th century architect, introduced the Neo-Classical style to English buildings and furniture, moving away from formal Palladianism. Vic Taylor examines his work and that of George Hepplewhite

A triumvirate of designers dominated the second half of the 18th century: Robert Adam (1728-1792), George Hepplewhite (d.1786), and Thomas Sheraton (1751- 1806); perhaps the firm of Gillow & Co of Lancaster should be added to the list.

Robert Adam was the second son of William Adam of Kircaldy, a well-respected architect of the Palladian style. He and his two brothers determined to create a new style of architecture which, although conforming to classical rules, would be lighter and more decorative than the rigid Palladian style of William Kent. Robert was far from modest: 'The massive entablature', he wrote, 'the ponderous compartment ceiling, almost the only species of ornament formerly known in this country, are now universally exploded, and in their place we have adopted a beautiful variety of light mouldings, gracefully formed, delicately enriched, and arranged with propriety and skill. We have introduced a great diversity of ceilings, friezes and decorative pilasters, and have added grace and beauty to the whole by a mixture of grotesque, stucco and painted ornament' *(The Works in Architecture of Robert and James Adam; 1773 and 1779).*

Obviously he was referring to architectural style, but the remarks applied equally well to his ideas for interiors and furniture. A visit to Italy, from which he returned to England in 1758, gave him the realization that the true interpretation of classical decoration was to use it as a basis for individual expression rather than as a set of rigid rules. This became the foundation of the Neo-Classical style.

Not everyone agreed with his interpretation: Horace Walpole, the creator of 'Strawberry Hill Gothic' and a scathing critic of everything under the sun, referred to 'all the harlequinades of Adam that never let the eye repose for a moment'. Sir William Chambers, who designed the pagoda in Kew Gardens and lived to regret it, sneered at Adam's 'filigrane toy-work' and Dr Johnson (another indefatigable critic) condemned some of the architecture at Kedleston Hall in Derbyshire: 'The pillars are very large and massy, they take up too much room, they were better away'.

Adam introduced several decorative motifs which had a lasting influence on the general design of furniture. Chief among them were gilding, painted furniture, the use of exotic timbers both as inlay and in the solid, and the fashioning of 'compo' (a malleable mixture of whiting, resin, and glue size) on wire skeletons to form tracery and filigree patterns. One design which he originated was the sideboard-table, flanked by a pair of pedestals which supported vases or urns used as receptacles for cutlery, bottles, plates, or water; this arrangement soon became fashionable and was widely copied.

At Osterley, Adam designed some painted armchairs in terracotta red and black on grey, (fig. 1); the backs are completely plain in contrast to the ornamented front parts, because the chairs were intended to stand with their backs against the wall so the centre of the room was left empty for the company to 'circulate'. The same consideration meant that dining tables were consigned to an anteroom and only brought in just before the meal.

Adam was fond of what he called 'grotesque' motifs; he explains that 'by grotesque, is meant that beautiful light style of ornament used by the ancient Romans in the decoration of their palaces, baths and villas'. His interpretation included fantastic human and animal figures, garlands, anthemion (honeysuckle), swags, scrolls, ram's heads, gryphons, *putti* (cherubs), and winged sphinxes; plus what are called 'trophies' or groupings of weaponry and military accoutrements.

Thomas Chippendale worked with Adam on several large houses, supplying the furniture for them to Adam's designs. Two such were Nostell Priory in Yorkshire, and Mersham-le-Hatch in Kent. Harewood House (also in Yorkshire) is often cited as another example of this collaboration, but it is almost certain that Chippendale designed the furniture himself in the Adam style (which he was quite capable of doing) since his bills for at least £3,000 of work have been traced, while there are none recorded for Adam.

A NEW PHENOMENON in the organisation of the manufacturing industries in the 18th century was the specialisation of labour, one of the basic tenets of Adam Smith's *The Wealth of Nations* (1776). A consequence of the growing strength of the Industrial Revolution, it was, perhaps, this specialisation that led to the rise of the designer *per se* as distinct from the craftsman-cum-designer. Thus there seems to be no actual furniture, or record of any, that was made personally by Chippendale himself, and the same can be said of both Hepplewhite and Sheraton. Indeed, the trend continues throughout the 19th century until we meet Sidney Barnsley (1865-1926), who was the archetypal craftsman-designer.

Joseph Aronson writes in his introduction to the Dover reprint of Hepplewhite's *The Cabinet Maker and Upholsterer's Guide:* 'The designer filled a place similar to that of a sawyer, joiner, turner, carver, and others. In modern practice, the classic book drawings would be considered mere sketches, wholly inadequate for production patterns, lacking precise dimensions and details. So it may be assumed that the training of the specialised

This rosewood sideboard table from Harewood House, near Leeds, was almost certainly made by Chippendale in his interpretation of the Adam style, c. 1775

Painted Pembroke table designed in the Etruscan style by Robert Adam for Osterley Park House, Middlesex, in 1770. Armchair by Adam also in the Etruscan style, also for Osterley Park House, in 1776: the frames are painted beech and the seats are caned to receive loose cushions (note the 'plinth' feet)

craftsman had attained such perfection that competence meant knowing to a hair the proper thickness and taper of a leg, the depth of carving, the provision for jointing.' Which applies equally to Chippendale, Sheraton, and others.

THE ONLY DOCUMENTED FACT we know about George Hepplewhite is that he died in 1786. His book *The Cabinet Maker and Upholsterer's Guide* was published posthumously by his widow, Alice, in 1788, followed a year later by a revised edition, and a third in 1794.

It is assumed he was born in the Lancashire area because he was apprenticed to Gillow and Company of Lancaster. In 1761 this company opened a shop in Oxford Street, London, and a few years afterwards Hepplewhite opened his shop in Red Cross Street, Cripplegate, London. After his death his widow carried on the business under the style of 'A. Hepplewhite and Co, Cabinet Makers'.

In the Preface to his book he states his aims: 'To unite elegance and utility, and blend the useful with the agreeable... we have exerted our utmost endeavours to produce a work which shall be useful to the mechanic, and serviceable to the gentleman'; and he mentions that 'English taste and workmanship have, of late years, been much sought for by surrounding nations...' This probably alludes to the export of furniture to America or the Netherlands, which by now had grown economically important.

The mention of the name 'Hepplewhite' immediately conjures up his 'shield-back' chair, also less romantically called a 'camel-back', from the humped shape in the top rail. It's by no means certain that he originated the design — that honour probably belongs to Robert Adam — but he certainly refined and developed it.

Hepplewhite designed other chairs, of course, among them what he called 'cabriole' chairs; he stipulates they should have stuffed backs, although one of the four designs in his book has an all-wood back! The term 'cabriole' has no connection with the leg, but was widely used at the end of the 18th century to describe an armchair 'stuffed all over' (Sheraton: *Cabinet Dictionary*, 1803); it was also employed to describe sofas.

Hepplewhite's principal achievement was to produce a range of comparatively plain utilitarian designs for the more mundane articles of furniture such as basin stands, bidets, pot cupboards, shaving tables, and the like. As a contrast he also produced 'Rudd's Table' which was 'the most complete dressing table made, possessing every convenience which can be wanted, or mechanism and ingenuity supply'. The lucky recipient of this paragon of tables was Margaret Caroline Rudd, a notable courtesan of the period. He was also the first designer to mention Pembroke tables, the elegant and useful little flap-tables which are still popular today (fig. 2). ∎

AXMINSTER POWER TOOL CENTRE

WOODWORKING SHOW

THE GUILDHALL AXMINSTER

DECEMBER
4th, 5th & 6th

FRIDAY 4th	**10am-6pm**
SATURDAY 5th	**10am-6pm**
SUNDAY 6th	**10am-4pm**

ADMISSION FREE CHILDREN UNDER 16 MUST BE ACCOMPANIED BY AN ADULT

DON'T MISS THIS RARE OPPORTUNITY TO MEET SO MANY MANU-FACTURERS AT ONE SHOW — COME AND SEE FOR YOURSELF THE MOST EXTENSIVE RANGE IN THE COUNTRY

NOBEX
MULTISTAR
TRITON
DeWALT
STARTRITE
CORONET
LUNA
LIBERON
WARCO
KITY
CRAFT SUPPLIES
ELU
HITACHI
MAKITA
RYOBI
SEALEY
HERMES
BOSCH
TOOLBANK
AEG
TAUNTON PRESS
LION
RIDGWAY
MULTICO
SCHEPPACH
TYME
CLICO
MINICRAFT
ELEKTRA
LEITZ
SPEAR & JACKSON
TITMAN
TREND
SHARPENSET

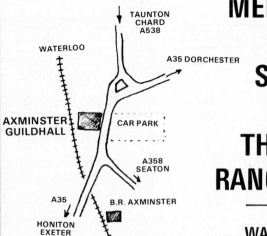

WAXES - FINISHES - BOOKS - VIDEOS
ABRASIVES - CHUCKS - CRAFT SUPPLIES
ALL ON SALE AT THE SHOW. ALL MACHINERY TO BE DELIVERED.

CHARD STREET, AXMINSTER, DEVON EX13 5DZ. 0297 33656

Bob Wearing's WORKSHOP

Custom-made frames for those special — or awkward — pictures

That special watercolour, photograph or drawing deserves something better than the run-of-the-mill ramin moulding or over-decorated plastic-faced framing, nailed together at the corners. In any case, for some subjects no suitable moulding exists; for example, a good watercolour behind a thick double mount, plus glass, plus hardboard backing will not fit into most commercial mouldings (fig. 1), and neither will mounted embroideries and collages.

Fortunately the small power router makes the production of individual mouldings relatively simple. English hardwoods in a natural finish — oak, ash, chestnut and sycamore — are all successful. The mahoganies too can be used for pictures of the right general colourings.

First measure the combined thickness of the various parts then draw out just the rebate to full size. The router can produce grooves, rebates, flats, quarter rounds and quarter hollows. The scratch tool can produce half rounds, fine grooves and reeds. Using both tools an immense range of mouldings can be built up. Most of the routing can be done on a routing table, but I prefer the Bosch POF 52 router mounted in a drill stand; this way, the whole operation can be clearly seen. Additionally, a ½in or ⅝in cutter can be used as a miniature thicknesser.

Some of the possible combinations are shown in fig. 2, but you could devise many more shapes.

Whatever the shape you want, the routine is similar. First you need to produce sufficient rectangular stock of appropriate dimensions, using whatever method you prefer. The rebate is quite straightforward; take out some of the waste with a circular saw, if you like, finishing with a rebate cutter using several gentle cuts.

Now you can shape the front, following through stages as in fig. 3. Cut a shallow decorative groove using a $\frac{1}{16}$ in slotting cutter in the router, then use a scratch tool to work the corner bead. If you like, you could lower the face very slightly with a rebate cutter, and then produce another small rebate, before using a cove or rounding cutter for the final cut.

Cut the mouldings close to the finished length then clean up with glasspaper previously glued to small wood blocks; use flat blocks for the flat and convex areas and pieces of suitable dowelling for the concave shapes. Mark the picture size plus in on the inside of the rebates and saw off, at 45°, slightly oversize. Now trim accurately to the marks using either a disc sander or a mitre shooting board (WW/Feb 1983). It is important that the block used on either side of these should be built up from plywood layers (fig. 4). A solid wood block will eventually shrink, causing the 90° angle to increase. (The 45° angle is not actually of enormous importance; what really matters is that the two angles together combine to make 90°). ▷

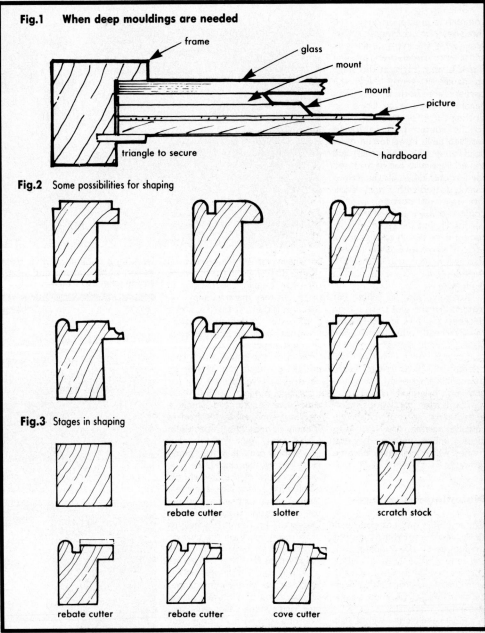

Fig.1 When deep mouldings are needed

frame · glass · mount · mount · picture · triangle to secure · hardboard

Fig.2 Some possibilities for shaping

Fig.3 Stages in shaping

rebate cutter · slotter · scratch stock

rebate cutter · rebate cutter · cove cutter

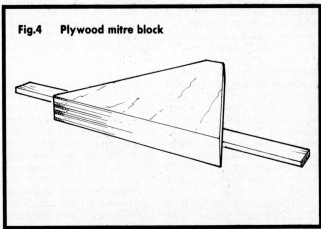

Fig.4 Plywood mitre block

Glue up the frame, using a commercial cramp, or one of the three described last month (*WW/ Nov 1987*). Clean off surplus glue and leave to harden overnight. The frame is very fragile at this stage so handle it gently. Now the corners are slotted, two slots generally being enough. Use a   in slotting cutter on an arbor fitted to the router. I use a special wooden table fitted for an overhead router (see photograph), and something similar can be arranged for a router table. Larger frames can be slotted with a small radial-arm saw, set horizontally. You could also use a table-saw with a vertical jig, but the guard must be removed for this so arrange some form of alternative guard. (A vertical jig is described in *Woodwork Aids & Devices*, Wearing, Unwin & Hyman).

Roughly saw a length of material for the slips to size, then thickness to a nice fit, either using the overhead router or by hand planing. Saw the slips off square and glue in place; glue in big and saw off later to avoid breakage. When thoroughly dry, saw off, plane flush and finish by further sanding.

For English hardwoods, finish with two thin coats of matt polyurethane varnish, easy to keep clean, unlike unfinished wood frames which eventually become grimy.

Mounting the picture

Watercolours and pastels in particular look best behind a cut-out mount, coloured artboard with the central area cut at 45°. These cuts are straightforward to make with one of the proprietary mount cutters available from shops supplying artists' materials.

You'll need picture-weight glass (2mm thick) and you can avoid measuring mistakes by taking the frame to the glazier. Special reflection-free glass is available, but it doesn't suit all subjects.

Hardboard is used for backing today, replacing the traditional cardboard that bowed and warped in time. Ideally, especially for small pictures, 2mm hardboard should be used; but this is not widely stocked, so you'll probably have to make do with ⅛in (3mm). Ensure a good tight fit. If the rebate is not deep enough, you can thin the hardboard edge down with a hand plane.

Clean and polish the glass both sides, dust the picture, then assemble, face down, with the

backing in place. Traditionally small wedge-shaped glazing sprigs were used for keeping the backing in place, but they make a lumpy finished job, and small panel pins aren't a lot better. Professional glaziers now use small sheet steel equilateral triangles with about 10mm sides, shot into place with a tool not unlike a staple gun. This would be an expensive tool to buy for occasional framing, but I have an alternative, if you can obtain a block of these triangles from a friendly glazier and separate them with a sharp knife.

I use a pair of water pump pliers to press them into place. The imperfect tips of the jaws should be filed flat and square, and use a strip of metal to prevent damage to the outside of the frame. During this process it may help to press down firmly on the triangle with a small screwdriver to ensure a really tight flat fit in the frame.

Finally, the whole assembly is kept dust free with gummed tape. Obtain a roll of 2in wide parcel tape, and cut the strips overlong. Wet one strip with a sponge, not by licking; wait a few moments for the glue to become tacky, then lay it in place. Press down well, using a paperhanger's hard rubber seam roller. Add the remaining strips. When all are dry, trim round with a cutting gauge set to about   in.

Fit suitably sized screw-eyes with split rings. Drill or bore for these, since if they're just forced into hardwood the screw-eyes tend either to break off or distort. Hang by twisted brass picture wire. Secure the ends very thoroughly, as sloppy twisting tends to unwind when the weight is applied.

Finally glue to the hardboard a label showing title, artist, date acquired and any other interesting details. ∎

Working a small decorative rebate with an overhead router, above. Below, slotting corner and inserting strengthening strip to obtain a strong, slim ash frame

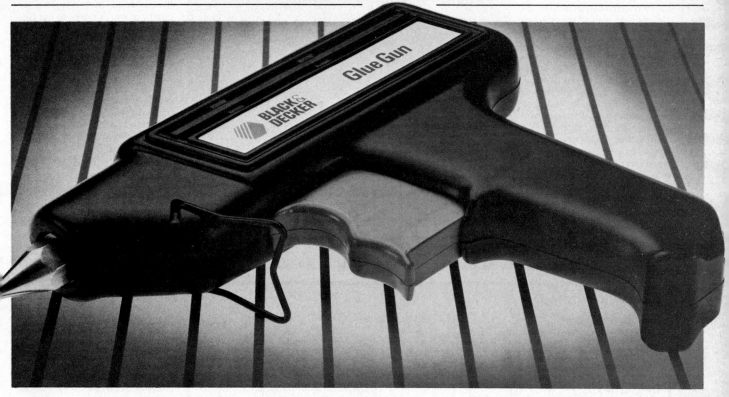
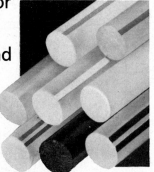

Every month the best idea for making any sort of woodwork quicker, more accurate, more profitable, easier and/or more enjoyable wins £60 worth of Sandvik tools. The other ideas we publish win a small fee. HOW TO ENTER: be as brief and clear as possible. Type (if you can) your entries double-spaced on one side of A4 sheets, and make your drawings as few and as well annotated as possible. Send to 'Hands On', WOODWORKER, I Golden Square, London WIR 3AB.

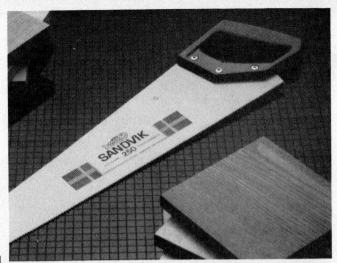

Win £60 worth of Sandvik tools!

Sandvik winner

Sizing/depth gauge

For a precisely cut recess for your expanding dovetail collets, use a plumber's hole cutter.

Grind off the cutting point and make it square to an 80° angle, the same as a scraper. Grind the centre point 3/16in further back than the cutting edge; this will act as a depth stop.

To cut your circle, just adjust the cutter to the required diameter, fit it up in the drill chuck and on to the tailstock, then rest the cutter on the toolrest to stop it turning when it comes in contact with the work. Cut out the centre, then cut the dovetail with a small skew chisel, and it's ready for the dovetail collet. The metal of these cutters is very hard so it should last a long time.

Derek Picken, Morecambe

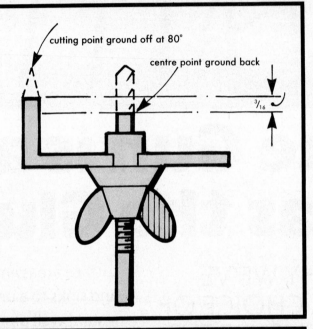

cutting point ground off at 80°

centre point ground back

3/16

Cutting rectangles in flexible sheet

If you don't have a jigsaw, or nearby power for one, to cut rectangles in (say) cabinet backs for socket outlets etc., simply stand the sheet in against a corner and bend it over so you can cut through it along the lines of your marked cut-out with a straight blade. Cut as much as you can of each of the four lines with a hand or tenon saw, then put it on the saw-horse or whatever to finish the corners off.

R.D. Clements, Wootton Bassett

Gluing and sanding

Two ideas; for getting glue into awkward places such as under lifted veneer, use 3in-long strips broken off an old steel measuring tape.

I use old packs of cards, wrapped around with masking tape, for nice, flexible, soft sanding blocks. The fewer cards in the pack, the softer the block.

D. Rogers, Shrewsbury

Clean stain applicators

Staining with a cloth is messy, and brushing it puts too much on. So take (say) a 2in length of plastic hosepipe and slit it lengthways. Cut a piece of 1/8in-thick felt about 2x1in, fold it double, and slide it into the slit in the hosepipe. Dip the felt, and away you go.

For corners and fiddly bits of moulding, roll up a small piece of felt as tight as you can, force it into the end of a narrow tube, then shape the end with scissors. You can use it like a large felt-tip pen.

Philip Holmes, Telford

▲ WOODWORKING WHEEZE OF THE MONTH ▲

Spindle-blank centre marker

I made this adjustable cradle out of ply scrap to mark the centres on the ends of a number of small blanks for spindle turning.

Make the slotted end-piece first, then mount it in position on the end of the cradle, which adjusts up and down in relation to the screw-point according to the size of the work. You do need comparatively consistently-sized blanks, though!

Ken Walters, Derby

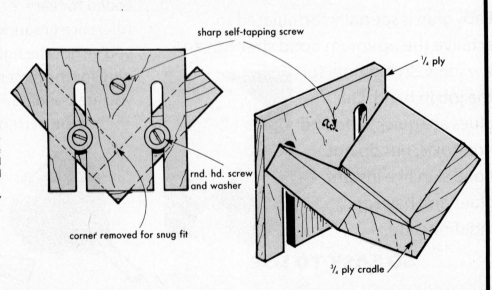

sharp self-tapping screw

1/4 ply

rnd. hd. screw and washer

corner removed for snug fit

3/4 ply cradle

Spindle-blank centre finder

The construction of this is obvious from the drawings. It can be used for finding the centres of already rounded workpieces, or even square ones as long as they are reasonably regular in size. Make a U-shaped frame from ½in ply, grooved to accept a large plastic draughting set-square; fix it together with the set-square in position. To find the centre, just mark across the diagonal of the workpiece one way, then roll it across the frame and mark the opposite diagonal. Make the frame (or frames) to suit the sizes of workpiece you work with most.

G.H. Wade, South Shields

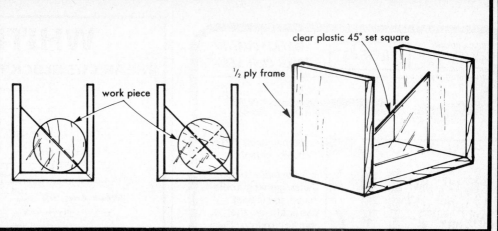

clear plastic 45° set square
½ ply frame
work piece

Bevelled-bead jig

This is a simple jig for use in the thicknesser to produce perfect same-size bevelled beads every time. You can adjust the sizes to your requirements, but I made mine from a 66x6¾in board and two 66in lengths of 1in-square lath. Mark the lengthwise centre of the board and bevel from the centre outwards, leaving a depth of ¼-⅜in, whichever you fancy. Glue and pin the laths to the outside edges of the board.

To make your beads, just set them up in the jig and pass the whole thing through the thicknesser. For short lengths you will need to make end-stops to hold them in.

Steven Bailey, Wakefield

lathe in position ready for thicknesser

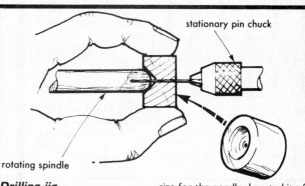

stationary pin chuck
rotating spindle

Drilling jig

I needed to drill a large number of spindles at one end to take a fine needle. I made a simple jig by turning a conical recess in a cylinder of close-grained timber and drilling into the centre with a drill the right size for the needle. I parted it off, then with the conical recess held against the spindle end and the little drill in a pin chuck, I fed the drill through the jig into the spindle centre as it revolved in the lathe.

D.G. Francis, Nottingham

NEXT MONTH

The WOODWORKER of January 1988 promises New Year treats for everyone, but it's the turners especially who'll like the look of this picture. Acknowledged giant of both the craft and art of woodturning, **David Ellsworth** was a big attraction for last August's Loughborough Seminar; now we have Liam O'Neill, leading Irish woodturner, in a conversation with David, plus lots of lovely colour pix of his work.

We visited John Corlyon, a north country joiner and cabinetmaker who is making lavishly decorated furniture for middle-eastern magnates on the grand scale to which they are accustomed; we have the design-and-make process of a simple but stylish Quaker Meeting House table; we have how to make your own expanding wooden collet chucks.

And of course, we have a massive report of the **London Woodworker Show** of 1987. More work, and to a higher standard, than ever before was the general judgement on the exhibits; more prizes too. Read all about what the lesser-known but nonetheless skilled woodworkers of Britain are doing — it's their showcase.

And the rest. All the features, regulars and projects that make WOODWORKER the best woodworking monthly the country has to offer; between us, we'll make it better for '88!

ON SALE 18 DECEMBER

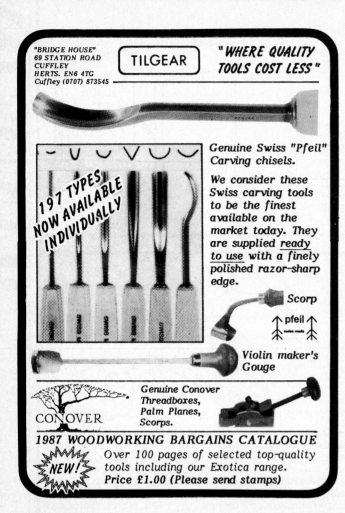
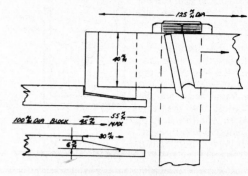

AXMINSTER POWER TOOL CENTRE

HORIZONTAL WETSTONE GRINDERS INC. VAT
OUR PRICE

JAPANESE Wetstone grinder **£129.00**
180G stone for above **£40.00**
1000G stone for above **£40.00**
6000G stone for above **£43.00**
PRECISION grinding jig **£43.00**
SHARPENSET Wetstone grinder **£240.00**
SHARPENSET 80g stone **£20.00**
SHARPENSET 150G stone **£18.40**
SHARPENSET 280G stone **£20.41**
SHARPENSET Green stone (TCT) **£18.40**
10" Planer Knife grinding jig **£65.00**
15" Planer Knife grinding jig **£78.00**
CHISEL grinding jig **£67.00**

VERTICAL WETSTONE GRINDERS
SCANGRIND 150 6" wetstone **£69.00**
SCANGRIND 200 8" wetstone **£88.00**
COMBI SC150 6" wet & dry **£89.00**
COMBI SC200 8" wet & dry **£112.00**
LUNA KIRUNA 11" wet & 4" dry **£118.00**
LUNA KIRUNA 14" wet & 5" dry **£184.00**

BENCH GRINDERS
ELU EDS163 6" 360W **£73.00**
ELU EDS164 7" 390W **£77.00**
ELU MWA149 6" Honer grinder **£90.95**
LEROY SOMER 5" 180W **£33.00**
LEROY SOMER 6" 250W **£44.00**
LEROY SOMER 6" with chuck **£49.00**
WARCO 5" 180W (European) **£33.00**
WARCO 6" 380W (European) **£43.00**
WARCO 8" 570W (European) **£69.00**

GRIND STONES (state bore size)
	5"	6"	7"
COARSE 36G	£6.60	£7.90	£11.40
FINE 60G	£6.60	£7.90	£11.40
WHITE 60G	£7.20	£8.50	£13.50
GREEN (TCT)	£7.20	£8.50	£13.50

JIGSAWS (Light Duty)
Bosch PST50 Single Speed **£29.95**
Bosch PST50E Var. Speed **£38.50**
Bosch PST60PEA Var. Speed Pend. **£65.00**
Hitachi FJ50SB Single speed **£31.95**
Hitachi FJ50VA Var. speed **£65.95**
Hitachi FCJ55V Var. Speed Pend. Act **£65.95**

JIGSAWS (Heavy Duty)
Elu ST142 2 speed **£101.00**
Elu ST142E Var. speed **£110.00**
Elu ST152 2 Speed **£98.00**
Elu ST152E Var. speed **£106.00**
Cases for above Jigsaws **£10.00**
Hitachi CJ65 2 speed **£104.95**
Hitachi CJ65VA Var. speed **£108.95**
Hitachi CJ65V Var. speed **£108.95**
Bosch 1581.7 Var. speed **£108.95**

DISC AND BELT SANDERS
Picador 10" Disc Sander **£219.00**
Warco BDS460 6" Disc 4" Belt **£86.00**
Warco BDS690 9" Disc 6" Belt **£179.00**
Luna Favourite 4" **£285.00**
Luna De-Lux Sander 4" **£599.00**
Luna YKV Pad Sander **£690.00**
Luna YK1500 Pad Sander 1PH **£1564.00**
Luna YK1500 Pad Sander 3PH **£1509.00**

CIRCULAR SAWS
HITACHI FC5SA 6" TCT 710W **£50.95**
BOSCH PKS46 6" TCT 600W **£53.50**
BOSCH PKS66 7⅛" TCT 1000W **£89.95**
HITACHI PSU6 6" 1050W HSS **£82.95**
HITACHI PSU7 7" 1600W HSS **£108.95**
HITACHI PSU9 9" 1759W HSS **£139.95**
HITACHI PSM7 7" 1200W TCT **£157.95**
HITACHI PSM9 9" 1600W TCT **£167.95**
ELU MH151 6" 850W TCT **£90.95**
ELU MH65 7" 1200W TCT **£131.95**
ELU MH85 9" 1600W TCT **£177.95**
ELU MH182 8" 1400W TCT **£148.00**
ELU 550 COMBI (for MH182) **£130.00**
ELU555 Snip saw (for 182) **£179.00**

FINISHING SANDERS
(DB Dust Bag)
Bosch PSS230 1/3rd Sheet **£29.95**
HITACHI FS10SA 1/3rd Sheet **£27.95**
HITACHI FS12 Sheet DB **£53.50**
BOSCH PS280A ½ Sheet DB **£59.95**
ELU MVS156 1/3rd Sheet DB **£73.00**
ELU MVS156E Var. speed DB **£85.95**
ELU MVS 94 ½ Sheet DB **£111.00**
ELU MVS47 ½ Sheet DB **£123.00**
HITACHI SV12 ½ Sheet **£121.95**
HITACHI SOD110 ½ Sheet DB **£98.95**
HITACHI SDO110 ½ Sheet **£89.95**
BOSCH 1288 9½ Sheet DB **£99.95**

DRILL STANDS
BOSCH S7 ..... **£21.00**
BOSCH S2 ..... **£52.00**
BOSCH S8 ..... **£25.00**
WOLFCRAFT 3403 ..... **£29.00**
WOLFCRAFT 5520 ..... **£59.00**

POWER TOOL WORK BENCHES
Post/Delivery £5.00
TRITON **£159.00**
Extension Tables **£69.00**
Stand **£29.00**
Router/Jigsaw Base **£39.00**
Wheel Kit **£9.50**
DUNLOP POWER BASE **£119.95**
Extension Table **£21.50**
Additional sole plates **£8.65**
WOLFCRAFT VARIOTEC **£45.00**
BOSCH MT92 Saw Table **£109.95**

POWER PLANES (Light Duty)
OUR PRICE INC. VAT

BLACK & DECKER DN710 ..... **£29.95**
BOSCH PHO100 82mm 450W **£46.95**
HITACHI FP20SA 82mm 320W **£44.55**
HEAVY DUTY
ELU MFF80 82mm 850W **£109.95**
ELU MFF80K (in kit box) **£127.95**
ELU MFF40 82mm 1000W **£189.95**
INVERSION Std. for MFF80 ..... **£20.95**
INVERSION Std. for MFF40 ..... **£29.00**
HITACHI P20SA 82mm 720W **£104.95**
HITACHI F30A 92mm 900W **£149.95**

BELT SANDERS
ELU MHB 157 3" 600W **£106.95**
ELU MHB 157E 3" var. speed **£119.00**
ELU 157 FRAME **£35.00**
ELU 157 inversion stand **£28.00**
ABRASIVE BELTS FOR MHB 157/pkt. 3
40G, 60G, 80G, 100G, 120G, 150G **£3.00**
BOSCH PBS75 3" 620W **£81.95**
ELU MHB 90 4" 850W **£193.95**
ELU MHB 90K With frame **£234.00**
HITACHI SB75 3" 950W **£122.95**
HITACHI SB10T 4" 950W **£147.95**
HITACHI SB10V 4" var. speed **£154.84**
MAKITA 9401 4" 1040W **£169.00**

BISCUIT JOINTER
ELU DS140 Biscuit Jointer **£197.00**
No. 10 Biscuits F.O.C.
No. 20 Biscuits (1000 off) **£19.95**
No. 10 Biscuits (1000 off) **£19.50**
No. 0 Biscuits (1000 off) **£18.63**
Mixed Box 0, 10, 20 (500 off) **£12.50**
DS140 saw blade 12T Std. **£29.95**
DS140 saw blade 30T Fine **£29.50**
DS140 Dust Tube adaptor **£5.95**
BOSCH Biscuit Jointer **£124.95**

★ ★ ★ SPECIAL OFFERS ★ ★ ★
HITACHI TR12 ROUTER
Powerful 1300w ½" Router in Metal
Carrying Case **£129.95** inc. VAT & P&P

RIDGWAY DRILL MORTICER
c/w Free Hitachi Drill ½" Chuck and
¼" Chisel and Bit
£186.00 inc. VAT and P&P

MARTEK DRILL SHARPENER
Excellent for Sharpening all Drill Bits
ONLY **£23.95** inc. VAT and P&P

★ CHAINSAW OWNERS ★ ★
25% off OREGAN SAW CHAINS
All chain Ex Stock By Return Post
State Type of Saw and Number of Links

POWER DRILLS (K-Kit box)
NEW ELU POWER DRILLS
ECD304K 420W V/S 10mm Compact **£73.95**
EMD400K 600W 2 Speed 13mm **£81.95**
ESD705K 320W V/S & Rev. 10mm **£102.95**
EMD403K 500W V/S/R Ham. 13mm**£90.95**
EMD406K 500W V/S/R Ham. 13mm**£114.95**
EMD406K 550W V/S Hammer 13mm**£106.95**
BOSCH 400-2 10mm 440W **£29.95**
BOSCH 500RLE 13mm 500W V/S Rev.**£49.95**
BOSCH 7002E 13mm 700W **£79.95**
BOSCH 850RLT 13mm 850W V/S Re**£111.95**
HITACHI FV12VA 13mm 420W V/S/R**£61.95**
HITACHI FDV16V 13mm 600W V/S/R**£61.95**
HITACHI FDV20VA 13mm 710W V/S/R**£83.95**
HITACHI VTP13K 13mm 2 Speed 460W**£79.95**
HITACHI VTP16AK 2 Spd. 800W ..**£122.95**
HITACHI FP20SA 82mm 320W **£44.45**

PALM GRIP SANDERS
(DB Dust Bag)
ELU MVS500 1/6th Sheet 135W DB**£60.95**
ELU MVS501 1/4 Sheet 135W DB ..**£60.95**
B&D P6301 1/6th Sheet 136W DB ..**£51.50**
B&D P6302 1/4 Sheet 135W DB **£51.50**
HITACHI SV12SA 1/4 Sheet 180W **£52.95**
MAKITA B045 10 1/4 Sheet **£48.95**

SWEDISH STEEL INDUSTRIAL BANDSAW BLADES
		¾₁₆	¼	⅜	½	⅝	¾
BURGESS	57"	£3.20	£3.30	£3.45	—	—	
DeWALT	59.5"	£3.20	£3.30	£3.45	—	—	
CORONET	67.5"	£3.43	£3.50	£3.70	—	—	
WARCO	70"	£3.60	£3.70	£3.80	—	—	
INCA	73"	£3.91	£3.70	£3.80	£3.90	£4.80	—
BIRCH	81"	£4.25	£4.35	£4.52	—	—	
DeWALT	82.5"	£4.75	£3.95	£4.10	£4.20	£5.11	£5.69
MINIMAX	86"	£4.10	£3.95	£4.10	£4.20	£5.11	£5.69
STARTRITE	88"	£4.10	£3.95	£4.10	£4.20	£5.11	£5.69
KITY	90.5"	£4.42	£4.14	£4.25	£4.42	£5.40	£5.90
STARTRITE	100"	£5.41	£4.66	£4.71	£4.86	—	£5.90
EVENWOOD	104"	£5.41	£4.66	£4.71	£4.86	—	£5.99
STARTRITE	112"	£5.06	£4.80	£4.90	£5.10	£6.30	£7.02
MINIMAX	144"	£6.46	£5.29	£5.46	£6.46	£7.13	£7.97

10% DISCOUNT WHEN ORDERING 10 OR MORE BLADES
POST PAID ON ORDERS £5.00 & OVER.

LIBERON WAXES
Waxes Sealers Stains Polishes Etc.
All Your Requirements In One
Send for Free Price List
GLUE POT ..... **£23.00** inc. P&P

CORDLESS DRILLS
OUR PRICE inc. VAT
HITACHI 10mm
DTC 10 6 cell 2 spd. & rev. **£79.95**
DRC10 as above torque adjustable**£104.95**
DTC10K 6 cell 2 spd. & rev. in case **£82.85**
D10DB 6 cell variable spd. & rev. . **£94.95**
D10DD 8 cell 2 spd. & rev. **£90.00**
D10D as above torque adjustable **£114.95**
DV10D 8 cell 2 spd. & rev. hammer **£125.95**

MAKITA 10mm
6012DWK 6 cell 2 spd. & rev. in case**£92.95**
6012HDW 8 cell 2 spd. torque adj. **£111.95**
8400DW 8 cell 1 spd. & rev. hammer**£119.95**
MAGNETIC Screwdriver kit 7 piece **£6.95**
REPLACEMENT BITS (state type) **£0.50**

MISCELLANEOUS POWER TOOLS
KEW HOBBY PRESSURE WASHER **£239.00**
DREMEL D576 FRETSAW **£69.95**
BOSCH WET 'n' DRY Vacuum cleaner **£110**
BOSCH 560 HOT AIR paint stripper **£39.00**
Steam Wallpaper stripper **£125.00**
NEW ELU DUST EXTRACTORS
EVE 938 **£229** EVE 948 ..... **£395**
BOSCH INDUSTRIAL PAINT STRIPPER**£82.95**
BELLE ELECTRIC CEMENT MIXER **£135.00**

KLEMSIA QUICK CLAMPS
SPAN	REACH	
200mm	110mm	£4.50
300mm	110mm	£4.80
400mm	110mm	£5.20
600mm	110mm	£6.00 (P&P £1.50)
800mm	110mm	£6.80
1000mm	110mm	£7.90
200mm	150mm	£7.50

RECORD CRAMP HEADS M130
1 off **£10.45** 5 off **£9.95** (P&P £1.50)

G CRAMPS (P&P £1.50 per order) may be mixed for quantity
RECORD 120-3" 1 off ..**£5.20** 5 off ..**£4.80**
120-4" 1 off ..**£5.50** 5 off ..**£4.90**
120-6" 1 off ..**£7.50** 5 off ..**£6.90**
120-8" 1 off **£11.00** 5 off **£9.80**
120-10" 1 off **£18.00** 5 off **£16.90**
RECORD DEEP THROAT 4" 1 off **£13.27**

PARAMO 3" 1 off ..**£5.30** 5 off ..**£4.60**
4" 1 off ..**£5.55** 5 off ..**£4.78**
6" 1 off ..**£7.76** 5 off ..**£6.60**
8" 1 off **£11.41** 5 off ..**£9.50**
10" 1 off **£16.90** 5 off **£15.77**
PARAMO DEEP THROAT 4" 1 off ..**£12.45**

SASH CRAMPS (P&P £2.00 per order) may be mixed for quantity
RECORD 135-18" 1 off ..... **£18** 5 off ..**£17**
135-24" 1 off ..... **£18** 5 off **£17.50**
135-36" 1 off ..... **£20** 5 off **£19**
135-42" 1 off ..... **£21** 5 off **£20**
135-48" 1 off ..... **£22** 5 off **£21**

RECORD 42" 1 off ..... **£35** 5 off **£32**
T bar 48" 1 off ..... **£36** 5 off **£34**
54" 1 off ..... **£37** 5 off **£35**
66" 1 off ..... **£40** 5 off **£38**
78" 1 off ..... **£47** 5 off ..**£45.00**

JAPANESE WATER STONES (P&P £1.00)
KING BRAND 800G WETSTONE **£8.00**
KING BRAND 1200G WETSTONE .. **£8.00**
Super Delux Finishing 8000G **£29**
Slipstones 100 × 50 × 12 1 or 4000G **£5.40**

SUPER FINISHING STONE 6000G ..**£8.90**
COMBINATION WATER STONE ..**£10.80**
SORBY Diamond honing system
(state Med. fine or Ex fine) **£14.00**

STANLEY HAND PLANES
(P&P £1.50/Order)
3	Smoothing 240 × 45mm	£23.60		03	Smoothing 240 × 45mm	£19.50
4	Smoothing 245 × 50mm	£20.00		04	Smoothing 245 × 50mm	£17.99
4½	Smoothing 260 × 60mm	£21.60		041/2	Smoothing 260 × 60mm	£18.99
5	Jack 355 × 50mm	£27.00		05	Jack 355 × 50mm	£21.99
5½	Jack 380 × 60mm	£28.00		051/2	Jack 380 × 60mm	£29.50
6	Fore 455 × 60mm	£37.80		06	Jointer 455 × 60mm	£33.99
7	Jointer 560 × 60mm	£39.40		07	Jointer 560 × 60mm	£39.75
78	Duplex Rebate	£18.50		778	Rebate 215 × 38mm	£30.80
10	Rebate 330 × 44mm	£33.00		010	Rebate 330 × 44mm	£39.50
80	Scraper	£9.50		020C	Circular Plane	£69.50
601/2	Block Plane	£21.00		0601/2	Block Plane	£16.50
92	Rebate Plane	£22.50		073	Shoulder Rebate	£42.50
CLIFTON Cap Iron 2" or 2⅜"		£5.00		RECORD 3 in 1 Plane		£39.00

MISCELLANEOUS HAND TOOLS (P&P £1.50 PER ORDER)
RECORD Dowel Jig ..**£34.00** 18" Extension Rods ..**£4.95** Drill Bushes ..**£1.90**
140 Corner Cramps **£12.00** 141 Corner Cramps **£19.40** Spare Collars **£3.20**
145 Hold Fast ..... **£12.90** 146 Hold Fast ..... **£14.70** Priory Bench Stop **£2.95**
Floorboard Cramp ..**£56.95** 169 Bench Stop ..**£7.50** STANLEY Web Clamp**£7.99**
Stanley Yankee Screwdrivers 13" ..... **£12.86** 20" ..... **£14.17** 27" **£18.50**

WORKSHOP VIDEOS (P&P £1.50)
Turning Wood (Raffan) **£29.95**
Bowl Turning (Stubbs) **£29.95**
Wood Finishing (Klausz) **£29.95**

Radial Saw Joinery **£29.00**
Router Jigs & Techniques **£29.95**
Small Shop Tips & Techniques **£29.95**

HANDSAWS
DISSTON D8 20" × 10pt ..**£23** D8 22" × 10pt ..**£24** D8 24" × 7pt ..**£26** D8 26" × 6pt ..**£27**
SPEAR & JACKSON PROFESSIONAL 22" × 10pt ..**£27** 24" × 8 ..**£28** 26" × 6pt ..**£30**
TENON SAWS S&J PROFF 8" × 20pt ..**£23** 10" × 15pt ..**£22** 12" × 15 ..... **£23**
Roberts and Lee Dorchester Dovetail Saw ..... **£27** RIDGWAY SPEEDSAW **£19**

SANDERSON KAYSER "PAX" HANDSAWS (P&P £1.50)
BRASS BACK TENNON SAWS 8" **£18.50** 10" **£19** 12" **£19.50** 14" **£20** D/Tail **£22**
HANDSAWS 20" × 10pt **£21** 22" × 6pt **£22** 22" × 8pt **£22** 22" × 10pt **£22** 24" × 6 **£22**
24" × 7pt ... **£23** 24" × 8pt ... **£??** 26" × 6pt ... **£23** 26" × 8pt ... **£23** 26" × 51/2pt ... **£23**

ABRASIVES (West German top quality P&P £1.00/Order)
SANDING BELTS resin bonded aluminium oxide cloth belts (price each)
Size (length width)	M/C	40G	60G	80G	100G	120G
75 × 480mm — 3" × 19"	(Elu)	£1.11	£1.08	£0.99	£1.05	£1.02
75 × 510mm — 3" × 20"	(B&D)	£1.14	£1.12	£1.03	£1.07	£1.02
75 × 533mm — 3" × 21"	(Bosch Hit)	£1.28	£1.17	£1.07	£1.09	£1.05
100 × 560mm 4" × 22"	(Elu 90)	£1.58	£1.43	£1.40	£1.37	£1.32
100 × 610mm 4" × 24"	(Wolf Hit)	£1.67	£1.53	£1.48	£1.43	£1.38
100 × 915mm — 4" × 36"	(Coronet)	£2.22	£1.99	£1.88	£1.85	£1.81
150 × 1090mm — 6" × 42"	(Coronet)	£4.20	£3.80	£3.65	£3.45	£3.40

★ ★ OTHER SIZES AVAILABLE ON REQUEST MANY IN STOCK ★ ★
★ ★ NEW ABRASIVES CATALOGUE/PRICE LIST OUT NOW ★ ★
Send for your free copy covers all belts discs sheets Etc.

WIRE WOOL
	0000 Fine	00/0 Medium	1/2 Coarse	3/4 V Coarse
1 KG ROLLS	£4.73	£4.35	£4.25	£4.13
250g ROLLS	£1.50	£1.45	£1.42	£1.38

ABRASIVE SHEETS (P&P £0.50 PER ORDER) state grit when ordering 100G and finer
Type	Description	60G/10	60G/50	80G/10	80G/50	100G+/10	100G+/50
PGF	GARNET FINISHING	£2.13	£8.90	£1.85	£7.70	£1.67	£6.94
GCAB	GARNET CABINET	£3.02	£12.59	£2.61	£10.90	£2.35	£9.82
PSF	SILICON FINISHING	£3.16	£13.17	£2.73	£11.40	£2.46	£10.27
WS	WET 'n' DRY	£6.19	£25.81	£5.28	£22.03	£3.59	£14.99

★SPECIAL OFFER★ 50 Sheets of asstd. Abrasives **£5.99** inc. P&P Garnet-Glass-W/Dry

---

DRILL BIT SETS
OUR PRICE INC. VAT
	Lip & Spur	HSS Std.
1/16"-1/2" × 64ths	—	£21.00
1/16"-1/2" × 32nds	£42.00	£17.00
1-13mm × 0.5mm	£54.00	£19.00
1-10mm × 0.5mm	£39.00	£11.00
1/8"-1/4" × 64ths	—	£4.50
1/16"-1/4" × 1/16ths		£2.00

WOODWORKING VICES (P&P £4.50)
RECORD 52½2 9" Quick Release **£50.00**
52½ED 9" Quick Release **£54.00**
53E 10" Quick Release **£69.00**
V150 6" Woodcraft **£11.50** (p&p £1.50)
V175 7" Woodcraft ..... **£12.95** (P&P £2.00)

CLIFTON HAND PLANES
CLIFTON 3 in 1 Rebate Plane **£67.00**
CLIFTON 410 Shoulder **£49.95**
CLIFTON 420 Rebate Plane **£57.00**
CLIFTON Multi-Plane **£189.00**

WOODWORKING BOOKS inc. P&P
MAKING WOODEN TOYS THAT MOVE**£7.95**
TRADITIONAL CABINETMAKING **£9.95**
WOOD FINISHING **£9.95**
FINISHING AND POLISHING **£2.50**
WOODWORKER GUIDE TO TURNING**£9.95**
TURNING PROJECTS (BOLTER) **£13.95**
Fine Woodworking Series
BENDING WOOD **£7.95**
SPINDLE TURNING **£7.95**
MARQUETRY & VENEER **£7.95**
THINGS TO MAKE **£7.95**
Many other titles available
FINE WOODWORKING TECHS **£15.95**
★ ★ ASK FOR NEW BOOK LIST ★ ★

PARAMO CRAMP HEADS
1 off **£10.00** 5 off **£9.00** (P&P £1.50)

SAVE 20% ON ALL HAND TOOLS SEND NOW FOR NEW HAND TOOL CATALOGUE £1.50 (REFUNDABLE ON 1st ORDER

0297 33656 5 Lines 24 Hour **CHARD STREET AXMINSTER DEVON** 6.30-9pm **34836**

MEALS
ON WHEELS

A seasonal offering to make cooking and eating your Xmas lunch — or any other meal, for that matter — extra special. Anthony Hontoir's preparation trolley is both practical and stylish

This food preparation trolley is a useful and attractive addition to the kitchen, and it's fully mobile, so you can easily take it into the garden, conservatory, or dining room. Built entirely from oak, its main features are a convenient worktop, three storage drawers for utensils (which can be opened from either side) and a pull-out tray beneath. Four sections of brass-coloured metal tubing prevent large items from sliding off the bottom shelf, and serve as handy towel rails. As an alternative to oak, you could choose ash or beech; the lighter hardwoods are most suitable.

Construction — top frame

Start by cutting to length the four legs from 38mm-square material, allowing an extra 19mm at the top for the tenon. Cut the two top end rails from 50x38mm timber, again allowing extra length so the mor-

tises can safely be cut without the risk of splitting at the ends.

Mark in the position of the mortises on the underside of both rails to receive the leg tenons. For this, the mortise gauge is set to 13mm between the two pointers, and the fence adjusted so they mark the wood centrally. Each mortise is then set in by 3mm from its inside edge and 9mm from the outside.

Cut all four mortises to a depth of 19mm. Mark out a corresponding tenon at the top of each leg saw, saw off the waste and trim the four shoulders of each tenon until the joints fit perfectly (fig. 2).

Cut the two top side rails from the same 50x38mm material, giving extra length to account for the tenon that will be prepared at each end.

Taking the board for the top shelf, accurately measure its thickness (it should be 13mm, but if you use veneered ply it might be a fraction more) and set the pointers of the mortise gauge to this measurement. Adjust the fence to 6mm from the nearest pointer, and mark in the groove that runs along the inside face of each top rail. When cut, these four housing grooves accommodate the top shelf (fig. 2).

The grooves are cut with an electric router and a 13mm cutter (you could use a plough plane),

with the cutter set to 9mm deep. The two top side rails should have the groove cut along their entire length, but the grooves in the two end rails are stopped 28mm from each end (fig. 2). This is why the router, being more accurate to control for a stopped groove, is the best tool for the job. You only then need to square off the rounded ends of the groove with a 13mm chisel.

The upper half of the outside faces of all four rails is chamfered, to add to the appearance. The areas of waste are firstly marked with the gauge; score a line halfway down the outside face, and set a line in by one-third of the

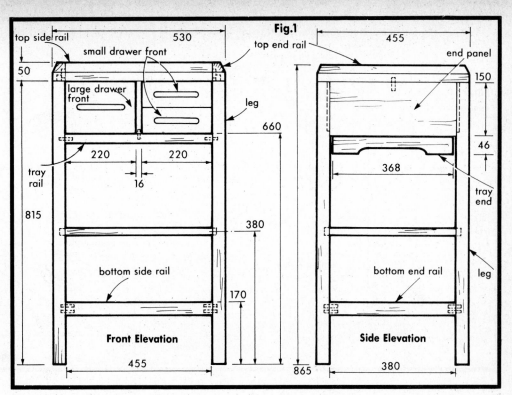

Fig.1

top side rail — small drawer front — large drawer front — leg — tray rail — bottom side rail

50 — 530 — 660 — 220 — 220 — 16 — 815 — 380 — 170 — 455

Front Elevation

top end rail — end panel — leg — tray end — bottom end rail — leg

455 — 150 — 46 — 368 — 865 — 380

Side Elevation

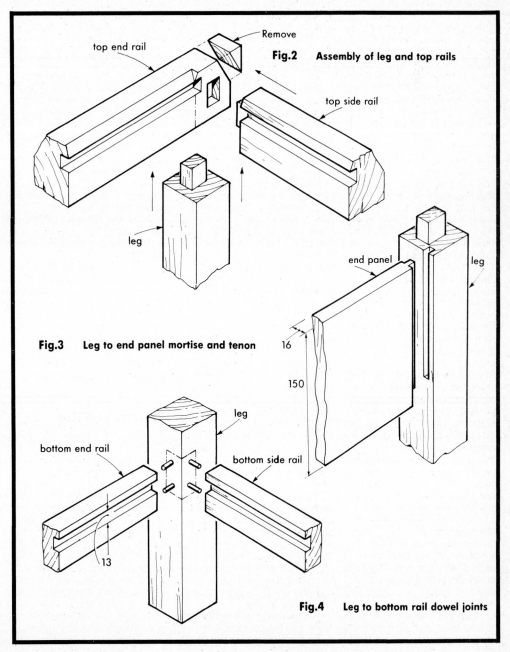

top end rail — Remove

Fig.2   Assembly of leg and top rails

top side rail

leg

Fig.3   Leg to end panel mortise and tenon

end panel — leg

16 — 150

bottom end rail — leg — bottom side rail

13

Fig.4   Leg to bottom rail dowel joints

thickness along the top edge. Clamp each piece firmly in the vice and plane off the waste.

The two end rails are attached to the two side rails with mortise-and-tenons, the mortises cut in the end rails and the tenons in the sides (fig. 2). A depth of 9mm for each joint is desirable — any more than that, and there is the risk of cutting into and weakening the leg joints. If 9mm seems rather shallow, remember that these joints are further strengthened by the top shelf, which is dowel-jointed into its four grooves.

Trim the four joints so the rails fit neatly together to make a frame for the top shelf. Mark in the sloped contour of both side rails against the two end rails where they have already been chamfered, and trim the end rails to their final length, copying the sloped face of the chamfer in the process.

Lightly chamfer the inside top edges of all four rails, working the bevel along the full length of the side rails, and stopping it short on the end rails where it coincides with the chamfering of the side rails. The end rail chamfering is best done with a spokeshave, and cleaned up with a sharp chisel so the bevels meet perfectly at the rail joints.

Check that the top shelf fits fully into its housing grooves, and tap the rail joints gently together, as a test to satisfy you that the components make a good assembly. For greater strength, the top shelf is dowel-jointed to the rails; drill a single dowel hole at the centre of each groove, and a corresponding hole dead-centre in each of the shelf's four edges; use a 6mm-diameter centre bit to a depth of 13mm.

Cut four 25mm-long pieces of 6mm dowel, running a shallow glue channel along their length with a tenon saw and bevelling the ends in a pencil sharpener. Brush wood glue well into the dowel joints, the grooves (if you're using ply) and the mortise and tenon joints. If you use solid wood for the top, don't glue the grooves or one end of the dowels. Tap the assembly together and cramp it firmly while the glue sets hard.

Leg frames

Fit the two top end panels to the legs with mortise and tenon joints (fig. 3). Each panel is 16mm thick, and mounted flush with the inside

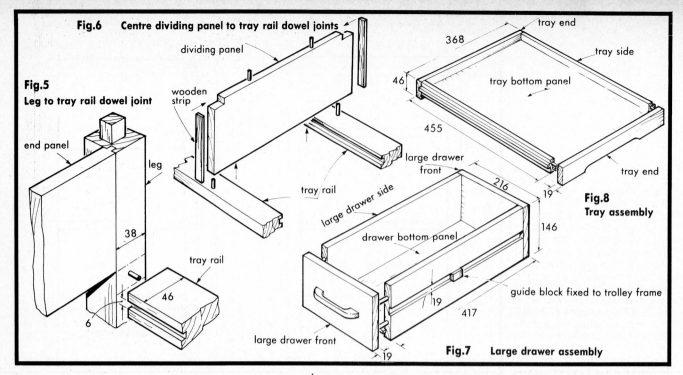

Fig.6   Centre dividing panel to tray rail dowel joints

dividing panel

Fig.5
Leg to tray rail dowel joint

end panel

leg

wooden strip

tray rail

38

tray rail

46

6

large drawer side

large drawer front

drawer bottom panel

large drawer front

19

19

417

Fig.7   Large drawer assembly

tray end

368

tray side

46

tray bottom panel

455

large drawer front

216

19

Fig.8
Tray assembly

tray end

146

guide block fixed to trolley frame

19

face of its two supporting legs. Each mortise is 6mm wide, set up by 13mm from the bottom edge of the panel. The corresponding tenon is marked centrally along both ends of the panel. Cut out the mortises with the router, fitted with a 6mm cutter set to 6mm deep. Stop the router at the point where the mortises end, and square off with a chisel.

Mark the tenons on the panels, using the same gauge setting, and remembering the 13mm haunch at the bottom (fig. 3). Cut the tenons with saw, router, chisel, or a combination of all three, and test them for fit in the long leg mortises. Drill a single 6mm dowel hole in the exact centre of each panel, 13mm deep.

Mark the positions of the 'brass' rails — 19mm if you have 19mm tube — in all four legs. This tube is not actually brass, but a bright-finished metal; you can use real brass, of course. Set the holes slightly off centre to the inside edges, and drill them out 13mm deep with a flat bit, brace and bit or Forstner bit (fig. 1).

Mark for the four bottom rails, which are dowelled to the legs with two dowels at each end (fig. 4). Cut the four bottom rails slightly oversize, and mark and cut the grooves for the shelf in the same way as you did for the top rails — as wide as the shelf is thick, set 6mm down from the top edge, and 9mm deep. Cut the rails to exact length and mark and drill accurately for the dowel holes in each end; before you drill, make sure you have the positions marked exactly in the legs too. A template the size of the rail end section would be useful here to marry the holes in legs and rails; now you can drill the dowel hole in the legs.

Cut and prepare 16 dowels 25mm long, and glue them into the rail ends. Allow a day for the

glue to set hard. Cut the brass tube to length, allowing for it to sit 9mm into each hole, and debur the ends.

Clamp each of the four legs vertically in the vice one at a time, bottom end uppermost, and drill a 9mm hole into the centre of the base to a depth of 38mm. Fit the cylindrical sockets that house the castor wheels, tapping them down with a mallet until the serrated shoulder grips the wood. Our trolley has a set of 75mm-diameter gold-coloured spoked wheels fitted with rubber tyres.

Mark in the position of the two tray rails on each leg — use another template, perhaps — and drill a single 6mm dowel hole, 9mm deep (fig. 5). Assemble the two ends, remembering to fit the 'brass' rails, gluing the joints together and cramping up.

Divider, tray rails and assembly

Cut the dividing panel that separates the drawers from one another to the same depth as the two end panels, notching it to fit round the top side rails and butt up against the underside of the top shelf assembly (fig. 6). The ends of this dividing panel don't lie flush with the outer faces of the top side rails or the tray rails; they stop 4mm short, leaving room to fit narrow strips of oak which cover the otherwise exposed endgrain.

Drill two dowel holes of 6mmdiameter to joint the dividing panel to the underside of the top shelf, and mark and drill the shelf as well; the divider is also dowelled to the tray rails, so drill for those dowels now. Then glue two short dowels in place in the top edge and fit the panel in position under the shelf.

Uncramp the two end assemblies, and temporarily fit the leg tenons into their mortises in the

top shelf frame assembly. This will give you the accurate length for the two tray rails. Cut these rails from 45x25mm material, marking in a groove along the 25mm-thick edge to receive the tongues of the tray. Scribe the grooves with the mortise gauge, its pointers set to a gap of 9mm, the fence adjusted to place them centrally. Cut the grooves to a depth of 6mm with the router, then trim both rails to the required length and drill dowel holes in their ends to match up exactly with the holes already marked and drilled in the legs. Drill for the dowels to match those in the under-edge of the divider.

Trim the bottom shelf to fit into its rail grooves, cutting small notches in the corners for a complete fit.

Apply glue to all the joints, slot the bottom shelf into its housing grooves, place the metal tubing in its holes and assemble all the dowel joints. Finally, join the four legs to the top shelf assembly, and cramp up tightly until the glue is dry. Upon removing the cramps, sandpaper the surfaces with medium and fine-grade paper.

Drawers and tray

All three drawers are designed to be opened from both sides, and there is a built-in limiter preventing them from pulling right out, which simply consists of the two guide-blocks fixed to the frame along which each drawer runs (fig. 7). The drawer sides are grooved to accept the blocks. But the drawer-fronts act as a stop to the grooves, so once they're assembled it's impossible to remove the drawers.

Cut all the drawer-fronts to size, giving a clearance of 2mm all round between their edges and

the trolley frame. Cut the drawer sides, matching each pair of sides to the same height as the drawer-fronts. Run a groove along the outside face of each side, exactly halfway down, cutting them 19mm wide and 4mm deep with the router.

Also run a groove along the lower inside face of the sides to receive the drawer bottom, measuring 6mm wide and 4mm deep. A corresponding groove is cut on the lower inside face of each drawer-front, stopped 6mm from both ends.

The drawer-fronts are assembled to the drawer sides with dowel joints; lapped dovetails may come to mind as an option, but they shouldn't be used here because it would be impossible to assemble the drawers properly — part of the assembly is carried out *in situ*.

Cut the drawer bottoms from 6mm ply, matching the colour as closely as possible to the oak.

Start by assembling the two sides to one drawer-front, and add the bottom. When dry, fit this part-assembly into the trolley and accurately mark the position of the two grooves on to the frame. Cut the blocks of wood for the drawer-guides and glue these in place halfway along the length of the end panels and the dividing panel, exactly on the line of the grooves in the sides.

Slide the half-completed drawer into position on the guide-blocks and fit the second drawer-front. Add green baize to the bottom of each completed drawer, and fit drawer handles — six in all.

The tray is of similar construction (fig. 8), except that the sides have a tongue worked on their outside faces to slot into the grooves cut in the tray rails. Both the tray ends are given a curved bottom edge for decoration. Grooves are cut for the bottom, and the sides are dowel-jointed to

Cutting list

Finished sizes

Legs	4	834mm x	38mm x	38mm	
Top side rails	2	473	50	38	
Top end rails	2	455	50	38	
End panels	2	392	150	16	
Dividing panel	1	447	178	16	
Tray rails	2	455	45	25	
Bottom side rails	2	455	38	19	
Bottom end rails	2	380	38	19	
Large drawer-fronts	2	216	146	19	
Small drawer-fronts	4	216	74	19	
Large drawer sides	2	417	146	13	
Small drawer sides	4	417	74	19	
Drawer bottoms	3	424	196	6	
Tray ends	2	368	46	19	
Tray sides	2	455	32	16	
Tray bottom	1	460	356	6	
Top shelf	1	470	395	13	
Bottom shelf	1	468	392	13	
Brass tube	2	473	19 dia.		
	2	398	19 dia.		

the ends. Once assembled, the tray slides into its grooves and can be pulled out from either end.

Finish the whole thing off with a semi-matt polyurethane varnish, which is hard-wearing and waterproof. Fit the four castor wheels into their sockets, and you have a practical and stylish piece of mobile kitchen equipment — just right to wheel in the turkey! ■

TRANSPORT OF DELIGHT

Photo R.S. Jones

What was once a tea hut is well on the way to its former glorious incarnation; horse-drawn tram enthusiast Rob Jones introduces his latest project

Horse-drawn tramcars had a relatively short lease of life. One I once helped to restore, 'Liverpool 43' had been built in 1892, but had been put to use as a potting shed in a garden only eight years later, in 1900.

More recently I've been involved in restoring an older tramcar in Southport. This particular car finished its days as a tea hut for coalyard workers, with a sloping roof added and even a chimney sticking out for a brazier. To consolidate the foundations, concrete had been poured into and around the wooden ▷

From potting shed, above, to restored glory: a previous horse-drawn tram restoration project

Photo A.H. Jacob

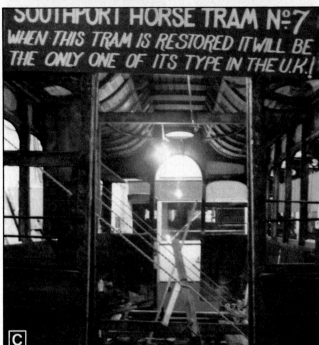

SOUTHPORT HORSE TRAM Nº 7
WHEN THIS TRAM IS RESTORED IT WILL BE
THE ONLY ONE OF ITS TYPE IN THE U.K.!

A Blockboard sandwich supports
pillars

B New underframe in place

C Tensioning ropes to straighten
frame

D Renewal of upper deck

E Fastening the canopy bend

F Looking like new: ornate
lining out and cut glass quarter
lights

G Almost complete

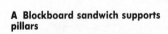

Craft Supplies Ltd.

The Home of wood turning.

The international mail order supplies company, based in beautiful Millers Dale in the Peak District, is renowned for its high quality and wide range. Both beginners and experts will find the very best in equipment, tuition, timber and demonstrations.

Choose from more than 40 types of wood in Craft Supplies' conditioned store plus 4,000 seasoned bowl blanks and squares.

For the right results you need high quality tools. Craft Supplies' in-house design team ensure that you have the most practical, easy-to-use tools and machinery in the market.

As the largest wood turning specialist in the world, Craft Supplies' extensive array of accessories, from barometers to bases, gives you the biggest choice possible.

Whether you are new to Wood turning or in need of a few expert tips, Craft Supplies' two and four day courses have a lot to offer. You can enjoy tuition from of the country's leading craftsmen.

Take advantage of the Derbyshire countryside by staying in one of Craft Supplies' comfortable cottages.

Woodturning demonstrations take place on the first Friday afternoon and all day Saturday of each month.

Send now for your full colour brochure. Only £2 from Craft Supplies, The Mill, 201 Millers Dale, Buxton, Derbyshire SK17 8SN. Telephone 0298 871636

CATALOGUE AVAILABLE FROM WHSMITH

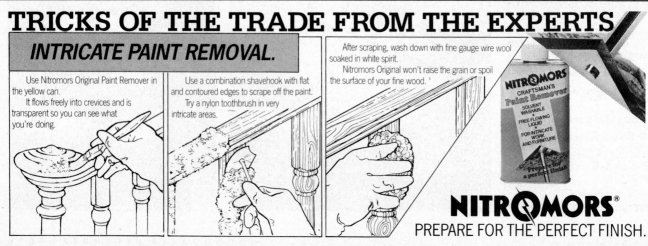

Photo H.G. Dibdin

Another tram in the same series

underframe, so when the tram was lifted away, the underframe remained in the concrete and the body was propped on the lorry on 'thin air'.

For the next 15 years the broken-down tramcar gathered dust in the working transport museum formed by the Southport Locomotive and Transport Museum Society; it looked as if it might collapse at any minute, and finally attracted my attention.

The first aim was to fix on a new underframe, replacing that which had been left in the concrete. Unfortunately, either the bases of the pillars were rotten or the ends of the tenons had snapped off. We spliced on new pillar stubs, using blockboard sandwiches (fig. 1) glued and screwed in place. We cut mortises in the underframe for the pillar stub tenons, reinforcing the joints with bolted-on steel brackets. We used secondhand pitch pine (from a Victorian church) for the underframe, as it would have been difficult to find — or afford — suitable hardwood.

But with the new underframe in place, the body couldn't be made vertical! The whole ceiling had shifted and the sides were falling over. So we attached four long loops of rope around the top of alternate pillars and, at the opposite side, around the underframe. A batten through the centre of the loop completed these 'Spanish windlasses' (fig. 2). Each rope was slowly tensioned and 'clamped off' using a longer batten and G-clamp: if you let go of one by accident you get a nasty crack from it — as we discovered...

The side pulled in very satisfactorily. At least we knew the car wasn't going to collapse like a pack of cards, as they seem to do in old silent films. Now we could tackle the large corner pillars which were just rotten timber from below waist height. This has to be cut well back and new pieces spliced in.

Because of the 'tumbling-home' sides there was a lot of waste on the Phillipine mahogany that we bought to replace the corner pillar bases — ash or oak were too expensive. We trimmed the 8x6in down with a Black & Decker bandsaw, resorting to chisel and mallet when it was too much for the machine. A long overlap on the joint of about 8in ensured plenty of gluing surface and also room for two large ½in coach bolts to pass through and secure it. These were countersunk, red oxided and the hole filled. Final shaping was done with the corner pillars in position, using a hand plane and that invaluable weapon, the spokeshave, before sanding. ▷

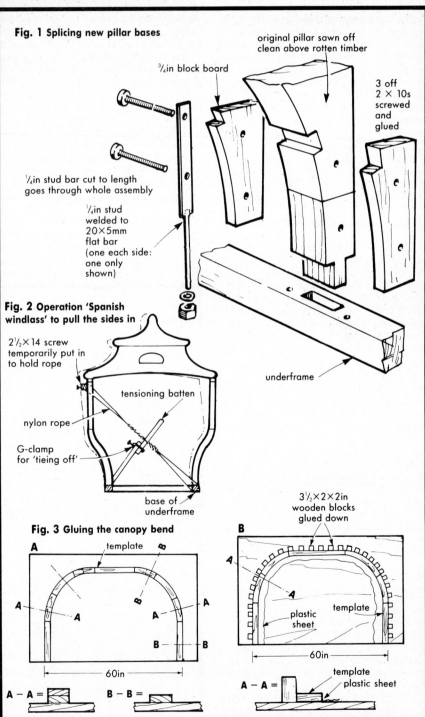

Fig. 1 Splicing new pillar bases

original pillar sawn off clean above rotten timber

¾in block board

3 off 2 × 10s screwed and glued

¼in stud bar cut to length goes through whole assembly

¼in stud welded to 20×5mm flat bar (one each side: one only shown)

underframe

Fig. 2 Operation 'Spanish windlass' to pull the sides in

2½×14 screw temporarily put in to hold rope

tensioning batten

nylon rope

G-clamp for 'tieing off'

base of underframe

Fig. 3 Gluing the canopy bend

A   template   B

A — A =   B — B =

60in

3½×2×2in wooden blocks glued down

A

plastic sheet

template

60in

template

A — A =   plastic sheet

Photo Steamport Railway Museum

Nearly completed

The canopy bend

An interesting joinery challenge was the making of a canopy bend. Originally this would have been made out of one piece of ash, 14x3x1½in, bent in a large steam chest: but we didn't have the money for the ash, nor could we find anyone with a big chest.

Our alternative was to laminate. We cut 8x4ft sheets of 4mm ply into 3½in strips lengthwise, acquired countless G-clamps, a half-gallon of PVA and hundreds of ½in and ¾in x 8 countersunk screws.

We bandsawed a template of the shape and placed it on a piece of ¾in plywood (fig. 3). We glued wooden blocks 3½x2x2in to the board on the outside of the template, weighting them down and putting extra blocks on the tight bends to take the greater strain. Then we removed the template, cut a piece of plastic sheet to approximate shape and stapled it to the board, butting up to the blocks to prevent the plywood slats sticking to the board. We drilled and countersunk the slats and the fun began. All hands were needed. We got glue everywhere as we put eight layers of the ply together and put in 400 screws per bend. Occasionally a screw was put in only to hit one lower down; we weren't worried, there were so many screws in it.

The canopy bend was over 10ft in length, so we took care to stagger the joins to avoid a line of weakness. We carefully marked out positions of screw-holes on the final layer of ply so that if they were visible, at least they would be neat.

The 3½in width for the laminations was purposely oversize, so that after gluing we could plane the bend to 3in, easily done with the Black & Decker electric planer. We finished off with a belt sander. The ends were run long, so we used a hacksaw to cut them square — cutting through screws as well as wood. The result was a very strong canopy bend!

Upper deck

A sloping roof had been put on the 'wreck' when the tramcar became a tea hut (fig. 5). We had to splice pieces of wood in to edges where the roof had rested; we planed these flush after the glue had dried. We also had to patch over a hole where a chimney for a brazier had come through — this dated from tea-hut, not tramcar, days.

We cut the bases for the seats to contour on a bandsaw, and covered the roof with canvas to look like new.

How old?

We wanted to know how old the tramcar was. Unfortunately, cutting the car through horizontally and 'counting the rings' proved an unacceptable method of establishing its age! When we started work we were told it was a 'Southport tram', which would date it from 1872. Later, while we were working on the roof, we found tickets from the Birkdale tramway company (Birkdale is the town next to Southport), which dated the car from 1883.

We hoped to find the route information and original style of painting when we started work on scraping the paint off the upper side panels. This laborious and painstaking work can be frustrating — one slip with the scraper blade, or the Nitromors is left on a few seconds too long, and the letters are gone. What made it more difficult was that when the car was re-painted the letters were 'flatted off' so they didn't show through on subsequent repaints. Only the faintest of pigment

had been left.

The first letters to be revealed were O and X: nowhere in Birkdale has an O and X in it! We went to the other end of the board and rubbed and rubbed away, and discovered the letters RRY: we couldn't think of anywhere in Birkdale with these letters either.

After many hours the full route 'OXTON, CLAUGHTON AND WOODSIDE FERRY' was revealed. This proved that the car originally began life in Birkenhead and was later sold to Birkdale, and is one of the oldest tramcars in the country.

We hope the tramcar will be completely restored by the end of 1987, and then we'll be looking at other restoration projects. ∎

● If anyone is interested in finding out more about the project, please contact: Rob Jones, British Horse Tram Enthusiasts, 59 Sherlock Lane, Wallasey, Merseyside L44 5TF. Donations towards PVA are always welcome!

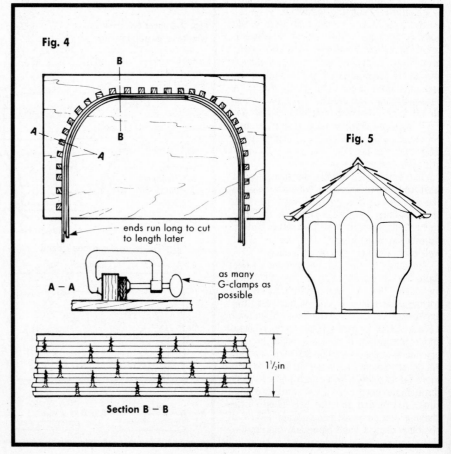

Fig. 4

B

A

A

B

A — A

ends run long to cut to length later

as many G-clamps as possible

Fig. 5

1½in

Section B — B

THE ESSENTIAL TOOL FOR ALL WOODWORKERS

£12.95

Woodworker Directory

Manufacturers & U.K. importers
Product specifications
Prices
Brand Names
Services
Timber suppliers
Local suppliers
Courses
Further sources of information

The essential tool for all woodworkers

AN ARGUS SPECIALIST PUBLICATION

Only £12.95 inc P&P (U.K. only)

If you buy woodworking equipment, materials or services, you need the **NEW 1988 WOODWORKER DIRECTORY.**

More than just a collection of names and addresses, the **WOODWORKER DIRECTORY** is the complete information service.

Included are: specifications and prices of hundreds of products and services, manufacturers and U.K. importers, timber suppliers, courses, services, plus a National Buyer's Guide.

Don't miss out. Order your copy now by returning the coupon below with your remittance to:
The Woodworker Directory, ASP Ltd., No. 1 Golden Square, London W1R 3AB. (Please allow 28 days for delivery.)
Published by **WOODWORKER** magazine.

- - - - - (PLEASE USE BLOCK CAPITALS) - - - - -

Please send me .... (copies) at £12.95 each plus P&P (U.K. Free, Overseas Airmail £3.00 each)

I enclose my cheque/postal order for £.................. (payments in sterling only) made payable to ASP Ltd. or debit £.................... from my Access/ Barclaycard No. ☐☐☐☐ ☐☐☐☐ ☐☐☐☐ ☐☐☐☐

valid from .... to ....

NAME (MR/MRS/MISS) .... Date ....

ADDRESS ....

.... POSTCODE ....

SIGNATURE .... Guild No. ....

SPECIAL OFFERS

▶ **More Master Class Video offers** ◀

Following our successful set of Xmas video offers last year, we are pleased to add six new titles to the list, from acknowledged woodworking video experts Taunton Press:

Making a mortise-and-tenon joint

Choosing the right joint: hand and machine techniques. 60 minutes. RRP inc. p&p £26.95; WOODWORKER price inc. p&p £24.
Order code WV7

Dovetail a drawer

Quick, masterly hand-cut dovetail joints; drawer-making from start to finish. 60 minutes. RRP inc. p&p £26.95; WOODWORKER price inc. p&p £24.
Order code WV9

Repairing furniture

Disassembling, choosing the right glue, mending and matching veneers, mouldings. 70 minutes. RRP inc. p&p £31.95; WOODWORKER price inc. p&p £28.
Order code WV11

Radial-arm saw joinery

Get the best from this versatile and popular machine. 110 minutes. RRP inc. p&p £31.95; WOODWORKER price inc. p&p £28.
Order code WV8

Carve a ball-and-claw foot

Scaling, bandsawing, laying out and carving this classic detail. 115 minutes. RRP inc. p&p £31.95; WOODWORKER price inc. p&p £28.
Order code WV10

Chip carving

Introduction to this direct and simple form of decoration. Incised borders, rosettes, lettering, free-form. 60 minutes. RRP inc. p&p £26.95; WOODWORKER' offer price inc. p&p £24.
Order code WV12

▶ **Same again** ◀

Bowl Turning with Del Stubbs — WOODWORKER price £28. Order code WV1

Carving Techniques and Projects — WOODWORKER price £28. Order code WV2

Wood Finishing — WOODWORKER price £28. Order code WV3

We are repeating last year's offer prices on the ever-popular first range of Taunton videos:

Router jigs and techniques — WOODWORKER price £24. Order code WV4

Turning wood with Richard Raffan — WOODWORKER price £28. Order code WV5.

Small shop tips and techniques — WOODWORKER price £24. Order code WV6

ASP Reader Services, PO Box 35, Wolsey House, Wolsey Rd, Hemel Hempstead, Herts HP2 4SS (0442) 41221.

SPECIAL OFFERS

A real Xmas special — we bring you a tempting range of quality goods at prices you'd be silly to ignore. Treat yourself, or drop some obvious hints!

British-made brass and stainless steel precision measuring tools

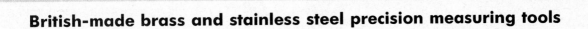

Dovetail gauge	Beam trammel	Plumbob set
A joy to use; two blades for 1:8 and 1:6 angles, plus full instructions. RRP inc. p&p £17.50; WOODWORKER **price inc. p&p £14.95.** Order code ROWW 10	Mark accurate circles: 12x¼in stainless steel bar, two adjustable brass heads, stainless steel pins. RRP inc. p&p £14.75; WOODWORKER **price inc. p&p £9.95.** Order code ROWW 11	A set of three solid brass plumbobs — 40, 80 and 130g; all supplied with twine. RRP inc. p&p £13.95; WOODWORKER **price inc. p&p £9.95.** Order code ROWW 12

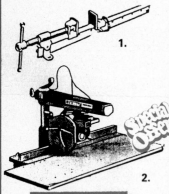

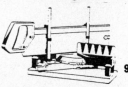

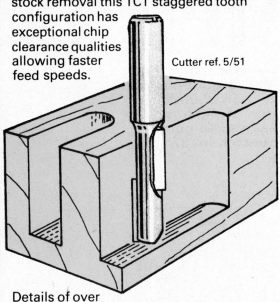

ARK DE TRIUMPH

A beautiful gift for some happy children this Christmas — Geoff King's gold-medal winning Noah's Ark sports an abundance of timbers and a number of child-safe features. But it's no mean task: get to work if you're to launch it in '87

Photo Ed Davis

After a new arrival in the family, I was asked if I could make a large and special toy. We decided upon a Noah's Ark, one toy that will never be out of date. It was a project I had been meaning to tackle for some time, so I was glad of the opportunity, and as it was in the family, I decided to make a special effort.

I wanted to make an ark that was somehow different from the traditional design, but still recognisable for what it was, so I set about designing it myself. I didn't stick to the recognised rules of proportion, I just followed my own feelings of what seemed aesthetically and functionally correct. I tried to incorporate unusual shapes so as to stimulate the child's imagination, but at the same time give the ark a solid and robust construction that will last for many years. I don't like limiting myself with strict plans to follow, because as a piece of work starts to take shape in three dimensions, I begin to get the feeling of the job and I spot improvements as I go along. Thus the design

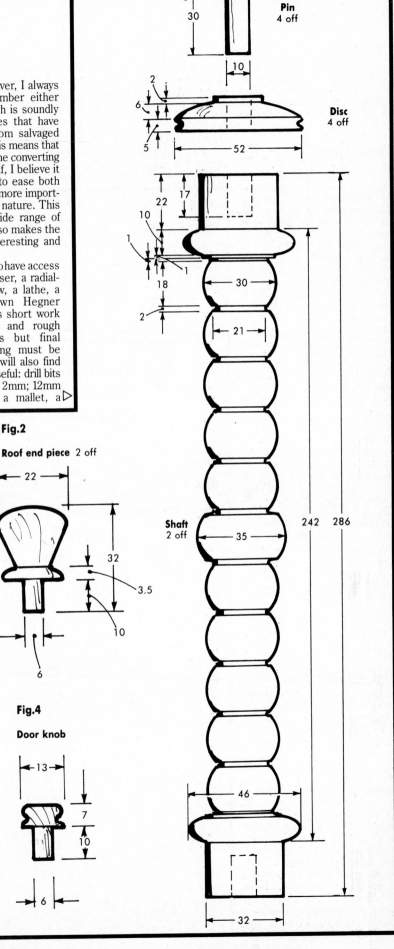

Fig.1 Handle

Pin
4 off

Disc
4 off

Shaft
2 off

changed slightly in the making with a few minor modifications and some added decorative detail. It is the finished version I have described here.

As the ark is constructed entirely from good solid hardwoods it is relatively large and heavy, so it's best used as a floor toy. It is quite easy for a child to push along on a carpeted floor, the two sides acting like 'skis'. There are two conveniently placed handles so an adult can pick it up when necessary. The large opening door at one end allows plenty of room for infant arms to explore the cavernous interior. A ramp, which hooks over the side, allows animal access to the upper storey and is easily stowed below deck. The roof of the cabin is loose fitting so it can be removed, turned on its side and used as temporary stalls for the animals or as a windbreak for Mr and Mrs Noah's picnic.

Being a nature lover, I always try to obtain my timber either from woodland which is soundly managed, from trees that have died naturally or from salvaged sources. Although this means that I have to do a lot of the converting and seasoning myself, I believe it is worth the effort to ease both my conscience and, more importantly, the burden on nature. This accounts for the wide range of woods I used and also makes the whole toy more interesting and educational.

I'm lucky enough to have access to a planer/thicknesser, a radial-arm saw, a bandsaw, a lathe, a router and my own Hegner fretsaw. This makes short work of all the cutting and rough shaping operations but final shaping and finishing must be done by hand. You will also find the following tools useful: drill bits of 10, 7, 6, 4.5, 3, and 2mm; 12mm and 6mm chisels, a mallet, a ▷

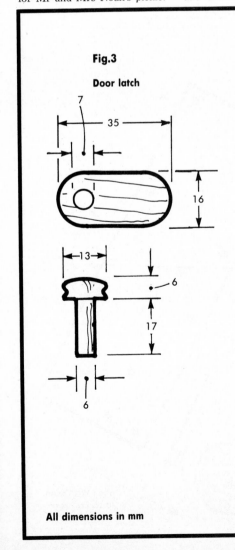

Fig.3

Door latch

Fig.2

Roof end piece 2 off

Fig.4

Door knob

All dimensions in mm

Construction

The main body of the ark is a bit like a sandwich, the sides acting as pieces of bread, between which are fitted the decks in slots and the handles in holes. The decks have rebated edges to give them extra gluing surface. The 'pins and discs' securing the handles add extra sideways strength as well as a decorative touch. The wood for the main carcase, cabin and roof should be as near quarter-sawn as possible to minimise the chances of the wood warping when it enters the centrally-heated home.

Turned pieces
(Figs 1, 2, 3 & 4)

Cut all the necessary pieces to size, allowing room for waste, mark the centres and turn them on the lathe to the profiles illustrated. Turned items are best sanded and finished on the lathe, but make sure you don't apply finish to any of the sections to be glued, as this will impair the adhesion of the glue.

Drill 10mm holes all the way through the centre of the four discs, and 17mm into both ends of each handle. As you've just turned the door knob and half the door latch you may as well make the other piece of the door latch now. Cut out the shape in fig. 3 from 9mm oak, and drill a 7mm hole in the middle of one end. Smooth off all the edges.

Side pieces (Figs 5 & 6)

Draw the outline of the side (fig. 5) on to a piece of ¼in or ⅜in plywood 245x680mm, and cut out the shape as accurately as possible with a fretsaw or bandsaw. Smooth the edges with a fine rasps and glasspaper to get the final shape. Use this as a template to mark the two sides of the ark onto the 22mm beech. Cut out these two shapes, again with a fretsaw or bandsaw and as accurately as possible. Mount each piece in turn in a bench vice and finish the shaping using a spokeshave, rasps and a cabinet scraper where necessary. Mark the centres for the handle-holes and cut them out with with a 32mm holesaw.

Using the template of the side

marking guage, 32mm and 38mm hole saws, rasps, rifflers, a cabinet scraper, a block plane, a jack plane, a dovetail saw and a whittling knife.

shape, make a template for the router to follow to cut the 8mm-wide slots shown in fig. 5. Remember to allow for the template-guide on the router. Stick the template to the side-piece with enough double-sided tape to hold it securely and rout out the slots to a depth of 9mm.

Turn the template over to make the slots on one face of the other sidepiece, so that it is a mirror-image of the first. With a sharp chisel cut out the waste left by the router in the corners and ends of the slots.

To round over the edges of the sidepieces, they must be securely

fixed horizontally to the bench so the router can be moved round the whole shape. You can either stick it to the bench with strong double-sided tape (you will need a lot of it) or secure it in a Workmate using two 20mm dowels through the handle-holes as stops (fig. 6). Once secured, use ▷

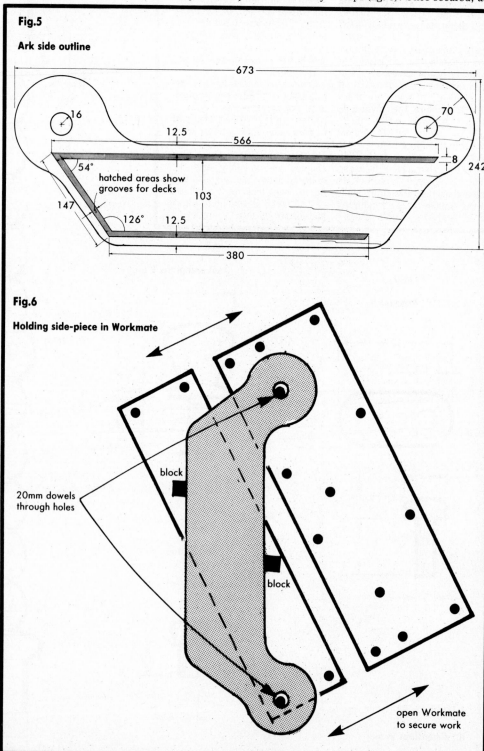

Fig.5

Ark side outline

hatched areas show grooves for decks

Fig.6

Holding side-piece in Workmate

20mm dowels through holes

block

block

open Workmate to secure work

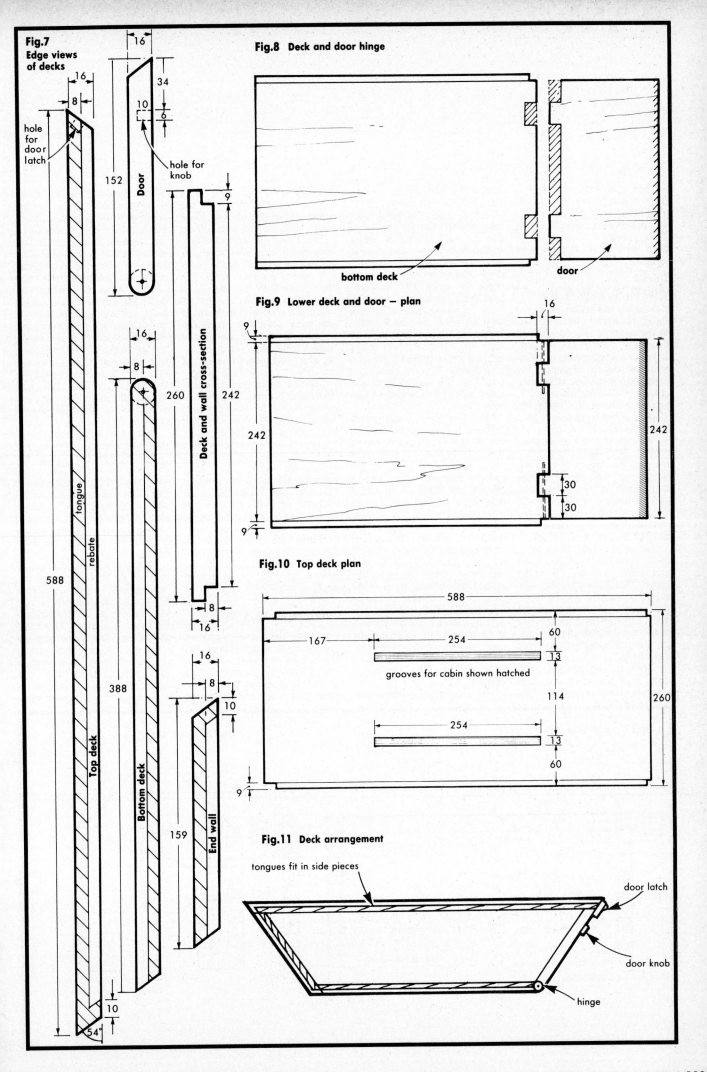

Fig.7
Edge views
of decks

16

16

8

hole for door latch

34

10

6

Door

152

hole for knob

tongue

rebate

588

Top deck

16

8

260

388

Bottom deck

10

Deck and wall cross-section

242

9

8

16

16

8

10

End wall

159

10

54°

Fig.8 Deck and door hinge

bottom deck

door

Fig.9 Lower deck and door — plan

9

16

9

242

242

30

30

9

Fig.10 Top deck plan

588

167

254

60

13

grooves for cabin shown hatched

114

260

254

13

60

9

Fig.11 Deck arrangement

tongues fit in side pieces

door latch

door knob

hinge

a 10mm rounding-over cutter in three or four passes all round the edge of the work. Turn the piece over and repeat on the other side. Then repeat the operation on both sides of the second sidepiece.

Decks
(Figs 7, 8, 9, 10 & 11)

Cut the top and bottom decks and the end wall from 260x16mm oak to the required lengths. Cut the door piece from 242x16mm oak. If you have a tilting-table or radial-arm saw, cut the angles on the ends in the same cut. Otherwise cut the pieces off square, accurately mark the angle and plane it off by hand with a good sharp plane.

With a router or a rebate plane remove 9mm wide, 8mm deep rebates from both edges of the topside of the top deck, the bottom side of the bottom deck and the outside of the end wall. This should leave a tongue 9mm wide and 8mm deep to fit into the slots on the sides of the ark.

Drill a 6mm hole, 8mm deep, in the centre of the angled door-end of the top deck at 90° to the angle. This is to take the door latch. Be careful not to break through the top surface of the deck. Cut two 13x13mm grooves in the top deck as shown in fig. 10. This is to take the cabin which fits on top.

The joint between the lower deck and the door forms a wooden hinge (figs 8 and 9). To make this, line up the bottom deck and the door, square end to square end, with the tongues on the deck and the ramp-slope of the door facing upwards. Mark the lower deck for two pieces to be cut out 30mm wide and 16mm deep, 30mm from each edge. Use these to mark the opposing knuckles of the hinge on the door. Make the saw-cuts on both pieces with a dovetail saw, back to the 16mm line. Round off both hinge ends with a rounding-over cutter in a router. Cut out the waste with a fretsaw or a sharp chisel and round off the shoulders of the hinge and the hinge and the edges of the door.

Fit the two components together, shaving off slithers with a sharp chisel if necessary, and fix them securely in a deep bench vice. Mark the centre of the hinge's diameter and drill a vertical hole 70mm deep with a 4.5mm drill bit. Insert a 75x4mm rod or dowel into the hole. Repeat for the other side of the hinge and test to see how well it works. At this stage you may have to sand off a few areas to get it to open and close without the two parts of the hinge rubbing. Remove the rods and disassemble the hinge until the final assembly.

Drill a 6mm hole, 10mm deep, in the centre of the outside of the door, 34mm from the angled end, and glue in the door knob. Before assembly, read the section on finishing.

It's advisable to dry-assemble the carcase first so that any minor adjustments can be made before gluing. Reassemble the door hinge and cut the pins off to length. Place one side of the ark, slots upwards, on the bench, fit and glue the tongues on the decks and the end wall into the appropriate slots (fig. 11). Then fit and glue the two handles into their holes. Fit and glue the other side piece on top, engaging the tongues in the slots and the handles in the holes. Try and keep the glue away from the door and any moving parts of the hinge.

Apply clamping pressure from both sides, ensuring there are no gaps where the decks meet. When it's dry, test the door to see if it opens and shuts easily enough. If not, sand the sides of it until it fits snugly. Clean off the ends of the handles where they come though the holes to make sure they're flush with the surface. Then fit and glue the 'pins and discs' to the ends of the handles.

Push the door latch-pin through the hole in the latch and glue the end of the pin into the hole in the door end of the top deck.

Cabin (Figs 12 & 13)

Cut to size the two sides and two ends of the cabin from 13mm oak. Cut two 45° angles on the cabin ends to form a right-angled point to take the roof, and round off the point so it clears the roof ridge.

Mark a line down one face of each of the sides 13mm from the edge, and plane a 45° angle to this line. Mark out the comb joints for all four corners of the cabin on both end walls and both sides. Make sure you leave the extra 13mm along the bottom of the cabin sides to fit the grooves in the top deck. Mark the sides first and use those markings to mark the cabin ends. Make the cuts with a fine dovetail saw on the waste side of the lines down to the 13mm mark. Cut out the waste with a fretsaw or a sharp chisel. Try to assemble the joints dry first and shave slithers off where necessary, with a sharp chisel, to ensure a good fit.

Mark the centre points of the three windows on the outside of both side pieces of the cabin, and cut them out with a 38mm hole saw. Mark the doorways in the two cabin ends and cut them out with a fretsaw. Use a 10mm rounding-over cutter in the router to round over over the outside edges of the window and door-holes.

Sand and scrape all four pieces until you get a satisfactory finish. Assemble the cabin round a block of softwood cut accurately to 1mm less than the inside dimensions of the cabin. This stops the cramping pressure from squeezing the doorways in. First, liberally smear the corners and corner edges of the softwood block with wax paste to stop the glue adhering to it, then glue and cramp the cabin

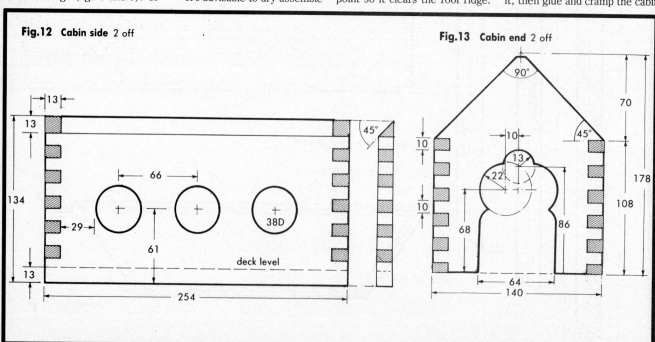

Fig.12 Cabin side 2 off

Fig.13 Cabin end 2 off

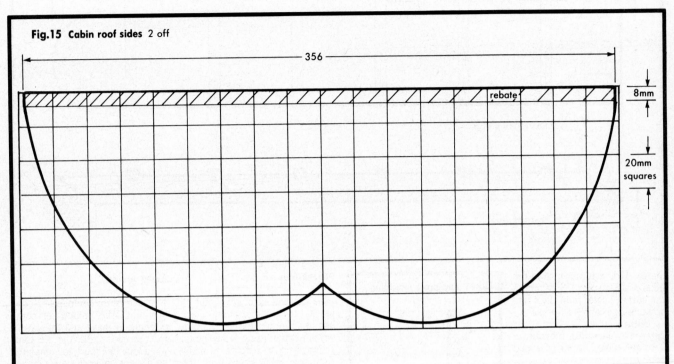

Fig.15 Cabin roof sides 2 off

356

rebate

8mm

20mm squares

Fig.14 Roof ridge section

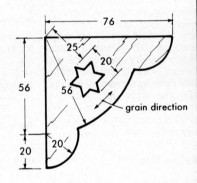

25

6mm × 10mm deep hole in each end

face 'A'

6

7

6

6

roof sides

Fig.16 Roof brace 3 off

76

25

20

56

56

grain direction

20

20

Fig.17 Position of roof braces

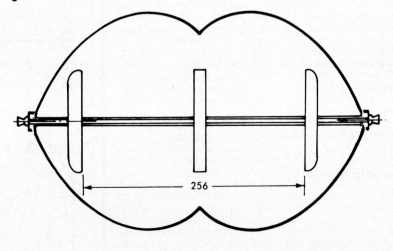

256

round it. When it's dry you should be able to knock the softwood block out with a mallet. Then fit and glue the cabin into the slots on the top deck.

Roof (Figs 14, 15, 16 & 17)

Cut the roof ridge to length from 25x25mm ash. Mark the centres in the ends, then drill a 6mm hole 10mm deep in each end. Using a 7mm straight cutter in a router, cut a slot along two adjacent faces of the ridge, 356mm long, 8mm deep and 12mm from the common edge, to take the roof sides. Stop the slots 9mm from each end. Use a plane, then rasps, files and glasspaper, to shape the roof ridge to the cross-section shown in fig. 14. Taper the last 50mm of each end of the two unslotted faces and the last 10mm at each end of the two slotted faces, so you form a 20mm-diameter circle centred on the drilled holes.

Cut an 8mm rebate, 7mm deep, from one edge of each of the pieces of 13mm oak for the roof sides. This should leave an 8x6mm tongue to go in the grooves in the roof ridge. Mark out the shapes for the roof sides as in fig. 15, and cut them out with a bandsaw or fretsaw. File and sand the edges to get rid of the saw marks. Mark and cut out the three roof supports from 13mm oak (fig. 16). File and sand the curved edges to remove saw ▷

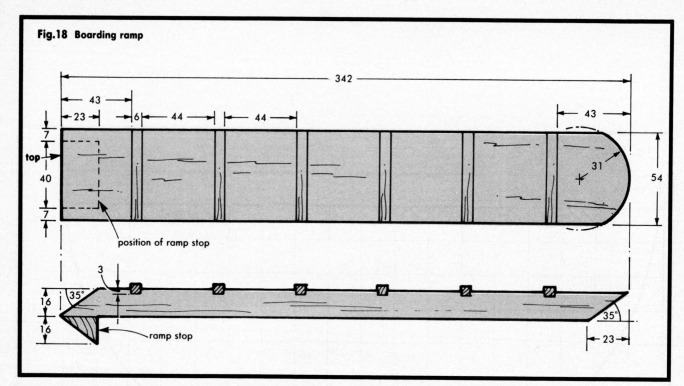

Fig.18 Boarding ramp

342

43
23
6
44
44
43

7
40
7
top

31

54

position of ramp stop

3
35°
16
16

ramp stop

35°

23

marks. Drill a 10mm hole in the middle of each piece, 35mm from the corner angle, then cut it into a star shape using a fretsaw.

With a 10mm rounding-over cutter and the router mounted in a router table, round over one edge of the curves on two roof braces and the outside edge of the curves of the roof sides, but remember to stop just before the rebate. Glue the two roof sides into the slots in the roof ridge, ensuring 90° between them. When it's dry glue in the roof braces, one in the middle and the other two so they will fit just outside the cabin ends with their rounded edges outwards (fig. 17). Glue the two turned pieces into the ends of the roof ridge.

Ramp (Fig. 18)

Cut the ramp to length from 54x 16mm oak. Cut the six 6mm wide by 3mm deep slots at right angles to the edge of the ramp using two passes of a radial-arm saw, and use a 6mm chisel just to clean them up. Plane a 35° angle off each end, but on opposite faces, and cut the bottom end of the ramp to shape. Make the six 6x6x 54mm steps and glue them into the slots. Then cut the ramp stop from an offcut of 16mm thick oak, plane off a 35° angle and glue it to the underside at the top end of the ramp.

Moulded strip (Fig. 19)

Cut a 242mm length from a piece of 20mm oak. Make the moulding down one 20mm-wide edge, then slice it off on a fine-cutting bandsaw to an 8mm-wide strip (including the moulding). Smooth the back of the strip to remove

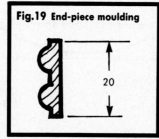

Fig.19 End-piece moulding

20

saw marks and glue it to the angle at the end of the top deck, just above the end wall. Secure the strip with three ⅜in brass pins through the middle of the moulding where it can't be seen.

Animals

I won't specify a wood type for each animal because this is a good opportunity to use up some of those offcuts you have been accumulating in boxes just in case you need them one day.

Copy the outlines of the animals shown in fig. 20 and use carbon paper to transfer them straight on to the wood. Be careful to take note of the recommended grain directions — you don't want legs and necks snapping off the first time they go into action. Drill all the eyeholes with a 2mm drill bit except for the elephants', where a 3mm bit is better. Cut out all the animal shapes as accurately as possible with a fretsaw and mark them for carving detail. Make sure the legs step different ways on opposite sides of each animal. Use a whittling knife to add the carving detail and to round-over all the outlines. Make the final shaping and even out the knife-cuts with rifflers and needle rasps, then sand them until they're smooth.

Finishing

I suggest you sand and scrape all pieces to a satisfactory finish before assembly, except where it will affect the fitting of any joints. I always try to remove as many scratches as possible from the wood, because once the finish is applied, there's a good chance the scratch will outlive you. It's also very important to smooth off all sharp edges and corners so there is nothing that could possibly injure the child. This point should be double-checked after final assembly.
All the finishing was done with three coats of sanding sealer (sanded between each coat), and three coats of non-toxic wax.

Last word

Because of its complicated construction, the amount of components to make and the care I took to do it right, the ark took me about 150 hours to complete, so it's not going to be a money-spinner. However, I feel any woodworker with enough time and patience will be well rewarded by the child's reaction to the ark, which must be worth as much as a gold medal at the Woodworker Show... and a merry Christmas to you and your family! ∎

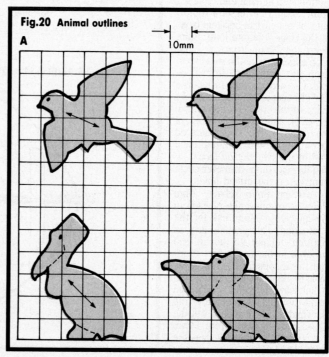

Fig.20 Animal outlines

A

10mm

Cutting list

Finished sizes, not allowing for waste

Carcase

Hinge pins	2	70mm	x	4mm dia.				Dowel or brass
Ark sides	2	673	x	242	x	22		Beech
Top deck	1	588	x	260	x	16		Oak
Bottom deck	1	388	x	260	x	16		Oak
End wall	1	159	x	260	x	16		Oak
Door	1	152	x	242	x	16		Oak
Moulding strip	1	242	x	20	x	7		Oak

Cabin

Roof sides	2	356	x	137	x	13		Oak
Cabin sides	2	254	x	134	x	13		Oak
Cabin ends	2	178	x	140	x	13		Oak
Roof ridge	1	375	x	25	x	25		Ash
Roof supports	3	76	x	76	x	13		Oak

Turned pieces

Roof end piece	2	32	x	22	x	22		Oak
Door latch-pin	1	23	x	22	x	22		Oak
Door knob	1	17	x	13	x	13		Oak
Handles	2	286	x	46	x	46		Ash
Discs	4	13	x	52	x	52		Oak
Pins	4	40	x	20	x	20		Ash
Door latch	1	35	x	16	x	9		Oak

Ramp

Ramp	1	342	x	54	x	16		Oak
Steps	6	54	x	6	x	6		Ash
Stop	1	40	x	23	x	16		Oak

Animals — Offcuts of oak, ash, sycamore, walnut, silver birch, yew, afrormosia etc.

Pigs	2	90	x	47	x	25	
Camels	1	74	x	80	x	25	
	1	86	x	38	x	25	
Walrus	2	128	x	48	x	25	
Giraffes	1	98	x	98	x	25	
	1	126	x	68	x	25	
Mr Noah	1	78	x	40	x	20	
Mrs Noah	1	66	x	30	x	20	
Cow	1	86	x	53	x	25	
Bull	1	105	x	68	x	25	
Rhinos	2	138	x	65	x	30	
Elephants	2	120	x	88	x	35	
Horses	1	89	x	72	x	25	
	1	74	x	82	x	25	
Lions	1	85	x	55	x	25	
	1	80	x	59	x	25	
Doves	1	55	x	46	x	15	
	1	55	x	50	x	15	
Pelicans	1	57	x	45	x	15	
	1	73	x	40	x	15	

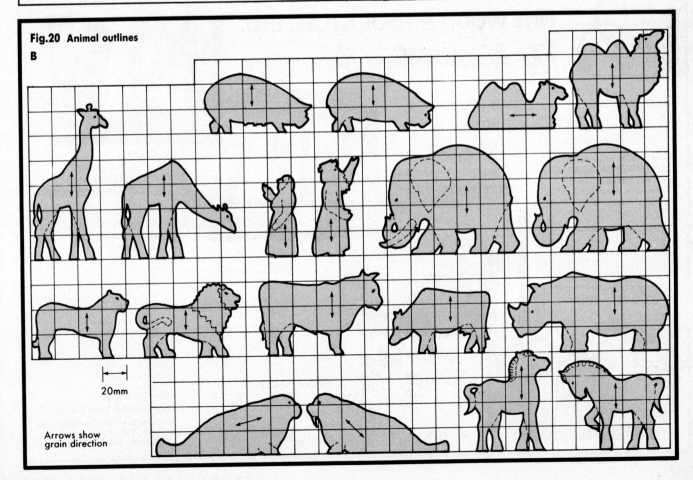

Fig.20 Animal outlines
B

20mm

Arrows show grain direction

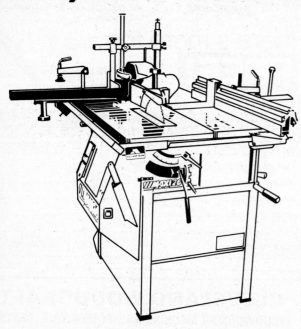

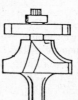

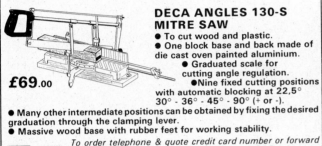

OLD TIMER TWO

The second half of Peter Manktelow's virtuoso clock-making project: the conclusion of the construction process, and time adjustment methods. Yes, it works

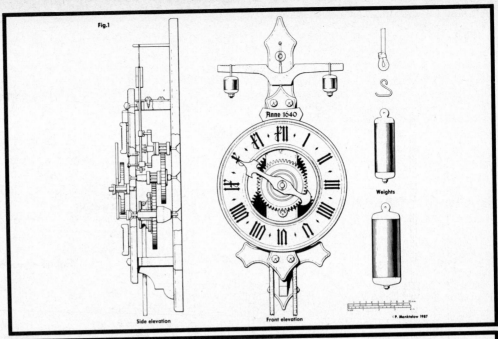

Fig.1

Anno 1640

Weights

Side elevation Front elevation

(P. Monktelow 1987)

L ast month I explained the calculations for the gearing of the single-handed replica Black Forest wooden clock, and the cutting of the gear wheels on my 'wheel cutting engine'. This month the rest of the construction is explained, with a few notes about timing, and alternative methods of making gear wheels.

Pinions

Because the arbor of my wheel cutting engine was of necessity ½in diameter, the wood arbors in the clock which were to receive the wheels were, of course, also partly turned to this dimension. The pinions (parts 3, 21 and 24, fig. 2: see also fig. 3), are of the 'lantern' type and are worthy of careful workmanship. I used box wood for their construction but any hard, close-grained wood will do. I did contemplate cutting solid pinions and my engine was conceived with this in mind, but as lantern pinions fascinated me, were traditional, looked the part and were self-clearing when exposed to dust, the matter was settled.

My method of making lantern pinions will cause some amusement amongst the experts, being somewhat crude to be sure — but no doubt so were the methods employed of old. The photographs show some of the processes. Turning the pinions in box wood was a straightforward task; I made them slightly oversize to be trimmed down later. I turned up a simple cup chuck to receive the pinions for boring the ends for the silver steel pivots; it was screwed ▷

The completed clock and the pieces it is made from, opposite. Below, boring the holes in a pinion 'bobbin' for the pivots. Below right, drilling the pinion bobbin for the 'trundles' or wires

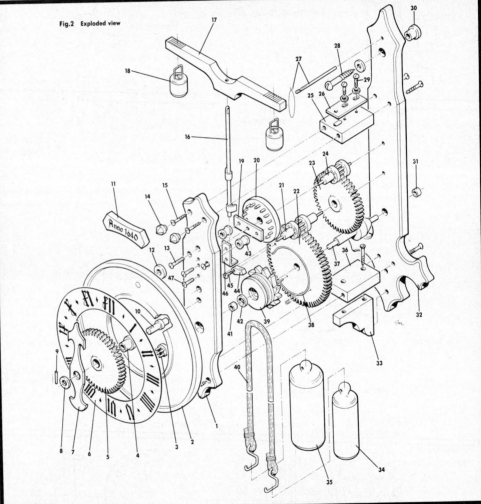

Fig.2 Exploded view

Anno 1640

Fig.3

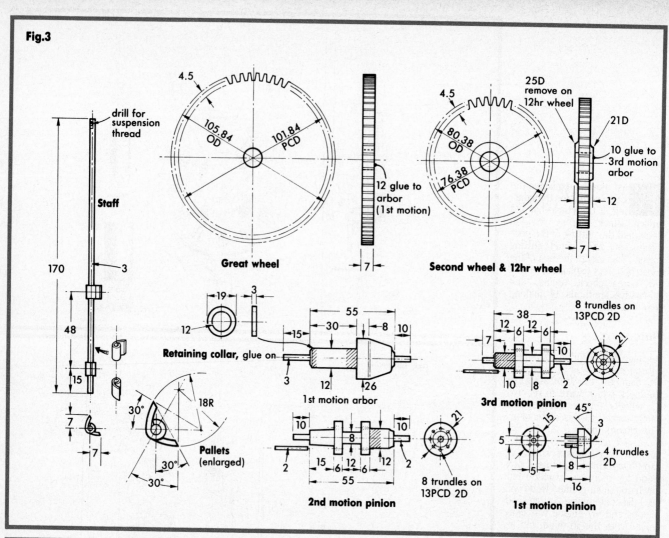

Great wheel — 4.5, 105.84 OD, 101.84 PCD, 12 glue to arbor (1st motion), 7

Staff — drill for suspension thread, 170, 3, 48, 15, 7, 7

Retaining collar, glue on — 19, 3, 12, 3

1st motion arbor — 55, 30, 8, 10, 15, 3, 12, 26

Pallets (enlarged) — 30°, 18R, 30°, 30°

Second wheel & 12hr wheel — 4.5, 80.38 OD, 76.38 PCD, 25D remove on 12hr wheel, 21D, 10 glue to 3rd motion arbor, 12, 7

3rd motion pinion — 38, 12, 6, 12, 6, 7, 10, 10, 8, 2, 8 trundles on 13PCD 2D, 21

2nd motion pinion — 10, 8, 10, 2, 15, 6, 12, 6, 12, 55, 8 trundles on 13PCD 2D, 21

1st motion pinion — 15, 45°, 3, 5, 5, 8, 16, 4 trundles 2D

Fig.4

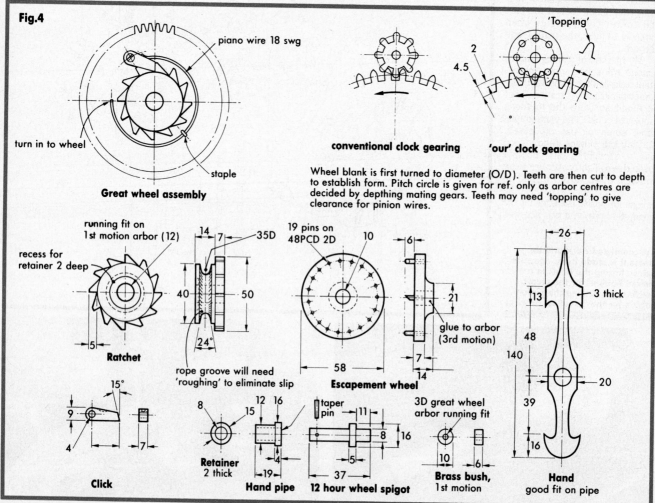

Great wheel assembly — piano wire 18 swg, turn in to wheel, staple

conventional clock gearing

'our' clock gearing — 'Topping', 2, 4.5

Wheel blank is first turned to diameter (O/D). Teeth are then cut to depth to establish form. Pitch circle is given for ref. only as arbor centres are decided by depthing mating gears. Teeth may need 'topping' to give clearance for pinion wires.

Ratchet — running fit on 1st motion arbor (12), recess for retainer 2 deep, 14, 7, 35D, 40, 50, 5, 24°, rope groove will need 'roughing' to eliminate slip

Escapement wheel — 19 pins on 48PCD 2D, 10, 6, 21, 7, 14, 58, glue to arbor (3rd motion)

Hand good fit on pipe — 26, 13, 3 thick, 48, 140, 20, 39, 16

Click — 15°, 9, 4, 7

Retainer 2 thick — 8, 15

Hand pipe — 12, 16, 4, 19

12 hour wheel spigot — taper pin, 11, 8, 16, 5, 37

Brass bush, 1st motion — 3D great wheel arbor running fit, 10, 6

Fig.5

Front bearing spacer (2)   12   25   2

Staff upper bearing 16swg brass   50   11   14   20   15

3 for staff   adjustment slots

12   2   40 24

3rd motion front bearing, brass   7   10 20 14   2   -24-   15   24 40   -35-   tap 2

56   30   10   10   30 58   32R   14R

56   12   56

Spacers   tap 2   12

16   8   3 for staff   14   15   8

2 for foliot suspension   36   32R   60

90   40   hole for grommet (screw)

Staff lower bearing 16swg brass

24   arbor centres are established by 'depthing' gears   50R   36   24   26   56

50   24

16   for staff lower bearing

490   Bush   236   76   50   306

24   24R   28R   72   40   44   40   50R   26   26   16   34   40R   84

85   26R   30   150   3   -24-

15   3   12

Rear plate   **Front plate**

---

to the faceplate of the lathe and bored to ensure a nice push fit for the pinions. The holes for the pivots were then bored undersize to ensure a good tight fit for the wires. After inserting the pivots I chucked one end in the lathe and supported the other end in a female centre in the tailstock. I then trued up the pinions to finished size and trusted that they would now run true between the plates.

Drilling the pinion flanges for the wires (the teeth — or trundes, to be precise) must be done with care and good judgement. No matter how well you have cut the teeth in your wheels, slipshod work here will nullify your efforts so far.

I made up two little clamps to hold the pinions vertically and dead centre on the drill table. This centring was checked with a wire in the drill chuck, and also by rotating the drill table until I had ironed out any trace of eccentricity. Only when I was satisfied that the pinion ran true on the table were the clamps tightened down. The drill table was then offset by an amount equal to the radius of the pinion wire centres and locked. Drilling for the wires, or trundles, now commenced; I used the index tape with the fixed pointer I had used for the 48-toothed wheels, explained last month. Every six marks gave me the eight pitches required. (Or every eight on the 64 index tape).

The eight wires were then cut for each pinion and with the drill used as a press, forced in and locked with a touch of epoxy. The final result was nice and satisfying.

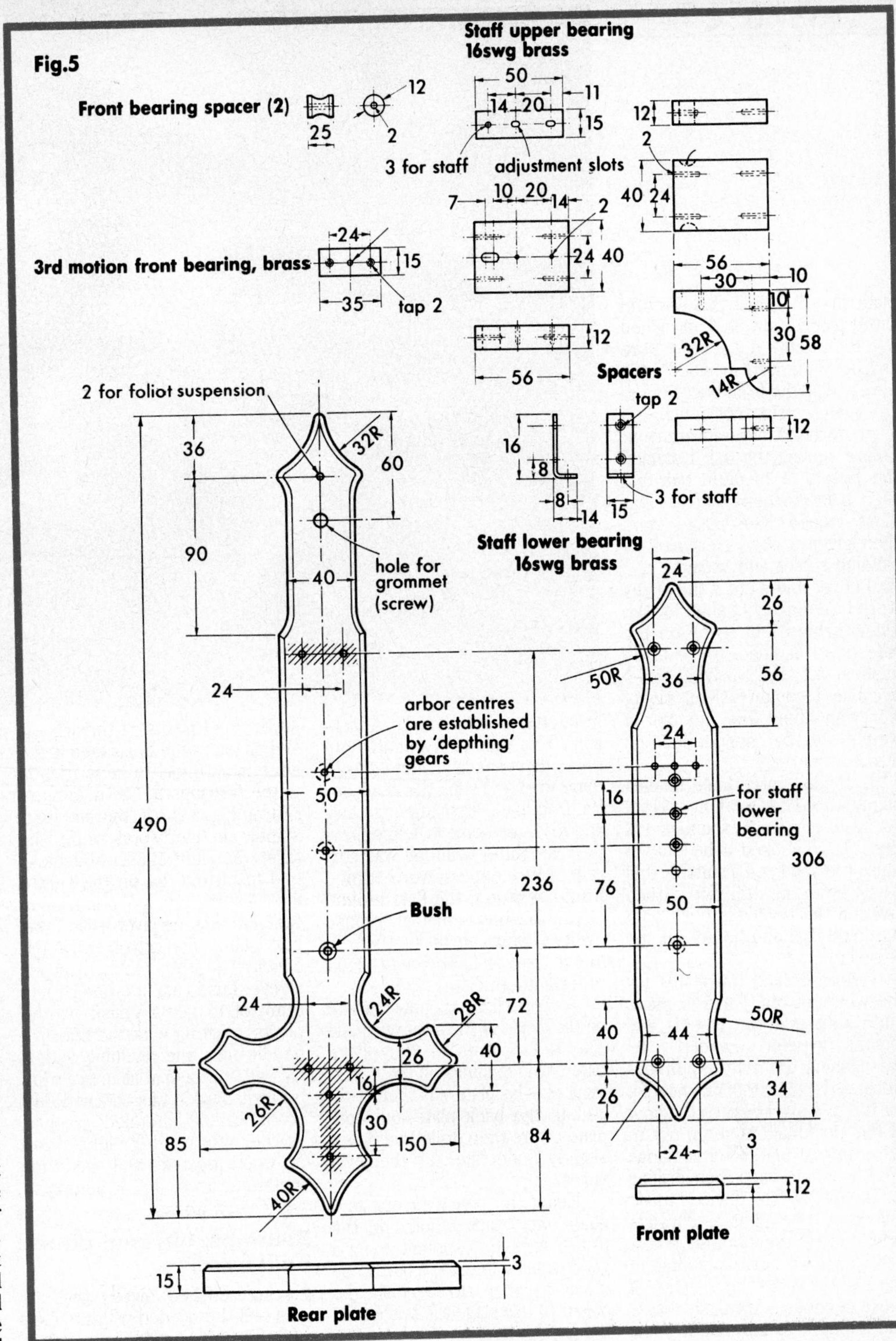

Wheels

The hub, or boss for the great wheel (figs 3 and 4) was turned from box wood and bored to receive the silver steel pivot which was duly locked in place. The great wheel seats on this hub; I secured it with wood glue, making sure everything ran nice and true. The drive pulley, combined with the ratchet wheel (fig. 4) was also turned from box and this was bored to run smoothly on the great wheel hub. The ratchet teeth were cut on my engine utilizing a special cutter I ground for the purpose. The click (fig. 4) was cut from oak and shaped to fit snugly into one of the teeth of the ratchet wheel. It is held in place on the great wheel

by a brass domed-head woodscrew. The click spring was made from 18swg piano wire which was pinned and glued in place, also on the great wheel.

The escape wheel disc was turned and then glued to its respective pinion and checked for concentricity. The assembly was now set up on the drill table and the 19 holes for the 'scape' pins were duly drilled using my patents pending — ie tape on drill table — method. The cut-to-length pins (for teeth) were then inserted in the holes and secured with epoxy resin. The drill was again used as a press, the drill stop giving constant height to the pins. The pins were then backed off at 45° to give the necessary clearance to the pallets. I have a small electric motor to which I attached a 1in-diameter emery wheel, which

when it's bench mounted is fine for hand-held grinding of small articles. I don't think it's necessary to rig up a grinding jig for mathematical accuracy here, but I do emphasise that accurate pitch and height to the pins is essential as this is the one item on our clock which governs all else and will be the source of trouble if workmanship is not sound. As a final assurance that the pins were all of equal height I mounted the wheel assembly back on the lathe between centres and with the wheel spinning at high speed touched up the pin ends with my portable (this time hand-held) grinder. It is vital too, that correct balance be achieved on this wheel as later events will show. One can set up two vertical plates and run the 'scape wheel along the edges of these plates, making certain

they are truly horizontal. Any imbalance should be remedied by attaching a small piece of lead on the rear face of the wheel where it will be out of sight, adjusting the weight until balance is achieved. Or a more workmanlike job would be to drill a hole, or holes, and fill flush with a slug of lead.

Framework and bushes

Being reasonably satisfied with the 'works' of my clock I could now proceed with a little more confidence on the basic woodwork. The frames, spacers and gusset were all made from wellseasoned oak that I cut from an old plan-chest drawer-front. Black Forest clockmakers would probably have used beech.

Not having a reasonable piece of oak wide enough for the rear ▷

Taking off arbor centres on the depthing tool

plate (fig. 5) I built this up from three pieces dowelled and glued together. Once the frames were shaped to outline I moulded a 45° bevel round the front edges of the two plates, using my bench drill in an overhead router incarnation; before sealing the oak I stained the bevels in medium oak and then painted them with a clear gloss laquer. The plates were then given a good treatment of sanding sealer and waxed.

I never found out if the plates were traditionally bushed for the wheel arbors, but to be on the safe side I decided to use brass bushes for the 'driving axle' because I couldn't sleep nights worrying about the amount of weight to be suspended on wooden bearings.

I couldn't turn these bushes on my wood lathe, so I improvised yet again using my ubiquitous drill (fig. 4). I chucked a bit of ¼in brass rod and fixed a suitable drill vertically in the drill vice. I then lowered the revolving bush onto the fixed drill and bored out the pivot hole.

Before drilling the plates for the wheel pivots, I had to make quite sure that the wheels and pinions meshed correctly, by establishing the centres' dimensions. A depthing tool was needed for the task, as I believe the best of the clockmakers seem not to rely on calculated dimensions upon which to base their drilling for the plates. The device I made (shown in the photo), consists simply of two sections with vertical portions corresponding to the plates of the clock. One of these sections is fixed to a base, and the other is movable to allow adjustment of the wheel centres. V-notches were cut on top of the vertical plates to receive the wheel arbors. A wheel with its corresponding pinion was laid on these Vs, and the centres adjusted until perfect running was established. The centres were then measured off with dividers and the correct reading transferred to the drawing as reference for drilling the holes in the plates.

If the wheels stick in one place — as mine did — it indicates some shoddy work somewhere. But if the fault lies in the cut teeth of the wheel, a little touch-up with a fine file should bring things to order. If the pinion is the offending item then the worst thing that can happen is that you have to make another pinion — as I had to.

The clock frame assembly was straightforward enough, with the front plate designed to be detachable. This will be on and off more times then you can count (at least mine was) so I sunk the heads for the front plate attachment screws and made up some little stoppers to cover them when all was correct. My stoppers were turned from hardwood, the flats ground off and finished in metallic bronze paint. If you can make them in metal they will, no doubt, look more authentic.

A centre line was now marked on the inside of the front plate and also the centres of the pivots taken from readings off the depthing tool. This plate was then clamped to the back plate and both plates were then drilled together, slightly undersize, for the pivot wires.

Using the pinion pivots as a guide the bearing holes in the plates were then opened up for a good running fit using a hardwood taper 'reamer' to burnish the holes. At this stage the bushes for the great wheel pivot were pressed and glued in their respective holes, checked with inserted wire to ensure alignment. The spacers were then assembled, screwed and glued to the back plate as a permanent fixture. I then inserted the 'works' between the plates to line everything up before drilling through the front plate into the spacers for the woodscrews. I then separated the plates and drilled clearance holes in the front plate and countersunk for the attaching screws. At this stage I also carefully countersunk the pivot holes to reduce bearing friction, ensuring that the pivot wires would just extend beyond the bearing surface. A final check was made to satisfy myself that subsequent assembly of the plates found all the pivot holes lined up true.

Before final assembly, the silver steel pivots of the wheels and pinions were burnished in the lathe in an effort to keep friction in the bearings to the minimum. I turned up a short 'morse taper' spindle in hardwood to fit the tailstock, then cut the business end to form a flat on the centre line. Then I cut a V-notch upon which to rest the pivot while I was burnishing. The driven end in the chuck was protected by a paper sleeve. I used any method I could think of to get a polish on the pivots, starting with the finest of needle files and finishing with a file with no teeth at all until a truly burnished finish was obtained. My pivots weren't hardened; graphite powder was used for lubrication of wood-to-wood and wood-to-metal surfaces, and it seems to work very well.

Bearings, bits and pieces: pallet staff

Having satisfied myself that all was well, I proceeded with the rest of it. The brass strip for the front bearing of the 'scape wheel (part 19, fig. 2; see also fig. 5) was cut from an old clock frame, and is supported (in my case) by turned pillars which are definitely non-standard Black Forest specification. But they look nice. A single piece of bent brass strip will serve just as well. Whatever you do here be careful to line up with the plate holes. The front plate hole is not used on the 'scape wheel, but is there to facilitate the line-up of this front bearing.

The top and bottom bearings of the foliot spindle (pallet staff — parts 26 and 46; see also fig. 5) were also cut from brass clock plate and offer a certain amount of adjustment for final set-up. The pallet staff (part 16) was made from 3mm-diameter silver steel and a flat was filed at the top end and drilled for the suspension cord. What shape, what material and how best to attach the pallets (fig. 3) to the staff was another major decision to be faced. I finally decided to make the pallets from sheet steel and these would be bent around the staff and, initially, left just tight enough for the thing to function. Adjustment at this stage would be vital while I experimented with angles and clearances, etc. Not unti I made the foliot (balance) also of oak, and satisfied myself that everything seemed to 'tick', the balance suspended with thread, did I secure the pallets with epoxy resin. This I did whilst everything was in place for fear of upsetting the adjustment. Silver soldering or brazing would have been much more professional here but I couldn't risk taking everything apart again without disturbing the pallets. So far things are holding up well so I see nothing much wrong in this unorthodox approach.

Timing adjustment

So it was time to see if there was any point going further with the project. I was getting impatient to see if the damn thing would function under proper weight drive, instead of the wheels being pushed round by hand. I sorted out a 6ft length of timber and clamped this upright to my bench. The clock was mounted at the top of this, resting on two protruding wood screws. The drive cord for the clock was given to me by a kind friend who said it had lain at the bottom of the case of his antique long-case clock for years and wouldn't be needed. So you need friends my friend. This cord, of course, served as a guide for

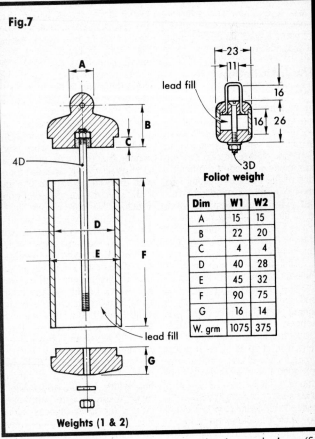

Fig.6

8 notches on 3mm pitch

200
6
40
12
tight fit on staff
30
10 · 30
10

Foliot

9

112 · 208

dowels 5D

Chapter ring

Fig.7

A

B

C

4D

D

E

F

lead fill

G

lead fill

Weights (1 & 2)

23
11
lead fill
16
16 · 26
3D

Foliot weight

Dim	W1	W2
A	15	15
B	22	20
C	4	4
D	40	28
E	45	32
F	90	75
G	16	14
W. grm	1075	375

the profile of the drive pulley; a slight taper to the groove, to eliminate slip, is required. So make yours to suit your rope.

I put some large steel washers on the foliot as temporary weights, and suspended something suitable as drive weight and compensating weight on the cord; just enough weight bias to get the thing in motion. To say that everything worked perfectly would be tantamount to deception. It transpired that I had worked to too close tolerances, not allowing wood to move as it is prone to, so everything had to come apart again for bearings to be freed and wheels to be thinned a bit to clear the walls of the lantern pinions. This was my biggest error in not making the pinion wires long enough; plenty of side play was the answer. My drawings reproduced here incorporate lessons learned, so see how lucky you are! Now everything worked fine after a little touch-up here and there with a file.

The great wheel was marked with chalk (no hand yet) and, with some trepidation, a check on timing was begun using a supply of washers on and off the foliot at varying radii. What was this?! Was my clock *that* slow? What happened to all my calculations? I went over them time and time again and still couldn't find anything amiss. Was there something I had forgotten, not taken into account? Suddenly light dawned. I was timing my clock against a minute hand from the *hour* wheel on my clock. Time I had a rest, I thought, and with my clock merrily clacking away, and in a much healthier state of mind, I went back indoors.

Hand, dial and weights

I made the hand from lime wood which is nice and light and easily cut. There is enough friction on the wheel boss to allow for adjustment, and the assembly, with the 12-hour wheel, is held from falling off by a hardwood taper pin and washer (part 9: see fig. 4). The hour drive pinion is no more than a hardwood boss with four 'teeth' secured with epoxy. The boss was drilled on the pillar drill for the pins in the same way as the other pinions, but the pitch can be measured direct tooth-to-tooth, and not round the circumference — which would be inaccurate with so small a number of teeth. The pinion was secured by epoxy to the front end of the great wheel

arbor after assembling the train and plates, making sure adequate clearance was maintained to allow easy running. The front plate was counterbored to allow for this. The 12-hour (hand) wheel was now offered up to the pinion and the centres established for correct location (and mesh) of the 12-hour wheel. With the wheel boss centre now established, the front plate was now drilled to receive it; the boss was secured with glue and gear meshing finally checked as correct. It had not been possible, up to this time, to properly fix the exact position of the dial but now this was established I could relax in the knowledge that the bulk of the work was behind me and I would soon know if my endeavours had been worthwhile. Right from the start I was reluctant to make the dial of the clock from plywood, feeling that it wasn't in keeping with Black Forest tradition. Nevertheless I doggedly went ahead and turned one up clamped to the outside of the headstock (I could only get 4in diameter between centres), but I didn't like it. I also had a go at turning one up from mahogany, but by the time I had achieved a reasonable finish the blessed thing was ½in down on diameter. Then I remembered some discarded pine bookshelves waiting to be put to good use; I'd never turned such soft wood before, but by this time I was ready to try anything. To my amazement the pine turned without trouble, finishing with a scraper; and with a touch of light oak stain, sealing and waxing, it looked the part.

The face of the dial (chapter ring) was drawn with india ink on to a sheet of good quality parchment paper — 'goat skin' on the water mark. It has a nice creamy appearance and with a bit of airbrushing on the inner and outer rim with vandyke brown oil colour, it looks quite well. The whole thing was given a fixing with a spray of clear matt laquer and then glued on to the dial. Dowels were glued on to the back of the dial and the assembly was offered to previously drilled holes in the front plate. A good push fit will suffice. To add a note of frivolity, a traditional date plaque of oak with incised lettering was made and glued in place above the dial. Purely decorative with no real significance.

The weights (fig. 7) were made from stock steel tubes of respective diameters that would

just clear each other when suspended. The only stipulation, I found, is that their length be kept to the minimum to achieve maximum drop per wind. My weights have end caps turned from a rolling pin. (It has not been missed yet to my knowledge). The top caps feature a knob drilled for the suspension hook, while the lower cap is bored to take the securing rod. The weights are filled to capacity with rolled-up sheet lead. My method

of securing the caps is shown (fig. 7) but this task can be varied according to one's fancy, or stock items used. Studding comes to mind but it must be of small diameter so as to get the maximum benefit from lead filling.

The foliot weights were made in a similar fashion to the drive weights but have suspension loops of wire as shown in fig. 7.

These wires are secured by spots of the proverbial epoxy. The steel tube parts of the weights ▷

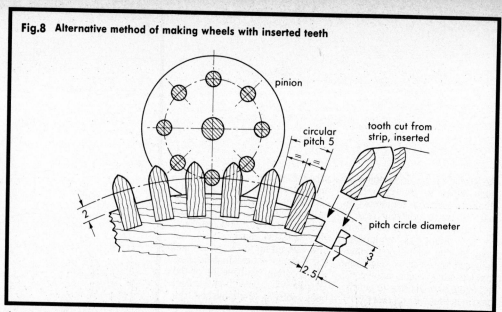

Fig.8 Alternative method of making wheels with inserted teeth

pinion

circular pitch 5

tooth cut from strip, inserted

pitch circle diameter

2

2.5

3

were painted matt black and waxed, while the wood caps were sealed and waxed while in the lathe. This arrangement is hardly 'Black Forest' I know, but a compromise is sometimes necessary. As it happened, some adjustment to the filling weight was necessary to achieve precise time regulation. They say these clocks originally had lumps of rock as weights but apart from the job of quarrying the correct shape, size and weight, and the prospect of further 'knapping' in order to get the weight right, I didn't really fancy this arrangement in the domestic scene; purely personal, mind you. Do as you please, for there is scope here for your imagination and if you have a metal turning lathe then you can go to town. I do, however, advocate loose lead filling because you will be doing a great deal of adjusting at first just as I did.

The installation

Having satisfied myself that everything was in order and the clock would keep going by winding every morning and every evening, a start was made for its domestic placement. Every effort was made to deaden the healthy tick of the clock by making sure the clock was suspended on rubber. The single securing screw goes into a rubber grommet secured into the back plate whilst the plate itself is held away from the wall by three rubber spacers.

All looked well with the clock suspended as high as was practical and plumbed. The cord was, and only at this stage, cut to length and the ends glued and copper wire bound on to their respective hooks. The weight was duly wound up as far as it would go under the clock ... and it went for only a few seconds. It continued to stop every 70-odd seconds and try as I might with every conceivable adjustment I could not coax the damn thing to go. The fault, of course, lay in the 'scape wheel, for that revolved once every 75 seconds. I discovered that the wheel was grossly out of balance, far too much to be overcome with the power available. A small piece of lead glued to the back outer rim of the offending wheel (out of sight) brought it into equilibrium and put the matter right. But why the clock went so well on the 'test bed', I just don't know. These thing are almost human, you know; treat them with care, give

them all the attention they deserve and they will respond. It probably preferred the friendly workshop environment!

More wheel cutting

There was only one thing about this clock that didn't look right. I was never really happy with the colour of the wheels; lignum vitae is too dark to show off all the work that had gone into them. All but the front 12-hour wheel were partly hidden, however, so they didn't matter too much, but something had to be done about the one in view. A lighter colour wood had to be found. A chance talk to a 'woodman' found me with a chunk of pearwood under my arm, having parted with more money than the whole project had cost up till now. However, I found this timber delightful to use and only wished I had chanced upon it before. No more cutting blanks from those 'wicked woods'. Blocks could be cut from the pear on my table saw and discs roughly cut by coping saw (a bandsaw would be better). The technique of successful gear cutting with this wood, because of the grain, is as follows: turn up the blanks dead to diameter but somewhat thicker than finished size. Bevel the back outer rim as this will help alleviate any tendency for the wood to break away on the cross grain, then spot face to correct hub width on the drill table. I found it essential to commence cutting the teeth (spaces) along the grain, where it is most favourable, to end up also on this favourable part of the grain. It's the last cut that is the most critical as up till now all the teeth have had solid wood support on one side. If you end up cutting a space across the grain you are sure to loose your last tooth — not helpful. After successfully cutting all the teeth don't get carried away by your work of art, for you have yet to turn down the disc to finished thickness. Secure your wheel back on the arbor in the lathe with what was the back

on the cutting engine now towards the tailstock. Very carefully bring down to correct thickness and watch you don't touch the outer rim of the teeth. Turn on a nice face design and very lightly sand — careful of those teeth — seal and wax. Remove the wheel from the arbor and then you can show your neighbour how clever you are.

When cutting teeth on wood blanks other than lignum vitae you may find it preferable to utilize a backing washer of hardboard to eliminate chipping on the back side of the teeth. One can, of course, cut several discs together, if they can be accommodated on the engine mandrel. We have two similar wheels on our Black Forest clock and there is no reason why these can't be cut together as flat discs. The bosses, if essential to the design, can be formed afterwards.

As an alternative method to the one I adopted for making wooden clock wheels from a solid blank, I can offer a suggestion which should make very accurate and chip-free wheels. Fig. 8 shows the process.

The wheel blank is finished-turned to a diameter corresponding to the root diameter of the teeth, and a little oversize on width. With the wheel-cutting engine and a suitable cutter or saw, slots are cut round the periphery of the blank to receive tooth inserts, which are glued in place and then trimmed up on the lathe when all is good and dry. For my teeth I cut and shaped a strip of suitable close-grained hardwood: apple, pear, maple or beech, for instance, to the tooth profile, plus a lug for keying into the wheel blank. The teeth are then parted off to width from this pre-formed strip and glued in place into the slots around the blank. The wheel can now be put on the lathe and trimmed to correct width and finished according to one's taste. A final finish to the teeth can best be done by hand filing or sanding. This method of making wheels entails more work,

of course, but the results can look quite effective if done with care and, by using contrasting woods, will show up the workmanship to perfection. True cycloidal tooth profiles are consequential to this *modus operandi*.

SO THERE IT IS

There was some light-hearted domestic quibble at first about having such a crude device by which to tell the time, but that's not what it's for, is it! Just in case you are wondering by now, does it really keep to time? Regulation, compared to that of a pendulum clock, is something of a tax on patience but by adjusting the position of the foliot weights, and the amount of lead in them, reasonable time-keeping can be achieved. On completion of your clock you will find that a 'running-in' period is an acceptance of the design and that it is wise to adjust the period a little slow to begin with, about ¼hr per day, I would say. The clock will gradually 'speed up' as the bearings and graphite work in and, with a little judicious attention to the weights, your clock will eventually keep reasonable time. Of course, a clock of this nature, as with all clocks with foliot escapement, are susceptible to weather and temperature changes and can never be made to run as accurately as a pendulum-controlled timepiece. Our clock here does have one thing in its favour, however, in that it is self-starting and doesn't need an initial push to set it going.

One soon gets used to reading the time — within five minutes anyway — with a clock having only one hand. Much to my surprise, over a five-day period, it keeps to time within five minutes, give or take a bit. Much better than expected. Now it's part of the family.

If I eventually get a useful metal-turning lathe, I will make a 'proper' clock. But will I enjoy the task as much as I have on this project? I doubt it very much.■

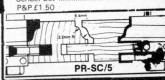

THE SEARCH FOR EFFICIENCY

Time is money when you're a professional, and you can't ignore the need to examine the way you spend it. Hugh O'Neill introduces the three aspects of making work easier (and quicker), Alan Peters explains his choice of machinery

MAKING WORK EASIER — HUGH O'NEILL

Efficiency costs money, and of course the knack is in ensuring that it saves or makes you more than it costs. The question of making work easy can be considered under three headings:

1 Using other people
2 Layout of the workplace
3 Mechanisation.

Other people

Obviously in some of these areas the costs can be considerable, so we need to make some careful calculations before we indulge in any efficiency exercise. Actually we need to do more. Probably the first thing to consider is just where our real skills lie, and you are right back to why you are running your own business in the first place.

If your interest is in a 'business' then perhaps it's time to consider whether you should still be at the workbench at all, or whether you should now be employing other people to handle the production. If you consider your greatest asset is your own craftsmanship and skill, then it's time you paid others to handle the business administration.

It's also worth considering not only where your skills lie and what you do well, but also to make an honest appraisal of what you do badly. As is often the case with craftsmen (I'm one of the worst examples) we are not very methodical about book-keeping. We leave it all until it's time to do the VAT return and then spend three days sorting it all out — and you can guarantee they'll be the very three days that you just have to complete a major order. So one of the first routes to efficiency can often be to get someone to do your books on a part-time basis.

Make a start by logging how many hours you spend on each of the total range of activities that you have to complete each week. Don't forget to make an allowance for the once-every-so-often tasks such as year-end accounts. Identify the key money-making activities of production, sales and marketing. Ask yourself: 'If I were to increase the time I spent upon these, and remembering that I have already covered all my overheads, could I make enough extra money to more than pay for help on the less enjoyable and/or "non-productive" tasks?'

With some items the equation is slightly more complex. There are some tasks you may wish to hive off where the use of a professional may actually save you money. A good ('creative') accountant can often reduce your tax bill.

The other piece of self-assessment you need to think about when you have logged the hours worked, is whether the total of hours is right. Most of us in our own businesses find that we never stop. You're in the workshop or talking to clients all day; then you do the books, put together the quotes, and write the letters in front of the TV at night. There comes a time when you have to say 'enough!' — we often don't notice how the family and the spouse are suffering until it's too late; not to mention our own health.

Here too there's a hidden element; we may not mind the hours but they do affect us. A diet of work without break soon leads to a lessening of creativity and a dulling of skilled performance. This can be imperceptible, but important long before we actually show signs of stress. Getting help has many benefits — it can actually improve our skills, and it can save more than it costs.

The second element of using help is in sub-contracting. It's interesting how many of the artist/craftsmen in the woodworking field are, in fact, only designer/assemblers. They have designed an attractive product, have all the components made by outworkers, even some of the sub-assembly done; and then they do the final putting together and finishing. One I know doesn't even do that — his assistant does.

The advantage of the outworker system, if you can square it with your conscience, is that you can often get quality work done at exceedingly low prices. A typical outworker is a housewife, retiree, or hobbyist who has no overheads; they often have useful skills, don't know how to value or price their time (never talk in terms of hourly rates, only in price per job), and are only too glad of something to do to earn a little pin money. But it does come perilously close to exploitation.

Workshop layout

Often this can be the least expensive area where we can increase efficiency. A basic fact of life is that the workshop is never going to be big enough. If it is you've got too much space and are probably wasting money on overheads. It's useful to have a little more space than you absolutely need, but not as much as you would like!

Being cramped makes you consider layout and use of space more carefully, but on the other hand it means you can't put things in their ideal position. A little bit of time-and-motion is useful. It can actually be worth getting a friend to make a log of your movements across a typical production day.

The principles are simple. Start by looking at your production flow-line: trace the sequence in which things are done, from raw materials in, to finished goods out; and note where there are holding periods (as in storage of sub-assemblies or glue-setting or seasoning periods). Try to lay out the workshop to provide a continuous through path.

Some machines may be used at more than one stage of the process. These should be made the focus point of a number of loops in the flow line. Arrange for the storage of working quantities of items where they're used. (This may mean having three or four points at which there is a supply of a particular screw). And the hand and power tools should be kept at the point at which they are most used, which may mean having different types of saw in different places in the shop. Sometimes it can even pay to have more than one of an item.

The wall display-mounting of tools is often much more efficient than keeping them in drawers or cupboards. And workbenches that aren't used frequently are a snare and a delusion — they soon get heaped up with things that have no proper place.

Probably the greatest contributor to overall efficiency is tidying up and cleanliness. No wonder the old apprentice masters were so insistent upon cleaning, sharpening and oiling of tools and restoring them to their proper position at the end of a day's work. It's no good starting on a new job, all fired up with ideas, only to find you have to locate or sharpen tools. But there's something worse — dropping a small tool into the mass of shavings left over from yesterday, then having to spend the next hour-and-a-half sifting through sawdust to find it.

We're all aware of the importance of having in stock the materials we need, and the absolute necessity of seasoning and so on. One of the greatest problems faced by most craftsmen is the storage of timber, and one of the biggest mistakes many make (some-

David Savage's workshop — room for multitudinous cramps

times because there's no choice) is to store the timber in the workshop itself. It always occupies too much space, it always gets in the way, it's always located where efficiency says that a particular operation should be carried out. A smaller workshop with a separate timber store is considerably better than a single combined unit.

Most of us also need to look at the placing of items within a location. Common sense says that in a stack you put the biggest at the bottom, gradually getting smaller and lighter. This may be wrong. Put nearest to hand those items that are used most frequently and put in the remote corners those things that are hardly ever picked up.

It's a very salutary exercise to re-appraise the workshop. Unless you have been in the business a long time and have recently formally redesigned the shop, then you are likely to find many things wrong. OK, it started out well; but over the years you have added bits, bought in new tools, fitted in new units where you could, and usually destroyed any rationality there was when you started. Stand back and look at what you now have — it can sometimes be worth while closing down for a couple of days and completely revamping the layout. At the same time put in a bin all those things you never use and take them to a car boot sale, and have a bonfire with all those bits and pieces you have kept 'in case they might be useful'. The squirrel mentality is the single greatest hindrance to workshop efficiency.

A related topic is that of stocks. In a well-run business you never run out of anything, nor do you have years' supplies of rarely-used items. Keeping an eye on stocks and replenishing in time usually means no interruption in production, not having to buy 50p packets from the local hardware store to keep going, and the facility for buying in carefully and at the best price.

Mechanisation

Here we can only talk in the most general of principles. Each type of woodwork business will have very different machinery requirements.

Machines make work easier, but particularly so if the machine has capacity beyond the requirements of the job, is easy to operate, and is reliable. (That it's also safe goes without saying).

Multi-function machines are compact and sometimes cheaper than a series of single-function units; but it may only be possible to use one function at a time — although this may not matter if there is only one of you in the shop. Also, some require adjustment and resetting when moving from one function to another.

When you're setting up you're usually watching the cash. You tend to buy the smallest machines you think you can work with — how soon you come to regret the choice! When I started turning seriously I bought a modestly priced but useful capacity German lathe and a 3in capacity bandsaw. The saw has only had one replacement blade — that's how little it has been used; and I am now on my fifth tool carriage with the lathe.

For me a second stage re-equipping had to come sooner than planned, but even then I made something of the same mistake. The big second-hand bandsaw still doesn't have the full capacity I now find I need. The lathe does, but to get it I had to go to a very large, old Wadkin (and now my workshop really *is* too small!).

To me efficiency in mechanisation is in having tools of surplus capacity, solid and accurate in use, that once set up require little adjustment, that never break down, that are single function, that are placed where they are needed in the work-flow, and above all that are so productive that their costs are recovered in months not years. If they meet that last criteria then the frequency with which they are used doesn't matter, provided they don't take space I could better use for something else.

Efficiency costs money, but it can and should save even more if it's truly 'efficient'. It takes a certain mentality to accept this.

There are some who'll tell you they can't afford it: 'I'm already working 18 hours a day to survive; I don't have the money to mechanise', or: 'I don't have the luxury of the space needed to re-organise', or: 'There's no way I could pay to have my books done'. And in their own minds they are right. In fact it's because of this attitude (rather than the true facts) that they'll always be locked in to the vicious, tail-chasing cycle of mere survival. My wife still can't forgive the fact that I borrowed money to pay for the 'new' lathe when the business wasn't doing all that well; the fact that the machine has paid for itself in increased and new sales isn't taken into consideration.

'You've got to speculate to accumulate'; the cliché is certainly true in terms of efficiency and making work easier — even if what you do speculate is a couple of days to assess the work you do and another two or three to revamp the workshop.   ▷

MACHINERY
ALAN PETERS

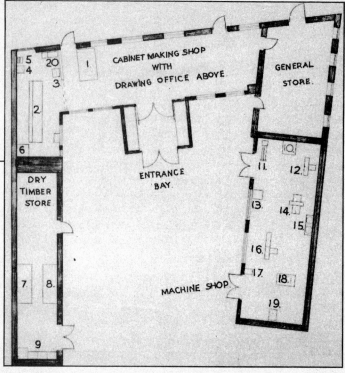

Despite some misgivings about the wider use of machinery and its implications for creative work, I know that I personally enjoy many of the machine operations. I like the speed with which the raw material can be transformed into workable sizes and components. I also like to exploit the potential for design that each new item of equipment I purchase throws up.

Here I must stress that many of my designs of recent years would not have been logical, sensible or even conceived without the equipment I have at my fingertips. Because I am chiefly engaged in working to commission, and therefore do much one-off work, machining takes up less than a fifth of my time and that of my assistants.

In order to have relative peace and quiet and a dust-free atmosphere for the remainder of our time, most of the machines are housed across the yard in a separate machine shop. Unfortunately, one item of equipment tends now to destroy this scheme and that is the portable router. For years I resisted its intrusion into our quiet world of cabinet-making, and never had one in the shop; eventually I relented, as its usefulness and versatility became all too apparent.

I do have now an overhead table router in the machine shop, which relieves some of the problem, but the portable one still gets picked up, and shatters the eardrums, simply because it is so easy to operate on the work-piece itself, rather than taking the work to the machine. Frankly, I still hate it and wish it had not been invented, although I have the quietest one on the market.

One of my next projects will be to develop an adjoining store into a soundproof area just to house this monster, and the work will just have to be carried in there and worked on. All this, of course, only becomes necessary when more than one person is using a workshop, for it is always the other guy's router which is irritating, not the one that you yourself are using.

The major decision one does have to make, however, on setting up and choosing equipment and machinery is whether you intend to concentrate on providing a service, the one-off shop, (whether it be reproduction, restoration or creative work, or working for other designers is immaterial), or whether it is a production workshop, producing in quantity either to your own or someone else's design. It is possible over the years to dabble a little in both, but I am convinced after 20 years that for success one must make this distinction and decide what your shop is really about.

If working in the former, you may well survive for several years with very little machinery, and sub-contract work like veneering and planing quite successfully, although this may depend on the location of your workshop. Secondly, although grant aid may change one's view, secondhand machines

are often quite adequate; in fact, it is often hard to justify installing expensive new equipment when most of it will be lying idle for much of the time. I have only recently replaced a secondhand panel saw that I purchased from a scrap merchant for £7.50 18 years ago with another secondhand machine.

In a one-off shop, it is far better, if space permits, to purchase a wide range of second-hand, separate machines rather than one expensive combination machine, which are nothing but a nuisance in a busy workshop. These are the items of equipment I have collected over the past 20 years, predominantly to assist me and my three assistants in providing a design and making service:

1 3-screw veneer press — secondhand, 1966; sited in cabinet shop.

2 10ft (3.05m) pad or stroke sander, built in 1928, which I bought for £100 in 1966, and which is sited in the finishing area of cabinet shop.

3 9in (228mm) precision saw bench situated in cabinet shop — new.

4 Floor-mounted drill press with various sanding attachments — new, 1966; sited in cabinet shop.

5 10in (254mm)-diameter separate disc sander — new, 1968.

6 Dust Collector for pad sander.

7&8 Floor-to-ceiling timber racks — one to house 8x4ft (2.44x1.22m) sheets; one to store timber in constant use, ½in (12mm) oak and cedar for drawer-making for example.

9 Timber racks for oddments, arranged in species.

10 Overhead router — secondhand.

11 Woodturning lathe — secondhand.

12 Planer grinder — secondhand.

13 Spindle moulder — secondhand.

14 21x9in (534x228mm) thickness planer — purchased secondhand in 1966 for £25.

15 Twin Dust Collector connected to both planers, spindle moulder and circular saw.

16 15x72in (380x1830mm) surface planer — purchased secondhand in 1980 for £150.

17 Hollow-chisel mortiser — secondhand.

18 12in (305mm) sliding table panel saw with tilting arbor — secondhand.

19 18in (456mm) bandsaw, new, replacing in

1981 my secondhand one bought in 1962.

20 Large Portable Dust Collector used on 9in (228mm) circular saw sanding disc, and as needed in the cabinet shop.

Power tools

Electric chainsaw — new.
Portable cross-cut — new.
Small portable router — new.
Small jigsaw — new.
3in (76mm) planer — new.
Compressor and spray gun — secondhand.

Now all this secondhand equipment, that has cost me relatively little over the years, does need nursing along, but it is perfectly adequate until one starts thinking in terms of quantity production. Its weakness is readily apparent as soon as any quantity of repetitive work is undertaken, where accuracy from the machines is of the utmost importance, and where any one machine may be working solidly for many hours non-stop.

This is why the decision as to what your shop is really about is so important. It is pointless and expensive to install, for example, a new 36in (915mm) planer if one is going to finish up making chairs or toast racks with a width of no more than 3 or 4in (76-100mm).

I am convinced that in cabinet work, as opposed to, say, country chair making, when quantity production is required one must not skimp on equipment. It must be sturdy, of the best make and preferably new, or at least comparatively so. Do-it-yourself toys and lightweight machines are fine for the amateur and useful in one-off shops, but they are completely unsuitable for any production work. Thus, anyone thinking in terms of batch production must allow for considerable outlay on equipment from the outset. ∎

● This extract from Alan Peter's book *Cabinetmaking — the Professional Approach* concludes our business series. We are grateful to the publishers, Stobart & Son, for permission to use the extract. Details of the book from Stobarts, 67-73 Worship St, London EC2A 2EL, 01-247 0501.

THE PROFESSIONAL'S CHOICE

Tame a TYME CUB

This Christmas with £££ Shavings!

CUB WOODTURNING LATHE

Manufactured to high standards from cast aluminium, cast iron and steel. Specifically designed to give the maximum capacity possible in a smaller lathe.

Features include ½ H.P motor with a no volt overload switch, 4 speeds (480, 800, 1250, 2000 RPM). Hollow tailstock for long hole boring, deep groove double sealed bearings. Bowl turning upto 15".

Available in 30" between centres **£319**

or 39" between centres **£331**

AVON WOODTURNING LATHE

The more professional woodturning lathe, features ¾ H.P motor, and a 23" bowl turning capacity.

Available in 36" between centres **£437**

or 48" between centres **£448**

VISA   Access

SAVE £50

This is an ideal set for anybody taking up woodturning. Consisting of a ¼", ⅜" and ½" spindle gouge, 1" skew chisel, ¾" roughing gouge, and ⅛" parting tool. We have chosen high speed steel, because of the superior edge life, giving up to 8 to 10 times more use. Without re-sharpening this will be a great asset until you get the knack of sharpening turning tools. Video tapes are available for purchase or hire on woodturning, contact your nearest stockist.

Our Christmas Offer

To compliment one of the best lathes on the market, we are offering a top quality sheffield made 6 piece high speed steel turning tool set normally sold for **£79.95** buy any Tyme lathe and it can be yours for only **£29.95**

WE GUARANTEE YOU WILL BE SATISFIED WITH OUR PRODUCTS

We have selected with care and have done our very best to describe the products honestly and accurately. However if you are not satisfied with your purchase for any reason just return the article to us within 14 days and we will promptly exchange it or send you a refund as you request. You can buy with confidence from us.

Members of the QUAL group of companies.

QUAL

QUAL TOOLS AND MACHINERY LIMITED

Watford Showroom and Mail Order
20 Market Street, Watford
Herts. WD1 7AD
Tel. Watford (0923) 50295

Reading Showroom
26-30 Kings Road, Reading
Berkshire
Tel. Reading (0734) 591361

THORCRAFT

THORCRAFT Hastings Showroom
181-182 Queens Road, Hastings, Sussex TN34 1RQ
Tel. Hastings (0424) 423072

WILLIAMS

WILLIAMS DISTRIBUTORS (TOOLS) LIMITED
Peterborough Showroom
108-110 Burghley Road, Peterborough, Camb. PE1 2QE
Tel. Peterborough (0733) 64252

Burch & Hills

BURCH & HILLS MACHINERY LIMITED

Aldershot Showroom
374 High Street, Aldershot
Hants. GU12 4NA
Tel. (0252) 334422

Southampton Showroom
7 Belvidere Road, Northam
Southampton, SO1 1RE
Tel. (0703) 332288

— **ALL OPEN MONDAY — SATURDAY** —

THE SLICE IS RIGHT

How were saw-cut veneers sawn? Lawrence Smith suggests a design for a hand-operated press

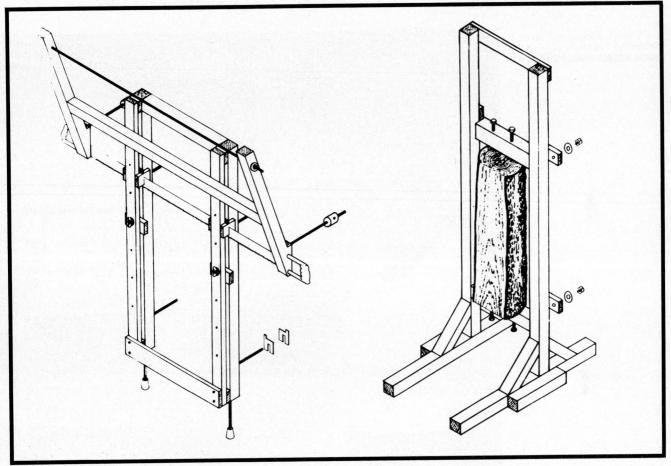

Sawing frame (left) bolts on to log-holding press (right)

One of my favourite points for pondering is how veneers were sawn in the long ago. I have come across an account of how they were done 'on a huge circular saw', along with a line drawing, but the whole idea fills me with dismay; the waste must have been terrific. And the spacing between first and fourth cut leaves would have produced wide variations in figure — they wouldn't have 'run on'.

John C. Rogers, in *English Furniture*, quotes from *New and universal dictionary of Arts and Sciences* (1756), with words that ring true: 'These slices or leaves were stated to be "about a line thick", cut from the blocks placed upright in a sawing press...' Mr Rogers gives the thicknesses as about $\frac{1}{16}$in for plain woods and slightly thicker for burrs. Thomas Sheraton confirmed that these veneers could, if they lay flat, be put down with a hammer.

I've never seen a drawing of a traditional veneer-sawing press, but I decided to design one that would cut vertical slices from green logs of up to 2ft diameter with great accuracy

and minimal waste. Remember that the log is green, so wet in fact that if it were cut on a circular saw we would be drenched with water thrown off its periphery. But wet wood is delightfully inert, doesn't snake, twist or bind in cutting because there are no stresses locked up inside it, so a thin saw with minimal set kept straight under great tension is not likely to be bent or deflected by green timber.

I have divided my design into two parts, the press, which holds the log clamped into it, and the frame which contains and guides the saw. The frame is bolted to the press by four bolts passing through lugs in the press. A stack of washers on each bolt separates the two parts, an equal number on each bolt, equal to the veneer thickness (about $\frac{1}{16}$in) plus the waste. After each leaf has been sawn the nuts are slackened and one washer removed from each bolt for the next cut.

The saw is guided by shoes which slide

freely but without much clearance down the long slots in the frame. The accuracy of the slot width is governed by spacers which are lowered and clamped as sawing proceeds. Metal weights fixed on top of the shoes ensure that they fall with the saw and maintain decisive guidance.

The tension and compression bars of the saw are angled away slightly to clear the work; two counterbalance weights offset this (alternatively the tension rod could slide against a light vertical bar). My design envisages a log capacity of 4x2ft diameter, with the press frame made from 4x4in. But a half size version of it would be cheap and interesting and still cut some useful sizes.

A veneer sawing press like this could be just what you need to make use of timber from unwanted garden trees, yielding some valuable and high quality thick veneer. ■

● If you know how veneers were sawn in the eighteenth century, Mr Smith would like to hear from you. Please write to Lawrence Smith, c/o Woodworker, 1 Golden Sq, London W1R 3AB.

MINIATURE MARVELS

Doll's houses and scaled-down replica furniture are fast becoming collectors' favourites and Den Young is famed for his Lilliputian manors and mansions. Michael Terry went to meet him

▲ **Den Young's stock model: an Elizabethan manor house**

▶ **Magnificent William and Mary mansion, recently completed for a collector at almost £1000 per room**

Den Young is living proof that you don't have to have certificates to become a master of your craft. Over the past 20 years he's made a good living and won international acclaim designing and building replica doll's houses and furniture exact in every particular — and without the benefit of any formal training.

He lives in Willingham, near Cambridge, and recently completed a scale model of a 23-roomed William and Mary mansion, commissioned by a woman in Miami for £20,000. Not only does Den look the part of the classic fairy-tale toymaker with pipe, and bushy grey sideburns, but he's also blessed with an

infectious laugh and an engaging manner. Sadly, he's not had any daughters or grand-daughters for the benefit of whom he could indulge his remarkable woodworking talents.

Den's attention to detail is obvious from the William and Mary mansion. The dome on its roof-lantern uses tiny, individual tiles made of real copper, the patterned parquet floor in the ballroom is made up of 1549 pieces of perfectly fitting wood and the symmetrical rows of miniature sash windows actually pull up and down.

It's a creation of epic proportions. Standing 69in tall, 66in wide and 34in deep, the model mansion was too large to fit inside Den's

workshop, so it had to take pride of place in the family garage.

The outside walls of the model convincingly simulate ochre blocks of Bath sandstone and the front and back facades both open to reveal the imposing interior. The front door leads into a spacious hall; the impressive staircase, with wrought-iron lamps on newel posts, took 200 hours to make. There's a delightful cast-iron kitchen range, toilets with cisterns and wooden seats — Den's vision is of a home lived in by the same family over two centuries — marble busts, fires that flicker and 42 lamps that light up. The wiring is skilfully concealed.

of Civil Service routine, he decided to take up full-time the spare-time hobby which had come naturally to him since he was given a tool set at the age of four — woodworking.

He then made a good living selling inlaid coffee tables, lamp standards and wooden bowls. Listening in his workshop one afternoon to BBC Radio's Woman's Hour, he heard an American woman's impassioned plea for someone to make decent miniature antique furniture for her doll's house. Den immediately wrote asking her to provide a list of her requirements. He's never looked back since.

His first doll's house was the prototype of what was to become his stock model: an Elizabethan manor house which now sells at around £2000. Den showed it at the ancient Cheese Show at Frome, Somerset, in 1964 and won first prize. He received plenty of local media publicity, including TV, and the enquiries started to flow in. The timing was impeccable. Den's discovery of his new craft coincided with a revival of interest in the serious collecting of replica doll's houses and miniature antique furniture.

Today it is a thriving world-wide market. In America it rates as the second most popular hobby for women. The model items, however, are never destined for nursery playrooms. They are collectors' pieces; heirlooms, skilfully fashioned works of art admired for their magical, microcosmic qualities. The collectors demand the very best in accuracy, quality of finish and durability and are prepared to pay top prices.

Den's workmanship is a case in point. Roofs on his model houses have lofts with authentic trusses, king posts, queen posts, rafters and joists. The thatch on one of his replica cottages has separate trusses of real straw all made to scale; and a 16th-century inn he made for a building contractor's wife who is assembling a model-village High Street has a miniature beer engine that actually works!

Even the joints on the model pieces of replica furniture Den builds are real mortise-and-tenons in miniature. Fragile though they may seem, Den gives his assurance that if four of his exquisite Windsor chairs were strategically placed, they would be strong enough to bear the weight of a man. To achieve such high standards requires hours of dedicated research and skilled craftsmanship, and it's the reason why commissions have poured in from as far afield as America, Canada and Australia. He's even doing his bit for British trade overseas with appearances at 'British Week' exhibitions at leading department stores in America and Japan.

But Den is very modest, some would say nonchalant, about his rare talent. 'Miniature work is merely about cutting, sticking and possessing a steady hand and good eyesight. All you need is an eye for scale and the ability to use simple carpentry tools.' Those in the know judge Den more seriously. Michal Prouse, owner of the specialist Covent Garden shop 'The Dolls' House' (and arguably the woman who set in motion Britain's post-war revival of interest in doll's houses) rates Den among the masters of his craft. Vivien Greene, wife of novelist and playwright Graham Greene, has congratulated him on his work. And given that Mrs Greene is President of the Doll Club of Great Britain, has two definitive histories of doll's houses

under her belt, and owns a priceless collection of doll's houses and contents, it is an accolade indeed.

Den operates out of a workshop at the back of his Willingham house and, as he says, basic carpentry tools are the order of the day. He uses a bandsaw, a Black-and-Decker electric hand-drill and a range of modelling knives. But his most important tool is his Myford ML8 lathe which he's had for 35 years and which he uses for turning pieces such as balusters and legs for furniture. The lathe has an adjustable saw-bench. He also has an array of specialist tools custom-made by him to meet specific tasks which relate to small-scale work, such as miniature beading on miniature chair legs.

The woods which he uses on his models are, where possible, those used in the period houses of the time — mahogany, oak, sycamore and teak are incorporated in the William and Mary mansion. But he's found that the ideal woods for small-scale work are those which are dense, strong, with very little grain visible and have an ability to absorb stain evenly.

Whereas Den meticulously researches the historical and technical details of the houses and furniture he builds, he uses no detailed drawings or set plans — not unless you include the occasional rough scribbles found on the back of old envelopes lying in his workshop. 'I've been blessed with an in-built sense of scale,' he claims. 'I just build as I go along.' His basic technique is to first cut and build the base, side walls and room divisions so that he has a hollow box with a grid in which to fit the pre-made floors, fittings and furniture.

And how does Den market his wares? He puts it down to word of mouth. But close questioning reveals that he also advertises in specialist-hobby magazines at home and abroad, attends crafts exhibitions and keeps the British Overseas Trade Board and his local tourist board fully informed. He also distributes through specialist shops in London and the regions.

But he makes the point that the essential characteristic of the market is that it is demand-led. It is the collectors who set the fashions and seek out craftsmen to build their orders. The doll's-house tradition in this country goes back 300 years when Anne Sharp, daughter of the then Archbishop of Canterbury, was given a doll's house by her godmother, the future Queen Anne. The house can still be seen in the Strangers' Hall Museum, Norwich.

Den Young joins a long line of practitioners which includes such eminent names as Sir John Vanburgh, the 18th century architect who built a magnificent example for the Yarburgh family of Yorkshire, and Sir Edward Lutyens who during the 1920s masterminded the world famous Queen Mary's doll's house. The present-day revival has also given rise to a fast-growing number of amateur builders who are gaining a reputation, even among experts such as Den, for the high standards of their skills and creativity.

In his time Den Young has made more than 40 doll's houses and thousands of individual pieces of miniature furniture. For him it's been 'fun, exasperation and being my own boss.' And his only regrets? 'That I didn't start 20 years earlier.' ■

Den reckons that the complete project will have taken 4000 painstaking hours. At a price which includes materials and therefore represents less than £5 per hour, the lady in Miami is not getting too bad a deal!

DEN, NOW IN his 60s, took up dolls'-house making 20 years ago by sheer chance. After service in the Second World War as an RAF sergeant flying Spitfires and Hurricanes on reconnaissance over North Africa, he became a GPO engineer in peace time. Then, tiring

WOODWORKING MACHINERY

5 Speed Lathe
This superb new lathe is fitted with many features found on machines twice the price ¾ h.p. motor, 5 speed, turning capacity 941mm (305mm diameter). Supplied with fence plate drive centre toolrests etc. Spindle protrudes to accept left hand face plate.
Price £139.00 inc. VAT/Delivery

Multipurpose light industrial, 3 speed, sealed bearings, ⅓ h.p. supplied with circle cutter, rip/mitre fence sanding belt and disc. Cut/Top 360mm, Cut depth 145mm, tilting table.
Price £164 inc. VAT/Delivery

PRICE £164 incl. VAT/Delivery

Heavy Duty Scroll Jigsaw
20" throat
Cast alloy surface
Adjustable arm
Two speeds
Professional machine
Supplied with many standard accessories
500mm throat
¼ HP Motor
45° Tilting Table
Price £249 inc. VAT/Delivery

10" Hobby Table Saw
Lightweight, powerful, compact sawbench, cast alloy table, 2 HP motor, rise and fall, tilting arbor, depth of cut 80mm.
PRICE £154 incl. VAT/Delivery

Lutz 14/16" Jumbo multipurpose saw bench. Powerful 3kw motor. Rise/fall tilting blade. Table Size 788mm x 562mm, Maximum cut 125mm.
Price £199.00 inc. VAT/Delivery

Heavy duty 12 speed bench drill
⅝" capacity
¾ HP motor
2 m/t chuck
Rack & pinion
Free mortising attachment with this unit
PRICE £199 incl. VAT/Delivery

Send SAE for colour brochures.
Many other woodworking machines available.

ABBEYCHAINS
Specialists in mail order. Supplies to Woodworkers

Unit 10/11, The Potteries Industrial Estate, Southend Lane, Waltham Abbey.
Tel: (0992) 714867/767426
(2 minutes from Junction 26, M25)

BEST EVER PRICE!

British made, cast iron, 1", H.D. chisel mortiser with **every practical advantage** – Now, direct from the makers at this best ever price:

THE CHARNWOOD 1"FCM FLOOR CHISEL MORTISER
JUST **£459!**
(PLUS £68.85 VAT)
(TOTAL £527.85)

THE CHARNWOOD 1"BCM BENCH MODEL MORTISER
£329!
(PLUS £49.35 VAT)
(TOTAL £378.35)

★ *Special discounts on all chisels etc.*

● **PROVEN PERFORMANCE**
The Charnwood range of mortisers have been in professional workshop use for more than 20 years. Its design has been consistently proved to give users the most successful combination of economy together with accuracy and speed of operation.

● **PRECISION & DURABILITY**
Principal components of the 1" FCM are machined from solid cast iron and steel to ensure a completely rigid relationship between the chisel and workpiece under load. In addition, all slideways are of dovetail section and feature full face, gib strip friction adjusters so that continuing smoothness and quality of cut-out are assured throughout the virtually unlimited future working life of each machine. **British motors are used on both the 1" FCM and 1" BCM.**

● **SUPERB SPECIFICATION**
Working advantages of the 1"FCM include its double action (push/pull) handwheel which engages a wormdrive for positioning the cross-slide with pinpoint accuracy or a toothed rack for rapid traverse control. The table is larger than average to give additional work support. Fully adjustable longitudinal, traverse, depth and haunch stops are fitted. Standard equipment also includes a full range of collets and bushes so that all sizes of chisel and auger can be used. **(Both the FCM and BCM mortisers accept tools from ¼" to 1")**

● **7 DAY DELIVERY**
We deliver to most mainland areas within 7 days of receipt of order. Your protection includes a **30 DAY FULL CASH REFUND**, if any unit supplied by us does not satisfy your requirements in every way and thereafter a **FULL 3 YEAR GUARANTEE.**

Prices are ex-works.

● **CONTACT US TODAY:-**

charnwood
1-3 ROWAN STREET, FOSSE ROAD NORTH LEICESTER, LE3 9GP
TEL: (0533) 511550

KNOWHOW PRODUCTIONS *Presents*

THE·VIDEO
CHRISTMAS OFFER

ACCLAIMED IN AMERICA

'...as for the tape itself, I thought it was outstanding. I have seen quite a number of films on woodturning, but I have never seen a film that shows the proper cutting techniques with such clarity and continual reinforcement. I am sure that this tape will be of benefit to turners on any level.'

DONALD E. GUNDRED, CALIFORNIA

DENNIS WHITE TEACHES WOODTURNING

AVAILABLE NOW
Turning between Centres
Turning Bowls
Boxes, Goblets and Screw Threads

COMING SOON
Novelties and Projects
Classic Profiles
Twists and Other Advanced Turning Techniques

SPECIAL CHRISTMAS OFFER

Send cheque or Postal order: made payable to:
KNOWHOW PRODUCTIONS LTD · PO. BOX 43
GREENFORD · MIDDLESEX · UB6 8TX
OR PHONE YOUR ACCESS NO. FOR IMMEDIATE DESPATCH
Tick Box for VHS · BETA or VIDEO 8
VHS ◇ BETA ◇ VIDEO 8 ◇ TEL: 01-578 8716

only £28·00 inc.P&P EACH

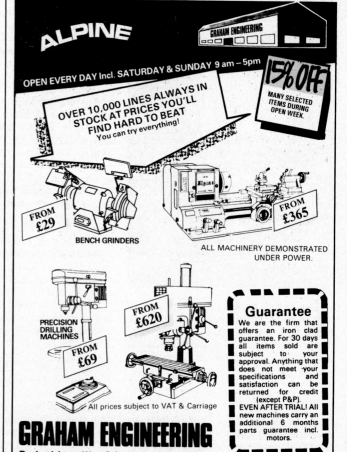

ALPINE

GRAHAM ENGINEERING

OPEN EVERY DAY Incl. SATURDAY & SUNDAY 9 am – 5pm

15% OFF MANY SELECTED ITEMS DURING OPEN WEEK.

OVER 10,000 LINES ALWAYS IN STOCK AT PRICES YOU'LL FIND HARD TO BEAT
You can try everything!

FROM £29
BENCH GRINDERS

FROM £365

ALL MACHINERY DEMONSTRATED UNDER POWER.

PRECISION DRILLING MACHINES
FROM £620
FROM £69

All prices subject to VAT & Carriage

Guarantee
We are the firm that offers an iron clad guarantee. For 30 days all items sold are subject to your approval. Anything that does not meet your specifications and satisfaction can be returned for credit (except P&P). EVEN AFTER TRIAL! All new machines carry an additional 6 months parts guarantee incl. motors.

GRAHAM ENGINEERING
Roebuck Lane, West Bromwich, Nr. Birmingham.
Telephone 021–525 3133   Telex 337676 GEM

Guild of WOODWORKERS

The Guild was set up by **WOODWORKER** to create a meeting ground for all those involved in working wood — professional, amateur and enthusiastic beginner. For further details send SAE to Guild of Woodworkers, 9 Hall Rd, Maylands Wood Est, Hemel Hempstead, Herts HP2 7BH.

Routing — Roy Sutton

12 March, 10-5, Herne Bay, Kent, £30 + VAT
Book early for this popular course. Starting from first principles, Roy covers housing, grooving, rebating, mortising, and rule joint and template work; he also deals with designing and setting up your own jigs.

Hand veneering — Bob Grant

19 March, 9.30-5, Oxford, £35 + VAT
Bob's courses are great favourites with Guild members. He'll be guiding you through each step of this traditional craft. You'll be laying a panel with veneer, mitring a cross-banding, inlaying lines round it, and applying a balancer veneer on the back. Bring a veneer hammer if you have one, but materials provided.

French polishing — Charles Cliffe

24-25 March, 10-4, Bexleyheath, £50
Charles Cliffe's courses are among the most successful run by the Guild. You'll learn about preparation, staining, and techniques of french polishing itself, with ample hands-on experience under Charles' expert tuition. You'll learn the correct way to sharpen a cabinet scraper, so bring yours along. He's also willing to offer advice on refinishing any small piece of furniture you bring.

Design and workshop drawing — Bob Grant

16 April, 9.30-5, Oxford, £30 + VAT
If getting your designs down on paper bugs you, here's the course to learn how, as many Guild members can testify. Bob will boost your confidence in freehand sketching, as well as teaching the use of a drawing board and other equipment.

Visit to Ashley Iles

The West Midlands group of the Guild hired a coach to visit the Lincolnshire factory of Ashley Iles during the summer. The 17-strong party was split into two groups to tour the factory and visit Ashley's 'Old Tool Store'. They saw every process from the initial annealing of the metal to the final marking and packing for despatch; 70% of the tools are exported. Everyone agreed it was a very enjoyable visit and hoped to have more in the future.

▲ **More new members' work: these rocking horses were made by David Kemsley of Chippenham**

Turning-in time: Mr C. Firth from Ipswich turned this clock face and goblet in oak ▼

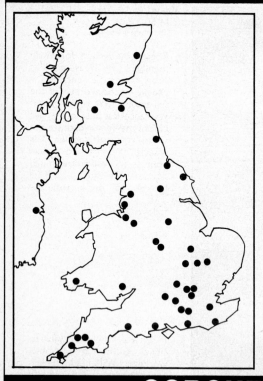

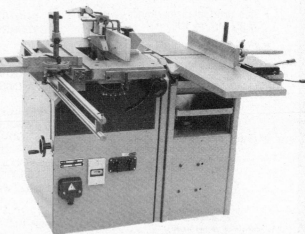

DISTINCTLY RATTLED

A turner's Xmas gift for the very young: Tobias Kaye tells you how to make a baby's rattle that's safe, beautifully shaped and noisy

Shaping the rattle — just before separation

A rattle, of course, should do just that. The free-ring type (fig. 1) is difficult for babies to get a sound out of, and so when I decided to make some rattles I looked for a design which would fit comfortably in a baby's hand, be safe to suck and chew, and make a noise at the slightest agitation to attract the baby's interest. The apple-core shape (fig. 1) seemed ideal for a baby's grasp and, because it's equally weighted, it wouldn't tip over the edge of a pram or cot.

The dimensions of the rattle make it small enough for a six-month baby, but large enough for a two-year-old to hold (fig. 2). The finish I decided on, after ruling out any sort of varnish and most commercial waxes and some oils — linseed is poisonous — was good quality salad oil and beeswax. I warm 20% beeswax together with 80% virgin cold-pressed olive oil, and don't use any solvent. This makes a good butter-hard paste which won't lose lustre as oil alone would.

Construction

The wood must be close-grained and splinter-free; it should be a non-poisonous, non-irritant species which will withstand constant sucking. Fruitwood is ideal (apple, some harder pear types, plum, cherry or almond), but boxwood, (holly, whitebeam, hornbeam) will also do. Avoid foreign exotics, as many are highly irritant.

Whenever I make a bowl from one of the above wood types, I cut all the offcuts into 2½in and ⅞in square strips (which shrink to about 1½in and ¾in) and stack it up to dry for rattles. Start with the smaller pieces for the plugs (fig. 3). It's best to cut the tapers with a sharp square scraper; the slight roughness helps to hold them in so they must be made accurately. (If the taper is too steep you'll have to glue it in (Cascamite) and set it aside to dry before finishing. Separate the ▷

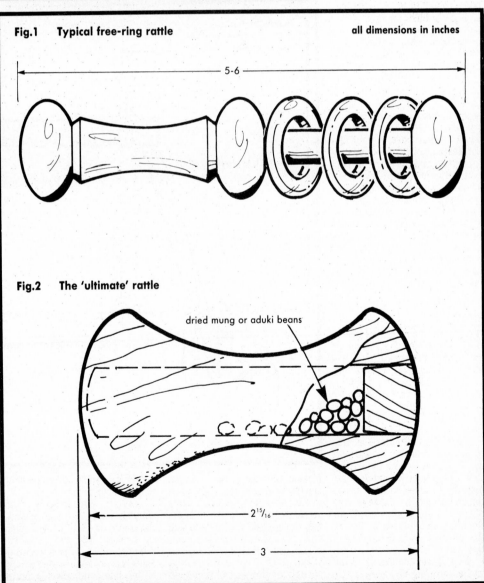

Fig.1 Typical free-ring rattle   all dimensions in inches

5-6

Fig.2 The 'ultimate' rattle

dried mung or aduki beans

2¹⁵/₁₆

3

plugs on the bandsaw carefully, holding the wood square, and use a push-stick to clear each plug as you cut it off so they can't roll back in front of the blade (fig. 4).

Now cut the rattle blanks, allowing enough extra on each blank for chucking by your chosen method, plus enough to get the tool in for final shaping and parting. I use a four-jaw self-centring chuck which means the square piece can be put straight in without any preliminary turning, but this is a highly dangerous chuck which can take the end off your finger if you're not carefree.

Once you've put the piece in the chuck, drill to the exact depth with the drill bit in the tailstock or a tailstock chuck. Don't use a flat bit, as it won't make accurate holes. You can get second-hand large twist bits (sometimes even with morse tapers) at steam fairs or car-boot sales — they're ideal for this sort of work as they cut much easier than saw-tooth bits.

After drilling the hole, stop the lathe and clear the dust. Then fill the rattle with 10-15 mung or aduki beans (available from wholefood shops), and fit the plug. I always use a plug of a contrasting colour wood from my timber list and the effect is much better than just a glue line. Smear a little Cascamite (which is water-resistant) around the plug to ensure it remains in place and tap it in lightly but firmly; too much pressure could cause splitting at a later stage, too little and it will come out during sanding or polishing. Now advance the tailstock to hold it in place and steady it.

Shaping

If you are using a four-jaw chuck, rough the blank down to round and mark out the depth of the drill hole with calipers. This is why accurate drilling to depth is important; you need to know for certain how deep the hole is — leave the end too thick and you'll mar the sound of the rattle.

Allow $\frac{1}{16}$ in beyond the line that marks the drill depth, and part into $\frac{5}{8}$ diameter with the parting tool. Cut a half core in the waste material to allow tool access to the end. Begin the shaping on the plug end leaving only enough for the tailstock to steady in, and on the left-hand end leaving most of the $\frac{5}{8}$in.

Now begin the curve of the 'apple core' (fig. 5). I use a $\frac{3}{4}$in roughing tool and take it carefully,

Fig.3   Row of plugs ready for sawing

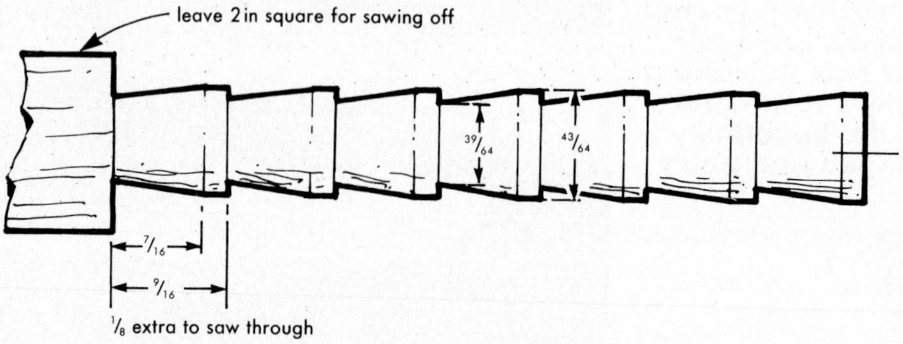

leave 2in square for sawing off

$\frac{39}{64}$ $\frac{43}{64}$

$\frac{7}{16}$

$\frac{9}{16}$

$\frac{1}{8}$ extra to saw through

Fig.4   Cutting plugs

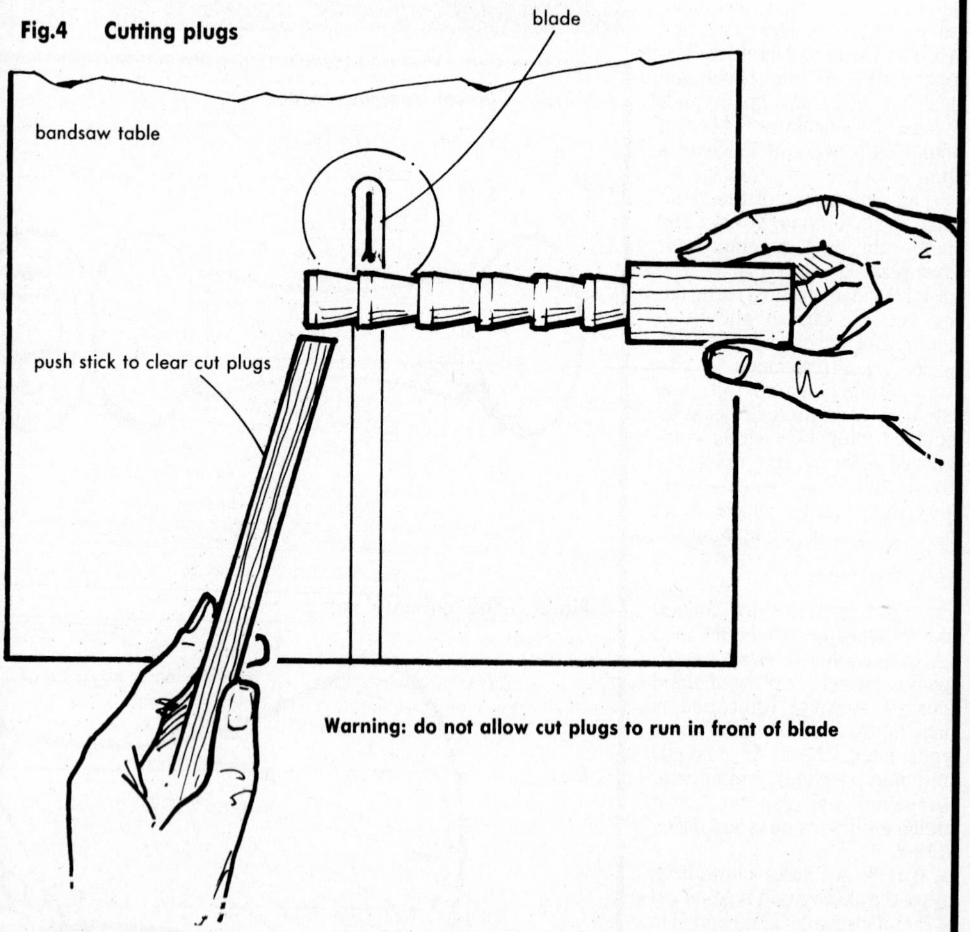

blade

bandsaw table

push stick to clear cut plugs

Warning: do not allow cut plugs to run in front of blade

making sure the curve is a nice smooth one. Take this right down to $\frac{3}{4}$in; leave it too fat and it won't sound very much at all. This is why drilling, plugging and shaping must all be done in one operation; if you drill the hole on a drill-stand, you'll never get it central enough for this sort of accuracy. Take the job down and re-chuck

it later, and you'll still find it likely to go out of true.

Those with really high standards will leave the walls of the rattle at this central point $\frac{1}{32}$ in thick, not the $\frac{1}{16}$ in I've recommended. This is what I do and it makes it just strong enough to be safe, and gives a better sound.

If you haven't two pairs of calipers (leaving them set speeds up repetition work) you can easily make a depth-marker-cum-diameter-tester in ply (fig. 6).

Now finish shaping the plug end and the left-hand end down to $\frac{1}{2}$in or $\frac{3}{8}$in. I start with 180-grit for these fine woods, then damp down with a wet rag

Photos Alasdair Gordon

to raise the grain and sand with 320-grit in reverse. This makes sure that any raised grain from sucking is minimal.

Now apply the oil and wax, separately or in the paste. Polish carefully so as not to break it off. The final shaping of the left-hand end is instead of parting off; a parting tool leaves a rough finish and can't be used to complete the shape properly. Rub this end with a little worn 320-grit to remove any fine ridges.

I grant you licence to make and sell these rattles *only* on condition that you make them to a high standard. Nice round curves; no rough finishes; no cheap polishes. Make them well and you'll delight young children. Make them badly and you'll cancel your licence and find yourself infringing my copyright!

Different combinations of coloured woods add interest to the rattles

Fig.5   Shaping

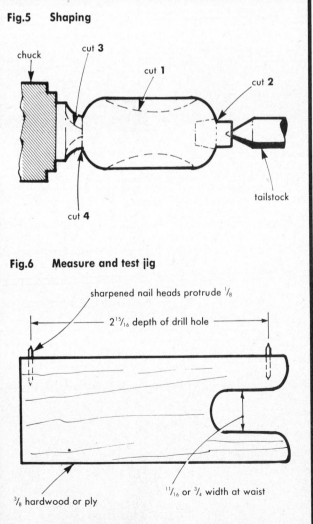

chuck

cut **3**

cut **1**

cut **2**

tailstock

cut **4**

Fig.6   Measure and test jig

sharpened nail heads protrude ⅛

2¹⁵⁄₁₆ depth of drill hole

⅜ hardwood or ply

¹¹⁄₁₆ or ¾ width at waist

This unusual toy has an intensely evocative air of the great sprint air races of the 1920' and '30s, the Schneider Trophy. It is (roughly!) modelled after the Supermarine winner, whose speed in those days, at above 200mph, was almost unheard of. Despite the everyday supersonic speeds of airplanes nowadays, there is still glory and glamour attached to these craft, and great stories of magnificent men in their flying machines will be inspired by the toy. It can hang from the ceiling or wall, and perhaps even be used in the bath!

A toy to please the maker and the player — this little seaplane looks simple, but it has a few tricks up its sleeve

UP IN THE

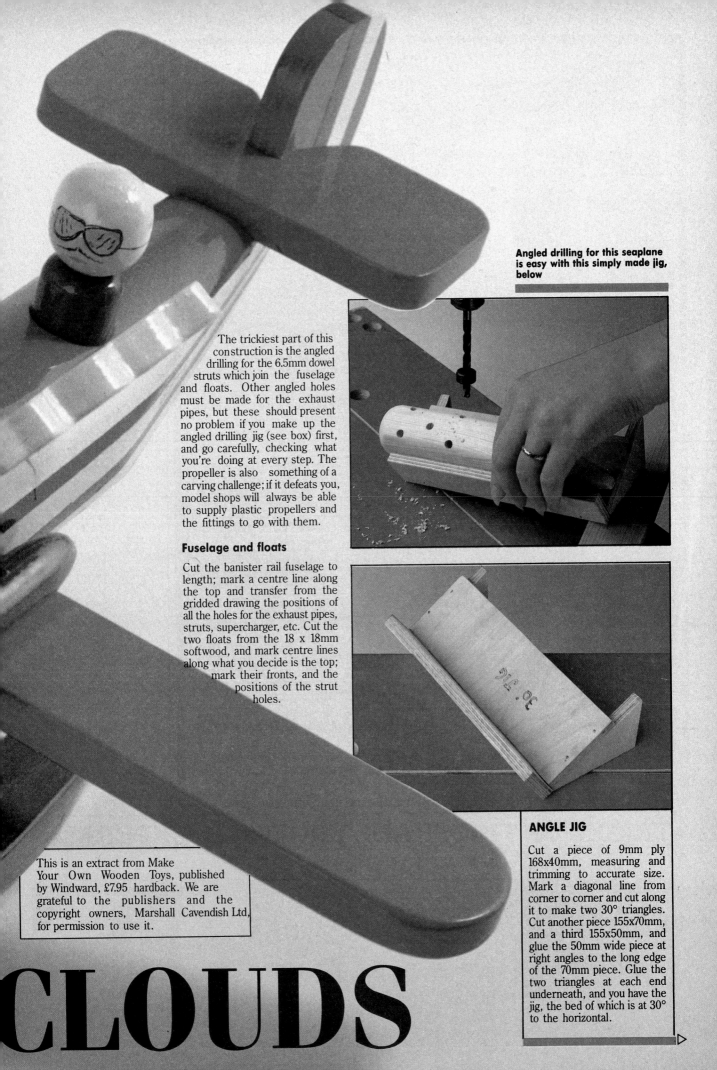

Angled drilling for this seaplane is easy with this simply made jig, below

The trickiest part of this construction is the angled drilling for the 6.5mm dowel struts which join the fuselage and floats. Other angled holes must be made for the exhaust pipes, but these should present no problem if you make up the angled drilling jig (see box) first, and go carefully, checking what you're doing at every step. The propeller is also something of a carving challenge; if it defeats you, model shops will always be able to supply plastic propellers and the fittings to go with them.

Fuselage and floats

Cut the banister rail fuselage to length; mark a centre line along the top and transfer from the gridded drawing the positions of all the holes for the exhaust pipes, struts, supercharger, etc. Cut the two floats from the 18 x 18mm softwood, and mark centre lines along what you decide is the top; mark their fronts, and the positions of the strut holes.

This is an extract from Make Your Own Wooden Toys, published by Windward, £7.95 hardback. We are grateful to the publishers and the copyright owners, Marshall Cavendish Ltd, for permission to use it.

ANGLE JIG

Cut a piece of 9mm ply 168x40mm, measuring and trimming to accurate size. Mark a diagonal line from corner to corner and cut along it to make two 30° triangles. Cut another piece 155x70mm, and a third 155x50mm, and glue the 50mm wide piece at right angles to the long edge of the 70mm piece. Glue the two triangles at each end underneath, and you have the jig, the bed of which is at 30° to the horizontal.

CLOUDS

ORDER TODAY and your new W250 will be working for you within the week! (Door-to-door delivery – £12)

W250 WOODWORKER

COMPLETE FOR JUST: **£259** + VAT £38.85

PAYMENT can be made by cash, cheque, credit card or on deferred terms. (E.g. Total order value £297.85 − Deposit £29.85 + 12 monthly payments of £26.31 = £345.57 total credit cost (A.P.R. 36.3%), or other terms to suit your requirements.)

WOODWORKER BRINGS YOU THE BEST. QUALITY AND QUANTITY NOW MORE THAN EVER. WE'VE GOT PLANS FOR ... YOU ...

The superb new "universal" R.A. saw that outclasses all competitors. Its unique construction ensures smooth, consistent performance and guaranteed precision in materials up to 3in thick.

PERFECT ACCURACY
Each of the 250's critical angle and alignment settings is determined by separate micro-adjusters that permit changes in arm and blade attitudes to be made in hundredths of a millimetre. Resetting after use at intermediate positions is simply done against hardened steel, "flip over" stops. The exceptional rigidity of the column, arm, sub-frame and yoke assemblies likewise ensure that inaccuracies due to flexing are eliminated.

MORE POWER
The 250 is designed not only to be used as a universal saw but also as the power source for moulding and planing operations where large quantities of material may be expected to be removed in a single pass. Motor output is therefore uprated to a full one and half horse power – 50% more than any similarly priced machine.

LARGER CAPACITIES
Timber sections of up to 3 in. in thickness can be crosscut or ripped through in a single operation with the 250. Also, because of the absolute precision with which the arm can be set, the normal crosscut capacity of just over 12in. can be doubled by reversing work to take a second cut from its opposite edge.

SIMPLER MAINTENANCE
Heavy duty bearings carry the 250's motor head along the radial arm and are easily accessible for cleaning or occasional adjustment. In addition to this the hardened steel bearing tracks themselves can be simply replaced by the user should this ever be necessary. "Smooth as silk" is no exaggeration when it comes to describing the 250's crosscut stroke.

GUARANTEES
We have absolute confidence that the WOODWORKER 250 is clearly and genuinely the best R.A. saw at its present price level or for very considerably more. In fact many important features contributing to its consistent reliability are not found on any other machine. We therefore guarantee it unreservedly for a full three years against any component failure due to manufacturing or material fault. We also invite you to take up our offer of a 30 day full cash refund if in any circumstances you are not entirely satisfied with the 250 and its performance.

CONFIDENCE
"CHARNWOOD" are British manufacturers and exporters of high precision framing saws, double mitre saws, guillotines and other woodworking machinery. The "WOODWORKER 250" is the latest development in R.A. saws from W. Raggiotti – the originator of most significant R.A. saw world patents on which all other R.A. saw designs are based.

WOODWORKER 250 R.A. SAW	(ex. VAT)	(inc. VAT)
COMPLETE MACHINE with 1 phase electrics (domestic), G.P. steel blade, tools, manual etc.	£259.00	**£297.85**
H.D. FLOORSTAND (Folding design)	£28.00	**£32.20**
T.C.T. MULTI-PURPOSE BLADE Fast, deep cutting, with good results in all materials.	£24.00	**£27.60**
T.C.T. SUPERFINE CUT BLADE for manmade boards and thin timber only	£36.00	**£41.40**
ECCENTRIC COLLARS (0-1/2in. throw)	£14.75	**£16.95**
COMB. PRESSURE GUARD/STOP	£18.00	**£20.70**
OTHER MAIN ACCESSORIES	(ex VAT)	(inc. VAT)
MOULDING FENCE ASSEMBLY with indep. micro-adjusting fences	£37.00	**£42.55**
83mm x 36mm **MOULDING BLOCK** (safety pattern) with rebating cutters	£33.00	**£37.95**
Pairs of profile cutters for above block (33 ptns. per pair)	£7.75	**£8.90**
Blank cutters (per pair)	£5.00	**£5.75**
90mm x 50mm **PLANER BLOCK** with 3 T.C.T. knives and scribing cutters for board edging etc.	£43.00	**£49.45**
HIGH SPEED ROUTER ATTACHMENT	£48.00	**£55.20**
Multi-profile T.C.T. cutters	£24.50	**£28.18**
SLIDING CARRIAGE	£29.50	**£33.93**
DRUM SANDER with one sleeve	£8.50	**£9.77**
Spare sleeves	.80	**.92**

charnwood®
1-3 Rowan Street,
Fosse Road Street,
Leicester LE3 9GP
Tel: (0533) 351735

Now comes the drilling, for which you should already have made the 30° angled jig as explained in the box. All the holes for the exhaust pipes are angled outwards, as are the lower holes for the undercarriage. For the floats, be sure that you are making one a mirror-image of the other — this is why the fronts should be clearly marked, so you get the cross-strut holes on the inside of each.

Lay the fuselage with its flat face on the bed and drill vertically all the 6.5mm holes for the exhaust pipes. Turn it round and drill them on the other side. Now turn it upside down and lay it with the flat face on top parallel to the jig bed. Drill the two 6.5mm holes for the front struts only.

Put the floats in the jig and drill the front strut holes in the tops at the 30° angle — be careful to make them left and right-handed. The rear holes in the fuselage and float for the joining struts are more tricky; cut a length of scrap and plane it to exactly 32mm wide, and lay it under one end of the jig; this will give you the double angle you need, 12° (approximately) one way and 30° the other. Drill with the drill vertical to the work surface and you should have no problems. If you are unsure it would be well worth cutting extra for the floats and doing a trial run.

When you have finished the angled drilling, set aside the jig and drill all the other holes in the fuselage and floats for the cross-struts, supercharger mounts, propeller shaft, tail fin and wing fixings. All these are 6.5mm deep. Also bore the 18mm hole for the pilot in the top of the fuselage.

Transfer the fuselage tapers to a full-size gridded drawing and then to card; cut it out and mark the tapering back first. Cut that and then mark and cut the rising line from the middle towards the raised back end. Mark and cut out the flat seating for the tailplane assembly. Shape the two floats with the same process — or you can measure from the printed drawing straight on to the wood with a ruler — and cut them out with the jig or coping saw.

Smooth with plane and glasspaper. Sand the floats and fuselage with medium and then fine glasspaper.

Measure and mark — from a gridded drawing or direct — the wing blank B, the tailplane C, the fin D and the exhaust fumes E on the 9mm ply, and cut them out. Drill the wing centrally, to a depth of 6.5mm with the 6.5mm drill for the fixing dowel, and also drill edge of the exhaust fumes after you have cut them out.

Propeller

Cut the 25x12mm softwood exactly to 127mm, and drill a 7mm hole through the centre of the wide face. Mark out the cutting lines, transferring from a full-size gridded drawing; then draw a line diagonally from corner to corner of the endgrain at both ends, then mark a line 2mm either side of that. Cut along that line and down along the marked shaped lines with the coping saw (don't use the jigsaw for this), sweeping out in a curve about 25mm down from the end, and coming out just above the middle. Do the same on the other side, and repeat it all from the other end. Cut the 'waist' either side of the hole, and clean it up with glasspaper.

Fixings

Cut all the lengths of 6.5mm dowel for the struts, supercharger mounts, and wing and tail fixings. Cut the 64mm length of 12mm dowel for the supercharger and 12mm of the same dowel for the propeller spinner N. Drill the mounting holes in the supercharger and the intake hole, and the mounting hole in the propeller spinner — all 6.5mm. Make the pilot peg person with the 18mm dowel, the 18mm ball or bead, and a length of 6.5mm dowel to hold them together.

Drill the centre of the 50mm wooden wheel that makes the cowling.

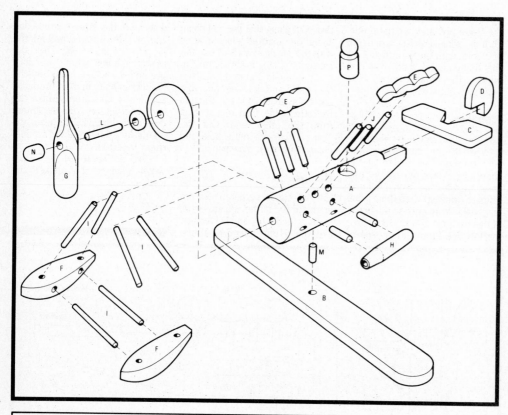

Painting and assembly

Dry-assemble all the parts, trimming and adjusting so that the plane sits square on the surface, the propeller spinner dowel spins easily in the nose of the fuselage, and everything is just right. Take it all apart again, give it a final sand, then paint it with varnish and enamels in that order, or acrylic paints and varnish in that order. Ordinary wood glue (PVA) is water-based, as are acrylic paints, so it will 'melt' them if you have painted a gluing area. Either mask gluing areas off, or use modelling enamels which are also non-toxic but much slower-drying. The alternative is to glue with epoxy, which you have to mix but which will stick painted parts.

Mask off the areas you want different colours, and rub down gently between coats of varnish with fine glasspaper.

You will find it easier to assemble the plane with tailfin and wing, supercharger and pilot as one unit, and the float structure as another.

Don't wait until the glue is dry in the floats, however, because you will almost certainly find yourself adjusting their positions. When the floats are on — the propeller spinner and dowel should already be glued together — fit the cowling and dowel together with some glue on the cowling; press it in position, then withdraw the propeller shaft and spinner so it won't get glued in. ∎

Materials

Ply sizes exact; softwood lengths exact, widths and thicknesses nominal

Birch faced ply

B Wing	1	280mm	x 42mm	x 9mm
C Tailplane	1	100	x 42	x 9
D Tail fin	1	50	x 42	x 9
E Exhaust fumes	1	75	x 18	x 9

Banister rail

A Fuselage	1	205	x 50	x 50

First quality (FAS) softwood (pine)

F Floats	2	108	x 18	x 18
G Propeller	1	127	x 25	x 12

Hardwood dowel

H Supercharger	1	64	x 12 dia.
N Spinner	1	12	x 12 dia.
I Struts	6	70	x 6.5 dia.
J Exhaust pipes	4	38	x 6.5 dia.
K Exhaust pipes	2	32	x 6.5 dia.
L Propeller shaft	1	38	x 6.5 dia.
M Fixings	5	12	x 6.5 dia.
P Pilot body	1	18	x 18 dia.
Pilot head	1	18mm dia. wooden bead	
Cowling	1	50mm dia. wooden wheel	

30° angle drilling jig — birch faced ply

Angles	1	168	x 40	x 9
Bed	1	155	x 70	x 9
Fence	1	155	x 50	x 9

Non-toxic acrylic or modelling enamel paints; non-toxic polyurethane varnish; glasspaper — medium, fine; wood glue or epoxy resin glue or both.

Cut the propeller with a coping saw on both sides before 'waisting' and final shaping

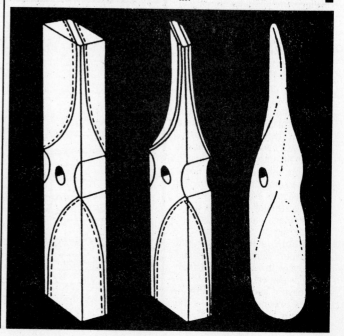

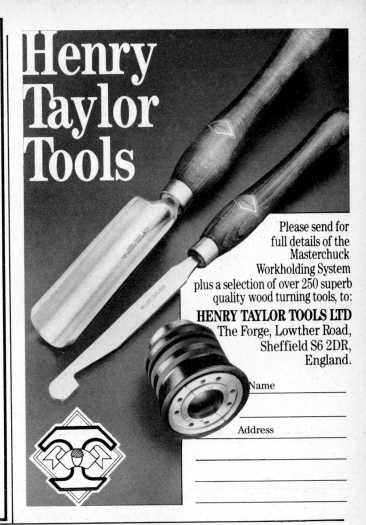
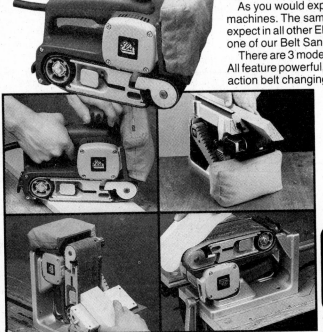

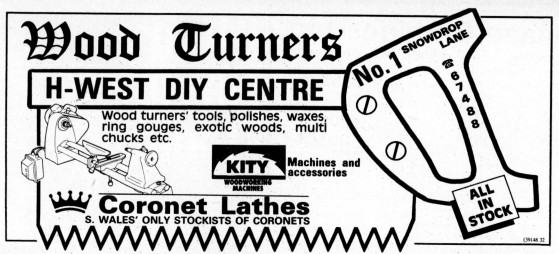
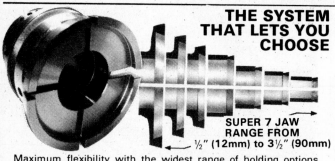

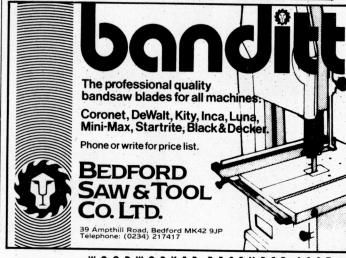

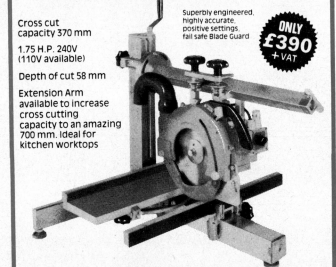

PHONE

Photos Ed Davis

PHANTASY

With its sparse lines, framed spaces and rich timbers, William Hepper's telephone cabinet is a design classic — and a cabinetmaking challenge

I t's not often that one is given the chance to indulge one's furniture-making fantasies to the full, so it was a delight when the opportunity came my way as the culmination of a one-year cabinetmaking course at the London College of Furniture. I set myself a brief to design and make a piece of furniture for the entrance hall in my parents' house. Functionally it needed a flat surface on which to put a telephone, a writing pad and an open phone book, with storage for about eight phone books, pencils and business cards.

As I thought about the project, I remembered seeing an oak desk, designed in 1896 by Charles Voysey, in the Victoria and Albert Museum; the distinguishing feature was that the legs ran from the floor up through the writing surface to the top, while the cabinet was suspended from the top, not actually touching the legs. I decided to base my design around this idea.

The space available allowed a maximum length up to 800mm while the height could be 1500mm. I utilized this full height in my first sketches, but felt it would look clumsy, given the size of the hall, and I settled for a normal worktop height of 850mm. I still wanted to use the full 800mm length. I decided to make the storage space fairly tightly to phone-book size, partly so the books would stand up properly, and also so the cabinet wouldn't be filled up with multitudinous household oddments; I thought a drawer or two would be useful for pencils, notebooks and essential paraphernalia.

My basic design consisted of front and back leg frames, each made up of two legs with rails across the top and middle (fig. 1). These frames were to be slipped on to the cabinet, front and back, and screwed in place. The top would then be fixed on top of them. Inside I wanted a vertical division down the centre and a drawer rail across the width, dividing the space into four with bookshelves below and drawers above, all concealed behind doors.

I toyed with the idea of making it entirely in solid timber, allowing the timber to move while the external structure remained stable. I changed my mind,▷

The doors were particularly satisfying to William : below right, detail of door opening

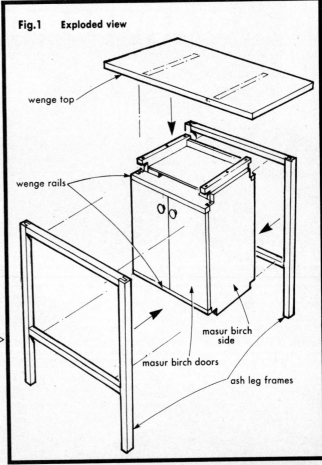

Fig.1   Exploded view

wenge top

wenge rails

masur birch side

masur birch doors

ash leg frames

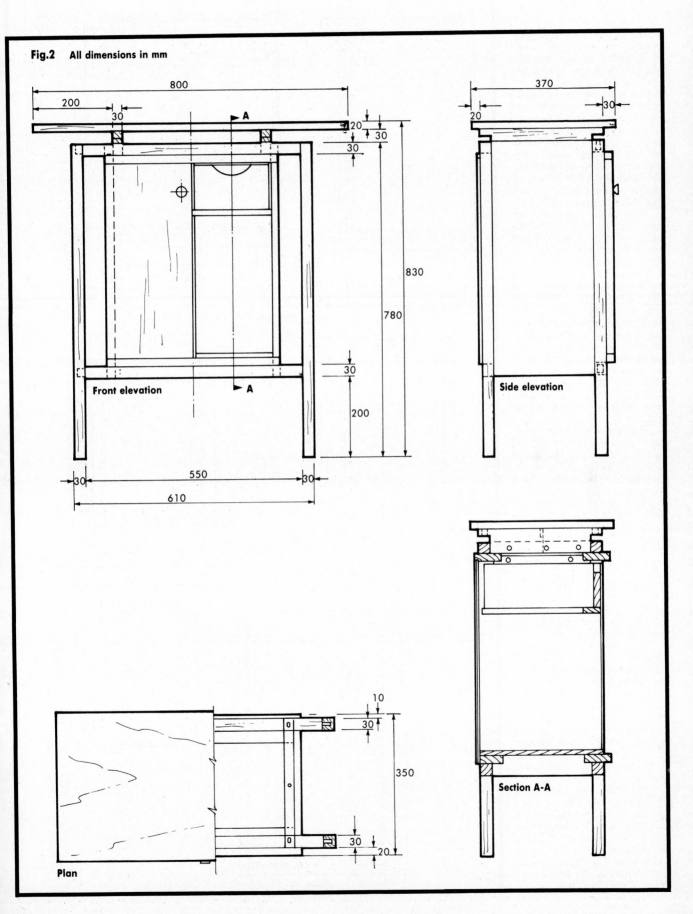

Fig.2   All dimensions in mm

800
200
30
A
20
30
30
830
780
Front elevation
A
30
200
30
550
30
610

370
30
20
Side elevation

10
30
350
30
20
Plan

Section A-A

however, after seeing some beautiful veneer work on a piece of furniture in the Brighton Museum by Jacques Ruhlmann, the French designer of the 1920's; the veneer was ambiogna, a beautiful rich reddish-brown. One exciting veneer that I had used successfully before was masur birch, and since I found the right quantity of the right-sized leaves with a particularly striking flame-like figure, I decided to base my choice of other timbers round that. As complements to the birch I chose ash, reflecting the lightness of the base colour of the birch, and wenge, a very rich dark brown colour, echoing the dark flecks in the birch.

I decided to specify solid ash for the top and leg frames, with the cabinet in blockboard veneered on the outside in masur birch, and top and bottom rails and handles in wenge. Inside I planned to use ash veneer predominantly, but with wenge for the drawer rail and as a wide lipping on the central division. The drawers would be solid ash with masur birch veneer on the front.

Having made working drawings, written a cutting list and selected the timber, I machined it all to within 5mm of the required dimensions, thus allowing for any movement in the dry workshop atmosphere where I stored it in stack. I machined each piece to final dimensions as required.

The making started with the two leg frames. I used stopped tenons on the lower rails, with dovetail tenons at the top for a bit of extra practice (fig. 3).

Next came the basic structure of the cabinet, two sides and four rails. The first step was to veneer the sides. I prepared the substrate out of 18mm blockboard, lipped in ash before veneering. Meanwhile the masur birch itself had dried out considerably, and got very brittle. Resuscitating it involved damping it and cramping it flat between newspaper and plywood.

After several hours I removed the veneer, trimmed it, book-matched the two halves and taped them together. Then I glued it up and hot-pressed it; this all had to be done quickly before the veneer started to dry out and cockle again. Once all the edges were trimmed and planed down to size,

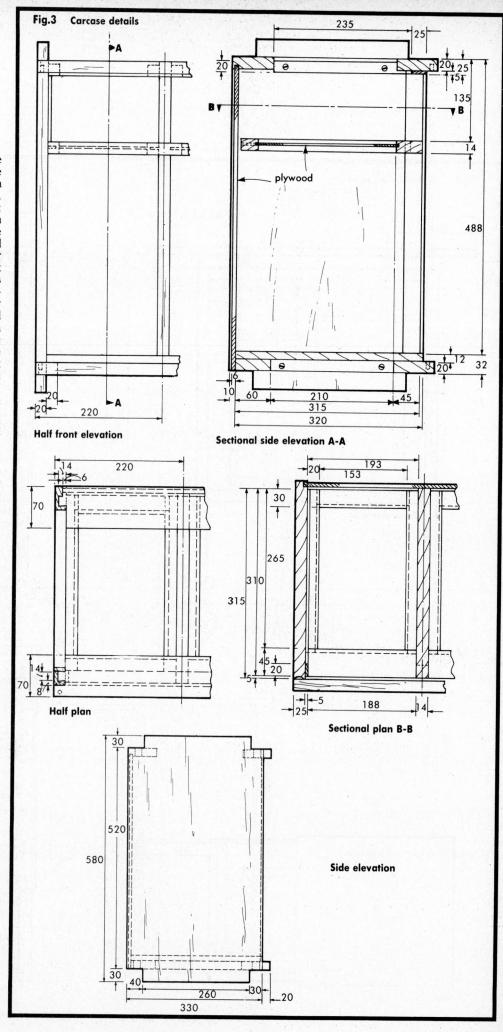

Fig.3   Carcase details

Half front elevation

Sectional side elevation A-A

Half plan

Sectional plan B-B

Side elevation

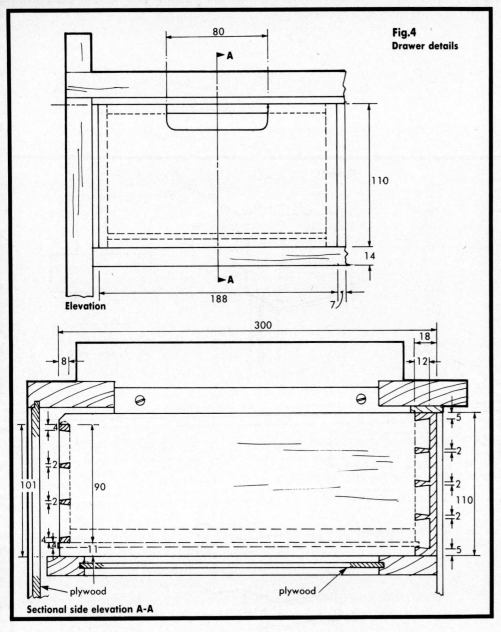

Fig.4
Drawer details

Elevation

Sectional side elevation A-A

work could start on the joints.

The jointing between the sides and the wenge rails was ridiculous. Basically it was a top dovetail, but for the tails to be pushed down on to the pins they first had to be inserted into a cavity above the pins, then pushed down on to them (fig. 5). After gluing, the cavity would be stopped up with a piece of ash. I think I will use mortise-and-tenons next time, but it was good practice!

IN CONSIDERING THE INTERNAL construction, the crucial thing was to make the gluing up as simple as possible. The plan was to fit the top and bottom rails and the drawer rail, tenoned in, first; then to slide the central divider into these from the back, housed in top and bottom with a cross-halving on the drawer rails. The back two rails could then be fitted, also housing the divider. The pot boards would be dropped in later in two halves and secured with screws through the bottom rails. The back could then be slid up grooves in the sides. In producing these components the only problem of interest that I encountered was on the central divider. In making this I cleaned up the wenge lipping flush with the veneer, and all was well until I applied the first coat of sanding sealer — which showed up the cloud of wenge dust that had settled in the ash grain. I had to scrape the sealer off and remove the worst effects with a pin.

As mentioned above, the drawers were to be enclosed behind doors. This created a problem of how to hang the doors. If they were hung internally the door would have to be opened 180° for the drawer to open, or 90° if the drawer were set away from the side by the thickness of the door. If they were hung externally, an ugly angle would be created between the back edge of the door and the side. Instead of these I opted to hang the door externally but pivoted on specially turned brass pins fitted in the top and bottom rails (fig. 6). This meant that the door, open at 90°, would remain flush with the side allowing the drawer to open. To make this work, however, involved making the edge of the carcase side concave, which I did with a home-made scratch-stock. It did the job, but was very awkward to use. Once the whole thing was together the doors

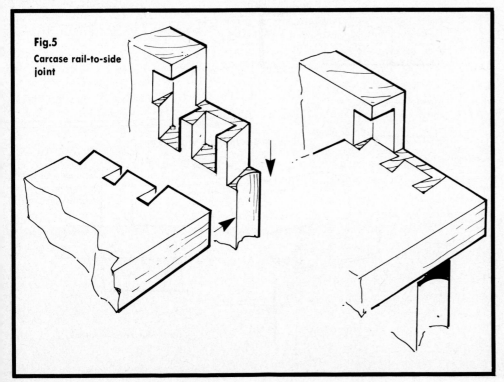

Fig.5
Carcase rail-to-side joint

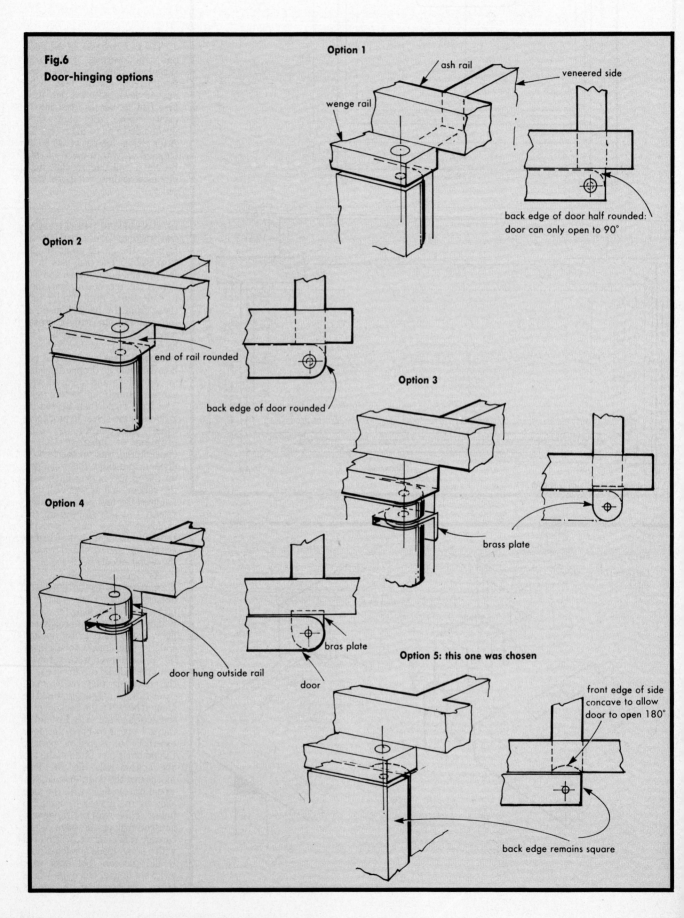

Fig.6
Door-hinging options

Option 1

ash rail

veneered side

wenge rail

back edge of door half rounded:
door can only open to 90°

Option 2

end of rail rounded

back edge of door rounded

Option 3

brass plate

Option 4

bras plate

door hung outside rail

door

Option 5: this one was chosen

front edge of side
concave to allow
door to open 180°

back edge remains square

worked very well, and for me are the most pleasing parts of the cabinet.

Having prepared all the components to be glued up, they needed cleaning and finishing. In the case of the wenge and ash this meant simply scraping, sanding and sealing the parts with shellac sanding sealer. The masur birch, however, was more tricky, because it was very pitted. The pits occurred in each of the dark flecks and needed filling with dark wax. Next the first coat of sealer was applied and cut back, which gave a shiny surface on which it was easy to see any remaining pits. These I filled with drops of sealer applied on a bradawl point. Finally the whole thing could be sealed to give a smooth surface.

With all the sealing finished gluing up could go ahead. Happily everything went without mishap and ended up, with the aid of a forest of sash cramps, near enough in square.

VENEERING THE DOORS involved basically the same processes as did the sides, only a little more care was needed to effect the triple book match with four leaves of veneer across the two doors. The back edge of the doors was also veneered, pressed under a timber bar and sash-cramps.

Hanging the doors was a matter of carefully marking and drilling the wenge rails to receive the brass pins. The doors were also drilled to receive small nylon bushes in which the pins rotated (fig. 7). A washer was needed around the lower pins to give the necessary 0.5mm clearance.

At this stage it was possible to fit the leg frames over the front and back of the cabinet and screw them in place. This gave some idea of the overall appearance and left two major constructional areas still to be finished — the top and the drawers.

The top was to be of 30mm solid ash, glued up out of three boards. Having cut it roughly to dimension I positioned it on the cabinet as planned. The result was terrible. The heavy expanse of bland, light ash totally overpowered the rich and subtle masur bitch. I mulled over a few solutions — chamfering the top, thinning it down, raising it, inlaying it with wenge, and so on. Eventually I scrapped it and made another, 20mm thick — and in wenge. Also I raised it up from frame by 30mm, continuing the idea of space around the cabinet.

The appearance was greatly improved.

The drawers were of traditional lap dovetail construction in ash, with the fronts veneered in masur birch. The drawer bottoms were ash-veneered 6mm plywood, fitted into drawer slips.

Finally, two important details needed dealing with — door handles and catches. I turned up some small round handles in wenge, and for catches used two ball catches. The catches themselves I sunk into the lower wenge rail while the plates were screwed to the bottom of the doors. This meant that only the two ball bearings are visible when the door is open and the ugly plates are out of sight altogether.

With everything together I gave it all another coat of sanding sealer and a rub down with flour paper; then a coat of wax applied with fine steel woo! and it was finished.

As I write the cabinet is downstairs and in use daily, and it works well. Visually I feel the proportions could be improved upon — the legs made thicker, for instance. But I'm satisfied that it's an object of quality that has received thought and care and includes a few interesting details. I enjoyed making it, and (I hope) learnt from it as well. ∎

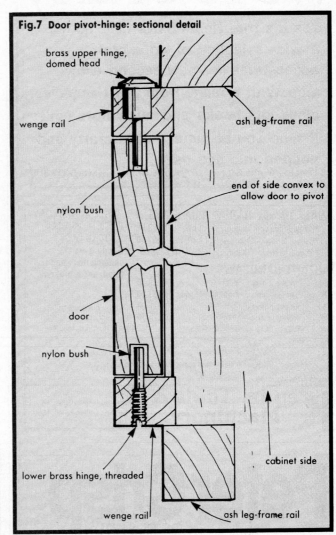

Fig.7 Door pivot-hinge: sectional detail

brass upper hinge, domed head

wenge rail

nylon bush

ash leg-frame rail

end of side convex to allow door to pivot

door

nylon bush

lower brass hinge, threaded

wenge rail

cabinet side

ash leg-frame rail

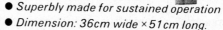

YOUR QUESTIONS

It's a Jiffy

Q I have recently acquired a Chalmers 'Jiffy' plane; all my enquiries have failed to reveal any ideas or clues as to its purposes. Is it a specialised tool for certain trades or tasks? There are four attachments, including a guide, as well as the 'base stock'.

H. Allen, Warley

A The Jiffy plane, patent No. 422596 is a 'fibre-board' plane designed to cut, slit, bevel or groove the soft, thick, wall-insulating board, made of felted wood or other vegetable fibre, which is now rarely used because of its fire hazard.

I don't know which were the special patented features of the 'Jiffy', made by Ernest Chalmers, of The Oval, Surbiton, but the patent number indicates a design of the 1930s and, using this number, it would be easy to find the precise details in the Patent Office's Volume of Abridgments kept in the libraries of Birmingham, Wolverhampton and several other industrial towns.

Other manufacturers made similar planes, for example the Stanley No. 193 which was sold from 1933 to 1958. Some of these planes had small, resharpenable cutters, with skew edges. Others used razor-blades which had to be clamped into the holder at an angle so that they would slit into the fibre-board, just as the cutter of a cutting gauge cuts into wood.

Philip Walker

● Philip Walker is a founder and former chairman of the Tool and Trades History Society.

Chair-seat shaping

Q I am copying a very old child's Windsor armchair (the chair, not the child), the seat of which is shaped as in this design. Can you tell me how this shaping was done originally, and how it can be best done today in a home workshop?

E. H. Ablitt, Aberdovey

A The familiar hollowing or 'saddling' of Windsor chairseats was traditionally done with an adze. This is a long-handled tool with a curved blade and the user, standing astride the seat blank, swung the adze down between the legs to scoop out the waste wood. Finishing was done with a travisher — a kind of curved spokeshave — and finally with a scraper.

The adze may still be used — if you can get one and have the courage to use it! — but there are other ways of using other tools. I have heard of sweeping cuts made with chainsaws and over the blade of a circular saw, but I dismiss these as far too dangerous. Some use a router and various jig arrangements but I have yet to try such methods. The two safe, hand methods I would suggest are:

1 Treat the seat as a shallow bowl and use a large carving gouge and mallet. A bent 'spoon' gouge is best to avoid digging in. Finish with a scraper and glass paper.

2 Use a tool called an inshave. This is a kind of curved drawknife which removes wood quite quickly when properly sharpened and used. It also leaves a good finish (which few of the other methods do) and I use the inshave from start to finish. Use it across the grain for roughing out and with light cuts with the grain to finish off. Methods 1 and 2 could be combined. Old inshaves (sometimes called scorps) can occasionally be found; new ones, made in Germany, are obtainable from specialist tool suppliers.

Jack Hill

● Jack Hill is an authority on green woodworking, an author and teacher.

Penetrating dyes

Q I found a lace bobbin turned from holly, one half of which has been dyed blue and the two pieces turned together. The blue dye seems to penetrate the holly fully — the original section must have been at least 4mm square.

Is it possible to achieve such penetration of a hardwood with ordinary dyes and equipment?

Eric Moseley, Solihull

A Charles Hayward's book *Staining and Polishing* is still one of the best in the market, if dated in places. The lace bobbin is curious on the face of it. It does appear to be made up of two pieces (one blue and one natural) with an undetectable joint, but inspection with a magnifying glass left me unsure. I can therefore only ask if you *know* it is made up of two pieces or are you assuming this because of its appearance?

You are correct in the observation that penetration of stains is pretty poor, and especially so in very dense hardwoods. To gain the penetration you would need for this bobbin is something of a task. I carried out an experiment on a piece of dowel which was left to soak in black water-stain. The stain penetrated both ends (up to approx. ½in) but not the sides. Wood is made up of tiny tubules and the penetration is the result of capillary action, but as this result took four days it's somewhat disappointing. Heating the stain (in effect boiling the wood in it) or applying pressure (as in a pressure cooker) will certainly improve matters and you may care to experiment here.

As I see it, there are two other options. The first is to use woods of contrasting colours but similiar densities (rosewood or sycamore). The second is an adaptation of the method to protect inlays while staining the background. The area which must not be stained is coated with a couple of layers of the final polish or given a single coat of Copydex. When the work is stained, the colour will not penetrate and ruin the inlay. Afterwards, the work is polished as normal. If Copydex has been used this is removed by peeling it off (being 'rubber', this is easy).

I also made a second experiment using a sycamore dowel. The natural part of the dowel was dipped into Copydex and allowed to dry for several hours before dipping into yellow spirit stain.

The demarcation line is clear, but not perfectly straight (more care needed). The Copydex was peeled off after the stain had dried. I also tried partially dipping a dowel in sanding sealer, drying it and dipping it in red water-stain. There was slight penetration in the grain, an effect also seen to a lesser degree in the bobbin.

Incidentally, water-stains are more penetrating than any other and this power is improved by adding a dash of ammonia — but not enough to make any difference to the rule of: once stained; don't sand!

Ian Hosker

● Ian Hosker is a professional restorer and Guild course tutor.

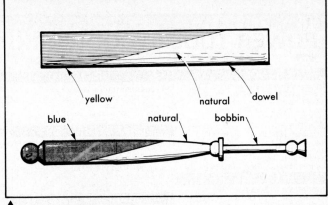

▲ **Stain penetration: Ian Hosker experiments**

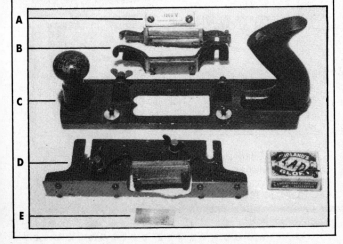

The Jiffy Plane

A — V-attachment takes two blades, fixes in centre of sole, adjusts for rise and fall at rear. **B** — Single attachment fixes to r/h side of centre hole vertical to sole. **C** — body. **D** — Guide attachment has cutter holder pivoted at front end, but allows lateral angle adjustment at rear. **E** — blade $1\frac{1}{2} \times \frac{11}{16} \times \frac{1}{16}$in approx, ground one long edge only

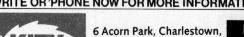

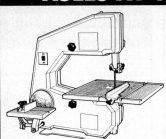

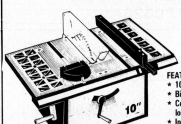

shopguide

AVON

BATH   Tel. Bath 64513
JOHN HALL TOOLS   ★
RAILWAY STREET

Open: Monday-Saturday
9.00 a.m.5.30 p.m.
H.P.W.WM.D.A.BC.

BRISTOL   Tel. (0272) 741510
JOHN HALL TOOLS LIMITED   ★
CLIFTON DOWN SHOPPING CENTRE
WHITELADIES ROAD
Open: Monday-Saturday
9.00 a.m.-5.30 p.m.
H.P.W.WM.D.A.BC.

BRISTOL   Tel. (0272) 667013
WILLIS   T
157 WEST STREET
BEDMINSTER
Open Mon.-Fri. 8.30 a.m.-5.00 p.m.

P.W.WM.D.CS.A.BC.

BERKSHIRE

READING   Tel. Littlewick Green
DAVID HUNT (TOOL   2743
MERCHANTS) LTD   ★
KNOWL HILL, NR. READING
Open: Monday-Saturday
9.00 a.m.-5.30 p.m.
H.P.W.D.A.BC.

READING   Tel. Reading 661511
WOKINGHAM TOOL CO. LTD   T
99 WOKINGHAM ROAD
Open: Mon-Sat 9.00 a.m.-5.30 p.m.
Closed 1.00-2.00 p.m. for lunch

H.P.W.WM.D.CS.A.BC.

SLOUGH   Tel: (06286) 5125
BRAYWOOD ESTATES LTD.   ★
158 BURNHAM LANE
Open: 9.00am-5.30pm.
Monday-Saturday.
H.P.W.WM.CS.A.

BUCKINGHAMSHIRE

MILTON KEYNES   Tel. (0908)
POLLARD WOODWORKING   641366
CENTRE   T★
51 AYLESBURY ST., BLETCHLEY
Open: Mon.-Fri. 8.30-5.30
Saturday 9.00-5.00
H.P.W.WM.D.CS.A.BC.   INCA

HIGH WYCOMBE   Tel. (0494)
ISAAC LORD LTD.   22221
185 DESBOROUGH ROAD   TK
Open: Mon.-Fri. 8.00 a.m. to 5.30 p.m.
Saturday 8.30 a.m. to 5.00 p.m.

H.P.W.D.A.WM.MF.

CAMBRIDGESHIRE

CAMBRIDGE   Tel. (0223) 63132
D. MACKAY LTD.   ★
BRITANNIA WORKS, EAST ROAD

Open: Mon.-Fri. 8.30 a.m.-1 p.m./2.00-
5.00 p.m. Sat. 8.30 a.m.-1.00 p.m.
H.P.W.D.T.CS.MF.A.BC.

CAMBRIDGESHIRE

CAMBRIDGE   Tel. (0223) 247386
H. B. WOODWORKING   TK
105 CHERRY HINTON ROAD
Open: 8.30 a.m.-5.30 p.m.
Monday-Friday
8.30 a.m.-1.00 p.m. Sat.
H.P.W.WM.D.CS.A.MF.BC.

CHESHIRE

NANTWICH   Tel. Crewe 67010
ALAN HOLTHAM   TK★
THE OLD STORES TURNERY
WISTASON ROAD, WILLASTON
Open: Tues.-Fri. 9.00 a.m.-5.30 p.m.
Sat. 9.00 a.m.-5.00 p.m. Closed Monday.
P.W.WM.D.T.C.CS.A.BC.

WIDNESS   Tel: 051 424 4545/7965
THE POWER TOOL CENTRE   T★
54/58 VICTORIA ROAD, WA8 7PJ
Mon.-Fri. 8.30am-5pm
Sat. 8.30am-4pm.

H.P.W.WM.D.CS.A.BC.

CLEVELAND

MIDDLESBROUGH   Tel. (0642)
CLEVELAND WOODCRAFT   813103
(M'BRO), 38-42 CRESCENT ROAD   TK

Open: Mon.-Sat. 9.15 a.m.-5.30 p.m.

H.P.A.BC.W.WM.CS.D.

CORNWALL

SOUTH WEST Power Tools

CORNWALL   Tel: Helston (03265) 4961
HELSTON AND LAUNCESTON   Launceston
(0566) 4781
  TK
H.P.W.WM.D.CS.A.

LISKEARD   Tel. (0579) 45307
D.R. WALKE BUILDING EQUIPMENT   ★
GREENBANK ROAD, LISKEARD
Open Mon.-Fri. 8.30 a.m. to 5.30 p.m.
Sat. 8.30 a.m. to 12.30 p.m.

H.P.W.WM.D.CS.A.   multico

CUMBRIA

CARLISLE   Tel. (0228) 36391
W. M. PLANT   T
ALLENBROOK ROAD
ROSEHILL, CA1 2UT
Open: Mon.-Fri. 8.00 a.m.-5.15 p.m.
Sat. 8.00 a.m.-12.30 noon
P.W.WM.D.CS.A.

DEVON

PLYMOUTH   Tel. (0752) 665363
F.T.B. LAWSON LTD.   T
71 NEW GEORGE STREET
PLYMOUTH PL1 1RB
Open: Mon.-Sat. 8.30 a.m.-5.30 p.m.

H.P.W.CS.MF.A.

DORSET

WEYMOUTH   Tel. (0305) 770303
WEYMOUTH HIRE & SALES LTD.   TK
5 KENT CLOSE
GRANBY INDUSTRIAL ESTATE
Open 7.30 a.m.-5.30 p.m. Mon.-Fri.
Sat. 8 a.m.-1 p.m.
H.P.W.WM.D.CS.A.K.

ESSEX

LEIGH ON SEA   Tel. (0702)
MARSHAL & PARSONS LTD.   710404
1111 LONDON ROAD   K

Open: 8.30 a.m.-5.30 p.m. Mon.-Fri.
9.00 a.m.-5.00 p.m. Sat.
H.P.W.WM.D.CS.A.

ILFORD   Tel. 597 7461
CUTWELL WOODWORKING   T★
776 HIGH ROAD
GOODMAYES IG3 8SY

H.P.W.WM.D.CS.A.

GLOUCESTER

TEWKESBURY   Tel. (0684)
TEWKESBURY SAW CO. LTD.   293092
TRADE ESTATE, NEWTOWN   K
  Telex No. 43382
Open: Mon-Fri 8.00 a.m.-5.00 p.m.
Saturday 9.30 a.m.-12.00 p.m.
P.W.WM.D.CS.

HAMPSHIRE

ALDERSHOT   **SOUTHAMPTON**
(0252) 334422   (0703) 332288
BURCH & HILLS POWER TOOL CENTRES
374 HIGH ST.   7 BELVIDERE RD.
Open Mon.-Fri. 8.30-5.30. Sat. 8.30-12.00
Closed for Lunch 1.00-2.00
H.P.W.WM.D.C.S.MF.BC.K.★   T

HEREFORDSHIRE

HEREFORD   Tel. (0432) 271366
WOODWORKING CENTRE   T
100 WIDEMARSH ST., HR4 9HG

Open: Mon.-Sat. 8 a.m.-5.30 p.m.

H.P.W.WM.D.CS.MF.A.T.

HERTFORDSHIRE

WARE   Tel: (0920) 870 230
HEATH SAWS   870 636
6 LEESIDE WORKS   K★
STANSTEAD ABBOTTS (near Ware) HERTS.
SG12 8DL.
Open: Mon.-Fri. 8.30 a.m.-5.30 p.m.
Sat. 8.30 a.m.-1 p.m. Sunday by appointment.
H.P.W.WM.D.T.CS.MF.A.BC.★K

HERTFORDSHIRE

ENFIELD   Tel. 01-363 2935
GILL & HOXBY LTD.   T
131-137 ST. MARKS ROAD ADJ.
BUSH HILL PARK STATION, EN1 1BA
Mon.-Sat. 8-5.30
Early closing Wed. 1 p.m.
H.P.A.M.MC.T.S.W.

HUMBERSIDE

HULL
HUMBERSIDE FACTORING/H.F.C.
SAW SERVICING LTD.
MAIN STREET
Open: Mon.-Fri. 8am-5pm.
Saturday 8am-12.00pm.
H.P.W.WM.D.CS.A.BC.K.

KENT

MAIDSTONE   Tel: (0622) 44350
HENSON AND PLATT
TOKE PLACE
LINTON
Open Mon.-Fri. 8.00 a.m.-5.00 p.m.
Saturday 8.00 a.m.-1.00 p.m.
H.P.W.T.CS.A.

MAIDSTONE   Tel. (0622) 50177
SOUTH EASTERN SAWS (Ind.) LTD.   ★
COLDRED ROAD
PARKWOOD INDUSTRIAL ESTATE
Open: Mon.-Fri. 8.00 a.m.-5.00 p.m.
Sat. 9.00 a.m.-12.00 a.m.
B.C.W.CS.WM.PH.

BIDDENDEN   Tel. (0580) 291555
THE TURNING POINT
BRITISH GATES AND TIMBER LTD.
BIDDENDEN, NR. ASHFORD TN27 8DD
Open: Mon.-Fri. 7.30 a.m.-5.30 p.m.
Sat. 8.30 a.m.-12.00 a.m.
H.P.W.D.T.CS.MF.A.BC.

LANCASHIRE

PRESTON   Tel. (0772) 52951
SPEEDWELL TOOL COMPANY   ★
62-68 MEADOW STREET PR1 1SU
Open: Mon.-Fri. 8.30 a.m.-5.30 p.m.
Sat. 8.30 a.m.-12.30 p.m.

H.P.W.WM.CS.A.MF.BC.

ROCHDALE   Tel. (0706) 342123/
C.S.M. TOOLS   342322
4-6 HEYWOOD ROAD   T★
CASTLETON
Open: Mon-Sat 9.00 a.m.-6.00 p.m.
Sundays by appointment
W.D.CS.A.BC.

LANCASTER   Tel. (0524) 32886
LILE TOOL SHOP   K
43/45 NORTH ROAD
Open: Monday to Saturday
9.00 a.m.-5.30 p.m.
Wed. 9.00 a.m.-12.30 p.m.
H.P.W.D.A.

DEVON

PLYMOUTH   Tel. (0752) 330303
WESTWARD BUILDING SERVICES   ★
LTD., LISTER CLOSE, NEWNHAM
INDUSTRIAL ESTATE, PLYMPTON
Open: Mon-Fri 8.00 a.m.-5.30 p.m.
Sat. 8.30 a.m.-12.30 p.m.
H.P.W.WM.D.A.BC.

LONDON

ACTON   Tel. (01-992) 4835
A. MILLS (ACTON) LTD.   ★
32/36 CHURCHFIELD ROAD W3 6ED
Open: Mon.-Fri. 8.32 a.m.-5.30 p.m.
Saturdays 9.00 a.m.-1.00 p.m.
H.P.W.WM.

LONDON   Tel. 01-723 2295-6-7
LANGHAM TOOLS LIMITED
13 NORFOLK PLACE
LONDON W2 1QJ

FULHAM   Tel. (01-636) 6109
I. GRIZARD LTD.
84a-b.c. LILLIE ROAD, SW6 1TL
Open: Mon.-Sat. 9.00-5.30 p.m.
Half day Thursday

H.P.A.BC.W.CS.WM.D.

MANCHESTER

MANCHESTER   Tel. (061 789)
TIMMS TOOLS   0909
102-104 LIVERPOOL ROAD   ★
PATRICROFT M30 0WZ
Weekdays 9.00 a.m.-5.30 p.m.
Sat. 9.00 a.m.-1.00 p.m.
H.P.A.W.

**Read Model Engineer
for a new angle on
construction and
design.**

MERSEYSIDE

LIVERPOOL   Tel. (051-207) 2967
TAYLOR BROS (LIVERPOOL) LTD.   TK
195-199 LONDON ROAD
LIVERPOOL L3 8JG
Open: Monday to Friday
8.30 a.m.-5.30 p.m.
H.P.W.WM.D.A.BC.

MIDDLESEX

RUISLIP   Tel. (08956) 74126
ALLMODELS ENGINEERING LTD.   ★
91 MANOR WAY

Open: Mon.-Sat. 9.00 a.m.-5.30 p.m.

H.P.W.A.D.CS.MF.BC.

NORFOLK

NORWICH   Tel. (0603) 898695
NORFOLK SAW SERVICES
DOG LANE, HORSFORD
Open: Monday to Friday
8.00 a.m.-5.00 p.m.
Saturday 8.00 a.m.-12.00 p.m.
H.P.W.WM.D.CS.A.

**Read Model Engineer
for a new angle on
construction & design**

NORFOLK

KINGS LYNN   Tel. (0553) 772443
WALKER & ANDERSON (Kings Lynn) LTD.   T
WINDSOR ROAD, KINGS LYNN
Open: Monday to Saturday
7.45 a.m.-5.15 p.m.

H.P.W.WM.D.CS.A.

NORWICH   Tel. (0603) 400933
WESTGATES WOODWORKING   Tx
61 HURRICANE WAY,   975412
NORWICH AIRPORT INDUSTRIAL ESTATE
Open: 9.00 a.m.-5.00 p.m. weekdays
9.00 a.m.-12.30 Sat.
P.W.WM.D.BC.   K

KINGS LYNN   Tel: 07605 674
NORFOLK WOODTURNING CENTRE   ★
UNIT A, HILL FARM WORKSHOPS
GREAT DUNHAM (Nr. Swaffham)
Tues.-Sat. 9.00am-5.30pm

H.P.W.D.T.MF.A.BC.

NOTTINGHAMSHIRE

NOTTINGHAM   Tel: (0602) 225979
POOLEWOOD   and 227064/5
EQUIPMENT LTD.   (06077) 2421 after hrs
5a HOLLY LANE, CHILLWELL
Open: Mon-Fri 9.00 a.m.-5.30 p.m.
Sat. 9.00 a.m. to 12.30 p.m.
P.W.WM.D.CS.A.BC.

OXON

WITNEY   Tel. (0993) 76431
TARGET TOOLS (SALES,   OXON
HIRE & REPAIRS)   T★
SWAIN COURT
STATION INDUSTRIAL ESTATE
Open: Mon.-Sat. 8.00 a.m.-5.00 p.m.
24 hour Answerphone
BC.W.M.A.

SHROPSHIRE

TELFORD   Tel. Telford (0952)
ASLES LTD.   48054
VINEYARD ROAD, WELLINGTON   K★

Open: Mon.-Fri. 8.30 a.m.-5.30 p.m.
Saturday 8.30 a.m.-4.00 p.m.
H.P.W.WM.D.CS.BC.A.

SOMERSET

TAUNTON   Tel. (0823) 335431
JOHN HALL TOOLS   ★
6 HIGH STREET

Open Monday-Saturday
9.00 a.m.-5.30 p.m.
H.P.W.WM.D.CS.A.

SUFFOLK

IPSWICH   Tel. (0473) 40456
FOX WOODWORKING   463884
142-144 BRAMFORD LANE   T★
Open: Tues.-Fri. 9 a.m.-5.30 p.m.
Sat. 9 a.m.-5 p.m.
W.WM.D.T.CS.MF.A.BC.K.*

SURREY

GUILDFORD   Tel. (0483) 61125
MESSINGERS FOR TOOLS   T
18-18 CHERTSEY ST.
(TOP OF NORTH ST.)
Open: Tues.-Sat. 8.30 a.m.-5.30 p.m.
H.P.W.CS.MF.A.BC.K.T.

SUSSEX

WORTHING   Tel. (0903) 38739
W. HOSKING LTD. (TOOLS &   KT★
MACHINERY)
28 PORTLAND RD, BN11 1QN
Open: Mon.-Sat. 8.30 a.m.-5.30 p.m.
Closed Wednesday
H.P.W.WM.D.CS.A.BC.

W. MIDLANDS

WOLVERHAMPTON   Tel: (0902)
MANSAW SERVICES   58759
WARD STREET, HORSELEY FIELDS   TK★
WOLVERHAMPTON, WEST MIDLANDS
Open: Mon.-Fri. 8.00 a.m.-6.00 p.m.
Saturday 8 a.m.-3 p.m.
H.P.W.WM.A.D.CS.

**All shops with an
asterisk ★
have a Mail Order
Service**

YORKSHIRE

THIRSK   Tel. (0845) 22770
THE WOOD SHOP   ★
TRESKE SAWMILLS LTD.
STATION WORKS
Open: Seven days a week 9.00-5.00

T.H.MF.BC.H.

SHEFFIELD   Tel. (0742) 441012
GREGORY & TAYLOR LTD.   K
WORKSOP ROAD
Open: 8.30 a.m.-5.30 p.m.
Monday-Friday
8.30 a.m.-12.30 p.m. Saturday
H.P.W.WM.D.

HARROGATE   Tel. (0423) 505328/
MULTI-TOOLS   66245
158 KINGS ROAD   K★

Open: Monday to Saturday
8.30 a.m.-6.00 p.m.

H.P.W.WM.D.A.BC.

STAFFORDSHIRE

**THIS COUNTY COULD
BE YOURS.
RING JULIE CAPSTICK
ON 01-437 0699 FOR
DETAILS.**

YORKSHIRE

HOLME UPON   Tel. (0696) 60612
SPALDING MOOR
CRAFT TOOLS AND TACKLE LTD.
HOLME INDUSTRIAL ESTATE
Open: Mon.-Fri. 9.00 am-5.30 pm
Saturday & Bank Holiday 9.00 am-4.30 pm
H.P.W.D.T.CS.MF.A.BC.

LEEDS   Tel. (0532) 574736
D. B. KEIGHLEY MACHINERY LTD.   ★
VICKERS PLACE, STANNINGLEY
PUDSEY LS2 86LZ
Mon.-Fri. 9.00 a.m.-5.00 p.m.
Sat. 9.00 a.m.-1.00 p.m.
P.A.W.WM.CS.BC.

YORKSHIRE

CLECKHEATON   Tel. (0274)
SKILLED CRAFTS LTD.   872861
34 BRADFORD ROAD   ★

Open: 9.00 a.m.-5.00 p.m. Monday
Saturday Lunch 12.00 a.m.-1.00 p.m.
H.P.A.W.CS.WM.D.

SCOTLAND

PERTH   Tel. (0738) 26173
WILLIAM HUME & CO.   TK
ST. JOHN'S PLACE
Open: Monday to Saturday
8.00 a.m.-5.30 p.m.
8.00 a.m.-1.00 p.m. Wednesday
H.P.A.BC.W.CS.WM.D.

EDINBURGH   Tel. 031-337-5555
THE SAW CENTRE   T
38 HAYMARKET TERRACE
EDINBURGH EH12 5JZ
Mon.-Fri. 8.30 a.m.-5.30 p.m.
Saturday 9.00 a.m.-1.00 p.m.
H.P.W.WM.D.CS.A.

PERTH   Tel: (0738) 36777
WORKMASTER POWER TOOLS LTD.   T★
8 SHORE ROAD, PH2 8BW
Mon.-Fri. 8.30 a.m.-5 p.m.
Sat. 9.00 a.m.-4 p.m.
Other times by appointment
H.P.W.WM.D.CS.A.

GLASGOW   Tel. 041-429-4444/
THE SAW CENTRE   4374 Telex: 777886
650 EGLINTON STREET   T★
GLASGOW G5 9RP
Mon.-Fri. 8.00 a.m.-5.00 p.m.
Sat. 9.00 a.m.-1.00 p.m.
H.P.W.WM.D.CS.A.

DUNDEE   Tel. (0382) 458918
FYFE DOUGLAS
119 CLEPINGTON ROAD
Open Mon.-Fri. 8.30 a.m.-5.00 p.m.
Sat. 8.30 a.m.-12.30 p.m.
Sunday 10.30 a.m.-4 p.m.
H.P.W.WM.D.A.BC.

KIRKCALDY   Tel. (0592) 260055
THOMSON BROS. LTD.
25 ESPLANADE
Open: Mon.-Sat. 8.30 a.m.-5.15 p.m.

H.P.W.WM.D.A.BC.

IRELAND

NEWTOWNARDS   Tel: 0247 819800
NORLYN MACHINERY   or 812506
UNIT 10, MALCOLMSON IND. EST.
80 BANGOR ROAD, CO. DOWN
Open: Mon.-Fri. 9.30am-5.30pm
(Closed 1-2pm for lunch)
Any other time by request.
H.W.WM.D.T.MF.A.   24 Hour Service K

PORTADOWN   Tel. (0762) 332546
LOCKE TOOLS   ★
50 WEST STREET BT62 3JQ
Mon.-Sat. 9 a.m.-5.30 p.m.
Any other time by request.
H.D.W.WM.D.CS.A.BC.

WOOD SUPPLIERS

WOOD SUPPLIERS

Classified Advertisements

FOR SALE

THE FINEST SELECTION ON DISPLAY IN SCOTLAND!

WOODWORKING & METAL WORKING MACHINERY POWER TOOLS HAND TOOLS

THE SAW CENTRE

LARGE STOCKS – COMPETITIVE PRICES. PHONE AND TRY US *NOW.*

Eglinton Toll, Glasgow G5 9RP
Tel: 041-429-4444

38 Haymarket Edinburgh EH12 5J2
Tel: 031-337-5555

OPEN Mon - Fri 8am - 5pm Sat 9am - 1pm

Yorkwire (Leeds) Ltd.
BRASS WIRE, ROD, STRIP & TUBE
Suitable for Miniature furniture, Clock Pendulums, Inlay work and many other Crafts.
SAE for Price List to:
Yorkwire (Leeds) Ltd.
34 Lupton Street,
Leeds LS10 2QW.
Tel: 0532 777472

MYFORD MLS LATHE, good condition 30" centres, rear turning 4", 8", 16" & 20" Rests. With Cabinate Stand. Some extras available, £500. Bristol (0272) 560995.

SECONDHAND saw/planer: Emco-Star Emco-Rex plus 17 attachments £650. Tel: 0602 877288.

CORONET MAJOR, maroon with 8" saw table, 4" planer/thicknesser, lathe, morticer and many extras £550. M. Hopton, Sutton. Tel: 07373 58096.

THE WHISTON CATALOGUE
Nuts, bolts, screws, washers, bar materials. In brass, alloy, steel, stainless steel, P.T.F.E., nylon, Tufnol, sheet material, electrical and mechanical items. We could go on and on! Better to send for free catalogue and see for yourself.
K. R. Whiston Ltd., Dept. WW, New Mills, Stockport, Cheshire. Phone: 0663 42028.

CARPENTER and Joiner's assistant Queen's Prize 1893. Good condition, offers from £120. Bailey, 17 Prince Rupert Court, Freshbrook, Swindon, SN5 8QQ. Tel: Swindon 871927.

SUPERB VALUE emigration forces sale of 3 barely used woodworking machines, 1. Luna L38 10" × 9" planer thicknesser £800. 2. Minimax T90 lathe with copier and accessories £600. 3. DeWalt 1370 Radial Arm Saw 12" TCT Blade £400. Tel: Godstone, Surrey 0883 842602.

BANKRUPT STOCK
Sandvik circular saw blades tungsten tipped
Hurry! Last few remaining
5", 5½", 6" **£4.00** each.
Any bore up to 30mm.
8¼" **£6.00** each.
Any bore up to 35mm.
P&P £1 extra per order.
Tel: 643 0244
Hannett, 11 Lind Road, Sutton, Surrey.

30 SECONDHAND bandsaws, 15 at 17 feet, 15 at 20 feet. Varying widths. Tel: Whitby 603509.

WOODCRAFT BOOKS: We can offer new out of print, secondhand and antiquarian books on every aspect of woodworking — for catalogues send 50p stamp to: Woodcraft Books, P.O. Box 58, Worcester WR8 0EL.

CLASSIFIED ADVERTISING TERMS & CONDITIONS

Woodturning Tools

A UNIQUE OPPORTUNITY TO ACQUIRE NEW, GOOD QUALITY TURNING TOOLS AT LOW PRICES
25% OFF LIST PRICE WHILE STOCKS LAST
Send 13p stamp for free brochure
ALEC TIRANTI LTD
70 High Street, Theale, Reading, Berks. RG7 5AR
Tel: Reading (0734) 302775
SALE

BOOKS & PUBLICATIONS

CORONET MAJOR, all accessories, saws, planes, drills, turns, joints, grinds, moulds. Offers I.R.O. £500. Mr Clegg, 35 Basingbourne Road, Fleet. Tel: Fleet 616074.

14" R+F Sawbench, 9" surface planer, £495 pair. Robinson 28" bandsaw £850. Wadkin/ Sagar spindle moulder £1200 plus VAT. All 3 phase. Tel: 0985 40686.

CONSORT UNIVERSAL woodworker, 8" circular saw, on a bench. All assembled and all accessories, 45° angle cut. Fitted with Gryphon 750 watt motor £200. Tel: 01 462 1361.

EMCO STAR universal woodworker, old type, with 6 basic functions, £500 o.n.o. Tel: Bristol 0272 556661.

Lathe ML8 £380 15LS Tools 2 collet chucks £60. B&D Router £50. Shopsmith 18" Jigsaw £150. Biggin Hill 73673.

VARIANT WOODTURNING LATHE, Burgess Bandsaw BK3 Plus. Both very good condition, £100 & £50 respectively. Bath 315973.

AMERICAN SINGLE sided razor blades — surgical steel — extra sharp 100 per £7.99 — all steel retractable holder £1.99, P&P £1.25. Allow 21 days delivery. Barlow, Primrose Cottage, Shere Road, Ewhurst, Surrey GU6 7PQ.

RE-EQUIPPING SALE Startrite T30 spindle, little used. £650.00. Multico TH3 12" Thicknesser. G.W.O. £450.00 — Old cast iron 9" plane £195.00. Sussex 082571 3120.

BLADES – for Machinery and Tooling
INCA EURO 260 motorised bandsaw	....£429.00
KITY K5 TCT planer knives	£18.00 each
125 x 40 x 30 Rebate block	£56.00
100 x 40 x 30 Profile block	£39.00
Prices include VAT & carriage UK mainland.
Send 18p large SAE for our new catalogue.
Saw & planer blades, spindle tooling etc.
BLADES, Dept. WW,
PO Box 27, Petersfield,
Hants. GU32 2NB.

BUSINESS OPPORTUNITIES

IDEAS/INVENTIONS WANTED. Call I.S.C. 01-434 1272 or write: Dept. ASP, 99 Regent Street, London W1.

QUALITY MOVEMENTS FOR QUALITY CASES
Eight Day Long case clock movements hand made of traditional design and very high quality, suitable for fitting in reproduction clock cases. These should appeal to the craftsman who requires the quality of the original Long Case movements. Dials and hands available made to your requirements. Brassware for clock cases including, capitals, escutcheons, etc. available.
Catalogue on castings + parts U.K. £1.25.
Overseas £2.50.
RICHARDS OF BURTON
Woodhouse Clockworks
Swadlincote Road, Woodville
Burton-on-Trent Tel: (0283) 219155

CORONET MAJOR 18" x 12", cast iron saw table. 10" TCT blade, £135 o.n.o. Haywards Heath, 451009, Sussex.

CORONET MAJOR Universal Woodworking machine in immaculate condition. Only used 8 hours since brand new. Including spare saws and extras, never been used. Further details please tel: (0749) 3299 weekdays, office hours (Somerset).

WANTED

WANTED for Myford ML8, mortising attachment and steady. Tel: (0407) 2763.

SPECIALIST TOOLS

UNIQUE SOLID BRASS TOOLS
Made by Richard Kell
Nine items in the range. All unique. Send for details:
67 Newbiggin Road, Ashington, Northumberland NE63 0TB.

RESTORATION

Furniture Restoration Materials
Everything you need to give your furniture that professional restoration look. Waxes, cleaners, alloy, french polishes, traditional upholstery supplies and many more items. Send sae for full price list:–
Furniture Restoration Supplies,
42 Acacia Avenue, Hale, Cheshire WA15 8QY. Tel: 061-928 3903.

BOOKS & PUBLICATIONS

LATHE CLASSICS AT BUDGET PRICES! Ornamental Turning by J. H. Evans £9.50. Simple Decorative Lathe Work by James Lunkin £8.50. Possibilities of Small Lathes by James Lukin £9.50. Lathe-Work by Paul Hasluck £11.50. Wood Turner's Handybook by Paul Hasluck £8.00. New woodcrafts bumper catalogue 60p stamps. Access/Visa orders by post/phone (24 hour) 01-579 7527. All orders post free. Mansard Press Ltd. (WW), 15 Princes Road, Ealing, London W13 9AS.

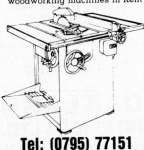

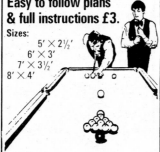

LETTERS

LETTERS TO THE EDITOR

If you are writing for publication, address your letter to 'Letters to the Editor', *Woodworker*, I Golden Sq, London WIR 3AB. We make every effort to keep the writer's individual tone intact, but reserve the right to edit and cut for brevity and clarity.

If you write to us for any other reason, we regret we cannot guarantee a reply if you do not enclose a stamped self-addressed envelope.

True chuck

I bought a Multistar chuck to use with my Tyme Avon Lathe, but it rotated very eccentrically, especially in the expansion mode, and repeated attempts by Multistar to solve the problem benefitted only the Post Office. Eventually a director came to see me from Colchester, but even he was baffled. But Multistar worked on the problem with true fighting spirit, and I now have received a new chuck. It runs as true as I could hope for, and I understand the precision modifications they made are now incorporated into their design.

Thank you Multistar — I'm glad to know there are still caring manufacturers around, even if they're the smaller ones.

Alan Gaskell, Cobham

Ban rust?

For many years I have kept my tools in 'Ban Rust' paper, the strong, oil-impregnated brown paper, but now I just can't find anyone to supply it. The shows in my area are unable to help me, even though the tools they sell come wrapped in a similar product. Does anyone know where I can get 'Ban Rust' or something like it? Please write direct:

F. T. Mann, 26 Swallowcliffe Gdns, Yeovil, Somerset BA20 IDQ

Reactions

I've been perusing the new-look WOODWORKER for some time now, and my thoughts are that it has definitely gone downmarket. The treatment of reader's queries and letters has taken a lot out of the magazine. True, the letters are separated a bit better, but that is no great advantage.

You seem to be dwelling more and more on the silly 'furniture' produced by the colleges — 'chairs' with 6ft-high backs and 'chairs' which are impossible to sit on for more than 10 seconds, etc etc. Most of these things are surely a waste of a valuable raw material and they have no purpose except ornamentation, which is NOT the prime purpose of furniture.

One final point — the ratio of advertisements to reading matter seems to have increased considerably. Advertisements are of some use, but they are not the reason I buy the magazine.

P. Ineson, Leicester

We aim to show what's going on in furniture design — we don't necessarily endorse or like the designs we publish in our College reviews. As for ads, our ratio of (approximately) 60% editorial, 40% advertising has stayed more or less the same. If we have more ad pages, we have more editorial pages — which is why last month's issues was the first 116-page WOODWORKER *in the magazine's 86-year history. Aidan Walker*

Ring-gouge sharpening

I was interested in the Sorby Ring Tool test in September's WOODWORKER, becaue I bought one of these a few months ago and decided the only way to sharpen it was with a variation of the old-fashioned gouge-honing guide. I made mine for about 40p from offcuts of ply and melamine-faced chipboard.

In use the right hand moves the oilstone to and fro underneath the ring, while the left hand moves the handle of the tool through an arc from 8 o'clock to 3 o'clock, slowly but continuously to avoid getting flats on the ring. It may look a lash-up, but it works and produces a satisfactory result, even with closed eyes!

T. H. Smallman, Crowborough

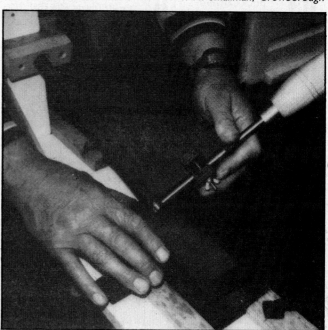

WOODWORKER, published every third Friday by **Argus Specialist Publications Ltd**
Editorial, Advertisting; I Golden Sq, London WIR 3AB, 01-437 0626
Editor Aidan Walker **Deputy editor** John Hemsley **Assistant editor** Kerry Fowler
Advertisment manager Trevor Pryer **Advertisement production** Andrew Selwood
Design ASP Art Studio **Technical illustrator** Peter Holland **Guild of Woodworkers**
John Hemsley, Kerry Fowler

We cannot accept responsibility for loss of or damage to unsolicited material. We reserve the right to refuse or suspend advertisements, and regret we cannot guarantee the bona fides of advertisers.

ABC UK circulation Jan-Dec '86 **32,849**

Back issues and subscriptions Infonet Ltd, 5 River Park Estate, Berkhamsted, Herts HP4 IHL, (04427) 76661-4
Overseas sales, non-newstrade sales Magazine Sales Dept., I Golden Sq, London WIR 3AB, 01-437 0626

Subscriptions per year 12 issues UK £15.60, Europe £22.80, Middle East £23, Far East £25.70, rest of the world £23.50 (USA $35). Airmail rates given on request.
UK Trade SM Distribution Ltd, 16-18 Trinity Gdns, London SW9 8DX, 01-274 8611
North American Trade Bill Dean Books Ltd, 151-49 7th Ave, PO Box 69, Whitestone, NY 11357, phone 1-718-767 6632
Printed by Chase Web, Plymouth **Typesetting** Project 3, Whitstable **Colour origination** Derek Croxson Ltd, Chesham, Bucks

© Argus Specialist Publications Ltd, 1987
ISSN 0043 776X
Second class postage paid at Rahway, NJ, USA. Postmaster: send address corrections to Woodworker, c/o Mercury Airfreight International Inc., 10B Engelhard Ave, Avenel, NJ 07001

ARGUS PRESS GROUP